Nineteenth-Century Literature Criticism

Guide to Gale Literary Criticism Series

For criticism on	Consult these Gale series
Authors now living or who died after December 31, 1959	*CONTEMPORARY LITERARY CRITICISM (CLC)*
Authors who died between 1900 and 1959	*TWENTIETH-CENTURY LITERARY CRITICISM (TCLC)*
Authors who died between 1800 and 1899	*NINETEENTH-CENTURY LITERATURE CRITICISM (NCLC)*
Authors who died between 1400 and 1799	*LITERATURE CRITICISM FROM 1400 TO 1800 (LC)* *SHAKESPEAREAN CRITICISM (SC)*
Authors who died before 1400	*CLASSICAL AND MEDIEVAL LITERATURE CRITICISM (CMLC)*
Black writers of the past two hundred years	*BLACK LITERATURE CRITICISM (BLC)*
Authors of books for children and young adults	*CHILDREN'S LITERATURE REVIEW (CLR)*
Dramatists	*DRAMA CRITICISM (DC)*
Hispanic writers of the late nineteenth and twentieth centuries	*HISPANIC LITERATURE CRITICISM (HLC)*
Native North American writers and orators of the eighteenth, nineteenth, and twentieth centuries	*NATIVE NORTH AMERICAN LITERATURE (NNAL)*
Poets	*POETRY CRITICISM (PC)*
Short story writers	*SHORT STORY CRITICISM (SSC)*
Major authors from the Renaissance to the present	*WORLD LITERATURE CRITICISM, 1500 TO THE PRESENT (WLC)*

ISSN 0732-1864

Volume 50

Nineteenth-Century Literature Criticism

*Criticism of the Works of
Novelists, Poets, Playwrights,
Short Story Writers, Philosophers, and Other
Creative Writers Who Died between 1800
and 1899, from the First Published Critical
Appraisals to Current Evaluations*

James E. Person, Jr.
Editor

**Catherine C. Dominic
Marie Lazzari**
Associate Editors

 **Gale Research**

An ITP Information/Reference Group Company

Changing the Way the World Learns

NEW YORK • LONDON • BONN • BOSTON • DETROIT
MADRID • MELBOURNE • MEXICO CITY • PARIS
SINGAPORE • TOKYO • TORONTO • WASHINGTON
ALBANY NY • BELMONT CA • CINCINNATI OH

∞™ This book is printed on acid-free paper that meets the minimum requirements of American National Standard for Information Sciences—Permanence Paper for Printed Library Materials, ANSI Z39.48-1984.

Library of Congress Catalog Card Number 84-643008
ISBN 0-8103-9291-7
ISSN 0732-1864
Printed in the United States of America

I(T)P™ Gale Research Inc., an International Thomson Publishing Company.
ITP logo is a trademark under license.

10 9 8 7 6 5 4 3 2 1

Contents

Preface vii

Acknowledgments xi

Preface

Since its inception in 1981, *Nineteenth-Century Literature Criticism* has been a valuable resource for students and librarians seeking critical commentary on writers of this transitional period in world history. Designated an "Outstanding Reference Source" by the American Library Association with the publication of its first volume, *NCLC* has since been purchased by over 6,000 school, public, and university libraries. The series has covered more than 300 authors representing 26 nationalities and over 15,000 titles. No other reference source has surveyed the critical reaction to nineteenth-century authors and literature as thoroughly as *NCLC*.

Scope of the Series

NCLC is designed to introduce students and advanced readers to the authors of the nineteenth century, and to the most significant interpretations of these authors' works. The great poets, novelists, short story writers, playwrights, and philosophers of this period are frequently studied in high school and college literature courses. By organizing and reprinting commentary written on these authors, *NCLC* helps students develop valuable insight into literary history, promotes a better understanding of the texts, and sparks ideas for papers and assignments. Each entry in *NCLC* presents a comprehensive survey of an author's career or an individual work of literature and provides the user with a multiplicity of interpretations and assessments. Such variety allows students to pursue their own interests; furthermore, it fosters an awareness that literature is dynamic and responsive to many different opinions.

Every fourth volume of *NCLC* is devoted to literary topics that cannot be covered under the author approach used in the rest of the series. Such topics include literary movements, prominent themes in nineteenth-century literature, literary reaction to political and historical events, significant eras in literary history, prominent literary anniversaries, and the literatures of cultures that are often overlooked by English-speaking readers.

NCLC continues the survey of criticism of world literature begun by Gale's *Contemporary Literary Criticism (CLC)* and *Twentieth-Century Literary Criticism (TCLC)*, both of which excerpt and reprint commentary on authors of the twentieth century. For additional information about *TCLC, CLC,* and Gale's other criticism series, users should consult the Guide to Gale Literary Criticism Series preceding the title page in this volume.

Coverage

Each volume of *NCLC* is carefully compiled to present:

- criticism of authors, or literary topics, representing a variety of genres and nationalities
- both major and lesser-known writers and literary works of the period
- 7-10 authors or 4-6 topics per volume
- individual entries that survey critical response to an author's work or a topic in literary history, including early criticism to reflect initial reactions, later criticism to represent any rise or decline in reputation, and current retrospective analyses.

Organization

An author entry consists of the following elements: author heading, biographical and critical introduction, list of principal works, excerpts of criticism (each preceded by an annotation and followed by a bibliographic citation), and a bibliography of further reading.

- The **Author Heading** consists of the name under which the author most commonly wrote, followed by birth and death dates. If an author wrote consistently under a pseudonym, the pseudonym will be listed in the author heading and the real name given in parentheses on the first line of the biographical and critical introduction. Also located at the beginning of the introduction to the author entry are any name variations under which an author wrote, including transliterated forms for an author whose language uses a nonroman alphabet.

- The **Biographical and Critical Introduction** outlines the author's life and career, as well as the critical issues surrounding his or her work. References are provided to past volumes of *NCLC* in which further information about the author may be found.

- Most *NCLC* entries include a **Portrait** of the author. Many entries also contain reproductions of materials pertinent to an author's career, including manuscript pages, title pages, dust jackets, letters, and drawings, as well as photographs of important people, places, and events in an author's life.

- The list of **Principal Works** is chronological by date of first publication and identifies the genre of each work. In the case of foreign authors with both foreign-language publications and English translations, the English-language version is given in brackets. Unless otherwise indicated, dramas are dated by first performance, not first publication.

- **Criticism** in each author entry is arranged chronologically to provide a perspective on changes in critical evaluation over the years. All titles of works by the author featured in the entry are printed in boldface type to enable the user to easily locate discussion of particular works. Also for purposes of easier identification, the critic's name and the publication date of the essay are given at the beginning of each piece of criticism. Unsigned criticism is preceded by the title of the journal in which it appeared. Publication information (such as publisher names and book prices) and parenthetical numerical references (such as footnotes or page and line references to specific editions of works) have been deleted at the editors' discretion to provide smoother reading of the text.

- Critical excerpts are prefaced by **Annotations** providing the reader with information about both the critic and the criticism that follows. Included are the critic's reputation, individual approach to literary criticism, and particular expertise in an author's works. Also noted are the relative importance of a work of criticism, the scope of the excerpt, and the growth of critical controversy or changes in critical trends regarding an author. In some cases, these annotations cross-reference excerpts by critics who discuss each other's commentary.

- A complete **Bibliographic Citation** designed to facilitate location of the original essay or book follows each piece of criticism.

- An annotated list of **Further Reading** appearing at the end of each entry suggests secondary sources on the author. In some cases it includes essays for which the editors could not obtain reprint rights.

Cumulative Indexes

- Each volume of *NCLC* contains a cumulative **Author Index** listing all authors who have appeared in Gale's Literary Criticism Series, along with cross-references to such biographical series as *Contemporary Authors* and *Dictionary of Literary Biography*. Useful for locating authors within the various series, this index is particularly valuable for those authors who are identified with a certain period but who, because of their death dates, are placed in another, or for those authors whose careers span two periods. For example, Fyodor Dostoevsky is found in *NCLC*, yet Leo Tolstoy, another major nineteenth-century Russian novelist, is found in *TCLC* because he died after 1899.

- Each *NCLC* volume includes a cumulative **Nationality Index** which lists all authors who have appeared in *NCLC*, arranged alphabetically under their respective nationalities, as well as Topics volume entries devoted to particular national literatures.

- Each new volume in Gale's Literary Criticism Series includes a cumulative **Topic Index**, which lists all literary topics treated in *NCLC*, *TCLC*, *LC 1400-1800*, and the *CLC* Yearbook.

- Each new volume of *NCLC*, with the exception of the Topics volumes, contains a **Title Index** listing the titles of all literary works discussed in the volume. In response to numerous suggestions from librarians, Gale has also produced a **Special Paperbound Edition** of the *NCLC* title index. This annual cumulation lists all titles discussed in the series since its inception and is issued with the first volume of *NCLC* published each year. Additional copies of the index are available on request. Librarians and patrons have welcomed this separate index: it saves shelf space, is easy to use, and is recyclable upon receipt of the following year's cumulation. Titles discussed in the Topics volume entries are not included in the *NCLC* cumulative index.

Citing *Nineteenth-Century Literature Criticism*

When writing papers, students who quote directly from any volume in Gale's Literary Criticism Series may use the following general forms to footnote reprinted criticism. The first example pertains to material drawn from periodicals, the second to material reprinted from books:

[1]T.S. Eliot, "John Donne," *The Nation and Athenaeum*, 33 (9 June 1923), 321-32; excerpted and reprinted in *Literature Criticism from 1400-1800*, Vol. 10, ed. James E. Person, Jr. (Detroit: Gale Research, 1989), pp. 28-9.

[2]Clara G. Stillman, *Samuel Butler: A Mid-Victorian Modern* (Viking Press, 1932); excerpted and reprinted in *Twentieth-Century Literary Criticism*, Vol. 33, ed. Paula Kepos (Detroit: Gale Research, 1989), pp. 43-5.

Suggestions Are Welcome

In response to suggestions, several features have been added to *NCLC* since the series began, including annotations to excerpted criticism, a cumulative index to authors in all Gale literary criticism series, entries devoted to criticism on a single work by a major author, more illustrations, and a title index listing all literary works discussed in the series.

Readers who wish to suggest authors or topics to appear in future volumes, or who have other suggestions, are cordially invited to write the editors.

Acknowledgments

The editors wish to thank the copyright holders of the excerpted criticism included in this volume and the permissions managers of many book and magazine publishing companies for assisting us in securing reprint rights. We are also grateful to the staffs of the Detroit Public Library, the Library of Congress, the University of Detroit Mercy Library, Wayne State University Purdy/Kresge Library Complex, and the University of Michigan Libraries for making their resources available to us. Following is a list of the copyright holders who have granted us permission to reprint material in this volume of *NCLC*. Every effort has been made to trace copyright, but if omissions have been made, please let us know.

COPYRIGHTED EXCERPTS IN *NCLC*, VOLUME 50, WERE REPRINTED FROM THE FOLLOWING PERIODICALS:

American Literature, v. XLIX, May, 1977. Copyright © 1977 Duke University Press, Durham, NC. Reprinted with permission of the publisher.—*The Centennial Review,* v. XXXIV, Fall, 1990 for "'Uncle Tom's Cabin': A Reappraisal" by Stephen J. DeCanio. © 1990 by The Centennial Review. Reprinted by permission of the publisher and the author.—*CLA Journal,* v. XVII, December, 1973. Copyright, 1973 by The College Language Association. Used by permission of The College Language Association.—*The Commonweal,* v. XXXVII, February 5, 1943. Copyright 1943, renewed 1971, Commonweal Publishing Co., Inc. Reprinted by permission of Commonweal Foundation.—*Criticism,* v. 6, Winter, 1964 for "'Hard Times' and F. R. Leavis" by David H. Hirsch. Copyright, 1964, renewed 1992, Wayne State University Press. Reprinted by permission of the publisher and the author.—*Dickens Studies Annual,* v. 18, 1989. Copyright © 1989 by AMS Press, Inc. Reprinted by permission of the publisher.—*The Dickensian,* v. LX, Winter, 1964 for "The Brother-Sister Relationship in 'Hard Times'" by Daniel P. Deneau. Reprinted by permission of the publisher and the author.—*ESQ: A Journal of the American Renaissance,* v. 38, Second Quarter, 1992 for "Failed Mothers and Fallen Houses: The Crisis of Domesticity" by Jennifer L. Jenkins. Reprinted by permission of the publisher and the author.—*History Today,* v. XXVIII, March, 1978. © History Today Limited 1978. Reprinted by permission of the publisher.—*The Indian Journal of English Studies,* v. XIII, 1972. © The Indian Association of English Studies 1972.—*The Monist,* v. 75, July, 1992. Copyright © 1992, The Hegeler Institute, LaSalle, IL 61301. Reprinted by permission of the publisher.—*New Literary History,* v. 23, Spring, 1992. Copyright © 1992 by *New Literary History*. Reprinted by permission of the Johns Hopkins University Press.—*New York Herald Tribune Books,* December 15, 1929. Copyright 1929, renewed 1957, New York Herald Tribune Inc. All rights reserved. Reproduced by permission.—*The New York Times Book Review,* December 1, 1929. Copyright 1929, renewed 1957 by The New York Times Company. Reprinted by permission of the publisher.—*Nineteenth-Century Fiction,* v. 32, June 1977 for "Hard Times: The News and the Novel" by Joseph Butwin. © 1977 by The Regents of the University of California. Reprinted by permission of the Regents and the author.—*Philological Quarterly,* v. 65, Fall, 1986 for "Christina Rossetti and the Poetry of Reticence" by Constance W. Hassett. Copyright 1986 by The University of Iowa. Reprinted by permission of the author.—*PMLA,* v. 84, May, 1969. Copyright © 1969 by the Modern Language Association of America. Reprinted by permission of the Modern Language Association of America.—*Proceedings of the American Philosophical Society,* v. 135, No. 3, September, 1991. Copyright © 1991 by the American Philosophical Society. Reprinted by permission of the publisher.—*Raritan: A Quarterly Review,* Vol. 2, Winter, 1983 for "Romance and Real Estate" by Walter Benn Michaels. Copyright © 1983 by *Raritan: A Quarterly Review*. Reprinted by permission of the author.—*The Review of Politics,* v. 16, July, 1954. Copyright, 1954, renewed 1982 by the University of Notre Dame. Reprinted by permission of the editors of *The Review of Politics* at The University of Notre Dame.—*The Saturday Review,* v. XXXIX, January 28, 1956. © 1956, renewed 1984, S.R. Publications, Ltd. Reprinted by permission of *The Saturday Review*.—*Southern Humanities Review,* v. IX, Summer, 1975. Copyright 1975 by Auburn University. Reprinted by permission of the publisher.—*Studies in the American Renaissance,* 1987, 1992. Copyright © 1987, 1992 Joel Myerson. All rights reserved. Both reprinted by permission of the publisher.—*The Times Literary Supplement,* n. 4316, December 20, 1985. © The Times Supplements Limited 1985. Reproduced from *The Times Literary Supplement* by permission.—*Victorian Poetry,* v. 17, Autumn, 1979 for "Sequence and Meaning in Christina Rossetti's Verses (1893)" by David A. Kent. Reprinted by permission of the author.

COPYRIGHTED EXCERPTS IN *NCLC,* VOLUME 50, WERE REPRINTED FROM THE FOLLOWING BOOKS:

Anna Laetitia Barbauld

1743-1825

English poet, essayist, editor, and children's writer.

INTRODUCTION

An eminent literary figure of the late eighteenth and earlier nineteenth centuries, Barbauld was known and admired by many prominent writers of her time, among them William and Dorothy Wordsworth, Samuel Taylor Coleridge, Frances Burney, Hannah More, and Elizabeth Montagu. After her death she was remembered primarily for her writings for children, but during the last quarter of the twentieth century, literary critics have begun to turn their attention to the essays, poems, and editorial work that helped secure her literary reputation among her contemporaries.

Biographical Information

Born Anna Laetitia Aikin in Leicestershire, Barbauld was the daughter of John Aikin, a Dissenting minister and headmaster of a boys' school, and his wife, Jane Jennings. Educated at home by her father, she studied Latin and Greek as well as modern languages. In 1758, her father took up a teaching position at Warrington Academy for Dissenters. Barbauld lived at Warrington for the next fifteen years, making the acquaintance of such prominent liberal intellectuals as Joseph Priestly, who also taught at the Academy, and Josiah Wedgwood. In 1772 she published several of her poems in a collection of essays by her brother, the physician John Aikin. The first collection of her poetry appeared in 1773; the same year, she and John published a volume of their essays entitled *Miscellaneous Pieces in Prose*. In 1774 she married Rochemont Barbauld, a clergyman educated at Warrington, and soon thereafter they adopted one of her nephews. Their marriage appears to have been one of considerable mutual affection and esteem, overshadowed in later years by Rochemont's increasing mental instability. Together they opened a successful academy for boys in Sussex, where Barbauld taught language and science to the younger students. While continuing to write and publish poetry, she also published several immensely popular volumes of lessons and prose pieces for young children. In 1785, citing ill health, the Barbaulds closed the school; the following year, they settled in Hempstead, where Rochemont headed a small congregation. A number of Barbauld's political essays and poems were written here; she also undertook an increasing amount of editorial and critical work. In 1802 the Barbaulds moved to Stoke Newington, where Anna Laetitia's brother also lived. Rochemont's mental condition continued to worsen, and on several occasions he tried to attack his wife. In 1808 he drowned, an apparent suicide. Barbauld continued to write

until her death, though she published little after the first decade of the nineteenth century. She died in Stoke Newington in 1825.

Major Works

Barbauld's poetry represents a wide variety of subjects and modes, including odes, satires, riddles, and hymns. Many of her poems draw their subjects and themes from the everyday matters of domestic life; these include "To Mr. Barbauld" (1778), a celebration of love and friendship in marriage; the mock-heroic "Washing Day" (1797); and "Life," a later poem that meditates on life, old age, and encroaching death. She also wrote on political subjects, often emphasizing the importance of personal and political freedom. Her early poem "Corsica" (1769) praises the spirit of Corsican nationalists in their long and ultimately unsuccessful battle for independence from France. The long poem *Epistle to William Wilberforce* (1791) expresses her firmly abolitionist stance, while *Eighteen Hundred and Eleven* (1812) predicts the decline of Great

Britain as a world power. Her liberal political convictions were also expressed in a number of widely read pamphlets. In 1790 she published *An Address to the Opposers of the Repeal of the Corporation and Test Acts,* a spirited attack on Parliament's refusal to revoke laws that limited the rights of citizens who were not members of the Established Church. *Sins of Government, Sins of the Nation* (1793), written in opposition to Britain's war with France, affirmed the duty of citizens to resist immoral acts by their government. Of her several collections of prose pieces for children, the most enduring was *Hymns in Prose for Children* (1781), which remained popular into the early years of the twentieth century. Sentimental, didactic, but elegantly wrought, her works for children set a new standard of writing for young readers. In the final twenty-five years of her life, much of her work was editorial in nature. She is particularly noted for editing Samuel Richardson's correspondence (1804) and a fifty-volume set of novels by British authors entitled *The British Novelists* (1810). Her introduction to the set and her essays on individual authors represent significant early literary and historical criticism of the novel.

Critical Reception

Barbauld's writing, particularly her poetry, was greatly admired by her contemporaries, and she was acknowledged throughout her lifetime as one of the leading intellectuals of her era. Yet by the late nineteenth century, she had come to be viewed as something of a footnote in literary history whose only lasting contribution was in the area of children's literature. Modern critics generally ascribe this rapid decline in her literary reputation to late nineteenth and early twentieth century prejudices against the poetry of the eighteenth century and against female authors. Critical interest in Barbauld began to revive in the 1970s, when scholars Paul Zall, Samuel Pickering, and Porter Williams suggested that many of the themes and images of the Romantic poets William Wordsworth and William Blake reflect their familiarity with Barbauld's writings for children. Since the mid-1980s, growing interest in writing by women has supported renewed attention to the larger canon of Barbauld's work. Ann Messenger and Marlon Ross have investigated relationships between gender and writing in her poetry, while Catherine E. Moore and Katharine M. Rogers have examined her contributions to the history and theory of the novel. The first modern edition of Barbauld's poems appeared in 1994.

PRINCIPAL WORKS

Poems [as Anna Laetitia Aiken] (poetry) 1773
Miscellaneous Pieces in Prose [as Anna Laetitia Aiken, with John Aiken] (essays) 1773
Lessons for Children. 4 vols. (essays) 1778-79
Hymns in Prose for Children (essays) 1781
An Address to the Opposers of the Repeal of the Corporation and Test Acts (pamphlet) 1790
Epistle to William Wilberforce, Esq., on the Rejection of the Bill for Abolishing the Slave Trade (poem) 1791

Sins of Government, Sins of the Nation (pamphlet) 1793
The Correspondence of Samuel Richardson. 6 vols. [editor] (letters) 1804
The British Novelists. 50 vols. [editor] (novels) 1810
Eighteen Hundred and Eleven (poem) 1812
The Works of Anna Laetitia Barbauld. 2 vols. (essays and poetry) 1825
The Poems of Anna Letitia Barbauld (poetry) 1994

CRITICISM

The Nation, **New York (essay date 1874)**

SOURCE: "Mrs. Barbauld," in *The Nation,* New York, Vol. XVIII, No. 456, March 26, 1874, pp. 206-07.

[*In the following excerpt, the writer summarizes Barbauld's contributions to English literature.*]

We fear that not many of our readers will have very distinct ideas suggested to their minds by the name of the excellent woman whose memory Mrs. Ellis has revived in the two handsome volumes noted below [*The Life and Works of Anna Laetitia Barbauld,* 1874]. Devout churchgoers may have noticed her name in their hymn-books as the author of some of the finest religious lyrics which they contain; and such of them as shall have passed the "mezzo del cammin" of life may rejoice that they encountered, at the outset of their pilgrimage, so gentle and wise a friend as she with her *Early Lessons* and with her contributions to her brother Dr. Aiken's excellent *Evenings at Home.* But of the younger generation, whose early days have fallen on times when the writing of children's books has become a trade instead of a religion, on whose infancy the flood-gates of trash have been opened, overwhelming it with slang, vulgarisms, and bad grammar, but few, we imagine, have much knowledge of her or of her works. It is observable that the best books for children, after the discovery of that lilliputian public, were the earliest, judged by the true test of their being good reading for grown people. Not counting *Robinson Crusoe,* which was meant for children of all growths and all ages, *Sandford and Merton* came first, the *Evenings at Home* next, and Miss Edgeworth's books afterwards. The stories for children of a later date, whether mawkishly "goody" or mischievously sensational, are a fit preparation for the reading furnished for their elders by the Braddon and Ouida crew. Dr. Johnson, who had a great contempt for children's books, is recorded by Dr. Burney as having declared that Mrs. Barbauld, as a suitable punishment for the *Early Lessons,* should be "sent to the Congress." Mrs. Barbauld would not have objected to this penalty, as she speaks in the highest terms of admiration of the Congress as it was then. Perhaps it were not an excessive castigation for the writers of later children's books to send them to the Congress as it is now. . . .

She was one of those fortunate writers who have their

good things in this life—an excellent time to have them—and she was better known and her writings more highly esteemed in her lifetime than since her death. They brought her more or less in contact with many eminent contemporaries, men and women. Her literary reputation brought her into occasional intercourse with Scott, Rogers, Horace Walpole, Sir James Mackintosh, Madame D'Arblay, Hannah More, Mrs. Montagu, the Edgeworths, Dr. Priestley, Joanna Bailey, Charles Lamb, and many other celebrities. . . . [Her letters] are extremely good reading, and very illustrative of her character. That her writings will occupy a very high place among the authors of her time is more than can be reasonably hoped for. Her voice is "lost among the throng of louder minstrels in these latter days." Her hymns, however, will keep her name fresh as long as sacred music is a part of divine worship, especially when a better morality shall have restored them from the mutilations of the villanous compilers of hymnbooks—wretches whose crimes should bring them within the penalties of the statute of cutting and maiming. These lyrics show that she possessed the spirit of genuine poetry, though it sometimes insensibly slipped into prose as it took form and pressure. Her fine poem of **"Life"** certainly bears the unmistakable impress of poetic genius, than the concluding stanza of which Rogers records that he "knew few lines finer"; which Wordsworth "wished he had written"; and which Madame D'Arblay repeated to herself every night before going to sleep:

> Life! we've been long together,
> Through pleasant and through cloudy weather;
> 'Tis hard to part when friends are dear;
> Perhaps 'twill cost a sigh, a tear;
> Then steal away, give little warning,
>   Choose thine own time;
> Say not Good Night—but in some brighter clime
> Bid me Good-Morning."

Anne I. Ritchie (essay date 1881)

SOURCE: "Mrs. Barbauld," in *Littell's Living Age,* Vol. XXXVI, No. 1955, December 10, 1881, pp. 579-93.

[*In the following excerpt, Ritchie discusses Barbauld's political convictions and reviews several of her poems and essays.*]

"The first poetess I can recollect is Mrs. Barbauld, with whose works I became acquainted—before those of any other author, male or female—when I was learning to spell words of one syllable in her story-books for children." So says Hazlitt in his lectures on living poets. He goes on to call her a very pretty poetess, strewing flowers of poesy as she goes.

The writer of this little notice must needs, from the same point of view as Hazlitt, look upon Mrs. Barbauld with a special interest, having also first learnt to read out of her little yellow books, of which the syllables rise up one by one again with a remembrance of the hand patiently pointing to each in turn. . . .

It is noteworthy that few of Mrs. Barbauld's earlier productions equalled what she wrote at the very end of her life. She seems to have been one of those who ripen with age, growing wider in spirit with increasing years. Perhaps, too, she may have been influenced by the change of manners, the reaction against formalism, which was growing up as her own days were ending. Prim she may have been in manner, but she was not a formalist by nature; and even at eighty was ready to learn to submit to accept the new gospel that Wordsworth and his disciples had given to the world, and to shake off the stiffness of early training.

It is idle to speculate on what might have been if things had happened otherwise; if the daily stress of anxiety and perplexity which haunted her home had been removed—difficulties and anxieties which may well have absorbed all the spare energy and interest that under happier circumstances might have added to the treasury of English literature. But if it were only for one ode written when the distracting cares of over seventy years were ending, when nothing remained to her but the essence of a long past, and the inspiration of a still glowing, still hopeful and most tender spirit, if it were only for the ode called **"Life,"** which has brought a sense of ease and comfort to so many, Mrs. Barbauld has indeed deserved well of her country-people and should be held in remembrance by them.

Her literary works are, after all, not very voluminous. She is best known by her hymns for children and her early lessons, than which nothing more childlike has ever been devised; and we can agree with her brother, Dr. Aikin, when he says that it requires true genius to enter so completely into a child's mind.

After their first volume of verse, the brother and sister had published a second, in prose, called *Miscellaneous Pieces,* about which there is an amusing little anecdote in Rogers's "Memoirs." Fox met Dr. Aikin at dinner.

> 'I am greatly pleased with your *Miscellaneous Pieces,* said Fox. Aikin bowed. 'I particularly admire,' continued Fox, 'your essay **"Against Inconsistency in our Expectations."**'
>
> 'That,' replied Aikin, 'is my sister's.'
>
> 'I like much,' returned Fox, 'your essay **"On Monastic Institutions."**'
>
> 'That,' answered Aikin, 'is also my sister's.'
>
> Fox thought it best to say no more about the book.

These essays were followed by various of the visions and Eastern pieces then so much in vogue; also by political verses and pamphlets, which seemed to have made a great sensation at the time. But Mrs. Barbauld's turn was on the whole more for domestic than for literary life, although literary people always seem to have had a great interest for her. . . .

Mrs. Barbauld was a Liberal in feeling and conviction; she was never afraid to speak her mind, and when the French Revolution first began, she, in common with many others, hoped that it was but the dawning of happier times. She was always keen about public events; she wrote an address on the opposition to the repeal of the Test Act in 1791, and she published her poem to Wilberforce on the rejection of his great bill for abolishing slavery:—

> Friends of the friendless, hail, ye generous
> band,

she cries in warm enthusiasm for his devoted cause.

Horace Walpole nicknamed her Deborah, called her the virago Barbauld, and speaks of her with utter rudeness and intolerant spite. But whether or not Horace Walpole approved, it is certain that Mrs. Barbauld possessed to a full and generous degree a quality which is now less common than it was in her day. . . .

It is possible that philanthropy, and the love of the beautiful, and the gratuitous diffusion of wall-papers may be the modern rendering of the good old-fashioned sentiment. Mrs. Barbauld lived in very stirring days, when private people shared in the excitements and catastrophes of public affairs. To her the fortunes of England, its loyalty, its success, were a part of her daily bread. By her early associations she belonged to a party representing opposition, and for that very reason she was the more keenly struck by the differences of the conduct of affairs and the opinions of those she trusted. Her friend Dr. Priestley had emigrated to America for his convictions' sake; Howard was giving his noble life for his work; Wakefield had gone to prison. Now the very questions are forgotten for which they struggled and suffered, or the answers have come while the questions are forgotten, in this future which is our present, and to which some unborn historian may point with a moral finger.

Dr. Aikin, whose estimate of his sister was very different from Horace Walpole's, occasionally reproached her for not writing more constantly. He wrote a copy of verses on this theme:—

> Thus speaks the Muse, and bends her brows
> severe:
> Did I, Lœtitia, lend my choicest lays,
> And crown thy youthful head with freshest
> bays,
> That all the expectance of thy full grown year,
> Should lie inert and fruitless? O revere
> Those sacred gifts whose meed is deathless
> praise,
> Whose potent charm the enraptured soul can
> raise
> Far from the vapors of this earthly sphere,
> Seize, seize the lyre, resume the lofty strain.

She seems to have willingly left the lyre for Dr. Aikin's use. A few hymns, some graceful odes, and stanzas, and *jeux d'esprit,* a certain number of well-written and orig-inal essays, and several political pamphlets, represent the best of her work. Her more ambitious poems are those by which she is the least remembered. It was at Hampstead that Mrs. Barbauld wrote her contributions to her brother's volume of *Evenings at Home,* among which the transmigrations of Indur may be quoted as a model of style and delightful matter. One of the best of her *jeux d'esprit* is **"The Groans of the Tankard,"** which was written in early days, with much spirit and real humor. It begins with a Virgil-like incantation, and goes on:—

> 'Twas at the solemn, silent noontide hour
> When hunger rages with despotic power,
> When the lean student quits his Hebrew roots
> For the gross nourishment of English fruits,
> And throws unfinished airy systems by
> For solid pudding and substantial pie.

The tankard now,

> replenished to the brink,
> With the cool beverage blue-eyed maidens
> drink,

but accustomed to very different libations, is endowed with voice and utters its bitter reproaches:—

> Unblest the day, and luckless was the hour
> Which doomed me to a Presbyterian's power,
> Fated to serve a Puritanic race,
> Whose slender meal is shorter than their
> grace.

Thumbkin, of fairy celebrity, used to mark his way by flinging crumbs of bread and scattering stones as he went along; and in like manner authors trace the course of their life's peregrinations by the pamphlets and articles they cast down as they go. Sometimes they throw stones, sometimes they throw bread. In '92 and '93 Mrs. Barbauld must have been occupied with party polemics and with the political miseries of the time. A pamphlet on Gilbert Wakefield's views, and another on *Sins of the Government and Sins of the People,* show in what direction her thoughts were bent. Then came a period of comparative calm again and of literary work and interest. She seems to have turned to Akenside and Collins, and each had an essay to himself. These were followed by certain selections from *The Spectator, Tatler,* etc., preceded by one of those admirable essays for which she is really remarkable. She also published a memoir of Richardson prefixed to his correspondence. Sir James Mackintosh, writing at a later and sadder time of her life, says of her observations on the moral of Clarissa that they are as fine a piece of mitigated and rational stoicism as our language can boast of. . . .

It was during the first years of her widowhood that she published her edition of the British novelists in some fifty volumes. There is an opening chapter to this edition upon novels and novel-writing, which is an admirable and most interesting essay upon fiction, beginning from the very earliest times.

In 1811 she wrote her poem on the king's illness, and also the longer poem which provoked such indignant comments at the time. It describes Britain's rise and luxury, warns her of the dangers of her unbounded ambition and unjustifiable wars:—

> Arts, arms, and wealth destroy the fruits they
>   bring;
> Commerce, like beauty, knows no second
>   spring.

Her ingenuous youth from Ontario's shore who visits the ruins of London is one of the many claimants to the honor of having suggested Lord Macaulay's celebrated New-Zealander:—

> Pensive and thoughtful shall the wanderers
>   greet
> Each splendid square and still untrodden
>   street,
> Or of some crumbling turret, mined by time,
> The broken stairs with perilous step shall
>   climb,
> Thence stretch their view the wide horizon
>   round,
> By scattered hamlets trace its ancient bound,
> And, choked no more with fleets, fair Thames
>   survey
> Through reeds and sedge pursue his idle way.

It is impossible not to admire the poem, though it is stilted and not to the present taste. The description of Britain as it now is and as it once was is very ingenious:—

> Where once Bouduca whirled the scythed car,
> And the fierce matrons raised the shriek of
>   war,
> Light forms beneath transparent muslin float,
> And tutor'd voices swell the artful note;
> Light-leaved acacias, and the shady plane,
> And spreading cedars grace the woodland
>   reign.

The poem is forgotten now, though it was scouted at the time and violently attacked, Southey himself falling upon the poor old lady, and devouring her, spectacles and all. She felt these attacks very much, and could not be consoled, though Miss Edgeworth wrote a warm-hearted letter of indignant sympathy. But Mrs. Barbauld had something in her too genuine to be crushed, even by sarcastic criticism. She published no more, but it was after her poem of *1811* that she wrote the beautiful ode by which she is best known and best remembered,—the ode that Wordsworth used to repeat and say he envied, that Tennyson has called "sweet verses," of which the lines ring their tender, hopeful chime like sweet church bells on a summer evening.

Madame d'Arblay, in her old age, told Crabb Robinson that every night she said them over to herself as she went to her rest. To the writer they are almost sacred. The hand that patiently pointed out to her, one by one,

the syllables of Mrs. Barbauld's hymns for children, that tended our childhood, as it had tended our father's, marked these verses one night, when it blessed us for the last time.

> Life, we've been long together,
> Through pleasant and through cloudy weather:
> 'Tis hard to part when friends are dear;
> Perhaps 'twill cost a sigh, a tear;
> Then steal away, give little warning,
> Choose thine own time.
> Say not good-night, but in some brighter clime,
> Bid me good-morning,

Mrs. Barbauld was over seventy when she wrote this ode. A poem, called **"Octogenary Reflections,"** is also very touching:—

> Say ye, who through this round of eighty years
> Have proved its joys and sorrows, hopes and
>   fears;
> Say what is life, ye veterans who have trod,
> Step following steps, its flowery thorny road?
> Enough of good to kindle strong desire;
> Enough of ill to damp the rising fire;
> Enough of love and fancy, joy and hope,
> To fan desire and give the passions scope;
> Enough of disappointment, sorrow, pain,
> To seal the wise man's sentence—"All is
>   vain."

There is another fragment of hers in which she likens herself to a schoolboy left of all the train, who hears no sound of wheels to bear him to his father's bosom home. "Thus I look to the hour when I shall follow those that are at rest before me." . . .

Sam Pickering (essay date 1975)

SOURCE: "Mrs. Barbauld's *Hymns in Prose:* 'An Air-Blown Particle' of Romanticism?" in *Southern Humanities Review,* Vol. IX, No. 3, Summer, 1975, pp. 259-68.

[*In the following excerpt, Pickering examines Barbauld's place in the history of children's literature and suggests that her writings influenced the development of English Romanticism.*]

Pinpointing the origins of the Romantic Movement is like tracing the evolution of man. New and embarrassing ancestors will forever turn up in isolated rifts in Kenya or in the backwaters of eighteenth-century journals. Wordsworth and Coleridge did not leap full grown from the forehead of Calliope, but were instead the poetic product of a long line of cultural ancestors. In this essay I want to make the case for eighteenth-century children's literature being among the progenitors of English Romanticism. Although many people wrote children's literature after 1780, I intend to focus on Anna Letitia Barbauld, whom Henry Crabb Robinson, the indefatigable diarist, compared to the angel Gabriel.

In 1802 Wordsworth wrote that the child was the father of the man. If this poetic description of human nature is accurate, then Mrs. Barbauld's influence upon nineteenth-century thought was incalculable. In 1781, Mrs. Barbauld published her *Hymns in Prose for Children*. Written for children aged 3 to 5, the *Hymns* were designed

> to impress devotional feelings as early as possible on the infant mind . . . to impress them by connecting religion with a variety of sensible objects, with all that he [a child] sees, all that he hears, all that affects his young mind with wonder or delight; and thus by deep, strong, and permanent associations, to lay the best foundation for practical devotion in future life.

The Hymns were a phenomenal success. In 1877 Mrs. Barbauld's biographer [Jerome March] wrote enthusiastically,

> where in the long catalogue of children's books, shall we find any to be compared with them? Many who heard them the first time at their mother's knee can trace to them their deepest, most precious convictions. A century has now passed since they were written; they have been largely used by all classes from the palace to the cottage, and still what a freshness and beauty in every page!

Even after allowance has been made for biographical afflatus, this was a remarkable tribute. Moreover it was repeated throughout the century. Not only were the *Hymns* translated into French, German, Italian, Spanish, and Hungarian, but they were construed into Latin hexameters. At Mrs. Barbauld's death in 1825, the *Christian Reformer* wrote that the *Hymns* were "beyond all praise" and accused the parent who did "not familiarize his children to these exquisite effusions of pious taste" of being "deficient in the first of duties."

During Mrs. Barbauld's lifetime, individuals were hardly less restrained than eulogists at her death. In "On the Living Poets," William Hazlitt reminisced that the "first poetess" he could recollect was Mrs. Barbauld. Recalling that she strewed "the flowers of poetry most agreeably round the borders of religious controversy," Hazlitt wrote nostalgically "I wish I could repay my childish debt of gratitude in terms of appropriate praise." In 1797 Coleridge called her "that great and excellent woman." On publication of the *Lyrical Ballads,* he instructed Thomas Longman to send complimentary copies to five people, one of whom was Mrs. Barbauld. According to Crabb Robinson, Wordsworth, who disapproved of Mrs. Barbauld's later political poetry, still thought her "the first of our literary women."

Not all judgments of Mrs. Barbauld's *Hymns* were favorable, but even those that were adverse underlined her influence. In describing his unhappy childhood, Ernest Pontifex remembered angrily that he had to learn Mrs. Barbauld's *Hymns* by heart. Charles Lamb objected to the *Hymns'* didacticism. He believed that fancy was the raw material from which literature was made and that

children would be better off imaginatively if they read "old wives tales." In 1802 he wrote Coleridge in exasperation, saying "Mrs. Barbauld's stuff has banished all the old classics out of the nursery, and the shopman at Newbery's hardly deigned to reach them off an unexplored corner of a shelf, when Mary [his sister] asked for them . . . Damn them!—I mean the cursed Barbauld Crew, those Blights and Beasts of what is human in man and child."

Thinking Mrs. Barbauld's works represented eighteenth-century rationalism, Lamb made an ill-founded criticism. With justice it could have been applied to some of Mrs. Barbauld's imitators, in particular Mrs. Trimmer, but not to Mrs. Barbauld herself, whose works freed rather than confined the imagination. For our purposes though, Lamb's statement that Mrs. Barbauld's works had filled the bookstore and had banished the "old classics out of the nursery" is important. In 1802 the *Guardian of Education* recounted the history of children's books in England. Before the reign of Queen Anne, the *Guardian* wrote, there were few children's books. During and after Queen Anne's reign, "the first period of Infantine and Juvenile Literature" began. During this time, Mother Goose's Fairy Tales, Esop's and Gay's Fables, and The Little Female Academy by Mrs. Fielding ("the learned translator of Xenophon") were prominent. "In general of a very harmless nature," these books "were most calculated to entertain the imagination, rather than improve the heart or cultivate the imagination." With Mrs. Barbauld's "introducing a species of writing, in the style of familiar conversation, which is certainly much better adapted to the capacities of young children than any that preceded it," the modern period of religious literature for children began. "The useful hints given by Mrs. Barbauld," the journal continued, were "generally adopted by her contemporaries, and many books have been supplied to the nursery by means of which children at an early age have acquired the rudiments of useful science, and even the first principles of Christianity with delight to themselves, and ease to their instructors." In banishing the fairy tales and establishing the general pattern of most English children's literature for at least forty years, Mrs. Barbauld was a moral Johnny-on-the-spot. Fortuitously her *Hymns* embodied the growing moral didacticism that later inspired widely-read writers like Legh Richmond and Hannah More.

In the preface to the *Hymns,* Mrs. Barbauld said that there were few books calculated to assist children in the devotional part of religion except Dr. Watts's verses. Although these were "in pretty general use," it was doubtful, Mrs. Barbauld argued, "whether poetry ought to be lowered to the capacities of children, or whether they should not rather be kept from reading verse, till they are able to relish good verse" (iii-iv). Behind Mrs. Barbauld's preface were the realizations that Watts's verses were pretty poor stuff and that poetic expression was beyond young children's understanding. However in evoking Watts, Mrs. Barbauld meant not only to be critical but also to establish herself as Watts's successor. First published in 1715, Watts's *Divine Songs Attempted in Easy*

Language for the Use of Children had been extremely popular in religious families. At the conclusion of the *Songs,* Watts included "a slight specimen of moral songs, such as I wish some happy and condescending Genius would undertake for the use of Children." "The Sense and Subjects," Watts urged, "might be borrowed plentifully from the *Proverbs of Solomon,* from all the common appearances of Nature, from all the occurrences in Civil Life, both in the City and Country, (which would also afford matter for other divine Songs). Here the Language and Measures should be easy and flowing, and without the Solemnities of Religion, or the sacred Names of God and Holy Things; that children might find Delight and Profit together."

After the publication of the *Hymns,* Mrs. Barbauld was recognized as Watts's "condescending genius." Written in "measured prose" instead of verse, her *Hymns* borrowed their subjects and sense from the common appearances of nature and were "nearly as agreeable to the ear as a more regular rhythmus." Moreover they conveyed Watts's delightful and profitable faith without confusing children with thorny doctrine or terrifying accounts of the wages of sin.

The *Hymns* were popular not only because of their literary merits but also because they embodied the moral concerns of the age. With the sermons of John Scott, Isaac Barrow, and John Tillotson serving as texts, the Church of England drifted towards latitudinarianism throughout the late seventeenth and early and mid eighteenth centuries. Charity replaced Christ, and good works rather than correct doctrine became the hallmark of the true Christian. For Scott personal benevolism was the Christian ideal. Christianity taught us, he wrote,

> to be benign and bountiful to the necessitous and distressed, and to endeavour according to our ability to allay their sorrows, remove their oppressions, support them under the calamities, and counsel them in their doubts, to be ready to every good work, and like the Fields of Spices to be scattering our Perfumes through all the Neighbourhood."

As latitudinarianism dominated the theology of the Established Church, so it pervaded literary criticism. Toward the end of the century, ethical criticism often led to a willing suspension of literary judgment. Journals such as the *Critical Review* wrote typically, "The author wishes to inculcate filial piety; and she has executed her design in a number of well-chosen pathetic tales.—In such a cause, Criticism smooths his brow and takes off his spectacles, willing to see no fault. She who would support the cause of piety and virtue cannot err." Supporting the cause of piety and virtue, Mrs. Barbauld's *Hymns* taught broad-church morality. Recognizing this, the two leading journals of the period, the *Monthly* and *Critical* reviews received the *Hymns* favorably, stating that Mrs. Barbauld gave young people "a proper idea of the Creator and his works."

A Unitarian at a time when Unitarians were respected rather than condemned, Mrs. Barbauld did not stress particular doctrines such as the atonement or the Trinity. This so broadened her appeal that even Calvinists conscientiously taught the *Hymns* to their children. When Hannah More and the Anglican evangelicals at Clapham began publishing their *Cheap Repository Tracts* for readers in "the lower and middling classes," the Calvinistic *Evangelical Magazine* advised them to imitate Mrs. Barbauld and avoid controversial political and theological doctrine.

The appearance of the *Hymns* in 1781 coincided with what J. R. Green in his *History of the English People* called "the beginnings of popular education." Although there had been previous fumblings forward, the Sunday School Movement made little headway until Robert Raikes began his school in Gloucester in 1780. In 1785 the Sunday School Society was founded; by 1792, it was estimated that there were five hundred thousand "Sunday Scholars." The phenomenal spread of Sunday Schools resulted, for the most part, from three factors: evangelical stress on man's responsibility for man, latitudinarian emphasis on personal benevolism, and the belief that a religious education would make society more stable. In the 1790's, Sunday Schools provided the only national system of education. After the Bell-Lancaster dispute in the first decade of the nineteenth century, other plans were adopted. But even so late as 1818 a parliamentary survey showed that 452,817 English children were being educated in Sunday Schools. This figure becomes significant for our purposes when we realize that Mrs. Barbauld's *Hymns* was one of the first works adopted as reading matter by Sunday Schools of all theological hues. Later, Lancaster used her books in his schools. Furthermore, with her *Easy Lessons for Children,* the *Hymns* established, in Fanny Burney's words, the "new walk" for children's literature, along which countless writers followed. For example, the *Easy Lessons* led Mrs. Trimmer to write *Easy Introduction to the Knowledge of Nature,* [1792] designed "to open the minds of children to a variety of information, to induce them to make observations on the works of nature, and to lead them up to the Universal Parent, the Creator of this world and all things in it."

Late eighteenth- and early nineteenth-century Englishmen believed that youthful reading made the man. Perhaps Dr. Johnson's friend, Anna Seward, known in poetry circles as the Swan of Lichfield, put it best, "it cannot be doubted that the understanding, and virtue, the safety, and happiness of those branches of Society which are raised above the necessity of mechanic toil depend much upon the early impressions they receive from books which captivate the imagination and interest of the heart." Today we are not so sure how influential childhood reading is in shaping adults, and, consequently, the influence of Mrs. Barbauld's works upon later writers must always remain in the hazy world of the history of ideas. Nevertheless, Mrs. Barbauld's poetics were Romantic. According to Henry James, the artistic sensibility is "a kind of huge spider-web of the finest silken threads suspended in the chamber of consciousness, and catching every air-blown particle in its tissue." In turn these particles were often converted into art. Certainly the *Hymns'* popularioty testified to the wind they stirred, and particles were blown into the nineteenth century. To say, however, that Mrs. Barbauld directly influenced Romantic poetry would be going too far. If, though, the artist does convert "the very pulses of the air into revelations," she may have had an indirect influence upon the Romantics. With the realization that I can reach no final conclusions, but can only furnish speculative matter for future thought, I want to examine some of the similarities between Mrs. Barbauld's poetry and that of Wordsworth, who read and admired her writings.

According to Pater, "the sense of a life in natural objects," which was rhetorical artifice in most poetry, was almost a "literal fact" for Wordsworth. "To him," Pater wrote [in *Appreciations,* 1911], "every natural object seemed to possess . . . a moral or spiritual life, to be capable of a companionship with man, full of expression, of inexplicable affinities and delicacies of intercourse." Wordsworth believed a spirit rolled through all thinking things and all objects of all thought. This spirit acted upon "certain inherent and indestructible qualities of the human mind," liberating it from the "degraded thirst after outrageous stimulation." Nature, as Emerson put it, conspired with the spirit to emancipate man from the long littleness of life. Lucy achieved immoratality when she became one with rocks and stones and tress, and her lover achieved a transcendent spiritual union when he took nature for the guardian of his heart and half-created the world about him. Wordsworth was not, of course, merely a sentimental naturalist. It was through nature, Pater wrote, that he approached the spectacle of human life and came to understand the burthen of the mystery. Mrs. Barbauld also resembles Wordsworth in her belief that natural objects possessed a moral or spiritual life which enabled them to emancipate man. For her, "every field" was "like an open book." "Every painted flower" had "a lesson written on its leaves," and "every murmuring brook" had "a tongue" (75). The universe was the living visible garment of God as nature taught man "to see the Creator in the visible appearance of all around him." Although Wordsworth's "Intelligence which governs all," was more complex than Mrs. Barbauld's God, the moral presences of both poets were cut from the same latitudinarian cloth and rarely descended to the doctrinaire.

Wordsworth and Mrs. Barbauld were poets of democracy and celebrated the degnity of the common man. Wordsworth's famous preface of 1800 championed democracy in poetry. The true poet was not a poetaster, appealing to an educated elite; neither was he an inspired prophet with his eye in a fine frenzy rolling. Instead, he was "a man speaking to men" in the "language really used by men." Poetry itself was "the spontaneous overflow of powerful feelings," not a frozen pastiche of "gaudiness and inane phraseology," which only the few could understand. In revolt, like Wordsworth, against poetic diction and eighteenth-century rationalism, Mrs. Barbauld used the language of a man speaking simply. Indeed, her simplicity fitted Wordsworth's definition of poetry better than his own verse. In **"Hymn II,"** Mrs. Barbauld wrote disarmingly,

Come let us go forth into the fields, let us see how the flowers spring, let us listen to the warbling of the birds, and sport ourselves upon the new grass. The winter is over and gone, the buds come out upon the trees, the crimson blossoms of the peach and the nectarine are seen, and the green leaves sprout. The hedges are bordered with tufts of primroses, and yellow cowslips that hang down their heads; and the blue violet lies hid beneath the shade . . . The butterflies flutter from bush to bush, and open their wings to the warm sun. The young animals of every kind are sporting about, they feel themselves happy, they are glad to be alive,—they thank him that has made them alive. They may thank him in their hearts, but we can thank him with our tongues; we are better than they, and can praise him better.

The simplicity of Mrs. Barbauld's poetic prose made the *Hymns* available to all children learning to read.

Her democracy, however, was not limited to language. Her poetic world was organic rather than atomistic, for, like Wordsworth, she believed that a spirit was "deeply interfused" through all things. As a result, the brotherhood of man was not a New Testament ideal but philosophic reality. Nature taught that all men from the "Negro woman . . . pining in captivity" to the "monarch ruling an hundred states" (60-61) were members of "God's family" (59). Trying to awaken children's sensibilities through lush descriptions, she attempted to enlarge their capacities for sympathy and love. Once children loved "all things because they are the creatures of God" (51), then "incidents and situations from common life" (Cumberland beggars, old leech gatherers, and idiot boys) could become worthy of serious thought.

Growth was the most prevalent theme in Wordsworth's and Mrs. Barbauld's poetry. For both, the child was the father of the man. As the subtitle of *The Prelude* was "Growth of a Poet's Mind" so the *Hymns in Prose* could have easily been subtitled "Growth of a Child's Mind." Wordsworth and Mrs. Barbauld believed that the mind developed through sense experience and reflection, Locke's sources of empirical knowledge. As she stated in the preface to the *Hymns,* by connecting religion with "sensible objects," Mrs. Barbauld hoped to control the "fair seed-time" of a child's soul. Accepting Locke's associationist view of behavior, she wanted "to lay the best foundation for practical devotion in future life." As important as empirical knowledge was, however, Wordsworth and Mrs. Barbauld also believed that intuition could play a major part in the learning process. For Wordsworth, one impulse could, but not necessarily would, invigorate "the discriminating powers of the mind." The ways of the worldly world, he wrote in the "Preface" of 1800, reduced men's minds to "almost savage torpor." The epiphanic moment could contribute to mental growth by moving vision beyond the actual object perceived to an object half-created by the imagination. Although Mrs. Barbauld wanted the epiphanic moment to lead to religious rather than imaginative perception, her emphasis upon the importance of impulse was similar to that of Wordsworth.

In so stressing impulse, she implicitly criticized eighteenth-century rationalism. Although their approaches were different, both poets thought imagination crucial to a child's growth. Book V of *The Prelude,* for example, celebrated the importance in childhood of "the open ground of Fancy." More pietistic and more openly critical of reason, the sixth "Hymn" was Mrs. Barbauld's Book V. In a catechistic section, she taught the importance of impulse and urged child readers to half-create the world about them. What Wordsworth later criticized as the "model child" was Mrs. Barbauld's "child of reason." She began the catechism by asking the child of reason where he had been and what he had seen. Lacking a creative imagination, the child replied that he had been in the meadow, looking at cattle and wheat. "Didst thou see nothing more?" she retorted.

> Didst thou observe nothing beside? Return again, child of reason, for there are greater things than these.—God was among the fields; and didst thou not perceive him? His beauty was upon the meadows; his smile enlivened the sun-shine. I have walked through the thick forest; the wind whispered among the trees; the brook fell from the rocks with a pleasant murmur; the squirrel leapt from bough to bough; and the birds sung to each other amongst the branches. Didst thou hear nothing, but the murmur of the brook? no whispers, but the whispers of the wind? Return again, child of reason, for there are greater things than these.—God was amongst the trees; his voice sounded in the murmur of the water; his music warbled in the shade; and didst thou not attend?

Mrs. Barbauld was not, as Arnold labelled Wordsworth, "one of the very chief glories of English Poetry." Preciously sentimental and didactically heavy-handed, her poetic prose has been neglected by contemporary criticism. Put into historical perspective, however, it becomes more interesting. "In the great poets," James Russell Lowell wrote, "there is an exquisite sensibility both of soul and sense that sympathizes like gossamer sea-moss with every movement of the element in which it floats." Mrs. Barbauld helped create the element in which the Romantic poets eventually floated. In 1803, a writer in the *Guardian of Education* said he had frequently heard the **Hymns** "recited by young children with such intelligence of countenance, and emphasis of delivery, as evidently proved that the sentiments of the writer were transfused into the minds of the little speakers." We can never know to what extent this "transfusion" contributed to the life-blood of Romantic poetry. There were similarities, as I have tried to point out, between Wordsworth's and Mrs. Barbauld's poetics. Indeed Wordsworth, as did probably most of the leading Romantic poets, read the **Hymns**. Beyond this, though, we cannot go; and the most we can conclude is that eighteenth-century children's literature, in particular Mrs. Barbauld's **Hymns in Prose,** was one of the progenitors of the English Romantic Movement.

Ann Messenger (essay date 1986)

SOURCE: "Heroics and Mock Heroics: John Milton,

Alexander Pope, and Anna Laetitia Barbauld," in *His and Hers: Essays in Restoration and Eighteenth-Century Literature,* The University Press of Kentucky, 1986, pp. 172-96.

[In the following excerpt, Messenger analyzes Barbauld's use of the mock-heroic mode in her satirical writings, particularly "The Groans of the Tankard" and "Washing-Day."]

Satire, that mode for which the earlier decades of the eighteenth century are so justly famous, fell into increasing disrepute [during the eighteenth century]. There had always been a few who protested against the ugliness of satire, suspicious that the satirist was ill-natured, grinding a personal axe, even unchristian. Addison and Steele's *Spectator* was uncomfortable with ridicule and irony as early as 1711, and they were far from the first. Practicing satirists routinely defended themselves against hostile opinion, attempting, like Pope in "An Epistle to Dr. Arbuthnot," to establish their credentials as disinterested moral exemplars. Toward the end of the century, Vicesimus Knox was very hostile indeed: "Ridicule . . . seems to become a weapon in the hands of the wicked, destructive of taste, feeling, morality, and religion." So much for the satirist as God's scourge on earth.

Stuart Tave, in *The Amiable Humorist* [1960], documents in detail this change in attitude, showing how good humor, good nature, and cheerfulness became the dominant desiderata, while the satirist, obviously lacking these virtues, retreated into outer darkness. Tave's analysis is accurate, but it is incomplete because he says almost nothing about women writers, who stood in a particularly problematic relationship to satire from the beginning. The very qualities that came to displace satire—good nature, good humor, and cheerfulness—had always been desirable in women; these qualities, along with submissiveness, made women pleasant creatures to have about the house. The very quality which lives at the heart of satire—the spirit of criticism—was consistently deplored when it raised its ugly head in a woman, especially when it took verbal form. As Lady Mary Chudleigh's Parson phrased the usual teaching: "Soft winning language will become you best; / Ladies ought not to rail, tho' but [that is, not even] in jest." Whatever women may have thought about satire as a mode of discourse, they knew they were asking for trouble if they wrote it. . . .

[One] female practitioner of satire dealt with the problems the mode created for her by adopting—twice—the mock heroic style, that style which can be taken as merely playful and so can serve as a protective cloak for the writer with something serious to say. . . .

Her first book, **Poems** (1773), is for the most part a quite conservative collection of pastoral songs, hymns, odes to wisdom, and paeans to female friendship. She strikes a public note in **"Corsica,"** a blank verse poem inspired by Boswell's book on Paoli and marked by lavish praise for freedom and the more rugged virtues. Comment on matters of public concern appears again in **"The Groans of** the Tankard" but this time disguised in light, bright, and sparkling mock heroics.

"The Groans of the Tankard" uses as its setting the dining room of the school in which Mrs. Barbauld's father taught. The silver Tankard, full of water and sitting on the sideboard, observes the scene and then delivers itself of a lengthy speech, bewailing its present condition and reminiscing about its glorious past. The poem is written in heroic couplets with Miltonic touches but is mainly Popeian in tone, at times alluding directly to *The Rape of the Lock.* Betsy Rodgers [in *Georgian Chronicles: Mrs. Barbauld and Her Family,* 1958] calls it "light verse," and it's great fun. When it first appeared, the *Monthly Review* was somewhat baffled by it. Praising virtually every poem in the book, the *Monthly* could say of **"The Groans of the Tankard"** only that it is "a kind of burlesque; in which the Writer has succeeded much beyond what could have been expected from her chastised and regulated genius."

The *Critical Review* came a bit closer to the mark. Less favorably inclined to the book as a whole, it could not "say much in commendation of **'The Groans of the Tankard'**." After doubting that the owner of such a tankard could confine himself to drinking water, the reviewer went on to grudging praise of the poet who acted "consistently enough" in praising abstemiousness, since she herself "resides among dissenters" rather than among "the sons of the church, who are supposed to indulge themselves in sacerdotal luxury." From its Establishment point of view, the *Critical Review* was beginning to get the point that this playful burlesque was, under the cloak of the mock heroic, a scathing indictment of the Establishment.

To begin at the beginning, the epigraph from Horace—"Dulci digne mero!"—is a nice piece of evidence that Mrs. Barbauld not only knew her Latin poets but responded, no doubt with glee, to the ironies in Horace that readers have sometimes overlooked. She is quoting from the Odes, Book III, number 13, a poem addressed to a spring or fountain, praising it and promising it a sacrifice. The poem begins: "Fount of Bandusia, shining more bright than glass, / Worth the sweetest of wine not without garlands crowned. . . . " That water should be "worth the sweetest of wine" ("Dulci digne mero") and be saluted by having wine poured into it is amusing enough. That the wine is called "mero," a substantive use of the adjective which means "pure, unmixed" (a common usage), makes the blending of wine and water even funnier. And that the phrase should head a poem in which a tankard filled with water argues for its worthiness to contain wine instead, an argument moreover that makes it the butt of the satire, is a wonderful joke.

The invocation to the Muse is couched in religious terms: "portents," "reverent," "faithful," "pious awe." The Muse is, of course, a goddess, but this much emphasis on the sacred is unusual. The ominous tone of the sacred terms prepares us for the supernatural—even Gothic—event of the speaking Tankard and for the abstemious religious atmosphere of the school dining room. If readers have not

responded to the exaggeration of the piety, they soon sense that they are engaged with a mock heroic poem rather than with the genuine heroic when they are told that "hunger rages with despotic power" at noon and when they meet a pun as "the lean student quits his Hebrew roots" to dine on "English fruits." The domestic detail of this part of the poem is peculiarly a woman's perception. However learned she was, Mrs. Barbauld knew that "solid pudding and substantial pie" had a more immediate value than "airy systems." Dr. Johnson, when he praised Elizabeth Carter for knowing how to make a pudding as well as translate Epictetus, was expressing his sense of what constituted a woman's worth; Mrs. Barbauld knows that a man's or boy's stomach is more demanding than his mind, which Johnson doesn't quite admit. The meal finished, the "decent grace" is spoken and the diners look toward the Tankard—"deep, capacious, vast, of ample size." This heroic vessel is filled with "the cold beverage blue-eyed Naiads drink," plain water. The allusive, circumlocutory designation of its contents is more Miltonic than Popeian, and the echoes of *Paradise Lost* continue as the mouth of the Tankard yawns to disclose "the deep profound," a tautological phrase not found in *Paradise Lost* in that form but reminiscent of the hundreds of uses of "deep," the "vast profunditie obscure" of Chaos, "this profound" of Hell, and many other phrases. Miraculously, the Tankard begins to speak, after breaking out in a cold sweat (as metal vessels full of cold liquid do).

That an inanimate object should speak shows that Mrs. Barbauld was not unacquainted with the conventions of the Gothic novel. Besides the regulation grating of rusty hinges, rattling of chains, and moaning of wind, Gothic novels are full of supernatural noises. *The Castle of Otranto* (1764), for example, is full of creaks and groans and even boasts a talking skeleton. By adding the Gothic to the mock heroic, Mrs. Barbauld doubles the fictiveness and the funniness of her poem, a lightening which balances the real seriousness of the satire.

For real seriousness there is. The Tankard begins its lament with "How changed the scene!"—directly quoting Thomson's "Summer" from *The Seasons,* a passage describing a sudden and violent storm of rain that blots out the sun, turning the smiling landscape to ominous gloom. For the Tankard, the school dining room is equally depressing. And water, in the form of rain or otherwise, holds no charms. Although the exact words are Thomson's, the Miltonic echoes are even more significant. In *Paradise Lost,* the newly fallen Satan faces a new scene when he opens his eyes on Hell and speaks for the first time, addressing Beelzebub: "O how fall'n! how chang'd . . . chang'd in outward lustre." The Tankard, sensing that, like Satan, it is being punished for something, asks, "for what unpardoned crimes / Have I survived to these degenerate times?" We have observed no degeneracy in the preceding passage. Instead, we have been shown lean, hard-working students eating a frugal meal, saying grace, and preparing to drink water. For the Tankard to regard this as a scene of degeneracy immediately puts it in the wrong and identifies it as the object of satiric attack. We will soon discover what the "unpardoned crimes" are.

Meanwhile, like Satan, the Tankard is lamenting a fall, though Satan fell from a true state of grace and the Tankard from a false one.

The Tankard goes on to describe the contents it was proud to hold in former days. The description is Miltonic with its exotic geographical references; it is Popeian in its echoes of Belinda's dressing table; it is accurately domestic in its recipe for what could be Wassail or Lambswool or Cold Tankard. With white froth on top and a Miltonic "brown abyss" below, made from the "golden store" of Ceres, we begin with beer or ale, made from wheat or barley. Sugar, "The dulcet reed the Western islands boast," was a standard ingredient. "Banda's fragrant coast" in Indonesia produced the nutmeg that was used in most if not all versions of the drink. Other spices varied, but most commonly ginger or cinnamon or both were added to the "Spicy Nut-brown Ale" (to quote Milton); "either India's shore," both India itself and the West Indies, produced and sold both of these spices in the eighteenth century. Perhaps Mrs. Barbauld was recommending water, but she knew the right ingredients for a liverlier beverage.

The elevated method of presenting the recipe may be compared to Milton's description of Eve preparing dinner for Raphael and Adam:

> . . . and from each tender stalk
> Whatever Earth all-bearing Mother yeilds
> In *India* East or West, or middle shoare
> In *Pontus* or the *Punic* Coast, or where
> *Alcinous* reign'd, fruit of all kinds, in coate,
> Rough, or smooth rin'd, or bearded husk, or
>   shell
> She gathers, Tribute large. . . .

Et cetera, et cetera. The recipe may also be compared to Belinda's toilette in *The Rape of the Lock,* presided over by her maid:

> The various Off'rings of the World appear;
> From each she nicely culls with curious Toil,
> And decks the Goddess with the glitt'ring Spoil.
> This Casket *India*'s glowing Gems unlocks,
> And all *Arabia* breathes from yonder Box.
> The Tortoise here and Elephant unite,
> Transform'd to *Combs,* the speckled and the
>   white.

Et cetera. Pope transforms the Miltonic goddess who deserves the whole world's tribute into the social beauty who does not; Mrs. Barbauld continues the process of reduction by collecting the spoils of the world in the belly of the Tankard, a beauty as proud of itself as ever Belinda was.

The Tankard is proud partly because it has officiated at City banquets, dispensing nectar to alderman and mayor, "the furry tribe." The epithet, while referring to the trimming on the official robes of office, also reduces the city men to animals, a state they regularly reached by overindulgence in the contents of the Tankard. . . . The country squire or "keen Sportsman," too, has been served by the Tankard. As it describes its patrons, the Tankard increasingly reveals its pride: the furry tribe declared its worth, but the sportsman was actually enabled by the Tankard to conquer land and sea. The Tankard has confused the power of its contents, and a spurious power at that, with its own powers, which are nil.

The next section of the poem reveals the full extent of the Tankard's hubris, although the Tankard itself seems superficially to be arguing simply for the proper decorum in the relationship of vessel to contents. A mere clay pot is good enough for water; fine china is suited to tea and coffee; but the Tankard, which is silver, claims "more exalted juice." The idea of a class structure and hence possibilities of disastrous misalliances between drinking vessels and their contents has a satiric edge to it, especially since it comes from a relatively egalitarian poet, a Dissenter outside the Establishment, who later supported the French and American revolutions and wrote pamphlets against the slave trade. This passage echoes two in *The Rape of the Lock.* First, "China's earth" and the "grateful flavour" of the tea recall the coffee-brewing scene: "From silver Spouts the grateful Liquors glide, / While *China*'s Earth receives the smoking Tyde." Second, the Tankard's account of its birth is a series of rhetorical questions, using the phrase "for this . . . ?" five times; the same phrase (four times) dominates the description of Belinda's hair-curling procedure, delivered by Thalestris:

> Was it for this you took such constant Care
> The *Bodkin, Comb,* and *Essence* to prepare;
> For this your Locks in Paper-Durance bound,
> For this with tort'ring Irons wreath'd around?
> For this with Fillets strain'd your tender Head,
> And bravely bore the double Loads of Lead?

The agonizing creation of Belinda's curls is paralleled to the mining, smelting, and stamping of the silver Tankard in the "torturing furnace." (We are now sure the Tankard is silver because its "native bed" is Potosi, a famous Bolivian source of that metal.) Both Belinda and the Tankard suffer for vanity, and both have their vanity punished, one by haircut and one by water. The two specific and detailed echoes of *The Rape of the Lock* at this point in the poem bring in Pope's whole world of frivolous aristocrats as the next stage in the progress of the satire, following the mayor and squire. There is a comic contrast in the ephemerality of Belinda's curls and the durability of the Tankard, but the moral point parallels Pope's.

The Tankard goes on to lament the day it was doomed to serve in a Presbyterian household, "Whose slender meal is shorter than their grace." The point of view here contrasts tellingly with that in the first part of the narrative frame, where the "short repast" is also called a "sober meal" and the grace has the adjective "decent." The phenomenon is the same but the attitudes are opposite. Mrs. Barbauld is a Dissenter but the Tankard is Church of England; it has "endur'd the fiery test" (Mrs. Barbauld deplored the Test Act) and is stamped "with Britain's lofty crest." Naturally, it has nothing but contempt for the temperance of the "moping sons" of the puritans. Nostalgically, the Tankard recalls its service among Anglican clergymen, whose notorious corruption Mrs. Barbauld is satirizing here. The dean may be an echo of Pope's "Of the Use of Riches," in which, while visiting Timon's chapel, he finds, "To Rest, the Cushion, and soft *Dean* invite, / Who never mentions Hell to Ears polite." In Mrs. Barbauld's poem, the cushions are soft while the dean is gouty, but he too looks like one not concerned with Hell. The prebend, on the other hand, is inspired, but only by the Tankard. The Dissenting satire on the shortcomings of the Anglican clergy is clear.

From alderman and mayor and squire, to Belinda, to Anglican dean and prebend, that is, from the civic governors to the aristocracy to the spiritual authorities, the satire has grown in seriousness under the comic surface of the poem. The final step of the satire is even more damning and, perhaps for that reason, more cautiously veiled. Here the Tankard reminisces about its former services to "Comus' sprightly train," those drinkers who do their reveling in "some spacious mansion, Gothic, old." One could take Comus simply as the Roman god of mirth and revelry, but Mrs. Barbauld's detailed knowledge of Milton makes a more particular association inevitable. Milton's Comus, however, worked his evil magic out in the woods and in a "stately Palace," not specifically in a Gothic mansion. Those drinkers who functioned in a Gothic mansion were in some ways nastier than Comus—the "monks" of Medmenham Abbey. The literary and the real corrupters may be conflated here at the climax of the satire.

It would be rash to claim that Mrs. Barbauld's Comus is necessarily a direct reference to the Order of Saint Francis, better but wrongly known as the Hell-Fire Club. There were various organizations, strict and loose, for riotous living in the eighteenth century. And, of course, she might have been thinking only of Milton's Comus and added the phrase about Gothic mansions because the whole episode of the speaking Tankard is on the Gothic side. But the Medmenham society is a possibility. Exactly when it was founded and how widely it was known about are matters for conjecture, but it gained a sudden notoriety in 1763 (when Mrs. Barbauld was twenty years old) because Wilkes, Churchill, and Lord Sandwich, fellow "monks" but political enemies, were at each others' throats in print and public speech. Newspapers and scandal sheets made the most of the story. Whether the society practiced Satanism or not is still debated, but all kinds of blasphemous religious practices, accompanied by sexual excesses and perversions, were popularly laid at the curiously ornamented door of the society.

That a great deal of drinking occurred is beyond question: the society's wine book, listing names, dates, quantities, and varieties, is still extant. The Tankard would have been kept busy. Furthermore, the architectural description— "some spacious mansion, Gothic, old"—fits Medmenham remarkably well. The twelfth-century abbey was largely ruined by the forces of Henry VIII, but a dwelling was constructed "without disturbing much of the original fabric," so it was simultaneously a Gothic heap and a spacious mansion. Sir Francis Dashwood, head of the order, improved upon this odd combination by installing stained glass windows and building "the pseudo-ruins of a tower" on a corner of the building. The practices of the society were also associated with the specially designed gardens surrounding the abbey (chapter 7) and were, at least in part, later transferred to chalk caves at West Wycombe (chapter 10); these other locations for alcoholic and venereal activities, if popularly known, could have reinforced the connection with Milton's primarily rural Comus.

Leaving aside the Medmenham conjectures, Milton's Comus supplies sufficiently serious hellfire to create the climax of Mrs. Barbauld's satire. The son of Bacchus and Circe, he carries about with him not a tankard but a crystal glass full of "orient liquor," which, like that in his mother's cup, turns the drinker into a "brutish form." Milton makes it clear that those who drink from this glass are indulging "fond intemperate thirst," which the Tankard specializes in satisfying, as we have seen. When Comus and his rabble get the Lady into the enchanted chair and she refuses his crystal glass, Milton treats us to a description of the drink less specific than Mrs. Barbauld's recipe for spiced ale but even more sensuous: "this cordial Julep here / That flames, and dances in his crystal bounds / With spirits of balm, and fragrant Syrops mixt." Like the Tankard, Comus sneers at "lean and sallow Abstinence" as he argues that the good things of nature were meant to be used. Those who "Drink the clear stream" do so merely in a "pet of temperance," he explains. But the Lady speaks up for Temperance, which causes Comus, like the Tankard, to break out in "a cold shuddering dew . . . all o're." He is, of course, dispatched by both the Lady's virtue and her brothers' force, but it takes Sabrina, the water nymph, to release the seated Lady from her enchantment, by sprinkling her breast with "Drops from my fountain pure." That the Tankard should be associated with Comus in the exercise of evil intemperance to the point at which men are turned to animals or, in Mrs. Barbauld's phrase, "Thought grows giddy," brings the growing seriousness of the satire to its climax.

Not Sabrina, the beautiful water nymph, but an "ancient Sibyl" concludes Mrs. Barbauld's poem. Perhaps this is the maidservant who waits on table in the school; perhaps it is a comic and self-deprecating reference to the poet herself, less than thirty years old but "sour and stern" from the Tankard's point of view. That she is called a Sibyl, a prophetess of Apollo, adds to the mock heroic tone of the poem. "Sibyl" also means "the will of God," and it is this power which silences the scandalous Tankard and causes it to break out in another "sudden damp." The Tankard is called "the conscious vessel" at this point, and various senses of "conscious" fit its state: "having guilty knowledge," "self-conscious," as well as "having internal perception or consciousness" (see the *Oxford English Dictionary*). The Tankard shuts up—literally— leaving only low murmurs, perhaps echoes, to "creep along

Warrington Academy, where Barbauld lived from 1758 to 1774.

the ground." And, in the final allusion to *The Rape of the Lock*, recalling Belinda's repeater watch (1:18), the air continues to vibrate with the "silver sound." We are back on the level of beautiful artifacts and petty vanities, leaving behind us grave corruptions of state, church, and spirit. But we have seen them. For all its fun, the poem has as much to say about real evil as does its model, *The Rape of the Lock*—perhaps even more.

Mrs. Barbauld dealt with serious matters in the playful **"The Groans of the Tankard."** The mock heroic mode can be merely playful or it can cloak concern with serious matters. Mrs. Barbauld was in a particularly vulnerable position as a woman and a Dissenter, so she wrapped her indictment of the Establishment in Popeian comedy and in the trivia of domesticity allowable in a woman. One could even see the pride of the Tankard as another cloak, pride being a conventional and acceptable target of satire. To some extent, that theme masks her more controversial concerns. Except for the slightly grumpy comments in the *Critical Review*, she seems to have gotten away with it.

When she turned to prose, Mrs. Barbauld donned other cloaks, especially the allegorical. She was always fond of witty indirection and sometimes used it for purposes other than self-protection. Her writing for children and young people is full of allegories, riddles, bits of mock heroic—playful circumlocutions of all sorts—as well as heavy piety. Sometimes her prose pieces for grownups are nearly as purely playful as some of her children's pieces. **"Zephyrus and Flora,"** for example, is a bright bagatelle in which a prudish lady writes a letter of warning to Flora's mother, cautioning her about the liberties that a young man, the breeze, is taking with the girl. The allegory here has no serious point to conceal. The tone is similarly comic in **"Letter of John Bull"** (1792), but this time the allegory conceals an attack on the growing jingoism of England and the prevalence of loyalty oaths as the Establishment reacted against the French Revolution. **"Dialogue in the Shades,"** on the surface a debate about ancient heroes, has an underlying antiwar theme. That theme is closer to the surface in **"The Curé on the Banks of the Rhone"** (1791), in which a clergyman describes true religion to a murderous revolutionary committee, which pays no attention to him. This piece is essentially tragic rather than comic satire, however, in the manner of Mark Twain's "War Prayer." But the satire is veiled: the whole story is presented as a letter from a friend and the final sentence is all that makes the satiric point.

In only one essay does the satiric vein dominate without some cloak such as fable or allegory. In the **"Letter on Watering-places,"** a male persona, carefully established as a virtuous but not puritanical character, satirizes the behavior of ladies at a fashionable seaside resort, criticizing their extravagance, hypochondria, snobbery, and other standard follies. Like Lady Winchilsea, Mrs. Barbauld spoke openly when she attacked silly women. She has made her speaker here a man, perhaps to give the criticism added authority, but there can be no doubt that she shared the speaker's values, as her temperate and strenuously useful life indicates. On such a subject, she had no need of a cloak.

The single overt satire among her poems is **"The Rights of Woman,"** undated but obviously an attack on Mary Wollstonecraft's "Vindication of the Rights of Woman" (1792). The poem begins, apparently supporting Mary Wollstonecraft, with a clarion call to "injured Woman" to arise and assert her rights. The tone soon grows questionable, however, as woman is urged to make man "kiss the golden sceptre of [her] reign," and to "Make treacherous Man [her] subject, not [her] friend." Soon woman becomes the "courted idol of mankind" on a "proud eminence," which has uncomfortable overtones of Satan on his "bad eminence" in *Paradise Lost* (2:6). But woman cannot stay on that eminence, the poem declares, because Nature will make her coldness and pride soften until "separate rights are lost in mutual love." The inevitability of love, and its destruction of maiden pride and scorn, is also the theme of Mrs. Barbauld's **"Song III,"** which is mildly comic. Here, in **"The Rights of Woman,"** she uses the same idea in the service of her satire, as she modulates from ironic agreement with Wollstonecraft through exaggerated claims for female sovereignty to the conclusion that Nature will simply cancel out such wrong thinking. There was no need to soften or conceal an attack on that hyena in petticoats, already established as the proper object for public scorn.

But when Mrs. Barbauld cast her satiric eye on men, indeed on the whole male sex, she donned again the cloak of mock heroic. In **"Washing-Day,"** using rolling Miltonic periods, she stuck a pin in the balloon of masculine pride and simultaneously glorified the endless drudgery of women.

Parodies of Milton's blank verse had long been popular, and the mode was flexible enough to serve a variety of purposes. John Philips's "The Splendid Shilling" (1701), for instance, has no particular point but offers a delightful compendium of Miltonic stylistic grandeurs applied to such low topics as the narrator's worn-out galligaskins. Philips turned again to Miltonics in "Cyder" (1708) and this time the style, coupled with imitation of Virgil's *Georgics,* dignifies the humble business of making cider and places it in a context of queens, heroes, and patriotism in general. Lady Winchilsea adopted the Miltonic mode in "Fanscomb Barn" (1713), but here a satiric point lurks below the surface of the imitation. Most of the poem is a long speech delivered by Strolepedon, a wandering beggar, to his wife, Budgeta. They have begged a drink and are slightly tiddly. Strolepedon regales Budgeta with a description of Fanscomb (which she can see perfectly well for herself at the time), a description decorated with classical allusions and couched in elevated Miltonic periods. As soon as his spiel makes reference to Morpheus, however, she falls asleep. Strolepedon comes across as as domineering, pompous, conceited ass, lording it over his wife. The satire also glances at *Paradise Lost* and Milton's own volubility, especially in Book VIII, where Eve, after putting up with Raphael's lengthy descriptions of the war in heaven and the creation for two and a half books, silently slips away to tend the garden. Eve has more stamina than Budgeta, but even she wilts at last. Milton is both model for and object of Lady Winchilsea's satire.

The same can be said of Mrs. Barbauld's **"Washing-Day,"** though the main focus of the satire lies elsewhere. The poem begins with an invocation to the "domestic Muse." The narrator, looking back on her childhood, traces the progress of the evil day from the arrival of the "red-armed washers," with speculations on the weather, through the dinner hour (pity the guest, if one should come on this day!), to her banishment from her usual company and her reception by the parlor fire, where the grandmother entertains her and the other little ones. As the poem ends, the children blow soap bubbles while they listen to the sounds of rinsing and starching and ironing.

Washing day was indeed a major event in seventeenth- and eighteenth-century households. Pepys records it regularly in the earlier volumes of his diary, often introducing the day's entry with a label, "washing day," something he always did for the "Lords day" and occasionally for his own birthday and the anniversary of Charles I's death. Other days are not labeled. Clearly, washing day was important to him. He notes on November 19, 1660, for example, that his wife stayed up until 2:00 A.M. so that she could wake "the wench" to start the washing on the twentieth—the day, he notes grimly, when he came home from the playhouse and alehouse only to find "the house in a washing pickle." On November 19, 1661, he found his wife alone in a small room with a gentleman caller, which roused his jealousy until he realized that it was washing day and there was no other room sufficiently warm and dry to sit in. On March 1, 1663, he skipped the usual family prayers at night because tomorrow was washing day, a day which he prudently spent away from home, but he still found the "house foul" on his return. On March 25, 1663, washing day was worse than usual because Susan, the maid, was sick, "or would be thought so," Pepys comments suspiciously. And so it went.

Despite some improvements in plumbing and other domestic conveniences, the day was still dire in Mrs. Barbauld's time. Its importance gives a doubleness to the mock heroic treatment it gets in her poem. Clearly, the events of such a day are not true epic matter: no pagan or Christian heroes wage war with Troy or Satan. The domestic is, by definition, less significant—so much so that one feels even Milton struggling to maintain his elevation of tone when Eve prepares a fruit salad for Adam and Raphael; bathetically, she has "No fear lest Dinner coole" when their protracted conversation makes them late. And yet washing day loomed as large on the domestic front as the siege of Troy or Heaven on the international or cosmic. It was a day when nothing else could be done, when the women of the family and their helpers reigned supreme and the husbands and fathers lurked in the shrubbery or went to the office, unwanted and unattended to.

Women had power on washing day. Here the sex of the author makes an important difference to the handling of the mock heroic. When Pope belittled Belinda for having hysterics over the haircut, one sees, for all the complexity of tone in that poem, the expected mock heroic gap between the littleness of the occasion, from the author's point of view, and the largeness of the language. In **"Washing-Day,"** however, the largeness of the language is both appropriate to the largeness of the events, from the woman's domestic point of view, and comically, mock heroically, inappropriate, because the domestic is considered necessarily trivial. Unless the house is in a pickle! Perhaps Mrs. Barbauld chose Milton rather than Pope as her model for this poem because, on one level, she wanted the grandeur of blank verse paragraphs (rather than the chime of couplets) to support the *real* importance of the occasion, to dignify the drudgery of women.

And yet, as in Lady Winchilsea's "Fanscomb Barn," Milton himself receives a light satiric lash in the poem. The Muses have discarded their tragic buskins and "Language of gods" for "slipshod measure loosely prattling on," a most uncomplimentary description of Miltonic blank verse and perhaps also a bit of self-deprecation here. But Mrs. Barbauld practices that versification with skill. She combines regularity and metrical freedom as Milton does; she sometimes uses a short line, the kind of dramatic breaking of the pattern which Milton used in *Lycidas* and *Samson Agonistes* though not in *Paradise Lost*. After the invocation, the poem is divided into three long verse paragraphs, the first devoted to the washerwomen, the second to the sufferings of unwanted menfolk and children, and the third to the musings of the child. Each paragraph has the true Miltonic sweep, as the thought moves logically but unconfined within the paragraph's general topic.

Mrs. Barbauld imitates Milton's language as well as his versification and paragraphing. She does not use epic sim-

iles, perhaps because her poem is relatively short, but she does use an occasional Latinism or archaism ("impervious," "welkin") and a few exotic names (Erebus, Guatimozin). She adopts the Miltonic trick of substituting one part of speech for another: "abrupt" for "abruptly," "indiscreet" as a noun. She uses apposition," "grandmother, eldest of forms," echoing Milton's "Night, eldest of things," and she leaves out the occasional "the." She also imitates that most Miltonic of devices, the inversion of natural word order. The device was controversial and was felt to be undesirable in excess. Both Addison and Johnson objected to overuse of it, which may be why it is dear to the hearts of imitators. Lady Winchilsea used it in "Fanscomb Barn"; Philips used it even more in "The Splendid Shilling." Mrs. Barbauld makes regular use of it: "From the wet kitchen scared and reeking hearth" is a fairly long mix-up, while "snug recess impervious" is simpler. The figure lends itself to another Miltonic device, that of repetition: "Or tart or pudding:—pudding he nor tart / That day shall eat . . . "; or, without inversion, "Cast at the lowering sky, if sky should lower." Milton's own repetitions are less formulaic than those of his imitators, but the formulaic repetitions certainly *feel* Miltonic, contributing to the heaviness and spurious dignity of the mock heroic style.

Mrs. Barbauld also imitates Milton, to some extent, in that she uses learned literary allusions. She begins her poem with an epigraph from *As You Like It,* lines from Jaques's speech on the seven ages of man, slightly misquoted. The same speech lies behind Mrs. Barbauld's line early in the poem, "By little whimpering boy, with rueful face"; Shakespeare's schoolboy is "whining" (he never used the word "whimpering") and his face is "shining" rather than "rueful," but his unwilling creeping would make one think of rueful feelings. The allusion is plain. Perhaps too Mrs. Barbauld was remembering *The Winter's Tale* when she mentioned "pleasant curds and cream" as a subject for the domestic Muse; in that play, Camillo dubs the lovely Perdita "the queen of curbs and cream." Homer's "rosy-fingered dawn" gets an ironic twist when Mrs. Barbauld's dawn produces a "gray streak" accompanied by "red-armed washers." She also alludes to Swift's mock heroic "A Description of a City Shower" when, amid speculations about rain, the unwanted master of the family cannot have his coat dusted; in the "Shower," Swift devotes several lines to the problems created by a mixture of dust and rain in the needy poet's "Sole Coat." The allusions to the "Shower" continue with the word "welkin" in the same paragraph and with the "impatient hand" that "Twitched" the apron off the shrubs "when showers impend"; Swift begins with a scene in which "Rain depends" (which means "impends") and describes "Brisk *Susan* [who] whips her Linen from the Rope."

What does it all add up to—the Miltonic versification and style, the learned references to Shakespeare and others, the application of the heroic mode to the domestic crisis that was washing day? The reference near the end of the poem to "Monglofier" (properly Montgolfier) is, I think, the clue. In June 1783, the brothers Montgolfier caused to rise from the ground in France a linen globe filled with hot smoky air from a fire made of chopped straw. Excitement was considerable, and a number of other balloon experiments were carried out in the same year, including one in which enthusiasm among the spectators ran so high that a violent downpour of rain drenched them all but did not dampen their interest. Among these experiments was another by the Montgolfiers before the king and queen, using a sheep, a cock, and a duck as the first passengers in a cage hung under the balloon. Silk was the material used in some balloons and human beings soon became the cargo. Smoky air was sometimes replaced by hydrogen. Aeronautics was born.

In **"Washing-Day,"** Mrs. Barbauld looks back to her childhood when she blew "and sent aloft" soap bubbles, "little dreaming then" that the "silken ball" of Montgolfier would "Ride buoyant through the clouds." But it did, and the mature poet adds the sardonic comment, "so near approach / The sports of children and the toils of men."

She had made the same point in an earlier poem, **"Written on a Marble"**:

> The world's something bigger,
>   But just of this figure
> And speckled with mountains and seas;
> Your heroes are overgrown schoolboys
> Who scuffle for empires and toys,
> And kick the poor ball as they please.
> Now Caesar, now Pompey, gives law;
>   And Pharsalia's plain,
>   Though heaped with the slain,
> Was only a game at *taw.*

In its witty brevity and its belittling of heroes, this poem is something like Lady Winchilsea's "Song Upon a Punch Bowl," in which Alexander the Great gets drunk and cries not for another world to conquer but for another bowl of punch. It is also consistent with several of Mrs. Barbauld's prose writings that, directly or indirectly, oppose war. The masculine world of glory and conquest did not win this woman's admiration.

Male pride has been the central focus of **"Washing-Day"** throughout, from the epigraph on the sixth age of man when the voice turns to "childish treble" to the nuisances that menfolk make of themeselves when women are engaged in the serious business of washing. The man "Who call'st thyself perchance the master" is dispossessed on washing day. Even more pointedly, his greatest exploits, imaged in the Montgolfier balloon, are reduced to the level of children's games. Not that Mrs. Barbauld was hostile to balloonists as such—indeed, in her letters she shows great interest in the whole business of ballooning. But the assumption that what men do is important and what women do is not, is turned upside down. The women's washing is heroic; the men's exploits are child's play.

Such a reversal of values was dangerous. In **"Written on a Marble,"** the idea could be dismissed as a brief joke or taken as serious criticism of war, but in **"Washing-Day,"**

with the explicit comparison between men's and women's deeds, the poet was taking a risk. She minimized that risk by using the mock heroic mode, which lends itself so well to the domestic and which could always be dismissed as merely playful. She also misquoted Shakespeare in her epigraph. She prints the lines thus: " . . . and their voice, / Turning again towards childish treble, pipes / And whistles in its sound." Shakespeare had written "his big, manly voice." "Their voice," however ungrammatical, blunts the sting. So does the second ending of the poem. After the lines comparing men to children, Mrs. Barbauld continues: "Earth, air, and sky, and ocean hath its bubbles, / And verse is one of them—this most of all." This final ending masks the announcement of the satiric point, which loses what would have been the place of most emphasis, the last line. The sting is further lessened by the claim that the poem is a mere bubble. The self-deprecating quality of the lines is enhanced by the poet-as-child blowing soap bubbles a few lines earlier and continuing to exhibit childishness, as she implies, by writing poetry. The self-deprecation becomes even stronger when one thinks of the usual reference to self at the ends of other poems: Pope's claim that "this Lock" will inscribe Belinda's name among the stars; Shakespeare's conclusion to Sonnet 18, "So long lives this, and this gives life to thee"; and all the other statements that the poet can confer immortality on his subject. Mrs. Barbauld says instead that her verse is a bubble, that most ephemeral of creations. Very few women writers make the claim that they can immortalize their subjects. Anne Killigrew does in "A Pastoral Dialogue"; Lady Winchilsea does in "Melinda on an Insippid Beauty." These are, however, rare instances of women making the claim that was routine for men.

And yet Mrs. Barbauld is not simply wallowing in self-deprecation in her final lines. For she has said "And verse is" a bubble, not just her own verse. And she has equated the most thrilling inventions of men with the sports of children, however much she has blunted the sting. Wearing her cloak, she got away with it.

Mrs. Barbauld was not only a writer of literature but also a literary critic, especially a critic of fiction, including satiric fiction. She edited a fifty-volume collection, *The British Novelists* (1810), which includes several texts that are satiric in whole or in part, among them books by women. In her prefaces to these books and her essay introducing the whole collection, she comments favorably on satire, without making any particular distinction between novels by men and by women. She relishes the mock heroic humor in Fielding and the satire in Fanny Burney: in *Evelina,* she finds that Miss Burney is "Equally happy in seizing the ridiculous, and in entering into the finer feelings," and she dubs the satirical Mrs. Selwyn "a wit and an oddity." She is glad that Cervantes' "immortal satire" drove romances out of fashion, and she delights in the best imitation of Cervantes, Charlotte Lennox's *The Female Quixote,* which she calls "an agreeable and ingenious satire." Indeed, the only thing wrong with *The Female Quixote* is that it is not satiric enough: the heavy sermon at the end which "recovers" the heroine is an error; that recovery should have been brought about by more satire, "the sense of ridicule . . . [or] some absurd mistake." Clearly, Mrs. Barbauld felt no distaste for the satiric mode and had no reservations about a woman's right to practice it.

And yet there is a hint, a slight suggestion, that women writers run particular risks. In her discussion of *Evelina,* Mrs. Barbauld comments on Fanny Burney's youth when that novel first appeared, and she generalizes, in nostalgic tones, about the joys of first authorship and the pleasures of success when a young writer is still "happily ignorant of all the chills and mortifications . . . , the ridicule and censure which fasten on vulnerable parts." The passage does not mention an author's sex nor does it specify satire as a "vulnerable part," but Mrs. Barbauld has chosen a preface to a woman's novel, a novel which contains an important element of satire, in which to lament the dangers of authorship. She could have had women satirists in mind.

She had herself experienced "chills and mortifications" when she had dared to speak out in critical tones on matters of public concern. Her early poem on Corsica, a public topic, had not been controversial or critical, and it escaped attack. But her prose pamphlet on the Corporation and Test Acts, published in 1790, was highly critical, even sarcastic in its ridicule of those parliamentarians who upheld the Acts. Although published anonymously, it earned her the titles "that virago Barbauld" and "Deborah" from Horace Walpole. When the Reverend Keate, attacking the same pamphlet, learned that it was written by a woman, he expressed shock and surprise that "'in soft bosoms dwells such mighty rage.'" Other controversial works met with varying receptions. Mrs. Barbauld suffered the strongest attack when she published *Eighteen Hundred and Eleven,* a narrative poem in which she imagines a visitor from the New World exploring the ruins of an England reduced to a primitive state by its immorality and decadence and its involvement with a long continental war. Although the poem glorifies the literature and philosophy of England, it was perceived as unpatriotic and the poet came under heavy fire.

Interestingly, in its comments on *Eighteen Hundred and Eleven,* the *Quarterly Review* attacked Mrs. Barbauld for becoming a satirist. Yet the poem contains none of the satirical techniques she had used elsewhere, no mock heroics, no irony, no ridicule, sarcasm, allegory, or fable, not even any witty clevernesses of language. It is sober, serious, elegiac in tone, prophesying doom. It is satire, of course, in that it expresses critical disapproval, and clearly the reviewer was reacting to the ideas in the poem. But he chose to criticize its mode, to abuse the woman for being a satirist, indeed, as he seems to think, for becoming a satirist for the first time:

> Out old acquaintance Mrs. Barbauld turned satirist!
> The last thing we should have expected, and, now that
> we have seen her satire, the last thing we could have
> desired. . . . we think she has wandered from the course
> in which she was respectable and useful, and miserably
> mistaken both her powers and her duty, in exchanging

the birchen for the satiric rod, and abandoning the "ovilia" of the nursery, to wage war on the "reluctantes dracones," statesmen and warriors, whose misdoings have aroused her indignant muse. . . . We had hoped, indeed, that the empire might have been saved without the intervention of a lady-author. . . . an irresistible impulse of public duty—a confident sense of commanding talents—have induced her to dash down her shagreen spectacles and her knitting needles and to sally forth. . . .

The hostility is obvious—the woman has left her proper sphere and trespassed on the affairs of men, specifically on the male preserve of satire. Indeed, the reviewer goes on to "take the liberty of warning her to desist from satire, which indeed is satire on herself alone. . . . " Mrs. Barbauld was so crushed by this and other reactions to her poem that she published no more during her lifetime.

As the eighteenth century drew to a close, satire grew steadily less acceptable and the satirist became an increasingly unattractive figure. But a female satirist, who had always been unattractive unless she was criticizing other women, was now entirely beyond the pale. Yet long before she was attacked for *Eighteen Hundred and Eleven,* Mrs. Barbauld had shown that she belongs to the mainstream of English literature when she so skillfully used that most central of satiric forms, the mock heroic. It's ironic.

Catherine E. Moore (essay date 1986)

SOURCE: "'Ladies . . . Taking the Pen in Hand': Mrs. Barbauld's Criticism of Eighteenth-Century Women Novelists," in *Fetter'd or Free? British Women Novelists, 1670-1815,* edited by Mary Anne Schofield and Cecilia Macheski, Ohio University Press, 1986, pp. 383-97.

[*In the following excerpt, Moore reviews Barbauld's essays on novelists and argues that she made important contributions to the history and theory of the novel.*]

A versatile woman—poet, essayist, polemicist, hymnwriter, children's writer, educator, critic—Anna Laetitia Barbauld (1743-1825) never wrote a novel. As an avid reader of novels, as well as a respected writer for nearly forty years, and the editor of Samuel Richardson's *Correspondence* (1804), she was well-qualified in 1810 to serve as editor of the fifty-volume *British Novelists, with an Essay and Prefaces, Biographical and Critical,* published that year. This collection includes twenty-one novelists, twenty-eight novels, and twenty essays by Mrs. Barbauld, including a long introductory essay, **"On the Origin and Progress of Novel-Writing."** The purpose of this edition, she says in her introduction, is to present a "series of the most approved novels, from the first regular productions of the kind to the present time." The titles offered in this collection confirm her judgment, for all the major eighteenth-century novelists (with the exception of Sterne—an unexplained omission) and many of the best and most popular minor novelists are represented. The essays, though varying in length and in thoroughness, collectively constitute a defense of novels as a genre and an attempt to define and illustrate literary principles in novel writing.

This useful collection of essays has received remarkably little attention over the past two centuries. Indeed, Lucy Aikin's reference to it as the "humbler offices of literature" may reflect the attitude of her aunt, Mrs. Barbauld, and certainly Aikin's explanation that the task was undertaken to assuage grief over Mr. Barbauld's suicide in 1808 points to something less than Mrs. Barbauld's total commitment to the project on its own merit. Since then, although scholars frequently have cited Mrs. Barbauld's prefatory remarks on novels in her edition of Richardson's *Correspondence,* few have ever alluded to the prefaces to **British Novelists**. Yet these are important for several reasons. Mrs. Barbauld has been justly praised for having written "the most complete and the most accurate history of [by Byron Hall Gibson, in a Ph. D. dissertation, 1931] prose fiction to appear during the years intervening between the publication of John Moore's *A View of the Commencement and Progress of Romance* (1797) and John Colin Dunlop's *History of Fiction* (1814)." Equally significant is her assertion of the artistic values of the novel at a time when the literary reputation of the genre had not yet entirely outgrown the widespread disapproval common in eighteenth-century criticism. A third important feature is her advocacy of women novelists, who as a group were yet to be taken seriously.

As historian and theoretician of the novel, Mrs. Barbauld synthesizes current ideas and information. She had been preceded not only by John Moore in 1797 but also by Clara Reeve, whose "The Progress of Romance" had appeared in 1785. Criticism of novels, however, was fragmented because most of it appeared incidentally in magazine reviews of individual novels. Nevertheless, from the scattered observations of authors and critics, a distinct body of criticism was emerging, and Mrs. Barbauld's achievement was to give coherent voice to it, through the introductory essay, which provides a historical background and a statement of principles, and through the individual prefaces, which draw upon those principles.

The work reveals Mrs. Barbauld's thorough assimilation of contemporary criticism of novels. J. M. S. Tompkins [in *The Popular Novel in England, 1770-1800,* 1961] says of the period from 1770 to the end of the century that "the two chief facts about the novel are its popularity as a form of entertainment and its inferiority as a form of art." The opening sentence of Mrs. Barbauld's introductory essay demonstrates her awareness of these facts: "A collection of Novels has a better chance of giving pleasure than of commanding respect." She even adopts the conciliatory tone which champions of the novel considered necessary to combat the moralistic opposition, as, for example, in her tentatively worded thesis: "It might not perhaps be difficult to show that this species of composition is entitled to a higher rank than has been generally assigned it." But concession is only a strategy which strengthens her defense of the novel. She addresses the main critical issues: defining the novel, defending it against

the moralists, and asserting its authenticity as a literary form. Her formal definition is obviously adapted from Fielding: "A good novel is an epic in prose, with more of character and less (indeed in modern novels nothing) of the supernatural machinery." But as Mrs. Barbauld traces the history of fiction, she reveals her bias in favor of realism—"the closer imitation of nature"—as the crucial trait of the "modern" novel. Thus, in England the "modern" novel begins with Defoe because he was the "first author amongst us who distinguished himself by natural painting." The account of the evolution of the novel has a twofold purpose: to show that "Fictitious adventures in one form or other, have made a part of polite literature of every age and nation" and to show that the popular contemporary form, the novel, has a superior moral advantage because of its closer imitation of nature. She argues, "If the stage is a mirror of life, so is the novel, and perhaps a more accurate one, as less is sacrificed to effect and representation." Moreover, she shrewdly connects the moral significance of the novel with its great popularity.

> Some perhaps may think that too much importance has been already given to a subject so frivolous, but a discriminating taste is no where more called for than with regard to a species of books which every body reads. It was said by Fletcher of Saltoun, 'Let me make the ballads of a nation, and I care not who makes the laws.' Might it not be said with as much propriety, Let me make the novels of a country, and let who will make the system?

On the other hand, Mrs. Barbauld is at odds with even the defenders of the novel in her defiant dismissal of the traditional idea that the "end and object of this species of writing" is "to call in fancy to the aid of reason, to deceive the mind into embracing truth under the guise of fiction" and in her personal endorsement of pleasure as the chief purpose of novels. "I scruple not to confess," she declares, "that when I take up a novel, my end and object is entertainment; and as I suspect that to be the case with most readers, I hesitate not to say that entertainment is their legitimate end and object."

On the subject of the art of fiction, Mrs. Barbauld suggests some theoretical principles, but without much elaboration. Her introductory essay seems to illustrate Frederick R. Karl's observation of the later eighteenth century that criticism of the novel "remained rudimentary" although "the novel was becoming an acceptable part of critical vocabulary" and thus "without any conscious development of novel theory, the novel [was entering] the literary consciousness. Mrs. Barbauld's summary of the required talents for a novelist implies what might be called rudimentary awareness of novelistic art. She simply lists "the invention of a story, the choice of proper incidents, the ordonnance of the plan, occasional beauties of description, and above all, the power exercised over the reader's heart by filling it with the successive emotions of love, pity, joy, anguish, transport, or indignation, together with the grave impressive moral resulting from the whole." On the other hand, her perception that the novel is an art form goes beyond the rudimentary. When she calls upon the novelist to attend to the truth of "real life and manners" because the novel must in "some respects give false ideas, from the very nature of fictitious writing," her concern is moral, but her subsequent comments are aesthetic:

> Every such work is a *whole,* in which the fates and fortunes of the personages are brought to a conclusion, agreeably to the author's own preconceived idea. Every incident in a well written composition is introduced for a certain purpose, and made to forward a certain plan. . . . it is a fault in *his* composition if every circumstance does not answer the reasonable expectations of the reader.

The "sagacious reader" actively "lays hold" on some "prominent circumstance" in the novel and interprets its meaning, often predicts the outcome of the story: "And why does he foresee all this? Not from the real tendencies of things, but from what he has discovered of the author's intentions." Fiction, then, is an ordered arrangement by the author, unlike real life, which is "a kind of chance-medley consisting of many unconnected scenes," and probability is not so much related to reality as it is to the successful execution of the novelist's design for the whole.

Not only is Mrs. Barbauld sensitive to artistic manipulation of material behind the illusion of reality, but she is also aware of some of the problems of narrative technique. In her earlier preface to Richardson's ***Correspondence,*** she had considered at length the methods of presenting the story, suggesting that the novelist has available three narrative points of view: (1) "narrative or epic," in which the "author relates himself the whole adventure"; (2) "memoirs," in which the "subject of the adventure relates his own story"; and (3) *"epistolary correspondence,* carried on between the characters in the novel." Her analysis displays considerable insight into the limits of each strategy. The omniscient narrator not only can "reveal the secret springs of action" and provide "knowledge which would not properly belong to any of the characters," but can also stand as a barrier between the fiction and the reader unless "he frequently drops himself and runs into dialogue." The method of the "memoirs" solves the problem of the too-intrusive narrator, communicates the "warmth and interest a person may be supposed to feel in his own affairs," and permits the narrator to "dwell upon minute circumstances which have affected him." Yet the first-person narration is most difficult, for the novelist must maintain a style suitable to the "supposed talents and capacity of the imaginary narrator," must write under the restriction that "what the hero cannot say, the author cannot tell," and also must create, in effect, "two characters"—the hero "at the time of the events to be related," and, simultaneously, the hero "at the time he is relating them." She concludes that the first-person point of view is the "least perfect mode." The epistolary method gives the illusion of immediacy; it is dramatic because all characters speak "in their own persons"; it can present multiple points of view; it can even supply information furnished by the omniscient narrator through such devices as omitted or lost letters and elaborations or digressions within

letters. Nevertheless, it is unlikely that letters should be so voluminously and conveniently produced and preserved so as to present a "connected story"; the "insipid confidant" is an irritating literary expedient; in sum, the epistolary method is "the most natural and the least probable way of telling a story." All her remarks reveal a preference for the technique that best permits the author to "drop himself"—unless the narrator is like Fielding, in whose narrative everything is "continually heightened by the contrast between the author's style and his view of things, and the characters he is holding up to ridicule." Theoretical discussions of the various narrative points of view were rare at the time, and, as Miriam Allott comments [*in Novelists on the Novel,* 1966]: "It says much for Mrs. Barbauld's perspicacity that subsequent novelists' views on narrative technique coincide at so many points with hers." Mrs. Barbauld does not repeat her theories on point of view in the introductory essay to ***British Novelists,*** but they are evident in practice in a number of the prefatory essays.

If, on the whole, Mrs. Barbauld pays more attention to defending the moral value of novels and less to novelistic theory in the introductory essay, she is at least addressing the most urgent problem her contemporaries saw in the novel. Moreover, she has more theoretical insight than one might expect. The individual prefaces to ***British Novelists*** similarly include much that is generalized and conventional in the way of criticism, but also a good deal that is specific and technical. Perhaps rudimentary as criticism, the prefaces also confirm Tompkins's observation that despite primary emphasis in later eighteenth-century criticism on the "moral, probability and characterization of a novel" and on style, there appeared "a growing interest in form." A summing up of Mrs. Barbauld's contribution to the theory of the novel must acknowledge that her views were mostly derivative and general, yet not entirely conventional and often quite perspicacious and pointed.

It is not especially surprising that a widely read, experienced writer like Mrs. Barbauld, once she had accepted her task, could sort out and unify critical assessments of her day, particularly on a subject as congenial as novels. Somewhat more surprising is the importance she accords women writers, for her reputation today—and in her time—is not that of an ardent feminist. A spokeswoman for radical dissenters in such human rights issues as movements to repeal the Corporation and Test Acts and to abolish the slave trade, she was not notably interested in specifically feminist causes, although she numbered a few women writers among her friends—Hannah More, Joanna Baillie, and Maria Edgeworth, particularly. Her own uncomfortable experience as a remarkably well-educated woman taught her that women "ought only to have such a general tincture of knowledge as to make them agreeable companions to a man of sense"; indeed, "to have a too great fondness for books is little favorable to the happiness of a woman." Her most direct comment on the feminist issue is a poem entitled "The Rights of Woman," which opens with an ironic address to "injured Woman" and concludes with the assertion that women ought to "abandon each ambitious thought" and accept the "soft maxims" of "Nature's school," which teach that "separate rights are lost in mutual love." Although Mrs. Barbauld was occasionally grouped with feminists, even her political enemies knew better, as a critic for the *Anti-Jacobin Review* indicated when he disputed her inclusion in a political satire upon certain "sisters in femality" and argued, quite correctly, that Mrs. Barbauld "must reprobate with me the alarming eccentricities of Miss Wollstonecraft." A. R. Humphreys [*in Modern Language Review,* 1946] has classified Mrs. Barbauld as belonging among conservative Bluestockings who "contented themselves with enhancing the prestige of women by a peaceful penetration of male preserves, rather than by blowing trumpets for independence." This estimate of her position seems much more accurate than a recent study which has included Mrs. Barbauld among those who "discriminated against [their] own sex."

In the **British Novelists**, if Mrs. Barbauld does not quite blow trumpets for the advent of women novelists, she comes very close to doing so. Not only does she recognize the dominance of women novelists, but she also welcomes it, as one paragraph, devoted to that point, states:

> And indeed . . . it may safely be affirmed that we have more good writers in this walk living at the present time, than at any period since the days of Richardson and Fielding. A very great proportion of these are ladies: and surely it will not be said that either taste or morals have been losers by their taking the pen in hand. The names of D'Arblay, Edgeworth, Inchbald, Radcliffe, and a number more, will vindicate the assertion.

Several features signify Mrs. Barbauld's efforts to do justice to the women novelists. Of the twenty-one authors in **British Novelists**, eight are women, and of the twenty-eight novels, twelve are by women. But it is not simply numerical apportionment that reveals her respect for these women, nor is her interest compelled by the common opinion she shares that the typical novel reader is female, often "a young woman in the retired scenes of life," for whom good novels proffer sound moral education, especially with respect to people "whom it is safer to read of than to meet." Rather, the evidence is in the prefaces, in which she evaluates the work of the writers, and to some extent in the account of the history of the novel.

The recognition of women in the history of the novel is a significant point in Mrs. Barbauld's long introductory essay. Assuming realism to be the distinguishing trait of the developing novel, she marks its beginning from the period when "a closer imitation of nature began to be called for." This landmark in the history of the novel is displayed by the work of Madeleine de Scudéry, along with that of La Calprenède, who "in the construction of the story, came nearer to real life." The next important figure of the developing genre is also a woman, Mme de la Fayette, whose fiction is the first to depict truthfully "the manners of cultivated life and natural incidents related with elegance" and thereby the first to "approach the modern novel of the serious kind." In England, of course,

she recognizes Defoe's realism as marking the beginning of the genre, after which "in the reign of George the Second, Richardson, Fielding, and Smollet, appeared in quick succession; and their success raised . . . a demand for this kind of entertainment." Nevertheless, she includes male and female novelists impartially, with no divisions by gender or even by such rankings as "major" and "minor." She mentions Mrs. Behn and Mrs. Manly, citing some moral objections to their novels; more approvingly, Mrs. Haywood, Mrs. Sheridan, Mrs. West, Miss Fielding, and Mrs. Opie; and most enthusiastically, Miss Edgeworth, Miss Burney, Mrs. Inchbald, and Mrs. Radcliffe.

While not discriminating against women writers, Mrs. Barbauld does ponder the differences between men and women novelists. Women, she observes, give a more "melancholy tinge" and less humor to their works than men. The chief reason, she thinks, is circumstance: "Men, mixing at large in society, have a brisker flow of ideas." In addition, she suggests that only "the stronger powers of man" have the ability to produce humor, the "scarcer product of the mind." The product of woman's mind, in contrast, is "sentiment," resulting from the societally imposed necessity to "nurse those feelings in secrecy and silence" which men usually experience only "transiently" and "with fewer modifications of delicacy." Women, therefore, unlike men, "diversify the expression of [feelings] with endless shades of sentiment." Thus, she perceptively notes, it is isolation that gives a distinctive color to the creations of the feminine imagination."

The women whose works are represented in the collection of novels—and who are thus treated more fully—are Clara Reeve, Charlotte Lennox, Frances Moore Brooke, Elizabeth Inchbald, Charlotte Turner Smith, Fanny Burney, Ann Radcliffe, and Maria Edgeworth—certainly a stellar group. Mrs. Barbauld deals with them justly and generously. In addition to biographical information, the prefaces include general assessments of the work of the authors and more detailed comments on a variety of matters such as structure and style and theme.

In each preface, usually at the beginning, Mrs. Barbauld summarizes in a few words the general reputation of the novelist. In the "Origin and Progress," though not applying any systematic rankings, she indicates that some novels are noteworthy for "excellence," some for "singularity," and some for moderate popularity "though not of high celebrity." These somewhat unequal categories roughly guide her overall assessments. Essentially they are subjective, but they also reflect popular critical opinions. Sometimes she evaluates in broad terms, as in the case of Clara Reeve who can claim only "a moderate degree of merit," or Charlotte Lennox, who is "very respectable," or even Fanny Burney, of whom she declares: "Scarcely any name, if any, stands higher in the list of novel-writers than that of Miss BURNEY." Maria Edgeworth is a novelist "fully in possession of the esteem and admiration of the public." In other cases, style is the telling trait, as with Mrs. Brooke and Mrs. Smith, whose novels are characterized by "elegance." Mrs. Barbauld also gives high marks for innovation. She admires Mrs. Inchbald's originality, and especially Mrs. Radcliffe's: "Though every production which is good in its kind entitles its author to praise, a greater distinction is due to those which stand at the head of a class; and such are undoubtedly the novels of Mrs. Radcliffe—which exhibit a genius of no common stamp." On the whole, Mrs. Barbauld's rankings hold good even today.

Mrs. Barbauld sometimes accords the individual elements of fiction the cursory treatment typical of the times, especially with respect to plot. For example, she complains that Frances Brooke's *Emily Montague* is not "interesting in the story" because descriptive passages predominate. But her criteria of coherence and unity are implicit in her praise of Brooke's *Lady Julia Mandeville* as a "simple, well connected story" and of Clara Reeve's *Old English Baron* as a "simple and well connected" story. By the same standard she censures as "a fault in the story" the "unravelling" of *The Mysteries of Udolpho,* which "depends but little on the circumstances that previously engaged our attention." Frederick R. Karl notes [in *The Adversary Literature,* 1974] that the concept of coherent plot structures in eighteenth-century novels evolved from the effort to counteract and control the episodic nature of earlier fiction, largely by focusing more on character than on events. Something of this attitude is evident in many of Mrs. Barbauld's remarks about plot. The objection to the loose episodic plot is clear in her criticism that *The Female Quixote* is "spun out too much." A feeling that plot should be subordinate to other elements lies behind her identification of the problem with stories characterized by the "strong charm of suspense and mystery," which is that at "the end of the story, the charm is dissolved, we have no wish to read it again."

Mrs. Barbauld's approval of the originality of the women novelists often focuses around their efforts to work out plots that center on character or theme more than events. She admires as "a new circumstance" the marital situation in Burney's *Cecilia* which "forms, very happily, the plot of the piece." She likes the characterization of the miser, Briggs, because "it is not the common idea of a miser . . . an originality is given to it" ("Miss Burney," 38:iv-v). Inchbald's "originality both in the characters and the situation" is illustrated by *A Simple Story,* which is not a *"simple story"* but "two distinct stories, connected indeed by the character of Dorriforth, which they successfully serve to illustrate."

Burney and Inchbald also represent laudable achievement in narrative technique. Significantly, both are praised for experimenting with points of view that conceal the authorial presence. Mrs. Barbauld praises Burney for dialogue "pointedly distinguished from the elegant and dignified style of the author herself." She is not simply addressing the issue of decorum. Fanny Burney's technique has the effect of drama: "every thing seems to pass before the reader's eyes." In *Cecilia,* for example, "We almost hear and feel the report of the pistol." Similarly, she finds it "a particular beauty" of the novels of Elizabeth Inchbald that they are "thrown so much into the dramatic form" that there is "little of mere narrative." What Mrs. Barbauld

likes is that "we see and hear the persons themselves; we are but little led to think of the author."

Another example of Mrs. Barbauld's interest in the developing techniques is her responsiveness to Inchbald's manipulation of time in *A Simple Story.* "The break between the first and second parts of the story has a singularly fine effect. We pass over in a moment a large space of years, and find everything changed. . . . This sudden shifting of the scene has an effect which no continued narrative could produce; an effect which even the scenes of real life could not produce." This is a remarkable concession from a proponent of realism.

Such a concession is, of course, prepared for by the discussion in the introductory essay of the novel as an aesthetic form, determined by the author's controlling hand in accordance with his or her design rather than the chance-medley of real life. Mrs. Barbauld's analysis of Ann Radcliffe's novels provides her the opportunity to illustrate her theory very clearly. As a rationalist, she always preferred sense to sensibility, and Gothic novels did not naturally appeal to her. Yet her recognition of Mrs. Radcliffe in one of her longer prefaces is accorded to a writer breaking new ground and carrying out successfully the design of the whole, no matter how different the design is from fiction which is based in realism or how jarring some elements seem in the execution.

She accepts readily the assumption that Mrs. Radcliffe "seems to scorn to move those passions which form the interests of common novels." Her purposes are otherwise: Radcliffe "alarms the soul with terror; agitates it with suspense, prolonged and wrought up to the most intense feeling." A consequence of these different purposes is clearly different methods. Mrs. Barbauld connects them with the idea of the sublime and, citing Edmund Burke, praises the novelist for being able "perfectly to understand that obscurity . . . is a strong ingredient in the sublime." This focus on obscurity is central; it is the reason for a setting of "vast uninhabited castles, winding staircases, long echoing aisles . . . lonely heaths, gloomy forests . . . the canvass and the figures of Salvator Rosa," or for an atmosphere of "solitude, darkness, low whispered sounds, obscure glimpses of objects." Characterization grows out of these assumptions, too: the "living characters correspond to the scenery:—their wicked projects are dark, singular, atrocious." Mrs. Barbauld's main criticism is aimed only at Mrs. Radcliffe's disruption of such unity, particularly manifest in this Gothic novelist's habit of finally revealing mysteries as merely natural phenomena. The reader is not only disappointed at the kind of explanation offered, but also resistant to any explanation, for the reader has been "affected so repeatedly, the suspense has been so long protracted, and expectations raised so high, that no explanation can satisfy, no imagery of horrors can equal the vague shapings of our imagination."

The criterion of "real life," nevertheless, weighs heavily in Mrs. Barbauld's judgment of other novelists. Thanks to a "discerning eye," Fanny Burney "draws from life, and exhibits not only the passions of human nature, but the manners of the age and the affectations of the day." A virtue of Charlotte Smith's novels is "that they show a knowledge of life," usually of "genteel life," but sometimes of "common life." Comments like these are more usual, partly because they reflect a basic tenet, partly because when selecting representative novels, Mrs. Barbauld chose novels grounded in realism.

Mrs. Barbauld's essays are full of comments on a miscellany of fictional elements, for she is not a systematic critic. She likes good beginnings, which, as in Radcliffe's *The Sicilian Romance,* remind her of "the tuning of an instrument by a skillful hand." She dislikes improbable or protracted endings, and she dislikes ambiguous endings, such as those in Fanny Burney's later novels, for though it is "true that in human life" one cannot "say whether the story ends happily or unhappily," in fiction there should be no doubt. On the other hand, though certainly a moralist herself, Mrs. Barbauld does not like novels that preach or teach too much, a fault she finds in Mrs. Inchbald's *Nature and Art,* which seems to her less a novel than a vehicle for "reflections on the political and moral state of society." Moreover, Mrs. Barbauld may seem to give first importance to the "very moral and instructive story of the *Harrels,*" for example, but her elaboration of the comment gives greater weight to Burney's ability to dramatize effectively the theme of "the mean rapacity of the fashionable spendthrift." Inappropriate tone jars Mrs. Barbauld's sensibility, as, for example, the "bitter and querulous tone of complaint" that pervades much of the unhappy Charlotte Smith's writings. Similarly, she objects to the "low humour" which "strongly characterizes, sometimes perhaps blemishes," Burney's "genius." She personally enjoys both the "beauties of description" and original verse at which some of these writers excel—Smith, Brooke, and Radcliffe, particularly—but she thinks these elements are a hindrance to "a novel of high interest." On the other hand, such decorative passages may be "very properly placed, at judicious intervals, in compositions of which variety rather than deep pathos, and elegance rather than strength, are the characteristics." Again, these elements are judged in terms of the whole design.

Mrs. Barbauld has never received adequate credit for her work as a critic. Yet she fully appreciated the novel and argued skillfully for its status as an important literary form. Although her theories about realistic representation of character, coherent plot structure, the design of the whole, dramatic narrative techniques, and moral tendency were not at all original, they were nowhere else at the time brought together; nor was there a single, extensive, thorough defense of the novel such as hers. But Mrs. Barbauld had always championed the novel, even as a young writer, for one of her earliest essays argues from the same premise that undergirds her later defense of the novel, that it "exhibits life in its true state" and that "every one can relish the author who represents common life because every one can refer to the originals from whence his ideas were taken." Her history of fiction is important as an attempt to give the novel the prestige of literary tradition, then still a relatively rare concept, and it is a creditable history, even by today's standards.

Finally, Mrs. Barbauld leaves no doubts about the significant role of women in the development of this still young and mistrusted literary form, which, nonetheless, calls upon "talents of the highest order." The introductory essay displays her appreciation of women writers throughout, not only by her references to English novelists, but also by her knowledgeable observations about various contemporary French women novelists, such as the Comtesse de Genlis, Sophie Cottin, Mme de Staël, Marie Jeanne Riccoboni, and Mme Élie de Beaumont. Subtly emphatic is her casual manner of giving the works of male and female novelists equal billing: "Many a young woman has caught from such works as *Clarissa* and *Cecilia,* ideas of delicacy and refinement." At other times she simply offers women novelists as typical examples of responsible authorship: "The more severe and homely virtues of prudence and oeconomy have been enforced in the writings of a Burney and an Edgeworth." Admirable, too, is Mrs. Barbauld's sensitivity to the different but powerful direction represented by Mrs. Radcliffe's novels. The more detailed analysis of the novels of Radcliffe and Burney signify the higher estimate she accords their work. She does a service, however, to all the women novelists, for she praises them freely and criticizes them seriously. She honestly ponders their distinctions both as novelists and as women novelists, and she grants them their own value as serious writers. Her introductory tribute to the work of the "ladies" who were "taking the pen in hand" is a fitting preamble to the critical and biographical prefaces which follow. They constitute a remarkable, enlightened, and even, to some degree, systematic criticism of the eighteenth-century novel and perhaps the first extended criticism of the woman novelist.

FURTHER READING

Biography

Le Breton, Anna Laetitia. *Memoir of Mrs. Barbauld Including Letters and Notices of Her Family and Friends.* London: Bell, 1874, 236 p.

    An account of Barbauld's life written by her grand-niece and including the texts of several of her poems and letters.

Oliver, Grace A. *The Story of the Life of Anna Laetitia Barbauld, with Many of Her Letters.* Boston: Cupples, Upham & Co., 1874.

    Biography based on Barbauld's correspondence and accounts by her contemporaries.

Rodgers, Betsey. *Georgian Chronicle: Mrs. Barbauld and Her Family.* London: Methuen, 1958, 298 p.

    Traces the history of Barbauld's family from the late seventeenth century through the mid-nineteenth century; includes bibliography and previously unpublished correspondence.

Criticism

"A Forgotten Children's Book." *The Hibbert Journal* 63,

No. 298 (Autumn 1964): 27-34.
> Discusses the publication history and contents of Barbauld's *Hymns in Prose for Children;* includes several facsimile pages.

McCarthy, William, and Elizabeth Kraft. Introduction to *The Poems of Anna Letitia Barbauld,* pp. xxi-xlii. Athens: University of Georgia Press, 1994.
> Reviews Barbauld's poetic works as well as contemporary and subsequent critical reception of her poetry.

Mishra, Vijay. "Gothic Fragments and Fragmented Gothics." In *The Gothic Sublime,* pp. 83-116. Albany: State University of New York, 1994.
> Defines the "Gothic fragment" as a distinct genre within the Gothic, taking Barbauld's "Sir Bertrand, A Fragment" as its archetypical text.

Rogers, Katharine M. "Anna Barbauld's Criticism of Fiction—Johnsonian Mode, Female Vision." *Studies in Eighteenth-Century Culture* 21 (1991): 27-41.
> Compares Barbauld's and Samuel Johnson's evaluations of the novel as a genre, paying particular attention to Barbauld's interest in woman readers and writers.

Ross, Marlon B. "The Birth of a Tradition: Making Cultural Space for Feminine Poetry." In *The Contours of Masculine Desire: Romanticism and the Rise of Woman's Poetry,* pp. 187-231. New York: Oxford University Press, 1989.
> Relates Barbauld's politics to the style and content of her poetry and to her attitudes towards her own writing.

Williams, Porter, Jr. "The Influence of Mrs. Barbauld's *Hymns in Prose for Children* upon Blake's *Songs of Innocence and of Experience.*" In *A Fair Day in the Affections: Literary Essays in Honor of Robert B. White, Jr.,* edited by Jack D. Durant and M. Thomas Hester, pp. 131-46. Raleigh, N.C.: Winston Press, 1980.
> Argues that Barbauld's *Hymns* exercised a small but significant influence on the style, imagery, and thematic structure of *Songs of Innocence.*

.

Zall, Paul M. "Wordsworth's 'Ode' and Mrs. Barbauld's *Hymns.*" *The Wordsworth Circle* 1, No. 4 (Autumn 1970): 177-79.
> Presents evidence that Barbauld's *Hymns in Prose for Children* influenced Wordsworth's poetic expression.

————. "The Cool World of Samuel Taylor Coleridge: Mrs. Barbauld's Crew and the Building of a Mass Reading Class." *The Wordsworth Circle* 2, No. 3 (Summer 1971): 74-9.
> Considers the contribution of Barbauld and other contemporary women writers for children to the spread of literacy in the late eighteenth century.

Additional coverage of Barbauld's life and career is contained in the following sources published by Gale Research: *Dictionary of Literary Biography,* Vols. 107, 109, 142.

Orestes Brownson

1803-1876

(Born Orestes Augustus Brownson) American clergyman, editor, essayist, and philosopher.

INTRODUCTION

Brownson's life and work were centrally concerned with the quest for religious truth and belief in justice and political liberty. Brownson's search for truth led him from Presbyterianism, Universalism, Unitarianism, and Transcendentalism to Catholicism. His political beliefs changed as frequently as his religious convictions, earning him a reputation among some critics as fickle and insincere. Despite these reservations, Brownson's works have been studied by twentieth-century scholars as thorough, insightful examinations of American government and religion.

Biographical Information

Born in Stockbridge, Vermont, Brownson and his twin sister were the youngest of six children. His father died not long after Brownson was born, and poverty forced his mother to send young Brownson to live with relatives in Royalton, Vermont. Several years later he was reunited with his family and at age 14 the Brownsons moved to upstate New York. At age 19, Brownson joined the Presbyterian Church, which he left two years later to join the Universalist Church, becoming an ordained Universalist minister in 1826. At about the same time, Brownson became a school teacher and fell in love with a student, Sally Healy; he and Healy were married in 1827 and, over the years had eight children. In 1831, Brownson left organized religion to become an independent preacher but he soon became a member and minister of the Unitarian Church. Following a move to Massachusetts in 1834 and meeting Henry David Thoreau the following year, Brownson became involved with the Transcendentalist movement and attended early meetings of the Transcendental Club. As Brownson's political and religious views continued to develop, he founded *The Boston Quarterly Review* in 1838, publishing his own essays on such topics as Presbyterianism, Unitarianism, and Christian socialism, as well as articles by various contributors, including Albert Brisbane and Margaret Fuller. During this time Brownson was also exploring the principles of Christianity and the life and work of Jesus Christ. His work in these areas led him to make his final religious conversion to Roman Catholicism in 1844. The same year, he began publishing *Brownson's Quarterly Review,* serving as its sole contributor. The essays, articles, and reviews he published therein reveal the shift in Brownson's political beliefs from his radical "denial of all authority except that of humanity" to the conviction that government is intended as an imitation of "Divine Providence" designed to protect humanity. His new political convictions led him to an unsuccessful run as the Republican candidate

in the 1862 Congressional election. Two years later, Brownson ceased publishing his *Quarterly Review* in order to begin writing what is perhaps his most well-known work, *The American Republic: Its Constitution, Tendencies, and Destiny* (1866). In his later years, Brownson's health rapidly deteriorated, though he continued to write for several church publications such as *Ave Maria* and *The Catholic World.* In 1873, in keeping with his wife's dying wish, Brownson revived his *Quarterly Review* and continued its publication until October, 1875. Less than a year later, Brownson died in Detroit, Michigan, where he was living with his son Henry.

Major Works

Brownson's most respected work, *The American Republic,* is a synthesis of its author's political thought. In it, Brownson examines such topics as the nature, authority, and necessity of government, as well as the destiny of the American republic. He discusses the divine origin of government and rejects his previously held views, which regarded the state as sovereign. Concerning the relationship between Church and state, Brownson argues that the two were united in principle and that neither should absorb the other. In 1854 Brownson wrote *The Spirit-Rapper: An Autobiography* in which he offers his reaction to critics who misunderstood his religious conversions and questioned his sincerity. However, the book was not a serious attempt to document his life and thought, and in 1857 Brownson completed his memoirs, *The Convert; or Leaves from My Experience.* The work chronicles his religious life through his conversion to Catholicism. Although noted for its candor and evidence of its author's rejection of earlier, radical beliefs, *The Convert* did little to earn Brownson the approval he sought.

Critical Reception

During his lifetime, Brownson's literary reputation was tainted by the radical shifts in his religious and political philosophies. Twentieth-century scholars, however, have reconsidered Brownson's work and have viewed it far more favorably than their nineteenth-century predecessors. This reexamination of Brownson as a noteworthy critical thinker extends to his religious thought as well as his writings on the American system of government. Brownson's logic and his powerful analyses, particularly as displayed in *The American Republic,* have been lauded by both Catholic and non-Catholic critics.

PRINCIPAL WORKS

Address on Intemperance (speech) 1833

New Views of Christianity, Society, and the Church (essays) 1836

The Mediatorial Life of Jesus (biography) 1842

Brownson's Quarterly Review (journal) 1844-64, 1873-75

Essays and Reviews, Chiefly on Theology, Politics, and Socialism (criticism) 1852

The Convert: or Leaves from My Experience (autobiography) 1857

The American Republic: Its Constitution, Tendencies, and Destiny (philosophy) 1866

Conversations on Liberalism and the Church (conversations) 1870

The Spirit-Rapper: and Autobiography (autobiography) 1854

CRITICISM

Henry F. Brownson (essay date 1882)

SOURCE: An introduction to *The Works of Orestes A. Brownson, Vol. I,* edited by Henry F. Brownson, Thorndike Nourse, Publisher, 1882, pp. v-xxviii.

[*In the following excerpt, one of the sons of Orestes Brownson provides an overview of this father's philosophical and religious beliefs.*]

It should be borne in mind that [Orestes Brownson] became a publicist at the age of only a little over twenty years, and for fifty years was before the public as a preacher, a lecturer, and a writer. Starting with a belief in the progressive perfectibility of the human race, and the denial of all authority except that of *humanity,* that is, of the people, or the masses, he did not claim that he was in possession of any truth to be taught, or that his views were either mature or sound. Humanity had outgrown the errors of its infancy and was moving on with an irresistible progress towards moral and intellectual truth; but as yet it had gone but a little way. Ages and ages were to elapse before it should attain its final destiny and its full development. The Christianity of to-day was far in advance of what it was as taught by Jesus, for it had grown and developed with eighteen centuries of the growth and development of the race. All that the friends of moral and religious progress could do to hasten this growth was to direct the attention of the masses to the great questions of life, its aims and its duties, in order to excite their thought to greater activity. On this theory it became the duty of every one who had views of his own to send them forth, right or wrong; the infallible instinct of humanity would preserve all that was good and true and the rest would perish. It was with this view Doctor Brownson began to preach and to write. His mind was almost constantly engaged with the great questions of philosophy, of religion, and of government, on which he published his views from day to day. Starting with no settled principles to direct his course he wandered from one doctrine to another, seeking for something to satisfy his mind, but meeting with disappointment after disappointment. To assert that all the writings of such a man were consistent would be to assert what every one knows must be false, and that he was as wise at twenty as he was at seventy. A careful study of all he wrote will, however, show that the changes in his opinions were never a departure from the truth once acquired, but a clearing away of the mists surrounding it in his own mind. They were a steady progress towards the clear perception of truth, and he is never found returning to an error he had once abandoned, or losing sight of a truth he had once perceived.

As fast as he detected an error in his own writings or those of another, he was anxious all the world should be warned against it, and he wrote in its refutation. If he caught a glimpse of a truth new to him, burning with the desire to communicate it to others, he wrote in its defence. His views being brought in this way before the public as they were forming in his own mind, he seemed to many that watched his course to be constantly changing, and those who saw not that these changes were but the successive abandonment of errors and the acquisition of additional truths, called him fickle and inconstant.

The great aim of Doctor Brownson's life was the attainment of truth in matters of religion. What must he do, what must he believe, in order to be saved? He saw that he must either accept revealed authority that would lead to the Catholic Church and follow it thither, or else reject supernatural revelation altogether and look for the truth in infidelity. Catholicity was the less reasonable alternative in the opinion of one who had formed his notions of Catholic faith and morals from Presbyterian misrepresentation and had no other knowledge of Catholics or their books. He, therefore, first tried infidelity,—under the forms of Universalism and Unitarianism,—and for twenty years he wrote and preached the religion of humanity, philanthropy, and progress. Towards the end of this time he began to learn that the progress and perfection of the race, of which he had dreamed, required other light and aid than the race itself furnished. As he expressed it, "A man cannot lift himself by his own waistbands," and so neither could the human race by its own efforts alone rise above its natural condition. Some extrinsic aid and light, something outside of and above nature must be communicated to it to elevate, perfect, and enlighten it. This something he could find nowhere except in the supernatural life and divine doctrine of the Catholic Church. He had never read but two Catholic books, Milner's *End of Controversy* and the *Catechism of the Council of Trent,* and even these only partially. He guessed at the Catholic doctrines from his knowledge of the Protestant doctrines opposed to them, and though he often guessed aright, he often blundered. Nevertheless, he had formed to himself an ideal Catholicity, demanded by his philosophy and sustained by it; and this ideal Catholicity he imagined was substantially what the Catholic Church believes, or really intends by her articles of faith. So he concluded that he was a Catholic, and had discovered a philosophy which would legitimate the Catholic Church, and give a scientific basis to all her doctrines. Such was the view he then took of the Church, that he fancied he might consistently, for a time, at least, stay outside of it, and labor to bring the Protestant public to right views of the Church in general. He thought he could do more good out of the Church than in it; and his dream was that he might by working in the bosom of the Protestant Churches, prepare them to return to the bosom of Catholic unity. But it was a brief dream. Logic demanded a plain, open avowal of Catholicity, and he always had a great horror of the sin of being inconsequent. Moreover, another question pressed hard, namely, the question of the salvation of his own soul. If the Catholic Church was the true Church, he could not be saved without being in her communion; for, admitting that the invincibly ignorant may be saved without being actually within her communion, the plea of invincible ignorance could not avail him, for he believed the Catholic Church to be the true Church. Then, again, he found himself in want of the helps that Church had to give. It was idle to contend for the necessity of the Church, if, standing outside of it, he could yet maintain the personal integrity, and attain to the holiness of life, for which the Church with her sacraments was especially instituted.

Dr. Brownson had already convinced himself of the insufficiency of Naturalism, Rationalism, and Transcendentalism; he had also convinced himself of the necessity of divine revelation, and of the fact that the Christian revelation was such a revelation. From this, by a process of reasoning which may be seen in the article **"The Church against no Church,"** he arrived infallibly at the Catholic Church. The process is simple and easy. It requires no

metaphysical subtilty, no long train of metaphysical reasoning. All it needs is good common sense, a reverent spirit, and a disposition to believe on sufficient evidence. Thus, after twenty years and more of wandering in search of a new and better way to the truth, he was forced to come back, to sit in humble docility at the feet of God's priests and learn of those sent by our Lord to teach. Fortunate was he in the teacher from whom he learnt Catholic doctrine and morals. Never again in the world did he find so true a friend, so patient and wise a teacher as his first instructor in the faith, the late Bishop Fitzpatrick of Boston. On being admitted into the Church Dr. Brownson wished to discontinue writing for the public until he should become more familiar with Catholic truth and Catholic habits of thought and expression. But Bishop Fitzpatrick urged him to continue to write on questions of theology, justly believing that he would be of great service to the Church in addressing the Protestant public, which he understood, and laboring to convince non-Catholics that what they wanted, life and truth, can be found in the true Church and nowhere else.

Those who may read the essays on political matters contained in these volumes, will not fail to note that the author's political opinions or views of government ran parallel with his religious or theological convictions. At first he was a radical, a believer in the majesty, the infallibility,—the divinity, I may say,—of the masses, placing the origin of all authority in the individual man, attempting to establish the association or community system of government; seeking the overthrow of all priesthood because it binds the conscience; of the banks, because they are in the interest of the business class or employers and opposed to the laboring class or employed; of the transmission of property by will or descent, because a man's right to his property ceased with his death, and he would have the State apportion it amongst the most needy. As he came to acknowledge the authority of God in matters of religion, he saw that power too was from him and thenceforth held that government was necessary for the preservation of order and the restraining of license, and although the political people are the means or channel through which the State derives its power, yet that power, whether monarchical, aristocratic, democratic, or mixed, is from God, and he that resists it resists God. Thus from a radical, a destroyer of all authority, he came to see in human Government a likeness and imitation of Divine Providence; not an evil to be hated and resisted, but a beneficent agent for the protection of right, the advancement of civilization, the aid of religion, science, art, and learning, and next to religion the greatest means by which man may attain his destiny, and as such to be loved, obeyed, and defended.

The essays of Dr. Brownson on theology, politics, and morals, are all based on his philosophy, according to which nature and grace, reason and revelation, the order of reality and that of science are brought into the harmony which for three hundred years had been the aim of thinking men.

The denial of authority in matters of revelation in the

fifteenth century was soon followed by a philosophical system which logically leads to scepticism,—atheism, or pantheism. The Cartesian philosophy had reduced all science to the science of the subject, and found its last logical results in Fichte's *Wissenschaftslehre,*—that the I is absolute and relative, in itself eternal, infinite, God; in its projections or manifestations only phenomenal. . . .

In his earlier philosophical writings, Dr. Brownson should be classed with the Eclectics. . . . In 1842 he disavowed Eclecticism and began to think out a philosophy for himself. The results of this attempt, so far as it went, may be seen in the articles on **"Schmucker's Psychology,"** the **"Synthetic Philosophy,"** and **"Philosophy of History."** But in these there is little that is original, and in his later years he had neither the time nor the inclination to produce a new system of philosophy. So far as the details are concerned, the usual philosophy taught in Catholic schools is satisfactory in the main. The great objection brought against the accepted philosophy was not on account of its method or its results, but that since Descartes philosophers have occupied themselves with method rather than principles. The great question has been to prove that science is science, that when we know we know that we know. Logic as an art is correctly taught and there is no improvement to be made in it; but logic as a science should be reformed. As now taught it is substantially pagan, based on the Aristotelian notion of matter and form, by the union of which all things are produced. He earnestly wished some competent person would reconstruct the philosophy now taught so that it shall conform to the truth, and shall assert that the object of thought is the real, and that what is not is not intelligible. The person to whom he suggested to undertake this labor has been for many years considering the plan to be pursued, and it is very possible that before long he will give to the public a text-book of philosophy based on the principles defended in Dr. Brownson's later writings.

It was by a slow process and severe study that the author worked out his philosophical conclusions. Yet in every one of his philosophical essays there seems to be an advance. In the essay on **"Philosophy and Common Sense"** the distinction is pointed out between direct and reflex thought, between intuition and reflection. Intuition is identified with common sense, while philosophy is shown to be the result of reflection on the matter furnished by common sense. In the criticism of Schmucker's *Psychology* the writer holds that the human mind is in intimate relation with the necessary and eternal truth which it perceives in perceiving the variable, the finite, and the contingent, not as an abstraction, but as the basis of the perception, or as expressed in his later essays, the intelligible or ideal element. In the **"Synthetic Psychology,"** the reality of the object of thought is established, and the author shows true philosophy must start not from the subject alone, nor from the object alone; but from their synthesis, the subject, the object, and the relation of both.

In his criticism of Kant the author has made an immense advance on his previous writings. He becomes clearer both in thought and expression, and at the same time more profound. He sees the absurdity of Kant's great problem of the possibility of science, which Kant denies, proving by science the impossibility of science. He shows that Kant, like most psychologists who seek for the object in the subject, errs in holding that in the fact of knowledge, the form under which the object is known, depends not on what the object is, but on the laws of the subject knowing it. In **"An a priori Autobiography"** the author demonstrates that we have direct and immediate intuition of real and necessary being; that abstractions are nullities; that ideas are not the product of the mind, but its real intelligible object, that they are in the Divine Reason, and are the Divine Reason. In the article on **"The Existence of God,"** it is proved from the fact of intuition of real being, which must be necessary and eternal, that we have intuition of that which is God; and therefore God is, and from this time on his philosophy is well settled in his own mind. At first he had held that all activity was in the subject; but when he reflected on the impossibility of the mind being its own object, or acting without the object, he easily proved the activity of the object presenting or affirming itself to the intellect, and then the reality of the object. Analyzing the object he finds the three elements: the ideal, without which the object would not be intelligible; the empirical, the fact of experience, the object as apprehended; and the relation of those two. In the ideal element he finds the necessary, the contingent, and their relation; the formula of which he makes: Being creates existences.

It would be presumptuous in me to attempt to prove the correctness of this analysis. Nothing can be added to the force of the arguments Dr. Brownson adduced in its proof. But the opponents of this formula who have reasoned against it, may not have understood exactly what Dr. Brownson meant by it. He did not maintain that the formula, as a formula, is intuitive, or given by intuition; but that it simply expresses what is given in ideal intuition. The formula itself is formed by reflection; or, in other words, the ideal formula is a formal and scientific statement of what is given intuitively as objective ideas, reduced by a mental process to a scientific formula or statement. There is nothing in it that supposes being or existences are not both presented to the mind as ideas. Indeed, it assumes that such is the fact, and this is wherefore the formula is termed ideal. It claims to embody in a complete formula the ideal element of all thought and what must be held by the mind as the condition of all science; and it maintains that this element, the principle and basis of all science, is given intuitively, in opposition to those who hold it to be innate, a form of the intellect, or obtained by the mind by its own action operating without ideas or principles. It has been misapprehended by having been confounded with the doctrine of the ontologists, from which it is essentially different; for the intuition they assert is not ideal, but a direct and immediate intuition of God. The formula itself is a synthesis of all that is given us in ideal intuition, and of the principles of all the real and all the knowable; but is not itself intuitive, and is obtained only by the most careful and profound analysis of the principles of thought, or of human cognition, and is the *primum philosophicum* only because it states what philosophy must recognize as given intuitively, in order to render thought, cognition, or empirical intuition possible and real.

It is a simple process from *Being creates existences* to demonstrate that God creates all that exists, and that the first cause must be the final cause, that the creative act is not completed in the initial order, but requires the teleological as its complement. Irrational creatures are created for the rational and these find their perfection as their origin in God. The beatitude or rational creatures is union with God. In the creative act of God is the foundation of ethics, of the moral law, and while this establishes the obligation to obey, it is sanctioned by the beatitude or misery which follows obedience or disobedience.

Many of the controversies in which **Brownson's Quarterly Review** took part were waged *fortiter in modo* as well as *in re* and susceptibilities were wounded and prejudices aroused. So far as those controversies were against the theological errors of infidels, Protestants, or of some within the Church, there is no apology to make. Truth is stern and uncompromising, and neither the Apostles nor the Fathers speak or write very *suaviter in modo* when combating heresy or immorality. But in the discussions of nationality just before the breaking out of the civil war, fault was found with our foreign-born citizens that they retained their foreign nationality and did not assimilate with the American people. Later Dr. Brownson thought they were Americanizing full fast enough, whether for the good of religion or the good of the nation. American national character, since the war, has not developed in a direction to make a natural-born citizen overproud of his American nationality. It is more necessary to guard Catholics of foreign birth against adopting the vices of the American character than it is to urge them to Americanize. The original American Constitution was a good one, worthy of the support of all good men, but as developed and applied by popular opinion and political parties, it can command the respect of no wise or thinking man. Much as he loved his country and venerated the Constitution as it was, he thoroughly detested the dominant radicalism, no matter of what party, which, if not checked, cannot fail to lead the nation to destruction, whither it is hastening with railroad speed.

In his earlier writings Dr. Brownson attempted to prove that the Church is compatible with American democracy; later he went further and insisted that without her, without her faith and discipline, her authority and influence, American democracy will go to destruction. No government, democratic, aristocratic, or monarchical, is or can be a good government if divorced from religion and moving on independently of the Church. No secular order suffices for itself or can sustain itself without the aid of the Catholic Church, nor even with her aid, if Catholics adopt the false maxim that their politics have nothing to do with their religion, or in politics act as if God had no rights and they no religion. The *Syllabus* condemns the separation of Church and State in the sense that the State is independent of the Church or spiritual authority, or that politics is not subject to the law of God. God is King of kings and Lord of lords, and the State, whatever its constitution, is subject to his supreme and universal law, and bound by his law as declared by his Church as much as is the individual himself. It is the forgetfulness of this great truth, or the neglect of courtly prelates to insist on it with due emphasis that has brought the old Catholic nations of Europe into their present deplorable condition.

For two or three years before the suspension of his **Review** in 1864, Dr. Brownson favored the tendencies of the liberal Catholics at home and abroad, but he never went all lengths with them. He steadily maintained two essential points finally settled by the Holy Council of the Vatican,—the supremacy of the Pope as head of the Church, and his infallibility in teaching and in determining all questions pertaining to faith. His **Review** steadily maintained that Our Lord founded the Church on Peter, and that the papacy is at the base as well as at the summit, the foundation as well as the crown of the edifice, that all power or authority in the Church is derived from Christ through him, and that bishops hold and exercise their authority in their respective jurisdictions from him as the successor of Peter and Vicar of Christ. He had been taught that Gallicans were Catholics, and that he could not assert papal infallibility as a Catholic dogma, but he held it as true, and was never able to defend the infallibility of the Church to his own satisfaction without asserting it. Consequently he hailed with joy the definition of the Council of the Vatican.

Another point he always maintained and gave great offence to liberal Catholics by doing so, is the supremacy of the Pope as representative of the spiritual order over temporal princes. He maintained that the power assumed by the Pope to depose the German Èmperors and other princes professing the Catholic faith belonged to him *jure divino,* not simply *jure humano,* that he held it not from the *jus publicum,* or by the consent of the nations, but as the Vicar of Christ and inherent in him as the divinely constituted representative of the spiritual order on earth or in human affairs. The popes no doubt exercised often an arbitratorship in disputes between sovereign and sovereign, and between sovereigns and their subjects by common consent; the Popes also exercised authority in several states as feudal suzerain, for those states had by their own consent and desire become fiefs of the Holy See. In neither of these cases did the **Review** ever pretend that the power exercised was held *jure divino.* Nor that in other cases, as in that of Henry IV. and Frederick II. of Germany, when the Pope was neither feudal suzerain nor simple arbitrator, though he held as Vicar of Christ the power to depose the prince and absolve his subjects from their allegiance, he was obliged to exercise it unless he believed it necessary for the interest of religion or to maintain freedom of conscience, and believed his sentence would be carried into effect. The Pope still holds the power, but there are no subjects on whom to exercise it. The Popes might as well have attempted to exercise it on the pagan emperors of Rome who persecuted the Christians of the Empire, as to attempt to exercise it on any of the sovereigns of the present day, for they have all emancipated themselves from the law of God.

Modern republicans were, no doubt, shocked at this doctrine, yet the republicans of England not only deposed, but beheaded their sovereign, Charles I. The republicans of France deposed and guillotined Louis XVI., deprived Louis Philippe of his crown, and declared the forfeiture of Napoleon III. The congress of the Anglo-American colonies deposed George III. as their sovereign, and absolved his subjects from their allegiance. Indeed, modern republicanism in both Europe and America asserts the sacred right of insurrection, and claims for any band of miscreants assuming to act in the name of the people, even more power than was ever exercised by the popes. This is natural enough, for the republicans of our day put the people in the place of God, and install demagogues as the ministers of the new religion.

There may have been little prudence, considering the state of the public mind, in broaching the doctrine, although true, but will those who object that it is inopportune, tell us how political atheism may be combated on Gallican principles, or how society may be protected from secularism and downright Godlessness, without asserting the supremacy of the spiritual over the temporal, or the law of God when human laws conflict with it? Gallicanism, which asserted the independence of the secular order, was a species of political atheism and contained the germ of communism or socialism; and it is worthy of remark that Professor Döllinger made it a grave charge against the definition of papal infallibility that it struck at the rights of the temporal power. We cannot, as Dr. Bownson said, obtain any practical safeguard against political atheism, the error that is ruining modern society, but in the recognition of the supremacy of the spiritual order, and consequently, of the Pope as its divinely instituted representative. Secularists, of course, were shocked; but truth is great and powerful, and to lack confidence in it, when fairly and honestly told, is to lack confidence in God, and is a dangerous as well as a cowardly species of infidelity.

In one respect Dr. Brownson never ceased to agree with Liberal Catholics. He differed from those Catholics who would restore Christendom on its old basis. He did not regard this as any longer practicable, or desirable even if practicable. All in that Christendom, which but too many confound with the Church, and which has now passed away, was not as the Church could wish, and under it, as now, she had to maintain an unceasing conflict with the powers of this world. There were princes who loyally served the Church, and with all their power executed her canons as far as they required the civil arm to enforce them, and willingly and faithfully protected her rights and interests; but there were many more who sought to destroy her independence, to subject her to their will, and to deprive her of her rights as the kingdom of God. The great Pope St. Gregory VII. had not an easier time than Pius IX., and the afflictions of Pascal II. were even greater, while his firmness was much less. Innocent III. found on his accession to the papal throne nearly the whole of Christendom in a state of revolt against the papacy, and Henry IV., Henry V., Henry VI., Frederick Barbarossa, and Frederick II. of Germany, the pretended successors of

Cæsar Augustus, were hardly less formidable enemies of the Church than Victor Emanuel, Prince Bismark, or the revolution these inaugurated. The Church can hardly suffer more from the internationalists, socialists, and communists than she has at times from the Kings and Kaisers of the West, and especially from the Emperors of the East.

The Christendom that has passed away, dating from the conversion of the Franks, was based on the monarchical principle, and the Church to a great extent held her relations with the faithful in each kingdom through their sovereign, instead of through her own prelates, with whom, latterly at least, the Pope could communicate, or who could communicate with him only by permission of the king. In France, Spain, Austria, and Italy, the Church under the monarchy that succeeded to feudalism, has been bound hand and foot by the secular powers, and it is to this fact we owe the dissolution of Christendom and the present condition of the Church in those nations, nay, the anti-Christian revolution now everywhere in progress. It is hardly possible, humanly speaking, for the sovereigns to arrest that revolution, or to reinstate Christendom on its old basis. The sovereigns have succeeded in alienating the affections of their subjects from the Church and bringing her into contempt with the people, and to maintain their crowns they are obliged, or believe themselves obliged to support the revolution in its war against her.

George Parsons Lathrop comments on Brownson's literary significance:

To whatever cause it be owing, Brownson is omitted from our manuals and histories of literature, or figures but slightly in them. Professor Richardson even affirms that the Catholic Church in the United States has "depended on foreign authorities in this line,"—meaning the literature of religion and morals; ignoring the fact that it has found here one of the most virile and accomplished exponents it possesses in any part of the world. In Stedman and Hutchinson's Library of American Literature only on extract from Brownson is given; and that one, relating to practical democracy, hints at but a single and least significant phase of the author's activity. Yet he was highly regarded and very prominent among his literary contemporaries, until the main current of his production flowed into Catholic channels. It seems to me that he merits a clearer and more grateful recognition, to-day, than he commonly receives. The large, Websterian cast of his mind, the cleancut massiveness of his thinking and his style, make him an interesting object of study. The very fact that in himself he formed so close a link between the Transcendental or other phases of American thought and those embodied in the Catholic Church adds to his significance; and he may well be commanded to all serious, fair-minded readers of the present and the rising generation as illustrating with strength and brilliancy the Catholic mind in the United States, and its relation to our national life.

George Parsons Lathrop, in
The Atlantic Monthly, *Vol. LXXVII,*
No. CCCCLXIV, June, 1896.

But the sovereigns in doing this are depriving themselves of all power to suppress the revolution which after using them to suppress the Church will cast them away. The Liberal Catholics, a party created by the unhappy La Mennais, urge the Church to abandon the sovereigns, who have abandoned her, make peace with the revolution, give it her blessing, and labor to reconstruct Christendom on a popular basis. These are opposed by another party who hold that it is necessary to labor to reconstitute Christendom on its old monarchical and aristocratic basis. So far as this party labor to reëstablish order and the independence of the Church Dr. Brownson was with them heart and soul, but he abhorred any alliance with the revolution, or any concession to it. He could see no reason, supposing the people Catholic, why the Church cannot be as free and independent with a Christendom based on the republican principle as she ever has been under the Christendom which no longer exists. The Church has no more necessary alliance with monarchy and nobility than she has with republicanism. She cannot make common cause with modern liberalism, nor bless the atheistic revolution; but there is nothing in her doctrine or constitution that prevents her from accepting a republican Christendom, or giving her blessing to a Christian republic, when once constituted. The people are not less trustworthy than Kings and Kaisers, and let it be remembered that the revolution originated with the sovereigns, not with the people.

Arthur M. Schlesinger, Jr. (essay date 1939)

SOURCE: "Orestes Brownson: An American Marxist Before Marx," in *The Sewanee Review,* Vol. XLVII, No. 3, Summer, 1939, pp. 317-23.

[*[Schlesinger is a prominent American historian and leading intellectual figure whose historical and political studies have won him both critical and popular acclaim. He was an influential figure in liberal politics, serving as a special assistant to Presidents John F. Kennedy and Lyndon Johnson. In addition, Schlesinger is considered one of the foremost scholars of Franklin D. Roosevelt's New Deal policies. In the essay that follows, Schlesinger argues that Brownson's theories on political economy presaged those of Karl Marx.*]

Conservatives, it has been earnestly pointed out, always confront change with the same war-cries. Throughout American history they have unfailingly demonstrated that every strange proposal, from inoculation to the TVA, is economically unsound, politically dangerous and morally calamitous. The species of novelty may vary, but the arguments against it rarely do—and demurrers from the right have thus become exceedingly unconvincing. Yet conservatives have no monopoly on denunciation by formula. Radicals behave with much the same regularity. They also lean on a set of arguments which apply equally to all situations. On both sides the arguments were probably invented in the critical Neanderthal days when conservatives and radicals battled over the infamous suggestion that huts were preferable to caves. They have proved useful ever since

in cloaking prejudice with the magic authority of logic. Today, the newspapers of the right show that Mr. Roosevelt's every gesture is a secret signal for collectivism to drive economic law, constitutional morality, national tradition and good sense into the night. With the same beautiful predictability, the pamphlets of the left disclose the class struggle to be nearing its climax and declare that Utopia is just across the barricades. Each depression, in fact, raises up its prophets who revive the arguments of the last one with the charming confidence that they are discovering them. Since conservatives are the more insistent in turning up bogeymen, their blanket indictment is by now well discredited for all but themselves. But radicals employ old arguments with the same unoriginality, even if the intervals between their outbursts deceive them into thinking that the arguments refer intrinsically to each new crisis.

Nearly all the current left-wing shibboleths were in use a century ago in the first major American depression. Overexpansion of credit had thrown the young economy off balance in 1837, and the insolvency of the Barings in England quickly led to bankruptcies, domino-fashion, all through the United States. In May the banks of New York City suspended; in the whole year over one hundred banks failed. Private banks were hopelessly discredited. Everywhere factories were closed, wages cut, men thrown out of work. The depression hit America with added force because of the concentration in cities of laborers with nothing of their own to fall back on. The suffering was new in the national experience.

Such a collapse in the nation's economy speedily produced its critics, of whom the most searching was Orestes A. Brownson, a Boston editor and minister. Brownson was then a man of thirty-five, tall, black-haired, vehement, unpolished and unruly. As a child, he had moved from his birthplace in Vermont to up-state New York. There, after a brief and unhappy experience with old-line Presbyterianism, he became a Universalist minister and then an associate of Robert Dale Owen in the New York Workingmen's Party. He later was attracted to Boston and Unitarianism because of the warm humanity of William Ellery Channing, the great Boston preacher. As the pastor in two small New England towns and finally of an independent society of his own in Boston, Brownson grew to be very important in Unitarianism and Transcendentalist circles. George Ripley, the founder of Brook farm, was his closest friend; Henry Thoreau spent a summer with Brownson which he afterwards regarded as "an era in my life, the morning of a new *Lebenstag*"; Emerson and Alcott, indeed, pondered for a time the notion of contributing to Brownson's journal, the *Boston Quarterly Review* instead of starting the magazine of their own which finally became the *Dial*.

But Brownson was not a man to be satisfied with the reveries of Transcendentalism. He devoted himself to problems that most of the group ignored. Living in Chelsea and preaching largely to workingmen, he saw abundant evidence of the impact of depression on the poor. While

Emerson and Thoreau worried about the remote evils of slavery, Brownson confronted the harsh and tangible question of capital and labor. He had once believed with Channing that reform was simply a matter of inner improvement; but such a belief could not easily survive the wretched misery that came in the wake of the Panic of 1837. Plainly it was not enough to be good, for the best intentions in the world must founder in the economic necessity of buying low and selling high. Brownson told Channing that he found more hatred of the rich than he expected. In face of this bitterness, which no appeals to the soul could placate or answer, he had to recast his plans of reform.

The analysis that Orestes Brownson arrived at is perhaps disconcerting to a generation which believes that Marx invented the Marxian theory of history. In 1838, a decade before the *Communist Manifesto,* Brownson interpreted history in terms of the inescapable conflict between those who profited by the existing order and those on whom its burden chiefly fell. "The war which is ever carried on between these two parties, whatever the name it may bear, or the forms it may assume is always, at bottom, a war of EQUALITY against PRIVILEGE." Elsewhere he wrote, "The feudal nobility is extinct, the *Bourgeoisie,* or middle class, is now on the throne." It is generally accounted the most virtuous class, he said—perhaps so: "it demands a laboring class to be *exploited,* but it loves order, peace, and quiet. These, however, it knows are incompatible with the existence in the community of an ignorant, vicious and starving populace; it, therefore, will attend to the wants of the lower classes up to a certain point." It "has a mission to execute, and when it shall have executed its mission it will then give way to the monarchy, not of a class, not of an order, but of Humanity." "All classes, each in its turn have possessed the government; and the time has come for all predominance of class to end; for Man, the People to rule."

Brownson thus obtained the historical warrant for his position; he had the set of doctrines—class conflict, the overthrow of the bourgeoisie, and the historic function of capitalism—which form so necessary an apparatus for enlightenment today. He went on to make the deductions which have become sacred through reiteration by each new generation. The class struggle has spread to letters, he pointed out. It was lawful to praise Irving in the respectable reviews; but Cooper, the critic of American folkways, was under the ban of all the quarterlies—save Brownson's; William Cullen Bryant, the liberal editor of the *Evening Post* could hardly hazard another volume of poems; William Ellery Channing, the pro-labor clergyman, was condemned as a Loco-foco with his eye on Congress; and George Bancroft, the unrepentant Jacksonian, was endured only because a Whig would be inherently incapable of writing American history. As the class lines grew tighter, Brownson decided that the want of a great social crisis explained the timidity and imitativeness of American literature. "The whole matter of wealth and labor . . . must come up, be discussed and disposed of," Brownson told the students at Brown in the fall of 1839. "In the struggle of these two elements, true American

literature will be born."

As America continued to flounder in the depths of depression, Brownson grew increasingly gloomy. In spite of a profound dislike for commitments of any kind, he joined the Democratic Party in 1839 because he thought it the only defense against the system of special legislation advocated by the Whigs, "which if not arrested, would bring us under the absolute control of associated wealth." The Constitution was not bad in itself, he thought, but it had been perverted under the pressure of the economic interests behind the Whig party. He was finally driven to remark, a century ahead of Lundberg, that economic legislation had fallen "under the control of, probably, less than two hundred individuals."

The advent of 1840, the election year, marked four years of intent thinking on the problem of capital and labor. The heat of the coming election suddenly ripened Brownson's conclusions and impelled him to give them to the public. In the July 1840 issue of the *Boston Quarterly,* just as the campaigns were swinging into action, he published the essay on **"The Laboring Classes."** This was an extraordinary performance, by far the best study of the workings of society written by an American before the Civil War, and probably for some time after. The exigencies of the day somewhat distorted the emphasis: Brownson's bitter anti-clericalism led him to exaggerate the villainy of the church, just as contemporary pamphleteers are moved by their hatred of newspaper owners to overrate the influence of the press. But the main lines of the diagnosis are straight and plausible. The class struggle had become acute, Brownson thought, and in England it would end inevitably in bloody war. The present wage system was intolerable. It was "a cunning device of the devil, for the benefit of tender consciences, who would retain all the advantages of the slave system, without the expense, trouble and odium of being slave-holders"; and the retreat of cheap land was putting the laborer even more at the mercy of his employer. Our duty, Brownson proclaimed, is "to emancipate the proletaries, as the past has emancipated the slaves."

All a bit familiar, of course, though today the same ideas are encrusted with a quasi-theological jargon, without which they can not be officially uttered. But the United States, in its first great depression, was in no mood to admire the brilliance of Brownson's analysis or to examine judicially his proposals for the future. The essay, crammed with social heresies and revolutionary appeals, was thrown into a savagely fought presidential contest and received as a pronouncement from a leading Democrat. The Whigs were suffering from that periodic disease of political parties—the passion to paint the opposition red; and they rushed to reprint **"The Laboring Classes"** as evidence of the radical leanings of the Democratic high command. The Democrats, suddenly embarrassed to find Brownson disrobing in public, were forced to repudiate him and make clear that he was in no way speaking for the party.

Brownson, however, was not to be deterred or intimidated, and in a second essay he filled in the outlines of his first inquiry into American society. The dominance of agriculture had thus far hindered the formation of classes, he wrote, but the day was now arrived when stratification could no longer be avoided. This provoked more whines of fear and more groans of impending disaster; but in November Van Buren—another New York aristocrat of Dutch ancestry who was condemned as a traitor to his class—went down to defeat, and the forces of Satan were driven from power.

Brownson was compelled by his inexorable logic to become a Catholic, and his name quickly dropped out of American history. But before he went over to Rome he anticipated virtually all the slogans and shibboleths that every depression since has resuscitated, and he applied the tool of economic analysis to the scene before him with a skill which few later commentators have attained. Some of his observations were so far ahead of the so-called science of political economy that his times passed them by without pausing. He pointed, for instance, to the defects of the "vicious method" of distributing the products of labor by which

> we destroy the possibility of keeping up an equilibrium between production and consumption. We create a surplus—that is, a surplus, not when we consider the wants of the people, but when we consider the state of the market—and then must slacken our hands till the surplus is worked off. During this time, while we are working off this surplus, while the mills run short time, or stop altogether, the workmen must want employment. The evil is inherent in the system.

The Panic of 1837 had to repeat itself half a dozen times before the professional economists achieved the idea of the business cycle.

Unhappily, few of Brownson's successors have had his remarkable perspicacity. These observations were sharp and fresh with him, but latterly they have grown into clichés, as stale and monotonous as the empty fear of the conservative that hell and Moscow always lie in wait for the person who takes two strides ahead. The United States has unaccountably lived through each depression which the logic of the crystal gazers ruled to be the last. The disappointed seers, in order to preserve the sanctity of their theory, have had to explain away each survival. For many years the free-land hypothesis was a favorite alibi: disaster, the story went, was detained because the unemployed moved away to the frontier instead of starving in the slums and growing class-conscious. Actually, as Brownson pointed out at the time, the workingmen had to stay in the slums, because they lacked money to get to the frontier, and, even if they had the money, few would have cared to exchange the city for the wilderness. In recent years, with the disappearance of the frontier, this convenient fiction has been washed up. Imperialism took its place for a while, but that too is now a dead issue. When the moment comes to explain why the present depression was not fatal, the radicals will hide their embarrassment by pointing to housing or the next war or the WPA and

will justify their choice in a highly persuasive theory which observes strictly the etiquette of logic.

But then another depression will come. The conservatives will swing into their well-rehearsed dirges at every suggestion of remedial measures. The American spirit, the iron laws of political economy and the dictates of horse sense will suffer continual insult. The Constitution will face fates worse than death, and communism will be just around the corner. The conservatives will believe that they are following rigorously the laws of logic and sound thinking, and that their arguments arise uniquely out of the conditions at hand. The radicals will point out gleefully that the people on the right are resurrecting old battle cries. Meanwhile, they will themselves engage in mystic communion with their sacred books, and will state solemnly that the class struggle is on its last phase. They will point out that the factors which staved off disaster in all previous depressions cannot possibly affect this one. They will look for a great literature to emerge, full-armored, from the turmoil. They will believe that they are following rigorously the laws of logic and sound thinking, and that their arguments arise uniquely out of the conditions at hand.

Radicalism, like capitalism, has its folklore.

Theodore Maynard (essay date 1943)

SOURCE: "Orestes Brownson, Journalist: A Fighter for Truth," in *The Commonweal*, Vol. XXXVII, No. 16, February 5, 1943, pp. 390-93.

[*In the following essay, Maynard favorably assesses Brownson's career as a journalist.*]

All his life long he was primarily a journalist, and of a kind that has probably never been surpassed in America and certainly never matched. That Brownson was a minister until he was forty-one was only incidental to his journalism, as was his lecturing. These things, indeed, were only spoken (and less effective) journalism, too. Though by practice he got rid of his early rusticity of manner, and developed a resonant voice, he was never quite at ease as a speaker. Young Isaac Hecker, who fell under his influence in 1841, noted that the tall (and as yet slim) Vermonter spoke without notes and with a logic and sincerity that appealed to those of a philosophical cast, but also noted that he came to grief when he attempted to be pathetic. It would seem that Brownson never acquired what is essential in a public speaker—the ability of getting at once into intimate touch with his audience. On the printed page everything was different; though even there he lacked (as he often acknowledged) the faculty of persuasion, he took his readers into his confidence; the editorial "we" and "us" never cloaked his burly and somewhat eccentric personality. He looked upon his readers as friends—as friends even when he was savagely fighting them. When he founded *Brownson's Quarterly Review* in 1844 he wrote in the first number, "This is *my* Review; I am its proprietor; its editor; intend to be its principal, if not its sole writer, and to make it the organ of my own view of truth." When thirty-one years later he at last gave it up, he was able to say, "Others may publish a quarterly review far more valuable than mine has ever been, but no other man can produce *Brownson's Quarterly Review*. . . . My Review must die when I cease to conduct it." Both statements were plain fact.

He had conducted magazines almost from the time he was ordained as a Universalist in 1826. And however much he moved from place to place or from denomination to denomination on his road to the Catholic Church, he was never long without a paper, though not until 1837 did he obtain just what he wanted in the *Boston Quarterly Review,* an organ in which he could fully expound his ideas. He expounded them at such length and was so very Brownsonian that when he offered his quarterly to the Transcendentalists as their medium of expression, Emerson and Margaret Fuller knew they would be swamped by him and so started the *Dial* instead. Upon which Theodore Parker commented, "Apropos of *The Dial:* to my mind it bears much the same relation to *The Boston Quarterly* that Antimachus does to Hercules . . . or a band of men and maidens daintily arrayed in finery . . . to a body of stout men in blue frocks, with great arms and hard hands, and legs like the Pillars of Hercules." When in 1842 he merged it with the *Democratic Review,* William Henry Channing declared it to have been the best journal this country has ever produced, Ripley and Bronson Alcott concurring. Fortunately Brownson lost the title by the merger; when he started again on his own, there was nothing for it but to call his magazine *Brownson's Quarterly Review*.

In the *Boston* he had printed contributions from Alcott, Ripley, Bancroft, Margaret Fuller, W. H. Channing and Albert Brisbane, the Fourierist and the father of the Hearst columnist. In *Brownson's Quarterly* nearly everything was Brownson. He had so much to say, and the Catholic contributors available were few. John Gilmary Shea was antagonized by having an article rejected, and the rival Catholic editors—especially McMaster and J. V. Huntington and Major—became bitter enemies. Poor Huntington was hurt by a review of one of his novels on which Brownson commented, "Every time he has occasion to introduce a woman [he stops to] give us a full-length portrait of her, the color of her hair, the form of her eyebrows, the cast of her features, the pouting or not pouting of her lips, the shape of her bust, the size of her waist, with remarks on the flexibility of her limbs, and the working of her toes." No wonder that Huntington was offended, just as Mc-Master did not like being told that it was no sin for a man to be unable to understand metaphysics but only a handicap when he insisted upon dealing with that subject.

Brownson did, in truth, have a wonderful faculty for treading heavily on other people's toes. The lion thought he was only playfully patting their heads when they felt that their skulls had been crushed. He did not realize his own strength, and he was completely devoid of tact. What he said about the Irish and the Jesuits was quite understandably taken by them as violent hostility.

Yet he had the best of intentions towards them. If he pointed out what he considered their short-comings, it was all for their own good. They did not have a truer friend than himself. He could not understand that most people are inclined to avoid a too candid friend. When Newman offered him a chair in his Irish university in 1854, it was soon made clear to him that he would have to rescind his offer. Brownson chose that moment to tell the Irish that their own conduct was largely responsible for the Know-nothing movement and that when they came to America they had better become Americans. For their part, they accused him of supplying their enemies with ammunition. His retort that the attempt to make the Catholic Church the Irish Church was damaging equally to the Irish and to the Church did little to help matters. As Van Wyck Brooks put it in *The Flowering of New England,* Brownson was too Catholic for the Yankees and too Yankee for the Catholics. The convert thought of himself as too Catholic for the Irish and they were enraged.

His quarrel with the Jesuits, such as it was, sprang largely out of philosophical differences. Whether or not he was the ontologist he is still often accused of being is too big a question to be discussed here. All that need be said was that Brownson was contemptuous of Scholasticism—at any rate as it was taught in the 'sixties and 'seventies— and that he bluntly said so. He had his own solution of the problem of knowledge, one which he believed was the only means of preservation from pantheism. As the scholastic philosophers did not accept it, he told them that they were outmoded. And though he afterwards said he wished he could recall some of the hard things he had said about the Jesuits, he never budged from his central position.

Brownson's were at once the merits and the defects of the self-made man. In youth he had had only a year or two of formal education. Yet as a young minister he had taught himself six languages, and as soon as he had mastered enough from a dictionary and grammar, he proceeded to the reading of abstruse tomes. At Brook Farm they told a story of how he paraded his Latin, distressing Bradford and Ripley with his false quantities. Ripley, whom he tried to drag into the Church, woke one night from a horrible dream. He had become a Catholic and had been to confession to Father Brownson. At the end the priest said to his penitent, "Now you will repeat after me the fifty-eighth psalm in the Vulgate," and Ripley cried out, "O Lord, my punishment is greater than I am able to bear!"

When Brownson came into the Church in 1844, Isaac Hecker fully expected him to bring into the Church with him hundreds and perhaps thousands of his former Transcendentalist associates. His failure to do so, and his abandonment of the line of approach that had brought him into the Church, Hecker attributed to the influence of Bishop Fitzpatrick of Boston. Fitzpatrick had, in fact, insisted that Brownson use the ordinary apologetic mode, with the result that the "liberal" Christians of Boston could see no nexus between what the prophet of the "Church of the Future" had held and what the Catholic Brownson affirmed. Not until he had moved from Boston to New York and had written his autobiography was his own road to Rome defined for the public. By then it was too late; he had lost his non-Catholic following.

Hecker blamed it all on Fitzpatrick. In the first of a series of articles written for the *Catholic World* in 1887, he called the Bishop "the hierarchical exponent of all that was traditional and commonplace in Catholic life." Of Brownson he said "that as a controversialist of the old school the fact that he so greatly distinguished himself only showed his versatility, and his versatility was in this his misfortune," I believe that Hecker's general apologetic method—that of building upon whatever truth a man already has instead of starting by correcting his errors—is to be preferred to the method Brownson chose to employ. But it was not versatility, or the dictation of Fitzpatrick, that determined Brownson's apologetic mode; it was his own make-up. For a while he tried to be conciliatory, as Hecker was conciliatory, and wrote in 1856 to Father Hewit, that his own method—that of logic—was the worst of all possible methods. In the abstract this may be so; as Newman once pointed out, men are not convinced merely by force of syllogism. But logic was the only method Brownson could handle. His was all the strength and all the weakness of the logician; he expected people to accept his logical demonstrations and could not understand it when they were not convinced. Perhaps they should have done so; but it does not require much knowledge of human nature to know that they rarely do so. Brownson had to give up his Protestant friends in despair and address himself to the task of strengthening Catholics in their faith.

For this reason most of his controversies were with Catholics. Those who imagined that he had entered the Church as a safe refuge from the storms of which he was tired, were as wide of the mark as those who imagined that, because he had belonged to several sects on the road to Rome, he would soon embrace Mohammedanism. He had to fight every inch of the way. The difference was that, whereas in the past he had fought to find truth, he now fought to uphold it. Wrong-headed he often was, though always worth listening to; yet on the main issues he is now seen to be right when the majority of the American Catholics were wrong. When he insisted on the indirect deposing power of the Pope, he alarmed many of the American bishops, who feared that his utterances would be quoted by the Church's enemies to prove that Catholics had a divided political loyalty. This, however, was hardly more than an academic point; what Brownson was really affirming was that the spiritual must be superior to the temporal, and that the sovereign people were not sovereign in an absolute sense but were in all things subject to God. As politics could not be divorced from morals, he did not shrink from the logic that maintained that it was for the Church to decide in moral issues. The mere affirmation of a "higher law," as in the case of the Abolitionists he loathed, set up a capricious private judgment in politics as well as religion and virtually abolished the force of the American constitution.

In this he was misunderstood inside the Church, as well as outside. Nevertheless he did a great deal to destroy the Gallican spirit at that time rampant in America, as it was also rampant elsewhere. Like Montalembert, a close friend by correspondence, he warned people against trusting Napoleon III. Most of the American bishops followed the lead of Veuillot in regarding the Emperor as a "second Saint Louis," where Brownson saw that the imperial protection of the Church involved its subjection to imperial domination. At the same time he began to suggest that, as the temporal power of the Pope was not essential to his spiritual sovereignty, it might be advisable for him voluntarily to forego what had become an anachronism in the modern world. That, too, of course got him into furious controversy, especially as he had an over-emphatic way of stating any case.

In 1855 he left Boston for New York, where he promptly got at loggerheads with Archbishop Hughes. While under Fitzpatrick he had submitted to Fitzpatrick's censorship. He had no intention of allowing Hughes to exercise the same control. As he wrote to Bishop Elder of Natchez, "I cannot accept the Archbishop of New York as my consultor. His advice I cannot respect, and I am not under his jurisdiction." To escape that jurisdiction he had transferred himself and his *Review* to Elizabeth, New Jersey, where Bishop Bayley—without always agreeing with him—allowed *Ursa Major,* as he called him, to have his say. From the other side of the Hudson, he fired his big guns at Hughes himself.

When the Civil War broke out, Hughes and Brownson found themselves in a new controversy. Hughes, knowing that the Irish were not at all enthusiastic about the liberation of the slaves, and fearing that they would not enlist in the defense of the Union if they came to believe that this was the object of the war, went so far as to offer a hypothetical case justifying even the slave trade. At once Brownson pounced on him: this was rank heresy; by flouting Gregory XVI's letter on slavery, the Archbishop had incurred the penalty of excommunication. Then with grimly humorous charity, he absolved Hughes; the Archbishop could not have meant what he had said. When next the two men met Hughes told him, "I will never write another word against you again."

Others did, however. Bishop Whelan of Wheeling cancelled his subscription to a review conducted by a "red Marat Republican." Brownson complained to Bishop Elder of Natchez that some members of the hierarchy, instead of making their representations to him direct, used their diocesan organs to rebuke him. "You may kill my *Review*," he added hotly, "but you cannot manage me through newspapers." On the other hand, he fiercely attacked the Catholic papers because of their disloyalty to the Union. Only two, he said in his *Review* for October, 1861, were decidedly loyal; two others were occasionally loyal; one was trying to straddle; all the others, whether avowedly or not, were Confederate. As his opponents were trying to silence him politically, by discrediting him philosophically, he announced in 1863 that he would prescind from the discussion of philosophy and theology to confine himself to public affairs.

Long before this he had lost all his subscribers in the South, and many that he had had in the North. Then by backing Frémont for the presidency—he had a low opinion of Lincoln—he was left without a party when Frémont withdrew. At the end of 1864 he ceased publishing his *Review*. It was his intention to devote the rest of his life to writing books. He listed them in a letter to Senator Summer, now his political bedfellow: the projected works were to be on the American Constitution, "to be followed by a work on Philosophy, another on Theology, another on the Church, and another on the Catholic and Protestant Controversy." Of these only his masterpiece, *The American Republic,* ever got written; and that was largely a revamping of former articles, some of them going back as far as 1843. This, like everything else that Brownson wrote, was really journalism—journalism of a superb kind.

He had had the reputation of being a very wild radical. Actually his basic political ideas were, from the start, far more conservative than those whom he startled supposed. Nor did he really change his social ideas, and here he was not so much a forerunner of Marx, as Mr. Schlesinger suggests, but a forerunner of the Papal encyclicals on labor. But when he gave up his postulation of the class war, as the only means of getting rid of capitalism, he could think of no other way of effectuating the deliverance of the working-man. Having no lead from the Church—the *Rerum Novarum* was still a long way off—he despairingly concluded that nothing much could be done. He did not abandon his hatred of industrialism.

The *Catholic World,* the *Ave Maria,* and the New York *Tablet* set him to the busy production of articles. With from four to six columns of copy to turn out every week—on top of his frequent lecturing—he had no time to spare for the books he wished to write. Much of his best work was done during this period, despite the gout in his hands and feet; but he did not feel happy without his own *Review*. As he was usually not allowed to sign his articles, few people knew their authorship. Those who did not, and were vaguely aware that Brownson was under some sort of a cloud, began to suppose that he had ceased to defend the Catholic cause; some of them even supposed that he had ceased to practice his religion.

He had several times thought of reviving his *Review,* if for no other purpose than that of clearing his name and of publicly repudiating the "liberalism" into which he had fallen. When his wife was on her death-bed in 1872 she urged him to do this, if only for a year. At the beginning of 1873 *Brownson's Quarterly Review* reappeared and continued until the end of 1875. In it he returned to all the most uncompromising positions he had once maintained; the world should not be left in any doubt as to his belligerent orthodoxy. If for several years he had tried to make Catholicism more palatable by softening it and toning it down, he now seemed to glory in stating it in the harshest possible terms. In particular he rammed down his interpretation of the doctrine that outside the Church there was no salvation. Give non-Catholics, he said, the slightest ground for hoping that they might obtain salvation, and none of them would ever become Catholics. Not even invincible ignorance would he admit as a valid plea. With the rigor that was a carry-over from his Puritan days, he tried to drive men to heaven with a pitchfork red-hot from hell.

In so far as the "Last Series" of his *Review* was intended to make his position clear, it amply succeeded. And there was little noticeable falling-off in power—none at all in logical power. But he began it when he was ill and he steadily grew more ill, until it was at last impossible for him to continue. In the issue for October, 1875, he wrote a moving valedictory. "Much of the time for the present year," he told his audience—his friends—"I have been unable to hold a pen in my hand." He had no secretary, and had written the whole of that last issue himself. Those familiar with his handwriting during those years must wonder how any compositor ever managed to read his manuscripts. He acknowledged that his memory was not what it had been, as he acknowledged again that he had never been able to realize his idea of what a Catholic review should be. "But I have done the best, being what I am, that I could." Others might have done better; editors of greater ability and prudence may arise. "Yet none will be found more sincerely Catholic, or more earnestly devoted to Catholic interests." He admits he has never been popular among some Catholics, but as he had never sought popularity that does not trouble him. As for wealth, "Why, what could I do with it, if I had it, standing on the brink of the grave?" In farewell to his readers, he asks their prayers, and concludes, "I have and desire to have, no home out of the Catholic Church. . . . My only ambition is to live and die in her communion."

A few months later he was dead. But before he died, the son who was to be his biographer and to edit his works in twenty volumes took him to his home in Detroit. There Brownson gathered notes for an autobiography he still hoped to write. But he was too worn out for that. All that he produced was a single article for the newly-established *American Catholic Quarterly Review.* He was never too tired, however, for an argument. On Holy Saturday he and his son had a long theological debate. When he had gone to his room and his daughter-in-law came up with his tray, he answered her knock with, "If that is Henry, I'm too tired to make it any plainer tonight." The next day, Easter Sunday, he was anointed. The following day, April 17, 1876, he died. Now thousands of young men every year pass over his body as it lies in the crypt of the church at Notre Dame University as they go to receive Holy Communion. It is a fitting place for him to rest.

A. Robert Caponigri (essay date 1945)

SOURCE: "Brownson and Emerson: Nature and History," in *The New England Quarterly,* Vol. XVIII, No. 3, September, 1945, pp. 368-90.

[*In the following excerpt, Caponigri analyzes the development of Brownson's Transcendentalist beliefs.*]

The career of Orestes Brownson possesses a unique interest for the student of American civilization. Alone of all the figures intimately associated with New England transcendentalism, he took the road to Rome which so many of his European contemporaries were taking. By what course of thought did he find himself compelled to take this step? The initial interest in this question is increased immensely by even a partial answer; for a cursory examination of his thought, in this connection, yields indubitable evidence that Brownson entered the Roman Catholic Church in the belief that it held the answer to the fundamental problem which he had found implicit in the whole Protestant tradition from which he came: the problem of nature and history.

That the problem of nature and history is the central problem of Transcendentalism is the axiom from which the thought of the most eminent Transcendentalists, and of Emerson in particular, proceeds. The history of western thought since the Reformation justifies this assumption. For this problem is dictated to Transcendentalism by its historical position at the close of the second phase of the historical career of the Protestant principle, and of this historical moment the problem of nature and history was the dialectical imperative.

The historical career of Protestantism manifested itself in two large phases which, upon the surface, may appear antithetical but are, in fact, logically continuous moments in the history of a single principle. In its first phase, Protestantism appears as a force for historical rectification. Operating as it did within the institutional framework of western Christendom, its ostensible purpose was to restore the historically authentic Christian spirit and form. Its real effect, inevitably, was nothing like its ostensible purpose—inevitably, because this purpose was intrinsically unfeasible. Its actual effect was to dissolve the unity of mediaeval Christendom and to multiply credal and institutional forms, all of which were more or less mimetic of the parent form and all of which bore indelibly the marks of their historical origin. The Protestant principle clearly operated, not to "rectify," but, as does every authentic historical principle, simply to "create" history. For such historical rectification is essentially impossible. To this end the irreversibility of history demands that one have recourse to an ahistorical principle, such as Protestantism did possess in the principle of private judgment. When this ahistorical principle is actually applied to the task of rectifying history, its effect is not to rectify, but to abolish history. Any ahistorical principle so applied must end by ultimately questioning the reality of history.

Such was the ultimate effect of the Protestant principle of private judgment. To the question of the historically authentic form of Christianity, another question inevitably succeeded. What is the need of any historical form for the Christian life? This new question was inevitable because the principle of private judgment is essentially a counter-principle and not a correlative to any principle of historical continuity. The second phase of the historical career of Protestantism is marked by the gradual emergence and

dominance of this new question and reaches its logical terminus in the assertion that the spiritual life of man is intrinsically independent of history because it is orientated not toward history, but directly toward the absolute spiritual principles of the universe, which are above and beyond history.

With the ascendency of this question the issue becomes strictly one of philosophy; for the imperative need is a philosophical, or more strictly speaking, an ontological principle which will substantiate this assertion of historical independence by demonstrating the direct orientation of the spiritual life of man toward absolute, trans-historical principles. Historically, the principle was at hand in the conception of nature as it underlies, on the one hand, scientific, and on the other, sentimental, naturalism in the modern world. In the fabric of both these forms of naturalism the concept of nature is such as to render history, if not ontologically impossible, then essentially illusory. Scientific naturalism comes to this end through the development of its concept of the absolute fixed laws of nature, while sentimental naturalism arrives at the same goal by way of its cult of the individual, of inspiration, of genius, of the divine indwelling in human nature. There emerges, inevitably, the antithesis, nature *versus* history. By the appeal to nature, scientist and sentimentalist alike try to emancipate themselves from history.

American Transcendentalism, viewed in historical perspective, is a moment in this second phase of the historical career of Protestantism. This is demonstrated by its preoccupation and its doctrine. Its preoccupation is the re-orientation of the spiritual life of man away from history toward absolute principles. It seeks to effect this re-orientation by the exploration and expansion of the concept "nature," which it derived from the new naturalism. . . .

Brownson's affinity to Transcendentalism is closest at the point of its ahistorical bias, and this affinity is the result of the movement of his own thought. In his early career, Brownson had recapitulated in his own experience the historical phases of Protestantism. His errancy among the available Protestant sects was dictated by the stupendous task which he had set himself and which was none other than the ostensible task of historical Protestantism itself: to ascertain, upon the principle of private judgment, the historically and doctrinally authentic form of Christianity. Disillusionment in the task was as inevitable for him as, historically, it had been for Protestantism, and disillusionment brought both to the same term, the questioning of history itself. It was at this moment, when in the depression of his first disillusionment he was prepared to challenge the meaning of history itself, that Brownson found himself in sympathy with Transcendentalism. Certain statements made by him at this time condemning the cult of the historical Jesus, asserting the universality of the Incarnation in all men, charging the historical church with obstructing the immediate communion of human nature with the eternal and absolute springs of goodness and divinity, might almost with indifference be ascribed to Emerson or Channing. Witness the words in which he arraigns the historical church:

> When she [the historical church] asserted the incarnation of the ideal in Jesus, she asserted the truth; when she asserted that it was and could be incarnated in him alone, she erred.

And again:

> The Church of the future will be based on two great principles . . . the generalization of the incarnation. . . .

At this very point of greatest affinity, however, a marked difference—a fundamental difference of intuition—between Brownson and Transcendentalism makes its appearance, and this difference first indicates to us the principles upon which Brownson will reconstruct, in constant dialectic with the ideas of Transcendentalism, his doctrine of nature and history. While asserting, on the one hand, the universal divinity of man and the human spirit's independence of history, Brownson nevertheless draws back from the extreme individualism and subjectivism to which these assertions appear to lead in Emerson. The crucial question is that of the immediacy of the relationship of the individual to the divine. To Emerson the doctrine of the divinity of man could mean but one thing, the divinity of every individual and, consequently, the immediate access of every individual to the plenitude of the divine in his own experience. Brownson, on the contrary, maintained from the beginning that the ascription of divinity must be made not in the first instance to the individual but to humanity. It is humanity which in the first instance is divine and the individual through his unity with humanity. This term, humanity, becomes a key term in his reconstruction of the doctrine of history.

And here it may be remarked, somewhat parenthetically, that Brownson's condemnation of individualism is not limited to this idea as it appears in Transcendentalism; he objects as strenuously to what appears to him to be the extreme and hampering individualism of the historical church. The basis for this rejection of individualism is the same in both cases: Brownson's sense of the solidarity of the individual with the group, and ultimately with the whole of manking in all its dimensions.

Brownson's intuition of the solidarity of the individual and the race—it is an intuition, similar to that "sense of dependence" which he employs in his theology and which allies him with the school of Schleiermacher—finds expression or formulation on several levels of human experience. It is this intuition, formulated and expressed on the level of truth and knowledge, which precipitates Brownson's attack upon the principle of private judgment and inspires his partial rehabilitation of the doctrine of tradition and universal consent as a criterion of certitude. In the act of knowing, he asserts, in direct opposition and with obvious reference to Emerson, the mind apprehends its object not in virtue of a radical identity but of an ultimate polarity. This polarity he conceives dynamically, as the actualization of the latent power of the individual to know by contact with an object which defines and realizes that power. The polarity, subject-object, is irreducible, while the actuality of knowledge is a synthesis in being of these polar elements. The principle of private judgment, consequently, in as far as it appears to involve an identity of the subject and object, is repugnant to experience.

Although the act of knowledge is realized in the individual, yet the individual mind neither constitutes its object nor apprehends it in virtue of a radical identity. Its object is the common world, which it shares with other minds. From this it appears clear to Brownson that the proper object of the mind is not addressed to the individual mind but to the intelligent faculty of the human nature in which the individual participates; concretely, to humanity. The testimony of universal assent, consequently, gains precedence in his mind over individual experience. Although he never examines either the structure or the implications of this doctrine with anything like the thoroughness of Lamennais or Newman, its influence upon him is great and he tries to employ it in his own thought; he was also able to comprehend immediately its temporal dimension, so that without further concern he speaks interchangeably of universal consent and of tradition. His philosophy of history leads him later to refine considerably on the concept of tradition.

In his epistemological discussions Brownson employs the concept of human nature as a real principle of Being, transcending the individual and defining his character. It becomes increasingly clear that the solidarity of the race depends upon the truth of this conception of human nature and the adequate explanation it can be given. Reviewing the work of the Saint-Simonian, Pierre Leroux, he writes with warm approval of the general line of that movement:

> Humanity is not an aggregate of individuals . . . humanity precedes individuals and is their origin and support. It is human nature, that is the human species, which makes individual men and women.

His method of exploring the empirical evidence for this principle follows the pattern set by his treatment of the problem of knowledge. Experience establishes that not only in respect to knowledge, but in regard to feeling and action, as well, the individual needs the "objective" in order to complete [or] actualize, his being.

> Leroux holds (and in this we coincide with him) that man taken alone is never competent to the task of his own manifestation. He remains in a latent virtual state till assisted to actualize himself by that which is not himself. . . . His whole life, whether intellectual, sentient, or sentimental is jointly in himself and in that which is not himself. His life is then at once subjective and objective.

Nature and society afford the individual the object elements of life; and since, without the objective element, his life and nature remain latent, in potency, in a state of non-being with respect to that which it might and should be, the dependence upon nature and society cannot be looked upon as accidental, but only as constitutive and essential.

> As he has need of living, so has he need of this communion, the indispensable condition of his life.

Since the solidarity of the individual with nature and society is so fundamental a principle, Brownson is led to examine its dimensions in full, and this inquiry leads him directly to the question of the reality of history as a principle of Being. So long as the relationship of the individual to the objective elements of his life is stated in general and abstract terms, such as nature and humanity, there might seem to be no particular occasion for the problem of history to arise. The actual orientation of the individual, Brownson warns, however, is not in the abstract, not toward mankind in general, nor toward nature as a vague concept or sentiment, but toward the concrete. The conditions under which solidarity, and the actuality of his life, are achieved by the individual are concrete, and he defines them as three: family, nation, and property. All these are fundamentally historical terms. The family most obviously, but the nation and property also quite clearly, define relationships with essential historical dimensions. The concrete conditions of life and actuality in the individual would seem therefore to be historical relations. The relevancy of the problem of history for Brownson is thus clear; he must face the question of the character of history as a principle of Being. He has been led inexorably to this point by the initial drive of his intuition of the solidarity of the individual and the group. Brownson formulates his answer to the problem of history in his doctrine of creation, by which he believes that he establishes the ultimate historical character of contingent Being itself.

Like Emerson's use of "nature," Brownson's term "creation" is one heavy with historical associations, which his own interpretation alters. Traditionally, the term "creation" has been used within the framework of the theistic position, which assumes the absolute transhistorical character of the first cause. As a consequence of this assumption, the theistic position had been beset by the problem of contingency, and in a form which to many has appeared critical. For if a first cause be assumed or proved to be absolutely outside history, the question cannot fail to arise, why historical and contingent Being exists at all, and by what mode it comes into being. Brownson, in his doctrine of creation, following Gioberti and, more remotely, Malebranche, is concerned with preserving the fundamentals of the theistic position; but is also concerned to escape the traditional embarrassments of the problem of contingency. And his point of departure is still the first intuition which has led him to this point: that of dependence, the sense of solidarity of the forms of Being.

Brownson's doctrine of creation is really the metaphysical or ontological projection or extension of his perception of the objective-subjective character of the life of individual man. The individual man, he has observed, is not autonomous, but needs the objective to actualize his latent humanity. The same is true of Being as a whole. Every form of Being needs its objective complement, the principle outside itself which will reduce its latent or potential power to actuality. The objective complement of the universe is its creative principle, the Creator. Creation is then the term which designates the objective-subjective character of Being in its ultimate terms, in terms of the universe and of God; it is the name of that real relation of dependency which defines the antecedent conditions of the actuality of the world which is given us in experience. In the light of this conception of the term, the problem of contingency in its traditional formulation appears spurious. The question, why does the Creator create, can never, in the true state of the problem, arise. For the first cause is known to us only as it manifests itself, that is only as creator, as the ultimate objective ground of the being of the universe. The actuality of the world postulates this objective principle as actual; it is inconceivable that the ultimate objective principle should not be that ultimate objective principle. There is no basis in reason or experience for the fantastic question whether the universe might not be, or its correlative, whether God is necessarily Creator. He is necessarily Creator in as far as it is given us to know him, i.e., as the objective principle of

Bust of Brownson by Samuel Kitson.

the universe; he is, further, necessarily Creator, if his nature be of that absolute character, which it is, that demands that all his relations be necessary and objective. In a word, creation is nothing else but the ultimate creative principle manifesting itself, God expressing himself, by an unquestionable necessity of his being.

The term *creation* is not the designation of a static relationship, but of a process which is essentially historical. For its end or term is the actually existent, which, Brownson holds, is always the concrete individual. But the Being of the creative principle can be imparted to the concrete individual only through the mediation of secondary causal principles, whose character it is to assure the concrete conditions for the actualization of the individual and whose mode of operation necessarily is successive, or progressive. For the end of creation is the expression of God's nature according to the conditions of actual concrete individual existence; but as the nature to be expressed is infinite, and the medium finite, succession or infinite progression interposes itself between the finite and the infinite as the only mode by which the expression of the one in terms of the others is possible. The complexus of secondary causes which mediate the expression of the infinite and absolute creative principle according to the conditions of individual concrete existence, constitute the order of nature, which is of necessity, historical.

Brownson illustrates this doctrine by his conception of species. The immediate object of the creative force is not the individual, he holds, but the humanity. Secondary causes operate historically, that is, in a causal sequence which induces temporal sequence. Human nature, for example, is precedent to the individual man not only logically, or conceptually, but actually, as a creative principle operating historically. The ultimate object of this activity is the actual individual, and the concrete historical form of the operation of the principle is, in this instance of man, the family. Nature, therefore, being itself in as far as given in nature, is essentially historical and history enters as a real principle of Being into the actuality of every individual substance.

What is the significance of this conclusion for Brownson's special problem, that of the access possessed by the individual to the divine? The complete denial of any immediate natural access and the quite unconditional assertion that the individual soul, in the nature of things, approaches the divine mediately, through the channels of history and tradition, just as it approaches the very well springs of Being through the mediation of historical natural causal forces.

At this point the severance of his affinity for the ahistorical element in Transcendentalism is completed. He has established, in complete antithesis to Emerson, the concept of nature as essentially historical, or the individual life as fundamentally dependent upon history in all its actuality, of the spiritual life of man as mediated by history. He is still far, however, from the acceptance of the historical claims of any form of Christianity to be the historical channel. The steps by which he comes to this

further term continue the process by which he has reached his rehabilitation of the doctrine of history, and the first step toward this ultimate goal is the formulation of the doctrine of the supernatural.

Brownson's treatment of the problem of the supernatural falls into two phases, the first prior to, the second succeeding, his conversion. With this second phase, in which he is concerned primarily with establishing the ontology of the supernatural and in which he ventures, without great success, into the labyrinth of scholastic metaphysics, we are not here concerned. In the first phase the supernatural appears as a principle of the philosophy of history, and Brownson's preoccupation is with the establishment of the supernatural as a fact of history. This preoccupation accords with his principle (formulated clearly only much later, but implicit in all his thought on the matter) that it is only from the fact of the supernatural that one can proceed to its rational explanation. It is in the light of this principle that he later, as a Catholic, attacks the traditional methodology of the treatise **"On The True Religion"** in which the procedure is to establish antecedently the possibility of the supernatural. The providential view of the philosophy of history which he expounds appears to him to have the merit of establishing the fact of the supernatural, as the basis for all speculation concerning its ontological character and mode of operation.

The providential theory of history, as Brownson conceives and expounds it, is a continuation of his doctrine of creation. Creation, it will be recalled, he has defined as the real nexus between absolute objective being and contingent subjective being. This nexus is necessarily historical and progressive, i.e., creation is a historical principle of Being, a continuous process.

The operation of the creative principle in history cannot be defined or limited by the fixed laws of nature alone, either analytically or empirically. For from the nature of the creative principle, infinite and absolute, fixed laws of its activity cannot be deduced. If fixed laws can be formulated for the operation of the creative principle in nature and history, their formulation must be inductive and empirical. Experience, however, as emphatically as analysis, forbids the description of fixed laws which preclude any special intervention of the creative principle. On the contrary it compels the postulation of such special intervention as the only rational explanation of indisputable facts of history.

> For ourselves, we confess our utter inability to explain the past history of the race on the theory of natural development or even on that of the supernatural inspiration which we believe to be common to all men. That history is all bristling with prodigies which are inexplicable save on the hypothesis of the constant intervention in a special manner of the ever-watchful father.

The special intervention of the creative force appears most clearly in providential men. These appear at every crisis in human affairs, and their powers and characters are such as to render impossible any account of them in the terms of ordinary human activity. The attempt to dissolve these semi-mythical personages into legendary embodiments of man's experience appears to him unsound. They can be accounted for only in terms of a specially intervening creative power and providence.

Providence itself he defines empirically as the order or *ratio* of this special intervention, and as such it constitutes the supernatural order whose actuality in history is empirical fact. This conception of the supernatural also affords the basis for at least a descriptive definition of it: it is nothing more or less than the divine creative force itself, immediately active at a point in time and history. It is God and what he does immediately.

This theory of the supernatural defines the basis upon which he is prepared to accept and finally does accept the historical claims of Catholicism: that there is a providential and supernatural intervention and agency in history, directed to some extraordinary and crucial historical end. The end toward which this supernatural agency and intervention is directed he recognizes as the healing of the rupture of original sin; and the succeeding steps in his movement toward the acceptance of the historical faith is his reconstruction of this doctrine and also that of the special mission of Christ and the historical necessity of its continuation through a historical principle or institution.

The reconstruction of the doctrine of original sin follows easily upon the sequence of Brownson's thought up to this point:—the doctrine of creation, of the historical character of nature and being, of the solidarity of the human race, the ontological character of the principle of mediation. These all conspire to establish the antecedent possibility of the doctrine because they demonstrate the reasonableness of its fundamental element: the transference of guilt. The unity of the race in Adam constitutes the ultimate ontological ground for this transference of guilt, while the doctrine of the unity of the race in Adam is itself a conclusion to be derived from the theory of creation and the mediated and historical character of Being.

The fact of original sin Brownson believes that he establishes by a trinity of arguments, from tradition, from scripture, and from experience. The doctrine of human depravity is universally held in one form or another by all mankind, he asserts; but such universal credence is an argument, at least a presumptive argument, for the truth of the idea, in accordance with the precedence which tradition has been shown to possess over the evidence of individual reason and experience. To the argument from Scripture he accords, at this point, an authority but little surpassing that of an element in the universal tradition. The experience of depravity he believes to be individual, immediate, and universal; and his description of this experience he derives from the dualism of the Pauline tradition.

The intrinsic character of this depravity is made clear to him by the opinion he has already reached. It is not indi-vidual, but generic, inhering in the common human nature, and pertaining to the individual only in the sense and to the extent to which he shares the common human nature as the basis for his own actuality. Further, it cannot be conceived of as a fall from original perfection, for such a fall appears to him intrinsically impossible. Man was created in the first instance imperfect, sharing thus the general imperfection of created nature, which itself derives from the impossibility of a finite realization of the infinite nature of God. In its innermost essence this original depravity of man can consist only in the deviation of the human race, as one dimension of creation, from the purpose of the whole creation, the progressive actualization or external realization of the perfection of God.

The fact of original sin established the necessity of redemption, the purpose and conditions of which are defined, on the one hand by the historical character of Being, and on the other by the intrinsic character of the original depravity. The latter indicates that the purpose of redemption must be the reintegration of the life of the human race with the primitive end of creation. This end of redemption can be actualized only by a special intervention of God himself, a historical incursion of his special activity, in the character of a providential agent, a mediator.

This historical mediator is Christ. Entirely reversing his previous position, namely, that Christ is to be looked upon as no more than one instance of the divine indwelling which is the natural gift of every man, Brownson now contends unreservedly for his special character and divine mission.

> It is impossible then to press Jesus into the category of ordinary men; he stands out as distinct, peculiar.

The unique historical incursion of the Mediator will not suffice, however, to the work of redemption. It must be historically perpetuated by an institution or principle which will continue and actualize its work on the historically successive planes of individual being. This historical perpetuation of the work of the mediator and redeemer is demanded by the historical character of nature itself. For, if the Redeemer is to impart to the human race a new life, that life must possess a historical dimension and principle. The church is the natural and inescapable principle perpetuating the Messianic or mediatorial work, and toward it the spiritual life of the individual must be orientated as toward that objective principle which alone can actualize it.

With this conclusion, the circle of Brownson's thought is complete. From his initial denial of the historical orientation of the spiritual life of man he has passed through the full cycle of reconstruction to its inescapable conclusion: the acceptance of the historical principle of the perpetual mediatorial work of Jesus as the imperative of the religious and moral life. And, with this complete reversion of his position, his affinity to Transcendentalism is completely dissolved. Now he stands upon the threshold of the ancient church, over which he did not hesitate to pass.

Chester A. Soleta (essay date 1954)

SOURCE: "The Literary Criticism of Orestes A. Brownson," in *The Review of Politics,* Vol. 16, No. 3, July, 1954, pp. 334-51.

[In the following essay, Soleta examines Brownson's views of nineteenth-century literature and his role as a literary critic.]

Literature was never central to Brownson's interests; indeed at times it was something he tolerated somewhat impatiently. He wrote about it regularly, however, and during his career filled over a thousand closely packed octavo pages on the subject. He could even use the cant of the journalist reviewer with professional facility. Of a novel called *Thorneberry Abbey,* for instance, he says, "It has one or two literary faults . . . efforts at fine writing, and wearisome descriptions of natural scenery, which . . . only interrupt the narrative." With variations in the details, this kind of formal gesture is repeated almost every time he reviews a novel. Moreover, the passage on *Thorneberry Abbey* appears towards the very end of a long review, introduced by the following candid admission: "But we have forgotten the little book before us." What precedes the remark is not primarily a literary discussion but rather a warning to Catholics against the dangers of unwary compromises with Protestantism. What follows the remark is literary in a perfunctory and conventional way and is quickly dropped in favor of more polemic discussion. Although this procedure is not true of every piece of criticism by Brownson, something like it happens often enough to make it characteristic. When he was accused of such irrelevance later in life, he defended himself vigorously: "The book introduced is regarded as little more than an occasion or a text for an original discussion of some questions which the author wishes to treat. . . . Books are worthy of no great consideration for their own sake, and literature itself is never respectable as an end, and is valuable only as a means to an end." In spite of this method, however, Brownson raised important critical questions and left a substantial amount of literary material.

To understand this material one must be aware of two difficulties. First, there is Brownson's instability of opinion. In some instances, however, what might appear to be a contradiction or perhaps a development in theory may turn out simply to be a change in the context of the discussion. In one review his anger or his fervor may carry him to an extreme position while in another he may be in a more pleasant and pliant mood: what appears to be a difference of view must be considered only a drop in temperature. At times the objections of his readers force him to make qualifications or explanations; at other times they only make him repeat himself with more vehemence. Thus, his definition of the novel is the same in 1847 and in 1875. In 1847 he shows mostly contempt for the form; in 1849, though less serious in his evaluation of the novel, he resigns himself to accept it as a legitimate and expedient form of entertainment; in 1856 he sees it as the real literary form of the nineteenth century which will

produce the great Christian masterpiece; in 1875, irritated by a Catholic feminist novel, he returns to his earlier surly contempt. But there are also real changes and developments: the development from his vague view of literature as ornament to his view of literature as representation; the change from a Jansenistic attitude in attacking the emotional elements of literature to a more Catholic respect for them.

The second important difficulty is Brownson's position as a social critic and reformer who was interested primarily in economic, moral, and theological problems and who judged all other things in relation to these main interests. The reversals in his appreciation of the novel, for instance, are to be explained either by his changing theological views or by a variation in the moral and social problems which formed the background of his reviews. Thus, although in this paper I shall try to mark the definite changes of his critical opinion, I feel justified in bringing together some statements which may have been separated in time only because the earlier context did not call for the later explicitness. Although I am also forced to introduce his social positions, I do this in a general way only to clarify his literary theories. It is necessary to introduce his social theories in order to understand his literary development, which can be divided into two parts: first, his speculation on a native American literature, which was to be the expression of a unique political institution; second, his practical concern with a literature for the Catholic minority in an atmosphere that was naturalistic rather than Protestant.

I

The publication of Emerson's "The American Scholar" in 1837 was the occasion for Brownson to begin his own speculation on the problem of an American literature in two pieces written in 1839, one a review of Emerson's essay, the other a lecture delivered at Brown University. In the review Brownson boldly asserted that a considerable American literature was already in existence.

> Our newspapers are conducted for the great mass of the people, by men who come immediately out of the bosom of the people. They constitute, therefore, in the strictest sense of the word, a popular literature. And scattered through our newspapers and popular journals may be found more fine writing, more true poetry, more genuine eloquence, vigorous thought, original and comprehensive views, than can be found in the classics of either France or England. Your most ordinary newspaper not unfrequently throws you off an essay that it would be impossible to match in the writings of Addison, Steele, or Johnson.

Seven months later in the academic atmosphere of Brown University, with greater restraint he said: "We have no literature that can begin to compare with the literature of England, the literature of Germany or that of France."

On the whole the two essays are consistent, each of them embodying a particular application of his proletarian social theories. He found fault with Emerson's plea for

American writers because it meant the creation of a specially privileged class of men. Setting aside a large number of men to work only in the spiritual and intellectual realm would impose "an extra amount of labor on the rest, for scholars have bodies and stomachs and require food and raiment as well as the drudges themselves. And in general of a somewhat superior order too." A literary class indeed would be as undemocratic and oppressive as an aristocratic, a sacerdotal, or a military caste.

Literature must come from the people themselves, and America's small achievement at that time was to be explained by the exhaustion of popular energy in the building of a new country. But in part this was exactly Emerson's objection: that the spiritual and intellectual were being neglected for the practical and external. Brownson's answer was simple and conventional; men must provide for the subsistence of life before they look for the embellishments. He goes no farther in defining literature—and what he calls the higher things—than to call it an ornament or an embellishment. These words are most insidious in the mouth of a purely utilitarian thinker like Locke or Thomas Huxley, and Brownson, though practical, was never utilitarian in their condescending and limited way. For him literature as embellishment is a perfection, which completes life and can be sought only after practical needs are satisfied, but then it must be sought "with similar intenseness in providing for the wants of the soul." Very near to agreement with Emerson on this point, he says that literature is not an object to be sought for its own sake but that it must rise naturally from some great movement. The souls of authors "must be swelling with great thoughts . . . , haunted by visions of beauty they are burning to realize." Men must be ambitious to make a new moral, religious, or social principle the basis of actual life for which speech, the essay, and song are necessary. In this one respect at least Brownson comes near being consistent in critical theory throughout his career. However much his social views changed, he held that great art developed from some great ideal almost by compulsion.

In 1839 this was the ideal of unlimited democracy. Our literature would have to be characteristically American, that is, a literature of the people.

> The struggle which is coming up here is not between the high-born and the low-born. . . . It is to be a struggle between the accumulator of wealth and the simple laborer who actually produces it; briefly a struggle between man and money. This struggle has not yet fairly commenced in the Old World, but it must come there and ultimately make the tour of the world.

This revolution will compel a great literature to rise from the American people, the highest moment of their genius. Both essays are written in a tone of almost boasting confidence that both the revolution and the great literature are to be realized almost immediately.

This was the period of Brownson's most radical thinking,

of his essay on **"The Laboring Classes,"** and of his ardent campaigning for Van Buren. But Van Buren lost the election. Brownson, shocked by the results, felt betrayed by the people. Gradually, he lost his confidence in them, and re-examining his position until he entered the Church, he also changed his social views, which in the end not only contradicted his proletarianism but also firmly asserted the need for an aristocracy of talent. A number of statements gathered from various essays between 1844 and 1847 show how complete the reversal was:

> The natural tendency of the newspaper is to bring literature down to the level of the tastes and attainments of the unreasoning, undisciplined multitude. . . . It must be adapted to the most numerous class of readers and win them by appeals to their prejudices or their passions. . . . We ask, indeed, for an educated class, and we ask it not for the benefit of its members but for the advancement of the general intelligence. . . . As to the charges of aristocracy, which socialists and demagogues may bring against these views, we treat them with scorn. . . . We care not for their barkings, come they from what quarter they may.

When he mentioned popular demonstrations against Catholics, he quoted with deep bitterness a former favorite axiom, *Vox Populi, vox Dei*. He now looked upon the popular mind as a conglomerate of sentimental impulses, and year after year he carried on an attack against popular literature because it catered to these impulses. The more impressive writers, especially the transcendentalists and the humanitarians, were merely afflicted with a more sophisticated form of the same malady.

Except for casual attacks on individual writers, Brownson did not take up the specific problem of a native American literature until 1856. Then, he announced that it was the mission of Catholics, and Catholics alone, to create this literature. In "The American Scholar" Emerson required three important qualities, among others, for an American literature: independence, originality, and spirituality—the last in opposition to the external and material concerns of the people. Brownson now held that only writers with Catholic grounds for political principles could achieve a harmony of American literature and American political institutions, which were really based on the freedom of the individual. The democracy of non-Catholic literature was based on the naturalism of European radical thinkers. The political principles of naturalism, however, presuppose "the absolutism of the one or the absolutism of the many." Though American art was to be created by Catholics, it must be written not for the cloister but for the world. It need not present Christian doctrine. Indeed it need not even advance the people spiritually or religiously. The literature must simply be native, philosophically in harmony with our political institutions, and its function must be to civilize in an American way.

Though independence as here discussed is not necessarily the same as originality, Brownson in 1864 complained that while originality was one of the obvious qualities of great literature it was absent from American work. Of Bayard Taylor's *Hannah Thurston* he said that "none but an American could have shown us the same evident effort to write like an Englishman." Taylor apparently was regarded as typical of all American authors, imitative of the English in manner and indebted to the French for their substance. But naturalism and imitativeness were not the only obstacles to a native literature; great writers need a "high, generous, and cultivated" audience, hardly to be found in a people dominated by the "mercantile spirit" and the pursuit of luxury. Brownson saw not only an opportunity but an obligation for Catholic writers, who in principle should be free of all these problems.

In his final thinking on a native literature, Brownson used three of Emerson's important terms but not in Emerson's sense. Independence is not to be identified with Emerson's individualism and self-reliance; it is Brownson's view that only God and not any human agency has the *right* to authority over man. Originality does not reduce itself to Emerson's ultimate isolation and incommunicability of individual experience; it is little more than the classical view that a work of art is at the same time unique and universal. Finally, Brownson's attack on the mercantile spirit has nothing of Emerson's transcendental quality but it simply asks for a cultivated audience. Actually, this late discussion of the problem is only a moment in Brownson's continually shifting discussion of Catholic literature.

II

Almost immediately after his conversion Brownson saw his position as one that carried with it the duty of protecting the doctrines of the Church against outside influence and against the mistakes of Catholics themselves. Almost all his thinking on the nature and purpose of literature occurs during this last and long period of his career. It became increasingly necessary for him to justify more and more completely the attacks he made regularly against certain kinds of writing. That literature is not to be sought for its own sake continued to be an assumption at least implied on almost every page of his critical writing. Christian doctrine was now to be the great ideal, which was to compel its own expression in art. At first he conceded a respectable place to literature with great reluctance. He once said of Irving and Hawthorne that they "are pleasant authors for the boudoir, or to be read while resting on the sofa after dinner. No man who has any self-respect will read either of them in the morning." At almost the same time he could give approval to the novel provided it was founded on Catholic doctrine, but he insisted strictly on this provision. "All that is profane, or not religious, is hurtful in a greater or less degree, and none is religious, save in so far as it embodies the supernatural life of religion, as the principle of the interest it excites." Indeed Brownson began by making a relentless distinction between the Catholic and the anti-Catholic with no middle ground. After commending one novel he says: "I only wish that Miss Duval had left the excellent Protestant lady out of the book."

As a premise of his critical thought he accepted the traditional metaphysical principle that truth and beauty are convertible. Along with the premise he adopted the method of separating form and content, focusing his discussion on the content and judging it almost exclusively on theological or philosophical grounds. He condemned Emerson's "Threnody," for instance, because of its theory of immortality, the merging of the individual with the world soul. Though he found *The Scarlet Letter* a work of powerful and fascinating genius, he attacked it because Hawthorne was "wholly ignorant of the Christian asceticism." The method of Brownson's judgment was simple. Truth is beauty and beauty is truth; it is not true that the individual merges with the world soul, etc. Therefore, the poem or novel is not beautiful and not a good work of art—at least not completely. In such instances the possible equivocation of *truth* does not seem to bother him. Both the premise and the method are retained by Brownson for the rest of his life. When he comes to accept novels which are not explicitly Catholic, it is not because he changes his criticism but because he re-examines his theological position on nature and supernatural grace.

He applied this method repeatedly to the question of the sensory and emotional elements of literature. Often, however, his argument is difficult to follow. He uses any one of several terms to identify these elements and makes no effort toward a discrimination of terms. They are easily identified with nature, at times explicitly called the corrupted nature of man. Though he did change his theory, he did not do it by any linear progression towards a final solution, but he shuttled back and forth between some degree of Jansenism and a more complete respect for nature. In a single review he may at first insist that he has no objection to sound feelings, but a few pages later he may inveigh against the feelings without any qualifications at all, not even from the context. However much he varies his attitude at the beginning, the problem is crucial. "The age in which we live is a sentimental age and sentimentalism is the deadliest enemy to true piety, and to all real strength or worth of character."

Brownson is likely to take up this problem in either one of two ways. At times he sees it as a problem of content and attacks a novel because it presents some sentimental theory of ethics. At great length, for instance, he attacks Lowell's "The Vision of Sir Launfall" because it explicitly puts spontaneous instinct above reasoned duty. He objects to many novels because they are written with the assumption that love is a fatal passion which overwhelms the soul. Most of the time, however, he uses a combined attack against both the content and the effect of the novel. In fact, the greater emphasis is on the power of the novels to excite the feelings of unregenerate nature. Novelists forget "the essential incongruity between nature and grace, and . . . [are] unaware that the affection of sentiment and imagination by natural causes is wholly repugnant to that supernatural affection which alone is religious." The distinction between natural and supernatural causes does not save him from a Jansenistic bias. On the next page he says that religion "is never that to which nature inclines, but it is always that from which it is averse, and which it resists." The most dangerous novels are not the obscene, for here disgust protects the reader; but the refined re-spectable novels which exploit the feelings subtly and break down the control of reason and will over nature.

Such pronouncements brought accusations of Jansenism from his readers and Brownson defended himself.

> Physically considered, man's nature has not been essentially altered by the fall, and is good now as well as when it came from the hands of the Creator. . . . By the fall we lost the supernatural grace . . . we before had, by which our nature was maintained in its integrity . . . , and in consequence of the loss of which our nature became turned away from God, so that we are now naturally averse to him.

Though more careful of the terms he used, he continued the attack against naturalism, which almost amounted to an attack against the novel as it then existed. Slowly the emphasis changed until his dominant belief was that grace and nature are compatible, that grace must elevate nature to a perfect human harmony. But even in Catholic novels he almost never found this harmony achieved. In his final stage he came to accept a novel which was purely natural, a complete reversal of his earlier position that an art is harmful when it is not based on supernatural problems. He asks of young Catholic writers a literature "which though natural, is pure and innocent; though secular and free, is inoffensive to Catholic truth and virtue." Evidence of his view that literature is not to be sought for its own sake becomes somewhat tenuous in contexts like this. Literature, nevertheless, is still for Brownson an expres-sion of his total Catholic belief. When, in his last reviews, he returns to attack certain novels, he does this not so much on theological grounds as on simple moral grounds. At least this is generally true. In 1875, only several months before his death, he showed another of his characteristic reversals and rejected novels entirely. "We set our face against all novels, especially against women's novels. They are all bad."

III

Partly because of his temperament and partly because of his own disillusionment with "sentimental" or subjectivist varieties of religion, Brownson was suspicious of the non-logical powers of the mind. He realized, too, how thin the logical content of the Catholic polemic and didactic nov-els really was. Moreover, he also realized by experience that when a novel was most like a novel, it neither de-pended on logic nor appealed to the reasoning parts of the mind. Forced therefore by the tradition of the Church and its use of art—he refers explicitly to music, painting, sculpture, and architecture—he had to admit that there "is no essential element of human nature that needs to be neglected or that may not be legitimately addressed." "It [poetry or the novel] addresses the sentiments, affections, imagination, rather than the understanding." Even though he found it practical to separate form from content and to evaluate the content in abstract isolation by Catholic theo-logical standards, he nevertheless needed clearer defini-tions of poetry and a more explicit statement of its rela-tions to the understanding and to other human interests.

In 1855 he began his review of Wordsworth's poetry by proposing to give the scientific foundations of criticism. He wanted to give poetry an ultimately divine origin and purpose at the same time that he wanted to avoid the romantic and transcendentalist view of the poetic act as a discovery of truth, especially ultimate truth, by a kind of imaginative and subjective possession. The truths pre-exist the poetic act and are a kind of matrix for the poetic activity. Thus, though Brownson used the contemporary term *creation,* he preferred the older term *imitation.* The poet imitates nature, not *natura naturata* but *natura na-turans,* that is, the creative energy in nature. Ultimately, creation is God's act and art is an imitation of divine causality. This is, of course, an extension of Brownson's ontologism. In art man finds another way of comprehend-ing God's causality. The theory is elaborated by an anal-ysis of the proposition, "God creates existences." There are here three parts: the subject, *God;* the copula, *creates;* and the predicate, *existences.* To fix the meaning of art, Brownson concentrates on the copula, *creates,* and shifts for a time from *imitation* to *contemplation,* accenting the intellectual quality of art but without changing the theory in any way. To contemplate the creative act "in its prima-ry revelation," that is, "the divine act at first hand," is to create in the strict sense the sublime; to contemplate its "pale reflex" in creatures, second causes, is to create only the beautiful in the strict sense.

This is an awkward, obscure, and impracticable distinc-tion. Shakespeare, Chaucer, Spenser, Milton, and Byron are the great poets, who apparently express the sublime. Wordsworth, his contemporaries, and successors, victims of nineteenth century *frivolezza,* are concerned with sec-ond causes and express at most the beautiful. "Hence it is that all modern art is feeble, wants grandeur of concep-tion, freedom and boldness in execution, and is admirable only in petty details." It is difficult to see how Chaucer and Shakespeare, highly dramatic poets, contemplate di-vine causality "at first hand." It is also difficult to see how the romantics, with all their anxiety about the infi-nite, express only the beautiful according to Brownson's definition—if they are successful at all as poets.

Even in the review of Wordsworth's poetry he did not carry out this theory completely. He dropped the distinc-tion between the sublime and the beautiful midway in the review as well as the peculiarly ontologistic aspects of his statement. He retained a fundamentally Aristotelian defi-nition of art as imitation of the ideal, in which both terms are important. This was the basis for his criticism of Wordsworth:

> He starts with the assumption, which we readily concede, that there is poetry in common everyday life; but when he undertakes to express the ideal revealed by that life, he copies or imitates its common everyday forms. Hence, he gives us every-day life itself, not its poetry. He imitates its expressions, not its ideal activity.

With less consistent precision of terms he keeps these two

concepts as assumptions in his criticism: that art is imitation and that it must imitate the ideal. He always insists that the purpose of art is pleasure, not instruction; that it is addressed to the imagination, not to the understanding. He does, however, frequently refer to its cognitive nature, calling it an expression or communication of life, which is achieved by a representation of its object. The function of such representation is to give a more intense awareness of life. Moreover, the object imitated must be the ideal. He objected to Trollope, Balzac, and Dickens, especially Dickens, because of their realism. In one instance he supplemented his Aristotelianism with Plato's distinction between the mimetic, copying of actuality, and the methetic, expression of the ideal. Some of his last reviews are extended attacks against the destruction of the feminine ideal by female novelists, who revealed to their male readers all the secret weaknesses, mischiefs, and even viciousness of women. Brownson was disturbed by the feminist woman and lamented the loss of the chivalric ideal, which used to create woman into an object of worship and mystery. This ideal was necessary for a great literature.

In general, this is an Aristotelian position acceptable to the Renaissance. It was effective enough in discriminating between truth as judgment and truth as artistic beauty. But Brownson's problem was twofold: to answer the contemporary claims for poetic imagination as a faculty which discovers truth, and to combat the sentimentalism of later nineteenth century literature. It was hardly enough to say that art is addressed to the feelings, affections, or imagination, and to reject a novel because it attracted the feelings, affections, and emotions. To speak of unsound and sound feelings was to change an aesthetic problem immediately into a moral problem. Some analysis of the role of the imagination and of the affective elements of the mind was necessary. I am not sure that Brownson ever solved this problem. But he did not fail in this alone. It was also the failure of every critic who fell back on the classical, humanistic view of art in the nineteenth century.

Conscious of his position as a Catholic social critic, using his critical assumptions with all their limitations, Brownson in his criticism of individual works gave most attention to the Catholic novel, especially the novel of conversion. Generally, he first attacked the apologetic novel on grounds of its structure, seeing it as a futile juxtaposition of two disparate elements: the sentimental love story and the theological argument. If the reader were interested in and capable of following the argument, he would turn to the more challenging formal treatise. If he were not, he would pass over the argument and submit himself to the sentiments of the love story. Brownson found a large complicated mistake in the whole strategy of trying to ambush the non-Catholic by theological reasoning hidden within a love story. First, the argument turned out to be a thin dilution of popular manuals of religion. Secondly, the arguments were usually out of date, directed against a fundamentalist kind of Protestantism, which no longer existed. Thirdly, to attract converts the arguments were so shaped that they tried to emphasize the similarities and to minimize the differences between the Catholic and Protestant, thus defeating their own purpose by convincing the Protestant that he had nothing to gain from conversion to the Church. Finally, it is always the part of the Church not only to win converts but above all to strengthen its own religious life. Brownson was able to see that the cultural and intellectual life of the Catholic minority was insecure in itself and not strong enough to attract converts. Hence, he often advised Catholics to write novels which were simply good novels. Such achievement would gain more respect for the cultural potential of the Church than any number of polemical novels or treatises. If there were any polemical problems, he was quite ready to take care of them himself.

He rejected the apologetic essays in novels because they were poor arguments and even more because they were not art, not "addressed to the imagination." But from the social critic's point of view, even when he turned to study the story, he found in it implied values which were disturbing. With shrewd penetration he recognized that the novels revealed a sense of inferiority and were unconscious compromises of the Church's doctrines. As Catholic grew more cultivated and wealthy, they lost their sympathy with humble poverty and at the same time, because of their religion found themselves isolated from what they believed was their own economic class in society. In the novels the converts are always intelligent, cultivated, and prosperous. Now, the church which attracts the best people, even when they have to make sacrifices, deserves to be socially respectable, and Catholics deserve to move in the best circles. In the review of one novel he changes the situation from a wealthy heroine in a large mansion to a simple kitchen maid in a poor cottage. Then he asks the reader how far the novel would carry his interest. Several times he is exasperated at the appeal which the parlors of the wealthy hold for the Catholic novelist. Perhaps the Catholic novel, after all, was idealizing values which were not Christian. Perhaps the novel of conversion was less a means of winning converts than of giving the Catholics themselves self-assurance and social importance.

His strictly literary analysis of the narrative element in the divided novel of conversion on the whole followed his critical premises. He often complained that the logical parts of the novel did not enter into the motivation of the narrative. "I would prefer to see Abel convinced by the Father's logic rather than the daughter's beauty." The sufferings of the heroine were simply the ordinary anxieties and fears of a young woman who is not sure of her lover. But the polemic novel so exaggerated them that they were turned into a martyrdom. This was unrealistic. The only possible motive for conversion was some personal gain, especially peace and spiritual security. Somehow this advantage was seldom developed in the novel. The problem and point of suspense was the following: will the young man marry the girl after her conversion? It was not, as it should be in a novel of conversion, a question of following conscience, a question of personal salvation or damnation. Moreover, there was no mention of the most important element in the situation, supernatural grace and its mysterious, intangible power. Thus, the novel of conversion turned out to be nothing more than a particular variety of the contemporary sentimental novel. This fact becomes the basis of most of Brownson's criticism of the form. His criticism follows the variations of his theological opinion on the feelings, from surly contempt through grudging tolerance to a complaint that both nature and supernature go their own ways, each following its own laws. With almost monotonous insistence he goes on warning the readers of the novel's moral effects. In a refined and subtle way it exploits the feelings and breaks down the control of reason over unregenerate nature. Towards the end of his career, looking back upon these Jeremiads written against third rate novels, he might have felt a little embarrassed and even ridiculous. With a touching tolerance and humor he wrote:

> We have said here nothing new; the parson in his sermon, has said it all, my dear, a hundred times. I have only given you the philosophy of his sermon, and shown you that it accords with the nature of things, save in accordance with which neither you nor I, however wise I am, or beautiful and angelic you are, can be happy, married or unmarried. So take what I have said kindly; for if I am old now, I have been young, and remember too well the follies of my youth.

It seems that personally Brownson did not have a great and consistent respect for literature. Objectively, however, he gave it considerable importance by holding that it was not to be sought for its own sake but only as an expression of some great ideal. Nevertheless, in his role as Catholic social critic he discussed popular literature most frequently. His hard practical sense prevented him from assuming an ideal reader. In fact, a large part of his writing is devoted to the formation of a competent reader. In most instances he finds certain books morally and intellectually debilitating and advises his readers not to read them. The background for such warnings is usually a discussion of feelings, sentiments, imagination, or unregenerate nature. Though he never solved the critical problem involved in this discussion, his intellectualist position enabled him to see the basic weaknesses of his own period and to emphasize the distinctive character of Christianity. This emphasis enabled him to anticipate an awakening which occurred in America only a few decades ago, that is, the decision of American Catholics to abandon their "state of siege," to develop their own philosophical and artistic potential without making continual apologies for their own existence. In this and in many other problems Brownson was without influence, and until recently literary criticism among Catholics in America had advanced little beyond this position. Actually, Brownson may have been asking for too much too soon. The kind of literature he wanted grows slowly out of a tradition. Indirectly he was part of that literary tradition.

Alvan S. Ryan (essay date 1955)

SOURCE: An introduction to *The Brownson Reader,* edited by Alvan S. Ryan, P. J. Kenedy & Sons, 1955, pp.

1-27.

[In the following excerpt, Ryan provides an overview of Brownson's Career as a journalist, examining the influence of his religious conversions on his writing and on his political beliefs.]

Brownson was born in Stockbridge, Vermont, September 16, 1803. He and his twin sister, Daphne, were the youngest among six children of Sylvester and Relief Metcalf Brownson. His father had come to Stockbridge from Hartford Country, Connecticut, where the Brownsons were among the earliest settlers, his mother from Keene, New Hampshire. Stockbridge was then a frontier town, having been first settled only twenty years before Orestes' birth, and had less than one hundred inhabitants. Orestes' father died when the boy was very young, and poverty forced his mother to send Orestes to live with foster parents in nearby Royalton, Vermont. Religious sects flourished here in this period of evangelical fervor—there were Congregationalists, Methodists, Baptists, Universalists, and a sect founded in 1800 which called themselves "Christ-yans." The stern Congregational morality of his foster parents made an indelible impression on the boy, though he was left to understand that conversion must come as a personal rebirth. His early schooling was acquired at home through his own reading of the Bible and the few English classics he found there or could borrow. The dominant impressions of his childhood were religious, and when very young he was imbued with the ambition to become a minister.

Moving at the age of fourteen to Ballston Spa in northern New York with his mother, he attended the local academy, and worked in a printing office as apprentice and then journeyman. At the age of nineteen he joined the Presbyterian Church, and for a time taught school in Stillwater, near Ballston Spa. Unable to reconcile himself to the doctrine of unconditional election, and convinced that to accept the Calvinistic teaching was to do violence to his reason, he rejected Presbyterianism and in 1824 became a Universalist. The next two years find him teaching school for a time near Detroit, Michigan, then in Elbridge, New York, where he fell in love with Sally Healy, one of his pupils in the country school. In the summer of 1826, in Jaffrey, New Hampshire, he was ordained a Universalist preacher. His marriage to Sally Healy occurred in June, 1827.

Brownson preached for short periods in New Hampshire and Vermont, then for longer periods in Ithaca and Auburn, New York. He first contributed to, and later edited, *The Gospel Advocate,* the chief publication of the Universalist society. It was soon apparent, however, that Brownson's Universalist career would not be long. The sensitivity to social injustice that makes his youthful diaries read so much like early Carlyle was quickened by his reading of William Godwin's *Political Justice.* Then, quite by chance, he heard Fanny Wright lecture in Utica, New York, in the fall of 1829. He was captivated by her eloquence and her Utopian schemes. She, in turn, saw in him a valuable ally. He became for a short time a contributing editor to the *Free Inquirer,* published in New York by Fanny Wright and Robert Dale Owen. For a brief period he was also a member of the Workingmen's party in New York, dedicated to social democracy. Brownson's socialistic enthusiasms did not please the Universalists. He was, in fact, preaching socialism rather than Christianity the last two years of his ministry, and later spoke of the years 1829—1831 as the most anti-Christian period of his life. His association with Fanny Wright had precipitated a crisis in his religious beliefs. Realizing that he no longer believed what he was expected to preach, he left the Universalists and in February, 1831, began preaching as an independent minister in Ithaca, New York. In his first sermon he declared: "I do not wish to be called a Universalist. Should I assume the name of any party, it should be Unitarian. . . . Unitarian discourses are mostly practical; their lessons inculcate charity, refined moral feeling, and universal benevolence."

Late in 1831, upon hearing a friend read to him a sermon by William Ellery Channing, the noted Boston Unitarian, Brownson's hitherto vague acceptance of Unitarianism was suddenly kindled to enthusiasm. In 1832 he applied for the Unitarian pulpit in Walpole, New Hampshire, and was accepted. The two years in Walpole were years of intensive study. He learned French, read the five octavo volumes of Benjamin Constant's *Religion Considered in Its Origin, Its Forms, Its Developments,* and found here confirmation of his own confidence in intuition. Thenceforth for many years French philosophy and social theory— Saint-Simon, Victor Cousin, Jouffroy—became one of his chief enthusiasms. Brownson's sermons and his intellectual vigor began to be recognized more widely. From Walpole he frequently traveled the ninety miles to Boston for Lyceum lectures, met Channing and George Ripley, with both of whom he exchanged pulpits, and so began to be known among the leading Unitarians around Boston. Ripley became his closest friend, and at Ripley's suggestion he moved to Canton, Massachusetts, in 1834 as Unitarian minister.

Brownson plunged into his work in Canton with prodigious energy. He often preached three or four sermons a week; he gave Lyceum lectures, and devoted especial attention to the situation of the workingmen around Boston. In fact, it was Brownson's earlier connection with the Workingmen's party that led Channing to believe him particularly fitted to win to Christianity the industrial workers of the city. In 1834, in *The Christian Examiner,* Brownson outlined his plan for his "Church of the Future," in which Christianity became essentially a doctrine of social reform. He was, as he said later in **The Convert,** working for "the progress of man and society, and the realization of a heaven on earth."

In 1836 he moved to Chelsea, across the Mystic River from Boston, where he would be even closer to the laboring men to whom he felt he had a special mission, and began to preach in the Lyceum Hall and the Masonic Temple. He also edited the *Boston Reformer.* "Even in Boston," wrote Harriet Martineau, "as far behind the country as that city is, a notable change has taken place. A

strong man, full of enlarged sympathies, has not only discerned the wants of the time, but set himself to do what one man may to supply them." The reference is to Brownson's discourse on **"The Wants of the Times,"** delivered in May, 1836, in which he declared the old churches to be failures. "All over the Christian world," Brownson declared, "a contest is going on . . . between the people and their masters, between the many and the few, the privileged and the underprivileged." In this contest, religion must ally itself with the cause of the people. Jesus is "the prophet of the workingmen." This was the doctrine of Brownson's "Church of the Future," and in July he established his Society for Christian Union and Progress as a beginning. In his first book, **New Views of Christianity, Society, and the Church** (1836), drawing heavily from Saint-Simon and Cousin, he attempted to show how the "Church of the Future" would combine the spirituality of Catholicism with the humanitarianism of Protestantism in a new synthesis. He was already, like so many of his associates, looking beyond Unitarianism.

This same year, 1836, saw the publication of Emerson's first notable work, the slim volume called *Nature,* and the appearance of Bronson Alcott's *Conversations.* In the fall at Ripley's home occurred the first meeting of the so-called Transcendental Club, or as Emerson always called it, for one of its members, F. H. Hedge, the "Hedge Club." Brownson attended several of the meetings, and some of them were held at his home in Chelsea. He was already recognized as one of the leaders of the new school, and his influence continued to increase in the next few years.

The establishment of the Club by no means signalized that the Transcendentalist group was thoroughly homogeneous. The movement assimilated myriad influences from Europe, while retaining its American flavor. Emerson, Alcott, Ripley, Brownson, F. H. Hedge, Convers Francis—each brought through personality, temperament, or background—a different emphasis to the movement. Dissatisfaction with the orthodoxy of Harvard Unitarianism was for many, at least, their point of departure. Emerson had left the ministry to become a lay prophet. Thoreau, who, after living with Brownson and tutoring his children for several weeks in 1836, had called these weeks "an era in my life—the morning of a new *Lebenstag*"—would go his way, and so of the others. They were more united in what they opposed than in what they professed. Philosophically, the enemy was eighteenth-century rationalism and the school of Locke, as it was with Coleridge and Wordsworth and many others of the English Romantic movement. Spiritual reality was deeper and richer than anything imagined by Unitarianism or by the rationalists.

Brownson's chief contribution to the movement was as the expositer of European philosophy and social thought, and as a leader in bringing religion to bear upon social problems. Whereas Emerson addressed the individual, and was suspicious of social reformers, Brownson became convinced that social institutions must be altered. In 1838 he founded the *Boston Quarterly Review* and for five years filled most of its pages with his own writing. Through these years Brownson's attempts to further his social ideals occupied nearly all of his energies. Religion was primarily a social evangel to be spread by independent Christians like himself who were dissatisfied with all existing churches. He became, much like Thomas Carlyle, whose influence on him during this period was pronounced, something of a lay prophet.

His essay on **"The Laboring Classes"** in the July, 1840, issue of his *Review* brought this phase of his thought to its climax. Carlyle's *French Revolution* had appeared in 1837. In it Carlyle had tried to show England an image of its own social conditions as in a glass, and to warn England of the imminent danger of revolution. Brownson had reviewed it enthusiastically. And when Carlyle's *Chartism* came out in Boston in 1840, Brownson made it the occasion of stating in the boldest terms his radical social doctrines. In England laboring men and factory workers were rioting; Chartism as a socialistic movement was short-lived but for a time threatened revolution. Carlyle in his pamphlet attacked *laissez-faire* economic theory vigorously, but saw no real solution in Chartism. Brownson, however, went far beyond Carlyle. He saw in the depression and panic of 1837 in America a parallel with what Carlyle called The-Condition-of-England-Question. The class war was entering an acute phase. Industrialism had brought on evils worse than those of slavery. "Wages," Brownson declared, "is a cunning device of the devil, for the benefit of tender consciences, who would retain all the advantages of the slave system, without the expense, trouble, and odium of being slave-holders." He ridiculed theories about freedom of opportunity in the factories and on the frontier. There was not even true *laissez faire;* the power had already passed to corporations. "The proletaries" must be emancipated, monopoly and privilege must go, the inheritance of property be abolished. On the positive side, what Brownson asked for was the restoration to the workingman of his dignity as a person, a return to genuine free competition, and the opportunity for every man to own shop or his own farm.

The essay created a sensation, coming as it did from an editor who had declared himself in this election year for the Democratic candidate, Van Buren. The Whig politicians used it skillfully as evidence of the socialistic leanings of the Democratic party, giving it wide distribution during the campaign.

Aside from the inadequacies of some of Brownson's positive suggestions, like Carlyle and Ruskin in England he saw early the gross injustices of the industrial system. Schlesinger calls the Brownson of this period "the nearest forerunner" of Marx in America. In the light of Brownson's conversion four years later, however, his indignation, if not his entire social theory, seems prophetic, for it should be remembered that neither in England nor in New England, where the factory system was developing most rapidly, had the Catholic Church yet developed any specific social program. The Catholic hierarchy was not even restored to England until 1850, and in New England Catholicism was still engaged in the vital mission of preserving the faith of immigrants who were beginning to

come here in vast numbers to escape oppressive conditions in the Old World. But by 1874 Cardinal Manning was delivering such addresses as his "Rights and Dignity of Labor," claiming for labor "not only the rights of property but the right of unionization, the right to strike, and the right to have recourse to the civil authorities." Not until 1891, however, with Leo XIII's *Rerum Novarum* do we have a positive and explicit Catholic social doctrine.

With the outcry against his essay on **"The Laboring Classes,"** Brownson began to re-examine his religious position. Both his Unitarian and Transcendental assumptions gradually gave way. His study of Leroux, he tells us, gave him the sense of hierarchy, which disposed him to look more favorably on the Catholic Church, and gave him also the doctrine of communion—that man lives by communion with realities outside himself, with nature, his fellow man, and God. For Brownson this meant a significant step beyond the subjectivism of his earlier religious views. It suggested to him, he says in *The Convert,* the Catholic doctrine of grace. Moreover, Leroux's treatment of the function of providential men led him to a different view of the historical church. **"The Mediatorial Life of Jesus"** (1842) is further testimony to Brownson's rejection of Unitarian doctrine. He now saw that his efforts to establish a new church as the foundation for a renewal of society were presumptuous. He was trying to lift himself by his own bootstraps. Man was no church builder. By April, 1844, he had concluded that "either there is already existing the divine institution, the church of God, or there are no means of reform." Nothing is more characteristics of Brownson than this indication that his "passion for reforming the world," to use Shelley's phrase, should lead him to examine the credentials of the Catholic Church.

Brownson tells the story of his conversion in *The Convert* and elsewhere, but even his own account is not entirely satisfying. To reconstruct the complex processes by which he was led to the Church is extremely difficult. As Maynard says, "it was an ecumenical council composed of such queerly assorted figures as William Godwin, and Robert Owen, and Benjamin Constant, and Saint-Simon, and cousin, and Leroux—all presided over by Dr. Channing—that gave Brownson his faith, in so far as this came from natural sources."

During these years prior to Brownson's conversion he was by no means concerned solely with his personal religious situation. His friend George Ripley inaugurated the Brook Farm venture, and while Brownson was not an ardent supporter of the project, he showed a wary interest in it, and visited the Farm often. But Brownson's true feeling may have been expressed in a letter he wrote in 1843 to Isaac Hecker, later the founder of the Paulist Congregation in America. Commenting on Hecker's stay at the Farm, he remarked, "after all, these communities are humbugs." Yet he sent his son Orestes there, and Hecker himself had gone there at Brownson's suggestion.

This period was also one of stormy political debates for Brownson. The year 1842 saw the end of the *Boston*

Quarterly and the start of Brownson's connection with J. L. O'Sullivan's *Democratic Review,* for which he wrote until he revived his own review, as **Brownson's Quarterly,** in 1844. His selection of metaphysical subjects for articles and his increasingly severe criticism of what he held to be myths as to the nature of democracy were no more pleasing to O'Sullivan, the editor, than was O'Sullivan's practice of appending objections to the essays to Brownson. And Brownson's admiration for John C. Calhoun and his states' rights doctrine was such that he was already working to insure the nomination of Calhoun as Democratic candidate for the presidency in 1844. In severing connections with the *Democratic Review* and establishing **Brownson's Quarterly,** he was able to put his own review behind Calhoun's candidacy.

Brownson saw Bishop Fenwick of Boston in the spring of 1844 and began taking instructions in the Catholic faith some time in May. The rapport between Brownson and the Bishop's coadjutor, Bishop Fitzpatrick, who gave him his instructions, was at first minimal. The steps by which Brownson had come to the door of the Church seemed of no interest to Fitzpatrick, who insisted that Brownson simply follow the traditional course of instruction. Difficulties were at length overcome, and Brownson was received into the Church October 20, 1844. Like Newman, whose conversion came a year later almost to the day, Brownson carried others with him, humanly speaking, into the Church. Isaac Hecker entered before Brownson, but largely because of his influence. Sophia Ripley, wife of George Ripley, the founder of Brook Farm, was another; and some others of the Brook Farm group owed their conversion to Brownson.

Though Brownson thought seriously of abandoning his review, now **Brownson's Quarterly Review,** and studying law, Bishop Fitzpatrick urged him to continue his work and as a Catholic journalist to bring Catholic principles to bear on the questions of the day. Brownson, a neophyte in the Church, without formal education in theology or philosophy, faced the prospect with misgivings. He was not prepared for such a task. Yet he became "a defender of the Catholic Faith, its champion in the printed word, two months after his conversion, without even a spiritual retreat in which to collect his thoughts."

Under Bishop Fitzpatrick's guidance, Brownson began an intensive study of St. Thomas, St. Augustine, and manuals of scholasticism. He virtually repudiated most of what he had written prior to his conversion, so intent was he to demonstrate his obedience. It is clear, however, that Brownson even then wished it might have been otherwise, and in retrospect he speaks of his attitude as mistaken. It was the Bishop who insisted that Brownson put aside all the thinking by which he had been led into the Church, and employ in his writing only the traditional arguments for belief. Thus Brownson tried, with the Bishop as censor of his theological articles, to make a new beginning. His old friends and readers saw no connection between his former and present opinions. In his *Fable for Critics* (1848) James Russell Lowell describes Brownson after Emerson and Alcott:

He shifts quite about, then proceeds to expound
That 'tis merely the earth, not himself, that turns
   round,
And wishes it clearly impressed on your mind
That the weathercock rules and not follows the
   wind;
Proving first, then as deftly confuting each side,
With no doctrine pleased that's not somewhere
   denied,
He lays the denier away on the shelf
And then—down beside him lies gravely
   himself.

Brownson had been, up to his conversion, in the main stream of American Protestantism, and a leading figure in the movement party of New England. He knew the Protestant mind as only one can who has himself passed through a series of religious crises on the road to Rome. It is not surprising, then, that immediately after his conversion he addressed himself to those outside the Church, and entertained great hope of leading them along the way he had traveled. What is surprising is the tone and the strategy of his appeal to Protestants. His tone was militant, his strategy was, in Schlesinger's words, to destroy "all the strongholds between atheism and Catholicity where Protestants might seek shelter." His method was chiefly logical, and his language was frequently the newly acquired terminology of scholastic philosophy, with which his readers were as unfamiliar as he had been a year earlier. He analyzed and refuted errors, often with devastating logic, when he might better have pointed out what Protestants held that was true. Years later, in 1856, he concluded in a letter to Father Hewit that his approach was mistaken. "My own conviction," he wrote, "is that our true policy in dealing with the American mind is to study first to ascertain, not its errors, but the truth it still maintains, and to show it that that truth can find its unity and its integrity only in the Catholic Church. . . . My own method, I believe, is the worst of all, that of logic."

His articles on Transcendentalism, brilliant and searching in many ways, failed to recognize that in many of those who still remained Transcendentalists there might be the same mental disposition of openness to the claims of the Catholic Church which was his own a few years earlier. In his criticism of Newman's *Development of Christian Doctrine* he charged Newman's theory with being "essentially anticatholic," insisting that Newman repudiate it now that he had embraced the Catholic Faith. Again, Brownson's interpretation of the doctrine "no salvation outside the Church" was frequently expressed in language that left little room for the necessary theological distinctions.

In all of this there was no effort on Brownson's part to say only what would please Catholics. On the contrary, his articles on Native Americanism and on the Know-Nothing party, while they opposed the injustice and bigotry of these movements in courageous fashion, succeeded in stirring up against him the wrath of many Irish Catholics. Henry F. Brownson suggests his father's situation under a crossfire of criticism during this period, when he says that Brownson defended against Americans his right to be a Catholic, and against Catholics, his right to be an American.

How much of Brownson's manner and method is to be attributed to his own judgment, and how much to Bishop Fitzpatrick's direction as censor of the *Review* is difficult to decide. Isaac Hecker in his articles after Brownson's death, and Brownson's son, Henry, in the biography, place much of the responsibility on the Bishop. Whatever the truth may be, Brownson had been requested to fulfill a most delicate function, and one for which he was not, nor could be expected to be, adequately prepared. He believed that on many issues it was his duty to present not his own ideas but rather the position of his Bishop, and as a recent convert he was not sufficiently aware that full acceptance of the teaching authority of the Church still left ample room for differences of opinion in the domain of prudential judgments. As he put it himself in 1862: "Having experienced the need of authority, having suffered more than we care to repeat for the lack of some infallible teacher, we thought, and could think, only of asserting authority in season and out of season." He had been for many years a liberal Christian in theology, and had virtually substituted a secular vision of the kingdom of God on earth for the supernatural life; his present harshness toward all merely secular reform programs was a repudiation of his own earlier social philosophy.

More important, Brownson saw, after becoming a Catholic, that while his own earlier social theories were neither inspired by nor tried to foment a hatred of the Catholic Church, these same theories on the continent of Europe were often so motivated. In his zeal to attack anti-Christian socialism, he seemed to lose sight also of what had once been his greatest hope: to bring Christian principles into a creative relation with the social problems of the time.

In the next ten years after his conversion, Brownson gradually regained for his *Review* a new reading public. A letter of general approbation from the American bishops for his work was signed in 1849, and appeared on the inside cover of the *Review* until 1855. Partly as a result of this recognition, and in spite of vigorous criticism of much that Brownson wrote, by 1853 his *Review* had a larger circulation than in 1845. In 1855, however, Bishop Kenrick of Baltimore, wishing to dissociate himself from some of Brownson's recent pronouncements, especially on the temporal power of the Church, suggested to Brownson that the Bishop's endorsement of 1849 be dropped, and later the Bishop of Pittsburgh asked that his name be omitted. Brownson complied, offended though he was by their attitude, and omitted the letter from subsequent volumes of the *Review*. As Maynard points out, the letter cut both ways in terms of Brownson's position. It set his *Review* apart from other Catholic publications, and probably aroused the jealousy of editors who were not so favored.

Favorable recognition came to Brownson from abroad. Late in 1853 Newman invited him to join the faculty of his new university in Ireland, though in the heat of the controversy in 1854 over Brownson's attitude on the issue of Native Americanism, Newman deemed it best to withdraw the invitation. An English edition of the *Review* began to be published in 1853, and in 1854 Pope Pius IX sent him his apostolic blessing for his work.

While Bishop Fitzpatrick was in Europe in 1854, Brownson's articles were censored by a substitute, but upon the Bishop's return, Brownson did not resume the practice of submitting his articles. The tension between them soon led him to reconsider Hecker's earlier suggestion that he move with his *Review* to New York, and in October, 1855, he did so. But soon he was having difficulties with his new Bishop, Archbishop Hughes. Brownson's articles of 1854 on the spiritual and temporal power of the Pope had not pleased Hughes, and he had written to Brownson on the subject. In 1856 Brownson published his essay on **"The Mission of America,"** developing the thesis, later presented at the close of *The American Republic* (1866), that America has a providential destiny "far higher, nobler, and more spiritual" than the "Manifest Destiny" usually spoken of—"the realization . . . of the Christian ideal of society for both the Old World and the New." Brownson's implication, in Maynard's words, "that a new sort of leadership was necessary for the Church in the United States" irked the Bishop, who suggested to Brownson that he stop agitating the question of Americanizing the Church.

While a change in emphasis and direction is apparent in Brownson's whole attitude during the 1850's, it is difficult to ascertain the specific causes for the change. His son calls it a gradual change, while Maynard says it began "the moment that Bishop Fitzpatrick sailed for Europe in 1854." Brownson himself self said in retrospect that at about this time he began to reassert his own identity. Actually the causes are complex and to be looked for both in the movement of events and in the progress of Brownson's own thought. He began to feel that, his apprenticeship now being over, he could reassess his earlier attitudes. By 1857, when he wrote *The Convert,* he had come to believe that he had been wrong to repudiate so completely in 1844 the philosophical, religious, and social thought which had led him to the Church. Indeed, Maynard makes very convincing his thesis that Brownson wrote *The Convert* largely to assert the validity of his personal approach to the Church. Maynard's interpretation is borne out by much that Brownson wrote in the 1850's and early 60's. In essay after essay he insisted on the distinction between Catholic tradition and the traditions of Catholics, and on the danger of confusing "what is of religion and what pertains only to the social life, nationality, or secular habits, customs, and usages of Catholics." He finds many Catholics "not up to the level of the church," but "merely men of routine, creatures of the traditions and associations inherited from their ancestors, and which they seldom ever dream of distinguishing from their religion itself."

Brownson's sympathies during this period were increasingly with those European Catholic thinkers whose political views were liberal. Add to this the fact that he had begun to criticize scholastic philosophy as not being adapted to meet the real philosophical problems of the age, and had begun to speculate in a way that brought upon him the charge of ontologism, and it can be understood why he was under suspicion in certain quarters for his theological, political, and social thought. Finally, when in 1860 Brownson wrote on the **"Rights of the Temporal"** in a way that seemed to some of his critics as minimizing the temporal power of the Church, his writings on the subject were referred to the Congregation *de Propaganda Fide.* Cardinal Barnabo, the Prefect of Propaganda, gave Brownson an opportunity to explain his position more clearly. No grounds for condemnation were found, and the matter was dropped.

In these years up to 1864, Brownson ventured into very troubled waters. This was just the time when in England, in Ireland, and on the Continent, Catholic reviews were involved in the great struggle between the liberal and conservative forces within the Church that took place during the papacy of Pius IX (1846—1878). Brownson's position is best understood when seen in this larger context. To state in simple terms relationships that were often complex, the *Dublin Review,* the French publication *Univers,* and in Rome the journal *Civiltà Cattolica* represented the extreme conservative position, while Montalembert's *Le Correspondant* and the reviews with which Newman was associated in an advisory capacity and briefly as editor—*The Rambler,* and *The Home and Foreign Review*—were liberal. A single statement by the editors of *The Rambler* will indicate the direction of their thought: "Modern society has developed no security for freedom, no instrument of progress, no means of arriving at truth, which we look upon with indifference or suspicion." Newman, for example, like Brownson during this period, saw the need of a review in which Catholic writers could address themselves freely to the philosophical, social, and political problems which critical minds were bound to consider, and he strenuously opposed the attitude of publicists like W. G. Ward who wanted every question settled authoritatively from Rome. But at the same time Newman was aware of the recklessness of the extreme liberals. He, like Montalembert, Lacordaire, and Bishop Dupanloup favored the liberal reviews, but he tried without success to moderate their tone. Papal censure would have terminated *The Rambler* had its editors not discontinued it, and did terminate *The Home and Foreign Review.* It is one of the great tragedies of this period that men who tried to make Catholicism a creative and revivifying force in every field of activity were too often silenced because of their errors, instead of being given the positive guidance that they looked for. Even in 1882 Newman writes in a letter of "what may be called Nihilism in the Catholic Body and in its rulers. They forbid, but they do not direct or create."

Brownson was by 1855 well aware of this struggle in Europe. He was with those Catholics who, like Newman, might be called the moderate liberals, but he certainly never for a moment defended religious liberalism. In his essay on **"Lacordaire and Catholic Progress"** (1862) he declared himself an ally of Lacordaire and Montalembert.

He wrote eloquently of their work and of that of Ozanam. "How often," he says of Lacordaire, "have we heard him traduced, denounced as a radical, a Jacobin, a socialist, concealing the *bonnet rouge* under the friar's hood. Yet he persevered, held fast to his integrity, held fast to his convictions, and continued on in the line of duty marked out for him, unshaken and unruffled, calm and serene. . . ." " And referring to what Montalembert called the Catholic renaissance in France, Brownson says: "Our own country presents a fair and open field for this *renaissance,* for the union of religion with civilization, and that new Catholic development which will restore to the church the nations she has lost, give her back the leadership of human intelligence, and secure her the willing obedience and love of mankind."

I have tried to illustrate by these quotations the direction of Brownson's thought during these years; I could quote from a dozen articles: **"Separation of Church and State," "The Rights of the Temporal," "Christian Politics," "Civil and Religious Freedom,"** and many others to indicate Brownson's position on the issues that were then so sorely dividing Catholic opinion. But Brownson's views were by now the object of widespread attack from ultra-conservatives. The time was not right for such ideas, and there is no denying that Brownson was at times far too blunt in his manner. Yet it is well to remember that even Newman, a far more moderate and restrained controversialist than Brownson, was about this time "denounced in Rome, and even delated to the Holy See, as the most formidable agent of Catholic Liberalism in England."

Even though Brownson's essays on European politics and on the relation of Church and state were the chief targets of criticism from Catholic quarters, he did not confine himself to such subjects during this period. On the contrary, the domestic issues raised by the Civil War occupied much of his attention, and he called the 1864 volume of the ***Review*** the "National Series" to emphasize its concern with domestic problems. Though he had little respect for Lincoln's statesmanship, Brownson's allegiance to the Union had led him to support Lincoln and the Republican party in 1860, and he continued throughout the war to defend the Union cause and to attack those sections of the Catholic press which he believed were lukewarm in the struggle. Finally, in 1864, after at first deciding to support Lincoln for re-election, he switched to General John C. Fremont, whose withdrawal from the campaign left Brownson stranded. Later Brownson said in a letter, "My Review died of Fremont. . . . I stopped it because I had sacrificed my position, and had no party to fall back upon." The Fremont fiasco certainly influenced, if it did not determine, Brownson's decision to suspend the ***Review.*** Under the pressure of criticism, Brownson, now sick and weary, his eyesight failing, his two sons recently killed in the war, ended his ***Review*** with the October, 1864, issue.

A few weeks later, December, 1864, Pope Pius IX handed down the encyclical *Quanta Cura* and had the *Syllabus of Errors* published at the same time. In such condemned theses as No. 80 of the *Syllabus:* "The Roman Pontiff can and ought to reconcile himself to, and agree with, progress, liberalism, and civilization as lately introduced," Brownson's critics thought they read a condemnation of his work of the past several years. The conclusion was undoubtedly false, but Brownson saw that his influence was at least temporarily destroyed. Moreover, he himself seemed to interpret the *Syllabus* as a condemnation of his most recent thought. Instead of examining it with his usual capacity for making distinctions, instead of recognizing it for what it was, an index of references to the various encyclicals and allocutions of recent decades—as did Bishop Dupanloup and Newman—Brownson capitulated to the critics who had opposed him for years, and from 1864 to the end of his life continued to do penance for his "liberal period." Nothing, in fact, more clearly reveals Brownson's loss of confidence after 1864 than to compare his understanding of the *Syllabus* with Newman's, as expressed in personal letters in 1864 and later in his *Letter to the Duke of Norfolk* (1875). Newman, for example, saw immediately the harm that would be done by extremists, both within and outside the Church, through misinterpretation of the *Syllabus,* and refused to be stampeded. Brownson, on the other hand, in taking the *Syllabus* as a condemnation of his writings of recent years, was really accepting the interpretation of it sanctioned by his opponents.

In the period immediately after the suspension of his *Review,* Brownson planned a whole series of volumes in which he hoped to give systematic expression to his thought. Of these, only one, *The American Republic* (1866), was brought to completion. Work on the others was deferred in favor of numerous essays he contributed to *The Catholic World,* the newly established *Ave Maria* at Notre Dame, and the New York *Tablet,* to the latter of which he was a regular contributor. Brownson was, to the end, a journalist, and he was unable in advanced years to change the writing habits of a lifetime. Nor was he, now that he was no longer in the editor's chair, happy about the revisions to which some of his essays were subjected. He wanted one more opportunity to speak out in his own review. His wife's request, just before her death in 1872, that he revive *Brownson's Quarterly Review,* was all that he needed, and in 1873 he began the "Last Series."

In the first issue of the revived *Review* Brownson wrote:

> I willingly admit that I made many mistakes; but I regard as the greatest of all the mistakes into which I fell during the last three or four years that I published my *Review,* that of holding back the stronger points of the Catholic faith, on which I had previously insisted. . . . I have no ambition to be regarded as a *liberal* Catholic. A *liberal* Catholic I am not, never was, save in appearance for a brief moment, and never can be. . . . What is most needed in these times. . . . is the truth that condemns, point-blank, the spirit of the age, and gives no quarter to its dominant errors. . . .

With this tone he carried on the *Review* for three years, until the autumn of 1875. As an affirmation of his orthodoxy and of his submission of all he had written to the judgment of the Church these last essays have some interest. But his best work had been done.

In the autumn of 1875, after the final number of his *Review* was finished, Brownson left Elizabeth, New Jersey, and went to live with his son Henry in Detroit, Michigan. He had been in poor health for more than fifteen years. Even as early as 1857 he had begun to suffer from gout of the eyes, and later his joints had been affected. Reading became difficult, and at times his hand was too crippled to hold a pen. He often had to dictate his articles, and in his last years even fell back on the re-publication of earlier essays to fill the pages of his revived *Review*. After moving to Detroit, Brownson was able to complete only one article, **"The Philosophy of the Supernatural."** From Christmas on into the spring the physical and intellectual energy that had sustained him through years of writing and lecturing waned rapidly. On Easter Sunday he received the Sacraments of Holy Communion and Extreme Unction. He died early the next morning, April 17, 1876, and was buried in Detroit.

Brownson had for many years known Father Edward Sorin, the first president of the University of Notre Dame. In 1862 Brownson had been invited to join the Notre Dame faculty, and though he declined at the time for reasons of health, his writings for the *Ave Maria* from 1865 to 1872 were the occasion of frequent correspondence with Father Sorin. In 1872, after the death of Brownson's wife, Father Sorin invited him to come to live at the University, but he had already decided to revive his *Review,* and felt it would be difficult to conduct it from there. Ten years after his death, Brownson's remains were removed from Detroit to Notre Dame, where they now repose in a crypt in the center aisle of the Brownson Memorial Chapel in Sacred Heart Church.

Brownson has been denounced by liberals for his conservatism; by conservatives for his liberalism. Liberals who acclaim his keenness of mind and courage in his early liberal period often look sadly upon his conversion as a retreat, and lament that one who was a "forerunner of Marx" in the 1830's should end as a reactionary Catholic. Conservatives who approve not only his *American Republic* (1866) but even his abandonment in old age of any interest in political and social reform seem too ready to place him among the ultra-conservatives within the Church whose influence he continued to oppose for nearly ten years prior to the publication of the *Syllabus*.

These, I believe, are gross oversimplifications. They ignore the whole context of Brownson's work: the hammering out of his thought in journalistic essays, the hazards and risks he took, perhaps too hastily at times, in laying before the public the very process of his own self-education, his development in the milieu of New England Protestantism, and then his entering the lists, so suddenly and so unprepared in many ways, as a champion of Catholic orthodoxy. More important, the isolation of what may loosely be called the two conservative or the two liberal phases of his thought from contemporary American and European movements makes his vacillations, as they are often called, far less understandable than they really are. The dialectic of Brownson's thought mirrors in many ways the intellectual dialectic of the middle half of the nineteenth century. And finally, to ignore the relation of Church history to these movements, and especially during the papacy of Pius IX, which, except for two years, covers Brownson's entire Catholic life, is at least to miss the drama of his intellectual changes.

Thomas R. Ryan (essay date 1976)

SOURCE: "The Continued Apostolate of the Pen," in *Orestes A. Brownson: A Definitive Biography,* Our Sunday Visitor, Inc., 1976, pp. 676-94.

[*In the following essay, Ryan, a Roman Catholic priest and educator, chronicles Brownson's contributions to several Catholic journals, discussing the author's religious motivation for writing.*]

Of all the works . . . that Brownson had speculated on writing after the suspension of his ***Review, The American Republic*** and his ***Essay in Refutation of Atheism*** are the only ones he ever completed. This is largely explained by the fact that other projects intervened in the meantime to claim his attention more immediately. His friend, Fr. Isaac Hecker, founded a monthly magazine in 1865, *The Catholic World,* and Fr. Edward Sorin, founder of Notre Dame University, also inaugurated in 1865 the *Ave Maria,* a weekly periodical dedicated to the promotion of devotion to the Blessed Virgin Mary. To both of these journals Brownson made significant contributions well-nigh up to the revival of his own ***Review*** in 1873. In 1867 he likewise began his contributions to the New York *Tablet* of which he was also editor.

Brownson's first contribution to the *Ave Maria,* beginning in 1865, was a series on the veneration Catholics pay the saints, especially the Queen of them all, the Blessed Virgin Mary, and on the veneration of relics and images. This ran for nearly half a year, and was followed by another series of articles on the moral and social influence of devotion to Mary, the Mother of God, in 1866. Fr. Sorin was ever endeavoring to prevail upon Brownson to write more for his magazine, and two truly elaborate articles, serially installed, were added later, one on **"Heresy and the Incarnation,"** 1867-1868, and the other on **"Religious Orders,"** 1871.

When Fr. Sorin first appealed to Brownson to enrich the pages of the *Ave Maria* with some of his thought on devotion to the Blessed Virgin Mary and the saints, Brownson was hesitant. He did not wear his deeper religious feelings on his sleeve, and "felt a little awkward about writing on the subject for the public, and he always preferred to be silent in his writings as to sentimental devotions and private feeling and practices of an emotional nature." But Fr. P. P. Cooney of Notre Dame, in a personal interview, assured him that he would not be expected to confine himself to mere sentiments on the subject, but that what would be looked for from him would be a philosophical explanation of the principle which underlies devotion to the Mother of God and the saints. It was with this understanding that Brownson accepted the invi-

tation to become a contributor. In his treatment of the subject, therefore, Brownson seldom or never gave way to emotionalism or sentimentality, but wrote rather as the philosopher who wished to show that the honor Catholics pay the Blessed Virgin Mary and the saints is warranted, and indeed called for, on the ground of the strictest theological reasoning. Speaking of his treatise, he said:

> In the whole series of saint-worship, if I have written indeed as a believer, I have aimed to write with all the sobriety and reason of the philosopher, I have rarely given way to emotional impulses of my own, or appealed to the devotional sentiments of my readers. I have no doubt appeared to most readers cold and insensible, a bold speculator to some, and a soulless logic-grinder to all. My aim has been to state and defend the naked truth to the unsympathizing understanding, and to show to the coolest and most exacting reason that the whole system and practice of saint-worship among Catholics is defensible on the most rigid theological reason, and must be accepted or Christianity itself be rejected as a delusion.

Although Brownson wrote his treatise largely to clear Catholics of any species of idolatry or superstition in their veneration of the saints, the title he used, saint-worship, might almost seem to confirm such a charge. He used the word "worship" in the case because it is the only word in the English language that fully expresses what is meant by the word *cultus,* the Latin word used by the Catholic Church in referring to the honor paid to the saints. The word "worship" is from the Anglo-Saxon *weorthscipe* which in general designates the honor paid to God, to a magistrate, or to any man because of his office, his acquirements, his possessions, or his virtues. Idolatry is not in rendering worship to men, but in rendering to them the worship that is due to God alone. That Protestants should regard Catholics as idolaters in their saint-worship, and rashly "brand the worship paid the Mother of God idolatry," Brownson did not find overly strange or surprising. "They seem not to be aware," he said, "that the supreme and distinctive act of worship to God is sacrifice, and that we offer never to a saint, never but to God alone. . . . Having rejected the sacrifice of the Mass, they have no sacrifice to offer, and therefore really no supreme distinctive worship of God, and their worship is of the same kind, and very little, if any, higher than that which we offer to the saints themselves. They see us give to the saints as high a worship as they render to God, and why, then, should they not regard us as idolaters?" His whole treatise was written of course to remove this false impression.

Although Brownson had in the previous years treated many of the most abstruse problems in the whole range of philosophy and Catholic theology, it is quite understandable to anyone who has read his treatise on saint-worship, that his son should tell us that nothing his father ever wrote gave him more labor, or required more thought, than this same extended treatise on saint-worship. But it was labor that turned out to be very rewarding to Brownson himself since he could say in conclusion: "If my articles have been profitable to no others, their preparation has been profitable to me, and have given me peace and serenity, quickened my love to Mary and the saints of our Lord, and rendered dearer both Catholic faith and worship."

Brownson's treatise, however, had almost been broken off before it really got started. In his second installment he had used the phrase, "as God is, in his essence, triune," and this led to disturbing trouble. The organ of "a latterly promoted archbishop" pronounced it "formal heresy." Fr. Sorin was considerably disturbed and said in a footnote to his letter to Brownson: "You gave me a distraction at High Mass this morning when I came to sing: 'et in essentia unitas.'" In a letter to Mother Angela Gillespie, foundress of the Congregation of the Sisters of the Holy Cross, and St. Mary's College, Notre Dame, Indiana—who had apparently already written him about the matter—Brownson remarked that he had consulted all the authorities on the point from St. Augustine down, and added: "For the life of me I cannot discover wherein my language is either unorthodox or inexact." To relieve his own mind about the matter, Fr. Sorin sent the respective article in which the phrase occurred to Cardinal Barnabò, Prefect of the Propaganda, Rome, who in turn submitted the matter for judgement to a group of Roman theologians. They declared the phrase was unusual, but that there was nothing in it not strictly orthodox.

While Brownson took the question raised over the orthodoxy of his phrase quite meekly, letters show that he was also quite upset over the affair. When Mother Angela learned of this, she took alarm as she was closely associated with the *Ave Maria,* and wrote to him an encouraging letter, dated December 3, 1865, in which she said in part:

> One of my strongest convictions is, that Our Blessed Mother needs you, has special work for you to do in her journal, and out of it also—and that in performing these works, as no other person in the United States can perform them, you have the greatest need of her assistance! Because you stand preeminent in the possession of rare intellectual gifts, and a great, generous, warm heart.

Mother Angela became the "unofficial editor" of the *Ave Maria* in 1866. She may have felt indebted to Brownson inasmuch as he had given her *Metropolitan Readers* a good boost in an article in 1862. This happy relationship between Brownson and Mother Angela explains the interest the late Sister Mary Rose Gertrude, a member of the same sisterhood, took in Brownson. She wrote an undocumented biography of him, *Granite for God's House, The Life of Orestes Augustus Brownson* (New York: Sheed and Ward, 1941). She used the pen name, Doran Whalen, the name of her father.

Although Fr. Sorin had innocently shied at the phrase Brownson had used touching on the Blessed Trinity, there can be no doubt about his great appreciation of Brownson's contributions to the *Ave Maria.* In a letter to Brownson in January 1867, he wrote:

> With regard to your course in the Ave Maria, of which

by the bye, the Most Reverend Archbishop of St. Louis was good enough to say that he considered it the best paper in the United States, I wish to say that you must consider yourself the representative of the American Catholics, speaking to his own people of the Mother of God, as you think they should be talked to. . . . It seems to me that no one better than yourself could tell the American people what our country has to gain by spreading such a devotion. . . . You have given us excellent articles, of which a number of persons have spoken in high terms, even the editor of the National Quarterly Review, Mr. Sears.

At practically the same time that Brownson began to write for the *Ave Maria,* he also began to write for the *Catholic World.* For a brief period he served as translator for that journal, and first appeared as the author of an article in the July 1866 issue. During the next half year, he contributed three more articles, and thereafter, until 1872, he generally had one or two articles in each issue. In his *History of American Magazines,* Frank Luther Mott remarked that during the first half century of the *Catholic World* Fr. Augustine Hewit, C.S.P., was the largest single contributor, and that "the leonine Orestes A. Brownson came next with seventy articles." Brownson's contributions, however, were confined to six years only, during which time he was also writing for the *Ave Maria,* and the New York *Tablet.* Most of his articles in the *Catholic World* have been incorporated into his collected *Works.*

Some of Brownson's articles were on such themes as **"The Independence of the Church," "Union of Church and State," "Rome and the World," "The School Question," "The Future of Protestantism and Catholicity,"** or themes of a similar genre. The political philosophy embodied in these treatises he summed up and presented rather pithily in an article on "Church and State" in 1870. To these particular essays were added progressively others of a wide variety—philosophical, controversial and scientific. His son remarks that they are of such high merit as to be ranked "among his most valuable writings, as they were by the Author and the Editor." The article on the church and state relationship appealed in particular to Fr. Augustine Hewit, who wrote in December 1870: "Your statement that the rights of man declared in our Declaration of Independence are the rights of God, is one of the pregnant principles that sum up a whole philosophy in a sentence and will live forever as an axiom. I borrowed some of your ideas for a lecture at St. Stephen's Church."

It was the most natural thing in the world that Brownson should have become a contributor to the *Catholic World,* newly founded by his old friend, Fr. Isaac Hecker—that is, after he had suspended his own *Review.* But it soon became apparent that all was not to go as smoothly as desirable between himself as contributor and the editors of the *Catholic World.* To set the stage a bit for what follows, a few points should be touched upon. Although Brownson had experimented with a liberal policy for a few years, as we have seen, he soon turned back, after the suspension of his *Review,* though gradually, into a rock-ribbed conservatism. And by contrast, the *Catholic World* seemed to him to become a trifle too liberal and conciliatory. He once wrote Fr. Hecker: "I protest against the *Catholic World* being put on the defensive." Nor could he agree with Fr. Hecker and Fr. Hewit on the best method for making converts. But worst of all, a goodly portion of the *odium theologicum* and the *odium philosophicum* was to bedevil the honest efforts of these three excellent men to understand each other and to work harmoniously, and each tried heroically. Brownson considered Fr. Hewit's views on original sin as set forth in his *Problems of the Age* as "unsound," and said so in the *Tablet*. When complaints were made, Brownson told Fr. Hecker in a letter, dated January 28, 1868, that his only objection in the matter was that Fr. Hewit gave what was only his theological opinion "as Catholic doctrine." The philosophical quarrel over ontologism was perhaps even more pronounced, not to say bitter. A part, too, of the difficulties was the fact that Brownson had a long career of editorship behind him, and quite naturally found it irksome to work under other editors. It is of course entirely understandable that a man of Brownson's international renown as a writer would be a little sensitive about how manuscripts would be handled which had been sent up to the editor.

There is an undated letter of complaint from Brownson to Fr. Hecker which no one apparently has ever attempted to date, even approximately, not even the preparator of the Brownson papers. But since Brownson mentioned at the end of the letter that he intended to address himself to a review of Professor J. W. Draper's works as soon as his eyes would permit, the letter must belong to the latter part of the year 1867 or the first part of 1868. For Brownson's review of Draper's works appeared in the May 1868 issue of the *Catholic World*. It is in this letter that Brownson expressed himself quite aggrieved over the mutilation of one of his manuscripts. He wrote in part:

> Very Rev. and Dear Father Hecker:
>
> . . . Hereafter I pray you to return my articles, when they do not suit you, with objectionable passages marked. I can bear the rejection of an article, but I find I cannot bear its mutilation by any hand but my own. I am too old a writer and too old an editor to be treated as a school boy writing his theme for his master.
>
> I think you have injured the article, but let that pass. . . . If you want me to write for the magazine you must allow me a reasonable freedom, and also try & not make me feel that my articles are accepted only as a favor to me. I think I have helped the magazine as much as it has helped me.
>
> With your purposes and general views I heartily sympathize, and I wish to cooperate with you to the best of my ability, but I can no more sink my individuality in another's than you can yours. I would not knowingly interfere with any of your plans, nor come in conflict with the Paulists, published or unpublished, but if you wish me to aid, you must let me feel that I am at home in the C.W. [*Catholic World*], and welcomed. I must feel that I am free to work in my own way or I cannot work at all. I say this simply, and in no ill humor.

It must have been in reference to this matter that Brownson wrote his son in February 1868, apparently after he and Fr. Hecker had had a visit together:

> Father Hecker and I have had a fight, but it is over now. It grew out of his rejecting one article, and mutilating another, because my views conflicted with some views on original sin by Father Hewit in the Problems of the Age. In the first instance, I did it ignorantly; in the second instance, I thought I had avoided the main objection, as I expressed my view in the words of the Council of Trent, I trusted it would pass. But no, Father Hewit might contradict the council, but nobody in the Catholic World must contradict Father Hewit, whose orthodoxy on more than one point is more than suspected. But after firing off several letters at Father Hecker I feel better. Father Hecker was sick for a week from the scolding I gave him, but we are good friends again. I shall not be surprised if Father Hewit, who is really a holy man, modifies at least the expression of his doctrine, which you will find in Vol. IV, pp. 528-530.

Whether or not there is any distinction to be made between mutilating a manuscript and correcting or revising it, Brownson did as a matter of fact acknowledge the right of the editor of the *Catholic World* to correct and revise as he saw fit the manuscripts he submitted. On January 29, 1868, he wrote Fr. Hecker:

> An editor is and always should be an autocrat. The whole responsibility is on you and your power should be absolute. Yet having been myself an autocrat for thirty years, I have some difficulty in making my mind work freely, if while I am writing, I am in doubt whether what I write will be accepted or not. I always write with the public before my eyes, & when you veil that public from my sight, I lose both my freedom & power of thinking and expression. It may be a weakness, but the habits of thirty years are too strong to overcome.

The great difficulty for Brownson, as indicated, was that his fear of running athwart the views of either Fr. Hecker or Fr. Hewit tended to paralyze his energy and verve and make it impossible for him to do his best writing. In a letter to Fr. Hecker on March 10, 1868, he said: "The harsh word Fr. Hewit said to me on the article that was rejected disturbed me, and feeling that I must meet his views as well as yours, I lack that confidence that enables me to put my whole soul into what I write."

It is evident that Brownson was striving earnestly for a harmonious working relationship between himself and Fr. Hecker, and it is just as evident that Fr. Hecker was equally concerned to achieve that same harmony. On March 19, Fr. Hecker replied to Brownson's letter, saying:

> It gives me great pleasure that your health is better and of your visiting us soon. I shall be glad to have the opportunity of settling the difficulties which have recently sprung up. Our opinions on the effects of the fall, and what is the best policy [in convert work], do undoubtedly differ, but not to the extent that we cannot

work together. This I think can be made evident when we talk it over together. I shall expect to see you at your earliest convenience.

No doubt these visits—there is no knowing how frequent they were over the years—did much to preserve a working relationship between the two. Results were more felicitous, however, when Brownson wrote on themes wherein Catholic doctrine was not so directly involved and a clash of views was less likely. Speaking of an article Brownson had written on the **"Woman Question,"** Fr. Hecker said on March 8, 1869:

> Your article on the subject is most welcome, and your treatment of it most satisfactory to my judgment. If you wrote the article under any restraint, Dear Doctor, in my opinion you never wrote better in your life. I say this in all sincerity. [And again, on June 7, 1869, he wrote Brownson:] You never wrote more finished articles than those on the Woman Question and Spiritism. The first took me quite by surprise—its gentle tone and polish did not at all abate your usual strength. The Archbishop of New York [McCloskey] expressed his complete satisfaction with those articles, and said you had never written better. He is not alone in this opinion.

But his relations with the *Catholic World* were not to continue smoothly overly long. On February 1, 1870, Fr. Hewit wrote Brownson complaining about some remarks Brownson had made in the *Tablet* concerning the *Catholic World,* and on his own doctrines in particular. He wrote:

> We have all of us in this house frequently felt ourselves very much aggrieved by various remarks made in the *Tablet* which we could not doubt proceeded from your pen, although officially you were not their acknowledged author. For myself, I have always thought it best to make no reply but that of silence. But, as the Catholic World has been twice associated with "Liberals" & "Liberalism" in the *Tablet,* I think it well to let you know that I consider this as likely to injure the character of the magazine and those connected with it, and to remonstrate with you on the subject. It may be useless, perhaps, to do so, and I have no wish to involve myself in a controversy. I beg you to consider the evil which ensues to the cause of God and his church from every word proceeding from a Catholic writer which lessens the reputation for soundness and loyalty to the church of those who are engaged in its defense. . . . If you think, nevertheless, that it is your duty to censure my doctrines or opinions as unsound, there is no recourse that I am aware of that is open to me, & I must submit to it patiently.
>
> I remain with great respect, your obedient servant in J.C.,
>
> Aug. F. Hewit

Brownson replied immediately on February 3, and said in part:

> I have written an article for the *Tablet* since receiving your letter in which I make as far as possible that

Amende honorable. I hope what I have said will be satisfactory, if not, send to the Tablet what you object, signed, editor of the Catholic World, and any apologies we owe shall be made, and no controversy opened. [Fair enough.]

> [Brownson continued:] Will write the article on Education you have requested, if my eyes get better, and you do not in your wrath countermand it. Father Hecker and I have had some doctrinal quarrels, and he has insisted that I should, in writing for the Tablet accord with the Catholic World. I have not considered that he has any right to control not only what I write for the Catholic World, but also what I write for the *Tablet.* I differ from you on the question of realism and nominalism, on original sin, and probably on the dogma of exclusive salvation. You follow the Jesuit theologians; I follow rather the Augustinians. But however that may be, whenever you feel aggrieved by anything I do or say, I shall always listen with profoundest respect to your remonstrances and as far as possible remove the grievance. I will simply add now, that I will henceforth refrain from all adverse criticisms of the *C.W.* [*Catholic World*] and will never allude to it in the *Tablet* save to commend. Do not run away with the notion that remonstrances are lost on me, especially if they come from yourself, whom I have so much reason to love as a friend and respect as a teacher. There is little, except abandoning principle, that you cannot make me do, if you try, for the truth you tell me even in wrath I will accept as if it was told in love.

In a letter of a few days later, dated February 9, Fr. Hewit articulated what had been his real grievance in the matter. He wrote in part:

> I do not complain of you for differing from me in theology. I admit that the Augustinian school tenets have not been censured. I have no objection to your defending your own opinions, and I have no right to complain of you for controverting mine or criticizing my arguments. My sole complaint is that you have applied the epithet "unsound," and other such terms to my writings which reflect upon my orthodoxy, and that you have also reflected on the Catholic World as tainted or suspected in the matter of Liberalism. For a priest, these suspicions are like doubts thrown on the virtue of a nun.

It must have been about this time that Fr. Hewit himself became editor of the *Catholic World.* Fr. Hecker had been invited to attend the First Vatican Council (December 8, 1869 through July 7, 1870), as procurator of the bishop of Columbus, Ohio, Sylvester H. Rosecrans. According to a letter of Fr. Hecker's to Brownson, dated January 12, 1870, it would seem that he did not set off for Rome until after that date, leaving Fr. Hewit editor in his absence. On February 4, 1870, Fr. Hecker wrote Brownson from Rome:

> I send you by mail Cantu's article on "Chiesa a Stato," which may serve if you wish as a basis for an article on Church and State, which I suggested for your pen. Cesare Cantu stands high in the esteem of the Pope and all sound Catholics of all parties. I formed his

acquaintance here; he resides in Milan, and has returned home.

In a letter to his son, Brownson wrote:

> Father Hewit wanted me to write an article on the School Question, and Father Hecker wrote me from Rome the outline of an article on Church and State for me to fill up for the *Catholic World.* These, with an article on Emerson, and the concluding one on the Abbé Martin, with my article for the *Tablet,* kept me so perplexed and busy that I have had hardly a moment in which to write you. I beg you to excuse me as well as you can, especially as my eyes are so bad that I ought not to write at all. . . . You may be sure I did not fill our Father H[ecker]'s outlines. I have written the article in my own way. I expressed my own views, which I think agree well enough with Father H[ecker]'s, if he only knew his own mind and could express it. And yet I am not sure it will be accepted or printed as I wrote it, as I have given *carte blanche* to Father Hewit, the editor at present.

In a letter to Fr. Hewit, dated February 22, 1870, Brownson remarked:

> Father Hecker suggested to me some time ago an article on Church and State, but I cannot recall his particular suggestions. He has written me from Rome requesting me to write the article. My doubt is, whether I have not anticipated it in the other article on Abbé Martin, and that just sent him on the School Question.

Brownson must have felt he might have been overdoing the subject to have another article on the church and state *ex professo.* And he asked Fr. Hewit's opinion on the matter. Fr. Hewit having overlooked to answer his question in a letter on February 24, Brownson replied immediately on February 25, saying: "I have, however, after reading Il Signor Cantu's article on the question, which Father Hecker sent me, begun the article," and he added with characteristic candor:

> My articles are of course subject, even when accepted, to your editorial revision and correction; but I am rather particular in my choice of terms, and a little sensitive to verbal changes, for the change of a single term is not unlikely to change my whole sense, and upset my logic. From what I have read of your writing, I think I am more nice and exact in the use of terms than you are yourself, and that you do not always attach the same value to single words that I do. I would more willingly submit to your doctrinal corrections than to your verbal changes, unless in cases where I have been careless and have obviously used an incorrect term.
>
> The *Catholic World* wants an editor, and an editor that has ample leisure to attend to it. Yet it suffers less than I should suppose it would. There is danger, however, of its becoming too heavy for a magazine, and it has too many feminine writers, whether they wear skirts or breeches. It wants as a whole, robustness, true manliness, which it might have without being less courteous or conciliatory. I do not dare put forth my

strength in writing for it, and feel nothing of the freedom that I do in writing for the *Tablet.* I feel that in writing for the *C.W.* I am only half a man, and that I must suppress the rough vigor of thought and expression that is natural to me. Father Hecker restrains me, and my mind does not, and will not work freely under his eye. He patronizes me, but treats me as an inferior. I can face-to-face converse more at ease with him than with you, but I can work more freely under you than under him. You do not disarrange my working gear, nor wound my *armour-propre.* But I have done my best things, and am only fit to be laid on the shelf. Have the charity to remember me in your prayers.

Father Hewit replied to this letter on March 3, 1870, saying in part:

> It is undoubtedly a great humiliation for you to be in any respect subject to one so much inferior to yourself in intellect and in most departments of knowledge. The only consolation I can give you under this trial is, that you have the opportunity of gaining great merit and making a sacrifice of the most difficult kind to God, and thus gaining an eternal crown of much greater value than any worldly glory. The powers which I must necessarily have and exercise, I always use with scrupulous respect toward every author who is master of his art, and to you especially, and never meddle with a word unless conscience or an evident reason of propriety requires it. If there is a difference of any sort, I have to act like Susan Nipper's conscientious goblin in the garret, and fulfill "the painful duty of my position."

After whipping the article on the church and state question into fair shape, Brownson wrote Fr. Hewit on March 8, 1870, to say: "I have written the article on Church and State, and shall finish and send it this week. It will take from 14 to 15 pages. I have modified the original plan in accordance with Father Hecker's suggestions. I have written my own views rather than his, but I do not think I have run athwart them."

This article on the church and state appeared in the May issue of the *Catholic World.* The general thought evolved by Brownson on the problem of church-state relationships is truly of remarkable prescience for the time in which he wrote. Speaking of Brownson's thought on this theme, the late Fr. J. P. Donovan, C.M., J.C.D., said: "His treatise on the nature of the civil power is in remarkable accord with the doctrine put forth fifty years later by the great authority appointed by Pope Leo to the first chair of public law in Rome, Cardinal Cavagnis. With a few changes in terminology Brownson would be in literal agreement with Cavagnis; yet Cavagnis was a specialist laboring at leisure and Brownson the general controversialist crowded with work."

Fr. Hewit had expressed his amazement in one of his letters at this time at the amount of work Brownson was doing. And it was truly remarkable in the face of his bodily infirmities. Gout had so crippled him that he could scarcely get a shoe on his foot, and he ventured out into his yard only now and then with the aid of crutches. Unable to go to church for the last two or three years, he received Holy Communion only when the parish priest brought the sacrament to his home. His eye trouble was critical, and the gout had also gnarled the fingers which held his pen—which helps to explain his almost illegible handwriting at this time. Already on April 12, 1867, he had written his son Henry: "I am still a cripple confined to the house. . . . Write me as often as you can, for my life is very lonely, & I cannot get out to see anybody. Besides, if I work too hard, it brings on the gout." To the surprise Fr. Hewit had expressed at the amount of work he was doing in spite of his infirmities, he replied in a letter of March 8, 1870:

But you overrate what I have done. I say unaffectedly that to me it seems I have done nothing, and that my life has been frittered away. I have not fulfilled my early promise, nor used the opportunities that I have had given me, and my only sadness is in the thought that it is now too late to redeem the time or to do anything now. Of all my mighty plans not one of them has been executed, and I cannot persuade myself that I have done or can do anything worth remembering. This is said as sincerely as in the confessional.

[He added:] There is no humiliation in being obliged to work under you and Fr. H[ecker]. The difficulty is that under Fr. H[ecker] my mind is restrained, and my faculties will not work freely. It is not that I cannot express freely my views, but that I cannot express them with the ease, *abandon,* or *verve* I wish.

Back in 1838 Brownson had written: "The oracle within will not utter his responses, when it depends on the good will of another whether they shall to the public ear or not."

Brownson's article on the school question, previously requested by Fr. Hewit, appeared in the May 1870 issue of the *Catholic World.* This article together with several others on the same theme in the *Tablet* were greatly appreciated at the time by Catholics generally. The bishop of St. Paul, Thomas L. Grace, took pen in hand to write his appreciation to the publishers of the *Tablet,* Messrs. Sadlier & Company, on March 23, 1870:

I was greatly disappointed with the lecture of the Rev. Mr. Preston. It was a very feeble statement of the Catholic view of the School Question, and in my opinion will injure rather than benefit the cause. A poor defense is worse than no defense. There is a writer in the *Tablet* that manifests a thorough knowledge and grasp of the subject in all its strongest points. He could do the subject perfect justice, and he would render a great and most needed service at this moment if he would present the Catholic view and grounds upon the School Question to take the place of Rev. Mr. Preston's pamphlet for general circulation.

Respectfully and sincerely

yours,

Thomas L. Grace, Bp. of

St. Paul

We have seen that Brownson's writing of the church-state article was attended by some friction, and it seems that the danger of clashing with the views of Fr. Hecker or Fr. Hewit, or both, was now becoming more and more the *bête noire* of his relations with the *Catholic World.* There is a letter of Brownson to Fr. Hecker, dated August 25, 1870, in which he laid all his cards on the table and called upon his old friend, Fr. Hecker, to decide whether or not there was any longer any use of trying to carry on together. He had by this time gone over completely to the conservative camp. After delineating at considerable length the views which really did divide them, particularly regarding democracy, he wrote:

You see, dear Father, where I stand. Can we work together or can we not? If not, it is useless to try; if you think we can, I will do the best I can for the Catholic World, and cease to grumble. Pray let me know your view of the matter.

I wish . . . you would write me expressly in answer to my question, or what is better, come & see me. I want if possible to identify myself with the *C.W.* & give it my best thoughts & my best labors, but if that is impossible, I wish to know it; but I trust, even in that case an old friendship will remain undiminished.

With the answer Fr. Hecker wrote him on August 30, 1870, Brownson expressed himself satisfied that "there is a deeper and more perfect sympathy between us than I have felt there was for years." Just the same, his letter of August 25, 1870, is plain evidence that he was beginning to despair at this time of working harmoniously with the *Catholic World.* What transpired during the visits between the two we do not of course know. But, in any case, it comes scarcely as a big surprise that a few months later Brownson seems on the point of discontinuing his contributions to the *Catholic World.* Brownson's son Henry says his father at this juncture wrote Fr. Hecker a note signifying his intention to discontinue, but I have been unable to find the note. However, Fr. Hecker's letter of January 30, 1871, with its solemn appeal to Brownson not to quit his contributions carries an evidence of its own that Brownson was on the point of discontinuing his contributions. His letter ran:

Dear Dr.:

. . . It seems to me that if you would continue to write such articles as you have done the last two years or more in refutation of the calumnies of the enemies of the church, in applying Catholic principles to the social and political questions of the day, in directing the young Catholic mind how to judge and act in the midst of existing difficulties, which were never greater or more threatening, and in boldly confronting and silencing the leading advocates of heresy and error, you would promote to the greatest degree Catholic interests, give the highest satisfaction to the hierarchy, and interest most readers of the magazine.

Believe me, Dear Dr., you have no idea of the great good which you have done by your pen employed in this direction. I, who am in more direct contact with the readers of the *Catholic World,* hear the satisfaction expressed on all sides and by all classes for articles of this nature, all rejoicing that in you they had found a champion of their faith and a master who teaches them how to harmonize their duties as Catholics with the best interests of society and the state.

Whatever value you attach to my judgment or sincerity to my friendship for you, believe me, that this is a matter of most serious consideration in the presence of God, before you leave this great field of doing good, and give up the privilege of leading and directing the Catholic mind of our country.

I have never known you to falter in what you considered to be your duty, and whatever may be your deliberate conclusion in this matter, the high esteem and sincere friendship which I have borne for you now nearly forty years, will be none the less, or in any way affected.

Ever yours faithfully and affectionately,

I. T. Hecker

By the time, however, that Fr. Hecker had written this letter, Brownson had decided to stay on anyhow with the *Catholic World,* for on this very date, January 30, he was already writing Fr. Hecker and proposing future articles. But he was apparently by no means at his ease. A little later, on March 25, 1871, he wrote his son:

The only trouble I have grows out of the fact that Father Hewit is not sound on the question of original sin, and does not believe that it is necessary to be in communion with the Church in order to be saved. He holds that Protestants may be saved by invincible ignorance, and that original sin was no sin at all except the individual sin of Adam, and that our nature was not wounded at all by it. Father Hecker agrees with him on these points, and is in fact a semi-pelagian without knowing it. So I am obliged to abstain from bringing out what I regard as the orthodox doctrine of original sin and of exclusive salvation. But in all other respects I am unrestrained.

Brownson had been chafing for some time now under the fact that he had to suppress his views on original sin when writing for the *Catholic World.* In a long letter to Fr. Hecker, dated January 24, 1868, he had argued against Fr. Hewit's views on original sin (with which Fr. Hecker seems to have agreed), and added: "Neither my opinion nor yours has been condemned, and neither can assert his own opinion as of Catholic faith. I believe mine [the Augustinian view] is the sounder opinion, and you believe yours the better opinion. The only fault I find on this point is that he [Fr. Hewit] gives the opinion of the school he follows as Catholic doctrine, which I humbly submit it is not."

However that may have been, Brownson was soon to utter a much deeper complaint. To an article he had submitted

on Dr. James McCosh's "Christianity and Positivism" (Dr. McCosh was president of Princeton), Brownson had appended a footnote explaining that it has been "erroneously supposed that Gioberti and himself maintained that the ideal intuition was formal intuition of Being." His footnote apparently contained his real doctrine on the point. This footnote was for him of great importance, for it was intended to set straight those who had misunderstood his philosophy. And all the more so since in those days articles in the *Catholic World* were unsigned. Fr. Hewit, however, did not see eye to eye with him in this matter. On August 2, 1871, he wrote Brownson:

My Dear Dr.:

Your two articles have been received. The first will go into the October number, as the September number was already full, and Fr. Hecker had left the list of contents here before his departure for Lake George, where he now is. I am very well satisfied with it, and think it a very able and thorough exposition of the topics handled. The note on Gioberti I think unnecessary and unadvisable. The real point is sufficiently brought out in the text, and will be understood by those capable of understanding a longer explanation. The rest may be left to their own forgetfulness. I have preserved the note, in case you may want to use it elsewhere.

The other article I have not yet read, and will take it up to Fr. Hecker. I have no doubt it is all right, as it must agree with your other articles in whose principles and doctrines I fully concur.

I wish you good health and the blessing of God, and remain yours very truly,

Aug. F. Hewit

To which Brownson replied at once on August 3, saying in part:

My dear Father Hewit:

I am not quite sure I like the omission of my note. I like to go to confession and get absolution, and never go on maintaining views as if I had never held the contrary. Others may forget, but I cannot. I have no doubt that in omitting the note you have done what was best for yourself, for you really had maintained a proposition which the Holy See had censured—immediate intuition of God, which I had never done, though accused of doing it. If I recollect aright, the ideal formula, in the sense ascribed to Gioberti and Dr. Brownson, is modified or rejected in the text, which leaves me in a false position without the explanation given in the note. I am apparently censured, or suffered in the text to lie under a false charge, for I never held any different view of ideal intuition from that given in the article with which you express yourself satisfied. If you strike out the note, it strikes me that you should strike out all allusion to Gioberti and to me in the text. I have never fallen, since a Catholic, on the point in question, into any error the Holy See has censured. My *Review* will show you that I was never an ontologist, and always held that true philosophy is a synthesis of the ontological and the psychological. But I will own to you that I had not sufficiently explained what I meant by *ideal intuition.* Perhaps I did not clearly understand myself, though I think I did, only I thought any further explanation unnecessary.

I have read carefully the propositions of the Louvain professors, M. Branchereau, and now Mgr. Hugonin. My **Review** censured them, as unsound, long before the Holy See censured them, but principally for their pantheistic tendencies. Fathers Ramière and Kleutgen show that ontologism is censured because it asserts immediate intuition or cognition of God, a point I did not hold, but on which I did not dwell. These Fathers are right in their assertion that ontologism is censured, but are we thence to conclude that ontology is no part of philosophy, and that philosophy is reduced, as Sir William Hamilton maintains, to psychology and logic, or with Cousin, that the ontological is logically deducible from the psychological? Because ontologism is censured, must we hold, with these good Fathers, that psychologism is approved and must be held? I wish to speak respectfully of them, but neither of them has any *ingegno filosofico,* or the slightest conception of the question to be solved, and in refuting McCosh I have virtually refuted them and their whole school. . . .

Yet you surprise me by approving my article on McCosh after having disapproved my article on Ontologists and Psychologists, for if I understand myself, both articles maintain one and the same philosophy, which is substantially that of St. Anselm in his *Proslogium.* I can really see no reason why you have approved the one, and reject the other, unless it be in the article on McCosh I have succeeded better in explaining what I mean by ideal intuition, and showing that it is simply intuition of the ideal or ideas, which reflection identifies and verifies as *ens necessarium et reale.*

With great respect and many good wishes for your health, I am,

Yours truly,

O. A. Brownson

In saying that Fr. Hewit had maintained immediate intuition of God, censured by the Holy See, Brownson referred to Fr. Hewit's *Problems of the Age.* In the course of a letter to Fr. Hecker, in September 1871, Brownson said:

The propositions condemned [i.e., by the Holy See] are of two classes. The one censured as pantheistic, & the other as asserting ontologism, or direct & immediate cognition of God, an objection you will remember I made to Fr. H[ewit]'s first article on the Problems of the Age at the time of its publication. [That letter of remonstrance to Fr. Hecker was written on April 28, 1866.]

[In this same letter of September, 1871, Brownson

went on to say of Fr. Hewitt:] . . . who I am sure has misapprehended both Gioberti and me, & supposed we agree with him when we did not. The censures of the Holy See strike him, but not me.

With the rest of the articles Brownson sent in for the last months of the year, both Fr. Hecker and Fr. Hewit expressed themselves well satisfied; if not enthusiastic in one or the other case. The year 1872, however, was to bring changed relations with the *Catholic World.* Both his articles, the one on **"Ontologism and Ontology,"** and the other on **"Reason and Revelation,"** were rejected. Fr. Hecker wrote him on January 8, 1872, to say that the article on the **"Necessity of Revelation"** clashed with the views held by both Fr. Hewit and himself. He added: "In my judgment it would seriously impair the influence of the C.W. to bring out in its pages conflicting views on such important subjects."

Brownson saw now more clearly than ever that the rift between his own theological and philosphical views and those represented by the *Catholic World* was too wide to be bridged over in any way. He sat down at once and wrote Fr. Hecker:

Dear Father Hecker:

You are the judge, not I, of what is suitable to your pages, and I regret that my philosophy and theology are under the ban of the *Catholic World.* I will be greatly obliged if you will return to me the two rejected articles. I have had Fr. Hewit's criticism [of the] Ontology article, and though it has surprised me, . . . I beg you to give him my thanks for it.

On the seventeenth of this same month he also wrote his son concerning this matter:

I have been prevented from writing sooner, by bad eyes, a lame foot, and an unusual press of work. I find I had undertaken more work than I could accomplish, that I could not write for the *Catholic World* and the *Tablet,* and have any time left to prepare the series of works I have, as you know, in contemplation. Consequently I have broken off my connection with the *C.W.* . . .

The immediate occasion of my doing it was the rejection of my article on Ontologism and Ontology, and another on Reason and Revelation. Both my theology and philosophy being under the ban of the *C.W.,* I thought it best to have nothing to do with it, and leave the Paulists to themselves. I shall hereafter devote my time to the *Tablet* and the preparation of my contemplated works.

The rejection of the two articles was, then, the occasion, not the cause of his withdrawal from the *Catholic World.* This, too, is what he emphasized in two other letters to Fr. Hecker, dated January 12 and January 31. He was also quite anxious lest "their long continued friendship" should in any way be interrupted or grow cool as he was not withdrawing "in a pet," as he said. Yet one wonders whether the relationship remained quite the same. There was apparently never any further correspondence between them. On the occasion of Brownson's demise (April 17, 1876), Fr. Hecker wrote his son Henry a very appropriate, if short, note. But more worthy of mention is the fine funeral service Fr. Hecker gave his old friend. Speaking of the memorial service given their father at the Paulist Church in New York, Sarah Brownson (Mrs. Tenney) wrote her brother Henry and said in a letter, dated April 27, 1876: "Yesterday at the Paulists it was done up in a style beyond anything the other churches could attempt. Printed invitations, the church heavily draped, solemn High Mass with innumerable ceremonies, priests beyond counting, and a funeral sermon by Fr. Hewit."

Despite doctrinal clashes, Brownson had remained quite affectionately disposed toward his old friend, Fr. Hecker, while a contributor to the *Catholic World*. He had favored him personally with such frequent mention in the *Tablet* that the publisher, James Sadlier, wrote him on June 3, 1868, to say that a continuance of such a practice would be poor policy. It is also to Brownson's credit that when contemplating a revival of his own *Review* and a consequent withdrawal from the *Catholic World*, he remarked to his son: "My only unwillingness to do it, is the injury Father Hecker may suffer from my withdrawal." Fr. Walter Elliott, C.S.P., in his "Personal Recollections" spoke, too, of the comradely visits Brownson used to make to the Paulist Convent, Fifty-ninth Street, New York, while he was a contributor to the *Catholic World*. On such occasions he would sometimes stay a day and a night, and there were long arguments lasting into the late hours of the night with the priests "about the more unknowable things of God." After which Brownson would seek out the novice-master of the Paulist Community, Fr. George Deshon, "to make his humble confession." Then as Fr. Elliott adds: "Next morning the noble-hearted, great-minded Champion of Holy Church would kneel among us novices and receive Holy Communion with us, as if glad to be one of us."

Brownson must have felt a real wrench in his severance from the *Catholic World*. But whatever the course of events, he turned ever with renewed vigor to the next project at hand. Fortunately, too, he was always receiving letters of reassurance to cheer him on his way. He received at this time, in March 1872, such a letter from William Seton, grandson of Mother Seton, who was studying in Munich, Bavaria. After deploring the political apathy and imbecility of Catholics generally in his letter, Mr. Seton wound up, saying:

> I will only add one thing more—but I do it with hesitation, for I hate flattery myself & never wish to flatter—and it is, if Catholics in my own country hold the position they now do, it serves them right. When years ago you were battling for the cause, they deliberately spiked your guns & turned you out to rust; they left you, like an old warhorse that had gone through the fights, to pasture in a stony lot, when they knew what you had sacrificed by leaving the company of Emerson, Holmes, Whittier & all those whose names

the American people cherish as household words.

> You will still be remembered—you will—and long years hence when people go wandering through Elizabeth they will point their fingers to a house and say: "There is where Brownson lived." Perhaps when the Jesuits have their headquarters in America instead of Rome, some future Father Becx will say: "Well, there was something in Brownson after all—but as we did not understand English, we did not find it out."

This is but one of quite a number of very interesting letters he received from William Seton and his sisters while they were studying abroad. Unfortunately we do not have his replies. It is but a part of the wide correspondence he continued to carry on during the years following the suspension of his *Review*. Not to mention his many letters to journals of the day on government and politics, especially those to the New York *Times*, he carried on a large personal correspondence with persons he had mostly never met, but who had written him for advice on one score or another. Such letters generally received close attention and were answered with care. Sometimes in the case of prospective converts, such as William G. Dix, the questions proposed in his many letters before becoming a Catholic called for replies well-nigh as extended as elaborate articles. But no labor was too great for Brownson where the cause of God and truth were at stake. In one of his letters, dated April 25, 1870, Mr. Dix assured Brownson that his writings were gradually working the destruction of Calvinism in New England. He wrote:

> Certainly, all Christians owe to you a great debt, which will be more acknowledged years hence than now, for aiding in that New England reaction, which in God's good time will make all this region as earnest for Catholicity, as it has been earnest for Calvinism, and for the earnest rebellion against Calvinism. I see many tokens the New England thinkers are getting tired of the sea of intellectual chaos, and are struggling back to dry land.

Another correspondent whose numerous letters to Brownson stretched over many years of this period was Mrs. Madeleine Dahlgren, wife of Rear Admiral J. A. B. Dahlgren. She was an accomplished lady living in Washington, D.C., a gifted translator and author, who felt great esteem and admiration for Brownson himself and his wife Sally. She made them godparents by proxy of her twin babies, a boy and a girl. She did so, she said, to express to them both "more than words can do my admiration, profound regard and real affection for you both. . . . May our boy emulate your long struggle for right and truth—and may our girl read as her mother has in the dove-like eyes of your dear wife the fairest womanly virtues which can adorn her sex."

Another brief but interesting correspondence Brownson had during these years was with Fr. Eugene M. O'Callaghan of Youngstown, Ohio, then in the Cleveland diocese. Fr. O'Callaghan's rectory was a perennial rendezvous for a numerous group of priests in the diocese who ran the full gamut in their discussions of diocesan and clerical matters. When a theological dispute arose which could not be resolved, it was to Brownson that Fr. O'Callaghan wrote as to a sort of a theological oracle. The question which divided the disputants concerned was whether or not it was repugnant to the sanctity of God to suppose an order of things in which it is possible for him to forgive a man one mortal sin upon the performance of certain prescribed acts of virtue accompanied by attrition, and at the same time to retain other mortal sins of which the man is guilty. In other words, is it possible to suppose a gradual return of the mortal sinner to God by a partial remission of his guilt?

To a second letter Fr. O'Callaghan had written him, Brownson replied on October 4, 1866, saying in part:

Rev. and dear Sir:

I have almost entirely forgotten what I wrote in reply to the question submitted for decision, but so far as I remember, I supposed the question to be substantially as you interpret it, viz: "Can there be a gradual return of a mortal sinner to God by a partial remission of guilt?" Is it compatible with the sanctity of God to forgive on attrition, confession, etc., a sinner guilty of a number of mortal sins, one of his mortal sins, while he retains the rest?

I think I answered the question, as you state it, and I repeat, in the negative. What I mean to say is this, that though the sinner's guilt undoubtedly augments in proportion to the number of his mortal sins, yet God cannot forgive one of the number without forgiving the whole; therefore the remission must be complete, or no remission at all. Did I not in my former letter so reply?

My reasons are that forgiveness on the part of God is not forensic or external justification, as Calvinists teach, but intrinsic, remitting not simply the penalty, but removing the sin, and receiving the sinner into Divine friendship, which is not possible so long as one or more mortal sins remain unforgiven and unremitted. With this view of remission I cannot understand in what would consist the remission of A.B.'s *fifth* sin while the *four* were retained. He is just as far from being grateful to God as ever. He who is guilty of one point is guilty of all. Not as guilty as if he had broken every point of the law, but just as far from justification. He may deserve less punishment, but he is just as far from the friendship of God, which is as effectually broken by one mortal sin as by a hundred. The man guilty of one mortal sin is just as effectually out of the state of grace as he who is guilty of the five you suppose; and as remission places the sinner in a state of grace, and restores the lost friendship of God, there can, in the nature of the case, be no remission for the other four. This seems to me to be conclusive.

This correspondence of Brownson with Fr. O'Callaghan takes on more interest now inasmuch as a biography of Fr. O'Callaghan has just been published. In many ways Fr. O'Callaghan seems to have been ahead of his times.

His biographer, Fr. Nelson J. Callahan, tells us that he was truly a prophet of the Church in America in the last third of the nineteenth century in working tirelessly for more humane procedures in the Church, in appealing for more dialogue between bishops and priests, in pleading that "due process" be established, so that a person accused would have the right to know the accusations, to face his accusers, to have a fair trial, and be given the right to appeal an unfavorable decision. In a day when canon law was in abeyance in missionary America, Fr. O'Callaghan believed there was too much arbitrariness in the exercise of authority on the part of American bishops, including those under whom he served. In his well-meant efforts to bring about a change, he published a series of letters (twelve in all) in the *New York Freeman's Journal* under the title, "The Status of the Clergy." He remained anonymous by signing simply as "Jus." His biographer says:

The "Jus Letters," as they were called, attracted immediate, and wide attention. They said with vigor and eloquence what many American priests felt regarding the relationship existing between priests and bishops, and about episcopal exercise of authority. . . . It was as Jus that Eugene O'Callaghan made a great contribution to the American Church in 1868-1870. The astonishing thing is that what he wrote then seems just as relevant and perhaps even more urgent today.

Whether or not Brownson knew anything about Fr. O'Callaghan's benevolent campaign for "due process," he most certainly would have been cordially in favor of it. He too deplored much arbitrariness in the exercise of authority in the Catholic Church, consequent on the fact that canon law did not apply to missionary America in his day. It was especially in the early 1860s that he was pleading for a reign of law rather than men. It is scarcely to be doubted that Fr. O'Callaghan took at least some of his ideas in his "Letters" from Brownson's *Review*.

Among Brownson's frequent correspondents, Sister Eulalia is also to be mentioned, who belonged to the Visitation nuns, and who founded the Academy of Mt. de Chantal, near Wheeling, West Virginia. She sought his advice on many matters, such as what textbook of philosophy to use in the academy, and often wrote words of encouragement to him through the years when he was in the thick of the fight for truth and justice. Some of the most revealing letters, however, which Brownson himself wrote, were addressed to his son Henry during the years 1860-1875—seventy-five in all. They are of particular interest insofar as he frequently consulted Henry on various topics. They bear the marks of genuine warmth and affection, but are not of course sentimental.

During the years he contributed to the *Catholic World,* the *Ave Maria* and the *Tablet,* Brownson also lectured now and then, but most notably at Seton Hall College, South Orange, New Jersey. Msgr. Michael A. Corrigan, vicar general of the Newark diocese, and president of the college, engaged him to come for the lectures. The preparation of the lectures cost him little time or energy, but the connections between Elizabeth and the college were extremely inconvenient. Msgr. Corrigan endeavored to settle the difficulty by getting Brownson a suitable residence in South Orange, but the price proving prohibitive, Brownson finally decided to discontinue the lectures.

It must have been a pleasure for Brownson to do such work in the diocese of Newark as the bishop there, James Roosevelt Bayley, was very well disposed toward him, though he professed himself a trifle chary of persons much given to philosophizing. It was he who dubbed Orestes Brownson, *Ursa Major,* the Big Bear. Commenting on this, Archbishop Robert J. Dwyer wrote:

> And for once the point of episcopal wit was not altogether wide of the mark. Big and bearish he was, towering over his contemporaries both in physical and intellectual stature, disposing of their trivialities with vast sweeping gestures and settling their hash with Johnsonian downrightness. His eyes burned below their bushy crags, calculated to strike terror in the hearts of friend and foe alike. . . .

> Even now, almost a century and a quarter since he trumpeted over the roofs of the world his conversion to the Catholic Church, we are just a little timid of his ghost, as though the Big Bear might suddenly rear up and maul us to death. Which is undoubtedly as good a reason as any why America's greatest convert is sedulously ignored.

Within three months of the time of his withdrawal from the *Catholic World,* Brownson had definitely decided to revive his defunct *Review.* It was in no sense at all a new idea to him. He had been, quite understandably, toying with the idea almost from the time he had suspended it. Already in June 1866 he had written to his son Henry (then in the armed forces) about the possibility of reviving *Brownson's Quarterly Review,* with Henry as proprietor and editor, and himself as a contributor. (This proposed arrangement was of course for reasons of policy.) A suggestion of this kind he again made to Henry in a letter written in March 1870, after he had published his booklet *Conversations on Liberalism and the Church.* He said he had put it out to the public as a "feeler." After all, he was still remembered by many as an apparent liberal of the early 1860s. But he had struck a new tack in this booklet, showing beyond doubt that he was one of the stalwarts in the conservative camp. He received many highly complimentary letters from various quarters on this treatise of the relation of the Catholic Church to liberalism. In his enthusiastic letter, Fr. Luke Wimmer, O.S.B., said: "I should like to point out this book to every sensible thinking man out of the Church, and say: `Take and read.'" In a letter of April 20, 1870, Fr. Hecker told Brownson that Fr. Hewit had suggested that he send a copy of the booklet to the pope. The *Dublin Review* hailed him "as our great old athlete of the faith," on this appearance before the public under his own name. Brownson had intended that the *Conversations* be published in the *Catholic World,* but Fr. Hecker decided against it. It was much more felicitous for Brownson that the treatise eventually

appeared under his own name.

The response to **Liberalism and the Church** was a decided encouragement to him at the time to revive his **Review.** It convinced him that the public would now again adequately support it. But it was of course the intervening events of the following years which led to his final decision. On March 25, 1872, he wrote his son Henry:

> I have finally resolved to revive my **Review, Brownson's Quarterly Review,** Last Series, Vol. I, beginning the year 1873. . . . There are looming up any number of questions on which I wish to have my say. . . . I want also to place myself *rectus in curia* before I die, for the sake of the cause, for the sake of my children and grandchildren, which I could not do in the *C.W.* [*Catholic World*], and cannot do in the *Tablet.* Do not try to discourage me, but speak

---

Robert Emmet Moffit on affinities between Brownson and Solzhenitsyn:

Brownson's startling conversion to Roman Catholicism in 1844, his acceptance of its authoritarian structure, spiritual austerity, discipline, and claim to infallibility in matters of faith and morals, was nothing less than a counterrevolutionary affirmation. He defied all the secularizing tendencies of his age. The Church unapologetically held for the superiority of the supernatural order and the supernatural destiny of man, against which all human actions would be judged. The Church claimed to stand as the divinely authorized, transhistorical bulwark of truth, amidst the fleeting confusions of the world. The Church claimed magisterial authority in the moral life, an authority for prince and pauper alike. This appeal to religious authority and the emphasis on man's transcendental destiny, this defiance of boundless secular authority, was not unlike that of Aleksandr Solzhenitsyn in our own day. For Brownson and Solzhenitsyn, despite radically different personal experiences, both pose the same question for modern men: Is it possible, in the face of the massive power of the modern state, to assert personal liberty without being antisecularist, or putting the question in institutional terms, to be anti-totalitarian without being pro-clerical?

Robert Emmet Moffit, in Modern Age,
Vol. XXII, Summer, 1978.

---

encouragingly.

There was one event in particular which had helped Brownson to come to this decision after having resolved "the matter for a long time" in his mind, and that was the dying wish of his wife Sally. She was a woman of deep piety, and in spite of increasing feebleness, she kept up her practice of attending Holy Mass daily, though the distance for her to walk was considerable. In a swirling January snowstorm she caught a cold that settled on her lungs, from which she never recovered. She died on April 19, 1872. One of the last wishes she expressed to her husband was that he revive his **Review,** "if only for a year, and prove to the world," as Brownson related later, "that my faith has never wavered; that I am still an humble but devoted son of the Church; that I am, as I always professed to be, an uncompromising Catholic and a thorough-going Papist." This wish of his dying wife became sacred to him, and he felt he could not do otherwise than comply with it. Never in this world did anyone ever receive sounder advice, and never did any man do a wiser thing than did Orestes Brownson in reviving his own *Review*. Only by so doing could the cloud which had hung over him in 1864 ever have been effectually dissipated.

The revival of his *Review* was for him a rather staggering undertaking. At his age it would have been so even under ordinary circumstances, but how much more so when we recall that he was still battling his old enemy, gout in the foot, gout in his eyes, and gout crippling the fingers which held the pen. Perhaps he was encouraged a trifle in the matter by the thought that his resurrected *Review* would mean more revenue for him. The fact is he had been living in varying degrees of poverty since the suspension of his *Review*. It was not at all that sufficient money had come to his hand, but that he was continually giving it away in goodly sums to those in need, mostly to relatives, often to indigent in-laws. This largehearted charity kept him rather permanently impoverished. For decades he had been frequently sending generous sums of money to his mother and to his sister Daphne for their support. But letters show that this period of his life was marked by more diffusive charities than ever. The result was that at times he did not have "decent clothes" to go about in. In a letter to his old friend George Bancroft, he remarked that he would like to visit him, "but my coat is too old and seedy for me to do so." Similar letters were written to his son Henry. In one he rejoices at the prospect that he shall get "a new hat & clothes, & appear once more like a gentleman." An increase in income would have been very convenient for him. Still, if such a thought ever crossed his mind, it could have had little influence in the matter of reviving his *Review*. The overshadowing reason that mattered was the cause he had embraced when he had become a Catholic, which remained ever dearer to him "than life itself."

Russell Kirk (essay date 1990)

SOURCE: "Christian Doctrine, Economic Order, and the Constitution," in *The Conservative Constitution*, Regnery Gateway, 1990, pp. 174-87.

[*An American historian, political theorist, novelist, journalist, and lecturer, Kirk is one of America's most eminent conservative intellectuals. Kirk's detractors have sometimes been skeptical of the charges he levels against liberal ideas and programs, accusing him of a simplistic, one-sided partisanship. His admirers, on the other hand, point to the alleged failure of liberal precepts—in particular those applied in the universities—as evidence of the incisiveness of Kirk's ideas and criticism. In the following essay, Kirk discusses Brownson's analyses of the Ameri-*

can constitution and economy.]

Any political constitution develops out of a moral order; and every moral order has been derived from religious beliefs. That truth, of which we have been reminded in recent decades by such historians as Christopher Dawson, Eric Voegelin, and Arnold Toynbee, was little regarded by the political economists of the first half of the nineteenth century.

Christian orthodoxy, nevertheless, has not forgotten the relationships among Christian doctrine, moral habits, political structures, and economic systems. In the United States, from the 1840s to the 1870s, the American constitution and the American economy were analyzed acutely by a Christian thinker of remarkable endowments, Orestes Brownson.

That philosopher and polemicist, whose quest for certitude had led him from Congregationalism successively to Presbyterianism, Universalism, humanitarianism, Unitarianism, Transcendentalism, socialism, atheism, and revolutionary plotting, at length—disillusioned with democratic politics and humanitarian notions of perfectibility—had entered the Catholic Church. As John Henry Newman (with whom he engaged in controversy) had set himself in opposition to the Utilitarian notions then being thrust upon England, so in America Brownson thundered against the materialism and the moral individualism of his countrymen.

I think it worth our while to pay attention, belatedly, to what Orestes Brownson said about constitutions and economic doctrines, for much of what Brownson predicted has come to pass. Before taking up Brownson, however, we may glance briefly at the economic circumstances of the United States during the middle decades of the nineteenth century.

A gigantic territorial expansion was in progress; and large commercial and industrial development paralleled the acquisition of territory—although not on such a scale, during the 1840s and 1850s, as was to occur shortly after the Civil War. This was the age of the coming of the railroads, the invention of a hundred instruments for efficient agricultural and industrial production, and thousands of important entrepreneurial successes.

. . . The corporate structure of business was given . . . [free] rein by Chief Justice Roger B. Taney—who, however, repeatedly declared that corporate charters should be granted only when they would be in the public interest, which overrode special interests. Not until after the Civil War, despite the striking increase in incorporations during the 1850s, would commercial corporations eclipse public-interest corporations and begin to supplant private proprietorships and partnerships in firms that required very large sums of capital.

America's booming prosperity, already envied in much of the world, was not primarily in consequence of natural resources; the beneficent influence of the federal Constitution loomed much larger as a cause. For the Constitution had made possible a national market, extending even by the 1840s over an area greater than that of Europe. The federal government's power to regulate interstate commerce, a principal objective of the Framers, had been meant to reduce barriers to trade among the several states; and Marshall's decisions had enforced such freedom of trade. Moreover, Congress' powers to grant patents and copyrights, to establish post offices and post roads, to issue money, to establish uniform bankruptcy laws, and to promote the general welfare—all these constitutional provisions encouraged investment and productivity. The federal system of courts, and the military strength of both federal and state governments, were guarantees of property and contract.

In such circumstances, hard work offered large rewards; so did extravagant speculation. Tocqueville describes American avarice, in the years when Orestes Brownson still was a radical and a leader of the dissidence of dissent: "A native of the United States clings to this world's goods as if he were certain never to die; and he is so hasty in grasping at all within his reach that one would suppose he was constantly afraid of not living long enough to enjoy them. He clutches everything, he holds nothing fast, but soon loosens his grasp to pursue fresh gratifications." The democratic character of American society encourages such economic appetites, Tocqueville remarks in another passage: "Democracy encourages a taste for physical gratification; this taste, if it becomes excessive, soon disposes men to believe that all is matter only; and materialism, in its turn, hurries them on with mad impatience to these same delights; such is the fatal circle within which democratic nations are driven round" [Alexis de Tocqueville, *Democracy in America,* edited by Phillips Bradley, 1948]. That fatal circle, one may comment, is grimmer still in the American of this year of our Lord 1990.

Democratic materialism had its clerical apologists. One thinks of the title of a book (published in 1836) by the Reverend Thomas P. Hunt: *The Book of Wealth: in Which It is Proved from the Bible that It Is the Duty of Every Man to Become Rich.* What Max Weber calls the Protestant Ethic was sufficiently evident in such publications. Only two delegates to the Constitutional Convention in 1787 had been Catholics, and by 1840, say, Catholics still had next to no influence upon American thought or policy—although the Irish had begun to pour in to build the railroads.

But in the year 1844, Orestes Brownson, becoming a Catholic communicant, began to criticize the American republic and the American economy in the light of Catholic moral and social doctrine. His arguments remain pertinent to our present discontents. To understand the nature of national constitutions, one ought to read Brownson's book *The American Republic,* published in 1866, and in print today. In that book and some of Brownson's other writings, one encounters a coherent application of Catholic moral and social teachings to the American Republic—an undertaking resumed, nearly two centuries

later, by Father John Courtney Murray, in his book *We Hold These Truths: Catholic Reflections on the American Proposition* [1960].

Brownson emphasizes that there exists in every nation, distinct from the formal constitution, an "unwritten" constitution made up of custom, usage, moral habit, and religious assumptions. Such an unwritten or informal constitution operates in the United States. If some new written constitution conflicts seriously with the old unwritten constitution of a country, that new formal constitution will be ineffectual. This is true in America, as elsewhere. Brownson points out in his little book **Liberalism and the Church** (written in 1869) that the Constitution of the United States is superior to the constitutions of other nations because it is founded upon a conviction (not mentioned in that written Constitution) of Christian origin, bound up with natural law:

> The peculiarity of the American Constitution," Brownson writes, " . . . is not merely in asserting the equality of all men before the law, but in asserting their equal rights as held not from the law, but from the Creator, anterior to civil society, and therefore rights which government is bound by its very constitution to recognize and protect to the full extent of its power. This view of rights you will not find in the Greek and Roman republics. Under them man was held to exist for the state, and had no rights but such as he held from it. You will not find it in the Roman Empire . . . .

Distinguishing between what he calls "the providential constitution of the people" and what he calls "the constitution of the government", Brownson proceeds in **The American Republic** to a close analysis of the written Constitution of the United States, and of Secession and Reconstruction. He finds the Constitution of 1787, joined with the providential or unwritten constitution of the American people, as good a constitution as any nation has known—nay, better than any other—for it maintains in balance or tension the claims of freedom on the one hand and of authority on the other. In Brownson's own sentences—

> No government, whose workings are intrusted to men, ever is or can be practically perfect—secure all good, and guard against all evil. In all human governments there will be defects and abuses, and he is no wise man who expects perfection from imperfection. But the American constitution, taken as a whole, and in all its parts, is the least imperfect that has ever existed, and under it individual rights, personal freedom and independence, as well as public authority or society, are better protected than under any other . . . .

But those sentences were written before "Reconstruction", engineered by the Radical Republicans, was imposed upon the states that had made up the Confederacy. Brownson had been an ardent opponent of slavery, a strong supporter of the Union, and at one time had called himself a Radical Republican. The ruinous measures vengefully thrust upon the South, however, roused Brownson's anger and sorrow. In the pages of *Brownson's Quarterly Review,* he denounced the Fourteenth and Fifteenth Amendments as destructive of the old Constitution's purpose. Those amendments had been unconstitutionally incorporated in the Constitution, and behind them loomed democratic despotism. As Brownson put it, "Fanatical humanitarianism triumphed, and the Union ceased to be a union of states. The people, irrespective of state organizations, became practically sovereign, and the federal republic became a consolidated republic, or centralized democracy, `one and indivisible.'"

To apprehend Brownson's argument, we need to digress for a few paragraphs concerning the Fourteenth and Fifteenth Amendments.

Drawn up by the Radical Republicans, dominant in Washington after their thrashing of President Andrew Johnson, the Fourteenth Amendment was a lengthy and most controversial addition to the Constitution. It was meant, among other purposes, to punish the people of the defeated Confederacy.

Section 1 of the Amendment declared that all persons born or naturalized within the United States are citizens of the United States "and of the States wherein they reside." This sentence guaranteed that Negroes would be treated as full citizens. The following sentence apparently was meant to provide that Negroes would receive equal treatment; but another motive of the Radical Republican politicians (or some of them) who backed this amendment was to extend the guarantees of the Fifth Amendment (previously applying only to the federal government) to the several states. This would mean that the federal government might restrain state regulation of trade and industry. The debatable passage runs as follows:

"No State shall make or enforce any law which shall abridge the privileges or immunities of citizens of the United States; nor shall any State deprive any person of life, liberty, or property, without due process of law; nor deny to any person within its jurisdiction the equal protection of the laws."

The federal courts did not at once proceed to interpret this "due process" clause of the Fourteenth Amendment to mean that the federal government might restrain state legislatures in their regulation of business; indeed, in the Slaughter-House Cases (1873), the Supreme Court firmly rejected the argument that the Fourteenth Amendment had extended the due process clause of the Fifth Amendment to the governments of the several states, in the sense of enlarging the jurisdiction of the federal government. Yet by 1884, the Supreme Court had changed its mind; and ever since then the federal courts have intervened in many economic concerns previously reserved to states' jurisdiction. As Edward S. Corwin summarizes this development in his analysis of the Fourteenth Amendment, "What induced the Court to dismiss its fears of upsetting the balance in the distribution of powers under the Federal System and to enlarge its own supervisory powers over state legislation were the appeals more and more addressed to

it for adequate protection of property rights against the remedial social legislation which the States were increasingly enacting in the wake of industrial expansion" [*The Constitution of the United States of America: Analysis and Interpretation,* 1953].

Although Brownson did not live to see the extention of the due-process clause to the state governments—at the urging of business interests—he gloomily expected such a result of the Fourteenth Amendment. "The great fault of our statesmen has been to make what should be a great agricultural and commercial people unnaturally a great manufacturing people," he wrote to his son in 1871. Reconstruction of the South had become reconstruction of the American economy by special interests: "The great industrial corporations have got the control and the government is simply its factor."

Dr. James McClellan, an able latter-day disciple of Justice Story, looks upon the Reconstruction Amendments much as Brownson did. "Beginning with the Reconstruction Amendments," McClellan writes, "which enlarged the powers not only of the federal courts but of Congress as well, the radical Republicans cut the heart out of federalism by stripping the states of their sovereignty respecting citizenship, state criminal procedures, and voter qualification. Using an interpretive device known as the doctrine of incorporation, the federal courts later used the Due Process Clause of the 14th Amendment to obliterate the reserved powers of the states respecting nearly all of the liberties enumerated in the Bill of Rights, thereby accomplishing a complete nationalization of all civil liberties and overturning the main purpose of the first ten amendments [James McClellan, "The Constitution from a Conservative Perspective," The Heritage Lectures, No. 157, 1988].

The centralizing Radical Republicans professed to be concerned for the liberties of black Americans. So they were, surely; men's motives are mixed. With few exceptions, the Radical Republicans were a self-righteous crew. All in all, despite its words about "due process", there is an unpleasant ring of arbitrary power about the Fourteenth Amendment. This was the first amendment to conflict clearly with the provisions of the original seven articles of the Constitution: for the whole tendency of Amendment XIV was to centralize political power in Washington and to favor the North over the South. With the Fourteenth Amendment, the powers of the several states began to dwindle. For the defeated eleven states that had joined the Confederacy to be readmitted to the Union, they were required first to ratify this Fourteenth Amendment, much though the people of those eleven states might dislike its provisions. Also there were loud complaints that political trickery and intimidation had been employed to secure ratification of the Amendment. About Amendment XIV, then, there still hangs a cloud; and Brownson, in the pages of his *Review,* parts vehemently with the dominant Republicans who framed that Amendment.

As for the Fifteenth Amendment, which deprived the states of power to determine who should vote and who should

<table>
<tr><td>

Peter J. Stanlis on the relevance of *The American Republic* today:

Not only does Brownson's ***The American Republic*** provide the norms by which to judge what has happened to the formal structure and spirit of the state-federal constitution, but its concept of the unwritten "Providential" constitution provides the principles by which Americans can regenerate their country. . . . If, as Brownson argued, politics is a branch of ethics, and ethics depeinds upon religion, the state cannot be all in all, and "the things that are Caesar's" cannot include the whole of public life. To secularized Americans the separation of church and state has meant the total subordination, and even the extinction, of the spiritual order in American society, in favor of the triumph of materialism. Such Americans, committed to descriptive, value-free sociology, have extended their denial of religious values even to human life itself. Brownson's unwritten providential constitution provides Americans in the Judaeo-Christian tradition with the normative principles which make the spiritual basis of American society a reality in the temporal order. Despite the enormous difficulties and complexities facing Americans in the Judaeo-Christian tradition, the best hope of a restoration of American freedom under constitutional law lies in Brownson's concept of the providential constitution of the American republic.

Peter J. Stanlis, in No Divided Allegiance: Essays in Brownson's Thought, *edited by Leonard Gilhooley, Fordham University Press, 1980.*

</td></tr>
</table>

not, Brownson thundered that this "is to destroy the state as a body politic." Of these two amendments combined, Brownson wrote, "They are revolutionary in their character and tendency, and destructive of the providential or unwritten constitution of the American people, according to which, though one people, they are organized as a union, not of individuals, but of states, or political societies, each with an autonomy of its own. . . . Give to congress or the Union the power to determine who shall or shall not be the political people of a state, and the state no longer exists; you merge the state in the Union, obliterate state lines, and convert the republic from a federal into a centralized or consolidated republic, or a pure democracy in which constitutions count for nothing, and the majority for the time have unlimited power."

Our present subject being the relationships between the Constitution and political economy, however, we must turn from Brownson's convictions about sovereignty and the franchise to his economic principles. What economic consequences did Brownson expect from the Reconstruction Amendments? And how would those consequences accord with the Church's teachings about social order?

Brownson had commenced his career as a polemicist when the doctrines of Bentham, the Philosophic Radicals, and the economists of Manchester were in the ascendant. In his early years as a political radical, and in his later years as a political conservative, he rejected Utilitarian economics. The reason for this is sufficiently given in some remarks by an imaginary priest in Brownson's late book

Liberalism and the Church.

"The political economists consider man only as a producing, distributing, and consuming machine, and seek only to get the greatest possible supply with the greatest possible demand," says Brownson's spokesman.

> I, by my profession, if not by my sympathy with my fellow-men, am led to look upon man as having a sentient, intellectual, and moral nature, and I seek for him the greatest possible sum of virtue and happiness. It is not likely, then, that the political economists and I should think alike. It adds not to the well-being of the poor that the aggregate wealth of a nation increases, if they are all the time growing poorer, and find it every day more difficult to supply their wants, or to obtain by honest industry their bread. Under the new system, it may be that wealth increases, but the tendency in the great industrial nations is to concentrate it in fewer hands, or in huge overgrown corporations, which in your country [the United States] are stronger than the government, and control, not always the elections, but the legislative assemblies, both state and national.

Here, as again and again in his writings, Brownson reaffirms the venerable doctrines of charity, family, community, and responsibility that the Church had enunciated over the centuries. His response to the evangels of the Dismal Science is like that of Coleridge and Southey in England. When we turn to the question of wants, we find Brownson reasserting the Christian teaching that is thoroughly forgotten in our age. (Of eminent economists nowadays, so far as I have noticed, only my Australian friend Dr. Colin Clark firmly upholds the Catholic doctrine about wants.) Brownson's imaginary priest from Europe, in **Liberalism and the Church,** rejects the liberals' notion that the gratification of wants is always a good:

"I was taught," continued the priest, "that to make a man happy we should study not to increase his stores, but to diminish his desires. The political economists study to increase a man's desires, and to develop new wants in him, in order to increase as much as possible consumption, which, in turn, will increase the demand, and the increased demand will stimulate increased production. The demand creates the supply, and the supply stimulates competition, which, in turn, creates an increased demand. This, if I understand it, is the essence of your modern science of political economy. But what is the gain to the laborer? . . . The more wants one has that he is unable to satisfy, the more he suffers."

The artificial stimulation of wants is an evil action, Brownson reminded his readers; while "poverty is no evil," he insisted. (Brownson himself had much practical experience of poverty, early and late in life.) Liberalism, obsessed by its economic calculations, leads mankind toward a materialistic hell in which the whole of life is an exercise in getting and spending.

These being Brownson's convictions, we need not wonder that the treatment of the southern states during Reconstruction, and the Fourteenth and Fifteenth Amendments, made him almost despair for the American Republic. He perceived in the measures of the Radical Republicans a design to crush the agricultural South; to employ the power and resources of the federal government for the stimulation of heavy industry; to concentrate power in a central government and in great profit-making corporations; to gratify special economic interests at the general expense.

The due-process clause of the Fourteenth Amendment, only eight years after Brownson's death, was being interpreted by the Supreme Court as binding upon the states in economic concerns—so, in effect, sheltering commerce and industry from the regulation of state legislatures. Brownson anticipated and scorned the twentieth-century American slogan that "the business of America is business." In the rich he would put no trust—not in those rich who meant to grow richer through speculation and misinterpretation of the Constitution.

As he had written in *The American Republic,* discussing enlargement of the franchise, "The men of wealth, the business men, manufacturers and merchants, bankers and brokers, are the men who exert the worst influence on government in every country, for they always strive to use it as an instrument of advancing their own private interests. They act on the beautiful maxim, 'Let governments take care of the rich, and the rich will take care of the poor,' instead of the far safer maxim, 'Let government take care of the weak, the strong can take care of themselves.'"

What Brownson expresses in these passages is not socialist ideology, not at all: really it is the Christian teaching of the common good. What Brownson preached to his countrymen was restraint of appetites and concern for the general welfare. The high exhortation often attributed to President John F. Kennedy, "Ask not what your country can do for you, but what you can do for your country," actually is borrowed from one of Brownson's addresses—borrowed by Mr. Arthur Schlesinger, Jr., whose first book had been about Brownson, and who wrote the President's inaugural address.

Few used such language during what Mark Twain called the Gilded Age, when speculation in gold and railway stocks might bring almost overnight wealth beyond the dreams of avarice: Henry Adams and Charles Francis Adams, Jr., describe most memorably the avarice of that age. But Orestes Brownson, when a radical and when a conservative, thought first of the laboring classes in any debate over the state of society.

Although Brownson's social and economic beliefs were rooted in Catholic doctrine, Brownson was no theocrat: he did not fancy that the Church should give marching orders to the captains and the kings. A passage in *Liberalism and the Church* might almost have been written by Father John Courtney Murray:

"The Church is not the state nor the farmer of its consti-

tution, and she has not and never has pretended to have temporal authority in the temporal order," Brownson wrote.

> She is a spiritual kingdom—the kingdom of God on earth—and she leaves to the civil and political order that which God himself leaves to it—human free will. She has always asserted the great principle which the American people more successfully than any other have carried out in their political constitution, but it has never been her mission to apply them practically out of her own order. Our Lord did not come as a temporal Messiah. The efforts to defend these principles, even in their spiritual application, has raised an almost universal clamor against her for encroaching on the province of the civil power, and are the basis of the principal charges her enemies even now allege against her. What then would have been the outcry, had she attempted to organize political society in accordance with these principles! The relation between Church and State here, which so well meets her wants, can subsist only where the state is founded on the recognition of the freedom of conscience, and the equal rights of all, which it is bound to protect and defend. Never in the Old World has it been humanly possible to found the state on the American doctrine of equal rights embodied in the American Constitution.

The Church's social teachings, then, are to work within and through the established political institutions of the United States—not advanced in a presumptuous spirit of hostility to the written or the unwritten constitution. "The American constitution is not founded on political atheism. Something of Christian tradition lives among us and is kept alive by the common law and the judicial department of the government." So Orestes Brownson wrote in his *Quarterly Review,* in the spring of 1873.

But would the swelling apparatus of the federal government—even the federal judiciary—remain friendly enough to the Church? Toward his end, Brownson had grave misgivings as to that. "The church wants freedom in relation to the state—nothing more," he had written in *The American Republic;* "for all her power comes immediately from God, without any intervention or mediation of the state." Just so; yet would that freedom endure?

Among the consequences of the Civil War and Reconstruction had been the enfeebling of the old Constitution, the subjugation of the agricultural economy, the corruptions of the Gilded Age, and the triumph of a secular order with Protestant roots but divested of faith in a transcendent order. Between 1860 and 1870 a revolution had been worked: and Brownson found that revolution to be an American variant of Jacobinism. This thoroughly secularized American state would not remain neutral on moral questions: as the general government should consolidate its power over the years, it would interfere increasingly with the concerns of the Church. Brownson's prediction is attaining fulfillment near the end of the twentieth century.

Might the Church withstand such pressures? Indeed, might the Church cohere long in the licentious American democracy with its ungoverned appetites and its revolt

Portrait of Brownson.

If, then, one must be a philosopher in order rightly to read the past and explain the course of history, one must also study the past, study history, and concentrate in himself, so to speak, his whole race in order to be a great philosopher. Our experiments must extend over nations and centuries.

—Orestes Brownson

It has recently been said that only since the 1930's has the notion of Christian philosophy become "an object of explicit discussion" [L. B. Gieger, "Christian Philosophy," *New Catholic Encyclopedia,* 1967]. No doubt the writer had in mind the lively controversy over the validity of the concept of Christian philosophy that came to a head in the historic conference on the subject sponsored by the *Société française de philosophie* in Paris in 1931. Contemporary discussions of the meaning and appropriateness of the notion often go back to the Parisian debate and the abundant literature *pro* and *con* that grew out of it. We should not think, however, that before the dispute of the 1930's there were no distinctly expressed differences of opinion about the meaning and validity of the term 'Christian philosophy'. The recently published *Christliche Philosophie im katholischen Denken des 19. und 20. Jahrhunderts* makes it abundantly clear that already in the nineteenth century philosophers and theologians throughout Europe were discussing these topics and adopting opposing views about them. It is remarkable that one of the most outspoken and articulate protagonists in the discussion was an American, Orestes Brownson. But then, Brownson by any account was a remarkable—if somewhat neglected—man. The present essay concerns his views on Christian philosophy and between philosophy and theology, which he formulated in opposition to the European Rationalists and Traditionalists.

Brownson's Career

Brownson stands out as one of the most knowledgeable and accomplished philosophers in America in the mid-nineteenth century. The recent revival of interest in his writings accords him an important role in the development of social, economic, political, philosophical, and theological ideas in his century. Born in 1803 in Stockbridge, Vermont, he had little formal education, but as a boy he read insatiably, including the then popular *Essay on Human Understanding* of John Locke. He knew the Bible, in the King James Version, almost by heart. Later, he learned Latin and Greek in order to read the Church Fathers and medieval scholastics, and German, French, Italian, and Spanish to keep abreast of European literature.

against authority? "There is a subtle influence at work which undermines the authority alike of the parent and of the magistrate, with Catholics as with non-Catholics," Brownson wrote to his son in 1870. "Catholics as well as others imbibe the spirit of the country, imbibe from infancy the spirit of independence, freedom from all restraint, unbounded license. So far are Catholics from converting the country, they cannot hold their own."

This question is more pressing still in the year 1990. And the endeavor to humanize the economy is as necessary nowadays as it was in Brownson's time. The American constitution of the government survives, with some alterations—or at least the Articles and the Amendments survive on paper, however courts may interpret them. Yet how much of the providential constitution, the unwritten constitution, still operates within American society? Is the providential constitution a ghost merely? If so, can the written Constitution be long for this world?

Armand Maurer (essay date 1992)

SOURCE: "Orestes Brownson and Christian Philosophy," in *The Monist,* Vol. 75, No. 3, July, 1992, pp. 341-53.

[In the following essay, Maurer, a Roman Catholic priest and educator, examines Brownson's views on Christian philosophy as evidenced by the author's writings.]

Raised in Congregationalism, his mind turned early to religion and he dedicated his life to its service. After joining successively various Protestant sects and passing through stages of agnosticism and socialism, he ended his religious pilgrimage in 1844 by conversion to the Catholic Church. By that time he was immersed in the political, philosophical, and theological disputes of the day, and he was leaving his mark on them by his depth of faith, rigor of logic, and philosophical acumen.

He avidly followed the contemporary intellectual movements in Europe and he lectured and wrote extensively—often critically—about them. He was searching for principles that might establish truth in matters of religion and social order, and, aware of the limited resources of the America of his day, he turned his gaze to Europe. He achieved an acquaintance with European philosophical ideas superior to that of any other American of the time, and he was an important channel by which they came to be known in the United States. He corresponded with some of the intellectual leaders in Europe and England and he was generally recognized by them for his philosophical ability. Victor Cousin (1792-1867), whose eclecticism initiated Brownson into the pathways of philosophy, knew his works well and thought so highly of them that he invited Brownson to lecture in Paris, an invitation Brownson could not accept. Newman (1801-1890) asked him to join the staff of his projected University of Ireland, though Irish patriots opposed the appointment. The French theologian Alphonse Gratry (1805-1872) wrote effusively and with blatant exaggeration of him: "I firmly believe that America is not proud enough of her Brownson. He is the keenest critic of the nineteenth century, an indomitable logician, a disinterested lover of the truth, more than a philosopher, a sage, as sharp as Aristotle, as lofty as Plato, the Newman of America." In 1903 a German periodical called him the greatest son the United States has given to the Catholic Church.

In his early career Brownson was attracted to the transcendentalist movement founded by Emerson in 1836. However, he soon became critical of the movement because of its lack of logical rigor and its identification of the individual soul with the universal soul or God. In later years, until his death in 1876, his quest for the true transcendental philosophy was shaped (but not without reservations) by the "ontologism" of Vincenzo Gioberti (1801-1852).

Reason and Faith; Philosophy and Theology

After his conversion to Catholicism Brownson was preoccupied with defining the relations between reason and faith and between philosophy and theology. While under the influence of Cousin he acquired a deep respect for human reason, but as a Christian he could not agree with the French philosopher's rationalism, which left no room for faith in a supernatural revelation or theology as a science based upon it. For Cousin, there is no truth transcending the natural order, no recognition of a supernatural order of divine revelation.

After his disenchantment with Cousin's eclectic philosophy and his embracing Catholicism, Brownson opposed all attempts to base philosophy on reason alone. He wrote in 1844: "We maintain, with Saint Augustine and John [Scotus] Erigena, the identity of religion and philosophy." However, as he matured in his Catholic faith he recognized the distinction between two orders of truths, one natural, the other supernatural. Ideally there should be no

disagreement between the two orders of truth, for the same God is the author of revelation and the human mind, but Brownson was realistic enough to realize that we do not have a philosophy that is thoroughly in accord with Christian faith. His aim was to bring reality a little closer to the ideal.

Another concern of Brownson was the freedom of the scientist and philosopher to pursue the truth. The only exception he made for the Catholic is that he must respect the dogmas of his faith. Aside from this, he is free to follow his own judgment. If someone disagrees with him, he has no right to quote the authority of any philosopher, ancient or modern, Catholic or non-catholic, "for in philosophy, reason, which is the same in all men, and in each man, is the only authority recognizable." The Catholic, Brownson continues, is apt to forget this and to introduce into philosophy the principle of authority that is valid in faith and theology. He astutely remarks, "The human mind, left to itself, seeks always to follow one and the same rule in all things." Catholics have the habit of deciding matters of faith by authority and they tend to carry this habit over into philosophy. The Protestant, on the contrary, with his principle of private interpretation, tends to appeal to natural reason as the authority in matters of faith. He inclines to rationalism, as the Catholic leans to supernaturalism, denying to reason its valid functions even in its own order.

In an essay on the freedom of science Brownson insists that science, and especially philosophy, must be free to follow their own laws, which are essential to their very existence. The Catholic must respect the freedom of science as its natural right. The freedom of scientific research is in the interest not only of science but also of the Church, for she wishes to show the agreement of science with faith, and this ideal cannot be reached by making science submissive to faith but only by putting faith to the test of a free and independent science.

Brownson is critical of contemporary education in philosophy in Catholic schools just because it does not respect the freedom of philosophy. "True," he writes, "there is something taught in our colleges and universities under the name of philosophy, but it is for the most part, as an eminent American prelate remarked to us one day in conversation, simply `some fragments of Catholic theology badly proved' . . . The principal cause of the present deplorable state of philosophy, is in the lack of free, independent thinkers,—in the fact that we philosophize not for the sake of truth, but for the sake of some philosophical theory, ancient or modern, and always more or less under the weight of authority." Catholic teachers generally profess to follow St. Thomas, Brownson remarks, adding with irony that some of them may have really read him, at least in part. He urges the profound study of St. Thomas, but cautions that we should not accept his philosophy on authority or be forbidden to dissent from his opinions. In sum, he writes:

> What we want . . . is not to substitute for the prevailing
> systems of philosophy a new system of our own, or

any new system at all. What we demand is, complete emancipation from all man-made systems, and room for the free and independent exercise of reason according to its own nature and laws. We want no official philosophy, no school system taught by authority, like theology, which our sons must get by rote, and which is ever after to cramp or encumber their intellect. We demand free intellectual development and culture.

Opposition to Traditionalism

Brownson's insistence on the rights of reason and the exclusion of external authority in philosophy was in conscious opposition to traditionalism, a movement that arose in France after the Revolution of 1789 to restore the Christian tradition and counteract the rationalism of the Enlightenment. Among the traditionalists were Louis de Bonald (1754-1840), Joseph de Maistre (1753-1821), Félicité de Lamennais (1782-1854), Louis Bautain (1796-1867), Augustin Bonnetty (1798-1879), and Gioacchino Ventura de Raulica (1792-1861). Though there were important differences in their philosophies, they all sought to base philosophy and metaphysical certitude on a primitive communication of truth from God to the human race. In short, they tended to rely on authority rather than on reason in philosophy.

Brownson did not deny the existence of a primitive revelation or the importance of tradition, but he rejected the traditionalists' notion of philosophy. He writes:

> Traditional philosophy is a misnomer. What rests on any other authority than reason is not philosophy. It may be faith, it may be history, it may be theology, and very true; but it is not philosophy in our modern use of the term, for philosophy is a purely rational science and only what rests on natural reason as its principle, or is cognizable by natural reason, can be included in it.

Brownson's main criticism of traditionalism was directed against the views expressed in the *Annales de Philosophie Chrétienne,* edited by Augustin Bonnetty. Bonnetty does not rate among the bright lights of the movement; he was more a publicist than a philosopher. But his *Annales* were among the chief organs for the dissemination of traditionalist ideas. Brownson sums up the position of the journal in these words: "This traditionalism, if it means any thing, denies philosophy to hold from reason as its principle, and seeks to place it on the same line with supernatural theology, as a discipline to be received on authority."

With his fellow traditionalists Bonnetty taught that as a consequence of the Fall of Adam and Eve human reason was so weakened that, left to itself, it cannot discover the existence of God or the moral laws. He argued on historical grounds that philosophers have fallen into grave errors in these matters and they have failed to reach a consensus about them. Whatever there is of value in their individual philosophies is a remnant of the primitive revelation made by God to Adam and transmitted to his descendants, who retained it with more or less purity. The pagan philosophers drew upon this traditional wisdom. The Jews preserved it more perfectly and God supplemented it with further revelations. The perfect and infallible embodiment of the traditional wisdom is the Catholic Church.

Bonnetty stresses the role of society in the handing down of this wisdom. We owe to society the beginnings of all our knowledge, which we accept on authority. Our parents taught us language, without which we cannot reason, and they gave us our first ideas. Indeed, we are formed by the traditions of the society in which we live. Later we may correct, improve, or add to these traditions, but whatever knowledge we may acquire presupposes traditional teaching, and ultimately the primitive revelation made by God to Adam.

In 1855 the Congregation of the Index issued a decree against traditionalism, requiring Bonnetty and his associates to subscribe to four propositions, two of which are of immediate concern to us: That reason can prove with certainty the existence of God (following St. Paul, Romans 1:20), and that the use of reason precedes faith and leads us to it through revelation and grace. Bonnetty accepted the propositions, while interpreting them in his own way. Thus, he claimed that reason can prove God's existence but only after his existence has been revealed and accepted from tradition. Human reason by itself cannot discover the existence of God, it can only confirm what it has already been taught.

Brownson saw clearly that this fails to do justice to the Roman decree. Tradition and authority are skill in command and reason follows in their wake. Reason is not given its full stature; when it proves any truth, its primary evidence or data is taken from tradition rather than from reason itself. What is here at stake is the competency of reason in its own order. Brownson at first was inclined to "an uncertain Traditionalism," but fuller study of the teachings of the Church and her theologians, such as Thomas Aquinas, convinced him that the Fall of the human race did not bring about the destruction of anything essential to human nature as such. Humanity was wounded, but the wound was the loss of supernatural gifts, which do not belong to pure human nature. Reason, after the Fall, remains substantially unchanged and retains its sufficiency in the natural order for all purely human purposes.

Attitude toward Christian Philosophy

If this is so, human reason has a valid function within its own order. It can philosophize from natural principles and data without having to accept its truths from faith or authority. To call philosophy Christian, then, as Bonnetty and other traditionalists do, is a confusion of the two orders of nature and supernature. Brownson writes caustically:

> Much, furthermore, is said about *Christian* philosophy, as was a few years ago about Christian architecture,

and is still about Christian art. M. Bonnetty calls his periodical the Annals of *Christian* Philosophy. All this has a pious and orthodox sound, as would have *Christian* coats and pantaloons, *Christian* hats and shoes. There is a Christian *use* of philosophy, but, correctly speaking, there is and can be no *Christian* philosophy. The Christian order, we take it, is the supernatural order, and in all that is peculiar to it included in the new creation, whose principle is grace; but philosophy belongs to the natural order, and is restricted to natural reason, essential to and inseparable from human nature itself, whether in Christians or non-Christians, and incapable without the aid of divine revelation, of attaining even to a conception of the supernatural. Christian philosophy, if it could mean any thing, would mean Christian theology, or the sacred science, of which St. Thomas speaks, a science constructed not by reason from its own *data,* but by the use of reason from *data* furnished by faith or revelation.

It will be noted that, while Brownson insists on the rationality of philosophy, he also recognizes a Christian use of philosophy in theology. All the great theologians, he tells us, used pagan philosophical notions in order to elucidate the mysteries of faith, and it is a striking fact that in doing so they philosophized better than when they philosophized for purely philosophical purposes. "There is in all the great theologians," he astutely observes, "a double philosophy, the philosophy they use as theologians, and the philosophy they set forth as philosophers," the former being superior to the latter. Brownson may have had in mind the excellence of the philosophy in St. Thomas's theological works in comparison with that in his commentaries on Aristotle. However that may be, he did not think the theologians as philosophers offered any original solutions to philosophical problems, but as theologians they were infinitely in advance of the pagan philosophers.

Thus theology can be a help to philosophy, according to Brownson, not in furnishing its data, but in placing natural reason in a position to perceive and to make better use of her own data. "In this sense," he writes, "tradition, both as to the natural and as to the supernatural, renders an important service in the development of reason, and in conducting us to philosophic truth." He explains how this is possible: "There may be truths of philosophy, that is, of the natural order, distinct from the truths of the supernatural order, or the new creation, which we could never by our natural intellect find out, but which when revealed to us we may discover to be evident to natural reason." An example he offers is the notion of creation. When this dogma is revealed and given to us in language, we find it to be really expressed in every one of our direct intuitions, and therefore it is also a truth of philosophy.

Thus, when faith enters the mind it "throws light on reason, or so employs reason that we better understand its use, and the problems really within its reach. The discussions occasioned by the great mysteries of faith, the Trinity, the Incarnation, the Real Presence, foreknowledge and predestination, free will and necessity in connection with

grace, the Beatific Vision, etc., have poured floods of light on both ontological and psychological science, and given to natural reason some of its finest developments." In this connection Brownson refers to the numerous passages in Thomas Aquinas where his theology throws light on his philosophy.

Limits of Reason and Philosophy

Does this not contradict Brownson's assertion that human reason is sufficient in the natural order to achieve its own ends? He has stressed, against the traditionalists, that philosophy belongs to the natural order; supernatural revelation is above philosophy and is no part or parcel of it. But he has rejected the rationalists' claim that reason is *all-sufficient* and that its powers are boundless. If the philosopher thinks deeply enough, Brownson says, he meets the inexplicable mysteries of our knowing and our existing, that no human power can deny or explain. So philosophy is not completely adequate and needs to be supplemented by revelation. Nature must be redeemed from the Fall and perfected by grace: "Let philosophy go as far as it can, but let the philosopher never for a moment imagine that human reason will ever be able to explain itself." Brownson points to ethics as a clear case in which reason is inadequate. Ethics should teach us the moral law and guide us to our destiny. But a purely natural ethics falls short of conveying to us the necessary rules of conduct revealed by God. Neither can it show us our actual destiny, which is the supernatural vision and love of God.

Our philosopher is steering a careful course between traditionalism and rationalism. While founding philosophy on reason and not on faith and authority, he leaves reason open to the influence of the higher light of revelation. In his view, Descartes made the fatal mistake of divorcing philosophy from faith and turning it into an independent science. Brownson sees this as something entirely modern. In antiquity neither Plato nor Aristotle separated themselves from their religious traditions. The fathers of the Church and the medieval scholastics never divorced reason from revelation. Thomas Aquinas, for example, did not think a complete philosophy in the natural order is possible without the light of revelation. Brownson concludes: "Revelation is not the basis of philosophy, but no philosophy of any value can be constructed without it." He avows that he would no more separate his own philosophizing from his religion than he would his politics or his private and social duties.

Brownson and Aeterni Patris

Brownson died in 1876, three years before the appearance of Leo XIII's encyclical *Aeterni Patris.* It would have captivated Brownson had he lived to read it. The first thing he would have done was to write an essay on it. He shared the encyclical's main concern to restore sound philosophy in Catholic schools. Like the Pope he urged a return to the traditional way of philosophizing in the Church, the uniting to the study of philosophy obedience to the Christian faith. The Pope called this Christian philosophy, a term which we have seen Brownson avoid in 1860 when engaged in controversy with the traditionalists, because at this time he identified the expression with the meaning they gave to it. Later, however, when he had distanced himself from the traditionalist dispute, he did not hesitate to use the term in a scholastic and thomistic sense. In an essay of 1869 he speaks approvingly of the scholastics, especially St. Thomas, transforming Aristotelian philosophy into a Christian philosophy. In this essay Aquinas has become for Brownson the greatest medieval doctor, "the Angel of the Schools." What did he mean by Christian philosophy at this time? We cannot say for sure, but presumably it was the way of philosophizing he had described at length, in which the Christian faith throws light on human reason in dealing with its most profound problems, and reason in turn aids in the understanding of faith. It should be noted that neither the Pope nor Brownson proposed as Christian philosophy a specific system of philosophy, but rather a way that Christians could use freely in their pursuit of the truth and a right use of reason in dealing with theological questions.

The encyclical calls the uniting to the study of philosophy obedience to the Christian faith the *best* way of philosophizing. Brownson goes further and contends that it is the *only* way to reach a sound philosophy. As we have seen, he did not think a worthwhile philosophy could be constructed without the Christian faith. Thus he writes:

> We are far from building science on faith or founding philosophy on revelation, in the sense of the traditionalists; yet we dare affirm that no man who has not studied profoundly the Gospel of St. John, the Epistles of St. Paul, the great Greek and Latin fathers, and the mediaeval doctors of the Church, is in a condition to write any thing deserving of serious consideration on philosophy.

As Joseph Owens says, the encyclical shows no tendency to absorb philosophy into theology. Brownson, on the contrary, identifies philosophy itself with the rational element of supernatural theology:

> We regard, as we often say, philosophy simply as the rational element of supernatural theology, never capable by itself alone of being moulded into a complete system even of natural truth, and never worthy of confidence when it aspires to disengage itself from revelation, and to stand alone as a separate and independent science. All we aim at is, to make a right use of reason in discussing those questions pertaining to reason which come in our way when defending Catholic faith and morals.

Brownson here identifies philosophy itself with philosophy at the service of theology. He does not recognize the possibility of a philosophy outside of theology, developed under the influence of Christianity, and yet not used as an instrument of theology. His insistence on the freedom of the philosopher to exercise reason according to its own nature and laws might have led him to envisage a Christian philosophy of this sort.

Brownson probably would not have been pleased with Leo XIII's giving special attention to Thomism. Though Brownson shows great respect for Thomas and his writings (of which he had neither an extensive nor profound knowledge), he did not think we should speak of a Thomistic philosophy but of a Thomistic theology. Thomas, he claims, never pretended to be a philosopher or to develop a philosophy of his own. The philosophy in his theological works is little more than Aristotelianism put to theological use. At times Brownson saw more in Thomas's philosophy than this, even elements of his own ontology. But he usually criticizes Thomas's philosophy for starting from the senses and external world and using premises that are only abstract conceptions. Brownson himself, following Gioberti, insisted that philosophy must begin with an intellectual intuition of being, a reality that on reflection can be shown to be God himself. He would likely have decried with his usual vehemence the wave of Thomism that swept through the Church in the wake of Leo XIII's encyclical, especially when it was erected as a philosophical system outside of theology and favored with a quasi-official status.

Brownson was far from the minds of the European participants in the debate over Christian philosophy in the 1930's. Had they known his works, however, they would have realized that, while he was not always happy about the term 'Christian philosophy', he in fact described and defended the same reality championed by Christian philosophers such as Jacques Maritain and Etienne Gilson. Like Gilson, he argued on historical grounds for the existence of a real and beneficial influence of Christianity on philosophy. In one of his earliest and clearest descriptions of Christian philosophy Gilson calls it "every philosophy which, although keeping the two orders formally distinct, nevertheless considers the Christian revelation as an indispensable auxiliary to reason." I do not think Brownson would have objected to this notion. As we have seen, he regarded reason and revelation as belonging to two distinct orders. As a rational pursuit, he defined philosophy solely in terms of natural reason; faith or revelation do not enter into its abstract concept. Philosophy is based on its own data and not even partially on those of faith. But, anticipating Leo XIII and later Christian philosophers, Brownson believed that a Christian can engage in a way of philosophizing and use of reason in theology that bring to human reason a new and higher light, enlarging and perfecting its rationality. It is noteworthy that in the mid-nineteenth century an American philosopher should have achieved this insight and added an important page to the history of the notion of Christian philosophy.

FURTHER READING

Biography

Brownson, Henry F. *Orestes A. Brownson's Life.* 3 vols. Detroit: H. F. Brownson, 1898-1900.

Exhaustive biography of Brownson compiled by his son,

Henry.

Lapati, Americo D. "Orestes A. Brownson: American Political Thinker (1803-1876)." In *Catholic Makers of America: Biographical Sketches of Catholic Statesmen and Political Thinkers in America's First Century, 1776-1876,* edited by Stephen M. Krason, pp. 163-86. Front Royal, Va.: Christendom Press, 1993.

> Detailed biographical essay discussing Brownson's political and religious views.

Maynard, Theodore. *Orestes Brownson: Yankee, Radical, Catholic.* New York: Macmillan, 1943, 456 p.

> Biography of Brownson which reevaluates his significance as an American writer.

Whalen, Doran [pseudonym of Sister Mary Rose Gertrude]. *Granite for God's House: The Life of Orestes Augustus Brownson.* New York: Sheed and Ward, 1941, 366 p.

> Biographical account of Brownson focusing on his theology.

Criticism

Butler, Gregory S. *In Search of the American Spirit: The Political Thought of Orestes Brownson.* Carbondale: Southern Illinois University Press, 1992, 278 p.

> In-depth discussion of Brownson's political and religious philosophy and analysis of his *The American Republic.*

Gilhooley, Leonard, ed. *No Divided Allegiance: Essays in Brownson's Thought.* New York: Fordham University Press, 1980, 193 p.

> Essays by eight Brownson scholars, including Russell Kirk, Peter J. Stanlis, C. Carroll Hollis, and Alvan Ryan, on Brownson's theology, political and economic philosophy, and theories on literary criticism.

Kirk, Russell. "Transitional Conservatism." In *The Conservative Mind: From Burke to Eliot.* 7th rev. ed., pp. 245-50. Chicago: Regnery Books, 1986.

> Discussion of Brownson's analysis of "the conservative power of Catholicism."

———. "Contending against American Disorder." In *The Roots of American Order,* pp. 441-78. Malibu, Cal.: Pepperdine University Press, 1978.

> Examination of Brownson's political and religious beliefs, including his thoughts on socialism, justice, and republicanism.

Lapati, Americo D. *Orestes A. Brownson.* New York: Twayne Publishers, 1965, 159 p.

> Discusses Brownson's theories on religion and literature and examines his efforts in the areas of political and social reform in the context of his search for truth.

Marshall, Hugh. *Orestes Brownson and The American Republic: An Historical Perspective.* Washington, D.C.: Catholic University of America Press, 1971, 308 p.

> Examination of Brownson's political thought in the context of his overall intellectual development.

Michel, Virgil G. *The Critical Principles of Orestes A. Brownson.* Washington, D.C.: Catholic University of America Press, 1918, 106 p.

> Critique of Brownson's ontological, aesthetic, and literary principles.

Schlesinger, Arthur M., Jr. *Orestes A. Brownson: A Pilgrim's Progress.* 1939. Reprint. New York: Octagon Books, 1963, 320 p.

> Examination of Brownson's achievements as a non-Catholic and analysis of his socio-economic views.

Lorenzo Da Ponte

1749-1838

Italian librettist, dramatist, poet, and memoirist.

INTRODUCTION

Da Ponte is renowned for having written the librettos for three of Wolfgang Amadeus Mozart's most acclaimed operas, *Le nozze di Figaro* (1786; *The Marriage of Figaro*), *Il dissoluto punito o sia il Don Giovanni* (1787; *Don Giovanni*), and *Così fan Tutte o la scuola delle amanti* (1790). As poet to the Italian Theatre in Vienna, he rose to become a favorite of Austrian emperor Joseph II, but fell from favor at court after Joseph's death, eventually becoming an unsuccessful bookseller in New York. Da Ponte led a life marked alternately by high levels of intrigue, betrayal, libertinism, piety, high accomplishment, and crushing failure. He recorded his life story in the entertaining, coyly self-centered *Memoire de Lorenzo Da Ponte da Ceneda* (1823-27; *Memoirs of Lorenzo Da Ponte*).

Biographical Information

Da Ponte was born Emanuele Conegliano in the Jewish ghetto of Ceneda, known today as Vittorio Veneto. As a young man he was baptized into the Catholic church, changed his name, and studied for the priesthood. Although he took major orders, he led a rakish life, running a brothel for a time; such activities led to his being expelled from a seminary position in 1776 and a fifteen-year banishment from Venetian territory three years later. Removing to Austria, Da Ponte made the acquaintance of poet-librettist Pietro Metastasio, and then, on the strength of a few poems, gained the position of Poet to the Italian Theatre. Becoming an influential favorite of Emperor Joseph II, he embarked on a career as a successful librettist, collaborating with such composers as Antonio Salieri, Vincenzo Righini, and (most importantly) Mozart, whom he met in 1783. Da Ponte was lionized for his successes as a librettists, but he also made several jealous, influential enemies. (One such enemy, on an occasion when Da Ponte was ill, tricked him into imbibing a "curative" which caused all his teeth to fall out—damaging Da Ponte's career as one of Vienna's more active libertines.) Upon the death of Joseph in 1790, he was forced to leave Vienna by the new emperor, himself heavily influenced by Da Ponte's enemies. With his wife and children, Da Ponte settled in England for some thirteen years, working for a time at Drury Lane Theatre as a librettist. But he incurred such heavy debts that he was forced by circumstances to flee to the United States, taking ship literally just a step ahead of the debt collector. He arrived in America in 1805, working successively as a grocer, medicine salesman,

bookseller, and—near the end of his life—the first professor of Italian literature at Columbia College (now University), to some extent through the influence of a close friend, author Clement C. Moore, a Columbia trustee. In this last position, he worked prodigiously to elevate the appreciation of Italian culture and literature in the United States. When he died in 1838, his *Memoirs* of a full life had been in print for several years, though available only in Italian.

Major Works

All of Da Ponte's libretti are forgotten today except those he wrote for Mozart: *The Marriage of Figaro, Don Giovanni,* and *Così fan Tutte.* This fact has been called a testimony to Mozart's ability to inspire the best from his librettist, and all three operas are performed to this day. *Memoirs of Lorenzo Da Ponte* is valued for its gossipy, insider's view of life at court in eighteenth-century Vienna, its confessions of sexual libertinism reminiscent of the author's friend, Giacomo Casanova di Seingalt, its recurrent theme of genius (the author's own) brought low by jealous rivals, and its view of nineteenth-century America through Italian eyes.

Critical Reception

Little in-depth criticism of Da Ponte's work in any genre exists. *The Marriage of Figaro* is based upon a work by Pierre-Augustin Caron de Beaumarchais and deemed a libretto which skillfully conveys the decline of the old European social order. Indeed, one critic, Herbert Weinstock, has written that *The Marriage of Figaro* by itself justifies the very existence of opera. *Don Giovanni*, written while Da Ponte was at work on two other libretti as well, is considered the weakest of the three, largely because of uneven characterization. *Così fan Tutte*, written at the emperor's request, is considered a superb example of comic opera, laden with sardonic wit. Criticism of *Memoirs of Lorenzo Da Ponte* tends to basically recount what the author has written and comment upon his believability. While *Memoirs* is valued for its vigor and insights, it is generally considered less valuable as such than the memoirs of Casanova, Giambattista Vico, and Carlo Gozzi.

PRINCIPAL WORKS

Il ricco d' un giorno (libretto) 1784
Il burbero di buon cuore (libretto) 1786
Le nozze di Figaro (libretto) 1786
Una cosa rara o sia bellezza ed onestà (libretto) 1786
L'arbore de Diana (libretto) 1787
Il dissoluto punito o sia il Don Giovanni (libretto) 1787
Cosi fan tutte o la scuola delle amanti (libretto) 1790
Storia compendiosa della vita de Loranzo Da Ponte (memoirs) 1807
Memoire de Lorenzo Da Ponte da Ceneda [*Memoirs of Lorenzo Da Ponte*]. 4 vols. (memoirs) 1823-27

CRITICISM

Da Ponte comments on his own accomplishment:

[In its initial performances] ***Don Giovanni*** did not please! And what did the Emperor say? He said:

"That opera is divine; I should even venture that it is more beautiful than ***Figaro***. But such music is not meat for the teeth of my Viennese!"

I reported the remark to Mozart, who replied quietly:

"Give them time to chew on it!"

He was not mistaken. On his advice I strove to procure frequent repetitions of the opera: at each performance the applause increased, and little by little even Vienna of the dull teeth came to enjoy its savor and appreciate its beauties, and placed ***Don Giovanni*** among the most beautiful operas that have ever been produced on any stage. . . .

Lorenzo Da Ponte, in his *Memoirs of Lorenzo Da Ponte*, edited by Arthur Livingston, translated by Elisabeth Abbott, J. B. Lippincott Company, 1929.

Emilio Goggio (essay date 1919)

SOURCE: "The Dawn of Italian Culture in America," in *The Romanic Review,* Vol. X, No. 3, July-September 1919, pp. 250-62.

[*In the excerpt below, Goggio summarizes Da Ponte's significance in introducing American college students to Italian language and literature.*]

Lorenzo da Ponte, a poet of renown and the well-known librettist of **Don Giovanni** and **Le Nozze di Figaro,** was also an exile, a satirical sonnet against Count Pisani having been the cause of his banishment from his beloved Venice. He first sought refuge in Austria and later migrated to the United States. In New York, where he finally settled, he opened a little book store and earned his livelihood by the sale of Italian books and wares. Moreover, being especially fond of literature, he thought of devoting part of his time to teaching, and began to offer private lessons in the language of his native country. This new enterprise turned out far better than he expected, for many young men and women of distinguished families profited by the occasion and applied for instruction. The gratifying success which he attained as a teacher is well brought out in the many letters in Italian which he received from his pupils and which he himself published with his **Memoirs**. When his students had been well drilled in the rudiments of the language, he passed to the literature and introduced them to the best Italian poets and prose writers, expounding to them the works of Dante, Petrarch, Boccaccio and of all the other great lights, including Alfieri and Metastasio. . . .

From 1826 to 1837 Da Ponte held a professorship at Columbia College, which, however, was in reality a private tutorship, carrying no salary from the college itself. Through his suggestion and cooperation, many Italian books of literature were given a place on the shelves of the college library and were made accessible to the student body of that institution. In 1833 Italian Grand Opera was auspiciously initiated in New York under his direction, and a new source of interest was thus created by him in the language of Italy.

Joseph Louis Russo (essay date 1922)

SOURCE: "How Da Ponte Became a Librettist" and "Glory and Downfall," in *Lorenzo Da Ponte: Poet and Adventurer,* Columbia University Press, 1922, pp. 41-58, 59-82.

[*Russo wrote the first full-length English-language study of Da Ponte in the twentieth century. In the following excerpt from that work, he offers a biographical and critical survey of his subject's rise and fall as a librettist. As the excerpt begins, Da Ponte has been banished from Venice and has entered Austrian territory, seeking refuge and his fortune.*]

Solely from his lyre the Poet hoped now to derive the

help he so badly needed. The Peace of Teschen. . . . had been negotiated and signed in the name of Maria Theresa by Count Johann Philipp von Cobenzl (1741-1810), whose father, the old Count Guido, was one of the leading noblemen of Gorizia. That the latter, evidently proud of his son's success, might welcome a poetical glorification of it, was at once perceived by Da Ponte, who accordingly wrote an ode eulogizing the aged Empress and her brilliant diplomat,—ode which he entitled *La gara degli uccelli*, (*The Birds' Rivalry*), an allusion to the Austrian and Prussian eagles.

Though on more than one occasion Lorenzo showed a paternal predilection for this offspring of his Muse, it is certainly not one of the best of his poems. Yet it sufficed to gain for him the protection of the wealthy patrician, who had it printed at his own expense, and generously rewarded its author. The reputation he thus acquired in the town procured him new favors. Count Rodolfo Coronini (1731-91) entrusted him with a translation into Italian verse of his *Liber primus fastorum Goritiensium*, a work of pretended historical erudition,—the *Fasti Goriziani* alluded to in the *Memorie*. Other families, all equally prominent, such as those of Strassoldo, Lantieri, Attems, Tuns and Torriani, opened their doors to him, and the young poet soon became a favorite in that society.

It happened, however, that his uncommon good luck aroused envy in another poet, Giuseppe de Colletti (1744-1815), whom Lorenzo describes in his autobiography with the bitterest animosity and against whom he wrote at that time a violent satire.

Meanwhile, at the request of a noble lady, he translated, probably through the French, a German tragedy for the use of a good Italian theatrical company which was giving performances in Gorizia. The play, he freely admits, proved a failure, but his reputation was somewhat restored when, shortly after, another production of his was presented,—this time the translation of a French tragedy. Admitted to an "Arcadic colony" which had just then been founded in Gorizia under the name of *Colonia Sonziaca* (a designation derived from that of the river Isonzo on which that city is situated), he had himself called *Lesbonico Pegasio*. Among the poems composed by him for that society, *Il capriccio* and *La gratitudine o sia la difesa delle donne* deserve to be remembered.

Yet, despite his remarkable success, it appears that he was far from happy, and in his heart he longed for a return to the City of the Lagoons. If he entertained any hope that his old protector, Giorgio Pisani, might grasp the reins of the Venetian government and recall him, that hope was rudely shattered by the news brought to him by Caterino Mazzolà, whom he had known in the house of Memmo, and who passed through Gorizia on his way to Dresden, where at the invitation of that Elector he was about to assume the position of Poet for the Opera House. . . .

Da Ponte offered to collaborate with Mazzolà in the composition of the plays which the latter was preparing for that Opera House, a help which it seems was gladly accepted. It was for our Poet, as he soon had occasion to discover, a sort of training for his future career.

But, apart from this work, his residence in Dresden and the close association with a pious man like Father Huber inspired him to compose a number of "psalms" which rank among his best poems. They are not, as some of his biographers have erroneously surmised, translations of the Psalms of David, but original compositions in varying meters, each having as a theme a passage from the Bible, such as *Miserere mei, Deus, quoniam infirmus sum,* or *Iustus es, Domine, et rectum iudicium tuum,* from which he developed the first two poems. For their austere simplicity coupled with unusual elegance of style, they were praised by many men of letters and, as Da Ponte with pardonable pride informs us, by no less an authority than Ugo Foscolo. Both Father Huber, to whom the verses were dedicated, and the Elector, who was presented with them by the learned clergyman, generously rewarded our Poet. . . .

Towards the end of [1782] having learned that the Emperor intended to establish an Italian theatre in Vienna, he boldly approached Salieri, asking that he be recommended for a position similar to that held by Mazzolà in Dresden. Salieri took the matter to heart, spoke to Count Olindo Orsini di Rosemberg (1725-96), High Chamberlain and intimate friend of Joseph II, and the request was granted.

In his account of his first audience with the Emperor, Da Ponte relates that he was asked whether he had ever written a drama. To his frank denial Joseph answered good-naturedly: "Never mind, we shall have a virgin Muse!"

The title conferred on him was that of "Poet to the Italian Theatre," and he received a yearly salary of 1200 florins, with the obligation of writing dramas, for which, according to usage, he was in addition to receive royalties.

To the poor man, whose life since his flight from Venice had been a daily struggle for existence, this sudden change bringing to him at the same time comforts and honors, must have seemed like a golden dream. He obtained at once access to the best homes of the Austrian capital and became acquainted with men elevated in rank or prominent in the fields of art, by whom he was treated with esteem and benevolence. It was at this early stage of his theatrical career that he met, in the house of Baron Wetzlar, the already famous Mozart.

It is curious to read in the *Memorie* of the difficulties which he encountered in writing his first melodrama, *Il ricco d' un giorno*. To quote his words, it seemed to him as though he had undertaken "to wield the club of Hercules with a child's hand." For many months he struggled with his subject, and only towards the end of 1783 was he able to submit the completed libretto to Salieri, who had to compose the music. . . .

The music of *Il ricco d' un giorno* was composed by Salieri during the early spring of 1784. Unfortunately the opera could not be given at that time, for the composer

Antonio Salieri, rival of Mozart and occasional musical collaborator with Da Ponte.

had to go to Paris for the first performance of his *Le Danaidi,* the score of which he had written in substitution for Gluck. To make matters worse, Casti, whose reputation as a poet was widespread all over Europe, came to Vienna from St. Petersburg in the beginning of May, followed soon after by Paisiello, whose fame in the field of music was at least as great as Salieri's, and the Emperor commanded an opera from them.

When, on August 23d, their *Re Teodoro a Venezia* was given, the great expectations of the sovereign and the public were realized; the opera obtained an extraordinary success, and, while Da Ponte would like us to believe that the applause was only for the music and the singers, it is certain that Casti's share in the triumph was recognized as well.

In the autumn, Salieri having returned, *Il ricco d' un giorno* was finally presented. It proved a complete fiasco. From Da Ponte's stanzas to Pietro Zaguri it appears that the hisses in the theatre were so insistent as to cause the performance to be suspended. Lorenzo, though frankly admitting the faults of his libretto, accuses Salieri of having mutilated it, claims that the music was worse than the words, and finally complains that the great artiste, Storace, being indisposed, her rôle had been entrusted to an incapable singer. There was probably some truth in these as sertions, but when Lorenzo goes so far as to accuse Casti of trying to ruin him in order to foster his own

ambitions, and of combining with all the adventurous poetasters who at that time crowded Vienna, in a conspiracy headed by no less a personage than Count Rosemberg, it seems that his imagination and his peculiar weakness for seeing rivals and enemies everywhere overpowered his better judgment.

Granting that Casti craved the place left vacant by the death of Metastasio, nothing forbade the simultaneous existence of a "Caesarean Poet" and a "Poet to the Italian Theatre," and therefore it is hard to see why the author of *Gli animali parlanti,* whose happy-go-lucky nature is well known, should have organized so devilish a plot. Even more absurd appears the accusation against Rosemberg (to whom, by the way, he owed his position) for the Count was too much of an Austrian courtier, as Nicolini opportunely remarks, to attempt to persecute a favorite of the Emperor, as Da Ponte undoubtedly was.

Nor is serious consideration due to the matter of a short dialogue in his praise and against Casti which Lorenzo inserted in his *Memorie,* and which is supposed to have taken place between Joseph II and Count Rosemberg the day after the performance of the unlucky opera; for the Venetian ambassador, Daniele Andrea Dolfin (1748-98), to whom the Emperor is said to have related it, and from whom it reached the ear of Da Ponte, was at that time representing the Republic of St. Mark at the Court of France and only on May 20th, 1786, came to Vienna to succeed Sebastiano Foscarini.

Be that as it may, Salieri took a solemn oath rather to allow his fingers to be cut off than again to write music for Lorenzo's verses. Nor were the singers more kindly disposed, for they wondered how they could have attempted to sing "those miserable lyrics." Satirical pamphlets were written against our Poet, to which he did not fail to answer with equal violence. The storm, however, was overcome, inasmuch as the Emperor retained him in his favor, and when, towards the beginning of the following year (1785), the two musicians, Stefano Storace and Vincenzo Martini, came to Vienna, he asked Da Ponte to write a libretto for the latter. . . .

Il burbero di buon cuore, an evident adaptation from the well known comedy of Goldoni, *Le Bourru bienfaisant,* set to music by Martini during the fall of that year, was finally produced on the evening of January 4th, 1786. That the opera was received with exceptional favor, is proved by the fact that for many years it continued to be played in Vienna and was also quite popular in Italy. It seems that Joseph II, on meeting the Poet immediately after the first performance, said to him with a smile: *Abbiamo vinto!*

And undoubtedly Lorenzo's prestige was restored. His popularity had grown overnight to such an extent that several of the foremost composers evidenced a desire to avail themselves of his services as a librettist.

One month later,—to be precise, on Februrary 7th,—in the Court Theatre of Schönbrunn, was produced the musical farce *Le parole dopo la musica,* which, according to a rather curious anecdote related by the Prince of Ligne, was written by Casti by order of the Emperor, after the music had already been composed by Salieri.

Michael Kelly (1762-1826), who sang the tenor rôle, gives in his *Reminiscences* an amusing account of the performance and, though by an evident error he attributes the music to Righini (spelled by him Rigini) and the words to Da Ponte, the facts related by him must be true since our Poet corroborates them in his ***Memorie.***

> "There was a character," he says, "of an amorous, eccentric poet, which was allotted to me. At that time, I was esteemed a good mimic, and particularly happy in imitating the walk, countenance and attitudes of those whom I wished to resemble. My friend the poet [Da Ponte] had a remarkably awkward gait, a habit of throwing himself (as he thought) into a graceful attitude by putting his stick behind his back and leaning on it; he had also a very peculiar, rather dandyish way of dressing; for, in sooth, the abbé stood mighty well with himself and had the character of a consummate coxcomb; he had also a strong lisp and broad Venetian dialect.

> "The first night of the performance, he was seated in the boxes more conspicuously than was absolutely necessary, considering he was the author of the piece to be performed. As usual, on the first night of a new opera, the Emperor was present, and a numerous auditory. When I made my *entrée,* as the amorous poet, dressed like the abbé in the boxes, imitating his walk, leaning on my stick, and aping his gestures and his lisp, there was a universal roar of laughter and applause; and after a buzz round the house, the eyes of the whole audience were turned to the place where he was seated. The Emperor enjoyed the joke, laughed heartily; the abbé was not at all affronted, but took my imitation of him in good part, and ever after we were on the best terms."

That speaks well for the good nature of our Poet; but his grudge against Casti was certainly aggravated by what he deemed a deliberate caricature of himself.

For Giuseppe Gazzaniga (1743-1819), judged by him "a composer of some merit, but of antiquated style," he had to prepare soon after a libretto, at the request of Count Rosemberg. The work, undertaken with little enthusiasm, was completed in a few days: it was *Il finto cieco*—an adaptation, as he says, of a French comedy—and was indifferently received.

But for this failure Da Ponte had opportunity soon after to console himself with a new work, the clamorous success of which brought him to the foremost position among living librettists, revealing at the same time the excellence as an operatic composer of that prodigious genius, Wolfgang Amadeus Mozart. . . .

Da Ponte met Mozart for the first time in the early part of 1783, at the home of Baron Wetzlar, a wealthy Jew with whom the great composer was then lodging. That they had already discussed on that occasion the possibility of collaborating on a new opera, appears from the following passage of a letter which Mozart wrote to his father, on May 7th of that year:

> A certain Abbé Da Ponte is our poet here; he has at present a great deal to do in theatrical revision, and has been charged *per obligo* to write a new libretto for Salieri. He will not be able to finish this for two months, after which he has promised to write one for me. But who can tell whether he can or will keep his word? You understand these Italian gentlemen; they are very charming on the surface, but—well, you know what I mean! If he fraternizes with Salieri, I may well wait for the rest of my life for a libretto from him. And yet I should be so glad to show what I can do in an Italian opera.

But Da Ponte, despite this rather pessimistic view, was faithful to his promise and as soon as he could he began to work on the libertto of *Le nozze di Figaro.* Free from any engagement with Salieri after the fiasco of his first production, and eager to gain credit and reputation, our Poet was keen enough to perceive the advantage of allying himself with the young German composer, who, though still a novice in the operatic field, enjoyed already a European renown in the other branches of music.

As he himself states, it was Mozart who suggested that he turn Beaumarchais' *Mariage de Figaro* into an opera. The idea probably originated from the fact that Paisiello's *Barbiere* had recently obtained an extraordinary success in Vienna. Furthermore, there is ground to believe that Mozart, knowing what excitement Beaumarchais' second comedy had created in Paris after having been prohibited for three years, foresaw that the curiosity of the Viennese public would be aroused by a presentation of it in operatic form, and that this would contribute to the success of his work.

The first difficulty which Da Ponte encountered in writing his libretto, was that of treating the subject in such a manner as to preclude the imperial censor from raising any objection to it. In this he showed uncommon ability, for, while eliminating whatever seemed too daring, he faithfully reproduced in his verses the vivacity and delightful humor of the original play.

In his ***Memorie*** he tells us that the score was written by Mozart almost as fast he handed him the words, and that the opera was completed in only six weeks. This explains the gap we find in Mozart's letters just at this period, and a note that Leopold Mozart wrote to his daughter on November 11th, 1785, not only enables us approximately to fix the time in which *Le nozze di Figaro* was composed, but also confirms Da Ponte's statement that the work which they had undertaken was pushed with feverish haste.

> "At last," the note says, "I have received a letter of twelve lines from your brother. He apologizes owing to the fact that he is up to his eyes in work finishing ***Le nozze di Figaro.*** In order to keep his mornings

free, he has put off all his pupils to the afternoons."

When the opera was completed Da Ponte undertook to secure the Emperor's consent for its performance. As was to be expected, the first objection made was to the subject; but this difficulty the crafty Poet easily overcame by pointing out that he had transformed Beaumarchais' violent satire into a harmless opera which could give offense to no one. The next obstacle was the fact that Joseph II, as was known, had a strong prejudice against Mozart and held him in slight esteem as an operatic composer. Here again Da Ponte showed his skill. With great tact and subtle diplomacy he informed the Emperor that the score was already completed and suggested that His Majesty, being himself so competent a musician, could form his own opinion as to the merits of the opera by ordering the composer to appear in his presence and play some excerpts.

Highly flattered, Joseph did as the Poet had advised, and the result was that the opera was ordered to be produced.

At this point in his *Memorie,* Lorenzo informs the reader that his "rivals," headed by Casti, who was powerfully protected by Count Rosemberg, tried by every means to spoil the success of the new opera; and he relates the following anecdote: Rosemberg, having learned that in the concluding scene of the third act the peasants assisting at Figaro's wedding were supposed to perform a little dance, took upon himself to interpret literally a command issued by the Emperor some time before, and in a rather blunt manner ordered the Poet to cut out that scene. Mozart was in despair. He intended to appeal directly to the Emperor and threatened to withdraw the score. Da Ponte had a hard time in calming him, and pretending to acquiesce in silence recurred to a clever stratagem in order to attain his purpose: in one of the principal rehearsals given in the presence of the Emperor, when the opera came to its finale and the forbidden scene had to be performed, the orchestra suddenly ceased playing, the singers became dumb and started gesticulating as in a pantomine.—"What's all this?" exclaimed Joseph, turning to Casti, who was sitting behind him.—"Perhaps the poet can tell you, Your Majesty," suggested Casti with a grin. And Lorenzo, summoned into the presence of the Emperor, without saying a word showed him the libretto from which Rosemberg had torn the dance scene. Count Rosemberg had an audience in his turn, was reproved for what he had done, and the ballet was restored.

Almost every biographer of Mozart and of Da Ponte has accepted this story as an actual occurrence; yet had it really taken place, is it not more than probable that Michael Kelly—who in his *Reminiscences* takes a particular delight in relating all kinds of anecdotes—would have recorded the incident in his book? Considering that he was one of the singers at the first performance of the opera, and that as such he would have taken an active part in the interpolated pantomime or at least have witnessed it, the fact that he makes no mention of it is indeed surprising.

The opera was presented for the first time at the Viennese Court Theatre on May 1st, 1786, with the following cast: Signora Laschi sang the part of the Contessa, Anna Storace that of Susanna, and Frau Gottlieb that of Barbarina, while the baritone Mandini took the rôle of Almaviva, Benucci that of Figaro, Michael Kelly those of Basilio and Don Curzio, and Bussani those of Bartolo and Antonio.

"Never," says Kelly again, "had one beheld such a triumph. The theatre was packed and so many numbers had to be repeated that the time of the performance was nearly doubled."

Yet, despite this immense enthusiasm, the popularity of **Le nozze di Figaro** was not of long duration, and, after nine performances during that season, the opera disappeared from the Vienna stage and was not mounted again until three years later, when, that is, the success of **Don Giovanni** had again brought Mozart into prominence. . .

With a care-free mind, Lorenzo redoubled his activity. He wrote at this time, for the composer Storace, the libretto of **Gli equivoci,** which he derived from Shakespeare's *Comedy of Errors* and in which, as Kelly remarks, "he retained all the main incidents and characters" of the original play.

But he attained a still greater success with the production, during the autumn of that same year, of **Una cosa rara,** set to music by Martini and undoubtedly the Spanish composer's masterpiece. The source from which Da Ponte took the plot of this opera is, as he states in his **Memorie,** the play *La luna de la Sierra,* which he erroneously attributes to Calderon, while it is by Luis Velez de Guevara, as pointed out by Arturo Farinelli in his exhaustive study on **Don Giovanni.**

Despite some intrigues on the part of the singers, related by our Poet with the usual amount of details which he employs whenever he dwells upon the obstacles he encountered, the new opera obtained a success that overshadowed that of **Le nozze.** Both Da Ponte and the composer became the favorites of Viennese society, while the ladies even adopted the vogue of dressing *à la Cosa Rara.*

Besieged now by several composers, Lorenzo hastily wrote for Righini **Il filosofo punito,** which was produced towards the end of 1786. It was received with marked indifference and, as Lorenzo facetiously remarks, it might better have been entitled "Both the maestro and the poet punished."

Another libretto which he prepared, shortly after, for the Sicilian composer Francesco Piticchio, that of **Bertoldo,** was even less fortunate. The opera, performed for the first time on June 22d of the following year, was a complete failure, and our Poet relates that Joseph II, on meeting him a few days later, gave him the advice not to write any more for composers who were not of the first rank.

The suggestion did not pass unheeded, and when Da Ponte

soon after set again to work, he started to write simultaneously a libretto for Mozart, another for Martini, and a third one for Salieri, who, after our Poet's recent triumphs, had reconsidered his former vow and had humbly begged that their past differences might be forgotten.

To the Emperor, who expressed his doubts as to the possibility of carrying out successfully such an arduous task, Lorenzo replied: "I shall try. I will work for Mozart at night and I will picture to myself that I am studying Dante's *Inferno;* I will devote my mornings to Martini and I will fancy that I am reading Petrarch; finally the evenings shall be given to Salieri and I will imagine that I am turning over the leaves of my Tasso."

This time it was he who selected the subject of the new libretto for Mozart and his choice fell on the legend of Don Juan; for Martini he began to write *L' arbore di Diana;* and for Salieri, *Axur, re d' Ormus.*

It is amusing to read how the Poet began his work:

> A bottle of Tokay on my right, the inkstand before me, and a box of Spanish snuff on my left, I sat at my table for twelve consecutive hours. My landlady's daughter, a pretty girl of sixteen (for whom I wish I could have felt only a paternal affection) came to my room whenever I called for her, which was very often, especially when it seemed to me that I was losing my inspiration. Now and again she brought me a cake or a cup of coffee, and sometimes only her winsome little face, always gay and smiling, as if created to inspire poetical fancies and witty ideas.

In the course of sixty-three days the libretti of *Don Giovanni* and *L' arbore di Diana* were completed, while only one-third of Salieri's opera remained unfinished.

Of the three works, the one which he esteemed the best was that written for Martini, the theme of which was the dissolution of monastic establishments by Joseph II, amusingly represented in an allegory in which Diana and her nymphs were outwitted by Cupid and Endymion.

It is more than probable that this plot was original; not so that of *Axur, re d' Ormus,* which, as he himself states, was an Italian adaptation of the libretto *Tarare,* written by Beaumarchais and unsuccessfully produced some time before by Salieri in Paris. As for *Don Giovanni,* hardly any doubt remains, especially after the already quoted study by Farinelli, that Da Ponte availed himself of other existing libretti, and in particular of that of Giovanni Bertati, who was his successor, some years later, as "Poet to the Italian Theatre," and against whom he directed some caustic remarks in his *Memorie.*

Yet this ought not entirely to deprive our Poet of the credit due to him, for, apart from the very selection of the subject which inspired Mozart's masterpiece, it is undeniable that the libretto has unusual qualities which ought to be taken into consideration.

"The common opinion," as one of Mozart's biographers

very appropriately remarks, "which considers the work of a librettist of small importance, is quite recent. At the time of Da Ponte, the relation between musician and poet was much closer than it is nowadays." Something similar to it can perhaps be found in the French comedy of the latter part of the last century where two authors coöperate in creating one play. The composition of the text of an opera was a specialty which required considerable study and gift, and which was held in great honor.

And, after what we know of Da Ponte's nature and adventurous life, is it not true that hardly another man could have been better qualified to treat the subject of *Don Giovanni?*

It was with keen insight, therefore, that Lamartine wrote, in his *Cours familier de Littérature,* after reproducing the passage of the *Memorie* in which Lorenzo describes how he started to work on his play:

> C' est ainsi que Don Juan devait être écrit, par un aventurier, un amant, un poète, un homme de plaisir et de désordre inspiré du vin, de l'amour et de la gloire, entre les tentations de la débauche et le respect divin pour l'innocence, homme sans scrupule, mais non sans terreur des vengeances du ciel. D' Aponte [*sic*], à l'impénitence près, écrivait le drame de sa propre vie dans le drame de Don Juan.

Of the three plays written by our Poet, *L'arbore di Diana* was the first to be produced. It was given on October 1st, 1787, on the occasion of the arrival in Vienna of the Archduchess Maria Theresa of Austria, bride of Prince Anthony of Saxony, as appears from the frontispiece of the libretto in its first edition. It was received with favor both by the public and the Emperor, who appreciated Da Ponte's flattering tribute to his policies and sent him a gift of one hundred sequins.

Nearly a month later—to be precise, on the 29th of October—*Don Giovanni* was staged in Prague. That public, known for its passionate love for music. and which the preceding year had received *Le nozze di Figaro* with unbounded enthusiasm, acclaimed the new opera a distinct triumph. Mozart, who came to direct it, was received with wild applause, which increased in volume after each number and soon seemed to threaten to break all bounds of restraint.

Da Ponte, unfortunately, was not present. He had come to Prague but, as he informs us, had been hurriedly recalled to Vienna, where Salieri, anxious to give his own opera, wanted him to finish the libertto for it.

From Mozart, we are told, he received immediately after the first performance the following note:

Our opera, *Don Giovanni,* was given last night before a very brilliant audience. The Princesses of Tuscany with their magnificent suites were present. It was received with such signs of approval that we could not have wished for more. Guardassoni [*the impresario*] came this morning to my room enthusiastically shouting: 'Long live Mozart! Long live Da Ponte! While these two live, impresari need not fear poverty!' Good-bye, my friend; prepare another opera for your MOZART.

It was not until six months later (May 7th, 1788) that the opera was performed in Vienna, where it met with an exceedingly cold reception. Salieri, whose Axur, re d' Ormus—given for the first time on January 8th—was enjoying immense popularity, endeavored to prevent its representation and it was only by the express command of the Emperor that *Don Giovanni* was given.

The interpretation, there is reason to suppose, was a very good one for the rôles were entrusted to first- rate artists: Benucci, who had created the part of Figaro, sang that of Leporello, Don Giovanni was the baritone Albertarelli, while the parts of Elvira and Anna were taken respectively by the Cavalieri and the composer's sister-in-law, Aloysia Lange. Yet, "How can I write it?" says Da Ponte in his *Memorie,*

> *Don Giovanni* was a failure! All, save Mozart, believed that something was lacking. We added a little, we changed some songs, and it was given again. Again it failed!—"The opera is divine," the Emperor asserted, "it is perhaps superior to *Figaro,* but it is not food suited to the teeth of my Viennese."—I related this to Mozart and he calmly replied: "Let us give them time to chew it."—He was right. I succeeded in arranging, by his advice, that the opera should be frequently repeated; at each performance the applause increased, and little by little the Viennese began to taste its beauty and to esteem *Don Giovanni* as one of the most beautiful operas ever produced for any stage.

About this time Italian opera in Vienna underwent a critical period. Lorenzo attributes this to the intrigues of certain singers, but it is more likely that Joseph II felt obliged to withdraw his support owing to the depletion of the State's finances resulting from the campaign then being waged against the Turks.

Da Ponte enlisted the support of private subscribers, and for some time managed to avert the necessity of discontinuing the performances. He wrote then for Salieri the libretto of *Il pastor fido,* taken from Guarini's drama. The opera was presented in the early part of 1789 and was indifferently received. Hardly a better success attended *La cifra,* written also for Salieri, and *Così fan tutte, o La scuola delle amanti,* which Mozart set to music. On the contrary, *Il pasticcio,* a kind of "revue" in which he introduced the best selections of all the operas heard in Vienna during the last few seasons, seemed to arouse a certain interest. "It was," the author informs us, "a rather witty and amusing criticism of the public, the impresari, the singers, the poets, the composers, and finally of myself."

The death of Joseph II, which occurred on February 20th, 1790, brought a sudden change in the fortunes of our Poet. Leopold II, who succeeded him, was quite a different type of man and he ascended the throne with the firm determination of pursuing a policy of restrictions and economy in contrast to his late brother's prodigality. . . .

Extremely busy with state affairs, Leopold ignored a *canzone* which Lorenzo wrote soon after his accession to the throne, mourning the death of Joseph and lauding in flattering hyperboles his successor. For a time, it seems, the old order of things remained unchanged, and when, towards the end of that year, Ferdinand IV of Naples came to Vienna, accompanied by his Queen and his two daughters, Princesses Maria Theresa and Maria Louise, brides respectively of the future Emperor Francis and of his brother Ferdinand, Lorenzo was asked to compose something in honor of the illustrious guests. He wrote then a *cantata* entitled *Flora e Minerva,* which was set to music by Joseph Weigl, and presented with great success, on January 17th, 1791, before the assembled court.

Another *cantata,* probably the one entitled *I voti della nazione napoletana,* for which Francesco Piticchio composed the music and which was given a month or so later, was written by Lorenzo at the request of the Neapolitan ambassador, Marquis Del Gallo. It was the last production of our Poet in Vienna, for the storm which had been gathering for some time burst upon him, resulting in his dismissal.

L. Collison-Morley (essay date 1926)

SOURCE: "Mozart's Librettist, Lorenzo Da Ponte," in *The London Mercury,* Vol. XIV, No. 82, August, 1926, pp. 401-10.

[*In the excerpt below, Collison-Morley surveys Da Ponte's career.*]

Of the many literary adventurers, knights of the pen rather than of the sword, who are so characteristic a feature of the life of eighteenth-century Italy, there is no more attractive figure than Lorenzo Da Ponte. Adventurers of all kinds were not uncommon at that day, when the national life was at its lowest ebb and there was no opening for men of such restless energy in their own country in any respectable sphere. The previous century had given them ample scope, for, with all its faults, the epoch of Spanish rule was not deficient in vigour. The adventurer enjoyed life for its own sake, for the adventures it threw in his way. Brigandage offered the most obvious outlet to a man of this type. But among the eighteenth-century adventurers are figures of outstanding ability who found it more amusing, more profitable, even more safe to exploit society while keeping their places in it. Of this type Casanova and Cagliostro are the most outstanding examples. Then there were the literary adventurers, like Goldoni, who calls himself an "avventuriere onorato," men of a more attractive pattern, often far more exploited than exploiting. It is to the adventurers that we owe the best memoirs of the time. There are Goldoni himself and Casanova, with that delightful Venetian spendthrift, Antonio Lungo, and last, but by no means least, Lorenzo Da Ponte.

Like Goldoni, he was a man of letters, and, though most of his troubles were due to his own fault, to the defects of character which no experience could teach him to overcome, they were thrust upon him rather than of his own seeking. . . .

[In 1782] we find him starting for Vienna with an introduction to Salieri, the chapel-master at Court. By a stroke of luck the Emperor was going to open an Italian theatre, being weary of his French actors and their grumblings and, at Salieri's suggestion, Da Ponte applied for and obtained the post of poet, the Emperor, Joseph II, being graciousness itself during the interview.

Da Ponte had never written an opera book in his life and, though the decline had set in, the libretto was of far greater importance than it has since become. It was expected to have a poetic value of its own, to be worth reading for its own sake. Da Ponte's first effort was not a success, and the famous Abbate Casti, who was in Vienna, a guest of Count Rosemberg, and hoping to step into Metastasio's shoes, went about saying that he could not write a book. But Joseph II met him out walking one morning in the Graben and said, "You know your opera is not as bad as they would have us think. Courage, you must give us

Unfinished portrait of Wolfgang Amadeus Mozart, for whom Da Ponte wrote three distinguished libretti.

another." We begin to hear a good deal of those enemies again, and doubtless there was a strong party who wished Casti to oust Da Ponte, but fortunately his second attempt was a success, and the Emperor said to him, "We have won."

Mozart was in Vienna, but hitherto jealousy had prevented him from writing anything. Da Ponte's pride is pardonable when he says that "it was due to my persistence and firmness that Europe, and indeed the whole civilised world, owes to a great extent the exquisite vocal compositions of this admirable genius." Mozart hesitated when Da Ponte made the suggestion, saying he did not think it would be allowed, but Da Ponte said he would answer for that. Mozart suggested Figaro as a subject. Unfortunately the Emperor had just prohibited a German version of the comedy, but Da Ponte undertook to submit the opera to the Emperor at a favourable opportunity. When he did so, the Emperor said Mozart had written only one opera, which had not been very successful. "Nor should I have written more than one, but for your Majesty's clemency," answered Da Ponte. And he gave his consent. Kelly (the Irish tenor) shows us Mozart, who was very like Garrick, directing the rehearsals in his red pelisse and gold-laced cocked hat. The opera was not a great success at Vienna, but it scored heavily at Prague, where musical taste was then in advance of that of the capital. Da Ponte's greatest success as a theatre-poet was *Una Cosa Rara,* with music by Martini, which finally established his position above all intrigue. He and Martini became the social lions of the hour. The book is entirely original. But, of course, Da Ponte owes his fame as a librettist to his association with Mozart.

His next two operas were for inferior composers and failed. Meanwhile, Martini and Mozart both asked him for operas, while Salieri requested him to provide him with a good book for his *Tarare,* the existing libretto being very poor. This year, 1787, was to be the culminating point in Da Ponte's career as a theatre-poet. For Mozart he chose *Don Giovanni,* a subject with which he was delighted. Martini was to have *Diana's Tree,* a theme thoroughly adapted to his style, and *Tarare* was to be duly revised for Salieri. The Emperor said he would fail. Da Ponte answered that he probably should:

> but I shall do my best. I shall write at night for Mozart when I intend to read Dante's *Inferno.* In the morning I shall write for Martini, when I propose to study Petrarch; in the evenings for Salieri and he shall be my Tasso.

The Emperor appreciated his comparisons and they parted. Da Ponte went straight home.

> I sat down at my desk and remained there twelve hours at a stretch, a bottle of Tokay on my right, an inkpot in the middle and a box of Seville snuff on my left. A lovely girl of sixteen (whom I should have preferred only to love as a daughter) was in the house also, helping her mother, who looked after the family. She came to my room whenever I rang the bell, and I am afraid I rang it rather frequently, especially when my inspiration began to flag. She would bring me a biscuit,

or a cup of coffee, or nothing but her own beautiful face, always bright and smiling, the very thing to inspire a poet and stimulate a weary brain. I continued working twelve hours a day, with short intervals, for two whole months and during all that time she remained in the next room, reading, sewing or embroidering, ready to come to me at the first sound of the bell. Sometimes she would sit by me without moving, almost without opening her lips or blinking her eyes. She would gaze at me fixedly, smile sweetly, sigh, and at times seem to be on the point of bursting into tears. In short, this girl was my Calliope for those three operas and in fact for all that I wrote during the next three years. At first I let her visit me in this way pretty often, but I was soon forced to limit her visits for fear of wasting too much time in love-making, an art of which she was a perfect mistress. On the first day, what with the Tokay, the Seville snuff, the coffee, the bell and the young Muse, I wrote the first two scenes of *Don Giovanni,* two of *L'Arbor di Diana,* and more than half of the first act of *Tarare.* In the morning I took these scenes to the composers, who could hardly believe their eyes when they saw them. The first two operas were finished in sixty-three days and nearly two-thirds of the last.

Doubtless we must not take this account too literally. Something it owes to Da Ponte's imagination and dramatic instinct. But could one conceive of a more ideal setting for the writing of the libretto of *Don Giovanni?* Anybody who has seen it given at the Old Vic. in Mr. Edward Dent's version, with the delightful moral ending there revived, will understand that the love affairs of Don Giovanni and Figaro are Da Ponte's love affairs, leaving no sense of tragedy behind them. His Don Giovanni is a character of comedy, not the latter-day Don Giovanni,

hopelessly seeking the ideal of womanhood through life, doomed for ever to disappointment.

L'Arbor di Diana was the first given and proved as great a success as the *Cosa Rara.*

Mozart, as we know, retired to write the *Don Giovanni* overture at midnight, asking his wife to make some punch and stay with him. She began by telling him fairy tales (which made him laugh till the tears ran down his cheeks) to keep him awake; but it was hopeless, and she persuaded him to sleep till five, when he set to work and had it ready by seven. But the copyists were slow and the music did not reach the theatre till 7:45, though the opera was timed to begin at seven. It was played by the brilliant Prague orchestra at sight, the sand still on the notes, and received with great enthusiasm by the critical audience. The whole performance was a triumph. But it actually failed at Vienna.

Don Giovanni is Da Ponte's masterpiece, and is considered the best libretto of the day after Metastasio's. Da Ponte always preferred *L'Arbor di Diana* because it was original, whereas *Don Giovanni* is based on an older libretto. Its excellence had not a little to do with inspiring Mozart, as Wagner pointed out. Da Ponte tried to deliver opera, says Masi, from the false heroic world of Metastasio and restore to it the intrigue and characteristics of comedy without falling into the worst trivialities of *opéra bouffe.* Of this some of his now forgotten books are even better examples. In *Don Giovanni* we see the culmination of the wild libertinage and gaiety of the old *régime* just before the *débâcle* of the Revolution. The story had, of course, to pass through a soul as great and sublime as Mozart's before it became the masterpiece we now possess. Yet its reckless impenitences, its diabolical gaiety, are always true comedy, and this is because, though Da Ponte's heart had been superficially seared by his vagabond life, his transparently open and kindly character was at bottom untouched, and remained so till the end, as we see on every page of the *Memoirs.* For Mozart he also wrote *Così fan Tutte.* . . .

[In 1825] he was made Professor of Italian at Columbia University, but as his professorship brought him neither pupils nor money, he soon threw it up in disgust. However, the students always invited him to the annual dinner. He even opened, when well over eighty, an Italian bookshop in Broadway. He was not often troubled by customers, but he had the satisfaction of seeing all that was smartest in the city going into the fashionable confectioner's next door. This is where his *Memoirs* end.

The *Memoirs* are written in a delightfully easy and unaffected style, very different from the elaborate periods then in vogue. This Da Ponte adopted deliberately, as he found the ordinary books of the day too difficult for beginners. They tend to be diffuse, but this is the only sign of age about them, except perhaps a little very natural querulousness at his treatment in England and America. Yet largely he sees that this was his own fault and his heart is always young. They bring the man before us to the life,

---

Arthur Livingston on the *Memoirs*:

Whatever Da Ponte may have been, he was not a liar. Despite the efforts to shake the veracity of his *Memoirs,* they stand there as the engaging record of a soul's labored and painful passage through this world, and a substantially accurate account of what that soul experienced here. Substantially, not absolutely: the *Memoirs* contain lapses of memory, misapprehensions, confusions. They show literary reworkings of fact, enlargements and reductions for the sake of interest—Da Ponte told his story so many times orally, and always, we may be sure, in such different ways, that in the end he hardly knew just what the truth was. On the polemical side, he was fighting now for an advantage, now for his reputation, now for his livelihood. Combat is combat: it is not an ethical exercise, and only rascals of the first class mentioned above pretend it is for the advantage there is in doing so. Presenting the argument for the defense in such cases, Da Ponte was under no obligations to present the argument, or collect the evidence, for the prosecution. As a historical document, therefore, the *Memoirs* of Lorenzo Da Ponte, like every other historical document the world has ever seen, need control.

Arthur Livingston, in *Memoirs of Lorenzo Da Ponte,* edited by Arthur Livingston, translated by Elisabeth Abbott, J. B. Lippincott Company, 1929.

and it is impossible not to admire his pluck and energy, his good heartedness, silly though it may often have been, his Micawber-like optimism, and the honesty with which he tells his story. We may smile at his vanity and laugh over his faults, as we do over those of Figaro or Cherubino, but he wins our affection. His mind was not profound, but he had a real lyric gift up to a point, and he can tell a story.

Leonard Woolf (review date 1929)

SOURCE: "From Mozart to Miss Stein," in *The Nation and the Athenaeum,* Vol. XLV, No. 17, July 27, 1929, p. 566.

[*Woolf is best known as one of the leaders of the Bloomsbury Group of artists and thinkers, and as the husband of novelist Virginia Woolf, with whom he founded the Hogarth Press. A Fabian socialist during the World War I era, he became a regular contributor to the socialist* New Statesman *and later served as literary editor of the* Nation and the Athenaeum, *in which much of his literary criticism is found. In the excerpt below, Woolf summarizes Da Ponte's* Memoirs *as the work of a failure and a rake, but intriguing as a portrait of the author's milieu.*]

Da Ponte's memoirs were well worth translating into English. He was born in 1740 at Ceneda in Venetia of Jewish parents, but he was baptized at the age of fourteen and soon became an Abbé. He is chiefly remembered as the librettist of Mozart's **Don Giovanni, Figaro,** and **Così fan tutte**. His early life was lived in Venice, and he was one of those eighteenth-century adventurers, of whom the greatest was his friend Casanova. But he was neither as great a scoundrel nor as great a character as Casanova. There is something very mean and unpleasant about the ego of Lorenzo da Ponte which, for all his efforts to conceal it, creeps about the pages of his biography. A wanderer, like all adventurers, from Venice to Gorizia, from Gorizia to Dresden, from Dresden to Vienna, from Vienna to Trieste, from Trieste to London, and from London to the United States, he was always meeting with misfortunes which he ascribed to the jealousy and malice of enemies, but which were really due to his own cantankerous follies and vices. When he died at the age of eighty-nine, Professor of Italian at Columbia, but in poverty and without a single pupil, dictating "tributary verses to his kind physician," he could look back over a life of failure in which his worst enemy had been his own ego. The merit of his memoirs is that they show us this ego creeping about the strange eighteenth-century world of Venice, Vienna, and London, and then again creeping on into the still stranger nineteenth-century world of New York and Philadelphia.

Walter Littlefield (review date 1929)

SOURCE: "Da Ponte, Adventurer and Librettist," in *The New York Times Book Review,* December 1, 1929, pp. 10, 50.

[*In the following excerpt from a review of two editions of Da Ponte's* Memoirs*-one edited by L. A. Sheppard, the other by Arthur Livingston-Littlefield emphasizes the rakish side of the noted librettist.*]

Knowledge of Lorenzo Da Ponte, Mozart's most celebrated librettist, Caesarean Poet to Emperor Joseph II of Austria and the first professor of Italian at Columbia College, great lover, pompous scholar, gentle, inspiring teacher, dominating poseur and impressive adventurer, is as persistently cumulative as is his fame.

Lorenzo Da Ponte was the greatest intellectual gift bestowed by the dying Ancien Régime of Europe on the young American Republic. The value of that gift, which included the first teaching of Italian here, the first exposition of Dante and the inauguration of Italian opera, has waited long for proper appraisement—so has the career of the remarkable man himself. When he died in this city in 1838, at the age of 89, after a residence of thirty-three years, some of his distinguished friends wrote intimate eulogies for the press followed by articles in the reviews. Their European vistas, however, were full of shadows and outlines. For this Da Ponte was chiefly responsible. He never imparted to his New York friends his original name or race, or the circumstances of his birth—naught but the fact that he had been educated under the patronage of a man of identical name, Mgr. Lorenzo Da Ponte, Bishop of Ceneda. This sole revelation gave rise to much peculiar gossip, which was not to be straightened out for nearly a century.

For Da Ponte, sublime egotist that he was, knew how to mystify his American friends as well as satisfy them—a satisfaction not felt by the following generations, particularly when it was gradually discovered what lay behind his casually expressed contacts with the great Moreover, his [*Memoirs*] written, rewritten, amplified, modified and polished in various editions from 1823 until the Autumn of 1830, showed that the writer was much more interested in his own fate than he was in the fate of empires—in the pretty daughter of his land-lady than in an Empress with whom he might have been conversing a few moments before. While he was living in Venice, Vienna and London the French Revolution gathered and broke, but he only mentions it because it prevented him from going to Paris with a letter to Queen Marie Antoinette. In England the threatened invasions of Napoleon meant no more to him than did the Emperor's expansion of power, his fall, exile and death, which took place while Da Ponte was in the United States. Napoleon, who remade Italy, is mentioned once—an anecdote told in 1798 by Da Ponte's father of General Buonaparte's visit to Ceneda two years before.

As has been said, knowledge in regard to Da Ponte has been cumulative:

Mr. Sheppard . . . incorporates in his introduction one important discovery. Just as Edouard Maynial in his "Casanova et son temps" demolished the tale of the greater adventurer's robbery of the Marquise d'Urfé as related with feverish gusto in the lesser adventurer's memoirs, so the latter's story as to how he left Venice is demolished by Mr. Sheppard with the aid of Fausto Nicolini working among the State archives of the old Adriatic republic. Da Ponte himself and all his biographers say that he was obliged to leave Venice purely on account of political reasons, against the background of which the widow Bellaudi, at whose house Da Ponte lodged; her daughter, Caterina, and her son, Cario, with his wife, Angioletta, move like shadows.

According to the Venetian archives, Da Ponte made love to Angioletta, forged a letter in her husband's hand which induced her to go away with him, and continued to harass the unfortunate Cario untill the latter dropped a renuncia, lion into the famous Lion's Mouth, which the Council of Ten received on May 28, 1779. Then the Esecutori contro la Bestemmia (Warders Against Blasphemy) began an investigation which lasted until September. Meanwhile Da Ponte, although feeling his once powerful friends alipping from him, continued to live with Angioletta in Venice until July, when he went to Treviso. On returning in September he learned that a warrant was out for his arrest and fled to Austrian territory. In December he was sentenced by default to the alternative of fifteen years' banishment or seven in prison.

It is fortunate that the enemies of Da Ponte in England and America, who even resorted to falsehood in order to blast his reputation here, did not have access to the Venentian archives. All the same, this "correction" is duplicated by episodes quite as romantic, if not quite so reprehensible, in other parts of the memoirs. Still, Lorenso was only 30 when he had to flee Venice. What is that in the life of a nonagenarian?

He now has a conspicuous place among those other Venetian erudite adventurers, Antonio Longo, Pietro Antonio Gratarol and Cario Goldoni, even with the famous Giovannl Jacope Casanova de Seingalt, his ever-suspicious friend, and, thanks to American scholarship, his memoirs are a distinctly valuable addition to Americana.

Harry Morgan Ayres (review date 1929)

SOURCE: "A Crowded Ninety Years," in *New York Herald Tribune Books,* December 15, 1929, p. 7.

[*In the following excerpt from a review of* Memoirs of Lorenzo Da Ponte, *Ayres offers a summary of the work, nothing that the focus falls recurrently upon Da Ponte's recognition of himself as a besieged genius brought low by his calculating inferiors.*]

If Da Ponte could have lived to be 180 instead of but a little less than half that span he would count this a wonderful year—n gala performance of his (and Mozart's) **Don Giovanni** at the Metropolitan, a professorship named after him in the university that furnished him alive neither stipend nor pupils, and finally his **Memoirs** done into an English he would admire. Here at once and at last come

Program of the first performance of Don Giovanni. *The names of Da Ponte and Mozart are buried in small print at the top.*

proper recognition of his literary talent (he did not claim to be a great poet, but he did know literature and the practicalities of the theater); recognition of his undoubted talents as a teacher, which he displayed in his earliest youth in the seminaries of the Veneto and again in his old age among his private pupils in New York; recognition of how grievously a sensitive, artistic soul may be made to suffer by the wicked of this world. Its cheats and its calumniators, until a man is all but beside himself and scarcely to be kept in his wits and in his pocket by the kindness of those patrons, all too few, who win immortal praise by recognixing his merits. Here in the **Memoirs** they are all set down—the calumniators who secured his expulsion from Venice, who caused his loss of imperial patronage at Vienna, who in New York impugned the purity of his Italian and disparaged his claim to be the first to reveal the beauties of Italian literature to Americans; the oheats, William-Taylor, the London impresario, whose notes Da Ponte indorsed, paid, bought in at ruinous discount, and on them recovered nothing; and sundry grocers and traffickers in small wares in Elizabeth, N. S., and Sunbury, Pa.; and the adored patrons, Joseph II of Austria, Thomas James Matthias, the London amateur of Italian letters, and Clement Moore in New York, generous as the Santa Claus of his own creation.

It was a crowded ninety years. Born in the ghetto of Ceneda (Vittorio Veneto), Da Ponte became the clever protege of the bishop who baptised him and whose name he assumed; thence to the seminaries, where he took orders and rapidly became an original and successful teacher of literature and an academic administrator, and then a Venetian amorist and gambler, till at the age of thirty even Venice cast him forth. So much for the first part of the *Memoirs*.

For the second the brilliant years at the Italian theater in Vlenna, for the third his marriage to Ann Grahl a clever and attractive English Jewess, and the years in London, with its opera, with bookselling and its usury, ending in disaster and flight to America. The fourth part recounts his ill-starred attempts to trade with the "Yankees" of New Jersey and Pennsylvania, and the fifth the serener years as a teacher in New York, exponent of European culture to a more innocent age. A sixth part, not added to the *Memoirs,* would have told of the attempts of an indomitable old man of eighty-three, now with no Ann to sustain or restrain him, to establish Italian opera in New York.

The *Memoirs* developed gradually under Da Ponte's hand. The original suggestion may well have come, as Professor Livingston suggests, from knowledge that his friend: Casanova was engaged in making copy of his own adventures. Hence the carefully worked-up accounts of the Venetian intrigues into something better than the plain facts at least. Later, in America, ugly rumors of his financial failures in London must have found corroboration in his mishandled affairs in New Jersey and Pennsylvania. Da Ponte therefore continues to write to justify himself and to confound his enemies. Still later, as a teacher in New York, Da Ponte finds himself and his work in a way to be submerged by a wave of Italian political refugees that followed the suppression of the Carbonari movement in the 1820's. It becomes necessary to assert his claims to the deanship of Italian letters abroad—and to see to it that there should be no diminution in the number of young ladies and gentlemen who frequented his classes and of the amateurs who dropped in upon him in his bookshop.

So conceived and written, the *Memoirs* are wholly Da Ponte, the adventures and the outcries of a living and suffering soul. Of background there is very little. The French Revolution, Napoleon, Post-Revolutionary New York society, of which he was always the courted guest, find scant mention in his pages. But atmosphere there is—both of an older Europe and of a younger America, somewhat wistfully and perplexedly aware of its discipleship.

Morris Bishop (review date 1930)

SOURCE: "Under the Fury of Destiny," in *The Saturday Review of Literature,* Vol. VI, No. 31, February 22, 1930,

p. 756.

[*In the excerpt below, Morris praises the* Memoirs *as a work which tells a fascinating story of a much-maligned but accomplished figure.*]

Lorenzo Da Ponte has at length come into his own in his adopted country. His memoirs, untranslated for a hundred years, have appeared in two excellent versions, furnished with much new information about his deeds and character. . . .

As one rereads the memoirs (have you noticed that the scholar never reads a book—he always rereads it?) one is impressed again by the excellence of the story as a story. "The most original memoirs which artistic Italy has ever offered public curiosity. . . . He writes as well as Goldoni, he is as sprightly as the chevalier de Grammont, as adventurous as Gil Blas, as amusing as Figaro, as unfortunate as Gilbert." said no less eminent a judge than Alphonse de Lamartine, in 1860. "But," continued the poet, "his Memoirs were buried in that American forest called New York. No one, I presume, has exhumed them over there, where the most brilliant manuscript will never weigh as much as a dollar."

Lamartine, lacking the results of modern research, could read the memoirs as the odyssey of the virtuous adventurer, ever at odds with hostile fate and human malevolence. Whoever can disregard footnotes may read them so today and find them rarely interesting. Da Ponte touched the world of his delightful day at many points; he tells us of life in Italian theological seminaries, in the perpetual masquerade of Venice, Europe's country club, in the operatic circles of Vienna, Dresden, and London, in the cultivated society of New York, and in the taverns and general stores of Sunbury, Pa., and the Reading Turnpike. He was the friend of Casanova, of Joseph II of Austria, of Mozart, and of how many others! And as the hero of his own story he is the embodiment of genius erect and indomitable under the fury of destiny. For one example of the quality of his spirit, at the age of eighty-four he built the first opera house in New York. It promptly failed, as was customary with da Ponte's enterprises. . . .

None of the revelations of da Ponte's failings have unsettled the important facts: that he was a man of real accomplishment in the most diverse fields, that he was a scholar and a literary artist, that his energy in battling with circumstances was a thing almost stupefying, and that he wrote one very good book.

Paul Nettl (essay date 1956)

SOURCE: "Casanova and *Don Giovanni,*" in *The Saturday Review,* New York, Vol. XXXIX, No. 4, January 28, 1956, pp. 44-5, 55, 57-8.

[*Nettl was a distinguished musicologist. In the essay below, he examines the influence of Casanova upon Da Ponte and upon the writing of* Don Giovanni.]

Of all the great figures of the eighteenth century, there is probably none that we more instinctively associate with the hero of Mozart's opera ***Don Giovanni*** than Giacomo Casanova. It is, indeed, one of the most curious coincidences in the history of art that this man, who was the incarnation of Don Juan in real life, should not only have been alive, but even have been in Prague when ***Don Giovanni*** was first produced in 1787. To find an appropriate parallel we almost have to imagine Hamlet rising out of his grave to be on hand for the first presentation of Shakespeare's great tragedy in London. Yet the extraordinary connection between Casanova and ***Don Giovanni*** is one which no historian of music has yet investigated seriously.

I still vividly recall the thrill I experienced years ago (1924) on discovering just how unusual this connection was. It was while I was searching through the Casanova papers that are stored near the little Bohemian town of Dux (northwest of Prague), in the castle of which the great Italian adventurer spent his last thirteen years as the librarian of Count Waldstein. At the time I visited Dux his papers were watched over by a vivacious little man called Bernard Marr, who, besides being a machine manufacturer, was a fanatical cabalist and admirer of Casanova, and had given such noted writers as Arthur Schnitzler, Stefan Zweig, and Max Brod invaluable information. Among the handwritten manuscripts that Marr showed me were two of quite exceptional interest. On examining them closely I realized that they were nothing less than a revision of part of the libretto of ***Don Giovanni***. It was apparent that Casanova had managed to study the libretto in detail, and that he had set out to revise some of it, or even to rewrite it entirely for Mozart or some other composer. This posed a fascinating riddle—just how had Casanova succeeded in getting hold of the text, and why had he done so?

The Casanova archives, which are now stored at Hirschberg, near Dux, are full of letters from Da Ponte, who bombarded the old Chevalier with accounts of his travels and with requests for aid and advice right up to the year of Casanova's death in 1798. There was even a time, in 1792, when Da Ponte, who was then in London and very much down on his luck, tried to get Casanova to procure him a sinecure from his own patron, Count Waldstein; a request which Casanova answered with characteristic cynicism by advising Da Ponte to live off his newly married wife's income. Furthermore, Da Ponte's memoirs, which he wrote in New York (after an unusual career as a grocer, distiller, language teacher, professor at Columbia, boarding-house owner, and impresario) contain a number of references to his old friend Casanova, whom he obviously considered one of the most remarkable men he had ever met.

To appreciate the extent of this influence it is necessary to know something of the background of the two men. Both were originally Venetians and began by leading somewhat parallel lives. Both belonged to that class of Italian adventurers who lived off their native wits and who could be found in the eighteenth century in all the royal courts and noble circles of the great European capitals. At one moment they would be living the life of cavaliers, driving about in four-horse carriages, throwing lavish parties, and moving in the company of beautiful women, only to find themselves in the next without a penny and forced to borrow from some old friend the money with which to pay for the previous night's lodgings. But with all this there was one important difference: Casanova was born in 1725 and was twenty-four years senior to Da Ponte, who was born in 1749, so that it was natural that the first should be a model for the second, rather than a contemporary rival.

In his memoirs Da Ponte tells us that he first met Casanova in 1777 in the palaces of the Venetian noblemen, Memmo and Zaguri, both of whom were patrons of the arts. At the time that Casanova and Da Ponte were living there Venice was at its most bewitching, and both revelled in the frenzy of its masked carnivals and nocturnal festivities. Like Casanova, the young, Lorenzo da Ponte had originally been destined to become an abbé in the Church, but he was soon expelled from the seminary he was teaching at for having written some public verses inspired by Rousseau. Even before his expulsion, however, his morals had run aground on the tempting reef of Venice's loose, glittering life, and his vow of chastity and celibacy had not restrained him from indulging in numerous love affairs and seductions. Once freed of his sacerdotal bonds he gave free rein to his amorous inclinations, and it was here, in a Venice where Casanova was Don Giovanni in the flesh, that Da Ponte imbibed that rich, erotic atmosphere which he later depicted with such mastery in Mozart's opera.

While Da Ponte's adventures in Venice were not as sensational as Casanova's, they were basically not so different. It was not long, indeed, before the gay city grew too hot for both of them. Thanks to the account of it he gives in his memoirs, Casanova's story of his imprisonment in the Doge's Palace and his escape over its leaden roofs has become world-famous. What occasioned it was his arrest by the Venetian Tribunal for spreading a tale about an affair between a nun and the French Ambassador (who later became Cardinal Bernis). Da Ponte's departure from Venice was not as dramatic, but he too was arraigned for trial and had to flee the city.

After passing some time in various European cities Casanova and Da Ponte met again in Vienna. In his reminiscences Da Ponte says that Casanova stayed several years in the Austrian capital, "though neither I nor anyone else knew what he was doing there, or what he was living on; I conversed with him frequently, and on every occasion he found my house and purse open to him. Although I could approve neither of his principles nor of his way of life, I nonetheless paid great heed to his counsels and precepts which truly—I perceive it now—were of the highest value, golden rules which I unhappily too little followed and from which I could have drawn the greatest advantage had I but put them into practice. . . . "

The importance which Da Ponte here attaches to Casanova and to his advice is an eloquent tribute to the older Italian's influence over the younger. But the friendship which ripened between them in Vienna is of special interest for another reason which has a direct bearing on the later composition of **Don Giovanni**. In his memoirs Da Ponte relates how one day, while he was strolling along a street in Vienna with Casanova "I saw him suddenly knit his brows, gnash his teeth, and begin to turn and twist, and uttering a yell and throwing up his hands to Heaven, rush away from me and hurl himself furiously upon a man he appeared to know, shouting at the top of his voice, `Assassin, now I have caught you!'" The "assassin" turned out to be a former servant of Casanova's called Costa, who for many years had been his companion and friend. But one day in France, immediately after Casanova had cheated an aging Marquise out of a small fortune in gold and jewels by administering a dose of laudanum in place of the magic elixir of life that he had enthusiastically promised her, this servant had decamped with the booty and not been seen again. Following the uproar in the street caused by Casanova's assault on him, Costa, who had now become the valet of a Viennese nobleman and something of a "poet" on the side, disappeared into a coffee-house and sent Casanova a poem of six lines:

> Casanova, make no fuss
> You stole and I did too.
> You were the master, I the pupil
> I learned your trade too.
> It was only tit for tat,

This incident is significant not only because it shows us another facet of Casanova's many-sided and versatile personality, but also because Da Ponte witnessed it personally. For this same Costa, the servant who had learned his master's tricks so well that he could one day use them against him, was destined to be the living model for Don Giovanni's servant, Leporello (rather different than Signarelle of Moliere's *Don Juan*).

The choice of Don Juan as the subject for a new, opera in Prague was Da Ponte's—so at least he tells us in his memoirs. Mozart, at any rate, was enchanted with the idea from the start. The theme, as it happened, was very much in the air. Though the Italian poet Goldoni had tried to make fun of the Don Juan legend some fifty years before by writing a dramatic extravaganza called *Don Giovanni Tenorio o sia Il Dissoluto,* the story of the dissolute hero from Seville had remained a popular one with the Italian stage. In fact, in the very year that Mozart and Da Ponte received their new commission, the Italian librettist Bertati and the composer Gazzaniga had written an opera on the Don Juan theme entitled *Il Convitato di Pietra.* First put on for the Venice carnival in February 1787 it had been an instantaneous "hit" and had conquered all of Italy in months, even though Goethe, who saw it during his trip to that country, thought it ridiculous.

Da Ponte may have been of the same opinion, for he set out to do better. He even undertook to write three operas

at once, and with typical verve he told Emperor Joseph II: "I shall write at night for Mozart as though I were reading Dante's *Inferno*; I shall write in the morning for Martini, and that will be like studying Petrarch. The evening will be for Salieri, and that will be my Tasso." The Emperor seems to have been amused by this scheme, though he doubted that Da Ponte could carry it out. In fact, of course, and notwithstanding Da Ponte's verbal flourishes, *The Divine Comedy* was only a minor source of inspiration to him in writing the text for **Don Giovanni**. To get in the right mood he set a bottle of Tokay on the right side of his desk and a Sevilla snuffbox on the left, and set out to work twelve hours a day, stopping every now and then to revive his poetic inspiration by carrying on an affair with the sixteen-year-old daughter of his housekeeper. He also helped himself liberally to whole chunks of Bertati's script, including the famous "Catalogue aria," in which Don Giovanni's servant lists his master's numberless seductions. But as he did so the vision of his old friend, Casanova, and his servant, Costa, might have hovered before his eyes and have inspired him to transform Bertati's pallid figures into the lusty, flesh-and-blood Don Giovanni and Leporello which, thanks to Mozart's music, have become for opera what Don Quixote and Sancho Panza are for literature.

After completing the text in Vienna Da Ponte arrived in Prague early in October to oversee the final preparations. He remained there a few days and was present at a number of rehearsals held at the National Theatre. But before the opera could be produced he was forced to return suddenly to Vienna. Mozart was thus left without an Italian librettist capable of making last-minute adjustments in the poetic text to suit the whims or the complaints of the singers. It is at this point that the mystery surrounding Casanova's involvement in the preparations of **Don Giovanni** begins.

The memorable premiere of *Don Giovanni* took place on October 29. There can be no doubt that Casanova was in Prague at the time, for on November 4 Count Lamberg wrote from Brunn to the Bohemian writer J. F. Opitz at Caslau that "Casanova is in Prague; his letter to me is of the 25th of October." He was in fact at that moment negotiating with his publisher, Schonfeld, about the publication of his novel *Icosameron*. He was also almost certainly in touch with Mozart. The subscription list to *Icosameron* (contained in the back of the first edition) includes a number of names that we encounter in Mozart's life—to mention but one: that of Count Pachta, for whom Mozart wrote the German Dances while in Prague.

None of the available scraps of evidence offer any conclusive proof that Mozart and Casanova met at this time. However, in his book *Rococcobilder (Scenes from the Rococco)*, which was published in 1871, the poet and historian Alfred Meissner claims that they did in fact meet at a party given by the singer Josephine Duschek (a friend of Mozart's) in her villa near Prague. The occasion was one of those famous "evenings" at the Duschek villa. Both Da Ponte and Casanova, Meissner says, were among the guests. All those present were disturbed by the unconcern of Mozart, who had still not finished the overture to **Don Giovanni,** though the dress rehearsal was due the next day and the first performance the day after.

The most important clue in this mystery is constituted by the two manuscript sheets which Bernard Marr and I discovered years ago in Dux. These two sheets represent a revision of the sextet that is sung in the second act of **Don Giovanni** when Donna Anna, Donna Elvira, Don Ottavio, Zerlina, and Masetto discover Leporello in the disguise of Don Giovanni, whom he has faithfully been trying to imitate by seducing Donna Elvira. In the second half of this scene, as Da Ponte wrote it, there is a bit of unaccompanied recetative in which Zerlina, Elvira, Ottavio, and Masetto threaten to punish Leporello, and this is followed by a G major aria beginning "Ah, pietà, Signori miel!" in which Leporello attempts to exonerate himself on the grounds that Don Giovanni had forced him to disguise himself.

The two Casanova fragments, which contain about thirty lines each, were both evidently written for formal musical accompaniment. Neither is numbered and each ends with the stage direction *fugge* (he escapes), which seems to indicate that they were written as alternative versions for the last part of the scene. They overlap with Da Ponte's text in that the first is a quintet, evidently intended to replace Da Ponte's recitative, and the second is an aria for Leporello.

In a second edition of his book *Mozart's Operas* (published after our discovery of the fragments) Professor Edward Dent has advanced the theory that at some moment during the rehearsals in Prague several of the singers may have complained about the lack of solo arias allotted to them, and that to satisfy them Mozart decided to introduce a scene after the sextet for Ponziana, who was singing the role of Leporello, and Baglioni, who had that of Ottavio. He therefore got Casanova, in Da Ponte's absence, to write the words for it. "Casanova," says Dent, "first sketches the aria for Leporello . . . , followed by an ensemble for all the characters except Donna Anna, who has left the stage at the end of the sextet. Mozart then probably points out that the audience already knows everything that Leporello says in this aria, and that another ensemble would be an anti-climax. Casanova rewrites the scene under Mozart's direction, making it much less formal and far more amusing and dramatic. As Mozart has taken away the sheet with the revised words, it is naturally lost; Casanova puts the rejected draft in his own pocket, and accident has preserved it. This reconstruction of what may have happened is purely conjectural."

Though conjectural, it is an ingenious theory. It does not tell us, of course, if the revised sheet that Mozart took away with him and which has been lost was ever used, or how it was fitted into the Da Ponte libretto as we know it, unless we are to suppose that Leporello's G major aria was the result of this revision, that is to say, that it was really written by Casanova and inserted into the final text. That is an entertaining notion to play with, but it seems highly unlikely that such a thing could have happened.

The libretto for **Don Giovanni** was definitely printed before Da Ponte left Prague. Furthermore, it had to be approved by the censor prior to the first performance. For this reason I doubt that any text of Casanova's, supposing that he wrote one for Mozart, was used at the premiere.

My own theory—and like Professor Dent's it is only a conjecture—is that Mozart may have asked Casanova to write a couple of additions to Da Ponte's text *after* the highly successful premiere, in order to satisfy the singers and particularly Ponziani (Leporello), who was the only singer in the opera who did not have two solo arias. (Lolli sang both the roles of Masétto and the Commendatore.) These additions may have taken the form of "prepared" improvisations, somewhat equivalent to what is known today as "encores." According to Luigi Bassi, who sang the first Don Giovanni, the opera director of Prague, Guardasoni, allowed quite a bit of such "impromptu" singing. It even seems that Mozart attached considerable importance to it, particularly in the dinner scene. Such

Austrian emperor Joseph II, protector and champion of Da Ponte.

improvisations were standard practice in Prague right up until fairly recent times, and I still recall old-timers of the Prague Opera House telling me years ago of how ***Don Giovanni*** always used to end with a chorus ensemble, culminating in "Evviva il immortale Maestro Mozart."

Regardless of what theory is advanced to explain the Casanova text, it differs significantly from Da Ponte's in both words and spirit. Casanova's is not only more formal and elaborate, as would be natural for words destined for a full musical accompaniment; it is more flamboyant in every way. Where, for example, Da Ponte has Zerlina, Elvira, Ottavio, and Masetto arguing as to who is to be the one to punish Leporello as he deserves, Casanova has them list all the dreadful fates that are about to overtake the hapless servant:

> Zerlina: *Ti vo mangiar le viscere* (I am going to eat your entrails).
> Masetto: *Vo divorarti l'anima* (I am going to devour your soul).
> Don Ottavio: *Appreso ad unpatibolo* (I'll bring you near a chopping block).
> Donna Elvira: *Pericolor lo spirito* (To scare the wits out of you).

Having thus emphasized the distinction between the rather grotesque chastisements envisaged by plebeians and the more sophisticated punishments of aristocrats, Casanova has all four join with Leporello in a lively quintet:

> All four: *Alla forca, alla forca, alla forca* (To the gallows, etc.).
> Leporello: *Ohibo, che morte sporca!* (Alas, what a dog's death!).
> All four: *In galera, in galera, in galera!* (To the galley, etc.).
> Leporello: *Remo, bussa, vita austera!* (Rowing, steering, austere life).
> All four: *Vada a scopar la piazza* (Go sweep the square).
> Leporello: *Sono di illustre razza* (I am of illustrious family).

In this last line Casanova has carried Leporello's effrontery in imitating his master to heroic heights—and we can only admire this lovely touch from the old boudoir buccaneer who had conferred on himself the high-flown title of Chevalier de Seingalt!

The same personal flavor can be found in Leporello's aria, as Casanova wrote it, in comparison with Da Ponte's. Whereas Da Ponte's presents a rather breathless Leporello trying to explain away his disguise and his presence in the courtyard of Donna Elvira's house, Casanova's Leporello appears much less intimidated, and even capable of philosophical reflections:

> *La colpa e tutta quanta* (The fault is all alone).
> *Di quel femineo sesso* (Of that feminine sex).
> *Che l'anima gl'incanta* (Which enchants the soul).
> *E gl'incantera il cor* (And will enchant the heart).
> *O sesso seductor!* (O seductive sex!).

Sorgente di dolor! (Source of sorrow!).

And he ends up on a really sublime note of insolence, crying:

> *Il solo Don Giovanni* (Don Giovanni alone).
> *Merita vostro sdegno* (Merits your indignation).
> *Iro a punir l'indegno* (I'll go punish the scoundrel).
> *Lasciatemi scappar . . . (fugge)* (Let me but escape [he flees]).

The whole "tone" of the two versions of the last part of the sextet is, in fact, quite different. Whereas Da Ponte's is graceful, reserved, urbane, and obviously written for a courtly audience, Casanova's text is uninhibited, exuberant, and at times almost improper. The contrast is the same that we find in their respective memoirs, the same that we find in their respective lives: the difference between two types of man—the one, Da Ponte, an accommodating man of letters, prepared on occasion to be a hypocrite and to draw a cloak of modesty over his more dubious escapades, the other: Casanova, a flamboyant exhibitionist, every ready to startle his listeners with some scandalous and unbelievably lascivious tale.

The Danish philosopher, Soren Kierkegaard, considered it a stroke of fortune that it should have fallen to a composer of Mozart's genius to exploit the unique material of the Don Juan theme, just as it fell to Homer to mould the stuff of the Trojan Wars into epic verse. For Kierkegaard, Mozart was the master of the erotic in music, and to prove his point he cites the amorous intoxication of Cherubino and the earthy simplicity of Papageno. To these we could add the coarse sensuality of Monastatos. It is in ***Don Giovanni*** that the "erotic age" finds its glorification, just as it is in Casanova's memoirs that it finds its definitive documentation. Not that the lasciviousness of Casanova's adventures can be lumped together in the same pot with Mozart's heavenly melodies; but both share a common ground and breathe the same air. The difference is that whereas with Casanova the spiritual is sensualized, with Mozart the sensual is made sublime.

Aram Bakshian Jr. (essay date 1978)

SOURCE: "Lorenzo Da Ponte: Mozart's Librettist," in *History Today,* Vol. XXVIII, No. 3, March, 1978, pp. 161-70.

[*In the following excerpt, Bakshian surveys Da Ponte's career.*]

On June 4th, 1805, the Transatlantic packet *Columbia,* fifty-seven days out of London, cast anchor in the harbour of Philadelphia. Included in the otherwise routine cargo of the *Columbia* was a distinguished if slightly threadbare Italian gentleman in his late middle years. Tall, with aquiline features and an oddly distinctive gait, half strut, half shuffle, with shoulders thrown back and chest thrust out, 'Signor Da Ponte' spoke fluent if heavily accented English with a slight lisp. When not speaking, his tight-lipped, feline smile concealed the fact that he was completely toothless. Like so much else connected with this newest immigrant to America, even the loss of his teeth had come about in a novel way—the result, according to their former owner, of poison administered by a jealous rival during one of his many love affairs in Vienna where he had briefly flourished as a Habsburg court poet.

The port official who examined Signor Da Ponte's meagre customs declaration (a violin, a tea urn, a carpet, a trunk of books and 'one box of fiddle strings and suspenders') can scarcely have suspected that this scanty inventory was all that remained of the European career and fortune of Mozart's greatest librettist, the artist who created the poetic and theatrical backdrops for the master's ***Marriage of Figaro, Così Fan Tutte*** and the work that many musicologists still consider the perfect opera, ***Don Giovanni.*** . . .

It was hardly an auspicious beginning; yet, at the age of fifty-six, Lorenzo Da Ponte, former Venetian Jew, renegade Catholic Priest, Viennese poet and English impresario, was about to launch a new career in the new world—a peripatetic and occasionally star-crossed thirty-three years which would see him become, among other things, a grocer, a distiller, a memoirist and one of the most important pioneers of Italian linguistic and literary studies in American academic life.

Da Ponte's memoirs alone, which some critics have compared favourably with those of his old friend and occasional fellow-swindler, Giacomo Casanova, entitle him to more lasting fame than has fallen his lot; but, even if he had died on the voyage to Philadelphia, his work as the most inspired (though strictly businesslike) collaborator of Mozart would have guaranteed him his permanent niche in the history of opera.

The preface to the posthumous 1860 Paris edition of Da Ponte's memoirs sums up both the character of the man and his opus with typical Gallic verve and contempt for foreign orthography:

> Here are the most original and anecdotal artistic Italian memoirs ever to be offered to a curious public. The memoirs of Benvenuto Cellini are neither more naif nor more amusing. In his memoirs, D'Aponte (sic) is as much of a writer as his compatriot Goldoni, as frivolously amusing as the Count de Grammont, as adventurous as Gil Blas, as droll as Figaro and as hapless as Gilbert.

All of which was, to a remarkable degree, true. . . .

[Da Ponte had arrived in Venice] in early 1782, just in time to have a private interview with Pietro Metastasio, the venerable Imperial Laureate. According to Lorenzo, the aged Laureate was enchanted with some of his verse, and we will have to take his word for it since no one else was present at the interview and Metastasio died shortly afterwards. He also met Salieri who expressed interest in

collaborating with Da Ponte on an opera.

But by far the most important acquaintance Da Ponte made at this time was the Emperor Joseph himself. Perhaps the most intelligent of all the Habsburgs, Joseph was a genuine intellectual with a well-developed artistic sense, and an enthusiastic love of music. Without the eccentricity of a Ludwig of Bavaria or the egomania of a Louis XIV, he was the ideal patron for a clever, gifted artist like Da Ponte. Emperor and poet seem to have hit it off immediately; even allowing for exaggeration on Da Ponte's part, it is a fact that so long as Joseph lived, Lorenzo was a significant figure in the artistic life of Vienna, and, soon after Joseph's death, the combination of jealous rivals, resentful court officials and his own excesses drove him from Vienna in eclipse. Da Ponte describes his first interview with the Emperor. He had never spoken to a monarch before, 'the cheery expression of his face, his suaveness of intonation, and above all the utter simplicity of his manner and his dress . . . not only restored my self-possession, but left me hardly aware that I was standing before an Emperor'. After a lengthy, pleasant conversation in which Joseph took his measure, he asked Da Ponte how many plays he had written:

> 'None, Sire.'

> 'Splendid! Splendid!' the Emperor replied smiling. 'We shall have a virgin muse.'

The initial result was *Rich for a Day,* a hastily-composed comic opera by Salieri with a hastily-written libretto by Da Ponte. It was neither quite a success nor quite a disgrace, and from it Lorenzo learned the crucial lesson that,

> . . . it was not enough to be a great poet to write a good play; that no end of tricks had to be learned—the actors, for instance, had to be studied individually so that their parts might fit; that one had to note the mistakes of others and one's own, and after two or three thousand booings, find some way to correct them. . . .

While Da Ponte studied and struggled to master the verbal side of opera, his future collaborator in greatness, Wolfgang Amadeus Mozart was contending with musical problems of his own. Although his German-language comic opera *Entführung aus dem Serail* had already been produced in Vienna with modest success in July 1782, Mozart still had to contend with the rivalry of other opera composers (including the officially-placed Salieri), and the Emperor's stubborn conviction that, while Mozart was a great composer of instrumental music, he was not cut out for the operatic genre ('Too fine for our ears, and an immense number of notes, my dear Mozart,' Joseph had commented after attending a performance of *Entführung*).

Thus it happened that the most brilliant composer of his generation and the ablest librettist of the time were thrown together by chance—because, ironically, both of them had time on their hands in the musical capital of the world. Mozart and Da Ponte met and agreed that an ideal vehicle for collaboration existed in the form of Caron de Beaumarchais' recent French comedy, *The Marriage of Figaro.* They were eager to work together, but there was a catch; the Emperor, very enlightened but even more despotic, had recently banned performance of the Beaumarchais play in Vienna as politically sensitive, with its thinly veiled attack on hereditary privilege. Mozart was convinced that Joseph would never consent to an operatic version of the banned play.

Da Ponte, who had a good deal of the fixer in his nature, was more sanguine. In the Spring of 1786 he convinced Mozart to join with him in creating an opera 'on speculation'—a tribute not only to Da Ponte's ability to inspire confidence as a librettist, but also to his plausibility as a salesman. In approximately two months of concentrated hard work (as usual, Lorenzo exaggerates, claiming in his memoirs that the work was done in six weeks) the manuscript was ready, and Da Ponte, going directly to the Emperor, made his pitch. When Joseph objected that he had already banned the Beaumarchais comedy, Da Ponte had an answer for him,

> . . . as I was writing a play to be set to music, and not a comedy, I have had to leave out many scenes and shorten many others, and I have eliminated whatever might offend the refinement and decorum of an entertainment at which Your Majesty presides. And as for the music, as far as I can judge, it is extraordinarily fine.

A copy of the score was then sent up to the palace, and Joseph, himself proficient at the harpsichord and cello, and quite a credible bass singer, immediately recognized the merit of the music. The opera was approved. Da Ponte's poetic gift had given Mozart a fine libretto; his diplomatic prowess saw it through to a performance. *Figaro* was such an enormous success that, as Michael Kelly, the Irish tenor who sang the roles of Don Curzio and Don Basilio, recalled in his own memoirs, 'at the end, I thought the audience would never have done applauding and calling for Mozart. Almost every piece was encored, which prolonged it nearly to the length of two operas, and induced the Emperor to issue an order on the second representation, that no piece of music should be encored.'

Mozart was well-launched as a master opera composer and Da Ponte as a master librettist. The reaction in Prague, the second city of the Habsburg realm, was even more enthusiastic, and when Mozart visited there at the beginning of 1787 he could write elatedly that, 'Here they talk of nothing else but—*Figaro!* The play, they sing, they whistle nothing but—*Figaro!*'

In his memoirs, Da Ponte himself is curiously modest about his role in the creation of the opera—but for essentially conceited reasons. His entire book is based on the assumption that *everything* about Da Ponte is interesting—not just the fact that on several occasions he happened to work with Mozart. Thus he dismisses his share of the triumph with acknowledgement that 'The libretto, too, was said to be beautiful. . . . '

But the triumph, however lightly he might shrug it off, led to further collaboration, and the greatest operatic achievement of Da Ponte's life—the libretto to ***Don Giovanni.*** Having agreed on the 'Don Juan' theme and informed the Emperor, Da Ponte went to work. His *modus operandi* had a distinctly Da Pontian flavour:

> I sat down at my table and did not leave it for twelve uninterrupted hours—a bottle of Tokay at my right, a box of Seville [snuff] to my left, in the middle an inkwell. A beautiful girl of sixteen—I should have prefered to love her only as a daughter, but alas!—was living in the house . . . and came to my room at the sound of the bell. To tell the truth the bell rang rather frequently, especially when I felt my inspiration waning.

Don Giovanni was rehearsed and produced in Prague. Da Ponte's old friend and fellow Venetian, Casanova—something of a Don Giovanni, himself—may have helped put a few finishing touches to the lyrics. This interesting possibility is backed up by at least one piece of physical evidence. Among the papers at the Castle of Dux, where Casanova spent his old age serving as librarian to Count Waldstein, were found notes in Casanova's hand rewriting parts of Act II of ***Don Giovanni.*** Considering Casanova's love life, he may have been brought into the project by Mozart and Da Ponte as a technical consultant.

The result, at any rate, was a resounding success in Prague. 'No one had ever before heard anything like it in this city,' a local newspaper declared. 'The unusually large audience applauded unanimously.' In Vienna, the opera was performed fourteen times and was reasonably well received, but the Emperor, while telling Da Ponte that he thought the work 'splendid,' added, 'but not for the likes of the Viennese'.

If the Viennese response to ***Don Giovanni*** was measured, history's has proven otherwise, and many great musicians of future generations would be inspired by this joint achievement of Mozart and Da Ponte. Tchaikovsky, to cite only one example, would write to his confidant, Frau von Meck, that, 'To me, the most beautiful opera ever written is ***Don Juan'.*** And Tchaikovsky's reasons were dramatic as well as musical. 'I am quite incapable of describing what I felt on hearing ***Don Juan,'*** he wrote, 'especially in the scene where the noble figure of the beautiful, proud, revengeful woman Donna Anna appears on the stage. Nothing in any opera ever impressed me so profoundly.'

One more collaboration remained for Da Ponte and Mozart, a frivolous eighteenth-century comedy theme with only six characters—***Così Fan Tutte,*** the tone of which might best be summed up by a few of Leporello's lines in Act I of ***Don Giovanni:***

> *A forza*
> *di chiacchiere, di vezzi e di bugie,*
> *ch'ho imparato si bene a star con voi,*
> *cerco d'intrattenerli.*

(With chattering
flattery and humbug,
which I've picked up so well in your
service, I tried to entertain them.)

Some Viennese were mildly shocked as well as entertained by *Così Fan Tutte* since the plot (a refined bit of what would today be called 'wife-swapping') bore a marked resemblance to a scandal that had recently shaken Viennese society. But, as the modern English music historian, Richard Rickett has written in his *Music and Musicians in Vienna*, 'From a purely musical point of view, *Così Fan Tutte* is arguably Mozart's finest opera,' and the late Sir Thomas Beecham once described the score as 'a long summer day spent in a cloudless land by a southern sea'.

Così Fan Tutte was produced on January 26th, 1790; in February Emperor Joseph died suddenly, and the artistic community in Vienna was turned upside down. Joseph's brother and successor, Leopold, had previously reigned as Archduke of Tuscany; he brought his own entourage to Vienna with him. In addition, many of Da Ponte's old enemies now united to pay off accumulated scores. Cabal was followed by counter-cabal, and Leopold at one point expressed his disgust with Da Ponte by exclaiming, 'To the Devil with this disturber of the peace!'

Ultimately, Lorenzo found himself out of funds and favour, and decided to decamp to Trieste, after asking an Italian friend for the loan of one hundred dollars. The answer was brief and to the point: 'My Dearest Da Ponte: To lend money is almost always to lose the money and the friend. I do not care to lose either. Good luck to you.' Da Ponte had the last word in his memoirs, however, noting of his fair-weather friend that, 'This good soul died young, and not in his bed,' which was Lorenzo's Italianate way of saying that the fellow was hanged by the Austrians in 1799.

Da Ponte's stay in Trieste is mainly remarkable for his meeting there with Ann Celestine Grahl, member of a Jewish family of chemists and moneylenders who had earned a fairly comfortable fortune discounting notes and dealing in drugs, spices and liquors. Twenty years younger than Lorenzo, Ann had been born in London and was a convert to Anglicanism. She was young, attractive and certainly much better off at the time than her ageing suitor, who was, by his own account, only one of several admirers. Da Ponte being Da Ponte, he carried the day and, on August 12th, the erstwhile priest and his pretty bride stepped into a calèche and set off on their honeymoon.

One of their first stops was at Dux, to visit Casanova, to whom Da Ponte may have introduced his bride as a mistress, for the sake of his reputation. The main purpose of the stop was to collect a few hundred florins owed by the senior to the junior scoundrel; but, not surprisingly, 'his purse was leaner than mine,' so all that the two exchanged during a four-day visit was reminiscences, some of which, in the form of excellent Casanovan anecdotes, found their

way into the pages of Da Ponte's memoirs. The old roué also gave Lorenzo a piece of valuable parting advice:

> . . . do not go to Paris—go to London . . . and when you get to London, never set foot inside the *Caffè degl' Italiani* and never sign your name to any bills!

'Happy me, had I religiously followed his advice!' a penitent Da Ponte would reflect in later years. He did follow it up to a point, however, settling in London in October 1792, where he spent, or misspent, the bulk of his remaining European years as a bookdealer, literary hack and theatrical impresario. It all ended in a desperate race to the gangplank of the packet *Columbia* in April 1805, one step ahead of the bailiffs, and the transatlantic voyage to rejoin his wife and growing family who had been shipped off to America in advance.

Despite occasional credit troubles, the Da Pontes (ultimately including two beautiful daughters, Louisa and Fanny, and two 'well-bred, well-mannered' sons, most of whom married well into socially prominent American families) flourished in America, though not before Lorenzo had tried his hand as a boarding house proprietor, a milliner, an itinerant pedlar, a licensed distiller, and had a few scrapes with the law. The two great achievements of his American years, however, dealt with his first love, words, in the form of teaching and writing.

Professor Arthur Livingston, who edited the first modern English translation of the Da Ponte memoirs, has admirably summed up Lorenzo's legacy as a teacher:

> There is no doubt at all that this [his teaching debut in New York in 1807] was an important moment for the American mind. Da Ponte made Europe, poetry, painting, music, the artistic spirit, classical lore, a creative classical education, live for many important Americans as no one, I venture, had done before. And his classical scholarship, his competence as a creative Latinist, dazzled quite as much as his fame as an Italian poet . . . A flare of real genius as a teacher Da Ponte had shown at Portogruaro and Treviso. Perhaps during this year, 1808, and again in the period of 1821 to 1826, Da Ponte was finding his real self. In my estimation it is a greater moment than his casual attachment to Mozart's fame. . . .

His teaching prowess ultimately won Lorenzo the appointment as Professor of Italian at Columbia University on September 5th, 1825, a title he retained until his death. The university still possesses an interesting portrait of Da Ponte in his old age, a pen clasped in his right hand and a classic folio in his left, his expression one of well-earned calm, as if he had finally found a place where he belonged.

Not content merely to teach existing Italian classics, Da Ponte also created one of his own during his American years. Although he may have begun work on his memoirs while still in Europe, the first edition was not published in America until 1823, supplementary editions or instalments appearing in 1826, 1827, 1829 and 1830. In 1830,

Clement C. Moore, author of "The Night before Christmas" and patron of Da Ponte in America.

at the age of eighty-one, he blithely announced that he was at work on yet another instalment, and there is still some doubt as to whether or not a 'lost' manuscript was written in his last years.

What has survived is quite enough, a masterpiece of mischief, good humour, grace, fact, invention and poetic licence—in short, a classic Italian (one had better say Venetian) memoir in the tradition of Casanova and Gozzi. If, like his two more illustrious compatriots, Da Ponte occasionally let malice or old grudges get the better of him in his account of events, he could well say, as Gozzi did in his *Useless Memoirs:*

> I have never singled out anyone for attack, apart from those who have directed attacks at me, and even then I have always used pleasantries of a moderate (sic) kind, not hurtful to their reputation.

If not true to the letter, this is certainly true to the spirit of Lorenzo Da Ponte. He died in New York in 1838 at the ripe old age of eighty-nine, and was buried in St John's Cemetery beside his beloved wife Ann, who had perished of pneumonia in 1831. Perhaps his most fitting epitaph could be drawn from the curtain lines of *Così Fan Tutte* which he had penned for his great collaborator, Mozart, almost half a century earlier:

> *Fortunato l'uom che prende*
> *Ogni cosi pel buon verso*

E tra i casi e le vicende
Da ragion guidar si fa.
Quel che suole altrui far piangere
Fai per lui cagion di riso
E del mondo in mezzo ai turbini
Bella calma trovera.

(Happy is the man who looks
At everything on the right side
And through trials and tribulations
Makes reason his guide.
What always makes another weep
Will be for him a cause of mirth
And amid the tempests of this world
He will find sweet peace.)

H. C. Robbins Landon (essay date 1985)

SOURCE: A foreword to *Lorenzo Da Ponte: The Life and Times of Mozart's Librettist* by Sheila Hodges, Universe Books, 1985, pp. ix-x.

[*In the excerpt below, Robbins Landon focuses upon the collaboration between Mozart and Da Ponte, noting that the story of the latter's extraordinary career arguably has more basis in fact than has been hitherto believed.*]

The collaboration between Wolfgang Amadeus Mozart and Lorenzo Da Ponte has often, and rightly, been compared to that between Richard Strauss and Hugo von Hofmannsthal; but whereas the latter collaboration is admirably documented, about the former we have only the tangible results in three of the greatest operas of all time—*Le nozze di Figaro, Don Giovanni* and *Così fan tutte.* But apart from this substantial and lamentable lacuna, we know quite a lot about the extraordinary Da Ponte, not least because of his fascinating memoirs, which he wrote in America when an old man. Many have seriously questioned the overall veracity of those memoirs: Da Ponte, it is asserted, has stretched the truth, tried to put himself in the best possible light, and so on. Recent research has, however, tended to show that Da Ponte was much more truthful than has been believed, and to illustrate the point, I would like to take the case of *Le nozze di Figaro.* Da

> **Steven Phillips on Da Ponte's foremost accomplishment:**
>
> Da Ponte, master craftsman and classicist, must have been pleased with *Così,* today generally considered the finest of his three efforts for Mozart. The plot was novel, if not entirely original, and amusing. Da Ponte observed all the rules of form and unity, restricting the cast to six characters, through which he created symmetry. Underlying the story is a moral of enlightenment, thoughtless idealism conquered by common sense.
>
> *Stephen Phillips, in* Opera News, *Vol. 46, February 27, 1982.*

Ponte describes the beginnings as follows:

> I set to work . . . , and as fast as I wrote the words, Mozart set them to music. In six weeks everything was in order. . . .

Naturally, it was seriously doubted that Mozart could have composed that very long opera—the printed score in the great new collection edition comprises 592 pages—in anything like six weeks. But the editor of that magnificent new edition, Ludwig Finscher, considers that, from information in Mozart's own letters and other authentic data (such as Mozart's own thematic catalogue, which contains many invaluable dates), it is likely that Mozart did indeed compose the 'short score' (i.e., without the instrumentation) within six weeks. The evidence of autograph manuscript—part of which belongs to the treasure trove recently rediscovered in Poland where it had been placed (in the Monastery of Grüssau, Silesia) for safekeeping by the German authorities in World War II—also confirms this almost incredible burst of enthusiasm and sheer hard work on Mozart's part (which resulted in headaches and stomach cramps, sure symptoms of nervous stress; see his letter of 14 January 1786).

We stress this rather pedantic affirmation of a small statement in Da Ponte's *Memoirs* simply to show that such a statement, even though unlikely when first considered, can be, and in this case has been, proved to be entirely accurate.

Da Ponte himself led a very unlikely life, moving from one country to another, often in circumstances less than pleasant, and ending his life as a respected and highly respectable Professor of Italian at Columbia University in New York. His life is fascinating, and it was high time that we had a new evaluation of this unbelievable man, whose achievements are considerable even apart from his connection with music's greatest genius. Da Ponte was a man of great subtlety and complexity. In *Figaro,* wrote the perceptive Hofmannsthal, there is "little to make one laugh and much to smile at': yes, indeed, and this wonderfully delicate pastel-like shade of colour is as much the merit of the libretto as the gift of the music that gave it life—a very *settecento* collaboration and result.

Sheila Hodges (essay date 1985)

SOURCE: An introduction and "Lorenzo Da Ponte," in *Lorenzo Da Ponte: The Life and Times of Mozart's Librettist,* Universe Books, 1985, pp. xi-xiv, 1-223.
[*Hodges is the author of a full-length, affirming biography of Da Ponte. In the following excerpt from that work, she favorably appraises Da Ponte's significance as a writer of libretti.*]

If, a century and a half after his death, Lorenzo Da Ponte could return to earth, it is likely that he would have mixed feelings about his twentieth-century image. First and foremost, though he would be astonished that the operas of Salieri, Martin y Soler and Winter, so famous in their

day, are now virtually forgotten, and the libretti which he wrote for them buried in the same grave of neglect, he would be immeasurably happy that, through his collaboration with Mozart, he has won the recognition for which he longed, and which he never found during his lifetime. In his memoirs and elsewhere he had much to say about the importance of the libretto in the success or otherwise of an opera, and he bitterly resented the low esteem in which the skilled librettist, as he knew himself to be, was held. So he would rejoice that today, wherever *Le nozze di Figaro, Don Giovanni* and *Così fan tutte* are performed, the name of Lorenzo Da Ponte is indissolubly linked with that of the genius whom he used to call 'the divine Mozzart'.

Nevertheless, it would grieve him that so little is remembered of his immense contribution to American culture during the thirty-three years which he spent in that country—through his dedicated teaching of Italian literature, through the many thousands of Italian books which he imported from Europe, and through his three valiant battles to establish Italian opera in the new world. All were of great and lasting importance in revealing to Americans the glorious literary and musical heritage of Italy, but, though during his lifetime they brought him the respect of a small yet important section of New York society, they have not given him the immortality which he felt to be his due.

Thirdly—and this would have produced thousands of words from his fluent and indignant pen—he would have been enraged at the comparison which is so often made between his life and memoirs and those of Casanova, with the scales of approval generally coming down on the side of the latter. Da Ponte has suffered much from posterity's view of him as a disreputable libertine, with a string of abandoned lady-loves in every town. In fact, apart from a short and extremely colourful period in Venice when he was still a young man, and again at the end of his Vienna period, his life was not that of an adventurer, if the word is taken to mean one who seeks adventures. By temperament and gifts a teacher whose great love for poetry, as he says, 'led him on a sudden to the dramatic field', through certain facets of his character—gullibility, vanity, the desire to be liked, a genuine wish to do everyone he met a good turn and (not least) his propensity to fall in love—for almost the whole of his eighty-nine years he was at the mercy of fate rather than in control of it, often tossed helplessly from adversity to adversity.

His life, like his nature, was full of contrasts and paradoxes, and this can be said too of the view which those who knew him or have written about him have formed of this elusive, gifted, fascinating man. Fausto Nicolini, joint editor of the standard Italian edition of the memoirs, described them as 'a jungle of lies, an apologia, coarse, badly strung together, unctuous, hypocritical, sentimental moralising', and, prejudiced and ill-judged though this comment is, nevertheless it reflects the opinion, less immoderately expressed, of other commentators. It is true that the accuracy of the memoirs cannot always be relied upon; like countless memoirists, Da Ponte prided himself overmuch on his excellent powers of recall, and with his lively mind, his black-and-white judgements of those who were for and those who were against him, and his skill in writing vivid dialogue, reconstructed from memory conversations which had, he claimed, taken place many years before. This is probably also true of some of the letters which he quotes verbatim, and which—if they ever existed—he would almost certainly have lost as he fled from the arms of the law or angry creditors. Later in life he wrote that he kept a scrapbook of notable things, but it is unlikely that he was able to carry many records from the past when he escaped to America. Equally, he is silent or untrustworthy about certain incidents which show him in a bad light. But the same accusation could be levelled at many other writers before and since—Rousseau, Cellini, Goldoni, Michael Kelly and Casanova amongst them— who are not scolded for their deviation from the exact truth. Often, when he is accused of inventing or exaggerating, careful examination of the documents shows that there is a solider basis for his narrative than he has been given credit for, and that, in the main, where it is possible to verify his statements the memoirs reflect the truth.

Karen Blixen wrote of the Africans whom she loved so dearly, 'They were never reliable, but in a grand manner sincere'; and though the word 'never' is much too harsh to apply to Da Ponte's memoirs, to some extent this is a just comment on their author. He was not a cheat or a liar, and was hurt, bewildered and outraged when he came across people who were, and who took advantage of his credulity. Testimonials from his contemporaries and from later writers bear witness to his sincerity, warmth of heart, generosity, and charity to those less fortunate than he was, even when his own fortunes were at a low ebb.

Nor, in general, are his courage and resilience sufficiently recognised. His long life took him successively to Venice in her last glittering years as a republic; to Vienna under the Emperor Joseph II, a brilliant centre of European culture to which many creative artists gravitated, and where the fight for imperial patronage was cut-throat and merciless; to the London of George III, bustling, elegant, yet in mortal terror of invasion by Napoleon; and finally to the new world, a land of scattered pioneers with little time as yet for the finer influences of European civilisation. In all four countries, each of them offering such a contrast to the others, he arrived a penniless fugitive, and everywhere, with optimism and enthusiasm, he built up a new life. Only in extreme old age, when the fame for which he longed began to seem unattainable, did despondence conquer—and even then never for long. Though the memoirs and his letters sometimes reflect a mood of defeat, his inextinguishable joy in life soon broke through; and the descriptions of his later years which have come down to us reflect a man who carried his immense vitality and exuberance to the end of his days.

Everywhere Da Ponte went he left traces of himself, above all in the state archives of Venice and Vienna and in the university libraries of the United States. Much of this material has appeared only in specialist journals in Italy and Austria; much has never been translated into English;

and a considerable amount—especially some of his American letters—has never been printed at all. Many of his libretti, too, are unfamiliar to those who have written about him. All this new material gives a very different picture from the one which is normally painted, showing Da Ponte as a man of erudition and talent, who produced some of the most skilful libretti that have ever been written, and who in his late years gained the respect and admiration of his contemporaries.

His memoirs, published between 1823 and 1830, provide the basis for any biography of Da Ponte; in addition, he wrote two short autobiographical forerunners, both published in America: ***Storia compendiosa della vita di Lorenzo Da Ponte,*** published in 1807 shortly after he reached New York, and ***An Extract from the Life of Lorenzo Da Ponte,*** which came out in 1819. Both are valuable sources of information. . . .

His libretti can be divided into four categories: translations, of which there are very few, and which are faithfully made; adaptations from 'straight' plays, especially those of Goldoni; adaptations from existing opera libretti; and original texts, which again constitute only a small part of his work. So by far the largest part of his output falls into the second and third classes, the adaptations. But nowhere does he slavishly copy, and often there is virtually no textual resemblance between the model and his libretto. His particular genius lies in his vast knowledge of classical and contemporary literature to which to go for his sources, his sense of stagecraft, his skill in turning prose into 'singable' verse, and his understanding of the relationship between words and music and of the music of words.

Da Ponte himself had strong views on this question of recourse to the work of earlier writers. In 1819 he wrote, 'If a writer of a theatrical piece does not deserve to be praised, or even noticed, when the subject of his composition is known, what praise is due to Shakespeare for all the pieces taken by him from Boccaccio, and Bandello's novels; what praise to Voltaire for his Merope; to Alfieri for his Antigone; to Metastasio for his Semiramide; to Monti for his Aristodemo, and to all those poets who, in common with them, not only wrote tragedies and dramas on well known subjects, but wrote them after having seen the performances of pieces on the same subjects?'

Also of crucial importance—and this is another reason why he is one of the greatest librettists who have ever lived—was his versatility. Opera at this time was sharply divided between *opera seria,* the older form, and *opera buffa,* which had developed as a reaction against *opera seria.* The composers and poets who worked within the earlier genre chose classical and mythological subjects, almost always with a Greek or Roman theme; emotions were formalised, ensembles were rare, and arias and *recitativo secco* (accompanied only by harpsichord or piano) predominated. *Opera buffa,* on the other hand, developed into a kind of social comedy, reflecting everyday life and characters whom the audience would recognise from their own experience. Aria and recitative were much more closely related, one leading naturally into the other, and the arias were more varied than was possible in *opera seria*. Da Ponte, with his quick wit, his ability to adapt to his ambience, the need to be liked which was always so strong a part of his nature, possessed a chameleon quality that enabled him to turn—as few other librettists were able to do—from the high tragedy and drama of *opera seria,* where gods and men lived within a close relationship and men were required to show themselves at their most heroic, to the domesticity of everyday life, and to plots concerned with intrigue, star-crossed lovers, stern fathers, jealous husbands and pretty chambermaids. . . .

Da Ponte was a complex man, full of contradictions, considerably larger than life, and perhaps influenced by his Jewish heritage to a far greater extent than he himself realised, or than he would have wished others to believe. Of himself he wrote, in his account of the Montresor venture:

> I believe that my heart is made of a different stuff from that of other men. A noble act, generous, benevolent, blinds me. I am like a soldier who, spurred by the longing for glory, rushes against the mouth of the cannon; like an ardent lover who flings himself into the arms of a woman who torments him. The hope of giving, *post funera,* immortality to my name, and of leaving to a nation which I revere a memory of me which will not be ignoble; the sweet allurement of arousing feelings of gratitude and goodwill in those who follow an art that was not disgraced by my pen; the desire to awaken love for the beautiful language which I brought to America, and love too for our ravishing music; the longing to see once again on the American stage some of the children of my youthful inspiration, which are still remembered in the theatres of the Thames, the Danube and the Elbe; and, finally, a sweet presentiment of joy, encouragement and honour, based on the integrity of my actions, the reliability of my promises and the happy success of a well-organised spectacle, were the powerful spurs which goaded me to this delightful undertaking, and from which nothing, so far, has succeeded in deterring me. I dreamt of roses and laurels; but from the roses I had only thorns, and from the laurels bitterness! So goes the world!

But in the end Da Ponte, librettist and teacher of genius, dedicated scholar, eloquent champion of his mother country, has found the immortality for which he craved; for as long as the operas of Mozart are performed Da Ponte, too, will be honoured.

April FitzLyon (review date 1985)

SOURCE: "Countering the Rumours," in *The Times Literary Supplement,* No. 4316, December 20, 1985, p. 1459.

[FitzLyon is the author of a biography of Da Ponte, The Libertine Librettist *(1957). In the following excerpt from a review of Sheila Hodges more recent biography, she provides a succinct overview of Da Ponte's accomplishment, concluding with a negative assessment of the* Memoirs.]

Lorenzo da Ponte has two considerable titles to fame: his collaboration with Mozart, when he was in his late thirties; and his self-appointed mission to introduce Italian culture to America, which he pursued with considerable energy and success from the age of seventy until his death at eighty-nine. . . .

Da Ponte's stay in Vienna, where Joseph II supported him, was the highlight of his career. He was poet to the Imperial Theatres, and his libretti for Salieri, for some other now-forgotten composers and for Mozart were a great success. At the time, he considered Martìn y Soler to be the greatest of these composers; but he later realized his mistake, and said of himself and Mozart, arrogantly but prophetically, "We are eternal". The few recorded facts about this collaboration are very well known; what we don't know is to what extent Mozart controlled and influenced his poet; judging from some of da Ponte's other libretti, it was probably a good deal. Be that as it may, *Le nozze di Figaro, Don Giovanni* adn *Così fan tutte* remain some of the best libretti ever written.

In America, da Ponte had a hard time; theatre poets were not much in demand when he arrived there in 1805. He had outlived his epoch, and entered a new civilization. But his desire to teach Americans to appreciate everything Italian, his zest and energy, and his real gifts as a teacher eventually won through. Not only was he made the first professor of Italian at Columbia College (now University), but it was due to his efforts that the first Italian Opera House was built in New York (1833). He had become a venerable and much appreciated old scholar; in order to maintain that reputation, and to counter unfortunate rumours about him spread by other Italian immigrants, between 1823 and 1830 da Ponte published his very unreliable memoirs. Much less diverting than those of his crony, Casanova, and very inferior to those of his contemporaries and compatriots, Goldoni and Carlo Gozzi, they tell us little of what we want to know—about Mozart, for example—and much that we could dispense with.

Luigi Sera (essay date 1990)

SOURCE: "Trans-Pontem: A Bridging between Europe and America by Lorenzo Da Ponte," in *Proceedings of the American Philosophical Society,* Vol. 135, No. 3, September, 1991, pp. 388-400.
[In the following essay, originally a paper read before the American Philosophical Society in 1990, Sera draws upon the Memoirs *and other sources in an "attempt to show how Lorenzo Da Ponte established a relevant link between Europe, and especially Italy, on one side, and the United States on the other."]*

The extraordinary human and literary experience of Lorenzo Da Ponte, experience eminently transversal and multifaceted, has already been for a long time the object of studies which, although numerous, often repeated one another. Until about ten years ago, with few exceptions, the figure and the work of Lorenzo Da Ponte have been flattened on the writing of Mozart's librettos and on a reductive homologation to eighteenth-century adventurism and libertinism. The publication in 1985 of the excellent work by Sheila Hodges, *Lorenzo Da Ponte: The Life and Times of Mozart's Librettist,* and the two conferences on Da Ponte held at Columbia University (1988) and in Vittorio Veneto (1989) have cast a new and more comprehensive light on the man from Ceneda. These recent studies by scholars in various fields from literary criticism to musicology, from biography to linguistics, by filling an excessively lacunose and at times superficial knowledge of Lorenzo Da Ponte, have recognized, by means of arguments of highly speculative and scientific dignity, the autonomous importance of Da Ponte's work. It seems that all that could be investigated has been investigated, but, in our time of late modernity, hermeneutics gives itself as a spy, ephemeral and vacillating, of textual and ontological complexities that are inexhaustible. In particular, the role and the function of Lorenzo Da Ponte in mediating Europe and its culture with the young American nation still offer room for new interpretations. This paper will attempt to show how Lorenzo Da Ponte established a relevant link between Europe, and especially Italy, on one side, and the United States on the other.

"Very little had I brought with me from London: a box of violin strings, a number of Italian classics of scant worth, several copies of a very fine Virgil, several of Davila's *History,* and from forty to fifty dollars in cash" writes Lorenzo in his **Memoirs,** making an inventory of what he had brought with him on his journey to America from which he would not return. In retrospect, the inventory makes itself to be read as a program of Da Ponte's existence in the New World, an existence under the banner of a predilection for music and literature, reified as average consumer goods for the modern civil society. The violin strings and the tomes of classics stand out on the vessel *Columbia* commanded by Abissay Hayden, "harpooner of whales," as degraded metonymies, as Platonic simulacra of a culture that has lost the statute of the perennial values and of the emancipating and progressive functions.

The eighteenth century had just ended. It had been a century of "magic and dazzling beauties, of extraordinary artists, of luminous and thundering ideologies, but also of violence, and of collective and individual tragedies, of wars and revolution" (L. Villari).

It had been the century of Arcadia and of the melodrama, of Goldoni and Mozart, of Tiepolo and Hogarth, of Newton and Kant, of the *Encyclopédie* and of Rousseau, of economists, jurists, travelers, memorialists, of Freemasonry, of the enlightened princes, of the Seven Years' War, of the American Independence, and of the French Revolution. It had been the century of the "crise de la conscience européenne" (P. Hazard), of the beginning of the Italian diaspora, of the "Italy outside Italy" (F. Venturi). It had been the century of what, in the conscience of many contemporaries, was felt as modernity.

Which was the actual encounter that Lorenzo Da Ponte

had with America? What kind of rapport did he interlace with the places of the New World, oscillating between utopia and hyperreality, archaic and modern, that literatus who had personally known the most sophisticated social and artistic milieux of Europe—from Venice, lively and resplendent in its twilight, to the elegant Vienna of the Hapsburgs, to the dynamic London of George III—who had worked in close contact with Mozart and other major composers and who, now that he was fifty-six, had on his shoulders a multiple existence of adventures and alternate situations?

The America in which Da Ponte landed was already a country institutionally set but still unresolved whether to opt for an economy predominantly agricultural, as Thomas Jefferson recommended, or mainly industrial, as it would happen in accordance with the program of Alexander Hamilton outlined in the famous "Report on Manufactures." At any rate, by then the ideology of an America, locus of natural simplicity and innocence of customs, nation of the palingenesis for the humanity of the future, had faded.

Throughout the eighteenth century, a plethora of dreams and utopias had nurtured the European *imaginaire.* Searching for happiness, an aspiration that had become philosophically legitimate, the European conscience discovered that it was divorced from itself and fragmented. It invented "elsewhere," the Golden Ages and the Arcadias irremediably lost because of the corrupting effects of civilization, as it was said then, or, as it is often said today, because of the effects of the continuous wars and famines, and because of the tiredness of a millenarian social organization, still mostly feudal. The apocalyptic idea of a *Mundus novus* or *novissimus* that would have, in time, supplanted the Old World had reemerged together with the gnostic concept of *ab oriente lux* interpreted as a symbol of the civilizations which follow the course of the sun, rising in the orient and moving toward the occident. Also in Italy many thinkers, writers, and travelers had narrated an America inhabited by strong and peaceful men, respectful of their peers, strenuous defenders of civic virtues and republican liberties. The American fashion had, moreover, crystallized the "Pensilvano" that would have been endowed with the innocence and industriousness of the Indians and the wisdom and temperance of the Quakers. In those ahistorical figurations, Philadelphia, with its etymology, evoked the actualizing of William Penn's Quaker project and of Benjamin Franklin's practical philosophy. At the turn of the century, however, the propaganda of the American utopia lost its appeal because the French Revolution and the Napoleonic "liberation" had shattered the ideals of equality and liberty. The young American nation watched from afar Napoleon's rise and the unending fight between England and France. On the other hand, the wars in Europe that committed the naval forces of the belligerent countries allowed the United States to become the greatest neutral maritime power and to start profitable trading, especially on the Pacific routes.

When Lorenzo Da Ponte arrived in 1805, Philadelphia, with its 68,000 inhabitants and an annual increase of 5 percent, was the most populous city in the United States. The city was still wearing the patriotic and civic halo of the former capital where the Declaration of Independence had been pronounced and the Constitution had been promulgated. It was an urban community of merchants, sailors, and shipbuilders involved in maritime activities that were at the acme. Called the Athens of America, it was the seat of the renowned American Philosophical Society. It boasted a public library, an art museum, a museum of natural history, bookstores, hotels, restaurants, theaters, and circuses. Between the Delaware River and Logan Square, houses were one next to the other with characteristic red bricks and white fences. Merchants and artisans lived above their stores and shops, and people of every social extraction inhabited totally integrated neighborhoods. There were private schools, elementary and secondary, for every religious group, and the University of Pennsylvania. The city had escaped the scourge of slavery, and every job was salaried. The census of 1790 registered fewer than 300 slaves for all Pennsylvania, and that of 1820 listed 3

slaves in Philadelphia and 4 in the suburbs. About 8,000 African-Americans were living in an environment free of racial tensions.

Although Da Ponte did not keep a good memory of his experiences in Philadelphia, the city was often a place of reference for him. He landed there after his uncomfortable Atlantic crossing, opened in it a millinery shop, traveled to and from it 72 times during his residence in Sunbury, and moved to it in August 1818.

> My intention was to settle there with my family and spread the language and literature of my country. . . . I began negotiations with the foremost men of letters . . . and with the directors of the public library, proposing that they buy books. . . . I offered a few books . . . through which a sample might be had of such beautiful literature.

Despite the strong support of Zaccheus Collins, a trustee of the Old Library Company and a prominent member of the American Philosophical Society, Da Ponte could not realize his projects. "I concluded that Philadelphia either did not care, or else was not able, to appreciate. . . . "

In April 1819, at the urging of Clement C. Moore, Da Ponte returned permanently to "the noble, populous, and . . . beloved, city of New York," concluding his American peregrinations which had taken him from his original settling in New York (1805) to Elizabethtown, NJ (1805-07), New York (1807-11), and Sunbury (1811-18). During these years, he embarked upon various business enterprises, including teaching, bookselling, running grocery stores and an emporium, trading in liquors and medicinals, land owning and farming, participating in a distillery partnership, and even attempting a trucking and carriage business. Embracing this range of enterprises, he showed the quintessential eighteenth-century disposition that had been made dignified and central by the figure of the *marchand philosophe.*

In the **Memoirs,** Da Ponte vividly details persons and places of the time he spent in Sunbury, when he extended his American experience beyond the merely urban. He spent almost eight years in that outpost of the Westward Movement that, in a few decades, would colonize and transform the immense territory extending to the Pacific. Lorenzo, who had been an Arcadian in Gorizia with the name of Lesbonico Pegasio, describes the environs of Sunbury on the banks of the Susquehanna River in—for him unusual—inspired terms, perhaps responding to nascent romantic sensibilities that were manifesting themselves in the contemporary writings of the American Transcendentalists. A prime example, of course, is the "pathetic fallacy," the sentiment of an infinite nature, as background to human emotions, which it absorbs and echoes. R. W. Emerson and H. Thoreau were singing nature on those modulations. Later, the Hudson River School took to the so-called luminescent style of representing light, piercing through clouds and forests, creating effects of mysterious atmospheres and impending events.

Holograph of a letter of Da Ponte.

One arrives at the foot of a mountain. . . . The roadsides are garlanded with bushes, shrubs and trees of every sort, splendid among which is an incredible quantity of wild laurel. . . . Brooks, cascades of water, hillocks, precipices, masses of white rock and multiform clumps of trees stretch away into two broad and deep valleys. . . . Here and there are little cottages, shepherds' cabins . . . and amid no end of deer, wild boars, partridges, pheasants . . . wolves, foxes, bears, and rattlesnakes, which . . . though they rarely attack the wayfarer, add nevertheless a certain delightful terror, a certain touch of solemnity, to that majestic solitude.

It is a "Symphony of the New World" composed by Lorenzo Da Ponte rather than by Antonin Dvorak, in honor of a landscape oblivious to history and inhabited until a few decades before only by Indians, similar to the places described by J. Fenimore Cooper, a New York acquaintance at the time Da Ponte was revising and publishing his autobiography.

What does Da Ponte's style reveal? In his *Memoirs,* he uses a language that, although interspersed with frequent Latin and Toscan idioms, shows lexical and syntactic simplicity. "I . . . deliberately chose a style that was simple, easy, natural, without affectations or flourishes." Rather than a fossil language, made such by long years of residence in foreign countries, Da Ponte's language is a relevant testimonial of a linguistic koine for a new and expanded public of readers that keeps the traces of the lingua franca of melodrama and opera.

An analysis of the structure of the *Memoirs* asks for the investigation of influences and the ascertainment of some theories. In such a way, it could be noted that J.-J. Rousseau, whose works Da Ponte frequented in the time of his teaching in Treviso, proudly had said, reflecting a new generally held view, that the obscure history of his own soul would be more interesting than that of the kings if only he could think more and better than they. Such a radical psychological change brought forth a reshaping of the narrative techniques and a democratization of the subject matter that entitled everybody to speak of himself. The passage from aristocratic to bourgeois autobiography took place by emphasizing the common man and his attributes which became something to be shown instead of dissimulated. As a consequence, the autobiography, by losing its character of exemplar, emerged as contiguous to the novel. Particularly, in the Venetian memoirs of L. Da Ponte, C. Goldoni, C. Gozzi, G. Casanova, the mobile subject/character that replaced the epical hero lived in the "immediacy of the present," as G. Poulet said referring specifically to Casanova, and moved in a time similar to the "time of adventure" that M. Bachtin detects in the Greek and Baroque novel. Da Ponte's autobiography, that shows a time dimension regulated around the author's events, also reflects the topoi of melodrama with which he had a proven rhetorical familiarity. Regarding this point, P. Brooks has said, quite convincingly, that the rise of modern melodramatic imagination conjures a structural collapse and failure of the numinous, the sacred, the supernatural of classical literatures by restricting the cos-

mic drama to the private and ordinary daily existence of the individual person.

More complex is the resolution, if a resolution has to be found, of the rapport *auctor/agens* which for some critics is irrelevant, while for others it must be maintained in the form of a strong author/character identity as outlined by P. Lejeune in his study of the "pacte autobiographique."

Rather than a "récit de carrière," a narration of a career, the existence of Lorenzo Da Ponte as recounted in his *Memoirs* appears as an imposed career, "una carriera subita" (F. Fido). "I was, therefore, trained after the manner of the priests, though inclined by taste and made by nature for different pursuits." By necessity, concealment is a defense. "Chi son io tu non saprai" (Who I am you will not know) says Don Giovanni/Da Ponte, wearing the mask that allows the change of identity and soul for an escape into fantasy while inviting the observer to inquire and discover. The man born in Ceneda in 1749 to a Jewish family found his original name Emanuele Conegliano changed to that of Lorenzo Da Ponte, the name of the bishop who baptized him when he was fourteen years old. " . . . [He is] the man *sine nomine* . . . professor *sine exemplo* . . . [Da Ponte's] self-portrait is constitutionally that of the man without."

The doxa of adventurer and libertine, expressed in terms of scandal and disapproval, has reduced and made opaque for a long time the collective works and experiences of Da Ponte. It goes back to the times of F. De Sanctis and G. Carducci and found a particularly biased condification in F. Nicolini, who while consecrating the literary fame of Da Ponte with the inclusion of his *Memoirs* in the famous Laterza collection *Scrittori d'Italia,* wrote" . . . there were [in him] a Jewish-priestly unctuousness and hypocrisy." In regard to this, quite appropriately, it has been recently written:

> That of Nicolini is the classic moralistic prejudice, to which perhaps racist connotations are not alien. . . . A deeper study, and not biased, of Da Ponte's biography brings today the majority [of scholars] to consider disproportionate the definition of adventurer and partially acceptable that of libertine, with a prevailing emphasis, for the latter, on the politico-philosophical connotation.

"An archetype of the Italian intellectual emigration to America" (P. M. Pasinetti), Da Ponte belonged to that diaspora, that destinal emigration elected for moral or intellectual reasons when most Italian states were governed by despotic or foreign monarchs, or simply for a longing to visit new places and mix in new societies, that started in the 1700s. Then, a constellation of Italian writers multiplied travels and social contacts, experiences and writings throughout Europe and also across the Atlantic. They were all from the peculiar entity that was Italy before the Unification, a nation-culture that had existed for centuries before it became a nation-state, and that through its expatriates and emigrants expressed an homogeneous cultural influence in the fields of arts, architecture, sciences, and jurisprudence of various countries of the West.

When, after his disastrous experiences in Pennsylvania, Da Ponte moved back permanently to New York in 1819, the city was set in the tumultuous expansion that in a few years would make it a financial and cultural magnet. Having lost its provincialism, it was looking openly and in a cleverly acquisitive way to European culture and arts. "My feet were treading once more the stones of this blessed city to me so dear." After his return to New York, until his death in 1838, Da Ponte glowed in a city where culture was establishing itself according to recognizable statutes and found cohesiveness and steadiness of purpose. Although in all his life, except for his short-lived Rousseauianism in Treviso, Da Ponte did not display interest in the political and social programs that brought to an end the "ancien régime," in New York he found a cause in publicly defending Italy and the Italians from the violent attack, headlined in the New York press, that, in connection with the celebrated divorce of the king and queen of England, the lawyer and councilman C. Phillips brought against practically everything Italian. As the oldest and most visible of the Italians in New York, Da Ponte felt that he had to intervene personally to dispel these denigrations. To this purpose, he rented a public lecture room where he delivered his "Apologetical Discourse on Italy" to an audience of more than 200 persons that the daily newspaper *Columbia* described as "one of the most numerous assemblages of wit and fashion which ever graced a lecture room in this city."

Da Ponte kept his pace to the frenzied rhythm of the city by corresponding and writing catalogues, memories, pamphlets, and lyrics, and by teaching hundreds of students— he was the first professor of Italian at Columbia College—importing thousands of books, promoting Italian opera. He was by then comforted by the ever-loyal and affectionate friendship of the Moores and the Livingstons; honored among the fashionable society; well acquainted with literati and intellectuals such as Washington Irving, Fitz-Greene Halleck, J. Fenimore Cooper, Henry W. Longfellow, Gulian Verplanck, Samuel Morse, John Francis, Pietro Maroncelli. In the last twenty years of his life, spent in New York, he was saddened by the death of two of his children and of his beloved wife, and he experienced the fatal advance of old age, but he kept busy to the very end. During this time, his involvement with theatrical enterprises was notable.

After the 1825 tournée of Manuel Garcia, considering that the times were ripe for Italian opera in America, he arranged the coming from Venice of his niece Giulia, who sang as prima donna in his revised "pasticcio" *Ape musicale,* set in the "Isole Fortunate," a clear metaphor for the island of Manhattan. Later he brought from Bologna the Montresor Company. Both ventures ended in disappointments and financial losses. Yet undaunted, at the age of eighty-four, he raised large funds among his wealthy friends and succeeded in establishing, at the cost of $150,000, the Italian opera house that was, according to the former mayor of the city, Philip Hone, "the neatest and most beautiful theater in the United States, and unsurpassed in Europe." After a year, the excessive costs of production and maintenance doomed Da Ponte's last attempt for success in the contemporary world of music and theater, but, thanks to him, the seeds of opera in America were planted. Despite the financial failures, these operatic ventures brought him considerable pleasure. In remembering Da Ponte, thirty years after his death, Henry T. Tuckerman wrote: "Some of our citizens yet describe his . . . handsome face at the opera . . . infecting others with enthusiasm, and serving as a vital bond between the musical strangers and the fascinated public."

In his last years, Da Ponte corresponded extensively with various persons in Italy, lamenting the disproportion between what he had done for the arts and the diffusion of Italian culture in America, and his present neglected condition, but this time his complaining was devoid of basis, at least partially, considering the affectionate care bestowed upon him at all times by his family and friends. When Lorenzo Da Ponte died, a few months before his ninetieth birthday, a large assembly of friends, former students, artists, and well-known representatives of the cultural establishment paid tribute to him with solemn obsequies and a large procession to the Roman Catholic cemetery on Second Avenue. Like Mozart, however, he was buried in an anonymous grave. The cemetery fell into disuse in 1851; to date, Da Ponte's remains have not been located.

Besides achieving an independently important position in the field of literature, Lorenzo Da Ponte, "a man considerably larger than life," has also achieved a definite recognition as a bearer and mediator of culture. The recognition of Da Ponte as a carrier of culture and precursor of Italian studies in America is supported by several authoritative sources of wide range, in time and personalities. On this occasion, one should like to quote Henry J. Anderson who, introducing Da Ponte to John Vaughan, president of the American Philosophical Society, in September 1829 wrote:

> Mr. Da Ponte is so well known in the literary world that I hardly think it necessary to speak to you of his professional qualifications. It is sufficient to say that he holds the highest rank among the literary men of Italy altho' so much of his life has been spent out of his native country. As an experienced and now veteran instructor, he still enjoys the honorable reputation of standing foremost alike in extent of literary acquirements and in ardent devotedness to the cause of Letters . . . An Apostle of the *bell' idioma.* . . .

And significantly, Clement C. Moore wrote: "So long as there remains a spark of taste among us for belles lettres, the name of Da Ponte will be held in veneration." Moreover, the first estimator of Da Ponte who was not his contemporary, Arthur Livingston, wrote: "There is no doubt at all that this was an important movement for the American mind. Da Ponte made Europe, poetry, painting, music, the artistic spirit, classical lore, a creative classical education, live for many important Americans as no one, I venture, had done before."

According to Sheila Hodges, Da Ponte was " . . . the indefatigable pioneer who gave to Americans an awareness of the literary and musical heritage of his native land, opening their eyes to splendors they had never seen or dreamt of before."

The man from Ceneda, twice diasporic, had lived in the Europe of the Age of Reason and in the America of the first democratic and pluralistic experiment without partaking of the fundamental ideologies of the Enlightenment and Romanticism. He had come from the Venice of the 1700s, par excellence *antiAufklärung,* city of carnivals and theaters, masks and libertines, where the least Italianate art was produced with the colorism of Canaletto, Longhi, Tiepolo and the desperate intellectualism of Guardi, where the funerary art of the neoclassic Canova was giving itself as a viaticum for the Angst of death. Venice the Oriental, metaphor by antiphrasis of the civilization of Italy, Abendland, Hesperia, land of the Occident, both marked by time and decline, where memories, traces, signs display the same motif of lucid distrust in reason and manifest the need to embellish, adorn, decorate the reasoning by aiming at the eccentric, the artificial, the spectacular. City where the mask is a device to transcend the internal "phantasma" and where modernity is already present in the eighteenth century with its apperceptions of transition, remembrance and ruin. Da Ponte in Philadelphia, Sunbury, New York brought with him the signs of the ancient wounds of the two imposed abjurations and asked for himself a normality that would always be denied to him, despite the normality of his human condition, recognized and accepted by today's standards, of being a traveler in time and an immigrant in the future, predecessor and posthumous of himself. In his experiences as a writer and as a man in the young America, rich of lures but also of defeats, land of hyperreality and of doing more than of *pietas* and being, Da Ponte revealed a submission to destiny that makes him common to the majority of the humans, and worthy of affection for his availability to be in the world and of the world. In America, Da Ponte embarked himself on commercial enterprises for which he felt the attraction of the new "homo americanus" who believes that everything is limitlessly possible. Like many who believed in the "American dream," he met the hard clog of the competition and of the economic cycles, and the failure behind the door, but as few did, he found in literature an energetic resource for renewed illusions and projects. With the passing of time, the distance between Da Ponte, cosmopolitan and eighteenth-century literatus, and the hosting country that has abandoned the egalitarian and universal ideals of the beginnings and has discovered its "unicity" and hegemonic vocation, becomes bigger and bigger. Having survived a time

definitely past, while he gathers one material failure after another, Da Ponte attains the ultimate success of an existence intensely lived until the very end and made glorious by a varied and light literature that offers itself as a dream and document of vanished graces and of modern and transient macrorealities. An authentic bridge between Europe and America, the figure and work of Lorenzo Da Ponte still transport across time and distance Venetian and Viennese levities and American intimations of a new modernity.

Further Reading

Biography

FitzLyon, April. *The Libertine Librettist: A Biography of Mozart's Librettist Lorenzo da Ponte.* New York: Abelard-Schuman, 1957.

    Detailed, informative biography.

Criticism

Mandel, Oscar. "Mozart, Da Ponte, and *Don Giovanni o il dissoluto punito,*" in *The Theatre of Don Juan: A Collection of Plays and Views, 1630-1963,* edited by Oscar Mandel, pp. 278-83. Lincoln: University of Nebraska Press, 1963.

    Short history of the collaboration of Mozart and Da Ponte upon *Don Giovanni,* recounting the opera's progress and first performance. Writing of Mozart, Mandel concludes, "The point that his music is perfect while Da Ponte's libretti are merely agreeable does not need to be labored; still, the two men, one a king and the other a vassal, were inhabitants of the same moral and intellectual realm."

Oulibicheff, Alexander. "An Imaginary Conversation between Mozart and Da Ponte." In *The World Treasury of Grand Opera: Its Triumphs, Trials and Great Personalities,* edited by George R. Marek, pp. 286-94. New York: Harper & Brothers, 1957.

    Reprints an imaginary conversation between Mozart and Da Ponte, with the two discussing a pending collaboration and each preening his own genius.

Rickett, Richard. "Wolfgang Amadeus Mozart." In his *Music and Musicians in Vienna,* pp. 14-30. Vienna: Georg Prachner Verlag, 1973.

    Contains dismissive comments concerning "a certain Lorenzo da Ponte," who is portrayed, in his collaborations with Mozart, as a scapegrace and a rascal.

Charles Dickens

Hard Times for These Times

The following entry presents criticism of Dickens's novel *Hard Times* (1854). For a discussion of Dickens's complete career, see *NCLC*, Volume 3.

INTRODUCTION

Perhaps the least-known of all Dickens's novels, *Hard Times* is a social-protest novel which attempts to lay bare the malignant impact of nineteenth-century industrial society upon the people living in English factory towns. It was poorly received upon its publication in hard cover and has been often overlooked in critical surveys of Dickens's works; still, *Hard Times* has acquired a growing critical following in the mid to late twentieth century, largely because of critical remarks by three key commentators.

Biographical Information

In early 1854, Dickens sought for ideas for a long story to be run in the magazine he edited, *Household Words*, which faced a shrinking circulation and falling profits. After some thought, he settled upon his theme: the condition of English factory life and its effects upon the laborers who were the victims of its unfairness, squalor, danger, and exhausting boredom. The idea for his yet-unwritten novel "laid hold of me by the throat in a very violent manner," Dickens wrote, and he vowed, in writing *Hard Times,* "to strike the heaviest blow in my power" for the English industrial worker. Having traveled to Preston in late January to experience life in an industrial city then in the midst of a twenty-three-week textile strike and having read of labor conditions in Manchester (upon which he modelled his Coketown), Dickens began writing his novel. *Hard Times* appeared in weekly installments in *Household Words* between April and August, a labor which left Dickens "three parts mad, and the fourth delirious, with perpetual rushing" but which also doubled (by one estimation, quadrupled) the circulation of *Household Words*. Exhausted upon finishing the novel in mid July, Dickens spent several days drinking heavily, later writing, "I have been in a blaze of dissipation altogether, and have succeeded (I think) in knocking the remembrance of my work out." Shortly afterward, *Hard Times* appeared in hardcover, published by the house of Bradbury and Evans and dedicated to another critic of British culture, Thomas Carlyle.

Plot and Major Characters

A schoolmaster at a utilitarian private school in industrial Coketown, Thomas Gradgrind insists that his students learn empirical facts alone; humor, music, and imagination are banished from his classroom and from the lives of his

children. The five Gradgrind children embody their father's philosophy, which was widely discussed and praised in early- to mid-nineteenth-century Britain. One day after school, Gradgrind is disturbed to discover his two eldest children, Tom and Louisa, attempting to peek through the walls of a circus tent; his displeasure increases when the two are unapologetic about this offense against the principles by which they have been raised. Puzzled by their behavior and determined to correct it, Gradgrind consults with a friend, Josiah Bounderby, a manufacturer and banker, who advises him that the children have been corrupted by a schoolmate, Cecilia ("Sissy") Jupe, the daughter of a circus rider. Before he can remove Sissy from his school and from his life, Gradgrind discovers that the girl's father has deserted her; moved by compassion and against the warnings of Bounderby and his own philosophy, he decides to raise Sissy in his own home and to allow her to continue attending his school. Years pass, the children grow up, and Bounderby sets his cap for Louisa, who agrees to marry this wealthy financier, thirty years her senior, to please her brother Tom, who has grown into a dissolute young man and now works at Bounderby's bank. The marriage rankles Bounderby's elderly housekeeper, Mrs. Sparsit, who mistrusts and begins spying on Louisa.

Meanwhile, Gradgrind, now in London as a member of Parliament, sends a young associate, James Harthouse, to Coketown to gather data on British economic and social life. Harthouse is directed to Bounderby's household, and while he finds Bounderby himself a self-aggrandizing blowhard, full of expansive talk about being a self-made man, he is smitten by pretty Louisa and sets about wooing her away from her husband and loveless marriage. He is successful, and soon he and Louisa are making plans to run away together—unaware that watchful Mrs. Sparsit is aware of their intent. Meanwhile, to the amazement of all, Bounderby's bank is robbed, and the authorities name one of Bounderby's employees, Stephen Blackpool, as their prime suspect. Blackpool, who had been mistreated by Bounderby, had been seen loitering in front of the bank shortly before it was robbed, in the company of an old woman known as Mrs. Pegler. The climax of the novel is reached when Louisa, having agreed to elope with Harthouse, chooses instead to return to her father's household; Mrs. Sparsit informs on Louisa and Harthouse, causing Bounderby to demand that Louisa return to him, which she does; Blackpool is cleared of all wrongdoing, Tom is found to be the real bankrobber; and Mrs. Sparsit, seeking to further ingratiate herself with Bounderby, tracks down Mrs. Pegler, who is revealed as Bounderby's own mother—who proceeds to publicly deflate Bounderby's claims of a Horatio-Algeresque career. Harthouse disappears. With the help of Sissy, Tom escapes Bounderby's vengeance, and Mrs. Sparsit is released by Bounderby for her meddlesomeness. Bounderby dies a few years later, and the Gradgrinds, bereft of all that makes life meaningful and pleasant, face long lives of boredom and misery.

Major Themes

Like the novels that preceded it—notably *Dombey and Son* and *Bleak House*—*Hard Times* is concerned with industrial society, but, as Edgar Johnson has written, "it is not so much a picture of its ramifications as a presentation of its underlying principles. It is an analysis and a condemnation of the ethos of industrialism." Rife with symbolism, the novel focuses upon characters not as human types but as products of the industrial age. Throughout the novel there is a tight, airless atmosphere informed by the utilitarian ethic; English life is no longer organic and whole but lived according to a poisonous theory which allows the rich and powerful to exert their will upon their employees and upon nature itself. The industrial city of Coketown is itself begrimed into colorlessness, shrouded in fumes and the unending plumes of reek arising from its many chimneys. The characters, with the exception of Sissy Jupe and members of the circus troupe, act less like human beings than like automata, programmed to respond to life and to each other by standards of measurable expediency alone. Freedom, humor, and art are symbolized by the circus performers; in glimpses of them (and thus, into the lives of characteristically humorous Dickensian characters), Dickens contrasts the life of imagination with the life of utility.

Critical Reception

Reviews of *Hard Times* marked it as a rare failure by Dickens. Critics found it variously misguided in its politics (Lord Macaulay found little but "sullen socialism" in the novel), largely humorless, hamhanded in plotting, marred by overdone caricatures, satirically off-target, divided in interest, and philosophically muddled. By the middle of 1855, less than a year after its appearance between hard covers, *Hard Times* lagged in sales far behind the three Dickens novels that immediately preceded it, trailing as well the author's minor *Child's History of England* (1852-54). The work's single critical accolade, met with widespread derision for a half century, appeared in 1860 in an article by John Ruskin, who wrote that he considered *Hard Times,* of all Dickens's works, "the greatest he has written." Numerous scholars, beginning with David Masson in his *British Novelist and Their Styles* (1859) and extending through Eleanor Graham's *Story of Charles Dickens* (1952) simply ignored *Hard Times* altogether in their discussions of Dickens, with others mentioning the novel in brief, sometimes chronologically inaccurate, asides. In the midst of its perpetual critical drubbing, Ruskin's remark was recurrently held up for curious examination, receiving no support until Bernard Shaw, in his preface to a 1913 edition, used Ruskin's comment as a springboard from which to find in *Hard Times* an "enormous" increase in Dickens's strength and intensity as a writer, adding that "the power that indicts a nation so terribly is much more impressive than that which ridicules individuals." Aside from this assessment, many critics during the first half of the twentieth century viewed *Hard Times* in a manner summarized by Stephen Leacock: that it "has no other interest in the history of letters than that of its failure." But a watershed in the critical history of *Hard Times* was reached in 1947 with F. R. Leavis's seminal essay "The Novel as Poem (I): *Hard Times*" in his periodical *Scrutiny*; this essay was reprinted with slight revisions as "*Hard Times*: An Analytic Note" the following year in Leavis's *The Great Tradition,* gaining wide attention. In this lengthy essay, Leavis sided with Ruskin and Shaw in writing that he considered the novel a "masterpiece" which, "of all Dickens's works . . . is the one that has all the strength of his genius, together with a strength no other of them can show—that of a completely serious work of art." By virtue of his critical stature as both a literary scholar in general and a Dickens scholar in particular, Leavis produced an essay that could not be ignored by subsequent commentators upon *Hard Times.* During the decades following the appearance of Leavis's "Analytic Note," scholars have scrutinized *Hard Times* through less jaundiced eyes, with several critics finding merit in the work (though not finding it Dickens's masterpiece, as had Leavis), while others—notably John Holloway and David H. Hirsch—attacking Leavis's position with thoroughgoing incisiveness, with Hirsch asking in conclusion, "For what, after all, can be more harmful to a genuinely great author's reputation than to insist that one of his dullest and least successful works is one of his greatest?" Critical essays of the 1970s through the 1990s have often moved beyond Leavis's essay and its critics to focus upon issues of gender, labor-capital relations, and politics in *Hard Times.*

CRITICISM

> **John Ruskin on the style of *Hard Times:***
>
> The essential value and truth of Dickens's writings have been unwisely lost sight of by many thoughtful persons, merely because he presents his truth with some colour of caricature. Unwisely, because Dickens's caricature, though often gross, is never mistaken. Allowing for his manner of telling them, the things he tells us are always true. I wish that he could think it right to limit his brilliant exaggeration to works written only for public amusement; and when he takes up a subject of high national importance, such as that which he handled in *Hard Times,* that he would use severer and more accurate analysis. The usefulness of that work (to my mind, in several respects, the greatest he has written) is with many persons seriously diminished because Mr. Bounderby is a dramatic monster, instead of a characteristic example of a worldly master; and Stephen Blackpool a dramatic perfection, instead of a characteristic example of an honest workman. But let us not lose the use of Dickens's wit and insight, because he chooses to speak in a circle of stage fire. He is entirely right in his main drift and purpose in every book he has written; and all of them, but especially *Hard Times,* should be studied with close and earnest care by persons interested in social questions.
>
> *John Ruskin, in* The Cornhill Magazine, *August, 1860.*

John Ruskin (letter date 1870)

SOURCE: A letter to Charles Eliot Norton on June 19, 1870, in *Letters of John Ruskin to Charles Eliot Norton, Vol. II,* Houghton, Mifflin and Company, 1904, pp. 4-6.

[*Ruskin was an English critic, essayist, historian, poet, novella writer, autobiographer, and diarist. Endowed with a passion for reforming what he considered his "blind and wandering fellow-men" and convinced that he had "perfect judgment" in aesthetic matters, he was the author of over forty books and several hundred essays and lectures that expounded his theories of aesthetics, morality, history, economics, and social reform. In the following excerpt from a letter written shortly after Dickens's death, he summarizes the achievement of Dickens, citing* Hard Times *as the single exception to his depicting the Dickensian hero as an "iron-master."*]

My dearest Charles,—I knew you would deeply feel the death of Dickens. It is very frightful to me—among the blows struck by the fates at worthy men, while all mischievous ones have ceaseless strength. The literary loss is infinite—the political one I care less for than you do. Dickens was a pure modernist—a leader of the steam-whistle party *par excellence*—and he had no understanding of any power of antiquity except a sort of jackdaw sentiment for cathedral towers. He knew nothing of the nobler power of superstition—was essentially a stage manager, and used everything for effect on the pit. His

Christmas meant mistletoe and pudding—neither resurrection from dead, nor rising of new stars, nor teaching of wise men, nor shepherds. His hero is essentially the iron-master; in spite of *Hard Times,* he has advanced by his influence every principle that makes them harder—the love of excitement, in all classes, and the fury of business competition, and the distrust both of nobility and clergy which, wide enough and fatal enough, and too justly founded, needed no apostle to the mob, but a grave teacher of priests and nobles themselves, for whom Dickens had essentially no word.

Edwin P. Whipple (essay date 1877)

SOURCE: "Dickens's *Hard Times*," in *The Atlantic Monthly,* Vol. XXXIX, No. CCXXXIII, March, 1877, pp. 353-58.

[*Below, Whipple suggests that some representative assessments of* Hard Times *fail to consider "the distinction between Dickens as a creator of character and Dickens as a humorous satirist of what he considers flagrant abuses." Whipple maintains that both Dickens's satirical and dramatic genius are evident in his portrayal of the characters and incidents of the novel.*]

Dickens established a weekly periodical, called *Household Words,* on the 30th of March, 1850. On the 1st of April, 1854, he began in it the publication of the tale of *Hard Times,* which was continued in weekly installments until its completion in the number for the 12th of August. The circulation of *Household Words* was doubled by the appearance in its pages of this story. When published in a separate form, it was appropriately dedicated to Thomas Carlyle, who was Dickens's master in all matters relating to the "dismal science" of political economy.

During the composition of *Hard Times* the author was evidently in an embittered state of mind in respect to social and political questions. He must have felt that he was in some degree warring against the demonstrated laws of the production and distribution of wealth; yet he also felt that he was putting into prominence some laws of the human heart which he supposed political economists had studiously overlooked or ignored. He wrote to Charles Knight that he had no design to damage the really useful truths of political economy, but that his story was directed against those "who see figures and averages, and nothing else; who would take the average of cold in the Crimea during twelve months as a reason for clothing a soldier in nankeen on a night when he would be frozen to death in fur; and who would comfort the laborer in traveling twelve miles a day to and from his work by telling him that the average distance of one inhabited place from another, on the whole area of England, is only four miles." This is, of course, a caricatured statement of what statisticians propose to prove by their "figures and averages." Dickens would have been the first to laugh at such an economist and statistician as Michael Thomas Sadler, who mixed up figures of arithmetic and figures of rhetoric, tables of population and gushing sentiments, in one odd jumble of doubtful calculations and bombastic declamations; yet Sadler is only an extreme case of an investigator who turns aside from his special work to introduce considerations which, however important in themselves, have nothing to do with the business he has in hand. Dickens's mind was so deficient in the power of generalization, so inapt to recognize the operation of inexorable law, that whatever offended his instinctive benevolent sentiments he was inclined to assail as untrue. Now there is no law the operation of which so frequently shocks our benevolent sentiments as the law of gravitation; yet no philanthropist, however accustomed he may be to subordinate scientific truth to amiable impulses, ever presumes to doubt the certain operation of that law. The great field for the contest between the head and the heart is the domain of political economy. The demonstrated laws of this science are often particularly offensive to many good men and good women, who wish well for their fellow-creatures, and who are pained by the obstacles which economic maxims present to their diffusive benevolence. The time will come when it will be as intellectually discreditable for an educated person to engage in a crusade against the established laws of political economy as in a crusade against the established laws of the physical universe; but the fact that men like Carlyle, Ruskin, and Dickens can write economic nonsense without losing intellectual caste shows that the science of political economy, before its beneficent truths come to be generally admitted, must go through a long struggle with benevolent sophisms and benevolent passions.

In naming this book Dickens found much difficulty. He sent the following titles to John Forster, as expressive of his general idea: 1. *According to Cocker.* 2. *Prove it.* 3. *Stubborn Things.* 4. *Mr. Gradgrind's Facts.* 5. *The Grindstone.* 6. *Hard Times.* 7. *Two and Two are Four.* 8. *Something Tangible.* 9. *Our Hard-Headed Friend.* 10. *Rust and Dust.* 11. *Simple Arithmetic.* 12. *A Matter of Calculation.* 13. *A Mere Question of Figures.* 14. *The Gradgrind Philosophy.* The author was in favor of one of three of these: 6, 13, and 14. Forster was in favor of either 2, 6, or 11. As both agreed on No. 6, that title was chosen. Yet certainly No. 14, *The Gradgrind Philosophy,* was the best of all, for it best indicated the purpose of the story. *Hard Times* is an extremely vague title, and might apply to almost any story that Dickens or any other novelist has written.

It is curious to note the different opinions of two widely differing men regarding the story itself. Ruskin says that "the essential value and truth of Dickens's writings have been unwisely lost sight of by many thoughtful persons, merely because he presents his truth with some color of caricature. Unwisely, because Dickens's caricature, though often gross, is never mistaken. Allowing for the manner of his telling them, the things he tells us are always true. I wish that he could think it right to limit his brilliant exaggeration to works written only for public amusement; and when he takes up a subject of high national importance, such as that he handled in *Hard Times,* that he would use severer and more accurate analysis. The usefulness of that work (to my mind, in several respects, the

greatest he has written) is with many persons seriously diminished because Mr. Bounderby is a dramatic monster instead of a characteristic example of a worldly master, and Stephen Blackpool a dramatic perfection instead of a characteristic example of an honest workman. But let us not lose the use of Dickens's wit and insight because he chooses to speak in a circle of stage fire. He is entirely right in his main drift and purpose in every book he has written; and all of them, but especially *Hard Times,* should be studied with great care by persons interested in social questions. They will find much that is partial, and, because partial, apparently unjust; but if they examine all the evidence on the other side, which Dickens seems to overlook, it will appear, after all the trouble, that his view was the finally right one, grossly and sharply told." This is the opinion of an eloquent thinker and writer who is most at variance with the principles which scientific economists consider to be scientifically established. On the opposite extreme we have the opinion of Macaulay, who records in his private diary, under the date of August 12, 1854, this disparaging criticism: "I read Dickens's *Hard Times.* One excessively touching, heart-breaking passage, and the rest sullen socialism. The evils he attacks he caricatures grossly and with little humor."

In judging the work, neither Ruskin nor Macaulay seems to have made any distinction between Dickens as a creator of character and Dickens as a humorous satirist of what he considers flagrant abuses. As a creator of character he is always tolerant and many-sided; as a satirist he is always intolerant and onesided; and the only difference between his satire and that of other satirists consists in the fact that he has a wonderful power in individualizing abuses in persons. Juvenal, Dryden, and Pope, though keen satirists of character, are comparatively ineffective in the art of concealing their didactic purpose under an apparently dramatic form. So strong is Dickens's individualizing faculty, and so weak his faculty of generalization, that as a satirist he simply personifies his personal opinions. These opinions are formed by quick-witted impressions intensified by philanthropic emotions; they spring neither from any deep insight of reason nor from any careful processes of reasoning; and they are therefore contemptuously discarded as fallacies by all thinkers on social problems who are devoted to the investigation of social phenomena and the establishment of economic laws; but they are so vividly impersonated, and the classes satirized are so felicitously hit in some of their external characteristics and weak points, that many readers fail to discover the essential difference between such realities of character as Tony Weller and Mrs. Gamp, and such semblances of character as Mr. Gradgrind and Mr. Bounderby. Whatever Dickens understands he humorously represents; whatever he does not understand he humorously misrepresents; but in either case, whether he conceives or misconceives, he conveys to the general reader an impression that he is as great in those characters in which he personifies his antipathies as in those in which he embodies his sympathies.

The operation of this satirical as contrasted with dramatic genius is apparent in almost every person who appears in

Hard Times, except Sleary and his companions of the circus combination. Mr. Gradgrind and Mr. Bounderby are personified abstractions, after the method of Ben Jonson; but the charge that Macaulay brings against them, that they have little of Dickens's humor, must be received with qualifications. Mr. Bounderby, for example, as the satirical representative of a class, and not as a person who could have had any real existence,—as a person who gathers into himself all the vices of a horde of English manufacturers, without a ray of light being shed into his internal constitution of heart and mind,—is one of the wittiest and most humorous of Dickens's embodied sarcasms. Bounderby becomes a seeming character by being looked at and individualized from the point of view of imaginative antipathy. So surveyed, he seems real to thousands who observe their employers from the outside, and judge of them, not as they are, but as they appear to their embittered minds and hearts. Still, the artistic objection holds good that when a man resembling Mr. Bounderby is brought into the domain of romance or the drama, the great masters of romance and the drama commonly insist that he shall be not only externally represented but internally known. There is no authorized, no accredited way of exhibiting character but this, that the dramatist or novelist shall enter into the soul of the personage represented, shall sympathize with him sufficiently to know him, and shall represent his passions, prejudices, and opinions as springing from some central will and individuality. This sympathy is consistent with the utmost hatred of the person described; but characterization becomes satire the moment that antipathy supersedes insight and the satirist berates the exterior manifestations of an individuality whose interior life he has not diligently explored and interpreted. Bounderby, therefore, is only a magnificent specimen of what satirical genius can do when divorced from the dramatist's idea of justice, and the dramatist's perception of those minute peculiarities of intellect, disposition, and feeling which distinguish one "bully of humility" from another.

It is ridiculous to assert, as Ruskin asserts, that *Hard Times* is Dickens's greatest work; for it is *the* one of all his works which should be distinguished from the others as specially wanting in that power of real characterization on which his reputation as a vivid delineator of human character and human life depends. The whole effect of the story, though it lacks neither amusing nor pathetic incidents, and though it contains passages of description which rank with his best efforts in combining truth of fact with truth of imagination, is ungenial and unpleasant. Indeed, in this book, he simply intensified popular discontent; he ignored or he was ignorant of those laws the violation of which is at the root of popular discontent; and proclaimed with his favorite ideal workman, Stephen Blackpool, that not only the relation between employers and employed, but the whole constitution of civilized society itself, was a hopeless "muddle," beyond the reach of human intelligence or humane feeling to explain and justify. It is to be observed here that all cheering views of the amelioration of the condition of the race come from those hard thinkers whose benevolent impulses push them to the investigation of natural and economic laws. Start-

ing from the position of sentimental benevolence, and meeting unforeseen intellectual obstacles at every step in his progress, Dickens ends "in a muddle" by the necessity of his method. Had he been intellectually equipped with the knowledge possessed by many men to whom in respect to genius he was immensely superior, he would never have landed in a conclusion so ignominious, and one which the average intellect of well-informed persons of the present day contemptuously rejects. If Dickens had contented himself with using his great powers of observation, sympathy, humor, imagination, and characterization in their appropriate fields, his lack of scientific training in the austere domain of social, legal, and political science would have been hardly perceptible; but after his immense popularity was assured by the success of *The Pickwick Papers,* he was smitten with the ambition to direct the public opinion of Great Britain by embodying, in exquisitely satirical caricatures, rash and hasty judgments on the whole government of Great Britain in all its departments, legislative, executive, and judicial. He overlooked uses, in order to fasten on abuses. His power to excite, at his will, laughter, or tears, or indignation was so great, that the victims of his mirthful wrath were not at first disposed to resent his debatable fallacies while enjoying his delicious fun. His invasion of the domain of political science with the palpable design of substituting benevolent instincts for established laws was carelessly condoned by the statesmen, legists, and economists whom he denounced and amused.

Indeed, the great characteristic of Dickens's early popularity was this, that it was confined to no class, but extended to all classes, rich and poor, noble and plebeian. The queen on the throne read him, and so did Hodge at the plow; and between the sovereign and her poorest subject there was no class which did not sound his praise as a humorist. Still, every student of the real genius of Dickens must be surprised at the judgment pronounced on his various romances by what may be called the higher, the professional, the educated classes, the classes which, both in England and in the United States, hold positions of trust and honor, and are bound, by the practical necessities of their posts, to be on a level with the advancing intelligence of the age in legislative, economic, and judicial science. By these persons *The Pickwick Papers* are, as a general thing, preferred to any other of the works of Dickens. The Lord Chief Justice (afterwards Lord Chancellor) Campbell told Dickens that he would prefer the honor of having written that book to the honors which his professional exertions had obtained for him, that of being a peer of Parliament and the nominal head of the law. All persons who have had a sufficiently large acquaintance with the men of practical ability who have risen to power in the United States, whether as judges, statesmen, or political economists, must have been impressed with the opinion of these men as to the superiority of *The Pickwick Papers* over all the successive publications of Dickens. Yet it is as certain as any question coming before the literary critic can be, that a number of the works that followed *The Pickwick Papers* are superior to that publication, not only in force of sentiment, imagination, and characterization, but in everything which distinguishes the individual genius of Dickens,—a genius which up to the time of *David Copperfield* deepened and enlarged in the orderly process of its development. The secret of this preference for *The Pickwick Papers* is to be found in the fact that the author had, in that book, no favorite theory to push, no grand moral to enforce, no assault on principles about which educated men had made up their minds. These men could laugh heartily at Mr. Buzfuz and Mr. Justice Stareleigh; but when, as in *Bleak House,* there was a serious attempt to assail equity jurisprudence, they felt that the humorist had ventured on ground where he had nothing but his genius to compensate for his lack of experience and knowledge. Thus it is that a work which, with all its wealth of animal spirits, is comparatively shallow and superficial considered as a full expression of Dickens's powers of humor, pathos, narrative, description, imagination, and characterization, has obtained a preëminence above its successors, not because it contains what is best and deepest in Dickens's genius, but because it omits certain matters relating to social and economical science, with which he was imperfectly acquainted, and on which his benevolence, misleading his genius, still urged him vehemently to dogmatize. His educated readers enjoyed his humor and pathos as before, but they were more or less irritated by the intrusion of social theories which they had long dismissed from their minds as exploded fallacies, and did not see that the wit was more pointed, the humor richer, the faculty of constructing a story more developed, the sentiment of humanity more earnest and profound, than in the inartistic incidents of *The Pickwick Papers,* over which they had laughed until they had cried, and cried until they had laughed again. They desired amusement merely; *The Pickwick Papers* are the most amusing of Dickens's works; and they were correspondingly vexed with an author who deviated from the course of amusing them into that of instructing them, only to emphasize notions which were behind the knowledge of the time, and which interfered with their enjoyment without giving them any intelligent instruction.

Still, allowing for the prepossessions of Dickens in writing *Hard Times,* and forgetting Adam Smith, Ricardo, and John Stuart Mill,—looking at him only as a humorous satirist profoundly disgusted with some prominent evils of his day,—we may warmly praise the book as one of the most perfect of its kind. The bleakness of the whole representation of human life proceeds from the Gradgrind Philosophy of Life, which emphasizes Fact and denounces all cultivation of the sentiments and the imagination. As a result of this system, Tom, the son of Mr. Gradgrind, becomes a selfish "whelp" and sneak thief; his daughter, Louisa, marries Mr. Bounderby under circumstances which point inevitably to a separation, either on account of adultery or incompatibility of temper and disposition; and young Bitzer, the plebeian product of the system, who glories in his own emancipation from all the ties of son, brother, and husband, who is eloquent on the improvidence of those who marry and have children, and who congratulates himself that he has only one person to feed, and that's the person he most likes to feed, namely, himself, is doomed to remain what he is, to the end of his life, a soulless, heartless, calculating machine, almost too

mean to merit even the spurn of contempt. The first person who stirs the family of Mr. Gradgrind to a vague sense that the human mind possesses the faculty of imagination is Mr. Sleary, the circus-manager; and, in the end, he is the person who saves Tom Gradgrind from the disgrace of being arrested and tried as a felon. Dickens shows much art in making a man like Sleary, who represents the lowest element in the lowest order of popular amusements, the beneficent genius of the Gradgrind family, inclosed as they are in seemingly impenetrable surroundings of propriety, respectability, and prosaic fact. In depicting Sleary, the author escapes from satire into characterization, and adds to the population of Dickensland one of his most humorously conceived and consistently drawn personages. While his hand is in he strikes off portraits of Master Kidderminster, Mr. E. W. B. Childers, and other members of the circus troupe with almost equal vigor and fidelity to fact. As a specimen of his humor, Sleary's description of the search which Merrylegs' dog made to find him, in order to inform him of his master's death, is incomparably good. Mr. Gradgrind, as a man of science, suggests that the dog was drawn to him by his instinct and his fine scent. Mr. Sleary shakes his head skeptically. His idea is, that the dog went to another dog that he met on his journey, and asked him if he knew of a person of the name of Sleary, in the horse-riding way,—stout man,—game eye? And the other dog said that he couldn't say he knew him himself, but knew a dog who was likely to be acquainted with him, and then introduced him to that dog. And you know, Sleary added, that being much before the public, a number of dogs must be acquainted with me that *I* don't know. And Sleary goes on to show that after fourteen months' journey, the dog at last came to him in a very bad condition, lame and almost blind, threw himself up behind, stood on his fore legs, weak as he was, and then he wagged his tail and died. And then Sleary knew that the dog was the dog of Merrylegs. We have not put the narrative into Sleary's expressive lisp, and can only refer the reader to the original account in the eighth chapter of *Hard Times*.

The relation between Mr. James Harthouse and Louisa is one of the best "situations" in Dickens's novels. Harthouse represents a type of character which was the object of Dickens's special aversion, the younger son of a younger son of family,—"born bored," as St. Simon says of the Duke of Orleans, and passing listlessly through life in a constant dread of boredom, but seeking distractions and stimulants through new experiences,—"a thorough gentleman, made to the model of the time, weary of everything, and putting no more faith in anything than Lucifer." Contrasted with this jaded man of fashion is Louisa Gradgrind, the wife of Mr. Bounderby. Far from being morally and mentally wearied by too large an experience of life, she has had no experience of life at all. Her instincts, feelings, and imagination, as a woman, have been forced back into the interior recesses of her mind by the method of her education, and are therefore ever ready to burst forth, with an impetuosity corresponding to the force used in their repression and restraint. Now Dickens, as an English novelist, was prevented, by his English sense of decorum, from describing in detail those sensuous and passionate elements in her nature which brought her to the point of agreeing to an elopement with her lover. A French novelist would have had no difficulty in this respect. Leaving out of view such romancers as Alexandre Dumas and Frédéric Soulié, with what pleasure would story-tellers of a higher order, like Théophile Gautier, Prosper Mérimée, George Sand, and Charles de Bernard, have recorded their minute analysis of every phase of passion in the breasts of the would-be adulterer and the would-be adulteress! As it is, the reader finds it difficult to understand the frenzy of soul, the terrible tumult of feeling, which rends the heart of Louisa as she flies to her father on the evening she has agreed to elope with her lover. Such madness as she displays in the culmination of passion might have been explained by exhibiting, step by step, the growth of her passion. Instead of this, we are overwhelmed by the sudden passage of ice into fire without any warning of the perilous transformation.

The method of the French novelists is doubtless corrupting in just the degree in which it is interpretative. Whatever may be said of it, it at least accounts, on the logic of passion, for those crimes against the sanctity of the marriage relation which all good people deplore, but which few good people seem to understand.

It is needless to add, in this connection, any remarks on the singular purity of the relation existing between Rachel and Stephen Blackpool. Any reader who can contemplate it without feeling the tears gather in his eyes is hopelessly insensible to the pathos of Dickens in its most touching manifestations.

Howells on Dickens as a writer of dialogue:

The vernacular of Dickens's people never seems to me quite trustworthy; he had not a good ear, and he had no scruple in perverting or inventing forms, if it suited his purpose. I fancy that his best and truest dialect writing is to be found in **Hard Times,** though he indulged in it everywhere in his novels.

William Dean Howells, in
Harper's Bazaar, *June, 22, 1895.*

George Gissing (essay date 1898)

SOURCE: "The Radical," in *Charles Dickens: A Critical Study,* Dodd, Mead and Company, 1912, pp. 255-82.

[*In the following excerpt from a work originally published in 1898, Gissing writes of* Hard Times *as a failed labor novel.*]

We do not nowadays look for a fervent Christianity in leaders of the people. In that, as in several other matters, Dickens was by choice retrospective. Still writing at a time when "infidelity"—the word then used—was becoming rife among the populace of great towns, he never

makes any reference to it, and probably did not take it into account; it had no place in his English ideal. I doubt, indeed, whether he was practically acquainted with the "free-thinking" workman. A more noticeable omission from his books (if we except the one novel which I cannot but think a failure) is that of the workman at war with capital. This great struggle, going on before him all his life, found no place in the scheme of his fiction. He shows us poor men who suffer under tyranny, and who exclaim against the hardship of things; but never such a representative wage-earner as was then to be seen battling for bread and right. One reason is plain: Dickens did not know the north of England. With adequate knowledge of a manufacturing town, he would never have written so unconvincingly as in his book **Hard Times**—the opportunity for dealing with this subject. Stephen Blackpool represents nothing at all; he is a mere model of meekness, and his great misfortune is such as might befall any man anywhere, the curse of a drunken wife. The book is a crude attack on materialism, a theme which might, of course, have entered very well into a study of the combatant working-class. But, as I have already pointed out, the working-class is not Dickens's field, even in London. For the purposes of fiction, it is a class still waiting its portrayer; much has been written about it in novels, but we have no work of the first order dealing primarily with that form of life. Mrs. Gaskell essayed the theme very faithfully, and with some success; but it was not her best work. I can recall no working-class figures in English novels so truly representative as those in Charlotte Brontë's second book. Given a little wider experience, the author of *Shirley* might have exhibited this class in a masterpiece such as we vainly look for.

G. K. Chesterton (essay date 1908)

SOURCE: *"Hard Times,"* in *The Collected Works of G. K. Chesterton: Chesterton on Dickens, Vol. XV,* Ignatius Press, 1989, pp. 357-63.

[*Regarded as one of England's premier men of letters during the first half of the twentieth century, Chesterton is best known today as a colorful bon vivant, a witty essayist, Catholic apologist, and as the creator of the Father Brown mysteries. His essays are characterized by their humor, frequent use of paradox, and chatty, rambling style. He was a lifelong Dickens enthusiast and wrote many essays on Dickens's works, including the introductions to each of the novels published in J. M. Dent's Everyman's Edition of Dickens's works. In the following essay, originally published in 1908 for the Everyman's Edition of* Hard Times, *Chesterton discourses on this novel as Dickens's harshest, a work strident in its emphasis upon egalitarianism.*]

I have heard that in some debating clubs there is a rule that the members may discuss anything except religion and politics. I cannot imagine what they do discuss; but it is quite evident that they have ruled out the only two subjects which are either important or amusing. The thing is a part of a certain modern tendency to avoid things because they lead to warmth; whereas, obviously, we ought, even in a social sense, to seek those things specially. The warmth of the discussion is as much a part of hospitality as the warmth of the fire. And it is singularly suggestive that in English literature the two things have died together. The very people who would blame Dickens for his sentimental hospitality are the very people who would also blame him for his narrow political conviction. The very people who would mock him for his narrow radicalism are those who would mock him for his broad fireside. Real conviction and real charity are much nearer than people suppose. Dickens was capable of loving all men; but he refused to love all opinions. The modern humanitarian can love all opinions, but he cannot love all men; he seems, sometimes, in the ecstasy of his humanitarianism, even to hate them all. He can love all opinions, including the opinion that men are unlovable.

In feeling Dickens as a lover we must never forget him as a fighter, and a fighter for a creed; but indeed there is no other kind of fighter. The geniality which he spread over all his creations was geniality spread from one centre, from one flaming peak. He was willing to excuse Mr. Micawber for being extravagant; but Dickens and Dickens's doctrine were strictly to decide how far he was to be excused. He was willing to like Mr. Twemlow in spite of his snobbishness, but Dickens and Dickens's doctrine were alone to be judges of how far he was snobbish. There was never a more didactic writer: hence there was never one more amusing. He had no mean modern notion of keeping the moral doubtful. He would have regarded this as a mere piece of slovenliness, like leaving the last page illegible.

Everywhere in Dickens's work these angles of his absolute opinion stood up out of the confusion of his general kindness, just as sharp and splintered peaks stand up out of the soft confusion of the forests. Dickens is always generous, he is generally kind-hearted, he is often sentimental, he is sometimes intolerably maudlin; but you never know when you will not come upon one of the convictions of Dickens; and when you do come upon it you do know it. It is as hard and as high as any precipice or peak of the mountains. The highest and hardest of these peaks is *Hard Times*.

It is here more than anywhere else that the sternness of Dickens emerges as separate from his softness; it is here, most obviously, so to speak, that his bones stick out. There are indeed many other books of his which are written better and written in a sadder tone. *Great Expectations* is melancholy in a sense; but it is doubtful of everything, even of its own melancholy. *The Tale of Two Cities* is a great tragedy, but it is still a sentimental tragedy. It is a great drama, but it is still a melodrama. But this tale of *Hard Times* is in some way harsher than all these. For it is the expression of a righteous indignation which cannot condescend to humour and which cannot even condescend to pathos. Twenty times we have taken Dickens's hand and it has been sometimes hot with revelry and sometimes weak with weariness; but this time we start a little, for it is inhumanly cold; and then we realise that we have

touched his gauntlet of steel.

One cannot express the real value of this book without being irrelevant. It is true that one cannot express the real value of anything without being irrelevant. If we take a thing frivolously we can take it separately, but the moment we take a thing seriously, if it were only an old umbrella, it is obvious that that umbrella opens above us into the immensity of the whole universe. But there are rather particular reasons why the value of the book called *Hard Times* should be referred back to great historic and theoretic matters with which it may appear superficially to have little or nothing to do. The chief reason can perhaps be stated thus—that English politics had for more than a hundred years been getting into more and more of a hopeless tangle (a tangle which, of course, has since become even worse) and that Dickens did in some extraordinary way see what was wrong, even if he did not see what was right.

The Liberalism which Dickens and nearly all of his contemporaries professed had begun in the American and the French Revolutions. Almost all modern English criticism upon those revolutions has been vitiated by the assumption that those revolutions burst upon a world which was unprepared for their ideas—a world ignorant of the possibility of such ideas. Somewhat the same mistake is made by those who suggest that Christianity was adopted by a world incapable of criticising it; whereas obviously it was adopted by a world that was tired of criticising everything. The vital mistake that is made about the French Revolution is merely this—that everyone talks about it as the introduction of a new idea. It was not the introduction of a new idea; there are no new ideas. Or if there are new ideas, they would not cause the least irritation if they were introduced into political society; because the world having never got used to them there would be no mass of men ready to fight for them at a moment's notice. That which was irritating about the French Revolution was this—that it was not the introduction of a new ideal, but the practical fulfilment of an old one. From the time of the first fairy tales men had always believed ideally in equality; they had always thought that something ought to be done, if anything could be done, to redress the balance between Cinderella and the ugly sisters. The irritating thing about the French was not that they said this ought to be done; everybody said that. The irritating thing about the French was that they did it. They proposed to carry out into a positive scheme what had been the vision of humanity; and humanity was naturally annoyed. The kings of Europe did not make war upon the Revolution because it was a blasphemy, but because it was a copy-book maxim which had been just too accurately copied. It was a platitude which they had always held in theory unexpectedly put into practice. The tyrants did not hate democracy because it was a paradox; they hated it because it was a truism which seemed in some danger of coming true.

Now it happens to be hugely important to have this right view of the Revolution in considering its political effects upon England. For the English, being a deeply and indeed excessively romantic people, could never be quite content with this quality of cold and bald obviousness about the republican formula. The republican formula was merely this—that the State must consist of its citizens ruling equally, however unequally they may do anything else. In their capacity of members of the State they are all equally interested in its preservation. But the English soon began to be romantically restless about this eternal truism; they were perpetually trying to turn it into something else, into something more picturesque—progress perhaps, or anarchy. At last they turned it into the highly exciting and highly unsound system of politics, which was known as the Manchester School, and which was expressed with a sort of logical flightiness, more excusable in literature, by Mr. Herbert Spencer. Of course Danton or Washington or any of the original republicans would have thought these people were mad. They would never have admitted for a moment that the State must not interfere with commerce or competition; they would merely have insisted that if the State did interfere, it must really be the State—that is, the whole people. But the distance between the common sense of Danton and the mere ecstasy of Herbert Spencer marks the English way of colouring and altering the revolutionary idea. The English people as a body went blind, as the saying is, for interpreting democracy entirely in terms of liberty. They said in substance that if they had more and more liberty it did not matter whether they had any equality or any fraternity. But this was violating the sacred trinity of true politics; they confounded the persons and they divided the substance.

Now the really odd thing about England in the nineteenth century is this—that there was one Englishman who happened to keep his head. The men who lost their heads lost highly scientific and philosophical heads; they were great cosmic systematisers like Spencer, great social philosophers like Bentham, great practical politicians like Bright, great political economists like Mill. The man who kept his head kept a head full of fantastic nonsense; he was a writer of rowdy farces, a demagogue of fiction, a man without education in any serious sense whatever, a man whose whole business was to turn ordinary cockneys into extraordinary caricatures. Yet when all these other children of the revolution went wrong he, by a mystical something in his bones, went right. He knew nothing of the Revolution; yet he struck the note of it. He returned to the original sentimental commonplace upon which it is forever founded, as the Church is founded on a rock. In an England gone mad about a minor theory he reasserted the original idea—the idea that no one in the State must be too weak to influence the State.

This man was Dickens. He did this work much more genuinely than it was done by Carlyle or Ruskin; for they were simply Tories making out a romantic case for the return of Toryism. But Dickens was a real Liberal demanding the return of real Liberalism. Dickens was there to remind people that England had rubbed out two words of the revolutionary motto, had left only Liberty and destroyed Equality and Fraternity. In this book, *Hard Times,* he specially champions equality. In all his books

he champions fraternity.

The atmosphere of this book and what it stands for can be very adequately conveyed in the note on the book by Lord Macaulay, who may stand as a very good example of the spirit of England in those years of eager emancipation and expanding wealth—the years in which Liberalism was turned from an omnipotent truth to a weak scientific system. Macaulay's private comment on *Hard Times* runs, "One or two passages of exquisite pathos and the rest sullen Socialism." That is not an unfair and certainly not a specially hostile criticism, but it exactly shows how the book struck those people who were mad on political liberty and dead about everything else. Macaulay mistook for a new formula called Socialism what was, in truth, only the old formula called political democracy. He and his Whigs had so thoroughly mauled and modified the original idea of Rousseau or Jefferson that when they saw it again they positively thought that it was something quite new and eccentric. But the truth was that Dickens was not a Socialist, but an unspoilt Liberal; he was not sullen; nay, rather, he had remained strangely hopeful. They called him a sullen Socialist only to disguise their astonishment at finding still loose about the London streets a happy republican.

Dickens is the one living link between the old kindness and the new, between the good will of the past and the good works of the future. He links May Day with Bank Holiday, and he does it almost alone. All the men around him, great and good as they were, were in comparison puritanical, and never so puritanical as when they were also atheistic. He is a sort of solitary pipe down which pours to the twentieth century the original river of Merry England. And although this *Hard Times* is, as its name implies, the hardest of his works, although there is less in it perhaps than in any of the others of the *abandon* and the buffoonery of Dickens, this only emphasises the more clearly the fact that he stood almost alone for a more humane and hilarious view of democracy. None of his great and much more highly-educated contemporaries could help him in this. Carlyle was as gloomy on the one side as Herbert Spencer on the other. He protested against the commercial oppression simply and solely because it was not only an oppression but a depression. And this protest of his was made specially in the case of the book before us. It may be bitter, but it was a protest against bitterness. It may be dark, but it is the darkness of the subject and not of the author. He is by his own account dealing with hard times, but not with a hard eternity, not with a hard philosophy of the universe. Nevertheless, this is the one place in his work where he does not make us remember human happiness by example as well as by precept. This is, as I have said, not the saddest, but certainly the harshest of his stories. It is perhaps the only place where Dickens, in defending happiness, for a moment forgets to be happy.

He describes Bounderby and Gradgrind with a degree of grimness and sombre hatred very different from the half affectionate derision which he directed against the old tyrants or humbugs of the earlier nineteenth century—the pompous Dedlock or the fatuous Nupkins, the grotesque Bumble or the inane Tigg. In those old books his very abuse was benignant; in **Hard Times** even his sympathy is hard. And the reason is again to be found in the political facts of the century. Dickens could be half genial with the older generation of oppressors because it was a dying generation. It was evident, or at least it seemed evident then, that Nupkins could not go on much longer making up the law of England to suit himself; that Sir Leicester Dedlock could not go on much longer being kind to his tenants as if they were dogs and cats. And some of these evils the nineteenth century did really eliminate or improve. For the first half of the century Dickens and all his friends were justified in feeling that the chains were falling from mankind. At any rate, the chains did fall from Mr. Rouncewell the Iron-master. And when they fell from him he picked them up and put them upon the poor.

Bernard Shaw (essay date 1913)

SOURCE: "Introduction to *Hard Times*," in *Shaw on Dickens,* edited by Dan H. Lawrence and Martin Quinn, Frederick Ungar Publishing Co., 1985, pp. 27-35.

[*Shaw is generally considered the greatest and best-known dramatist to write in the English language since Shakespeare. During the late nineteenth century, he was also a prominent literary, art, music, and drama critic, and his reviews were known for their biting wit and brilliance. Like his friendly rival, Chesterton, Shaw was a longtime enthusiast of Dickens's work, primarily because of its value in the literature of class struggle, an emphasis which appealed strongly to the Fabian Shaw. In the following introduction to the Waverley subscription edition (1913) of* Hard Times, *Shaw finds the novel to portray the realism and social criticism that emerged in mid-nineteenth-century literature.*]

John Ruskin once declared **Hard Times** Dickens's best novel. It is worth while asking why Ruskin thought this, because he would have been the first to admit that the habit of placing works of art in competition with one another, and wrangling as to which is the best, is the habit of the sportsman, not of the enlightened judge of art. Let us take it that what Ruskin meant was that **Hard Times** was one of his special favorites among Dickens's books. Was this the caprice of fancy? or is there any rational explanation of the preference? I think there is.

Hard Times is the first fruit of that very interesting occurrence which our religious sects call, sometimes conversion, sometimes being saved, sometimes attaining to conviction of sin. Now the great conversions of the XIX century were not convictions of individual, but of social sin. The first half of the XIX century considered itself the greatest of all the centuries. The second discovered that it was the wickedest of all the centuries. The first half despised and pitied the Middle Ages as barbarous, cruel, superstitious, ignorant. The second half saw no hope for mankind except in the recovery of the faith, the art, the

humanity of the Middle Ages. In Macaulay's *History of England,* the world is so happy, so progressive, so firmly set in the right path, that the author cannot mention even the National Debt without proclaiming that the deeper the country goes into debt, the more it prospers. In Morris's *News from Nowhere* there is nothing left of all the institutions that Macaulay glorified except an old building, so ugly that it is used only as a manure market, that was once the British House of Parliament. **Hard Times** was written in 1854, just at the turn of the half century; and in it we see Dickens with his eyes newly open and his conscience newly stricken by the discovery of the real state of England. In the book that went immediately before, *Bleak House,* he was still denouncing evils and ridiculing absurdities that were mere symptoms of the anarchy that followed the industrial revolution of the XVIII and XIX centuries, and the conquest of political power by Commercialism in 1832. In *Bleak House* Dickens knows nothing of the industrial revolution: he imagines that what is wrong is that when a dispute arises over the division of the plunder of the nation, the Court of Chancery, instead of settling the dispute cheaply and promptly, beggars the disputants and pockets both their shares. His description of our party system, with its Coodle, Doodle, Foodle, etc., has never been surpassed for accuracy and for penetration of superficial pretence. But he had not dug down to the bed rock of the imposture. His portrait of the ironmaster who visits Sir Leicester Dedlock, and who is so solidly superior to him, might have been drawn by Macaulay: there is not a touch of Bounderby in it. His horrible and not untruthful portraits of the brickmakers whose abject and battered wives call them "master," and his picture of the now vanished slum between Drury Lane and Catherine Street which he calls Tom All Alone's, suggest (save in the one case of the outcast Jo, who is, like Oliver Twist, a child, and therefore outside the old self-help panacea of Dickens's time) nothing but individual delinquencies, local plague-spots, negligent authorities.

In *Hard Times* you will find all this changed. Coketown, which you can see to-day for yourself in all its grime in the Potteries (the real name of it is Hanley in Staffordshire on the London and North Western Railway), is not, like Tom All Alone's, a patch of slum in a fine city, easily cleared away, as Tom's actually was about fifty years after Dickens called attention to it. Coketown is the whole place; and its rich manufacturers are proud of its dirt, and declare that they like to see the sun blacked out with smoke, because it means that the furnaces are busy and money is being made; whilst its poor factory hands have never known any other sort of town, and are as content with it as a rat is with a hole. Mr. Rouncewell, the pillar of society who snubs Sir Leicester with such dignity, has become Mr. Bounderby, the self-made humbug. The Chancery suitors who are driving themselves mad by hanging about the Courts in the hope of getting a judgment in their favor instead of trying to earn an honest living, are replaced by factory operatives who toil miserably and incessantly only to see the streams of gold they set flowing slip through their fingers into the pockets of men who revile and oppress them.

Clearly this is not the Dickens who burlesqued the old song of the "Fine Old English Gentleman" [anti-Tory lampoon published in *The Examiner,* August 7, 1841], and saw in the evils he attacked only the sins and wickednesses and follies of a great civilization. This is Karl Marx, Carlyle, Ruskin, Morris, Carpenter, rising up against civilization itself as against a disease, and declaring that it is not our disorder but our order that is horrible; that it is not our criminals but our magnates that are robbing and murdering us; and that it is not merely Tom All Alone's that must be demolished and abolished, pulled down, rooted up, and made for ever impossible so that nothing shall remain of it but History's record of its infamy, but our entire social system. For that was how men felt, and how some of them spoke, in the early days of the Great Conversion which produced, first, such books as the Latter Day Pamphlets of Carlyle, Dickens's **Hard Times,** and the tracts and sociological novels of the Christian Socialists, and later on the Socialist movement which has now spread all over the world, and which has succeeded in convincing even those who most abhor the name of Socialism that the condition of the civilized world is deplorable, and that the remedy is far beyond the means of individual righteousness. In short, whereas formerly men said to the victim of society who ventured to complain, "Go and reform yourself before you pretend to reform Society," it now has to admit that until Society is reformed, no man can reform himself except in the most insignificantly small ways. He may cease picking your pocket of half crowns; but he cannot cease taking a quarter of a million a year from the community for nothing at one end of the scale, or living under conditions in which health, decency, and gentleness are impossible at the other, if he happens to be born to such a lot.

You must therefore resign yourself, if you are reading Dickens's books in the order in which they were written, to bid adieu now to the light-hearted and only occasionally indignant Dickens of the earlier books, and get such entertainment as you can from him now that the occasional indignation has spread and deepened into a passionate revolt against the whole industrial order of the modern world. Here you will find no more villains and heroes, but only oppressors and victims, oppressing and suffering in spite of themselves, driven by a huge machinery which grinds to pieces the people it should nourish and ennoble, and having for its directors the basest and most foolish of us instead of the noblest and most farsighted.

Many readers find the change disappointing. Others find Dickens worth reading almost for the first time. The increase in strength and intensity is enormous: the power that indicts a nation so terribly is much more impressive than that which ridicules individuals. But it cannot be said that there is an increase of simple pleasure for the reader, though the books are not therefore less attractive. One cannot say that it is pleasanter to look at a battle than at a merry-go-round; but there can be no question which draws the larger crowd.

To describe the change in the readers' feelings more precisely, one may say that it is impossible to enjoy Gradgrind or Bounderby as one enjoys Pecksniff or the Artful Dodger or Mrs. Gamp or Micawber or Dick Swiveller, because these earlier characters have nothing to do with us except to amuse us. We neither hate nor fear them. We do not expect ever to meet them, and should not be in the least afraid of them if we did. England is not full of Micawbers and Swivellers. They are not our fathers, our schoolmasters, our employers, our tyrants. We do not read novels to escape from them and forget them: quite the contrary. But England is full of Bounderbys and Podsnaps and Gradgrinds; and we are all to a quite appalling extent in their power. We either hate and fear them or else we *are* them, and resent being held up to odium by a novelist. We have only to turn to the article on Dickens in the current edition of the *Encyclopedia Britannica* to find how desperately our able critics still exalt all Dickens's early stories about individuals whilst ignoring or belittling such masterpieces as **Hard Times,** *Little Dorrit, Our Mutual Friend,* and even *Bleak House* (because of Sir Leicester Dedlock), for their mercilessly faithful and penetrating exposures of English social, industrial, and political life; to see how hard Dickens hits the conscience of the governing class; and how loth we still are to confess, not that we are so wicked (for of that we are rather proud), but so ridiculous, so futile, so incapable of making our country really prosperous. *The Old Curiosity Shop* was written to amuse you, entertain you, touch you; and it succeeded. **Hard Times** was written to make you uncomfortable; and it will make you uncomfortable (and serve you right) though it will perhaps interest you more, and certainly leave a deeper scar on you, than any two of its forerunners.

At the same time you need not fear to find Dickens losing his good humor and sense of fun and becoming serious in Mr. Gradgrind's way. On the contrary, Dickens in this book casts off, and casts off for ever, all restraint on his wild sense of humor. He had always been inclined to break loose: there are passages in the speeches of Mrs. Nickleby and Pecksniff which are impossible as well as funny. But now it is no longer a question of passages: here he begins at last to exercise quite recklessly his power of presenting a character to you in the most fantastic and outrageous terms, putting into its mouth from one end of the book to the other hardly one word which could conceivably be uttered by any sane human being, and yet leaving you with an unmistakable and exactly truthful portrait of a character that you recognize at once as not only real but typical. Nobody ever talked, or ever will talk, as Silas Wegg talks to Boffin and Mr. Venus, or as Mr. Venus reports Pleasant Riderhood to have talked, or as Rogue Riderhood talks, or as John Chivery talks. They utter rhapsodies of nonsense conceived in an ecstasy of mirth. And this begins in **Hard Times**. Jack Bunsby in *Dombey and Son* is absurd: the oracles he delivers are very nearly impossible, and yet not quite impossible. But Mrs. Sparsit in this book, though Rembrandt could not have drawn a certain type of real woman more precisely to the life, is grotesque from beginning to end in her way of expressing herself. Her nature, her tricks of manner, her way of taking Mr. Bounderby's marriage, her instinct for hunting down Louisa and Mrs. Pegler, are drawn with an unerring hand; and she says nothing that is out of character. But no clown gone suddenly mad in a very mad harlequinade could express all these truths in more extravagantly ridiculous speeches. Dickens's business in life has become too serious for troubling over the small change of verisimilitude, and denying himself and his readers the indulgence of his humor in inessentials. He even calls the schoolmaster M'Choakumchild, which is almost an insult to the serious reader. And it was so afterwards to the end of his life. There are moments when he imperils the whole effect of his character drawing by some overpoweringly comic sally. For instance, happening in *Hard Times* to describe Mr. Bounderby as drumming on his hat as if it were a tambourine, which is quite correct and natural, he presently says that "Mr. Bounderby put his tambourine on his head, like an oriental dancer." Which similitude is so unexpectedly and excruciatingly funny that it is almost impossible to feel duly angry with the odious Bounderby afterwards.

This disregard of naturalness in speech is extraordinarily entertaining in the comic method; but it must be admitted that it is not only not entertaining, but sometimes hardly bearable when it does not make us laugh. There are two persons in *Hard Times,* Louisa Gradgrind and Cissy Jupe, who are serious throughout. Louisa is a figure of poetic tragedy; and there is no question of naturalness in her case: she speaks from beginning to end as an inspired prophetess, conscious of her own doom and finally bearing to her father the judgment of Providence on his blind conceit. If you once consent to overlook her marriage, which is none the less an act of prostitution because she does it to obtain advantages for her brother and not for herself, there is nothing in the solemn poetry of her deadly speech that jars. But Cissy is nothing if not natural; and though Cissy is as true to nature in her character as Mrs. Sparsit, she "speaks like a book" in the most intolerable sense of the words. In her interview with Mr. James Harthouse, her unconscious courage and simplicity, and his hopeless defeat by them, are quite natural and right; and the contrast between the humble girl of the people and the smart sarcastic man of the world whom she so completely vanquishes is excellently dramatic; but Dickens has allowed himself to be carried away by the scene into a ridiculous substitution of his own most literary and least colloquial style for any language that could conceivably be credited to Cissy.

"Mr. Harthouse: the only reparation that remains with you is to leave her immediately and finally. I am quite sure that you can mitigate in no other way the wrong and harm you have done. I am quite sure that it is the only compensation you have left it in your power to make. I do not say that it is much, or that it is enough; but it is something, and it is necessary. Therefore, though without any other authority than I have given you, and even without the knowledge of any other person than yourself and myself, I ask you to depart from this place to-night, under an obligation never to return to it."

This is the language of a Lord Chief Justice, not of the

dunce of an elementary school in the Potteries.

But this is only a surface failure, just as the extravagances of Mrs. Sparsit are only surface extravagances. There is, however, one real failure in the book. Slackbridge, the trade union organizer, is a mere figment of the middle-class imagination. No such man would be listened to by a meeting of English factory hands. Not that such meetings are less susceptible to humbug than meetings of any other class. Not that trade union organizers, worn out by the terribly wearisome and trying work of going from place to place repeating the same commonplaces and trying to "stoke up" meetings to enthusiasm with them, are less apt than other politicians to end as windbags, and sometimes to depend on stimulants to pull them through their work. Not, in short, that the trade union platform is any less humbug-ridden than the platforms of our more highly placed political parties. But even at their worst trade union organizers are not a bit like Slackbridge. Note, too, that Dickens mentions that there was a chairman at the meeting (as if that were rather surprising), and that this chairman makes no attempt to preserve the usual order of public meeting, but allows speakers to address the assembly and interrupt one another in an entirely disorderly way. All this is pure middle-class ignorance. It is much as if a tramp were to write a description of millionaires smoking large cigars in church, with their wives in low-necked dresses and diamonds. We cannot say that Dickens did not know the working classes, because he knew humanity too well to be ignorant of any class. But this sort of knowledge is as compatible with ignorance of class manners and customs as with ignorance of foreign languages. Dickens knew certain classes of working folk very well: domestic servants, village artisans, and employees of petty tradesmen, for example. But of the segregated factory populations of our purely industrial towns he knew no more than an observant professional man can pick up on a flying visit to Manchester.

It is especially important to notice that Dickens expressly says in this book that the workers were wrong to organize themselves in trade unions, thereby endorsing what was perhaps the only practical mistake of the Gradgrind school that really mattered much. And having thus thoughtlessly adopted, or at least repeated, this error, long since exploded, of the philosophic Radical school from which he started, he turns his back frankly on Democracy, and adopts the idealized Toryism of Carlyle and Ruskin, in which the aristocracy are the masters and superiors of the people, and also the servants of the people and of God. Here is a significant passage.

"Now perhaps," said Mr. Bounderby, "you will let the gentleman know how you would set this muddle (as you are so fond of calling it) to rights."

"I donno, sir. I canna be expecten to't. Tis not me as should be looken to for that, sir. Tis they as is put ower me, and ower aw the rest of us. What do they tak upon themseln, sir, if not to do it?"

And to this Dickens sticks for the rest of his life. In *Our*

Mutual Friend he appeals again and again to the governing classes, asking them with every device of reproach, invective, sarcasm, and ridicule of which he is master, what they have to say to this or that evil which it is their professed business to amend or avoid. Nowhere does he appeal to the working classes to take their fate into their own hands and try the democratic plan.

Another phrase used by Stephen Blackpool in this remarkable fifth chapter is important. "Nor yet lettin alone will never do it." It is Dickens's express repudiation of *laissez-faire.*

There is nothing more in the book that needs any glossary, except, perhaps, the strange figure of the Victorian "swell," Mr. James Harthouse. His pose has gone out of fashion. Here and there you may still see a man—even a youth—with a single eyeglass, an elaborately bored and weary air, and a little stock of cynicisms and indifferentisms contrasting oddly with a mortal anxiety about his clothes. All he needs is a pair of Dundreary whiskers, like the officers in Desanges' military pictures, to be a fair imitation of Mr. James Harthouse. But he is not in the fashion: he is an eccentric, as Whistler was an eccentric, as Max Beerbohm and the neo-dandies of the *fin de siècle* were eccentrics. It is now the fashion to be strenuous, to be energetic, to hustle as American millionaires are supposed (rather erroneously) to hustle. But the soul of the swell is still unchanged. He has changed his name again and again, become a Masher, a Toff, a Johnny and what not; but fundamentally he remains what he always was, an Idler, and therefore a man bound to find some trick of thought and speech that reduces the world to a thing as empty and purposeless and hopeless as himself. Mr. Harthouse reappears, more seriously and kindly taken, as Eugene Wrayburn and Mortimer Lightwood in *Our Mutual Friend.* He reappears as a club in The Finches of the Grove in *Great Expectations.* He will reappear in all his essentials in fact and in fiction until he is at last shamed or coerced into honest industry and becomes not only unintelligible but inconceivable.

Note, finally, that in this book Dickens proclaims that marriages are not made in heaven, and that those which are not confirmed there, should be dissolved.

Stephen Leacock (essay date 1934)

SOURCE: "*Bleak House* and Social Reform," in *Charles Dickens: His Life and Work,* 1934. Reprint by The Sun Dial Press, Inc., 1938, pp. 152-72.

[*A respected Canadian professor of economics, Leacock is best known as one of the leading humorists of the first half of the twentieth century. He is also the author of biographies of Twain and Dickens. In the excerpt from the latter which appears below, Leacock sketches the plot and details the "failure" of* Hard Times.]

The story **Hard Times** has no other interest in the history of letters than that of its failure. At the time, even enthusiastic lovers of Dickens found it hard to read. At present they do not even try to read it. A large part of the book is mere trash; hardly a chapter of it is worth reading today: not an incident or a character belonging to it survives or deserves to. The names of Mr. Gradgrind and Mr. Bounderby are still quoted, but only because they are felicitous names for hard, limited men, not because the characters in the book are known or remembered. Not a chapter or a passage in the book is part of Dickens's legacy to the world.

This may well seem strange. If the book had been written at the outset of its author's career, its faults could have been laid to immaturity; if at the close, to the waning powers of age; if written ten years later—as was *Our Mutual Friend*—it could have been explained away as the product of a wearied body and an over-taxed mind. But this book was written at the height of Dickens's power, with *David Copperfield* and *Bleak House* just in front of it, and *A Tale of Two Cities* and *Little Dorrit* still to follow.

It may be, of course, that the added exertion involved in assuming the editorship of *Household Words* had already overstrained the abounding energy of Charles Dickens. There are complaints at this time of uncertain health, passed off as "hypochondria." But there was as yet no so such cruel strain of either mind or body as could involve such a literary collapse as this. It may be also that the form of publication week by week in *Household Words* was unfortunate, that it unduly "breaks" the story. But there is really very little to break.

The scene of the book is laid in a factory town (Coketown) intended as typical of the new industry and the new tyranny that went with it. Its leading characters represent the soulless employers of the age, applying the ruthless philosophy of *laissez faire* and the survival of the fittest; and against this, the angelic suffering of the working class. The book is thus an amalgam of Jack the Giant Killer, Ricardo's *Political Economy,* and the Sermon on the Mount; the whole of it intermingled with a comic strain which fails to come off.

The book can be explained only in terms of the old adage that even Homer nods at times. It is the result, perhaps, of oversuccess and overencouragement. You encourage a comic man too much and he gets silly; a pathetic man and he gets maudlin; a long-winded man and he grows interminable. Thus praise and appreciation itself, the very soil in which art best flourishes, may prompt too rank a growth.

In the case of Dickens, failure was likely to be as conspicuous as success. He thought in extreme terms and wrote in capital letters. There are no halfway effects in the death of Little Nell and the fun of Mr. Pickwick. Hence, any of his characteristic methods—comic, pathetic, impressive, or rhetorical—could be strained to the breaking point. This book strains them all: the humour is forced, the rhetoric is rodomontade, and the pathos verges on the maudlin.

But the principal fault of the book is that the *theme* is

wrong. Dickens confused the faults of men with the faults of things; hardness of heart with hardness of events. In attacking the new industrial age of factories and machinery that was transforming England, Dickens directed his attack against the wickedness and hardness of his Gradgrinds and his Bounderbys, his brutal employers of labour. Did he really think that they were any wickeder than other people? Mankind at that period had been caught in the wheels of its own machinery and was struggling vainly for salvation; just as it has been caught again and struggles at the present moment. But Dickens insists on regarding the poor and the working class as caught in the cruel grasp of the rich, which was not so, or only in a collective sense, impossible for the individual employer to remedy on the spot. It was the grasp of circumstance and not the hand of tyranny.

At the time the tremendous prestige of Dickens was sufficient to float the book along, and at least to guarantee its sale. But Lord Macaulay, in a well-known phrase, damned it as "sullen socialism." Even John Ruskin, whose ideas it is supposed to reflect, sees the weakness of it as art. In a note to his first essay in *Unto This Last* he says, "I wish he could think it right to limit his brilliant exaggeration to works written only for public amusement. The usefulness of the work, *Hard Times,* is with many persons seriously diminished because Mr. Bounderby is a dramatic monster, instead of a characteristic example of a worldly master: and Stephen Blackpool a dramatic perfection, instead of a characteristic example of an honest workman."

These are the judgments of the moment, of contemporaries among whom Dickens towered as a living reality. With the lapse of time the book has found the place it deserves.

But the inferiority of this book does not in any way detract from a proper estimate of Dickens's genius. In art one must judge a man by his best, never by his worst; by his highest reach, not by his lowest fall.

Lewis Harrison (essay date 1943)

SOURCE: "Dickens's Shadow Show," in *The Dickensian,* Vol. XXXIX, No. 268, Autumn, 1943, pp. 187-91.

[*In the essay below, Harrison profiles the characters in* Hard Times, *each of whom is "the ghost of some greater creation," appearing in a "great book" which is "no less a piece of artistry than* Copperfield."]

I

In the good old days of my Victorian childhood there were two forms of entertainment, forerunners of the cinema, which have dwelt in my memory.

The first was the "Penny Reading," when the Vicar read to a (more or less) enthralled audience some work of (also more or less) merit and interest. How this species of enjoyment was developed and transcended by Charles

Dickens everyone knows.

The Shadow Show was the other diversion. The performers, themselves unseen, were behind a white sheet and between it and a powerful light, so that their shadows were cast upon the screen. Much skill was needed on the part of actors and producer. Well managed, an excellent and amusing performance resulted. It was possible to accomplish much on the transparent curtain that could not be done upon the actual stage itself. A swordsman could most effectively run his adversary through without in the least incommoding him, and an angry termagant could empty a basin of gluey tapioca pudding over her husband without the victim being in any way inconvenienced. As Dickens glorified the Penny Reading into a magnificent and thrilling feast of laughter and tears, so, though he suspected it not, he achieved one of the greatest of all Shadow-shows. For that great book, *Hard Times,* is a Pantomime of Phantoms.

That "great book"? Yes; for although I do not love it as I do the other novels, I consider it to be a great literary and artistic triumph. It is quite unnecessarily apologised for by some Dickensians who proclaim it "Dickens's one failure." It is a success! no less a piece of artistry than *Copperfield.*

Hard Times is a greater achievement than it would otherwise be, since not a single character in it is real, but is only the ghost of some greater creation. Some are the foreshadowings of full-blooded beings. Others are ghosts of earlier personalities. Their very voices are echoes of other and richer voices from the past, or speak in proleptic tones words of those whose forerunners they are.

Let us marshal them in ghostly array. Who first shall peer through the horse-collar? Who, indeed, but the hero and heroine.

That raises the question: Who is the hero, and who the heroine, of *Hard Times*? There are two pairs of claimants, yet neither pair with any very valid claims to the titles.

First, then, Stephen Blackpool and Rachael. Poor Stephen is only the very pallid ghost of Ham Peggoty; and while we admire his rugged honesty, and deplore his sorrows, his is so joyless an existence, unrelieved by any gleam of humour, that we do not warm to him as we do to the hearty, good-humoured, though equally tragic, Yarmouth fisherman.

I am going to be very immoral, though not in such fashion as to bring a blush to the cheek of the young person, even though she be so susceptible as Miss Podsnap. If only Stephen had actually broken into the bank, broken Bitzer's head for him, and stolen a hundred and fifty of the best—which old Bounderby could well have afforded to lose—I should have liked him better! Surely he could have escaped safely with his Rachael to some foreign land? There he could have saved the life of some millionaire who had no encumbrances such as relatives. Once in possession of the fortune of the grateful Croesus, whom Dickens could have caused to depart this life at a convenient season, Stephen could have returned the sum forcibly borrowed, together with a like sum in recognition of the accommodation! But he just fades out of the picture, without the glory with which Ham made his exit. He has the high character of Ham, however, and we are forced to admire him. Dickens's indictment of that old-time Divorce Law, which was so unequal for rich and poor, was justified, and without doubt, played its part in the changing of it.

Rachael is but a sorrowful Harriet Carker, minus Harriet's education and her Mr. Morfin. The two women have the same gentle patience, and believing as I do that "thoughts are things," I am sure that certain ideas utilised in the presentation of Harriet Carker, were still floating in the author's mind when he evolved Rachael. Hers is a stronger spirit than most, and even rather overshadows Harriet. Perhaps she is the most substantial, or, shall I say, the least unsubstantial, figure in *Hard Times*. She is heroic, and could have been made the outstanding personage of the book.

Who are our other candidates for the rôle? Who but Mr. and Mrs. Bounderby. They are the only legitimate lovebirds apart from Stephen and Rachael. And the love of the latter pair, though innocent, was illicit.

II

Enter, then, Josiah and Louisa. Like Mr. Dombey, whom he resembles in his commerciality and in his love of power but in little else, old Bounderby wanted a presentable wife to preside at his table and over his household. Like him, too, he sought to domineer when things went wrong, and, copying his predecessor, tried to humble his wife by the presence of a masterful and prideful housekeeper. This was a rather favourite device of Dickens. You will recall that Mr. Murdstone used his sister to browbeat poor little Mrs. Copperfield "as was" into obedience.

Josiah Bounderby still exists. He is at the moment a town councillor in a borough well known to some of us. He shows his superiority by being familiar and rude to everybody who doesn't suit him.

Dickens's Josiah, however, was no Dombey (in which Mrs. Chick would even him with Florence, I suppose!). Josiah Bounderby was like another Joey B., old Josh, that plain red herring with a hard roe, sir, J. Bagstock.

I do not despise or share the common contempt for the old Major, I must confess. I have come into fairly close touch with army men, from General to Bugler Boy, and I have found many of the Bagstock breed among them. Put them in a club after retirement on half-pay, or whatever it is, and they are blustering, bullying, bellicose, and all that's objectionable with a B or any other letter. Boastful braggarts; vain-glorious; gluttonous; self-seeking; how their fellow-clubmen often loathe them! Opinionated bores! But let us not dismiss the Bagstock breed so summarily.

Put them on the battlefield against your Hitlers, Mussolinis, Rommels, and they'll prove the Bagstock breed to be the true British bulldog type; fighting to the last drop of their blood; never conscious of defeat, so never beaten. And because they never speak of their real and often glorious achievements, but only boast and exaggerate almost imaginary exploits, we are apt to sneer at old Josh and his like. For the Bagstocks of to-day, as well as for men of finer calibre, let us be grateful! Hats off to those grand old officers who, unable because of age to rejoin at their old rank, are content to do humbler yet equally noble work.

The Bounderby breed we can well spare. Josiah had the same sort of pride as had the Major, and like him was always boosting and puffing J. B. But since he could not boast of his high connections, he bragged of his low ones. If you are a psychologist you will perfectly understand the reason. Some folk must have limelight. If they have no merit and no high connections they make a merit of their demerit and exalt themselves in their very degradation. To such, to be proven commonplace or mediocre, is humiliating. So in the failure of the much be-lauded "my friend Dombey, sir," Joey B. lost face. In the proving that he was respectable in origin and not disreputable, the other J. B. too, lost face. The Bounderbys of this world, though often good business men—not so much by reason of talent as of bounce—are insufferable bores and bounders. Josiah, like Mr. Gabriel Parsons (surely the least offensive of the clan) "mistook rudeness for honesty . . . Many besides Gabriel mistake bluntness for sincerity." Bounderby, however, didn't care a "demnition" whether he was thought sincere or not. He was just blunt and brutal, because he thought it signified power. He and the Major were supreme egoists and egotists.

Bounderby's wife doesn't move us to any emotion whatsoever. She just leaves us cold. We know she is only a puppet, made in the likeness of Lizzie Hexam, who is at least warm-blooded. Loo Bounderby was never intended to be a wife, and even after her freedom from J. B. Dickens has no future as wife and mother for her. She was never intended for sweetheart or wife. She was essentially a sister. The relationship of brother and sister is the one Dickens best understood, and he has given us notable examples in most of his works. Sometimes the twain are both bad, as witness the Murdstones, and Sampson and Sally Brass. We find examples of the good brother and good sister in Paul and Floy, the Pinches, Nicholas Nickleby and Kate. Good brother and bad sister Dickens practically declines to acknowledge, but in the reverse he excels. This latter state of affairs we find exemplified in Little Dorrit and Tip, Charlie Hexam and Lizzie, Tom and Loo Gradgrind.

In Tom and Louisa we see Charlie and Lizzie Hexam reflected. Like Lizzie, Louisa sacrifices herself nearly always to her brother's interests. Like Lizzie, Loo saw pictures in the fire. Unlike Lizzie, she did not realise that such sacrifice could become a form of selfishness, involving the sacrifice of others; also that it could be a curse instead of a blessing even to the object of her affection. Like a wise girl Lizzie refused to marry Bradley Headstone just to please her brother; but Loo married Mr. Bounderby simply to please her father and to make things easy for the "whelp." She really deserved to be miserable, sorry for her though we are.

This brother and sister affection is a reflection of Dickens's own family life, and is worthy of much closer examination than we have time to expend upon it at the moment. Few have equalled and none has surpassed Charles Dickens in depicting this tie.

III

What of the villain? That pallid study which afterwards developed into Henry Gowan, artist—James Harthouse (an anœmic James Steerforth, with a "whelp" instead of a "daisy" for hero-worshipper) is unworthy the dignity. Gowan *did* marry Pet, and that was worth living for, for Pet was really one of the few lovable Dickens girls. His description of her is in but a few words, yet how well the portrait is drawn. Harthouse, however, achieved nothing. He had all the indecision of Cousin Rick without his charm and amiability. Harthouse hadn't the gizzard to be a "willin."

But Mrs. Sparsit! Ah, there I grant you we have a very pretty villainess. I adore Mrs. Sparsit (the wicked old marplot), though I'm glad she laddered her stockings and grazed her aristocratic conk through her nosey-parkering. But I love her because she was a Powler. My grandmother was a Powler. At least she was a de la Moth, and could never forget it—nor allow anybody else to forget it. She was a grand old snob, in a kindly way, and Mrs. Sparsit was a grand old snob in an unkindly way. I'm a snob, too. I'm proud that I'm a de la Moth, a de Port, a St. John and a Fortescue, and that I have the right—the *right,* mark you—to the title Esquire; also that I have the right, moreover, to place the picture of a bar of iron with knobs on on my carriage door (had I a carriage still), and to cause my coachman to wear a sort of black cauliflower, yclept a cockade, in his top hat. So as a de Regis (I'd forgotten him!) I willingly kowtow to Mrs. Sparsit for her merit in being a Powler. Nevertheless the old dear was a feline, and a feminine canine, and I'm glad she had to return to old Lady Scadgers—a fattened Lady Tippins. Of course Mrs. S. was just the ghost of Mrs. Pipchin minus her bombazeen and the Peruvian mines. She was also a lesser Mrs. General, and the shade of "The Old Soldier" (Mrs. Markleham).

The bride's parents next claim our attention. Thomas Gradgrind was a mere study for the great Mr. Podsnap. Podsnap was a man of Fact—the fact that Great Britain is not America. Gradgrind was a man of facts. Podsnap was the finished picture; Gradgrind the charcoal outline.

Mrs. Gradgrind is a weak after-image of Mrs. Nickleby. She is the one really comic character (the Powler apart) in *Hard Times.* Her admonition to her children to "run away and be something-ological, at once," is real Dickens, and comparable with Mrs. Nickleby's suggestion that

some agreement be made with old Mr. Snawley that young Mr. Snawley (or Slammons, or Smike) should have "fish twice a week, and a pudding twice, or a dumpling, or something of that sort."

Her death-bed, had Dickens not hurried over it (*Hard Times* alone, of all his novels, shows signs of impatience), would have been a little like that of old John Willett, and we should have expected her to "Go to the Ologies" as old John went to the "Salwanners." But the author was weary of her. Her colourlessness bored him. So, though he gives us just a touch of the grisly passing of Mrs. Skewton, he doesn't follow it up.

The bridegroom's widowed mother must be noticed. Mrs. Pegler was only good Mrs. Brown washed and brushed up and spoiled in the process. Mrs. Brown had an undutiful daughter; Mrs. Pegler an undutiful son. One mother was mercenary, the other self-sacrificing, but they are unfinished sketch and completed etching respectively.

IV

Of the lesser lights, Sissy Jupe is Esther Summerson's Charley. She is the only attractive girl in the book. Kidderminster and "the revolving Bailey" are one. E. W. B. Childers's conversational style—toward Mr. Bounderby anyway—is that of Rogue Riderhood toward his daughter. Mr. Jupe has no more real being, so far as the story is concerned, than has Mrs. Harris. We strongly suspect "there ain't no sich a person."

Slackbridge, though his oratorical style is that of Chadband, is a Roger Riderhood in his sneaking, underhand ways; his betrayal of Stephen is akin to Riderhood's denunciation of "Gaffer."

Miss Peecher's pet pupil finds her opposite number in the model Bitzer. The same model must have sat for certain characteristics of both "the lightest of porters," and the eminently respectable Mr. Littimer. M'Choakumchild is of the Bradley Headstone type of pedagogue; a type which the new science of psychology has caused largely to die out. He was practical, but not so practical as Mr. Squeers, who, having extracted from a student a definition of a horse scarcely equal to that of Bitzer, sends him to gain a further knowledge of that friend of man by grooming him. Mr. M'C. did not teach; he crammed. Squeers did teach, and was the better educationalist of the two!

Mr. Sleary was one of Dickens's charming asthmatics. Though in this respect of the Omer clan, he is really Vincent Crummles, half-resuscitated. Sleary was grandfather to a male Infant Phenomenon. Crummles was the father of the female I.P.

In Mrs. Blackpool we are not at all interested. She was what poor Nancy might have became, but without Nancy's excuses. Emma Gordon and Josephine Sleary might have been anybody or nobody and have their counterparts as walkers-on in various other tales.

V

A *great* novel? Yes. A picture of sordid places and stodgy people whose loves and hates and commonplace lives do not thrill us over-much, but a picture true to life. It is a book that makes us think, and makes us realise that life can be very commonplace and yet abound in tragedy and misery. A lesson that we ought to be—*must* be—interested in the unattractive dull people whom we meet, as well as in those who are attractive and brilliant.

The picture of a factory can be a great work of art, and we only expect blacks, greys, and dingy browns. Only a fool would complain that there are not seen gorgeous sunset and palms, and camels.

"What is terewth, my friends?" If I should read a book of facts, factories and fools, and should say, "Lo, it is not a good book; it hath no crystal fountains, no champagne and oysters, would that be terewth?" And echoes answer, it would be dem'd foolishness.

Hard Times is a great book, the greater for being enacted entirely by phantoms. It is Charles Dickens's Shadow Show.

F. R. Leavis (essay date 1948)

SOURCE: "*Hard Times:* An Analytic Note," in *The Great Tradition,* Doubleday & Company, Inc., 1954, pp. 273-99.

[*Leavis was an influential twentieth-century English critic. His methodology combines close textual criticism with predominantly moral and social concerns; however, Leavis is not interested in the individual writer per se, but rather with the usefulness of his or her art in the scheme of civilization. The essay reprinted below, which appeared in its present form in 1948, is widely considered the seminal (and most controversial) essay on* Hard Times *published in the twentieth century. Here, elaborating on claims made in decades past by Ruskin and Shaw, Leavis presents a case for perceiving* Hard Times *as Dickens's greatest novel. This essay has been answered by numerous critics during the past forty years, notably by John Holloway (1962) and David H. Hirsch (1964).*]

Hard Times is not a difficult work; its intention and nature are pretty obvious. If, then, it is the masterpiece I take it for, why has it not had general recognition? To judge by the critical record, it has had none at all. If there exists anywhere an appreciation, or even an acclaiming reference, I have missed it. In the books and essays on Dickens, so far as I know them, it is passed over as a very minor thing; too slight and insignificant to distract us for more than a sentence or two from the works worth critical attention. Yet, if I am right, of all Dickens's works it is the one that has all the strength of his genius, together with a strength no other of them can show—that of a completely serious work of art.

The answer to the question asked above seems to me to bear on the traditional approach to 'the English novel.' For all the more sophisticated critical currency of the last decade or two, that approach still prevails, at any rate in the appreciation of the Victorian novelists. The business of the novelist, you gather, is to 'create a world,' and the mark of the master is external abundance—he gives you lots of 'life.' The test of life in his characters (he must above all create 'living' characters) is that they go on living outside the book. Expectations as unexacting as these are not when they encounter significance, grateful for it, and when it meets them in that insistent form where nothing is very engaging as 'life' unless its relevance is fully taken, miss it altogether. This is the only way in which I can account for the neglect suffered by Henry James's *The Europeans,* which may be classed with **Hard Times** as a moral fable—though one might have supposed that James would enjoy the advantage of being approached with expectations of subtlety and closely calculated relevance. Fashion, however, has not recommended his earlier work, and this (whatever appreciation may be enjoyed by *The Ambassadors*) still suffers from the prevailing expectation of redundant and irrelevant 'life.'

I need say no more by way of defining the moral fable than that in it the intention is peculiarly insistent, so that the representative significance of everything in the fable—character, episode, and so on—is immediately apparent as we read. Intention might seem to be insistent enough in the opening of **Hard Times,** in that scene in Mr. Gradgrind's school. But then, intention is often very insistent in Dickens, without its being taken up in any inclusive significance that informs and organizes a coherent whole; and, for lack of any expectation of an organized whole, it has no doubt been supposed that in **Hard Times** the satiric irony of the first two chapters is merely, in the large and genial Dickensian way, thrown together with melodrama, pathos and humour—and that we are given these ingredients more abundantly and exuberantly elsewhere. Actually, the Dickensian vitality is there, in its varied characteristic modes, which have the more force because they are free of redundance: the creative exuberance is controlled by a profound inspiration.

The inspiration is what is given in the title, **Hard Times.** Ordinarily Dickens's criticisms of the world he lives in are casual and incidental—a matter of including among the ingredients of a book some indignant treatment of a particular abuse. But in **Hard Times** he is for once possessed by a comprehensive vision, one in which the inhumanities of Victorian civilization are seen as fostered and sanctioned by a hard philosophy, the aggressive formulation of an inhumane spirit. The philosophy is represented by Thomas Gradgrind, Esquire, Member of Parliament for Coketown, who has brought up his children on the lines of the experiment recorded by John Stuart Mill as carried out on himself. What Gradgrind stands for is, though repellent, nevertheless respectable; his Utilitarianism is a theory sincerely held and there is intellectual disinterestedness in its application. But Gradgrind marries his eldest daughter to Josiah Bounderby, 'banker, merchant, manufacturer,' about whom there is no disinterestedness whatever, and nothing to be respected. Bounderby is Victorian 'rugged individualism' in its grossest and most intransigent form. Concerned with nothing but self-assertion and power and material success, he has no interest in ideals or ideas—except the idea of being the completely self-made man (since, for all his brag, he is not that in fact). Dickens here makes a just observation about the affinities and practical tendency of Utilitarianism, as, in his presentment of the Gradgrind home and the Gradgrind elementary school, he does about the Utilitarian spirit in Victorian education.

All this is obvious enough. But Dickens's art, while remaining that of the great popular entertainer, has in *Hard Times,* as he renders his full critical vision, a stamina, a flexibility combined with consistency, and a depth that he seems to have had little credit for. Take that opening scene in the school-room:

> 'Girl number twenty,' said Mr. Gradgrind, squarely pointing with his square forefinger, 'I don't know that girl. Who is that girl?'

> 'Sissy Jupe, sir,' explained number twenty, blushing, standing up, and curtsying.

> 'Sissy is not a name,' said Mr. Gradgrind. 'Don't call yourself Sissy. Call yourself Cecilia.'

> 'It's father as call me Sissy, sir,' returned the young girl in a trembling voice, and with another curtsy.

> 'Then he has no business to do it,' said Mr. Gradgrind. 'Tell him he mustn't. Cecilia Jupe. Let me see. What is your father?'

> 'He belongs to the horse-riding, if you please, sir.'

> Mr. Gradgrind frowned, and waved off the objectionable calling with his hand.

> 'We don't want to know anything about that here. You mustn't tell us about that here. Your father breaks horses, don't he?'

> 'If you please, sir, when they can get any to break, they do break horses in the ring, sir.'

> 'You mustn't tell us about the ring here. Very well, then. Describe your father as a horse-breaker. He doctors sick horses, I dare say?'

> 'Oh, yes, sir!'

> 'Very well, then. He is a veterinary surgeon, a farrier, and horse-breaker. Give me your definition of a horse.'

> (Sissy Jupe thrown into the greatest alarm by this demand.)

> 'Girl number twenty unable to define a horse!' said Mr. Gradgrind, for the general benefit of all the little

pitchers. 'Girl number twenty possessed of no facts in reference to one of the commonest animals! Some boy's definition of a horse. Bitzer, yours.'

. . . . .

> 'Quadruped. Graminivorous. Forty teeth, namely, twenty-four grinders, four eye-teeth, and twelve incisive. Sheds coat in the spring; in marshy countries, sheds hoofs too. Hoofs hard, but requiring to be shod with iron. Age known by marks in mouth.' Thus (and much more) Bitzer.

Lawrence himself, protesting against harmful tendencies in education, never made the point more tellingly. Sissy has been brought up among horses, and among people whose livelihood depends upon understanding horses but 'we don't want to know anything about that here.' Such knowledge isn't real knowledge. Bitzer, the model pupil, on the button's being pressed, promptly vomits up the genuine article, 'Quadruped. Graminivorous,' etc.; and 'Now, girl number twenty, you know what a horse is.' The irony, pungent enough locally, is richly developed in the subsequent action. Bitzer's aptness has its evaluative comment in his career. Sissy's incapacity to acquire this kind of 'fact' or formula, her unaptness for education, is manifested to us, on the other hand, as part and parcel of her sovereign and indefeasible humanity: it is the virtue that makes it impossible for her to understand, or acquiesce in, an ethos for which she is 'girl number twenty,' or to think of any other human being as a unit for arithmetic.

This kind of ironic method might seem to commit the author to very limited kinds of effect. In *Hard Times,* however, it associates quite congruously, such is the flexibility of Dickens's art, with very different methods; it cooperates in a truly dramatic and profoundly poetic whole. Sissy Jupe, who might be taken here for a merely conventional *persona,* has already, as a matter of fact, been established in a potently symbolic rôle: she is part of the poetically-creative operation of Dickens's genius in *Hard Times*. Here is a passage I omitted from the middle of the excerpt quoted above:

> The square finger, moving here and there, lighted suddenly on Bitzer, perhaps because he chanced to sit in the same ray of sun-light which, darting in at one of the bare windows of the intensely whitewashed room, irradiated Sissy. For the boys and girls sat on the face of an inclined plane in two compact bodies, divided up the centre by a narrow interval; and Sissy, being at the corner of a row on the sunny side, came in for the beginning of a sunbeam, of which Bitzer, being at the corner of a row on the other side, a few rows in advance, caught the end. But, whereas the girl was so dark-eyed and dark-haired that she seemed to receive a deeper and more lustrous colour from the sun when it shone upon her, the boy was so light-eyed and light-haired that the self-same rays appeared to draw out of him what little colour he ever possessed. His cold eyes would hardly have been eyes, but for the short ends of lashes which, by bringing them into immediate contrast with something paler than themselves, expressed their form. His short-cropped hair might have been a mere continuation of the sandy

freckles on his forehead and face. His skin was so unwholesomely deficient in the natural tinge, that he looked as though, if he were cut, he would bleed white.

There is no need to insist on the force—representative of Dickens's art in general in *Hard Times*—with which the moral and spiritual differences are rendered here in terms of sensation, so that the symbolic intention emerges out of metaphor and the vivid evocation of the concrete. What may, perhaps, be emphasized is that Sissy stands for vitality as well as goodness—they are seen, in fact, as one; she is generous, impulsive life, finding self-fulfilment in self-forgetfulness—all that is the antithesis of calculating self-interest. There is an essentially Laurentian suggestion about the way in which 'the dark-eyed and dark-haired" girl, contrasting with Bitzer, seemed to receive a 'deeper and more lustrous colour from the sun,' so opposing the life that is lived freely and richly from the deep instinctive and emotional springs to the thin-blooded, quasi-mechanical product of Gradgrindery.

Sissy's symbolic significance is bound up with that of Sleary's Horse-riding, where human kindness is very insistently associated with vitality. Representing human spontaneity, the circus-athletes represent at the same time highly-developed skill and deftness of kinds that bring poise, pride and confident ease—they are always buoyant, and, ballet-dancer-like, in training:

> There were two or three handsome young women among them, with two or three husbands, and their two or three mothers, and their eight or nine little children, who did the fairy business when required. The father of one of the families was in the habit of balancing the father of another of the families on the top of a great pole; the father of the third family often made a pyramid of both those fathers, with Master Kidderminster for the apex, and himself for the base; all the fathers could dance upon rolling casks, stand upon bottles, catch knives and balls, twirl hand-basins, ride upon anything, jump over everything, and stick at nothing. All the mothers could (and did) dance upon the slack wire and the tight-rope, and perform rapid acts on bare-backed steeds; none of them were at all particular in respect of showing their legs; and one of them, alone in a Greek chariot, drove six-in-hand into every town they came to. They all assumed to be mighty rakish and knowing, they were not very tidy in their private dresses, they were not at all orderly in their domestic arrangements, and the combined literature of the whole company would have produced but a poor letter on any subject. Yet there was a remarkable gentleness and childishness about these people, a special inaptitude for any kind of sharp practice, and an untiring readiness to help and pity one another, deserving often of as much respect, and always of as much generous construction, as the everyday virtues of any class of people in the world.

Their skills have no value for the Utilitarian calculus, but they express vital human impulse, and they minister to vital human needs. The Horse-riding, frowned upon as frivolous and wasteful by Gradgrind and malignantly scorned by Bounderby, brings the machine-hands of Coke-town (the spirit-quenching hideousness of which is hauntingly evoked) what they are starved of. It brings to them, not merely amusement, but art, and the spectacle of triumphant activity that, seeming to contain its end within itself, is, in its easy mastery, joyously self-justified. In investing a travelling circus with this kind of symbolic value Dickens expresses a profounder reaction to industrialism than might have been expected of him. It is not only pleasure and relaxation the Coketowners stand in need of; he feels the dreadful degradation of life that would remain even if they were to be given a forty-four hour week, comfort, security and fun. We recall a characteristic passage from D. H. Lawrence.

> The car ploughed uphill through the long squalid straggle of Tevershall, the blackened brick dwellings, the black slate roofs, glistening their sharp edges, the mud black with coal-dust, the pavements wet and black. It was as if dismalness had soaked through and through everything. The utter negation of natural beauty, the utter negation of the gladness of life, the utter absence of the instinct for shapely beauty which every bird and beast has, the utter death of the human intuitive faculty was appalling. The stacks of soap in the grocers' shops, the rhubarb and lemons in the greengrocers'! the awful hats in the milliners all went by ugly, ugly, ugly, followed by the plaster and gilt horror of the cinema with its wet picture announcements, 'A Woman's Love,' and the new big Primitive chapel, primitive enough in its stark brick and big panes of greenish and raspberry glass in the windows. The Wesleyan chapel, higher up, was of blackened brick and stood behind iron railings and blackened shrubs. The Congregational chapel, which thought itself superior, was built of rusticated sandstone and had a steeple, but not a very high one. Just beyond were the new school buildings, expensive pink brick, and gravelled playground inside iron railings, all very imposing, and mixing the suggestion of a chapel and a prison. Standard Five girls were having a singing lesson, just finishing the la-me-do-la exercises and beginning a 'sweet children's song.' Anything more unlike song, spontaneous song, would be impossible to imagine: a strange bawling yell followed the outlines of a tune. It was not like animals: animals *mean* something when they yell. It was like nothing on earth, and it was called singing. Connie sat and listened with her heart in her boots, as Field was filling petrol. What could possibly become of such a people, a people in whom the living intuitive faculty was dead as nails, and only queer mechanical yells and uncanny will-power remained?

Dickens couldn't have put it in just those terms, but the way in which his vision of the Horse-riders insists on their gracious vitality implies that reaction.

Here an objection may be anticipated—as a way of making a point. Coketown, like Gradgrind and Bounderby, is real enough; but it can't be contended that the Horse-riding is real in the same sense. There would have been some athletic skill and perhaps some bodily grace among the people of a Victorian travelling circus, but surely so much squalor, grossness and vulgarity that we must find Dickens's symbolism sentimentally false? And 'there was a remarkable gentleness and childishness about these people, a special inaptitude for any kind of sharp practice'—that, surely, is going ludicrously too far?

If Dickens, intent on an emotional effect, or drunk with moral enthusiasm, had been deceiving himself (it couldn't have been innocently) about the nature of the actuality, he would then indeed have been guilty of sentimental falsity, and the adverse criticism would have held. But the Horse-riding presents no such case. The virtues and qualities that Dickens prizes do indeed exist, and it is necessary for his critique of Utilitarianism and industrialism, and for (what is the same thing) his creative purpose, to evoke them vividly. The book can't, in my judgment, be fairly charged with giving a misleading representation of human nature. And it would plainly not be intelligent criticism to suggest that anyone could be misled about the nature of circuses by *Hard Times*. The critical question is merely one of tact: was it well-judged of Dickens to try to do that—which had to be done somehow—with a travelling circus?

Or, rather, the question is: by what means has he succeeded? For the success is complete. It is conditioned partly by the fact that, from the opening chapters, we have been tuned for the reception of a highly conventional art—though it is a tuning that has no narrowly limiting effect. To describe at all cogently the means by which this responsiveness is set up would take a good deal of 'practical criticism' analysis—analysis that would reveal an extraordinary flexibility in the art of *Hard Times*. This can be seen very obviously in the dialogue. Some passages might come from an ordinary novel. Others have the ironic pointedness of the school-room scene in so insistent a form that we might be reading a work as stylized as Jonsonian comedy: Gradgrind's final exchange with Bitzer (quoted below) is a supreme instance. Others again are 'literary,' like the conversation between Gradgrind and Louisa on her flight home for refuge from Mr. James Harthouse's attentions.

To the question how the reconciling is done—there is much more diversity in *Hard Times* than these references to dialogue suggest—the answer can be given by pointing to the astonishing and irresistible richness of life that characterizes the book everywhere. It meets us everywhere, unstrained and natural, in the prose. Out of such prose a great variety of presentations can arise congenially with equal vividness. There they are, unquestionably 'real.' It goes back to an extraordinary energy of perception and registration in Dickens. 'When people say that Dickens exaggerates,' says Mr. Santayana, 'it seems to me that they can have no eyes and no ears. They probably have only *notions* of what things and people are; they accept them conventionally, at their diplomatic value.' Settling down as we read to an implicit recognition of this truth, we don't readily and confidently apply any criterion we suppose ourselves to hold for distinguishing varieties of relation between what Dickens gives us and a normal 'real.' His flexibility is that of a richly poetic art of the word. He doesn't write 'poetic prose'; he writes with a poetic force of evocation, registering with the responsiveness of a genius of verbal expression what he so sharply

sees and feels. In fact, by texture, imaginative mode, symbolic method, and the resulting concentration, *Hard Times* affects us as belonging with formally poetic works.

R. C. Churchill on Dickens's descriptions in *Hard Times*:

Like Cobbett, [Dickens] was concerned not only for the welfare of the poor but for their dignity; unlike Cobbett, he did not see the remedy in economics. Probably he saw no remedies at all, save the fundamental Christian or moral one. In *Hard Times,* his most impressive statement of the problems of poverty, he insists merely upon a better understanding between the conflicting parties; not only between the maltreated labourer and the would-be reformer. "In an England gone mad about a minor theory," says Chesterton, "he reasserted the original idea—that no one in the state must be too weak to influence the state." It is a mistake to look in Dickens's writings for "solutions"; in *Hard Times* the view he takes is too long, and in *The Uncommercial Traveller* probably too short, to suit either the economist or the politician. It is the *presenting* of the case which we should naturally expect from a novelist embarked upon this theme, and *Hard Times* does that for us, unforgettably. The description of Coketown at the beginning of the book owes nothing to sentimentality:

Let us strike the key-note, Coketown, before pursuing our tune. It was a town of red brick that would have been red if the smoke and ashes had allowed it . . . It was a town of machinery and tall chimneys, out of which interminable serpents of smoke trailed themselves for ever, and never got uncoiled. . . . It contained several large streets all very like one another, and many small streets still more like one another . . . You saw nothing in Coketown but was severely workful; the jail might have been the infirmary, the infirmary might have been the jail, the town-hall might have been either . . . .

R.C. Churchill, in Scrutiny, *Summer 1942.*

There is, however, more to be said about the success that attends Dickens's symbolic intention in the Horse-riding; there is an essential quality of his genius to be emphasized. There is no Hamlet in him, and he is quite unlike Mr. Eliot.

> The red-eyed scavengers are creeping
> 　　From Kentish Town and Golders Green

—there is nothing of that in Dickens's reaction to life. He observes with gusto the humanness of humanity as exhibited in the urban (and suburban) scene. When he sees, as he sees so readily, the common manifestations of human kindness, and the essential virtues, asserting themselves in the midst of ugliness, squalor and banality, his warmly sympathetic response has no disgust to overcome. There is no suggestion, for instance, of recoil—or of distance-keeping—from the game-eyed, brandy-soaked, flabby-surfaced Mr. Sleary, who is successfully made to figure for us a humane, anti-Utilitarian positive. This is not sentimentality in Dickens, but genius, and a genius that should be found peculiarly worth attention in an age when, as D. H. Lawrence (with, as I remember, Mr. Wyndham Lewis immediately in view) says, 'My God! they stink,' tends to be an insuperable and final reaction.

Dickens, as everyone knows, is very capable of sentimentality. We have it in *Hard Times* (though not to any seriously damaging effect) in Stephen Blackpool, the good, victimized working-man, whose perfect patience under infliction we are expected to find supremely edifying and irresistibly touching as the agonies are piled on for his martyrdom. But Sissy Jupe is another matter. A general description of her part in the fable might suggest the worst, but actually she has nothing in common with Little Nell: she shares in the strength of the Horse-riding. She is wholly convincing in the function Dickens assigns to her. The working of her influence in the Utilitarian home is conveyed with a fine tact, and we do really feel her as a growing potency. Dickens can even, with complete success, give her the stage for a victorious *tête-à-tête* with the well-bred and languid elegant, Mr. James Harthouse, in which she tells him that his duty is to leave Coketown and cease troubling Louisa with his attentions:

> She was not afraid of him, or in any way disconcerted; she seemed to have her mind entirely preoccupied with the occasion of her visit, and to have substituted that consideration for herself.

The quiet victory of disinterested goodness is wholly convincing.

At the opening of the book Sissy establishes the essential distinction between Gradgrind and Bounderby. Gradgrind, by taking her home, however ungraciously, shows himself capable of humane feeling, however unacknowledged. We are reminded, in the previous school-room scene, of the Jonsonian affinities of Dickens's art, and Bounderby turns out to be consistently a Jonsonian character in the sense that he is incapable of change. He remains the blustering egotist and braggart, and responds in character to the collapse of his marriage:

> I'll give *you* to understand, in reply to that, that there unquestionably is an incompatibility of the first magnitude—to be summed up in this—that your daughter don't properly know her husband's merits, and is not impressed with such a sense as would become her, by George! of the honour of his alliance. That's plain speaking, I hope.

He remains Jonsonianly consistent in his last testament and death. But Gradgrind, in the nature of the fable, has to *experience* the confutation of his philosophy, and to be capable of the change involved in admitting that life has proved him wrong. (Dickens's art in *Hard Times* differs from Ben Jonson's not in being inconsistent, but in being so very much more flexible and inclusive—a point that seemed to be worth making because the relation between Dickens and Jonson has been stressed of late, and I have known unfair conclusions to be drawn from the comparison, notably in respect of *Hard Times*.)

The confutation of Utilitarianism by life is conducted with great subtlety. That the conditions for it are there in Mr. Gradgrind he betrays by his initial kindness, ungenial enough, but properly rebuked by Bounderby, to Sissy. 'Mr. Gradgrind,' we are told, 'though hard enough, was by no means so rough a man as Mr. Bounderby. His character was not unkind, all things considered; it might have been very kind indeed if only he had made some mistake in the arithmetic that balanced it years ago.' The inadequacy of the calculus is beautifully exposed when he brings it to bear on the problem of marriage in the consummate scene with his eldest daughter:

> He waited, as if he would have been glad that she said something. But she said never a word.

> 'Louisa, my dear, you are the subject of a proposal of marriage that has been made to me.'

> 'Again he waited, and again she answered not one word. This so far surprised him as to induce him gently to repeat, 'A proposal of marriage, my dear.' To which she returned, without any visible emotion whatever:

> 'I hear you, father. I am attending, I assure you.'

> 'Well!' said Mr. Gradgrind, breaking into a smile, after being for the moment at a loss, 'you are even more dispassionate than I expected, Louisa. Or, perhaps, you are not unprepared for the announcement I have it in charge to make?'

> 'I cannot say that, father, until I hear it. Prepared or unprepared, I wish to hear it all from you. I wish to hear you state it to me, father.'

> Strange to relate, Mr. Gradgrind was not so collected at this moment as his daughter was. He took a paper knife in his hand, turned it over, laid it down, took it up again, and even then had to look along the blade of it, considering how to go on.

> 'What you say, my dear Louisa, is perfectly reasonable. I have undertaken, then, to let you know that—in short, that Mr. Bounderby . . .'

His embarrassment—by his own avowal—is caused by the perfect rationality with which she receives his overture. He is still more disconcerted when, with a completely dispassionate matter-of-factness that does credit to his *régime,* she gives him the opportunity to state in plain terms precisely what marriage should mean for the young Houyhnhnm:

> Silence between them. The deadly statistical clock very hollow. The distant smoke very black and heavy.

> 'Father,' said Louisa, 'do you think I love Mr. Bounderby?'

> Mr. Gradgrind was extremely discomforted by this unexpected question. 'Well, my child,' he returned,

'I—really—cannot take upon myself to say.'

'Father,' pursued Louisa in exactly the same voice as before, 'do you ask me to love Mr. Bounderby?'

'My dear Louisa, no. I ask nothing.'

'Father,' she still pursued, 'does Mr. Bounderby ask me to love him?'

'Really, my dear,' said Mr. Gradgrind, 'it is difficult to answer your question—'

'Difficult to answer it, Yes or No, father?'

'Certainly, my dear. Because'—here was something to demonstrate, and it set him up again—'because the reply depends so materially, Louisa, on the sense in which we use the expression. Now, Mr. Bounderby does not do you the injustice, and does not do himself the injustice, of pretending to anything fanciful, fantastic, or (I am using synonymous terms) sentimental. Mr. Bounderby would have seen you grow up under his eye to very little purpose, if he could so far forget what is due to your good sense, not to say to his, as to address you from any such ground. Therefore, perhaps, the expression itself—I merely suggest this to you, my dear—may be a little misplaced.'

'What would you advise me to use in its stead, father?'

'Why, my dear Louisa,' said Mr. Gradgrind, completely recovered by this time, 'I would advise you (since you ask me) to consider the question, as you have been accustomed to consider every other question, simply as one of tangible Fact. The ignorant and the giddy may embarrass such subjects with irrelevant fancies, and other absurdities that have no existence, properly viewed—really no existence—but it is no compliment to you to say that you know better. Now, what are the Facts of this case? You are, we will say in round numbers, twenty years of age; Mr. Bounderby is, we will say in round numbers, fifty. There is some disparity in your respective years, but . . . '

—And at this point Mr. Gradgrind seizes the chance for a happy escape into statistics. But Louisa brings him firmly back:

'What do you recommend, father?' asked Louisa, her reserved composure not in the least affected by these gratifying results, that 'I should substitute for the term I used just now? For the misplaced expression?'

'Louisa,' returned her father, 'it appears to me that nothing can be plainer. Confining yourself rigidly to Fact, the question of Fact you state to yourself is: Does Mr. Bounderby ask me to marry him? Yes, he does. The sole remaining question then is: Shall I marry him? I think nothing can be plainer than that.'

'Shall I marry him?' repeated Louisa with great deliberation.

'Precisely.'

It is a triumph of ironic art. No logical analysis could dispose of the philosophy of fact and calculus with such neat finality. As the issues are reduced to algebraic formulation they are patently emptied of all real meaning. The instinct-free rationality of the emotionless Houyhnhnm is a void. Louisa proceeds to try and make him understand that she is a living creature and therefore no Houyhnhnm, but in vain ('to see it, he must have overleaped at a bound the artificial barriers he had for many years been erecting between himself and all those subtle essences of humanity which will elude the utmost cunning of algebra, until the last trumpet ever to be sounded will blow even algebra to wreck').

Removing her eyes from him, she sat so long looking silently towards the town, that he said at length: 'Are you consulting the chimneys of the Coketown works, Louisa?'

'There seems to be nothing there but languid and monotonous smoke. Yet, when the night comes, Fire bursts out, father!' she answered, turning quickly.

'Of course I know that, Louisa. I do not see the application of the remark.' To do him justice, he did not at all.

She passed it away with a slight motion of her hand, and concentrating her attention upon him again, said,

'Father, I have often thought that life is very short.'— This was so distinctly one of his subjects that he interposed:

'It is short, no doubt, my dear. Still, the average duration of human life is proved to have increased of late years. The calculations of various life assurance and annuity offices, among other figures which cannot go wrong, have established the fact.'

'I speak of my own life, father.'

'Oh, indeed! Still,' said Mr. Gradgrind, 'I need not point out to you, Louisa, that it is governed by the laws which govern lives in the aggregate.'

'While it lasts, I would wish to do the little I can, and the little I am fit for. What does it matter?'

Mr. Gradgrind seemed rather at a loss to understand the last four words; replying, 'How, matter? What matter, my dear?'

'Mr. Bounderby,' she went on in a steady, straight way, without regarding this, 'asks me to marry him. The question I have to ask myself is, shall I marry him? That is so, father, is it not? You have told me so, father. Have you not?'

'Certainly, my dear.'

'Let it be so.'

The psychology of Louisa's development and of her brother Tom's is sound. Having no outlet for her emotional life except in her love for her brother, she lives for him, and marries Bounderby—under pressure from Tom—for Tom's sake ('What does it matter?'). Thus, by the constrictions and starvations of the Gradgrind *régime,* are natural affection and capacity for disinterested devotion turned to ill. As for Tom, the *régime* has made of him a bored and sullen whelp, and 'he was becoming that not unprecedented triumph of calculation which is usually at work on number one'—the Utilitarian philosophy has done that for him. He declares that when he goes to live with Bounderby as having a post in the bank, 'he'll have his revenge.'—'I mean, I'll enjoy myself a little, and go about and see something and hear something. I'll recompense myself for the way in which I've been brought up.' His descent into debt and bank-robbery is natural. And it is natural that Louisa, having sacrificed herself for this unrepaying object of affection, should be found not altogether unresponsive when Mr. James Harthouse, having sized up the situation, pursues his opportunity with well-bred and calculating tact. His apologia for genteel cynicism is a shrewd thrust at the Gradgrind philosophy:

> 'The only difference between us and the professors of virtue or benevolence, or philanthropy—never mind the name—is, that we know it is all meaningless, and say so; while they know it equally, and will never say so.'

> 'Why should she be shocked or warned by this reiteration? It was not so unlike her father's principles, and her early training, that it need startle her.

When, fleeing from temptation, she arrives back at her father's house, tells him her plight, and, crying, 'All I know is, your philosophy and your teaching will not save me,' collapses, he sees 'the pride of his heart and the triumph of his system lying an insensible heap at his feet.' The fallacy now calamitously demonstrated can be seen focussed in that 'pride,' which brings together in an illusory oneness the pride of his system and his love for his child. What that love is Gradgrind now knows, and he knows that it matters to him more than the system, which is thus confuted (the educational failure as such being a lesser matter). There is nothing sentimental here; the demonstration is impressive, because we are convinced of the love, and because Gradgrind has been made to exist for us as a man who has 'meant to do right':

> He said it earnestly, and, to do him justice, he had. In gauging fathomless deeps with his little mean excise rod, and in staggering over the universe with his rusty stiff-legged compasses, he had meant to do great things. Within the limits of his short tether he had tumbled about, annihilating the flowers of existence with greater singleness of purpose than many of the blatant personages whose company he kept.

The demonstration still to come, that of which the other 'triumph of his system,' Tom, is the centre, is sardonic comedy, imagined with great intensity and done with the sure touch of genius. There is the pregnant scene in which Mr. Gradgrind, in the deserted ring of a third-rate travelling circus, has to recognize his son in a comic negro servant; and has to recognize that his son owes his escape from Justice to a peculiarly disinterested gratitude—to the opportunity given him by the non-Utilitarian Mr. Sleary, grateful for Sissy's sake, to assume such a disguise:

> In a preposterous coat, like a beadle's, with cuffs and flaps exaggerated to an unspeakable extent; in an immense waistcoat, knee breeches, buckled shoes, and a mad cocked-hat; with nothing fitting him, and everything of coarse material, moth-eaten, and full of holes; with seams in his black face, where fear and heat had started through the greasy composition daubed all over it; anything so grimly, detestably, ridiculously shameful as the whelp in his comic livery, Mr. Gradgrind never could by any other means have believed in, weighable and measurable fact though it was. And one of his model children had come to this!

> At first the whelp would not draw any nearer but persisted in remaining up there by himself. Yielding at length, if any concession so sullenly made can be called yielding, to the entreaties of Sissy—for Louisa he disowned altogether—he came down, bench by bench, until he stood in the sawdust, on the verge of the circle, as far as possible, within its limits, from where his father sat.

> 'How was this done?' asked the father.

> 'How was what done?' moodily answered the son.

> 'This robbery,' said the father, raising his voice upon the word.

> 'I forced the safe myself overnight, and shut it up ajar before I went away. I had had the key that was found made long before. I dropped it that morning, that it might be supposed to have been used. I didn't take the money all at once. I pretended to put my balance away every night, but I didn't. Now you know all about it.'

> 'If a thunderbolt had fallen on me,' said the father, 'it would have shocked me less than this!'

> 'I don't see why,' grumbled the son. 'So many people are employed in situations of trust; so many people, out of so many, will be dishonest. I have heard you talk, a hundred times, of its being a law. How can *I* help laws? You have comforted others with such things, father. Comfort yourself!'

> The father buried his face in his hands, and the son stood in his disgraceful grotesqueness, biting straw: his hands, with the black partly worn away inside, looking like the hands of a monkey. The evening was fast closing in; and, from time to time, he turned the whites of his eyes restlessly and impatiently towards his father. They were the only parts of his face that showed any life or expression, the pigment upon it

was so thick.

Something of the rich complexity of Dickens's art may be seen in this passage. No simple formula can take account of the various elements in the whole effect, a sardonic-tragic in which satire consorts with pathos. The excerpt in itself suggests the justification for saying that *Hard Times* is a poetic work. It suggests that the genius of the writer may fairly be described as that of a poetic dramatist, and that, in our preconceptions about 'the novel,' we may miss, within the field of fictional prose, possibilities of concentration and flexibility in the interpretation of life such as we associate with Shakespearean drama.

The note, as we have it above in Tom's retort, of ironic-satiric discomfiture of the Utilitarian philosopher by the rebound of his formulae upon himself is developed in the ensuing scene with Bitzer, the truly successful pupil, the real triumph of the system. He arrives to intercept Tom's flight:

> Bitzer, still holding the paralysed culprit by the collar, stood in the Ring, blinking at his old patron through the darkness of the twilight.
>
> 'Bitzer,' said Mr. Gradgrind, broken down, and miserably submissive to him, 'have you a heart?'
>
> 'The circulation, sir,' returned Bitzer, smiling at the oddity of the question, 'couldn't be carried on without one. No man, sir, acquainted with the facts established by Harvey relating to the circulation of the blood, can doubt that I have a heart.'
>
> 'Is it accessible,' cried Mr. Gradgrind, 'to any compassionate influence?'
>
> 'It is accessible to Reason, sir,' returned the excellent young man. 'And to nothing else.'
>
> They stood looking at each other; Mr. Gradgrind's face as white as the pursuer's.
>
> 'What motive—even what motive in reason—can you have for preventing the escape of this wretched youth,' said Mr. Gradgrind, 'and crushing his miserable father? See his sister here. Pity us!'
>
> 'Sir,' returned Bitzer in a very business-like and logical manner, 'since you ask me what motive I have in reason for taking young Mr. Tom back to Coketown, it is only reasonable to let you know . . . I am going to take young Mr. Tom back to Coketown, in order to deliver him over to Mr. Bounderby. Sir, I have no doubt whatever that Mr. Bounderby will then promote me to young Mr. Tom's situation. And I wish to have his situation, sir, for it will be a rise to me, and will do me good.'
>
> 'If this is solely a question of self-interest with you—' Mr. Gradgrind began.
>
> 'I beg your pardon for interrupting you, sir,' returned Bitzer, 'but I am sure you know that the whole social system is a question of self-interest. What you must always appeal to is a person's self-interest. It's your only hold. We are so constituted. I was brought up in that catechism when I was very young, sir, as you are aware.'
>
> 'What sum of money,' said Mr. Gradgrind, 'will you set against your expected promotion?'
>
> 'Thank you, sir,' returned Bitzer, 'for hinting at the proposal; but I will not set any sum against it. Knowing that your clear head would propose that alternative, I have gone over the calculations in my mind; and I find that to compound a felony, even on very high terms indeed, would not be as safe and good for me as my improved prospects in the Bank.'
>
> 'Bitzer,' said Mr. Gradgrind, stretching out his hands as though he would have said, See how miserable I am! 'Bitzer, I have but one chance left to soften you. You were many years at my school. If, in remembrance of the pains bestowed upon you there, you can persuade yourself in any degree to disregard your present interest and release my son, I entreat and pray you to give him the benefit of that remembrance.'
>
> 'I really wonder, sir,' rejoined the old pupil in an argumentative manner, 'to find you taking a position so untenable. My schooling was paid for; it was a bargain; and when I came away, the bargain ended.'
>
> It was a fundamental principle of the Gradgrind philosophy, that everything was to be paid for. Nobody was ever on any account to give anybody anything, or render anybody help without purchase. Gratitude was to be abolished, and the virtues springing from it were not to be. Every inch of the existence of mankind, from birth to death, was to be a bargain across the counter. And if we didn't get to Heaven that way, it was not a politico-economical place, and we had no business there.
>
> 'I don't deny,' added Bitzer, 'that my schooling was cheap. But that comes right, sir. I was made in the cheapest market, and have to dispose of myself in the dearest.'

Tom's escape is contrived, successfully in every sense, by means belonging to Dickensian high-fantastic comedy. And there follows the solemn moral of the whole fable, put with the rightness of genius into Mr. Sleary's asthmatic mouth. He, agent of the artist's marvellous tact, acquits himself of it characteristically:

> 'Thquire, you don't need to be told that dogth ith wonderful animalth.'
>
> 'Their instinct,' said Mr. Gradgrind, 'is surprising.'
>
> 'Whatever you call it—and I'm bletht if I know what to call it'—said Sleary, 'it ith athtonithing. The way in

which a dog'll find you—the dithtanthe he'll come!'

'His scent,' said Mr. Gradgrind, 'being so fine.'

'I'm bletht if I know what to call it,' repeated Sleary, shaking his head, 'but I have had dogth find me, Thquire . . . .'

—And Mr. Sleary proceeds to explain that Sissy's truant father is certainly dead because his performing dog, who would never have deserted him living, has come back to the Horse-riding:

> he wath lame, and pretty well blind. He went round to our children, one after another, ath if he wath a theeking for a child he knowed; and then he come to me, and throwed hithelf up behind, and thtood on his two fore-legth, weak as he wath, and then he wagged hith tail and died. Thquire, that dog was Merrylegth.

The whole passage has to be read as it stands in the text (Book III, Chapter VIII). Reading it there we have to stand off and reflect at a distance to recognize the potentialities that might have been realized elsewhere as Dickensian sentimentality. There is nothing sentimental in the actual effect. The profoundly serious intention is in control, the touch sure, and the structure that ensures the poise unassertively complex. Here is the formal moral:

> 'Tho, whether her father bathely detherted her; or whether he broke hith own heart alone, rather than pull her down along with him; never will be known now, Thquire, till—no, not till we know how the dogth findth uth out!'

> 'She keeps the bottle that he sent her for, to this hour; and she will believe in his affection to the last moment of her life,' said Mr. Gradgrind.

> 'It theemth to prethent two thingth to a perthon, don't it, Thquire?' said Mr. Sleary, musing as he looked down into the depths of his brandy-and-water: 'one, that there ith a love in the world, not all Thelf-interetht after all, but thomething very different; t'other, that it hath a way of ith own of calculating or not calculating, whith thomehow or another ith at leatht ath hard to give a name to, ath the wayth of the dogth ith!'

> Mr. Gradgrind looked out of the window, and made no reply. Mr. Sleary emptied his glass and recalled the ladies.

It will be seen that the effect (I repeat, the whole passage must be read), apparently so simple and easily right, depends upon a subtle interplay of diverse elements, a multiplicity in unison of timbre and tone. Dickens, we know, was a popular entertainer, but Flaubert never wrote anything approaching this in subtlety of achieved art. Dickens, of course, has a vitality that we don't look for in Flaubert. Shakespeare was a popular entertainer, we reflect—not too extravagantly, we can surely tell ourselves, as we ponder passages of this characteristic quality in

their relation, a closely organized one, to the poetic whole.

Criticism, of course, has its points to make against *Hard Times*. It can be said of Stephen Blackpool, not only that he is too good and qualifies too consistently for the martyr's halo, but that he invites an adaptation of the objection brought, from the negro point of view, against Uncle Tom, which was to the effect that he was a white man's good nigger. And certainly it doesn't need a working-class bias to produce the comment that when Dickens comes to the Trade Unions his understanding of the world he offers to deal with betrays a marked limitation. There were undoubtedly professional agitators, and Trade Union solidarity was undoubtedly often asserted at the expense of the individual's rights, but it is a score against a work so insistently typical in intention that it should give the representative rôle to the agitator, Slackbridge, and make Trade Unionism nothing better than the pardonable error of the misguided and oppressed, and, as such, an agent in the martyrdom of the good working man. (But to be fair we must remember the conversation between Bitzer and Mrs. Sparsit:

> 'It is much to be regretted,' said Mrs. Sparsit, making her nose more Roman and her eyebrows more Coriolanian in the strength of her severity, 'that the united masters allow of any such class combination.'

> 'Yes, ma'am,' said Bitzer.

> 'Being united themselves, they ought one and all to set their faces against employing any man who is united with any other man,' said Mrs. Sparsit.

> 'They have done that, ma'am,' returned Bitzer; 'but it rather fell through, ma'am.'

> 'I do not pretend to understand these things,' said Mrs. Sparsit with dignity. ' . . . I only know that those people must be conquered, and that it's high time it was done, once for all.')

Just as Dickens has no glimpse of the part to be played by Trade Unionism in bettering the conditions he deplores, so, though he sees there are many places of worship in Coketown, of various kinds of ugliness, he has no notion of the part played by religion in the life of nineteenth-century industrial England. The kind of self-respecting steadiness and conscientious restraint that he represents in Stephen did certainly exist on a large scale among the working-classes, and this is an important historical fact. But there would have been no such fact if those chapels described by Dickens had had no more relation to the life of Coketown than he shows them to have.

Again, his attitude to Trade Unionism is not the only expression of a lack of political understanding. Parliament for him is merely the 'national dust-yard,' where the 'national dustmen' entertain one another 'with a great many noisy little fights among themselves,' and appoint commissions which fill blue-books with dreary facts and futile statistics—of a kind that helps Gradgrind to 'prove that the Good Samaritan was a bad economist.'

Yet Dickens's understanding of Victorian civilization is adequate for his purpose; the justice and penetration of his criticism are unaffected. And his moral perception works in alliance with a clear insight into the English social structure. Mr. James Harthouse is necessary for the plot; but he too has his representative function. He has come to Coketown as a prospective parliamentary candidate, for 'the Gradgrind party wanted assistance in cutting the throats of the Graces,' and they 'liked fine gentlemen; they pretended that they did not, but they did.' And so the alliance between the old ruling class and the 'hard' men figures duly in the fable. This economy is typical. There is Mrs. Sparsit, for instance, who might seem to be there merely for the plot. But her 'husband was a Powler,' a fact she reverts to as often as Bounderby to his mythical birth in a ditch; and the two complementary opposites, when Mr. James Harthouse, who in his languid assurance of class-superiority doesn't need to boast, is added, form a trio that suggests the whole system of British snobbery.

But the packed richness of **Hard Times** is almost incredibly varied, and not all the quoting I have indulged in suggests it adequately. The final stress may fall on Dickens's command of word, phrase, rhythm and image: in ease and range there is surely no greater master of English except Shakespeare. This comes back to saying that Dickens is a great poet: his endless resource in felicitously varied expression is an extraordinary responsiveness to life. His senses are charged with emotional energy, and his intelligence plays and flashes in the quickest and sharpest perception. That is, his mastery of 'style' is of the only kind that matters—which is not to say that he hasn't a conscious interest in what can be done with words; many of his felicities could plainly not have come if there had not been, in the background, a habit of such interest. Take this, for instance:

> He had reached the neutral ground upon the outskirts of the town, which was neither town nor country, but either spoiled. . . .

But he is no more a stylist than Shakespeare; and his mastery of expression is most fairly suggested by stressing, not his descriptive evocations (there are some magnificent ones in **Hard Times**—the varied *décor* of the action is made vividly present, you can feel the velvety dust trodden by Mrs. Sparsit in her stealth, and feel the imminent storm), but his strictly dramatic felicities. Perhaps, however, 'strictly' is not altogether a good pointer, since Dickens is a master of his chosen art, and his mastery shows itself in the way in which he moves between less direct forms of the dramatic and the direct rendering of speech. Here is Mrs. Gradgrind dying (a cipher in the Gradgrind system, the poor creature has never really been alive):

> She had positively refused to take to her bed; on the ground that, if she did, she would never hear the last of it.

Her feeble voice sounded so far away in her bundle of shawls, and the sound of another voice addressing her seemed to take such a long time in getting down to her ears, that she might have been lying at the bottom of a well. The poor lady was nearer Truth than she ever had been: which had much to do with it.

On being told that Mrs. Bounderby was there, she replied, at cross purposes, that she had never called him by that name since he had married Louisa; and that pending her choice of an objectionable name, she had called him J; and that she could not at present depart from that regulation, not being yet provided with a permanent substitute. Louisa had sat by her for some minutes, and had spoken to her often, before she arrived at a clear understanding who it was. She then seemed to come to it all at once.

'Well, my dear,' said Mrs. Gradgrind, 'and I hope you are going on satisfactorily to yourself. It was all your father's doing. He set his heart upon it. And he ought to know.'

'I want to hear of you, mother; not of myself.'

'You want to hear of me, my dear? That's something new, I am sure, when anybody wants to hear of me. Not at all well, Louisa. Very faint and giddy.'

'Are you in pain, dear mother?'

'I think there's a pain somewhere in the room,' said Mrs. Gradgrind, 'but I couldn't positively say that I have got it.'

After this strange speech, she lay silent for some time.

. . . . .

'But there is something—not an Ology at all—that your father has missed, or forgotten, Louisa. I don't know what it is. I have often sat with Sissy near me, and thought about it. I shall never get its name now. But your father may. It makes me restless. I want to write to him, to find out, for God's sake, what it is. Give me a pen, give me a pen.'

Even the power of restlessness was gone, except from the poor head, which could just turn from side to side.

She fancied, however, that her request had been complied with, and that the pen she could not have held was in her hand. It matters little what figures of wonderful no-meaning she began to trace upon her wrappers. The hand soon stopped in the midst of them; the light that had always been feeble and dim behind the weak transparency, went out; and even Mrs. Gradgrind, emerged from the shadow in which man walketh and disquieteth himself in vain, took upon her the dread solemnity of the sages and patriarchs.

With this kind of thing before us, we talk not of style but

of dramatic creation and imaginative genius.

Edgar Johnson (essay date 1952)

SOURCE: "Critique of Materialism-Criticism: *Hard Times*," in *Charles Dickens: His Tragedy and Triumph, Volume Two,* Simon and Schuster, 1952, pp. 801-19.

[*Johnson is one of the most prominent Dickens scholars of the mid to late twentieth century, and his two-volume* Charles Dickens: His Tragedy and Triumph *(1952) is considered an essential text on Dickens and his work. In the excerpt below, he provides a detailed examination of Dickens's anti-Utilitarian stance in* Hard Times, *noting that the novel's final scenes "hold . . . the essence of his defense of art."*]

Hard Times brings to a culmination an orderly development of social analysis that extends in Dickens's work from *Dombey and Son* through *Bleak House.* That development has its roots, indeed, far earlier, and is to be found, although fragmentarily, in the social attitudes underlying *Oliver Twist* and the prison scenes of *Pickwick Papers.* With *Dombey and Son,* however, Dickens achieved his first clear picture of the workings of a monetary society; and even while he was still writing that story he underlined his hostility to Mr. Dombey's world through Scrooge and the fantasy of *A Christmas Carol.* Although *David Copperfield* is mainly an exploration of personal emotion, the social comment is an organic part of its pattern. It lurks in the legal morasses of Doctors' Commons and runs through the conscienceless exploitation of child labor in the bottling warehouse; its emphasis on money is as clear in the ostentatious display of Mr. Spenlow as in the mean rapacity of Uriah Heep; its spiritual essence is painted in Steerforth's cynical middle-class indifference to the humanity of the poor and the callousness of his seduction of Little Em'ly.

Bleak House carries on that analysis to a detailed examination of the rotten workings of the social system in almost every major institution and activity of society. Except for one: the operations of that colossus of mechanized industry that had swollen its dominion until it had almost all of modern society subjected to its power. That power Dickens saw as an inhuman, life-denying tyranny. *Bleak House* reveals the monstrous tentacles of acquisitive power in general, crushing human fulfillment in its foggy coils. *Hard Times* deals with industrial power, but is not so much a picture of its ramifications as a presentation of its underlying principles. It is an analysis and a condemnation of the ethos of industrialism.

These facts partly explain why *Hard Times* has been unpopular with many readers and has been disliked by most critics. People could laugh unrestrainedly at Dick Swiveller and Pecksniff and Micawber, who can only amuse, not hurt us, but no such irresponsible mirth is possible with Bounderby and Gradgrind, who have the world appallingly under their control. In Dickens's earlier novels it had been easy to think of him as a warm-heart-ed, unphilosophic humanitarian indignant at individual cruelties. Even in *Bleak House* the reader might not realize the total meaning of the indictment, and could comfort himself by imagining that Dickens was merely prejudiced against some groups in society—lawyers, moneylenders, members of the aristocracy, politicians. But there is a desperate endeavor among commentators to ignore or belittle the dark masterpieces of Dickens's maturity because they will not let us close our eyes on the clamorous problems that threaten us with disaster. The harsh truth of Mr. Merdle and the Circumlocution Office in *Little Dorrit* is dismissed as "twaddle," and *Our Mutual Friend*'s astringent satire on Podsnap and the Veneerings as mere clowning in a dusty desert of a book. Except for a few critics such as F. R. Leavis, who do not care for Dickens's earlier work, only radicals and revolutionaries like Ruskin and Bernard Shaw have praised *Hard Times*.

For in *Hard Times* there is no mistaking Dickens's violent hostility to industrial capitalism and its entire scheme of life. Here he is proclaiming a doctrine not of individual but of social sin, unveiling what he now sees as the real state of modern society. "This," Shaw says, "is Karl Marx, Carlyle, Ruskin, Morris, Carpenter, rising up against civilization itself as a disease, and declaring that it is not our disorder but our order that is horrible; that it is not our criminals but our magnates that are robbing and murdering us; and that it is not merely Tom-all-Alone's that must be demolished and abolished, pulled down, rooted up, and made for ever impossible so that nothing shall remain of it but History's record of its infancy, but our entire social system." "Here you will find," Shaw continues, "no more villains and heroes, but only oppressors and victims, oppressing and suffering in spite of themselves, driven by a huge machinery which grinds to pieces the people it should nourish and ennoble, and having for its directors the basest and most foolish of us instead of the noblest and most farsighted." And thus, he summarizes, the indignation with which Dickens began "has spread and deepened into a passionate revolt against the whole industrial order of the modern world."

The change that reaches its climax in *Hard Times,* however, is not only in revolutionary thought, it is in method as well. And this disturbs still another group of Dickens's readers, grown used to a profusion of comic episode and a tremendous crowded canvas thronged with characters almost as numerous as life itself, all painted in vivid contrasting scenes of light and dark with a brilliant external realism. This is the method of *Dombey* and of *Bleak House,* those complicated and elaborate literary structures like some enormous medieval building whose bays and wings and niches are filled with subordinate figures and with bright genre groups of all kinds clustering in a hundred patterns ranging from grotesque fancy to portraits from nature.

Had Dickens been following this method in *Hard Times,* he would have had scenes among the clerks in Bounderby's bank like those in Mr. Dombey's countinghouse and scenes among the hands in Bounderby's factories like those of pasting on the labels in Murdstone and Grinby's warehouse. He would have had scenes of a cotton spinner getting tangled in the threads of his loom as comic as the marchioness smiting herself on the chin with her corkscrew, and extended scenes of clamorous industrial activity as vivid as the brief glimpses of glaring furnace mouths in Little Nell's nocturnal wanderings through the Black Country. He would have had scenes of the home lives of the factory laborers as warm as those of the Toodle family, and as grim as those of the brickmakers in *Bleak House*. All this would have been no less easy for Dickens's creative vitality, perhaps even easier, than the technique he did follow. Dictated partly, no doubt, by the need of compressing his story into a short novel of brief weekly installments, that technique was even more determined by Dickens's resolution to make it a formidable and concentrated blow against the iniquity of a heartless materialism.

In consequence, **Hard Times** is a morality drama, stark, formalized, allegorical, dominated by the mood of piercing through to the underlying *meaning* of the industrial scene rather than describing it in minute detail. Therefore Coketown, which might be Hanley, Preston, Birmingham, or Leeds, or, for that matter, Fall River or Pittsburgh, is drawn once for all in a few powerful strokes:

> It was a town of red brick, or of brick that would have been red if the smoke and ashes had allowed it; but as matters stood it was a town of unnatural red and black like the painted face of a savage. It was a town of machinery and tall chimneys, out of which interminable serpents of smoke trailed themselves for ever and ever, and never got uncoiled. It had a black canal in it, and a river that ran purple with ill-smelling dye, and vast piles of buildings full of windows where there was a rattling and a trembling all day long, and where the piston of the steam-engine worked monotonously up and down like the head of an elephant in a state of melancholy madness. It contained several large streets all very like one another, and many small streets still more like one another, inhabited by people equally like one another, who all went in and out at the same hours, with the same sound upon the same pavements, to do the same work, and to whom every day was the same as yesterday and tomorrow, and every year the counterpart of the last and the next.

> The streets were hot and dusty on the summer day, and the sun was so bright that it even shone through the heavy vapour drooping over Coketown, and could not be looked at steadily. Stokers emerged from low underground doorways into factory yards, and sat on steps, and posts, and palings, wiping their swarthy visages, and contemplating coals. The whole town seemed to be frying in oil. There was a stifling smell of hot oil everywhere. The steam-engines shone with it, the dresses of the Hands were soiled with it, the mills throughout their many stories oozed and trickled with it. The atmosphere of those Fairy palaces was like the breath of the simoom: and their inhabitants, wasting with the heat, toiled languidly in the desert. But no temperature made the melancholy mad elephants more mad or more sane. Their wearisome heads went

up and down at the same rate, in hot weather and cold, wet weather and dry, fair weather and foul. The measured motion of their shadows on the walls, was the substitute Coketown had to show for the shadows of rustling woods; while, for the summer hum of insects, it could offer, all the year round, from the dawn of Monday to the night of Saturday, the whir of shafts and wheels.

> Seen from a distance, in such weather, Coketown lay shrouded in a haze of its own, which appeared impervious to the sun's rays. You could only know the town was there, because you knew there could have been no such sulky blotch upon the prospect without a town. A blur of soot and smoke, now confusedly tending this way, now that way, now aspiring to the vault of Heaven, now murkily creeping along the earth, as the wind rose and fell, or changed its quarter: a dense formless jumble, with sheets of cross light in it, that showed nothing but masses of darkness:—Coketown in the distance was suggestive of itself, though not a brick of it could be seen.

Every packed detail of this entire setting is surcharged with significant emotional and intellectual comment, and every character among the small unified group, symbolic and stylized, who act out their drama in the gritty industrial world, serves to deepen and intensify the meaning. Josiah Bounderby, banker and manufacturer, is its blatant greed and callous inhumanity in action. Thomas Gradgrind retired wholesale hardware dealer, man of facts and figures, is the embodiment of utilitarian economic theory and its endeavor to dry up life into statistical averages. Young Thomas Gradgrind, devoted first and only to his own advantage, is the mean product of the paternal theories—"that not unprecedented triumph of calculation which is usually at work on number one." The daughter Louisa is their predestined tragic victim going to her doom, in her face "a light with nothing to rest upon, a fire with nothing to burn." The consummate achievement of Mr. Gradgrind's system is represented by Bitzer, one of the pupils graduated from the day school founded by Gradgrind: for Bitzer everything is a matter of bargain and sale, accessible to no appeal except that of self-interest.

In contrast to these, Sissy Jupe, the strolling juggler's child, spending her childhod among the acrobats and equestrians of Sleary's Horse-riding, symbolizes everything in human nature that transcends the soul-crushing hideousness and mere instrumentalism of Coketown: she is vitality, generosity, uncalculating goodness. It is significant that she has been born and nourished among a people whose activities are not dominated by pure utility, but have at least some association with those of art, self-fulfilling, self-justified, and containing their ends within themselves. The contrast between her "dark-eyed and dark-haired" warmth, glowing with an inward sun-filled luster, and Bitzer's cold eyes and colorless hair and etiolated pallor, renders in pure sensation, as F. R. Leavis points out, the opposition between "the life that is lived freely and richly from the deep instinctive and emotional springs" and "the thin-blooded, quasi-mechanical product of Gradgrindery."

Nor does Dickens concern himself in *Hard Times* with any of the small tricks of verisimilitude in speech. The characters express themselves in a stylized idiom that is as far removed from everyday diction as it is true to the inward essence of their natures. Louisa speaks in a solemn poetry filled from the beginning with vibrant forewarnings of her destiny, and Sissy, the stroller's child, confronts Harthouse, the smart, sarcastic worldling, with the stern justice of an angelic messenger. Bounderby's housekeeper, Mrs. Sparsit, with her Roman nose and Coriolanian eyebrows, has a grotesque and mournful dignity of utterance fitting to a world of mad melodrama. And in the wild exuberance of his humor, Dickens allows Mr. Bounderby to talk with the extravagant absurdity of a figure in an insane harlequinade. When Mrs. Sparsit, rendered inarticulate by an inflamed throat and pathetic with sneezes, is trying in vain to tell Mr. Gradgrind that Louisa has deserted Bounderby for Harthouse, the aggrieved husband seizes and shakes her. "If you can't get it out, ma'am," he exclaims, "leave *me* to get it out. This is not a time for a lady, however highly connected, to be totally inaudible, and seemingly swallowing marbles."

In all Dickens's previous novels there had been scenes in which the characters burst into a theatrical diction of an ornate dignity or talked a gabble fantastically ridiculous. Nicholas and Ralph Nickleby assail each other in words of purple rhetoric and Edith Dombey addresses both her husband and Mr. Carker in the accents of a tragedy queen, but the successes Dickens achieves in such passages are won in the teeth of their language. And with Mrs. Nickleby, Sampson Brass, Pecksniff, Sairey Gamp, Captain Cuttle, Mr. Toots, and Jack Bunsby he had risen to heights of triumphant nonsense. "But now," as Shaw remarks, "it is no longer a question of passages;"—or even of an occasional character—"here he begins at last to exercise quite recklessly his power of presenting a character to you in the most fantastic and outrageous terms, putting into its mouth from one end of the book to the other hardly a word which could conceivably be uttered by any sane human being, and yet leaving you with an unmistakable and exactly truthful portrait of a character that you recognize at once as not only real but typical."

In the same way, the overtones of symbolism and allegory had always moved through Dickens's earlier novels, in solution, as it were, and only at times rendered in definite statement. They are implicit in the social myth of Little Nell's mad grandfather and his mania for the "shining yellow boys" seen against the stock-market-gambling fever of the 1840's. They glimmer in the Christmas pantomime transformation-scenes that end *Martin Chuzzlewit*, with old Martin as the beneficent Prospero bringing the pageant to a close. They are symmetrically balanced in the ice and frozen cupids of Mr. Dombey's dinner table and the warmth of the Little Midshipman where Florence and Captain Cuttle are the wandering princess and the good monster of a fairy tale. They emerge again in the image of Uriah Heep as an ugly and rebellious genie and Betsey Trotwood as the fairy godmother. They underlie that entire symbolic bestiary of wolves, tigers, cats, captive birds, flies, and spiders that moves among the fog

and falling tenements and self-consuming rottenness of *Bleak House*. But in these novels, except for the last, the symbolism always lurked below the surface or played over it in a fanciful and exuberant embroidery of metaphor. Even in *Bleak House* symbolism had never taken charge, nor determined and limited every detail in the structure.

. . . . .

Hard Times opens, significantly, in a schoolroom. Here the children are to be indoctrinated in the tenets of practicality, encouraged to think of nothing except in terms of use, crammed full of information like so many "little vessels . . . ready to have imperial gallons of facts poured into them until they were full to the brim." "Now, what I want," Mr. Gradgrind tells the schoolmaster, "is, Facts. Teach these boys and girls nothing but Facts. Facts alone are wanted in life. Plant nothing else and root out everything else. You can only form the minds of reasoning animals upon Facts: nothing else will ever be of service to them. This is the principle on which I bring up my own children, and this is the principle on which I bring up these children. Stick to Facts, sir!"

In the Gradgrind world there are to be no imagination, no fancy, no emotion, only fact and the utilitarian calculus. When Sissy Jupe—"Girl number twenty," Mr. Gradgrind calls her, obliterating human identity itself in the blank anonymity of a number—defends her taste for a flowery-patterned carpet by saying, "I am very fond of flowers . . . and I would fancy——" the government inspector of schools pounces upon her triumphantly: "Ay, ay, ay! But you mustn't fancy. That's it! You are never to fancy"; and "You are not, Cecilia Jupe," Mr. Gradgrind repeats sepulchrally, "to do anything of that kind." "Fact, fact, fact!" says the government official. "Fact, fact, fact!" echoes Thomas Gradgrind.

For Sissy's loving humanity, though, this bleak factuality is quite impossible. "'Here are the stutterings,'" she misquotes her school-teacher—"Statistics," corrects Louisa—of a town of a million inhabitants of whom only twenty-five starved to death in the course of a year. What does she think of that proportion? "I thought it must be just as hard on those who were starved whether the others were a million, or a million million." So "low down" is Sissy in "the elements of Political Economy" after eight weeks of study, that she has to be "set right by a prattler three feet high, for returning to the question, 'What is the first principle of this science?' the absurd answer, 'To do unto others as I would that they should do unto me.'"

Mr. Gradgrind's stand at school is the stand he takes among his own children at home.

> No little Gradgrind had ever seen a face in the moon; it was up in the moon before it could speak distinctly. No little Gradgrind had ever learnt the silly jingle, Twinkle, twinkle, little star; how I wonder what you are! No little Gradgrind had ever known wonder on the subject, each little Gradgrind having at five years old dissected the Great Bear like a Professor Owen, and driven Charles's Wain like a locomotive engine-

driver. No little Gradgrind had ever associated a cow in a field with that famous cow with the crumpled horn . . . or with that yet more famous cow who swallowed Tom Thumb: it had never heard of these celebrities, and had only been introduced to a cow as a graminivorous ruminating quadruped with several stomachs.

But the facts in which Gradgrindery is interested are only the cut-and-dried facts of intellectual definition, not the facts of living and breathing reality. It wants to learn nothing about the behavior of horses and how they are trained, which Sissy Jupe knows from Sleary's Horse-riding: "You musn't tell us about the ring, here." Instead, it trots out Bitzer's "definition of a horse": "Quadruped. Graminivorous. Forty teeth, namely twenty-four grinders, four eye-teeth, and twelve incisive. . . . Hoofs hard, but requiring to be shod with iron. Age known by marks in mouth."—"Now girl number twenty," says Mr. Gradgrind, "you know what a horse is."

The factual education approved by Mr. Gradgrind is identical in spirit with that which was inflicted upon John Stuart Mill and which left him in his young manhood despairingly convinced that his emotional and imaginative nature had been starved to death. Mr. M'Choakumchild, the schoolmaster, has been "turned out," with

> some one hundred and forty other schoolmasters . . . in the same factory, on the same principles, like so many pianoforte legs. . . . Orthography, etymology, syntax, and prosody, biography, astronomy, geography, and general cosmogany, the sciences of compound proportion, algebra, land-surveying and levelling, vocal music, and drawing from models, were all at the ends of his ten chilled fingers. He had worked his stony way into Her Majesty's most Honourable Privy Council's Schedule B, and had taken the bloom off the higher branches of mathematics and physical science, French, German, Latin, and Greek. He knew all about all the Water Sheds of all the world (whatever they are), and all the histories of all the peoples, and all the names of all the rivers and mountains, and all the productions, manners, and customs of all the countries, and all their boundaries and bearings on the two and thirty points of the compass. . . .

> He went to work in this preparatory lesson, not unlike Morgiana in the Forty Thieves: looking into all the vessels ranged before him, one after another, to see what they contained. Say, good M'Choakumchild. When from thy boiling store, thou shalt fill each jar brim full by-and-by, dost thou think thou wilt always kill outright the robber Fancy lurking within—or sometimes only maim him and destory him!

The principles that dominate Mr. Gradgrind's school are the principles that dominate Coketown and its industry. His hard-facts philosophy is only the aggressive formulation of the inhumane spirit of Victorian materialism. In Gradgrind, though repellent, it is honest and disinterested. In Bounderby, its embodiment in the business world,

with his bragging self-interest, it is nothing but greed for power and material success, Victorian "rugged individualism" in its vulgarest and ugliest form. And Bounderby is nothing but the practice of that business ethos, for which "the relations between master and man were all fact, and everything was fact between the lying-in hospital and the cemetery, and what you couldn't state in figures, or show to be purchaseable in the cheapest market and saleable in the dearest, was not, and never should be, world without end, Amen."

The wonderful wit and insight with which Dickens withers laissez-faire capitalism is not to be lost sight of "because he chooses to speak," as Ruskin says, "in a circle of stage fire." Carlyle never voiced a more burning denunciation of the dismal science of classical economic theory or the heartlessness of "cash-nexus" as the only link between man and man. The hundred years that have passed since *Hard Times* was written have done hardly more to date the cant with which businessmen defend industrial exploitation than they have to brighten the drab and brutal thing. Laboring men who protested wanted "to be set up in a coach and six and to be fed on turtle soup and venison, with a gold spoon"; the laboring class "were a bad lot altogether, gentlemen," "restless," "never knew what they wanted," "lived upon the best, and bought fresh butter; and insisted upon Mocha coffee, and rejected all but prime parts of meat, and yet were eternally dissatisfied and unmanageable." As for the Labor unions: "the united masters" should not "allow of any such class combinations."

One more cluster of these sardonic clichés recalls the capitalists of our own day who were going to dispose of their businesses and go to Canada if Franklin Delano Roosevelt were re-elected. The Coketown industrialists, Dickens observes dryly, were always crying that they were ruined:

> They were ruined, when they were required to send labouring children to school; they were ruined when inspectors were appointed to look into their works; they were ruined, when such inspectors considered it doubtful whether they were justified in chopping people up with their machinery; they were utterly undone when it was hinted that perhaps they need not always make quite so much smoke. . . . Whenever a Coketowner felt he was ill-used—that is to say, whenever he was not left entirely alone, and it was proposed to hold him accountable for the consequences of any of his acts—he was sure to come out with the awful menace that he would 'sooner pitch his property into the Atlantic.' This had terrified the Home Secretary within an inch of his life, on several occasions.

> However, the Coketowners were so patriotic after all, that they never had pitched their property into the Atlantic yet, but, on the contrary, had been kind enough to take mighty good care of it.

The only weaknesses in Dickens's handling of the industrial scene are his caricature of the union organizer Slackbridge and his portrayal of that noble but dismal representative of the laboring classes, Stephen Blackpool. Slackbridge, with his windy and whining rhetoric ("Oh my friends and fellow-countrymen, the slaves of an iron-handed and a grinding despotism! Oh my friends and fellow-sufferers, and fellow-workmen, and fellow-men!") is a figment of imagination. "He was not so honest," Dickens says, as the workers he addressed, "he was not so manly, he was not so good-humoured; he substituted cunning for their simplicity, and passion for their safe solid sense. An ill-made, high-shouldered man, with lowering brows, and his features crushed into an habitually sour expression, he contrasted most unfavourably, even in his mongrel dress, with the great body of his hearers in their plain working clothes."

Such a description is a piece of sheer ignorance, not because union leaders cannot be windbags and humbugs as other politicians can, but because labor organizers are not like Slackbridge and do not talk like him, and did not do so in Dickens's day any more than in ours. Dickens knew

---

Lionel Trilling on the liberal principles expounded in *Hard Times*:

When [John Stuart] Mill urged liberals to read Coleridge, he had in mind not merely Coleridge's general power of intellect as it stood in critical opposition to the liberalism of the day; he had also in mind certain particular attitudes and views that sprang, as he believed, from Coleridge's nature and power as a poet. Mill had learned through direct and rather terrible experience what the tendency of liberalism was in regard to the sentiments and the imagination. From the famous "crisis" of his youth he had learned, although I believe he never put it in just this way, that liberalism stood in a paradoxical relation to the emotions. The paradox is that liberalism is concerned with the emotions above all else, as proof of which the word happiness stands at the very center of its thought, but in its effort to establish the emotions, or certain among them, in some sort of freedom, liberalism somehow tends to deny them in their full possibility. Dickens' *Hard Times* serves to remind us that the liberal principles upon which Mill was brought up, although extreme, were not isolated and unique, and the principles of Mill's rearing very nearly destroyed him, as in fact they did destroy the Louisa Gradgrind of Dickens' novel.

Lionel Trilling, in The Liberal Imagination: Essays on Literature and Society, *Viking Press, 1950.*

---

human nature too well not to know that fundamentally laboring men were like all men, and he knew domestic servants and artisans working for small tradesmen, but of the class manners and behavior of industrial laborers he had made no more than a superficial observation in some half-dozen trips through the Midlands. He had attended only one union meeting in his life, during the Preston strike in January, 1854. "It is much as if a tramp," Shaw comments with witty but not untruthful exaggeration, "were to write a description of millionaires smoking large cigars in church, with their wives in low-necked dresses and diamonds."

There is a possibility, to be sure, that the brief chapter in which Slackbridge appears was designed to reassure a middle-class audience that might otherwise grow restive and worried over the radical sound of the book. Dickens's own personal support of the labor movement, however, is unequivocally clear. He had already stated in *Household Words* his belief that laborers had the same right to organize that their employers had, and shortly after the conclusion of *Hard Times* he was to appeal to working men to force reforms from the Government. *Hard Times* itself burns with indignant sympathy for the injustice under which the workers suffered and is violent in its repudiation of Bounderby's career and Gradgrind's philosophy.

Hardly less typical of the laboring class than Slackbridge is the independent workman Stephen Blackpool, who is ostracized by his fellow workers for not joining the union and blacklisted by Mr. Bounderby for having the courage to defend their cause. Stephen's isolated stand cuts him off from the support of his own class and the patronage of the factory owners. For all this, it is in Stephen's mouth that Dickens puts a dark summation of the life of the industrial workers: "Look round town—so rich as 'tis—and see the numbers o' people as has been broughten into bein heer, for to weave, an to card, an to piece out a livin', aw the same one way, somehows, twixt their cradles and their graves. Look how we live, an wheer we live, an in what numbers, an by what chances, an wi' what sameness; and look how the mill is awlus a goin, and how they never works us no nigher to ony dis'ant object—'ceptin awlus Death."

And to Stephen, too, Dickens gives a denunciation of laissez faire and the hostile division it creates in society: "Let thousands upon thousands alone, aw leading the like lives and aw faw'en into the like muddle, and they will be as one, and yo will be as anoother, wi' a black unpassable world betwixt yo, just as long or short a time as sitch-like misery can last. . . . Most o' aw, rating 'em as so much Power, and reg'latin 'em as if they was figures in a soom, or machines: wi'out loves and likens, wi'out memories and inclinations, wi'out souls to weary and souls to hope—when aw goes quiet, draggin' on wi' 'em as if they'd nowt o' th' kind, and when aw goes onquiet, reproachin 'em for their want o' sitch human feelins in their dealins wi' you—this will never do't, sir, till God's work is on-made."

When Stephen's crushed body is brought up from Old Hell Shaft, into which he had stumbled, his dying words are as if the crushed people themselves were speaking from the pit into which the modern world had fallen:

> I ha' fell into the pit . . . as have cost wi'in the knowledge o' old fok now livin, hundreds and hundreds o' men's lives—fathers, sons, brothers, dear to thousands an thousands, an keeping 'em fro' want and hunger. I ha' fell into a pit that ha' been wi' th' Firedamp crueller than battle. I ha' read on't in the public petition, as onny one may read, fro' the men that works in the pits, in which they ha' pray'n and pray'n the lawmakers for Christ's sake not to let their work be

murder to 'em, but to spare 'em for th' wives and children that they loves as well as gentlefok loves theirs. When it were in work, it killed wi'out need; when 'tis let alone, it kills wi'out need. See how we die an no need, one way an another—in a muddle—every day!

And, in the end, as if from the depths of Old Hell Shaft, Dickens sounds once more a prophetic warning to the "Utilitarian economists, skeletons of schoolmasters, Commissioners of Fact, genteel and used-up infidels, gabblers of many little dog's eared creeds," lest "in the day of [their] triumph, when romance is utterly driven out" of the souls of the poor, "and they and a bare existence stand face to face, Reality will take a wolfish turn, and make an end of you."

. . . . .

Within this larger sweep of *Hard Times* and its social-economic criticism there is a no less significant spiritual core. That core involves a demonstration of the way in which the Gradgrind philosophy denudes and devastates the life of Mr. Gradgrind himself. Not a bad man, "an affectionate father, after his manner," "Mr. Gradgrind, though hard enough, was by no means so rough a man as Mr. Bounderby. His character was not unkind, all things considered; it might have been very kind indeed if only he had made some mistake in the arithmetic that balanced it years ago." Instead, he has gone astray in the aridities of a crude mechanistic theory of human nature, and spends his time in the "parliamentary cinder-heap in London" proving "that the Good Samaritan was a Bad Economist."

His kindness in taking Sissy Jupe under his care enables Dickens to bring in a contrasting picture of the circus folk in Sleary's Horse-riding. They symbolize art, and their position in the eyes of Mr. Gradgrind and Mr. Bounderby implies the position of art in Victorian England, just as Gradgrind and Bounderby themselves symbolize the orthodox respectability of that society. For them, art is reduced to the status of mere entertainment, and the artist is a useless Bohemian of dubious respectability, whose work they frown on as frivolous and wasteful, utterly valueless for the utilitarian calculus. Nevertheless, that work ministers to vital human needs and, debased and degraded though it is in social estimate, represents one of the few clear links Coketown has with the life of disinterested achievement and the enrichment of experience.

> There were two or three handsome young women among them . . . and their eight or nine little children, who did the fairy business when required. The father of one of the families was in the habit of balancing the father of another of the families on the top of a great pole; the father of a third family often made a pyramid of both those fathers . . . ; all the fathers could dance upon rolling casks, stand upon bottles, catch knives and balls, twirl hand-basins, ride upon anything, jump over everything, and stick at nothing. All the mothers could (and did) dance upon the slack wire and the tight rope, and perform rapid acts on bare-backed steeds; none of them were at all particular in respect

of showing their legs; and one of them, alone in a Greek chariot, drove six-in-hand into every town they came to.

The circus people are also vessels of those simple virtues of sympathy and helpfulness to others for which Mr. Gradgrind's philosophy had no use and Mr. Bounderby's hardened heart no room. When Bounderby harshly tells Sissy that her father has deserted her, "They cared so little for plain Fact, these people," Dickens writes, "and were in that advanced state of degeneracy . . . that instead of being impressed by the speaker's strong common sense, they took it in extraordinary dudgeon. The men muttered 'Shame!' and the women 'Brute!'"—a reaction leading Sleary to give the visitors a hasty warning that they were in danger of being pitched out of the window.

There is no sentimentality in this portrayal of the circus strollers. Dickens admits that "they were not very tidy in their private dress" and grants that they were sometimes rather disorderly in their private lives. He knows the dirt and squalor of their surroundings. He sees Sleary exactly as he is, with his flabby body, game eye, wheezing voice, and brandy-soaked state of never being quite sober and never quite drunk. But he knows that the qualities they exemplify are just as real as those in Mr. Gradgrind, and that they are quite as likely to be found in jugglers and acrobats as in bankers and businessmen.

So the two worlds confront each other, the world of generous feeling and the world of rationalized greed. It is through his heartless philosophy that Mr. Gradgrind is to be struck down, and through his inconsistent deed of kindness that he and his family are ultimately to be saved. Through his blindness to imagination, his failure to understand the life of the emotions, the mechanical crudity of his philosophy, his son becomes a selfish sneak and thief, and Louisa, his favorite child, suffers a dark emptiness in her heart. The love that her father always ignores, the devotion to which he denies any reality, she directs with all her starved and thwarted intensity upon her scapegrace brother. For his sake she accepts the proposal her father brings from Bounderby and prostitutes herself in marriage to a man she does not love.

The scene in which she receives that proposal is a triumph of dramatic subtlety. Her dispassionate chill is disconcerting even to the father who has consistently urged treating every situation in terms of fact. With intervals of silence between them punctuated by the hollow ticking of a "deadly statistical clock," she subjects her father to a cold questionnaire: "Father, do you think I love Mr. Bounderby?" "Father, do you ask me to love Mr. Bounderby?" "Father, does Mr. Bounderby ask me to love him?"

The embarrassed man tries to escape into the realms of abstract definition; the reply, he says, depends "on the sense in which we use the expression." Mr. Bounderby does not do either Louisa or himself "the injustice of pretending to anything fanciful, fantastic, or (I am using synonymous terms) sentimental." Let them reduce the question to one of Fact: "Does Mr. Bounderby ask me to marry him? Yes, he does. The sole remaining question then is: Shall I marry him?"

Throughout the conversation Louisa has been regarding her father fixedly. "As he now leaned back in his chair, and bent his deep-set eyes upon her," Dickens writes, "he might have seen one wavering moment in her, when she was impelled to throw herself upon his breast, and give him the pent-up confidences of her heart. But, to see it, he must have overleaped at a bound the artificial barriers he had for so many years been erecting, between himself and all those subtle essences of humanity which will elude the utmost cunning of algebra . . . The barriers were too many and too high for such a leap. With his unbending, utilitarian, matter-of-fact face, he hardened her again; and the moment shot away into the plumbless depths of the past, to mingle with all the lost opportunities that are drowned there.

"Removing her eyes from him, she sat so long looking silently towards the town, that he said, at length: 'Are you consulting the chimneys of the Coketown works, Louisa?'

"'There seems to be nothing there but languid and monotonous smoke. Yet when the night comes, Fire bursts out, father!' she answered, turning quickly.

"'Of course I know that, Louisa. I do not see the application of the remark.' To do him justice, he did not, at all."

How beautifully this conversation, in reducing each question to one of "Fact," empties it of all meaning! No philosophic analysis could puncture the calculus of fact with more deadly effectiveness. And with what power it conveys the emotional tensions beneath the dialogue, Louisa's yearning for sympathy and understanding and the obtuse, well-meaning father missing it all, even the allusion to those unquenchable fires of human passion, so often hidden, that burst out in the dark night of despair. An uncomfortable sense of something not quite right, however, Mr. Gradgrind does have, and he questions his daughter whether she has any other attachment.

"Why, father," she replies with fathomless irony, "what a strange question to ask *me!* The baby-preference that even I have heard of as common among children, has never had its innocent resting-place in my breast. You have been so careful of me, that I have never had a child's dream. You have dealt so wisely with me, father, from my cradle to this hour, that I have never had a child's belief or a child's fear." "What do *I* know, father, of tastes and fancies; of aspirations and affections; of all that part of my nature in which such light things might have been nourished? What escape have I had from problems that could be demonstrated and realities that could be grasped?"

As Louisa speaks these words, she unconsciously closes her hand, "as if upon a solid object," and slowly opens it, "as though she were releasing dust or ash." Mr. Grad-

grind is "quite moved by his success, and by this testimony to it."

When Louisa's disastrous marriage to the braggart Bounderby ends in flight back to her father, all his past blindness recoils upon his head. "How could you give me life," she reproaches him, "and take from me all the inappreciable things that raise it from the state of conscious death? Where are the graces of my soul? Where are the sentiments of my heart? What have you done, O father, what have you done," and she strikes herself with both hands upon her breast, "with the garden that should have bloomed once, in this great wilderness here!"

"I never knew you were unhappy, my child."

"Father, I always knew it. In this strife . . . my dismal resource has been to think that life would soon go by, and that nothing in it could be worth the pain and trouble of a contest. . . . I do not know that I am sorry, I do not know that I am ashamed, I do not know that I am degraded in my own esteem. All that I know is, your philosophy and your teaching will not save me. Now, father, you have brought me to this. Save me by some other means!"

And as he clasps her to prevent her falling, and then lays her down upon the floor, he sees "the pride of his heart and the triumph of his system, lying, an insensible heap, at his feet."

The next day he entreats Louisa to believe that he had meant to do right. "He said it earnestly, and to do him justice he had. In gauging fathomless deeps with his mean little excise-rod, and in staggering over the universe with his rusty stiff-legged compasses, he had meant to do great things. Within the limits of his short tether, he had tumbled about, annihilating the flowers of existence with greater singleness of purpose than many of the blatant personages whose company he kept."

But in the crisis of his life, Mr. Gradgrind, unlike Sir Austin Feverel, is able to choose love and his child, not the pride of his system. And she finds her comfort and he finds his redemption through the uncalculated and inconsistent deviation from the system that had led to his taking into his household the strolling juggler's child. Sissy Jupe's affection has been twining through that utilitarian home the ministrations of a loving heart, and on her gentle strength both the father and the daughter in the end come to repose. Through Sissy, too, and Sleary's non-utilitarian gratitude for Mr. Gradgrind's kindness to her, comes the resolution of the remaining part of the story, the escape of young Tom, that other "triumph" of Mr. Gradgrind's system, from going to jail for robbing Bounderby's bank.

This conclusion to the demonstration is trenchant satire. Sulky to the last, disguised as a comic servant with black face and a grotesquely ludicrous livery, the whelp grumblingly defends himself in his father's own jargon: "So many people are employed in situations of trust; so many people, out of so many, will be dishonest. I have heard you talk, a hundred times, of its being a law. How can I help laws? You have comforted others with such things, father. Comfort yourself!"

Swift upon this confrontation arrives Bitzer, the real success of the system, determined to drag Tom back to Coketown and clinch his own succession to Tom's job in the bank. To the anguished father's pleas, Bitzer's replies, with mordant irony, throw in his face every one of his old arguments. Has he a heart? Mr. Gradgrind asks. "Smiling at the oddity of the question," Bitzer retorts with brisk factuality that the circulation couldn't be carried on without one. "If this is solely a question of self-interest with you," Mr. Gradgrind begins. But Bitzer interrupts. "I am sure you know that the whole social system is a question of self-interest." Nor can he be bribed; his advancement at the bank is worth more than any sum Mr. Gradgrind can offer. Mr. Gradgrind tries to appeal to Bitzer's gratitude for his schooling. "My schooling was paid for," says Bitzer; "it was a bargain; and when I came away, the bargain ended."

"It was a fundamental principle of the Gradgrind philosophy," Dickens notes, "that everything was to be paid for. Nobody was ever on any account to give anybody anything, or render anybody any help without purchase. Gratitude was to be abolished, and the virtues springing from it were not to be. Every inch of the existence of mankind, from birth to death, was to be a bargain across the counter. And if we didn't get to Heaven that way, it was not a politico-economical place, and we had no business there."

Bitzer is prevented from giving the alarm and young Tom is smuggled out of the country by a fantastic plot involving the services of the circus's dancing horse and educated dog. Mr. Sleary, no economist to the last, refuses any financial reward, although a collar for the dog and a set of bells for the horse, he agrees, he will be glad to take. "Brandy and water I alwayth take." And privately, to Mr. Gradgrind, over his glass of grog, he makes a final revelation and pronouncement. Sissy's father is dead: his performing dog, who would never have deserted him, had returned to the circus months ago, worn out and almost blind, and there died.

It seems to suggest, Mr. Sleary observes musingly, that there is a love in the world, not all self-interest after all, but something very different; and that love has a way of its own of calculating or not calculating, to which it may be hard to give a name.

And, as for the circus artists and Mr. Gradgrind's former disapproval of them, Mr. Sleary says in his preposterous lisp: "Thquire, thake handth, firtht and latht! Don't be croth with uth poor vagabondth. People mutht be amuthed. They can't be alwayth a learning, nor yet they can't be alwayth a working, they ain't made for it. You *mutht* have uth, Thquire. Do the withe thing and the kind thing too, and make the betht of uth; not the wortht!"

Seen in all its implications against the background of the story, these final scenes hold in solution Dickens's entire indictment of nineteenth-century industrial society and the essence of his defense of art. Against the monstrous cruelty of mine and mill and pit and factory and counting-house, against the bleak utilitarian philosophy with which they were allied, what power could there be except the flowering of the humane imagination and the ennoblement of the heart?

Monroe Engel (essay date 1959)

SOURCE: "Addenda: The Sports of Plenty," in *The Maturity of Dickens,* Cambridge, Mass.: Harvard University Press, 1959, 169-89.

[*In the following excerpt, Engel favorably appraises* Hard Times, *focusing upon its economy of presentation and emphasis upon the need for imagination—not utility alone—to make life bearable and full.*]

The recent marked increase in the reputation of *Hard Times* has come at the expense of Dickens' general reputation. Satisfaction with this one sport of his genius has been used as a basis on which to denigrate that genius in its more characteristic manifestations. *Hard Times* satisfies the modern taste (in the arts alone) for economy—in fiction, for spare writing and clearly demonstrable form. Dickens was capable of both, but they were not natural or congenial to him, and he chose to employ them only under the duress of limited space. Curiously enough, *Hard Times* grants a scant measure of the very quality for which it argues, imaginative pleasure. Its seriousness is so scrupulous, plain, and insistent that the reader moves along with simple, too rarely surprised consent, and it is worth noting that at one point Dickens considered calling the novel "Black and White."

Yet it is silly to prolong the arbitrary see-saw between *Hard Times* and the rest of Dickens' work. It is more to the point to see that the greatest virtues of *Hard Times* are Dickens' characteristic virtues, but less richly present in this book than in many others.

Hard Times is least interesting as an exploitation of its avowed subject, the inadequacy of the Benthamite calculus. The crude but forceless simplicity of Gradgrind can scarcely be said to represent the complexity and solidity of Bentham's influential contributions to English thought. Gradgrind is the merest of straw men. But it may well be that in writing *Hard Times* Dickens was impelled as much by a need to dissociate himself fully and publicly from the Benthamites as by any need to attack them for themselves. The chief grounds on which he attacks the Benthamites, however, are well taken grounds—are, in fact, the very grounds on which Mill himself was to attack them two decades later in his *Autobiography*. Mill had to discover poetry in order to recover from the ravages of the Benthamite education imposed on him by his father; and the ultimate deficiency of the Gradgrind system, too, is that it ignores or condemns the imagination.

More interesting than the attack on the Benthamites, then, though it is laid out almost as obviously, is the defense of fancy and imagination. The necessity for imagination becomes clear only when the inadequacy of reason and of rational social action to deal completely with the unalterable aspects of existence is recognized. The death of fancy is linked to the threat of revolution:

> The poor you will always have with you. Cultivate in them, while there is yet time, the utmost graces of the fancies and affections, to adorn their lives so much in need of ornament; or, in the days of your triumph, when romance is utterly driven out of their souls, and they and a bare existence stand face to face, Reality will take a wolfish turn, and make an end of you.

It is only imagination, too, that can bridge the gulf of difference between the classes, only imagination that can merge immediate and divergent self-interests in an ultimate common self-interest. "The like of you don't know us, don't care for us, don't belong to us," Rachael says to Louisa, and the "facts" of Coketown amply support her contention, though in Louisa's case the birth of her imaginative powers is accompanied by a growing realization of and sympathy for the condition of the poor.

Fancy is the progenitor of charity, in the Christian rather than the philanthropic sense, and it is the lack of fancy in her childhood that makes it impossible for Louisa to approach her mother's deathbed with full feeling, with better than "a heavy, hardened kind of sorrow." This recognition immediately precedes one of Dickens' most brilliant and functional death scenes, the death of Mrs. Gradgrind with only Louisa present.

> "But there is something—not an Oology at all—that your father has missed, or forgotten, Louisa. I don't know what it is. I have often sat with Sissy near me, and thought about it. I shall never get its name now. But your father may. It makes me restless. I want to write to him, to find out for God's sake, what it is. Give me a pen, give me a pen."

> Even the power of restlessness was gone, except from the poor head, which could just turn from side to side.

> She fancied, however, that her request had been complied with, and that the pen she could not have held was in her hand. It matters little what figures of wonderful no-meaning she began to trace upon her wrappers. The hand soon stopped in the midst of them; the light that had always been feeble and dim behind the weak transparency, went out; and even Mrs. Gradgrind, emerged from the shadow in which man walketh and disquieteth himself in vain, took upon her the dread solemnity of the sages and patriarchs.

Here, as usual with Dickens, death is the control by which reality is measured—and, in this case, by which the Gradgrind system is discounted. In the vivid imaginative rendering of the scene, we comprehend what forces are at work on Louisa to pierce her trained incapacity, as we do

too when her hazard at the devices of James Harthouse is rendered in an extraordinary sexual image: "The figure descended the great stairs, steadily, steadily; always verging, like a weight in deep water, to the black gulf at the bottom."

It is finally the brief, largely figurative renderings of experience in this novel, far more than the rather mechanical working out of the plot, that most effectively accomplish the destruction of the "hard facts" point of view. We know best what is wrong with Coketown not from the facts we are told about it, nor from the picture of Bounderby's hypocritical oppression, nor even so much from the scene of the union meeting, as from the descriptive imagery of serpents and elephants. In a sense, imagination makes its own best case for itself.

The great virtues of the novel are in disquieting part incidental virtues—incidental, that is, to the main line of development of the story, though absolutely essential to its impact. The questions this raises are peculiar questions concerning the forced restriction of the play of imagination or fancy in a novel that has chiefly to do with the necessity for the free life of the imagination. It seems almost Gradgrindian therefore to prefer **Hard Times** to, say, *David Copperfield* or *Our Mutual Friend!*

A. O. J. Cockshut (essay date 1961)

SOURCE: *"Hard Times*-Dickens's Masterpiece?" in *The Imagination of Charles Dickens,* Collins, 1961, p. 137-42.

[*In the essay below, Cockshut seeks to demonstrate*—contra *F. R. Leavis—that* Hard Times *is not Dickens's masterpiece. He does, however, consider it a novel of high accomplishment.*]

Dr. Leavis has performed a valuable service by focusing attention on **Hard Times,** an important and neglected work. Those of us who do not quite agree with him about its quality are nevertheless grateful.

The leading idea of the book is proclaimed in the contrast between its subject, industrial society, and the titles of its three sections—Sowing, Reaping and Garnering. The intention, carried out at times with great subtlety and at times with a rather weary obviousness, was to show inherent life and growth conquering theory and calculation. This approach tends to break down the stock distinctions between town and country, between industry and agriculture, between science and intuition. From the first brilliant description of the factory world, where the elephants' heads represent the movements of machinery, the factory is treated as a living thing. Thus industrial smoke is linked with the horrors of hypocrisy and deception. "A blur of soot and smoke, now confusedly tending this way, now that way, now aspiring to the vault of Heaven, now murkily creeping along the earth, as the wind rose and fell, or changed its quarter: a dense formless jumble, with sheets of cross light in it, that showed nothing but masses of darkness: Coketown in the distance was suggestive of itself, though not a brick of it could be seen." And in a notable passage the fire of the furnaces is compared to the fire of human passions. When she is considering Bounderby's proposal, Louisa is asked by her father, "Are you consulting the chimneys of the Coketown works?" and she replies, "There seems to be nothing there but languid and monotonous smoke. Yet when the night comes, Fire bursts out."

Coketown and its people are living mysteries, not facts. The process of inner growth is never absent from the author's mind. It dominates even casual phrases: "to pretend . . . that they went astray wholly without cause, and of their own irrational wills, was to pretend that there could be smoke without fire, death without birth, harvest without seed." This, in part, is the meaning of Stephen Blackpool's fall into the disused mine, which causes his death. The creature of industrial society, the mine, does not cease to influence events when it is uncontrolled and forgotten—a point which Stephen's own words underline: "When it were in work, it killed wi'out need; when 'tis alone, it kills wi'out need."

Now it seems that two of the three main targets at which Dickens directed his criticism, were well chosen. Bounderby and Harthouse, each in his odd, inverted way, illustrate the principle of inner life and growth. Bounderby's story of character and industry triumphant is a sham; and his mock humility about being brought up in the gutter is a form of snobbery and pride. His relations with Mrs. Sparsit perfectly illustrate the real source of his feelings and his lies. The important point is that the low "down-to-earth" materialistic attitude takes its origin in an idealistic illusion. Harthouse, on the other hand, has adopted the dogmas of political economy out of boredom, out of that weary assumption of originality, which is always a mark of dullness of mind. (How well Dickens understood this *avant-garde* type. Gowan in *Little Dorrit* is a different and equally interesting version of it.) Also Harthouse knows in advance that the devotees of political economy will be secretly impressed with his upper-class connections. Therefore he will carry more weight in their councils than he would in circles more accustomed to enjoying aristocratic support. His pose is one of cynicism. "The only difference between us and the professors of virtue or benevolence, or philanthropy—never mind the name—is, that we know it is all meaningless, and say so; while they know it equally and will never say so." But this sincere-insincerity is itself insincere. He has no real interest in the cynical principles of the political economists; his cynicism is only an attractive line. He is the ancestor of a long line of "brutally frank and courageously outspoken" publicists of the twentieth century; and it can be fairly claimed that Dickens may well have been the first person to understand and analyse the type.

Altogether it is a beautifully-planned contrast between Bounderby and Harthouse. But the third term is surely weaker than Dr. Leavis allows. Gradgrind seems to belong to the world of pure moral fable—which in its main outlines **Hard Times** most certainly is not. So we are

uneasy whenever Gradgrind has dealings with Bounderby and Harthouse. They are not the same kind of creature at all, and so can only communicate, as it were, through the author's mind. And so there is no reserve of dramatic force to play with at the time of Gradgrind's conversion; the conversion itself, accordingly, is almost trivial.

Of course, the atmosphere of the moral fable, or even of the fairytale is introduced deliberately at times. We cannot doubt that when we read a sentence like this: "Stephen, whose way had been in a contrary direction, turned about, and betook himself as in duty bound to the red brick castle of the giant Bounderby." It is deliberate, but is it always judiciously used? Neither Bounderby nor Blackpool really deserves this aura of fairytale. Each has his own psychological truth; and each has characteristics which could not occur in any pre-industrial society.

There is a similar difficulty about the circus. Dr. Leavis says, most aptly, of the scene where Sleary finally points the book's moral: "Reading it there we have to stand off and reflect at a distance to recognise potentialities that might have been realised elsewhere as Dickensian sentimentality. There is nothing sentimental in the actual fact." The crucial importance of Mr. Sleary and the circus is obvious. The circus is at the beginning and the end. From it comes Sissy Jupe to save the Gradgrind family; and Tom, the disgraced product of a politico-economical education returns to it to make his escape.

But here again we meet the difficulty, are we reading a fable or a novel? In a semi-realistic work of this sort we can hardly be satisfied with the circus as a simple undifferentiated alpha and omega, like Kafka's castle or the lake from which Arthur's sword appeared and to which it returned. We are bound to look for some positive wisdom in Mr. Sleary and I cannot help feeling that Dr. Leavis is too enthusiastic when he speaks of "the solemn moral of the whole fable, put with the rightness of genius in Mr. Sleary's asthmatic mouth." Sleary belongs, of course, to a long tradition of the wise or holy fool. To speak of genius here is surely to place Sleary among the finest representatives of this tradition, to put him in the company of the Fool in *Lear* and Dostoevsky's Myshkin. He will scarcely stand the comparison; and the passage Dr. Leavis quotes will hardly support his claim:

> "Thquire, you don't need to be told that dogth ith wonderful animalth."
>
> "Their instinct," said Mr. Gradgrind, "is surprising."
>
> "Whatever you call it—and I'm bletht if I know what to call it"—said Sleary, "it ith athtonithing. The way in which a dog'll find you—the dithtanthe he'll come."
>
> "His scent," said Mr. Gradgrind, "being so fine."
>
> "I'm bletht if I know what to call it," repeated Sleary, shaking his head, "but I have had dogth find me, Thquire. . . . "

It is generally acknowledged by Dr. Leavis and others that the Trade Union scenes are not satisfactory; though Dickens achieved one stroke of prophetic insight, when, in Bounderby's interview with Blackpool, he showed the subconscious sympathy between owners and Trade Unions linked against individualistic workers.

The parallel between Bounderby's and Blackpool's matrimonial troubles is unconvincing; and one feels that probability, psychology and everything else had been sacrificed to symmetry. The last chapter summarises in a few hundred words events which might fill a whole novel. Here Dickens's sense of the superiority of life to fact, which is the guiding star of the novel, up to this point, seems ironically to have deserted him. Gradgrind could almost have written the chapter himself.

There are then, it seems to me, sound reasons against considering *Hard Times* a masterpiece. But it remains a work of great distinction, which performed for the first time the very important imaginative task of integrating the factory world into the world of nature and of humanity. And I end with a quotation designed to show this process at work. It is like a new pastoral tradition miraculously beginning, in which the Industrial Revolution can really share: "They walked on across the fields and down the shady lanes, sometimes getting over a fragment of a fence so rotten that it dropped at a touch of the foot, sometimes passing near a wreck of bricks and beams overgrown with grass, marking the site of deserted works. They followed paths and tracks, however slight. Mounds where the grass was rank and high, and where brambles, dockweed, and such like vegetation, were confusedly heaped together, they always avoided; for dismal stories were told in that country of the old pits hidden beneath such indications."

John Holloway (essay date 1962)

SOURCE: *"Hard Times: A History and a Criticism,"* in *Dickens and the Twentieth Century,* edited by John Gross and Gabriel Pearson, Routledge and Kegan Paul, 1962, pp. 159-74.

[*The essay below, along with David H. Hirsch's "Hard Times and F. R. Leavis" (1964), represents the most trenchant critical response to Leavis's famous 1948 essay championing* Hard Times *as Dickens's most accomplished novel.*]

I

'With his unbending, utilitarian, matter-of-fact face', Dickens writes of Mr. Gradgrind. That *Hard Times* is a novel which embodies a moral problem, an issue between ways of living, is by now familiar knowledge; and so is it, that one side of the issue, in some sense or another, is 'Utilitarianism'. But the ideas and attitudes which that word most readily calls up today prove not to be those which were most prominent in Dickens's own mind or own time; and to trace the exact contour of significance which ran

for Dickens himself, as he wrote the book, through the material he handled, will turn out to be a more than merely historical accumulation of knowledge: it determines the critical position which one must finally take with regard to the novel.

Hard Times itself provides the necessary clues plainly enough. But they do not point to Utilitarianism as an ambitious philosophical theory of enlightened and emancipated thinking or of comprehensive social welfare and reform; nor to the genuine (if challengeable) idealism and dedicated high-mindedness of such an education as James Mill designed for his son (Greek at the age of three, and something that could at least pass as the full circle of human knowledge by adolescence). What Dickens seems to have had in mind was something much less far-reaching, and much more mundane and commonplace. The point comes out at once from Dickens's list of possible titles for the novel. This included: 'Two and Two are Four'; 'Simple Arithmetic'; 'A Mere Question of Figures'; and, the first of all, 'According to Cocker'. The last is William Cocker, the seventeenth-century author whose *Arithmetic* was still in use as a school text. 'The celebrated Mr. Cocker', Dickens called him in a speech the year after *Hard Times* appeared.

That Mr. Gradgrind stands for the utilitarian seen not philosophically but arithmetically is made plain elsewhere. 'Let us strike the key-note again . . . ' Dickens opens Bk. I, Ch. 8, ' . . . by means of addition, subtraction, multiplication, and division, settle everything'. The very next chapter indicates what kind of arithmetic is in question. 'Mr. M'Choakumchild said he would try me again . . . "What is your remark on that *proportion?* (of population dying from starvation); . . . What is the *percentage?*" (of sea-voyagers drowning, etc.)' And at the beginning of this chapter, Mr. Gradgrind is explicit: Dickens's concern is with the often naïve enthusiasm of the earlier nineteenth century for undigested statistics of economic and social advance. ' . . . the necessity of infinite grinding at the mill of knowledge as per system, schedule, blue book, report, and tabular statements A to Z'.

That there was something naïve in the use of statistics during the period is not only confirmed by such a modern authority as Schumpeter, but will be clear, even to the comparative layman's eye, from a glance at the tabular statistics of such an author as J. R. McCulloch. In *Hard Times,* in fact, Utilitarianism largely means 'Manchester School' political economy: 'Utilitarian economists, skeletons of schoolmasters, Commissioners of Fact'—there is an implicit reference back to the 'unlucky infants' who are told to 'take everything on political economy'.

Dickens had views about McCulloch. Six months before he began *Hard Times* he wrote that a piece submitted for his magazine *Household Words* was *'dreadfully dull . . .* I should have thought the greater part of it by McCulloch edited by Rintoul'. R. S. Rintoul was editor of the *Spectator* from 1828 and (as the *D.N.B.* has it) was 'a model of exact journalism' who 'soon brought round him men like Bentham (and) Mill'. McCulloch is important in the field of political economy not only for his *Principles* (1st ed., 1825)—to which this discussion must revert: it was the standard work until Mill's book of the same name replaced it in 1843—but also, and perhaps still more, for encyclopaedic productions like the *Descriptive and Statistical Account of the British Empire.* In these two enormous volumes, amid the laboured elegance of McCulloch's style, and the laborious superabundance of his figures, one may find both what sets the scene for Dickens's novel, and what brings one back to some of the attitudes (those of Bounderby, say) depicted in it. 'Lancashire is the grand seat of the cotton manufacture . . . Manchester, now the second town in the empire, is the principal centre of the manufacture; but it is also carried on, to a great extent, and with astonishing success, at Preston (etc.).' Immediately before this, McCulloch records of the county of Lancashire, ' . . . average rent of land in 1842-3, 28*s.* 11½*d.* an acre'. This cotton manufacture is 'by far the most wonderful triumph of mechanical genius and invention that the world has ever seen'. In another of McCulloch's encyclopaedias, the *Practical, Theoretical, and Historical Dictionary of Commerce and Commercial Navigation* (1832), we find that for the Lancashire cloth to undersell Indian handloom weavers, though using raw material brought from India, was again 'the greatest triumph of mechanical genius'. *The Dictionary, Geographical, Statistical and Historical, of the Various Countries, Places and Principal Natural Objects of the World* (2 vols., 1841-2), happens to bring out another fact relevant to **Hard Times.** Until only a very few years before this novel was written, no town north of Preston was served by rail from London: Dickens, visiting the town early in 1854 to get first-hand impressions of the cotton lock-out, was indeed penetrating deep into the Other World of the industrial north.

I have given the full titles of these works of McCulloch, because even by themselves they enable one to glimpse the world of naïve but encyclopaedic fact against which Dickens was reacting. As the picture is completed, it leads the attention not towards men of greater intellectual distinction than McCulloch, but towards men still more commonplace, towards now forgotten figures of mid-Victorian popularization. One of these was Charles Knight, Secretary of the Society for the Promotion of Useful Knowledge, and like McCulloch a great compiler of encyclopaedic dictionaries. Knight was for many years a personal friend of Dickens, who was willing to view his factual compilations sympathetically. In 1854 Knight sent him a copy of his *Knowledge is Power,* which was a kind of elementary (and enthusiastic) guide to contemporary processes of commerce and more particularly manufacture; and said he was afraid that Dickens, then busy writing **Hard Times,** would set him down as 'a cold-hearted political economist'. Dickens's reply provides useful confirmation of what is now being argued as the issue in the novel: 'My satire is against those who see *figures and averages, and nothing else*—the representatives of the wickedest and most enormous vice of this time— . . . Bah! What have you to do with these?'

J. T. Boulton has already suggested that (in spite of this

disclaimer on Dickens's part) *Knowledge is Power* should be seen as the kind of work which Dickens had in mind in his critique of factualism. But Dickens's ideas must have been fully formed before he saw a copy of this work, and a much earlier compilation by Knight, his *Store of Knowledge,* seems far more to the point. Indeed, it seems certain that one of the articles in the *Store of Knowledge* directly influenced Dickens in respect of **Hard Times.** This is the piece by William Youatt entitled, baldly, 'The Horse'. On the first page of this we find a paragraph which begins, 'The teeth of the horse require some lengthened consideration . . . '; and explains that the discussion which follows, some 750 words in length, is of value because the horse's mouth is a sure guide to his age. There seems reason to think that this must have given Dickens the ideas for Bitzer's egregious 'definition of a horse':

> Quadruped. Graminiverous. Forty teeth, namely twenty-four grinders, four eye-teeth, and twelve incisive. . . .
> Age known by marks in mouth.

Moreover, another article in the *Store of Knowledge* may also have contributed something to the novel. This is the piece entitled 'Schools' by Dr. Beard, for it contains a remarkable passage from the evidence given before the 1838 Committee on Education: a passage which cannot but recall, in detail, the visit of Mr. Gradgrind and the 'third gentleman' to the school in the opening scene of the novel. This is the visit which produces Bitzer's model performance, and the discomfiture of Sissy Jupe:

> . . . certain children are brought prominently forward . . . these frequent exhibitions to strangers visiting the school have all an injurious effect upon the mind of the child, and also an injurious effect upon the minds of the other children, discouraging and disheartening them.

A careful reading of Beard's article, however, begins to reveal the complexities of the situation Dickens was moving in; for it closes with what is in some ways a most humane and enlightened account of how the education of children should proceed; envisaging it, almost after the manner of *Émile,* as a following of nature and a gradual unfolding of the child's inner powers. I think that this makes clear how one cannot see the issue as a simple one between a humane and enlightened novelist and rigid and hide-bound compilers. That the enlightenment is not on one side only is confirmed by some words of McCulloch's on the subject; words which hint at some of the intricacies of meaning in the word 'utilitarian' itself:

> To render education productive of all the utility that may be derived from it, the poor should, in addition to the elementary instruction now alluded to, be made acquainted with the duties enjoined by morality and religion . . .

The context of these remarks is thoroughly 'Manchester School', and has its unenlightened side. But the reference to 'utility' gives a little help towards rightly understanding what has often been not understood at all: the standpoint which Dickens takes up in the latter part of the schoolroom scene, the discussion that deals, improbably enough one cannot but remark, with wallpapers and carpets.

II

The fact is, that (as K. J. Fielding has in part made plain, but not, I think, fully enough), Dickens in this section of his book is far from taking up a position which is enlightened. In fact, it is much easier to argue that his satire was directed against the contemporary forces of enlightenment (the whole scene is rich in contemporary reference) and is written from the standpoint of the mid-Victorian middle-class Philistine. This, broadly speaking, is the Dickens who wrote with a low-brow vulgarity about Millais's 'Christ in the Carpenter's Shop' in the Pre-Raphaelite exhibition. The naïveté, in fact, is now on his side. The 'third gentleman' (as Fielding points out) represents the views of the 'Department of Practical Art' organized under the Board of Trade in 1852. But it did not use the word 'Practical' through no-nonsense fact-and-nothing-but-fact Philistinism: it did so because it sought to function as a growing point in the decorative arts and in industrial design. Those whom it drew together—John Bell, head of the Normal School of Design at Somerset House; Owen Jones, the forerunner of Morris in wallpaper design; M. Digby Wyatt, Secretary of the Executive Committee of the Great Exhibition; Ralph Wornum, compiler of the 1846 National Gallery catalogue; Richard Redgrave; and Henry Cole, Secretary of the Department of Science and Art from 1853 to 1873, and (since he was a civil servant) pseudonymous designer of 'Summerly's Art Manufactures' from 1847 on—were the most enlightened men in their field at the time. What they stood for was a repudiation of the crude and vulgar photographic realism of ignorant factory design—what might with justice be called 'Bounderby art'—and its replacement by designs which recognized what would nowadays be universally accepted as first principles of informed, professional work: the stylization necessary in decorating a flat surface, the preservation of a proper balance between empty and filled spaces, and so on. What they opposed was what Professor Pevsner, writing of design such as Dickens is defending, called 'the riotous effect of large bouquets of flowers, rank ferns, and thick whorls'—the carpets, as another designer having affinities with this group was later to describe them, 'on which ponds of water were drawn with water-lilies floating upon them, and other absurdities equally offensive to good taste'.

Professor Giedion's important discussion of this group does much to bring out their contemporary affinities and their essential quality. First, he points out that in their basic principle of design, fitness for purpose, 'the intellectual outlook of the circle is more or less in keeping with Utilitarianism as expounded in its philosophical and economic aspects by J. S. Mill', a view which does less to damn the designers than to remind one that Utilitarianism, at its best, had itself some claim to rank as part of a high civilization. Second, he mentions that another name

must be added to those given above: that of Gottfried Semper. Semper is a forerunner of twentieth-century standards of design. In 1855 Semper left England to become Professor to the Technische Hochschule in Zürich. His main work, *Style in the Technical and Tectonic Arts* (1860-3) was a fundamental work in the theory of design; and by 1910 'the German reform movement in the decorative arts, which took fitness to purpose as its final criterion, regarded him as a basic authority'. Through Semper, the circle which Dickens satirized counts among the forerunners of the Bauhaus.

Like Charles Kent, Henry Cole, perhaps the most active member of the group, was a personal acquaintance of Dickens; and this perhaps explains the difference between the latter's scornful if covert attack on the Department in the novel, and the explicit discussion, in *Household Words,* of the 'Chamber of Horrors', the room full of prize examples of disastrous mid-Victorian taste, which Cole organized for a short time at Marlborough House. Dickens's extent of disagreement with the principles of design represented by Marlborough House is a limited one; and in fact, it would be fair to say that he hardly knows where he stands: 'the whole Hog and nothing but the whole Hog . . . is a little indigestible'. The importance of this article (as of the rather sheepishly inconclusive sentence just quoted) is that it enables one to see the level of thought at which Dickens was operating. Certainly, in both novel and article, he stands in a general way for human feeling against what is doctrinaire and rigid. But there is a sense in which his disagreement is partial or even casual: it does not penetrate to the fundamental issues involved, and one cannot deny that there is at least a hint of the Philistine about it.

III

At present, the reputation of **Hard Times** stands high, and the suggestion that lack of depth, even something of the middle-class Philistine, shows elsewhere in how the book works out its scheme of values, will not carry immediate conviction. The assertion requires proof, of course, with regard to what is in the text itself. Nothing takes the place of that. But it may prove easier to see clearly what is there, if one notices the elements of compromise, of an amiable but casual grasp of the realities, in Dickens's outlook as we can trace it generally at the very time it was being written. The deficiencies of McCulloch, for example, transpired in his tone—'wonderful triumph of mechanical genius', 'grand seat of the cotton manufacture . . . astonishing success', as much as in his '28s. 11½d.'; we are reminded too closely of the complacent bombast of Mr. Roebuck as Arnold pillories him in *The Function of Criticism at the Present Time*. But it is not easy to find a Roebuckism which excels the following:

> To that great compact phalanx of the people, by whose industry, perseverance, and intelligence, and their result in money-wealth, such places as Birmingham, and many others like it, have arisen—to that great centre of support, that comprehensive experience, and that beating heart—Literature has turned happily . . .

and this is Dickens himself, at a civic dinner in Birmingham exactly a year before he began writing *Hard Times*. All in all, Dickens stood much too near to what he criticized in the novel, for his criticism to reach a fundamental level. This is not a matter of his having a balanced view of the whole situation as between manufacture, labour, and capital; but of his sharing the somewhat naïve enthusiasms, and with them to some extent the brusque middle-class hostilities and presumptions, of those whom he thought he was criticizing. *Household Words,* throughout the early 1850's, is full of enthusiastic accounts of the wonders of Victorian manufacture. Even in February 1854, almost the very moment when he was beginning *Hard Times,* Dickens could write:

> Mighty, indeed, are the dealings of these cotton monarchs. Complicated are their transactions; numberless the interests they affect; and far away and strange the lands they give vitality to, the mouths they feed, the forms they clothe.

A year before, writing then too of the Lancashire mills, he wrote:

> the factory itself is certainly not a 'thing of beauty' in its externals. But it is a grand machine in its organization—the men, the fingers, and the iron and steel, all work together for one common end.

The article concludes with a eulogy of the 'captain of industry' (Mr. Titus Salt) who was building new model factories at Saltaire. 'Captain of industry' is of course a phrase of Carlyle's. Dickens dedicated *Hard Times* to that fiery and apocalyptic bourgeois, and assured him that there was nothing in the book with which he would disagree. It is plain that Dickens's whole love-hate relation to Victorian industry was deeply influenced by the writings of the older man.

If this is true, though, how does it show in the novel? It shows in Dickens's treatment of the main situation of the book. For all his opposition to the 'hard fact men' like McCulloch, he subscribes out and out to McCulloch's principle of an ultimate identity of interest between men and masters. 'Those whose interests must be supposed to be identical or must be destroyed', he writes; and the effect of this on the novel is barely less than deliberate falsification of what Dickens knew, from his visit to Preston, to be the facts. For Slackbridge, the 'O my friends' stump-orator (it is wholly in place to appropriate Carlyle's scornful term in *Latter Day Pamphlets*) is based upon a 'professional speaker' whom Dickens actually witnessed on his visit to Preston during the 1853-4 lockout. He, however, so far from dominating the meeting and getting his way at it, was on Dickens's own testimony suppressed by the Chairman; and when Dickens wrote of that meeting in *Household Words,* what he did was praise the men's

> . . . astonishing fortitude and perseverance; their high sense of honour among themselves; the extent to which they are impressed with the responsibility that is upon

them of setting a careful example, and keeping their order out of any harm and loss of reputation. . . .

IV

If we seek to assess the level of seriousness and insight at which Dickens is working in the novel, it cannot be without significance to notice what he sets against the world of 'addition, subtraction, multiplication, and division' which he rejects. His alternative is neither the determined individuality and, in a certain degree, genuine cultivation of the best masters (as Charlotte Brontë saw this when she depicted Hunsden in *The Professor,* or as Mrs. Gaskell did with John Thornton in *North and South* or indeed, to some extent, Dickens himself with Mr. Rouncewell in *Bleak House*); nor the desperate need, communal feeling, and strengthening responsibility which he saw for himself among the 'hands'. His alternative was something which lay altogether outside the major realities of the social situation with which he dealt: the circus world of Mr. Sleary.

In principle, perhaps, this world could indeed carry the weight of that 'vital human impulse' to which Dr. Leavis refers as counterpart to the 'utilitarian' ethos that for him is one pole of the novel. The comparison between *Hard Times* and Picasso's 'Saltimbanques' has been made (though it seems obviously extravagant); and occasionally, a phrase in the novel (such as the reformed Mr. Gradgrind's reference to 'the right instinct'—supposing it for the moment to be some quality of that nature) looks as if it could support so ambitious and life-giving an interpretation. Again, however, general indications of how Dickens's mind was working in the period of composition help us to detect the chief impact lying within the text, the main thing which he is setting up in opposition to the 'hard fact men'. It does not seem to be anything even remotely Lawrentian (this was, after all, a pre-Nietzsche novel). On the contrary, it too, like its opposite, operated (for all its obvious common sense and its genuine value) at a relatively shallow level of consciousness, one represented by the Slearies not as vital horsemen but as plain entertainers.

In fact, the creed which Dickens champions in the novel, against Gradgrind's, seems in the main to be that of 'all work and no play makes Jack a dull boy'. How unwilling many will be to admit this! Yet Dickens's letter to Charles Knight when he was writing *Hard Times* takes just this point of view, and turns out to have simply been reworded in the novel.

> I earnestly entreat your attention to the point (I have been working upon it, weeks past, in *Hard Times*) . . . the English are, as far as I know, the hardest-worked people on whom the sun shines. Be content if, in their intervals of pleasure, they read for *amusement* and do no worse. They are born at the oar, and they live and die at it. Good God, what would you have of them!

In *Hard Times* this becomes

I entertain a weak idea that the English people are as hard-worked as any people upon whom the sun shines. I acknowledge to this ridiculous idiosyncrasy, as a reason why I would give them a little more *play.*

With which one may usefully compare Mr. Gradgrind's 'annihilating the flowers of existence' with his excise-rod and compasses, and Louisa's lament to her brother:

I don't know what other girls know. I can't play to you, or sing to you. I can't talk to you so as to enlighten your mind, for I never see any *amusing* sights or read any amusing books that it would be a *pleasure or a relief* to you to talk about, *when you are tired.*

One may compare also the decisive closing paragraph of the novel, about the main survivor of the book, Sissy Jupe:

. . . thinking no *innocent and pretty* fancy ever to be despised; trying hard to . . . *beautify* . . . lives of machinery and reality with . . . imaginative graces and delights.

and the concluding words of Mr. Sleary, with their emphasis not on art or gracious vitality, but amusement:

. . . Don't be croth with uth poor vagabonth. People mutht be amused. They can't alwayth be a learning, nor yet they can't be alwayth a working, they an't made for it. You *mutht* have uth, Thquire. Do the withe thing and the kind thing too, and make the betht of uth; not the wurtht!

From outside the text of the novel, *Household Words* and the *Letters* readily confirm this interpretation. The letter, already quoted, about the 'dreadfully dull' article ran: 'some *fancy* must be got into the number': fancy (the 'tender light of Fancy', as the novel has it was the necessary antidote to McCulloch and Rintoul. Finally, the *Household Words* article on the Preston lockout makes the same point, and one must bear in mind that it is one entirely characteristic of Dickens from Mr. Pickwick on:

there must enter something of feeling and sentiment, something which is not to be found in Mr. McCulloch's Dictionary . . . political economy is a mere skeleton unless it has a little human covering and fitting out, a little human bloom on it, and a little human warmth in it.

V

What this discussion seems to me to issue in is a view of the novel's moral intention which accords with the quality and development of Dickens's whole mind. He was not a profound and prophetic genius with insight into the deepest levels of human experience; but (leaving his immense gifts aside for a moment) a man whose outlook was amiable and generous, though it partook a little of

the shallowness of the merely topical, and the defects of the bourgeois—the word is not too harsh—Philistine. Ruskin, generations ago, gave the necessary lead over **Hard Times:** 'in several respects the greatest (novel) he has written', he said, the author is 'entirely right in his main drift and purpose', but Ruskin himself wishes that he had used 'a severer and more accurate analysis'.

Turn to the detailed presentation, and it is clear that when Dickens is most preoccupied with his 'idea that laid hold of me by the throat in a very violent manner', he usually fails. The point is made, and as it transpires, the life fades away. Sissy's spontaneous, childish compassionateness becomes a smart debating point:

' . . . in a given time a hundred thousand persons went to sea on long voyages, and only five hundred of them were drowned or burned to death. What is the percentage? . . . And I . . . said it was nothing.'

'Nothing, Sissy?'

'Nothing, Miss—to the relations and friends of the people who were killed. . . . '

In the conversation between Louisa and her father when Bounderby has proposed, it is apparent at once that neither character is a true embodiment of the standpoint—or predicament—which is their allotted rôle; they are creatures of stick, arguing a case or (with Gradgrind) obligingly but unconvincingly tongue-tied:

'Father . . . Where have I been? What are my heart's experiences?'

'My dear Louisa,' returned Mr. Gradgrind . . . 'you correct me justly . . . I merely wished to discharge my duty.'

'What do *I* know, Father . . . of tastes and fancies; of aspirations and affections; of all that part of my nature in which such light things [the word "light" should not be overlooked] might have been nourished? What escape have I had from problems that could be demonstrated, and realities that could be grasped?' As she said it, she unconsciously closed her hand, as if upon a solid object, and slowly opened it as though she were releasing ash.

'My dear,' assented her eminently practical parent, 'quite true, quite true.'

How, frankly, can writing like this (the forced rhetoric, the lack of interchange, the banal image) retain our attention, unless we are enticed by problems but indifferent to art?

Two moments in the working out of the fable seem especially to deserve attention. The first is the moment of anagnorisis for Gradgrind. The scene is peculiarly significant. It is the resolution of the whole first movement of the fable (and as will become clear, it is fair to say that there is no real second movement). What is the response of a Gradgrind to the moment of discovering that his system is no system at all?—indeed, that it does not even represent what must always have meant most to him, his love for his daughter. Even as we put the question, we notice the extraordinary bias of emphasis which Dickens has given to the chapter. All its weight goes to Louisa. Gradgrind does, and says, virtually nothing. His response to the moment of truth is no response. Mill, in the *Auto-biography,* was later to describe such a moment—of total disillusion with the life of the unmitigated intellect—though seen with an amplitude and depth which Dickens did not command, and which (I have argued) was no part of his main intention on the politico-economic side of his book. *Hard Times* does not begin to depict it, and I believe that the limit of the book's achievement is never clearer than it is here. George Eliot, when she showed Rosamund Vincy humiliating herself before Dorothea in the matter of Ladislaw, showed that she had the entry to this world of tortured and intricate psychology. Dickens did not.

It is easy to see the closing chapters of *Hard Times* as an example of what is so common among imperfect novels: the continuation of the plot (after the central idea of the work has been resolved) at the level merely of crisis and adventure. This, however, would do Dickens less than justice. The gradual degeneration of Tom, until the superb moment when, in his ridiculous and degrading disguise, 'he came down, bench by bench [like a monkey] until he stood in the sawdust', is barely (as in fact it is treated) related to Dickens's major problems in the book, though it is one of its best things. But Mr. Sleary's decision to stand by Tom, and compound the felony which Bitzer will not compound, is a major landmark in the whole fable, and the second of the two 'moments' which I mentioned above. For, after all, it is the key point (along with the 'discovery' of Bounderby's mother and her devotion) at which the fable creates its picture of the lengths to which untutored kindness and unreasoned feeling can go, and how they look as they go to these lengths. It is, or could be, the second great test of the values of the book. Yet Dickens does not come up to the scratch; nor, after all, has Mr. Sleary ever been a character that his creator could really hope to steer through a revelatory moral crisis. The moment is left as one of lively, but not meaningful, excitement.

> The Thquire thtood by you, Thethilia, and I'll thtand by the Thquire. More than that: thith ith a prethiouth rathcal, and belongth to that bluthering Cove that my people nearly pitht out o' winder. It'll be a dark night. . . .

As a 'moral fable' *Hard Times* is a vigorous and good-hearted book, but if 'shallow' is unduly severe with regard to the level of insight with which it proceeds, Dr. Leavis, in writing that here 'the creative exuberance is controlled by a *profound* inspiration' has conceded just the word which requires to be withheld.

At which point, when the smugness that too easily attends passing critical *fiats* is (it may be) about to descend, we open the novel at random and find, it may be, this:

> ' . . . she never had a lover, and the governor proposed old Bounderby, and she took him'.

> 'Very dutiful in your interesting sister,' said Mr. James Harthouse.

> 'Yes, but she wouldn't have been as dutiful, and it would not have come off as easily,' returned the whelp, 'if it hadn't been for me.'

> The tempter merely lifted his eyebrows; but the whelp was obliged to go on.

> '*I* persuaded her,' he said, with an edifying air of superiority. 'I was stuck into old Bounderby's bank . . . and I knew I should get into scrapes . . . so I told her my wishes, and she came into them . . . It was very game of her, wasn't it?'

> 'It was charming, Tom!'

> 'Not that it was altogether so important to her as it was to me,' continued Tom coolly, 'because my liberty and comfort, and perhaps my getting on, depended on it . . . but still it was a good thing in her.'

> 'Perfectly delightful. And she gets on so placidly.'

> 'Oh,' returned Tom . . . 'She's a regular girl. A girl can get on anywhere . . . I have often known her sit and watch the fire—for an hour at a stretch.'

> 'Ay, ay? Has resources of her own,' said Harthouse, smoking quietly.

> 'Not so much of that as you may suppose. . . .'

How splendid that is, in its crisp vitality and observation, and how copiously yet exactly it contributes, at every point, to the movement of the book! The hint of theatricality that is never quite absent in Dickens seems here only to add to the energy. Elsewhere, too, Harthouse figures in scenes which the author manages admirably—as in the critical conversation between him and Louisa:

> 'I will confide to you my doubt whether he has had many advantages. Whether—forgive my plainness—whether any great amount of confidence is likely to have been established between himself and his most worthy father.'

> 'I do not,' said Louisa, flushing with her own great remembrance in that wise, 'think it likely.'

> 'Or, between himself, and—I may trust to your perfect understanding of my meaning, I am sure—and his highly-esteemed brother-in-law.'

> She flushed deeper and deeper, and was burning red

when she replied in a fainter voice, 'I do not think that likely, either.'

The moment of the decisive revelation runs:

> ' . . . When I married, I found that my brother was even at that time heavily in debt. Heavily for him, I mean. Heavily enough to oblige me to sell some trinkets. They were no sacrifice. I sold them very willingly. I attached no value to them. They were quite worthless to me.'

> Either she saw in his face that he knew, or she only feared in her conscience that he knew, that she spoke of some of her husband's gifts. She stopped, and reddened again. If he had not known it before, he would have known it then. . . .

No one can miss the mounting emotion, created in the increasing bluntness, of the very words of Louisa's speech; nor the shrewd insight into psychology, and dexterous use of it for drama, in the author's comment which follows.

Perhaps the most vividly memorable part of the whole novel is that of Mrs. Sparsit spying on Louisa and Harthouse, and following the fleeing Louisa, through the thunderstorm, to the railway station and to Coketown. It is the culmination of one of the great imaginative strokes of the book, Dickens's likening of her temptation to the descent of a great staircase, into chaos at its foot. He extracts the image, with great skill and economy, from Louisa's own 'What does it matter?' then imposes it on Mrs. Sparsit, and modulates it, with a truly poetic movement, into the 'deep water' and universal deluge of the railway scene. This whole scene of the flight, in its fluent modulation of imagery and its melodrama charged with human weight, is Dickens at his most characteristic and his best.

In fact, if what is best in this novel is reviewed generally, it cannot but suggest reflections which extend beyond itself. For the passages in *Hard Times* where Dickens most shows his genius, is most freely himself, are not those where he is most engaged with his moral fable or intent (if we think, mistakenly, that he is so at all) on what Dr. Leavis called 'the confutation of Utilitarianism by life'. Rather, they appear when he comes near to being least engrossed with such things; when he is the Dickens who appears throughout the novels: the master of dialogue that, even through its stylization, crackles with life, perception, and sharpness, the master of drama in spectacle and setting and action. And one possibility that the novel suggests is that we can pay too high a price for the moral fable, for such undertakings as 'the confutation of Utilitarianism'. We can pay the price of impairing a large free-ranging consciousness of the outward spectacle and psychic life of men. We assume, it may be, as we turn from the picturesqueness and picaresqueness of Dickens's earlier work to a novel like *Hard Times,* that in organizing his work round a moral issue he will enjoy a deeper apprehension and produce a richer result. On second thoughts, this may prove the reverse of true. The 'pecu-

liarly insistent moral intention' (the words are again Dr. Leavis's, and to me they seem wonderfully disquieting and unacceptable) is one thing; and a moral because simply a total apprehension on the writer's part, a capacity in him to consume and register, in full, the buoyant abundance and endless variation of reality, is another. Henry James has already made the point: 'The essence of moral energy is to survey the whole field . . . try to catch the colour of life itself'. Perhaps we are too much inclined to demand the all-embracing moral structure in fiction, to take its mere presence as its success, to forget that what is all-embracing may also be all-consuming, and in some measure to forgo the free life, the unconstrained movement, the inexhaustible wealth of fiction, for the chiaroscuro of moralism and tyranny of theme.

David H. Hirsch (essay date 1964)

SOURCE: "*Hard Times* and F. R. Leavis," in *Criticism,* Vol. 6, No. 1, Winter, 1964, pp. 1-16.

[*The essay below represents one of the two most notable critical responses to F. R. Leavis's seminal 1948 essay on* Hard Times, *the other being John Holloway's* "Hard Times: A History and a Criticism" (1962). *Hirsch finds* Hard Times "*One of the dullest and least successful*" *of Dickens's works, despite the author's "most commendable" purpose.*]

The inability of Dickens scholars to agree in their evaluations of particular novels has become one of the commonplaces of Dickens criticism. *Hard Times,* especially, has had a checkered career. On the one hand, it has been completely ignored as a novel (F. G. Kitton excluded it from his book *The Novels of Dickens*). On the other hand, such men as John Ruskin and George Bernard Shaw considered it Dickens's best book. In recent years, largely on the basis of the critical brilliance of F. R. Leavis, it is the latter view that has prevailed.

Dr. Leavis's close reading and perceptive analysis seem to have set the book's reputation, once and for all, on firm aesthetic ground. Hence, Edgar Johnson, the most important recent biographer of Dickens, accepts Leavis's evaluation wholeheartedly, concluding that the low evaluations of the book are not the result of aesthetic failure on Dickens's part, but are to be explained by the fact that the book "is an analysis and a condemnation of the ethos of industrialism." For literary critics to condemn a book on such non-aesthetic grounds is deplorable, but it is equally deplorable for literary critics to attempt to praise a work of art on such grounds. And yet, this is just what defenders of the book, including the new-critical Dr. Leavis, have done.

In the first chapter of *The Great Tradition,* Dr. Leavis writes, "The adult mind doesn't as a rule find in Dickens a challenge to an unusual and sustained seriousness. I can think of only one of his books in which his distinctive creative genius is controlled throughout to a unifying and organizing significance, and that is *Hard Times*. . . . "

The tendency of Dr. Leavis's criticism is revealed in the words "genius is controlled throughout to a unifying and organizing significance." To put Dr. Leavis's point a little less eloquently, *Hard Times* is praiseworthy because it has a clearly intended and clearly expressed moral purpose. This is the "unifying significance" that Dr. Leavis speaks of. And the reader's consciousness of Dickens's moral purpose is, I suspect, what he means by the challenge to sustained seriousness. What I shall try to show is that both the "challenge" found by the "adult mind" and the "sustained seriousness" of *Hard Times* are negligible, not because Dickens's analysis of the ethos of capitalism is too penetrating and his condemnation too convincing, but because he does not succeed in converting his very commendable moral intentions into first-rate fiction.

Dr. Leavis (and since later critics do no more than echo him, I will limit myself to his critical analysis of the book) states that in *Hard Times* "the fable is perfect; the symbolic and representative values are inevitable, and, sufficiently plain at once, yield fresh subtleties as the action develops naturally in its convincing historical way." Fable has become a highly honorific word these days; yet there still exists some legitimate question as to whether "perfect fable" is synonymous with "great art." There is, too, a touch of ingeniousness in Dr. Leavis's using the adjective "perfect" to describe, at least by implication, a work of art; first because it is possible for a work to be "perfect" of its kind and yet at the same time of questionable significance, but more basically because even the most objective of our aesthetic criteria are so fluid that it is impossible to agree on any sort of fixed standard against which aesthetic "perfection" can be measured. And as for the clause, "the symbolic and representative values are inevitable," it is meaningless till Dr. Leavis tells us first what he imagines those values to be, and secondly what he takes to be the origin and direction of their inevitability. Does he mean an "inevitability" that grows out of the original premises of the work, or one that grows out of "real" life, out of "actual" laws of probability?

I suspect that Dr. Leavis himself is not certain, for this inability to distinguish what is in the work from what is outside of it later clogs his entire analysis. Even in the passage just quoted, the inconsistencies are patent. To maintain, for example, that "symbolic . . . values are inevitable and sufficiently plain," and to say this in commendation, is to posit and accept a supposed simplicity in the relationship between a symbol and a "something" symbolized that does not and cannot exist. Dr. Leavis's concept of the way in which symbolism and fiction operate with regard to each other is naive. Even his adjectives are confused. If it is necessary or possible to make a distinction between what is "historical" and what is "symbolic" in fiction, then it seems that the first must refer to values and the second to action. That is, as the symbolic action develops it tests (whether to affirm or deny) "historical" values.

The full extent of all this confusion is plain enough the moment Dr. Leavis starts to deal with the book itself. For instance, he tries to justify the portrayal of Sissy Jupe

(one of the most insipid portraits in Dickens's generally splendid gallery) by contending that "Sissy Jupe, who might be taken here for a merely conventional *persona,* has already, as a matter of fact, been established in a potently symbolic role: she is part of the poetically-creative operation of Dickens's genius in *Hard Times*." But one of the things that makes Sissy so untenable and unpalatable as a character is the fact that she never does achieve what is in the truest sense "a potently symbolic role." That Dickens has attempted to create a symbolic character in Sissy is obvious, but that he has failed completely is equally obvious.

Karl Jaspers, in a profound monograph called *Truth and Symbol,* comments that

> Thinking of symbols through an "other" explains them genetically and dissolves them. Geniune symbols cannot be interpreted; what can be interpreted through an "other" ceases to be a symbol. On the other hand, the interpretation of symbols through their self-presentation encircles and circumscribes, penetrates and illuminates. . . . The symbol is not passed over by being understood, but is deepened and enhanced by being meditated upon.

> The modes of interpretation are, therefore, to be tested as to their meaning, whether they destroy by explaining or whether they enhance by penetrating.

But precisely what Dr. Leavis tries to do, and succeeds in doing, with regard to Sissy Jupe, is to explain her in terms of an "other" without dissolving her. He says, quite rightly, that Sissy "stands for vitality as well as goodness." Exactly. She "stands for." She does not at once embody and illuminate these qualities, as she would if she achieved existence as a genuine symbol. Sissy as a "symbol" presents no problem and no dimension. It is not only not necessary but not possible to "think" through Sissy. Her "meaning" is neither deepened nor "enhanced" by being meditated upon. The fact is that Sissy's "symbolic significance" is non-existent. If Dickens, as Leavis recognizes, intended her as a symbol, then he surely failed. And the extent of his failure is the measure of Sissy's proximity to an ordinary soap-opera heroine.

The same kind of failure, too, is perceivable in Dickens's portrayal of Sleary's Horse-riding. Leavis claims that "Sissy's symbolic significance is bound up with that of Sleary's Horse-riding, where human kindness is very insistently associated with vitality. Representing human spontaneity, the circus-athletes represent at the same time highly developed skill and deftness of kinds that bring poise, pride and confident ease—they are always buoyant, and, ballet-dancer-like, in training. . . ."

As in his exposition on Sissy, the nature and tone of Dr. Leavis's diction are more revealing than his intended meaning. The Horse-riding "represent," they do not embody or encompass. Moreover, there is no question of penetrating or illuminating the symbol through interpretation. As in the case of Sissy, a very superficial interpretation is possible. The Horse-riding, like Sissy, are simplistically associated (by Dickens and Leavis) with pure goodness. And this is to say that they are sentimentalized in the same way that Sissy is. Dr. Leavis cites the following passage in support of his contention that Sissy Jupe has "been established in a potently symbolic role":

> The square finger, moving here and there, lighted suddenly on Bitzer, perhaps because he chanced to sit in the same ray of sun-light which, darting in at one of the bare windows of the intensely whitewashed room, irradiated Sissy . . . Sissy . . . came in for the beginning of a sunbeam, of which Bitzer . . . caught the end. But, whereas the girl was so dark-eyed and dark-haired that she seemed to receive a deeper and more lustrous colour from the sun when it shone upon her, the boy was so light-eyed and light-haired that the self-same rays appeared to draw out of him what little colour he ever possessed. His cold eyes would hardly have been eyes, but for the short ends of lashes which by bringing them into immediate contrast with something paler than themselves, expressed their form. His short-cropped hair might have been mere continuation of the sandy freckles on his forehead and face. His skin was so unwholesomely deficient in the natural tinge, that he looked as though, if he were cut, he would bleed white.

Dr. Leavis is all but carried away by what he takes to be the sheer poetry of this passage. He comments as follows:

> There is no need to insist on the force—representative of Dickens's art in general in *Hard Times*—with which the moral and spiritual differences are rendered here in terms of sensation, so that the symbolic intention emerges out of metaphor and the vivid evocation of the concrete. . . . There is an essentially Laurentian suggestion about the way in which "the dark-eyed and dark-haired" girl, contrasting with Bitzer, seemed to receive a "deeper and more lustrous color from the sun," so opposing the life that is lived freely and richly from the deep instinctive and emotional springs to the thinblooded, quasi-mechanical product of Gradgrindery.

Of course there is no need to insist. That is just the trouble. The entire passage is embarrassingly obvious. The force of the imagery must certainly be granted. But this very force falsifies Dickens's "message." In its gross oversimplification of the complexity of human moral problems, the description rings a resoundingly false note. Sissy, who represents vitality, is kindled by the ray of sunlight. From the source of all life the girl who lives instinctively draws sustenance. Bitzer, who represents the antithesis of vitality, has his pallor intensified by the very same sunbeam. Operating on the boy who lives by fact, the lifesource underlines his sterility. Moral problems, however, as we all know from reading the great nineteenth-century novels, do not precipitate out of solution so easily. Nor can it be argued that Dickens had to preserve a clear distinction between light and dark, good and evil, in order to realize his symbolic intention, for this is only to say in other words that at this point in his career Dickens was incapable of creating truly symbolic fiction. When one thinks of the heights that Herman Melville had

reached three years earlier in his potently imaginative use of white and black color imagery in *Moby-Dick,* then Dickens's failure is obvious.

Dr. Leavis's inability to see the superficiality and thinness of Dickens's imagery and symbolism is a clue to the weakness of both his aesthetic and moral criticism. It is not that morality has no place in the novel, but that Dr. Leavis's perception, or at least articulation, of the dynamic relationship between moral and artistic problems is hazy. Had Dickens truly succeeded in his imagery and symbolism, then the problem of good and evil, vitality and sterility would have been set immediately and eternally in its full complexity and ambiguity. Whiteness would not have become a convenient tab, as it is, for Bitzer, but an inscrutable mystery to be penetrated, as it is in *Moby-Dick*. And Sissy would not merely have "represented" vitality, she somehow would have encompassed it and have been encompassed by it at the same time.

Jaspers points out that

> already in the "sign" as a symbol essential reality is rudimentarily and inherently implicit. In the unfolding of the symbol-content of the sign into a work of art, the symbol does, to be sure, become rich through consistent contemplation but in the fullness of spirit it becomes empirically less effective. The sign compels and puts everything upon me. The work of art is guidance through contemplation and by means of its external form awakens and presents in definite, pregnant articulations what is lying in readiness within.

But Sissy and the Horse-riding never become more than empty signs without "symbol-content." They contain no potential richness to be realized through contemplation; whatever effectiveness they have remains always empirical and therefore, as symbol, minimal. If we consider for a moment the richness and suggestiveness of Pearl as a symbol in *The Scarlet Letter* (whatever one may think of her empirical presentation as a "realistic" portrait) the banality of Sissy becomes immediately evident. It is the myriad meanings, frequently contradictory, that cluster around Pearl that make her a viable and truly fertile symbol in a way that Sissy is not.

Dr. Leavis's inadequacy in dealing with symbols in fiction is demonstrated again when he tries to establish that Sissy and the Horse-riding not only have symbolic significance but are successfully drawn "realistic" portraits as well. Dr. Leavis makes his point by way of anticipating, as he says, the following objection: "Coketown, like Gradgrind and Bounderby, is real enough; but it can't be contended that the Horse-riding is real in the same sense. There would have been some athletic skill and perhaps some bodily grace among the people of a Victorian travelling circus, but surely so much squalor, grossness and vulgarity that we must find Dickens's symbolism sentimentally false?"

To begin with, it seems that in expressing the objection, Dr. Leavis actually should have used the word "believable" instead of "real." The question is not one of whether Coketown and Bounderby have a different kind of "reality" than the Horse-riding, but of whether they are more believable, for it is possible to contend that in all cases the "reality" is the texture of words that Dickens has created. It may, of course, be objected that this is the merest quibbling over terms, that in proportion as a functional creation is "real" it is credible, and the more "unreal" it is, the less believable. But the way in which Dr. Leavis uses "real" here is indicative, it must be insisted, of a certain *naïveté*. He is unwilling to distinguish between "historical reality" and fictional reality, between the empirical fact and the symbolic artifact.

What Dr. Leavis seems to mean when he says that Coketown is "real enough" is that there is some empirical or historical referent (Manchester in the nineteenth century?) against which the accuracy of Dickens's description can be judged. And he extends this meaning of "real" to Bounderby and Gradgrind when he lumps them in with Coketown. Apparently, they are "real" because they represent "historical" personages in the same way that Coketown resembles a "historical" city. But the Horse-riding, Dr. Leavis continues in his imaginary objection, is not real in the same sense. The implication, then, is that the "unreality" of the Horse-riding is a reflection of its lack of historicity. The next sentence, however, indicates that what Dr. Leavis (in the role of objector) means by the "unreality" of the Horse-riding is not a lack of historicity but a lack of "roundedness," an insufficiency of human qualities. In short, they are, as every reader (including Dr. Leavis) must recognize, "too good to be true." Dr. Leavis concludes that if the Horse-riding does not contain these "rounding" qualities of "squalor, grossness, and vulgarity," then "we must find . . . the symbolism sentimentally false."

The straw man conjured up by Dr. Leavis shows the same confusion that Dr. Leavis himself has demonstrated. If the Horse-riding are lacking in certain human qualities, as they surely are, then their convincingness as a "realistic" portrayal is diminished. They do not, that is, resemble people we have known in "real" life. But this should not necessarily *falsify* their symbolic function. As Jaspers points out, a symbol does not rely for its truth on fidelity to empirical observation, though it is always related to empirical observation.

> If we inquire about the source of the symbols [he asserts] we obviously discover their original essence to be without source. It is not possible to get behind them. The question of their source is answered in a penetrating realization of their originality. . . . The material of their appearance stems from the world of sensuous observations and of conceivabilities. But to lead the symbols back to this material is to misunderstand their essence and becomes a genetics which dissolves them.

Leavis, however, conceives the Horse-riding as symbol, and yet, at the same time tries to lead the symbol back to "the world of sensuous observations and conceivabilities,"

a procedure which is inevitably self-contradictory and self-defeating.

It will not do, either, to claim that the confusion cannot be attributed to Dr. Leavis, but must be imputed to the imaginary skeptic who makes the protest. For in answering the anticipated objection, Dr. Leavis accepts the false premises that are the source of all the difficulty. His reply is that

> If Dickens, intent on an emotional effect, or drunk with moral enthusiasm, had been deceiving himself . . . about the nature of the actuality, he would then indeed have been guilty of sentimental falsity, and the adverse criticism would have held. But the Horse-riding presents no such case. The virtues and qualities that Dickens prizes do indeed exist, and it is necessary for his critique of Utilitarianism and industrialism, and for (what is the same thing) his creative purpose, to evoke them vividly.

What Leavis says here is more or less true. The virtues Dickens prizes probably do exist, and Dickens certainly did have to locate them somewhere, if not for aesthetic then for thematic purposes. But the anticipated objection—that the Horse-riding is not real in the same sense that Coketown, Gradgrind, and Bounderby are real—remains unanswered. For one thing, the question is not whether the virtues Dickens prizes "exist," but whether Dickens has dramatized them convincingly in the novel. Furthermore, Dr. Leavis makes the error of trying to justify the symbol by a return to "sensuous observation." As a result, what Dr. Leavis shows, finally, is not that Coketown, Gradgrind, Bounderby, the Horse-riding, and Sissy are real in the same way, but that they are fictional in the same way. As fictive creations, they are all what E. M. Forster calls "flat" characters. Just as the Horse-riding has no human vices (and are thereby less human), so Bounderby has no human virtues. All are, to use Forster's definition of a flat character, "constructed around a single idea or quality." And it does not help very much to insist that the virtues and vices they do have "exist," or that Bounderby's portrait is based on a "real-life" capitalist and Gradgrind's on the actual upbringing of John Stuart Mill.

Flat characters, as Forster points out, are not necessarily "bad" art. What plays the mischief in **Hard Times,** however, is that Dickens tries to give these characters a function that they simply cannot fulfill. "A serious or tragic flat character," comments Forster, "is apt to be a bore. . . . It is only round people who are fit to perform tragically for any length of time and can move us to any feelings except humour and appropriateness."

And yet, precisely what Dickens tries to do is to use these flat "humours" characters to project a serious theme. The result is not only a bore, it is a catastrophe. The serious theme is finally ludicrous, for the characters degenerate into a hodgepodge of sentimental clichés. In his refusal to allow the existence of this sentimentality in the book, Dr. Leavis is perverse. We have already seen him extolling what he imagines to be the symbolic potency and reality of Sissy Jupe and the Horse-riding. He extends his praise further to Louisa and Tom Gradgrind; in the latter instance, however, commending the "sound psychology" of the portraits rather than the symbolism or reality:

> The psychology of Louisa's development and of her brother Tom's is sound. Having no outlet for her emotional life except in her love for her brother, she lives for him and marries Bounderby—under pressure from Tom—for Tom's sake. . . . Thus, by the constrictions and starvations of the Gradgrind *régime,* are natural affection and capacity for disinterested devotion turned to ill. As for Tom, the *régime* has made of him a bored and sullen whelp. . . .

But what Dr. Leavis is talking about here is not so much psychology as ideology. Louisa is a convenient example of the ruin that "Gradgrindism" brings upon a basically good girl; Tom is an example of the way in which the same philosophy corrupts completely a basically bad boy. But as far as any serious attempts to probe the dynamic interrelationship between the "basic" character and the environment, to consider the problematic nature of self-love and conscience, Utilitarian philosophy as opposed to the Christian ideal of self-sacrifice as ways of working on basic human substance, such efforts are totally absent.

The absence is revealing, for it underlines the weakness of characterization in the book. It is no wonder that Leavis feels compelled to insist so vigorously and so repeatedly that the characterization is "potently symbolic" and "realistic" and "psychologically sound" and "wholly convincing." In showering praise on what is hardly praiseworthy a loud voice is a necessary substitute for careful, painstaking analysis. Hence, Leavis, instead of turning his perspicuous mind to close analysis of the book, wastes his great subtlety in devising strategies for presenting his argument convincingly. He concedes, for example, that Stephen Blackpool, a minor character, is drawn in the sentimental vein, but then goes on to insist that "Sissy Jupe is another matter. A general description of her part in the fable might suggest the worst, but actually she has nothing in common with Little Nell; she shares in the strength of the Horse-riding. She is wholly convincing in the function Dickens assigns to her."

Yet it is obvious to anyone who has read the book that Sissy, as she is therein portrayed, is as dismal a failure on a literal level as she is on the "symbolic" level. She does resemble Little Nell and she does resemble Stephen Blackpool. And while it is true, too, that she has something in common with the Horse-riding, it is not strength she shares with them but weakness. To demonstrate his point that Sissy is not sentimentalized, Dr. Leavis cites the following lines from a climactic scene between Sissy and James Harthouse, Louisa's would-be seducer:

> She was not afraid of him, or in any way disconcerted; she seemed to have her mind entirely preoccupied with the occasion of her visit, and to have substituted that consideration for herself.

Dr. Leavis comments, almost ecstatically: "The quiet victory of disinterested goodness is wholly convincing." Surely this is nonsense. How can these lines inform us whether the "victory" is wholly convincing or not? They are merely expository prose, an assertion by the author; and out of dramatic context they are no more convincing than any other direct assertion the author may make. The fact is that the lines are wholly unconvincing, for they indicate Dickens's own suspicion that the dramatization does not carry its own weight. And Dickens is right, too. It does not.

At the crux of this scene, Sissy pleads with and then commands Harthouse:

> "Mr. Harthouse," returned Sissy, with a blending of gentleness and steadiness that quite defeated him, and with a simple confidence in his being bound to do what she required, that held him at a singular disadvantage, "the only reparation that remains with you, is to leave here immediately and finally. I am quite sure that you can mitigate in no other way the wrong and harm you have done. I am quite sure that it is the only compensation you have left in your power to make. I do not say that it is much, or that it is enough; but it is something, and it is necessary. Therefore, though without any other authority than I have given you, and even without the knowledge of any other person than yourself and myself, I ask you to depart from this place to-night, under an obligation never to return to it."

> If she had asserted any influence over him beyond her plain faith in the truth and right of what she said; if she had concealed the least doubt of irresolution, or had harboured for the best purpose any reserve or pretence; if she had shown, or felt, the lightest trace of any sensitiveness to his ridicule or his astonishment, or any remonstrance he might offer; he would have carried it against her at this point. But he could as easily have changed a clear sky by looking at it in surprise, as affect her.

To insist that something is convincing or unconvincing is to become hopelessly involved in solipsistic argument. What convinces one man readily, invariably fails to convince another. And while it is probably true that few men have as much right as Dr. Leavis does to indulge in this kind of personal criticism, nevertheless I must insist that there is much in the scene cited to arouse the reader's skepticism and to justify his questioning its "convincingness." To begin with, Sissy's speech is entirely out of character for her. She is conceived initially as a "natural" character. Her naturalness is closely associated with her vitality and is one of the characteristics that identifies her. Her first speech in the book comes in answer to Mr. Gradgrind, who has just insisted that she call herself Cecilia, not Sissy: "'It's father as calls me Sissy, sir,' returned the young girl. . . .'" Subsequently we learn that she cannot define a horse, that she confuses "natural prosperity" and "National Prosperity," that she can never distinguish between "statistics" and "stutterings," and so on.

To all this, one need not particularly object. Dickens wants to use Sissy's inherent natural goodness and simplicity as a foil against fact-filled and heartless Gradgrindism. Her inability, in all her "vitality," to learn dry facts stands against and emphasizes the sterility of Gradgrind's factual system. The device is somewhat clumsy and oversimplified, but legitimate nonetheless.

However, no sooner does Dickens need Sissy for a different purpose—to cow the degenerate Harthouse with her unsullied (and untried) virtue—than he changes her character without the least justification. Now the simple girl who previously was unable to string three syllables together, and who has shown herself completely incapable of being schooled, now this same simple girl speaks fluently in the flowery rhetoric of a cultured and refined eighteenth-century heroine. The words "reparation" and "mitigate," "compensation" and "obligation" flow from her lips with a readiness that Clarissa herself would have envied. And now the girl who once said "It's father as calls . . ." has, in spite of her copiously demonstrated inability for learning, achieved perfect control of vocabulary, syntax, and grammar. She is no longer the sentimentalized waif so dear to the nineteenth century, but the sentimentalized heroine so familiar to the eighteenth. Sissy now speaks the language of the sentimental romance of seduction, and her diction is complemented by all the clichés of that genre. Purity and virtue indignantly confront shamed depravity; the former triumph magnificently, the issue never having been in doubt. Innocence expands in the glow of its own resplendence; villainy gloomily retreats to its murky, miasmatic lair. Incorruptible maid subdues vile seducer.

Dickens's inability to break out of these trite sentimental formulae must be a key to the artistic failure of the book. And it is not merely a failure of diction or of characterization that we are dealing with, it is a failure of imagination. Everywhere we look we see patches of threadbare melodrama. Whenever we stop to listen we hear the sickly glissandos of a street fiddler. Another climactic scene (good melodrama always has a few) will demonstrate my point. Louisa, torn between a purely mechanical loyalty to the husband she detests and the desire to be seduced by the unctuous and persistent Harthouse, suffers a nervous breakdown which comes in good soap-opera fashion: Gradgrind "tightened his hold in time to prevent her sinking on the floor, but she cried out in a terrible voice, 'I shall die if you hold me. Let me fall upon the ground.' And he laid her down there, and saw the pride of his heart and the triumph of his system, lying, an insensible heap, at his feet."

On awaking, the next morning, Louisa learns from her sister that Sissy has brought her into her old room. Another short exchange with her father reveals that Mr. Gradgrind no longer believes in his system. He has finally learned that "heart" can be as important as facts. He states the discovery in his own pompous way:

> "Some persons hold," he pursued, still hesitating, "that there is a wisdom of the Head, and that there is a wisdom of the Heart. I have not supposed so; but, as I have said, I mistrust myself now. I have supposed the head to be all-sufficient. It may not be all-sufficient. . . ."

Finally, the scene reaches its climax with the entrance of Sissy. At first, Louisa, still ashamed of her weakness, and her heart still hardened by the Gradgrindian ordeal, repels Sissy. But Sissy humbly persists in tolerating abuse and radiating disinterested love until Louisa, utterly overcome, is moved to confess:

> "I am so unhappy, and all that should have made me otherwise is so laid waste, that if I had been bereft of sense to this hour, and instead of being as learned as you think me, had to begin to acquire the simplest truths, I could not want a guide to peace, contentment, honour, all the good of which I am quite devoid, more abjectly than I do. Does not that repel you?"
>
> "No!"
>
> In the innocence of her brave affection, and the brimming up of her old devoted spirit, the once deserted girl shone like a beautiful light upon the darkness of the other.
>
> Louisa raised the hand that it might clasp her neck and join its fellow there. She fell upon her knees, and clinging to this stroller's child looked up at her almost with veneration.
>
> "Forgive me, pity me, help me! Have compassion on my great need, and let me lay this head of mine upon a loving heart!"
>
> "O lay it here!" cried Sissy. "Lay it here, my dear."

This should be a moving scene, for it suggests the power of Christian self-sacrifice, humility, and love to overcome the ruin wrought by a sterile materialism. As the scene materializes, however, it is actually ludicrous. The language is excessive, trite, and empty. The same is true of the gestures. No doubt Dickens intends the laying of Louisa's "head" on Sissy's "loving heart" to bristle with symbolic significance. But any significance is lost in the tiredness of the sentimental rhetoric. Christian and human love is triumphant, all right. But over what? Louisa has yet to do any evil. Worse, she has yet to suffer. Certainly, her rapid recovery is remarkable. And as for Sissy, she has yet to make any real sacrifice. What we get, then, in place of potently moving Christian passion and the cataclysmic struggle between the forces of good and evil is twitches of sentiment: no power, no mystery, no engagement of the moral imagination; only wallowing in the aqueous effusions of a pair of frustrated females.

The scene is a failure because the suffering is hollow. And the suffering is hollow because the characters are. At one point, Louisa and her brother, both in their adolescence, sit before the fire and converse. Louisa says,

. . . As I get older, and nearer growing up, I often sit wondering here, and think how unfortunate it is for me that I can't reconcile you to home better than I am able to do. I don't know what other girls know. I can't play to you, or sing to you. I can't talk to you so as to lighten your mind, for I never see any amusing sights or read any amusing books that it would be a pleasure or a relief to you to talk about, when you are tired.

Ostensibly, Louisa is stating the case for the arts against the mechanical monotony of stern Gradgrindian facts. But it is soon clear that for her the arts are a genteel pastime, something with which to while away the wearisome hours, something to titillate a tired mind. She is not so much concerned with the beauty or passion or power, or even the heuristic possibilities of art. Rather, she laments only the fact that the two secular opiates of the middle class—light literature and pop music—have been denied her and her brother. It is not a question of enlightening the mind, but of "lightening" it. In short, she sounds like a forerunner of the modern apologists for commercial television Westerns. Her Art-to-mesmerize-the-bourgeois position is, in fact, something of an ironic comment on Dr. Leavis's insistence that art must have a serious moral purpose, and on his commendation of *Hard Times* for supposedly having one.

What is so utterly appalling about Louisa's speech is its brainlessness. Dickens intends this, of course. And yet, so feeble-minded do the "good" characters become at times that it is ultimately impossible to take them at all seriously. Eventually everything is enveloped in the general inanity. Sissy, for example, describes the one instance in which she has seen her father angry:

> Father, soon after they came home from performing, told Merrylegs to jump up on the backs of the two chairs and stand across them—which is one of his tricks. He looked at father and didn't do it at once. Everything of father's had gone wrong that night, and he hadn't pleased the public at all. He cried out that the very dog knew he was failing, and had no compassion on him. Then he beat the dog, and I was frightened, and said, "Father, father! Pray don't hurt the creature who is so fond of you! O Heaven forgive you, father, stop!" And he stopped, and the dog was bloody, and father lay down crying on the floor with the dog in his arms, and the dog licked his face.

The problem here is not only sentimentalism, but bad writing and bad taste. If there is any ingenuity or inventiveness it is in Dickens's managing to cram so many clichés into one paragraph: the failing performer (Let's have a benefit for Judy Garland), the abused pet, the cruel-then-repentant master, the kindly long-suffering daughter, the invocation to Heaven, the cruel-kind master-father grovelling wetly in his own tears being licked by his bleeding dog!

Tears, idle tears. And yet, these bitter orgies of tears are the only alternative that Dickens seems to have to offer to fact-grubbing Gradgrindism. That is why it is so difficult to agree with the overly-enthusiastic critics who claim that the book is a highly effective attack on the evils of industrialism and Utilitarianism. Edgar Johnson asks, "Against the monstrous cruelty of mine and mill and pit and factory and countinghouse, against the bleak utilitarian philosophy with which they were allied, what power could there be except the flowering of the humane imagination and the ennoblement of the heart?" The answer may be the power of *true* mind *and* heart, for in attempting to ennoble one at the expense of the other, what Dickens accomplishes is to debase both.

I have no doubt that Dickens's purpose was most commendable. But it seems quite clear that his achievement, unfortunately, did not match it. And my quarrel, let me make clear, is not with Dickens or even with Dickensian "sentimentalism," but with unkind criticism that gives this particular book so eminent a position in the Dickens canon. For what, after all, can be more harmful to a genuinely great author's reputation than to insist that one of his dullest and least successful works is one of his greatest?

Daniel P. Deneau (essay date 1964)

SOURCE: "The Brother-Sister Relationship in *Hard Times*," in *The Dickensian*, Vol. LX, No. 342, January, 1964, pp. 173-77.

[*In the essay below, Deneau details incestuous overtones in relations between Tom and Louisa Gradgrind in* Hard Times.]

One of Dickens's major concerns in *Hard Times* is to display the disastrous results of an educational system which is exclusively factual, rational, utilitarian. As all readers of the novel immediately recall, Bitzer, a product of Mr. Gradgrind's school, dramatically reveals how well he has learned the utilitarian principle of self-interest and how little he knows of gratitude and human sympathy. More to the point, Tom Gradgrind, after being carefully educated according to his father's system, becomes a thief and attempts to escape the consequences of his crime by casting suspicion on an innocent man; and Louisa, his sister, painfully discovers that her education has ill-equipped her to cope with a loveless marriage and a beckoning lover. But this is not all. Isolated and schooled as they are, Tom and Louisa experience an abnormal brother-sister relationship. To my knowledge, F. R. Leavis has come the closest to identifying the nature of this relationship; in his well-known "Analytic Note" in *The Great Tradition,* he explains: "The psychology of Louisa's development and of her brother Tom's is sound. Having no outlet for her emotional life except in her love for her brother, she lives for him, and marries Bounderby—under pressure from Tom—for Tom's sake . . . Thus, by the constrictions and starvations of the Gradgrind *régime,* are natural affection and capacity for disinterested devotion turned to ill." Although Dr. Leavis puts the case well, he stops short and fails to examine the matter as fully as it deserves.

Moulded in the school of self-interest, young Tom Gradgrind develops into "that not unprecedented triumph of calculation which is usually at work on number one"—that is to say, a self-indulgent, ungrateful egoist, or a "whelp" as Harthouse and Dickens repeatedly label him. Instead of cherishing and responding normally to his sister's love, he actually uses her proffered love for whatever advantages it can bring to him.

A somewhat more detailed charting of his relationship to Louisa is instructive, though I caution that one must return to the text itself to appreciate all the implications. During the first two occasions when brother and sister converse privately, Tom plays the active role, Louisa remaining passive and pensive. The first of these dialogues occurs at an unspecified period, sometime, however, after the appearance of Sissy Jupe and during the adolescence of Tom and Louisa. On this occasion Tom repeatedly singles out Louisa for his special regard; for instance, as the conversation opens, "the unnatural young Thomas Gradgrind" declares to Louisa that "'I hate everybody except you.'" But before the conversation concludes, we—and probably Louisa as well—are aware that Tom's affection for his sister is subordinate to his interest in self: he looks forward to the day when Louisa's affection for him can be translated into goodwill and leniency from Mr. Bounderby. The second of these conversations occurs on the evening before Louisa accepts Bounderby's offer of marriage; Tom, now actively at work for "number one," visits Louisa with the intention of insinuating Bounderby's coming proposal and of assuring himself of Louisa's willingness to sacrifice herself (prostitute herself, as Edgar Johnson says). During the scene Tom seems intent on making Louisa aware of his physical presence: " . . . encircling her waist with his arm, [he] drew her coaxingly to him," and shortly later "he pressed her in his arm, and kissed her cheek." More importantly, he elicits from her an avowal of her affection, reminds her of the "'great deal of good'" she is capable of doing him, and, apparently clever enough to put his suit in language most calculated to make an impression on Louisa, says as follows: "'We might be so much oftener together—mightn't we? Always together, almost—mightn't we?'" It is possible to hear the tones of a lover in these words; but the speech, I believe, reflects more clearly the desire of Louisa rather than that of Tom; for during the same scene she twice complains of his failing to visit her frequently enough, and as later events prove, Louisa's proximity is not what Tom desires. Once Tom has accomplished his goal of transforming his sister into Mrs. Bounderby, he takes few pains to offer expressions of his affection. He receives money from Louisa, acts the braggadocio when explaining to Harthouse the cause of Louisa's marriage, and eventually grows cold and sullen to her when he feels that she fails to supply him with adequate funds, and still more distant yet when the revelation of his crime grows closer. In the final big scene at Sleary's circus, Tom completely repulses Louisa, blaming her for his downfall, and crying: "'Pretty love that. You have regularly given me up. You never cared for me.'"

In the last chapter of the novel, a typical Victorian epilogue which supplies glimpses into the future, we read that Tom eventually learns "that all the treasure in the world would be cheaply bartered for a sight of her [Louisa's] dear face," and upon his deathbed his last word is Louisa's name.

Although Tom's robbery and subsequent actions speak emphatically of his character—the robbery is also an important piece of plot mechanism—I believe that his reaction to his sister is an equally persuasive way of revealing the effects of his education and of clarifying his moral status. Certainly when at the end Dickens wishes us to understand that Tom experiences a redemption, that he becomes for the first time something near an emotionally and morally healthy human being, it is not, say, through an act of benevolence that the point is made, but rather through his expression of genuine love for Louisa. In short, through Tom's relationship to Louisa we learn how the Gradgrind educational régime dams up normal channels of affection and produces an abnormal love of self.

The "constrictions and starvations of the Gradgrind régime" do not successfully dry up the emotional and imaginative spring of Louisa's feminine nature; she is conscious that she has been deprived of the poetry of life, and locked within her are confused, half-formed longings. Louisa's education creates in her a dull unhappiness and an indifference towards everyone and everything, except her scapegrace brother, who apparently has been her closest companion in the long, dreary pursuit of "ologies." Abundant evidence of her sisterly affection appears in the novel. At the time of her greatest emotional crisis, she explains to her father that Tom "'had been the subject of all the little tenderness of my life'"; and it is through the "tenderest sentiment" of her heart, her love for Tom, that Harthouse begins to establish his rapport with her. It is, however, after she sacrifices herself in the marriage to Bounderby that her love for Tom seems to become more intense; although Dickens does not comment pointedly on the subject, we may speculate that her marriage is so emotionally and physically unsatisfying that she clings with renewed vigour to her emotional attachment to her brother. When Harthouse first sees Louisa, he wonders if there is anything which will move her face:

> Yes! By Jupiter, there was something, and here it was, in an unexpected shape. Tom appeared. She changed as the door opened, and broke into a beaming smile.

> A beautiful smile. Mr. James Harthouse might not have thought so much of it, but that he had wondered so long at her impassive face. She put out her hand—a pretty little soft hand; and her fingers closed upon her brother's, as if she would have carried them to her lips.

> "Ay, ay?" thought the visitor. "This whelp is the only creature she cares for. So, so!"

Louisa's reaction at this point seems less passive than during the earlier scenes before her marriage.

The third and final private conversation between Tom and Louisa occurs on the night after the disclosure of the bank robbery. Already suspecting Tom's guilt, Louisa proceeds to her brother's bedchamber and unsuccessfully attempts to persuade him to confide in her. The details of the scene are so telling that a long quotation must be supplied; in what follows I omit the brief and unresponsive replies of Tom.

> Then she arose, put on a loose robe, and went out of her room in the dark, and up the staircase to her brother's room. His door being shut, she softly opened it and spoke to him, approaching his bed with a noiseless step.

> She kneeled down beside it, passed her arm over his neck, and drew his face to hers . . .

> "Tom, have you anything to tell me? If ever you loved me in your life, and have anything concealed from every one besides, tell it to me." . . .

> "My dear brother," she laid her head down on his pillow, and her hair flowed over him as if she would hide him from every one but herself, "is there nothing that you have to tell me? . . . You can tell me nothing that will change me. O Tom, tell me the truth!" . . .

> "As you lie here alone, my dear, in the melancholy night so you must lie somewhere one night, when even I, if I am living then, shall have left you. As I am here beside you, barefoot, unclothed, undistinguishable in darkness, so must I lie through all the night of my decay, until I am dust. In the name of that time, Tom, tell me the truth now!" . . .

> "You may be certain," in the energy of her love she took him to her bosom as if he were a child, "that I will not reproach you. You may be certain that I will be compassionate and true to you. You may be certain that I will save you at whatever cost. O Tom, have you nothing to tell me? Whisper very softly. Say only 'yes' and I shall understand you!"

> She turned her ear to his lips, but he remained doggedly silent . . .

> "You are tired," she whispered presently, more in her usual way.

In spite of Tom's insistence that he has nothing to tell Louisa, she presses the matter with a peculiar urgency, even passionately. A "yes," as I read the scene, is really the answer Louisa desires; she seems intent on establishing a type of mental intimacy with her brother—on sharing a secret about a dark matter, a not-to-be-revealed crime. Moreover, Dickens's reference to "a loose robe" and Louisa's more pointed reference to her state of undress—"'barefoot, unclothed'"—are pretty insistent details. I suggest, in fact, that sexual overtones hover over the scene, or, more plainly, that the scene has the atmosphere of a seduction. And still another emotional current is estab-

lished when we are told that Louisa takes Tom "to her bosom as if he were a child." For a moment at least (notice that after a time she returns to speaking "more in her usual way") Tom seems to become for Louisa an object of both sexual and maternal love. Though writing obliquely enough not to offend Victorian propriety, Dickens nonetheless brings his attentive reader to the realisation that, as a result of a lopsided education, Louisa reaches a point where her affection for Tom is not merely superlative sisterly affection. When Bounderby comes to inquire about his missing wife, her father stammers that "'there are qualities in Louisa, which—which have been harshly neglected, and—and a little perverted.'" The words are truer than Mr. Gradgrind suspects.

On the night of her collapse Louisa tells her father that possibly she has loved and still loves Harthouse, but her declaration is not very convincing. Through the symbolic image constructed in Mrs. Sparsit's mind, an image of Louisa racing down a long staircase towards an abyss, Dickens attempts to suggest Louisa's dangerous movement towards adultery; but the image, after all, is Mrs. Sparsit's, and neither Louisa's actions nor thoughts clearly inform us of any lover-like response to Harthouse. No mention is made of Louisa's reaction to his disappearance (she is still declaring her love for Tom at the moment of his flight); apparently when Harthouse vanishes from Coketown he vanishes from Louisa's mind. Louisa's relationship to Tom, then, is much more central in the novel; and it is this relationship, rather than that to Harthouse, which most clearly suggests Louisa's emotional and even moral confusion.

In **Hard Times** Dickens moves with undeviating progress towards his goal: and that, simply stated, is a plea for the poetry rather than the prose of life. As part of his design, he speaks of an educational system which is capable of subverting a normal human relationship. At first glance, Tom's robbery and Louisa's unsuccessful marriage may seem to be Dickens's sole way of depicting their failures, and in turn the failure of the system and philosophy which moulded them; a closer look, however, makes clear that Dickens uses a more subtle, a more psychological means of asserting the moral dangers of Gradgrindism, namely, an abnormal brother-sister relationship.

David Lodge (essay date 1966)

SOURCE: "The Rhetoric of *Hard Times*," in *Language of Fiction: Essays in Criticism and Verbal Analysis of the English Novel,* Routledge and Kegan Paul, 1966, pp. 144-63.

[*Lodge is an English novelist and dramatist who is also highly regarded for his work as a literary critic and as the editor of several works on nineteenth- and twentieth-century British authors. In the following essay, he evaluates Dickens's rhetorical strategies, which he believes form the polemical basis of* Hard Times.]

'It is the least read of all the novels and probably also the least enjoyed by those who read it,' said Humphrey House of *Hard Times* in *The Dickens World* (1941). The first part of this statement, at least, has probably not been true since *The Great Tradition* was published (1948). Of *Hard Times,* it will be remembered, Dr Leavis said, ' . . . of all Dickens's works, it is the one that has all the strength of his genius, together with a strength no other of them can show—that of a completely serious work of art'.

There are of course two propositions here: one, that *Hard Times* is a complete and satisfactory work of art; and two, that this novel is the crown of Dickens's achievement. The latter proposition has had the greater notoriety, yet it is essentially an aside which Leavis does not attempt to argue through. The first proposition is far more susceptible of fruitful critical discussion, and as John Holloway's recent article, *'Hard Times,* a History and a Criticism' [*Dickens and the Twentieth Century,* 1962], is the most interesting expression of dissent it has provoked, I shall take the article as a starting point.

Holloway's case can be summarized as follows: that the Utilitarian philosophy Dickens claims to be representing in the novel is a crude travesty of the reality, shallowly conceived as a mere blind faith in statistics; that it is opposed by an equally shallow plea for 'play' and 'fancy', represented by the Slearies 'not as vital horsemen but as plain entertainers'; that Dickens's attitude to Trade Unions and labour problems is unenlightened; that, in short, the novel as a whole is the product of a mind not prophetic and profound, but bourgeois and philistine. There is considerable force in all these arguments, and in some respects they merely consolidate points previously made by Humphrey House [in *The Dickens World*] and Raymond Williams [in *Culture and Society 1780-1950,* 1961]. There are two interconnected grounds for caution in accepting Holloway's arguments, however: they are extensively documented with external evidence—such as contemporary Utilitarian works and Dickens's journalism; and they tend towards an assessment of the novel itself even lower than Holloway wishes to reach. Thus he is compelled to make a divorce between the achievements of the novel and Dickens's manifest intentions:

> The passages in *Hard Times* where Dickens is most freely himself, are not those where he is most engaged with his moral fable or intent (if we think, mistakenly that he is at all) on what Dr. Leavis has called 'the confrontation of Utilitarianism by life'.

While agreeing that 'life' (with the special resonances Dr Leavis gives to that word) is far too grand a term for the values which Dickens opposes to the world of Gradgrind and Bounderby, I suggest that Dickens's achievements in the novel can no more be separated from his polemical intention than can his failures.

On every page *Hard Times* manifests its identity as a polemical work, a critique of mid-Victorian industrial society dominated by materialism, acquisitiveness, and ruthlessly competitive capitalist economics. To Dickens, at the time of writing *Hard Times,* these things were represented most articulately, persuasively, (and therefore dangerously) by the Utilitarians. It is easy to abstract the argument behind the novel, and to demonstrate its logical and practical weaknesses. The argument has two stages: (1) that the dominant philosophy of Utilitarianism, particularly as it expresses itself in education, results in a damaging impoverishment of the moral and emotional life of the individual; and (2) that this leads in turn to social and economic injustice, since individuals thus conditioned are incapable of dealing with the human problems created by industrialism. On the level of plot (1) is expounded in terms of the Nemesis which punishes Gradgrind through his children and (2) is expounded in terms of Stephen Blackpool's sufferings. That Dickens makes a connection between the two propositions and the two areas of the plot is made clear in the scene where Blackpool confronts Bounderby and Harthouse, and is challenged to offer a solution for the 'muddle' he is always complaining about. Stephen expresses himself negatively. He repudiates the employers' exploitation of their power (' the strong hand will never do't'); their reliance on *laissez faire* ('lettin alone will never do't'); their withdrawal from social contact with the working classes ('not drawin nigh to fok, wi' kindness and patience an' cheery ways . . . will never do't'); and, 'most of aw', their mental habit of regarding the workers as soulless units in the economic machine while inconsistently accusing them of ingratitude if they protest:

> 'Most o'aw, rating 'em as so much Power, and reg'lating 'em as if they was figures in a soom, or machines; wi'out loves and likens, wi'out memories and inclinations, wi'out souls to weary and souls to hope—when aw goes quiet draggin' on wi' 'em as if they'd nowt o' th'kind, and when aw goes onquiet, reproachin' 'em for their want o' sitch humanly feelins in their dealins wi' yo—this will never do't, Sir, till God's work is onmade.' (II, v)

It is clear that Dickens is speaking through Stephen here, and what the speech amounts to in positive terms is a plea for generosity, charity, imaginative understanding of the spiritual and emotional needs of humanity.

While these values have an obvious relevance to the field of personal relations (the Gradgrind-Bounderby circle) they are less viable as a basis for reform of the body politic, because there are no sanctions to ensure their application. They are not—apart from Louisa's abortive attempt to help Stephen—shown in action in the novel vertically through the class structure: Stephen's martyr-like death bears witness to this. Yet Dickens could only offer a disembodied and vaguely defined benevolence as a cure for the ills of Coketown because he had rejected all the alternatives. In his hostile portrait of Gradgrind, Dickens repudiated not only the narrowest kind of Utilitarian rationalism, but also, as House and others have pointed out, the processes by which most of the great Victorian reforms were carried out—statistical enquiry, commissions, reports, acted on by Parliamentary legislation. In his hostile portrait of Slackbridge, and his account of Stephen's ostracism because of his refusal to join the Trade Union,

Dickens repudiated the workers' claim to secure justice by collective bargaining. Dickens is, then, opposed to any change in the political and economic structure of society, and places his hopes for amelioration in a change of heart, mind, and soul in those who possess power, who will then disseminate the fruits of this change over the lower echelons of society. Dickens's ideal State would be one of 'benevolent and genial anarchy' [House].

This is an insecure basis from which to launch a critique of society, and its insecurity becomes all the more obvious when we look outside *Hard Times* to Dickens's journalism of the same period, and find him enthusing over the wonders of Victorian manufacture and expressing surprised admiration for the Preston cotton-workers' conduct of their strike in 1854.

And yet, when all this has been said, and the contradictions, limitations, and flaws in Dickens's argument extrapolated, *Hard Times* remains a novel of considerable polemical effectiveness. The measure of this effectiveness, it seems to me, can only be accounted for in terms of Dickens's rhetoric. This approach should recommend itself to the author of *The Victorian Sage,* a study which shows how many key Victorian writers, disarmed of logic by their opponents, resorted to non-logical methods of persuasion in order to communicate their ideas. In the criticism of fiction we have learned, . . . to use 'rhetoric' as a term for all the techniques by which a novelist seeks to persuade us of the validity of his vision of experience, a vision which cannot usually be formulated in abstract terms. But in a novel like *Hard Times,* which can be called a *roman à thèse,* rhetoric functions very nearly in its traditional rôle as the vehicle of an argument.

There is another reason why rhetoric seems a particularly useful term in discussing Dickens's work. Not only is the 'author's voice' always insistent in his novels, but it is characteristically a public-speaking voice, an oratorical or histrionic voice; and it is not difficult to see a connection between this feature of his prose and his fondness for speech-making and public reading of his works.

I shall try to show that *Hard Times* succeeds where its rhetoric succeeds and fails where its rhetoric fails; and that success and failure correspond fairly closely to the negative and positive aspects, respectively, of the argument inherent in the novel.

The very first chapter of *Hard Times* affords an excellent illustration of Dickens's rhetoric, and it is short enough to be quoted and analysed in its entirety.

HARD TIMES

BOOK THE FIRST. SOWING

CHAPTER I

THE ONE THING NEEDFUL

'Now, what I want is, Facts. Teach these boys and girls nothing but Facts. Facts alone are wanted in life. Plant nothing else, and root out everything else. You can only form the minds of reasoning animals upon Facts: nothing else will ever be of any service to them. This is the principle on which I bring up my own children, and this is the principle on which I bring up these children. Stick to Facts, Sir!'

The scene was a plain, bare, monotonous vault of a schoolroom, and the speaker's square forefinger emphasised his observations by underscoring every sentence with a line of the schoolmaster's sleeve. The emphasis was helped by the speaker's square wall of a forehead, which had his eyebrows for its base, while his eyes found commodious cellarage in two dark caves, overshadowed by the wall. The emphasis was helped by the speaker's mouth, which was wide, thin, and hard set. The emphasis was helped by the speaker's voice, which was inflexible, dry, and dictatorial. The emphasis was helped by the speaker's hair, which bristled on the skirts of his bald head, a plantation of firs to keep the wind from its shining surface, all covered with knobs, like the crust of a plum pie, as if the head had scarcely warehouse-room for the hard facts stored inside. The speaker's obstinate carriage, square coat, square legs, square shoulders—nay, his very neckcloth, trained to take him by the throat with an unaccommodating grasp, like a stubborn fact, as it was—all helped the emphasis.

'In this life, we want nothing but Facts, Sir; nothing but Facts!'

The speaker, and the schoolmaster, and the third grown person present, all backed a little, and swept with their eyes the inclined plane of little vessels then and there arranged in order, ready to have imperial gallons of facts poured into them until they were full to the brim.

This chapter communicates, in a remarkably compact way, both a description and a judgment of a concept of education. This concept is defined in a speech, and then evaluated—not in its own terms, but in terms of the speaker's appearance and the setting. Dickens, of course, always relies heavily on the popular, perhaps primitive, assumption that there is a correspondence between a person's appearance and his character; and as Gradgrind is a governor of the school, its design may legitimately function as a metaphor for his character. Dickens also had a fondness for fancifully appropriate names, but—perhaps in order to stress the representativeness of Gradgrind's views—he does not reveal the name in this first chapter.

Because of the brevity of the chapter, we are all the more susceptible to the effect of its highly rhetorical patterning, particularly the manipulation of certain repeated words, notably *fact, square,* and *emphasis.* The kind of education depicted here is chiefly characterized by an obsession with facts. The word occurs five times in the opening speech of the first paragraph, and it is twice repeated towards the end of the second, descriptive paragraph to prepare for the reintroduction of Gradgrind speaking—'"we want nothing but Facts, sir—nothing but Facts"'; and it occurs for the tenth and last time towards the end of the last paragraph. In Gradgrind's speeches the word is capital-ized, to signify his almost religious devotion to Facts.

> **Whether [the first chapter of *Hard Times*] represents fairly any actual educational theory or practice in mid-nineteenth-century England is really beside the point. It aims to convince us of the *possibility* of children being taught in such a way, and to make us recoil from the imagined possibility.**
>
> *— David Lodge*

Gradgrind's concept of education is further characterized in ways we can group into three categories, though of course they are closely connected:

(1) It is authoritarian, fanatical and bullying in its application.

(2) It is rigid, abstract and barren in quality.

(3) It is materialistic and commercial in its orientation.

The first category is conveyed by the structure of the second paragraph, which is dominated by 'emphasis'. This paragraph comprises six sentences. In the first sentence we are told how the 'speaker's square forefinger empha-sised his observations'. The next four, central sentences are each introduced, with cumulative force, by the clause 'The emphasis was helped', and this formula, translated from the passive to the active voice, makes a fittingly 'emphatic' conclusion to the paragraph in the sixth sen-tence: 'all helped the emphasis'. This rhetorical pattern has a dual function. In one way it reflects or imitates Gradgrind's own bullying, over-emphatic rhetoric, of which we have an example in the first paragraph; but in another way it helps to *condemn* Gradgrind, since it 'em-phasises' the narrator's own pejorative catalogue of de-tails of the speaker's person and immediate environment. The narrator's rhetoric is, as it must be, far more skilful and persuasive than Gradgrind's.

The qualities in category (2) are conveyed in a number of geometrical or quasi-geometrical terms, *wide, line, thin, base, surface, inclined plane* and, particularly, *square* which recurs five times; and in words suggestive of bar-ren regularity, *plain, bare, monotonous, arranged in or-der, inflexible*. Such words are particularly forceful when applied to human beings—whether Gradgrind or the chil-dren. The metamorphosis of the human into the non-hu-man is, as we shall find confirmed later, one of Dickens's main devices for conveying his alarm at the way Victo-rian society was moving.

Category (3), the orientation towards the world of com-merce, is perhaps less obvious than the other categories, but it is unmistakably present in some of the boldest tropes of the chapter: *commodious cellarage, warehouse room,*

plantation, vessels, imperial gallons.

The authoritarian ring of *'imperial'* leads us back from category (3) to category (1), just as *'under-scoring* every sentence with a *line'* leads us from (1) to (2). There is a web of connecting strands between the qualities I have tried to categorize: it is part of the rhetorical strategy of the chapter that all the qualities it evokes are equally applicable to Gradgrind's character, person, ideas, his school and the children (in so far as he has shaped them in his own image).

Metaphors of growth and cultivation are of course com-monplace in discussion of education, and we should not overlook the ironic invocation of such metaphors, with a deliberately religious, prophetic implication (reinforced by the Biblical echo of the chapter heading, 'The One Thing Needful') in the title of the Book, 'SOWING', later to be followed by Book the Second, 'REAPING', and Book the Third, 'GARNERING'. These metaphors are given a further twist in Gradgrind's recommendation to 'Plant nothing else and root out everything else' (except facts).

If there is a flaw in this chapter it is the simile of the plum pie, which has pleasant, genial associations alien to the character of Gradgrind, to whose head it is, quite superfluously, applied. Taken as a whole, however, this is a remarkably effective and densely woven beginning of the novel.

The technique of the first chapter of **Hard Times** could not be described as 'subtle'. But subtle effects are often lost in a first chapter, where the reader is coping with the problem of 'learning the author's language'. Perhaps with some awareness of this fact, sharpened by his sense of addressing a vast, popular audience, Dickens begins many of his novels by nailing the reader's attention with a display of sheer rhetorical power, relying particularly on elaborate repetition. One thinks, for instance, of the fog at the beginning of *Bleak House* or the sun and shadow in the first chapter of *Little Dorrit.* In these novels the rhetoric works to establish a symbolic atmosphere; in **Hard Times,** to establish a thematic Idea—the despo-tism of Fact. But this abstraction—Fact—is invested with a remarkable solidity through the figurative dimension of the language.

The gross effect of the chapter is simply stated, but anal-ysis reveals that it is achieved by means of a complex verbal activity that is far from simple. Whether it repre-sents fairly any actual educational theory or practice in mid-nineteenth-century England is really beside the point. It aims to convince us of the *possibility* of children being taught in such a way, and to make us recoil from the imagined possibility. The chapter succeeds or fails as rhetoric; and I think it succeeds.

Dickens begins as he means to continue. Later in the novel we find Gradgrind's house, which, like the school-room, is a function of himself, described in precisely the same terms of fact and rigid measurement, partly geometrical and partly commercial.

A very regular feature on the face of the country, Stone Lodge was. Not the least disguise toned down or shaded off that uncompromising fact in the landscape. A great square house, with a heavy portico darkening the principal windows, as its master's heavy brows overshadowed his eyes. A calculated, cast up, balanced and proved house. Six windows on this side of the door, six on that side; a total of twelve in this wing, a total of twelve in the other wing; four and twenty carried over to the back wings. A lawn and garden and an infant avenue, all ruled straight like a botanical account-book. (I, iii)

It has been observed [by Randolph Quirk in "Some Observations on the Language of Dickens," *Review of English Literature,* II (1961)] that Dickens individualizes his characters by making them use peculiar locutions and constructions in their speech, a technique which was particularly appropriate to serial publication in which the reader's memory required to be frequently jogged. This technique extends beyond the idiosyncratic speech of characters, to the language in which they are described. A key-word, or group of key-words, is insistently used when the character is first introduced, not only to identify him but also to evaluate him, and is invoked at various strategic points in the subsequent action. Dickens's remarkable metaphorical inventiveness ensures that continuity and rhetorical emphasis are not obtained at the expense of monotony. The application of the key-words of the first chapter to Mr Gradgrind's house gives the same delight as the development of a metaphysical conceit. The observation that Mrs Gradgrind, 'whenever she showed a symptom of coming to life, was invariably stunned by some weighty piece of fact tumbling on her' (I, iv), affords a kind of verbal equivalent of knock-about comedy, based on a combination of expectancy (we know the word will recur) and surprise (we are not prepared for the particular formulation).

Bounderby offers another illustration of Dickens's use of key-words in characterization. He is first introduced as 'a big, loud man, with a stare, and a metallic laugh' (I, iv). The metallic quality is shortly afterwards defined as 'that brassy speaking-trumpet of a voice of his' (*ibid.*). His house has a front door with 'BOUNDERBY in letters very like himself) upon a brazen plate, and a round brazen door-handle underneath it, like a brazen full stop' (I, xi). Bounderby's bank 'was another red brick house, with black outside shutters, green inside blinds, a black street door up two white steps, a brazen door-plate, and a brazen door-handle full-stop' (II, i). The buildings Bounderby inhabits take their character from him, as Gradgrind's do from him. But here the emphasis is on the brass embellishments which, by the use of the word *brazen* (rather than *brass* used adjectivally) epitomize several facets of his character: his hardness, vanity, crude enjoyment of wealth, and, most important of all, the fact that he is a brazen liar. (We do not know for certain that he is a liar until the end of the novel; the 'brazen' fittings reinforce other hints which prepare us for the revelation.)

The failures of characterization in *Hard Times* are generally failures in using rhetorical strategies which Dickens

elsewhere employs very successfully. The portrait of Slackbridge, the trade union demagogue, for instance, seeks to exploit a relationship between character and appearance in a way which is familiar in Dickens and well exemplified in the first chapter; but it does so crudely and clumsily:

Judging him by Nature's evidence, he was above the mass in very little but the stage on which he stood. In many respects he was essentially below them. He was not so honest, he was not so manly, he was not so good-humoured; he substituted cunning for their simplicity, and passion for their safe solid sense. An ill-made, high shouldered man, with lowering brows, and his features crushed into an habitually sour expression, he contrasted most unfavourably, even in his mongrel dress, with the great body of his hearers in their plain working clothes. (II, iv)

Apart from the vividness of 'crushed', the description of Slackbridge is carelessly vague, and we miss the metaphorical inventiveness that characterizes Dickens's best descriptions of people. But the main error of the passage is the ordering of its material. The rhetorical strategy announced by the opening sentence is that Slackbridge's character is to be read in his appearance. But in fact the character is read *before* we are given the appearance. It is as if Dickens has so little confidence in his own imaginative evidence that he must inform us, over-explicitly, what conclusions we are to draw, before we come to the evidence. We know from external sources that Dickens was in a confused state of mind about the trade union movement at the time of writing *Hard Times,* and we can rarely expect to receive a balanced account of organized labour from any middle-class Victorian novelist. However, the failure of understanding here reveals itself in the first place as a failure of expression; the portrait of Gradgrind, on the other hand, though it probably derives from an equivalent misunderstanding of Utilitarianism, succeeds.

Another, more significant failure of Dickens's rhetoric is to be observed in the treatment of Tom Gradgrind. In this connection, I must register my disagreement with John Holloway's opinion that 'the gradual degeneration of Tom . . . is barely (as in fact it is treated) related to Dickens's major problems in the book, though it is one of its best things'. It is gradual (though not very extensively treated) up to the beginning of Book II, by which point we have gathered that Tom, so far from drawing strength of character from his repressive and rationalist upbringing, is turning into a selfish young man prepared to exploit others for his own advantage. He is still a long way, however, from the depravity that allows him to connive at the seduction of his own sister and to implicate an innocent man (Stephen Blackpool) in his own crime. This moral gap is rather clumsily bridged by Dickens in the second chapter of Book II, where he suddenly introduces a key-word for Tom: 'whelp'.

The Bounderbys are entertaining James Harthouse to dinner. Louisa does not respond to Harthouse's attempts to flirt, but when Tom comes in, late, 'She changed . . . and broke into a beaming smile. . . .'

'Ay, ay?' thought the visitor. 'This whelp is the only creature she cares for. So, so!'

The whelp was presented, and took his chair. The appellation was not flattering, but not unmerited. (II, ii)

The chapter ends very shortly afterwards, but Dickens contrives to use the word 'whelp' three more times, and the title of the following chapter (II, iii), in which Tom betrays Louisa's situation to Harthouse, is entitled 'The Whelp'.

'Whelp' is a cliché, and it will be noticed that the word is first used by Harthouse, and then adopted by the novelist in his authorial capacity. When a novelist does this, it is usually with ironical intent, suggesting some inadequacy in the speaker's habits of thought. Dickens plays on Gradgrind's 'facts' to this effect. But in the case of Harthouse's 'whelp' he has taken a moral cliché from a character who is morally unreliable, and invested it with his own authority as narrator. This gives away the fact that Tom is being forced into a new rôle halfway through the book. For Tom's degeneration *should* be related to the major problems with which Dickens is concerned in **Hard Times**. According to the overall pattern of the novel, Tom and Louisa are to act as indices of the failure of Mr Gradgrind's philosophy of education, and should thus never be allowed to stray outside the area of our pity, since they are both victims rather than free agents. But Tom's actions do take him beyond our pity, and diminish the interest of his character.

Perhaps Dickens was misled by feeling the need to inject a strong crime-interest into his story, of which Tom was a handy vehicle; or perhaps he lost his head over the preservation of Louisa's purity (the somewhat hysterical conclusion to Chapter iii, Book II, 'The Whelp', seems to suggest this). Whatever the explanation, 'the whelp', unlike those key-words which organize and concentrate the represented character of individuals and places, acts merely as a slogan designed to generate in the reader such a contempt for Tom that he will not enquire too closely into the pattern of his moral development—a pattern that will not, in fact, bear very close scrutiny.

In the conduct of his central argument, Dickens explicitly calls our attention to a 'key-note'. The first occasion on which he does so is when introducing the description of Coketown, in Chapter v of Book I, entitled 'The Keynote':

COKETOWN, to which Messrs. Bounderby and Gradgrind now walked, was a triumph of fact; it had no greater taint of fancy in it than Mrs Gradgrind herself. Let us strike the key-note, Coketown, before pursuing our tune.

It was a town of red brick, or of brick that would have been red if the smoke and ashes had allowed it; but as matters stood it was a town of unnatural red and black like the painted face of a savage. It was a town of machinery and tall chimneys, out of which interminable serpents of smoke trailed themselves for ever and ever, and never got uncoiled. It had a black canal in it, and a river that ran purple with ill-smelling dye, and vast piles of building full of windows where there was a rattling and a trembling all day long, and where the piston of the steam engine worked monotonously up and down like the head of an elephant in a state of melancholy madness. It contained several large streets all very like one another, and many more small streets still more like one another, inhabited by people equally like one another, who all went in and out at the same hours, with the same sound upon the same pavements, to do the same work, and to whom every day was the same as yesterday and tomorrow, and every year the counterpart of the last and the next.

[In "The Dickens World: a View from Todgers's," *The Dickens Critics,* 1961] Dorothy Van Ghent has commented on the effects Dickens gains by investing the inanimate with animation and vice versa. 'The animation of inanimate objects suggests both the quaint gaiety of a forbidden life, and an aggressiveness that has got out of control. . . . The animate is treated as if it is a thing. It is as if the life absorbed by things had been drained out of people who have become incapable of their humanity.' The description of Coketown illustrates this process. The buildings and machinery of Coketown are invested with a sinister life of their own, the life of savages, serpents, and elephants (the serpent and elephant images are reiterated at least five times in the novel). The people of Coketown, on the other hand, take their character from the architecture of the town non-metaphorically conceived— 'large streets all very like one another, and many small streets still more like one another'. They are reduced to indistinguishable units caught up in a mindless, monotonous, mechanical process, superbly represented in the droning repetition of sound and syntax in the last sentence of the passage quoted.

In the rest of this chapter Dickens goes on to say that, despite the efficiency of the town, it was afflicted by *malaise,* social and moral: drunkenness, idleness, irreligion. 'Is it possible,' he asks, 'that there was any analogy between the case of the Coketown populace and the little Gradgrinds?' He goes on to suggest that in both 'there was fancy in them demanding to be brought into healthy existence instead of struggling on in convulsions'.

The antithesis of 'fact and fancy' introduces the chapter (see the quotation above). It has been previously introduced in the schoolroom chapters, where Cissy Jupe's words, 'I would fancy————', are rudely interrupted by the government official:

'Ay, ay, ay! But you mustn't fancy,' cried the gentleman, quite elated by coming so happily to his point. 'That's it! You are never to fancy. . . . You are to be in all things regulated and governed . . . by fact. . . . You must discard the word Fancy altogether.' (I. ii)

A very similar interruption establishes the same antithesis in slightly different terms in Chapter viii, Book I, 'Never

Wonder', where Dickens again proposes to strike the key-note:

> LET us strike the key-note again, before pursuing the tune.

> When she was half a dozen years younger, Louisa had been overheard to begin a conversation with her brother one day, by saying 'Tom, I wonder'—upon which Mr. Gradgrind, who was the person overhearing, stepped forth into the light, and said, 'Louisa, never wonder!'

> Herein lay the spring of the mechanical art and mystery of educating the reason without stooping to the cultivation of the sentiments and affections. Never wonder. By means of addition, subtraction, multiplication and division, settle everything somehow, and never wonder. Bring to me, says M'Choakumchild, yonder baby just able to walk, and I will engage that it shall never wonder.

The antithesis between fact and fancy (or wonder), is, then, the dominant key-note of **Hard Times**. It relates the public world of the novel to the private world, the *malaise* of the Gradgrind—Bounderby circle to the *malaise* of Coketown as a social community; and it draws together the two stages of the central argument of the book: the relationship between education in the broad sense and social health. In this respect Dickens is not so very far removed from the position of the Romantic critics of industrialist society. Compare [Shelley's *Defence of Poetry*, 1840]:

> We have more moral, political and historical wisdom than we know how to reduce into practice; we have more scientific and economical knowledge than can be accommodated to the just distribution of the produce which it multiplies. The poetry, in these systems of thought, is concealed by the accumulations of facts and calculating processes. . . . We want the creative faculty to imagine that which we know. . . . To what but a cultivation of the mechanical arts in a degree disproportioned to the presence of the creative faculty, which is the basis of all knowledge, is to be attributed the abuses of all invention for abridging and combining labour, to the exasperation of the inequality of mankind? From what other cause has it arisen that the discoveries which should have lightened, have added a weight to the curse of Adam? Poetry, and the principle of Self, of which money is the visible incarnation, are the God and Mammon of the world.

There is a real community of feeling between Shelley and Dickens here: one might almost think that **Hard Times** takes its cue for the criticism of 'the accumulation of facts', 'calculating processes', and 'the principle of Self' from the *Defence*. But whereas Shelley opposes to these things poetry, imagination, the creative faculty, Dickens can only offer Fancy, wonder, sentiments—though he does so with the same seriousness and the same intentions as Shelley, as a panacea for the ills of modern society. It is tempting to relate the inadequacy of Dickens's concept of Fancy to the discussions familiar in Romantic criticism of

Fancy and Imagination. But it is on the rhetorical level that the inadequacy of Dickens's concept manifests itself. In the first 'key-note' chapter, the authorial voice inquiries, with heavy irony, whether we are to be told 'at this time of day'

> that one of the foremost elements in the existence of the Coketown working-people had been for scores of years deliberately set at nought? That there was any Fancy in them demanding to be brought into healthy existence instead of struggling on in convulsions? That, exactly in the ratio as they worked long and monotonously, the craving grew within them for some physical relief—some relaxation, encouraging good humour and good spirits, and giving them a vent— some recognized holiday, though it were but for an honest dance to a stirring band of music—some occasional light pie in which even M'Choakumchild had no finger—which craving must and would be satisfied aright, or must and would inevitably go wrong, until the laws of the Creation were repealed? (I, v)

The rhetorical questions here impede and confuse the argument. The parallelism of 'which craving must and would be satisfied aright, or must and would inevitably go wrong' is tired and mechanical. A mathematical image is enlisted in arguing *against* the mathematical, calculating faculty: it is precisely Dickens's case in the novel as a whole that the 'laws of Creation' are not accountable in terms of 'ratios'. The vagueness of '*some* relaxation', '*some* recognized holiday' is by no means clarified by the unexciting offer of an 'honest dance' or a 'light pie' as specific palliatives for the people of Coketown.

Dickens is struggling to assert, here, the existence of a universal need in humanity, a need which arises from quite a different side of man's nature from that which is occupied with the mechanical processes of industrialism, a need which must be satisfied, a need distantly related to that need for poetry which Shelley asserts. But whereas Shelley's 'poetry' is a faculty which involves and enhances and transforms the total activity of man—'We must imagine that which we know'—Dickens's Fancy is merely a temporary escape from what is accepted as inevitably unpleasant. It is 'relief', 'a vent', 'a holiday'. To be cruel, one might say that Dickens offers the oppressed workers of Coketown bread and circuses: bread in the metaphorical 'light pie' and circuses in the 'honest dance'—and, of course, in Mr Sleary's circus.

The realm of Fancy is most vividly evoked by the rhetoric of **Hard Times** in what might be called the 'fairy-tale' element of the novel. Many of the characters and events are derived from the staple ingredients of the fairy-tale, and this derivation is clearly revealed in the language.

Louisa and Tom first figure as the brother and sister who often appear in fairy-tales as waifs, exiles, victims of circumstance, hedged about with dangers (the Babes in the Woods, etc.). As they sit by the fire of their room, 'Their shadows were defined upon the wall, but those of the high presses in the room were all blended together on the wall and on the ceiling, as if the brother and sister were overhung by a dark cavern' (I, viii). In their childhood their father wears the aspect of an 'Ogre':

> Not that they knew, by name or nature, anything about an Ogre. Fact forbid! I only use the word to express a monster in a lecturing castle, with Heaven knows how many heads manipulated into one, taking childhood captive, and dragging it into gloomy statistical dens by the hair. (I, iii)

Later, Louisa becomes the enchanted princess with a heart of ice, while Tom takes on the rôle of the knave. Harthouse is the demon king, popping up suddenly in the action with mischievous intent, in a cloud of (cigar) smoke:

> James Harthouse continued to lounge in the same place and attitude, smoking his cigar in his own easy way, and looking pleasantly at the whelp, as if he knew himself to be a kind of agreeable demon who had only to hover over him, and he must give up his whole soul if required. (II, iii)

Sissy tells Mr Gradgrind that she used to read to her father 'About the fairies, sir, and the dwarf, and the hunchback, and the genies' (I, vii); and the circus folk in *Hard Times* are comparable to the chorus of benevolent, comic, grotesque, half-supernatural creatures who inhabit the world of romance and fairy-tale. They are persistently associated with legend and myth—Pegasus (I, v), Cupid (*ibid.*), Jack the Giant Killer (III, vii), etc. Mr Bounderby's mother, Mrs Pegler, 'the mysterious old woman' (III, v) is the crone who figures in many fairy-tales and who brings about a surprising turn in the action. Mr Bounderby refers to her as 'an old woman who seems to have been flying into the town on a broomstick now and then' (II, viii). But the proper witch of the story, and Dickens's most effective adaptation of a stock-figure from fairy-tale, is Mrs Sparsit. 'Mrs Sparsit considered herself, in some sort, the Bank Fairy', we are told, but the townspeople 'regarded her as the Bank Dragon, keeping watch over the treasures of the mine'. Her heavy eyebrows and hooked nose are exploited for vivid effects of cruelty:

> Mr Bounderby sat looking at her, as, with the points of a stiff, sharp pair of scissors, she picked out holes for some inscrutable purpose, in a piece of cambric. An operation which, taken in connexion with the bushy eyebrows and the Roman nose, suggested with some liveliness the idea of a hawk engaged upon the eyes of a tough little bird. (I, xvi)

She flatters Bounderby to his face, but secretly insults his portrait. She wills Louisa into Harthouse's clutches, figuring Louisa's progress as the descent of a 'Giant's Staircase', on which she keeps anxious watch (II, x). The boldest treatment of Mrs Sparsit as a witch occurs in the scene where she steals through the grounds of Mr Gradgrind's country house, hoping to catch Louisa and Harthouse together.

> She thought of the wood and stole towards it, heedless

of long grass and briers: of worms, snails, and slugs, and all the creeping things that be. With her dark eyes and her hook nose warily in advance of her, Mrs Sparsit softly crushed her way through the thick undergrowth, so intent upon her object that she would probably have done no less, if the wood had been a wood of adders.

Hark!

> The smaller birds might have tumbled out of their nests, fascinated by the glittering of Mrs Sparsit's eyes in the gloom. . . . (II, xi)

When a thunderstorm bursts immediately afterwards, Mrs Sparsit's appearance becomes still more grotesque:

> It rained now, in a sheet of water. Mrs Sparsit's white stockings were of many colours, green predominating; prickly things were in her shoes; caterpillars slung themselves, in hammocks of their own making, from various parts of her dress; rills ran from her bonnet, and her Roman nose. (II, xi)

Traditionally, witches are antipathetic to water. It is appropriate, therefore, that the frustration of Mrs Sparsit's spite, when she loses track of Louisa, is associated with her ludicrous, rain-soaked appearance (see the conclusion to II, xi).

We may add to these examples of the invocation of fairy-tale, the repeated description of the factories illuminated at night as 'fairy palaces' (I, x; I, xi; II, i, *et passim*), and Mr Bounderby's often expressed conviction that his men 'expect to be set up in a coach and six, and to be fed on turtle soup and venison and fed with a gold spoon' (I, xi; I, vi; II, i, *et passim*). These phrases contrast ironically with the actual drab environment and existence of the Coketown people.

It is, indeed, as an *ironic* rhetorical device that the fairy-tale element operates most successfully. On one level it is possible to read the novel as an ironic fairy-tale, in which the enchanted princess is released from her spell but does not find a Prince Charming, in which the honest, persecuted servant (Stephen) is vindicated but not rewarded, and in which the traditional romantic belief in blood and breeding, confirmed by a discovery, is replaced by the exposure of Bounderby's inverted snobbery.

In other respects, however, the fairy-tale element sets up unresolved tensions in the novel. It encourages a morally-simplified, non-social, and non-historical view of human life and conduct, whereas Dickens's undertaking in *Hard Times* makes quite opposite demands. Mr Sleary's ruse for releasing Tom from the custody of Bitzer, for instance (III, viii), is acceptable on the level of fairy-tale motivation: he returns Mr Gradgrind's earlier good deed (the adoption of Sissy) and scores off an unsympathetic character (Bitzer). But the act is essentially lawless, and conflicts with Dickens's appeals elsewhere in the novel for justice and social responsibility. As long as the circus-folk represent a kind of life that is anarchic, seedy, socially disreputable, but cheerful and humane, they are acceptable and enjoyable. But when they are offered as agents or spokesmen of social and moral amelioration, we reject them. The art they practice is Fancy in its tawdriest form, solemnly defended by Mr Sleary in terms we recognize as the justification of today's mass entertainers:

> 'People mutht be amuthed. They can't be alwayth a learning, nor yet they can't be alwayth a working, they an't made for it. You *mutht* have uth, Thquire. (III, viii)

Sissy is meant to represent a channel through which the values of the circus folk are conveyed to the social order. But her one positive act, the dismissal of Harthouse (III, ii), depends for its credibility on a simple faith in the superiority of a good fairy over a demon king.

In other words, where Dickens invokes the world of fairytale ironically, to dramatize the drabness, greed, spite and injustice which characterize a society dominated by materialism, it is a highly effective rhetorical device; but where he relies on the simplifications of the fairy-tale to suggest means of redemption, we remain unconvinced.

If Dickens's notion of Fancy was attached mainly to fairytale and nursery rhyme (cf. the allusions to the cow with the crumpled horn and Peter Piper in I, iii), his own art is very much one of Fancy in the [sense invoked in S. T. Coleridge's *Biographia Literaria,* 1817]: 'Fancy has no other counters to play with, but fixities and definites. The Fancy is indeed no other than a mode of Memory emancipated from the order of time and space. . . .' This seems an appropriate description of Dickens's method in, for instance, the first chapter of *Hard Times,* or in the description of Coketown, or in the treatment of Mrs Sparsit as a witch. To appreciate this, is to feel that Coleridge was wrong to depreciate Fancy as a literary mode; but it is also to understand why Dickens's greatest achievement as a novelist was his depiction of a disordered universe in which the organic and the mechanical have exchanged places, rather than in his attempts to trace moral and emotional processes within the individual psyche.

In *Hard Times,* Dickens expounds a diagnosis of the ills of modern industrial society for which no institutions can supply a cure: society, represented by a group of characters, must therefore change itself, learning from a group outside the social order—the circus. But Dickens's characters are incapable of change: the language in which they are embodied fixes them in their 'given' condition. They can only die (like Stephen Blackpool) or be broken (like Mr Bounderby). Mr Gradgrind may lose his 'squareness', but he is left a shadow: he cannot become a Michelin Man, all circles and spheres. Louisa when her heart has been melted is a far less convincing character than Louisa with a heart of ice. (This can be quickly seen by comparing the scene of her interview with Gradgrind to discuss Bounderby's proposal (I, xv), rightly singled out for praise by Leavis, with the parallel scene at the end of the book where she returns to her father to reproach him for her upbringing, and where she is given the most

embarrassing lines in the novel to speak (II, xii).) Dickens falters in his handling of the character of Tom Gradgrind precisely because he uses a device for fixing character (*whelp*) to express a process of change.

If *Hard Times* is a polemical novel that is only partially persuasive, it is because Dickens's rhetoric is only partially adequate to the tasks he set himself.

Clifton Fadiman on Dickens's anti-politicism:

[There] is something that bids us pause before accepting the easy view of Dickens as the revolutionary whose socio-economic libido was insufficient to make him fall in love with the proletariat. To be even an unconscious revolutionary one's temper must be dominantly political—and the feeling comes over one that Dickens was not only nonpolitical, but anti-political. *Hard Times* is full of sympathy for the oppressed factory-worker, though hardly for the union. Yet its central theme is not political but, in a sense, poetical: at bottom *Hard Times* is a plea, not for the claims of the worker but for the claims of the imagination. Its anger is directed against Gradgrindism. Gradgrindism is a state of mind that may prevail in any society, capitalist or communist, and indeed tends to flourish much more tropically under communism.

Clifton Fadiman, in Party of One: The Selected Writings of Clifton Fadiman, *The World Publishing Company, 1955.*

David Sonstroem (essay date 1969)

SOURCE: "Fettered Fancy in *Hard Times,*" in *PMLA,* Vol. 84, No. 3, May, 1969, pp. 520-29.

[*In the following essay, Sonstroem identifies conflict between Fact—dry statistics and empirical definitions—and Fancy—variously identified with imagination, romance, wonder, and nonsense—as central to the structure of* Hard Times.]

In 1948 F. R. Leavis threw down the gauntlet, proclaiming *Hard Times,* hitherto "passed over as a very minor thing," to be a "masterpiece." Dickens' achievement, according to Leavis, was the production of "a richly poetic art of the word. He doesn't write 'poetic prose'; he writes with a poetic force of evocation, registering with the responsiveness of a genius of verbal expression what he so sharply sees and feels. In fact, by texture, imaginative mode, symbolic method, and the resulting concentration, *Hard Times* affects us as belonging with formally poetic works." His study has drawn vigorous counterstatements critical of the book, the most telling retort being that its characters are "creatures of stick": John Holloway finds neither Louisa nor her father "a true embodiment of the standpoint—or predicament—which is their allotted rôle." W. W. Watt describes Louisa as speaking "fustian." David H. Hirsch notes, "so feeble-minded do the 'good' characters become at times that it is ultimately impossible to take them at all seriously." As early as 1912 George

Bernard Shaw had described Sissy Jupe as speaking "'like a book' in the most intolerable sense of the words." In short, Leavis pointed to the novel's success as poetry—its symbolic or imagistic structure—whereas the other critics point to the novel's failure as drama—its failure to produce believable, attractive characters who can act out the meanings entrusted to them.

If one avoids the polar atmosphere of the controversy, it is entirely possible to share both views of the book. I find *Hard Times* to be a truly impressive achievement of meaningful symbolic structuring, but weak dramatically, because the personalities of certain characters do not support their full symbolic charge. The key to both aspects of the novel lies in the cause that it champions: Fancy. Through an examination of the novel's concept of Fancy—its meanings and employments—I hope to show precisely why *Hard Times* succeeds and fails as it does. My purpose is not really to serve as critical mediator (the critical conflict merely calls attention to the area of my consideration) but rather to get at the heart of the book and the somewhat conflicting impulses that moved Dickens as he wrote it.

The first sentence of *Hard Times* discloses the villain of the piece: Facts—narrow, dry statistics and definitions imperiously presented as a sufficient, and the only sufficient, explanation of the world and all living things. Not so obvious is the beleaguered alternative that Dickens champions. The predominant word for it is Fancy, but what he means by it is decidedly sweeping and variable, and therefore unclear. Dickens himself must have felt the need to explain his meaning, for he frequently links the word with synonyms: Thomas Gradgrind describes Josiah Bounderby as not "pretending to anything fanciful, fantastic, or (I am using synonymous terms) sentimental." Elsewhere Fancy is linked with "romance," "wonder," "nonsense," and "tastes, aspirations, and affections." Implicitly synonymous terms are "imaginative graces and delights," "childish lore," "Faith, Hope and Charity," and "Heart."

Two areas of meaning emerge from this cluster. The one is imaginative play: mental play unhindered by the strictures of reality. The other is fellow feeling: compassion, sentiment. That imaginative play and fellow feeling are quite different activities seems sufficiently obvious (it is easy to imagine a dull-witted bleeding heart or a thick-skinned dreamer of dreams). It is equally obvious that the two activities might be joined to form the attractive human faculty that we commonly call the sympathetic imagination—the faculty that permits one human being to enter into the mind and circumstances of another. But I will postpone consideration of Dickens' relationship between imaginative play and fellow feeling in order to treat separately the relationship of each to their common enemy, Fact. For Dickens employs each as a weapon in its own defense.

The first kind of Fancy—imaginative play—is ably and almost exclusively represented by the zestful and defiantly imaginative narrative personality, who uses Fancy against Fact in several direct and very effective ways.

First, the narrator's *jeux d'esprit* are living proof that Fancy does exist, that it can be great fun, and that it contributes to a personality that is more charming, lively, and powerful than that of Gradgrind, the straw man of Fact. There is evident enjoyment in conceiving the description of Gradgrind as "a kind of cannon loaded to the muzzle with facts, and prepared to blow them clean out of the regions of childhood at one discharge." or of Bounderby as "a commercial wonder more admirable than Venus, who had risen out of the mud instead of the sea." Some of the joy is transferred to the reader, who accords the narrator the victory in the battle of personalities.

Second, the narrator rides circles of Fancy around the Gradgrinds of the world to make them dizzy. Machines become elephants; smoke becomes a snake; a factory becomes a fairy palace; a face, a medallion. No tabular mentality can achieve control in such a verbal environment, but the narrator and we, who are used to such talk (we equestrians, who can keep our balance in a living, changing world), can appreciate the imaginative spin, and the discomforting of the enemy.

Third, he shows that Fancy is not only more enjoyable and mobile than Gradgrind's Fact, but also more applicable; it comes closer to tracing the twists and complexities of the world as it is, and consequently is more accurate in representing reality. M'Choakumchild, we are told, "had taken the bloom off the higher branches of mathematics"; the narrator revivifies a dead metaphor, even as he mocks the kind of mind that petrified it in the first place. He sees something that M'Choakumchild would not. Later he tells us that Gradgrind was "looking about for a suitable opportunity of making an arithmetical figure in Parliament"; the fanciful phrase, beyond Gradgrind's tabular comprehension, succinctly expresses both his aspiration and his devotion to scientific method, as well as the ridicule the narrator heaps upon his pretensions. Such language expresses truths elusive of graphs, yet it rivals them in conciseness and precision.

A fourth employment of image-play against Fact deserves extensive elaboration, and will form the main body of this study. Dickens uses imagery to show that the world he presents is interrelated, with each part resembling and depending upon every other part. The curse of the Gradgrind system is that it separates and alienates, achieving a theoretical order at the expense of actual order. The disjointed nature of the Gradgrind family; the many lonely pits, both figurative and literal, into which various characters fall; the ostracism of Stephen; the metaphor in the name Slackbridge; and the fact that there is not one true marriage portrayed in the whole book, are expressions of Dickens' sense of the pervasive separation among human beings. In contemporary pronouncements outside the novel, Dickens revealed the same fear that "the System" was imposing estrangement upon man. He condemned a labor dispute for "the gulf of separation it hourly deepens between those whose interests must be understood to be identical or must be destroyed." Elsewhere he wished for "the fusion of different classes, without confusion . . . the bringing together of employers and employed . . . the creating of a better common understanding among those whose interests are identical, who depend upon each other, and who can never be in unnatural antagonism without deplorable results." By explicitly encouraging the reader to draw literary analogies, Dickens reveals his belief that the exercise of Fancy could prove very useful in apprehending and encouraging true union: "Is it possible, I wonder, that there was any analogy between the case of the Coketown population and the case of the little Gradgrinds?" Literary analogies like this one could be used to assert the interrelationship, the interdependence, that exists in the world. A tissue of imaginative links could give the reader a sense of that harmonious world which Dickens feared Facts were destroying. Of course, by composing a novel that uses imagery to suggest analogy and, ultimately, to achieve unity, he does what every other novelist does. The noteworthiness lies in his treating imaginative play as an object as well as a vehicle for consideration, and in employing it in its own defense.

The governing distinction in the imagery of *Hard Times* is that between life and lifelessness. The primary symbols of life are flowers and horses. Flowers represent the passive aspects of life: its tenderness, delicacy, and helplessness. In the first scene, in the schoolroom, flowers are presented as objects that crush and wither when trampled on with heavy boots. The irony of the situation lies in the fact that the three teachers of Fact are stamping out the flower-like fancies of little children (who are themselves described in plant imagery) even as the teachers preach against stepping upon figurative flowers. The connotation of vulnerability is reinforced throughout the book: Mr. M'Choakumchild (as we have seen) had "taken the bloom off the higher branches of mathematics"; Mr. Bounderby tears up a flower garden to plant cabbages; Tom, Jr., moodily tears roses apart even as he contributes to the destruction of the lives of his sister and Stephen; and his father is described as "annihilating the flowers of existence."

The active side of life is represented by horses, which connote vitality, spiritedness, and movement. The circus people, who look and act as if they are "always on horseback," are repeatedly described as engaged in energetic action: they "perform rapid acts," and, in Sleary's words, "they're accuthtomed to be quick in their movementh." Sissy Jupe, in saying of her father that "he belongs to the horse-riding," quite accurately presents him as engaged in an activity rather than a profession. The nobility of the horse image is enhanced through mythic suggestion: One circus performer, Mr. Childers, is described as a centaur, and the whole troupe lives at the Pegasus's Arms, in "the upper regions." The horse image represents a force to be reckoned with, a force worthy to oppose the powers of Fact and all that it represents. Although Bounderby claims to have "eaten in his youth at least three horses," and has brought under his control "so many hundred horse Steam Power," it is the horse that triumphs ultimately. Bitzer is obviously deluded in thinking that he has captured the true beast in his definition of a horse at the beginning of the novel, but the thing itself turns the tables by capturing Bitzer at the end of the book.

Lesser forms of life are nicely defined by measurement against the horse image. Merrylegs, Signor Jupe's performing dog, symbolizes him, in a way: The dog is clever and quick on his feet, like all the circus animals, but he is smaller than they. Like Signor Jupe, he does not quite measure up. Tom describes himself as a donkey and a mule, and the narrator, following the lead of Harthouse, calls him "the whelp." In his humiliating disguise, Tom's hands look "like the hands of a monkey." And, beast that he is, he is engaged in biting straw. The machinery of Coketown is described as "melancholy mad elephants," more powerful, but less spirited than horses. In a delightful image, Mrs. Sparsit netting—a form of needlework involving looping some of the threads round the lady's shoe—is described as "easily ambling along," "in a side-saddle attitude, with one foot in a cotton stirrup." She is poised beautifully between her own idea of herself (a lady fair on horseback) and her actual occupation (cloth-making for Bounderby, like everyone else in Coketown). Comparison with the livelier and less dignified bareback riders of the circus is also invited. Another extension of the animal imagery is Gradgrind's conception of the circus people as "noisy insects," and Bounderby's reference to his workmen as "pests of the earth." Both expressions are grossly unfair to the people they are supposed to describe, and so serve to mark the imperceptiveness toward others of the two men of Fact. With a greater show of justice the narrator likens Bitzer to an insect, and Bounderby calls himself a maggot.

A third major image indicative of life is the sun. In his provocative essay, Leavis calls our attention to a descriptive passage in which "Sissy, being at the corner of a row on the sunny side, came in for the beginning of a sunbeam, of which Bitzer, being at the corner of a row on the other side, a few rows in advance, caught the end. But, whereas the girl was so dark-eyed and dark-haired that she seemed to receive a deeper and more lustrous colour from the sun, when it shone upon her, the boy was so light-eyed and light-haired that the self-same rays appeared to draw out of him what little colour he ever possessed." What might appear, in the absence of sunlight, to be darkness in Sissy is here apprehended as "deeper and more lustrous colour." What seems to be light according to the crepuscular illumination of Gradgrindism is shown up by the sunbeam as unhealthy paleness, bloodless white. Ironically, Bitzer will become a "light porter" who carries no light. That Bitzer stands only to lose from affiliation with the source and symbol of life reveals his contrariety to it. The imagery shows him to be a negative force in the book, whereas it shows Mrs. Gradgrind, for example, in a passage reminiscent of this one, to be a cipher: Mrs. Gradgrind "looked . . . like an indifferently executed transparency of a small female figure, without enough light behind it." Neither she nor the sun affects the other in any significant way.

Elsewhere Dickens pursues the imagery in a very conventional manner. When Stephen unwillingly returns to his home, now occupied by his besotted wife, Rachael's face unexpectedly "shone in upon the midnight of his mind." Later Rachael herself wanted "no brighter light to shine on their sorrowful talk" than Sissy. Sissy is a sun to Louisa, also: "the once deserted girl shone like a beautiful light upon the darkness of the other." Conversely, Coketown's "blur of soot and smoke," satanically "aspiring to the vault of Heaven," makes the city "impervious to the sun's rays."

Fire as a symbol for life may be considered an extension of the sun imagery. Whereas the sun represents life in its purest, most elemental form, fire represents life—liveliness—as it manifests itself in actual and imperfect people. Consequently it can be quenched (Louisa is forever watching fires dying out). And it can be a force for evil as well as for good: Louisa's resentment of Sissy's pity "smouldered within her like an unwholesome fire," and when her scheming brother misleads Stephen, "his breath fell like a flame of fire on Stephen's ear, it was so hot"; but when Sissy obtains rescuers to pull Stephen from the shaft, "their spirits were on fire like hers." The fires in the furnaces of Coketown present us with a larger image, representing the passions, and sometimes specifically the resentments, of its inhabitants. Of course fire is anathema to the forces of Fact: there is "a row of fire-buckets" in Bounderby's bank. But more often than not, these men are incapable of seeing it; they do not know that it is there. We first meet Bounderby with his back to the hearth, obliviously enjoying its warmth, and blocking off its benefits from others. Gradgrind looks directly at the fire, and yet does not understand why young Tom and Louisa would wish to see a circus. As Louisa stares into the hearth, her more corrupt brother tells her, "You seem to find more to look at in it than ever I could find." Gradgrind's blindness to the fires of life is best revealed in the passage in which he conveys Bounderby's marriage proposal to his daughter:

> "Are you consulting the chimneys of the Coketown works, Louisa?"

> "There seems to be nothing there but languid and monotonous smoke. Yet when the night comes, Fire bursts out, father!" she answered, turning quickly.

> "Of course I know that, Louisa. I do not see the application of the remark." To do him justice he did not, at all.

His blindness to the analogy is due to his blindness to passionate life. Bounderby's blindness is put in similar terms, but more humorously. As the suspicious Mrs. Sparsit strains her eyes to observe Louisa and Mr. Harthouse strolling in the garden, Bounderby asks, "What's the matter, ma'am? . . . you don't see a Fire, do you?"

Smoke is an image that links images of life with those of lifelessness. An unpleasant derivative of fire, it is even farther removed from the sun, and is symbolically an enemy of the life represented by fire. It is repeatedly linked with the serpent—an obnoxious form of life and the foe

of life at its prelapsarian best. Smoke is dirty, and it covers everything; it turns Coketown into "the painted face of a savage"—an image that links industrial progress with the jungle, and prepares us for Tom (that triumph of the System) in blackface. The serpentine coils of smoke that enfold Coketown symbolize disorder, the "muddle" of which Stephen complains. Smoke produces a narcotic effect, which blinds its victims and prevents them from acting in a prudent manner. We see this effect not only in the misguided factory workers, but also in "the whelp," his wits addled by the heady smoke of Harthouse's rich tobacco.

We find opposed to the images of life those of destruction, and usually violent destruction. In reading *Hard Times* one senses a pervasive violence which the action of the book cannot completely account for—which can be explained only in terms of the book's imagery. The names of the antagonists point the way to Dickens' intentions: grind in Gradgrind; bound in Bounderby (Dickens' working plans for *Hard Times* show that Bounderby was first to be called Mr. Bound, until Dickens hit upon the happier elongation); choke in M'Choakumchild; nick (and Old Nick) in Nickits; bite (and horse's bit) in Bitzer. But we hardly need the names to appreciate the destructiveness of Fact and its practitioners: Gradgrind is a "cannon loaded to the muzzle"; the "third gentleman" was a "professed pugilist" who was "certain to knock the wind out of common sense"; Bounderby is frequently a destructive wind, or a windbag at the breaking point (cf. the fire in Louisa, which threatens to flare out); M'Choakumchild will either "kill outright the robber Fancy" or "only maim him and distort him"; Mrs. Gradgrind, frequently "stunned" by "collision" with some Fact, habitually "dies away"; Tom would like to blow up all Facts with "a thousand barrels of gunpowder"; the loom at which Stephen works is a "crashing, smashing, tearing piece of mechanism," and Stephen has within himself a similar violence that he comes close to directing against his wife; Mrs. Sparsit, in carrying the news to Mr. Bounderby of Louisa's passionate flight, "exploded the combustibles with which she was charged, and blew up." Chapters are entitled "Gunpowder" and "Explosion." The reader soon realizes that the flowers of Fancy must find root in soil no more nourishing than gunpowder.

Destruction includes self-destruction. Even as Gradgrind chokes off Fancy in the little children, he is himself throttled by his own necktie, "trained to take him by the throat with an unaccommodating grasp." Bounderby has a self-destructive streak too, although his has more to do with turbulence than constriction: "One might have fancied," with regard to the scantiness of his hair, that "he had talked it off; and that what was left, all standing up in disorder, was in that condition from being constantly blown about by his windy boastfulness." We see self-destructiveness even in the more restive votaries of Fact: after being kissed by Bounderby, Louisa rubs the spot on her cheek until it is red. Tom cautions her that she will rub a hole in her face, to which she replies, "You may cut the piece out with your penknife if you like." Later we see Tom engaged in similar behavior, "chafing his face on his coatsleeve, as if to mortify his flesh, and have it in unison with his spirit."

Specific images of lifelessness that find frequent expression, besides those connected with gunpowder and fisticuffs, are the following: (1) Bounderby's windiness, which is not to be confused with the airy qualities of the circus folk. (2) Starvation: related to the Coketowners, who live in material poverty, is Louisa, who is described several times as being imaginatively and emotionally starved. (3) The inorganic in general, which we see in the machinery of Coketown, the "metallic laugh" of Bounderby, the inflexible divorce laws, and the equally inflexible concepts of Gradgrind. (4) The pit: Old Hell Shaft, into which Stephen falls; the ditch out of which Bounderby describes himself as arising; the well into which Mrs. Gradgrind seems to have sunk as she approaches death; and the "dark pit of shame and ruin" that lies at the bottom of the staircase erected by Mrs. Sparsit for Louisa's expected moral lapse. All the pits owe their existence to Fact and all that the word entails: In effecting his rise in the world, Bounderby has thoughtlessly dug the pit for Stephen. Just as thoughtlessly, Gradgrind has prepared the "dark pit" for his daughter. And in his digging around in the "National dustbin" of Parliament, Gradgrind is only preparing further pitfalls for the innocent and unwary.

The greatest confrontation of the two classes of imagery—life and lifelessness—occurs in the first two chapters, the schoolroom scene. Here we find age versus youth—an opposition that is picked up elsewhere in the book, as we realize from the names "Kidderminster" and "Childers," the pervasive "peterpantheism" (to borrow W. W. Watt's word) among the circus characters, and the precipitate maturity or old age among the characters associated with Fact. We also find the organic opposed to the inorganic—more specifically, human beings described sometimes as plants, sometimes as vessels. Gradgrind himself is appropriately described principally in terms of the latter category, terms of enclosure. His "eyes found commodious cellarage in two dark caves"; his head is a "warehouse." Everything about him is hard and square, like the "square wall" of his forehead. (Incidentally, his squareness forms a geometric opposition to the round world of the circus.) The students are also described in similar terms—they are "little vessels," "little pitchers," and "jars"—but the expressions are ridiculously inappropriate when applied to them, and obviously represent the terms in which Gradgrind thinks of them: creatures with no value or bent of their own, mere containers. The alternative imagery for them, plants, is supplied in the exemplary flowers that must not appear on wallpaper; in the divisional title, "Sowing"; and in Gradgrind's own injunction, "Facts alone are wanted in life. Plant nothing else, and root out everything else." A measure of Gradgrind's wrongheadedness is his seeing Facts, not children, as plants, and children as the pots to put them in. The wide disparity between the two images applied to children goes far in making Gradgrind look ridiculous.

The book's confrontation of imagery is beautifully concentrated in the two paper horses that we find in this scene. The one is the representation of a horse with which the more natural of the pupils would paper a room. The other is the definition of a horse supplied by Bitzer but emanating originally from Gradgrind. The one is no less a paper horse than the other, and the inability of the three adults to appreciate this fact dramatizes their foolishness. (The point that they are unable to distinguish between an object and a depiction of the object is reiterated when the third gentleman, in his conceptual blindness, professes that he would not step on a representation of flowers for fear of destroying them, whereas Sissy realizes that they would be "pictures" only and therefore would not "crush and wither.") The great difference between the two paper horses lies in their relationship to life. Sissy would be *adding* a semblance of life to an otherwise lifeless wall (the narrator does much the same thing in his treating prosaic objects, people, and events in more exotic terms: elephants, snakes, fairy palaces, a griffin, Morgiana, Blue Beard, the Sultan, and so forth), whereas Gradgrind, in preferring the definition to the real thing, is *denying* life that actually exists.

Thus does Dickens build bridges of imagery within each of two domains: that of life and Fancy, and that of lifelessness and Fact. The gulf between them is a real one, and members of one domain cannot really touch upon the other. Sissy is curiously unaffected by school or Stone Lodge. Peeping Tom and Louisa can only glimpse the circus horses' hoofs, and Mrs. Sparsit sees little more in her spying upon Louisa and Harthouse. Bounderby is as disruptive a presence in the Pegasus's Arms as Stephen is at Bounderby's home. But the gulf, though real enough, is not a necessary one. Even as Dickens presents it he throws bridges of imagery across it, to indicate the fundamental relationship between the two domains.

For example, people on both sides are ever rising and falling. We remember the pits, wells, and shafts mentioned earlier. The black ladder of the undertaker symbolizes a descent that characters on both sides of the gulf must undertake. Bounderby has risen in life, like the bag of hot air that he is, but the circus people, those denizens of the upper regions, also spend much of their time aloft. Kidderminster suggests the similarity in referring to Bounderby as being "on the Tight-Jeff." The narrator also suggests the similarity in calling Bounderby a circus balloon. Louisa and Tom "abase" themselves to watch the circus; so Gradgrind commands them to "rise." Yet he himself must plunge "into the howling ocean of tabular statements, which no diver ever got to any depth in and came up sane." An important feature of this imagery is that no fixed meaning or value is implied by up or down. When Bounderby remarks, "Queer sort of company . . . for a man who has raised himself," Kidderminster retorts, "Lower yourself, then. . . . Oh Lord! if you've raised yourself so high as all that comes to, let yourself down a bit"—and we see this as good advice. The ambivalence is just one more way in which Dickens upsets an oversimplified system to further the cause of Fancy. Louisa descends Mrs. Sparsit's staircase only to find herself in a saner, "higher" situation than before. Mrs. Sparsit, in making her last exit from Bounderby, "swept disdainfully past him, and ascended the staircase," although it is really a lower, more miserable life she goes to. The sharp separation between men of Fact and Children of Fancy is softened by the recognition that both are caught up in the common vicissitudes of life.

A more direct relationship between the two domains shows the circus to be another business, not unlike Bounderby's factory. Bounderby and Sleary, the two owners, are alike in being rotund and in being described in wind imagery, the chief difference in the imagery being that Sleary is a "*broken* old pair of bellows" italics mine). On several occasions Sleary refers to the "fairy-*business*" (italics mine). He is no more apt to confuse representations of fairies with real fairies than Sissy is apt to confuse real and paper horses. A responsible position in the circus must be prepared for with an apprenticeship, just like its Coketown counterpart. Both the circus workers and the mill workers deal with "elephants" of one kind or another. And both classes of workers can be injured by their elephants: Rachael's sister was killed by a machine, and Emma Gordon, an informal foster mother to Sissy, lost her husband in "a heavy back-fall off a Elephant." The circus folk, the practitioners of Fancy, have their hard times as surely as the victims of Fact. The real difference between factory and circus is not that between labor and idleness, as Bounderby would have it, but rather that between self-seeking, exploiting management and kindly, paternalistic management. The difference is an accidental one, and shows factory and circus to be more closely related than one might at first expect.

Conversely, the domain of Fact partakes heavily of Fancy; it is the Fact people who are actually the shameless fictionalizers. Harthouse's older brother made his reputation in Parliament with his cow-and-cap fantasy, a patently false, although humorous, reconstruction of a disastrous railroad accident, an account that his hardheaded fellow M.P.'s were willing to accept as truth simply because it reinforced their prejudices. Although Bounderby's highly imaginative account of his sorry youth is pure fiction, he manages to persuade everyone, including himself, of its truth. Mrs. Sparsit's conception of the meaning that the world attaches to "Scadgers" and "Powler" is equally fanciful. And Dickens is ever referring to "prevalent fictions" among the mill owners of Coketown: industries, like fragile chinaware, easily ruined; workers desirous of turtle soup, to be eaten with a gold spoon; dissatisfaction in a worker a sign of utter criminality. We see that the domain of Fancy holds no exclusive rights to Fancy. The basic distinction would seem to be rather that the Sissys and Slearys, in accepting both Fact and Fancy, are able to tell them apart, whereas the no-nonsense Gradgrinds and Bounderbys, in refusing to recognize Fancy, engage in it unawares. Their greatest Fancy is that they do not entertain any. But again, our chief response to the realization that the proponents of Fact are at least as fanciful as anyone else is to see the gulf between the two basic domains of the book as diminished.

My intent in the previous pages has been to convey in detail a sense of the elaborate imaginative webbing or

bridging that Dickens applied to the book—to show that Dickens took great pains to make **Hard Times** a unified imaginative whole. His doing so was no mere matter of course, but a necessity, for the tactics of the book demanded that he answer the Gradgrindian world view with the narrator's world view: a conception of imaginative links showing all parts of the world to be interrelated and answerable to one another. A primary activity of the narrative personality, then, is imaginative play—just one of the two meanings that Dickens attaches to the word Fancy.

The second meaning that Dickens attaches to Fancy, it will be remembered, is fellow feeling, "an untiring readiness to help and pity one another." The book is full of scenes of sympathy: Rachael "alone appeared to have compassion on a degraded, drunken wretch of her own sex." When Sissy learns of her abandonment, Josephine Sleary kneels "down on the floor to nurse her, and to weep over her." Louisa tells Tom, when she suspects him of foul play, "You may be certain that I will be compassionate and true to you," although she later must ask, "Where are the sentiments of my heart?" Troubled Louisa pleads with Sissy, "Forgive me, pity me, help me! Have compassion on my great need, and let me lay this head of mine upon a loving heart!" To which Sissy replies, "O lay it here! Lay it here, my dear." Even Gradgrind comes to plead for fellow feeling from Bitzer—"Pity us!"—although his search for heart is not so successful as his daughter's. Bitzer's reply to Gradgrind's question, "have you a heart?" namely, "The circulation, Sir . . . couldn't be carried on without one," reveals through the divergent meanings that can be applied to the same word the hopeless difference between the sensibility of Fact and that of Fancy. The sensibilities are no closer to touching than the meanings.

Like imaginative play, fellow feeling has a force and strength of its own, which is directed against Fact. Dickens' intentions are manifest in a note from his working plans, or "Mems.," for **Hard Times**: "Carry on Sissy—Power of affection." We see this power in her ingenuous jousting with her schoolmasters, where headless heart is pitted against heartless head: "I thought it must be just as hard upon those who were starved, whether the others were a million, or a million million. And that was wrong, too." The two great confrontations between Fact and Feeling are that between Bitzer and the largehearted circus folk, and that between Sissy (speaking in Louisa's behalf) and Mr. Harthouse, in which she, supported only by "my love for her, and her love for me," completely routs the man-of-the-world and sends him packing. The military motif that is carried throughout the conversation underlines the victory of heart over heartlessness. The happy and fruitful marriage forecast for Sissy at the end of the book shows the ultimate might of the values that she represents.

In these several ways Dickens pits both imaginative play and fellow feeling against Fact. If we are not entirely satisfied with the victory of these allies, the reason may be that the two components of Fancy are not always in league, and in fact work somewhat at cross-purposes. It is time to examine their relationship to each other.

That they do not always go together well is indicated by the narrator's curious paucity of compassion. For all his imagination, he displays remarkably little imaginative sympathy. In fact, as E. P. Whipple observes, "Bounderby becomes a seeming character by being looked at and individualized from the point of view of imaginative antipathy" [Dickens's *Hard Times, The Atlantic Monthly,* March, 1877]. Whipple goes on to criticize Dickens for his failure of sympathy toward Bounderby, and I would apply his remarks even more generally throughout the book:

> When a fictional character is conceived, he shall be not only externally represented but internally known. There is no authorized, no accredited way of exhibiting character but this, that the dramatist or novelist shall enter into the soul of the personage represented, shall sympathize with him sufficiently to know him, and shall represent his passions, prejudices, and opinions as springing from some central will and individuality. This sympathy is consistent with the utmost hatred of the person described; but characterization becomes satire the moment that antipathy supersedes insight and the satirist berates the exterior manifestations of an individuality whose interior life he has not diligently explored and interpreted.

It should be said in Dickens' behalf that Whipple is too absolute and categorical. He touches upon a characteristic practice that Dickens puts to good use in many of his novels, including this one. Dickens' flat characters and his mode of handling them are rich fare indeed, and count generally as one of his strengths. But Whipple's remarks, applied as they are to *Hard Times,* are fair insofar as they point up an inconsistency within this book: A narrator with a mind and heart closed to certain characters is strangely out of place in a novel that pretends to champion fellow feeling.

The narrator extends his antipathy toward others besides Bounderby. He (and through him, Stephen) displays not the first sign of fellow feeling for Stephen's drunkard wife. Such expressions as "brutish instinct," "debauched features," "greedy hand," and "insensate grasp" show that the narrator is as anxious as Stephen to keep her at a great distance. Stephen's past efforts to abide with her do not entirely atone for his present revulsion; and the kindness of Rachael (who loses at least as much as Stephen because of her) shows up both Stephen and the narrator as callous in their evasive treatment of the wife. (The argument for divorce is oddly out of place in a work celebrating the compassionate bridging of interpersonal gulfs.) Thus would the narrator *limit* the reader's fellow feeling, by extending to Stephen alone the pity that rightfully applies to both husband and wife. Another telltale sign of antipathy is the narrator's customarily referring to Tom, Jr., as "the whelp." It is a trick of his to highlight the inappropriateness of a designation uttered by one character about another by repeating the offensive expression in his own person (e.g., "young rabble," "Jupe," "Miss Gradgrind"). When he does the same with "the whelp" we take

it as another criticism of Harthouse's inability to appreciate what a thing is a man. But then the narrator takes the expression as his own, applying it again and again to Tom. Thus does the narrator, apparently inadvertently, come to share an unsympathetic outlook with Harthouse. Other characters whose plights do not receive their due of sympathy from the narrator are Mrs. Sparsit, Bitzer, and (except, perhaps, at her death) Mrs. Gradgrind. The "sneer of great disdain" on the face of the despised Slackbridge is unexpectedly reflected on his own.

Another, converse indication of cross-purposes between imagination and compassion is the lack of imaginative play on the part of the virtuous, compassionate characters: Stephen, Rachael, Louisa, the circus folk, and especially Sissy Jupe. They show up very badly against the villainous characters: Bounderby, with his magnificent imaginative reconstruction of his past, and with such expressions as, "I didn't four seven one. Not if I knew it" and "if she takes it in the fainting way, I'll have the skin off her nose, at all events!"; Mrs. Sparsit, with her staircase and her view of herself as the Bank Fairy; and even young Tom, with his "jolly old—Jaundiced Jail." These characters make the virtuous ones seem very dull indeed. Although the depiction of a wheezy lisp or colorful circus argot may save Dickens from the charge of dullness, there is no imagination required of the circus characters themselves to produce such talk; so they still emerge with dull personalities. They do not produce imaginative leaps and turns to match their physical ones. Stephen's living over a toy shop may be supposed to carry a symbolic charge, but his situation does not reverberate in his personality. Sissy, whose father specialized in "chaste Shaksperean quips and retorts," and—a superb image for the exercise of fantasy—in "forming a fountain of solid iron in mid-air," whose mother was a dancer, and whose childhood reading consisted of highly imaginative literature, turns out to be pedestrian enough to have been the daughter of Gradgrind. In fact, she has as little imagination as any character in the novel. I think that what is lacking in the virtuous characters—what the critics, quoted in my first paragraph, are objecting to—can be narrowed down precisely to lack of Fancy, in the first sense of the word: lack of imaginative play. Dickens denies his characters one aspect of the very quality that they represent. Their personalities lack one half of their symbolic meaning.

Thus the bifurcation of the two components of Fancy is consistently preserved: The narrator has all the imagination and none of the sentiment; the Sissy Jupes have all the sentiment and none of the imagination. The distinction between imaginative play and fellow feeling, which was educed at the beginning of this essay from Dickens' synonyms for Fancy, is seen to hold, even in implicit ways, throughout the novel.

Yet Dickens would seem to be desirous of having fantasy and sentiment come together into one harmonious activity or state of being. This intention is made clear in his treating the two concepts as synonymous—in his regarding them both as Fancy. It is also made clear, as we have seen, in his ascribing both to the virtuous characters of the book, imaginative play being ascribed to them symbolically, through the narrator's imagery, and fellow feeling, dramatically, through the characters' behavior.

In practice *Hard Times* relates the concepts to each other, but the connection is not really a synonymous or equivalent one. Their true relationship is implicit in Louisa's words to her father upon her returning to Stone Lodge after her near seduction: "Father, if you had known . . . that there lingered in my breast, sensibilities, affections, weaknesses capable of being cherished into strength . . . would you have robbed me . . . of the immaterial part of my life, the spring and summer of my belief, my refuge from what is sordid and bad in the real things around me? . . . Yet, father, if I had been . . . free . . . to exercise my fancy somewhat . . . I should have been a million times wiser, happier, more loving." Both concepts are referred to: "sensibilities, affections" on the one hand, "the immaterial part of my life, the spring and summer of my belief" (that is to say, childhood fantasies, imaginative play) on the other. The function of the latter concept (referred to directly here as "fancy") is to provide a "refuge from what is sordid and bad in the real things around me." In other words, the proper function of imaginative play is to provide a protective atmosphere of delusion, within which a child's fellow feeling can grow to strength without being blighted by the "sordid and bad" aspects of reality. Thus is fantasy to foster compassion.

The relationship between the two components of Dickens' Fancy is elaborated further in an earlier passage: as Louisa returns to Stone Lodge and her dying mother,

> Neither . . . did any of the best influences of old home descend upon her. The dreams of childhood—its airy fables; its graceful, beautiful, humane, impossible adornments of the world beyond: so good to be believed in once, so good to be remembered when outgrown, for then the least among them rises to the stature of a great Charity in the heart, suffering little children to come into the midst of it, and to keep with their pure hands a garden in the stony ways of this world, wherein it were better for all the children of Adam that they should oftener sun themselves, simple and trustful, and not worldly-wise—what had she to do with these?

The "dreams" and "airy fables" of fantasy rise to "a great Charity in the heart"; imagination leads to sentiment, and the relationship of the previously quoted passage is reasserted. What is especially revealing about the present passage is its likening the "airy fables" of imagination to a Garden of Eden, cut off from "the world beyond," "the stony ways of this world," and the "worldly-wise." Imagination is seen to be a refuge characterized by profound innocence; "little children" and "pure hands" enforce this connotation. We remember the aura of childhood that surrounds the virtuous characters of the novel—the "wonderful kind of innocence" that surrounds Sleary, for example.

Innocence tends to display a self-protective offishness, which is clearly observable in a few telling gestures in the novel. One is Sissy in full flight from Bitzer. Sensing her natural enemy, she runs away from him. Sissy must remain inviolably innocent; she cannot know Bitzer, even mentally or imaginatively. So she flees. Another such gesture is that of Rachael, in answer to Stephen's attempt to express his darker feelings about his wife:

> " . . . I thowt, 'How can *I* say what I might ha' done to myseln, or her, or both!'"
>
> She put her two hands on his mouth, with a face of terror, to stop him from saying more.

Rachael can permit herself to know only the gentle side of Stephen's nature. Knowledge of his other side would compromise her innocence, so she instinctively silences him. Finally, there is Sissy's visit to Harthouse; the innocent enters the lair of the man-of-the-world: "She was not afraid of him, or in any way disconcerted; she seemed to have her mind entirely preoccupied with the occasion of her visit, and to have substituted that consideration for herself." I would suggest that it is not herself that she is ignoring here but Harthouse, the embodiment of worldliness. In fact the success of her visit comes about precisely because she never really notices, understands, or is touched by him—because "her mind looked over and beyond him": "if she had concealed the least doubt or irresolution, or had harboured for the best purpose any reserve or pretence; if she had shown, or felt, the lightest trace of any sensitiveness to his ridicule or his astonishment, or any remonstrance he might offer; he would have carried it against her at this point. But he could as easily have changed a clear sky by looking at it in surprise, as affect her." His every statement "had no effect on Sissy." Her success against him is seen to depend on her absolute lack of "sensitiveness" toward him. Again, to know him would be to be polluted by him, but she resists his charm, remaining as impersonal and distant as the sky itself.

And thus we come to the heart of the problem of *Hard Times*: Dickens' apparent failure to realize that he has allotted two, contrary roles to the imagination, because he is championing two somewhat conflicting causes: fellow feeling and innocence. On the one hand (as we have seen), through the narrator's imaginative play—his complex pattern of imagistic analogies—Dickens develops a model of a highly interrelated world, to contradict the world of separation and alienation that the Gradgrind system was imposing upon man. On the other hand, through self-delusive imaginative play, the book's innocent characters are able to insulate themselves from "what is sordid and bad" in "the world beyond." The function of the imagination is now to build bridges, now to build buffers. Dickens seems uncertain whether to work toward a coherent, interdependent world, or toward a scattering of islands of innocence. His uncertainty is due to his cross-purposes as to whether one's heart should go out in fellow feeling for others, or whether it should harden itself in self-protection. Is "the world beyond" to be truly known, or avoided? In his double advocacy of fellow feeling and innocence, Dickens does not seem to realize that either can be achieved only at some expense to the other.

The result of Dickens' cross-purposes is a series of compromises. What he gives on one hand he takes away on the other. True imaginative sympathy—imaginative play working in tandem with fellow feeling—is nowhere to be found in the novel. But we do find unimaginative sympathy—blind compassion—on the part of the virtuous characters, and imaginative antipathy on the part of the narrator. Each is given one quality that permits him to reach out toward others, and another that permits him to fend off those of evil nature. In addition, the innocents are permitted to know only other innocents, or to be touched only by what is congenial to innocence in mixed characters, like Louisa and Stephen. The more observant and adult narrator yet holds his ground within the "garden," denying all sympathy with the "worldly-wise," perhaps out of nostalgia, perhaps the better to protect the innocents. Fancy is decidedly fettered in one way or the other. Because the forces of Fancy are so confused, there is no clear, attractive alternative to the Facts of Gradgrindism. The self-confidence of the narrator is felt to be largely bluster, and the victory over Facts, a paper one. But the greatest defeat in the book is suffered by the elaborately and extensively interrelated imaginative world view that the narrator posits opposite the tabular one of Gradgrind. Dickens himself betrayed it because it showed the things and people of the world to touch in a way and to an extent that he, protective of innocence, was not ready to accept.

N. K. Banerjee (essay date 1972)

SOURCE: "*Hard Times:* A Note on the Descriptive Titles of Its Books," in *The Indian Journal of English Studies,* Vol. XIII, 1972, pp. 22-28.

[*In the following excerpt, Banerjee explores the relation between the tripartite structure of* Hard Times—*"Sowing," "Reaping," and "Garnering"—and Dickens's development of the novel's themes.*]

'Sowing', 'Reaping', and 'Garnering' are three descriptive words which appear at the head of each of the three books of *Hard Times*. These words are connected with an activity which is universal and eternal. They are all the more curious in the context they are used. Being a novel set in an industrial area, Coketown, and about people connected with it, Dickens's application of the expressions is deliberate and figurative. The division of the novel in terms of the three clear-cut phases of agricultural activity has the effect of drawing pointed attention to three distinctive stages of the linear progression and of providing a commentary upon each of them. Moreover, by stressing the organic unity of the process, it invites us to view the development as a whole. If there is any treatment of this feature of the novel in any critique of *Hard Times* it has escaped me. This [essay] attempts to find out if the imaginative division made by Dickens has any bearing upon the structure and overall vision of the novelist.

By way of indicating the ground covered in significant criticism of this novel, mention may be made of a few important approaches. In speaking of the motive force behind this novel, F. R. Leavis asserted [in *The Great Tradition*] that ' . . . in *Hard Times* he is for once possessed by a comprehensive vision, one in which the inhumanities of Victorian civilisation are seen as fostered and sanctioned by a hard philosophy, the aggressive formulation of an inhumane spirit.' Stated thus, few critics disagree with Leavis's finding. With regard to *Hard Times,* the presence of 'a comprehensive vision' is readily admitted by most critics. But critical treatment differs in diagnosing the nature of and the emphasis on 'the inhumanities' and consequently, on the 'formulation of the inhumane spirit'. To this may be added the divergence over Dickens's mode of approach and its effect upon readers.

Few today go so far as Edgar Johnson in claiming [in *Charles Dickens*] that the novel expresses 'Dickens's violent hostility to industrial capitalism and its entire scheme of life.' Nor do many critics agree with T. A. Jackson [in *Charles Dickens*] in regarding *Hard Times* as a 'frontal attack upon the ethics of capitalism as represented by the Manchester School.' Such tall claims on Dickens's behalf are rejected by Humphrey House who asserts [in *The Dickens World*]: 'On the question of theory there is no real difference between Dickens and W. R. Greg: he is not in the least a Socialist.' House bases his observation on Dickens's rejection of the Trade Union solution of the dispute. While it is not difficult to see how the particular evil of industrialism came to be regarded as the worst form of inhumanity of the age, other critics have found an even more powerful and pervasive inhumanity in a systematic neutralization of imagination from life in demand of a hard philosophy. As K. J. Fielding says [in *Charles Dickens*], 'That mere fact, or logic, that leaves half of our lives out of account—any method of ruling our conduct or affairs that lacks sympathy, love, and understanding between human beings—is, in the end, not merely sterile, but bitterly destructive of all moral virtues, beauty, and everything that is best.'

Whatever the specific nature of the evil exposed or the cause thereof, there is general agreement about regarding the novel as being under the perfect intellectual control of the novelist. The fact that it was originally serialized may have obliged Dickens to be economical and mindful of its overall structure. By calling it a 'moral fable', F. R. Leavis testifies to its neat structure because intention is insistent enough everywhere in the novel. K. J. Fielding, on the other hand, believes that 'In many ways, even, the story is to be read less as a fable than as a parable, or a tract for the times.' The structural compactness and unity may be equally well believed as being conceived in terms of 'sowing', 'reaping', and 'garnering' as indicated in the plan of contents of the book.

Several interesting aspects of the novel come to light when viewed in terms of the agricultural process. What is being sown, evidently, are ideas in the minds of people in the novel. The outcome of the sowing has to be traced necessarily and this is done in the book entitled 'reaping'. 'Garnering' likewise is intended to work out the net yield.

In the first chapter of Book I Gradgrind outlines his ideal:

> Now, what I want is, Facts. Teach these boys and girls nothing but Facts. Facts alone are wanted in life. Plant nothing else, and root out everything else. You can only form the minds of reasoning animals upon Facts: nothing else will be of any service to them.

The remarks of Gradgrind are intended to instruct the instructors of his Model School. The interesting part of the address is the image of planting and rooting out. Teaching is equated with planting, also of pulling out everything else which are not facts. By a mixture of metaphors, the planting is to be done in the 'minds' of 'reasoning animals'. As Book I progressively reveals, 'facts' it is that are sown in the minds of Bitzer, Tom, Louisa and even Sissy.

Bitzer's demonstration of his prowess in recapitulating facts is indeed formidable. If anyone is likely to illustrate the triumph of the cult of Fact, it is he. The implication of the operation of sowing is no less remarkable, even in relation to others. In the case of Tom and of Louisa, it is of dubious advantage to either. As for Sissy, it must be accounted a complete failure. Even so, there are many minds which are denied the benefit of facts being sown. Stephen Blackpool and Rachael and the disreputable Circus people are a few. They are too old to go to school and in any case they form no part of the experiment. In one sense, however, no one is excluded, not even Gradgrind and Bounderby, Mrs Sparsit and James Harthouse. While applying the agricultural image, Dickens could hardly be unaware of the implication of popular saying, such as 'as you sow, so you reap', or 'Sowing the wind, and reaping the whirlwind'. In either of the senses, facts or no facts, each may be regarded as reaping what each has sown.

It would be an over-simplification to treat the novel as a demonstration of the Fact-Fancy antithesis or of Capital-Labour relation grounded in a hard philosophy of the day. Each character is locked up in a private battle with his own self and a more public one with the outer world. The experience of a lifetime is crystallized in their utterance. Thus Mrs. Gradgrind:

> But there is something—not an Ology at all—that your father has missed, or forgotten.

Nothing in the novel reveals the collapse of the 'system' and the spiritual bankruptcy of the age as the accusation of Louisa:

> How could you give me life, and take from me all the inappreciable things that raise it from the state of conscious death? Where are the graces of my soul? Where are the sentiments of my heart?

And her agonized wail:

> All that I know is your teaching and your philosophy will not save me. Now, father, you have brought me to this. Save me by some other means.

Stephen Blackpool, without the benefit of either the Gradgrind philosophy or the Sleary philosophy, learns from experience: ''Tis a muddle.' Called upon by Bounderby to suggest a solution to the muddle, he can only fall upon the 'identity of interest' recipe of orthodox economists. The very fact that he is cast out both by his fellow workers and by the employer shows his failure to establish his identity with the world. His rejection is the negation by the world, of any transcendent spiritual power behind the material world.

The death of Mrs. Gradgrind, the departure of Stephen and the flight of Louisa are conceived as the outstanding development of Book II—Reaping. They are the first to be cut down as weaklings and failures from the point of view of the given conditions and expected yield. They go down feeling, as their pronouncements indicate, that in the act of living, something has gone wrong either with them or the world around them. The process of reaping, however, spares Tom, Bitzer, Harthouse, and the rest.

Intention, as Leavis says, may be insistent enough everywhere in the novel, but nothing like its full force can be appreciated until the pattern is complete. Book III, which completes the design in Dickens's mind, is appropriately entitled—Garnering. These chapters contain significant statements which have a bearing upon the total meaning and justify the overall agricultural image. Gradgrind's peroration on the planting of facts and rooting out everything else from the minds of reasoning animals in the very first chapter, is put to the test by Dickens upon some of the pupils of the Model School within the framework of the test of life in which sowing, reaping and gleaning go on with many things else.

In operation-gleaning, the wisdom gleaned by Gradgrind ironically reverses his own hard philosophy of facts:

> Some persons hold that there is a wisdom of Head, and that there is a wisdom of the Heart. I have not supposed so; but, as I have said, I mistrust myself now. I have supposed the head to be all-sufficient. It may not be all-sufficient.

Tom's bitter and cynical elucidation of the same philosophy, as applied to his own case, counterpoints his father's lifelong stand:

> So many people are employed in situations of trust; so many people, out of so many, will be dishonest. I have heard you talk, of its being a law. How can I help laws? You have comforted others with such things, father. Comfort yourself.

Of this kind of wisdom Bitzer's is the deadliest:

> . . . but I am sure you know that the whole social system is a question of self-interest. What you must always appeal to, is a person's self-interest. It's your only hold. We are so constituted.

Such is the harvest gleaned from the planting of facts in

Book I—Sowing. But the fact that Dickens does not confine himself to the demonstration of the experiment with facts but lets many others who get involved articulate their philosophy also, suggests that the novel's structure, in its entirety, with all the characters, is conceived in the image of a full-scale agricultural operation. It is this aspect of the novel which gives it its larger dimension. Thus, even James Harthouse who was to be nothing more than the wicked aristocratic villain, once cynically admitted, 'I am not a moral sort of fellow.' While accepting defeat, he remains unregenerate to the end, as he says,

> I cannot say that I have any sanguine expectation of ever becoming a moral sort of fellow, or that I have any belief in any moral sort of fellow whatever.

Even Mrs. Sparsit, of the Coriolanian nose, is given leave to speak her mind for once. An undoubted caricature of the humbled gentry by Dickens, she endears herself permanently by her estimate of that 'bully of humility'—Bounderby:

> Nothing that a noodle does, can awaken surprise or indignation; the proceedings of a noodle can only inspire contempt.

Accurate or not, such a description assuages our outraged sense of decency in spite of the exaggeration and inaccuracy. Much of Stephen's dying speech and Sleary's moralizing could be mistaken for and dismissed, and rightly so, as sheer Dickensian and Victorian sentimentality. But one portion of the latter's speech, better even than the one approvingly quoted by Leavis, is,

> Don't be croth with uth poor vagabondth. People mutht be amused. They can't be alwayth a-learning, nor yet they can't be alwayth a-working, they an't made for it. You mutht have uth, Thquire. Do the withe thing and the kind thing too, and make the betht of uth; not the wurtht!

The sentiment is not particularly profound, but it is common sense. It takes all sorts to make the world. Some will be ne'er-do-wells and good-for-nothings by material standards. In fact, there may be something of this in all of us. Consequently, we cannot be serious all the time. We must relax, we must unbend. The best thing to do is to accept this unpalatable truth. This reminder, not to take our ego too seriously, is salutary. It is fatally easy to slip into the mould of a readymade ideal or identity.

Keeping in view the structuring of the novel in terms of the agricultural operations of sowing, reaping, and garnering, it is time to see if it helps us to appreciate the novel any better. 'Dickens's novels,' declares Hillis Miller [in *Charles Dickens*], 'are a transposition into fiction of his assimilative way of living in the real world.' The real world to Dickens is usually the city, Coketown in this instance. Of its numerous people, Dickens has chosen a few through whose efforts to realize themselves, he presents a picture of the world. Like the agricultural operation it has a recurring pattern. The harvest is at all times variable and uncertain, depending upon many factors.

Robert Barnard (essay date 1974)

SOURCE: *"Hard Times,"* in *Imagery and Theme in the Novels of Dickens,* Humanities Press, 1974, pp. 77-90.

[*In the following excerpt, Barnard discusses Dickens's treatment of industrial unrest and his characterizations of Gradgrind and Bounderby in* Hard Times.]

> "I am afraid I shall not be able to get much here."

Dickens's disappointment in the Preston power-loom strike was obvious: the town was quiet, the people mostly sat at home, and there were no hints whatsoever from which he could work up one of his big set-pieces. He would have been much happier, artistically, with something of a more French-revolutionary nature:

> I am in the Bull Hotel, before which some time ago the people assembled supposing the masters to be here, and on demanding to have them out were remonstrated with by the landlady in person. I saw the account in an Italian paper, in which it was stated that 'the populace then environed the Palazzo Bull, until the padrona of the Palazzo heroically appeared at one of the upper windows and addressed them!' One can hardly conceive anything less likely to be represented to an Italian mind by this description, than the old, grubby, smoky, mean, intensely formal red brick house with a narrow gateway and a dingy yard, to which it applies.

One suspects Dickens would have liked to take the Italian view of the incident rather than the English. But he obviously felt there was nothing to be done with industrial action as such: "I have no intention of striking", he wrote to Mrs. Gaskell. The decision changed not only the direction of the plot, but the whole tone and texture of the novel. If Dickens had found what he was hoping to find, [*Hard Times*] would surely have been at once more melodramatic and more "popular". As it is, the emotional key of the novel is low.

In most respects the decision was a fortunate one. At this period Dickens adopted the pusillanimous view that workers had a right to strike but were unwise to use that right, and his presentation would probably have been slanted as well as sensationalised. Dickens knew very little about the Northern industrial scene, and the North and the South are two nations. A brief visit was far from sufficient to understand the industrial worker and the stand he was taking. Again, in such a terse, compact novel the interest could not be widely diffused, and the comparative thinness of the Trade Union side of the novel enabled him to concentrate his attention relentlessly on the Hard Fact men (though even here Butt and Tillotson note that Dickens intended to establish an identity between the Gradgrind view of life and the "dandy", dilettante view, so roundly castigated in *Bleak House,* but was unable to find space for it).

Nevertheless, the discontent of the workers, and their banding together in Trade Unions could not be ignored altogether, and it is in the treatment of these themes that the reader is brought up against the major false note in the book. As many commentators have observed, the professional speaker from a nearby town whom Dickens saw addressing the striking workers during his visit to Preston becomes the Slackbridge of *Hard Times,* with the difference that in Preston the man was received with scant sympathy by the men, and was prevented from stirring up trouble by "the persuasive right hand of the chairman", whereas in *Hard Times* he gets a sympathetic hearing and brings about the ostracisation of Stephen.

The point is not as trivial as it might seem. Of course Dickens is under no obligation to be exact in his reporting; a misrepresentation of detail which allowed the better presentation of a wider truth about the industrial situation would have been understandable. But in this case Dickens makes the change in order to misrepresent the wider situation. Either to placate his middle-class readers, or else because a preconceived plot-line forced the falsification on him, he depicts the workers as intelligent men misled by mischievous agitators—just the very line taken up towards the new Trade Unions by the faint-hearted who baulked at offending either side. Edgar Johnson's heading for his chapter dealing with the writing of *Hard Times*—"The heaviest blow in my power"—is distinctly misleading. Dickens used the phrase in a letter written 16 years before the visit to Preston. As far as the treatment of industrial unrest in this novel is concerned, the "blow" Dickens strikes is a muffled, misdirected one.

The importance of his misrepresentation of the situation is not merely extra-literary, for the falseness of Dickens's approach is quite evident in the text itself:

> As he stood there, trying to quench his fiery face with his drink of water, the comparison between the orator and the crowd of attentive faces turned towards him, was extremely to his disadvantage. Judging him by Nature's evidence, he was above the mass in very little but the stage on which he stood. In many great respects he was essentially below them. He was not so honest, he was not so manly, he was not so good-humoured; he substituted cunning for their simplicity, and passion for their safe solid sense. An ill-made, high-shouldered man, with lowering brows, and his features crushed into an habitually sour expression, he contrasted most unfavorably, even in his mongrel dress, with the great body of his hearers in their plain working clothes. Strange as it always is to consider any assembly in the act of submissively resigning itself to the dreariness of some complacent person, lord or commoner, whom three-fourths of it could, by no human means, raise out of the slough of inanity to their own intellectual level, it was particularly strange, and it was even particularly affecting, to see this crowd of earnest faces, whose honesty in the main no competent observer free from bias could doubt, so agitated by such a leader.

It does indeed appear strange; in fact nothing Dickens says can make it anything but inexplicable. Nor is he helped by the quality of his writing in the Trade Union section of the novel which at times ("no competent observer free from bias") resembles that of a leader-writer defending a distinctly dubious proposition.

The first consequence of making the workers malleable by such hands as Slackbridge is that Dickens's no doubt genuinely admiring descriptions of them and their attitudes no longer ring true. His comment that "age, especially when it strives to be self-reliant and cheerful, finds much consideration among the poor" sounds condescending, where similar tributes to the brick-makers' wives in *Bleak House* seem perfectly natural. Nor can one convincingly laud the intelligence of men who are persuaded by the eloquence of a windbag to persecute an admirable and unfortunate fellow-worker. And the second consequence is that, if he devalues and disowns the Trade Union movement, he is forced to look elsewhere for a panacea, since this is a novel which cries out for some sort of positive statement—seems, in fact, almost to have presented itself to Dickens as the means of bringing his testimony on the subject to the public's notice. And thus he is forced into the drivelling fatuity of Stephen's "'dyin prayer that aw th'world may on'y coom toogether more, an' get a better unnerstan'in o' one another'". Stated so baldly this message would be feeble in any industrial novel. In one that includes Bounderby it is patently ludicrous. Is it suggested that the "honest", "manly" and "good-humoured" workers should sort out their troubles amiably by getting together with this hectoring, lying bully? As far as the Trade Union section is concerned, this novel refutes its own thesis.

But in the parts of the novel concerning the Hard Fact men Dickens is much more at home. If the scenes involving Stephen and Rachael seem thinly written, superior padding, the Gradgrind-Bounderby scenes are hard-hitting and rich in layer upon layer of implication. The first impression these scenes give is of a powerful imagination holding itself in, of an almost painful discipline being exercised over an unruly creative urge. The descriptions of character are brief, forceful; the "key-notes" of the various sections are struck with admirable directness. Most of the chapters begin succinctly, even brutally: "Thomas Gradgrind, Sir. A man of realities. A man of facts and calculations"; or "The Gradgrind party wanted assistance in cutting the throats of the Graces." What would be matter for a page in Dickens's normal style is compressed to a three or four line paragraph in the new, telegraphic style necessary for the short episodes of a weekly serial:

> Mr. James Harthouse began to think it would be a new sensation, if the face which changed so beautifully for the whelp, would change for him.

or

> I entertain a weak idea that the English people are as hard-worked as any people upon whom the sun shines. I acknowledge to this ridiculous idiosyncrasy, as a reason why I would give them a little more play.

The idea that Dickens is a writer incapable of artistic self-control is a discredited one; no novel proves its untruth so well as this one. The letters of the time and the notes for the novel testify to the severity of the discipline which he kept himself under, but the reader also senses that he is consciously trying not to squeeze out entirely the exuberance and fluency of his mature style—hence the occasional latitude he allows himself in the depiction of, for example, the circus people and Bounderby.

Dickens's use of imagery in *Hard Times* is similarly spare, similarly effective. In the larger novels the aspects which acquire in the course of the novel symbolic overtones—be they weather, landscapes, buildings or whatever—are thoroughly, hauntingly established early on, and then subjected to elaboration and modification as the book progresses. The significance of the symbol, and the ramifications of that significance are gradually opened up to the reader; the emotional and intellectual effects that Dickens aims at are cumulative. No such technique was possible for *Hard Times*. There is nothing in this novel comparable to the prison in *Dorrit* or the river in *Our Mutual Friend*. Here Dickens's method is to strike a keynote, then remind the reader of it by constant repetition. For example, the key-note Coketown is struck in Chapter 5 in three pages which suggest, with a wealth of illustrative example, emotional and imaginative repression, uniformity, spiritual death. The key features of the physical description are the "interminable serpents of smoke" from the chimneys and the piston of the steam-engine which looked like "the head of an elephant in a state of melancholy madness". Later, in Chapter 10, we are told that from the express trains the lights in the factories made them look like fairy palaces. Whenever we need to be reminded of the emotional stagnation inherent in the Coketown system later in the book, Dickens simply mentions the serpent, the elephant and the fairy palaces, normally with no alteration or elaboration, none of the extravagances one might expect from him, given such material. Never has he made his points so economically.

A similar self-discipline is evident in the use of the staircase image, symbol of Louisa's gradual slipping into an adulterous relationship with Harthouse. It is first foreshadowed in Chapter 7 of Book II, where Dickens mentions Louisa going "step by step, onward and downward, towards some end, yet so gradually, that she believed herself to remain motionless." Later we hear that she has fallen into a confidential alliance with Harthouse "by degrees so fine that she could not retrace them if she tried." By this time the image, and its usefulness in depicting a process which he himself had not space to trace in detail was clear to Dickens, and he decided to present the image as an authorial gift to Mrs. Sparsit:

> Now, Mrs. Sparsit was not a poetical woman; but she took an idea in the nature of an allegorical fancy, into her head. Much watching of Louisa, and much consequent observation of her impenetrable demeanour, which keenly whetted and sharpened Mrs. Sparsit's edge, must have given her as it were a lift, in the way of inspiration. She erected in her mind a mighty Staircase, with a dark pit of shame and ruin at the bottom; and down those stairs, from day to day and

hour to hour, she saw Louisa coming.

From this point on Mrs. Sparsit becomes suitably single-minded in her idea until the moment when, she believes, Louisa "falls from the lowermost stair, and is swallowed up in the gulf". In the author's hand this image would have needed considerable elaboration and expansion; without that it would have seemed too rigid and unsympathetic as a symbol of the downward course of an unhappily married woman, desperately seizing the chance of a love she has never had, and would have suggested a too conventional moral judgement of her actions. As a figment of Mrs. Sparsit's imagination, however, it is perfect, and further develops the woman's combination of prurient curiosity and dreary respectability.

Hard Times is a reaffirmation of belief in fancy. Its targets are not Utilitarianism or Political Economy, but some aspects of Utilitarianism, some results of Political Economy. The book is aimed, in fact, at all the tendencies of the age to repress the free creative imagination of men, to stifle their individuality, to make them cogs in a machine—mere numbers in a classroom, or "hands" without bodies or minds. That Dickens was unfair to the Utilitarians, and in particular to their achievements in the great national cinder-heap, is only important if we agree with House that Gradgrind is satirised as an "intellectual", that Dickens was taking on a philosophy. If this were true, then we might agree that he "did not understand enough of any philosophy even to be able to guy it successfully." But Utilitarianism plays the same role in Gradgrind's mind as, say, religion in Mrs. Clennam's: it acts as a formidable prop to traits of character which were formed quite independently of it. Just as religion was not a part of Dickens's early conception of Mrs. Clennam, so one can imagine Gradgrind without the overlay of Utilitarianism, and still see him as a significant and relevant comment on his age. Dickens's target was not a philosophy but a frame of mind, and a very nineteenth-century frame of mind. It is not often noted that much of what he says about Gradgrind and the education of his children repeats in almost identical terms what he had recently said about Grandfather Smallweed and the education of his grandchildren, who "never owned a doll, never heard of Cinderella, never played at any game" and "could as soon play at leap-frog, or at cricket, as change into a cricket or a frog". It was inevitable that he should be thought at the time to be "taking on" the political economists, but he is in fact only concerned with certain of their attitudes which he regarded as symptomatic of attitudes generally current at the time. His message was little more than "we must not neglect the imagination"—a familiar one from Dickens, but an extremely timely one.

Inevitably in a novel with such a theme mathematical and mechanical imagery plays a large part. In many superb, ironical phrases Dickens salutes mechanised, dehumanised man in his mechanised, de-naturised environment. For example Gradgrind's house is a "calculated, cast up, balanced, and proved house", with a "lawn and garden and an infant avenue, all ruled straight like a botanical account-book". Gradgrind's judgement of human beings and relationships, which is the core of the novel's message, is similarly mathematical, though faced with the extraordinary grace and vitality of a Sissy Jupe he has to admit that "there was something in this girl which could hardly be set forth in a tabular form". "Gradgrind himself is a "galvanizing apparatus" and life at Stone Lodge—like life in the Clennam household, which practises a similar repression of emotion and imagination—goes "monotonously round like a piece of machinery". The "mechanical art and mystery of educating the reason" is served in his school by a master who is one of a hundred and forty "lately turned at the same time, in the same factory, on the same principles, like so many pianoforte legs". Time is the "great manufacturer" and, in a series of images in Chapter 14, turns out a number of human products, varying in their satisfactoriness. In this environment, love—or rather courtship—wears a "manufacturing aspect": "love was made on these occasions in the form of bracelets". All is profit and loss, input and output. Mass production extends to people: "thousands upon thousands . . . aw leading the like lives", says Stephen, as usual a mouthpiece for the author, with the masters "'rating 'em as so much Power, and reg'latin 'em as if they was figures in a soom, or machines'".

And yet fancy, rigorously excluded by the front door, pushes its way brazenly in at the back. Butt and Tillotson note the intrusion of fancy through Bounderby's assumption of low origins and Mrs. Sparsit's assumption of gentility. Even more insistent is the imagery of the novel, with its constant reference to fables, fairy tales, and the stuff of childhood and adolescent reading. Everything that was lacking in the upbringing of Louisa and Tom is present in Dickens's treatment of their story, and the Hard Fact men, who sternly outlaw fancy and emotion from their lives, become, paradoxically, the stuff of fairytales—mere ogres. Dickens makes the point very explicitly early on:

> Almost as soon as they could run alone, they had been made to run to the lecture-room. The first object with which they had an association, or of which they had a remembrance, was a large black board with a dry Ogre chalking ghastly white figures on it.

> Not that they knew, by name or nature, anything about an Ogre. Fact forbid! I only use the word to express a monster in a lecturing castle, with Heaven knows how many heads manipulated into one, taking childhood captive, and dragging it into gloomy statistical dens by the hair.

And of course here and later he goes on to emphasise the imaginative deprivation of the young Gradgrinds, cut off—like the appalling young Smallweeds—from nursery rhymes, fairy tales, and the usual nourishers of childhood fancy.

But fancy has its revenge, and Coketown and its inhabitants are covered with a patina of myth and fable. Stephen, for example, betakes himself at one point to "the red brick castle of the giant Bounderby." Mrs. Sparsit, whose classical features are of the "Coriolanian style", is surrounded by Roman references drawn from the sort of story once considered suitable for schoolboy reading. She goes down to meet Mr. Harthouse "in the manner of a Roman matron going outside the city walls to treat with an invading general"; as she takes tea with Bounderby she "rather looked as if her classical countenance were invoking the infernal gods"; her position in that gentleman's household is that of "captive Princess" in attendance on his car in state-processions. Inevitably, after her drenching during the pursuit of Louisa, she is compared to a classical ruin. Not particularly fanciful herself, Mrs. Sparsit is the source of fancifulness in Dickens, and is rich in a number of other imaginative comparisons of a fabulous nature: she is a griffin, she is the "Bank Dragon keeping watch over the treasures of the mine" (though she thinks of herself as the Bank Fairy), she trails Louisa "like Robinson Crusoe in his ambuscade against the savages". Similarly Coketown, as well as being full of fairy palaces, is "red and black like the painted face of a savage". The more repulsively unimaginative the subject, the more exotic and fantastic the imagery Dickens lavishes on it, always with rich comic effect. Mr. Bounderby, for example, is a "Venus . . . risen out of the mud"; by banging his hat he becomes an oriental dancer who eventually puts her tambourine on her head. Indeed, his own description of the aspirations of the Coketown hands—"to be set up in a coach and six, and to be fed on turtle soup and venison, with a gold spoon" is drawn from the world of childish fantasy, reminding one of the young Pip's lies about Miss Havisham. Thus in all these ways Dickens drives home his message that the irrational and life-giving world of fancy cannot be suppressed, *will* be heard; as Sleary says to Gradgrind: "You *mutht* have uth, Thquire . . . make the betht of uth; not the wurtht.'"

The fancy is not the only quality that is suppressed in Coketown and has its revenge by devious means. Religion too is perverted and slighted, yet emerges fitfully as one of the few forces that can save men from the living death which is Coketown. Dickens's religion, as it shows itself in this novel, is the same uncomplicated, unintellectual religion of good works and the heart's affections which it always had been. He is moved by the story of the Good Samaritan and the Woman Taken in Adultery more than by any Christian doctrine, however vital and central the theologians might judge it. But if he never goes beyond the "common stock of Christian phrases" which House notes as being all he has at his command, he uses it with telling force, for he sees the Political Economists as erecting a new religion, full of doctrine and empty of love. He can hardly mention the views of the "hard Fact tribe" without tacking on an ironical religious phrase to emphasise the barrenness of their philosophy:

> The M'Choakumchild school was all fact, and the school of design was all fact, and the relations between master and man were all fact, and everything was fact between the lying-in hospital and the cemetery, and what you couldn't state in figures, or show to be purchaseable in the cheapest market and saleable in the dearest, was not, and never should be, world without end, Amen.

One senses in all the religious references the desperation of one who sees the comfortable and comforting faith which he has taken for granted all his life, and which he has believed to be the natural religion of mankind in general, being extinguished all around and being replaced by something brutal and materialistic. The masters in Coketown take up a god-like stance, rule with "a sort of Divine Right", and the Gradgrind party regale their "disciples" with "little mouldy rations of political economy". Faith, Hope and Charity, the cornerstones of his faith, are being ground in the "dusty little mills" of the Political Economists; existence is becoming a "bargain across a counter" and "if we didn't get to Heaven that way, it was not a politico-economical place, and we had no business there." In similar vein Mr. Gradgrind, at the moment when his daughter is about to burst in upon him to confront him with the terrible consequences of his system, is writing in his room what Dickens conjectures to be a study proving that the Good Samaritan was a bad political economist. For Bitzer, that superbly mechanised product of the system, the "whole duty of man" can be calculated as a matter of profit and loss, and when Mr. Gradgrind becomes an M.P., he is described as the Member for

> . . . ounce weights and measures, one of the representatives of the multiplication table, one of the deaf honourable gentlemen, dumb honourable gentlemen, blind honourable gentlemen, lame honourable gentlemen, dead honourable gentlemen, to every other consideration. Else wherefore live we in a Christian land, eighteen hundred and odd years after our Master?

And if the masters deny the Christian message, or twist it to their own ends, the Union leaders do the same. It is perhaps a sign of the shaky balance which Dickens saw it as his mission to maintain that this should be so. Slackbridge is a slightly more secular Chadband, and what Dickens christens "the gospel according to Slackbridge" contains frequent references to Judas Iscariot, the serpent in the garden and the "God-like race" of workers. Slackbridge always talks of himself in terms of a Miltonic God punishing our first fathers: "I hurled him out from amongst us: an object for the undying finger of scorn to point at . . . etc." It is characteristic of Dickens that Stephen should answer him with a reference to the Good Samaritan. Dickens rather frequently uses the God of the New Testament to shame the God of the Old.

For in spite of perversions and suppressions, Dickens's religion of the heart does manage to establish itself as a yardstick by which the newer, harsher creeds are measured and found wanting. Partly, of course, it makes itself felt in this novel through Stephen, and this is unfortunate. Dickens establishes, from the moment the keynote Coketown is struck, that whoever belongs to the eighteen religious denominations which had established chapels like "pious warehouses" in Coketown, "the labouring people did not". Stephen, therefore, is untypical of his class not merely in the promise he made to Rachael not to join a Union (that inexplicable promise which she didn't want him to make and apparently doesn't insist that he keep)

but also in his conviction that "'the heavens is over me ahint the smoke'". He is, as Leavis observes, a white man's nigger, and it is a measure of Dickens's lack of confidence in his power to handle the subject of the industrial worker that he has to remove Stephen so far from the average or typical before he can consider it appropriate to demand sympathy for him from the reader. The laboured allegory of his end in the "Old Hell" shaft, squeezed so dry of all emotional impact by the dreary, obvious moralising as Stephen approaches the "God of the poor", is feeble beyond belief, and one feels that it required considerable audacity on Dickens's part to write such a scene shortly after complaining about Mrs. Gaskell's characters, that he wished they would be "a little firmer on their legs." Stephen's fall down Old Hell Shaft and his long wait for hearers for his dying words amount to wanton and sadistic sentimentality. He is butchered in order to bring home to the masters and men a wholly inadequate—indeed a thoroughly false—moral.

Nevertheless, not even Stephen's blankness as a character and wrongness as a representative can totally rob his words of their force. It is wonderful how Dickens, in this brief novel, makes his moral equations almost mathematically precise but still generally manages to make them convincing. Stephen accuses his work-mates of being like the Levite who ignored the man who fell among thieves ("'if I was a lyin parisht i' th' road, yo'd feel it right to pass me by, as a forrenner and stranger'" just as Mr. Gradgrind had proved to himself that the Good Samaritan was a bad economist. At the end of the book Gradgrind's appeal to Bitzer for compassion and that young machine's reply recall, but without seeming pat or unconvincing, Sissy Jupe's version of the first principle of Political Economy: "To do unto others as I would that they should do unto me." Sissy's quotation is the stuff of which Dickens's homely, kindly religion was made, as is Rachael's "'Let him who is without sin among you cast the first stone at her!'" Totally unmystical, generous, practical, tinged with sentimentality yet capable of rising to extraordinary insights. It is not always realised how closely interwoven into his thought and range of reference the Bible and its message are. It comes to his mind almost automatically when he is confronted by the brutality and materialism of his age. The philosophy of the toady Pockets, the commercial arrogance of Dombey, the greed that Merdle plays on, the stifling in children of fancy in favour of fact—the immediate response to all these is to use, or to pervert ironically, the Bible, to emphasise the shabbiness and selfishness of the proceedings. "Murdering the Innocents" is the title of the chapter which deals with Gradgrind's school.

And the third irrational force which the Philosophers fail to suppress is, of course, passion, the affections—that love which is the basis of Dickens's philosophy of life—as well as the more dangerous and destructive expressions of the sexual instinct. The whole direction of the novel is an exposition of this failure, and though this theme is dealt with less frankly and less exhaustively than the related suppression of "fancy", the crime of the attempt is clearly, in Dickens's eyes, as heavy.

In no one is the suppression completely successful. Mr. Gradgrind himself may not be conscious of any gap in his life, any dissatisfaction with the pale transparency of a wife whom he married because she was "most satisfactory as a question of figures", but he unconsciously seeks a compensation through his love for his daughter, a love which he disastrously fails to disentangle from the figures and percentages which preoccupy his conscious mind. Even Bitzer, that triumphant product of the system, on one occasion is found relieving his irrational impulses by tormenting Sissy Jupe. Though in Coketown "Nature was as strongly bricked out as killing airs and gases were bricked in", we have a sense throughout this novel of an uneasy, deceptive calm, of suppressed forces which are in danger of becoming, by that very suppression, perverted and destructive forces.

The images Dickens uses to suggest these unused powers are related to fire and water. The fires of Coketown are mirrored in the fires of Louisa's nature, where, unobserved by her father, there is "a light with nothing to rest upon, a fire with nothing to burn". In the striking scene—obviously prefiguring the similar ones in **Our Mutual Friend** involving Lizzie Hexam and Charlie—when Tom first explicitly suggests that Louisa might use her sexual hold over Bounderby to his, Tom's, advantage, she gazes into the fire, thinking her "unmanageable thoughts". When Tom leaves her after a later scene, she stands at the door gazing out over the lurid lights from the fires at Coketown and trying to establish their relationship to "her own fire within the house". All the suppressions involved in the Coketown system are related. Fire is the image she herself uses in that extraordinary and suggestive moment during the crucial interview with her father over the Bounderby proposal, he uneasily fingering his paper-knife, she gazing with a restlessness she herself only half understands over the tall chimneys of Coketown: "'There seems to be nothing there but languid and monotonous smoke. Yet when the night comes, Fire bursts out, father!'" The image is further developed when, later in the book, Dickens has to describe Louisa's resentment at Sissy Jupe's pity for her. The fire which has been suppressed is now all the more likely to rage destructively:

> A dull anger that she should be seen in her distress, and that the involuntary look she had so resented should come to this fulfilment, smouldered within her like an unwholesome fire. All closely imprisoned forces rend and destroy. The air that would be healthful to the earth, the water that would enrich it, the heat that would ripen it, tear it when caged up.

The frequent use of water imagery and one powerful scene involving water have a similar purpose, but the instincts suggested by the comparison are deeper, gentler, more fruitful. In Coketown the factual and the superficial are relentlessly cultivated at the expense of the irrational, subconscious forces, but nevertheless Dickens has to suggest the depths of a nature like Louisa's, unplumbed, neglected, unaroused though they are. Of course, he only has to suggest, for there is nothing in Coketown that will ever be able to bring them to the surface:

> To be sure, the better and profounder part of her character was not within his [Harthouse's] scope of perception; for in natures, as in seas, depth answers unto depth.

For all his love and genuine desire to do right her father entirely fails to understand her nature—he has merely been "gauging fathomless deeps with his little mean excise-rod." The whole process of education for Louisa has been nothing more than "the drying up of every spring and fountain in her young heart as it gushed out." Dickens never develops the conventional image of life as a voyage—as he does in other novels—but phrases associated with such an image come naturally to his mind when he considers the waste of Louisa's life, and the perilous suppression of her best feelings. "It is the drifting icebergs setting with any current anywhere, that wreck the ships" he notes of Harthouse. In the desperate scenes with her father when she confronts him with the consequences of his system, she is described as "cast away"—for "she had suffered the wreck of her whole life upon the rock". Her descent down the staircase towards adultery is "like a weight in deep water, to the black gulf at the bottom". The powerful and suggestive scene between Tom and Harthouse, where Tom plucks to pieces rose-buds and scatters them onto the lake below is, in its level of suggestion, too subtle and complex to respond readily to analysis, but clearly it suggests among other things the wanton sacrifice not only of Louisa's virginity but also of her whole life on the altar of Tom's selfishness. In its feeling of waste and constraint the whole scene is a brilliant epitome of the book as a whole.

David Craig (essay date 1974)

SOURCE: "*Hard Times* and the Condition of England," in *The Real Foundations: Literature and Social Change,* Oxford University Press, Inc. 1974, pp. 109-31.

[In the following essay, Craig details Dickens's use of cultural and popular elements in Hard Times.*]*

Dickens's flair for expressing matters of common concern *in their own style* shows in the very title of the novel in which, for once, he dealt with the average life of his time. Most of the twenty-five possible titles for **Hard Times** and the fourteen he short-listed suggest, usually by a cliché or a pun, the theme of human life ground down by calculation and routine: for example, 'According to Cocker', 'Prove It', 'Hard Times', 'Hard Heads and Soft Hearts', 'A Mere Question of Figures'. 'Hard Times' stands out in that it was the phrase which came most naturally, when weariness or hardship had to be voiced, to the people with whom the novel is concerned: the men, women and children whose lives were being transformed by the industrial revolution. It is very much a vernacular phrase, common in folk songs especially between 1820 and 1865 but not in pamphlets, speeches, or the papers, however popular or radical. 'Hard times' (or 'tickle times', 'weary times', 'bad times') usually meant a period, often a slump, when scanty food and low wages or unemployment bore particularly hard. Much less often it could mean the more pervasive state in which people felt that the essential and permanent conditions of their lives hemmed them in inflexibly, as in the refrain of a song from the knitting mills of South Carolina around 1890:

> Every morning just at five,
> Gotta get up, dead or alive.
> It's hard times in the mill, my love,
> Hard times in the mill.
>
> Every morning just at six,
> Don't that old bell make you sick?
> It's hard times in the mill, my love,
> Hard times in the mill. . . .
>
> Ain't it enough to break your heart?
> Have to work all day and at night it's dark.
> It's hard times in the mill, my love,
> Hard times in the mill.

The rightness of Dickens's judgement lay in his seizing on the popular phrase and using it for a novel which is not about a time of special neediness but rather about a kind of bondage to routine and calculation so integral to the culture of industrial societies that much of it is still with us.

Both theme and title, then, are typical at once of Dickens's fellow-feeling for the mass of people and of his flair for sharpening the topical to a pitch of memorable art. His novels in general, and *Hard Times* more than any other, are so saturated in the habits, social forms, and events of his own age, and enter so directly into its struggles, that we can best understand why such works appeared at just that juncture if we consider the trends in his own development and in English literature as a whole that had led up to the situation at mid-century. Dickens himself was notable for not drawing much on the art-literature that came before him. He delighted in and owed much to the hearty comedians among eighteenth-century novelists, especially Smollett, but it is at least as relevant to note that he began his career as a reporter, writing against time on breathless journeys around the country from one political meeting to another; that he was famous among the journalists in the gallery of the House of Commons, where he reported for seven years, for the extraordinary speed and fullness of his reports; that his first wish artistically was to act at Covent Garden because 'I believed I had a strong perception of character and oddity, and a natural power of reproducing in my own person what I observed in others'; and that his first novel, *Pickwick Papers*, began as the letterpress for a series of 'cockney sporting-prints' issued in monthly parts. He thus differs in kind from Jane Austen, who carried on from Johnson and Sheridan, and George Eliot, who carried on from Jane Austen and Dickens. Dickens raised an established form, the novel, to new levels by fusing all manner of popular elements and new cultural media, and this is typical of how an art grows at a time of rapid, drastic social change, when artists must take in and digest the startling new experiences, assailing them from all sides, which the con-

ventional art of the time finds it hard to cope with.

Dickens also arrives after a prolonged lull or barren phase in British writing. By 1824 Shelley, Keats, and Byron are dead, and Wordsworth's powers have failed him; Jane Austen dies in 1817, Maria Edgeworth publishes nothing of interest after 1812, and Scott's best vein is quite done by 1824. The Twenties and Thirties are thus, in literature, a flat calm, stirred only by the faint ripples of Tennyson's first books; and when energy returns to literature it is in the form of an urgent concern with what came to be called the 'Condition-of-England question'. From about 1838 Dickens is brusquely modernising the novel, driven by his sense of the topical, his consuming fascination with his own times. His modernity is extraordinary: how many people faced with these words—'plain to the dark eyes of her mind, as the electric wires which ruled a colossal strip of music-paper out of the evening sky were plain to the dark eyes of her body'—would place it in the 1850s? Yet it is from *Hard Times*. Clearly the 'accident' of Dickens's individual genius is crucial in modernising fiction at that juncture, just as the 'accidental' deaths of those leading Romantic poets were crucial in causing the lull. Yet the lull also corresponds with what contemporaries called the Thirty Years' Peace (from 1815 to 1848), and what ends the lull is the upheaval that includes the outcry against the New Poor Law of 1834 (an ingredient in *Oliver Twist*), the Chartist campaign from 1838 onwards (an ingredient in Disraeli's *Sybil*), and the Year of Revolutions, 1848 (an ingredient in the radicalism of Elizabeth Gaskell and George Eliot). Altogether it is as though our [English] culture (including folk song, political parties, and trade unions as well as the main arts) had been cudgelling its brains for ways of dealing with the new life—life dominated by the industrial system—and had now found what was needed.

The historical image of this period—the breakneck growth of the railways, the congested towns and great oblong mills swarming across Lancashire—is so familiar that we can't pretend to keep it out of our minds as we read *Hard Times*. Equally, it would be wrong—a failure to drink in what Dickens offers—if the novel were allowed to trail after that history, used merely to attach a few picturesque personifications and episodes to a body of material we *think we already know*. But it would be another kind of missed opportunity not to use the novel as a source of insights into a specific phase in that long train of social experience which has brought us to where we are. Dickens himself was writing with this purpose—to incite thought and help mould attitudes to burning problems; and *Hard Times* is 'about' a specific time, the Forties, whereas others even of his most social novels tend either to satirise types that could have been found at many a time (e.g. the stony-hearted businessman in *Dombey and Son*) or else to draw historical elements freely from several different times (as in *Bleak House*). In *Hard Times* Dickens was striving to articulate the parts of a civilization, with a minimum of flights down fanciful by-ways, and with an insistence on the typical and even the average which suited the industrial and mass aspects of that age. It was the age in which cities like the original of Coketown multiplied by three within a lifetime and Britain 'changed over from a rural to an urban civilization' inside two generations. It happened fast enough to cause actual bewilderment. We can read in the diary of a man who must have been very much like Stephen Blackpool how when he set out on Good Friday 1860 to walk through his native parts of twenty-eight years before—the industrial villages around the eastern side of Manchester—he found that 'everything was changed':

> Villages have grown into large towns, and country places where there was nothing but fields are now covered with streets, and villages and large factories and workshops everywhere. I made enquiries [at] many a place after people who had lived there, but they were either dead or gone to America or gone somewhere else. I only saw one woman whom I knew, but she did not know me and would not believe me when I told her I was very tired.

Again, from the Black Country comes a song with the refrain 'I can't find Brummagem'. Once, this sense of being literally lost in the new surroundings would have been confined to London with its uniquely fast development in the eighteenth century. Now it was widespread. According to the Census taken three years before *Hard Times* was written, of the 3,336,000 adults living in London and 61 other English and Welsh towns, little over one-third had been born in the town where they now lived.

Of course many things could be made of such material. But one broad approach that we can now see, from its frequent occurrence, to have been positively enjoined upon artists by the life of those times is a radical or humane concern with hard conditions, a vehement desire to bring home to public opinion, in terms both compassionate and warning, that it was *not tolerable* that the ordinary conditions of living for so many should be damaging to physical and psychological well-being or that rich and poor, employers and working people, should live at such different standards and be arrayed against each other in class struggle. This is the 'Condition-of-England question', so named by Carlyle in his essay 'Chartism' of 1839—Carlyle to whom *Hard Times* was dedicated and a quotation from whom was printed on the balance-sheet of the fund collected for unemployed workers during week fourteen of the Preston lock-out which Dickens went to report when gathering copy for the novel.

Dickens had thus found his way to a subject from the heart of industrial civilization quite early in his artistic maturity. It is surely the novels in which social institutions are turned into rich and ramifying dramatic symbols that are in Dickens's *oeuvre* what the tragedies are in Shakespeare's, and the series of these novels starts with *Dombey and Son* in 1846-8. It is a measure of the urgency and directness of Dickens's concern in *Hard Times* that whereas in *Dombey* the business that dominates Dombey's life is scarcely typical of English commercial activity at that stage, and is vaguely specified into the bargain, for *Hard Times* Dickens was so bent on 'getting it right' that he went to Preston (in January 1854) for

material. Much of what he saw there he turned straight into fiction: for example, the 'coldly and bitingly emphatic' master or owner on the train north, who extolled Political Economy and insisted on the total irrelevance of human sympathy to questions of labour or production; or the professional speaker whom Dickens heard at a Sunday meeting of locked-out cotton workers and whom in his article he dubbed 'Gruffshaw'. It must also be said that Dickens had to go and gather copy because he had never known the industrial heartlands at first hand (apart from an occasional visit to relatives in Manchester). Both aspects, his real concern and his comparative inexperience in this field, must be kept in mind when we are pondering the truth of the novel as an image of the life centred on the factory system.

To put it in this way is not to beg the question of whether or not *Hard Times* really is an 'industrial novel'. My opening discussion of its title should already have shown that Dickens's concern entailed his dealing in the same breath, continually, with both the immediate facts of mill-town life and the less direct, the all-pervading *cultural* effects of the new intensive production. The novel is about the ways in which iron conditions were felt to have closed round people's lives. I say 'felt' as though the matter were not clear-cut, for it is a fact that people were often making heavy weather of perfectly convenient new arrangements: for example, Dickens was fascinated by transport, and people tended to grumble about the sheer punctuality and orderliness of the railways compared with the old coaching. Yet many contemporaries were not being captious or just torpidly averse to change when they expressed concern at the condition of England and considered they were beset by unprecedented troubles. Dickens was writing towards the climax of a phase during which, it can now probably be said, the standard of living for large sections of the people fell, as the first manic onset of the industrial revolution took its toll and had not yet yielded its compensating benefits. We have also to remember that encroachments on freedom of behaviour aroused militancy quite as readily as evils like wage-cuts or the price of flour. The many petitions against the enclosing of common and waste ground were only the first of many protests against the process whereby the actual scope or room in which to live was curtailed. Dickens's lifetime saw the beginning of the end for the old cottage industry. The family which in the time of, say, Defoe had carded, spun, and woven, washed and bleached as a team was now scattered from home out into the mills, there to be knit together again as a class no longer based on blood-ties—the Hands of Bounderby and Gradgrind. Instead of work following the rhythms of close personal relations— work until the piece was finished, a journey to sell it, and then perhaps a long week-end until the money was finished—now the men, women, and children must submit to a rigid time-table laid down by a management avid that every minute should be worked to the full. Experience narrowed. The surroundings of the work and the work itself were the same day in day out. Where once a man might have had several jobs—for example, the German iron miners who wore their furnace-skins of white calf's hide while haymaking in their own meadows, now each person was likely to work at one job only and his sole means of livelihood was the sale of his power to work at that job.

The point is not that the quality of life deteriorated in some absolute way: so general a matter is impossible to decide for or against, and even if one breaks it down into seemingly verifiable parts, it turns out that, for example, the notorious horrors of the early factories were parallelled by the physically vile conditions in which many handloom weavers worked at home. The point for *Hard Times* is that people had become less a law unto themselves, the stuff of their lives less variegated, and it is this sense of lives clamped under a grid that haunts Dickens throughout his work, whether he is writing about imprisonment itself or about the more impalpable sorts of bondage that are the theme of *Hard Times*. In such matters it is necessary to hear the testimony of the people who lived at the point of change: for example, the following verse from a song about the transition to powered weaving (staple industry of Coketown), written by the Gorton weaver John Grimshaw:

> So, come all you cotton-weavers, you must rise
> up very soon,
> For you must work in factories from morning
> until noon:
> You mustn't walk in your gardens for two or
> three hours a-day.
> For you must stand at their command, and keep
> your shuttles in play.

Grimshaw was a notable songster, but singing was precisely what the mill-owner felt obliged to forbid in case it interfered with production. The handloom weaver had either talked or sung while he worked: 'When not talking he would be humming or singing snatches of some old ballad.' And in a weaving-shop before steam came in, 'let only break forth the healthy and vigorous chorus "A man's a man for a' that", the fagged weaver brightens up. His very shuttle skytes boldly along, and clatters through in faithful time to the tune of his merrier shopmates!' By mid-century this was forbidden: in mill after mill placards were up with such rules as 'Any person leaving their work and found Talking with any other work-people shall be fined 2d. for each offence', and similarly for 'Talking with any one out of their own Ally', or 6d. (the equivalent of £1 today in terms of real wages) for 'talking to another, whistling, or singing'. Here is the policing and hemming-in of the human being that moved Dickens to his reiterated message, put into Sleary's mouth in *Hard Times:* '"People mutht be amuthed. They can't be alwayth a learning, nor yet they can't be alwayth a working, they an't made for it."' In *Hard Times* the rigid system that cages people in is located squarely in or rather is seen actually to consist of the mill-town itself, especially in that passage from Chapter 5 that sets the keynote or fixes the image of the dominant scene:

> It was a town of red brick or of brick that would have
> been red if the smoke and ashes had allowed it. . . .
> It was a town of machinery and tall chimneys, out of

which interminable serpents of smoke trailed themselves for ever. . . . It had a black canal in it, and a river that ran purple with ill-smelling dye. . . . It contained several large streets all very like one another, and many small streets still more like one another, inhabited by people equally like one another . . .

In face of this insistence on a specific real location, it seems wilful to rarefy the novel's theme along metaphysical lines: 'Coketown with its troubles is merely the purgatory in which individuals suffer.' What Dickens is intent upon is a specific society which had become unbearable for historical (and therefore remediable) causes.

In stressing the directness of the links between the novel and mill-town life, one is not somehow missing or coarsening its thematic subtlety. Certainly Dickens did not intend an 'industrial novel' if by that one means a barely-fictive report on troubles in, say, Manchester or Sheffield: for example, he decided against depicting a strike. This led to disappointment among early reviewers who evidently assumed that he should have written a straight industrial piece and not made this aspect 'subordinate and incidental' to the educational aspect. But Dickens was shirking nothing. To be as trenchant as he was about the owners and their pet schools was itself to take sides and declare one's commitment in the matter of the condition of England. Dickens was writing at a time when the periodicals could smell radicalism a mile away, and in the most unlikely places. *Jane Eyre* had been censured for 'moral Jacobinism' and anti-Christian 'murmuring against the comforts of the rich and against the privations of the poor', although I would have thought that Charlotte Brontë had leaned as far back to square with conventional taboos as a remarkable artist well could without sinking herself entirely. Charles Kingsley's *Alton Locke, Tailor and Poet* (1850) had just been given hostile reviews in *The Times, Blackwood's,* the *Edinburgh Review,* and the *Quarterly* for advocating socialism cunningly disguised as Christianity. Philanthropic cotton-masters were warning village institutes about the tendencies implicit in *Mary Barton.* Indeed the trenchancy of Dickens's social criticism now began to jeopardize his reputation, throughout the second half of his career, in the eyes of both the conservative and the go-ahead, from Macaulay with his objection to the 'sullen socialism' of *Hard Times* to an American, Whipple, who considered it childish to oppose 'the established laws of political economy', which he considered on a par with those of the physical universe. It took artistic determination to come as near the heart of the industrial matter as Dickens did, and equally it led to several swerves into evasion as the good-hearted radical novelist strove to come near the truth without committing himself too ruinously.

The stress on schooling is certainly no evasion. This linking of classroom and mill turns out to be one of Dickens's most telling ways of composing his sense of English civilization into a coherent, many-sided image. Both school and town were owned, or at least controlled, by the same men, the masters, some of whom were fanatically eager to try out on the populace the theoretical social systems which they had drawn up on strict Utilitarian principles. Some of the first efforts to redeem the hell of what Mumford calls the 'insensate industrial town' went into restoring the common land in the form of parks, beginning with Dickens's Coketown, Preston, in 1833-5. But the spirit of the movement was distinctly Gradgrind. The park at Derby, for instance, was 'tastefully laid out in grass intersected by broad gravel walks, and planted with a great variety of trees, shrubs, and flowers botanically arranged'—admission free on Sunday *except* during hours of church service, or 6d. (equivalent to £1 now) on weekdays. Here was what the Hands got in place of the two- and three-hundred acre commons on which townsfolk a generation before had run races, played at knur and spell, or courted among the bushes. Again and again the trouble with the 'utilitarian economists and Commissioners of Fact' satirized by Dickens is not so much their basic aims as the detailed arrangements they thought necessary to achieve them—the fanatical tidy-mindedness which had so little sense of the freedom, the room for free movement, that we need as organic, sentient beings. Under the Poor Law of 1834, which was engineered by Edwin Chadwick (former secretary to the founder of Utilitarianism, Jeremy Bentham), a destitute man could get no poor-relief unless he entered a workhouse (and more than a quarter of a million had done so by the Forties). To discourage people of low moral fibre from succumbing to the lure of an easy life, Chadwick and company worked out 'a discipline so severe and repulsive as to make them a terror to the poor': 'minute and regular observance of routine', for example silence during meals; confiscation of all personal possessions; total separation of men and women; and separation of husbands and wives, if still fertile, partly to make easier *'the requisite classification'* (my italics). And all this was grafted onto the economic system favoured by the Utilitarians—*laissez-faire,* which in its tendency to produce uncontrolled slumps might have been designed to turn able-bodied and industrious workmen into paupers. Dickens was never more surely in touch with rightful popular feeling then when, in this particular novel, he made rigid systematism the centre of his target rather than the more glaring sorts of material evil. In the words of a contemporary, the attempt to apply the New Poor Law 'did more to sour the hearts of the labouring population than did the privations consequent on all the actual poverty of the land'.

Why did Dickens dwell so much on the educational forms taken by the new fanaticism? Partly because it was there, among the young, that one could see most strikingly how the still plastic human being was forced into an iron mould; partly because the schooling systems favoured by go-ahead cotton masters were themselves like living satires on Utilitarianism in practice, even before Dickens had recreated them in the mode of satire. The Gradgrind model school with its regimen of pure fact is in no way an allegory or symbol of what a cult of fact would run to if carried to an extreme. It has been suggested that what Dickens is really getting at is the Victorian fascination with compendiums, encyclopedias, statistical accounts, etc., and that Bitzer's 'definition of a horse' owes something to what could be found in publications like Charles Knight's *Store of Knowledge.*

The fact is that the first two chapters of the novel are an almost straight copy of the teaching system in schools run by the two societies for educating the poor. In the Manchester Lancasterian School a thousand children were taught in one huge room, controlled by a kind of military drill with monitors and a monitor-general, and taught by methods derived from the Catechism. Groups of facts, mechanically classified, were drummed in by methods that might have been meant to squash forever the children's urge to find out or understand anything for themselves:

> A lesson on natural history would be given thus. The boys would read: 'Ruminating Animals. Cud-chewing or ruminating animals form the *eighth* order. These, with the exception of the camel, have no cutting teeth in the upper jaw, but their place is supplied with a hard pad. In the lower jaw there are eight cutters; the tearers, in general, are absent, so that there is a vacant space between the cutters and grinders. The latter are very broad, and are kept rough and fit for grinding the vegetable food on which these animals live, by the enamel being disposed in crescent-shaped ridges . . . '

> MONITOR. What have you been reading about?
> BOY.   Ruminating animals.
> MONITOR. Another name for ruminating?
> BOY.   Cud-chewing.
> MONITOR. What is the root of the word?
> BOY.   'Rumen', the cud . . .
> MONITOR. You read in the lesson *the enamel is disposed in crescent*
>   *shaped ridges.* What is the enamel?
> BOY.   The hard, shining part of the tooth.
> MONITOR. What part of our tooth is it?
> BOY.   The covering of that part that is out of the jawbone.
> MONITOR. What do you mean by disposed?
> BOY.   Placed.
> MONITOR. The root?
> BOY.   'Pono', I place . . .

> (*Bleak Age*)

This of course is precisely Bitzer's '"Quadruped, Graminivorous. Forty teeth, namely twenty-four grinders"', and so on. It only remains to add that the inventor of this system, Joseph Lancaster (a Quaker), claimed to have 'invented, under the blessing of Divine Providence, a new and mechanical system of education', and that the inventor of a similar rival system, Andrew Bell (an Anglican), called his 'the STEAM ENGINE of the MORAL WORLD'. Given this kind of thing Dickens had no need to invent: the satire was already there in life, and not on some lunatic fringe but in a widespread, dominant, and much-admired system. (On grounds of authenticity alone, apart from deeper considerations, this aspect has not lost its relevance. I was present, as teacher, in a class in a Scottish city school in 1959 when one of Her Majesty's Inspectors spent twenty minutes trying to get the boys to define a table. As he was about to leave, he turned and asked them to repeat the hard-won definition. None of them could remember it.)

Dickens was not seizing on a very unusually glaring or ludicrous part of the culture and making more of it than it signified. There were the closest links between heartless schooling and worse than heartless factory discipline. One of the worst sides of the early factories was the hours and conditions of work for very young children. It turns out that some of the atrocious punishments added to the already draconic routine were copied from Lancaster:

> Lancaster worked out an elaborate code of rewards and punishments among which was 'the log', a piece of wood weighing four to six pounds, which was fixed to the neck of the child guilty of his (or her) first talking offence. On the least motion one way or another the log operated as a dead weight on the neck. Needham [owner of a cotton mill in the Peak district of Derbyshire] clearly tried to copy this progressive idea of the age. More serious offences found their appropriate punishment in the Lancasterian code; handcuffs, the 'caravan', pillory and stocks, and 'the cage'. The latter was a sack or basket in which more serious offenders were suspended from the ceiling. Needham clearly borrowed this idea, too, though his children are alleged to have been suspended by their arms over the machines.

That will not surprise anyone aware of what the factory system was like in its early days. But few, I think have realized that schools too went in for that kind of inhuman forcing. Lancaster laid down that classroom offenders should walk backwards round the room with the yoke of wood on their necks, and a child who was kept in was tied to his desk to save the expense of keeping a teacher on to supervise him. 'What impressed the governing classes was the orderliness that prevailed.'

If Dickens had been topical only, instead of topical, far-sighted, and profound, he might have concentrated on specific abuses: for example, physical hardships that could quite easily be remedied. The Nottingham spinners whose bones were deformed, joints inflamed, and limbs ulcerated with long hours standing at the machine were presently given chairs to sit on, the thousand children stupefied by the Lancasterian drill were curtained off in 'classrooms' of fifty each (on the advice of a Utilitarian). But hardship was not the only trouble and might not even be the case: in the Preston cotton mills themselves, according to the inspecting surgeon, health was generally better than among the other townsfolk. Dickens was concerned rather to question the intrinsic nature of industrial organisation in which the worker has nothing to do but mind a machine, with no variety of work or psychological outlet in the form of some say in the running of the concern, and in which productivity is pursued at the expense of the human satisfaction it is supposed to serve. The industrial image that haunts ***Hard Times*** is of machinery that runs itself, as though without the volition of the human beings it nevertheless compels to attend it:

> Time went on in Coketown like its own machinery: so much material wrought up, so much fuel consumed, so many powers worn out, so much money made . . . the piston of the steam-engine worked monotonously up

and down like the head of an elephant in a state of melancholy madness . . . all the melancholy-mad elephants, polished and oiled up for the day's monotony, were at their heavy exercise again . . . no temperature made the melancholy-mad elephants more mad or more sane. Their wearisome heads went up and down at the same rate, in hot weather and cold, wet weather and dry, fair weather and foul. The measured motion of their shadows on the walls was the substitute Coketown had to show for the shadows of rustling woods; while, for the summer hum of insects, it could offer, all the year round, from the dawn of Monday to the night of Saturday, the whirr of shafts and wheels.

The complement to the machines are the workers—whole humans reduced to Hands:

> A race who would have found more favour with some people, if Providence had seen fit to make them only hands, or, like the lower creatures of the seashore, only hands and stomachs. . . . A special contrast, as every man was in the forest of looms where Stephen worked, to the crashing, smashing, tearing piece of mechanism at which he laboured. . . . So many hundred Hands to this Mill; so many hundred horse Steam Power.

This compound insight is in the classic line of labour analysis: in literature, from Blake and Dickens through Robert Tressell to Alan Sillitoe; in discussion, from Cobbett and Hodgskin, Engels and Marx, Ruskin and Morris, through Kropotkin to the Workers' Control and Work Enlargement movements at the present time. Engels puts the thing with characteristic lucidity: factory work 'is, as the manufacturers say, very "light", and precisely by reason of its lightness, more enervating than any other. The operatives *have little to do'* (my italics). Marx rises to images of industrialism whose scalding force and richness of physical evocation draw, it seems to me, on Carlyle and Dickens as well as on his own genius. In 1829 Carlyle wrote in 'Signs of the Times': 'On every hand, the living artisan is driven from his workshop, to make room for a speedier, inanimate one. The shuttle drops from the fingers of the weaver, and falls into iron fingers that ply it faster.' (Note the impersonal passive there.) We have seen what Dickens wrote in 1854. In 1867 Marx wrote in the first volume of *Capital:*

> [Manufacture] seizes labour-power by its very roots. It converts the labourer into a crippled monstrosity, by forcing his detail dexterity at the expense of a world of productive capabilities and instincts; just as in the States of La Plata they butcher a whole beast for the sake of his hide or his tallow. Not only is the detail work distributed to the different individuals, but the individual himself is made the automatic motor of a fractional operation, and the absurd fable of Menenius Agrippa, which makes a man a mere fragment of his own body, becomes realized. . . . Here we have, in the place of the isolated machine, a mechanical monster whose body fills whole factories, and whose demon power, at first veiled under the slow and measured motion of his giant limbs, at length breaks out into the

fast and furious whirl of his countless working organs.

This, in its sheer openness to the newly released energies, its sense of their mingled enormity and potency, is akin to passage after passage in Dickens where he evokes the pace, the swarming detail, and the potentiality for good and ill of his age.

Given this deep and manifold rootedness of *Hard Times* in its age, it may seem less presumptuous to offer to assess the truth of its image of the life that centred on the factory system. This can be done, so long as we approach through the kind of art that is there in the novel; for presumably if there is a flaw in the *truth* of its image, this will show as failure or uncertainty in the art. I take it that something like the following would be generally acceptable as an account of how the novel works: By creating motifs and *personae* distinguished by a few bold, vivid, and repeated traits, far-flung and complex forces are organised into one homogeneous 'fable'. This simplifying mode is no doubt something that must be 'accepted', by which I really mean that we may well have to take it as a mixed blessing, something which, after all, is clearly a condition of the vitality—the trenchant social attack, the whole-hearted humour, and the graphic presentation—of Dickens's kind of art. It is surely a less repressible impatience that we feel with the outstanding weakness in the novel: that is, the Stephen Blackpool part, the mixture of sentimentality and melodrama in the giving of his life and his unacceptability as representative worker (the sole representative apart from Rachael, and she is only a female replica of him). The question is whether this element—which could be written off as the usual Victorian tear-jerking, obligatory and easy to disregard—flaws the truth of the total image of life centred on the factory system.

Presumably there is no need to show in detail that Stephen and Rachael are too good to be true and that their sufferings are exploited for maudlin purposes. It is the more insidious aspects of Stephen's role that call in question Dickens's managing of the political aspect. Saddling Stephen with a monstrous drunken spouse is in keeping with that Victorian way of martyring the hero or heroine (compare Janet's husband in George Eliot's 'Janet's Repentance' or Rochester's wife in *Jane Eyre*). But the special effect here is to isolate Stephen as much as possible from his work-fellows, and this is geared to the trade-union theme through a decision not to subscribe to the union regulations which is so flimsily motivated that no credible or even intelligible account of it ever comes out. Stephen's reasons are meant to be given in two speeches from Chapters 4 and 6 of Book II: '"I ha' my reasons—mine, yo see—for being hindered; not on'y now, but awlus—awlus—life long!"', and Louisa's statement and question to Rachael, which is never answered: '"He fell into suspicion with his fellow-weavers, because he had made a promise not to be one of them. . . . Might I ask you why he made it?"' This blur makes us begin to think that Dickens is not even implying an adverse judgement of trade-unionism but is sliding out of dealing with it at all. Stephen, by being singled out as a lonely martyr, has been made easy to pity; the well-to-do reader could take

his part without being drawn for a moment into discomfiting thoughts of a whole martyred *class*. The figure of Slackbridge completes the unsatisfactoriness: his foaming rhetoric is done with splendid *brio,* but his extravagant denunciation of a highly personal decision is not credible, and his only other appearance is when he is trotted on (in Book III, Chapter 4) purely to abuse Stephen again, on the occasion of Bounderby's poster offering a reward for his arrest.

This part of the novel is thus peculiarly shaky; and its upshot is to imply that working-class militancy and working-class decency are mutually exclusive. On this [F.R.] Leavis comments [in his *The Great Tradition,* 1948] that 'when Dickens comes to the Trade Unions his understanding of the world he offers to deal with betrays a marked limitation. . . . Trade Unionism [is shown] as nothing better than the pardonable error of the misguided and oppressed, and, as such, an agent in the martyrdom of the good working man.' To leave it at that, however, and to insist that 'Dickens's understanding of Victorian civilisation is adequate for his purpose; the justice and penetration of his criticism are unaffected' is to postpone the disturbing question: how could Dickens have felt free to travesty so important a movement? That it is a travesty, a mere echo of popular and stubborn misconceptions, is easily proved: [Humphrey] House shows it in some useful pages of *The Dickens World,* and we know that much the commonest kinds of union meeting were not to hound individuals but to decide when and where to put in wage claims, to hear information and messages of support from other branches or unions, to hand out strike pay, and the like. Indeed what Dickens wrote from Preston makes it sound as though it was partly his disappointment at finding the town in so uninflamed a state that led him both to make little of the union aspect and to graft on some extraneous excitement when he did present it. But the damage done to the novel is, in my view, minimised if one sees it as a failure of sociological accuracy. For one thing, does an artist have quite this obligation to known facts? True, he will fail to arouse our deepest interest if he diverges wildly from, while plainly basing himself on, a familiar state of affairs. But may he not hit off a *general* type—for example, the huffing-and-puffing sort of demagogue—while colouring in only enough topical detail to make the *persona* come alive? The main problem is more subtle, and leads to deep-rooted factors in Dickens's view of social life. Let us rephrase the question already put and ask: why did Dickens pick *that* side of his theme for his exhibition of Virtue and Pathos? Or (to take the matter beyond guesswork and into the realm of verifiability): were there really no possibilities or makings, in the area from which Dickens got his material, for an image of industrial man as *fully human though sore-pressed?*

This area was Preston in the winter of 1853-4. The city was a heartland of radicalism: it so happened that all male townspeople had the vote and it therefore attracted one radical leader after another to fight the constituency. Great numbers had welcomed Cobbett when he fought an election there in 1826, and Henry Hunt, the 'matchless orator' was its M.P. (thus breaking a virtually feudal monopoly of the seat) from 1830-32. The Preston employers had long been known for their opposition to unions and as late as 1860 it was said that 'increases in wages are sometimes granted elsewhere, in Preston never'. Four strikers had been shot dead by troops in 1842. 1853 was, nationally, a year of intensive labour activity which won wage rises and shortened working hours, and in June there started what became 'by far the biggest industrial struggle in the cotton trade since the general "turn out" of 1842'. The power-loom weavers asked the employers to restore a 10 per cent wage cut enforced in 1847 on the weaving of all fabrics. Most of the masters refused even to meet the workers' representatives, and many of them were fired. To support these men and further the wage claim, unions were re-formed and at some mills strikes were started. The Masters' Association of Preston locked out their workers from September, declared they would not re-employ them unless they renounced trade-union membership, and launched prosecutions against the union leaders to help break the strike (the charges were then dropped). To help the workless, funds were raised in many places (including London) by specially-formed Trades' Committees, which are presumably what Dickens is getting at under the gratuitously pompous coinage 'United Aggregate Tribunal'. As late as April, three weeks after *Hard Times* began to run as a serial, strikes were still breaking out all over mid-Lancashire, at Wigan, Burnley, Bacup, Padiham.

The reader of Dickens (as of most well-known treatments of Victorian working-class life with the exception of Elizabeth Gaskell's *North and South*) would imagine that the workers who were putting up this struggle and going through this ordeal were a wretched, sullen lot, cowed by factory and city life unless they were inflamed by trouble-makers from outside. The first-hand reports of behaviour and morale show that the prevailing tone was one of resilience, self-reliance, solidarity. In a town where between twenty and thirty thousand had been workless for twenty-three weeks, the spirit of meetings was good-humoured determination. When delegates from the (left-wing) Labour Parliament asked to be heard, the weaver chairman would say that money or constructive comment were welcome but not '"politics and differences among us when what we want is 'armony, brotherly love, and concord"'. When a professional speaker got up and began in exactly Slackbridge's 'O my friends' vein to denounce plots involving a neighbouring town's alleged failure to contribute, 'the persuasive right hand of the chairman' fell gently on the man's shoulder and at once stopped him. Yet in his novel Dickens conveys that organised labour was so much self-deceiving agitation, which in passing squashed the rights of individuals, and that its platforms were hogged by mere politicoes. He knew that it was not so, for the above eye-witness account is his own, from his article 'On Strike'.

Notice that my point is not the question of simple truth to life but rather the question as to whether the essential springs of humanness were failing under industrial conditions. In that key Coketown passage early in the novel, Dickens writes that the 'many small streets still more like

another' were 'inhabited by people equally like one another', and this, taken with his treatment of the Horse-riders, suggests that it is only among the travelling people, the rovers from outside settled and disciplined society, that the full humanness of spontaneity, togetherness, wholehearted fun, and tenderness can still thrive. It turns out (again from Dickens's own account and also from many other sources) that the Preston spinners and weavers had a whole culture, and a traditional and rooted culture, of fun and imagination and common effort, which they kept up in the heart of, and indeed adapted to, the industrial struggle. 'Behind the chairman,' at the Preston meeting, 'was a great crown on the top of a pole, made of parti-coloured calico, and strongly suggestive of May-day.' Comic poems were written to drum up contributions to the unemployed fund, people contributed under playful nicknames ('The chirping blacksmith, six pence'), and humour was used especially to prod laggards into paying up. On the handbills we read:

> If that fiddler at Uncle Tom's Cabin blowing room does not pay, Punch will set his legs straight.

> If that drawer at card side and those two slubbers do not pay, Punch will say something about their bustles . . . .

> If squinting Jack of Goodairs does not pay up in future, Punch will stand on his corns.

> If those piecers at Dawson's new mill do not pay better, young Punch (old Punch's urchin) will come and break their ends . . .

> If that young spark, Ben D., that works at Baxter's Mill does not pay to his trade, Punch will tell about him eating that rhubarb pudding that was boiled in a dirty night cap.

> If Roger does not pay, Punch will tell about her robbing the donkey of its breakfast to stuff her bustle with.

When we come upon the first bits of circus slang in Chapters 5 and 6 of *Hard Times,* we quicken at once, after the bullying formalities and dry precisian assertions of the Gradgrind set. Plainly the author himself is enjoying the quirky idiom of Sleary's troupe (and we also notice that Bounderby is affronted by its outlandishness). The perspective of the novel would have been transformed, and brought still nearer to the real currents of life under industrial conditions, if Dickens had been able to allow that there were kindred things to enjoy and an unquenched capacity for enjoyment at the heart of Coketown. The more we find out what actually happened at that time, the more we realise that militancy was a lifeline—a well-spring of hope, a channel for popular energies, as well as an indispensable lever—amidst the direst conditions. Preston at Hunt's election in December 1830: the radicals, "in a high state of exaltation', paraded the streets with 'music, flambeaux, a lighted tar-barrel and three flags, one of them tri-coloured'. Glasgow during the Reform campaign of 1831: 'The whole people in that place and in the adjoining towns walked in procession into the Green, divided into their crafts, societies, villages, and parishes, with colours and emblems . . . with about 500 flags and 200 bands of music.' Leeds at the start of Chartism in 1838: 'At the demonstrations the Moor [Hartshead Moor, then called Peep Green] was like a fair, with huts erected for the sale of food and drink, and wives and families accompanying their menfolk. From Bradford, Huddersfield, Halifax, Dewsbury, and other towns in the West Riding the delegates marched in formation—often several thousands strong—with banners flying and bands playing.' But the Preston high spirits in 1854 are all the more impressive for bubbling up, after that long workless winter, on occasions that were not special or stirring.

The relevance for *Hard Times* can be put in two ways. We may say that Dickens excelled when satirising the employers' habit of discrediting every rightful demand of the Hands (as in that ludicrous recurring image of Bounderby's about 'turtle soup and venison, with a gold spoon') but tended to waver into the sentimental or unconvincing when obliged to focus on the Hands either as private people or as a class liable to take social initiatives. Or we may go further and say that it was *not possible* to write well when taking the line that militancy was a kind of aberration. On this crucial issue he repeatedly veils radical indecision under a kind of fair-mindedness typical of the gentleman of his time (or the liberal today) who sees much too clearly to deny clamant injustice but cannot commit himself to any course of action that might end it. When Dickens assures us that 'these men [the Coketown workers], through their very delusions, showed great qualities' even when they 'went astray' by combining, or that 'every man felt his only hope to be in his allying himself to the comrades by whom he was surrounded; and that in this belief, right or wrong (unhappily wrong then), the whole of that crowd were gravely, deeply, faithfully in earnest', he is speaking with a usual voice of the middle class. It is the voice of Elizabeth Gaskell in chapter 3 of *Mary Barton,* blaming John Barton's bitterness at the death of his starving child partly on 'those who, either in speech or in print, find it their interest to cherish such feelings in the working class', and of *The Times* leader on Peterloo which generously condoled with those massacred in spite of the folly of the 'half employed and half starved' in letting themselves get 'puffed up by prodigious notions of their strength, and inflamed by artful pictures of their grievances'. Indeed it turns out that the notion of politics as an imported disease, with its implication that, left to themselves, masters and men would live in harmony, was precisely the line of the Bounderbys—the Preston cotton masters. In their manifesto of 15 September 1853 they deplored the 'designing and irresponsible body' who were interfering 'with the relation between master and servant' and creating 'where it does not exist . . . a feeling of dissatisfaction and estrangement'.

Dickens, it seems, repeatedly leans to the mass of the people, then draws back, because to commit himself would have been to wake up from the dream of harmony between classes. His criticism of a desperately harsh and unequal society is weakened to make it less uncomfort- able, whether to himself or to the reader, and Stephen's latent function turns out to be to suggest that the right way to take the inevitable suffering is with dignified restraint, and alone. His dying words about the murderous condition of the mines are at once given the cast of something to be wished or prayed for rather than struggled about by his still later plea (clearly a message from the author) that '"aw th' world may on'y coom together more"'. In specific situations this could only mean that the mill workers should give up their struggle, with its hard-won momentum and solidarity, in favour of arbitration (the suggestion that ends 'On Strike'), or that they should give up politics—the 'froth' and 'unsound counsel called the People's Charter'—in favour of agitation on practical matters like clean streets and cholera epidemics, all of which would somehow give rise to good government and 'a better understanding between the two great divisions of society'. Do not the first-hand records of militant activity—the songs, memoirs, and union documents—show that so much spirit, so rich a human nature, flowed into struggle that to pooh-pooh it or opt out of it by setting up some ideal above the battle was to risk one's art going soft and blurred? In taking for his subject the very core of industrial civilisation—its consequences for people's upbringing, feelings and relationships, and life's work—Dickens had set himself the most exacting test of ability to see truly. In the struggle to live humanly, the working people were exerting every kind of intelligence, courage, and elasticity, the masters were blocking, curbing and denying their humanness at point after point. In such a situation all are stultified, and Dickens embodies this most memorably in Louisa and her relationship—the lack of it—with her father. But more was needed, and if one tried to imagine the great industrial novel that never did get written, one might suggest that the masters cried out to be satirised, the mass of the people to be presented with clear-eyed realism. In so far as Dickens fails in the latter, his novel sags; in so far as he excels in the former, it succeeds, and thereby earns the currency which has made 'Coketown' the classic name for the early industrial city.

Joseph Butwin (essay date 1977)

SOURCE: *"Hard Times:* The News and the Novel," in *Nineteenth-Century Fiction,* Vol. 32, No. 1, June, 1977, pp. 166-87.

[*In the following essay, Butwin examines* Hard Times *as a novel of social reform and compares it with social-reform journalism of the period.*]

Modern criticism tends to judge the novel that aims at social reform by standards that are appropriate to another kind of novel. This tendency is typified by Virginia Woolf's rejection of the novels of Arnold Bennett, H. G. Wells, and John Galsworthy according to standards that she derives from the novels of Laurence Sterne and Jane Austen:

What odd books they are! Sometimes I wonder if we

are right to call them books at all. For they leave one with so strange a feeling of incompleteness and dissatisfaction. In order to complete them it seems necessary to do something—to join a society, or, more desperately, to write a cheque. That done, the restlessness is laid, the book finished; it can be put upon the shelf, and need never be read again. But with the work of other novelists it is different. *Tristram Shandy* or *Pride and Prejudice* is complete in itself; it is self-contained; it leaves one with no desire to do anything, except indeed to read the book again, and to understand it better. . . . But the Edwardians were never interested in character in itself; or in the book in itself. They were interested in something outside. Their books, then, were incomplete as books, and required that the reader should finish them, actively and practically, for himself.

Woolf acknowledges two kinds of fiction; if we continue to judge one by the standards of the other, then her dissatisfaction is justified. But if we trace the novel of social reform back to its mid-Victorian practitioners, we find a literature that certainly deserves to be studied in its own terms and according to the special demands that it made on its original audience. Readers of **Hard Times** were asked to turn their attention away from the novel. Dickens's valediction in the last paragraph of the novel makes this intention clear: "Dear reader! It rests with you and me, whether, in our two fields of action, similar things shall be or not. Let them be!" He sets out to initiate "action" in a reader who is seen as something other than just a reader of novels. The novel of social reform completes itself outside the novel in a multitude of acts that may include the joining of societies and the writing of checks. It is also likely to include *further* reading as opposed to *re*reading. In the case of **Hard Times** the original readers were encouraged to see the novel as a form of journalism to be read continuously with *Household Words,* the weekly magazine in which it appeared. The novel of social reform exists in a continuum with journalism and defines its audience within the general public rather than among the community of "ideal readers" of fiction whose response justifies most literary criticism. The concept of an isolated reading public exercising no other function than the perusal of novels merely reflects the isolation of the Flaubertian artist who has become the archetype of the European novelist since Dickens.

Critical study of the novel of social reform must begin with an understanding of its differences. A great deal of the difference lies outside the novel itself within a context established by journalists, in a format congenial to journalism written for an audience that is prepared to see itself as a social force. In this essay I will re-create the journalistic milieu of **Hard Times,** which I take to epitomize the novel of social reform in England. This does not mean that the problems of the novel can be explained away by an outside appeal. On the contrary, **Hard Times** presents certain critical problems which stem precisely from Dickens's understanding of his genre and which I will try to explain in terms appropriate to the genre.

Hard Times was first read by a public which tended to take its newspapers more seriously than its novels. Abundant testimony in the 1850's locates a new source of power in public opinion, and over and over opinion is linked with the press. When novelists set out to enlist public opinion on social issues they generally understood that they were following the lead of the journalists. In an early venture of this kind Dickens follows Oliver Twist into the Magistrate's Court and shifts into the present tense that he reserves for the observation of continuous social abuse in that novel:

> Although the presiding Genii in such an office as this, exercise a summary and arbitrary power over the liberties, the good name, the character, almost the lives, of Her Majesty's subjects, especially of the poorer class; and although, within such walls, enough fantastic tricks are daily played to make the angels blind with weeping; they are closed to the public, save through the medium of the daily press.

Critical reception of novels more strictly given over to social issues in the 1840's indicates that they were being read as something other than novels. The *Edinburgh Review* justified W. R. Greg's long (and largely unfavorable) review of Elizabeth Gaskell's *Mary Barton* with the running head: "*Not to be regarded as a mere Novel.*" Similarly the *Manchester Guardian* (28 February 1849) identified the book as a form of current history or journalism masquerading as a novel: "There are popular works published in the form of novels that depict either important historical events of bygone years, or the passing realities of the present, in such an intense manner that the impression conveyed is stamped more vividly and indelibly on the mind . . . than from the study of history properly so-called." This, of course, is just what the novelists of social reform intended. Greg and the *Guardian* reviewer were protecting the domain of journalism. Both criticized the novel for errors in fact and analysis. The novelists themselves understood that they were entering that domain and in some cases improving upon it. Charles Kingsley praised *Mary Barton* "for the awful facts contained in it." He saw that there are certain functions served by novelistic "facts" that may even surpass the instructive powers of the press. "In spite of blue-books and commissions, in spite of newspaper horrors and parliamentary speeches, Manchester riots and the 10th of April, the mass of higher orders cannot yet be aware of what a workman's home is like in the manufacturing districts." Again, his eye is on facts and their impact on public opinion which he locates among "the higher orders." The interest of this kind of criticism then turns to the distribution of the novel and consequent action on the part of the readership, neither of which has anything to do with the criteria described by Virginia Woolf in her essay on the Edwardians. The reviewer in this case is also a preacher and a publicist and a novelist of social reform. He begins his review of *Mary Barton* with a call to action: "Had we wit and wisdom enough, we would placard its sheets on every wall, and have them read aloud from every pulpit, till a nation, calling itself Christian, began to act upon the awful facts contained in it, not in the present peddling and desultory manner, but with an united energy of shame and repentance proportionate to the hugeness of the evil." Kingsley's own novel, *Yeast,* had just concluded its six-month run in *Fraser's* where the review of *Mary Barton* appeared. By this time the periodical press had become the ideal vehicle for the news and the novel.

Ever since the success of *Pickwick* had allowed Dickens to leave the *Morning Chronicle* in 1836, it had been his ambition to unite the functions of the newspaper and the novel. *Bentley's Miscellany, Master Humphrey's Clock,* and the *Daily News* all failed to satisfy that impulse before 1850 when all of his ideas jelled around a journal of social reform. His earliest intentions for *Household Words* included the idea that it should provide the proper context for novels like *Mary Barton.* Immediately he wrote Gaskell: "There is no living English writer whose aid I would desire to enlist in preference to the authoress of *Mary Barton* (a book that most profoundly affected and impressed me). . . . all will seem to express the general mind and purpose of the journal, which is the raising up of those that are down, and the general improvement of our social condition."

Dickens's public declaration in the "Preliminary Word" to the first number of *Household Words* (30 March 1850) would appear at a glance to have a quite different aim in mind. He celebrates "Fancy" and the "imagination" and promises to reveal the "thousand and one tales" too often obscured by the smoke of the factories and their flaming chimneys. One might ask how the Condition of England is to be improved by the telling of tales. Through the agency of fancy and the imagination a whole class may be able to adopt the experience of another class. In order for the facts of industrial life to take hold they must be bodied forth in a fanciful way. Then something akin to Romantic sympathy may be made to prick the conscience of a class. But this activation of middle-class sympathy is not to be confused with "class consciousness" on the part of the beneficiaries of that sympathy. Dickens knows that this mixture of fact and fancy could become extremely volatile. At the end of his introduction he moves without apparent transition into a denial of revolutionary intention:

> Some tillers of the field into which we now come, have been before us, and some are here whose high usefulness we readily acknowledge, and whose company it is an honour to join. But, there are others here—Bastards of the Mountain, draggled fringe on the Red Cap, Panders to the basest passions of the lowest natures—whose existence is a national reproach. And these, we should consider it our highest service to displace.

The Dickensian impression of the "Red Cap" and the "Mountain" had recently been kindled by events in France. The radical press in England self-consciously followed the French example. Julian Harney called himself "L'ami du peuple" in the *Red Republican,* a weekly journal published from June 1850 to July 1851, and Dickens makes it clear from the start that he is no Harney, certainly no Marat, and that his audience are not *sans-culottes.*

A journal dedicated to "the raising up of those that are down" finds its ideal audience among those who are not down. Dickens's other contribution to the first number of *Household Words* begins with the favorite formula of the middle-class reformer: "As one half of the world is said not to know how the other half lives, so it may be affirmed that the upper half of the world neither knows nor greatly cares how the lower half amuses itself." The article, called "The Amusements of the People," affirms for the lower orders the right that Sleary claims for all people in *Hard Times:* "We believe that these people have a right to be amused." Amusement—in this case vaudeville theater—is also education. For the education of the poor Dickens rejects the "Polytechnic Institution in Regent Street" in favor of the theater because "there is a range of imagination in most of us, which no amount of steam-engines will satisfy." The "amusements" and the instruction of the poor are not served by print. Joe Whelks, as Dickens calls the man of the people, "is not much of a reader, has no great store of books, no very commodious room to read in, no very decided inclination to read, and no power at all of presenting vividly before his mind's eye what he reads about." In other words, he is telling his audience, if you are reading this article you are not a part of "the other half." His audience is thus identified as a reading public to whose amusement and instruction is added the responsibility of reform.

Dickens initiated *Household Words* in 1850 with many of the ideas that would animate the writing of *Hard Times* four years later. The novel represents the principles of the journal as they are stated in its first issue—its belief in the redemptive power of fancy, especially in the industrial milieu, its defense of popular amusement, and its warning not to confuse middle-class reform with demagoguery.

Six months after the conclusion of *Hard Times,* as an introduction to the eleventh volume of *Household Words,* Dickens restates the principles of his journal in a leading article called "That Other Public." The threats of the "Red Cap" have receded and been replaced by the corruption of successful politicians and entrepreneurs. The machinations of both tend to render the public sluggish and recalcitrant on issues of reform. The means of both are essentially the same: they manipulate the press through the contrivance of favorable publicity. During the busy first week of February 1855 when Palmerston was to become Prime Minister, several papers reported that he had hired a few disreputable journalists to convince the American press of his pacific international policy. Without naming names Dickens condemns a politician who would "purchase remote puffery among the most puff-ridden people ever propagated on the face of the earth." Since the time of his visit to the United States in 1841, the American example would bring to Dickens's mind the worst excesses of the press and of the promoters who habitually misuse it. From Palmerston he turns to the unnamed author "of a little book of Memoirs" lately published. The list of impostures shows the subject to be P. T. Barnum:

> Does the "smart" Showman, who makes such a

Mermaid, and makes such a Washington's Nurse, and makes such a Dwarf, and makes such a Singing Angel upon earth, and makes such a fortune, and, above all, makes such a book—does *he* address the free and enlightened Public of the great United States: the Public of State Schools, Liberal Tickets, First-chop Intelligence, and Universal Education? No, no. That other Public is the sharks'-prey.

In many ways Barnum's Dwarf and Angel—Tom Thumb and Jenny Lind—fulfill the needs that Dickens describes in his articles on "The Amusements of the People" and in *Hard Times*. A nation governed by Gradgrinds would seem to need its Barnums. Unfortunately, Barnum asks too high a price. All of his tricks, pranks, and promotions represent the utter perversion of the art that Dickens was cultivating in *Household Words*. Dickens's fictions become Barnum's lies; the public's willingness to absorb fantasy becomes downright credulity. Barnum represents the self-serving publicist whose aim is not to inform but to advertise. In his autobiography Barnum describes the way the press serves the purposes of the entrepreneur:

> Whatever your occupation or calling may be, if it needs support from the public, *advertise* it thoroughly and efficiently, in some shape or other, that will arrest public attention. . . . In this country [the United States], where everybody reads the newspapers, the man must have a thick skull who does not see that these are the cheapest and best mediums through which he can speak to the public, where he is to find his customers. Put on the *appearance* of business, and generally the reality will follow.

Household Words included no commercial advertisement beyond the announcement of its own future publication, the continuation of a serial or the appearance of separate volumes. When a distributor slipped a sheet of advertisement into one of the issues and angry readers complained to the *Times*, Dickens traced the "disgraceful effusion" to its source and reported his findings in a letter to the editor (*Times*, 10 and 20 July 1852). Dickens shared Carlyle's disdain for the new art of advertisement with its seven-foot hats and quack medicines.

The kind of advertisement practiced by Barnum taps what Dickens recognized as a basic human need, the need to be amused. By the time he undertook the editorship of *Household Words* Dickens had begun to interpret the old injunction to amuse and instruct as a mandate for social reform that could be best fulfilled through the medium of journalism. Much of what he writes in *Household Words* amounts to the definition and education of a good, responsive, and politically responsible public that would counter the false appeal of the Barnum breed and establish a firm constituency for the Dickensian enterprise. In *Hard Times* Dickens seeks a public that has been trained to respond to journalism. Various stylistic devices encourage readers to verify and test the fiction outside the novel. When the novel is made to stand alone, its weakness lies in an editorial policy that defers specific issues out of the mouths of novelistic characters and into the

journalistic setting where the middle-class public is encouraged to turn from spurious demagogues and entrepreneurial boosters to the reliable guidance of the journalist.

The installments of *Hard Times* are the only signed articles in *Household Words*. The name "Charles Dickens" appears above each one, and readers are invited to take the novel as the editor's own comment on the "times." Each installment seems to enjoy both the status of a leading article and the special identity of a signed novel inserted into the journal. The reader who meets the novel in the journal comes away with a quite different impression of the meaning of the fiction than the reader of the hardcover volume called *Hard Times for These Times*. In *Household Words* it is simply *Hard Times*. The reader of the journal did not need the expanded title. Every article appeared under the sign of novelty; all was news, all was timely. Having read the installment, the reader continues into other reports, equally timely. Regular readers of *Household Words* might recall an article on the Manchester library, "Manchester Men at Their Books," when in the 22 April 1854 issue they read in *Hard Times* about a library in Coketown; other articles about the London poor or the Preston strike are likely to linger in the mind of the reader of the novel. It is not so much that the reader will transfer knowledge directly from one sphere to another, from fact to fiction and back again, as that he reads with the inclination to do so. Other novels that invoke the facts of historical or contemporary life do not necessarily encourage verification. *Hard Times,* by virtue of its format, does. The fiction leads the reader to the threshold of fact; the threshold is easily crossed within the same journal. The inquisitive reader will go further. Within the text of the novel Dickens encourages these excursions outside the novel. He teases the reader with fictions that retain the latent authority of fact.

The facts of industrial life are bound to represent opinions, and it is Dickens's reluctance to lodge fully developed opinions within the text that renders *Hard Times* incomplete as a novel of social reform. As we shall see, in one significant deletion he takes words out of the mouth of a character, Stephen Blackpool, and lets them live in a series of reports on factory safety that appeared before and after the run of the novel. The reformer who characterizes his enemies as revolutionaries—"Bastards of the Mountain"—cannot let his hero wear a red cap. Deletions and swift allusions send the reader back into the journal and locate the source of social improvement as middle-class opinion guided by a responsible reformer-journalist. The reader is led out of the novel into the journal. This process begins with the substitution of fact for fiction.

Hard Times is generally read as a denigration of "hard facts" but at the same time it may be seen as Dickens's attempt to renew rather than reduce the status of fact. He sets out to reclaim fact from the hands of the statisticians by showing that much of what passes for fact in Coketown is really fiction. A master says "that he would 'sooner pitch his property into the Atlantic'" if he is "not left entirely alone" to do as he pleases with his own. "Another prevalent fiction," says Dickens. Any worker who saves his money can become a master or at least a rich man. "This, again, was among the fictions of Coketown." The by-play of "fact" and "fiction" is especially evident when the novel is read in the journal. An article in *Household Words* calls the image of marital bliss that hides the legal inequality of man and woman "One of our Legal Fictions." On the last page of the article a discreet advertisement announces the appearance of "the SIXTH PORTION of a New Work of Fiction called *Hard Times*." Fiction is a pejorative word only in a world self-consciously governed by fact. Dickens writes in both worlds.

Both as a novelist and a journalist Dickens contrives fictional proper nouns as a masquerade of fact. Outside the novel Dickens resisted any attempts to identify "Coketown." Literal identification would "localize" and therefore narrow the application of the story. But within the text he invites his readers to ask whether or not a real town exists behind the pseudonym: "Stone Lodge was situated on a moor within a mile or two of a great town— called Coketown in the present faithful guide-book," "A mile or two from Coketown" or even "a mile or two from a great town called Coketown" is a defensible fiction. Knowledge of English geography would reveal no Coketown. But phrased as it is, the town invites identification, especially when we remind ourselves that for its first readers the "present faithful guide-book" was *Household Words,* a journal filled with factual descriptions of conditions in real factory towns. The reader is always on the edge of the fact in the installments of *Hard Times*. At any point the author might break through as he does in "One of our Legal Fictions" to say "this is a true story." Charlotte and Robert Desborough (in that article) could be identified. The emergent meaning of the fiction is always validated by the constant possibility of fact. The journalist stands behind the novelist, and the power of the press is brought to bear on a novel whose purpose is "the general improvement of our social condition."

The literal identification of Oldham or Preston or Wigan would mean nothing. Dickens frequently makes his point by making up names. Coketown is more descriptive and evocative than Preston. In "On Strike," which we take to be a factual, journalistic report of a trip to Preston, Dickens meets a nasty (but convenient) antagonist "whom I had already began [sic] to call in my own mind Mr. Snapper, and whom I may as well call by that name here as by any other." Snapper is a straw man; he serves a purpose but he is not a real, historical person. A reader accustomed to modern, "objective" journalism is less prepared to accept Dickens's identification of an obnoxious potential demagogue as "Gruffshaw" when other, reliable reports reveal only a "Grimshaw" among the leaders of the strike. Gruff is a nice replacement for grim. A reader might recognize the hand of the novelist in this anonymous report. A few months earlier, in another article about Preston, a well-known leader of the workers named Cowell is misidentified as Cowler. In this case the change of name is meaningless and a little careless. The author was James Lowe, a journalist who knew Preston well. Lowe corrected himself six years later in his report to the Social Science Association where he names both Cowell and

Grimshaw. When we look back to 1853 and 1854, I think that we can safely say that Lowe just made a mistake, but that Dickens deliberately mixed newsmaking and novel writing in order to gain the best of both in *Household Words*.

Together the techniques of the novelist and the journalist can be made to serve the rhetorical function of persuasion. And yet in a novel that is so harsh on other forms of rhetoric—Slackbridge's oratory, Bounderby's self-aggrandizement, and Sleary's advertisement—Dickens is unable to create a worthy spokesman for the poor. Stephen Blackpool, for one, is almost mute. Thanks to a significant deletion from an early speech, Stephen is barely allowed to give specific designation to the complaint of the factory workers, and thanks to the same deletion we never know why it is that he is unable to join the union. His public declaration leaves questions unanswered: "But I ha' my reasons—mine, yo see—for being hindered; not on'y now, but awlus—awlus—life long!" As it happens, he has made a vow to Rachael, but that vow is hidden in the deleted passage. In chapter 13 Stephen is sitting a night watch over his drunken wife. He very nearly allows her to poison herself with an unprescribed dose of medicine when Rachael wakes up and takes the matter in hand. In the dialogue that follows she alludes to a dead sister whose death is explained by Stephen in a passage that made it through the manuscript into the corrected proofs before it was cancelled:

> "Thou'st spoken o' thy little sister. There agen! Wi' her child arm tore off afore thy face." She turned her head aside, and put her hand [up]. "Where dost thou ever hear or read o' us—the like o' us—as being otherwise than onreasonable and cause o' trouble? Yet think o' that. Government gentlemen come and make's report. Fend off the dangerous machinery, box it off, save life and limb; don't rend and tear human creeturs to bits in a Chris'en country! What follers? Owners sets up their throats, cries out, 'Onreasonable! Inconvenient! Troublesome!' Gets to Secretaries o' States wi' deputations, and nothing's done. When do we get there wi' our deputations, God help us! We are too much int'rested and nat'rally too far wrong t'have a right judgment. Haply we are; but what are they then? I' th' name o' th' muddle in which we are born and live and die, what are they then?" "Let such things be, Stephen. They only lead to hurt, let them be!" "I will, since thou tell'st me so. I will. I pass my promise."

Why delete? Dickens was certainly pressed throughout the writing of *Hard Times* to cut it down to fit twenty short installments, but it is hard to believe that a passage of such brevity and such importance had to be sacrificed for space. It may be that at the last moment he decided that this was simply bad drama, that Rachael's arbitrary prohibition was weaker than Stephen's unexplained mystery.

Let us say that Dickens rids himself of one dramatic gaffe; he also avoids a subtle connection with the rest of the novel and a major statement of a specific industrial complaint coming from a factory worker. At the end of the last chapter four paragraphs describe the future of the survivors. Each ends with a similar refrain: "Such a thing was to be. . . . Such things were to be. . . . Such a thing was never to be. . . . These things were to be." Only the last of these confirms a cheerful future that is dependent on "no fantastic vow, or bond . . . or pledge" but on Sissy's dutiful promotion of "childish lore . . . imaginative graces and delights" among her children. It is then that Dickens in the final paragraph enjoins the reader to promote "similar things. . . . Let them be!" Taken as an affirmation of responsible action, this last "Let them be" is a repudiation of the cynical carelessness of the Harthouse philosophy, "What will be, will be," which is another way of saying "laissez-faire." Stephen calls this policy on the part of the manufacturers "lettin alone." The final allusion to vows and pledges seems to imply a freedom from the unreasonable constraint by which Stephen was bound doubly in promises to Rachael and to his wife. The last "Let them be" is an ironic reflection on Rachael's opposite use of the phrase. In the deleted passage she had said, "Let such things be, Stephen" in a way that means "Let them alone. Desist." The final "Let them be" means "Let them exist. Act in such a way that these lessons will prevail." It is an injunction to action on the part of his readership. Now it may be that Dickens foresaw a problem and was unwilling to allow any ironic reflection on Stephen's promise to Rachael. The uncorrected version could be taken to mean that workers are wrong to "let such things be" in Rachael's sense. When one considers the truth (and simple eloquence) of Stephen's complaint in the deleted passage along with his pathetic fate, the vow that he makes to Rachael can be made to look at least as unfortunate as his marriage vow—to evoke shades of the red cap and the mountain and a kind of working-class activism that Dickens truly means to avoid. If there is to be any political initiative, it is to be taken not by the working class but by the reading class to whom he safely returns responsibility in the last paragraph of the book.

Stephen's complaint on the subject of preventable accidents is not entirely lost to the novel. It is deferred to a highly elliptical passage in his last speech, spoken as he lies dying beside the Old Hell Shaft. Of course, Stephen's physical condition at this point does not allow a developed argument. Stephen reminds Rachael that the Old Hell Shaft has caused many deaths and been the subject of many petitions from the miners unheeded in Parliament. "When it were in work, it killed wi'out need; when 'tis let alone, it kills wi'out need." Stephen's death becomes another industrial accident. Now, to complete his argument, Rachael's little sister is resurrected in a brief allusion which is not likely to have much resonance in a novel in which she has only been mentioned once, two hundred pages or two months earlier not (thanks to the deletion) as an industrial victim but simply as a dead child among the angels. Now her death is explained not as a result of brutal amputation but as a result of "sickly air":

> "Thy little sister, Rachael, thou hast not forgot her. . . .
> Thou know'st . . . how thou didst work for her, seet'n all

> day long in her little chair at thy winder, and how she died, young and misshápen, awlung o' sickly air as had'n no need to be, an' awlung o' working people's miserable homes. A muddle! Aw a muddle!"

The reader jumps from the immediate situation into the question of preventable accidents in the mines and the unwillingness of legislators to act. From there we follow the weak link of Rachael's forgotten sister into conditions in the factories and the cities which, presumably, might also be amended by legislation and enforcement. A reader who has only the novel in hand may well be perplexed.

This digression does not seem to serve the immediate demands of the story of Stephen's attempt to clear himself of guilt or to say a few last words to the woman he loves. As a political prescription this mingling of open pits and petitions, a misshapen sister and miserable homes is somehow incomplete, no more than a "muddle." Dickens certainly does not wish to limit his comment here to a suggestion that unused mine shafts should be fenced off. A reader familiar with contemporary controversy would have heard the description of a man whose life has been "mangled . . . out of him" in an unfenced "shaft" as an allusion to the factory as well as the mine.

The Factory Act of 1844 required the fencing of open shafts that housed dangerous machinery, but inspection had always been inadequate and the owners unwilling to sacrifice the expense necessary for safety. In 1854 and 1855 the inspectors, with support from the Home Secretary and an informed public, began to enforce regulation. As we shall see, articles in *Household Words* contributed to the making of a public policy that would draw the masters out into the open.

The ellipses in Stephen's argument in *Hard Times* can be filled in by further reading in *Household Words*. In the number that included the fourth installment of the novel, an article by Henry Morley called "Ground in the Mill" also appeared (22 April 1854). The article is really an extended statement of the complaint that Dickens would delete from Stephen's speech three weeks later. Within that passage Dickens had inserted a footnote directing the reader back to "Ground in the Mill." Footnotes frequently refer to other articles in *Household Words*. In this case the note was deleted with the passage, and the modern editor assumes that it was done because an "intrusion of this kind of documentation would distract his readers from the realities of his fictional world." As editor of *Household Words* Dickens himself was not intent on maintaining the inviolability of his fictional world. Different political intention rather than the different status of fact and fiction may have prompted Dickens to reduce the association between the opinions of fictional characters and the editorial stance of *Household Words*. Within the novel the specific complaints of the workers are abbreviated, and attention is diverted from the novel to the journal where the editorial voice suggests action on the part of the middle class rather than the working class. An eloquent Stephen would be as unreliable as Slackbridge. Neither Morley nor Dickens advises initiative on the part of the workers; both hold the owners responsible, but neither expects much response from the owners without coercion. The owners speak directly to the Home Secretary through their "deputations." Their victims have no voice but that of their middle-class sympathizers whose effective power resides in public opinion.

In 1854 the reading public was prepared to consider conditions in the factories. The strikers at Preston were just about to give up their long and well-publicized struggle when *Hard Times* began to appear in the April issue of *Household Words*. Soon news from Crimea would seem to drive the Condition of England into oblivion, but journalists remained "to show the evils of that carelessness, which, in great matters and little matters, from Balaklava to the Lancashire coal-pits, is undoubtedly becoming a rather remarkable feature of our national character." If we take the monthly reviews and daily press to be both a gauge and a guide of public opinion, we may measure the relative impact of the novel of social reform and the journal in which it was placed. As we might guess, since Dickens allowed the journal to absorb the most pressing issues related to the industrial theme, it was the journal and not the novel that made itself felt in the press and on the platforms of public debate.

By the mid-1850's a press that was generally hostile to the claims of labor was ready to acknowledge as wholesome the appeal that the new, national unions were making to the court of public opinion. "It is public opinion, and that only which can assist the workmen in the recovery of their 'rights' if any such have been lost. From this all-controlling force manufacturers are no more exempt than any other classes in the kingdom" (*Times,* 2 January 1852). But until the renewal of the debate of the factory acts in 1854 the manufacturers were not inclined to consult public opinion. Strikes could be suppressed quietly, and the strikers' claim to higher wages could never wholly penetrate a community still dominated by the laws of a free and open market. It was the high incidence of preventable accidents in the factories that would fix the attention of middle-class reformers and finally draw the masters into the public arena. Here economic arguments meant less, and the humanitarian argument could hold its own. And in this case legislation and enforcement could be retained as a middle-class enterprise without the necessity of intervention from the beneficiaries. (It was not until 1882 that a working man, J. D. Prior of the Amalgamated Carpenters, was made an Inspector.) Factory safety, the latent basis of Stephen Blackpool's complaint in *Hard Times,* would become the favored crusade of Dickens and Morley in *Household Words*.

All of the emotional appeal of Rachael's little sister "wi' her child arm tore off afore thy face" is released in the first of Morley's articles. He begins the argument of "Ground in the Mill" with little vignettes of children who are caught in moments of play and punished by the machines:

> "Watch me do a trick!" cried such a youth to his fellow, and put his arm familiarly within the arm of the great

iron-hearted chief. *"I'll* show you a trick," gnashed the pitiless monster. A coil of strap fastened his arm to the shaft, and round he went. His leg was cut off, and fell into the room, his arm was broken in three or four places, his ankle was broken, his head was battered; he was not released alive.

Another is "caught as he stood on a stool wickedly looking out of window at the sunlight and the flying clouds." Imprisoned children punished, a taste for freedom and play quelled. No question of circuses here, and, for that matter, no question of polytechnic education. In conclusion Morley describes a factory school (also provided by the Act of 1844) which is flawed by complete carelessness and irregularity rather than by the rigors of the school room in *Hard Times*. The novel describes the price paid by children of the middle class rather than the working class. Rachael's sister is the only factory child mentioned in *Hard Times*. "Ground in the Mill" is dense with examples, and all are true. Twenty-six examples of death and mutilation have almost no statistical force, but they argue strongly when described one by one. Dickens and his writers replace one kind of fact with another, and as journalists they are unrelenting. One can follow the fate of their agitation in the press and what one finds is a public that reads, responds, reacts in decidedly nonliterary ways. This then was the public for the novel as well.

In an article called "Fencing With Humanity," written a year after "Ground in the Mill," Morley describes the campaign mounted by the manufacturers since that time. The Home Secretary has ordered enforcement and "instantly a large number of millowners fly to the platform, deliver and hear angry orations, form deputations, and declare themselves a slaughtered interest." This is Stephen's deleted speech cleansed of dialect: "What follers? Owners sets up their throats, cries out, 'Onreasonable! Inconvenient! Troublesome!' Gets to Secretaries o' States wi' deputations." The novel moves toward a statement that is made in the journal. Together they seek the same public, and in this case the effect can be measured by the response of competitive publicists. "Fencing With Humanity" is dated 14 April 1855, a Saturday. It appeared for sale on the preceding Wednesday (11 April). On the following Tuesday (17 April) a meeting of manufacturers calling themselves The National Association for the Amendment of the Factory Law met in Manchester. They would enlist public opinion which, they recognized, had recently turned against them. *Household Words* was selected by the chairman as an example of the most obvious opposition.

The chairman was the ubiquitous W. R. Greg, and the meeting was given thorough coverage in the next day's *Guardian*. According to Greg, the current troubles of the manufacturers are a result of "the amount of ignorance and prejudice and ill-will towards them on the part of the community-at-large." He produces an example of this ill-will:

> Dickens's *Household Words*—(hear, hear)—a paragraph from which he would read to them, and

which had been very good-naturedly put into the London morning papers only a few days ago. He would read it not merely to give an idea, if proof were necessary, of the ignorance and prejudice existing against them, but because in it were stated facts, partial facts, but still facts, on which were grounded, no doubt, the general feeling against the millowners which pervaded the community, and the abuse which was then lavished upon them as a body.—(hear, hear). (*Manchester Guardian,* 18 April 1855)

After reading an especially unflattering paragraph from Morley's article of the preceding week, Greg launches into his own statistics. The government, he says, finds time to prosecute factory owners for the death of one worker in 70,000 when thanks to its own neglect men are dying in Crimea at the rate of 1000 per week. And more in that vein. Greg is seconded by a Mr. Turner who knows the value of these awesome numbers in the making of public opinion. He only hopes that the chairman's words will "travel throughout the length and breadth of the land, and prove an antidote to the trash, the poison, published on Saturday in *Household Words.*" He attacks "philanthropic writers": "They wished, of course, not only to write works which might create a popularity for themselves, but the publishers of twopenny publications wished to add grist to their mill—and so the one wrote and the other published for the prejudices of the people." Dickens is accused of barnumizing. After receiving support from a speaker with the charmingly Dickensian name of Holdforth, Turner enjoins his fellows to "charge the enemy, and they would soon beat down his ranks."

Four weeks after the meeting in Manchester, Morley responded to the assault on "twopenny publications [written] for the benefit of pseudo-philanthropists." The response, titled "Death's Cyphering-Book," is a fairly faithful record of the transactions at Manchester accompanied by a commentary that clearly bears the mark of Dickens's own repugnance for "arithmetical" calculation of life and death. Greg's statistics were supposed to reduce the threat of unfenced machinery. Through a series of imaginative counterexamples Morley reduces to absurdity "the assumption that arithmetic will ever work out questions of moral right and wrong. By such calculation a man who spends only five minutes out of a long lifetime as a murderer cannot be found guilty, especially when he could have had so many more victims. "Our pseudo-philanthropic readers" are left to decide the question.

However they are labeled, these readers are Dickens's intended audience, a morally responsive middle class whose collective power is embodied in public opinion. In one of his few vocal outbursts, Stephen Blackpool is allowed to aim his attack not at bad working conditions but at bad publicity. Stephen complains to Bounderby:

> "Look how you considers of us, an writes of us, an talks of us, and goes up wi' yor deputations to Secretaries o' State 'bout us, and how yo are awlus right, and how we are awlus wrong, and never had'n no reason in us sin ever we were born."

If Stephen cannot speak for himself—and Dickens says that he cannot—others will. Stephen's speech to Bounderby invites the appearance of a spokesman who never appears in the novel. Whatever was to be said in his behalf as a specific complaint that might require specific reform would be said in the editorial columns of the journal.

When *Hard Times* was published as an independent volume immediately after its conclusion in *Household Words,* it was bound to appear incomplete, even to those readers who came to it with the correct expectation of a novel that would answer pressing social questions. Reviewers in both *Blackwood's* and the *Westminster Review* declared that the public was cheated out of a timely statement on the industrial theme. "The name of the book and the period of its publication alike deluded the public. We anticipated a story . . . of the unfortunate relationship between masters and men which produced the strike of Preston; and this most legitimate subject, at once for public inquiry and for the conciliating and healing hand of genius, to whom both belligerents were brothers, might have well employed the highest powers." Both reviewers are perplexed by the turn to the educational theme which strikes them as fanciful and irrelevant.

Dickens, if he had wished to, could have justified himself by pointing to *Household Words.* Another novelist of social reform would be less inclined to let the reader wander beyond the text. In *North and South,* which began in serial form (2 September 1854) a month after the completion of *Hard Times,* Elizabeth Gaskell reopens the industrial theme with a fully articulate working man, Nicholas Higgins, who reads books and responds to them, who explains the rationale of the strike and who understands the value of "public opinion" and knows how it is to be won. Higgins meets a master, John Thornton, who is stubborn but intelligent and eventually willing to change. Before the novel is over, Higgins and Thornton have begun to reconcile their differences and have embarked on a cooperative enterprise. It may be that *North and South* is too pat, too perfect. In this case Gaskell is less willing than Dickens to recognize that the novel of social reform takes a modest position in the literary and political processes of a world that refuses to perfect itself.

Barbara Hardy (essay date 1977)

SOURCE: "The Late Novels," in *Charles Dickens: The Later Novels,* edited by Ian Scott-Kilvert, Longman Group Limited, 1977, pp. 13-34.

[*In the excerpt below, Hardy examines* Hard Times *as one among several novels in which Dickens chose not to affirm a sure solution to the social problems he addressed.*]

Hard Times, Little Dorrit, A Tale of Two Cities and *Great Expectations* limit their concluding demands on the reader and do not expect us to settle down and see everything and everyone as now prospering after all that pain. The sense of reality begins in *Hard Times* (1854), with a toughening of moral humours in the two chief women characters. Sissy Jupe is a more subdued type of womanly virtue than Esther [in *Bleak House*] and we are asked to concentrate not on Sissy but on Louisa, a close study in moral psychology who also does not task our credulity or our faith. Like Edith Dombey, to whom she is related, Louisa is a case of repressed passion and vision. She sees the highest, but pride, self-contempt and doubt drive her into following the lowest. She perversely represses her capacity for virtue, and tries to act out the utilitarian disregard for feeling which her education has held up as a model. She is also moved by her love for her brother, and does not follow Edith's earlier course of punishing herself and her male aggressors, and is indeed moved by Harthouse (and he by her, and by Sissy) as Edith never is by Carker. Harthouse is a less stagey and a more compressed version of Carker, a study in perverted *ennui* who is a sketch for Eugene Wrayburn. Louisa is also exposed to experience not simply as a victim, like Esther Summerson, but as a susceptible and malleable human being who has a capacity for damnation.

Though the treatment of the working-class characters and industrial problems is sentimental and crass, the virtue of **Hard Times** lies in a new kind of truthfulness about social conditioning of character. We do not find, as in *Bleak House,* the anatomy of destructiveness followed by a small-scale model of construction. The humours of the self-made man *gloriosus,* in Bounderby, and of the convertible Utilitarian, in Gradgrind, are incisive and spirited, very much in the manner of those Jonsonian humours whose very narrowness produces a pressure of vitality. The presentation of the circus with its symbols of pastime, joy and goodhearted sleaziness is effective within the limits of the fable and, in spite of its embarrassing lisping innocence, responds adequately enough to the counter-symbol of the fact-choked and fact-choking schoolroom. The novel lacks a proper adult paradigm for the imaginative and sensual life denied by Gradgrind, but so much of the focus is on the child's education that this passes almost without notice. That it does not escape entirely without notice is perhaps a tribute to the delineation of passion, repression and conflict in Louisa. Dickens cannot really be said to explore her inner life, but he manages very skilfully, as with Dombey, to imply it.

Louisa does not go right down to the bottom of Mrs Sparsit's gloatingly imagined moral staircase, but her redemption is treated with some sternness and there is no falsely triumphant climax. The anatomy of a heartless education and a heartless industrialism, linked by the criterion of efficiency, concludes with no more than a sad and sober appraisal:

> Herself again a wife—a mother—lovingly watchful of her children, ever careful that they should have a childhood of the mind no less than a childhood of the body, as knowing it to be even a more beautiful thing, and a possession, any hoarded scrap of which, is a blessing and happiness to the wisest? Did Louisa see this? Such a thing was never to be.

The last words to the Dear Reader, which recall the end of *The Chimes,* though discussing the possibility of remedy, is free from optimistic flights: 'It rests with you and me, whether, in our two fields of action, similar things shall be or not'. Dickens looks forward to rebirth—in the lives of children still unborn and in deathbed repentance—but he denies Louisa a brave new life; the quiet and almost matter-of-fact language is true to the experience of the novel. His liking for cheers and congratulations at the end is subdued, as he suggests that Louisa's future will be undertaken 'as part of no fantastic vow, or bond, or sisterhood . . . but simply as a duty to be done'. It is particularly satisfying that Dickens avoids the pendulum-swing so grossly offensive in *Bleak House;* he does not offer the language and symbolism of strong feeling and vivid fancy in reaction to the world and values of hard fact. He matches heartless rationality with a rational warmth. The very last words of the novel are placed in a context of age and death: 'We shall sit with lighter bosoms on the hearth, to see the ashes of our fires turn grey and cold.' The image of dying fires is wholly sensitive to Coketown, and remembers its ashes, in contrast to the way that Esther's little 'Bleak House' depended on ignoring the larger bleakness.

Harland S. Nelson (essay date 1981)

SOURCE: "The Meaning of Dickens," in *Charles Dickens,* Twayne Publishers, 1981, pp. 190-209.

[*In the following excerpt, Nelson cites* Hard Times *and incidents in its plot in the course of illustrating the importance of life's mystery and diversity as presented in Dickens's works.*]

Though there is little of nature in Dickens, . . . there is a significant touch in that description of Bleak House: the "still older cottage-rooms in unexpected places, with lattice windows and green growth pressing through them" imply an original and intimate connection with nature, and the irregularity of the house makes it seem a living organism which has developed a form answering to the setting and the needs of the people of the house. Human order, when it is wrong, is quite unlike this. Thomas Gradgrind's house in **Hard Times** is "a very regular feature on the face of the country":

> Not the least disguise toned down or shaded off that uncompromising fact in the landscape. A great square house, with a heavy portico darkening the principal windows, as its master's heavy brows overshadowed his eyes. A calculated, cast up, balanced, and proved house. Six windows on this side of the door, six on that side; a total of twelve in this wing, a total of twelve in the other wing; four-and-twenty carried over to the back wings. A lawn and garden and an infant avenue, all ruled straight like a botanical account-book.

Part of the point Dickens is making, of course, is how boring the straight lines and the symmetry are. But why are they? Because there are no straight lines in nature, nor is there symmetry. To get straight lines and symmetry you leave some things out and rearrange others. E. M. Forster's image of Western order is the plan of the British sector of Chandrapore, with its regular grid of streets intersecting at right angles. "It charms not, neither does it repel" (*A Passage to India*, 1). In his story, most kinds of reality (and it is suggested, the most meaningful kind) fall through such a net. Straight lines and regularity mean the same in Dickens. Mr. Gradgrind "meant to do great things," but "in gauging fathomless deeps with his little mean excise-rod, and in staggering over the universe with his rusty stiff-legged compasses," he had, "within the limits of his short tether . . . tumbled about, annihilating the flowers of existence. . . ."

Contrasted to the irregularity and variety that Dickens favors, and that seem to imply the natural order of things, straight lines suggest a counter-order, Gradgrindian dryness and meagerness instead of the infinite variety of creation. Interestingly enough, Hablot Browne's illustration of Pecksniff and his daughters in their living room shows the wall at the rear hung with four pictures in a perfectly symmetrical arrangement, each of them portraying a perfectly symmetrical and straight-lined design (three buildings and a memorial to some hero), while in the shadows at the left rear the bust of Pecksniff appears to gaze approvingly. Symmetry and straight lines are here also connected to fraud and hypocrisy. There is something else about Pecksniff that fits here, too: his very moral throat. "You saw a good deal of it. You looked over a very low fence of white cravat (whereof no man had ever beheld the tie, for he fastened it behind), and there it lay, a valley between two jutting heights of collar, serene and whiskerless before you. It seemed to say, on the part of Mr. Pecksniff, 'There is no deception, ladies and gentlemen, all is peace, a holy calm pervades me'." That kind of insistence on perfect plainness and openness, concealing devious criminality, also appears in the short story "Hunted Down" (1859), in Mr. Sampson, a man whom the narrator distrusts on the instant of meeting (correctly, as it turns out). He parts his hair "straight up the middle," and he makes his hair-part stand for candor: as if he were to say in so many words, "You must take me, if you please, my friend, just as I show myself. Come straight up here, follow the gravel path, keep off the grass, I allow no trespassing." Harold Skimpole, too, affects openness, along with his inflexible claim of childlike innocence. Esther says, "The more I saw of him, the more unlikely it seemed to me, when he was present, that he could design, conceal, or influence anything; and yet the less likely that appeared when he was not present . . . "; and of course her skepticism is right, for he does nothing else. In *Our Mutual Friend* Eugene Wrayburn imposes on his friend Mortimer Lightwood in a similar way, protesting that he simply doesn't know whether anything in particular has been on his mind lately that would account for a change Mortimer thinks he has noticed in him. (There has been something on his mind, increasingly—Lizzie Hexam.) "So much of what was fantastically true to his own knowledge of this utterly careless Eugene, mingled with the answer, that Mortimer could not receive it as a mere evasion. Besides, it was given with an engaging air of openness, and of special exemption of the one friend

he valued, from his reckless indifference." Here, too, the appearance of openness and simplicity is itself a deception.

All this hangs together. Like Forster, Dickens makes regularity and geometricity images of intellect, and like him too he shows, supremely in **Hard Times**, how much the intellect leaves out. Coketown has no place for the knowledge belonging to the fancy; Sleary's traveling circus (to which Gradgrind finally owes much) must set up on the outskirts of the city, and the pointedly named Pegasus's Arms where the circus people stay is "a mean little public-house, . . . as haggard and as shabby, as if, for want of custom, it had itself taken to drinking, and had gone the way all drunkards go, and was very near the end of it." But where Forster suggests reason is simply inadequate to net the world's truth, Dickens indicates it may also be a positive fraud. Reality is *not* open and plain; it is charged with mystery. Representations of it by the reason are utterly inadequate at their well-meaning best, and fraudulent at their criminal worst. To apprehend it fully is the work of imagination.

George Orwell on Dickens's political gradualism:

[In *David Copperfield*] David escapes from the warehouse, but Mick Walker and Mealy Potatoes and the others are still there, and there is no sign that this troubles Dickens particularly. As usual, he displays no consciousness that the *structure* of society can be changed. He despises politics, does not believe that any good can come out of Parliament—he had been a parliamentary shorthand writer, which was no doubt a disillusioning experience—and he is slightly hostile to the most hopeful movement of his day, trade unionism. In **Hard Times** trade unionism is represented as something not much better than a racket, something that happens because employers are not sufficiently paternal. Stephen Blackpool's refusal to join the union is rather a virtue in Dickens's eyes. Also, as Mr Jackson has pointed out, the apprentices' association in *Barnaby Rudge,* to which Sim Tappertit belongs, is probably a hit at the illegal or barely legal unions of Dickens's own day, with their secret assemblies, passwords and so forth. Obviously he wants the workers to be decently treated, but there is no sign that he wants them to take their destiny into their own hands, least of all by open violence.

George Orwell, in The Collected Essays,
Journalism and Letters of George Orwell: An Age
Like This, 1920-1940, *Harcourt Brace
Jovanovich, 1968.*

That is one reason why Dickens has no grand programs to offer: Orwell was right. To Dickens system is the child of intellect, and the complexity of the world is beyond the manipulative grasp of reason. But reason is inadequate not only because it cannot know enough. Love is required for any solution to the world's problems, and reason does not love. Love belongs to imagination—plausibly enough, when imagination includes the power to identify with, rather than merely to describe and anatomize. The explicit link between love and imagination is in *Hard Times,* in the character Sissy Jupe, who is one of Dickens's love-bearers and who comes from Sleary's circus. It is she who ministers to Louisa when Louisa flees from Hart-house, and who sends Harthouse away, and who has made a better home for Louisa's younger sister than Louisa did, and to whom Louisa turns in her trouble; and who does so miserably in M'Choakumchild's school, unable to tell whether a nation with fifty millions of money is a pros-perous nation unless she knows who has them, and taking into account, in computing the percentage of accidental deaths, the intensity of the survivors' grief. M'Choakumchild's star pupil is Bitzer, whose heart "is accessible to Reason . . . and to nothing else." and Sissy's place in the schoolroom as well as her coloring empha-size her contrast with him. She sits at the end of a row diagonally across the room from Bitzer, and further back, so that she is also higher up than he is, and the sunbeam that strikes her ends at him. "But, whereas the girl was so dark-eyed and dark-haired that she seemed to receive a deeper and more lustrous colour from the sun, when it shone upon her, the boy was so light-eyed and light-haired that the self-same rays appeared to draw out of him what little colour he ever possessed." Sissy is far from Bitzer in the schoolroom, and in every other way too: higher up and nearer the natural light (and by the same token far-ther from the factual lectern) which confirms her fullness of being as it reveals Bitzer's deficiency.

No grand program then, but what Sissy has to offer, is what the world needs; and there needs no system for that. Perhaps this explains why Dickens was a radical but no revolutionary: why overturn an imperfect system to set up another? deflate a blustering manufacturer like Bounderby so that a windy labor leader like Slackbridge may swell into his place? What is required is personal determination to make things right within one's own radius; "if men would behave decently the world would be decent." Dickens recognizes the powerlessness of most people to set things right, but does not therefore absolve those "born expressly to do it"—the -oodles and -uffys, "my lords and gentlemen," "Right Reverends and Wrong Reverends of every order"; those Mr. Plornish, one of the helpless, means—"He only know'd that it wasn't put right by them what undertook that line of business, and that it didn't come right of itself"; or those addressed by the narrator in *Our Mutual Friend:* "My lords and gen-tlemen and honourable boards, when you in the course of your dust-shovelling and cinder-raking have piled up a mountain of pretentious failure, you must off with your honourable coats for the removal of it, and fall to work with the power of all the queen's horses and all the queen's men, or it will come rushing down and bury us alive."

Roger Fowler (essay date 1983)

SOURCE: "Polyphony and Problematic in *Hard Times,*" in *The Changing World of Charles Dickens,* edited by Robert Giddings, Vision and Barnes & Noble, 1983, pp. 91-108.

[*Here, Fowler discusses Dickens's use of language and dialect in* Hard Times *as a tool for characterization and "unresolved ideological complexity."*]

The polarization of critical response to *Hard Times* is familiar enough to make detailed reporting unnecessary, but since this polarization is a fact relevant to my argu-ment, I will recapitulate it briefly.

Popular reception of the novel has been largely antago-nistic or uninterested. The character of the earlier novels has led to the formation of a cheerful and sentimental 'Dickensian' response which finds *Hard Times,* like the other later novels, cold and uncomfortable, lacking in the innocent jollity, sentimentality and grotesquery of the earlier writings. When Dickens's anniversary was men-tioned in a T.V. spot on 7 February 1983, the novelist was identified through a list of his works which totally excluded the later 'social' novels.

In other circles, there has been a keenly appreciative re-sponse to *Hard Times:* in some quarters more academic, and in some quarters more socialist. Committedly posi-tive evaluation is found as early as 1860 in Ruskin and then in this century in Shaw, whose appreciation of the book as 'serious social history' initiated a line of evalu-ation more recently reflected in, for example, Raymond Williams and in David Craig. Then there is a famous and extravagant essay by Leavis:

> Of all Dickens's works it is the one that has all the strength of his genius, together with a strength no other of them can show—that of a completely serious work of art. [*Culture and Society 1780-1950,* 1968]

If Leavis was over-enthusiastic, others, some such as John Holloway and David H. Hirsch provoked by Leavis's surplus of commendation, have insisted on faults in the novel both as art and as social history. Even that majority of modern academic critics who accept and praise *Hard Times* concede some faults. Among the flaws cited by both camps are the following. A failure of a documentary kind is the presentation of the demagogue Slackbridge— 'a mere figment of the middle-class imagination. No such man would be listened to by a meeting of English factory hands' (Shaw). Similarly, the use of a professional circus to represent Fancy as opposed to Fact has been faulted on the grounds that Dickens might have found Fancy in the native recreations of working people (Craig). A more 'ideological' criticism would allege that Dickens's *con-cept* of Fancy was, judging from the symbols by which he represented it, too trivial to weigh effectively against the Fact of Utilitarian economic theory and philosophy of education (Holloway, Lodge). Other critics have admitted faults of characterization—the girl Sissy is sentimentally presented and emerges as inadequate: her childhood at-tributes do not ground her later strength on Louisa's be-half. Again, Stephen and Rachael are said to be too good to be true; Stephen's martyrdom to a drunken wife is a cliché; his refusal to join the union is not motivated and therefore puts him into a weak, contradictory position in relation to his fellow-workers. Now these allegations of faults of construction are not naïve 'Dickensian' complaints. There is real evidence that many things are not quite right with the book, for whatever reason: because of the unfamiliar constraints of small-scale writing for weekly parts, because of the secondhand nature of Dickens's experience?

Since *Hard Times* has gained a very positive reputation in this century, we should beware of condemning it by totting up 'faults'. Perhaps the yardstick which we unconsciously apply, the tradition of the humanistic novel already well established by 1850, is not entirely relevant. It might be preferable to revise our conception of what type of novel this is, or at least to suspend preconception. *Hard Times* is problematic for the critics, and that response itself is perhaps evidence of peculiarities of form. And what we know about the genesis of the novel suggests that it was problematic for Dickens too, involving him in compositional innovations. By this I do not refer merely to the structural consequences of weekly serialization (a discipline he had experienced only once before, in writing *Barnaby Rudge* (1841)), though this mode undoubtedly imposed constraints on episodic and thematic structure, and demanded compression. I mean by 'compositional innovations' new and defamiliarizing dispositions of language in response to new themes and unprecedented *and unresolved* ideological complexity.

A possible model for the structure of *Hard Times* is provided by Mikhail Bakhtin's theory of the 'polyphonic' novel; a theory which has the great benefit, for my purpose, of being interpretable in linguistic terms [in *Problems of Dostoyevsky's Poetics,* transl. by R. W. Rotsel, 1973]. In a complex argument, partly theoretical and partly historical, Bakhtin proposes that there have existed two modes of representational fiction: monologic on the one hand and polyphonic or dialogic on the other. The monologic novel, which he claims has been the dominant traditional form, is authoritarian in essence: the author insists on the particular ideology which he voices, and the characters are 'objectified', dependent on the authorial position, and evaluated from the point of view of that position. In the polyphonic novel, on the other hand, the characters (or the 'hero', according to Bakhtin) are more liberated: they achieve voices, and points of view, which challenge the validity of the authorial position. The musical metaphor of polyphony refers to the co-presence of independent but interconnected voices. 'Dialogue' means implicit dialogue, not turn-by-turn speeches: it refers to the fact that one person's speech-forms reflect consciousness of the actual or potential response of an interlocutor, orientation towards a second act of speech. But there is a stronger meaning which Bakhtin seems to have in mind for 'dialogic', and that is 'dialectical'. The dialogic relationship confronts unresolved contrary ideologies, opposing voices in which conflicting world-views resist submersion or cancellation. The dialectical nature of Bakhtin's aesthetic can best be seen in his discussion of *carnival,* which was in his view the medieval forerunner of the polyphonic novel [*Rabelais and His World,* transl. by H. Iswolsky, 1968]. Carnival, with its boy kings and other multifarious travesties, mediates opposites, associates

them while preserving their autonomous identities. It rejoices in extremes, negation, inversion, subversion, antithesis. The rhetorical figures generated by the logic of carnival are clear: they include prominently hyperbole, litotes, negation, syntactic inversions, paradox, contradiction. In social terms, the carnivalistic dialectic is the tension between mutually supportive but antithetical partners such as ruler and subject, employer and worker, teacher and pupil, husband and wife. And we would expect these differences of role, and antagonisms, to be articulated in the language of carnivalistic structures.

At a superficial level, the application of these ideas to *Hard Times* seems well justified. Three of the role-clashes just mentioned (employer/worker, teacher/pupil, husband/wife) figure directly and importantly in the plot. Then the novel contains a large number of diverse characters and groups of characters of very different social origins and affiliations, putting forward many and clashing points of view. The circus performers are an almost literal case of carnival: their diversity and deviance are strongly emphasized, as is their challenge to the authority of Gradgrind and Bounderby (Bk. I, Ch. 6). But polyphonic or dialogic structure is by no means limited to these circus artistes, but exists in the ensemble of numerous voices of opinion and conflict: Slackbridge, Bounderby, Stephen Blackpool, Harthouse, Louisa, Sissy, etc. The task for the analyst who wishes to make sense of this medley of voices is twofold. First, it is necessary to show in detail the linguistic and semiotic characteristics of the various voices (including the narrating voice) which participate in the dialogic structure. Second, the polyphonic structure, the multiplicity of voices, needs to be interpreted in terms of the author's ideology. A plurality of voices does not in itself mean a non-authoritarian narrative stance.

Turning to language itself, Bakhtin does not give a very clear guide as to how the structure of language contributes to the dialogic aesthetic. In fact, he appears to be quite negative on the dialogic value of stylistic variety. But this caution is strategic. He has to concede that Dostoyevsky, his main subject, is stylistically flat, but he must claim, of course, that his thesis works even in this linguistically undifferentiated case. He observes that marked linguistic individuation of fictional characters may lead to an impression of closure, a feeling that the author has definitively analysed a character and placed a boundary around its imaginative or moral potential: 'characters' linguistic differentiation and clear-cut "characteristics of speech" have the greatest significance precisely for the creation of objectivized, finalized images of people.' This seems to me not so much a limitation as an illumination, specifically an insight into our response to Dickens's grotesques: Peggotty, Micawber, Mrs. Gamp, and here, Slackbridge. All such characters seem to be clearly delineated, completely known, striking but uncomplicated. But we also need Bakhtin's more positive concession concerning the dialogic potential of speech styles; this potential is effective under certain conditions:

> the point is not the mere presence of specific styles,
> social dialects, etc., . . . the point is the dialogical

angle at which they . . . are juxtaposed or counterposed in the work . . .

and

> dialogical relationships are possible among linguistic styles, social dialects, etc., if those phenomena are perceived as semantic positions, as a sort of linguistic *Weltanschauung.*

That is to say, speech styles need not be just caricaturing oddities, but to transcend caricature they must encode characters' world-views as dialectical alternatives to the world-view of the author and/or, I would suggest, other characters. Thus we might investigate whether, say, Stephen Blackpool's speech, or Bounderby's, encodes in its specific linguistic form a world-view, a set of attitudes; and how the two attitudes relate—in this case, antithetically. Similarly, and perhaps easier to demonstrate, we can look at the dialogic relationships between Gradgrind and Sleary on the one hand, and Gradgrind and the author on the other.

How to proceed in this project? The examples just mentioned are merely striking instances of many, perhaps dozens, of semiotically significant stylistic oppositions which permeate *Hard Times*. To provide a full account would require a book, not [an essay]. As essential as space, however, is analytic methodology. Bakhtin provides no tools for analysing linguistic structure, but there is one linguistic theory which explicitly covers Bakhtin's condition that speech styles should be treated as embodying world-views: M. A. K. Halliday's 'functional' theory of language. I must send my readers elsewhere for details [*Halliday: System and Function in Language,* ed. G. R. Kress, 1976, and *Language as Social Semiotic,* 1978], but Halliday's main premise is that linguistic varieties within a community, or 'registers', encode different kinds of meaning, different orientations on experience. Halliday offers a number of analytic systems such as 'transitivity', 'mood', 'cohesion', 'information structure' which I and others have found very valuable in analysing texts for the world-views which they embody. I will use some of these categories below, but my analysis is constrained by space to be largely untechnical.

A list of distinct speech styles in the novel would show that there is an exceptional range of clearly differentiated voices: Sissy, Sleary, Slackbridge, Harthouse, Childers, Bounderby, Stephen, Gradgrind, etc. The length and diversity of the list are of less importance than the specific meanings of the voices and of their structural relationships, but sheer diversity is of some significance for the notion of polyphony. It could be argued merely on the basis of this multiplicity and variousness of voices and people that *Hard Times* makes a *prima facie* claim to be a polyphonic novel. The case would be putative as a global observation, more concrete and demonstrable in relation to specific sections which are explicitly carnivalistic in conduct. The best instance of the latter is the scene at the Pegasus's Arms in Book I, Chapter 6, when Gradgrind and Bounderby, in search of Sissy's father, are confronted by the members of the circus troupe, who speak 'in a variety of voices' and who are combative and subversive in their address to these gentlemen. This scene, which is both challenging and farcical, threatens an anarchic overriding of utility and authority, and touches on antitheses which are more thoroughly debated elsewhere in the book.

I shall now look more closely at how the multiple languages of *Hard Times* signify and intersect by examining samples under three headings: *idiolect, sociolect,* and *dialogue.*

An idiolect is the characteristic speech style of an individual. Like dialect, it is a set of background features of language, supposedly constant and permanent characteristics which distinguish a person linguistically. In its most sophisticated realization it is the complex of features, mostly phonetic, by which we recognize our acquaintances' voices on the telephone. Now idiolects apply to literature in two ways. First, the elusive 'style of an author' might be thought of as an idiolect. I mention this only to observe that *Hard Times* had no consistent authorial idiolect (unlike, to cite a comparable example, Mrs. Gaskell's *North and South*). Second, in fiction foregrounding of idiolect produces caricature; and although caricature is a fixing, objectifying process as Bakhtin has indicated, it is a device for making statements, and that is something we are looking for in *Hard Times*. The two sharp instances in this novel are the union demagogue Slackbridge and the circus-master Sleary. Each has a mode of speech which is quite idiosyncratic (with a qualification in the case of Sleary, below) and absolutely self-consistent.

Slackbridge conducts himself with a violent, biblical rhetoric:

> Oh my friends, the down-trodden operatives of Coketown! Oh my friends and fellow countrymen, the slaves of an iron-handed and a grinding despotism! Oh my friends and fellow-sufferers, and fellow-workmen, and fellow-men! I tell you that the hour is come, when we must rally round one another as One united power, and crumble into dust the oppressors that too long have battened upon the plunder of our families, upon the sweat of our brows, upon the labour of our hands, upon the strength of our sinews, upon the God-created glorious rights of Humanity, and upon the holy and eternal privileges of Brotherhood!

It has been objected that no trades unionist of the time would have spoken like that (although, apparently, this is not beyond question). But fidelity to the language of the delegates' platform is only part of the issue. The point is that Dickens does not represent *any* social role in a focused way. He has created a symbolic language for his conception of 'Slackbridges', but this language signifies nothing precise: it is a generalized bombast which might inhabit the pulpit, the House of Lords, or any kind of political or public meeting. Conventionally, of course, this sort of language connotes vacuousness and insincerity, and presumably it does so here; but Slackbridge's appearance is an intervention in a complex moral dilemma

(Stephen's refusal to 'combine', and his subsequent ostracism by the work-mates who know and respect him) and the signification of his speech style is inadequate to the situation. So Dickens is forced to comment directly on what Slackbridge represents:

> He was not so honest [as the assembled workmen], he was not so manly, he was not so good-humoured; he substituted cunning for their simplicity, and passion for their safe solid sense.

These judgements cannot be read off from the language in which Slackbridge is presented. His role remains puzzling, and since he is dramatically foregrounded as the main speaker against Stephen in this scene, the troubling nature of the scene (stemming largely from the unclarity of Stephen's motives and therefore of his relations with others at the meeting) remains provocatively unresolved.

Sleary is the second linguistic grotesque in the novel. Whereas Slackbridge's language is dominated by a bombastic rhetoric, Sleary's speech is submerged under brandy-and-water. Sibilants are drowned: . . . all reduce to a sound spelled *th:*

> Tho be it, my dear. (You thee how it ith, Thquire!) Farewell, Thethilia! My latht wordth to you ith thith, Thtick to the termth of your engagement, be obedient to the Thquire, and forget uth. But if, when you're grown up and married and well off, you come upon any horthe-riding ever, don't be hard upon it, don't be croth with it, give it a Bethpeak if you can, and think you might do wurth. People mutht be amuthed, Thquire, thomehow, . . . they can't be alwayth a working, nor yet they can't be alwayth a learning. Make the betht of uth; not the wortht.

But Sleary's function in the plot and in the thematic structure of the novel make him more than a comic drunk. In his first appearance (Bk. I, Ch. 6), he is a firm leader of the circus-people in their challenge to the bullying of Gradgrind and Bounderby, and effectively presides over the passage of Sissy into the care of Gradgrind. At the end of the novel, he has been harbouring Gradgrind's criminal son Tom, and (carnivalistically, through the good offices of a dancing horse) manages Tom's flight from apprehension. He is then given virtually the last word, an almost verbatim repetition of the sentiment just quoted. His interventions in the story are directly implicated in Gradgrind's fortunes, and he is the philosophical antithesis to Gradgrind's utilitarian educational thesis: Sleary's Horse-Riding stands for Fancy. This notion of Fancy may well be too trivial for Dickens's purpose, as has been conceded; but at least Sleary is so constituted as to demand attention. The idiolect is insistently defamiliarizing: it 'make[s] forms difficult . . . increase[s] the difficulty and length of perception' as Shklovsky puts it [*Russian Formalist Criticism,* ed. and transl. by Lee T. Lemon and Marion J. Reis, 1965]. It takes effort to determine what Sleary is saying, because of the completeness and the whimsicality of the phonological transformation which has been applied to his speech. The reader is compelled to decipher a radical, and not entirely consistent, code which

deforms everyday English words into momentarily unrecognizable spellings: *bitterth, prentitht.* These difficulties do not guarantee that what Sleary says is of any great interest; but the fact that Dickens has placed these difficulties in our way indicates that Sleary is *meant* to be listened to, that he is designed as a significant voice against Gradgrindism in the polyphonic structure of the book.

There is another interesting aspect of Sleary's speech, and one which further distinguishes his discourse from that of Slackbridge. Beneath the idiolect, there are markers which suggest a social dialect or sociolect. Dickens builds into Sleary's speech hints of working-class morphology and lexis: eathy (easily), ath (who), wouldn't . . . no more, took (taken), plain (plainly), winder, lyin', etc., (plus some odd spellings which suggest deviance from the middle-class code, but obscurely: natur, fortun, wurthst, conwenienth); and slang and oaths: morrithed (morrissed, 'fled'), cut it short, damned, mith'd your tip (missed your tip, 'jumped short'), cackler, pound ('wager'), etc. These characteristics link Sleary with the working class—in this novel, the interests of the 'hands'—and with the circus fraternity—the spokespeople for Fancy. These links not only 'naturalize' Sleary by providing him with social affiliations, but also broaden the basis of opposition to the Utilitarian philosophies embodied in Gradgrind (whom Sleary first meets in a confrontation).

The novel contains many other contrasts of speech style, and on the whole they can be explained sociolectally rather than idiolectally: Dickens seems to have accepted the principle that now provides the theoretical basis for Hallidayan linguistics, namely that registers of language characterize social groups and encode their values. Consider, for example, the contrasting speech of Harthouse and of Stephen Blackpool. The former is first introduced as an idle waster ('carelessly lounging') with a languid, verbless, fragmented speech (Bk. II, Ch. 1). When he is established in Louisa's favours, however, this affectation is replaced by the syntax of 'elaborated code':

> Mrs. Bounderby, though a graceless person, of the world worldly, I feel the utmost interest, I assure you, in what you tell me. I cannot possibly be hard upon your brother. I understand and share the wise consideration with which you regard his errors. With all possible respect both for Mr. Gradgrind and for Mr. Bounderby, I think I perceive that he has not been fortunate in his training. Bred at a disadvantage towards the society in which he has to play, he rushes into these extremes for himself, from opposite extremes that have long been forced—with the very best intentions we have no doubt—upon him. Mr. Bounderby's fine bluff English independence, though a most charming characteristic, does not—as we have agreed—invite confidence. If I might venture to remark that it is the least in the world deficient in that delicacy to which a youth mistaken, a character misconceived, and abilities misdirected, would turn for relief and guidance, I should express what it presents to my own view.

Hypotaxis—the use of multiple subordinate clauses—dominates the syntax, which is further complicated by parenthetical clauses such as '—as we have agreed—'. Main clauses are delayed by preposed adjective clauses ('Bred at a disadvantage . . .') and by suspect protestations of diffidence or sincerity ('If I might venture . . .'). Nouns are liberally modified by adjectives, many of them evaluative and evocative of extremes (*graceless, worldly, utmost, wise, opposite, very best,* etc.). Modals are also prominent, emphasizing the speaker's claim to epistemic and deontic involvement in what he says: *cannot possibly, all possible, very best, no doubt, most, least.* Touches of rhetoric of more identifiable origin than Slackbridge's are present: 'a youth mistaken, a character misconceived, and abilities misdirected' is a literary, educated form associated with writing, not oratory—the key to this literariness being the inverted structure N + Adjective (there is only one inversion, Verb + Subject, in all of Slackbridge's speeches. Harthouse's speech in this episode is marked as middle-class, elaborated, evasive.

At the other pole, socio-economically and linguistically, is Stephen Blackpool. There is a detailed effort to make Stephen's language indicate his representativeness of a class. A number of different features of his language combine to make his language suggest the regional, uneducated and oral properties of the language of the Hands. He is first shown in an intimate conversation with Rachael, an introduction which makes an immediate point that his speech style is shared, not idiosyncratic. I must quote a sizeable extract, including some commentary by the narrator which offers a clear contrast of style:

> 'Ah, lad! 'Tis thou?' When she had said this, with a smile which would have been quite expressed, though nothing of her had been seen but her pleasant eyes, she replaced her hood again, and they went on together.

> 'I thought thou wast ahind me, Rachael?'

> 'No.'

> 'Early t'night, lass?'

> ''Times I'm a little early, Stephen; 'times a little late. I'm never to be counted on, going home.'

> 'Nor going t'other way, neither, t'seems to me, Rachael?'

> 'No, Stephen.'

> He looked at her with some disappointment in his face, but with a respectful and patient conviction that she must be right in whatever she did. The expression was not lost upon her; she laid her hand lightly on his arm a moment, as if to thank him for it.

> 'We are such true friends, lad, and such old friends, and getting to be such old folk, now.'

> 'No, Rachael, thou'rt as young as ever thou wast.'

> 'One of us would be puzzled how to get old, Stephen, without t'other getting so too, both being alive,' she answered, laughing; 'but, any ways, we're such old friends, that t'hide a word of honest truth fro' one another would be a sin and a pity. 'Tis better not to walk too much together. 'Times, yes! 'Twould be hard, indeed, if 'twas not to be at all,' she said, with a cheerfulness she sought to communicate to him.

> ''Tis hard, anyways, Rachael.'

> 'Try to think not; and 'twill seem better.'

> 'I've tried a long time, and 'ta'nt got better. But thou'rt right; 'tmight mak fok talk, even of thee. Thou hast been that to me, through so many year: thou hast done me so much good, and heartened of me in that cheering way, that thy word is a law to me. Ah lass, and a bright good law! Better than some real ones.'

> 'Never fret about them, Stephen,' she answered quickly, and not without an anxious glance at his face. 'Let the laws be.'

> 'Yes,' he said, with a slow nod or two. 'Let 'em be. Let everything be. Let all sorts alone. 'Tis a muddle, and that's aw.'

A minimum of deviant spellings here serves to hint at the vowel sounds and the elisions of a northern accent. Elsewhere, Dickens indicates the accent by a more radical set of orthographic, lexical and morphological peculiarities:

> 'My friends,' Stephen began, in the midst of a dead calm; 'I ha' hed what's been spok'n o' me, and 'tis lickly that I shan't mend it. But I'd liefer you'd hearn the truth concernin myseln, fro my lips than fro onny other man's, though I never cud'n speak afore so monny, wi'out bein moydert and muddled.'

Detailed analyses of these dialect notations are unnecessary. Different novelists (e.g. Mrs. Gaskell, Emily Brontë) use different notational devices: some use more archaisms, others more 'non-standard' morphology, and there is variation in the spelling conventions for vowels. There are two simple points to grasp in all such cases. First, these are not to be judged as realistic transcriptions where fidelity might be an issue—they are simply conventional signals of socio-linguistic difference. Second, only a very slight deviance, as in the conversation between Stephen and Rachael, is needed to persuade middle-class readers that they are in the presence of a social group below their own.

More significant is the syntax, which is in sharp contrast to Harthouse's elaborated forms. Halliday maintains that speech and writing have different information structures, and therefore different modes of syntactic organization. Writing, which can be scanned and re-scanned for complexities and qualifications of meaning, is a medium which can accommodate the kinds of indirections which we noted in Harthouse's language. Speech, according to Halliday, is more straightforwardly linear, and it releases its meanings in a sequence of short chunks or 'information units'; these units are segmented off by intonation patterns, rises and falls in the pitch of the voice. Syntactically, they need not be complete clauses, but are often phrases or single words, and often loosely linked by apposition or concatenation. The overall style is not strictly speaking paratactic, because the conjoined constituents are not clauses of equal weight; but in its avoidance of clause subordination it is much more like parataxis than hypotaxis.

Once the existence of this mode of speech has been pointed out, it takes no great analytic expertise to recognize that the description fits the conversation of Stephen and Rachael. The point is that Dickens has—in *writing,* of course—deliberately constructed a very *oral* model of language for these two humble characters, contrasting with the formal, written model used for some unsympathetic middle-class speakers such as Harthouse. I think there is a contrast of values intended here: solidarity and naturalness on the one hand, deviousness and insincerity on the other. I cannot prove this by reference to the language alone; I simply suggest that Dickens is using speech style stereotypes to which his readers, on the basis of their socio-linguistic competence and of their knowledge of the novel's plot, assign conventional significances.

So far I have offered examples of significant individual voices, and of speech styles which seem to take the imprint of social values ('social semiotic' in Halliday's term). Other examples could be discussed; together they would assemble a picture of a text articulated in a multitude of voices. These voices are, overall, discordant and fluctuating in the kaleidoscope of views they express. Furthermore, the opposing points of view do not neatly align. Though Sleary confronts Gradgrind directly, so that the symbol of Fancy and that of Fact are in direct opposition, Harthouse and Stephen are not immediately opposed, nor many other significant antitheses of voices. Dickens's intellectual scheme for the book does not seem to have been symmetrical: his socio-linguistic symbols embodied in characters do not relate diagrammatically, and so the relationships among theoretical issues such as factual education, exploitive capitalism, statistics, social reform, play, etc., are not dramatized neatly in the linguistic or narrative relationships between the characters. The story and the language figure the ideological debates in an unsettled, troubled way. I think this raggedness is a strength. But before commenting on it directly, I want to refer to other areas of linguistic instability, different from the 'unpatternedness' of the global canvas. These areas involve dialogue, explicit or implicit, and figure shifting organization in the style of the voice.

Stephen Blackpool visits Bounderby's house on two occasions, and each time finds himself in a stand-up argument. The debates start with each speaker using his characteristic speech style. Bounderby is blustery and bullying, his speech packed with commands and demands:

> Well Stephen, what's this I hear? What have these pests of the earth being doing to *you?* Come in, and

speak up. . . . Now, speak up! . . . Speak up like a man. . . .

Bounderby continues in this register (which is his constant idiolect, or a major part of it), while Stephen's responses begin quiet and polite, in a language heavily marked for the dialectal phonology, and based on the short information units noticed earlier:

> 'What were it, sir, as yo' were pleased to want wi' me?' . . .
>
> 'Wi' yor pardon, sir, I ha' nowt to sen about it.' . . .
>
> 'I sed as I had nowt to sen, sir; not as I was fearfo' o' openin' my lips.'
>
> 'I'm as sooary as yo, sir, when the people's leaders is bad. They taks such as offers. Haply 'tis na' the sma'est o' their misfortuns when they can get no better.' . . .

Pressed to state how he would solve the troubles of the weaving industry, Stephen moves into a sequence of five long speeches; their sheer length is a sign of departure from character, against the norm of his conversation with Rachael. The spelling peculiarities are maintained to a large degree, as is the syntax of spoken information; this from the third long speech:

> Look round town—so rich as 'tis—and see the numbers of people as has been broughten into bein heer, fur to weave, an to card, an to piece out a livin', aw the same one way, somehows, twixt their cradles and their graves.

The fifth of these speeches has Stephen, under intense provocation, voicing sentiments of 'man' against 'master' which on independent evidence, as well as the evidence of the novel, can be associated with Dickens's own humanitarian point of view. Stephen cannot say what will right the world, but he can say what will not: the strong hand of the masters, *laissez-faire,* lack of regard for the humanity of the mill-workers, and so on. When Stephen gives voice to these sentiments, the overall structure of his language changes to the parallelistic rhetoric of a public speech: a succession of balanced sentences, steadily increasing in length, is used to enumerate his arguments; here are two of them:

> Not drawin' nigh to fok, wi' kindness and patience an cheery ways, that so draws nigh to one another in their monny troubles, and so cherishes one another in their distresses wi' what they need themseln—like, I humbly believe, as no people the genelman ha seen in aw his travels can beat—will never do't till th'Sun turns t'ice. Most of aw, ratin 'em as so much Power, and reg'latin 'em as if they was figures in a soom, or machines: wi'out loves and likeins, wi'out memories and inclinations, wi'out souls to weary and souls to hope— when aw goes quiet, draggin on wi' 'em as if they'd nowt o' th'kind, an when aw goes onquiet, reproachin 'e, for their want o' sitch humanly feelins in their dealins wi' you—this will never do't, sir, till God's

work is onmade.

Some of the elaborated syntax noticed in Harthouse's language can be found here in the internal structure of clauses, in the qualifications and self-interruptions. And the overall format of repetitive structure recalls the insistent harangue of the book's opening scene, in the schoolroom.

When Stephen engages with the moral issues which concern Dickens centrally, then, his language deviates sharply from what had earlier been offered as his own characteristic socio-linguistic style. I do not point this out as an inconsistency of characterization, but as an application of the dialogic principle in the language through which Stephen is constituted. The stylistic shift shows strain in Dickens's use of a voice to express an ideological position that has become problematic through being assigned to that speaker. Stephen as originally set up by Dickens is inadequate to occupy the place in debate in which he has become situated: his language strains towards the rhetoric of a more public form of disputation than his social role warrants.

Surprising shifts of register occur in the speech of other characters, although none so remarkable as the transformation from tongue-tied weaver to articulate orator. I have no space to demonstrate any more of these changes; nor, most regrettably, can I show any selection of the range of styles of the narrative voice. Dickens ranges from subversive parody (Bk. I, Ch. 1, on Gradgrind on Fact), to complex animating and de-animating metaphors (Bk. I, Ch. 5, the superb evocation of Coketown) to pathos, and to simple direct judgement ('He was a good power-loom weaver, and a man of perfect integrity'). David Lodge has analysed some varieties of the narrative rhetoric of *Hard Times* in an excellent chapter of *Language of Fiction:* analysis which readers can consult to fill out this gap in my account. Lodge also relates these variations to uncertainties in Dickens's own position, as I do. But his judgement is essentially based on a monologic norm: '*Hard Times* succeeds where its rhetoric succeeds and fails where its rhetoric fails.' Generally, Lodge argues, this rhetoric is successful when Dickens is being antagonistic or ironic, but fails when he is trying to celebrate his fictional positives.

But it is more complex than that. The various styles are not just 'successful' or 'failed', but transcend a two-term set of values: it is the plurality of codes, their inconstancy, and their frequent stridency, which all together constitute a fruitful and discordant polyphony. Any account of Dickens's 'argument' in this novel is bound to come to the conclusion that he attacks an unmanageably large and miscellaneous range of evils (utilitarianism in education and economics, industrial capitalism, abuse of unions, statistics, bad marriage, selfishness, etc.); that he mostly over-simplifies them (e.g. fails to see the beneficial relationship between some fact-gathering activities and real social reforms); that he is unclear on what evil causes what other evil. On the other side, his proposed palliatives are feeble, misconceived in terms of purely individ-

ual initiatives and responsibilities, and sentimentally formulated. Most of this conceptual muddle stems from the crucial inadequacy of Dickens's idealized solution of tolerant rapprochement of the two parties to the industrial situation:

> 'I believe,' said I, 'that into the relations between employers and employed, as into all the relations of this life, there must enter something of feeling and sentiment; something of mutual explanation, forbearance, and consideration; something which is not to be found in Mr. McCulloch's dictionary, and is not exactly stateable in figures; otherwise those relations are wrong and rotten at the core and will never bear sound fruit.'

Translation of all Dickens's insecurely based theses and antitheses into elements and structural relationships of this novel's form has produced the asymmetries and dissonances which my stylistic analysis has begun to display. But few people today would condemn *Hard Times* as a ragged failure. The inconsistencies and discords are an indication of the problematic status of the social and theoretical crises in question for a great imagination like Dickens who could not articulate unequivocally in fiction the (unknown to him) facile solutions which were consciously available to him as theory. The novel's lack of monologic authority fits Bakhtin's description, I believe; and the stylistic polyphony is provocative and creative, compelling the reader to grapple uneasily with the tangle of issues that Dickens problematizes.

Juliet McMaster (essay date 1987)

SOURCE: *"Hard Times:* 'Black and White'," in *Dickens the Designer,* The Macmillan Press Ltd, 1987, pp. 177-92.

[*In the following essay, McMaster examines how Dickens uses color imagery in* Hard Times *to reinforce its characterizations and themes.*]

In *Hard Times* Dickens made colour a major feature of design. One of the titles he considered for it was 'Black and white.' The novel is patterned on a progression between the two most powerful scenes: the first in the 'intensely whitewashed' schoolroom at the beginning, with its albino star pupil, Bitzer, so pale that he looks as though he would 'bleed white,' and the second set in Sleary's darkened circus ring at the end, with Tom Gradgrind disguised as a blackamoor clown, his face 'daubed all over' with a 'greasy composition' of black make-up.

But the world of *Hard Times* is not all just black and white, and that tentative title, like 'Two and two are four,' 'Stubborn things,' and 'Fact,' which appear in the same working list, was intended to indicate what was wrong with the world according to Gradgrind, and how much was missing in it. As it is a novel that treats of imagination, grace, instinct, and feeling, as well as of the utilitarian system that tries to reject them, so it is concerned with the modulation *between* black and white, the various tones of grey, and with brighter colours. Pigmentation is one of Dickens's recurring images, and he uses it consistently to furnish incidents for his fable and to reinforce his theme.

With a vision of a world, like Dickens's, threatened with the loss of colour and romance, Keats in 'Lamia' had produced a comparable set of associations:

> Do not all charms fly
> At the mere touch of cold philosophy?
> There was an awful rainbow once in heaven:
> We know her woof, her texture; she is given
> In the dull catalogue of common things.
> Philosophy will clip an Angel's wings,
> Conquer all mysteries by rule and line,
> Empty the haunted air, and gnomed mine.

For Dickens the philosophy that clips an angel's wings is Utilitarianism, and the attempt to 'conquer all mysteries by rule and line' is realized in Mr. Gradgrind's 'gauging fathomless deeps with his little mean excise-rod, and . . . staggering over the universe with his rusty stiff-legged compasses.' Gradgrind would certainly have expected his children and the pupils at his school to study the woof and texture of a rainbow, among their other Ologies. (One can imagine Bitzer's definition of a rainbow.) Dickens doesn't use the rainbow as an image, but he summons instead flowers, butterflies, peacock feathers and fire, and, instead of Keats's 'gnomed mine' that is opposed to 'the dull catalogue of common things' ('facts and calculations,' as Gradgrind would call them), he provides Sleary's circus. Like Keats he here sees evil as the tendency to drain and nullify the sources of bright colour. Colours, if not rainbows, are essential to his composition, as the mitigation of the stark black and white terms of the Gradgrind universe.

Black and white in *Hard Times* do not represent polar opposites in a moral scale: so much is clear from the fact that Bitzer, 'the colourless boy,' and Tom Gradgrind, whom we last see appropriately besmeared with black, are products of the same educational system. Dickens is in fact explicitly rejecting the light-dark moral contrast that he had exploited, say, in *Oliver Twist,* and he gives us a villain not a Fagin or a Quilp or a Carker, who all have feet more or less cloven, but a James Harthouse, 'aweary of vice, and aweary of virtue, used up as to brimstone, and used up as to bliss.' Black, as with Tom in blackamoor make-up, does have some of its customary associations with evil; but it is characteristically a pigmentation applied from without, and connotes a social degradation rather than innate evil. And white is not a positive attribute of virtue, but rather a negative quantity, an absence of imagination or passion, an absence of colour.

Dickens develops a number of unpleasant associations for whiteness and pallor. The earliest remembrance of the Grandgrind children is of 'a large black board with a dry Ogre chalking ghastly white figures on it.' Similarly—another parallel between the schoolroom and the town at large—the signs and public inscriptions in Coketown are all painted alike, 'in severe characters of black and white.' Black and white are like facts and figures, unaccommodating, undifferentiating, inhumane. The schoolroom in Mr. Gradgrind's school is bare and undecorated and 'intensely whitewashed,' and his children's playroom looks like 'a room devoted to hair-cutting'—that is, presumably, hygienic and sterile, and probably whitewashed too.

But it is in Bitzer that Dickens most memorably depicts whiteness, or lack of pigmentation, as repellent:

> The boy was so light-eyed and light-haired that the self-same rays [of the sun] appeared to draw out of him what little colour he ever possessed. His cold eyes would hardly have been eyes, but for the short ends of lashes which, by bringing them into immediate contrast with something paler than themselves, expressed their form. His short-cropped hair might have been a mere continuation of the sandy freckles on his forehead and face. His skin was so unwholesomely deficient in the natural tinge, that he looked as though, if he were cut, he would bleed white.

Dickens's bad characters in other novels, and Bounderby in this one, are apt to be all too 'colourful'—that is, they tend to make the good characters such as Oliver and Nell seem by contrast pale and vapid. But in Bitzer for once he produced a thoroughly nasty character with no colour at all, and his nastiness resides in his colourlessness. 'I [hate] that white chap,' Tom Gradgrind complains of him; 'he's always got his blinking eyes upon a fellow.' The whiteness is like the lean and hungry look of Cassius, Jingle and Stiggins—it expresses the beholder's sense of evil and danger. Even when Bitzer exerts himself, as in pursuit of Tom, he gathers no colour: 'For, there was Bitzer, out of breath, his thin lips parted, his thin nostrils distended, his white eyelashes quivering, his colourless face more colourless than ever, as if he ran himself into a white heat, when other people ran themselves into a glow.' A fit profession for the grown Bitzer is as the 'light porter' at the bank—'a very light porter indeed.' Dickens seems to have considered this avocation something of an inspiration, for in his working-plan for the number he noted, 'Bitzer light porter? *Yes.*' He may, I think, have been playing on the catch-phrase of Utilitarianism, 'enlightened self-interest,' for Bitzer is the supremely successful product of the Gradgrind educational system. His self-interest is complete, and enlightened—besides the light colouring—strictly to the extent that he will avoid breaking the law because breaking the law would get him into trouble. It is not surprising that F. R. Leavis [in his *'Hard Times:* An Analytic Note,' 1948,] should have admired the characterization of Bitzer, for he is a very Lawrentian conception[5]—one of the effete and bloodless products, like Clifford Chatterley, of a civilization that has lost contact with the physical and instinctual sources of life. Bitzer is a successful utilitarian, but at the price of losing his humanity. His blood is white, and he has no heart—none, that is, except for the physiological organ that pumps his corpuscles around his bodily frame after the manner described by Harvey.

The other colourless product of utilitarian principles is Mrs. Gradgrind, though she is by no means so successful in the pursuit of self-interest as Bitzer. Rather she seems the result of the enlightened self-interest of others, her husband's in particular. Mrs. Gradgrind is 'a little, thin, white, pink-eyed bundle of shawls, of surpassing feebleness, mental and bodily; who was always taking physic without any effect, and who, whenever she showed a symptom of coming to life, was invariably stunned by some weighty piece of fact tumbling on her.' Again, her colourlessness is an essential aspect of Dickens's conception of her. As for Bitzer he had noted in his working-plan 'Pale winking boy,' so he saw in advance Mrs. Gradgrind as a 'badly done transparency without enough light behind.' This very precise visual image, with its suggestion of the latest in the audiovisual aids market, is one he maintains consistently for poor insipid Mrs. Gradgrind. Bitzer is unwholesomely pale and white, but at least he is opaque. She is even more washed-out in colour than he. The image, when worked up into the text of the novel, becomes, 'Mrs. Gradgrind, weakly smiling, and giving no other sign of vitality, looked (as she always did) like an indifferently executed transparency of a small female figure, without enough light behind it.' We are to understand that she has been so crushed and ground by Gradgrind facts that she is scarcely alive, and Dickens has never so successfully depicted a low ebb of life: a starved amoeba would be a dynamo to her. When Louisa is summoned to her deathbed she finds her 'as nearly dead, as her limited capacity of being in any state that implied the ghost of an intention to get out of it, allowed.' And her death itself is announced with the familiar image: 'the light that had always been feeble and dim behind the weak transparency, went out.' In keeping with his larger design, the term Dickens chooses for the rendering of her fractional existence is an insufficient infusion of pigment.

Deprived of love, and dosed with an exclusive diet of hard facts, she is pathetically ignorant of what is absent in her life, the 'something—not an Ology at all,' that her husband has missed. She has no access even to her own physical being: when Louisa asks her, at her deathbed, 'Are you in pain, dear mother?,' she can only reply, 'I think there's a pain somewhere in the room, . . . but I couldn't positively say that I have got it.' As Melvyn Haberman comments [in his "The Courtship of the Void: The World of *Hard Times*," 1975,] 'So withdrawn is she from her self, so vacant her being, that she cannot experience her own pain.' At her death, we are reminded of the relation between transparent Mrs. Gradgrind, victim of facts, and Bitzer, who is so constituted that he can thrive on them. Bitzer is the 'fit colourless servitor at Death's door when Mrs. Gradgrind knocked.'

The lady who is most fully opposed to Mrs. Gradgrind in the colour-scheme of the book (and it is a one-way opposition, for Mrs. Gradgrind wouldn't oppose anybody) is Mrs. Sparsit. Here there is no shortage of pigment infusion. With her definite views and her no-nonsense attitudes, she is rather like the black-and-white inscriptions in Coketown. Bounderby imagines her when young as dressed 'in white satin and jewels, a blaze of splendour,' but at the time of life in which we meet her the black predominates in her colouring. She wears white stockings, but, as a widow, presumably a black dress. Much is made of her 'dense black eyebrows,' and subsequently of her 'black eyes.' As befits her character as witch, her black eyes are black in more than their own blackness: they see evil, and, to the extent of their power, determine it. In her jealousy of Louisa she wills her into an affair with Harthouse: 'she kept her black eyes wide open, with no touch of pity, with no touch of compunction, all absorbed in interest. In the interest of seeing [Louisa], ever drawing, with no hand to stay her, nearer and nearer to the bottom of this new Giant's Staircase.' She watches eagerly, with 'gratified malice,' as Louisa proceeds to compromise herself, and draw nearer to the dark abyss that her imagination has prepared for her. As she follows Louisa on the train after spying on the assignation with Harthouse, she continues to cast dark spells to bring about the evil she longs for:

> All the journey, immovable in the air though never left behind; plain to the dark eyes of her mind, as the electric wires which ruled a colossal strip of music-paper out of the evening sky, were plain to the dark eyes of her body; Mrs. Sparsit saw her staircase, with the figure coming down. Very near the bottom now. Upon the brink of the abyss.

Mrs. Sparsit, sufficiently black herself, seeks to blacken others. It is her mission to denigrate.

In the colouring of Mr. Gradgrind, Dickens suggests the need for some modulation between the stark blacks and whites that prevail in the signs of Coketown and in his children's education. For the most part he is dissociated from colour, just as he outlaws fancy, and spends his life 'annihilating the flowers of existence.' The one colour that is briefly associated with him is blue, but it is not a very vivid blue, and is cleared immediately from any romantic associations: 'Although Mr. Gradgrind did not take after Blue Beard, his room was quite a blue chamber in its abundance of blue books.' This library of the dismal science is itself sufficiently dismal, being 'a stern room, with a deadly statistical clock in it, which measured every second with a beat like a rap upon a coffin-lid.' Gradgrind is to be changed by the disasters that his educational system causes in his children's lives; and his reform, and movement towards increased humanity and understanding, is marked by his going grey. After Louisa's marriage is shattered, and he begins to suspect Tom's responsibility for the bank robbery, we hear, 'His hair had latterly begun to change its colour. . . . He leaned upon his hand again, looking grey and old.' The touch might be only a passing one, but Dickens gives it weight by including 'grey' in the final image of the book—words which he had again thought out in advance. The narrator connects humane endeavour with the effort 'to beautify . . . lives of machinery and reality with those imaginative graces and delights, without which . . . the plainest national prosperity figures can show, will be the Writing on the Wall.' This is the lesson that the Gradgrinds of the world, with their tabulation of black and white facts and figures, need to learn. Then there is a final apostrophe to the reader:

> Dear reader! It rests with you and me, whether, in our two fields of action, similar things shall be or not. Let them be! We shall sit with lighter bosoms on the hearth, to see the ashes of our fires turn grey and cold.

The fire imagery has been consistent, and this ending connects it with the colour motif, and suggests a consonance between the imaginative endeavour and modulation between the uncompromising extremes of black and white.

It is characteristic of Dickens's presentation of colour here, and in keeping with movements in painting, that he should differentiate between colour that is innate in the object or person, and colour that is the effect of external context, like lighting, or the kind of deposits caused by contaminated air, as in *Bleak House*. Although, in the colourless world as projected by Gradgrind, any infusion of colour might be seen as good, the pigment imposed from without, as on Tom's face or on the cinder-blackened buildings of Coketown, is nearly always seen as evil. The face and the town are aligned in the initial description of Coketown:

> It was a town of red brick, or of brick that would have been red if the smoke and ashes had allowed it; but as matters stood it was a town of unnatural red and black like the painted face of a savage. It was a town of machinery and tall chimneys, out of which interminable serpents of smoke trailed themselves for ever and ever, and never got uncoiled. It had a black canal in it, and a river that ran purple with ill-smelling dye.

The imposition of pigment on pigment, black on red, black in stagnant canal, purple in running water, is unnatural and degrading, like Tom's circus make-up, which is already intimated in the comparison of Coketown with 'the painted face of a savage.' This is no longer the colourless world of utilitarian theory and enlightened self-interest, but the soiled world of utilitarian practice: industrialism, *laissez-faire,* and every man for himself. The gross trailing serpents of smoke and pollution are the agents of corruption by which a potentially fair city falls to being an industrial slum. 'Coketown did not come out of its own furnaces, in all respects like gold that had stood the fire,' we hear. It is overlaid, tarnished and blackened. In its environs, 'the besmoked evergreens were sprinkled with a dirty powder.' Seen from a distance, it tarnishes and blackens the landscape too, as a 'sulky blotch upon the prospect . . . A blur of soot and smoke . . . murkily creeping along the earth.' And, as the action moves into the countryside surrounding Coketown, we find similar suggestions that the landscape too has been spoiled and soiled by some outside agency, and that what was innocent has been made ugly and dangerous by an external application of black dirt. When Sissy and Rachael take their walk in the countryside, natural greens and blues are threatened by the encroaching blackness of industrial detritus: "Though the green landscape was blotted here and there with heaps of coal, it was green elsewhere, and there were trees to see, . . . and all was over-arched by a bright blue sky. In the distance one way, Coketown showed as a black mist.' Though colour and nature seem to prevail, and the women can take pleasure in their walk, presently it emerges that the landscape has not only been overcast by the black mist, but literally undermined as well: 'Before them, at their very feet, was the brink of a black ragged chasm hidden by the thick grass.' In this black chasm Stephen Blackpool, the victim and martyr of Bounderby's utilitarian practice, lies dying.

Stephen's name, and the place of his death, associate him with the blackness of Coketown. In the street where he lies, we hear, the undertaker keeps, as a timely convenience, 'a black ladder, in order that those who had done their daily groping up and down the narrow stairs might slide out of this working world by the windows.' This black ladder, the grim *memento mori* of the working-class neighbourhood, receives some emphasis. Stephen's face, as compassionately described by Rachael, is 'so white and tired.' He belongs, then, to the prevailing black-and-white colour scheme of the tentative title, but he is not judged as responsible for this joyless pattern, as Gradgrind is, and he already has the 'iron-grey hair,' the sign of his ability to accept modulation and shades of difference, which Gradgrind must painfully acquire. The dark colours associated with him suggest rather that his life has been shadowed and darkened by inescapable suffering than that he is smeared and soiled, or morally tainted. His dipsomaniac wife, however, is another matter. She is one member of the working classes for whom the narrator has no compassion, and her degradation is again signalled by external application of dirt. Her hands are 'begrimed,' and she is 'a creature so foul to look at, in her tatters, stains and splashes, but so much fouler than that in her moral infamy, that it was a shameful thing even to see her.'

But the character who is the most memorable instance of externally applied pigmentation as a signal of moral infamy is of course Tom Gradgrind. Tom, like the colourless Bitzer, is a product of his education, but, whereas the system makes of Bitzer a successful machine, it makes of Tom an unsuccessful brute. Both are less than human, but Bitzer has no passions and no physical temptations, whereas Tom has both, without any training in how to control them.

> It was very remarkable that a young gentlemen who had been brought up under one continuous system of unnatural restraint, should be a hypocrite; but it was certainly the case with Tom. It was very strange that a young gentleman who had never been left to his own guidance for five consecutive minutes, should be incapable at last of governing himself; but so it was with Tom. It was altogether unaccountable that a young gentleman whose imagination had been strangled in his cradle, should be still inconvenienced by its ghost in the form of grovelling sensualities; but such a monster, beyond all doubt, was Tom.

His grovelling sensualities lead him to pander his sister to a man she finds repulsive, to embezzle funds from the bank, and to throw suspicion on an innocent man. When these crimes have caught up with him, and Sleary has disguised him as a blackamoor clown to help him to escape the law, Tom is at least shown, so to speak, in his true colours. This is a passage that most critics quote, for it is one of the most powerful in the book. But much of its force derives from the build-up that Dickens has provided, in marking the contrast as well as the parallel between Bitzer and Tom, and in training the reader in the moral infamy of externally applied pigmentation.

> In a preposterous coat, like a beadle's, . . . with seams in his black face, where fear and heat had started through the greasy composition daubed all over it; anything so grimly, detestably, ridiculously shameful as the whelp in his comic livery, Mr. Gradgrind never could . . . have believed in.

As Tom proves to his father over again that his teaching is responsible for his downfall—the statistical probabilities decree that 'so many people, out of so many, will be dishonest. . . . How can *I* help laws?'—the degrading blackening receives more emphasis still. Dickens rubs in the effect:

> The father buried his face in his hands, and the son stood in his disgraceful grotesqueness, biting straw: his hands, with the black partly worn away inside, looking like the hands of a monkey. . . . From time to time, he turned the whites of his eyes restlessly and impatiently towards his father. They were the only parts of his face that showed any life or expression, the pigment upon it was so thick.

The passage is one of Dickens's triumphs in rendering a moral condition visible. And, to complete the pattern of black and white, he now produces Gradgrind's pupil, the 'colourless' Bitzer in a 'white heat,' eager to break his educator's heart by preventing his son's escape. Gradgrind is to be punished, crucified, by the black and white, the unmodulated declaration of facts that he had always advocated.

There is another and more comic instance of the external application of pigment as a vehicle for poetic justice. Mrs. Sparsit is by no means lacking in dark colour herself, as we have seen, but, black as she is, there is a further daubing she is to undergo that will announce her infamy, though there is no one but the reader to see it. In her zeal to catch Louisa in the wrong she creeps through shrubbery and braves thunderstorms, collecting on the way a coating of verdure and worse: 'Mrs. Sparsit's white stockings were of many colours, green predominating; prickly things were in her shoes, caterpillars slung themselves, in hammocks of their own making, from various parts of her dress.' So much she endures unflinching while success, and Louisa's downfall, are in sight, but, when she has lost her in the crowd, and is weeping in frustrated malice, we are allowed to rejoice in the spectacle of Mrs. Sparsit properly punished, and daubed over, like Tom, with the vis-

ible signals of her villainy: 'Wet through and through: . . . with a rash of rain upon her classical visage; . . . with a stagnant verdure on her general exterior, such as accumulates on an old park fence in a mouldy lane.' To be reduced to an old park fencepost, encrusted with lichen and mould, is the appropriate come-uppance for the highly connected Mrs. Sparsit, once a Powler.

Brighter colours than the black and white of the Gradgrind and Bounderby world also have their place in the design of ***Hard Times***. Colour, as in Sissy Jupe and the circus, generally suggests feeling, imagination and vitality; but there are some exceptions to this rule, which need considering first. For, though one would expect Bounderby to be mainly black, as he rejoices in the smoke of Coketown—'That's meat and drink to us. It's the healthiest thing in the world in all respects, and particularly for the lungs', he boasts—he is actually vividly coloured. He is always talking about the workers' propensity to 'expect to be set up in a coach and six, and to be fed on turtle soup and venison, with a gold spoon,' and in his own complexion he is as gaudy as anyone in the novel: at his final rage at the end of his marriage we see him 'with his very ears a bright purple shot with crimson,' a veritable mandrill. But the coloration is not so inappropriate after all. For one thing the explosive pressure signalled by his crimson and purple features completes the main terms of his characterization as windy, inflated, explosive—a Braggadocio. But, besides this, the colourful imagery that differentiates him from the black-and-white world of Gradgrind is an early signal of his true nature as a creator of fiction. For, however he may disapprove of 'idle imagination' in others, he has fancifully invented a past for himself as romantic as Dick Whittington's. Colour erupts in him, in spite of his Utilitarian principles, as fire erupts in Louisa and in the factory hands, for 'all closely imprisoned forces rend and destroy.' As Warrington Winters shows [in his 'Dickens's *Hard Times*,' 1971], Bounderby and his fictional past belong to Dickens's major theme in serving 'to demonstrate that we cannot live by facts alone, that the imagination must have an outlet.'

All the same, as Bounderby is differentiated from the black-and-white Gradgrind world on the one hand, so is his livid coloration distinct from the colour of Sissy Jupe's world, which symbolizes feeling and the power of the imagination. Bounderby's fiction is not a saving myth, but a self-aggrandizing lie. Likewise his colouring is crude and forced. He lives 'in a red house with black outside shutters, green inside blinds, a black street door, up two white steps, BOUNDERBY (in letters very like himself) upon a brazen plate, and a round brazen door-handle underneath it, like a brazen full-stop.' This loudly declarative arrangement of rectangles, squares and circles recalls the 'third gentleman's' disquisition on taste in the schoolroom scene. In confounding Sissy, who says she would enjoy representations of flowers in carpets as 'pretty and pleasant, and I would fancy—', he cuts her off with the command that she must never fancy, but must be regulated in all things by fact:

> 'You don't walk upon flowers in fact; you cannot be

allowed to walk upon flowers in carpets. You don't find that foreign birds and butterflies come and perch upon your crockery; you cannot be permitted to paint foreign birds and butterflies upon your crockery. . . . You must see', said the gentleman, 'for all these purposes, combinations and modifications (in primary colours) of mathematical figures which are susceptible of proof and demonstration. . . . This is fact. This is taste.'

Bounderby's domestic décor would live up to these standards. For him colour is best regimented, separated, and arranged in hard-edged shapes. It is no surprise to find that his bank has exactly the same exterior as his house—red brick, black shutters, green blinds, and so forth, all 'strictly according to pattern.' These colours become, in fact, not very different from the Gradgrind black and white, inasmuch as their tendency is to eliminate differences and shades, to confound the individual with the aggregate, and so to dehumanize.

Sissy Jupe, with her allegiance to flowers, butterflies and fancy, is the representative of both colour and goodness. In the definitive schoolroom scene, she is contrasted with the colourless Bitzer, who sits in the same ray of sunshine: 'But, whereas the girl was so dark-eyed and dark-haired, that she seemed to receive a deeper and more lustrous colour from the sun, when it shone upon her, the boy was so light-eyed and light-haired that the self-same rays appeared to draw out of him what little colour he ever possessed.' Leavis has memorably pointed out 'the force . . . with which the moral and spiritual differences are rendered here in terms of sensation,' but he has not noticed how this contrast is part of a dominant visual pattern in the novel at large. The scene continues to emphasize her colour, particularly that which comes from within. She 'would have blushed deeper, if she could have blushed deeper than she had blushed all this time.' When she is grown we are reminded of her 'rich dark hair' and of her propensity to blush: 'Her colour rose,' and 'Sissy flushed and started.' Such are the gestures which keep her colouring before us. Her fondness for flowers distinguishes her from Gradgrind, who annihilates the flowers of existence, from M'Choakumchild, who 'had taken the bloom off the higher branches' of science, and from Tom, whom we see literally tearing roses to pieces in one scene.

Her place of origin, Sleary's circus, is more colourful still. The circus people too cherish flowers, and the 'graceful equestrian Tyrolean flower-act' is one of their recurring numbers. They foregather at the Pegasus's Arms, where there is a theatrical Pegasus 'with real gauze let in for his wings, golden stars stuck on all over him, and his ethereal harness made of red silk.' Her father the clown wears as part of his clown's outfit a 'white night-cap, embellished with two peacock's feathers,' and the diminutive Master Kidderminster, who aspires to her hand, plays the role of Cupid made up with 'white bismuth, and carmine.' (Make-up, incidentally, is not degrading to the circus people as to Tom, for impersonation and clowning are their immemorial and legitimate business.)

Louisa Gradgrind's moral evolution, in gravitating from Gradgrind's world to Sissy's, is also signalled by the colour scheme. Her father intends to bring her up according to the colourless Bitzer pattern, quelling all fancy and feeling in her and devoting her entirely to fact. But the young Gradgrinds are not as bloodless and passionless as Bitzer. We have seen what happens to Tom. His inability to control his 'grovelling sensualities' causes him to become besmeared with pigment from the outside. Even little Jane Gradgrind, who is to be saved for humanity by Sissy, must have her native fancy and childish cheeks daubed over by the prevailing white—she falls asleep over vulgar fractions with a composition of white clay on her features, manufactured from 'slate-pencil and tears.'

Louisa, in spite of being a docile child, early shows signs of not belonging in the Gradgrind world. She is caught, 'red and disconcerted,' peeping through a loophole at the 'graceful equestrian Tyrolean flower-act!' In her face 'there was a light with nothing to rest upon, a fire with nothing to burn, a starved imagination keeping life in itself somehow.' The redness recurs, and in her it is the signal of feeling and passion, though she is not even aware of them in herself, nor can she give them a name. There is a poignant little incident of her adolescence, when the fifty-year-old Bounderby, stirred with lust, kisses her cheek.

> He went his way, but she stood on the same spot, rubbing the cheek he had kissed, with her handkerchief, until it was burning red. . . .
>
> 'What are you about, Loo?' her brother sulkily remonstrated. 'You'll rub a hole in your face.'
>
> 'You may cut the piece out with your penknife if you like, Tom. I wouldn't cry!'

The incident sharply suggests the appalling violation—though one that she could not explain or analyse—that is practised on her in giving her to Bounderby in marriage. Having no access to her own instincts and feelings, and no knowledge that she has them, she makes no strong objection. But Bounderby's polluting kiss, so fiercely disgusting to her, is the preview of her wedding-night. And the knowledge that Tom gains of her feelings in this kiss scene shows him as doubly depraved in pushing her into the marriage.

Her father's transfer of her to Bounderby, the progress from the theory to the practice of Utilitarianism, sets her on the same path as Tom, and there is the same suggestion of denigration from without. Louisa's state of mind has been consistently associated with the fires and fumes of Coketown, and as Gradgrind proposes the match we hear of 'The distant smoke very black and heavy.' She is on her way to becoming grimed over, like the red brick of Coketown and the painted face of her brother. But her symptomatic interest in fires and the light of imagination prevails over the smoke, and the more vivid colouring asserts itself. As she warns her father, 'when the night comes, Fire bursts out.'

It is Harthouse's sensual mission to awaken the dormant passion in Louisa; and he goes a long way towards succeeding. Harthouse, though not moved by strong passion himself, takes a connoisseur's delight in being the object of passion. That is, as his name implies, having no heart (he has a 'nest of addled eggs' in 'the cavity where his heart should have been') he wants to become the home for Louisa's. He specialises in arousing passion, not feeling it. Or, to use Dickens's colour metaphor, he is 'the very Devil' at 'the kindling of red fire.' As we have seen, Dickens was to develop the association of red with unleashed passion further still in *A Tale of Two Cities*, with the prominent red caps of the revolutionaries, and the red wine spilled in the streets that is the preview of the bloodbath of the Reign of Terror. Colour is Dickens's shorthand for aroused emotion in Louisa. Her love for Tom, the one feeling she is conscious of, first signals to Harthouse her capacity for passion, and he covets it. He sees that 'Her colour brightened' for Tom, and he begins to think 'it would be a new sensation, if the face which changed so beautifully for the whelp, would change for him.' Presently, by pretending interest in Tom, he has inveigled himself into her confidence, and proceeds on the assumption not only of her love for Tom but also of her absence of love for her husband. The signals are encouraging. She is 'flushing,' and then 'She flushed deeper and deeper, and was burning red.' Next, when she betrays that she has sold her husband's gifts to pay her brother's debts, 'She stopped, and reddened again.' Now she varies her normally numb response to her husband's blustering by facing him 'with a proud colour in her face that was a new change.' Harthouse has indeed been successful in kindling the red fire.

Louisa goes so far as to hear his urgent proposal that she should elope with him, and to be tempted by it. So much we may infer from her flight in the tempest on the train, amidst 'Fire and steam, and smoke, and red light.' But she flees not to her lover but to her father, and by the time she gets to him she is appropriately purged of pigment: 'so colourless, so disshevelled, so defiant and despairing, that he was afraid of her.'

Within the bounds of a brief fable, Louisa undergoes an emotional education. Though we are not to approve of Harthouse, he provides the means by which she discovers her own heart. Out of touch with her instincts and emotions, like her mother, and alienated from her self, she is not fully alive, and allows herself to be handed over to Bounderby like a parcel of goods, hardly even knowing that it matters. Harthouse causes an awakening of passion and consciousness; but her newly vivid colouring, like Tom's, is not integrated with moral imagination, and must be exorcised, leaving her torpid and colourless again. It is only the deep-hued Sissy (who has meanwhile changed little Jane's chalk-smeared countenance to 'a beaming face') who can reconcile her to her self. Under her influence Louisa, at the conclusion of the novel, is 'trying hard to know her humbler fellow-creatures, and to beautify their lives of machinery and reality with those imaginative graces and delights, without which the heart of infancy will wither up.' Leaving behind the black-and-white Gradgrind world, she has come to the Jupe philosophy that rejoices in flowers, butterflies and circuses, the 'imaginative graces and delights.'

Hard Times is not a complex novel, and its colour motif is simple too. The directive we receive on the appropriate colouring of imagination and pleasure in our lives is the adage, *Not too little* (like the absence of pigment in Bitzer and Mrs. Gradgrind), *not too much* (like the artificially applied coloration of Tom, Coketown and Mrs. Sparsit), *but just right* (like the organic colouring of Sissy Jupe and, eventually, Louisa). This essentially simple and consistent scheme serves Dickens well, and furnishes some memorable scenes and characterizations. Artistically, he has been most successful in the negative extremes, the black and white of his tentative title: in the slug-like pallor of Bitzer and the daubed-over blackness of Coketown and Tom, who wear their pigment like tar and feathers. These are memorable figures, and for good reason commentators keep coming back to them. Sissy Jupe, once she has left behind the schoolroom and her childhood, is only intermittently successful. But Louisa, cut off from access to her own feelings and instincts and a stranger to her self, is a figure of considerable psychological interest, and Dickens has made the colour-scheme tell in the development of her character too. Though its design is less elaborately developed than that of *Bleak House*, **Hard Times** equally gains in impact and coherence from a dominant visual motif.

Jean Ferguson Carr (essay date 1989)

SOURCE: "Writing as a Woman: Dickens, *Hard Times,* and Feminine Discourses," in *Dickens Studies Annual,* Vol. 18, 1989, pp. 161-78.

[*In the essay below, Carr assesses Dickens's "sympathetic identification with feminine discourses in the 1850s" as exemplified in* Hard Times.]

In his 1872 retrospective essay on Dickens, George Henry Lewes presents Dickens as an exemplary figure whose career has upset the balance between popular taste and critical judgment. The essay depends on what seems initially an aesthetic opposition between show and Art, between "fanciful flight" and Literature, but these critical terms also demark class and gender boundaries that preserve the dominant literary culture. Dickens becomes "the showman beating on the drum," who appeals to the "savage" not the "educated eye," to "readers to whom all the refinements of Art and Literature are as meaningless hieroglyphs." He works in "delft, not in porcelain," mass producing inexpensive pleasure for the undiscerning reader, but is found wanting by the "cultivated" reader of "fastidious" taste. The essay attempts to contain Dickens' impact by identifying him as lower-class, uneducated, and aligned with feminine discourses, but it also suggests the difficulty of accounting for Dickens' influence and the importance of investigating the "sources of that power." Despite Lewes's isolation of Dickens as a "novelty" or as a madman, he concedes that he "impressed a new direction on popular writing, and modified the Literature of his age, in its spirit no less than in its form."

Dickens' admirers, following John Forster, have responded to the essay as mistaken and insulting. As John Gross wrote, the essay "still has the power to irritate," with its innuendo about hallucinations and lower-class vulgarity, and its casual anecdotes about the author's inadequate library. Lewes's class bias and his narrow definition of education have undermined the influence of his critique of Dickens for modern readers, but his subtle positioning of Dickens in relation to women writers and his articulation of the categories by which novels will be judged has been more durable. When, for example, Gordon Haight concludes that "Dickens was a man of emotion, sentimental throughout; Lewes was a man of intellect, philosophical and scientific," he is echoing the gender-based oppositions of Lewes's argument.

The essay on Dickens is part of the broader attempt begun by Lewes in the 1840s to serve as arbiter of the emergent literary class and of its premier form, the novel. Like Lewes's 1852 essay "The Lady Novelists," it seeks to position those literary newcomers who threaten the status and boundaries of nineteenth-century literary territory, to control the impact of a broader-based literacy and of women's emergence into more public spheres. The critique of Dickens depends on polarities that usually mark gender differences in nineteenth-century criticism, as, for example, the difference between feeling and thinking, between observing details and formulating generalizations. "Dickens sees and feels," Lewes intones,

> but the logic of feeling seems the only logic he can manage. Thought is strangely absent from his works.... [K]eenly as he observes the objects before him, he never connects his observations into a general expression, never seems interested in general relations of things.

Lewes makes still more explicit his identification of Dickens with this secondary realm of women's writing in this backhanded compliment:

> With a fine felicity of instinct he seized upon situations having an irresistible hold over the domestic affections and ordinary sympathies. He spoke in the mother-tongue of the heart, and was always sure of ready listeners.

Dickens is thus identified with the feminine, as instinctual and fortunate, as seizing rather than analyzing, as interested in "domestic affections and ordinary sympathies." He "painted nothing ideal, heroic," Lewes explains. "The world of thought and passion lay beyond his horizon."

Lewes evokes many of the same oppositions when instructing Charlotte Brontë on the "proper" realm for women writers, when cataloguing the "lady novelists" of the day, or when marking the novel as the particular "department" of women, the form that values "*finesse* of detail, . . . pathos and sentiment." His acknowledgment that Dickens is "always sure of ready listeners" rehearses

a charge often made against nineteenth-century women writers, that the financial success and popularity of their work, its very attentiveness to audience concerns, marks it as "anti-" or "sub-literary," concerned with sales not posterity. Dickens thus joins the company of writers like Fanny Fern and Mary Elizabeth Braddon who, as one critic put it, discovered: "a profitable market among the half-educated, . . . giving the undiscriminating what they wanted to read." The use of a category like the "subliterary" works to regulate the effects of the novel as a newly-positioned literary discourse that challenges the cultural hegemony of upper-class men of letters.

In July 1845, Dickens described the aim and rhetorical stance of a proposed journal, *The Cricket:* "I would at once sit down upon their very hobs; and take a personal and confidential position with them." In 1850, he finally established a periodical to fulfill the role of domestic comrade, that aspired "to live in the Household affections, and to be numbered among the Household thoughts, of our readers." In establishing a journal to be "familiar in their mouths as Household Words" (as the motto read), Dickens was making use of a feminine guise, privileging the intimate, private, and informal qualities usually associated with women over the social, public, and authoritative powers usually associated with men. But he was also disrupting the conventional wisdom that sharply divided the domestic and public spheres, for his journal insisted on the interpenetration of these realms.

This gesture of cultural cross-dressing is part of a recurring exploration by Dickens in the 1850s of the discourses usually identified as feminine. Michael Slater has argued that in the decade 1847 to 1857 Dickens was "apparently preoccupied with women as the insulted and injured of mid-Victorian England," and that the novels in this period feature more women characters in more prominent positions than do other of his novels. But he also sees Dickens as "voicing no general condemnation of prevailing patriarchal beliefs and attitudes." I do not find it surprising that Dickens did not "voice" a "general condemnation" of the ideology within which he wrote. What I want to investigate is why his interest hovers at the edge of articulation, why it goes so far and then retreats, or goes so far and then is silent. Why is Dickens simultaneously empathetic with oppressed women and insistent on the constraints and stereotypes that restrict them? What does his practice suggest about how women are rendered silent in Victorian culture and novels, how their perspective is undermined or preempted? To use Pierre Macherey's terms, such issues become part of what is "unvoiced," "unspoken" both in the novels and in Dickens' public postures. The issue is not so much, then, whether Dickens crafted complex psychological women characters along the lines of George Eliot or Charlotte Brontë, but how women are positioned in the powerful discourses of the novels as in contemporary social practices. In Dickens' novels, the notion of "writing as a woman" is problematic, as opposed to the confident assumptions Lewes makes of what it means "to write as women," of what the "real office" is that women "have to perform," of the "genuine female experience." Dickens' experimentation suggests that much is unknown, even to the women who "experience" their lives and desires, that there is no ready language for what women wish to "write." Although Dickens himself certainly does not articulate a program of women's liberation, and indeed deploys many cultural tropes that restrict women as "relative creatures," his novels often make the "commonsense" notions of Lewes untenable.

The proliferation of child-wives in his novels and his portrait of Esther Summerson's strained narrative have often been cited by critics as signs of Dickens' preference for coy, idealized, and subservient women. His advocacy of the domestic values of hearth and home has similarly been dismissed as a sign of a peculiar weakness, a bourgeois sentimentality aimed at pleasing or appeasing his readers. Along with his taste for melodrama and Christmas morality, such quirks are explained away as a cultural disguise the master assumed to protect his more radical designs. The more critically acceptable Dickens provides cynical and witty analysis of cultural conventions and hypocrisies from a disengaged position. In other words, Dickens is valued as a prototype of the (male) modern artist as rebel and cultural critic; he is embarrassing in his assumption of what we label (female) "Victorian" values. Like Lewes, then, we perpetuate the stigma of writing as a woman, associating feminine discourse with a lack of analysis and rigor, with pandering to "cheap" tastes. And we resist identifying Dickens with either its problems or its effects.

When Dickens' experimentation with "writing as a woman" is examined within this contest for literary territory and power, it involves more than merely being a woman writer or adopting a feminine persona. By aligning himself with terms and oppositions usually associated with women (for example, fancy vs. reason or fact, the personal vs. the institutional), Dickens, in effect, explores how his own position as a writer of fiction is marked off as suspect or inferior. He experiments with writing that traverses opposed realms and deploys narrative tropes that mark breaks in discursive power—stuttering, deception, metaphor, eccentricity, strain of voice or prose, interruptions. In this context, for example, Dickens' insistence on a linkage between "romance" and familiar things is more than a personal credo or a rehearsal of a romantic ethos. The preference in *Hard Times* of the devalued term "fancy" over the more culturally respectable term "imagination" locates his argument in a contemporary ideological contest, rather than as a repetition of an earlier aesthetic debate. The problematic position of women characters and writers functions as a figure of Dickens' own position in a culture suspicious of fancy and wary of claims to "domestic" power. Deflecting the unease of his position onto women as an oppressed class allows Dickens to be more extreme and critical than he could if he were evaluating his own position directly.

I would like to focus on what has usually been cited as a negative portrait of women, the failure to create a strong, likable heroine or a credible mother figure in *Hard Times* (1854). The novel itself is an instance of the conditions of feminine discourse, written not in any expansive artistic mode, but under the urgency of periodical publishing, as a project his printers hoped would attract readers to *Household Words*. Dickens disliked the conditions of weekly publication and deplored as "CRUSHING" the consequent lack of "elbow-room" and "open places in perspective." But the process must have underscored the constraints embedded in the social and material production of discourse. Indeed much of the novel explores what cannot be said or explained, what cannot be portrayed. The women of this fictional world in particular are restricted by and to their social positions, defined within narrow ideological bounds that afford little relief. The characters do not operate primarily in personal relationships to each other, nor do they "forget" their social positioning, or the polarities that operate in Coketown. They are constructed in oppositions, as women and men, mothers and daughters, middle-class thinkers and lower-class workers. The usual cultural positions for women remain curiously unpopulated, incomplete, present but not functioning as they ought. This schematic underdevelopment need not be explained away as a technological effect of the novel's weekly form, or as a style of abstraction. The ideological and technical constraints also create the possibility for Dickens to write as if from within the realm that Lewes marks off for women writers—a realm of fancy, romance, ordinary events, and mass production; a realm that remains apart from what fastidious or learned readers will value.

The novel is constrained from the beginning by the powerful social discourse of the Gradgrind system, which exists in the novel as what Bakhtin called "the word of the fathers." Bakhtin argues that such a word need not be repeated or reinforced or even made persuasive, but has "its authority already fused to it":

> The authoritative word demands that we acknowledge it, that we make it our own; it binds us, quite independent of any power it might have to persuade us internally; we encounter it with its authority already fused to it. . . . It is, so to speak, the word of the fathers. Its authority was already *acknowledged* in the past. It is a *prior* discourse. It is therefore not a question of choosing it from among other possible discourses that are its equal.

Against such a word, opposition or argument is already preempted, made secondary or unhearable. Unlike the opposing terms of "wonder" and "fancy," which require constant justification in the novel, the simplest reference to "fact" evokes the authority of learning and scientific knowledge. The effect of such an authority is to make all private exchanges in the book dependent on arguments that cannot be imagined within the novel's authorized categories, so that the characters speak a kind of shadow dialogue.

The effect of this social construction is especially destructive to the transparent figure who serves as the heroine's mother. In a more self-consciously "feminist" novel, Mrs. Gradgrind might be expected to suggest the alternative to patriarchal discourses. In *Hard Times,* the mother is comically ineffectual and trivial, represented not as a person but as an object, as a "feminine dormouse," and a "bundle of shawls." Yet she is not even a particularly satisfactory object. Her central representation, repeated three times, is as a "faint transparency" that is "presented" to its audience in various unimpressive attitudes:

> Mrs Gradgrind, weakly smiling and giving no other sign of vitality, looked (as she always did) like an indifferently executed transparency of a small female figure, without enough light behind it.

A transparency is an art form popularized by the dioramas in which a translucent image painted on cloth is made visible by backlighting. Its fragility and potential for varying production make the transparency a felicitous medium to suggest Mrs. Gradgrind's ambivalent positioning. The failure of the transparency renders her almost invisible in the novel, making her neither a pleasing image nor one that is easily readable. But the particularity of the image insists on a producer as well as a product, raising the issue of what painter "executes" her so indifferently, what producer withholds the light that might have made her more substantial, in other words, why she has been neglected as a cultural formation. Vaguely discernible through the translucent object, the producer remains a shadowy, unnamed, prior force, whom we know by traces and effects. At Mrs. Gradgrind's death, for example, we are told of an effect, but not of a cause—"the light that had always been feeble and dim behind the weak transparency, went out." And the physical depiction of her as recumbent, "stunned by some weighty piece of fact tumbling on her" leaves unnamed the force that stuns her with its weight and carelessness. We are left with an authorless piece of evidence, a "piece of fact"; but in *Hard Times* "fact" is easily traced back to the Gradgrind system. When we are told that finding herself alone with Gradgrind and Mr. Bounderby is "sufficient to stun this admirable lady again, without collision between herself and any other fact," we know what constitutes her as an object of its gaze. It is under her husband's "wintry" eye that Mrs. Gradgrind becomes "torpid again"; under Sissy Jupe's care or even in Louisa's presence, she can be "rendered almost energetic." Both fact and its proponents are equally capable of rendering Mrs. Gradgrind nonexistent, a product of a careless fancy: "So, she once more died away, and nobody minded her."

Mrs. Gradgrind has been so slighted as a "subject" that she is surprised when Louisa asks about her: "You want to hear of me, my dear? That's something new, I am sure, when anybody wants to hear of me." And the outcome of such a lifetime of being constituted by others is that she cannot even claim to feel her own pain; when Louisa asks after her health, she answers with what the narrator calls "this strange speech": "I think there's a pain somewhere in the room . . . , but I couldn't positively say that I have got it." She is certainly slighted by Dickens, appearing in only five of the novel's thirty-seven chapters, and then usually in the final pages or paragraphs. Even her introduction seems almost an afterthought, located not in the chapter with Mr. Gradgrind, the children, or even the

house, but in a parenthetical position as audience for Mr. Bounderby (ch. 4). But if Dickens is cavalier about her presence, he strongly marks her absence from that nineteenth-century site for Mother, as idealized figure in her children's memories or in their imaginative dreams of virtue. Mrs. Gradgrind's expected place as her children's earliest memory has been usurped by the father who appears as a "dry Ogre chalking ghastly white figures" on a "large black board." Louisa's return "home" for her mother's death evokes none of the "dreams of childhood—its airy fables" and "impossible adornments" that Dickens describes as "the best influences of old home"; such dreams are only evoked as a lengthy litany of what her mother has *not* provided for her child.

Mrs. Gradgrind does not offer a counter position—covert or otherwise—to the world of fact and ashes. She cannot overtly defy her husband, nor can she save herself from her daughter's scorn. Her advice to Louisa reflects this helplessness, and its incomprehension of the accepted referents makes her ridiculous in her child's eyes: "Go and be somethingological directly," she says, and "turn all your ological studies to good account." When she is dying, Mrs. Gradgrind tries to express her loss—of something and of words with which to articulate it—to her daughter:

> But there is something—not an Ology at all—that your father has missed, or forgotten, Louisa. I don't know what it is. . . . I shall never get its name now. But your father may. It makes me restless. I want to write to him, to find out for God's sake, what it is. Give me a pen, give me a pen.

To the transparent Mrs. Gradgrind, all authoritative knowledge must come from the father, yet she worries that he has missed or forgotten something. She does not imagine herself finding or naming it, but remembers it as unsaid. The outcome of this "insight" is invisible to the patriarchal eye; it disappears as "figures of wonderful no-meaning she began to trace upon her wrappers." When Louisa tries to fashion a meaning of her mother's words, her aim is to "link such faint and broken sounds into any chain of connexion," in other words, to translate her mother into the Gradgrind discourse. Mrs. Gradgrind emerges "from the shadow" and takes "upon her the dread solemnity of the sages and patriarchs"—she "hears the last of it"—only by dying, not as a living speaker addressing her daughter knowingly and directly. She remains stubbornly unincorporated by the novel's powerful discourses, a no-meaning that can be neither heard nor reformed.

But the mother is ridiculous, rather than tragic, only within the father's terms of judgment—terms which a society divided into opposites cannot unimagine or unspeak, and against which the lower-class opposition of fancy and heart will have little impact. The mother's very imprecision undercuts the authority of the father's discourses, making them a lesson imperfectly learned and badly recited. The novel cannot construct an imagined alternate culture, in which Mrs. Gradgrind would "discover" the language to define the "something missing," in which "ological" would not be required as an ending that validates an object's existence. Instead it unfolds the boundaries and effects of such a system. Louisa learns painfully that Mrs. Gradgrind's point-of-view has been confined to its position of "no-meaning" by concerted efforts by her father and his system of definition. Towards the end of the novel, Louisa reverses the charge of "no-meaning" and demands that her father justify instead what his "meaning" has produced: "Where are the graces of my soul? Where are the sentiments of my heart? What have you done, O father, what have you done, with the garden that should have bloomed once, in this great wilderness here!" In this confrontation, Louisa recognizes the contest her father has suppressed and her mother has barely suggested, a contest for how to determine the shape and value of the social realms:

> I have grown up, battling every inch of my way. . . . What I have learned has left me doubting, misbelieving, despising, regretting, what I have not learned; and my dismal resource has been to think that life would soon go by, and that nothing in it could be worth the pain and trouble of a contest.

The novel presents several scenes between Louisa and her father in which this authority is examined and questioned, scenes which pointedly exclude Mrs. Gradgrind, as someone whose objections or interests are irrelevant. The chapter "Father and Daughter" opens with an oblique questioning of the absolute value of such authority, but only once the "business" is resolved does Gradgrind suggest, "now, let us go and find your mother." Yet the exploration of Gradgrind's power makes an obscure and unacknowledged connection between his power and her mother's "death" from the novel. By what seems a frivolous word-game on the part of the narrator, Gradgrind's governmental blue books (the emblem of his power) are associated with an infamous wife-killer: "Although Mr Gradgrind did not take after Blue Beard, his room was quite a blue chamber in its abundance of blue books." The narrator denies that this "error" has any meaning, thus resisting the implication that Gradgrind's intellectual system of power has something to do with the oppressed status of his wife. The blue books are accorded the power of fact, which is to prove "usually anything you like," but the narrator's flight of fancy is not to prove anything. It refers, not to the authoritative realms of statistics and science, but to fairy-tales; it is not a "fact" derived from texts, but is "something missing," an association produced by the unconscious. It remains, at best, as a kind of insider's joke, in which readers can remember that its "power" derives from texts with which Dickens was aligned, both in general (fiction and fairy tale), and explicitly (Blue Beard is the basis for Dickens' Captain Murderer, whose tale he published in 1860 as one of his "Nurse's Stories").

The reference to the wife-killer, Blue Beard, who charms all with his show of courtesy and devotion before devouring his wives in the privacy of their home, is an "error" that suggests the gap between public and private, between acknowledged power and covert violence. Like the marginalized tensions created by Mrs. Gradgrind throughout

the novel, this slip of the pen provokes despite its claim to marginality. The error is allowed to stand, thereby suggesting what would otherwise be too bizarre to consider. It reminds us that Gradgrind has been a social "wife-killer," obliterating his wife's role as mother to her daughter and keeping her from fuller participation in the daughter's narrative. He has "formed his daughter on his own model," and she is known to all as "Tom Gradgrind's daughter." He has isolated Louisa in his masculine realm, depriving her of any of the usual female resources with which to oppose his power; as Tom mentions with devastating casualness, Louisa "used to complain to me that she had nothing to fall back upon, that girls usually fall back upon." The reference to Blue Beard reminds us that Gradgrind's realm is *not* absolute except by force and mystification, that his "charmed apartment" depends on the exclusion of a more powerful, more resistant "other." The rest of the chapter teases out the possibilities that his power can be questioned. Through a series of fanciful images—that make the narrator not an unworthy companion of Mrs. Gradgrind—the absolute value of his authority is obliquely undermined. Gradgrind is presented as needing to enforce his positions with military might, relying on his books as an "army constantly strengthening by the arrival of new recruits." His solutions persist because they are isolated within a necromancer's circle, protected from critique or even outside knowledge. From his enclosed, abstracted fortress, he orders the world as if "the astronomer within should arrange the starry universe solely by pen, ink and paper, . . . could settle all their destinies on a slate, and wipe out all their tears with one dirty little bit of sponge." All these questions about Gradgrind's power are delivered as amusing details, as arguments the novelist is not able to give serious articulation. Yet the details attack not the effect of Gradgrind's power, as Louisa does with hopeless inertia, but the claim to power, its genealogy and maintenance.

It is not surprising that Louisa and her mother, and even Dickens, cannot find words for what is missing from their lives, words having been usurped as the tools of the Gradgrind system, defined and delimited by male authority. Mrs. Gradgrind does not articulate an opposition, nor does the novel openly pursue the traces of her petulant complaints. *She* remains unaware that her headaches and worries are symptoms of a cultural dissatisfaction, although she knows that her head began "to split" as soon as she was married. She complains to Louisa about the trouble that comes from speaking—"You must remember, my dear, that whenever I have said anything, on any subject, I have never heard the last of it; and consequently, that I have long left off saying anything," but the ideological implications of these remarks are shortcircuited by the personal contexts in which she declines to speak. These scenes do not transform Mrs. Gradgrind into a covert rebel, but represent her as willful and self-absorbed, betraying Sissy and Louisa by her silence and diverting attention from their more pressing needs.

In fact, Mrs. Gradgrind seems to exist primarily as the cautionary exemplum of the Gradgrind system, having been married for the "purity" of being as free from nonsense "as any human being not arrived at the perfection of an absolute idiot, ever was." She proves her usefulness to the system, admirably serving as the negative against which the father seems more caring, more responsive than he seems in isolation. Her mother seems unsympathetic to Louisa's discontent, worrying over it as "one of those subjects I shall never hear the last of." And she serves as the agent who reinscribes the ideological positions of the Gradgrind system, who insists on reality being defined as what is kept "in cabinets" or about which one can "attend lectures." Louisa is scolded for running off to look at the forbidden circus by her mother, not by the father whose prohibition it is and who has caught her in the crime. The hapless Mrs. Gradgrind "whimpers" to her daughter; "I wonder at you. I declare you're enough to make one regret ever having had a family at all. I have a great mind to say I wish I hadn't. *Then* what would you have done, I should like to know." Yet in this pathetic effort to enforce her husband's laws, Mrs. Gradgrind has unknowingly allied herself with her child's rebellion. Her words give her away: she has "wondered" (a crime against reason), she has "regretted" (a crime against fact), and she has "wished" (a crime against her husband). Dickens notes that "Mr. Gradgrind did not seem favourably impressed by these cogent remarks." Yet what seems initially a silly, self-indulgent speech has deflected the father's wrath from his daughter and has suggested the terms for opposition—wonder, regret, desire.

Hard Times appears to authorize an oppositional discourse of fancy, which is lisped by the circus-master Sleary and represented in Sissy Jupe, the substitute mother whom Gradgrind praises as the "good fairy in his house" who can "effect" what 10,000 pounds cannot. Gradgrind's approval, and the conventionality of Sissy's depiction as a house fairy, devalues her status as an opposition figure. Indeed Sissy rarely speaks in opposition, or at all. Her power is cited by men like Harthouse and Gradgrind, and by the narrator. Unlike Mrs. Gradgrind, Sissy cannot be mocked for "cogent remarks," but simply *looks* at Louisa "in wonder, in pity, in sorrow, in doubt, in a multitude of emotions." Her effect is largely due to the novelty of her discourse, a novelty produced by her status as an outsider who does not understand the conventions of the system. "Possessed of no facts," girl number twenty does not recognize that "fancy" is a significant term, but uses it unthinkingly. She silences the cynical Harthouse by presenting "something in which he was so inexperienced, and against which he knew any of his usual weapons would fall so powerless; that not a word could he rally to his relief." Sissy insists on her words to Harthouse remaining a "secret" and relies on a "child-like ingenuousness" to sway her listener. And what Harthouse notices is her "most confiding eyes" and her "most earnest (though so quiet)" voice. Sissy's "wonder" is powerful only as long as she does not "speak" it in her own right, but presents it in her disengaged role as go-between. Her "power" depends on "her entire forgetfulness of herself in her earnest quiet holding to the object"—depends, in other words, on a strenuous denial of herself as a contestant for power. The narrator comments that "if she had shown, or felt the slightest trace of any sensitiveness to

his ridicule or astonishment, or any remonstrance he might offer; he would have carried it against her at this point."

Sissy's discourse derives its power, not from any essential woman's knowledge that Louisa and her mother could share, but from her experience as a working-class child who knows counter examples and a different word than "fact." Louisa acquires from Sissy not the power to be "a mother—lovingly watchful of her children" but to be "learned in childish lore; thinking no innocent and pretty fancy ever to be despised." The opposition Sissy seems to represent—of imagination, emotion, questioning of patriarchal discourses—stands like the circus-master's fancy, a fantastic dream that amuses children but does not displace Gradgrindian fact. It has no ability to construct a shared feminine discourse that can alter the rigid polarities of fact and fancy, meaning and no-meaning. When Louisa tries to inquire about such forbidden topics as love, she is on her own, pursuing a "strong, wild, wandering interest peculiar to her; an interest gone astray like a banished creature, and hiding in solitary places."

In her dramatic confrontation with her father, Louisa tries to construct a realm outside the powerful sway of reason and logic. Yet she can imagine this realm only as the "immaterial part of my life," marking it as that which has no material existence or is irrelevant. She thereby perpetuates the construction of her world as absolute in its polarities—as world that is either material or immaterial, fact or fancy, reason or nonsense. To use Bakhtin's terms, she remains "bound" to "the authoritative word" in its totality; she cannot "divide it up," or "play with the context framing it" or "play with its borders." She suggests she might have come closer to a desired end "if I had been stone blind; if I had groped my way by my sense of touch, and had been free, while I knew the shapes and surfaces of things, to exercise my fancy somewhat, in regard to them." Passionate as this scene is, Louisa's specific argument shows the difficulty of evading the power of patriarchal discourse; she can only "prove" the worth of an oppositional realm by the tools she has learned from her father. Her vision remains defined as "no-meaning," as existing only in opposition to what persists as "meaning." Louisa tries to imagine a realm "defying all the calculations ever made by man, and no more known to his arithmetic than his Creator is," but ends up describing herself as "a million times wiser, happier." Like her mother, her power lies in speaking the father's word imperfectly, making her father's statistical practices meaningless by her exaggerated application. Like her mother, Louisa's complaints refer only to "something" missing; there are no words for what might be gained. The Gradgrind system is too powerful to allow Louisa or her mother to break away or to communicate very well with each other. All they can do, in their separate ways and unbeknownst to each other, is to disrupt the functioning of the father's word, and to indicate a lack, an incompleteness.

The schematic quality of *Hard Times* indicates a broader lack or incompleteness in the authoritative discourses of Dickens' social and literary world. Like Louisa and Mrs. Gradgrind, Dickens must articulate his valuing of "fancy" and his concern about crossing proscribed boundaries in language devalued by the patriarchal discourses of reason and fact. That Lewes sees him as hallucinating a world no wise man would recognize indicates the disturbing effect of this crossing of boundaries. Both Lewes and Dickens identify the disturbance as somehow connected with women, seeing women as touched by issues that more successfully acculturated males do not notice. Lewes saw much of Dickens' power—and what made him a disturbing novelist—as the ability to represent something that could not otherwise be acknowledged. "What seems preposterous, impossible to us," he wrote in 1872, "seemed to him simple fact of observation." Writing as a woman places Dickens in a position to observe what seems "preposterous, impossible."

At the same time, of course, for a powerful male novelist like Dickens, the position of outsider is exaggerated. Dickens can be seen as exploiting the exclusion and material oppression of women and the poor when they serve as analogies for his own more temperate marginality as a lower-middle class writer of fiction in a literary culture that preferred educated reason over experienced fancy. For male writers like Dickens and Trollope, writing "as a woman" brought literary respect and considerable financial return, whereas a writer like Charlotte Brontë was censured for her unwomanly productions and underpaid by her publisher. Unlike women who transgress the boundaries of the literary establishment, Dickens could signal his difference as significant rather than ridiculous. Unlike the poor with whom he was so closely identified, Dickens had access to the means of publication; he had the influence and position to pressure contemporary methods of production and dissemination of literary and social discourse. Such was his influence as spokesman of social discontent, that women writers of the nineteenth century, in both England and America, had to come to terms with his boundaries and codes, with his literary conventions for observing the social world and its institutions. Writers like Mary Elizabeth Braddon, Elizabeth Gaskell, Elizabeth Stuart Phelps, and Rebecca Harding Davis both quote and revise his portrayal of women's writing and social position. Their attempts to write as women are circumscribed within Dickens' example and within the audience that he so powerfully swayed.

This assessment of Dickens' sympathetic identification with feminine discourses in the 1850s returns to the intertwined, ideological interests involved in any attempt to write "as a woman," in any project that *assumes* the position of an outsider, of an other. Dickens' experimentation with excluded positions of women and the poor provided him with a way of disrupting the status quo of the literary establishment. But, ironically, his experimentation also helped him capitalize on his status as an outsider in that literary realm. The inarticulate masses became, in effect, his constituency and his subject matter, supporting his powerful position within the literary and social establishment as arbiter of how to write about cultural exclusion. Dickens' growing influence as an editor and public spokesman for the literary world make his representations of women's writing dominate the literary scene. His ex-

ample carves out a possible space for women writers in his culture, but it also takes over that space as its own. His assumed position as outsider complicates assumptions about gender difference in writing and problematizes what Lewes so confidently called "genuine female experience." It disrupts and forces out into the open the literary establishment's defensive cultural narratives, and, in the process, constructs its own protective practices and standards. In writing as a woman, in speaking for a silenced group, Dickens both makes possible and makes complicated a challenge to "the father's word" by those who use "the mother-tongue."

FURTHER READING

Criticism

Butt, John, and Tillotson, Kathleen. "*Hard Times:* The Problems of a Weekly Serial." In their *Dickens at Work,* pp. 201-21. London: Methuen & Co., 1963.

> Systematic examination of *Hard Times* in the light of the conditions under which Dickens wrote it. Butt and Tillotson draw upon Dickens's working notes and week-by-week record of the novel's serialization.

Cowles, David L. "Having It Both Ways: Gender and Paradox in *Hard Times*." *Dickens Quarterly* VIII, No. 2 (June 1991): 79-84.

> Illustrates how Dickens undermines many of his own thematic assertions regarding gender issues by "playing both sides of irreconcilable contradictions." "Yet he does so in ways harmonious with his time, sex, and class (and therefore largely invisible to his contemporary readers) through conceptual languages he could not escape any more than we can escape our own linguistic and interpretive limitations."

Dyson, A. E. "*Hard Times:* The Robber Fancy." In his *The Inimitable Dickens: A Reading of the Novels*, pp. 183-202. London: Macmillan, 1970.

> Appraises *Hard Times* as "a powerful fiction" which "triumphantly survives," despite its unrelenting grimness and purposefulness.

Ford, George, and Monod, Sylvère, eds. *Hard Times,* by Charles Dickens. New York: W. W. Norton & Co., 1966, 378 p.

> The Norton Critical Edition, containing an authoritative text, backgrounds, sources, and criticism on the novel from Ruskin through Daniel P. Deneau.

Friedman, Stanley. "Sad Stephen and Troubled Louisa: Paired Protagonists in *Hard Times*." *Dickens Quarterly* VII, No. 2 (June 1990): 254-62.

> On the way in which Dickens shows, through the lives of Stephen Blackpool and Louisa Gradgrind, how "men and women in diverse social strata may suffer greatly in a nation marked by an insensitivity to basic emotional needs."

Green, Robert. "*Hard Times:* The Style of a Sermon." *Texas Studies in Literature and Language* 11, No. 1 (Spring 1969): 1375-96.

> Seeks "to show the existence of a close relationship between the details of Dickens' style and his overall purpose in writing *Hard Times*, and then to draw a few parallels between the language of this novel and the stylistic devices of a piece of nonliterary English that was contemporary with Dickens' novel," that being the sermons of John Cardinal Newman.

Hornback, Bert G. "*Hard Times* and *A Tale of Two Cities:* Two Late Fables." In his *"Noah's Arkitecture": A Study of Dickens's Mythology*, pp. 111-24. Athens: Ohio University Press, 1972.

> Reads *Hard Times* as a moral fable told through a sermon, the text for which being the "mad world" and the lesson of which being "that love is the only thing that can save us, and that art and the works of the imagination, however strange and impractical and useless they may seem, are intimately connected with the life of love."

Howells, W. D. "Dickens's Later Heroines." In his *Heroines of Fiction*, Vol. I, pp. 148-60. New York: Harper & Brothers, 1901.

> Cites *Hard Times* as having "more affinity with the actual world than most other novels of Dickens," though "the means of any effect to be accomplished are so far beyond the requisite that one is inclined to ask with the Irishman challenged to astonishment at the prodigious fall of water at Niagara, "What's to hinder it?"

Kearns, Katherine. "A Tropology of Realism in *Hard Times.*" *ELH* 59, No. 4 (Winter 1994): 857-81.

> Suggests that the language and plot in Dickens's novel function as an examination of two kinds of realism: fictional realism and the industrial-based realism that eliminates fanciful elements from the lives of the workers portrayed in the novel.

Lodge, David. "How Successful Is *Hard Times*?" In his *Working with Structuralism: Essays and Reviews on Nineteenth- and Twentieth-Century Literature*, pp. 37-45. Boston, Mass.: Routledge and Kegan Paul, 1981.

> Reads *Hard Times* as an artificial, "moralized theatricality," in which Dickens seeks, through techniques borrowed from the theater and fairy tales, to "defamiliarise not merely the subject-matter of the story, so that we perceive it freshly, but also the method of presentation itself, so that instead of lapsing into a passive story, we are compelled to recognize its artificiality and to consider its ideological implications."

Michie, Elsie B. "'Those That Will Not Work': Prostitutes, Property, Gaskell, and Dickens." In her *Outside the Pale: Cultural Exclusion, Gender Difference, and the Victorian Woman Writer*, pp. 113-41. Ithaca, N.Y.: Cornell University Press, 1993.

> Feminist examination of the connection between economics and sexuality in mid-Victorian discussions of prostitution and in Elizabeth Gaskell's and Dickens's novels of the mid-1850s, with recurrent reference to *Hard Times*.

Rounds, Stephen R. "Naming People: Dickens's Technique in *Hard Times.*" *Dickens Studies Newsletter* VIII, No. 2 (June 1977): 36-40.

> Demonstrates how, in *Hard Times*, "names are more than just keys to the characters of their holders; but here they are sources of power and dominance."

Stevenson, Lionel. "Dickens's Dark Novels, 1851-1857." *The Sewanee Review* LI, No. 3 (July-September 1943): 398-409.

> Surveys the three "least read" of Dickens's novels (*Bleak House, Hard Times,* and *Little Dorrit*), finding that in *Hard Times* "the essential conflict of capital and labor is presented so baldly, the complacency of the *laissez-faire* industrialists and the utilitarian cant that masks their rapacity, are contrasted so persistently with the nobility of the honest working man, that the story has a machine-made effect, totally devoid of those inconsistent human traits that give verisimilitude to even the most exaggerated characters and episodes in all [Dickens's] other books."

Additional coverage of Dickens's life and career is contained in the following sources published by Gale Research: *Nineteenth-Century Literature Criticism,* **Vols. 8, 18, 26;** *Short Story Criticism,* **Vol. 17;** *World Literature Criticism, Concise Dictionary of Literary Biography,* **1832-1890;** *Dictionary of Literary Biography,* **Vol. 21, Victorian Novelists Before 1885; Vol. 55, Victorian Prose Writers Before 1867; Vol. 70, British Mystery Writers, 1860-1919;** *Major Authors and Illustrators for Children and Young Adults;* **and** *Something About the Author,* **Vol. 15.**

Margaret Fuller

1810-1850

(Full name Sarah Margaret Fuller) American essayist, critic, travel writer, translator, and poet.

For additional information on Fuller's life and career, see *NCLC,* Volume 5.

INTRODUCTION

Fuller was a distinguished literary and social critic and pioneering feminist. As a founding editor of the Transcendentalist journal the *Dial* and a contributor to other influential periodicals, she was instrumental in introducing European art and literature to the United States. In addition, her *Woman in the Nineteenth Century* (1855) is an important early American feminist treatise.

Biographical Information

Fuller was the first of nine children born to a lawyer and his wife. She received an extensive private education and became active in intellectual circles made up of Harvard and Cambridge students and faculty, later forming longstanding personal and professional relationships within the Transcendentalist movement, including friendships with Amos Bronson Alcott, Ralph Waldo Emerson, Horace Greeley, Nathaniel Hawthorne, and Henry Wadsworth Longfellow. She participated in various liberal educational and social experiments, including Alcott's progressive Temple School and the Fruitlands and Brook Farm communal living experiments. Fuller's efforts to involve women in the country's intellectual life included a series of "Conversations" between 1939 and 1842, lectures on history, art, literature, and culture during which Fuller encouraged questions, discussion, and independent thought. Contemporary records, including the letters and diaries of the women who participated, attest to Fuller's brilliance as a speaker. Fuller worked closely with Emerson in developing editorial policy for the *Dial* magazine and served as its unpaid editor for its first two years of publication; the *Dial* failed within a year after Emerson assumed the editorship in 1842. After publishing literary criticism, social commentary, and travel essays in Greeley's *New York Daily Tribune,* Fuller obtained the post of literary editor of that journal in late 1844. Traveling to Europe in 1846, Fuller sent back firsthand accounts of the Risorgimento, the Italian liberal independence movement, to the *Tribune,* thus becoming one of the United States' first foreign correspondents. Fuller met and may have married Giovanni Ossoli in 1847; she was returning to the United States in 1850 with Ossoli and their son when her ship sank within sight of shore. Her body was never recovered.

Major Works

Fuller is best remembered for *Woman in the Nineteenth Century,* an acute assessment of the personal, social, professional, and political status of American women. Highly controversial in its time, particularly in calling for all professions to be open to women, this treatise was often condemned on religious grounds: Fuller's argument for equality between the sexes was held to controvert divine intent. Her travel essays and social commentary, first published periodically, were gathered and published in *Papers on Literature and Art* (1846), *Summer on the Lakes, in 1843* (1844), and several posthumous collections. These works included vibrant landscape descriptions, discussion of the living conditions of Native American tribes, investigation into the treatment of incarcerated women, and feminist commentary. The dispatches that Fuller submitted from Europe to Greeley's *New York Daily Tribune* during the Risorgimento are generally acclaimed to contain some of her finest written work; in these firsthand accounts of the Italian fight for independence, Fuller demonstrated facility with vivid, terse, and profoundly moving reportage.

Critical Reception

Most assessments of Fuller's writing note that with the exception of her foreign correspondence from Italy, her literary style is overly ornate, allusive, and convoluted. Fuller's contemporaries reacted as much to her forceful personality as to her literary accomplishments, and commented more on her character and conversation than on her published works. Meaningful evaluation of her life and works was impeded when William Henry Channing, James Freeman Clark, and Ralph Waldo Emerson produced a heavily edited volume of posthumous *Memoirs,* seriously misrepresenting Fuller, revising passages from her letters and diaries as well as from works written for publication. Her reputation suffered further when Hawthorne based his portrayal of the alluring but strident and manipulative Zenobia in *The Blithedate Romance* on Fuller. The distortions of the more famous male associates who outlived Fuller colored popular impression of her for many decades. More balanced evaluation began in 1927 when Vernon Louis Parrington offered an evaluation of her written works in his *Main Currents in American Thought.* Since the late 1970s, scholarship and reinvestigation by primarily feminist critics has resulted in far more accurate estimation, acknowledging Fuller's contribution to the cultural life of nineteenth-century America and as a commentator on, and crusader to improve, the status of women.

PRINCIPAL WORKS

Summer on the Lakes, in 1843 (travel essays) 1844
Woman in the Nineteenth Century (essay) 1845
Papers on Literature and Art (criticism) 1846
Woman in the Nineteenth Century and Kindred Papers Relating to the Sphere, Conditions, and Duties of Woman (essays) 1855
At Home and Abroad; or; Things and Thoughts in America and Europe (essays and letters) 1856
Life Without and Life Within (essays and poetry) 1860
The Writings of Margaret Fuller (essays, criticism, letters, poetry, memoirs) 1941
The Letters of Margaret Fuller. 6 vols. (letters) 1983-94

CRITICISM

Orestes Brownson (essay date 1845)

SOURCE: A review of *Woman in the Nineteenth Century,* in *Brownson's Quarterly Review* Vol. 2, No. 2, April, 1845, pp. 249-57.

[*An American clergyman, editor, and essayist, Brownson was a prolific writer whose work was centrally concerned with the quest for religious truth and belief in justice and political liberty. In the following review, he charges that* Woman in the Nineteenth Century *possesses neither style nor structure, and rejects on religious grounds Fuller's call for women's equality.*]

Miss Fuller belongs to the class . . . of *Transcendentalists,* of which sect she is the chieftainess. She has a broader and richer nature than Mr. [Theodore] Parker, greater logical ability, and deeper poetic feeling; more boldness, sincerity, and frankness, and perhaps equal literary attainments. But at bottom they are brother and sister, children of the same father, belong to the same school, and in general harmonize in their views, aims, and tendencies. Their differences are, that he is more of the theologian, she more of the poet; he more of the German in his taste, she more of the Grecian; he the more popular in his style of writing, she the more brilliant and fascinating in her conversation. In the Saint-Simonian classification of the race, he would belong to the class of *savans,* she to that of *artistes.*

But Miss Fuller is an *artiste* only in her admiration of art, for she has little artistic skill. Nothing is or can be less artistic than the book before us [*Woman in the Nineteenth Century*] which, properly speaking, is no book, but a long talk on matters and things in general, and men and women in particular. It has neither beginning, middle, nor end, and may be read backwards as well as forwards, and from the centre outwards each way, without affecting the continuity of the thought or the succession of ideas. We see no reason why it should stop where it does, or why the lady might not keep on talking in the same strain till doomsday, unless prevented by want of breath.

The title gives no clew to the character of the work; for it is no part of its design to sketch, as one would suppose, the condition of woman in the nineteenth century. Indeed, we do not know what is its design. We cannot make out what thesis or what theses it does or does not maintain. All is profoundly obscure, and thrown together in "glorious confusion." We can attempt no analysis of its contents. As talk, it is very well, and proves that the lady has great talkative powers, and that, in this respect at least, she is a genuine woman.

As we read along in the book, we keep constantly asking, What is the lady driving at? What does she want? But no answer comes: She does not know, herself, what she wants. She has an ugly feeling of uneasiness, that matters do not go right with her; and she firmly believes that if she had—I know not what—all would go better. She is feverish, and turns from one side of the bed to the other, but finds no relief. The evil she finds, and which all her class find, is in her, in them, and is removed by no turning or change of posture, and can be. She and they are, no doubt, to be compassionated, to be tenderly nursed and borne with, as are all sick people. It is no use attempting to reason them out of their crotchets; but well people should take care not to heed what they say, and especially not to receive the ravings of their delirium as divine inspirations.

Seriously, Miss Fuller does not know what she wants, any

more than does many a fine lady, whom silks, laces, shawls, dogs, parrots, balls, routs, jams, watering-places, and despair of lover or husband and friends have ceased to satisfy. She even confesses her inability to formula her complaint. She has a strange gnawing within, an indefinable craving for what she has not, does not know how to get, where to find,—a very unpleasant condition, no doubt, but not an uncommon one. Poor girl!/ hers is but the common lot of all her Protestant and infidel sisters, and brothers too; for her brothers are hardly less subject to the vapors than her sisters. They are all seeking they know not what, craving what they have not, find not,—now seizing on this bawble, now on that,—a bonnet, ribbon, shawl, cravat, coat, minister, sect, association; but all to no purpose. The craving remains; nothing satisfies; the aching heart nothing fills. Cook the vegetable oyster as they will, serve it up with what condiments, flanked by what sauces, they please, it is never the genuine oyster.

"O, give us something to love!" exclaim a bevy of dear, sweet, enchanting creatures. "Give us something to love; we were made to love"; and round they look with fond eyes and loving hearts, but as ever there is the gnawing, the aching void within. Love is the be-all, the cure-all, the end-all; but, alas, there is nothing to love; no one knows how to love; no one knows how to respond to the true, fond, loving heart. Try again,—again,—another,—another, and still another;—'t is vain. The heart is not met; is not filled; is emptier than ever. Surely there is some mistake. The Creator committed a blunder when he made the world, especially when he made man and woman. Man and woman, it is true, as says our authoress, are but "two halves of one thought"; but the right halves do not come together, or do not match. They get mismatched. Mrs. Jones has got my other half, and I have got Mrs. Peter Smith's,—or am cheated out of it altogether. All this is very provoking, no doubt. To be made capable of loving, to have this free, pure, rich heart, full to overflowing with love, containing a whole ocean of love, large as the Atlantic, nay, as the five oceans together, and warm enough to thaw out either pole, and no one I can love,—nobody but Jim Jones or Peter Smith,—'t is intolerable.

The terrible evil here set forth Miss Fuller thinks is confined exclusively to her own sex. Men have the advantage; with them it is not so bad. There she is wrong. There are those who have beards on their faces, as well as those who have none, who have these cravings, these hearts full of love, such as it is, and an aching void in these same full hearts, because there is no one for them to love. They cannot love Bridget or Sukey, and all but the Bridgets and Sukeys are—not for them. Men are not much more easily satisfied than women; and if women are forced to take to tea, scandal, philanthropy, evening-meetings, and smelling-bottles, men are forced to take to trade, infidelity, sometimes the pistol, and even to turn *reformers,* the most desperate resort of all. All this is sad enough, and really under all this is a grievous evil, of which no seriousminded man will make light. But what is the remedy?

Miss Fuller, so far as we collect her thought from her interminable prattle, seems to think this evil is to be remedied by having it understood that woman has an immortal soul, and by securing her free scope to develope herself. But what change this implies, or would introduce, Yankee as we are, we are unable to guess. Understand that woman has an immortal soul! Why, we are far beyond that already. Read our poets, listen to our philanthropists, abolitionists, Fourierists, Saint-Simonians, dietetic reformers, and other reformers of all sorts and sizes, of all manner of things in the universe, and some others, and you shall find that she is already a divinity, and adored as such. Who has not heard of the "divine Fanny," or not been eager to adore as she made his heart jump by her capers and pirouettes? Not her soul only, but woman's body, is held to be divine, divine from head to foot, and we go into ecstacy of devotion at sight of a "divine ankle." In our ordinary prosaic language, is not woman an "angel," "an angel of purity," of "loveliness," and "too holy for earth"? and they who scorn to bend the knee before their Maker, are they not ready to prostrate themselves at her feet, and kiss the very ground on which she stands?

"The more fools they. But this is not what we want. This is sickening, disgusting." And yet there are comparatively few women seriously offended at it, if they themselves are its object, even though offered by those they have good reasons for believing are double-distilled villains. But enough of this. There are evils, great evils, no doubt, to which both men and women are subject. Neither sex is what it should be, or finds always the fair weather and smooth sea the heart may crave; but we have yet to be convinced that woman's lot, compared with that of man's, is one of peculiar hardship. She is not always the victim, and examples of suffering virtue may be found amongst men as well as amongst women. No doubt, there are evils enough to redress, but we do not think the insane clamor for "woman's rights," for "woman's equality," "woman's liberation," and all this, will do much to redress them. Woman is no more deprived of her rights than man is of his, and no more enslaved. Woman as to her moral and spiritual nature has always been emancipated by Christianity, and placed as a human being on the same platform with man. She is treated, and always has been treated, by Christianity as having an immortal soul, and as personally accountable to her Maker. In this respect man has no claims, and is allowed no preëminence, over her; and what more can she ask?

In the distribution of the several spheres of social and domestic action, woman has assigned to her one sphere, and man another; both equally important, equally honorable. This therefore is no cause of complaint.—But who assigned her this sphere? Has she given her consent to be confined to it? Has she ever been consulted? her assent asked?—And what if not? Who assigned man his sphere? was his assent asked or obtained? Their appropriate spheres are allotted to man and woman by their Creator, and all they have to do is to submit, as quietly, and with as good a grace, as they can. Miss Fuller thinks it is man who has crowded woman one side, and refused her full scope for self-development; and although the sphere in which she moves may really be that most appropriate to her, yet man has no right to confine her to it, and forbid her to take another if she prefer it. She should be as free to decide her own destiny as man is his. All very plausible. But God, and not man, has assigned her the appropriate sphere; and, moreover, we must be ungallant enough to question Miss Fuller's leading doctrine of the perfect social and political equality of the sexes. She says man is not the head of the woman. We, on the authority of the Holy Ghost, say he is. The dominion was not given to woman, nor to man and woman conjointly, but to the man. Therefore the inspired Apostle, while he commands husbands to love and cherish their wives, commands wives to love and *obey* their husbands; and, even setting aside all considerations of divine inspiration, St. Paul's authority is, to say the least, equal to that of Miss Fuller.

Miss Fuller would have all offices, professions, callings, pursuits thrown open to woman as to man; and seems to think that the lost Eden will not be recovered till the petticoat carries it over the breeches. She is quite sure the ancient heathens understood this matter better than we do. They had a juster appreciation of the dignity of woman. Their principal divinities were goddesses, and women ministered in the fane, and gave the responses of the oracles. She is greatly taken with Isis, Sita, Egyptian Sphinx, Ceres, Proserpine. Would she recall these ancient heathen deities, their ancient worship, filled with obscene rites and frightful orgies? Would she restore the Isiac worship? revive that of Syrian Astarte? reëstablish the old custom which prevailed at Babylon; according to which every woman, on a certain festival, must prostitute herself to the first comer in honor of the goddess? readopt the old Phænician method of obtaining marriage portions for dowerless daughters? have carried again in public procession certain pleasant images which Roman dames were eager to crown with wreaths of flowers? or reproduce the wild Bacchantes with loosened tresses and loosened robes, and lascivious satyrs? These and far worse obtained in the worship of those female divinities, and where woman served the fane, and gave the responses of the gods. Has it never occurred to our learned and philosophic lady to ask, if there was not some relation of cause and effect between the part women took in these ancient religions, and these filthy rites and shameful practices?

We ask not this last question because we would imply that women are less pure, or more easily corrupted, than men. We are not likely to fall into the common herd of libellers of women, and sneerers at female virtue. We have lived too long, or been too fortunate in our acquaintances, to think lightly of woman's worth, or woman's virtues. We remember too vividly the many kind offices we have received from her hand, the firmness with which she has clung to us in adversity, when all the world had deserted us, and also the aid which her rapid intuitions and far-glancing sense has afforded us in our mental and moral progress, if we have made any, to be in danger of this. It has been our good fortune to have experienced all woman's tenderness, all her sympathy when we were in sorrow and destitution, her joy when the world bright-

ened to us, her generous self-forgetfulness and self-sacrifices for the beloved of her heart, and the sweet and gentle companionship in intellectual pursuits and in moral duties which seems to double man's power and to make virtue thrice more amiable; and we do not feel, that, so long as we retain our memory, we can be in danger of speaking lightly of woman, or of doing her injustice. But though we say all this; and could say much more, we still say the two sexes cannot mingle in certain spheres, and on the terms Miss Fuller proposes, without the mutual corruption of both. The fault is not woman's more than man's, perhaps not so much; but the fact is no less certain. While we live in the flesh, restraint and mortification are our law,—whether for men, or for women. The things which look to us so enchanting, which even are not bad within certain limits, the glowing pictures of our innocent imaginations, the bright ideals of our youth,—alas! human nature is rotten, trust it not. They who imposed the restraints against which Miss Fuller protests, who separated the sphere of the sexes, and assigned to each as far as possible a separate line of duty, if they were men, must have known all too well what they were about. They may have been men who had lost their innocency; but if so, they had gained—experience.

The first mistake which Miss Fuller commits is the mistake committed by all reformers,—from him who undertook in the Garden to reform God's commandment to our first parents, down to the author of the "Orphic Sayings,"—that the true moral and social state is to be introduced and secured by the free, full, and harmonious development of human nature. This mistake is committed everywhere. Go where we will, out of the Catholic world, we meet it. We find it with Deists and Atheists, with German Rationalists and American Transcendentalists, in the fanciful theories of Gall and Spurzheim, in the dreams of Charles Fourier and Saint-Simon. It is the settled doctrine, and only settled doctrine, of modern philosophy, and apparently the fixed creed of the whole Protestant and infidel worlds,—exception to be made, perhaps, in favor of the Puseyites, and the few remnants of the old Calvinistic sects. It is embraced and hotly defended by hundreds and thousands who have no suspicion of its direct and glaring hostility to experience and revelation. Nothing can be falser or more dangerous than this delusion. Nature does not suffice. Nature cannot be trusted. Away with your wretched cant about "faith in man, in man's nature," his "lofty capacities," "glorious affinities," and "Godlike tendencies." Nature, we repeat, is rotten; trust it not. The fairest, sweetest, purest, dearest affections nature ever knows lead us most wofully astray, and will do so, if not restrained, whatever your moral codes or social arrangements. There is no such thing as a harmonious development of nature. Cultivate nature as you will, observe the nicest balance between all its tendencies, and, before you know it, before you can dream of it, one rascally passion has suddenly gained the mastery, and all is confusion and anarchy within. Nature is cursed. For six thousand years you have cultivated it, and it has yielded you only briers and thorns; cultivate it as you will for six thousand years to come, and it will yield you nothing else. "He that soweth to the flesh shall of the flesh reap corruption."

Another mistake, not less fatal, is also committed by our reformers. They see there are evils, that men and women suffer, and suffer horribly. Their sympathies are awakened, and they seek if relief cannot be found. All this is well, commendable even. But they assume that relief is to come here, and the good craved, but found not, is to be realized in this world, in this probationary life. "The highest ideal man can form of his own powers," says Miss Fuller, "that he is destined to attain." And this ideal is to be attained here. But Eden, the terrestrial paradise, is lost, never to be regained. Man forfeited it, and has been driven forth from it, never to repose again in its fragrant bowers, or beneath its refreshing shades. The earth is cursed; do what you will, rebel as you please, the curse is irrevocable. This world is a prison-house, and escape you cannot till death sets you free. The sooner you come to this conclusion, the better for you, the better for all. This life is and must be a discipline, a probation, a warfare. You must stand on your guard, always in arms, sleepless, and fight, fight for your life, with enemies from all quarters, and of all sorts and sizes, till you are called home to enjoy the victory and the triumph.

We know this is an unpalatable truth to our zealous philanthropists, and we know the scorn and derision with which they will treat it. But the realization of a heaven on earth is not the end for which the Gospel was given us. Our Maker has not abandoned us; far from it. He has prepared something far better for us than a terrestrial paradise. He has prepared heaven and its eternal beatitude for us. But we can enjoy that here only through faith and hope. It is ours here only by promise. It is set before us as a glorious prize, as an exceeding rich reward; but it is not to be gained without the dust and heat of the race; nor will it be bestowed till the race is run, till the battle is fought, till the victory is won. Consolations we may have, consolations which the world knows not, cannot give, cannot take away. Angels will minister unto us and revive our fainting strength; but happiness, the full freedom and joy of the soul, are tasted not till the songs and harps of angels welcome us home to our Father's house.

True wisdom consists in fixing our eyes on this heavenly reward, and throwing off all that we may win it. We must count the sufferings of this present life not worthy to be compared with the glory hereafter to be revealed, we must despise the joys of this life, and trample the world under our feet. *Beati pauperes spiritu.* We must despise riches and honors, we must joy in poverty and destitution, and count all things as mere dross for the sake of Chist. This is the law imposed upon us, and no reforms which come not from obedience to this law will avail us aught. Here the struggle, the warfare; there the triumph, the joy.

But we have no room to proceed. As much as we dislike Miss Fuller's book, as pernicious as we regard the doctrines or notions it contains, as utterly as we are forced to condemn the whole race of modern, reformers,—all who are seeking to recover the lost Eden on earth, from the harmonious development of nature alone,—we can still believe, without difficulty, that she may be a pure-minded woman, honestly and earnestly struggling to obtain a greater good for suffering humanity. Taking her starting-point, we should arrive at her conclusion. Believing a terrestrial paradise possible, we should strive for it; believing the free, full, and harmonious development of human nature the means and condition of obtaining it, we should protest against whatever restrains nature in woman as well as in man. We believe Miss Fuller wholly in the wrong, but we see no occasion for the kind of animadversions on her or her book, which we have noticed in some newspaper criticisms. She has done or said nothing which should be regarded as a sin by her Protestant brethren. In our remarks we have designed nothing personal against her. We are able, we trust, to distinguish between persons and doctrines. For persons, however, far gone they may be in error, or even in sin, we trust we have the charity our holy religion commands, and which the recollection of our own errors and sins, equal to any we may have to deplore in others, requires us to exercise. But for erroneous doctrines we have no charity, no tolerance. Error is never harmless, and in no instance to be countenanced.

The Christian Examiner and Religious Miscellany (essay date 1845)

SOURCE: A review of *Woman in the Nineteenth Century,* in *The Christian Examiner and Religious Miscellany* Vol. XXXVIII, No. 1, May, 1845, pp. 416-17.

[*In the following review, the critic asserts that* Woman in the Nineteenth Century *lacks formal structure and rigorous analysis of a clearly stated thesis, but commends the intelligence and eloquence found throughout the book.*]

On the whole, we have been disappointed in this book as we like to be disappointed. A woman here vindicates the cause of her own sex without a very large infusion of special pleading—an achievement not slightly meritorious, and deserving no small praise. We took up the volume,—we are willing to confess it candidly,—expecting to find in it a considerable amount of mannerism, affectation, eccentricity and pedantry. It gives us all the more pleasure therefore, to acknowledge that our suspicions were, to a great extent, unjust. The number of inverted sentences, *outré* ideas, far-fetched comparisons and foreign idioms, is more limited than we had feared. Of pedantry, indeed, perhaps there is not an entire absence. Classical characters, and references to mythological fables, are introduced with a frequency which the best taste would hardly sanction; but the error is often committed with a gracefulness and appositeness which partially redeem it. We just notice these faults the more readily, because we believe Miss Fuller might easily be rid of them, and would gain greatly by the change. We observe that exactly in proportion as she becomes thoroughly in earnest, her style becomes straightforward and natural. An honest thinker, who occasionally wields the good Anglo-Saxon phrase so energetically, and with so much directness as she, ought to abandon at once all seeking after the novel, the strange and the startling. Like the class of writers to which she belongs, much read in the authors of another nation, and much delighted with them, she sometimes puts herself under a yoke, while she longs above all things to be free; adopts a constrained air, while particularly ambitious of unrestraint; and while aiming at a healthful exercise of the faculties, falls into a habit of thought that is morbid, inharmonious, without symmetry, and so, of course, unattractive, if not disgusting. Moreover,—to finish cleanly this ungrateful work of censure,—the book lacks method sadly, and should have been relieved to the reader by the kindly intervention, here and there, of a sectional or capital division. It is rather a collection of clever sayings and bright intimations, than a logical treatise, or a profound examination of the subject it discusses.

Whether Miss Fuller's ethical code would correspond precisely with our own, we should be able to declare with more confidence if she had made it perfectly clear to us what that code is. The same may be said of her standard of manners. But of the general spirit of the essay we can, and we must, speak with sincere and hearty approbation. There is a noble and stirring eloquence in many of the passages, that no susceptible person can fail to be affected by. Great, lustrous thoughts break out from the pages, finely uttered. The pervading sentiment is humane, gentle, sympathetic. Miss Fuller says in one place, "I wish woman to live, first, for God's sake;" and she seems to be possessed by the reverential, devout feeling indicated by this remark. She casts a deserved contempt on the miserable trifling so often exhibited by men in their conversation and deportment with women, a custom that depreciates and openly insults their character. For our own part, we have often wondered at their patient toleration of the indignity, implied so palpably in this sort of bearing. Mean topics and flippant discourse are perpetually introduced in society for their entertainment, as if they were capable of comprehending nothing else. She urges in respectful terms their rights, both in property, and, as mothers, to their children, suggesting some worthy thoughts for law-makers. She would have woman respectably employed. She would elevate the purposes of their lives, and by dignifying their position and character, restore the ancient chivalrous respect paid them by every manly heart. Her notions do not seem *ultra* nor extravagant. She does not ask that woman may be thrust into man's sphere, but that she may have a right and honorable sphere of her own, whether as sister, daughter, mother, or "old maid." And, for ourselves, we admire the noble appeals, near the close of the work, in which she rebukes vice, and entreats for it a wise but prompt consideration. She has discussed a delicate topic delicately and fearlessly; without prudish folly, without timidity, as a true woman should. No tongue will dare to cavil at her. She is too evidently above all small criticism in this quarter, far up out of its reach. What she has said needed to be said, and, if the age has any necessity, needs, we firmly believe, to be repeated, felt and acted upon. The "nineteenth century" has a mission to woman, as well as she to the nineteenth century.

Henry James (essay date 1903)

SOURCE: "The Siege of Rome," in *William Wetmore Story and His Friends: From Letters, Diaries, and Recollections, Vol. 1,* Houghton Mifflin & Co., 1903, pp. 93-163.

[*James was an American novelist and short story writer valued for his psychological acuity and complex sense of artistic form. He also wrote literary criticism in which he developed his artistic ideals and applied them to the works of others. In the following excerpt, taken from a reminiscence of the period during which Fuller was living in Rome, James muses on Fuller's place in literary and intellectual history and in the personal histories of those who knew her.*]

The unquestionably haunting Margaret-ghost, looking out from her quiet little upper chamber at her lamentable doom, would perhaps be never so much to be caught by us as on some such occasion as this. What comes up is the wonderment of *why* she may, to any such degree, be felt as haunting; together with other wonderments that brush us unless we give them the go-by. It is not for this latter end that we are thus engaged at all; so that, making the most of it, we ask ourselves how, possibly, in our own luminous age, she would have affected us on the stage of the "world," or as a candidate, if so we may put it, for the cosmopolite crown. It matters only for the amusement of evocation—since she left nothing behind her, her written utterance being naught; but to what would she have corresponded, have "rhymed," under categories actually known to us? Would she, in other words, with her appetite for ideas and her genius for conversation, have struck us but as a somewhat formidable bore, one of the worst kind, a culture-seeker without a sense of proportion, or, on the contrary, have affected us as a really attaching, a possibly picturesque New England Corinne?

Such speculations are, however, perhaps too idle; the *facts* of the appearance of this singular woman, who would, though conceit was imputed to her, doubtless have been surprised to know that talk may be still, after more than half a century, made about her—the facts have in themselves quite sufficient colour, and the fact in particular of her having achieved, so unaided and so ungraced, a sharp identity. This identity was that of the talker, the moral *improvisatrice,* or at least had been in her Boston days, when, young herself, she had been as a sparkling fountain to other thirsty young. In the Rome of many waters there were doubtless fountains that quenched, collectively, any individual gush; so that it would have been, naturally, for her plentiful life, her active courage and company, that the little set of friends with whom we are concerned valued her. She had bitten deeply into Rome, or, rather, *been,* like so many others, by the wolf of the Capitol, incurably bitten; she met the whole case with New England arts that show even yet, at our distance, as honest and touching; there might be ways for her of being vivid that were not as the ways of Boston. Otherwise what she would mainly prompt us to interest in might be precisely the beautiful moral complexion of the little circle of her interlocutors. That is ever half the interest of any celebrated thing—

taking Margaret's mind for celebrated: the story it has to tell us of those for whom it flourished and whose measure and reflection it necessarily more or less gives. Let us hasten to add, without too many words, that Mme. Ossoli's circle represented, after all, a small stage, and that there were those on its edges to whom she was not pleasing. This was the case with Lowell and, discoverably, with Hawthorne; the legend of whose having had her in his eye for the figure of Zenobia, while writing *The Blithedale Romance,* surely never held water. She inspired Mrs Browning, on the other hand, with sympathy and admiration, and the latter, writing of her in 1852, after the so lamentable end of her returnvoyage, with her husband and child, to America—the wreck of the vessel, the loss of father, mother and small son in sight of shore—says that "her death shook me to the very roots of my heart. The comfort is," Mrs Browning then adds, "that she lost little in the world—the change could not be loss to her. She had suffered, and was likely to suffer still more." She had previously to this, in December 1849, spoken of her, in a letter to Miss Mitford, as having "taken us by surprise at Florence, retiring from the Roman world with a husband and child above a year old. Nobody had even suspected a word of this underplot, and her American friends stood in mute astonishment before this apparition of them here. The husband is a Roman marquis appearing amiable and gentlemanly, and having fought well, they say, at the siege, but with no pretension to cope with his wife on any ground appertaining to the intellect." The "underplot" was precisely another of the personal facts by which the lady could interest—the fact, that is, that her marriage should *be* an underplot, and that her husband, much *decaduto,* should make explanation difficult. These

---

W. H. Channing on Fuller's conversation:

When her turn came, by a graceful transition she resumed the subject where preceding speakers had left it, and, briefly summing up their results, proceeded to unfold her own view. Her opening was deliberate, like the progress of some massive force gaining its momentum; but as she felt her way, and moving in a congenial element, the sweep of her speech became grand. The style of her eloquence was sententious, free from prettiness, direct, vigorous, charged with vitality. Articulateness, just emphasis and varied accent, brought out most delicate shades and brilliant points of meaning, while a rhythmical collocation of words gave a finished form to every thought. She was affluent in historic illustration and literary allusion, as well as in novel hints. She knew how to concentrate into racy phrases the essential truth gathered from wide research, and distilled with patient toil; and by skilful treatment she could make green again the wastes of commonplace. Her statements, however rapid, showed breadth of comprehension, ready memory, impartial judgment, nice analysis of differences, power of penetrating through surfaces to realities, fixed regard to central laws and habitual communion with the Life of life.

W. H. Channing, in Memoirs of Margaret Fuller Ossoli, *edited by Ralph Waldo Emerson, William Henry Channing, and James Freeman Clarke, Phillips, Sampson, 1852.*

---

things, let alone the final catastrophe, in short, were not talk, but life, and life dealing with the somewhat angular Boston sibyl on its own free lines. All of which, the free lines overscoring the unlikely material, is doubtless partly why the Margaret-ghost, as I have ventured to call it, still unmistakably walks the old passages.

Paula Blanchard (essay date 1978)

SOURCE: "Conversations and *The Dial,*" in *Margaret Fuller: From Transcendentalism to Revolution,* Delacorte Press/Seymour Lawrence, 1978, pp. 139-62.

[*In the following excerpt, Blanchard discusses the series of "Conversations," paid seminars combining elements of entertainment, instruction, and intellectual development for women which Fuller conducted in Boston beginning in 1838. Blanchard also examines Fuller's development and editorship of the Transcendentalist journal the* Dial.]

[Margaret Fuller's] conversation, Emerson said simply, was the most entertaining in America. And it may very well have been during one of the bookstore discussions that someone suggested that the most entertaining conversation in America might be worth paying for. In an era earnestly bent on self-culture, when almost anyone who wanted to give a speech on free will, cold baths, or the bumps on the human head could fill a lecture hall, the idea was not farfetched. In fact, [Bronson] Alcott had already begun to augment his income by holding conversations in private homes in the suburbs. (Being Alcott's, they were not so much conversations as monologues on a single, never-exhausted subject, punctuated occasionally by approving noises from his audience.) Elizabeth Peabody too had held conversational teaching sessions in the homes of friends. To be paid for doing what she liked best to do while living where she liked best to live seemed far too easy to Margaret, whose Fuller ancestry led her to regard this life as a series of ordeals set by the Lord to purify the soul. But several of her woman friends promised among them to form the solid core of a group: the Peabody sisters, Anna Barker, Eliza Farrar, Sophia Ripley, Sarah Clarke, Caroline Sturgis, and her sister Ellen Hooper. It would not be difficult to find eleven more to make up a group of twenty, and if each paid $20 for a series of ten conversations (a high fee for those days) she could support herself this way for several months. Elizabeth generously offered the use of the bookstore as a meeting place.

Men were excluded not out of any lack of interest on their part or false sense of propriety on Margaret's, but because her purpose in the Conversations had to do with changing the status of women. She did not want primarily to entertain or instruct (though she hoped to do both), but to alter the image women had of themselves. This was the purpose she had half-realized in her evening classes and in her classes in Providence, and it was this that had made the idea of opening a school in Cincinnati briefly attractive. In spite of the liberal rhetoric about universal equality, and in spite of scattered gestures that were being made toward higher education for women, individual women found it difficult to believe that their minds were equal to men's. She herself was not free from self-doubt, in spite of the brave show she made. Her own education had been reversed in the middle, and her intellectual self-assurance drew heavily on her experience as a young child; her social experience whenever she stepped out of her own circle, and sometimes even within it, demonstrated to her in a thousand little ways that insofar as she was bright she was not quite a whole woman. She wanted to help women overcome the double educational and social handicap by forcing them to fully engage their minds in an atmosphere that was as free as possible from censure. Women were taught a great many subjects in school, but they were not really expected to remember them. Except in a few academies, they were not required to reproduce what they had learned in examinations as men were; nor, except for teachers, were they required to do so in vocational life. Margaret hoped to induce them to systemize their thought and express themselves boldly as they had never been asked to before. She hoped to sharpen their thinking habits, but beyond that, and more important, she hoped to bring them to an understanding that their inadequacies were not innate, but were the result of superficial education and the attitude of self-deprecation instilled by social custom. If she could do this much, a small revolution might begin in Boston. And if such a plan failed in Boston, she told Sophia Ripley, it could not succeed anywhere in America.

Margaret Fuller hoped to bring women to an understanding that their inadequacies were not innate, but were the result of superficial education and the attitude of self-deprecation instilled by social custom. If she could do this much, a small revolution might begin.
— *Paula Blanchard*

The Conversations were very popular and continued for four years, with two series a year, one beginning in November and the other in March. Twenty-five women joined the first series, and in subsequent series the number rose to thirty-five or more, although all the members were never there at one time. The ***Memoirs*** list about forty women who participated at one time or another. Some, like Jane Tuckerman, were former students. Others were friends who had to travel some distance: Lidian Emerson, Sarah Alden Ripley, Almira Barlow, and Elizabeth Hoar. Lydia Maria Child came, and her fellow abolitionist Louisa Loring. But the list itself as given in the ***Memoirs,*** with its frequent omission of the women's Christian names and its allusions to their male relations, suggests how strongly these women were overshadowed by fathers, husbands, and fiancés. There are Shaws, Russells, Higginsons, Lees—all daughters and wives of the mercantile Boston aristocracy. Mrs. George Bancroft attended; Mrs. Theodore Parker; Maria White (the fiancée of James Russell Lowell); Mrs. Josiah Quincy; Mrs. Charles Newcomb (his mother, not his wife); Marianne Jackson (sis-

ter-in-law of Oliver Wendell Holmes); and Mary Channing, who, as Higginson explains, was Dr. Channing's only daughter. Most of those who were married or engaged had been singled out by their men because, among other reasons, their intelligence made them very satisfactory attendant spirits. Having the money and leisure to attend the Conversations, they also had very good cause.

The topics were deliberately broad, so as to allow everyone to participate without special preparation. One series was devoted to "Education," under which they discussed "Culture," "Ignorance," "Vanity," "Prudence," "Patience," and "Health." Another was on the Fine Arts. But Margaret's favorite topic, often repeated, was Greek Mythology, or rather the universal themes of will, reason, understanding, love, beauty, and so on, as objectified by the Greeks and other cultures. This may seem to be a more specialized subject than the others, but even women customarily received the rudiments of a "classical" education, and Margaret told them they need know only what they had learned from Homer and the fine arts.

The Conversations were usually held on Saturdays at 11:00 A.M. The members would sit in a semicircle and Margaret would stand in front of them, dressed in one of the full-sleeved, long-waisted gowns of the period, sometimes with a bowl of yellow chrysanthemums on the table beside her. Around her neck she wore a lorgnette, which she raised from time to time in order to see the people in the back of the room. At the beginning of the session she would give an introductory statement on the subject of the day, and then she would ask for comments. If none were forthcoming, she would ask for written statements to be read at the beginning of the next session. But apparently this seldom happened; the response of the group was enthusiastic, and she usually had no more to do than guide the conversation once it was under way. Even among this group she did not entirely escape the old criticism that she was too domineering, but it was limited to a few. The majority would have agreed with the description of one of the sessions written by a member to a friend:

Christmas made a holiday for Miss Fuller's class, but it met on Saturday, at noon. As I sat there, my heart overflowed with joy at the sight of the bright circle, and I longed to have you by my side, for I know not where to look for so much character, culture, and so much love of truth and beauty, in any other circle of women and girls. The names and faces would not mean so much to you as to me, who have seen more of the lives, of which they are a sign. Margaret, beautifully dressed (don't despise that, for it made a fine picture,) presided with more dignity and grace than I had thought possible. The subject was Beauty. Each had written her definition, and Margaret began with reading her own. This called forth questions, comments, and illustrations, on all sides. The style and manner, of course, in this age, are different, but the question, the high point from which it was considered, and the earnestness and simplicity of the discussion, as well as the gifts and graces of the speakers, gave it the charm of a Platonic dialogue. There was no pretension or pedantry in a word that was said. The tone of remark and question was simple as that of children in a school class; and, I believe, every one was gratified.

The main defect of the plan seems to have been that since the subjects were so general (general enough to be thought grandiose by the critical), the women were not in fact called upon to reproduce what they had learned, or at least not what they had formally studied. But they were obliged to formulate opinions on subjects which they had been led to believe they could have no opinions about. Margaret demanded that they "lay aside the shelter of vague generalities, the art of coterie criticism, and the 'delicate disdains' of *good society,*" and be "willing that others should think their sayings crude, shallow, or taste-less." It was only by acquiring the courage to do so, she told them, that they could "attain the real health and vig-or, which need no aid from rouge or candlelight, to brave the light of the world."

There are no accurate records of any of the sessions, al-though Elizabeth Peabody wrote some general summaries from memory. The one attempt made to record the Con-versations on the spot was a failure, although in justice to the writer, Caroline Dall, it must be said that the series itself was a failure. In 1841 Margaret decided to include men in the discussion and she gave a Monday evening series open to all. The men present included Emerson, Alcott, Ripley, Hedge, Clarke, Jones Very, William Wet-more Story, Messrs. Mack of Belmont and Shaw of Bos-ton, and Charles Stearns Wheeler, the only one of the group who could claim to be a Greek scholar. But the spontaneity of the other series was missing. The women were intimidated by the very presence of men and lapsed into deferential silence, except for a few brave spirits like Elizabeth Peabody and Caroline Sturgis. The men picked up the abandoned discussion and made off with it wher-ever they chose, the worst offender probably being Bron-son Alcott. Margaret's attempts to round them all up again were only momentarily successful. Emerson seems to have made himself deliberately obtuse, as he sometimes did, making his idealism seem more rigid than it actually was and pronouncing his opinions with a finality that left no room for compromise. Afterward, trying to be contrite in a letter to Margaret, he succeeded only in being petulant:

> The young people wished to know what possessed me to tease you with so much prose, and becloud the fine conversation? I could only answer that it was not an acute fit of Monday evening, but was chronic and constitutional with me, and I asked them in my turn when they had heard me talk anything else? . . . You, instead of wondering at my cloistered and unfriendly manners, should defend me if possible from friendship, from ambition, from my own weakness which would lead me to variety, which is the dissipation of thought. You and those others who are dear to me should be so rightly my friends as never to suffer me for a moment to attempt the game of wits and fashionists, no nor even that of those you call Friends. . . .

The following year the Conversations reverted to the orig-inal plan and were as successful as ever, in the way Margaret had intended. To discover that they actually were

able to think and speak for themselves on subjects outside their "sphere" had an intoxicating effect on many of the women, unlike anything they had ever experienced. Much of this overflowed into a feeling for Margaret herself which was close to adulation, especially among the young. Mrs. Dall herself, then in her teens, was an example:

> Our last talk, and we were all dull. For my part, Bacchus does not inspire me, and I was sad because it was the last time that I should see Margaret. She does not love me; I could not venture to follow her into her own home, and I love her so much! Her life hangs on a thread. Her face is full of the marks of pain. Young as I am, I feel old when I look at her.

This kind of uncritical devotion was widespread, not only among the girls in the Conversations but among Marga-ret's other students. "Had she been a man," Elizabeth Hoar once told Emerson, "any one of those fine girls of sixteen, who surrounded her here, would have married her; they were all in love with her, she understood them so well." Emerson says some of the girls complained that "she quite reduced them to satellites" with her "burly masculine existence"; yet women all over Boston "were eager to lay their beauty, their grace, the hospitalities of sumptuous homes, and their costly gifts, at her feet." She was all the more idolized by her teen-age students be-cause they had convinced themselves that she was doomed to an early grave. (This is not as preposterous as it seems. People died all the time of ailments that seemed no worse than migraine headache, and Margaret herself did not believe she would reach old age.) Nor was the feeling Margaret inspired limited to the very young. Elizabeth Peabody, herself no melting sixteen-year-old, wrote of the Conversations: "It is sometimes said, that women never are so lovely and enchanting in the company of their own sex, merely, but it requires the other to draw them out. Certain it is that Margaret never appears, when I see her, either so brilliant and deep in thought, or so desirous to please, or so modest, or so heart-touching, as in this very party." She was brilliant in any group, but when she was with other women she discarded the mask she more or less consciously assumed in everyday life and actually became that warmer, less cerebral person she would have liked to be all the time.

The object of such adulation was bound to provoke crit-icism, even if she were not engaged in a radical enter-prise. But the most memorable shot against Margaret, as against Bronson Alcott, came from England. Harriet Martineau had not said all she had to say about America in her earlier book. Miss Martineau's *Autobiography,* published long after Margaret's death, added to the dis-tortions and half-truths clustered about her memory:

> The difference between us was that while she was living and moving in an ideal world, talking in private and discoursing in public about the most fanciful and shallow conceits which the transcendentalists of Boston took for philosophy, she looked down upon persons who acted instead of talking finely, and devoted their fortunes, their peace, their repose, and their very lives to the preservation of the principles of the republic.

> While Margaret Fuller and her adult pupils sat "gorgeously dressed," talking about Mars and Venus, Plato and Göthe, and fancying themselves the elect of the earth in intellect and refinement, the liberties of the republic were running out as fast as they could go, at a breach which another sort of elect persons were devoting themselves to repair; and my complaint against the "gorgeous" pedants was that they regarded their preservers as hewers of wood and drawers of water, and their work as a less vital one than the pedantic orations which were spoiling a set of well-meaning women in a pitiable way.

Miss Martineau had no firsthand knowledge of the Conversations, having left the country four years before they were begun; but clearly Margaret's letter about Alcott had rankled, although the two women were still corresponding affectionately during the 1840s. The remark about "gorgeousness" is traced by Higginson to a comment by one of Margaret's admirers that she "used to come to the conversations very well dressed, and altogether looked sumptuously." Since Margaret's income hardly allowed her to buy anything more sumptuous than calico and bombazine, her reputation for dressing well rested entirely on her knowing what to do with them. As for her "looking down" on activists, more than half the members of the Conversations were abolitionists, and Mrs. Child and Mrs. Loring were leaders of the movement. Margaret herself, though put off by the shrill rhetoric of the abolitionists and the violence many of them advocated, sympathized with the cause and in later years wrote effectively in its support. Miss Martineau was still unable to see the close relationship between Transcendentalism and abolitionism, and ironically, she was also blind to the contribution these discussions were making to the emancipation of her own sex. Beyond that, her comments are a typical illustration of the vituperative tone Margaret's critics assumed, and of the way her eccentricities could easily be fashioned into a one-dimensional, larger-than-life symbol of whatever bugaboo it was her detractors most hated and feared.

During the four years of the Conversations, Margaret supplemented her income by teaching private pupils, occasionally having one or two boarding with her. The remainder of her time she had intended to devote to her Goethe biography, but during the summer of 1839 another project took shape which was to shoulder her book aside and prevent her completing it. At a September meeting of the Transcendentalist Club the idea of a journal, which had first been proposed in 1835 by Henry Hedge, was revived. Since the "Divinity School Address" it had been almost impossible for members of the circle to publish except at their own expense, and Alcott pointed out to them the modest success a similar journal, *The London Monthly Review,* was enjoying in Britain. Why, Alcott wanted to know, could not New England have such a review? In fact Emerson had been trying to persuade Carlyle to edit a journal in America for some time, but Carlyle's evasiveness had at length crystallized into refusal. Unless one counted the Unitarian *Christian Register,* or Orestes Brownson's erratic *Quarterly Review,* the only literary journal in New England was the stolidly conservative *North American Review* ("the snore of the Muses," Emerson called it). The *North American*'s editors, George Bancroft and Edward Everett, may well have lain awake nights ruing the day they had helped introduce German literature to America.

Everyone agreed that the journal was a fine idea, but of course no one wanted to edit it, Emerson—the obvious choice—least of all. Henry Hedge, who had suggested it five years before, then had no inkling of the distance some of his friends would put between themselves and the liberal church. Now among the most conservative of the group, he could not be considered as editor of a review which would espouse George Ripley's associationism, William Henry Channing's socialism, and what many believed to be Waldo Emerson's pantheism. The person chosen would have to be one whose sympathies were broad enough to include all these, whose convictions were strong without being narrow, and whose literary background was firm. None seemed better qualified than Margaret, and after careful thought she accepted on the condition that George Ripley take care of the business arrangements. It was hoped that enough subscriptions could be obtained to pay her $200 a year after the publisher received his share. They decided to call the journal the *Dial,* after a portion of Alcott's diaries.

Margaret's expectations of the *Dial* were realistic. She did not propose to establish a new standard of literary quality, but rather to bring a freshness of thought and style to the stale atmosphere of literary convention. It was important to shake off the Nay-saying strictures of the past, whether they were represented by the division between the elect and the damned, the lines between social classes, the hard rows of benches in the schoolroom, or the neat little enclosure of the heroic couplet. She realized that much of the writing would be rough, but all pioneering was rough; it would be up to those who came later to smooth the edges. A beginning had to be made if American literature, like American women, was to find its own identity. She expressed her limited hopes for the journal to W. H. Channing while she was preparing the first issue:

> A perfectly free organ is to be offered for the expression of individual thought and character. There are no party measures to be curried, no particular standard to be set up. A fair calm tone, a recognition of universal principals will, I hope pervade the essays in every form. I hope there will neither be a spirit of dogmatism nor of compromise. That this periodical will not aim at leading public opinion, but at stimulating each man to think for himself, to think more deeply and more nobly by letting them [sic] see how some minds are kept alive by a wise self-trust. . . . I am sure we cannot show high culture. and I doubt about vigorous thought. But I hope we shall show free action as far as it goes and a high aim. It were much if a periodical could be kept open to accomplish no outward object, but merely to afford an avenue for what of free and calm thought might be originated among us by the wants of individual minds.

As for her own part in it, she expected mainly to "urge on the laggards and scold the lukewarm, and act Helen MacGregor to those who love compromise, by doing my little best to sink them in the waters of oblivion!!" The date for the first issue was tentatively set for April 1840. Emerson, Ripley, and Alcott could be depended on to write, and she asked Hedge, W. H. Channing, and James Freeman Clarke for contributions. Thoreau promised to send something and Emerson wrote to another of his protégés, William Ellery Channing (who had left Harvard and was living by himself in a hut in Illinois) asking for permission to publish some of his verses. Theodore Parker promised some of his workmanlike prose. Caroline Sturgis and her sister Ellen Hooper put the poems they had written in their journals at Margaret's disposal, with the prim condition that not even the other Transcendentalists be told who had written them. (Public anonymity was not an issue, since periodical articles usually were left unsigned.) Emerson selected passages from the journals of his dead brothers and verses written by his first wife, Ellen Tucker Emerson.

But by spring there was not nearly enough material for the 136 pages agreed on with the publisher. Margaret set about writing as much as she could herself, and her attempts to coax the more shy Transcendentalists out of their winter dens became a little desperate. Shyest of all was Henry Hedge:

> Henry, I adjure you, in the name of all the Genii, Muses, Pegasus, Apollo, Pollio, Apollyon, ("and must I mention"——) to send me something good for this journal before the 1st May. All mortals, my friend, are slack and bare; they wait to see whether Hotspur wins, before they levy aid for as good a plan as ever was laid. I know you are plagued and it is hard to write, just so it is with me, for I also am a father. But you can help, and become a godfather! if you like, and let it be nobly, for if the first number justify not the magazine, it will not find justification; so write, my friend, write, and paint not for me fine plans on the clouds to be achieved at some future time, as others do who have had many years to be thinking of immortality.

> I could make a number myself with the help Mr. E[merson] will give, but the Public, I trow, is too astute a donkey not to look sad at *that*.

Hedge, however, was appalled at the guise in which his own suggestion had returned to haunt him, and now flatly refused to have anything to do with the *Dial*, though he later relented enough to contribute to the second issue and one or two after that. James Freeman Clarke, newly married and living in Pennsylvania, also disappointed her for the first issue. Emerson sent two poems and the family selections he had promised, and wrote most of the introduction. Otherwise he kept aloof, content to let the *Dial* be stillborn rather than divert his attention from the preparation of his first book of *Essays*. He urged Margaret to take the same view of it, and not to run down her health, which was worse as it always was in winter. But she developed a stubborn affection for the *Dial,* or at least for the idea of the *Dial,* and she kept scribbling away, the old distaste for writing dragging at her pen. She told Channing,

> I have myself a great deal written, but as I read it over scarce a word seems pertinent to the place or time. When I meet people I can adapt myself to them, but when I write it is into another world, not a better one perhaps, but one with very dissimilar habits of thought to this where I am domesticated. . . . What others can do, whether all that has been said is the mere restlessness of discontent, or there are thoughts really struggling for utterance will I think be tested now.

When the first issue at last appeared, Margaret was by far the largest contributor. Others, besides the Emerson family, were Parker, Ripley, John Sullivan Dwight, Christopher Cranch, H. D. Wilson, Alcott, Ward, Ellen Hooper, Sarah Clarke, and Thoreau, who sent the poem "Sympathy." The literary quality in this as in later issues was uneven, the most solid pieces being Parker's on "The Divine Presence in Nature and the Soul," Ripley's discussion of the writings of Brownson, and Margaret's own **"Essay on Critics."** The verse in the *Dial,* notwithstanding poems by Thoreau and Emerson, was always its weakest feature: American Transcendentalism, which had seemed to offer a fertile field for poetry, proved a veritable quagmire. But the prose was often good, sometimes memorable, and in its primary purpose of giving expression to the spirit of democratic idealism at its best, the Dial was a success. It was a rallying point for the young, as Emerson pointed out in defending it to Carlyle:

> If the direction of these speculations is to be deplored, it is yet a fact for literary history, that all the bright boys and girls in New England, quite ignorant of each other, take the world so, and come and make confessions to fathers and mothers,—the boys that they do not wish to go into trade, the girls that they do not like morning calls and evening parties. They are all religious, but hate the churches: they reject all the ways of living of other men, but have none to offer in their stead. Perhaps, one of these days, a great Yankee shall come, who will easily do the unknown deed.

The *Dial* was greeted with whoops and chortles by those already disposed to be its natural enemies. "It is, to us, humble uninitiated sinners, yet ignorant of the sublime 'mysteries,' one of the most transcendentically (we like big words) ridiculous publications," sneered the editor of the *Boston Times*. None of those who had worked to bring it about were satisfied with it, although their reasons were sometimes poles apart. The most frequent criticism was the most justified: it was ethereal, abstract, and precious. "Too much of a soul," growled Carlyle, while Alcott thought it did not have soul enough: "It is but a twilight 'Dial'," he wrote sadly to an English friend. Ripley thought it was "not *prononcé* enough"; instead of sporting "hoofs and horns," it was "gentle as any sucking dove." All the same, he noted happily, "the Philistines, who dare show out, are wrathy as fighting-cocks." Not surprisingly, its shortcomings were occasionally blamed on the fact that it had a woman editor. Carlyle's objections seem to have been at least partly on this score: "[The *Dial*] is all spirit-like, aeriform, aurora-borealis like. Will no *angel* body himself out of that; no stalwart Yankee *man*, with colour in the cheeks of him, and a coat on his back!" Theodore Parker, whose personal distrust of aggressively intellectual women did not interfere with his being Boston's most eloquent preacher on behalf of human equality, remarked that the chief thing wrong with the *Dial* was that it needed a beard. But the new journal was generally well received by the readers for whom it was meant.

Margaret was editor of the *Dial* for two years. Her editorial policy was set forth in her **"Essay on Critics,"** in the first issue. She did not believe that a work of art should be measured against some ideal, inflexible standard, but thought that the critic should encourage talent as well as genius, while clearly distinguishing between them. She encouraged freshness and vitality in the *Dial,* even though the writing might be technically flawed. In this she differed from Emerson, who would have tightened up the literary quality even though it meant excluding more writers. The difference was probably more theoretical than actual, for the *Dial* changed little after Emerson took it over in 1842, and Margaret was firm in trying to bring her writers (including Emerson himself) up to the mark. She offended Alcott by discontinuing his "Orphic Sayings"—apothegms taken from his diaries which were much parodied in the establishment press. And she wounded Thoreau's pride by returning several of his pieces for revision.

Emerson and Parker continued to be the heaviest contributors after Margaret herself, Emerson assuming a large share of the writing after the first issue. Parker was very popular with the readers, and it is doubtful that the journal could have survived without him. Besides Margaret and the Sturgis sisters, women who ventured into print in the *Dial* included Elizabeth Peabody, Sarah Clarke, Lydia Maria Child, and a follower of Emerson's from Dorchester named Eliza Thayer Clapp.

The *Dial* soon absorbed nearly all of Margaret's working hours, and she was forced to set aside her Goethe biography, promising herself she would return to it when she had time. But the succeeding years offered no such opportunity, and all that remains of the book is a detailed outline of the early chapters and a collection of notes. For her *Dial* editing she never received a salary, since the journal barely supported itself. In 1814 its printers went bankrupt and refused to return the subscription list without payment for it. An arrangement was reached, and Elizabeth Peabody printed the *Dial* on her own press until it was placed with the company of James Munroe. But its financial position went from bad to worse, and in 1843 Emerson paid for the last few issues out of his own pocket.

As editor Margaret was largely spared the financial haggling over the journal, but she shouldered the responsibility for its contents. Contributors continued dilatory, and she made up the missing copy herself. She wrote more than half the October 1841 issue, her essays on **"Lives of**

the Great Composers" and Bailey's **"Festus"** numbering eighty-five pages. Christmas of the same year found her racing the printer in order to finish the January issue: "I am in a state of extreme fatigue," she wrote her mother, who was in Canton. "This is the last week of the *Dial,* and as often happens, the copy did not hold out, and I have had to write in every gap of time. Marianne J., and Jane [two of her pupils] have been writing for me extracts etc., but I have barely scrambled through, and am now quite unfit to hold a pen." In July 1842, anxieties over her income, her family, and her health forced her to resign the editorship; Emerson carried it on for two more years.

Margaret's writing for the *Dial* varies widely in quality. This reflects partly the conditions of haste, fatigue, and pain under which it was produced, and partly her reluctance to write instead of talk. But these years were a valuable apprenticeship for her, and some of her *Dial* writing is as good as anything she did. She still lapses into sentimentality and digression, and she is clearly out of her depth in her discussions of art and music; her article on **"The Great Composers,"** for example, suffers from the common Romantic fallacy of equating esthetic and moral excellence. Passionately loving the music of Beethoven, she concluded that he must have been an altogether admirable human being and elevated him to chief position in her own private pantheon. No more enlightened, for similar reasons, are her discussions of sculpture and painting, which are almost entirely concerned with the physiognomy of the models (noble brows and pure eyes lifted heavenward, etc.). Having very little technical knowledge of these subjects and a great deal about literature, she is at her best in the latter field. Her *Dial* essay on Goethe contributed significantly to an acceptance of the great German poet in this country, and her **"Essay on Critics"** signals the beginning of her development as one of America's first two literary critics worthy of the name, the other being Poe.

But Margaret's most important contribution to the *Dial* was published in the July 1843 issue under the ponderous title, **"The Great Lawsuit: Man vs. Men. Woman vs. Women."** This article, the most radical feminist document yet produced in America, brings together the liberal thought she had distilled from years of study and the bitter contradictions and disillusionment she had experienced, not only in her own life but in the lives of literally dozens of other women who had confided in her as in no one else. She wrote it while she was still conducting the Conversations, having constantly before her the contrast between the heady sense of freedom a few women could achieve for two hours once a week, and the carefully limited reality to which they went home afterward. Among the various benevolences to which the Unitarian and Transcendentalist movements had contributed—abolitionism, educational reform, the amelioration of conditions for the poor, the insane, and the criminal—feminism was the last to be recognized because it was the most fundamental of all. To radically change the status of their wives and daughters (especially their wives) was a challenge from which even the most dedicated Transcendentalists inwardly shrank, no matter how generously they maintained the justice of it on an intellectual plane. To face squarely the changes in domestic life which were implied by that equal education they so cheerfully promulgated was so difficult that they closed their eyes to it, as had Timothy Fuller when he set out to educate his small daughter. The male liberal would lend his books to the intellectual woman and invite her to his discussions; he would congratulate her on how accomplished she was, "for a woman." He would even accept her as editor of a journal for which he wrote. But she remained apart from the mainstream of society; she was seen as an anomaly. With rare exceptions men did not marry such women, because the vocation of wife excluded all others. (No better example of liberal male doublethink can be found than the exclusion of woman delegates from the 1840 World Anti-Slavery Convention, which would not have been possible without the efforts of women.)

"The Great Lawsuit: Man vs. Men. Woman vs. Women," brings together the liberal thought she had distilled from years of study and the bitter contradictions and disillusionment she had experienced, not only in her own life but in the lives of literally dozens of other women who had confided in her as in no one else.
—*Paula Blanchard*

In three years of existence (two of them admittedly under Margaret's direction) the *Dial* had touched on the "woman question" only once before, in an 1841 article by Sophia Ripley titled simply "Woman." But Mrs. Ripley had not led her men friends any further than they were already willing to go. After expressing with some force her complaint that a woman loses her individuality in marriage and becomes "an appendage . . . the upper nurse," she goes meekly back to her corner: a woman should be educated so that she will not lean on her husband, but will "attend on him as a watchful friend." Only then can she pursue her "high vocation of creator of a happy home." There was nothing here to alarm the menfolk, and at Brook Farm later that year Sophia Ripley stayed indoors, cooked, taught the children, and worked long hours in the laundry; it would not have occurred to her to go out in the fields and hoe corn.

Margaret's article, on the other hand, is deeply, basically radical. Beginning with the premise that all souls are equal before God, and its application to Negroes and American Indians, she goes on to claim the same equality for women: "We would have every arbitrary barrier thrown down. We would have every path laid open to women as freely as to man." She asks for educational equality, but not for the same stultifying education that is available to men; rather she asks for new institutions of higher learning specifically for women, and run by women. She goes on to appeal for that vocational equality which follows from equal education, and for legal and political equality as well, including by implication the right to vote, though she stops short of

advocating it in so many words. **"The Great Lawsuit"** suffers from a digressive style, and once Margaret betrays her own inner conflict about whether women can become first-rate artists: "More native to her is it to be the living model of the artist, than to set apart from herself any one form in objective reality, more native to inspire and receive the poem than to create it." But immediately she goes on to recognize the androgynous nature of the individual mind: "There is no wholly masculine man, no purely feminine woman. . . . Man partakes of the feminine in the Apollo, woman of the masculine as Minerva." She defends women's right to remain unmarried, if they choose, without social penalty. Above all, she would not have them defined by relationships to men:

> A profound thinker has said "no married woman can represent the female world, for she belongs to her husband. The idea of woman must be represented by a virgin." But that is the very fault of marriage, and of the present relation between the sexes, that the woman does belong to the man, instead of forming a whole with him. Were it otherwise there would be no such limitation to the thought. Woman, self-centred, would never be absorbed by any relative; it would be only an experience to her as to man. It is a vulgar error that love, *a* love to woman is her whole existence. . . .

Deceptively gentle in tone, **"Lawsuit"** undermined even the most liberal assumptions of the day. It was a courageous statement, and it brought Margaret to the notice of a wider public, while it brought her Transcendentalist friends face to face with their own ideals.

Marie Mitchell Olesen Urbanski (essay date 1980)

SOURCE: "Genesis, Form, Tone." In *Margaret Fuller's "Woman in the Nineteenth Century": A Literary Study of Form and Content, Of Sources and Influence,"* Greenwood Press, 1980, pp. 128-45.

The first impression a reader may get from a hasty perusal of Margaret Fuller's **Woman in the Nineteenth Century** is one of effusiveness and formlessness. Containing a display of erudition that is impressive, it is prolix, as was the work of many transcendentalists and other writers of the past century. In the April 1845 issue of his *Quarterly Review,* Orestes Brownson observed that **Woman** has "neither beginning, middle, nor end, and may be read backwards as well as forwards." In his satire, Brownson expressed aspects of the organic living quality of the work, but he did not discern its form. In the midst of its verbosity, it is still possible to see more of a pattern in **Woman** than has been maintained. Its basic structure is that of the sermon, which is appropriate, because **Woman's** message is hortatory. Its complexity and apparent lack of form are due to its dual nature. Within the sermon framework, **Woman** partakes of the major characteristics of transcendental literary art. But before analyzing **Woman** as a literary work from the standpoint of form, tone, and use of rhetorical devices, it is necessary to examine its genesis. If a study can be made of its genesis from an early draft, then some insight may be obtained as to the way in which Fuller's ideas were developing and thus a clearer perception of her composition of *Woman* is possible.

Woman developed from **"The Great Lawsuit.—Man *versus* Men; Woman *versus* Women,"** which was published in the July 1843 issue of the *Dial,* a year after Fuller had relinquished its editorship to Emerson. In her preface to *Woman,* she explained that she had prepared her expanded version for publication in compliance with wishes expressed from many quarters. Then she discussed her change of title. She conceded that the meaning of the original title is puzzling—"it requires some thought to see what it means." Her preference, she told her readers, was to retain the first title in her enlargement, but she was dissuaded from doing so by friends. Although awkward, her early biographer Higginson explained, the original title was intended "to avert even the suspicion of awakening antagonism between the sexes." Nevertheless, this title does sound antagonistic because it suggests court action. But why is the title worded "man versus men" instead of "man versus woman," or vice versa, which is the usual order in the battle of the sexes? Fuller's intention was not to write a long history of woman's grievances against the tyranny of the male sex. Instead she keynoted the grievance of the individual man or woman whose aspirations were thwarted by the multitude, or by himself or herself, from becoming the developed soul he or she might become. She explained:

> I meant by that title to intimate the fact that, while it is the destiny of Man, in the course of the ages, to ascertain and fulfil the law of his being, so that his life shall be seen, as a whole, to be that of an angel or messenger, the action of prejudices and passions which attend, in the day, the growth of the individual, is continually obstructing the holy work that is to make the earth a part of heaven. By Man I mean both man and woman; these are the two halves of one thought. I lay no special stress on the welfare of either. I believe that the development of the one cannot be effected without that of the other.

She developed this concept in *Women* by adding to **"Lawsuit"** her dual epigraphs. Then, by rephrasing them, she made them applicable to men as well. What she had to say applied to the men and women; her message was not ambivalent but hortatory, and its significance, again referring to her original title, was "great."

It appears at first glance that *Woman* is much longer than **"Lawsuit,"** but a line-by-line examination of the content indicates that the number of words per page in **"Lawsuit"** is much greater than that in *Woman*. The first 130 pages of the 179-page text of *Woman* are a close adaptation of the 47 pages of **"Lawsuit."** In most instances, Fuller used a verbatim transcription of **"The Great Lawsuit"** in *Woman*. Occasionally she changed a few words to clarify or modify the meaning of a sentence, but she did very little polishing of her original text. For example, in the original essay she wrote, "Is it not enough, cries the sorrowful trader," and in her second version she changed *sorrowful* to *irritated*. In the original version she wrote,

"But our doubt is whether the heart does consent with the head, or only acquiesces its decrees." In the second version, she changed *acquiesces* to *obeys* and then added to her sentence, "with a passiveness that precludes the exercise of its natural powers, or a repugnance that turns sweet qualities to bitter, or a doubt that lays waste the fair occasions of life." Another word changed to clarify meaning is *incessant,* which in *Woman* becomes *frequent:* "Shrink not from frequent error in this gradual, fragmentary state" (p. 19). She deleted a phrase or a sentence a few times, but mostly she developed and elaborated on points she had already made. In her discussion of property rights for widows, she said that the wife "inherits only a part of his fortune" and then inserted in her second version the phrase "often brought him by herself" after "fortune." In her treatment of illustrative old maids— "No one thinks of Michael Angelo's Persican Sibyl, or St. Theresa, or Tasso's Leonora, or the Greek Electra, as an old maid"—she added, "more than of Michael Angelo or Canova as old bachelors," in order to give her sentence and idea balance. Sometimes she added discussions of writers whom she had not included before, such as Charles Fourier and Walter Savage Landor. Furthermore, she tended to add capital letters and italics for emphasis and occasionally corrected punctuation.

There are forty-nine pages of new material. The portion she added contains the most daring subject matter in the book because much of it was contemporary application of her thesis. Her new material contained some frank discussions of sex; an example of an incompatible marriage: "I have known this man come to install himself in the chamber of a woman who loathed him, and say she should never take food without his company"; the double standard of morality: "Let Sir Charles Grandison preach to his own sex"; the notorious trial of Amelia Norman; a mother's sadness when she gives birth to a daughter; the father's kidnapping of his own children as a means of coercing his wife; problems of older women—a well-preserved woman at forty who is spoken of "upholstery-wise"; property rights for married women; and her idea that ladies are responsible for rehabilitating prostitutes. More trenchant social criticism was used to supplement her earlier points: "Those who think the physical circumstances of Woman would make a part in the affairs of national government unsuitable, are by no means those who think it impossible for negresses to endure field-work, even during pregnancy, or for sempstresses to go through their killing labors." Also included in her enlargement was her remark about letting women be sea captains. Although she added the ancient belief that a baby's body was inherited from his mother and his soul from his father, in general her new material contained less spiritual transcendentalism until the peroration. Therefore the most controversial writing in *Woman* was that which she added to **"The Great Lawsuit."** The importance of the earlier draft is that it gave Fuller the courage to treat inflammatory subject matter. Because the reception of **"The Great Lawsuit"** was on the whole favorable among the *Dial*'s small coterie of readers, she became more outspoken. One criticism she did receive about her earlier draft, as she herself explained, was that she did not make her "meaning sufficiently clear." Consequently, she may have been guilty of repetition. And in order to make her meaning unmistakable, less of it is veiled in metaphor.

The residue of a trial from **"The Great Lawsuit"** remains. The thinking man or woman, who has not yet become the enlarged soul he or she would become, is admonished to perfect himself despite all obstructions. Once this extraordinary person frees himself from ordinary frailty, then this individual could become the king or queen she seeks to lead and to inspire his waiting adversaries.

The broadest structural framework of *Woman* reflects the sermon, which she mentioned both in her introduction—"sermons preached from the text"—and in her statement in the conclusion that she would retrace her design "as was done in old-fashioned sermons." Closely akin to the sermon is the oration, and *Woman* contains elements of both forms. Fuller began her work with the classic exordium in a vague way so her thesis is not clear for several pages. Using caution, Latin and German quotations, and preliminary conciliation, she did not introduce her *propositio* until the tenth page: woman needs her turn, and improvement of her lot would aid in the reformation of men, too. Then she stated her sermon topic: "Be ye perfect." Having established her thesis at last, she proceeded with *partitio* or analysis of her subject, which is done in a debate style by raising the popular arguments men used with which to oppose women's rights, and then rebutting them. She began with the conversational method of questions and answers characteristic of the speaker who wishes to dramatize a point. A husband asks:

> "Is it not enough," cries the irritated trader, "that you have done all you could to break up the national union, and thus destroy the prosperity of our country, but now you must be trying to break up family union, to take my wife away from the cradle and the kitchen-hearth, to vote at polls, and preach from a pulpit? Of course, if she does such things, she cannot attend to those of her own sphere. She is happy enough as she is. She has more leisure than I have,—every means of improvement, every indulgence."

> "Have you asked her whether she was satisfied with these *indulgences?*"

> "No, but I know she is."

Fuller ended this dialogue by saying that liberating measures are proposed to ascertain truth. Objectively, she continued: "Without enrolling ourselves at once on either side, let us look upon the subject from the best point of view which to-day offers." She debated the issue with rebuttals that accelerated in strength until she concluded, "We would have every arbitrary barrier thrown down."

Then in a long *digressio* composed of sermon-style exemplar, she considered all that is known of woman, delineating her story in myth, folklore, the Bible, poetry, fiction, history, and in her own time. Beginning with an extensive analysis of the institution of marriage, she examined the life cycle of a woman. She sought women whose lives she found inspiring such as Queen Isabella of Castile, or Marina, the Indian woman who accompanied Cortez, but she evaluated the lives of other women, such as Queen Elizabeth and Mary Stuart, lauding their strengths and castigating their weaknesses. Interwoven in her examples is an attempt to buttress her argument with authority using the views of recognized authors to support her position. She conceded that women have always had some power, but they want freedom from men to learn the secrets of the universe alone. Within her narrative in a form suggestive of the *reprehensio* is admonition to men, who refuse to grant women freedom and who call strong women "manly," and to women, who misuse what power they have. Scornfully she recognized that a coquette, a shrew, or a good cook could have lifelong sway.

Fuller inculcated within her discussion a realistic assessment of the options open to women in various societies, ancient and modern. Reasonably enough, since most women would marry, she spent a lot of time examining the institution of marriage. She contrasted idealized concepts of courtly love in which the lady served as inspiration with the reality of arranged marriages of convenience. It is no surprise that she advocated not only a marriage of love but a spiritual union of two souls on a common pilgrimage. She also discussed other options women have, such as women who write, women who are mothers, and women who do not marry, as well as the problems of women in middle and old age. She praised women abolitionists brave enough to speak on the platform but warned that they must work for measures not only favoring slaves but also for themselves. In her all-inclusive discussion of a woman's life cycle, she discussed the child toward the end of this section, lamenting the father who stunts his daughter's education for fear she will not find a husband. Again pointing out that a woman must work alone and use her special gifts of intuition, she mentioned a crisis at hand and prophesied a new Jerusalem, which the prophets Swedenborg, Fourier, and Goethe foretell. Then her sermon became more direct as she preached about the problems of prostitutes and polygamy and warned that men must be as pure as women. In an accelerating evocative vision of the future in which both men and women rule their passions by reason, she placed her hope with the young—"harbingers and leaders of a new era." Triumphantly she concluded her long narrative by proclaiming her expectation that a young "Exaltada" would serve as an "example and instruction for the rest."

The structural pattern of *Woman* next takes the sermon form of an *applicatio* in a departure from the main thrust of the argument and moves from the visionary future to the prosaic present. Fuller sighed over books recently published in which the chief point was to fit a wife "to please, or, at least, not to disturb a husband" (p. 158). She recognized the dilemmas women faced and completed this section by admonishing American women to use their moral power and not to let themselves be intimidated by aspersions on their modesty. Her application of her sermon, therefore, is that women must act to save themselves.

From practical application of the sermon, the form of *Woman* soars back to the sublime world of the spirit. In a peroration, Fuller outlined the major points of her argument and of her vision of the harmonious world that an ideal relationship between men and women would bring. Then, like a minister ending a sermon, she addressed a prayer to God: "Thou, Lord of Day!" After a cold winter, she prophesied a distant day of glory. With a final hortatory admonition to cherish hope and act, she concluded with poetry that echoed the Bible: "Persist to ask, and it will come." With an allusion to her epigraphs, she envisioned—"So shalt thou see, what few have seen, / The palace home of King and Queen"—and thus gave structural and thematic wholeness to her work.

The structure of *Woman* does seem to fit loosely the sermon-oration form. What tends to obscure its pattern is Fuller's use of writing techniques derived from transcendentalism. According to precepts generally accepted by the transcendentalists, a work of literature grows out of experience and hence is organic. As Coleridge, a romantic, wrote: "The organic form is innate; it shapes, as it develops itself from within." And Keats, using a nature metaphor, explained that good poetry grew as naturally as the leaves on a tree. Emerson later used this concept, saying a poem is "a thought so passionate and alive that like the spirit of a plant or an animal it has an architecture of its own." The basic assumption of transcendental art is of the "superiority of the spirit to the letter." Art as inspiration meant that the word became one with the thing. Ultimately, the "transcendental theory of art is a theory of knowledge and religion as well." Hence transcendental expression must coalesce the seer and spectacle into one, an organic whole. Margaret Fuller, the observer, united the spectacle—her experience—with that of all other women into the final fusion of *Woman in the Nineteenth Century*.

As early as 1826 Sampson Reed published his "Observations on the Growth of the Mind," setting forth transcendental literary theory. He wrote: "Syllogistic reasoning is passing away," leaving nothing behind but a demonstration "of its own worthlessness." Both Julia Ward Howe and Arthur W. Brown pointed out that there was no systematic parallelism in *Woman;* however, Fuller did not intend that there should be. By not following a rigidly organized pattern of syllogistic reasoning, she was merely demonstrating that she had accepted the transcendentalist aesthetic theory that, as a member of the club, she had helped to shape. The movement of her treatise is not parallel but soaring and circular. Its dominant mode of composition is an unfolding from the subconscious in a form of spiraling thought patterns. One of her recurrent themes is an optimistic refrain that appears in a mood of confidence, disappears in a burst of admonition, and later reappears in a form of wavelike undulation characteristic of transcendental writing. Moreover, the polarities of optimistic expectation (symbolized by the epigraph, "The Earth waits for her Queen") and impatient anger (symbolized by, "Frailty, thy name is Woman") have an ebb and flow rhythm to them. She may begin in a lull with a mundane matter such as the problem of a poor widow

whose husband has died leaving no will and accelerate in intensity to the sublime "ravishing harmony of the spheres," or start at the crest of the wave as it flows back to the sea. From practical application of her sermon, the thought patterns of *Woman* soar back to the world of the spirit. Instead of syllogistic reasoning, order comes from the authority that the certitude of intuition brings.

A characteristic of transcendental literature, which *Woman* reflects, is subjectivity—the individual as the center of the world. At times this method suggests a free association of ideas. One authority requires that another be included; one mythological figure suggests another. Ultimately the thought patterns lead from the conscious, to the subconscious mind, to the transcendental wellspring of truth, the divine intuition. Fuller used her own experience as representative of the experience of all women—that indeed the lot of woman is sad, that all women need and, in fact, should aspire to the same self-culture and fulfillment that she herself had desired. She began *Woman* by using the conventional "we" but she changed to "I" after only fifteen pages. Later she alternated between "we" and "I." She gave an account of her youthful education by her father under the guise of the persona, Miranda, as an example of an independent girl who was respected for being self-reliant. Fuller told this story by means of an imaginary conversation in which the "I" takes the role of the foil to Miranda's explanation of her youthful training in self-reliance, so unusual for a girl of that day. In her subjectivity there are times when she almost linked herself with the queen that the earth awaits. If not the queen directly, she associated herself in her description of Miranda with the woman of genius, possessor of the magnetic electrical element (intuition), who has a contribution to make to the world—"a strong electric nature, which repelled those who did not belong to her, and attracted those who did." At another time in the discussion of woman's power of intuition, she wrote: "Women who combine this organization with creative genius are very commonly unhappy at present. They see too much to act in conformity with those around them, and their quick impulses seem folly to those who do not discern the motives." By looking into her own soul, she saw reflected there the problems and the frustrated aspirations of other women: "but what concerns me now is, that my life be a beautiful, powerful, in a word, a complete life in its kind. Had I but one more moment to live I must wish the same." Starting from her own angle of vision, she unfolded her hopes to the world, and she concluded her treatise as a prophet:

> I stand in the sunny noon of life. Objects no longer glitter in the dews of morning, neither are yet softened by the shadows of evening. Every spot is seen, every chasm revealed. Climbing the dusty hill, some fair effigies that once stood for symbols of human destiny have been broken; those I still have with me show defects in this broad light. Yet enough is left, even by experience, to point distinctly to the glories of that destiny; faint, but not to be mistaken streaks of the future day.

Thus her subjectivity became universal as she linked her own experience to that of the experience of all women and prophesied that in the future life would be better for them.

The tone of *Woman* reinforces the idea that Fuller was writing a didactic work. At times the tone admonishes the audience to act; at other times it is declamatory, but dominantly it is conversational. Although its voice patterns are conversational, the archness of Fuller's diction and tone is transcendental. Today, the mannerism of Fuller's speaking style may sound affected. Nevertheless, many people who knew Fuller said that her chief talent was as a speaker, so it is not surprising that instead of syllogisms, many phrases contain the emotive power of a conversation, of which she would have been the star. Her writing technique included both questions and answers in a debate form, but it also revealed the hallmark of the accomplished conversationalist: a flair for the dramatic. At best her conversational technique suggests breathless ejaculations rather than sentences. In a kind of accelerating excitement, she used the hortatory style: "Let us be wise, and not impede the soul. Let her work as she will. Let us have one creative energy, one incessant revelation. Let it take what form it will, and let us not bind it by the past to man or woman, black or white. Jove sprang from Rhea, Pallas from Jove. So let it be." Then her tone changes to one of intimacy. Her writing sounds as if she were talking to a small group and studying the reaction of her audience.

In the following passage, she revealed that she was a perceptive performer who could quickly adapt an argument to match the mood of her imaginary audience by modifying, explaining, and then hammering home at the proper psychological moment the point she intended to make in the first place:

> If it has been the tendency of these remarks to call Woman rather to the Minerva side,—if I, unlike the more generous writer, have spoken from society no less than the soul,—let it be pardoned! It is love that has caused this,—love for many incarcerated souls, that might be freed, could the idea of religious self-dependence be established in them, could the weakening habit of dependence on others be broken up.

Her excuse for her stand was love. In effect, she seemed to be anticipating objections. Her most famous suggestion combines a speaking conversational style with her flair for dramatization: "But if you ask me what offices they may fill, I reply—any. I do not care what case you put; let them be sea-captains, if you will." Her frequent use of dashes suggests the pause used by accomplished speakers.

Other passages in *Woman* combine the dramatic method of composition with an aphoristic technique: "Tremble not before the free man, but before the slave who has chains to break"; "Whatever abuses are seen, the timid will suffer; the bold will protest." In her dramatization of her thesis, she used an aphoristic method of attracting attention by reversing sex roles, beginning with her sug-

gestion that the time had come for "Eurydice to call for an Orpheus, rather than Orpheus for Eurydice." Again she wrote: "Presently she [nature] will make a female Newton, and a male Syren." "But Penelope is no more meant for a baker or weaver solely, than Ulysses for a cattle-herd." Later she suggested, not unlike semantic changes in vogue today, that the title given to a party abroad, "Los Exaltados," be changed to "Los Exaltados, Las Exaltadas." This stylistic device of sex role reversal is used to advocate one of her central ideas—that there is no "wholly masculine man, no purely feminine woman"— which culminates in the "sea-captain" passage.

Whether that of a preacher, orator, or confidante, the tone of *Woman* expresses the spoken word. Hence many of Fuller's images relate to sound. Perhaps here she echoes Shelley, whom she admired: "And, if men are deaf, the angels hear. But men cannot be deaf." She used music as a means of expressing the divine: "Then their sweet singing shall not be from passionate impulse, but the lyrical overflow of a divine rapture, and a new music shall be evolved from this many-chorded world." Or she saw woman as a bird with clipped wings that desires to fly and sing: "no need to clip the wings of any bird that wants to soar and sing." That she frequently preferred sound imagery to that of sight is again indicated by her final poem:

> For the Power to whom we bow
> Has given its pledge that, if not now,
> They of pure and steadfast mind,
> By faith exalted, truth refined,
> *Shall* hear all music loud and clear,
> Whose first notes they ventured here.

Another type of rhetorical device that Fuller often used is imagery derived from organicism, which implies movement, growth, expansion, or fruition. Her argument rested on the "law of growth." She used phrases such as *ampler fruition, fruitful summer,* or *plants of great vigor will always struggle into blossom.* She liked movement related to the life force symbolized by the heart: "I must beat my own pulse true in the heart of the world; for *that* is virtue, excellence, health." And the cycles of nature—the flowing of streams, the waxing moon, and noon-morning-dawn imagery—are favorites.

Yet despite her frequent choice of auditory and organic imagery, her work's salient characteristic is its great use of references to literature, history, religion, and mythology. These references are used primarily as an exemplar for her readers to emulate, as recognized authority to support her topic, or as allusions to Holy Writ.

Since the structure of *Woman* is sermon-like, Fuller used biblical allusions as the major support for her near-rhapsodic religious vision of the great potentialities of men and women. She derived her thematic exhortation—"Be ye perfect"—from Matthew 5:48, from which she deleted "therefore." On occasion she quoted directly from the Bible: "This is the Law and the Prophets. Knock and it shall be opened; seek and ye shall find." Another way that she used biblical sources was to reshape a scriptural passage. Matthew 5:13 reads: "Ye are the light of the world. A city that is set on a hill cannot be hid. Neither do men light a candle, and put it under a bushel, but on a candlestick; and it giveth light unto all that are in the house." Fuller changed the meaning: "The candlestick set in a low place has given light as faithfully, where it was needed, as that upon the hill." In this passage, she incorporated biblical allusions and Christian concepts: "Love has already been expressed, that made all things new, that gave the worm its place and ministry as well as the eagle; a love to which it was alike to descend into the depths of hell, or to sit at the right hand of the Father." She used a clause such as *a love that cannot be crucified* or commonly used biblical terms as *future Eden, lamb, green pastures, Prince of Peace,* and *Holy Child* to symbolize hope and renewal. From traditional Christian theology she derived a reference to the deadly sin of sloth. Phrases that connote Calvinism, such as "doomed in future stages of his own being to deadly penance," can be found in **Woman**. Elements of the providential doctrine appear: "Yet, by men in this country, as by the Jews, when Moses was leading them to the promised land, everything has been done that inherited depravity could do, to hinder the promise of Heaven from its fulfillment."

She found inspiration in the figure of the Madonna, whom she mentioned several times: "No figure that has ever arisen to greet our eyes has been received with more fervent reverence than that of the Madonna." She referred to the Virgin Mary's powerful influence to reinforce her idea that women are born not only to nurture and alleviate the loneliness of men but also are prossessors of immortal souls.

But it was to the Old Testament that she turned for the woman who would redeem mankind. Adam, she wrote somewhat ironically, "is not ashamed to write that he could be drawn from heaven by one beneath him,—one made, he says, from but a small part of himself." Adam "accuses" Woman—through her "Man was lost, so through woman must Man be redeemed" by "Immortal Eve."

Fuller employed biblical and religious allusions in the usual way to clarify meaning and as the wellsprings of her treatise. In addition, she cited contemporary writers—feminists, socialists, and transcendentalists—to buttress her argument that women could play a broader role in society. Her use of allusions to outstanding women from all recorded time, however, was complex. Their use is not an affectation but an intrinsic part of her way of thinking and the rhetorical method she adopted in order to make her point. Her allusions not only clarify her meaning but also serve as models of conduct to inspire or instruct women. Examples used as affirmations are taken from poetry, such as Britomart; from history, such as Aspasia; from mythology, such as Isis and Iduna or Sita in the *Ramayana;* from folklore, such as Cinderella; or from more contemporary life, such as the Polish Countess Emily Plater. Instead of cataloging lists of words, as Emerson suggested and Whitman did, her technique was to catalog women. She barely escaped creating an encyclopedic ef-

fect because she appears not to have wanted to leave anyone out. She admitted she "may have been guilty of much repetition." It could be argued that Fuller should have been more selective, but on the other hand, through sheer weight of numbers, the women cited from the ages become a catalog that is an evocation, a challenge to men to remove "arbitrary barriers" through proof that women can succeed. Thus she explained her use of her numerous examples: "I have aimed to show that no age was left entirely without a witness of the quality of the sexes in function, duty, and hope." As Fuller said, the function of her examples is to serve as a witness. Her citation of women from history and women from fiction finally blends into women from mythology. Her search led her to delve beyond patriarchal Hebrew-Christian society to the prototype mythic woman—an earth mother who was recognized as a powerful figure, a priestess with powers of intuition and serving as a medium to the divine. Fuller's figures become in themselves the incarnation of concepts. Cassandra and Iphigenia serve as witnesses to her argument that not only are women enslaved in Western civilization but that they are not allowed to use their special gifts of "electric or magnetic powers" with which they could be enriching the world. She cited the Seeress of Prevorst and "a friend" as examples of contemporary women whose gift of psychic power was wasted. Summarizing this concept, she asked: "Grant her, then, for a while, the armor and the javelin. Let her put from her the press of other minds, and meditate in virgin loneliness. The same idea shall reappear in due time as Muse, or Ceres, the all-kindly, patient Earth-Spirit." It was to classical mythology that Fuller turned for models to illustrate her ideas of the possibilities of the feminine principle.

In her search for an ideal of feminine virtue, she considered many of Shakespeare's heroines. She preferred his portrait of Cordelia, whose virtue she greatly admired. She also discussed the quality of the marriages he portrayed and found the marriage of Portia and Brutus superior to those in *Cymbeline* and *Othello*. Nevertheless, she used the relationship between Portia and Brutus as an example of the way women were neglected in ancient Rome. She thought Shakespeare was a genius with greater poetic power than John Ford and Philip Massinger, whom she also cited, but believed he did not portray women as heroic as they did or as did Spenser:

> Shakespeare's range is also great; but he has left out the heroic characters, such as the Macaria of Greece, the Britomart of Spenser. Ford and Massinger have, in this respect, soared to a higher flight of feeling than he. It was the holy and heroic Woman they most loved, and if they could not paint an Imogen, a Desdemona, a Rosalind, yet, in those of a stronger mould, they showed a higher ideal, though with so much less poetic power to embody it, than we see in Portia or Isabella.

Her main interest in her evaluation of Shakespeare's female characters was whether their images were heroic.

Of all of the authors in British literature, Fuller chose Edmund Spenser as the one who gave the best portraits of female characters: "The range of female character in Spenser alone might content us for one period" (p. 66). Britomart was her choice for an ideal woman not only because she was virtuous but also because she was strong and independent. Having mentioned Britomart several

---

An excerpt from *Woman in the Nineteenth Century*:

Male and female represent the two sides of the great radical dualism. But, in fact, they are perpetually passing into one another. Fluid hardens to solid, solid rushes to fluid. There is no wholly masculine man, no purely feminine woman.

History jeers at the attempts of physiologists to bind great original laws by the forms which flow from them. They make a rule; they say from observation, what can and cannot be. In vain! Nature provides exceptions to every rule. She sends women to battle, and sets Hercules spinning; she enables women to bear immense burdens, cold, and frost; she enables the man, who feels maternal love, to nourish his infant like a mother. Of late she plays still gayer pranks. Not only she deprives organizations, but organs, of a necessary end. She enables people to read with the top of the head, and see with the pit of the stomach. Presently she will make a female Newton, and a male Syren.

Man partakes of the feminine in the Apollo, woman of the masculine as Minerva.

What I mean by the Muse is the unimpeded clearness of the intuitive powers which a perfectly truthful adherence to every admonition of the higher instincts would bring to a finely organized human being. It may appear as prophecy or as poesy. It enabled Cassandra to foresee the results of actions passing round her; the Seeress to behold the true character of the person through the mask of his customary life. (Sometimes she saw a feminine form behind the man, sometimes the reverse.) It enabled the daughter of Linnæus to see the soul of the flower exhaling from the flower. It gave a man, but a poet man, the power of which he thus speaks: "Often in my contemplation of nature, radiant intimations, and as it were sheaves of light appear before me as to the facts of cosmogony in which my mind has, perhaps, taken especial part." He wisely adds, "but it is necessary with earnestness to verify the knowledge we gain by these flashes of light." And none should forget this. Sight must be verified by life before it can deserve the honors of piety and genius. Yet sight comes first, and of this sight of the world of causes, this approximation to the region of primitive motions, women I hold to be especially capable. Even without equal freedom with the other sex, they have already shown themselves so, and should these faculties have free play, I believe they will open new, deeper and purer sources of joyous inspiration than have as yet refreshed the earth.

Let us be wise and not impede the soul. Let her work as she will. Let us have one creative energy, one incessant revelation. Let it take what form it will, and let us not bind it by the past to man or woman, black or white. Jove sprang from Rhea, Pallas from Jove. So let it be.

Margaret Fuller, in
Woman in the Nineteenth Century, *1845.*

---

times, Fuller eventually began to compare her with contemporary women. She believed that Madame Roland was as valiant as Britomart and that Mary Wollstonecraft and George Sand would not have become outlaws had there been "as much room in the world for such, as in Spenser's poem for Britomart." When a character like Britomart satisfied her expectations, Fuller sounded as if she were speaking of a real person and began to mix fictional with historical women.

According to Fuller, having a woman monarch (whatever Elizabeth's quality as a ruler) had its value in inspiring Spenser's creation of epic women characters: "Unlike as was the English queen to a fairy queen, we may yet conceive that it was the image of *a* queen before the poet's mind that called up this splendid court of women." If Queen Elizabeth helped to inspire Spenser, any strong woman inspired Fuller. She used her outstanding women—dead or alive, literary or historical or mythical—to witness the capabilities within women when they rely on themselves. Figures as disparate as Lady Godiva, Cinderella, George Sand, Mrs. Hutchinson, Cassandra, Eve, Hagar, and Venus served as testimonials in her sermons on the power within women.

This plethora of examples represents a remarkable amount of scholarship, and Fuller delved into countless sources in her search for answers. Although written in nineteenth-century language with some words as outmoded as *purity* and *delicacy* and a conversational style that might be considered affected, her work is surprisingly modern in its concepts. Her brilliant treatise presents and prefigures such modern ideas as the need for role models. Fuller searched beyond Judeo-Christian patriarchy for the feminine principle and the earth mother. She posited an androgenic quality in all people, a need to do away with sexual stereotyping. In essence, Fuller's creation becomes the archetype of woman, of "The Woman in the Nineteenth Century," and of any woman who has aspired, who has wondered and been thwarted but who has still refused to compromise. Fuller's archetypal woman knows that in any compromise, she compromises not only herself but everyone else as well; and that men who become exploiters suffer and lose their humanity themselves.

As with all scholarly and complex literature, reading *Woman* calls for active participation from readers. Also, since *Woman* is a highly suggestive work, readers must be receptive to its message. Both Edgar Allan Poe and Henry David Thoreau said that Fuller's writing and speaking voice were one. A careful scrutiny of *Woman* reveals the dynamism and insights that Fuller's conversation praised, and readers who are willing to become engaged in the profundity of her thought processes will be amply rewarded.

Essentially *Woman* is an affirmation, a witness to the possibilities within women and men who discover within themselves their spirituality and permit it to grow. It is a call for excellence. The first obstruction, the self, is on trial. Beginning with the individual, who must take responsibility for her or his own life, *Woman* envisions a world that would correspondingly reflect this changed self. Ultimately, *Woman* transcends the issue of woman's rights. Paradoxically, after preaching self-reliance for women, it becomes a philosophic message on the interdependence of all people.

Woman in the Nineteenth Century's philosophic framework is predicated on universals; principles of right and wrong do indeed exist. Margaret Fuller was not ashamed to preach because she believed an individual could re-shape her or his life—in fact, could approach perfection. And her sermon had effect. Early feminists were inspired to action by *Woman in the Nineteenth Century*. Three years after its publication, they called the first woman's rights convention in Seneca Falls, New York.

Stephen Adams (essay date 1987)

SOURCE: "'That Tidiness We Always Look for in Woman': Fuller's *Summer on the Lakes* and Romantic Aesthetics," in *Studies in the American Renaissance,* 1987, pp. 247-64.

[*In the following essay, Adams proposes that when assessed by Romantic literary aesthetics, Fuller's seemingly aimless travel narrative possesses an identifiable structure.*]

From its publication, critics have been disturbed by the apparent disunity, randomness, and padding of Margaret Fuller's *Summer on the Lakes, in 1843*. Even the favorable reviewers stressed its heterogeneous nature. In describing the book as "a remarkable assemblage of sketches," Edgar Allan Poe echoed *James Freeman Clarke, who had earlier called it* "a portfolio of sketches." Caleb Stetson was bothered by the inclusion in it of "things connected by no apparent link of association with the objects which seem to fill her eye and mind. . . . Tales also unexpectedly appear—such, for instance, as the German story of the 'Seeress of Prevorst'—which have no connexion with the scenes she visited, except the accidental fact that they occurred in the course of her reading or were called up from the depths of her memory by some mysterious association." Orestes Brownson was hardest on the book and on Fuller herself, whom he described as "a heathen priestess, though of what god or goddess we will not pretend to say." Brownson was upset not only by the book's corrupting heresies but also by its "slipshod style": "Miss Fuller seems to us to be wholly deficient in a pure, correct taste, and especially in that tidiness we always look for in woman.

Recent criticism, what little there is, dispenses with the sexist stereotyping but remains troubled by the apparent incoherence and occasionally bewildering content of the book. According to Arthur W. Brown, "*Summer on the Lakes* lacks systematic arrangement. Its only order is a loose kind of chronology, and its form shows the episodic qualities of the journal upon which it is based" [*Margaret Fuller*]. Lawrence Buell relates the book to other experi-

iments in Transcendentalist literary excursion, but he insists that, unlike Whitman and Thoreau, who "prophesy" in their excursions, "Margaret Fuller is largely content to remain on the level of description and anecdote." [*Literary Transcendentalism: Style and Vision in the American Rengissance*]. Margaret Allen discovers more substance in the book, but she still finds it "self-consciously literary, episodic, and rambling"; she maintains that "Fuller never solved the problem of form for herself and never found the best vehicle for her expression" [*The Achievement of Margaret Fuller*]. Madeleine B. Stern and Annette Kolodny argue for thematic unity in the book, but they do not analyze its structure [in an Introduction to a 1972 edition of *Summer on the Lakes* and in *The Land Before Her,* respectively].

I would like to propose here that the book is more coherent and controlled than most readers have contended and that its experimental form can be described in some detail. Perhaps its structure, however loose, is deliberately planned rather than the unfortunate result either of Fuller's self-admitted difficulty with form or of the traditionally diffuse, meandering nature of travel writing. Perhaps the letters, tales, poems, extracts from books, and other materials ostensibly unrelated to the trip do not merely pad out an otherwise skimpy narrative, but help control and direct the book's shape and major themes.

In her own literary criticism Fuller joined contemporary calls for new structures that would suit the new matter of America. Imitations of British literature, she insisted, do not express the fresh American race "with ample field and verge enough to range in and leave every impulse free, and abundant opportunity to develope a genius, wide and full as our rivers, flowery, luxuriant and impassioned as our vast prairies." She looks forward to a time when "our literature [shall] make its own laws, and give its own watch-words." As Bell Gale Chevigny notes, Fuller's literary stance is related to her political—and specifically feminist—radicalism: "She appears to have . . . associated the strictness of literary forms with the confining social forms and to have resented what both cost her in vitality" [*The Woman and the Myth: Margaret Fuller's Life and Writings*].

> I would like to propose that *Summer on the Lakes* is more coherent and controlled than most readers have contended and that its experimental form can be described in some detail. Perhaps its structure, however loose, is deliberately planned rather than the unfortunate result either of Fuller's self-admitted difficulty with form or of the traditionally diffuse, meandering nature of travel writing.
>
> —*Stephen Adams*

According to Fuller, Emerson comes closest to realizing a form free, flexible, and rich enough for new American discoveries in the "life without and life within." She writes of Emerson's detractors, "They were accustomed to an artificial method, whose scaffolding could easily be retraced, and desired an obvious sequence of logical inferences. They insisted there was nothing in what they had heard, because they could not give a clear account of its course and purport. They did not see that Pindar's odes might be very well arranged for their own purpose, and yet not bear translating into the methods of Mr. Locke." Although she is sympathetic to Emerson's experiments in forms ordered by other than classically logical means, she joins his critics in demanding greater unity and coherence: "in no one essay [of *Essays: Second Series*] is the main stress so obvious as to produce on the mind the harmonious effect of a noble river or a tree in full leaf. Single passages and sentences engage our attention too much in proportion. These Essays, it has been justly said, tire like a string of mosaics or a house built of medals." Such criticism seems ironic from one whose own works were denounced for incoherence and lack of unity, but Fuller was just as hard on herself. In passages published in her *Memoirs,* she claimed: "I shall never be an artist; I have no patient love of execution; I am delighted with my sketch, but if I try to finish it, I am chilled. Never was there a great sculptor who did not love to chip marble. . . . For all the tides of life that flow within me, I am dumb and ineffectual, when it comes to casting my thought into a form. No old one suits me. If I could invent one, it seems to me the pleasure of creation would make it possible for me to write."

She reveals uneasiness about the structure specifically of *Summer on the Lakes.* In its last chapter, after an extended series of excerpts from other books, she wishes for "a thread long enough to string on it all these beads that take my fancy"—a metaphor closer to the "string of mosaics or a house built of medals" than to the organic unity of a river or tree. And Higginson quotes a journal entry in which Fuller expresses dissatisfaction especially with the "last part": "I ought to rewrite the Indian chapter, were there but time! It will, I fear, seem desultory and ineffectual, when my materials are so rich; *owre* rich, perhaps, for my mind does not act on them enough to fuse them." But although it may have fallen below her aims, *Summer* does represent an attempt more successful than has been acknowledged at the new form and the fused, harmonious whole that she longed for in Emerson's work and her own.

As does much Romantic and post—Romantic writing, the book offers hints about the aesthetic by which it should be judged. Fuller insists that "we must learn to look at [the new Western form of life] by its own standard," and she argues for a "new, original, enchanting" kind of elegance for Western women. This repeated theme can be applied to her book, too; perhaps *Summer* should be judged by new standards rather than by outmoded literary rules. "What is limitless is alone divine," Fuller says, implying that her book will not be bound within conventional limits. And as an alternative to the structural metaphor of a string of beads, she offers the figure of a "dexterous weaver" who "lets not one color go, till he finds that which matches it in the pattern; he keeps on weaving, but chooses his shades" maybe the book is not so much unrelated sketches strung loosely together as a skillful pattern composed of consciously matched threads.

In the first chapter of *Summer,* Fuller records her disappointment in Niagara Falls, a sense of anticlimax brought on by her familiarity with pictures and travel literature. Reading about them has removed all freshness and surprise from her own visit to the falls. We might expect, then, that she would attempt a new kind of travel writing, one that avoids conventional objective description and that precludes standard response from the reader. Indeed, Fuller presents a highly subjective excursion that focusses on the perceiver more than the objects perceived and that is designed to make the reader an active participant in the excursion. She offers not the usual guidebook but a "poetic impression of the country at large; it is all I have aimed to communicate." She gives her travel narrative a sense of drama and spontaneity by suggesting that she is composing it in the very process of her travels, rather than ordering and evaluating the whole after the fact. Thus, she speaks in the first sentence of "the, as yet, unknown drama" of the trip. As she goes along, she shows herself deciding what to include and leave out of her book, letting us in on the process of its making.

She uses, also, other techniques to make her book unconventional and to "defamiliarize" her material. She varies the standard structure of a voyage out and back by breaking off her narrative before she has returned to her point of departure. In this way the book—like so many other Romantic works—is essentially a fragment. *Summer on the Lakes* is fragmentary in other important ways, too. In her poetic epigraphs, Fuller speaks of the book as the product of a broken reed—as some significant fragments left from her trip West. She challenges her readers to create for themselves a magical narrative out of what she has salvaged. In her comments on books about Indians, she returns to the theme of the creative reader generating a valuable work from a flawed text: "it is easy to make images from his hints," she writes of Murray's travels; about Schoolcraft's *Algic Researches* she says, "We can just guess what might have been there, as we can detect the fine proportions of the Brave whom the bad taste of some white patron has arranged in frock-coat, hat, and pantaloons." And in calling attention to the "hidden vortex" of the Niagara Falls whirlpool, Fuller hints at a similar center in her own book: "the slight circles that mark the hidden vortex, seem to whisper mysteries the thundering voice above could not proclaim,—a meaning as untold as ever." Maybe her readers are to supply the untold meaning not explicitly proclaimed in *Summer on the Lakes*.

Fuller provides other hints about the active role of the reader in the process of her work. By including in it dialogues, extracts from her reading, and letters, poems, and anecdotes from others, she establishes that *Summer* is the result of creativity shared by a number of people.

She borrows an observation on Titian's "Venus and Adonis" that is pertinent to her own book: "like all beautiful works, it gains by study." She quotes Justinus Kerner on the freedom of the reader: "I give facts; each reader may interpret them in his own way." Finally, in her closing poem **"The Book to the Reader,"** she not only requests her readers' sympathy and cooperation but also challenges us to experience for ourselves the Western "fruit" that is one subject of her book.

The context of Fuller's loose, fragmented, heterogeneous travel narrative is a period of Romantic experimentation with new forms and aesthetic principles. To convey their sense of complex, unstable, manifold reality, the Romantics developed a dramatic, explorative literature of process—an art that generates moments of insight caught from fleeting, often contradictory perspectives. They frequently employed a loose narrative spine (often some kind of voyage out and back), from which they could branch off at will for imaginative excursions in a number of directions. The focus shifts from the landscape through which the protagonist travels to the protagonist himself or herself—from objective or outer to subjective or inner exploration (Thoreau's "home cosmography"). The resulting works (e.g., *The Prelude, Childe Harold's Pilgrimage,* "Song of Myself," *Walden, Moby-Dick*) move away from traditional unity toward a looser coherence based on the writer as protagonist and on interconnecting patterns of related images, moods, and themes. These works are not "formless," as anti-Romantic critics have charged, but are purposely flexible, digressive, and encyclopedic. Thus, in place of works structured according to classical rules and patterns, Augustus Wilhelm Schlegel argues for "a deeper, more intrinsic, and more mysterious unity . . . the Unity of interest." To convey this new sense of unity and structure, Schlegel uses the metaphor of "a mighty stream" which springs from different sources and receives various tributaries (compare Fuller's metaphor for structure quoted earlier, "the harmonious effect of a noble river"): "Why should not the poet be allowed to carry on several, and, for a while, independent streams of human passions and endeavours, down to the moment of their raging junction, if only he place the spectator on an eminence from which he may overlook the whole of their course? And if this great and swollen body of waters again divide into several branches, and pour itself into the sea by several mouths, is it not still one and the same stream?"

Romantic works, then, strive for a deep unity beneath the surface disjointedness, digressiveness, and fragmentation. That surface itself is crucial because it functions to defamiliarize the reader—to prevent stereotyped responses and encourage novelty of perception. The Romantics complicate, disrupt, fragment, and otherwise alter straightforward narrative structures to involve the reader. The fragment, which D. F. Rauber calls "the ultimate Romantic form," becomes "a peculiarly potent means of eliciting active imaginative response." That the Romantics wanted active response from their readers is clear from their pronouncements. Emerson contends in "The American Scholar" that books "are for nothing but to inspire" and that "one must be an inventor to read well. . . . When the

mind is braced by labor and invention, the page of whatever book we read becomes luminous with manifold allusion. Every sentence is doubly significant, and the sense of our author is as broad as the world." At the end of *A Week,* Thoreau declares, "A good book is the plectrum with which our else silent lyres are struck. We not unfrequently refer the interest which belongs to our own unwritten sequel, to the written and comparatively lifeless body of the work. Of all books this sequel is the most indispensable part." And Whitman sums up the new Romantic aesthetic theory under his concept of "Suggestiveness": "I round and finish little, if anything; and could not, consistently with my scheme. The reader will always have his or her part to do, just as I have had mine. I seek less to state or display any theme or thought, and more to bring you, reader, into the atmosphere of the theme or thought—there to pursue your own flight."

Given its contex of Romantic aesthetic experimentation, then, *Summer on the Lakes* should not be expected to be unified in conventional ways but rather in a looser, more flexible Romantic manner. Besides the structural spine of the (almost) round trip from New York to the upper Midwest, Fuller uses recurrent images, themes, and moods that the cooperative reader weaves together to make a whole fabric from threads apparently unrelated to the trip itself. Those repeated, partially developed images and themes contribute to the suggestiveness noted by early critics. Clarke called the book "full of suggestion, rich in matter, to be read again and again, and to appear new with each new reading." Stetson evaluated the same quality negatively; he complained of "underground associations, unintelligible to those who are not in the secret of her thoughts." But Fuller does, I think, furnish sufficient clues throughout the book to indicate the drift of her thought. Margaret Allen points to one underlying, directing concern: "the theme of Summer is nature and civilization, and their interaction." This theme certainly pervades the work, but it does not appear to encompass such important "digressions" as the stories of Captain P., Mariana, or the Seeress of Prevorst. Perhaps the underlying theme is broader and more inclusive. In parts of the book devoted to nature and civilization (e.g., those on the Indian and on the relation of whites to the land), Fuller stresses the wider theme of an ideal junction of opposites that cannot last—that ends in disappointment, anticlimax, and wasted potential. This wider theme extends, also, to the frequent examples in the book of unhappy relationships between women and men. The recurrent elements of wasted resources, disjunction, and disappointment occur also in the personal, autobiographical segments of the book, especially in the central story of Mariana. Selfishness, materialism, prejudice, conformity, extremism, inflexibility—the forces that destroy the Indians, scar the new land, and inhibit the growth of women are the same forces that blight Mariana. Occasional glimpses of an ideal emerge—hints of harmonious junction in the national, social, and personal spheres—but these glimpses soon vanish, only to emphasize the distance we are from attaining the ideal. Beneath the surface light tone common to travel works, a prophetic, fatalistic vision pervades the whole, as Fuller indicates her sense of great potential that will never be fulfilled.

Finally, besides its unity of theme and mood, *Summer on the Lakes* reveals a tighter architectonic structure than critics have claimed for it. Fuller arranges parallels, contrasts, and cross-references to create a series of paired chapters around the physical, thematic, and emotional center in Chapter IV:

Poetic Epigraphs (pp. 1-2)

Chapter I (pp. 3-13)

Chapter II (pp. 14-42)

Chapter III (pp. 43-69)

Chapter IV (pp. 70-108)

Chapter V (pp. 109-168)

Chapter VI (pp. 169-236)

Chapter VII (pp. 237-255)

Concluding Poem (pp. 255-256)

The epigraphs introduce both the theme of disappointment and a challenge to the active involvement of the reader. Fuller counts herself with the "moderns" who "their tale can only tell / In dull words, with a poor reed / Breaking at each time of need"). She hints that her book is fragmentary, incomplete—an unsatisfactory attempt to convey the summer excursion. But, she claims, despite its shortcomings, the book can be redeemed—can be understood and appreciated—by careful readers: "those to whom a hint suffices." These readers will create a coherent whole from the hints and fragments that Fuller provides. The second epigraph again stresses disappointment and failure: "I give you what I can, not what I would . . . In our dwarf day we drain few drops, and soon must thirst again." Once more she talks of fragments, the hints which readers must use to create their own experience in the process of reading. Among those fragments are "an eagle's feather which adorned a Brave, / Well-nigh the last of his despairing band." Fuller thus introduces two motifs (eagle and Indian) that recur as important threads in the tapestry of *Summer* and that come to symbolize opportunities lost and nobility and vitality now destroyed.

The opening epigraphs create a frame with the concluding poem **"The Book to the Reader."** Here, too, Fuller emphasizes the failure of her book, which can offer only remnants of her experience in the West. She likens *Summer* to a "dish of homely sweets," "blackberry jam" that will not taste as good as berries that we could pick fresh ourselves. Again she invites our active participation—first in the direct experience of the West ("But the best pleasure such a fruit can yield, / Is to be gathered in the open field") and also in reading the book that she has made of her experiences. "Read me, even as you would be read," she says, since the book does become a collaboration between her and her readers.

Chapter I begins with some conventional thoughts about Niagara Falls (a spectacle "great enough to fill the whole life, and supercede thought"). Yet immediately Fuller confesses, "We have been here eight days, and I am quite willing to go away." One problem is that she experienced no surprise at the falls; prepared by books, drawings, and the panorama, "I knew where to look for everything, and everything looked as I thought it would." She does feel a moment of "undefined dread" proper to conventional appreciation of this sublime scene, but her main impression is one of anticlimax: "When I arrived in sight of them I merely felt, 'ah, yes, here is the fall, just as I have seen it in picture'." She finds herself "provoked with my stupidity in feeling most moved in the wrong place"— that is, at the rapids before the falls instead of at the falls themselves. "Happy were the first discoverers of Niagara," she writes, "those who could come unawares upon this view and upon that, whose feelings were entirely their own." This is her first experience of disjunction, as civilization keeps her from fully enjoying a natural spectacle. She cannot look at the falls with the fresh vision or surprise and astonishment that Father Hennepin recounts.

Her experience of Niagara is diminished by other irritants, too. The man who appropriates the falls to his own use by spitting into them symbolizes an age obsessed by utility. Although Fuller hopes that such is not "truly the age or truly the America," her subsequent discoveries diminish that hope considerably. Also, Jack Downing, who views the falls as "his great water-privilege," told her "all about the Americanisms of the spectacle; that is to say, the battles that have been fought here"—to which she responds, "It seems strange that men could fight in such a place." These misuses of a natural resource are followed by another—the chaining and tormenting of an eagle, which Fuller links to a chained eagle from her childhood that elicited her intense sympathy.

Disappointment and anticlimax also pervade the last chapter of *Summer on the Lakes*. The rapids at Sault St. Marie parallel in impressiveness those at Niagara, yet Fuller is again let down by her experience. After "shooting" these rapids in a canoe, she "was somewhat disappointed in this being no more of an exploit than I found it." She also found "quite a disappointment" the launching of the "noble boat, the Wisconsin . . . which could not be made to stir." Perhaps her chief disappointment was that "I shall not see the Pictured Rocks, their chapels and urns. It did not depend on me; it never has, whether such things shall be done or not." This incident prompts an outburst of protest that extends beyond this one, apparently minor, opportunity lost: "My friends! may they see, and do, and be more, especially those who have before them a greater number of birthdays, and of a more healthy and unfettered existence." She thus looks back to the fettered eagle of Chapter I and she crystallizes in this one occasion the other disappointments and lost opportunities recorded in the previous chapters. She had already mentioned reading books "in anticipation of a canoe-voyage on Lake Superior as far as the Pictured Rocks," thereby pointing her narrative forward to this anticlimax. Yet remembering her disillusionment after reading about and then seeing Niagara Falls, we must wonder if a trip to the Pictured Rocks would not in any case have been disappointing. Her various frustrations inspire Fuller's longing for another world, a motif that recurs throughout the book: "Bear me to thy better world . . . Take me to that far-off shore, / Where lovers meet to part no more."

Besides the themes of disappointment and anticlimax, other parallels and contrasts link I and VII as framing chapters. For example, the fantasy at Niagara Falls of literary, Cooper-style Indians—"naked savages stealing behind me with uplifted tomahawks"—contrasts with the pitiful reality that Fuller confronts at Sault St. Marie: the "broken and degraded condition" of real Indians, their "greatness, unique and precious" now vanished. The deformation that some see in the buildings at Niagara Falls parallels the "blemishes" that the begging Indians leave behind at the Sault. The section on Niagara as a battlefield anticipates the discussion of General Hull's surrender of Detroit in the War of 1812. In both chapters Fuller refers to "a dream within a dream." Finally, Fuller's praise of novelty and her lament over lacking any sense of freshness and wonder at Niagara find parallels in the last chapter. She writes,

> We get the better [of the Indians] because we do
> "Look before and after."
> But, from the same cause, we
> "Pine for what is not."

Books and art let her "look before" at what previous visitors saw at Niagara, thus preventing the novel experience that she then pines for. In a related passage, a ship captain sees for the first time the ruins of an old English fort on Point St. Joseph's, although he has sailed by them many times: "He presented a striking instance how men, for the sake of getting a living, forget to live." Just as one product of civilization (books and art) interferes with Fuller's appreciation of Niagara, another manifestation of civilization (business or busyness) prevents the captain from appreciating a beautiful landscape available to him. The incident prompts Fuller to restate an ideal which she has mentioned in several previous chapters: "We want a more equal, more thorough, more harmonious development, and there is nothing to hinder from it the men of this country, except their own supineness, or sordid views."

Fuller sets up II and VI as another pair of matched chapters by including in them another series of cross-references, parallels, and contrasts. In Chapter II she arrives at Mackinaw too late to go ashore but promises that "I shall see it to more purpose on my return"; she thus points forward to Chapter VI, where she does explore the island at length. In Chapter II she glimpses her first Indians and briefly reviews books about them; most of Chapter VI is devoted to Indians and consists of extracts from the Indian books. In both chapters, too, she refers to the Wickapee flower, which she associates with Indian culture.

More substantially, in these paired chapters she presents examples of an ideal—of harmonious junction and growth on individual, social, and regional levels—but she then goes on to suggest that the ideal will not be fulfilled, despite the wonderful opportunities that the West offers. Chapter II begins and ends with glimpses of an ideal union of opposing energies. In the opening dialogue, Fuller assumes the role of gnome, which she portrays as an alchemist and poet. Rejecting J.'s condemnation of gnomish materialism, M. (Margaret) sees the gold that the gnomes produce as "the last expression of vital energy" and the earth, the gnomes' dwelling, as "spirit made fruitful,—life." This junction of the material and spiritual is crucial for this chapter and the entire book. She concludes the chapter with a tour through land that seems another union of the earthly and spiritual, of the human and divine. The section is pervaded by images of heaven, fairyland, and harmony.

Glimpses of ideal, harmonious landscapes and of opposites joined appear also in Chapter VI. Fuller finds at Mackinaw "an old French town, mellow in its coloring, and with the harmonious effect of a slow growth, which assimilates, naturally, with objects around it. The people in its streets, Indian, French, half-breeds, and others, walked with a leisure step, as of those who live a life of taste and inclination, rather than of the hard press of business, as in American towns elsewhere." She writes that, for the Indians, "All places, distinguished in any way by nature, aroused the feelings of worship." She thus associates herself with the Indians; in Chapter II she described the trees of Ross' grove as "large enough to form with their clear stems pillars for grand cathedral aisles. There was space enough for crimson light to stream through upon the floor of water which the shower had left. As we slowly plashed through, I thought I was never in a better place for vespers." She gives two important examples of white men living in concord with Indians: Alexander Henry, "who combines some of the good qualities of both [races]; . . . the sentiment and thoughtfulness of the one, with the boldness, personal resource, and fortitude of the other," and Governor Everett of Massachusetts, whose address to the Indian chiefs features various images of harmony between the races (e.g., "they are all one branch, one family. . . . May the oak and the sapling flourish a long time together").

But these glimpses of harmony and junction are overwhelmed by evidence in both Chapter II and VI that the potential ideals will not be realized—that opportunities for combining the best of opposites are being wasted and will not come again. Fuller sees indications of failure from the very start of her trip West. She writes of the people on her boat, "It grieved me to hear these immigrants who were to be the fathers of a new race, all, from the old man down to the little girl, talking not of what they should do, but of what they should get in the new scene. It was to them a prospect, not of the unfolding nobler energies, but of more ease, and larger accumulation. It wearied me, too, to hear Trinity and Unity discussed in the poor, narrow doctrinal way on these free waters." The theme of the old narrow theology coming West and diminishing chances of genuine renewal appears again in the corresponding Chapter VI. Here Fuller condemns "the stern Presbyterian, with his dogmas and his task-work," for failing to integrate the Indian and his values into the changing order of the West, and thereby destroying an opportunity to make him "a valuable ingredient in the new state." Most whites, she maintains, are religious "only to mask their iniquity" against the Indians. Even those who are sincere in their religion do wrong to impose that religion on the Indians.

In both chapters, the glimpses of a slow, organic growth that joins the natural and manmade in harmony give way to visions of ugly "mushroom growth": "The march of peaceful is scarce less wanton than that of warlike invasion. The old landmarks are broken down, and the land, for a season, bears none, except of the rudeness of conquest and the needs of the day, whose bivouac fires blacken the sweetest forest glades." Although in Chapter II Fuller says, "I trust by reverent faith to woo the mighty meaning of the scene, perhaps to forsee the law by which a new order, a new poetry is to be evoked from this chaos," she finds in subsequent chapters little justification for that faith and hope. Rather, the emphasis remains on destruction rather than valuable new construction. She talks in Chapter II of the "fire-ships" (steamboats), the "demons of a new dynasty," that have stripped the Manitou Islands of their best trees; in Chapter VI she links the disappearance of the Indian with the felling of forests and she quotes a traveller's observation that "the atmosphere of the trees does not agree with Caucasian lungs; and it is, perhaps, in part, an instinct of this, which causes the hatred of the new settlers towards trees."

Even the Indian encampments that first seemed symbols of harmony contain evidence of disjunction between white and red. Fuller includes in her picturesque descriptions reminders of "ignominious servitude and slow decay" and of the "firewater" with which whites are subverting the Indians. The ideal union of white and red represented by Everett and Henry will not occur. Fuller sees little likelihood of an amalgamation that would combine the best qualities of both races. As a rule, she says, mixed breeds are inferior, and, anyway, the callous, materialistic, self-righteous whites that she describes in Chapter VI are more likely to exterminate than incorporate the Indians. She points to the shameless treatment of the civilized Cherokees: "There was a chance of seeing what might have been done, now lost forever." As a result, man "loses in harmony of being what he gains in height and extension; the civilized man is a larger mind, but a more imperfect nature than the savage."

Finally, among the other images of disjunction and failed relationships in these paired chapters are a corresponding set of disastrous marriages. In Chapter II Fuller tells the story of Captain P., a "spiritual" man tragically mismatched to the "hard and material" Fanny; in Chapter VI she recounts the Indian myth of the marriage between an Indian brave and a she-bear—"a poetical expression of the sorrows of unequal relations." In both stories, the junction of opposites leads not to ideal, harmonious growth but to tragedy and wasted potential.

Chapters III and V are also related by specific cross-references and common themes. Both focus on the (ultimately unrealized) ideal of joining heaven and earth, nature and mankind, with particular attention to women. Chapter II opens with three days in "Elysium," the Rock River area of Illinois, which Fuller describes in terms of heaven and Eden. She draws heavily on the literature of landscape gardening, turning Illinois into a garden monument to the harmony between man and nature: "But Nature all-astonished stands, to find / Her plan protected by the human mind."

This Edenic, harmonious landscape represents the opportunities offered by the West—"a new country and a new life." But, according to Fuller, "the great drawback upon the lives of these settlers, at present, is the unfitness of the women for their new lot . . . a lot which would be full of blessings for those prepared for it." Because of their upbringing in the East, in a society that does not use their potential, women cannot take advantage of the opportunities that the West offers. They are hampered by "reference to European standards" which prevent original growth in the new Western soil. Their education, especially, unfits them for the new life and contentment they might otherwise enjoy." Another hindrance to the ideal union of heaven and earth, man and nature, is the narrow materialism of most settlers, people who "had no thought beyond satisfying the grossest material wants." Despite the elysian setting of their homes, Fuller finds the typical settler's house "repulsive"; she is struck by "the slovenliness of the dwelling and the rude way in which objects around it were treated, when so little care would have presented a charming whole." Once again she contrasts the whites and Indians, using new imagery: "Wherever the hog comes, the rattlesnake disappears; the omnivorous traveller, safe in its stupidity, willingly and easily makes a meal of the most dangerous of reptiles, and one whom the Indian looks on with a mystic awe."

Alongside this imagery appropriate to the region are references to the classical myths of Ganymede and Hyacinth. Both myths concern a union of the earthly and divine. Ganymede is the mortal boy chosen by Zeus and granted a glimpse of heaven, which now torments him in his earth-bound condition as he longs for the junction that cannot yet be. Hyacinth is the mortal loved by both Apollo and Zephyrus and killed through the latter's jealousy. In both cases, the potential union of human and divine is frustrated, just as the western settlers fail to realize their heaven on earth because of their materialism and failure to fulfill the potential of women.

Chapter V is linked explicitly to Chapter III. Fuller compares Milwaukee, the setting of V, with the Rock River region of III: "I saw not those majestic sweeps, those boundless distances, those heavenly fields; it was not the same world." Parallel to Ganymede and Hyacinth is the story here of Venus and Adonis, another brief junction of the human and divine which ends in "the tragedy of a breaking tie." Just as Black Hawk returned to what once was his Illinois home, an Indian returns to his former home in Milwaukee, thereby angering the new white owner of the land. Just as the Edenic settings of Illinois reveal, upon closer inspection, houses that Fuller finds out of character with their environment, she now happens upon a "very Eden" which turns out actually to be ravaged by sickness, care, and labor. Just as she earlier enjoyed the hospitality of an Irish gentleman's mansion, she now accepts shelter with the destitute Pottawattamies. And just as she saw most Illinois women unfit for Western life and therefore miserable, she discovers in Wisconsin "a contented woman, the only one I heard of out there"; the others "found their labors disproportioned to their strength, if not to their patience; and, while their husbands and brothers enjoyed the country in hunting or fishing, they found themselves confined to a comfortless and laborious indoor life."

Much of Chapter V is devoted to the Seeress of Prevorst, a "digression" which many readers have found disturbing. If this section were included only because Fuller happened to read about the German spiritualist while she was at Milwaukee, *Summer on the Lakes* might well suffer from incoherence and padding. But the story picks up and develops many of the threads that Fuller has all along been weaving through her tapestry. By way of a preface to the Seeress, Fuller (here taking the role of "Free Hope") urges "apprehending the infinite results of every day," and she claims, "All my days are touched by the supernatural." She thus offers in her own example and that of the Seeress the junction of earth and heaven that appears throughout *Summer* as a tantalizing but infrequently realized ideal. She finds the Seeress a "strong contrast with the life around me." Unlike the materialistic Western settlers, the Seeress reveals "the development of the spiritual in the fleshly eye . . . the faculty for prophetic dreams and the vision of spirits." Her "peculiar inward life" and "inward state" contrast with the merely external life of the settlers. Yet, like the other women in *Summer,* the Seeress becomes the victim of an oppressive social system. Upon her marriage, "she was obliged hourly to forsake her inner home, to provide for an outer, which did not correspond with it." Unfitted as she is for her new life— as are most of the women Fuller finds in the American West—she breaks down physically even as she grows spiritually.

The Seeress thus becomes another example of disjunction. In leading "an almost disembodied life," she moves away from Fuller's ideal of the harmonious conjunction of opposites. In the Seeress "spirit and soul seemed often divided, and the spirit to have taken up its abode in other regions, while the soul was yet bound to the body." She provides a counterbalance to the western settlers, but does not herself represent the ideal because she goes too far in the opposite direction. As Fuller argues in her summation of the Seeress, "the functions should be in equipose, and when they are not, when we see excess either on the natural . . . or the spiritual side, we feel that the law is transgressed."

The Seeress provides, then, yet another example of potential not realized—of an ideal not maintained or developed. Her own life, along with the ghosts that she sees, illustrates once again Fuller's recurring theme of opportu-

nities lost: "The Hades she imagines is based in fact, for it is one of souls, who, having neglected their opportunities for better life, find themselves left forlorn, helpless."

Chapter IV is the central chapter of the book numerically and thematically. It is unusual in that it has, explicitly, very little to do with Fuller's trip West. Back in Chicago, she does not write about the places and people there but inserts poetry and letters received from friends, fills most of the chapter with the story of Mariana, and then closes with material from her reading. In a letter to Emerson, Fuller describes the chapter as a grab-bag or miscellany: "I shall bring in with brief criticisms of books read there, a kind of letter box, where I shall put a part of one of S. Ward's letters, one of Ellery's and apropos to that July moon beneath whose influences I received it, a letter containing Triformis." While this chapter, even more than the others, might seem to justify criticism of *Summer on the Lakes* for incoherence and padding, Fuller may have tighter control here than critics have suggested.

First, she includes materials from other writers as part of her Romantic program for demonstrating that any work of art is a collaboration. As David Luke argues, letters, especially, represent "an appeal for shared creativity as an expression of friendship." Second, the materials that she includes in this central chapter are not random or unrelated to the rest of the book. Rather, they recapitulate and focus major images and themes from the whole work.

J. F. Clarke's poem "Triformis," for example, is another expression of disappointment in the relationships between men and women. The affair that begins as a potential "treasure" of "undeveloped destinies" ends with "miles of polar ice" parting the two lovers. The poem typifies the pattern that Fuller has been varying throughout *Summer on the Lakes:* a glimpse of an ideal, followed by disillusion when that ideal is not realized. The letter from the painter, too, picks up important themes from previous chapters and looks forward to later ones. The painter sketches himself as an archetypal Traveller driven by "insatiable desire" for the secrets of "a far-off world" and for a "pathway to a world beyond." The Traveller thus represents an urge to leave this world for a better, a theme that Fuller also treats in sections devoted to the Lorelie, Ganymede, the Seeress of Prevorst, and some of her own moods. Again through the painter's letter, Fuller returns to the theme of ideal organic, harmonious progress opposed to the "rapid progress here" in the West.

The center of the chapter and the book—and perhaps its "hidden vortex"—is the story of Mariana. This fictionalized autobiography would be entirely out of place in travel writing before the Romantic period, with its conventions of objectivity and impersonality. With Romantic literary experimentation, however, travel writing changed significantly. Subjectivity now replaced objectivity as a standard. A reviewer for *Putnam's* summarized the change of taste: "It is not the things seen, nor the difficulty surmounted, but the man and the hero who sees and surmounts, that interests us." More recently, William C. Spengemann insists that the "true Romantic travel narrative has dispensed with physical travel." Thus, if *Walden* is Thoreau's record of inward travel and exploration (see especially the first two paragraphs of "Conclusion"), *Summer on the Lakes* is Fuller's account of internal as well as external travel and so appropriately centers on "Mariana." As Stetson wrote in his review, the book is "in a high degree subjective . . . evidently she is much more occupied with what is passing in her own soul, than with the objective realities which present themselves to the senses."

The story of Mariana illustrates the book's central themes of disappointment, disjunction, and opportunities lost. We learn from the start that "Mariana, so full of life, was dead." In the first part, Fuller pictures her idealized alter ego as an energetic, imaginative child with a "touch of genius and power." Through the envy and malice of her classmates, who cannot tolerate her nonconformity, Mariana becomes a "genius of discord among them." She recovers her ability to love, however, and once more brings her classmates together, united in their love for her. In this first section, Fuller links Mariana to the Seeress by references to her poetic abilities, sleepwalking, and "strong convulsions"; the Seeress herself is a sleepwalker, poet, and victim of "convulsions and spasm." Mariana resembles the Seeress in the second part of her story, too, as her energies are wasted and her inner life disrupted by her own excesses and marriage to a one-dimensional businessman. "Sylvain became the kind, but preoccupied husband, Mariana, the solitary and wretched wife." Mariana comes to typify "a fine sample of womanhood" who is "born to shed light and life on some palace home" but who instead wastes away in a frustrating domestic captivity. Like the Traveller at the beginning of the chapter and the other defeated questers in the book, she laments that "love passed me by," leaving her with a "thirst that none can still."

Fuller argues that "such women as Mariana are often lost, unless they meet some man of sufficiently great soul to prize them." This is a transition to the last part of the central chapter, devoted to Philip Van Artevelde and Morris Birkbeck. Both represent types of men who might have redeemed Mariana by letting her grow and live up to her full potential. Van Artevelde becomes for Fuller a symbol of the ideal conjunction of opposite qualities. "When will this country have such a man?," she asks; "It is what she needs; no thin Idealist, no coarse Realist, but a man whose eye reads the heavens while his feet step firmly on the ground, and his hands are strong and dexterous for the use of human implements . . . [Such men possess] prescience, as the wise man must, but not so far as to be driven mad to-day by the gift which discerns to-morrow [an allusion, perhaps, to the Seeress]. When there is such a man for America, the thought which urges her on will be expressed."

Birkbeck, too, functions as an ideal, the answer for both Mariana and America: "Freedom, the liberty of law, not license; not indolence, work for himself and children and all men, but under genial and poetic influences;—these were his aims. How different from those of the new set-

tlers in general!" Yet such men as Van Artevelde "come not so often as once an age," and as for Birkbeck, "death prematurely cut short his plans." The central chapter ends on a note of frustration and pessimism, of ideals unrealized and opportunities lost.

The book as a whole ends on much the same note. Returning to Buffalo, Fuller encounters a "shabbily dressed phrenologist" whose phony spiritualism contrasts with the true inner dimension of a Seeress of Prevorst or Morris Birkbeck. She sees "knots of people gathered here and there to discuss points of theology," just as on the boat out she heard "Trinity and Unity discussed in the poor, narrow doctrinal way." Apparently their trip west has not given these people the new vision that Fuller had hoped for. Instead of taking advantage of the freedom and novelty afforded by the West, they are more likely to establish in the West the old narrow notions that they brought with them. Fuller is buoyed up a little to hear some people "discussing the doctrines of Fourier." But, she remarks, "It seemed pity they were not going to, rather than from, the rich and free country where it would be so much easier, than with us, to try the great experiment of voluntary association." (Three years after the publication of *Summer,* the collapse of Fourierist Brook Farm confirmed her fears.) Fuller concludes her book with this last indication of possibilites that will not likely be realized— of disappointment over opportunities missed.

Summer on the Lakes possesses, then, if not the tidiness that Orestes Brownson looked for in woman, at least a greater degree of unity and coherence than it has been

Drawing of Fuller by James Freeman Clarke, circa 1831.

credited with. Brownson seems correct, however, in describing *Summer* as "a sad book." We might justly apply to it Fuller's own remark about Goethe's *Elective Affinities:* "There is indeed a sadness, as of an irresistible fatality, brooding over the whole."

Horace Greeley on Fuller's journalism:

I think most of her contributions to the *Tribune,* while she remained with us, were characterized by a directness, terseness, and practicality, which are wanting in some of her earlier productions. Good judges have confirmed my own opinion, that, while her essays in the *Dial* are more elaborate and ambitious, her reviews in the *Tribune* are far better adapted to win the favor and sway the judgment of the great majority of readers. But, one characteristic of her writings I feel bound to commend,—their absolute truthfulness. She never asked how this would sound, nor whether that would do, nor what would be the effect of saying anything; but simply, 'Is it the truth? Is it such as the public should know?' And if her judgment answered, 'Yes,' she uttered it; no matter what turmoil it might excite, nor what odium it might draw down on her own head. Perfect conscientiousness was an unfailing characteristic of her literary efforts.

Horace Greeley, in "New York," in Memoirs of Margaret Fuller Ossoli, *by Margaret Fuller, The Tribune Association, 1869.*

Jeffrey Steele (essay date 1992)

SOURCE: "Freeing the 'Prisoned Queen': The Development of Margaret Fuller's Poetry," in *Studies in the American Renaissance,* 1992, pp. 137-75.

[*Steele is an American educator and critic who here applies to Fuller's poetry biographical interpretations that he considers crucial to an understanding of her emotional and intellectual development. He divides Fuller's poetry into three chronological periods: an early period (1835-38) consisting primarily of occasional pieces and poems to a close friend; a middle period (1839-1843) that charts a spiritual crisis in Fuller's life; and a mature period in 1844, during which Fuller wrote nearly all of her notable poems. The following excerpt is taken from Steele's discussion of poems from this final period.*]

We will probably never know the exact causes of Fuller's *annus mirabilis*—1844. In the space of a little over eight months, she finished her two most important books—*Summer on the Lakes* and *Woman in the Nineteenth Century*—and managed to write thirty-eight poems, most of which rank among her best compositions. Then, accepting a position as book reviewer with Horace Greeley's *New-York Tribune,* she moved to New York to embark on a new career as cultural arbiter and public reformer. It is all too easy to say that 1844 closed one chapter in Fuller's life because in 1845, in New York, she had finally arrived. As a literary celebrity with increasing political power, she had a forum from which to advocate reform—a position enjoyed by few other women in America. At this moment, the obsessive, mythical quality simply disappears from Fuller's writing—either because she was too busy to indulge earlier moods or because she had simply outgrown them. In March 1845 Fuller noted the change in her position as a shift from "personal relations" to a "public career": "I have given almost all my young energies to personal relations. I no longer feel inclined to this, and wish to share and impel the general stream of thought."

But the recognition that 1844 is the watershed year in Fuller's emotional and imaginative development does not explain what happened that year. Again, the best evidence is contained in the poems that document a remarkable progression through a sequence of psychological and mythic encounters. Fuller was never to come this close again to achieving in her art a consciousness of her private demons and angels. We might read the poems of this year as a progressive act of exorcism—a psychological healing that once and for all closed the door on many of Fuller's deepest obsessions. Whatever the truth of the matter, a number of the poems she composed rank among her finest artistic achievements.

A note of anguish is struck by what are probably the earliest of Fuller's 1844 poems—**"I wish I were where Helen lies"** and **"Death opens her sweet white arms."** Written on 22 April, these poems strike a chord of despondency that brought Fuller as close as she was to come to thoughts of suicide. In the first, the Poet contrasts her desolate position with that of a "lover in times of old" who laments the death of Helen. The bereft lover, she argues has at least known happiness; for "Who wholly loves has known the whole, / The wholly loved doth truly live." In contrast, the Poet's situation is one of loveless solitude:

> But some, sad outcasts from this prize,
> Wither down to a lonely grave,
>   All hearts their hidden love despise
> And leave them to the whelming wave.
>
>   They heart to heart have never pressed,
> Nor hands in holy pledge have given,
>   By father's love were ne'er caressed,
> Nor in a mother's eye saw heaven.
>
>   A flowerless and fruitless tree,
>   A dried up stream, a mateless bird,
>   They live, yet never living be,
>   They die, their music all unheard.

"Loved passed me by," the Poet laments, portraying herself as a homeless child doomed to wander in a forbidding world. A "lost lover," she becomes the "prey and spoil" of others who use her rather than comforting her.

Cut off from the world of human love, her only hope is

the promise of divine charity:

> But oh this thirst that none can still
> Save those unfounden waters free;
> The angel of my life should fill
> And soothe me to Eternity.

As we shall see, the movement from human to divine love is the course that Fuller takes during this pivotal year.

On the same manuscript sheet, a second poem offers an even starker portrait of Fuller's condition:

> Death
> Opens her sweet white arms and whispers,
>   peace!
> Come say thy sorrows in this bosom! This
> Will never close against thee; and my heart
> Though cold cannot be colder much than man's.

We can surmise that a number of factors contributed to Fuller's depression: a general malaise and discontent that seems to date from her 1843 trip to the west, her ill health the following winter, and the second distribution of her father's estate in March. But perhaps the deepest wound resulted from the pregnancies of Fuller's sister Ellen, Hawthorne's wife Sophia, and Emerson's wife Lydia. In December 1842, Fuller had written that "the darkest hue on my own lot is that I have neither children, nor yet am the parent of beautiful works by which the thought of my life might be represented to another generation." Fuller's comments in her letters and in her published writings make it clear that she did not see motherhood as the only option for women. She noted, for example, in a July letter to Emerson that "the saddest position in the world must be that of some regal dame to whom husband, court, kingdom, world, look in vain for an heir!" But at the same time, it is clear that the pregnancies and childbirths of three of her women friends touched her very deeply.

On one level, they seem to have awakened a complex set of associations that embodied some of her deepest feelings about birth and death. When Ellen's child was born in late May, Fuller was reminded of an earlier birth that became a death: "Our youngest brother Edward, who died while I held him, was born on my eighteenth birthday, and given to me. . . . If this child dies, too, her uncle will be grown to about the angelic size in the other world and can take care of her." Fuller herself was a "parent" on 23 May (to recall the terms of her 1842 letter): she completed the composition of *Summer on the Lakes* on that date (her birthday) and then visited Mount Auburn Cemetery and "walked gently among the graves." This conjunction of birth and death, of creativity and mourning, is typical of Fuller's imaginative rhythms. Echoing the terms of her 1840-41 spiritual crisis, it suggests that once again Fuller was returning to mourning as a gateway to her deepest psychological energies. Striking a prolonged note of melancholy, her 1844 journals displace the act of mourning from external figures entirely onto Fuller's self-image. Depicting herself as a bereft and loveless maiden, Fuller begins to work through the anguish she felt at her

inability to occupy a traditional female role. Although Fuller's catastrophic infatuation with James Nathan in 1845 revealed the persistent lure of the Muse/true woman role, after 1844 she was able to play the part of the unconventional woman (Minerva) without falling into the abyss of melancholy. This is tantamount to saying that, during 1844, Fuller finally started to become "Minerva"—the unconventional, unmarried woman "betrothed to the sun."

Significantly, the childbirths surrounding Fuller during this period resonate with a set of images in her letters that depict her experiencing an analogous process of pregnancy and birth. "As fire lays open, and the plough awakes a virgin soil," she writes in October 1843, "successions of seeds are called into development, which the powers of nature had generated in different moods." In November, she remarks that "after preparation of unknown length beneath the soil, an unexpected plant springs up and shadows all the remaining scene." Writing to Anna Barker Ward the next month, she imagines stirring within herself "the tree born to lift its head" in order to bless with many a blossom the struggles of its root to establish itself in the cold dark earth." In January 1844, she writes Emerson that "I have enjoyed a consciousness of inward ripening"—a phrase that could easily be applied to an expectant mother's consciousness of the quickening of her fetus. Finally, in what could be interpreted as a powerful womb image, Fuller writes Caroline Sturgis in August that "Life opens again before me, longer avenues, darker caves, adorned with richer crystals!"

Characteristically, Fuller translates her own ambivalences about motherhood into powerful mythic images of maternity. Cut off by personal circumstances from the actual experience of bearing and nurturing a child, she is still able to imagine herself as sharing maternal qualities. In May 1844, Fuller sends her friend Anna Loring a pin bearing the image of Raphael, "who, beyond all others, was worthy to depict the holy Virgin, the Mother of a holy child." Several weeks later, in a revealing slip of the pen, she suggests a maternal relationship to her younger brothers by observing in a letter to Caroline Sturgis: "I did not know then I should have such a large family of sons." In the letter to Channing (previously cited) in which Fuller enjoins him to preserve her "flower-pieces," she clearly ties her self-image with the image of her mother. Fuller's adoption of a maternal role is also evident in the letter she wrote Sarah Shaw in September. "If you can feel towards me as a Mother, after knowing me so long," she writes, "I should not be afraid to accept the sacred trust." But in the most striking passage of all, Fuller compares herself to the goddess Ceres seeking for her lost child, Persephone. Commenting on the possibility that Caroline Sturgis may not be able to visit her in New York, she observes: "But if not so, Ceres is well accustomed to wander, seeking the other Magna Dea, and to be refused the cup of milk by the peasant."

It is easy enough to assert that, during 1844, Fuller felt stirring within the gestation and birth of creative powers that manifested themselves in her writing. On one level, this rings true. But the reference to "Ceres" and "Magna

Dea" above compels us to examine these images more deeply. Corresponding to such passages in the letters are numerous poetic evocations of powerful goddesses or archetypal female powers: the waxing moon, Virgin Mother, Leila, Diana, Hecate, Sphinx, and Isis. Such mythic figures suggest the forces welling up from Fuller's unconscious, at the same time they point outward from Fuller's expanding self to a wider circle of reference. Given Fuller's actions by the end of 1844—her visits with female prisoners at Sing-Sing, her growing commitment to the plight of abandoned and imprisoned women, her comments on the position of women in *Woman in the Nineteenth Century*—we can see that these goddess-figures both symbolize her own creative power and bond her with other women. Summoning the goddess, Fuller both reveals a hidden part of herself and releases myths that embody an ideal of Woman for her forgotten sisters. Once she recovered the goddess in 1844, Fuller was able to turn the next year to new roles that enabled her to manifest in public ways the nurturing qualities that she had found through Her.

Two poems written in early May demonstrate the powerful mythic material that Fuller was uncovering. The first, enclosed in her 3 May letter to Caroline Sturgis, returns to one of the central symbols orienting her 1840-41 spiritual crisis. "I live, I am—*The carbuncle is found,*" Fuller had written ecstatically to Sturgis on 8 September 1840. Then, on 22 October of that year, she presented the carbuncle as the goal of her quest: "I would now steal away over golden sands, through silent flowery meadows father still through darkest forests 'full of heavenly vows' into the very heart of the untrodden mountain where the carbuncle has lit the way to veins of yet undreamed of diamond." Now in 1844, she returns to the carbuncle as a mystical talisman that might defend a close friend:

> Slow wandering on a tangled way
> To their lost child pure spirits say
> The diamond marshal thee by day;
> By night the carbuncle defend
> Hearts-blood of a bosom friend. . . .

Read in relation to the poem **"I wish I were where Helen lies,"** written two weeks before, the image of the "lost child" is revealing. In the earlier poem, Fuller had portrayed herself as a lost child wandering in a hostile world; here she imagines a source of protection, a talisman that connects the lost child to a realm of protecting spirits. Many of Fuller's poems during the next seven months seem to perform a similar talismanic function. Relieving her of the burdens of isolated selfhood, they link her with a region of transcendent spiritual power.

In a poem written just two days later, on 5 May, Fuller locates that region in the depths of the psyche. "Four times the form upon the dreamer's eye / Has dawned," she begins, recounting four similar dreams that struck her as moments of revelation. The first moment came to her as **"The Revelation of all Poesy"**; the second, recalling the 1835 poem to Anna Barker, is an escape from "crushing dull despair." In the poem to Barker (discussed above),

Fuller portrayed herself reaching up frantic arms toward a benevolent figure "with soft eyes, beaming the tenderest love." Here, the same figure returns, but with an important amplification—she has started to take on the lineaments of the Virgin Mother:

> My eyes were upward turned, when
>   downward bent
> A gaze met mine; Oh of such love benign,
> Such melting love, such heavenly human love,
>   As mothers feel when in their virgin hearts
> First stirs the folded dove. . . .

Anticipating the exultant Christianity of poems to be written later that summer—works such as **"Virgin Mother Mary mild"** and **"Sub Rosa-Crux"**—this image suggests one direction Fuller's imagination was carrying her—toward images of a nurturing goddess-figure who would eventually combine aspects of the Virgin Mother with those of Diana and Isis. Again, we notice the displacement and sublimation of the image of pregnancy into a spiritual context: the "folded dove" stirring within the Mother who reaches down toward her lost daughter.

Fuller presents the third moment of revelation as a feeling "Of intimate communion far more full / Than ever known before in any hour." But the account of the fourth dream is the most striking, because of Fuller's vivid dramatization of her spiritual and psychological condition:

> I had walked forth alone, seeking in vain
>   After dull days of many petty cares,
> Of petty, seemingly of useless cares,
>   To find again my nobler life,—again
> To weave the web which, from the frosty
>   ground,
>   Should keep the tender feet of prisoned Queen,
> Or wrap the breast of weeping beggar child,
>   Or curtain from the saint a wicked world,
> Or,—if but rightly woven were this web
>   For any, for all uses it were fit:
> But I had lost the shuttle from my hand. . . .

Again, the image of the lost child appears; but here, the Poet imagines herself as once capable of achieving a "nobler life" of creative expression that might protect her from such vulnerability. She has woven the protecting "web"; she might do so again, if she can find the lost "shuttle." After such a preface, Fuller's account of the fourth dream, a moment that "left a deep calmness in my heart" presages a return to queenly power. Significantly, Fuller last portrayed herself as a queen in 1840. Now, she senses a renewed accession of regal power—a power that seems linked to the lesson that her fourth dream provides her: "Flow with thy Destiny, and serve thy Fate."

Fuller's poetry during the month of May reverberates around the two poles defined in "Four times the form upon the dreamer's eye." Images of solitude, loss, and isolation are matched by an increasingly articulated vision of an ideal realm that becomes Fuller's "Fate." In "When no gentle eye beam charms," she contrasts the absence of hope and comfort with a "better world" where "The star of love shall set no more." Another poem, written just a few days later, concludes with a prayer:

> The heart of stone in me renew
> A heart of marble pure and white,
> Sculptured with characters of light
> For when all souls all love may know,
> And their true core time's falseness show
> Then hard and soft together flow
> And marble melting like the snow
> With sunset rays shall roseate glow.

Imagining her self transfused with a glowing radiant spirit, Fuller evokes a moment of grace that redeems her present isolation.

This vision of grace is amplified in **"The temple soared"**—a poem that Fuller later revised and included in *Woman in the Nineteenth Century*. "In the inmost shrine," she writes, "Stands the image divine / Only seen / by those whose deeds have worthy been." This vision, Fuller concludes, is offered by "truth" who "assumes the wand of Love." This truth is attired either in a "robe of green" or "Winter's silver sheen," a "White, pure as light" that "Is fit alike for bridal vest, or gentle shroud." The disturbing conflation of life and death, bridal veil and shroud, is matched by the imagery of another poem written at about the same time, "Boding raven of the breast." The Poet has been haunted by a "boding raven," a "vulture"; yet she maintains the hope that the "vulture may become a Dove." This spiritual transformation will be enacted through a ritual that combines aspects of baptism, burial, and marriage:

> Let the humble linnet sing
> Of the assured, if distant Spring;
> While I baptize in the pure wave,
> Then prepare a deep safe grave.
> Where the plighted hand may bring
> Violets from that other spring.
> Whence the soul may take its flight
> Lark-like spiral seeking light
> Seeking secure the source of light.

While the precise referents of these images are impossible to determine—what is that other spring?—it is clear that this poem enacts a ritual burial associated with the past (a burial of the past?). The Poet's "plighted hand," presumably a sign of her marriage to the spirit, similar to the "woman betrothed to the sun" in *Woman in the Nineteenth Century*, strews flowers upon a grave—a ritual of mourning that becomes a spiritual release, freeing her soul to a "lark-like spiral seeking light."

"To the Apollo on my pin" depicts an analogous process of transformation. Composed 3 June and later revised and copied into Fuller's letter of 3 November, this poem imagines Apollo as a heavenly singer who achieves a larger consciousness of life" through the sublimation of disappointed love into artistic creation. Although Apollo "loved in vain so many lovely forms" and was left with nothing "but his song," his losses were compensated by the flowing of love "into genius," a process through which Apollo was "baptized in his own life's fire." An image of the process Fuller herself was experiencing in 1844, this poem promises the insight of poetry as the replacement for lost love.

As Fuller explored the transformative powers that were surfacing in her poetry, she attended as well to the external forces that threaten to impede the progress of enlightenment. Ultimately, these two themes were blended in *Woman in the Nineteenth Century,* which founded an enlarged conception of female selfhood on the power of myth at the same time that it analyzed the cultural pressures imprisoning women. In one of her most unusual poems, **"On the boundless plain careering,"** Fuller created a striking allegory of the ways in which a free being (in this case, a wild horse named Konic) was captured and emotionally shackled by the "tyrant"—man. Opening with a vista of the "untamed" Konic galloping on the "boundless plain," this poem portrays his transformation from a creature who knows "no servile moment" to one whose spirit has been broken. Suddenly, Konic is frightened by the appearance on the horizon of "Centaur forms"—broken horses bearing their riders. Portrayed as "enslaved brethern" (l. 16), these creatures endure the "bit & whip of tyrant scorn" as their riders hasten "To make new captives as forlorn." The terrified Konic is roped and then released. He gallops off, filled with the illusion that he is once again free.

But it is the pathos of Konic's illusory freedom that becomes the focus of Fuller's poem. For although his body seems free, his psyche has been marked as indelibly as the brand that he now carries:

> Never again, upon the mead
>   Shalt thou a free wild horse feed.
>   The mark of man doth blot thy side
> The fear of man hath dulled thy pride
>   Thy master soon shall on thee ride.

Refering ostensibly to a broken horse, these lines resonate unmistakenly as a representation of the psychological position of any dominated group—American slaves or American women. Although it seems likely that Fuller intended this piece as a commentary on slavery, the gender reference is unmistakable. After a number of intervening years, the "captor re-appears" to find Konic with "broken pride." At that moment, the Poet comments, "Thou'rt *wedded* to the sad estate." And then in lines that Fuller's brother later suppressed, she makes the connection explicit:

> Sometime, on a fairer plain
>   May those captives live again
>   Where no tyrant stigmas stain.
> Marriage will then have broke the rod
>   Where wicked foot has never trod
>   The verdure sacred to a God.

Someday, the Poet hopes, free and untyrannical relationships will be possible in a world where marriage will no longer be modeled upon a pattern of domination.

During the remainder of June and early July, as Fuller pursued the goal of personal and psychological freedom, she reached a level of inspiration that led to the composition of six of her best poems: **"To Sarah," "Leila in the Arabian zone," "Double Triangle, Serpent and Rays," "Winged Sphynx," "My seal ring,"** and **"Sistrum."** (A seventh poem, **"Virgin Mother Mary mild,"** introduces a vein of Christian imagery that Fuller was to exploit more fully later in the summer.) The importance that Fuller attributed to these poems is evident from the letter she wrote Emerson on 13 July. Although she feels that Emerson's literary "excellence . . . is of a kind wholly unattainable to me," she too has been writing—creating "flowers and stones" that might "have a hieroglyphical interest for those of like nature with me." Unable to "polish my marbles" as Emerson does, Fuller defines her production as the expression of "unimpeded energy." Their truth is the truth of feeling; for "Whatever is truly felt has some precious meaning." Fuller then refers to the poems she has been working on (I have added titles in brackets):

> The horse, konic belongs to Frank Shaw [**"On the boundless plain careering"**]. S. Ward it was who likened Sarah to the sweet fern [**"To Sarah"**]. The Sistrum [**"Sistrum"**] I have shown you, and I believe the Serpent, triangles, and rays [**"Double Triangle Serpent and Rays"**] which I had drawn for me. The other two emblems were ascribed to me by others, and the Winged Sphynx [**"Winged Sphynx"**] I shall have engraved and use, if I ever get to look as steadily as she does. Farewell, O Grecian Sage, though not my Oedipus.

The significance of these poems is most evident in their mythic imagery. Leila, the goddess animating Fuller's most important mystical essay, reappears after a three-year absence. At the same time, the figure of Leila is deepened and enriched by a complex weave of mythical reference. Io, Isis, Diana, Mercury, the Sphynx are all evoked—a mythical panoply that links directly with the myths underpinning Fuller's "idea of Woman" in *Woman in the Nineteenth Century*.

"Our friend has likened thee to the sweet fern," the poem "To Sarah" opens, evoking the sweet "fragrance" exuded by Fuller's intimate, Sarah Clarke. Comparing the influence of her friend to the calming effect of plants, Fuller goes on to equate her soothing power to that felt one restless day when she fled from the "dull ebb after emotion's shocks" to the retreat of a secluded wood. Spreading for herself a bed of "sweet bay," she found

> an hour of pure tranquillity
> Like to the autumn sweetness of thine eye
>   Which pries not, seeks not, & yet clearly sees,
>   Which woos not, beams not, yet is sure to
>   please.

Defining an ideal of female support and nurturance, the poem concludes by contrasting Sarah's "green" world with the Poet's "dim wood of regret," a realm that "Was made the one to rhyme with Margaret." Rather than embodying the sweetness of laurel (bay), the Poet identifies herself as "Leila." *Her* world is one of painful aspiration, not sweet being:

> But, since I know that Leila stands for night,
> I own that sable mantle of the sky
>   Through which pierce, gem-like, points of
>   distant light.
> "As sorrow truths, so night brings out her stars."

Aspiring in solitude toward "points of distant light," the Poet embodies what Fuller in *Woman in the Nineteenth Century* calls the role of "Minerva": she is the self-reliant spiritual quester. In contrast, her friend Sarah—with all of her emotional nurturance—is the more traditional true woman, the "Muse."

During the next few months, Fuller was exploring the realm of Minerva—a figure whose realm, she jokingly suggested in a letter to Emerson, lay far outside the dominion of masculine power. Chiding Emerson in July about his insensitivity to the sources of her inspiration, Fuller commented on the distance between his and her own creative positions: "But what is this pathos compared to that perceptible in the situation of a Jove, under the masculine obligations of all sufficinyness, who rubs his forehead in vain to induce the Minerva-bearing headach! Alas! his brain remains tranquil, his fancy daughterless!" Judging from the poetry that Fuller was writing at this time, her fancy was far from "daughterless." Instead, she was uncovering a pantheon of daughters, as in the following remarkable poem:

>   Leila in the Arabian zone
> Dusky, languishing and lone
>   Yet full of light are her deep eyes
> And her gales are lovers sighs
>
>   Io in Egyptian clime
> Grows an Isis calm sublime
>   Blue black is her robe of night
> But blazoned o'er with points of light
>   The horns that Io's brow deform
> With Isis take a cresent form
>   And as a holy moon inform.
> The magic Sistrum arms her hand
>   And at her deep eye's command
>   Brutes are raised to thinking men
> Soul growing to her soul filled ken.
>
>   Dian of the lonely life
>   Hecate fed on gloom and strife
>   Phebe on her throne of air
>   Only Leila's children are.

Assuming the role of the goddess Leila, a figure "languishing and lone," Fuller expands her being to encompass the attributes of Io, Isis, Dian, Hecate, and Phebe. Of all these, the figure of Isis is most important. Her "magic Sistrum" (a rattle) possesses a transformative power on the opposite sex: "Brutes are raised to thinking men / Soul growing to her soul filled ken." The Goddess, Fuller suggests (in an argument she will amplify in *Woman in the Nineteenth Century*), embodies an ideal of spiritual fulfillment that transcends the gender divisions marking the unequal relationships of American culture.

Fuller's next poem, **"Double Triangle, Serpent and Rays,"** symbolizes the transfiguration of gender difference through the powerful symbol of androgynous union, the "hieros gamos" or mystical marriage sought by numerous hierophants as the final consummation of consciousness. The significance of this symbol for Fuller is indicated by the drawing that accompanies this poem in her 1844 Commonplace Book. This design—interlocking triangles, surrounded by a serpent swallowing its tail and rays—was later used by Fuller to preface the 1845 edition of *Woman in the Nineteenth Century*.

> Patient serpent, circle round,
> Till in death thy life is found;
>   Double form of godly prime
> Holding the whole thought of time,
>   When the perfect two embrace,
> Male & female, black & white,
>   Soul is justified in space,
> Dark made fruitful by the light;
>   And, centred in the diamond Sun,
>   Time & Eternity are one.

"Male and female represent the two sides of the great radical dualism," Fuller had written the previous summer near the end of **"The Great Lawsuit."** "But, in fact, they are perpetually passing into one another. Fluid hardens to solid, solid rushes to fluid. There is no wholly masculine man, no purely feminine woman." Now, as she expanded her earlier essay into *Woman in the Nineteenth Century,* Fuller returned to an even more profound realization of this theory of androgyny. Her assertion the previous year sounds theoretical; but the poems of 1844 take that theory and concretize it in moving articulations of spiritual aspiration. Praying for a wholeness that has eluded her, Fuller defines a talisman, a mandala, that might resolve for her the contradictions of her existence.

"Winged Sphynx" maintains the image of spiritual quest. Here, Fuller adopts the persona of a sphynx who has progressed through a period of renunciation, when she maintained "an aspect Chaste, Serene," to a moment of fulfillment. The imagery of this poem connects Fuller's spiritual awakening of 1844 with her crisis during the winter of 1840-41. The earlier crisis is now interpreted as a necessary station on the poet's journey. The fragments of her life are now seen to cohere into a pattern of spiritual progression:

> Through brute nature upward rising,
>   Seed up-striving to the light,
> Revelations still surprising,
>   My inwardness is grown insight.
>   Still I slight not those first stages,
> Dark but God-directed Ages;

> In my nature leonine
> Labored & learned a Soul divine;
>   Put forth an aspect Chaste, Serene,
> Of nature virgin mother queen;
>   Assumes at last the destined wings,
> Earth & heaven together brings;
>   While its own form the riddle tells
> That baffled all the wizard spells
>   Drawn from intellectual wells,
> Cold waters where truth never dwells:
>   —It was fable told you so;—
>   Seek her in common daylight's glow.

"Yes, others are purer, chaster, kinder than I," Fuller once wrote, "but none more religious. All my life is aspiration." Both this assertion and the poems Fuller was writing in 1844 remind us of the mistake of defining her literary accomplishments in secular, intellectual terms. Fuller's deepest moments of introspection, as well as her most effective political actions, were directed by a fervent—although unorthodox—faith. In biographical terms, this insight reminds us that the winter of 1840-41 and the summer of 1844 are two of the most critical moments in Fuller's life; for, during these two periods, she came closest to defining the vision of a central spiritual power that shaped many of her pursuits.

"My seal ring" continues the argument of **"Winged Sphynx."** Here, Fuller asserts that one must follow the lead of Mercury, who has "cast aside / The signs of intellectual pride" to accept "the soul." Only in this way can one become "wholly human," "A spotless radiant ruby heart" who has learned to control or cast out each "serpent thought." Expanding the imagery of **"Double Triangle, Serpent and Rays"** (as well as that of the early poem **"Drachenfels"**), this poem defines the expansion of soul as a conquest over serpent energies, the power of instinct that Fuller associated with the dragons of the Rhine legend as well as with the image of Typhon in the myth of Isis and Osiris. It is not surprising that Fuller's next poem, **"Sistrum,"** celebrates the rattle of Isis, which—in Plutarch's myth—was used to frighten away Typhon. Only through maintaining the "ceaseless motion" of the sistrum, the Poet argues, can one escape from the petrifaction of "dead devotion." By controlling the serpent (dragon/Typhon/devil), one preserves an image of purity and spiritual fulfillment. The alternative is to lapse into the sensuality and even depravity evoked throughout *Woman in the Nineteenth Century*.

The intensity of symbolism, the archetypal energy, of Fuller's 1844 poems suggests the power of the forces she was encountering. A sense of anguish, and even despair, lurks just beneath the surface of many of them, as if their lines were charms or talismans preserving a precarious psychological equilibrium. As the summer of 1844 progressed, Fuller's poetry balanced between assertions of an increasingly militant faith and eruptions of personal doubt and bitterness. **"July Fourth 1844"** represents the latter impulse. Questioning the patriotic celebrations that surround her, Fuller contrasts the levelling tendencies of contemporary America with the heroism that she finds in ancient Rome. The men around her seem filled with a noisy, but pointless, energy that falls far short of earlier nobility:

> I know you have no king,
>> But have you noblemen?
>> Or have you gentlemen?
>> Far more, have you *Men*?
> No! Why then, Ameriky,
>> I pray you tell to me
>> Why you make such a noise
> With rockets, guns, and boys!—

"All the use of earth," the Poet continues, "Is to good men to give birth." But few of the men surrounding Fuller have that inherent divinity.

If this vision of masculine heroism defines one side of Fuller's temperament, the other side is evoked by the maternal imagery of a succeeding poem—**"Here comes the night." Day brought no delight,"** the Poet laments, "Welcome Mother night." But the maternal embrace provides only a temporary and unsatisfactory comfort: "she with dark soft charms / Calls to her arms / Yet with no heat warms." Another poem written at this time also balances masculine and feminine qualities. In **"Lead lunar ray,"** Fuller portrays a longing for the emergence of an "armed knight," the Poet's champion," who might help her to reach the "throne" of her "phoenix king." But these masculine images contrast with feminine images of gestation and nurturance that evoke the other side of the Poet's personality. She prays that the rain will "Free from their pain / Plants which still in earth / Are prisoned," 9), a growth that is equated with the emergence of the "Soul . . . *Cradled* in the will" (emphasis added). Fed by *"mother thought,"* the infant "Birds" of the Poet's thought will eventually sprout strong "wings."

But as the year progressed, the balance between sun and moon, king and queen, seemed harder and harder to maintain. From July to November 1844, this vision of harmony was periodically threatened by moments of despair, loneliness, and unfulfilled desire. **"Lonely lady tell me why,"** for example, directly addresses the anxiety, the "dull despair, that threatens to "bind" the Poet's "heaven-born, heaven-seeking mind." The Poet bids the lonely Lady of the poem (Fuller) to discipline her heart to relinquish the lure of secular love in favor of a "nobler part." But the emotional sacrifice of this spiritual discipline seems almost too much to bear:

> No more to thee, no more, no more.
> Till thy circling life be oer,
>> A mutual heart shall be a home,
> Of weary wishes, happy tomb.

In a surprisingly explicit poem, **"Is it not great—this feat of Fate,"** Fuller even more directly confronts her sense of unfulfilled desire. She longs for the "Diver" who can "Break the spell / Of the slimy oyster shell, / Showing a pearl beyond all price so / round and clear." "Swift as the dart," this "joyous deliverer" will "bathe in the

stream / Which of him doth endlessly dream." Like "Rama," he will fill the "gold cup" of "His Sita."

But Fuller's best poems sublimate longing into symbol, transform pain into myth. In **"Leaving Fishkill for New York,"** Fuller wonders if her position might be that of an Ariadne deserted by Theseus. Here, too, the union between masculine and feminine threatens to dissolve:

> For if this fail, alone I stand
> To watch the sail on desert strand
> And if a Theseus so forsake
> Is there no God will pity take
> On the sad maiden motherless,
> On the lost maiden fatherless!
> A widowed bride, more comfortless.

But during the second half of 1844, Fuller was to write five poems that celebrated the pursuit of that harmony of spirit she termed a "sacred marriage."

Each of these poems—**"Sub Rosa-Crux," "Raphael's deposition from the cross," "To the Face seen in the Moon," "For the power to whom we bow,"** and **"The Sacred marriage"**—overcomes the sense of abandonment by imagining existence as a spiritual quest. Fuller's syncretism is revealed by the rich blend of symbols that are held up for worship. Images of Christ, carbuncle, Leila, moon, and marriage evoke a sense of quest that mingles aspects of Christian vocation, alchemical process, and mystical mediation. Fuller never came closer to defining the spiritual discipline that oriented much of her life and writing. Written during the period she was completing *Woman in the Nineteenth Century,* these poems express both the enthusiasm underlying that work and its mythological/religious substratum.

"Sub Rosa-Crux," a poem celebrating the worship of Jesus, seems to be the most traditional of these poems. But here images of Christian quest merge into an evocation of a private spiritual discipline—a transformation later prompting Emerson's observation that Fuller invented her own mythology. We have lost, Fuller laments, the strict devotion of the "Knights of the Rosy Cross" who wore "within the heart" a secret fire corresponding to the "glistening ruby" they bore without. Although we "wear the cross of ebony and gold," we have lost the capacity to "feed an undying lamp." Instead, our "hope" is a "starry promise in a frequent night." Yet, the Poet holds forth the promise that spiritual aspiration, the faithful mining of "the vein of gold" might lead to transfiguration:

> And, by that lovely light all truth revealed,
> The cherished forms which sad distrust
>> concealed
>> Transfigured, yet the same, will round us
>> stand,
>> The kindred angels of a faithful band;
> Ruby and ebon cross both cast aside,
> No lamp is needed for the night has died.

Happiness, the Poet asserts, is the reward of those who

maintain this vision even in the face of adversity. "Be to the best thou knowest ever true" is their "creed." Even if they themselves are "over borne," they know the satisfaction of "marshal[ing] others on the way." In contrast to Fuller's poems of despair and solitude, pain here is sublimated into an *imitatio Christi* that justifies suffering for the sake of illumination, solitude as the means of spiritual discipline.

Fuller's finest poem, **"Raphael's deposition from the cross,"** expands the meditation upon Christian symbolism by evoking Mary's pain at the moment of Christ's death. Returning to an imaginative situation that had obsessed her as early as the fall of 1839, Fuller focuses Mary's grief as that of a mother lamenting a dead child. The poem echoes the grief occasioned by the death of Emerson's first child Waldo, a loss that had been reawakened by the birth in 1844 of his second son. But more importantly, it confronts Fuller's own pain and grief for "the heavenly child, / Crucified within my heart." As in the spiritual crisis of 1840-41, a process of grief-work prepares the way for vision. Only by accepting and working through her sense of loss can the Poet rediscover her deepest spiritual and creative energies. "Let me to the tomb repair," she prays, "Find the angel watching there, / Ask his aid to walk again. . . . " The goal she longs for is a moment of death and rebirth, purification and apotheosis—her old self dying into a renewed being:

> Fan again the Parsee fire,
> Let it light my funeral pyre
> Purify the veins of Earth,
> Temper for a Phenix birth.

Returning in the second part of this poem to the image of the mourning Virgin, the Poet begins to realize that "power" is only reached through the "deepest of distress." The Christian message of death and resurrection is evident, but combined with the Christian theme is a psychological truth as well—that the resurrection of the self depends upon the acceptance, and not the avoidance, of pain. Only by focusing upon the "blight" hidden in the "coffin." can one "escape and bathe in God."

The concluding stanzas evoke the accession of spiritual insight and power:

> Margaret! shed no idle tears;
> In the far perspective bright
>   A muse-like form as thine appears
> As thine new-born in primal light.
>   Leila, take thy wand again;
> Upon thy arm no longer rest;
>   Listen to the thrilling brain;
> Listen to the throbbing breast;
>   There nightingales have made their nest
> Shall soothe with song the night's unrest.

Recapturing the elusive image of Paria in **"River of beauty flowing through the life"** (1841), the Poet recovers her muse. Fulfilling the promise of "Lead, lunar ray," she finds a nest for the birds of her heart. As in the earlier

1844 poem **"Leila in the Arabian zone,"** the figure of Leila reappears after a three-year absence from Fuller's writing. Fuller's most profound image of her muse, Leila embodies unconscious energies that have been transformed from dragonish instinct into creative power. Leila appears in Fuller's writing when the disruptive power of the dragon/serpent/Typhon has been controlled and transformed.

At the same time, death in this poem ceases to be spectre—the hiding place of either father or muse—but rather a source of release:

> "Maiden wrap thy mantle round thee"
> Night is coming, starlit night,
>   Fate that in the cradle bound thee,
> In the coffin hides thy blight;
>   All transfused the orb now glowing,
> Full-voiced and free the music growing
>   Planted in a senseless sod
>   The life is risen to flower a God.

At this triumphant moment, all sense of entrapment, frustration, and enclosure falls away. Resurrected from the ashes of her former existence, the Poet rises with a godlike power. Fulfilling the Transcendentalist dream of the "God within," she manifests the essential divinity of the self.

But as most poets have realized, consummation is much more difficult to portray than aspiration. Despite the triumph of the conclusion of **"Raphael's deposition from the cross,"** it is presented as a moment of potential atonement—as an image of longed-for perfection. Three other poems written in the autumn of 1844 strike this note of spiritual desire, but do so in strikingly different terms. Rather than using the familiar imagery of Christianity, they analyze the healing of the self as a harmonizing of masculine and feminine, sun and moon, or king and queen. The first of these poems, **"To the Face seen in the Moon,"** sets the terms for this resolution by mapping the Poet's identity in gendered terms. The poem opens by evoking a solace familiar from Fuller's other poems—the "soft Mother's smile" of the consoling moon. But as she meditates, the Poet realizes that this maternal strength, part of her own personality, is matched by another side.

> But, if I stedfast gaze upon thy face
> A human secret, like my own, I trace,
>   For through the woman's smile looks the male
>   eye
> So mildly, stedfastly but mournfully
>   He holds the bush to point us to his cave,
> Teaching anew the truth so bright, so grave
>   Escape not from the middle of the earth
> Through mortal pangs to win immortal birth,
>   Both man and woman, from the natural womb,
> Must slowly win the secrets of the tomb. . . .

In order to realize the "worthy Angel of a better sphere," the androgynous "angel of Swedenborg" that—in the words of ***Woman in the Nineteenth Century***—"considers man and woman as the two-fold expression of one thought," the Poet must allow the "Man from the Moon" side of her personality to express his "secret heart."

It is revealing that this process is portrayed as winning "the secrets of the tomb." Having released herself from the burden of mourning her father, Ward, Barker, Emerson—all those that have been "lost" to her—Fuller depicts her heart as a tomb, a crypt, that can be reopened to reveal both masculine and feminine power:

> And then, together rising fragrant, clear,
> The worthy Angel of a better sphere,
>   Diana's beauty shows how Hecate wrought,
>   Apollo's lustre rays the zodiac thought. . . .

At this moment of release, both "Moon and Sun" rise from their grave. But in order to achieve that consummation, the Poet must wed the "Man in the Moon," her "Apollo." In other words, she must acknowledge and express both her masculinity and her femininity. Only when the man hidden inside her is released can the "union" of the self be realized—a moment of ecstatic communion from which

>   shall spring
>   The promised King
> Who with white sail unfurled
> Shall steer through the heaven
>   Of soul—an unpolluted world.

And ultimately, the Poet hopes, that kingly power will meet "on his hard won throne a Juno / Of his own."

"For the Power to whom we bow," a poem later printed in *Woman in the Nineteenth Century,* continues this promise of an androgynous union of masculine and feminine qualities. This "Power," the Poet promises, "Has given" its pledge that "They of pure and stedfast mind" shall hear the music first "ventured" in Fuller's book. The way to such revelation, she cautions, will be arduous; for "rabble rout may rush between, / Beat thee senseless to the ground." Commenting upon Fuller's own position as a pioneer among America's gender theorists, the image of threatening "rabble" suggests as well the horde of fears, anxieties, and uncertainties that she must weather before reaching the tranquillity of self-reliance. But in contrast to Emerson's assertion that self-reliance involves the realization of power, light, and instinct through the expansion of the self, Fuller defines the process as entrance into a dwelling where masculine and feminine powers both rule—"the palace home of King and Queen." This is an enlargement of one's habitation, a harmonious balancing of disparate qualities that leads to a more regal sense of self. But, significantly, it is not—as Emerson imagined—an aggressive process of "dominion." Self-fulfillment, Fuller suggests, does not come through conquest but rather as a result of accepting and assimilating qualities that others repress.

Fuller achieves her most direct expression of this ideal in the poem **"The Sacred Marriage,"** which she placed at the conclusion of *Woman in the Nineteenth Century*. If this position emphasizes the significance of this poem, its importance for Fuller is underscored by the existence in her journals of the draft of nineteen stanzas that are not included in the published version. Although these lines lack the polish of Fuller's finished verse, they maintain resonance, especially in the light of the poems Fuller had been writing in 1844. For example, the image of the tomb recurs, as the Poet longs for "Each thought" to "be planted in a fruitful grave." But as important as this release from the burden of mourning is the Poet's realization that her self is constelled of disparate powers that must be balanced and harmonized:

> And as the One to vent his rays divine
> Needs many orbs in stellar wreath to shine
> And motions may join and recombine
>
> So with some souls like ours the lot may be
> A constellation be their destiny
> An every varying various destiny

Near the end of this unfinished fragment, Fuller proposes that "wedded love may give / All that self centring for which we strive." But marriage, she knows full well, is a course that she has not followed. The fragment ends, as if blocked by the realization that Fuller's destiny (at least for the next five years) was to explore a self that was married only to the intuition of its own power.

While the published version of **"The Sacred Marriage"** suggests as well that the highest fulfillment comes through another, here the image of marriage is replaced by a more general articulation that includes "wedded love," "parent love," and—one assumes—the love of friends such as Fuller and Anna Barker. The important thing is the sharing of "mutual aims and tasks, ideals bright," a mingling of "Twin stars that mutual circle in the heaven." It is through "Mutual light," the Poet argues, that one is able "to draw out the powers." Through a sharing of "mutual moods" and of "mutual action," one is able to achieve "A Home in Heaven,—the Union in the Soul."

Although Margaret Fuller—in the following years—had to struggle to achieve the harmony that her poetry promised, she seems to have reached a moment of personal reconciliation in the autumn of 1844. Embodying her deepest anxieties and her most cherished dreams, her poems both enabled her to articulate a theory of selfhood that animated her most famous book, *Woman in the Nineteenth Century,* and gave her the courage to leave New England for New York City. An existence of more expansive political action awaited her. In November, for example, she addressed the female prisoners at Sing-Sing, telling them that "Your angels stand forever there to intercede for you; and to you they call to be gentle and good. Nothing can so grieve and discourage those heavenly friends as when you mock the suffering." This note of compassion, which was to characterize her *New-York Tribune* essays, represents one of the most important fruits of Fuller's years of turmoil. Having wrestled with her own demons, Fuller was now ready to help those less fortunate ones who seemed to have perished in the battle.

> **Margaret Fuller on writing:**
>
> When I write, it is into another world, not a better one perhaps, but one with very dissimilar habits of thought to this where I am domesticated.
>
> *Margaret Fuller, in a letter of 1840.*

Bell Gale Chevigny (excerpt date 1994)

SOURCE:An introduction to *The Woman and the Myth: Margaret Fuller's Life and Writings,* revised edition, Northeastern University Press, 1994, pp. 3-15.

[*In the following excerpt, Chevigny comments on the quality of Fuller's writing.*]

[It] is appropriate to remark on the quality of Fuller's writing. While it can be argued that certain social prejudices blocked her contemporaries from perceiving some of its virtues, still many modern readers have difficulty with it. At the worst, they find the style overblown, the form rambling and repetitious, the tone self-indulgent or arrogant, and the whole effect unremittingly intense. Although such difficulties cannot be explained away, it is important to try to understand them. An occasionally purple style and a form that follows where whimsical thought may lead characterize much of the writing of an age which placed a premium on spontaneity and feeling. In Fuller's case, her need to feel (and/or convince others) that she was a woman while engaging in the intellectual pursuits of men may unconsciously have dictated a vehement and impulsive style rather than one more logical, cool, spare, and cerebral. The same instinct may have fed her tendency to digression; we often feel the insistent personal presence of the woman in these intimate asides. In a defense of the excesses of her life style, Fuller herself implies a related explanation of her writing style: "In an environment like mine, what may have seemed too lofty or ambitious in my character was absolutely needed to keep the heart from breaking and enthusiasm from extinction." Her argument is that a woman seeking free action in nineteenth-century America must overdo to do at all. Applied to her writing, it may be her best defense. The rhetorical extravagance of the sentence quoted diminishes in proportion to the credence we lend to her thought. She appears to have similarly associated the strictures of literary forms with the confining social forms and to have resented what both cost her in vitality. She wrote that no old form suited her, and in writing as in life experimented and invented. Fuller was anything but vain about her writing, and her own dissatisfaction or modesty about it was so explicit and so often excessive that she herself has contributed to the low esteem in which it has been held.

Though Fuller's writing has passages of great force and beauty, my chief interest is in what it reveals of her remarkable development. In her stylistic excesses one can read the struggle she had to create the appropriate tone, or rather to generate an authentic self who could command an attentive audience. Until experience completed that self, she was obliged to try on, like many costumes, the rhetorics to which she had access.

Donna Dickenson (essay date 1994)

SOURCE:An introduction to *Woman in the Nineteenth Century and Other Writings* by Margaret Fuller, edited by Donna Dickenson, Oxford University Press, Oxford, 1994, pp. vii-xxix.

[*In the following introduction to her edition of a collection of Fuller's writings, Dickenson surveys Fuller's life, thought, and works.*]

> 'My dear Sir,' I exclaimed, 'if you'd not been afraid
> Of Margaret Fuller's success, you'd have stayed
> Your hand in her case and more justly have rated her.'
> Here he murmured morosely, 'My God, how I hated her!'
>
>   [Amy Lowell, 'A Critical Fable']

Margaret Fuller was privileged in her lifetime—as a woman editor, essayist, political journalist, and arts critic in an otherwise largely male domain—because she was one of the first of her kind. When women began entering the literary lists in greater numbers, after Fuller's death and partly through her inspiration, she became a greater threat, to be excoriated and exorcised. Yet throughout her life she herself was ambivalent about her critical and creative abilities, saying of herself, 'I have no art'. Such diffidence was further ammunition against her after her death: she was taken at her own modest word by male successors who 'came to praise but also, perhaps uncon-

> **Contemporary feminists mourn Fuller:**
>
> The first national women's rights convention was called for October 23-24, 1850, in Worcester, Massachusetts. In an account of this convention, the president, Paulina Wright Davis, wrote:
>
> One great disappointment fell upon us. Margaret Fuller, toward whom many eyes were turned as the future leader in this movement, was not with us. The "hungry ravening sea," had swallowed her up, and we were left to mourn her guiding hand—her royal presence. To her, I at least, had hoped to confide the leadership of this movement. It can never be known if she would have accepted it; the desire had been expressed to her by letter; but be that as it may, she was, and still is, a leader of thought; a position far more desirable than a leader of numbers.
>
> *Paulina Wright Davis, in* History of Woman Suffrage, *edited by Elizabeth Cady Stanton, Susan B. Anthony, and Matilda Jocelyn Gage, Fowler 4 Wells, 1881.*

sciously, to bury her' [Bell Gale Chevigny, *The Woman and the Myth: Margaret Fuller's Life and Writings*].

Fuller was the emblematic woman of her time. The American critic Norman Podhoretz has suggested that at most only one woman of her generation and place is allowed to be the 'Dark Lady', the intellectual superstar of her sex. This female lead in the mid-twentieth-century United States was taken first by Mary McCarthy, and then by Susan Sontag. Elaine Showalter has identified Margaret Fuller as the Dark Lady of the American Renaissance. Showalter also suggests that the Dark Lady is inevitably punished for accepting the eminence thrust upon her, citing recent harsh criticism of Sontag's previously influential work. Could this also help to explain the volte-face in Fuller's reputation?

What befell Fuller's reputation has happened to that of many other women writers, in the manner documented for a later period by Sandra M. Gilbert and Susan Gubar [in *No Man's Land: The Place of the Woman Writer in the Twentieth Century, Vol. I—The War of the Words*]; but it happened to her first. Fuller wrote her own life by living it. She wove it into a tapestry of epic proportions, a new *Aeneid* of Rome's refounding by an outsider. But after her early death alterations were made: the garment of her life was refashioned by male tailors—primarily Emerson and Hawthorne—to suit the prevailing female fashion. The mode which they chose was less than flattering: the styles on which they modelled her garb were the female invalid, the cerebral spinster, the vestal devotee.

Yet Fuller's life and death were heroic. She made her life not into the Gothic tale which women's novels of the time portrayed, but into a Latin epic: beginning from a youth steeped in the Latin texts from which most girls were barred, she spent the three last and most vital years of her life supporting the Roman revolution and running a hospital for the wounded during the siege of Rome. Earlier, she had edited the magazine which was to epitomize the Transcendentalist movement (*The Dial*), written criticism and social-policy articles for the *New York Daily Tribune,* worked with prostitutes at Sing Sing Prison in Ossining, New York, and visited the Native American women on Mackinac Island in the Great Lakes.

Fuller's most influential publication, *Woman in the Nineteenth Century* (1845), sold out within a week. *Woman* was based on Fuller's earlier work on the Woman Question, '**The Great Lawsuit: Man *versus* Men. Woman *versus* Women**' (*The Dial,* July 1843), but the book was much more politically minded than the earlier essay. Bringing to the fore such issues as prostitution, employment, and marriage reform, *Woman* helped to set the tone, if not the precise agenda, for the Seneca Falls convention of 1848 and the American women's movement. (Fuller did not explicitly advocate women's suffrage, which did become a focus of the movement: the *Tribune* editor Horace Greeley, who sponsored the publication of *Woman,* was an inveterate foe of votes for women.) After her death 'Margaret Fuller Clubs' sprang up all over America. Elizabeth Cady Stanton and Susan B. Anthony judged that

Fuller 'possessed more influence upon the thought of American women than any woman previous to her time'.

Fuller's personal life, too, was heroic in the best woman's way: caring for her mother and seven younger siblings, then later enduring her own first childbirth without family support in Italy, and with no one who could so much as speak her language. Even her death—in a hurricane, fifty yards off the coast of Fire Island, returning to America from Italy with her Italian husband and 22-month-old son—was tragic rather than merely poignant.

It was Ralph Waldo Emerson who began the process of mythologizing Fuller into obscurity after her death. As one of three editors of her posthumous *Memoirs,* together with James Freeman Clarke and William Henry Channing, friends of Fuller's youth, he rewrote the heroic epic which she had lived as a minor novelette. The three editors' names did not even appear on the title-page of the *Memoirs* which re-invented Fuller in their preferred image. Nevertheless, Emerson sold more copies of Fuller's *Memoirs* than of any work of his own: his *Nature* (1836) took seven years to clear an edition of 500 copies. Fuller's *Woman in the Nineteenth Century* sold out an edition twice that size in one week.

The 'best possible motives' with which Emerson and his fellow editors were generally acknowledged to have acted—saving Fuller's sexual reputation—absolved them of any blame for finishing the 'autobiography' which her premature death had stopped short. They rewrote her life, apparently with her own posthumous permission.

Added to the editors' prurience about Fuller's Italian years—when she had a baby by Marchese Giovanni Angelo Ossoli, to whom she may or may not have been married at the time of their son Nino's birth in 1848—was their fear of what might be revealed about their own idiosyncrasies when Fuller's correspondence with them was printed. Fuller had a talent for inspiring confidences. Very soon after her death Emerson wrote in his journal: 'When I heard that a trunk of her correspondence had been found and opened, I felt what a panic would strike all her friends, for it was as if a clever reporter had got underneath a confessional and agreed to report all that transpired there in Wall street.' What he had to fear appears to have been less any sort of sexual innuendo than the embarrassing revelation that Fuller could actually make the august sage of Concord laugh. He recorded of their first meeting in July 1835:

> She had a dangerous reputation for satire, in addition to her great scholarship . . . her talk was a comedy in which dramatic justice was done to everybody's foibles. I remember that she made me laugh more than I liked . . . . She had an incredible variety of anecdotes, and the readiest wit to give an absurd turn to whatever passed; and the eyes, which were so plain at first, soon swam with fun and drolleries, and the very tides of joy and superabundant life.

Emerson also lays great stress on Fuller's alleged ugliness—accepted as fact by subsequent critics, though feminists have pointed out that Thoreau's horsey nose and Emerson's fishy eyes have never been held against *them*. The abiding image of Fuller has been the one Emerson paints: bulging eyes, half-closed in perpetual sibylline contemplation; dishwater-blond locks; and a stooped posture. 'It is to be said that Margaret made a disagreeable first impression on most persons, including those who became afterwards her best friends, to such an extent that they did not wish to be in the same room with her.'

Male bitchiness about Fuller's appearance has continued. Henry James imagined her as 'glossily ringletted and monumentally breastpinned'; the modern editor and critic Perry Miller, as 'phenomenally homely', her hair 'not quite blond, stringy and thin'. But the most salacious have been her admirers: 'At thirteen her breasts were so developed that she seemed eighteen, or twenty . . . Her hair was blond, fine and softspun, reflecting light like buckwheat honey when poured from a pottery jar. Her mouth was soft and curving. . . .'

A similar male prurience pervades Nathaniel Hawthorne's characterization of the Fuller-figure Zenobia in *The Blithedale Romance* (1852). Although in life Fuller counted Hawthorne more 'a brother to me, than ever . . . any man before', Hawthorne fulminated after her death against 'a damned mob of scribbling women'. More woundingly, he created in *The Blithedale Romance* a character widely assumed to be Fuller, with implications which were less than flattering. Throughout the novel the narrator makes openly sexual remarks about Zenobia, admitting to imagining her in 'Eve's earliest garment'.

> She should have made it a point of duty, moreover, to sit endlessly to painters and sculptors, and preferably to the latter; because the cold decorum of the marble would consist with the utmost scantiness of drapery, so that the eye might chastely be gladdened with her material perfection in its entireness . . . what was visible of her full bust,—in a word, her womanliness incarnated,—compelled me sometimes to close my eyes, as if it were not quite the privilege of modesty to gaze at her.

Whether or not Hawthorne intended Zenobia really to *be* Fuller, the novel ends with her drowning, and most readers took that to be more than coincidence. Most unpleasantly of all, Hawthorne wrote in his notebooks—later published by his son with great damage to Fuller's remaining reputation—that she was better off dead.

> She was a great humbug; of course with much talent, and much moral reality, or else she could not have been so great a humbug . . . tragic as her catastrophe was, Providence was, after all, kind in putting her and her clownish husband, and their child, on board that fated ship.

But however bitter Hawthorne's personal feelings about Fuller, modern critical opinion has begun to explore the idea that he was greatly influenced by *Woman in the*

Nineteenth Century. Hawthorne may have been more angered by Fuller's disclosure of her sexuality through her affair with and marriage to Ossoli than was Emerson, more 'disappointed' in her, because of the two men he actually shows the greater awareness of the Woman Question. In chapter 14 of *The Blithedale Romance*, 'Eliot's Pulpit', Hawthorne demonstrates quite a sophisticated understanding of the conflicting pressures on Zenobia. Though the eloquent advocate of her sex, she can only win the orator Hollingsworth's heart by letting him monopolize her speech and belief. Hawthorne parodies Hollingsworth's tired arguments about male superiority: woman is made to be protected by man, Hollingsworth asserts, and if she doesn't recognize that, by God, she should be beaten into it. It is worth noting that Hollingsworth is often taken to be Emerson.

Some critics also see in Hawthorne's *Scarlet Letter* the influence of Fuller's 'apocalyptic feminism', particularly in this passage from the novel's conclusion:

> Women . . . in the continually recurring trials of wounded, wasted, wronged, misplaced, or erring and sinful passion,—or with the dreary burden of a heart unyielded, because unvalued and unsought,—came to Hester's cottage demanding why they were so wretched, and what the remedy . . . She assured them of her firm belief, that, at some brighter period, when the world should have grown ripe for it, in Heaven's own time, a new truth would be revealed, in order to establish the whole relation between man and woman on a surer ground of mutual happiness. Earlier in life, Hester had vainly imagined that she herself might be the destined prophetess, but had long since recognized the impossibility that any mission of divine and mysterious truth should be confided to a woman stained with sin, bowed down with shame, or even burdened with a lifelong sorrow. The angel and apostle of the coming revelation must be a woman, indeed, but lofty, pure and beautiful; and wise, moreover, not through dusky grief, but the ethereal medium of joy; and showing how sacred love should make us happy, by the truest test of a life successful to such an end!

In *Woman* Fuller anticipates Hawthorne's belief that the female Messiah must herself be pure (though not his extraneous assumption that she must also be beautiful), remarking, in an otherwise adulatory passage about George Sand: 'Those who would reform the world must show that they do not speak in the heat of wild impulse; their lives must be unstained by passionate error; they must be severe lawgivers to themselves'.

Underlying this sentiment was the political need for Fuller to placate the devotees of the then dominant discourse, what has since been termed the 'Cult of True Womanhood'. Earlier, in the late eighteenth and early nineteenth centuries, American thought on the woman question was actually more progressive than in Fuller's period. What the feminist historian Jane Rendall calls 'the rhetoric of republican motherhood' had elevated educational aspirations for women, though without challenging their confinement to the domestic sphere. In that realm—through boycotting tea, producing cloth for the revolutionary army's uniforms, and bearing the burden of billeting troops—American women had shown themselves worthy. The popular heroines 'Molly Pitcher' (Mary Hays), who carried water to American troops at the Battle of Monmouth, and Betsy Ross, who sewed the new republic's flag, epitomized this combination of patriotism and domesticity during the War of American Independence.

Some women, like the poet and playwright Mercy Otis Warren (1728-1824), had also used their pens to denounce the corruption of the old order and proclaim the glories of the new republic. These women writers of the late eighteenth and early nineteenth centuries saw no contradiction between female independence of spirit and domestic harmony. The successful novelist and poet Susanna Rowson (1762-1824) urged husbands to treat their wives as intelligent and free beings if they wanted peace at home. Her patriotic comedy, *The Slaves in Algiers, or, a Struggle for Freedom,* centres on a group of American women held for ransom by Barbary Coast pirates. A parable of liberty from the former colonial oppressor whose privateers still ravaged American shipping on the seas, Rowson's text has one of the women say: 'I feel that I was born free, and while I have life, I will struggle to remain so.'

In an essay, 'On the Equality of the Sexes', written in 1779 and published in 1790 in the *Massachusetts Magazine,* Judith Sargent Murray had urged her fellow Americans to instil republican virtues into new generations of women. Coincidentally Murray's essay described the education given to a girl called 'Margaretta' by 'Mrs Vigilius'. Timothy Fuller, Margaret's father, likewise chose to indoctrinate his daughter in the republican virtues of Rome as well as those of America. Margaret's first extant essay, written at the age of about 12 for her father, showed that the cult of republican virtue had a new convert. 'Resolved, united hearts freed America . . . [I]t is not in the power of circumstance to prevent the earnest will from shaping round itself the character of a great, a wise, or a good man.'

From an early age Margaret learned Latin, French, logic, rhetoric, and a little Greek. One of her first letters to her father, written at 7, shows that she was being fed on a diet of warrior kings:

> I have been reviewing Valpy's Chronology [of ancient and English history]. We have not been able to procure any books [on] either Charles 12th of Sweden or Philip IId of Spain but Mama intends to send to Uncle Henry. I hope to make greater proficuncy [*sic*] in my Studies I have learned all the rules of Musick but one.

By 9 she was writing letters to Timothy in Latin and working her way through the fifth book of Virgil, whom she had begun memorizing at 6, along with passages from Plutarch and Ovid. She had ingested not only the language but also its agonistic spirit, smarting inwardly because one Mary Elliot had finished her Virgil in thirty days. The ambition which she expressed openly all her life was already alive in a letter to her father of 3 February 1820. There she reiterated her determination to best Mary Elliot's record and sealed her resolve with the Lord's Prayer in Latin. In reply, Timothy wrote: 'I would not discourage you, my girl, by being too critical and yet I am anxious to have you admit to one *fault,* which you will remember I have often mentioned, as the source, the very fountain of others—carelessness.'

In *Woman* Fuller still shows her father's influence: when she is overly pedantic, when her recital of historical evidence becomes interminable, it is as if she is still trying to forestall any possible accusations of carelessness or lack of scholarship. Timothy Fuller, who took sole charge of his daughter's early education, had been adamant:

> You must not speak, unless you can make your meaning perfectly intelligible to the person addressed; must not express a thought, unless you can give a reason for it, if required; must not make statements, unless sure of all particulars—such were his rules. 'But', 'if', 'unless', 'I am mistaken', and 'it may be so', were words and phrases excluded from the provinces where he held sway.

Fuller was taught to talk like a man. This alone would account for why many men found her so insufferable, and her erudition so dismaying, as this English comment makes pungently plain:

> Margaret Fuller was one of those he-women, who, thank Heaven! for the most part figure and flourish, and have their fame on the other side of the Atlantic. She was an intellectual Bloomer of the largest calibre. She understood Socrates better than Plato did, Faust better than Goethe did, Kant Philosophy [*sic*] better than Kant did . . . but alack the difference between an encyclopaedia bound in calf and an encyclopaedia moving in blue stockings. Every fact, word, thought, idea, theory, notion, line, verse, that crowded in the cranium of Margaret Fuller was a weapon. They shot from her like pellets from a steam gun. She bristled all over with transcendentalism, assaulted you with metaphysics, suffocated you with mythology, peppered you with ethics, and struck you down with heavy history . . .

But between Fuller's assault-course education in girlhood, and her maturity, there had been a 'backlash'. The Roman constancy of will and purpose which the young Fuller so much admired played no part in the increasingly dominant cult of the True Woman, which celebrated submissiveness, piety, and passivity as the 'genius' of the female. The Cult of Republican Motherhood had allowed women a sturdy independence: but that of True Womanhood saw her as fully absorbed in her vocation, purifying and restoring fallen Man. Selfishness of any kind was the prime sin for women, and independence was a kind of selfishness. In return for abjuring all autonomy of thought and action, the 'True Woman'—the epitaph on the tombstone of Margaret's mother, Margarett Crane Fuller—could expect worship. As an article of 1830 in the *Ladies' Magazine* put it: 'A halo of glory encircles her, and illumines her whole orbit. With her, man not only feels safe, but is actually renovated. For he approaches her with an awe, a reverence, and an affection which before he knew not that he possessed.'

This conservative backlash began at the turn of the nineteenth century—with the victory of the Federalist party in 1796 and the puritanical American reaction to the publication of the frank *Memoirs of Mary Wollstonecraft* by her husband, William Godwin, after her death in 1797. (The damage done to Wollstonecraft by Godwin—who was her rival as well as her survivor—neatly parallels that done to Fuller by Emerson and the other editors.) Although conservative reaction to women's advancement was initially less pronounced in America than in England or France, it drew extra strength from the rise of religious evangelicalism, the narrowing of female employment opportunities outside the home, and concern for family cohesion on the Western frontier. True Womanhood was now held to be largely incompatible with the virtues of self-reliance and critical thought, though a partial exception would be made for female moral education.

In the political sphere, too, the early nineteenth century was a period of retreat for women. During the American Revolution enthusiasm for the logical consequences of the idea that all *men* are created equal had undermined the common-law position inherited from England, that married women had no legal, economic, or political existence. Women married to Tories who had been exiled, and their property confiscated, were sometimes able to regain their own share if they swore loyalty to the new republic. This implied that married women's property rights were not entirely subsumed in those of their husbands, and that women's political commitment could have some meaning, even if they were not full citizens. In 1790 the state of New Jersey even went so far as to adopt a franchise statute referring to voters as 'he or she'. In the aftermath of the Revolution divorce, overruled by the Privy Council in 1773 as contrary to the law of England, also became a right for those women in the New England and mid-Atlantic seaboard states whose legislatures had legalized it.

With the end of the Revolution and no further need for female support in the war effort, and the rise of an entrepreneurial capitalism which confined women's economic activity more closely to the home, these political and economic gains were generally short-lived. By the 1830s and 1840s, ironically the high tide of individualistic liberalism, the political and economic rights of American women had never been fewer. At the same time that white. American men had gained near-total control over their wives' property, they were benefiting from the abolition in almost all states of property requirements for the franchise. Rhode Island, for example, one of the few states which still limited white male suffrage to freeholders, extended the vote to all native-born men after the Dorr rebellion of 1842. The contrast between the sexes was sharper in America than in England, where the 1832 Reform Act still left lower middle-class and working-class men disenfranchised. (There, too, however, the forces of misogyny were in the ascendant: the 1832 Act specified for the first time in statue form that the voter must be male.)

For women Jacksonian America was not the land of opportunity: rather the land of *shrinking* opportunity. Early revivalists of the Great Awakenings had allowed women to take a key part in meetings and to lead prayers; but by 1823 they were forbidden to do either in a pamphlet on 'Female-Influence', published by the Presbyterian Utica Tract Society and typical of the changes in the hotbed of evangelicalism, the Burnt-Over District of western New York State. In the repressive 1820s and 1830s even maternal and moral-reform societies were beginning to be thought suspect. To step outside the domestic sphere, hardliners argued, would sully the purity which alone gave women the right to call themselves morally superior to men, and capable of the other sex's moral reform.

Education was the last of the partial exemptions which remained intact—and indeed flourished—in the early 1840s. Improvement of the female intellect was acceptable as a means to an imperative end. As Fuller herself enunciated the dominant view, American daughters were exhorted to strive constantly for spiritual and intellectual perfection, not only for the sake of their own salvation, but for the good of their fathers, brothers and beaux—whose contact with the sharp world of business excused them from any such strictness with themselves. 'Improvement in the daughters will best aid the reformation of the sons of this age', she wrote in **Woman**. (This jars oddly with Fuller's assertion that 'Not one man in the million, shall I say? no, not in the hundred million, can rise above the belief that Woman was made *for* Man . . . ', and her complaint that 'So much is said of women being better educated, that they may become better companions and mothers *for men*'.

Catharine Beecher, founder of the Hartford Female Seminary and later of the Western Female Institute in Cincinnati, had justified female education by women's aptitude as natural missionaries, spreading a civilizing influence from the holy hearth. This imperial role for women was given a patriotic force by Philo Stewart, co-founder of Oberlin, the first college to educate men and women together. 'The work of female education', wrote Stewart, 'must be carried on in some form, and in a much more efficient manner than it has been hitherto, or our country will go to destruction.'

In the Cult of True Womanhood a strong religious component coexisted more or less peacefully with what might appear the ideological opposite, the philosopher John Locke's doctrine of the mind as a *tabula rasa* or blank slate. Since the child's personality was entirely a reflection of what the educator put into it, mothers as principal child-rearers bore a ponderous responsibility. Both the true man and the true woman were formed by their mothers. This perilous power in women's hands had to be tamed, by educating them to be reliable propagandizers. The 'concession' made in favour of education was not so much a privilege afforded to women as a further mechanism of control. Education was certainly not intended to prepare women for the professions and public life; it was meant to make them more reliable stewards of the master's most important resources, his children.

But by operating within the constraints of the acceptable, early nineteenth-century reformers had secured some educational advancement for women. Colluding with the doctrine of separate spheres, 'domestic feminists' such as Catharine Beecher helped to breed a class of educated heretics within the Cult, women who would *not* accept separate spheres. Further, the legitimacy of evangelical fervour, and the partial exceptions made in favour of philanthropic caused and education, had allowed some women a taste of life outside the home. Ladies' societies gave women experience in drawing up regulations, electing officers, corresponding with other charitable organizations, and overseeing accounts. The rise of 'Moral Reform' (the movement against prostitution) and of the abolitionist movement presented further opportunities for public participation, though women's increased activity on the platform was met by intense and sometimes violent male resentment.

It was in this situation of simulataneous male backlash and female backlash *against* male backlash that *Woman in the Nineteenth Century* appeared. The language and conclusions of 'The Great Lawsuit'—and to a lesser degree of *Summer on the Lakes* and *Woman in the Nineteenth Century*—reflect the baleful influence of the Cult of True Womanhood. That this was so should not be surprising, or a cause for castigating Fuller, as some of her earlier feminist biographers tended to do. In order to reach her intended audience, Fuller had to speak their language, and that was the diction and discourse of the True Woman. The 'hegemony' of a cultural discourse, in the term used by the Italian social philosopher Antonio Gramsci, affects not only the woman writer's audience, but also her own opinions.

A similar set of Gramscian ideas has been applied to the English Victorians by Deirdre David [in *Intellectual Woman and Victorian Patriarchy: Harriet Martineau, Elizabeth Barrett Browning, George Eliot*], who judges that Elizabeth Barrett Browning, George Eliot, and Harriet Martineau were 'neither ideological slaves to patriarchal thought, nor distinctly separate from patriarchal culture. They were both collaborateurs and saboteurs in the world that enabled their very existence as women intellectuals.' Is this also true of Margaret Fuller? Is it the price a woman writer must pay for being allowed to play the Dark Lady?

It would be unfair, I think, to say that Fuller was partly colluding in her own oppression, as David implies of Barrett Browning, Eliot, and Martineau. Her attitudes towards women *were* considerably more radical than those of any of these three, though she is closest to Eliot. But it is certainly true that Fuller must be judged against the background of her time as well as that of her own personal development.

It is also perfectly true that Fuller's high abstraction and individualistic, self-reliant solutions to women's social disadvantage are still cast in the Emersonian mould. As his disciple, Fuller used all the arguments that Emerson promulgated about the individual and applied them to

women. **'The Great Lawsuit',** and the first two-thirds of *Woman* (which largely reproduces 'Lawsuit') are hymns to women's equal powers of self-reliance with men.

Indeed, self-reliance was the story of Fuller's life, and of her death. Fuller had to be economically independent— and to provide for her father's children from the limited means available from a woman's profession, teaching. It did her health no good, and probably caused her death. The boat on which she went down, the *Elizabeth,* was an old-fashioned wooden-bottomed merchantman; Fuller could not afford a modern steamer or packet ship. When the *Elizabeth* foundered on a sand-bar off Fire Island, the bottom ruptured under the cargo of Italian marble and a statue of John Calhoun—that advocate of nullification, states' rights to self-reliance.

In her dispatches written during the Roman Revolution of 1849, when she ran a hospital and her husband Ossoli served in the Civic Guard, Fuller became much more practical, more communitarian, and quite radically socialist. But **'The Great Lawsuit'** is marred by the Transcendentalist tendency to see reality through the lens of symbols. Although it contains striking and powerful statements, it also carries a heavy freight of vagueness and conceptual sloppiness.

Similarly, *Woman in the Nineteenth Century* reflects not only Timothy Fuller's educational influence and the spell of the Cult of True Womanhood, but also the ideals of the New England Transcendentalist movement. Transcendentalist literary theory consciously rejected syllogistic reasoning and systematic analysis. In accord with these dictates which she had helped to set as editor of the movement's canon-forming journal, *The Dial,* Fuller conceived *Woman* as an organic, subjective composition, a free association of ideas.

Although Fuller's writing could be quite pungent and down-to-earth—as in much of *Summer on the Lakes*— *Woman* is often high-blown in the Transcendentalist style, which was characterized by 'inchoate structure, prodigal imagery, wit, paradox, symbolism . . . and a manifesto-like tone'. Part of the difficulty was that 'the Transcendentalists were exceedingly weak in the genres most in favor today (poetry, drama, prose fiction)', but were attempting to revive styles little known at present, and to create new genres. In *Woman* Fuller welds sermon and conversation into such a form, one which may seem archaic to modern readers but which struck her contemporaries as powerful and new. Even Henry David Thoreau, who 'never liked anything', according to Emerson, considered **'The Great Lawsuit',** the earlier essay which Fuller drew on in compiling the book length *Woman,* to be 'rich extempore writing . . . talking with pen in hand'.

The Transcendentalist, consciously literary manner departs about two-thirds of the way through *Woman,* however— the point (marked in the Explanatory Notes to this edition) at which the recycled 'Lawsuit' essay ends and the pages penned exclusively for the book begin. Between the publication of **'Lawsuit'** in July 1843 and the final editing of *Woman* in November 1844, Fuller's thought had become more concrete and more radical, particularly on the subjects of slavery, Native American women, and prostitution. In all three cases she now saw, as she put it in *Summer on the Lakes,* 'the aversion of the injurer for him he has degraded'.

'[T]here exists in the minds of men a tone of feeling toward women as toward slaves', she wrote in *Woman.* Indeed, slavery is more honest: 'In slavery, *acknowledged* slavery, women are on a par with men'. Fuller was not the first to make this uncomfortable comparison. Drawing on ideas first advanced by the Irish feminist Anna Wheeler (b. 1785), William Thompson's *Appeal of One-Half the Human Race* (1825) likewise remarks:

> As little as slaves have had to do in any part of the world in the enacting of slave-codes, have women in any part of the world had to do with the partial codes of selfishness and ignorance, which everywhere dispose of their right over their own actions and all their other enjoyments, in favour of those who made the regulations; particularly that most unequal and debasing code, absurdly called the contract of marriage . . . From regulating the terms of this pretended contract, women have been as completely excluded as bullocks, or sheep, or any other animals subjugated to man, have been from determining the regulations of commons or slaughter-houses.

Earlier still, Charles Brockden Brown, writing in the 1790s, had identified marriage as a 'compact of slavery'. But there is no firm indication that Fuller had read Thompson or Brown by the time she wrote her texts on women's position; and in the climate of the 1840s, such sentiments were much more shocking—particularly when they came from a woman. Even more controversial was Fuller's scepticism about the arguments put forward by white men to justify their political and economic dominance: that women, or slaves, are incapable of fiscal wisdom or political *nous*. These, she judged, are only psychological mechanisms which the dominant sex, or race, must use in order to justify its own arbitrary power to itself.

Fuller was not an active abolitionist at this time, but the examples of slaves and Native Americans had galvanized her thought on women. In 1843 she had made a journey to Niagara Falls and the Great Lakes with her friends Caroline Sturgis, Sarah Ann Clarke, and Clarke's brother William. The book which resulted, *Summer on the Lakes in 1843* (1844), represents a forward hop, if not a leap, in both style and thought. Although the book lacks what Fuller admired—'the Spartan brevity and sinewy grasp of Indian speech'—it is liberally sprinkled with Thoreauvian salt:

> [At Niagara] what I liked best was to sit on Table Rock, close to the great fall. There all power of observing details, all separate consciousness, was quite lost. Once, just as I had seated myself there, a man came up to take his first look. He walked close up to the fall, and, after looking at it for a moment, with an air of thinking how he could best appropriate it to his own use—he spat into it.

The range of Fuller's thought on women was stretched by the example of the squaws of Mackinac Island, among whom she was able to wander freely. Unlike the Enlightenment, which explored various constellations of domestic power relations—matrilineal Iroquois society, polyandry among the Nairs of Malabar, collective marriage in eastern Iran—the early nineteenth century lumped together all 'uncivilized' women's positions as barbarous. Fuller agreed that Native American women were lumbered with drudgery: their 'peculiarly awkward gait, and forms bent by burthens . . . so different from the steady and noble step of the men, [mark] the inferior position they occupy'. But she also observed more tenderness towards children among Native American braves than among white men, and considerable respect for matrons who were mothers of warriors. Native American children were called by the mother's name, and divorce was easy, more advantageous to women than men. On the boat for Sault St Marie, Fuller met a Native American woman (with whom she quite markedly did *not* identify, since she says that she was the only lady on board the ship). The woman had left her husband because he drank and wasted their earnings; she earned a living for herself and her child as a chambermaid. 'Now and again, she said, her husband called on her, and asked if he might live with her again, but she always answered, no. Here she was far freer than she would have been in civilized life'.

But if *white* western women were not freer than eastern, Fuller thought it was probably their own fault. Still unable to see women's position as socially conditioned, in *Summer* Fuller remains within the True Woman tradition by looking to western women for their own salvation.

> It is . . . evident that . . . the women have great power at home. It can never be otherwise, men being dependent upon them for the comfort of their lives. Just so among ourselves, wives who are neither esteemed nor loved by their husbands, have great power over their conduct by the friction of every day, and over the formation of their opinions . . . This power is good for nothing, unless the woman be wise to use it aright. Has the Indian, has the white woman, as noble a feeling of life and its uses, as religious a self-respect, as worthy a field of thought and action as man? If not, the white woman, the Indian woman, occupies an inferior position to that of man. It is not so much a question of power, as of privilege.

Individual before social reform remains Fuller's creed in *Woman,* even though she is considerably more aware of social ills than she showed herself to be in **'Lawsuit'**. The particular target on which she expends most firepower is prostitution, with marriage a close second. The remaining selections in this volume, particularly the review of George Sand's novel *Consuelo* (1843) and the excerpt from Fuller's story **'Aglauron and Laurie'**, often bear witness to Fuller's concerns about sexual politics. It was the politics of sexuality which roused Fuller's interest in the politics of politics. In **'The Great Lawsuit'** Fuller had preached the Emersonian creed of self-reliance. But when 'we women have no profession except marriage, mantua-making and school-keeping', to be *economically* self-reliant without following one of these three 'trades', or the working-class equivalents of service and factory work, could only mean one possibility: the enterprise which the women of Sing Sing had pursued. Realization of this anomaly in her own thought combined with Fuller's detestation of hypocrisy—'Give me truth, cheat me by no illusion'—to ignite her fiery denunciation of the double standard.

It was prostitution which emblematized all other social ills, and which propelled Fuller into her increasing public concern and sympathy for socialism. Evangelical writers conflated prostitution with other forms of social chaos, including socialist radicalism; conversely, Owenite socialists saw prostitution as the paradigm of exploitation in industrial capitalism.

Fuller's concern about prostitution was by no means unique, nor was her analysis as systematic or programmatic as that of existing activists. The New York Female Moral Reform Society, founded in 1834 to convert prostitutes to evangelical Protestantism, had proposed to keep vigil at brothels and to publish a list of clients in the society's journal, the *Advocate of Moral Reform*. By the 1840s the American Female Moral Reform Society, as it became, had over 500 branches, providing cannon fodder for intensive political lobbying of the legislature to make seduction imprisonable—and succeeding in their demands by 1848. The Society also pilloried the male monopoly of the professions and claimed that low wages for women caused prostitution. (Many working-class girls used casual prostitution to eke out low earnings or get through periods of unemployment.)

What made the double standard particularly pernicious in the nineteenth century was the decline of the New England communitarian ideal in favour of the deracinated, deregulated market-place. Among the Puritans each member of the community, man or woman, had been responsible for the moral health of the group as a whole. This legitimized prying into what the more private-minded nineteenth century would regard as nobody else's business. Such institutionalized nosiness had meant that Puritan men's misdeeds were as likely to be uncovered as women's, even if they might be less strictly punished. But disestablishment of the Protestant churches after the Revolution lessened the religious imperative to uncover a neighbour's nakedness. Ironically, the nineteenth-century ideology of domesticity, retreating into the sancity of the private home, also covered up male mis-steps *outside* the home. The wife's blissful domestic ignorance would be threatened if a husband's wrong-doing were revealed, it could be argued.

A new ideal of female 'passionlessness' emerged in Anglo-American culture in the late eighteenth century. The *natural* woman was sexless; prostitutes were unnatural. Both male and female writers began to stress female chastity as protection for both the individual woman and society as a whole, and evangelical fervour heightened the imperative. Vestiges of the older joy in sexuality remained:

Peter Gay has documented, at least in private sources such as diaries, that eroticism between loving partners was as great in the nineteenth century as ever or as now. But at least formally the ideology *did* change. As the early nineteenth century came to reject the Ideal of Republican Motherhood in favour of the Cult of True Womanhood, it replaced more egalitarian notions about male and female sexuality with what Bram Dijkstra calls 'the cult of the Household Nun'. The purity of the Angel in the House required a demon outside to service male sexuality. This accentuated the divide between good and 'fallen' women, but also legitimized male libido. Prostitution was a boon to society, and the whore the upholder of the wife's chastity.

Further, the dominant discourse only applied to native-born white middle-class women; women of colour, immigrants, and working-class women were not regarded as passionless, but as fair sexual game. Native American women were also thought debased: the heroic figures of Pocahontas and Sacajawea, both of whom saved men, were replaced by accounts in mid-nineteenth-century travel journals of 'dirty little squaws' leading male adventurers astray.

Fuller's view, never conditioned by prejudice against immigrant or Native American women, travels far beyond this dominant discourse, yet also begins from a starting-point in the Cult of the True Woman. Prostitution posed a particular problem for anyone who accepted, as Fuller did, that women were different from men in nature: a basic premiss of the Cult as well. Fuller writes in *Woman*:

> The especial genius of Woman I believe to be electrical in movement, intuitive in function, spiritual in tendency. She excels not so easily in classification, or recreation, as in an instinctive seizure of causes, and a simple breathing out of what she receives that has the singleness of life, rather than the selecting and energizing of art.

Men's especial nature apparently included being more *immoral*. In the Cult of True Womanhood: 'Passionlessness was on the other side of the coin which paid, so to speak, for women's admission to moral equality' [Nancy F. Cott, 'Passionlessness: An Interpretation of Victorian Sexual Ideology, 1790-1850', *Signs*, 4, 1978]. But prostitutes were sexual women. Either Fuller could accept that prostitutes were passionless victims of male predatory sexuality—or she could prove the rule by the exceptions, denigrating prostitutes as false to all that True Womanhood stood for. Both strategies would have confirmed the Cult by ratifying asexuality in the 'normal' female. Instead, Fuller asks: 'Why can't a man be more like a woman?' She extends the True Womanly ideal of chastity to men: 'We shall not decline celibacy as the great fact of our age.'

In the end Fuller stands the Cult of the True Woman on its head: female moral nature, rightly reconstituted in the case of aberrant specimens such as prostitutes, can and should instruct male. It follows the Cult to its own logical conclusions, uncomfortable for men though they may actually turn out to be.

This aspect of Fuller's thought was *not* typical of her time, but it can be seen in later feminists. English campaigners against the Contagious Diseases Acts of 1864, 1866, and 1869 likewise rejected the mere regulation of prostitution as benefiting men only. They, too, called for an abolition of the sexual double standard and the establishment of a single joint code of sexual behaviour. If the prostitute was the unwitting guardian of the domestic hearth, this root-and-branch stance—which Fuller shares—means a radical willingness to see conventional marriage die the death. In contrast, Emerson wrote: 'We cannot rectify marriage because it would introduce such carnage in our social relations'.

In her 1875 lecture 'Social Purity', Susan B. Anthony argued: 'There is no escape from the conclusion that, while woman's want of bread induces her to pursue this vice [prostitution], man's love of the vice leads him there. For every abandoned woman, there is always *one* abandoned man and oftener many more.' This is pure Fuller.

In our own century, Fuller's relational feminism, her belief in separate male and female natures, prefigures an important strand in women's studies. Unlike Mary Wollstonecraft, whose 'rationalist' feminism is primarily rights-oriented and education-minded, Fuller's 'romantic' feminism seeks liberation mainly through psychological means. Second-wave feminism embodied this striving in consciousness-raising groups. Further, much modern feminist writing, particularly in psychology and educational theory, has confirmed the idea of 'a different voice', the concept—central to Fuller—that male and female moral personalities are not the same.

Fuller is a romantic feminist in contending that the content of girls' education should be *affirmatively* different, not merely a watered-down version of the classic texts fed to boys. Having been privileged to learn the father speech, Latin, she need not worship the priestly tongue mindlessly. Romanticism values diversity and assigns positive value to gender differences. It does not define female nature solely in contrast to male. This is the impetus behind Fuller's description of female nature as electrical, vital, magnetic, full of life. It is intended as the most affirmative of descriptions, not the mere negative of masculine identity. *Life* is what Fuller writes into her definition of woman.

Fuller's feminism is romantic in another sense: it emphasizes self-help and self-assertion, another strand in modern feminism. *Woman* is ambivalent as to whether women will achieve freedom through each other's support or their own individual striving, but it is clear that they will not achieve it in league with men. 'Men do *not*

look at both sides, and women must leave off asking them.' This is another reason why political lobbying— of an all-male legislature—can have little effect, to Fuller's way of thinking. But although Fuller is not primarily remembered as a political activist, she targeted most of the inequities that would preoccupy later feminists: marriage as slavery, sex and sexuality, and women's poverty.

Fuller's attempt to state a vibrant and positive ideal of femaleness borrows from the Cult of True Womanhood, but ultimately transcends it. The qualities which Fuller claims for women by nature and right are too dynamic to sit comfortably in the hands-in-lap posture of the True Woman.

FURTHER READING

Bibliography

Myerson, Joel. *Margaret Fuller: An Annotated Secondary Bibliography.* New York: Burt Franklin & Co., 1977, 272 p.

> Lists and annotates critical writings, as well as poems dedicated to Fuller, and stories, novels, and poems which feature characters thought to be based on her. Important manuscript collections by and about Fuller are also listed.

———. *Margaret Fuller: A Descriptive Bibliography.* Pitts-burgh: University of Pittsburgh Press, 1978, 163 p.

> Extensive primary bibliography. Myerson provides analytical descriptions of Fuller's book-length publications and lists her known contributions to newspapers, magazines, and collections. The source features many photographs and reproductions of important editions.

Biography

Alcott, A. Bronson. "Margaret Fuller." In his *Concord Days,* pp. 77-9. Boston: Roberts Brothers, 1888.
> Appreciation of Fuller as a thinker and an advocate for women.

Berkson, Dorothy. "'Born and Bred in Different Nations': Margaret Fuller and Ralph Waldo Emerson." In *Patrons and Protégées: Gender: Friendship, and Writing in Nineteenth-Century America,"* edited by Shirley Marchalonis, pp. 3-30. New Brunswick: Rutgers University Press, 1988.

> Suggests that "Fuller's relationship with Emerson lies at the center of any effort to reexamine her work and reassess her reputation," and examines major areas of difference and agreement between them.

Capper, Charles. *Margaret Fuller: An American Romantic Life, Volume 1—The Private Years.* New York: Oxford University Press, 1992, 423 p.

Biography described by Capper as an "act of historical recovery" and an exploration of Fuller's life and thought as well as works. This volume treats Fuller's life through 1840.

Cargill, Oscar. "Nemesis and Nathaniel Hawthorne." *PMLA* LII, No. 3 (September 1937): 848-62.

Exploration of the various friendships, familial relationships by marriage, and tensions between Fuller, Hawthorne, Elizabeth Peabody, Sophia Peabody (who married Hawthorne), and Ellery Channing (who married a sister of Fuller's). After Fuller's death, Hawthorne based the character of Zenobia in *The Blithedale Romance* on her, while Channing participated with Ralph Waldo Emerson and James Freeman Clarke in the extensive censorship and revision of her posthumous papers. This article is rebutted by Austin Warren (below).

Dickenson, Donna. *Margaret Fuller: Writing a Woman's Life.* New York: St. Martin's Press, 1993, 247 p.

Biographical and critical study. Dickenson begins with an exploration of Fuller's posthumous treatment: the heavily censored and revised edition of her work and the negative assessments published by her friends and professional associates. Dickenson writes that her treatment of Fuller's life is informed by insights provided by recent works of feminist scholarship.

Fuller, Frederick T. "Hawthorne and Margaret Fuller Ossoli." *The Literary World* XVI, No. 1 (10 January 1885): 11-15.

A nephew of Fuller's addresses Nathaniel Hawthorne's posthumously published excoriation of her. The critic quotes extensively from diary entries written by both Hawthorne and Fuller during the course of their relationship.

Hawthorne, Julian. "The Old Manse." In *Nathaniel Hawthorne and His Wife: A Biography, Volume 1*, pp. 243-303. Boston: Houghton Mifflin and Co., 1884.

Includes a diary extract in which Hawthorne receives as fact scurrilous gossip regarding Fuller and articulates his own negative assessment of her character.

Higginson, Thomas Wentworth. *Margaret Fuller Ossoli.* Boston: Houghton Mifflin, 1884, 323 p.

Early, appreciative biography that addresses the distortions introduced by the editors of the *Memoirs.*

von Mehren, Joan. *Minerva and the Muse: A Life of Margaret Fuller.* University of Massachusetts Press, 1995, 526 p.

Biography that offers analysis of Fuller's political sentiments.

Warfel, Harry. "Margaret Fuller and Ralph Waldo Emerson." *PMLA* L, No. 2 (June 1935): 576-94.

Account of Fuller's relationship with Emerson that adheres to a largely discredited perception that Fuller was forever in the position of acolyte to the more learned Emerson. Warfel includes an account of Fuller's

editorship of the *Dial* magazine.

Warren, Austin. "Hawthorne, Margaret Fuller, and Nemesis." *PMLA* LIV, No. 2 (June 1939): 615-18.

Notes that in his account of the relationship between Fuller and Hawthorne, Oscar Cargill (cited above) "offers conjectures as authoritative, and advances 'views' necessarily unprovable."

Criticism

Barbour, Frances M. "Margaret Fuller and the British Reviewers." *New England Quarterly* (December 1936): 618-25.

Assesses coverage of Fuller in the British press from 1846 to 1852. Barbour notes that the majority of British commentators on Fuller focus on her personality rather than her writing.

Brown, Arthur W. *Margaret Fuller.* New York: Twayne Publishers, 1964, 159 p.

Balanced account of Fuller's life and works. This was one of the first published studies to credit Fuller for her pioneering journalism.

Chevigny, Bell Gale. *The Woman and The Myth: Margaret Fuller's Life and Writings.* Rev. ed. Boston: Northeastern University Press, 1994, 574 p.

Revised and expanded edition of a study that interposes Fuller's own writings with Chevigny's commentary. The book is divided into six sections corresponding to Chevigny's division of Fuller's written works into broad categories: "The Problem of Identity and Vocation," "The Friend," "The Transcendentalist: Teacher, Editor, Literary Critic," "The Feminist," "The Social Critic and Journalist," and "The Radical in Italy."

Myerson, Joel, ed. *Critical Essays on Margaret Fuller.* Boston: G. K. Hall, 1980, 289 p.

Collects previously printed critical essays on Fuller.

Smith, Bernard. "The Criticism of Romance." In his *Forces in American Criticism: A Study in the History of American Literary Thought*, pp. 66-113. New York: Harcourt Brace Jovanovich, 1939.

Favorable appraisal of Fuller as a literary critic.

Steele, Jeffrey. "The Call of Eurydice: Mourning and Intertextuality in Margaret Fuller's Writing." In *Influence and Intertextuality in Literary History*, edited by Jay Clayton and Eric Rothstein, pp. 271-97. Madison: University of Wisconsin Press, 1991.

Explores the supposition that Fuller underwent a process of transformed self-identity during the winter of 1840-41, suggesting that she came to a full identification of herself as a woman and a writer through the process of mourning for her father.

———. Introduction to *The Essential Margaret Fuller,* by Margaret Fuller, edited by Jeffrey Steele, pp. xi-xlix. New Brunswick: Rutgers University Press, 1992.

Overview of Fuller's intellectual growth and development and survey of her major literary works.

Tuttleton, James W. "Margaret Fuller, the American Minerva." *The New Criterion* 13, No. 6 (February 1995): 24-9.
   Outline of Fuller's life and career occasioned by the publication of several new biographies.

Watson, David. *Margaret Fuller: An American Romantic.* Oxford: Berg, 1988, 123 p.
   Critical biography divided into three sections, treating Fuller's life, her works, and her reputation.

Additional coverage of Fuller's life and career is contained in the following sources published by Gale Research: *Nineteenth-Century Literature Criticism, Volume 5,* and *Something about the Author,* Volume 25.

Christina Rossetti

1830-1894

(Also wrote under the pseudonym Ellen Alleyn) English poet, short story writer, and prose writer.

For additional information about Rossetti's life and caeer, see *NCLC*, Volume 2.

INTRODUCTION

Rossetti is ranked among the finest English poets of the nineteenth century. Closely associated with Pre-Raphaelitism—an artistic and literary movement that aspired to recapture the vivid pictorial qualities and sensual aesthetics of Italian religious painting before the year 1500—Rossetti was equally influenced by the religious conservatism and asceticism of the Church of England. Scholars find in her poetry an enduring dialectic between these disparate outlooks, as well as an adeptness with a variety of poetic forms.

Biographical Information

Rossetti was born in 1830, four years after her father, an Italian exile, settled in London and married Frances Mary Polidori. Demonstrating poetic gifts early in her life, Rossetti wrote sonnets in competition with her brothers William Michael and Dante Gabriel, a practice that is thought to have developed her command of metrical forms. At age eighteen, Rossetti began studying the works of Italian poet Dante Alighieri, who became a major and lasting influence on her poetry, as evidenced in her many allusions to his writing. As a young woman, Rossetti declined two marriage proposals because her suitors' failed to conform to the tenets of the Anglican Church. Rather than marry, she chose to remain with her mother, an equally devout Anglican. Rossetti's poetic production diminished as she grew older and increasingly committed to writing religious prose. A succession of serious illnesses strongly influenced her temperament and outlook on life; because she often believed herself close to death, religious devotion and mortality became persistent themes in both her poetry and prose. In 1871 she developed Graves's disease and, though she published *A Pageant, and Other Poems* in 1881, she concentrated primarily on works of religious prose, such as *The Face of the Deep: A Devotional Commentary on the Apocalypse*, published in 1892. That same year she was diagnosed with cancer; she died two years later.

Major Works

Rossetti's first published poem appeared in the *Athenaeum* when she was eighteen. She became a frequent contributor to the Pre-Raphaelite journal *The Germ*, which her brother Dante Gabriel founded. The title poem of her first collection of poetry, *Goblin Market, and Other Po-*

ems (1862), relates the adventures of two sisters who are tempted by the fruit of the goblin merchants of Elfland. The poem has been variously interpreted as a moral fable for children, an erotic fantasy, and an experiment in meter and rhyme. In 1874 Rossetti published a collection of prose for children, *Speaking Likenesses*. The book consists of three fantasy stories which are told to five sisters by their aunt. The title poem of *The Prince's Progress, and Other Poems* (1866) relates a prince's physical, moral, and spiritual journey to meet his bride. Rossetti's later volumes of poetry consist primarily of reprinted poems from her first three volumes and other sources. The first authoritative collection of her work *The Poetical Works of Christina Georgina Rossetti* (1904), was edited by her brother William and contains most of Rossetti's highest esteemed and frequently studied works. Rossetti's devotional verse explores humanity's relationship with God and the nature of life in the afterworld. It also celebrates Rossetti's denial of human love for the sake of religious purity, as in the sonnet sequence "Monna Innominata," included in *A Pageant, and Other Poems. Time Flies: A Reading Diary* (1885), offers for each day of the year a thought or passage designed to provoke spiritual reflection. In *The Face of the Deep*, Rossetti explores, verse by verse, the entire *Book of the Revelation of St. John.* Throughout Rossetti's verse and prose, the themes of isolation and unhappiness recur.

Critical Reception

Critics generally consider Rossetti's poetry superior to her later nonsecular prose works but observe that much of her most highly regarded verse was also inspired by her deeply held religious beliefs. Faulted by some critics for an alleged indifference to social issues, she is praised by others for her simple diction, timeless vision, and stylistic technique. Although she is remembered by many merely as the ethereal symbol of Pre-Raphaelitism evoked in Dante Gabriel Rossetti's paintings, Rossetti also produced a unique body of work that transcends the limits of any single movement. Rossetti's work continues to inspire scholarly study and debate. Modern critics, including Constance Hassett and W. David Shaw, have focussed recent studies of Rossetti on what is unsaid or alluded to in her work. Others, such as Antony Harrison, have explored the feminist aspects of Rossetti's work, and in doing so challenge their nineteenth-century predecessors and their twentieth-century peers who have focussed their examinations of Rossetti on the poet's reticence and her renunciation of this world in favor of the afterlife.

PRINCIPAL WORKS

Goblin Market, and Other Poems (poetry) 1862

Poems (poetry) 1866

The Prince's Progress, and Other Poems (poetry) 1866

Commonplace, and Other Short Stories (short stories) 1870

Sing-Song: A Nursery Rhyme Book (children's verse) 1872

Speaking Likenesses (children's stories) 1874

Seek and Find (religious prose) 1879

Called to be Saints: The Minor Festivals Devotionally Studied (religious prose) 1881

A Pageant, and Other Poems (poetry) 1881

Time Flies: A Reading Diary (religious prose) 1885

The Face of the Deep: A Devotional Commentary on the Apocalypse (religious prose) 1892

Verses (poetry) 1893

New Poems (poetry) 1896

Maude: Prose and Verse (children's stories and verse) 1897

The Poetical Works of Christina Georgina Rossetti (poetry) 1904

The Complete Poems of Christina Rossetti: A Variorum Edition 3 vols. (poetry) 1979-90

CRITICISM

Littell's Living Age (essay date 1866)

SOURCE: "Miss Rossetti's Poems," in *Littell's Living Age,* Vol. XC, No. 20, August 18, 1866, pp. 441-42.

[*In the following review of Rossetti's poems collected in the volume* The Prince's Progress, and Other Poems, *the critic praises Rossetti's unaffected style.*]

If an illustration of the unsatisfactoriness of Robertson's definition of poetry—"the natural language of excited feeling"—were necessary, it could be found nowhere better than in the productions of Miss Rossetti. On the other hand, however, the definition, when applied to the volume now before us, contains a kind of half truth, for Miss Rossetti, though never excited, is always natural. It would be difficult to find a selection of poems so thoughtful and serious, yet so devoid of that frenzy which is often inseparably associated with the notion of true poetry—such as Miss Rossetti's really is. In all she writes there is a certain element of tranquillity and repose. Calm and subdued herself, she imparts to her reader's mind a kind of grateful quiet. Poetical authorship evidently is with her no field for the display of brilliantly sensational ability. She applies herself to the composition of a poem in the same way, and probably for much the same reasons, that many persons would read the most reflective passages of Wordsworth in solitude; but that solace which others find in reception, comes to her through the exercise of her creative powers. For this reason, if for no others, Miss Rossetti's writings cannot fail to be interesting; whatever imperfections of style and expression we meet with, we cannot help feeling all along that we are contemplating the workings and processes of a mind of no common order. Tranquil in her joy, she is not over demonstrative in her grief. We can perceive that her whole being mourns, but we can perceive, too, very plainly the presence of a self-disciplined heart. Strictly speaking, it is to herself alone that she sings—always sweetly, and always as her passing emotions prompt her utterance. Hence she is to a certain extent inclined to an almost morbid habit of introspection; but behind this there is, as it were in the distance, a faint background of peaceful happiness and satisfaction, which prevents any one of her poems from being gloomy. Perhaps there is no better instance of this than in one of her "Devotional pieces"—all Miss Rossetti's poems are full of the spirit, though not the technicality, of devotion—entitled **"Dost Thou not Care?":**—

> Lord, it was well with me in time gone by,
> 　That cometh not again,
> When I was fresh and cheerful: who but I?
> 　I fresh, I cheerful: worn with pain,
> Now out of sight and out of heart;
> 　O Lord, how long?—
> *I watch thee as thou art,*
> 　*I will accept thy fainting heart, be strong.*

But Miss Rossetti can be sportive as well as serious; in the **"Queen of Hearts"** a good idea is well worked out, and lightly handled. Of the poem which gives its name to the present volume, we do not think that it is altogether the best. Miss Rossetti pleases us most in her short lyrical thoughts—we use the latter word advisedly. There are some minds to whom sustained effort is painful, or rather, whose emotions are best expressed in short, detached pieces, and it is to this class that Miss Rossetti seems to us to belong. A poem of thirty pages wants some strong prominent figure to which other figures are subordinate, and in the **"Prince's Progress"** too much strength is spread equally over a somewhat enlarged surface. But we are treated to some delicious glimpses of scenery:—

> By willow courses he took his path,
> Spied what a nest the kingfisher hath,
> Marked the fields, green to aftermath,
>   Marked where the old brown field-mouse ran,
> Loitered awhile for a deep-stream bath,
>   Yawned for a fellow man.

Much, too, would it please us to quote at length the **"Bride Song"** at the end of this poem, the rhythm of which is well managed, the sound and sense accompanying each other perfectly.

We are almost sorry that one or two pieces have not been omitted—**"Eve,"** for example perhaps, and **"Maiden Song."** Occasionally, too, Miss Rossetti deals in conceits which she would have done well to avoid. These, however, are minor defects, and detract but little from the merits of the pleasantest volume of verse which this year has given us. On the whole, we feel inclined to assign the first place to **"Life and Death."** It is not only, to our mind, the best poem in the book, but the most characteristic as well. In the contemplation of death, the writer carefully, or we should rather say instinctively, avoids looking at the gloomy and terrible side. To her, to die is nothing more than to become unconscious of a world of sweet sounds and sights, and that at a time when one has become weary of the earth:—

> Life is not sweet. One day it will be sweet
>   to shut our eyes and die:
> Nor feel the wild flowers blow, nor birds dart by
>   with flitting butterfly;
> Nor grass grow long above our heads and feet;
>   Nor hear the happy lark that soars sky high;
> Nor sigh that spring is fleet and summer fleet,
>   Nor mark the waving wheat,
> Nor know who sits in our accustomed seat.

There is nothing here of the horrors of dissolution and the pangs of a tortured eternity. Miss Rossetti has so happily expressed her conception of cessation of existence—death seems almost too stern a name—that there is left upon the mind a strange feeling of indistinctness as to whether it is sorrow or grief that is left for ever. It would be absurd to compare Miss Rossetti's poems to *"Vers de Société,"* yet in one point, at least, there is a similarity between W. M. Praed and the present authoress. Each is able to bring out into the strongest relief the gentle, and for this reason the lighter, side of human feeling: the difference, of course, is, that with the one it is the levity of comedy, with the other it is the levity of seriousness.

To a host of readers Miss Rossetti's poems will deservedly be very popular. Possessing just that tinge of melancholy which it may be assumed, is as indispensable to beauty as, according to the Baconian canon, is a corre-

sponding "strangeness," their melancholy never mars their picturesqueness. Rather is it subordinate to it, yet subordinate in such a manner that it is always sincere, always heart-deep, never affected, and never false. Hers is never the voice of sorrow only; to quote her own words—

> Her voice is sweeter than that voice;
> *She sings like one who grieves.*

It is because Miss Rossetti is so entirely free from affectation, so true to nature, and so true to herself, that we welcome her poems so heartily. At a time when in verse, as in everything else, the glare, and glitter, and tinsel of pseudo-sentiment are often painfully discernible, it is a positive pleasure and relief to meet with poetry the music of which is as melodious as its truthfulness is deep. We cannot, perhaps, discover many traces of originality; but it is far better to be simply and easily natural than to be ever hankering after the creation of some novel and striking effect. Like most other poetical writers of the present time, Miss Rossetti frequently causes us to remember that she lives under the Tennysonian dynasty; but it would be as absurd to suppose that minor poets could be dead to the influence of the great contemporary masters of song, as it would be to assert that these in their turn were not affected by the influences of the times in which they lived; nor does this fact prevent Miss Rossetti's new volume from being the most acceptable of recent contributions to English poetry.

The Catholic Review (essay date 1867)

SOURCE: "Christina G. Rossetti," in *The Catholic World,* Vol. IV, No. 24, March, 1867, pp. 839-46.

[*In the following review of the verses collected in* Poems, *the anonymous critic analyzes the defects in Rossetti's poetry.*]

We had heard some little of Miss Rossetti, in a superficial way, before reading this her book. Various verses of hers had met our eye in print, and if they themselves left no very decided mark upon the memory, yet we had the firm impression, somehow, that she was one more of the rising school of poets. Accordingly we thought it well to take a retrospect of a few post-Tennysonians—Mrs. Browning, Owen Meredith, Robert Buchanan, Jean Ingelow, and so on—supposed fellow disciples—so as to be tolerably sure of ranking the new-comer rightly. On reading this volume we find our labor lost through an entirely unforeseen circumstance. Unfortunately, it does not appear that Miss Rossetti is a poetess at all. That there are people who think her one, we infer from the fact that this is in some sort a third edition; why they think so, we are at a loss to see. The book will not answer a single test of poetry. The authoress's best claim to consideration is, that she sincerely, persistently, fervently *means* to be a poetess. Only the most Demosthenian resolve could have kept her writing in face of her many inherent unfitnesses. For imagination, she offers fantasy; for sentiment, sentimentality; for aspiration, ambition; for originality and thought, little or nothing; for melody, fantastic janglings of words; and these, with all tenderness for the ill-starred intensity of purpose that could fetch them so far, are no more poetry than the industrious Virginian colonists' shiploads of mica were gold.

The first cursory impression of this book would be, we think, that its cardinal axiom was "Poetry is versified plaintiveness." The amount of melancholy is simply overwhelming. There is a forty-twilight power of sombreness everywhere. Now, criticism has taken principles, not statistics, to be its province; but we could not resist the temptation to take a little measurement of all this mournfulness. Limiting our census strictly to the utterly irretrievable and totally wrecked poems, with not a glimmering of reassurance, we found no less than forty-nine sadnesses, all the way from shadow to unutterable blackness—*"nfernam Iumbram noctemque perennem."* There is the sadness decadent, the sadness senescent, the sadness bereft, the sadness despondent, the sadness weary, the sadness despairing, the sadness simply sad, the grand sadness ineffable, and above and pervading all, the sadness rhapsodical. They are all there. Old Burton will rise from his grave, if there be any virtue in Pythagoreanism, to anatomize these poems. What it is all about is strictly a secret, and laudably well kept; which gives to the various sorrows that touching effect peculiar to the wailings of unseen babies from unascertained ailments. So sustained is the grief, indeed, that after protracted poring, we hang in abeyance between two conclusions. One is that Miss Rossetti, outside of print, is the merriest mortal in the United Kingdom; the other, that her health is worse than precarious. That one or the other must be right, we know. There is no other horn to the dilemma, no *tertiary quiddity,* no choice, no middle ground between hilarity and dyspepsia.

Perhaps the reader can judge for himself from these lines, which are a not unfair sample:

"May."

I cannot tell you how it was;
But this I know: it came to pass
Upon a bright and breezy day,
When May was young; ah, pleasant May!
As yet the poppies were not born,
Between the blades of tender corn;
The last eggs had not hatched as yet,
Nor any bird foregone its mate.
I cannot tell you what it was;
But this I know: it did but pass.
It passed away with sunny May,
With all sweet things it passed away,
And left me old and cold and gray.

We may be very unappreciative, and probably are sinfully suspicious, but the above sounded at the first and sounds at the present reading, exactly like a riddle. We certainly don't know how it was nor what it was. There is a shadowy clue in its passing away with sunny May,

but we are far too cautious to hazard a guess. If there be any conundrum intended, all we have to say is, we give it up.

We do but justice, however, in saying that amid much mere lugubriousness there is some real and respectable sadness. The following, in spite of the queer English in its first lines, sounds genuine, and is moreover, for a rarity of rarities, in well-chosen and not ill-managed metre:

I have a room whereinto no one enters
    Save I myself alone:
There sits a blessed memory on a throne,
    There my life centres.

While winter comes and goes—Oh! tedious
        comer!
    And while its nip-wind blows;
While bloom the bloodless lily and warm rose
    Of lavish summer;

If any should force entrance he might see there
    One buried, yet not dead,
Before whose face I no more bow my head
    Or (*sic*) bend my knee there;

But often in my worn life's autumn weather
    I watch there with clear eyes,
And think how it will be in Paradise
    When we're together.

Here is one of a trite topic—nearly all the good things in this book are on themes as old as moonlight—but with a certain mournful richness, like autumn woods:

Life is not sweet. One day it will be sweet
    To shut our eyes and die:
Nor feel the wild flowers blow, nor birds dart by
    With flitting butterfly;
Nor grass grow long above our head and feet,
Nor hear the happy lark that soars sky high,
Nor sigh that spring is fleet, and summer fleet,
    Nor mark the waxing wheat,
Nor know who sits in our accustomed seat.
Life is not good. One day it will be good
    To die, then live again;
To sleep meanwhile: so not to feel the wane
Of shrunk leaves dropping in the wood,
Nor hear the foamy lashing of the main,
Nor mark the blackened bean-fields, nor where
        stood
    Rich ranks of golden grain,
Only dead refuse stubble clothe the plain:
Asleep from risk, asleep from pain.

This is one of her best poems in point of style. The "waxing wheat" we are just a shade doubtful about; but the mellowness of the diction is much to our liking, and it is unmarred by any of the breaks of strange ill taste that flaw nearly all these poems. If not poetry nor novelty, at least we find it sadly agreeable verse.

Our professor of rhetoric once astonished his class by a heterodoxy, which we have since thought sound as well as neat. "Walter Scott," said he, "writes verse as well as a man can write and not be a poet." We are sorry we cannot say as much for Miss Rossetti; she has considerable faults as a writer. The chief of these has elsewhere been carped at—her laborious style of being simple. The true simplicity of poets is not a masterly artifice, but a natural and invariable product where high poetic and expressive powers combine. The best thought is always simple, because it deals only with the essences of things: the best expression—the machinery of thought—is simple, just as the best of any other machinery is. But the grand, obvious fact to the many is that the best poetry is admired for being simple. Writing for this market, Miss Rossetti and unnumbered others have more or less successfully attempted to achieve this crowning beauty of style by various processes that are to the inspiration of real simplicity as patent medicines to vigorous vitality. Almost all hold the immutable conviction that Saxon words are an infallible recipe for the indispensable brevity. Accordingly the usual process is by an elaborate application of Saxon—if rather recondite or even verging on the obsolete, so much the more efficacious—to a few random ideas. Of course, with such painful workmanship, one must not expect the best material. Original, or even well defined thought seldom thrives in the same hot-house with this super-smoothness. But without pursuing the process into results at large, we have only to take Matthew Arnold's distinction as to Miss Rossetti:—she tries hard for *simplicité,* and achieves *simplesse.* But there is no such thing as hard work without its fruits. This straining after effect crops painfully out in a peculiar baldness and childishness of phrase that is almost original. The woman who can claim The Lambs of Grasmere as her own has not lived in vain. This production, with its pathetic episode of the maternal

> Teapots for the bleating mouths,
> Instead of nature's nourishment,

has already been noticed in print, and duly expanded many visages. We pause rapt in admiration of the deep intuition that could select for song the incident of feeding a sheep with a teapot. It carries us back, in spirit, to the subtle humor and delicate irony of "Peter Bell," and "We are Seven." What a burst of tenderness ought we to expect, if Miss Rossetti should ever chance to see stable-boys give a horse a bolus! . . . . We shall not cite examples of this *simplesse;* those who like it will find it purer and more concentrated in the bard of Rydal; or if they must have it, they are safe in opening this book almost anywhere.

Of the individual poems, the two longest, **"The Goblin Market"** and **"The Prince's Progress,"** are rivals for the distinction of being the worst. All the best poems are short, excepting one, "Under the Rose." The story is of an illegitimate daughter, whose noble mother takes her to live with herself at the inevitable Hall, without acknowledging her. There are able touches of nature in the portrayal of the lonely, loving, outlawed, noble heart, that, knowing her mother's secret, resolves never to betray it,

even to her. In the following passage, the girl, alone at the castle, as her mother's favorite maid, describes her inner life:

> Now sometimes in a dream,
> My heart goes out of me
> To build and scheme,
> Till I sob after things that seem
> So pleasant in a dream:
> A home such as I see,
> My blessed neighbors live in;
> With father and with mother,
> *All proud of one another,*
> *Named by one common name;*
> *From baby in the bud*
> *To full-bloun workman father;*
> It's little short of Heaven.

>   . . . . .

> Of course the servants sneer
> Behind my back at me;
> Of course the village girls,
> Who envy me my curls
> And gowns and idleness,
> Take comfort in a jeer;
> Of course the ladies guess
> Just so much of my history
> As points the emphatic stress
> With which they laud my Lady;

> The gentlemen who catch
> A casual glimpse of me,
> And turn again to see
> Their valets, on the watch
> To speak a word with me;—
> All know, and sting me wild;
> Till I am almost ready
> To wish that I were dead,—
> No faces more to see,
> No more words to be said;
> My mother safe at last
> Disburdened of her child
> And the past past.

"The Convent Threshold"—the last words of a contrite novice to her lover—has touches of power. There is an unusual force about some parts, as for example here:

> You linger, yet the time is short;
> Flee for your life; grid up your strength
> To flee; the shadows stretched at length
> Show that day wanes, that night draws nigh;
> Flee to the mountain, tarry not.
> Is this a time for smile and sigh;
> For songs among the secret trees
> Where sudden blue-birds nest and sport?
> The time is short, and yet you stay:
> To-day, while it is called to-day,
> Kneel, wrestle, knock, do violence, pray;
> To-day is short, to-morrow nigh:
> Why will you die? why will you die!

>   . . . . .

How should I rest in Paradise,
Or sit on steps of Heaven alone?
If saints and angels spoke of love,
Should I not answer from my throne,
'Have pity upon me, ye, my friends,
For I have heard the sound thereof?'
Should I not turn with yearning eyes,
Turn earthward with a pitiful pang?
Oh! save me from a pang in heaven!
By all the gifts we took and gave,
Repent, repent, and be forgiven.

The lines called **"Sound Sleep,"** p. 65, we like very well for very slight cause. It says nearly nothing with a pleasant flow of cadence that has the charm of an oasis for the reader. Much better is **"No, Thank You, John!"** which strikes into a strain of plain sound sense that we could wish to see much more of. The style, as well as the sense, seems to shuffle off its affectations, and the last two stanzas especially are easy, natural, and neat.

A strange compound of good and bad is the singular one called

"Twice."

I took my heart in my hand,
   O my love, O my love!
I said, "Let me fall or stand,
   Let me live or die;
But this once hear me speak,
   O my love, O my love!
Yet a woman's wonds are weak;
   You should speak, not I"

You took my heart in your hand,
   With a friendly smile,
With a critical eye you scanned,
   Then set it down
And said: "It is still unripe—
   Better wait a while;
Wait while the skylarks pipe,
   Till the corn grows brown."

As you set it down it broke—
   Broke, but I did not wince;
I smiled at the speech you spoke,
   At your judgment that I heard:
But I have not often smiled
   Since then, nor questioned since,
Nor cared for corn-flowers wild,
   Nor sung with the singing-bird.

I take my heart in hand,
   O my God, O my God!
My broken heart in my hand:
   Thou hast seen, judge thou.
My hope was written on sand,
   O my God, O my God!
Now let thy judgment stand—
   Yea, judge me now.

This, contemned of a man,
   This, marred one heedless day,
This heart take thou to scan
   Both within and without:
Refine with fire its gold,
   Purge thou its dross away;
Yea, hold it in thy hold,
   Whence none can pluck it out

I take my heart in my hand—
   I shall not die, but live—
Before thy face I stand,
   I, for thou callest such;
All that I have I bring,
   All that I am I give,
Smile thou, and I shall sing,
   But shall not question much,

This poem, we confess, puzzles us a little to decide upon it. The imitation is palpable at a glance, but it is a very clever one: the first three stanzas above all catch the mannerism of their model to admiration. But the whole is a copy, at best, of one of the archetype's inferior styles; and yet we fancy we can see, under all the false bedizening, something of poetry in the conception, though it is ill said, and only dimly translucent. There is art, too, in the parallelism of the first and last three verses. But we do not like the refrain in the fourth verse—somehow it jars. Perhaps the best we can say of it is, that Browning, in his mistier moments of convulsiveness, could write worse.

There is another imitation of Browning in this book, that is the most supremely absurd string of rugged platitudes imaginable—**"Wife to Husband,"** p. 61. The last verse is sample enough:

Not a word for you,
   Not a look or kiss
     Good-by.
We, one, must part in two;
   Verily death is this,
     I must die.

The metre generally throughout this book is in fact simply execrable. Miss Rossetti cannot write contentedly in any known or human measure. We do not think there are ten poems that are not in some new-fangled shape or shapelessness. With an overweening ambition, she has not the slightest faculty of rhythm. All she has done is to originate some of the most hideous metres that "shake the racked axle of art's rattling car." Attempting not only Browning's metrical dervish-dancings, but Tennyson's exquisite ramblings, she fails in both from an utter want of that fine ear that always guides the latter, and so often strikes out bold beauties in the former. Most of Miss Rossetti's new styles of word mixture are much like the ingenious individual's invention for enabling right-handed people to write with the left hand—more or less elever ways of doing what she don't wish to do. What possible harmony, for instance, can any one find in this jumble, which, as per the printer, is meant for a "song":

There goes the swallow—
Could we but follow!
Hasty swallow, stay,
Point us out the way:
Look back, swallow, turn back, swallow, stop,
swallow.

There went the swallow—
Too late to follow,
Lost our note of way,
Lost our chance to-day.
Good-by, swallow, sunny swallow, wise
swallow.

After the swallow—
All sweet things follow;
All things go their way,
Only we must stay,
Must not follow; good-by, swallow, good
swallow.

Where on earth is sound or sense in this? Not a suggestion of melody, not a fraction of a coherent idea. People must read such trash as they eat *meringues à la crême:* we never could comprehend either process.

Truth to tell, we have in this book some of the very choicest balderdash that ever was perpetrated; worthy to stand beside even the immortal "Owl and Goose" of Tennyson. There is a piece at p. 41 which we would give the world to see translated into some foreign language, we have such an intense eagerness to understand it. Its subject, so far as we have got, seems to be the significance of the crocodile, symbolically considered. We glanced over, or rather at it once, and put it by for after reading, thinking the style probably too deep for love at first sight. On the second perusal we fell in with some extraordinary young crocodiles that we must have missed before. They had just been indulged in the luxury of being born, but Miss Rossetti's creative soul, not content with bestowing upon them the bliss of amphibious existence, made perfect their young beauty by showing them "fresh-hatched perhaps, and—*daubed with brithday dew."*

We are strong of head—we recovered from even this— we became of the very select few who can say they have read this thing through. There was a crocodile hero; he had a golden girdle and crown; he wore polished stones; crowns, orbs and sceptres *starred his breast* (why shouldn't they if they could); "special burnishment adorned his mail;" his punier brethren trembled, whereupon he immediately ate them till "the luscious fat distilled upon his chin," and "exuded from his nostrils and his eyes." He then fell into an anaconda nap, and grew very much smaller in his sleep, till at the approach of a very queer winged vessel (probably a vessel of wrath), "the prudent crocodile rose on his feet and shed appropriate tears (obviously it is the handsome thing for all well-bred crocodiles to cry when a winged ship comes along) and wrung his hands." As a finale, Miss Rossetti, too nimble for the unwary reader, anticipates his question of "What does it all mean?" and triumphantly replying that she doesn't know herself, but that it was all just so, marches on to the

next *monumentum aere perennius.* In the name of the nine muses, we call upon Martin Farquhar Tupper to read this and then die.

There are one or two other things like this *longo intervallo,* but it is reserved for the Devotional Pieces to furnish the only poem that can compete with it in its peculiar line. This antagonist poem is not so sublime an example of sustained effort, but it has the advantage that the rhyme is fully equal to the context. Permit us then to introduce the neat little charade entitled

"Amen."

It is over. What is over?
  Nay, how much is over truly!—
Harvest days we toiled to sow for;
  Now the sheaves are gathered newly,
  Now the wheat is garnered duly.

It is finished. What is finished?
  Much is finished known or unknown;
Lives are finished, time diminished;
  Was the fallow field left unsown?
  Will these buds be always unblown?

It suffices. What suffices?
  All suffices reckoned rightly;
Spring shall bloom where now the ice is,
  Roses make the bramble sightly,
  And the quickening suns shine brightly,
  And the latter winds blow lightly,
And my garden teems with spices.

Let now the critic first observe how consummately the mysticism of the charade form is intensified by the sphinx-like answers appended. Next note the novelties in rhyme. The rhythmic chain that links "over" and and "sow for" is the first discovery in the piece, closely rivalled by "ice is" and "spices" in the last verse. But far above all rises the subtle originality of the three rhymes in the second. A thousand literati would have used the rhyming words under the unpoetical rules of ordinary English. Miss Rossetti alone has the courage to inquire "Was the fallow field left *un*sown? Will these buds be always *un*blown?" We really do not think Shakspeare would have been bold enough to do this thus.

But despite this, the religious poems are perhaps the best. They seem at least the most unaffected and sincere, and the healthiest in tone. There are several notably good ones: one, just before the remarkable **"Amen,"** in excruciating metre, but well said; one, **"The Love of Christ which Passeth Knowledge,"** a strong and imaginative picture of the crucifixion; and **"Good Friday,** a good embodiment of the fervor of attrite repentance. The best written of all is, we think, this one (p. 248):

"Weary in Well-doing."

I would have gone; God bade me stay;
  I would have worked; God bade me rest.

He broke my will from day to day,
  He read my yearnings unexpressed
    And said them nay.

Now I would stay; God bids me go;
  Now I would rest; God bids me work.
He breaks my heart, tossed to and fro,
  My soul is wrung with doubts that lurk
    And vex it so.

I go, Lord, where thou sendest me;
  Day after day I plod and moil:
But Christ my God, when will it be
  That I may let alone my toil,
    And rest with thee?

This is good style (no *simplesse* here) and real pathos—in short, poetry. We do not see a word to wish changed, and the conclusion in particular is excellent: there is a weariness in the very sound of the last lines.

It is remarkable how seldom *thought* furnishes the motive for these poems. With no lack at all of intelligence, they stand almost devoid of intellect. It is always a sentiment of extraneous suggestion, never a novelty in thought, that inspires our authoress. She seems busier depicting inner life than evolving new truths or beauties. Nor does she abound in suggestive turns of phrase or verbal felicities. In fact, as we have seen, she will go out of her way to achieve the want of ornament. But there is one subject which she has thought out thoroughly, and that subject is death. Whether in respect to the severance of earthly ties, the future state, or the psychical relations subtly linking the living to the dead, she shows on this topic a vigor and vividness, sometimes misdirected, but never wanting. Some of her queer ideas have a charm and a repulsion at once, like ghosts of dead beauty: *e.g.* this strange sonnet:

"After Death"

The curtains were half-drawn, the floor was
  swept
  And strewn with rushes; rosemary and may
  Lay thick upon the bed on which I lay,
Where through the lattice ivy-shadows crept.
He leaned above me, thinking that I slept
  And could not hear him; but I heard him say,
"Poor child, poor child!" and as he turned away
Came a deep silence, and I knew he wept;
      He did not touch the shroud, or raise the
  fold
  That hid my face, or take my hand in his,
Or ruffle the smooth pillows for my head;
He did not love me living, but once dead
  He pitied me, and very sweet it is
    To know he still is warm though I am cold.

There is some *chiaro-oscuro* about this. Under all the ghastliness of the conception, we detect here a deep, genuine, unhoping, intensely human yearning, that is all the better drawn for being thrown into the shadow. We do not know of a more graphic realization of death. Miss

Rossetti seems to be lucky with her sonnets. We give the companion piece to this last—not so striking as the other, but full of heart's love, and ending with one of the few passages we recall which enter without profaning the penetralia of that highest love, which passionately prefers the welfare of the beloved one to its own natural cravings for fruition and fulfilment:

"Remember."

Remember me when I am gone away,
  Gone far away into the silent land;
  When you no more can hold me by the hand
Nor I half turn to go, yet turning stay.
Remember me when no more, day by day,
  You tell me of our future that you planned;
  Only remember me; you understand
It will be late to counsel then or pray.
Yet if you should forget me for a while
  And afterwards remember, do not grieve;
  For if the darkness and corruption leave
A vestige of the thoughts that once I had,
  Better by far you should forget and smile
  Than that you should remember and be sad.

Another marked peculiarity often shadowed forth is our authoress's sharply defined idea that the dead lie simply quiescent, neither in joy nor sorrow. There are several miserable failures to express this state, and one success, so simple, so natural, and so pleasant in measure, that we quote it, though we have seen it cited before:

When I am dead, my dearest,
  Sing no sad songs for me;
Plant thou no roses at my head,
  Nor shady cypress-tree:
Be the green grass above me
  With showers and dew-drops wet;
And if thou wilt, remember,
  And if thou wilt, forget.

I shall not see the shadows;
  I shall not feel the rain;
I shall not hear the nightingale
  Sing on as if in pain;
And dreaming through that twilight
  That doth not rise nor set,
Haply I may remember,
  And haply may forget.

Such bold insight into so profound a subject says more for the soul of an author than a whole miss's paradise of prettinesses.

In singular contrast with this religious fervency and earnestness, the sincerity of which we see no reason to impeach, comes our gravest point of reprehension of this volume. We think it fairly chargeable with utterances—and reticences—of morally dangerous tendency; and this, too, mainly on a strange point for a poetess to be cavilled at—the rather delicate subject of our erring sisters. Now, we are of those who think the world, as to this matter, in a state little better than barbarism; that far from feeling the first instincts of Christian charity, we are shamefully like the cattle that gore the sick ox from the herd. The only utterly pitiless power in human life is our virtue, when brought face to face with this particular vice. We hunt the fallen down; hunt them to den and lair; hunt them to darkness, desperation, and death; hunt their bodies from earth, and their souls (if we can) from heaven, with the cold sword in one hand, and in the other the cross of him who came into the world to save, not saints, but sinners, and who said to one of these: "Neither do I condemn thee. Go, and now sin no more."

But there is also such a thing as misdirected mercifulness; a dangerous lenity, all the more to be guarded against for its wearing the garb of charity; and we think Miss Rossetti has leaned culpably far in this direction. Two poems are especially prominent examples—**"Cousin Kate,"** and **"Sister Maude."** In each the heroine has sinned, and suffered the penalties of discovery, and in each she is given the upper hand, and made a candidate for sympathy, for very bad reasons. There is no word to intimate that there is anything so very dreadful about dishonor; that it may not be some one else's fault, or nobody's fault at all—a mere social accident. A few faint hinting touches there may be of conventional condemnation, but somehow Miss Rossetti's sinners, *as sinners,* invariably have the best of the argument and of the situation, while virtue is put systematically in the wrong, and snubbed generally. **"The Goblin Market"** too, if we read it aright, is open to the same criticism. We understand it, namely, to symbolize the conflict of the better nature in us, with the prompting of the passions and senses. If so, what is the story translated from its emblematic form? One sister yields; the other by seeming to yield, saves her. Again there is not a syllable to show that the yielding was at all wrong in itself. A cautious human regard for consequences is the grand motive appealed to for withstanding temptation. Lizzie tells Laura, not that the goblin's bargain is an evil deed in the sight of God, but that Jennie waned and died of their toothsome poisons. She saves her by going just so far as she safely can. What, if anything, is the moral of all this? Not "resist the devil and he will flee from you," but "cheat the devil, and he won't catch you." Now, all these sayings and silences are gravely wrong and false to a writer's true functions. With all deference then, and fully feeling that we may mistake or misconstrue, we sincerely submit that some of these poems go inexcusably beyond the bounds of that strict moral right, which every writer who hopes ever to wield influence ought to keep steadily, and sacredly in view. We are emboldened to speak thus plainly, because we have some reason to believe that these things have grated on other sensibilities than our own, and that our stricture embodies a considerable portion of cultivated public opinion.

In conclusion, we repeat our first expressed opinion, that Miss Rossetti is not yet entitled to take a place among to-day's poets. The question remains, whether she ever will. We do not think this book of hers settles this question. . . . She has done nothing in poetry yet of any consequence. These verses may be as well as she can do. They contain poetical passages of merit and promise, but they show also a defectiveness of versification, a falseness of ear, and occasionally a degree of affectation and triviality that, we can only hope, are not characteristic. To borrow a little of the style and technology of a sister branch of thought, the case, as now presented, can be accounted for as in essence a simple attack of the old and well-known endemic, *cacœthes scribendi.* Probably it befell her at the usual early age. Only instead of the run of gushing girls, we have Dante Gabriel Rossetti's sister, Jean Ingelow's

---

Algernon Charles Swinburne, in a poem to Rossetti:

A BALLAD OF APPEAL.

TO CHRISTINA G. ROSSETTI.

Song wakes with every wakening year
  From hearts of birds that only feel
Brief spring's deciduous flower-time near:
  And song more strong to help or heal
  Shall silence worse than winter seal?
From love-lit thought's remurmuring cave
The notes that rippled, wave on wave,
  Were clear as love, as faith were strong;
And all souls blessed the soul that gave
  Sweet water from the well of song.

All hearts bore fruit of joy to hear,
  All eyes felt mist upon them steal
For joy's sake, trembling toward a tear,
  When, loud as marriage-bells that peal,
  Or flutelike soft, or keen like steel,
Sprang the sheer music; sharp or grave,
We heard the drift of winds that drave,
  And saw, swept round by ghosts in throng,
Dark rocks, that yielded, where they clave,
  Sweet water from the well of song.

Blithe verse made all the dim sense clear
  That smiles of babbling babes conceal:
Prayer's perfect heart spake here: and here
  Rose notes of blameless woe and weal,
  More soft than this poor song's appeal.

Where orchards bask, where cornfields wave,
They dropped like rains that cleanse and lave,
  And scattered all the year along,
Like dewfall on an April grave,
  Sweet water from the well of song.

Ballad, go bear our prayer, and crave
Pardon, because thy lowlier stave
  Can do this plea no right, but wrong.
Ask nought beside thy pardon, save
  Sweet water from the well of song.

Algernon Charles Swinburne, in A Midsummer Holiday and Other Poems, *Chatto & Windus, Piccadilly, 1884.*

intimate friend, and a young lady of intelligence and education, constantly in contact with real literary society, and—what is thoroughly evident in this book—read in our best poets. Add all these complicating symptoms, and is there not something plausible about the diagnosis? We do not say, observe, and do not mean to say, that this is Miss Rossetti's case; only all she has done so far seems explicable on this hypothesis. For ourselves, we lean to the view that she will do more. We judge hers a strong, sensuous, impulsive, earnest, inconsiderate nature, that sympathizes well, feels finely, keeps true to itself at bottom, but does not pause to make sure that others must, as well as may, enter into the spirit that underlies her utterances, and so buries her meaning sometimes beyond Champollion's own powers of deciphering. But her next book must determine how much is to be ascribed to talent, and how much to practice and good models; and show us whether genius or gilt edges separate her from the οἱ πολλοί.

The Dial (essay date 1895)

SOURCE: "Christina Georgina Rossetti," in *The Dial,* Chicago, Vol. XVIII, No. 206, January 16, 1895, pp. 37-9.

[*In the following unsigned essay, the critic praises three of Rossetti's volumes of poetry, comparing her literary achievement to that of Elizabeth Barrett Browning.*]

The last day of the year just ended brought news of the death of Miss Rossetti, the youngest of that famous quartette of brothers and sisters of whom Mr. W. M. Rossetti is now left the sole survivor. Maria Francesca, who died in 1876, was the oldest of the four, having first seen the light in 1827. Then came Dante Gabriel in 1828, William Michael in 1829, and Christina Georgina in 1830. Miss Rossetti gave early evidence of her poetic talents, as is shown by the privately-printed volume of *Verses,* dated 1847. In 1850, with her brothers, she wrote for the famous *Germ,* over the pseudonymous signature of "Ellen Alleyne." It was not, however, until 1862 that she took her destined place among the greater Victorian poets, with *Goblin Market and Other Poems.* That volume was followed, in 1866, by *The Prince's Progress and Other Poems,* and, in 1881, by *A Pageant and Other Poems.* It is upon the contents of these three collections that Miss Rossetti's reputation must rest, although she did a considerable amount of other literary work. Before discussing the character of her poems, we may dispose of the other books by a simple enumeration. *Commonplace and Other Short Stories* (1870) and *Sing-Song: A Nursery Rhyme-Book* (1872) are titles that speak for themselves. *Speaking Likenesses,* a volume of "quasi-allegorical prose," and *Annus Domini: A Prayer for Every Day in the Year,* both bear the date 1874. *Seek and Find, Called to the Saints,* and *Letter and Spirit,* three religious works in prose, date from 1879, 1881, and 1883, respectively; while *Time Flies,* a reading diary in alternate verse and prose, appeared in 1885, and was, we believe, her last published volume. These devotional books, which have both found

and deserved a large and appreciative audience, are distinctly out of the common, but the spirit which finds expression in them finds utterance still more intense and rapturous in the three volumes of song to which we now turn.

It is not the least of the glories of English poetry that two women should be numbered among the singers whom we most love and honor. It is perhaps idle to inquire whether Mrs. Browning or Miss Rossetti is to be esteemed the greater poet; the one thing certain is that no other English woman is to be named in the same breath with them. These two stand far apart from the throng, lifted above it by inspiration and achievement, and no account of the greater poetry of our century can ignore them. If there is something more instinctive, more inevitable in impulse, about the work of Mrs. Browning, there is more of restraint and of artistic finish about the work of Miss Rossetti. The test of popularity would assign to the former the higher rank, just as it would place Byron above Keats and Coleridge, or above Wordsworth and Shelley; but the critic has better tests than the noisy verdicts of the multitude, and those tests lessen, if they do not quite do away with, the seeming disparity between the fame of the two women.

The longer pieces which introduce Miss Rossetti's three volumes are not the most successful of their contents. It is rather to the lyrics, ballads, and sonnets that the lover of poetry will turn to find her at her best. Who, for example, could once read and ever forget such a sonnet as **"Rest"**?

> O Earth, lie heavily upon her eyes;
>   Seal her sweet eyes weary of watching, Earth;
>   Lie close around her; leave no room for mirth
> With its harsh laughter, nor for sound of sighs.
> She hath no questions, she hath no replies,
>   Hushed in and curtained with a blessed dearth
>   Of all that irked her from the hour of birth,
> With stillness that is almost Paradise.
> Darkness more clear than noonday holdeth her,
>   Silence more musical than any song;
> Even her very heart hath ceased to stir:
>   Until the morning of Eternity
>   Her rest shall not begin nor end, but be;
> And when she wakes she will not think it long.

Or who could escape the haunting quality of such a lyric as this:

> When I am dead, my dearest,
>   Sing no sad songs for me;
> Plant thou no roses at my head,
>   Nor shady cypress-tree;
> Be the green grass above me
>   With showers and dewdrops wet;
> And if thou wilt, remember,
>   And if thou wilt, forget.
>
> I shall not see the shadows,
>   I shall not feel the rain;

I shall not hear the nightingale
  Sing on, as if in pain:
And dreaming through the twilight
  That doth not rise nor set,
Haply I may remember,
  And haply may forget.

The poem just quoted can hardly fail to recall, in feeling, thought, and measure, Mr. Swinburne's "Rococo," and thus emphasizes the spiritual relationship of the author to the poets of the group sometimes styled "Pre-Raphaelite." Similarly, the perfect lyric called **"Dream-Land"** is clearly akin to "The Garden of Proserpine," and it is not difficult to discern the same sort of kinship between Miss Rossetti's **"Up-Hill"** and Mr. Swinburne's "The Pilgrims." Now the point to be noted is that all three of Miss Rossetti's poems were published in the volume of 1862, while the three Swinburnian poems date from several years later. There is, of course, no question of imitation—in each case what remains a simple theme with the one poet is elaborated into a symphony by the other—but it is difficult to escape the conclusion that the man was influenced by the woman in all three of the cases. Particularly with **"Up-Hill"** and "The Pilgrims," we note the common use of the dialogue form and the absolute identity of the austere ethical motive.

Miss Rossetti's verses sometimes suggest those of other poets, but we always feel that her art is distinctly her own. The divine simplicity of Blake is echoed in such a stanza as

What can lambkins do
  All the keen night through?
Nestle by their woolly mother,
  The careful ewe.

The melting, almost cloying, sweetness of the Tennysonian lyric meets us in these verses:

Come to me in the silence of the night;
  Come in the speaking silence of a dream;
Come with soft rounded cheeks and eyes as
  bright
    As sunlight on a stream;
      Come back in tears,
O memory, hope, love of finished years.

As for the influence of the great Italian, which shaped so powerfully the thought of every member of the Rossetti family, it is less tangible here than in the work of her greater brother, yet to it must be attributed much of the tenderness and the pervasive mysticism of her poems. It is perhaps most apparent in the two sonnet-sequences, **"Monna Innominata"** and **"Later Life,"** both included in the volume of 1881. And the influence of that brother who bore the sacred name of the Florentine is likewise intangible but pervasive. We get a glimpse of it in **"Amor Mundi,"** for example, and in many a *vanitas vanitatum* strain. But we must repeat that Miss Rossetti's genius was too original to be chargeable with anything more than that assimilation of spiritual influence from which no poet can hope wholly to escape, and which links together in one golden chain the poetic tradition of the ages.

If in most of the provinces of the lyric realm Miss Rossetti's verse challenges comparison with that of our greater singers, it is in the religious province that the challenge is most imperative and her mastery most manifest. Not in Keble or Newman, not in Herbert or Vaughan, do we find a clearer or more beautiful expression of the religious sentiment than is dominant in Miss Rossetti's three books. In this respect, at least, she is unsurpassed, and perhaps unequalled, by any of her contemporaries. In her devotional pieces there is no touch of affectation, artificiality, or insincerity. Such poems as **"The Three Enemies"** and **"Advent"** in the first volume, **"Paradise"** and **"The Lowest Place"** in the second, and many of the glorious lyrics and sonnets of the third, will long be treasured among the religious classics of the English language. Perhaps the poet's highest achievement in this kind is the **"Old and New Year Ditties"** of the first volume. Some such claim, at least, has been made by no less an authority than Mr. Swinburne for the closing section of the poem.

Passing away, saith the World, passing away;
Chances, beauty, and youth sapped day by day;
Thy life never continueth in one stay.
Is the eye waxen dim, is the dark hair changing
  to gray
That hath won neither laurel nor bay?
I shall clothe myself in Spring and bud in May:
Thou, root-stricken, shalt not rebuild thy decay
On my bosom for aye.
Then I answered: Yea.

Passing away, saith my Soul, passing away;
With its burden of fear and hope, of labor and
  play;
Hearken what the past doth witness and say:
Rust in thy gold, a moth is in thine array,
A canker is in thy bud, thy leaf must decay.
At midnight, at cock-crow, at morning, one
  certain day
Lo, the Bridegroom shall come and shall not
  delay:
Watch thou and pray.
Then I answered: Yea.

Passing away, saith my God, passing away:
Winter passeth after the long delay;
New grapes on the vine, new figs on the tender
  spray,
Turtle calleth turtle in Heaven's May.
Though I tarry, wait for Me, trust Me, watch
  and pray.
Arise, come away, night is past, and lo it is day,
My love, My sister, My spouse, thou shalt hear
  Me say.
Then I answered: Yea.

It is peculiarly fitting that the author of these fervid and solemn verses, written for one New Year's season, should herself have passed away on the very eve of another.

Mackenzie Bell (essay date 1898)

SOURCE: "Devotional Prose," in *Christina Rossetti: A Biographical and Critical Study,* fourth edition, Haskell House Publishers Ltd., 1971, pp. 285-318.

[In the following excerpt, first published in 1898, Bell surveys Rossetti's works of devotional prose.]

Annus Domini, which was issued in 1874, through the publishing house of Messrs. James Parker & Co., Oxford and London, is the first in point of date of Christina Rossetti's devotional prose works, and deserves particular attention, as it presents many features showing the inception of her later devotional prose style. *Annus Domini* is called on the sub-title page 'a prayer for each day of the year, founded on a text of Holy Scripture.' Following the title-page is a brief commendatory note by the Rev. William Henry Burrows. . . . Next comes a short Prefatory Note by the author, and then two pages occupied by what she names a 'Calendar' wherein the numbers are given of certain of the prayers which presumably she considered appropriate to memorable periods of the Christian year, such as Advent, Christmas, Epiphany, Septuagesima, Lent, Passiontide, Holy Week, Easter, Ascension, Whitsuntide, Holy Trinity, Saints' Days, Feast of the Blessed Virgin, S. Michael and All Angels, Ember Weeks, and Rogation Days. Each prayer is addressed to Christ. These prayers are not so imaginative as Christina's later devotional work. Perhaps this restraining of the imagination may have arisen on her part from her deep reverence for prayer as prayer, and her feeling, once or twice expressed to me, that no human creature, however skilful, ought wantonly to embroider with his own ability petitions to the Almighty. It may also have arisen partly from the fact that her symbolism became more developed in later life. But even in this book we find her remarkable power of evoking spiritual sublimity from Biblical passages which at first sight do not appear to contain it in a great degree. As an example of her writing here page 354 may be quoted in its entirety:

Rev. xv. 4.

"Who shall not fear Thee, O Lord, and glorify Thy Name? for Thou only art Holy."

O Lord Jesus Christ, Who only art Holy, forgive, I implore Thee, forgive and purge the unholiness of Thy saints, the unholiness of Thy little ones, the unholiness of Thy penitents, the unholiness of the unconverted, the unholiness of me a sinner. God be merciful to us sinners. Amen.

Occasionally we see the influence of the Book of Common Prayer and it is not too much to say that she has sometimes caught much of its well-ordered grandeur. Perhaps there is almost an excessive realism in these words, part of a petition to Christ:

By virtue of Thy victory give us also, I entreat Thee, victory. Let Thy pierced Heart win us to love Thee, Thy torn Hands incite us to every good work, Thy wounded Feet urge us on errands of mercy, Thy crown of thorns prick us out of sloth, Thy thirst draw us to thirst after the Living Water Thou givest: let Thy life be our pattern while we live, and Thy death our triumph over death when we come to die. Amen.

But how beautiful, how full of the true rhythm of the finest English prose is the following:

O Lord Jesus Christ, King of Kings, draw, I beseech Thee, all Kings of the earth to come and worship before Thee. Bless them who for our sakes are burdened with responsibility and cares; teach us to reverence, love, and obey them in all things lawful; and in the next world of Thy goodness give them with us rest. Amen.

Seek and Find was published in 1879, and on the title-page is termed by its author 'A double series of short studies of the Benedicite.' In a 'Prefatory Note' on the succeeding page, she tells us that in writing her book she consulted the *Harmony* by the late Isaac Williams (presumably his work entitled *A Harmony of the Four Evangelists*). She goes on to say that, as she is unacquainted with either Hebrew or Greek, any 'textual elucidations' were obtained from 'some translation,' and that she discovered 'many valuable alternative readings' 'in the Margin of an ordinary Reference Bible.'

Following the 'Prefatory Note,' under the general heading of 'The Benedicite,' are five pages of small type setting forth the contents of the volume, each of the five pages being divided into three columns. . . .

The 'first series' of 'studies,' called on the sub-title-page 'Creation,' occupy one hundred and fifty-three pages; while the 'second series,' termed 'Redemption,' fill one hundred and fifty-nine pages.

In a letter to Christina, (October 8, 1879), her brother Dante Gabriel says that he finds *Seek and Find* 'full of eloquent beauties,' and then adds:

I am sorry to notice that—in my own view—it is most seriously damaged, for almost all if not for all readers, by the confusion of references in the text, which they completely smother. Surely these should all have been marginal, and not nearly so numerous. [Mr. Frederic] Shields, who was of course much interested in seeing the book, took quite the same view in this.

The volume might certainly have been better arranged. But, this objection stated, little but praise ought to be given to a work that contains so many noble prose sequences. 'It is the Spirit that quickeneth'—Christina Rossetti, without knowing Hebrew and Greek, was, nevertheless, frequently able to flash light on a Scriptural phrase, or series of phrases, owing to a devout use of her poet's intuition, for, generally speaking, she approaches even her prose work from the standpoint of a poet. Throughout *Seek and Find* her characteristic inclination towards symbolism is everywhere displayed and mainly with happy effect, although once and again, as in her disquisition on the connection between fishes and men, she appears to carry her symbolism a little too far. Perhaps the finest disquisition in the book is that on angels—a disquisition valuable not only for the ideas set forth therein, but because some of these ideas seem to be more fully the outcome of her personal experience than is usual even with Christina Rossetti. The excerpt that follows, sets forth some of these ideas:

> Since we believe that even in this life we dwell among the invisible hosts of angels,—since we hope in the life to come to rejoice and worship without end in their blessed company, let us collect what we already know of these our unseen fellows, that by considering what are their characteristics, we ourselves may be provoked unto love and to good works. (Heb. x. 24).

Seek and Find is not one of Christina Rossetti's great books, but it is not unworthy of her, and is further noticeable as exhibiting her great knowledge of the Bible.

Called to be Saints: The Minor Festivals Devotionally Studied, was published in 1881. The saints and festivals dealt with in the volume are St. Andrew, 'Apostle'; St. Thomas, 'Apostle'; St. Stephen, 'Deacon'; St. John, 'Apostle and Evangelist'; The Holy Innocents; St. Paul, 'Apostle'; The Presentation and Purification; St. Matthias, 'Apostle'; The Annunciation; St. Mark, 'Evangelist'; St. Philip and St. James the Less, 'Apostles'; St. Barnabas, 'Apostle'; St. John, 'Baptist'; St. Peter, 'Apostle'; St. James the Great, 'Apostle'; St. Bartholomew, 'Apostle'; St. Matthew, 'Apostle and Evangelist'; St. Michael and All Angels; St. Luke, 'Evangelist'; St. Simon and St. Jude, 'Apostles'; and All Saints.

Prefixed to the volume is **'The Key to my Book,'** a short essay ending with the lyric 'This near-at-hand-land' to which reference has been made at the beginning of Chapter VII. To each of the saints a separate section is given. Each of these sections is again sub-divided into brief dissertations, and in the contents each of these has a separate heading. The first of these headings is always styled 'The Sacred Text'; the second, 'Biographical Additions'; the third, 'A Prayer,' a composition written wholly by Christina Rossetti, and partly based on the characteristics of the especial saint commemorated. Then comes what is designated as 'A Memorial.' These 'memorials' are noteworthy in many ways, and are often of considerable length, the memorial of St. Andrew, for example, extending to ten pages of fairly close type. They show their author's intimate acquaintance with the Bible, and her great power in bringing the passages she cites to bear on the particular subject she has in hand. Each of the pages in these 'memorials' is divided midway into two portions. At the opening of the left-hand column are the first words of some brief commentary matter, supplied by Christina Rossetti, and printed in block type, and these commentatory words are interspersed in the left-hand column of the 'memorials' throughout the book. For purposes of example this commentatory matter in the first three pages of the memorial to St. Andrew has been given below, and

printed consecutively, but, to save space, more closely than in the author's text, asterisks being placed where breaks occur in the original:

> St. Andrew of Bethsaida * * * learns of St. John Baptist, follows Christ and abides with him that day, * * * brings to our Lord his brother, * * * on whom a new name is bestowed, * * * is called from the nets to be fisher of men, * * * is ordained Apostle.

Following each of these detached phrases, and set in the same type as the rest of the volume, are Scripture passages relating either to the Saint's history, or mainly interpreting it. In the right-hand column are text from the Bible also in usual type illustrative of, but not directly referring to, the saint. Further there is a little treatise, often most delicately phrased, relating to some flower, and to each of the saints she appropriates some particular flower. To St. Andrew, for instance, she appropriates the daisy. She adds likewise, in the case of the Apostles, a short disquisition on each particular precious stone with which she associates them, the disquisitions in their case being suggested by Rev. xxi. 14:

> And the wall of the city had twelve foundations, and in them the names of the twelve apostles of the Lamb.

She follows the order of the precious stones given in the same chapter of Revelation, verses 19 and 20, and, adopting the Ecclesiastical Calendar in the assignment of the stones, gives the jasper to St. Andrew and, proceeding in regular order, gives the amethyst, the last of the stones mentioned, to St. Jude—the latest apostle in the Ecclesiastical Calendar. Scattered throughout the prose text moreover are some of her most exquisite and solemn lyrics, fervid and intense in their piety, ecstatic in their rapture, but these, as they are discussed in Chapter VII., need not be referred to in detail here.

Following Rev. iv. 7:

> And the first beast was like a lion, and the second beast like a calf, and the third beast had a face as a man, and the fourth beast was like a flying eagle,

and the traditions of many centuries, she appropriates the fourth living creature, the eagle, to St. John, with a few words charged with fitting symbolism; while in a similar manner she gives the first living creature, a lion, to St. Mark; the third living creature, an angel, to St. Matthew; and the second living creature, an ox, to St. Luke.

The prose of **'The Key to my Book'** is full of that rhythmical beauty noticeable especially in much of her devotional prose,—perhaps because the mental qualities required in order to write such prose with a high degree of excellence, were precisely the qualities she possessed. Her simple yet sensuous mind—a mind stored with poetic imagery—found in such work a stimulus to lofty achievement. Nor, in her case, is this lofty achievement ever gained by elaborate artifice. Her arrangement and choice of words are as unartificial as the wild flowers of England, which she prefers to associate with the saints she loves, rather than the flora of Palestine. Very tender and touching are these opening words:

> How beautiful are the arms which have embraced Christ, the hands which have touched Christ, the eyes which have gazed upon Christ, the lips which have spoken with Christ, the feet which have followed Christ.

> How beautiful are the hands which have worked the works of Christ, the feet which treading in his footsteps have gone about doing good, the lips that have spread abroad his name, the lives which have been counted loss for him.

Her description of 'Hepaticas' which she allocates to Matthias is an excellent example of her admirable power of idealising a merely botanical description. Work such as this is exceedingly difficult. If ordinary language be used, then the effect is commonplace and dull. If over-much symbolism be employed, then the result seems strained and unreal. In this instance, however, the result is most successful. The passage which follows is especially pretty and fanciful:

> Hepaticas favour a light soil, and love to meet the morning sun rather than to endure a more continuously sunny exposure. They do not well bear moving, or at the least they bear it not always with indifference: an instance is quoted of one changing from blue to white when transplanted, whilst on returning to its former soil the enduring plant resumed its original tint. Humble in height, the hepatica may be termed patient in habit; for during one whole year the blossom, perfect in all its parts, lurks hidden within the bud.

> This plant belongs to the family of Anemones or Wind-flowers; and, as a wind-flower, seems all the more congruous with St. Matthias; . . . When, the lot having already fallen on him, "suddenly there came a sound from heaven as of a rushing mighty wind," that wind which "bloweth where it listeth," and on him as on the rest the Fiery Tongue of consecrating power lighted and sat.

> Kindly as the hepatica thrives amongst us, it yet is no native of England, but comes to us from Switzerland. Thus if hepaticas prefer repose, they yet submit to transference, blooming cheerfully in their allotted sphere.

Mention may be made of an exquisite little homily on violets; of her **'Prayer for Conformity to God's Will'**; and of her disquisition on **'Arbutus and Grass,'** which she designates as 'great and small,' and assigns to All Saints Day. In the discourse last-named there is one of the autobiographical touches which, when they occur in her work, are always interesting.

> Often as I have let slip what cannot be regained, two points of my own experience stand out vividly; once, when little realising how nearly I had despised my last

chance, I yet did in bare time do what must shortly have been for ever left undone; and again, when I fulfilled a promise which beyond calculation there remained but scant leisure to fulfil.

As to this passage Mr. William Rossetti has sent me the following communication:

> [Concerning] those references made by Christina in *Called to be Saints*. As to "doing in bare time what would shortly have been un-do-able," the natural inference seems to be that she did something or other in relation to a person who soon afterwards died. As to a promise which was fulfilled, but only just in time, a similar inference again suggests itself. It is just as likely as not that the incidents were in themselves of the very slightest consequence possible; for C[hristina] often bore such matters in mind, if any sort of principle seemed to be involved in them.

The last quotation that shall be made from *Called to be Saints* is from her meditation on St. Michael and All Angels, and may be said to be a complement to the passage concerning angels in *Seek and Find* lately referred to. The extracts which here follow show how deep was the spirituality of her nature.

> Now of all which is, that which is made known unto us is undoubtedly made known for our profit. Let us not fail to love God all the more because He hath given His Angels charge concerning His own to keep them in all their ways; because the armies of heaven pitch their camp around the faithful when need arises; because blessed spirits minister to the heirs of salvation; because they rejoice over one sinner that repenteth:—for all this we know assuredly, whether or not with a multitude of pious souls we solace ourselves by the thought of one Angel guardian assigned to each baptised person. . . . When it seems (as sometimes through revulsion of feeling and urgency of Satan it may seem) that our yoke is uneasy and our burden unbearable, because our life is pared down and subdued and repressed to an intolerable level: and so in one moment every instinct of our whole self revolts against our lot, and we loathe this day of quietness and of sitting still, and writhe under a sudden sense of all we have irrecoverably foregone, of the right hand, or foot, or eye cast from us, of the haltingness and maimedness of our entrance (if enter we do at last) into life,— then the Seraphim of Isaiah's vision making music in our memory revive hope in our heart.

Probably with the single exception of *The Face of the Deep, Called to be Saints* is more thoroughly and beautifully built up through symbolism than any other of Christina Rossetti's devotional books.

Lady Mount-Temple 'found joy in' *Called to be Saints* (to use Mr. Shields's happy phrase). He told this to Christina who, in a letter to him now before me, expresses her great satisfaction at hearing it.

Letter and Spirit: Notes on the Commandments, published in 1883, is dedicated

To
My Mother
in thankfulness for her
dear and honoured
example.

—a dedication specially interesting in view of some words to Mr. Shields, which may here be inserted. Writing from 'Church Hill, Birchington-on-Sea,' under date August 23, 1883, Christina says:

> Thank you for welcoming *Letter and Spirit*—my Mother's life is a far more forcible comment on the Commandments than are words of mine.

As its title is doubtless meant to indicate, *Letter and Spirit* is a treatise on the inner meaning of the Commandments. Christina places in full on the first page of her book Christ's exposition of the Decalogue as it is given in Mark xii. 28-30, and Matt. xxii. 39-40, and then quotes the entire Decalogue itself, the rest of the work being an exposition of it. The volume ends with a Harmony on I. Corinthians xiii. and in the right column parallel sayings of Jesus culled from the Gospels.

On a first glance at this book one is apt to think that, in form at least, it partakes too much of the character of the ordinary religious commentary. Not till we have looked further into it do we perceive it filled with the same qualities which have made her other devotional prose remark-

The frontispiece to Goblin Market, *from an engraving by Dante Gabriel Rossetti.*

able—the qualities I mean of symbolism and a chastened form of imagination. The original manuscript of *Letter and Spirit* is now in the possession of Mr. Fairfax Murray, and he has been good enough to allow me to examine it with some care. Like many other of her manuscripts, particularly the manuscripts of her later prose works, it is written on ordinary blue paper, quarto size, and in somewhat large handwriting, with considerable space between the lines, and with comparatively few erasures.

Letter and Spirit is the only one of her books, except *Seek and Find,* and *Speaking Likenesses,* which contains no verse of her own. It is likewise noteworthy from the fact that only two lines of verse of other writers are quoted—the lines of Bishop Heber:—

> Richer by far is the heart's adoration,
>   Dearer to God are the prayers of the poor.

Seldom in her books did she quote the verses of other poets. Probably this was because, in her case, it was so easy to write verse. But was there another reason? It is a somewhat interesting field of speculation. . . .

Nothing is more unreasonable than the opinion so often expressed and apparently truly felt that the poetic mind is deficient in practical attributes. The exact reverse is not seldom the case with the higher types of poetic genius, and certainly nothing could be more practical than the exhortations of Christina Rossetti in this book. She refers to England by name, and is persuaded 'that our national honour, wealth, credit, already impaired' probably implies, 'unless we repent' the commencement 'of our chastisement.' By and by she remarks that it is 'no light offence to traduce the dead.' If we believe that every man and woman born into the world since its beginning still lives a life unbroken by death—still retains 'one continuity of individual existence from birth to this moment, from this moment to the Day of Judgment'—if we feel assured that, with them, we shall ourselves be judged, then must we realise in full that to cherish 'malice' towards them is 'simply devilish'—then must we realise what 'a solemn thing it is to write history'; and she concludes by this personal reference, striking in its graceful homeliness:

> I feel it a solemn thing to write conjectural sketches of Scripture characters; filling up outlines as I fancy, but cannot be certain, may possibly have been the case: making one figure stand for this virtue and another for that vice, attributing motives and colouring conduct. Yet I hope my mistakes will be forgiven me, while I do most earnestly desire every one of my personages to be in truth superior to my sketch.

We have likewise some carefully thought out remarks on the arrangement of daily life; on the relative importance of rest and work; and on what really constitutes work, what rest.

The beautiful *Harmony,* alluded to already, opens with a little note, in which she tells her readers that it 'was in part if not wholly suggested to me,' and though the person who made the suggestion is not certainly known, it was most probably her sister Maria.

She approaches, as said before, in ***Letter and Spirit*** more nearly than in her other writings to theological disquisition. She was not a professed theologian. She had too distinct a bias to the symbolical—to the poetic—and was too little touched by the merely intellectual, to excel in theological disquisition. Occasionally, however, particularly in her prose devotional works, we come upon passages in which her natural commonsense and her natural eloquence enable her to deal with themes more or less theological with much power.

Time Flies: A Reading Diary, with the appropriate motto 'A day's march nearer home' from James Montgomery, was published in 1885. It was dedicated thus:

To
My Beloved Example, Friend,
MOTHER.
'Her children arise up, and call her blessed.'

Time Flies has the distinction of containing more frequent personal references than any other of her books, unless it be ***The Face of the Deep.*** Indeed it may almost be called a kind of spiritual autobiography. For even when there are no obvious personal allusions many of the original thoughts and pregnant sayings that enrich the book must have had their root in her own spiritual experience. Probably having to write something about each day in the year, something that must necessarily be short, and that ought also to be concise and pithy, she fell back, unconsciously, on her own wide experience, wide, not in the outer but in the inner sense. Be this as it may, what has just been said gives an added and peculiar value to ***Time Flies,*** altogether apart from the remarkable literary merit of the book.

As showing Christina Rossetti's breadth of mind and ample charity, despite her firm and unwavering faith not only in religion but in dogma, it is worthy of note, that very often in the course of these books we encounter passages which none could have written but a woman who had thought for herself, and who had not reached her present standpoint without much deep meditation. Seldom does she allow her passion for symbolism to carry her too far, and thus her symbolism rarely becomes, as we have often seen it become in the hands of lesser writers, something almost ridiculous. This in itself is a great achievement. For, as may easily be imagined, in a volume of brief devotional essays such as this 'reading diary' is in effect, it is most difficult to discuss in a few words, and without a sense of the ridiculous, such questions, for instance, as whether the association of 'tapers and bonfires' with St. Blaise arose or did not arise out of a quibble on his name. To January 24, she allocates the sonnet beginning:

> 'Give Me thy heart.' I said: Can I not make
>   Abundant sacrifice to Him Who gave
>   Life, health, possessions, friends, of all I have,
> All but my heart once given?

terming the sonnet 'devotional.' She further adds that a 'friend' gave it to her many years before, and that she now reproduces it from memory. The 'friend' was James Collinson.

Sometimes Christina Rossetti introduces in a characteristic manner her opinions respecting subjects only indirectly connected with the theme which she is treating at the moment. Thus under date of February 5, and in relation to the Feast of St. Agatha, Virgin Martyr (who is supposed to have 'suffered death' about the year 251) she tells how Catania and Palermo claim to be the birthplace of 'this heroine of piety'; how Quintianus, 'Consular of Sicily' loved Agatha; and how, when he found that Agatha remained a Christian and repelled his overtures, his affection towards her became repugnance. She narrates further how he 'exhausted cruelty and torture' on her in vain, and how subsequently Agatha died in prison. Then she discusses anew, with simplicity and force, the familiar problem of how far a man or a woman may differ on important points and yet love one another. Her conclusion is that much real affection may exist despite important differences of opinion, and she closes her remarks by quoting St. Paul's words at Athens 'I found an altar with this inscription, "To the Unknown God." '

Time Flies contains many sayings of Christina's full of striking commonsense such as this: 'For many are they of whom the world is both "not worthy" and ignorant,' or this under date of February 18, where she adduces some excellent lessons from the 'quaint remark' of a friend who said, concerning her own—not Christina Rossetti's—feet, that it was a good thing they were so large for thus anyone could wear her boots. Then we have a neat and sensible little homily, with considerable freshness, on the 'square man in a round hole.' Later we have a cheerful little exhortation on the subject of 'dirt' as the symbol of 'something out of place.' Still later there is a timely disquisition on the relative duties of hospitality in which she points out that

> In many cases the person who annoys and the person who is annoyed are both in the right, or (if you please) are both in the wrong—

illustrating her proposition by the differing standards of courtesy of an Arab chief and his English guest.

In response to an enquiry as to whether the poem allocated to February 15 beginning

> My love whose heart is tender, said to me,

and ending

> And still she keeps my heart and keeps its key,

refers to her sister, her younger brother writes to me:

> I certainly regard it as applying to Maria. The 2nd line, "a moon lacks light" &c., is conclusive to me. Maria had a very round face, and Christina was much

in the habit of calling her Moon, Moony, &c. I have no doubt that Maria on some occasion made this her cue for saying something very like what appears in the poem. However I never knew her to call C[hristina] her "Sun," or anything of the sort.

At February 8 are some subtle and carefully differenti-ated remarks respecting heaven and music, in the course of which Christina points out that music to be music must not be monotonous, and that therefore 'a heaven of music,' even if that conception of heaven be not some-what narrow and unreasonable, would be a place of variety, not of monotony. Under date of March 28 and April 16, she shows conclusively that, what she aptly calls physical 'grievous besetments,' may not relatively be disadvantageous; she also at the second date avers how even our most cherished opinions almost inevitably are modified by time, drawing therefrom this cheerful moral:

> If even time lasts long enough to reverse a verdict of time, how much more eternity?

> Let us take courage, secondary as we may for the present appear. Of ourselves likewise the comparative aspect will fade away, the positive will remain.

At March 7 we meet with a few words about Vivia Per-petua, the martyr, on the subject of whose pathetic career the author of *Nearer my God to Thee* wrote a drama full of force and poetical enthusiasm. Christina Rossetti's special powers of reasoning are admirably used in her moralisings on the Feast of St. George, Martyr. The entry under May 8 has peculiar interest, and reveals her love of William Blake:

> There is a design by William Blake symbolic of the Resurrection. In it I behold the descending soul and the arising body rushing together in an indissoluble embrace: and the design, among all I recollect to have seen, stands alone in expressing the rapture of that reunion:

—an opinion worth quoting when we recollect how great, apparently, was the influence of Blake on her own work, though it is right to add what Mr. William Rossetti tells me:

> It would I think be an error to suppose that C[hristina] at any time read B[lake] much or constantly—certainly she prized the little she did read.

The entry under May 8 closes with a suitable quotation from Cayley's translation of Dante's 'Paradise,' Canto XIV.

Under date of August 30 tact is discussed shrewdly. Her entry for the following day, (where she dwells on the resemblance, once pointed out to her, between a grey parrot and an elephant) seems at first sight to have a quality akin to humour, were it not for the grim seriousness of the words with which she concludes:

> It is startling to reflect that you and I may be walking about unabashed and jaunty, whilst our fellows observe very queer likenesses amongst us.

> Any one may be the observer: and equally any one may be the observed.

> Liable to such casualties, I advise *myself* to assume a modest and unobtrusive demeanour.

> I do not venture to advise *you.*

In a right sense she had a fearlessness, almost a contempt of current opinion, and, under date of September 30, she recalls with approval the saying of Jerome to the lady Asella: 'I know we may arrive at heaven equally with a bad, as a good name.' There is deep spiritual teaching in the following words which occur under date of December 20:

> St. Thomas doubted.

> Scepticism is a degree of unbelief: equally therefore it is a degree of belief. It may be a degree of faith.

> St. Thomas doubted, but simultaneously he loved. Whence it follows that his case was all along hopeful.

The Face of the Deep: a Devotional Commentary on the Apocalypse has as motto 'Thy judgments are a great deep'—Psalm xxxvi. 6. It was dedicated

To
MY MOTHER
for the first time
to her
beloved, revered, cherished memory,

and was published in 1892 by the Society for Promoting Christian Knowledge.

In the simple and touching account given by Mr. Will-iam Rossetti (in his memoir of Dante Gabriel) of the early education of his brother and sisters we are told how their good mother instructed them in the Bible, and in this connection the Apocalypse is especially men-tioned. There is therefore fair ground for supposing that Christina Rossetti's knowledge of the Book of the Rev-elation, and her fondness for it, had their origin in very early days, probably, in Mr. William Rossetti's opinion, by the age of eight or nine. Should such be the case, and the inference is just, it is striking and beautiful to think that her last, and in some respects her greatest literary achievement, was a commentary on the Book she had loved as a child.

The Face of the Deep deals systematically with the entire *Book of the Revelation of St. John,* a chapter in the com-mentary being devoted to each Chapter of the Book. One, two, or three verses of the chapter under consideration are placed in block type, being followed by a paragraph or paragraphs of comment.

Two and a half, or perhaps three years elapsed between the date at which she first commenced to write her treatise and the date on which she handed the completed manuscript to her publishers.

The commentary, as indicated by the sub-title, is of course largely devotional. No effort of set purpose is made on the author's part to expound prophecy, nor does she make any fixed attempt at exegesis. Throughout, the reader is impressed by her childlike humility and by her unconsciousness of the fact that she possessed, in addition to her other gifts, no small share of miscellaneous learning. Very frequently when a word or phrase suggests something to awaken her lyrical gift, she breaks forth into snatches of exquisite song. Throughout the commentary we have also many noble prose litanies (to use the apt word by which Mr. Shields spoke of them to me). In these sequences her rich diction and fine ear for the rhythm of prose enable her to excel. Some of these, indeed most of them, are choice examples of rhythmically-balanced and delicate prose. Once and again, indeed, she reaches such a high level of style that her work is comparable with the finest masterpieces of prose composition in the English language—with the work, for example, of the translators of the authorised version of the English Bible of James the First's time—of the compilers of *The Book of Common Prayer*—and with great writers like Hooker and Jeremy Taylor.

Her 'Prefatory Note,' with its reference to her sister Maria, . . . is couched in that characteristic vein of dignified humility (the phrase is used for lack of a better) with which students of her writings are familiar. This, indeed, is the secret of her wide influence. Very original likewise are the opening words wherein she implies that if she cannot 'dive' and 'bring up pearls' she may at least 'collect amber.' 'Though,' she adds, 'I fail to identify Paradisaical "bdellium," I still may hope to search out beauties of the "onyx stone." ' These words are the keynote of the entire commentary.

Of a commentary of such considerable length as *The Face of the Deep,* (extending to five hundred and fifty-two pages) it is manifestly undesirable, even if space permitted, to give a full and detailed analysis. . . .

She bases her opening sentences on the first two verses of chapter i. of the Revelation, and writes:

> "Things which must shortly come to pass."—At the end of 1800 years we are still repeating this "shortly," because it is the word of God and the testimony of Jesus Christ; thus starting in fellowship of patience with that blessed John who owns all Christians as his brethren (*see* ver. 9),'

so emphasising anew what she regards as the central idea of the book. In the course of her remarks on Rev. i. 12-16, we have one of the first outbursts of devotional feeling which, noticeable in all Christina Rossetti's religious works, are especially so in *The Face of the Deep*. And these outbursts of devotional—of ecstatic feeling grew in intensity as she proceeded in the writing of this treatise—as the sublimity of her theme gradually took a deeper hold of her mind. Nothing shows more clearly her essential sanity, her essential commonsense—qualities in which her mind was akin to the greatest minds of all ages—than that never throughout *The Face of the Deep* has she once departed either from sanity or commonsense. And remembering the temptations which the obscurity, as well as the abounding symbolism of the theme, must have had for her, who was at once so devout, so poetic, and so prone to symbolism, to say this of *The Face of the Deep* is to say much, and yet not to laud it unduly.

Paul Elmer More (essay date 1904)

SOURCE: "Christina Rossetti," in *The Atlantic Monthly,* Vol. 94, No. 6, December, 1904, pp. 815-21.

[*In the following essay, More extols Rossetti's "feminine genius" as displayed in her poetry.*]

Probably the first impression one gets from reading the *Complete Poetical Works* of Christina Rossetti, now collected and edited by her brother, Mr. W. M. Rossetti, is that she wrote altogether too much, and that it was a doubtful service to her memory to preserve so many poems purely private in their nature. The editor, one thinks, might well have shown himself more "reverent of her strange simplicity." For page after page we are in the society of a spirit always refined and exquisite in sentiment, but without any guiding and restraining artistic impulse; she never drew to the shutters of her soul, but lay open to every wandering breath of heaven. In comparison with the works of the more creative poets her song is like the continuous lisping of an Æolian harp beside the music elicited by cunning fingers. And then, suddenly, out of this sweet monotony, moved by some stronger, clearer breeze of inspiration, there sounds a strain of wonderful beauty and flawless perfection, unmatched in its own kind in English letters. An anonymous purveyor of anecdotes has recently told how one of these more exquisite songs called forth the enthusiasm of Swinburne. It was just after the publication of *Goblin Market and Other Poems,* and in a little company of friends that erratic poet and critic started to read aloud from the volume. Turning first to the devotional paraphrase which begins with "Passing away, saith the World, passing away," he chanted the lines in his own emphatic manner, then laid the book down with a vehement gesture. Presently he took it up again, and a second time read the poem through, even more impressively. "By God!" he exclaimed at the end, "that's one of the finest things ever written!"

> Passing away, saith the World, passing away:
> Chances, beauty, and youth, sapped day by day,
> Thy life never continueth in one stay.
> Is the eye waxen dim, is the dark hair changing
>   to gray,
> That hath won neither laurel nor bay?
> I shall clothe myself in Spring and bud in
>   May:

Thou, root-stricken, shalt not rebuild thy decay
On my bosom for aye.
Then I answered: Yea.

Passing away, saith my Soul, passing away:
With its burden of fear and hope, of labor and
    play,
Hearken what the past doth witness and say:
Rust in thy gold, a moth is in thine array,
A canker is in thy bud, thy leaf must decay.
At midnight, at cockcrow, at morning, one cer-
    tain day
Lo the Bridegroom shall come and shall not
    delay;
Watch thou and pray.
Then I answered: Yea.

Passing away, saith my God, passing away:
Winter passeth after the long delay:
New grapes on the vine, new figs on the tender
    spray,
Turtle calleth turtle in Heaven's May.
Though I tarry, wait for Me, trust Me, watch
    and pray:
Arise, come away, night is past and lo it is day:
My love, My sister, My spouse, thou shalt hear
    Me say.
Then I answered: Yea.

And Swinburne, somewhat contrary to his wont, was right. Purer inspiration, less troubled by worldly motives, than these verses cannot easily be found. Nor would it be difficult to discover in their brief compass most of the qualities that lend distinction to Christina Rossetti's work. Even her monotone, which after long continuation becomes monotony, affects one here as a subtle device heightening the note of subdued fervor and religious resignation; the repetition of the rhyming vowel creates the feeling of a secret expectancy cherished through the weariness of a frustrate life. If there is any excuse for publishing the many poems that express the mere unlifted, unvaried prayer of her heart, it is because their monotony may prepare the mind for the strange artifice of this solemn chant. But such a preparation demands more patience than a poet may justly claim from the ordinary reader. Better would be a volume of selections from her works, including a number of poems of this character. It would stand, in its own way, supreme in English literature,—as pure and fine an expression of the feminine genius as the world has yet heard.

It is, indeed, as the flower of strictly feminine genius that Christina Rossetti should be read and judged. She is one of a group of women who brought this new note into Victorian poetry,—Louisa Shore, Jean Ingelow, rarely Mrs. Browning, and, I may add, Mrs. Meynell. She is like them, but of a higher, finer strain than they . . . , and I always think of her as of her brother's Blessed Damozel, circled with a company of singers, yet holding herself aloof in chosen loneliness of passion. She, too, has not quite ceased to yearn toward earth:—

And still she bowed herself and stooped
    Out of the circling charm;
Until her bosom must have made
    The bar she leaned on warm,
And the lilies lay as if asleep
    Along her bended arm.

I have likened the artlessness of much of her writing to the sweet monotony of an Æolian harp. The comparison returns as expressing also the purely feminine spirit of her inspiration. There is in her a passive surrender to the powers of life, a religious acquiescence, which wavers between a plaintive pathos and a sublime exultation of faith. The great world, with its harsh indifference for the weak, passes over her as a ruinous gale rushes over a sequestered wood-flower; she bows her head, humbled but not broken, nor ever forgetful of her gentle mission,—

And strong in patient weakness till the end.

She bends to the storm, yet no one, not the great mystics nor the greater poets who cry out upon the sound and fury of life, is more constantly impressed by the vanity and fleeting insignificance of the blustering power, or more persistently looks for consolation and joy from another source. But there is a difference. Read the masculine poets who have heard this mystic call of the spirit, and you feel yourself in the presence of a strong will that has grasped the world, and, finding it insufficient, deliberately casts it away; and there is no room for pathetic regret in their ruthless determination to renounce. But this womanly poet does not properly renounce at all, she passively allows the world to glide away from her. The strength of her genius is endurance:—

She stands there like a beacon through the
    night,
    A pale clear beacon where the storm-drift is—
She stands alone, a wonder deathly-white:
She stands there patient, nerved with inner
    might,
    Indomitable in her feebleness,
Her face and will athirst against the light.

It is characteristic of her feminine disposition that the loss of the world should have come to her first of all in the personal relation of love. And here we must signalize the chief service of the editor toward his sister. It was generally known in a vague way, indeed it was easy to surmise as much from her published work, that Christina Rossetti bore with her always the sadness of unfulfilled affection. In the introductory Memoir her brother has now given a sufficiently detailed account of this matter to remove all ambiguity. I am not one to wish that the reserves and secret emotions of an author should be displayed for the mere gratification of the curious; but in this case the revelation would seem to be justified as a needed explanation of poems which she herself was willing to publish. Twice, it appears, she gave her love, and both times drew back in a kind of tremulous awe from the last step. The first affair began in 1848, before she was eighteen, and ran its course in about two years. The man was one James

Collinson, an artist of mediocre talent who had connected himself with the Preraphaelite Brotherhood. He was originally a Protestant, but had become a Roman Catholic. Then, as Christina refused to ally herself to one of that faith, he compliantly abandoned Rome for the Church of England. His conscience, however, which seems from all accounts to have been of a flabby consistency, troubled him in the new faith, and he soon reverted to Catholicism. Christina then drew back from him finally. It is not so easy to understand why she refused the second suitor, with whom she became intimately acquainted about 1860, and whom she loved in her own retiring fashion until the day of her death. This was Charles Bagot Cayley, a brother of the famous Cambridge mathematician, himself a scholar and in a small way a poet. Some idea of the man may be obtained from a notice of him written by Mr. W. M. Rossetti for the *Athenæum* after his death. "A more complete specimen than Mr. Charles Cayley," says Mr. Rossetti, "of the abstracted scholar in appearance and manner—the scholar who constantly lives an inward and unmaterial life, faintly perceptive of external facts and appearances—could hardly be conceived. He united great sweetness to great simplicity of character, and was not less polite than unworldly." One might suppose that such a temperament was peculiarly fitted to join with that of the secluded poetess, and so, to judge from her many love poems, it actually was. Of her own heart or of his there seems to have been no doubt in her mind. Even in her most rapturous visions of heaven, like the yearning cry of the Blessed Damozel, the memory of that stilled passion often breaks out:—

> How should I rest in Paradise,
> Or sit on steps of heaven alone?
> If Saints and Angels spoke of love,
> Should I not answer from my throne,
> Have pity upon me, ye my friends,
> For I have heard the sound thereof?

She seems even not to have been unfamiliar with the hope of joy, and I like to believe that her best-known lyric of gladness, "My heart is like a singing bird," was inspired by the early dawning of this passion. But the hope and the joy soon passed away and left her only the solemn refrain of acquiescence: "Then I answered: Yea." Her brother can give no sufficient explanation of this refusal on her part to accept the happiness almost in her hand, though he hints at lack of religious sympathy between the two. Some inner necessity of sorrow and resignation, one almost thinks, drew her back in both cases, some perception that the real treasure of her heart lay not in this world:—

> A voice said, "Follow, follow:" and I rose
>   And followed far into the dreamy night,
>   Turning my back upon the pleasant light.
> It led me where the bluest water flows,
> And would not let me drink: where the corn
>   grows
>   I dared not pause, but went uncheered by
>   sight
>   Or touch: until at length in evil plight

> It left me, wearied out with many woes.
> Some time I sat as one bereft of sense:
>   But soon another voice from very far
>   Called, "Follow, follow:" and I rose
>   again.
>   Now on my night has dawned a blessed
>   star:
>   Kind steady hands my sinking steps sus-
>   tain,
> And will not leave me till I go from hence.

It might seem that here was a spirit of renunciation akin to that of the more masculine mystics; indeed, a great many of her poems are, unconsciously I presume, almost a paraphrase of that recurring theme of the Imitation: "Nolle consolari ab aliqua creatura," and again: "Amore igitur Creatoris, amorem hominis superavit; et pro humano solatio, divinum beneplacitum magis elegit." She, too, was unwilling to find consolation in any creature, and turned from the love of man to the love of the Creator; yet a little reading of her exquisite hymns will show that this renunciation has more the nature of surrender than of deliberate choice:—

> He broke my will from day to day;
> He read my yearnings unexprest,
> And said them nay.

The world is withheld from her by a power above her will, and always this power stands before her in that peculiarly personal form which it assumes in the feminine mind. Her faith is a mere transference to heaven of a love that terrifies her in its ruthless earthly manifestation; and the passion of her life is henceforth a yearning expectation of the hour when the Bridegroom shall come and she shall answer, Yea. Nor is the earthly source of this love forgotten; it abides with her as a dream which often is not easily distinguished from its celestial transmutation:—

> O dream how sweet, too sweet, too bitter sweet,
>   Whose wakening should have been in Para-
>   dise,
> Where souls brimful of love abide and meet;
>   Where thirsting longing eyes
>   Watch the slow door
> That opening, letting in, lets out no more.

> Yet come to me in dreams, that I may live
>   My very life again though cold in death:
> Come back to me in dreams, that I may give
>   Pulse for pulse, breath for breath:
>   Speak low, lean low,
> As long ago, my love, how long ago.

It is this perfectly passive attitude toward the powers that command her heart and her soul—a passivity which by its completeness assumes the misguiding semblance of a deliberate determination of life—that makes her to me the purest expression in English of the feminine genius. I know that many would think this preëminence belongs to Mrs. Browning. They would point out the narrowness of Christina Rossetti's range, and the larger aspects of woman's nature, neglected by her, which inspire some of her rival's best-known poems. To me, on the contrary, it is the very scope attempted by Mrs. Browning that prevents her from holding the place I would give to Christina Rossetti. So much of Mrs. Browning—her political ideas, her passion for reform, her scholarship—simply carries her into the sphere of the masculine poets where she suffers by an unfair comparison. She would be a better and less irritating writer without these excursions into a field for which she was not fitted. The uncouthness that so often mars her language is chiefly due to an unreconciled feud between her intellect and her heart. She had neither a woman's wise passivity nor a man's controlling will. Even within the range of strictly feminine powers her genius is not simple and typical. And here I must take refuge in a paradox which is like enough to carry but little conviction. Nevertheless, it is the truth. I mean to say that probably most women will regard Mrs. Browning as the better type of their sex, whereas to men the honor will seem to belong to Miss Rossetti; and that the judgment of a man in this matter is more conclusive than a woman's. This is a paradox, I admit, yet its solution is simple. Women will judge a poetess by her inclusion of the larger human nature, and will resent the limiting of her range to the qualities that we look upon as peculiarly feminine. The passion of Mrs. Browning, her attempt to control her inspiration to the demands of a shaping intellect, her questioning and answering, her larger aims, in a word, her effort to create,—all these will be set down to her credit by women who are as appreciative of such qualities as men, and who will not be annoyed by the false tone running through them. Men, on the contrary, are apt, in accepting a woman's work or in creating a female character, to be interested more in the traits and limitations which distinguish her from her masculine complement. They care more for the *idea* of woman, and less for woman as merely a human being. Thus, for example, I should not hesitate to say that Thackeray's heroines are more womanly than George Eliot's,—though I am aware of the ridicule to which such an opinion lays me open; and for the same reason I hold that Christina Rossetti is a more complete exemplar of feminine genius, and, as being more perfect in her own sphere, a better poet than Mrs. Browning. That disconcerting sneer of Edward FitzGerald's, which so enraged Robert Browning, would never have occurred to him, I think, in the case of Miss Rossetti.

There is a curious comment on this contrast in the introduction to Christina Rossetti's **"Monna Innominata,"** a sonnet-sequence in which she tells her own story in the supposed person of an early Italian lady. "Had the great poetess of our own day and nation," she says, "only been unhappy instead of happy, her circumstances would have invited her to bequeath to us, in lieu of the *Portuguese Sonnets,* an inimitable 'donna innominata' drawn not from fancy, but from feeling, and worthy to occupy a niche beside Beatrice and Laura." Now this sonnet-sequence of Miss Rossetti's is far from her best work, and holds a lower rank in every way than that passionate self-revelation of Mrs. Browning's; yet to read these confessions of the two poets together is a good way to get at the division between their spirits. In Miss Rossetti's sonnets all those

feminine traits I have dwelt on are present to a marked, almost an exaggerated, degree. They are harmonious within themselves, and filled with a quiet ease; only the higher inspiration is lacking to them in comparison with her **"Passing Away,"** and other great lyrics. In Mrs. Browning, on the contrary, one cannot but feel a disturbing element. The very tortuousness of her language, the straining to render her emotion in terms of the intellect, introduces a quality which is out of harmony with the ground theme of feminine surrender. More than that, this submission to love, if looked at more closely, is itself in large part such as might proceed from a man as well as from a woman, so that there results an annoying confusion of masculine and feminine passion. Take, for instance, the twenty-second of the *Portuguese Sonnets,* one of the most perfect in the series:—

> When our two souls stand up erect and strong,
> Face to face, drawing nigher and nigher,
> Until the lengthening wings break into fire
> At either curvèd point,—What bitter wrong
> Can earth do to us, that we should not long
> Be here contented? Think. In mounting
>   higher,
> The angels would press on us, and aspire
> To drop some golden orb of perfect song
> Into our deep, dear silence. Let us stay
> Rather on earth, Beloved,—where the unfit
> Contrarious moods of men recoil away
> And isolate pure spirits, and permit
> A place to stand and love in for a day,
> With darkness and the death-hour rounding it.

That is noble verse, undoubtedly. The point is that it might just as well have been written by a man to a woman as the contrary; it would, for example, fit perfectly well into Dante Gabriel Rossetti's *House of Life.* There is here no passivity of soul; the passion is not that of acquiescence, but of determination to press to the quick of love. Only, perhaps, a certain falsetto in the tone (if the meaning of that word may be so extended) shows that, after all, it was written by a woman, who in adopting the masculine pitch loses something of fineness and exquisiteness.

A single phrase of the sonnet, that "deep, dear silence," links it in my mind with one of Christina Rossetti's not found in the **"Monna Innominata,"** but expressing the same spirit of resignation. It is entitled simply **"Rest:"**—

> O Earth, lie heavily upon her eyes;
>   Seal her sweet eyes weary of watching, Earth;
>   Lie close around her; leave no room for
>   mirth
> With its harsh laughter, nor for sound of sighs.
> She hath no questions, she hath no replies,
>   Hushed in and curtained with a blessed
>   dearth
>   Of all that irked her from the hour of birth;
> *With stillness that is almost Paradise.*
> *Darkness more clear than noonday holdeth her,*
>   *Silence more musical than any song;*
> Even her very heart has ceased to stir:

Until the morning of Eternity
Her rest shall not begin nor end, but be;
   And when she wakes she will not think it
     long.

Am I misguided in thinking that in this stillness, this silence more musical than any song, the feminine heart speaks with a simplicity and consummate purity such as I quite fail to hear in the *Portuguese Sonnets,* admired as those sonnets are? Nor could one, perhaps, find in all Christina Rossetti's poems a single line that better expresses the character of her genius than these exquisite words: "With stillness that is almost Paradise." That is the mood that, with the passing away of love, never leaves her; that is her religion; her acquiescent Yea, to the world and the soul and to God. Into that region of rapt stillness it seems almost a sacrilege to penetrate with inquisitive, critical mind; it is like tearing away the veil of modesty. I will not attempt to bring out the beauty of her mood by comparing it with that of the more masculine quietists, who reach out and take the kingdom of Heaven by storm, and whose prayer is, in the words of Tennyson:—

Our wills are ours, we know not how;
Our wills are ours, to make them Thine.

It will be better to quote one other poem perhaps her most perfect work artistically, and to pass on:—

"Up-Hill."

Does the road wind up-hill all the way?
   Yes, to the very end.
Will the day's journey take the whole long
     day?
   From morn to night, my friend.

But is there for the night a resting-place?
   A roof for when the slow dark hours begin.
May not the darkness hide it from my face?
   You cannot miss that inn.

Shall I meet other wayfarers at night?
   Those who have gone before.
Then must I knock, or call when just in sight?
   They will not keep you standing at that door.

Shall I find comfort, travel-sore and weak?
   Of labor you shall find the sum.
Will there be beds for me and all who seek?
   Yea, beds for all who come.

The culmination of her pathetic weariness is always this cry for rest, a cry for supreme acquiescence in the will of Heaven, troubled by no personal volition, no desire, no emotion, save only love that waits for blessed absorption. Her later years became what St. Teresa called a long "prayer of quiet;" and her brother's record of her secluded life in the refuge of his home reads like the saintly story of a cloistered nun. It might be said of her, as of one of the fathers, that she needed not to pray, for her life was an unbroken communion with God. And yet that is not

all. It is a sign of her utter womanliness that envy for the common affections of life was never quite crushed in her heart. Now and then through this monotony of resignation there wells up a sob of complaint, a note not easy, indeed, to distinguish from that *amari aliquid* of jealousy, which Thackeray, cynically, as some think, always left at the bottom of his gentlest feminine characters. The fullest expression of this feeling is in one of her longer poems, **"The Lowest Room,"** which contrasts the life of two sisters, one of whom chooses the ordinary lot of woman with home and husband and children, while the other learns, year after tedious year, the consolation of lonely patience. The spirit of the poem is not entirely pleasant. The resurgence of personal envy is a little disconcerting; and the only comfort to be derived from it is the proof that under different circumstances Christina Rossetti might have given expression to the more ordinary lot of contented womanhood as perfectly as she sings the pathos and hope of the cloistered life. Had that first voice, which led her "where the bluest water flows," suffered her also to quench the thirst of her heart, had not that second voice summoned her to follow, this might have been. But literature, I think, would have lost in her gain. As it is, we must recognize that the vision of fulfilled affection and of quiet home joys still troubled her, in her darker hours, with a feeling of embittered regret. Two or three of the stanzas of **"The Lowest Room"** even remind one forcibly of that scene in Thomson's *City of Dreadful Night,* where the "shril! and lamentable cry" breaks through the silence of the shadowy congregation:––

In all eternity I had one chance,
   One few years' term of gracious human life,
The splendors of the intellect's advance,
   The sweetness of the home with babes and
     wife.

But if occasionally this residue of bitterness in Christina Rossetti recalls the more acrid genius of James Thomson, yet a comparison of the two poets (and such a comparison is not fantastic, however unexpected it may appear) would set the feminine character of our subject in a peculiarly vivid light. Both were profoundly moved by the evanescence of life, by the deceitfulness of pleasure, while both at times, Thomson almost continually, were troubled by the apparent content of those who rested in these joys of the world. Both looked forward longingly to the consummation of peace. In his call to *Our Lady of Oblivion* Thomson might seem to be speaking for both, only in a more deliberately metaphorical style:—

Take me, and lull me into perfect sleep;
   Down, down, far hidden in thy duskiest cave;
While all the clamorous years above me sweep
   Unheard, or, like the voice of seas that rave
On far-off coasts, but murmuring o'er my
     trance,
   A dim vast monotone, that shall enhance
   The restful rapture of the inviolate grave.

But the roads by which the two would reach this "silence more musical than any song" were utterly different. With an intellect at once mathematical and constructive, Thomson built out of his personal bitterness and despair a universe corresponding to his own mood, a philosophy of atheistic revolt. Like Lucretius, "he denied divinely the divine." In that tremendous conversation on the river-walk he represents one soul as protesting to another that not for all his misery would he carry the guilt of creating such a world; whereto the second replies, and it is the poet himself who speaks:—

> The world rolls round forever as a mill;
> It grinds out death and life and good and ill;
> It has no purpose, heart or mind or will. . . .
>
> Man might know one thing were his sight less
>   dim;
> That it whirls not to suit his petty whim,
> That it is quite indifferent to him.

There is the voluntary ecstasy of the saints, there is also this stern and self-willed rebellion, and, contrasted with them both, as woman is contrasted with man, there is the acquiescence of Christina Rossetti and of the little group of writers whom she leads in spirit:—

> Passing away, saith the World, passing away. . . .
> Then I answered: Yea.

David A. Kent (essay date 1979)

SOURCE: "Sequence and Meaning in Christina Rossetti's *Verses* (1893)," in *Victorian Poetry,* Vol. 17, No. 3, Autumn, 1979, pp. 259-64.

[*In the following essay, Kent argues that Rossetti's devotional verses must be read as a whole, as the poet intended, in order to fully comprehend their structure and meaning.*]

Thanks to such critics as Robillard, Fredeman, and Baker, Dante Gabriel Rossetti's *The House of Life* is no longer thought to lack "systematic arrangement" or a "principle of grouping," as even a sympathetic estimation had earlier asserted. The stubborn ghost of biographical criticism has been successfully exorcized, and the poet's conscious artistry in his sonnet sequence rediscovered and more fully appreciated. The devotional poetry of Christina Rossetti has, unfortunately, never benefited from any comparable redemption. If her religious poems are not completely ignored by today's readers, they are probably regarded with the same kind of patronizing condescension that Dorothy Stuart voiced fifty years ago: "Her devotional verses can be as trite as the quatrains on a Christmas card, as stuffy as the smell of pitchpine and red baize." However, a brief examination of *Verses* (1893), her major collection of devotional poetry, demonstrates that the sister did inherit a concern for the meaningful arrangement of lyrics similar to that of her brother.

Christina Rossetti's interest in the poetic possibilities of ordered structures for shorter poems should be almost self-evident from the numerous examples of linked poems (e.g., "Three Stages" or "Three Nuns") and sonnet sequences (e.g., "Monna Innominata" and "Later Life") within her total body of writings. And, to indicate the poet's firm convictions on this question of arrangement, Lona Mosk Packer has already cited her reply in 1883 to a correspondent who wanted to anthologize some of her lyrics. Her opposition to any disruption in her own arrangement is unambiguous and the stern rebuke, from a normally reticent woman, notable:

> I do not mind what piece you select, subject only to your taking any piece in question *in its entirety;* and my wish includes your *not* choosing an independent poem which forms part of a series of group,—not (for instance) one . . . of "Passing Away" or one Sonnet of "Monna Innominata." Such compound work has a connection (very often) which is of interest to the author, and which an editor gains nothing by discarding.

The identical sentiment recurs in a letter of November 24, 1886, in which she comments on a possible reprinting of *Goblin Market*. She will give permission, she states, "on no account if any portion whatever is to be omitted. . . . I now make a point of refusing extracts, even in the case of my Sonnet of Sonnets some of which would fairly stand alone." Evidently Christina Rossetti was all too aware that her lyrics tempted editors to arbitrary selection and to a neglect of the "compound work" in which her poems were sometimes embedded. The regretful irony is that she voiced these strictures too privately, and that the "extracts" she so vigorously opposed during her life have actually governed the editorial treatment of her poetry ever since her death.

The Society for Promoting Christian Knowledge first published Christina Rossetti's *Verses,* a collection of 331 religious lyrics disposed in eight sections, late in 1893. By the spring of 1894 the volume had passed into its third edition; the SPCK in fact continued to issue it well into the present century. The decisive date in its history came in 1904, though, when William Michael Rossetti edited *The Poetical Works of Christina Georgina Rossetti*. This edition effectively subsumed all earlier publications of her poetry, and it has since remained authoritative. The precedent Rossetti set for subsequent editors has, however, not been entirely beneficial to his sister's reputation as a poet. The overriding problem with his edition is that chronology, the "order of date," is the criterion by which he arranges his sister's poetry. The result insofar as *Verses* is particularly concerned is nothing less than disastrous. His chronological procedure, quite simply, completely disrupts the original order of the eight sections. He thus creates the following sequence for her devotional poems: instead of the authorial order of 1 . . . 8, the reader is given 8, 3, 6, 7, 2, 1, 4, 5—with miscellaneous poems wedged between most of the sections as well. Because of this radical dismemberment of *Verses* for the 1904 edition, few critics—if any—have ever read Christina Rossetti's devotional poetry in the sequential order she designed for it. The time is therefore long overdue for according her last publication the kind of reading she intended it to receive.

Christina Rossetti's *Verses* contains no "original" compositions because all of the poems had been previously published by the SPCK in three books of devotional prose: *Called to be Saints: The Minor Festivals Devotionally Studied* (1883), *Time Flies: A Reading Diary* (1885), and *The Face of the Deep: A Devotional Commentary on the Apocalypse* (1892). And although the poems in these texts are normally subordinate to other devotional aids (such as exegesis of Scripture, explanations of tradition, or the citation of Psalms and Biblical passages), these facts do not in themselves mean that *Verses* is merely the product of perfunctory compilation. Indeed, collation of the poems in the prose texts with their state in *Verses* shows clearly that the collection is the result of much conscientious revision. Christina Rossetti made over 800 individual changes in the more than 300 religious lyrics as she prepared *Verses* for publication. What is of even more importance here, however, is that she also fashioned a unified poetic sequence out of this mass of heterogeneous materials.

The eight sections of *Verses* dramatize the spiritual pilgrimage of the poet-speaker, who begins in confessions of guilt, "self-contempt and blame," and who gradually achieves understanding of, and faithful resignation to, God's will. The sequence can best be described as having two major movements, or two quatrains of thematic focus. The first four sections center on the speaker's personal growth, while the second quatrain of sections shifts to a more cosmic, impersonal vantage point; in the second half of the sequence, then, the important issues are the more universal questions of the fallen world, time, and eternity. The two halves of *Verses* have almost the same number of poems: the first half contains 168 poems, the second half, 163.

The title of section I, **"Out of the Deep have I called unto Thee, O Lord,"** is drawn from Psalm 130, and the tone of these seventeen poems is consistently plaintive. Each "humble hopeful quiet psalm," furthermore, is a sonnet, a form particularly appropriate to the speaker's loving but ardent complaints. Insistent petitioning to the "Lord," for the moment distant and detached, finally stops when the speaker recognizes that she can only wait attentively: "Lord, drop Thou in the counterscale alone / One Drop from Thine own Heart, and overweigh / My guilt, my folly, even my heart of stone." Section II, **"Christ our All in all,"** dramatizes in a series of dialogues Christ's merciful response to the suppliant. Intimate communion thus supplants separation, and communicative exchanges replace the lonely, penitent monologues of I. In section II itself, reassurance and counsel ease the speaker's oscillations between encouragement and paralyzing shame, awe and complaint, and by the end of II—certain that God "hast not forgotten" and "wilt not forget"—the speaker can conquer her vacillation. Section III, **"Some Feasts and Fasts,"** then places the personal relationship with God within the larger context of the church's corporate life of worship because, for Rossetti, it is there that the

pilgrim receives the necessary nourishment to carry on in the world. This grouping of poems surveys the church year and consists of the poet-speaker's meditations on the major feasts and fasts. All of the various elements of the spiritual life—praise, confession, supplication, declarations of faith—take their place within the formalized order of the liturgical year. Whereas section II dramatizes the gracious intervention of Christ into the individual's heart, section III traces the consequences of Christ's historical intervention into time as it is recreated and commemorated annually by the church. The dominant concern of the following section, **"Gifts and Graces,"** is with the qualities of spiritual discipline that the pilgrim needs in this life. Reconciled with her God, the speaker aims to justify His ways to men by celebrating the gifts He bestows. One such gift is hope, "the counterpoise of fear," and the speaker is now able to perceive even anguish and suffering, when rightly used, as "potential bliss." The quiet acceptance and confident faith characteristic of IV testify to the speaker's personal growth in the sequence to this point as well as signal the conclusion of the first movement. Although section IV ends, as section I had begun, with supplicatory prayers, the speaker is no longer desperate and anxious. Christ's intervention in II, a strengthening circuit of the church year in III, and a revaluation of God's gifts in IV all help to make her closing entreaties the expression of a ripened faith.

Section V, **"The World. Self-Destruction,"** marks an abrupt transition to the second half of *Verses,* the second quatrain of thematic focus where more universal terms of reference replace the earlier emphasis on the individual's relationship with God. The violent *contemptus mundi* sentiment that explodes in V counterpoints dramatically the preceding calm and underlines the sudden shift in perspective. Denunciations of the world as a "hollow thing" conclude with a warning that the fate of the "Self-slain" is death to the comfortless tolling of a bell. In section VI, **"Divers Worlds. Time and Eternity,"** these funereal bells reappear in more positive terms in the very first poem: although man is "out of tune with daily bells," paradise "accords the chimes / Of Earth and Heaven." The promise of eternity, grounded in the oxymoronic "evidence of faith," restores the lost harmony between man and time, reconciles the speaker to life amid "death and ills," and helps section VI to initiate an ascending movement that culminates in section VII. The special thematic tension of VI is the antithesis between time and eternity, the "world of sin" within and the "world of righteousness" above which the second lyric of the section describes. Section VII, **"New Jerusalem and its Citizens,"** is free of this tension; as its title suggests, it celebrates and focuses primarily upon the joys awaiting the pilgrim in paradise. The visions of the "lovely city" in section VII contrast sharply with the nihilistic tenor of V. Yet, as in the first half of the sequence, hellish separation from God (I and V) has been bridged by renewed hope and faith (II and VI), and the picturing of endless praise and worship in eternity (VII) parallels the performance by the church of the same rites in this world in the analogous section of the first half (III). Section VIII, **"Songs for Strangers and Pilgrims,"** provides a fitting conclusion both to the second half of *Verses* and to the whole sequence by recapitulating all the major themes and gestures of the preceding sections. The plaintive petitions of section I, the dialogue poems, the poems on the saints and on the nature of pilgrimage, the occasional lapses into despair, the assertions of final reward, and more visions of the New Jerusalem all recur in this massive section comprising ninety poems. As a closing witness of faith to "Strangers" and another act of dedication on behalf of all "Pilgrims," section VIII ends with a victorious glance backward: "Looking back along life's trodden way." Endowed with the authority of experience, the speaker recognizes, and can convey to her readers, how "Evening harmonizes all to-day." The pilgrimage of *Verses* is completed, and the speaker stands ready to meet her God.

If Christina Rossetti's devotional poetry seemed to Dorothy Stuart to lack the "thrust and counter-thrust of image and ideation" that critic once claimed for the best religious poetry, then much of the reason for that impression is that the sequential structure the poet had designed for her devotional verse has been totally ignored. The only critical treatment of *Verses* in its original order is by Mackenzie Bell, and his impressionistic remarks (e.g., "How expressive are the lines . . . ") do nothing to illuminate the poet's larger intentions. I have tried to outline the main contours of sequential meaning in Christina Rossetti's arrangement of her religious poems. That *Verses* needs closer scrutiny from editors and critics of the poet seems obvious. That her sequence has been overlooked for so long is the legacy of careless attention to the poet's concern with ordered structures for short lyrics and to her stated intentions about how she wished her poetry to be handled and read. Just as her brother Dante Gabriel Rossetti's *The House of Life* has been accorded careful study out of respect for its wholeness, so students of Christina Rossetti need to reconsider her devotional poetry in light of the fact that *Verses* is "compound work" to be read *"in its entirety."*

Kathleen Blake (essay date 1983)

SOURCE: "Christina Rossetti's Poetry: The Art of Self-Postponement," in *Love and the Woman Question in Victorian Literature: The Art of Self-Postponement,* The Harvester Press, Sussex, 1983, pp. 3-25.

[*In the following excerpt, Blake examines the themes of time, waiting, and "balked desire" in Rossetti's poetry.*]

"Hope deferred"—Christina Rossetti repeats this phrase from Proverbs 13.12 over and over again in her poetry. A discouraging phrase, it emphasises and extends the postponement already implied by hope. No other poet returns so often to words like lapse, slack, loiter, slow, tedious, dull, weary, monotonous, long. She plays on the relation between long and longing; long gets longer in a favourite word, lengthening. A poet with a "birthright sense of time", she usually counts time as slow suspense, suspense so slow that it loses almost the eagerness of suspense. By contrast, **"Goblin Market"** (1862, written 1859) displays

vividness and speed, luscious fruits and an "iterated jingle". Her most famous poem, in her first volume, is an anomaly, except for establishing the sensuous underlay of her austerity and the native alacrity painfully strung out in the bulk of her work. Or, if the story of the girl nearly fatally insatiate for goblin fruits treats "passionate yearning" and "balked desire", so does the rest of Rossetti's poetry. Only the emphasis shifts from the passion to its balking.

The poet is in slow suspense because she is a Christian. She draws upon her experience as a woman to embody this condition.

According to *The Face of the Deep* (1892), her commentary on the Apocalypse, suspense characterises the state of humanity as it awaits the second coming. This state is pictured in the angels' tensed stillness at the four corners of the earth as they hold back the winds in the prolonged moment before the Day of Judgement. Rossetti says the angels may be there now. But now lasts a long time, and Christ is long in coming. The earth must meanwhile endure "the drips / Of Thy slow blood". The opening sentence of *The Face of the Deep* invites us to consider the 1800 years that the faithful have had to wait for things "shortly" to come to pass, and Rossetti calls *patience* an exclusively New Testament word.

Traditionally, also, *patience* is a feminine word. Christina Rossetti is traditional—she disassociated herself from the suffrage movement and thought women's rights and Christianity were at odds. At the same time she treats the maddening, martyring dullness of feminine patience. Her purpose is neither social analysis nor criticism. She simply shows postponement as it becomes, in her brother's phrase characterising her own life, "self-postponement". There is nowhere better to study the style, the very tempo, as well as the content of this feminine state of mind.

Rossetti offers a number of reflections on feminine mentality. A woman particularly ponders the fact that time passes but doesn't get anywhere, so that "woman's looking-glass" forms "wisdom's looking-glass". Here is a weary wisdom:

> It's a weary life, it is, she said:—
> Doubly blank in a woman's lot:
> I wish and I wish I were a man:
> Or, better than any being, were not.

The poem **"In Progress"** sounds like a comment on the poet's own life, described by William Michael Rossetti as a "hushed life-drama", "a life which did not consist of incidents". It gives the quality of a woman's patience:

> Gravely monotonous like a passing bell.
> Mindful of drudging daily common things,
> Patient at pastime, patient at her work,
> Wearied perhaps, but strenuous certainly.

According to Rossetti's unpublished notes on Genesis and Exodus, the penalty of death has been laid on men and of life on women, and, for her, continuance exacts as great a penalty as extinction. Thus in a number of poems she as passionately commiserates Christ for his endurance of life as of death, and she adds onto his six hours of agony the foregoing thirty-three years. A parallel may be drawn between Christ-like and feminine longsuffering.

And yet there is a difference between the patience of Christ and the patience of a woman, because in Christ inheres his own eventual glory, whereas the woman must wait for grace to come to her. Of course, this is true for all Christian souls. But in a very significant statement in *The Face of the Deep* Rossetti makes the woman in love the emblem of radical insufficiency and dependence on an external dispensation: "Eve, the representative woman, received as part of her sentence 'desire': the assigned object of her desire being such that satisfaction must depend not on herself but on one stronger than she, who might grant or might deny". This passage offers a key to Rossetti's love and devotional poetry. She returns again and again to the experience of one who loves but cannot act on that love, which constitutes the woman's relation to the man, in her view, and the soul's to God. Initiative and saving grace lie on the other side.

The poem **"Twice"** describes the unnatural and futile seizure of initiative by the woman:

> I took my heart in my hand,
> (O my love, O my love),
> I said: Let me fall or stand
> Let me live or die,
> But this once hear me speak—
> (O my love, O my love)—
> Yet a woman's words are weak:
> You should speak, not I.

The man coolly rebuffs her advance. With a friendly voice and a critical eye he says, "Better wait awhile". Waiting is the role of the woman in love, as it is of the soul who loves Christ: Loving Lord, accept us in good part; / And give me grace to wait".

Throughout her poetry and prose devotional writing Rossetti uses the figure of the Bride who awaits the Bridegroom, drawn from the Song of Solomon and from the parable of the wise and foolish virgins in Matthew 25. 1 - 13. The Bride is the Church, the collective faithful, or the individual soul, and the Bridegroom is Christ, the "Heavenly Lover", "Husband, Brother, Closest Friend to me". Rossetti addresses the lover/saviour with erotic longing: "I am sick of love in loving Thee. / But dost Thou love me? Speak and save". But the consummation is deferred to heaven: "There God shall join and no man part, / I full of Christ and Christ of me". Sometimes she imagines an alternative travesty marriage and even a grisly procreation, as in the love-death vision of the grave in **"Two Thoughts of Death"**, where the worms will be "flesh of her flesh" and will be "born of her from nothingness". There is no certainty of desired fulfilment since, in her phrase, hope signifies no more than fear viewed on the sunny side. Sometimes she cries out against the sus-

pense. In the poem "Why" the soul asks, "Lord, if I love Thee and Thou lovest me, / Why need I any more these toilsome days? / Why should I not run singing up Thy ways / Straight into heaven?" Christ answers, "Bride whom I love . . . Thou needs must choose My Likeness for thy dower: / So wilt thou toil in patience, and abide". Christ the Bridegroom admonishes the soul in another poem: "Though I tarry, wait for Me". Rossetti therefore customarily resolves to "keep silence, counting time", and to "meditate / Our love-song while we wait". The image of the Bride above all embodies tense, waiting patience, as feminine as it is Christian.

A number of Christina Rossetti's longer poems treat the waiting bride in her secular aspect shading toward spiritual allegory. Most notable is the title poem of her second volume, *The Prince's Progress* (1866, written 1861-5). The emotional impact of this work does not derive from the prince's progress as such, nor from his difficulties, detours and backslidings along the way. That is, the poem does not follow the Red Crosse Knight model. Rather, Rossetti views the prince's movements from the stationary position of the bride to whom he journeys. The poem begins and ends with the princess. She waits till she is dead. The prince comes too late. He is delayed by one thing and another, a witch-like milkmaid, a stagnant, wasteland terrain, and a hermit-like old man in the desert. Weak-purposed and slow in setting out, "Lagging he moved and apt to swerve". His waystations can be interpreted, and such interpretation comprises the usual critical approach to the poem. But more important than why he delays is the delay itself. Rossetti isn't especially interested in what keeps him; she says, "He did what a young man can". She is more interested in what it means to sit and hope that he will come at last. From the first stanza the poem sounds the stretched-out music of monotony:

> Till all sweet gums and juices flow
> Till the blossoms of blossoms blow,
> The long hours go and come and go;
> The bride she sleepeth, waketh, sleepeth,
> Waiting for one whose coming is slow:—
> Hark! the bride weepeth.

The stanza opens with a time word, Till. Time is to be filled; time is to be fruitful only later. The repetitions of words forgo novelty—Till, till, blossoms of blossoms, go, go, sleepeth, sleepeth. "Go and come and go" restores the cyclical meaning to the stock phrase "come and go"; and also makes it longer. Cyclical meaning is carried too by "sleepeth, waketh, sleepeth". "Slow" expresses the prevailing idea; its long vowel suits the meaning and therefore suitably furnishes the prevailing rhyme sound. The falling cadence of the "feminine" ending trails effectively, especially with the unstopped "th" sound. The meter is mostly tetrameter, with a signable flow. As Rossetti says elsewhere, "There's music of a lulling sort in words that pause between.' And yet the overall effect is not only lulling. Line three counters the lulling rhythm; it lengthens and stops it both. The princess experiences time passing in regular units of hours of sleeping and waking, but for her time is also long, and also sometimes, so to speak, stuck. Line three can be read in regular tetrameter. But the monosyllables "long hours go" cry out for a stress each, and such stresses break and slow the rhythm, make it more tolling that lulling, and stretch the line to five beats.

Intermittently throughout the poem we return to the princess and her patient attrition. The prince makes painfully gradual progress, and the princess undertakes the minimum of movement: "We never heard her speak in haste; / Her tones were sweet, / And modulated just so much / As it was meet . . . There was no hurry in her hands, / No hurry in her feet; / There was no bliss drew nigh to her, / That she might run to greet". For her the only movement is found in the revolution of seasons, of night and day; one year, five years, ten years pass; she sleeps, wakes, sleeps, dreams, weeps, waits, dies. It is a poem about a princess out of the action, dependent on the prince's action. It is highly kinetic poem about the sense of motion of someone who sits still.

"Goblin Market" contrasts to "The Prince's Progress" in being often a hurrying poem, with goblins "Flying, running, leaping / Puffing and blowing / Chuckling, clapping, crowing". The tempted sister, Laura, shows no inclination to wait like the princess. She is in only too great a hurry to close with the little men. The goblins offer satisfaction of desire in the form of fruits bearing the additional erotic connotation of "joys brides hope to have", for which Laura's friend Jeannie had been unwilling to wait. The shortness and shifting irregularity of the poem's lines produce a breathless tempo. Yet the whole point is to warn against over-eagerness. Jeannie had died of seizing her desire. Patience is the lesson. If it is not the cheerful sort like the patience of good sister Lizzie, who resists the goblins by enduring to go hungry, it is desperate like the patience forced on Laura. Once having tasted forbidden fruit, she is left longing impotently for the goblins to come back with more:

> Day after day, night after night,
> Laura kept watch in vain
> In sullen silence of exceeding pain.
> She never caught again the goblin cry,
> "Come buy, come buy;"—
> She never spied the goblin men
> Hawking their fruits along the glen:
> But when the noon waxed bright
> Her hair grew thin and grey;
> She dwindled as the fair full moon doth turn
> To swift decay and burn
> Her fire away

No strict meter regulates this passage, but the pace is certainly slowed down from that of the jaunty goblins. The prevailing line lengths are irregularly mixed tetrameter and trimeter, suggestive of ballad measure thrown off its even flow. Two lines have five beats, but line 10 is stretched even further to six (or possible seven) beats, expressive of Laura's drawn-out ordeal, and the spondaic "fair full moon" is very leisurely. The line length then emblematically dwindles to match the dwindling of the

moon and the maiden. Although Laura languishes for illicit joys brides hope to have and not for an authorised princely bridegroom, let alone Christ, this stanza evokes very much the same psychological condition as that of the waiting princess, the Christian Bride, and many another wearily tense Rossetti heroine.

"The Lowest Room" makes women's needlework the emblem of ennui, as do other poems, like "Repining" and one of the "Sing-Song" nursery rhymes. "The Lowest Room" (1856) shows two sisters at their needles, talking. One is dexterous and unflagging, while the other is disgusted with her aimless life. She has been reading Homer and wishes she could have lived in that time of passion and action. She is attracted by the fighting heroes, and she hold that even the women were happier at their embroidery of glowing scenes of battle than the two sisters are as stitch follows stitch "Amid that waste of white". The elder sister is content while the younger frets, because the elder has something happening in her life besides sewing and reading. She has a lover. He arrives while the two sit there, and the elder sister gets up to go outside into the garden with him. "While I? I sat alone and watched". This is what Christina Rossetti's heroines do, with sedentary, more or less impotent yearning. This poem explores the bad temper of the watcher, though she pacifies herself by transferring her expectations from an earthly lover to the archangelic trumpet-burst, meanwhile accepting the "lowest room" of the title.

According to Rossetti's introduction, the sonnet cycle "Monna Innominata" (before 1882, pp. 58-64) expresses what the troubadour's lady would have had to say for herself, that is, the feminine viewpoint on romantic love. The romantic love tradition, which flourishes on separation, divides Dante from Beatrice and Petrarch from Laura. The introduction invokes this tradition and promises an unhappy affair. But if Dante and Petrarch pant, aspire, and follow after their ladies, Christina Rossetti treats the ladies' case, which is to await the lovers' doubtful arrival. The first sonnet opens, "Come back to me, who wait and watch for you", and the entire poem counts time by a man's coming or not coming. The time seems long before he comes; it lags while he's away. Hope waxes and wanes. The lady thinks always of "when he comes, my sweetest 'when'", and the same hyperconsciousness of time intensifies her sense of the pastness of past youth and joy, and even forecasts pastness into the future, since every meeting precedes farewells, and then the waiting begins again.

A number of other shorter poems treat the woman "watching, weeping for one away". The absent one is the lover, bridegroom or husband on far travels or across the ocean or sometimes in his grave, as in "The Ghost's Petition", "Twilight Night", "Hoping Against Hope", "A Fisher-Wife", "Songs in a Cornfield", and "Song". One of the "Sing-Song" nursery rhymes describes Minnie waiting for her Johnny to come home from the sea: she watches the church clock, but it hardly seems to go.

Occasionally Rossetti treats the joy of the lover's arrival, as in her most rarely jubilant poem, "A Birthday": "Raise me a dais of silk and down; / Hang it with vair and purple dyes; / Carve it in doves and pomegranates, / And peacocks with a hundred eyes; / . . . Because the birthday of my life / Is come, my love is come to me" (1857). More characteristic is the torment of an almost-arrival. The poem **"Autumn"** pictures a sort of Lady of Shalott living alone in a tower by a river that flows down to the sea (1858). Boats sail on the river, and she hears lovesongs across the water, but no friend comes to her. The lady is full of longing. This is a poem about fulfilment in sight but out of reach and passing by. The frustration is exquisite when the wind flags, the love vessels lie bacalmed in sight of the lady's strand. Those on board cannot hear her moan, but their amorous songs rouse echoes in her lonely land. Yet the imagery of calm winds is also an imagery of languor. The maidens on the boats are lulled and languid. The erotic energy slackens. When the wind rises, it both rouses the lovers and carries them away, leaving the lady alone with her longing again.

It is interesting that one poem depicts the bridegroom who waits for the bride to sail from a far land. The situation is the same but different from the usual in a Rossetti love poem. There is the customary waiting tension, but the difference is that when the bride's ship sinks and she does not arrive, the bridegroom blithely marries someone else (**"A Birds-Eye View,"** 1863). The woman in love and not the man typifies indefinite patience.

One of Rossetti's best-known poems bridges the erotic and the religious with a variant of the Bride/Bridegroom motif which shows that the waiting continues even after death. **"A Pause"** pictures a woman who lies dead (1853). Flowers are heaped on her bed, and she does not hear the birds about the eaves or the reaper in the field. She is dead but not insensate, which means that she can still keep watch: "Only my soul kept watch from day to day, / My thirsty soul kept watch for one away". This represents the extreme of powerless suspense. She is waiting, typically, for her lover, for his step on the stair, Earthly and spiritual consummation are confounded in the poem. At the sound of the step and the turning lock, her spirit flies free, it scents the air of paradise, and the waiting is over: "then first the tardy sand / Of time ran golden; and I felt my hair / Put on a glory, and my soul expand".

Rossetti is fascinated by the possibilities of consciousness after death because of her characteristic fascination with long-drawn-out patience and suspense. Her famous **"Song"** (1848) wonders whether the living lover will remember or forget; this is less odd than to raise the same question about the one who lies in the grave: "Haply I may remember, / And haply may forget". Rossetti builds poems on both contingencies. In **"Rest"** the dead woman enjoys blissful release from irksome consciousness. In **"After Death"** she is aware of her lover's tears and gratified by them. **"Life Hidden"** proposes a paradoxical combination of unconsciousness and consciousness: "She doth not see, but knows; she hears no sound, / Yet counts the flight of time". Rossetti does not stop counting, even after death. This typifies her temporal obsession. She sometimes uses grave time to imagine the contrast that defines

earthly time. In the grave, time may lose tension, as in **"Dream Land"** and **"Rest":** "Rest, rest at the heart's core / Till time shall cease"; "Her rest shall not begin nor end, but be / And when she wakes she will not think it long". Suspense eases to suspension at least.

A theological tenet underlies Rossetti's interest in the equivocal state of mind of the dead. Death does not insure an end because some interim, long or short, still divides the burial day of the faithful from Christ's second coming, when the dead arise for final judgement. Though she makes the grave a relatively quiet waiting place, Rossetti is never one to minimise the stretch of time that must pass. It is thus purely appropriate that in her devotional tract *Seek and Find* (1879) as well as in her Exodus notes she should contemplate with interest the great temporal extension by evolutionary science of the orthodox six days of creation. She can easily imagine a "day" as a vast geological period, just as she can imagine lengthy residence in the grave. This is because there is nothing swift about earthly days for Christina Rossetti or for one of the waiting brides about whom she so often writes.

In 1850 Rossetti wrote what her brother deemed a **"Tale for Girls"**. It is called **"Maude"**, and it examines feminine long-suffering, stripping it of charm and almost of merit. It is a less pious and a more clinical story than it has been taken to be. This time not even a lover presents, or absents, himself, and yet Maude pines. The tale poses the question—why is Maude so depressed? What does she find to reproach herself with such that she writes broken-hearted verses at the age of fifteen and feels so much need of chastisement by sickness and suffering that she dies willingly before she is twenty? In introducing the story William Michael Rossetti sounds a bit nonplussed by Maude's sense of sin since the only misdeeds she can claim are valuing her own poetry, enjoying church services, and missing the sacrament when she feels unworthy of it. He sets her self-reproaches down to Christina Rossetti's over-fine scruples. However, the story itself scrutinises such scruples.

Maude's misdeeds may look awfully innocent, but Rossetti is more interested in her state of mind. Acute feminine innocence breeds its own betrayers: ennui and irritability. The story opens by describing Maude as pale, tired and headachy. Her mother is used to her inattention. She is abstracted because everything bores her except writing. The languor and resignation of her sonnets—characteristic Christina Rossetti sonnets—are both Christian and highly specific to Maude's life. For instance, the sentiment of one of them, "To do is quickly done; to suffer is/Longer" is desentimentalised by the context in which it appears. After writing it Maude yawns and wonders how she is going to fill the time until dinner. On a visit to her conventional cousins in the country, Maude gladly hears the clock announcing bedtime; this means the first day is over. She hates facing a dreary social visit, the evening drags intolerably, the meal seems endless, the small talk dies, and yawns have to be suppressed. Maude is annoyed by the two ladies who insist on gushing over her verses. In this context the soulful note of Maude's poetry sounds almost querulous—"To-day is still the same as yesterday"—or just wretchedly tired—"let us wait the end in peace". These lines come from poems that appear independently as devotional pieces in William Michael Rossetti's collected edition of his sister's work. As originally placed in **"Maude"** they illustrate the source of a particular religious mood in the particulars of a young woman's life.

Maude is stultified. She would like a little unsaintly variety, such as to go to balls, where she could watch people, or to the theatre, except that no one offers to take her. She is restive, and that constitutes her spiritual problem. From the dismal social evening she returns home in a fret of dissatisfaction with her circumstances, her friends, and herself. What she calls her "impatient fits" explain her bad conscience. Rossetti makes clear that she overdoes her contrition and that in banishing herself from communion she performs a misplaced penance, more hurtful than what it punishes. She draws a portrait of an altogether sickly and overwrought mentality, and an altogether feminine one. Maude's cross is her dull girl's life, her sin to find it a cross; it makes her cross.

Rossetti captures the lack of content, in both senses of the word, of a life like this, which, without being innocent, has to strain to find reasons for its sense of sin. She doesn't beatify her heroine. Maude is the most unglamorous of martyrs. Her suffering is out of proportion to what she has to suffer, so that actual illness and death are necessary to restore some correlation. It is a relief to have done. Maude finds an essentially negative delivery from life, like the dead woman in Rossetti's **"Rest"**: "Hushed in and curtained with a blessed dearth / Of all that irked her from the hour of birth; / With stillness that is almost Paradise". "Irked" stands as the important word here. It is not a word much expected in poetry, and not perhaps expected from Christina Rossetti, by reputation lovely, lachrymose, saintly, morbid, feminine. All true enough, but also irked to death.

Christina Rossetti remarks of Dante Gabriel Rossetti's paintings of Elizabeth Siddall that "every canvas means / The same one meaning", and something similar might be said of her own writing. The painful sense of time so often figured by feminine waiting and irksome tedium is the same one meaning that finds expression in a number of ways throughout her work, both in content and form. Even when Rossetti titles a devotional tract *Time Flies* (1885), she doesn't mean that time flies. She means that, though we may rejoice that no day lasts longer than twenty-four hours, we cannot afford to wish the time shorter in which to receive Christ; it means that mortal life is the vigil, and death is the festival. *Time Flies* is cast as a journal that works its way through the ecclesiastical year, and it belongs with other prose and poetic sequences that display in their formal structures Rossetti's habit of counting off time. She is a repetitious poet, in her themes, in her words, phrases, rhythms, sounds. Always "hope deferred", and hence "Our long and lengthening days", "these long still-lengthening days", "Yesterday, this day, day by day the Same", "Time lengthening, in the lengthening

seemeth long", "Oh long re-echoing song! / O Lord, how long?" Inventive novelty would be lost on a poetry of ennui. And yet changes can be rung on sameness. There is enough variation in Rossetti's ways of conceiving the pains of time for her to be able to keep on saying what she has to say.

Time can drag, or move restlessly, or stand still. She captures these temporal experiences in several emblems, besides drawing from a woman's life the image of the Bride waiting for the earthly or divine Bridegroom. Some (like the Bride/Bridegroom motif) represent waiting, and come supplied with closure, though necessarily to Rossetti's outlook, not close at hand. These are the repeated emblems of days and seasons. Night drags awaiting morning; winter drags awaiting spring. More final and fulfilling is the longed-for harvest of souls of the Apocalypse: "Is not time full? Oh put the sickle in, / O Lord, begin!" She also employs a journey motif. With this she shifts from the stance of stationary waiting, but the emotional difference is negligible because the soul struggling toward God hardly seems to move, the way is so far, as it makes its "long-drawn straining effort across the waste", "As the dry desert lengthens out its sand". Often the emphasis falls more on lasting out the time than covering ground: "Will the day's journey take the whole long day?" The extraordinary strain of this line comes from the questioning of a foregone certainty, since a day's journey must take a day.

Other emblems emphasise restlessly cycling time, hopeless of an end. These are the surging sea and the waxing and waning moon. "The stir of the tedious sea" is especially depressing. "The things that were shall be again; / The rivers do not fill the sea, / But turn back to their secret source". For all of its motion, the sea makes no progress because of "the under / Drain of ebb that loseth ground". Rossetti figures the sea as aspiring to be full but never full. It typifies unappeasable craving, just as the waxing and waning moon typifies "a fire of pale desire in incompleteness". She thereby suggests the frustration of a circle aspiring to linear direction and goal.

An interesting aspect of Rossetti's concern for time as cycle lies in her preternatural sensitivity to memory and foreknowledge: "So tired am I, so weary of to-day, / So unrefreshed from foregone weariness, / So overburdened by foreseen distress"; "I am sick of where I am and where I am not, / I am sick of foresight and of memory". This explains her prevision of the grave and her projection of time even there. It also explains the pain mixed even with meeting in the love poetry of **"Monna Innominata"**; because she can remember, she can forecast the parting.

Rossetti has another version of radical reiteration. She presents identity as perpetual re-enactment: "I am not what I have nor what I do; / But what I was I am, I am even I. / Therefore myself . . . My sole possession every day I live, / And still mine own despite Time's winnowing". This dogged persistence in identity resembles that of Lazarus: "I laid beside the gate am Lazarus; / See me or see me not I still am there / . . . Dog-comforted and

A photograph of Rossetti and her mother taken in 1863 by Lewis Carroll

crumbs solicitous / . . . And, be I seen or not seen, I am thus". These poems render the dignified part of what Rossetti elsewhere calls her "tedious dignity".

Other poems explain the tedious part, the making and remaking of the same old self: "Wearied of sinning, wearied of repentance, / Wearied of self". **"Three Stages"** (1854) shows the effort of will required perpetually to reiterate the self, which the time sense casts more as a treadmill than as a steadfast rock. The poem describes life experienced as stages, actually more than the three of the title, which don't lead anywhere except to the point of beginning over again. Succeeding one another are desire, then consciousness of hope deferred, watching and waiting, continued effort felt to be useless, regret for useless effort, a haunting sense of what else one might have done, sickening and resignation, endurance, and near lapsing into the condition of sleep, but then awakening and a renewed pulse of life, with full awareness that these must again pass, while "I . . . yet nerve myself to give / What once I gave, again". The poem "Memory" (1857/1865) is also about being one's past by constantly re-enacting it, a wearing sort of integrity: "None know the choice I made; I make it still. / None know the choice I made and broke my heart, / Breaking mine idol: I have braced my will /

Once, chosen for once my part". Anaphora figures effectively in a poem about repetition. The repeated "once" is ironic because not even the word happens once, just as once is now too; the choice is singular but not the choosing. For the love she crushed still forms the centre of the woman's life, and she has to keep crushing it. Great effort goes into remaining the same, and the only change in the poem lies not in any change from what she was, but in her growing exhaustion in choosing what she chose.

Time moving round and round grows as tiring in its way as time lagging and sluggish. I have already discussed some examples of Rossetti's metrical slowing in **"The Prince's Progress"** and **"Goblin Market",** for she is a poet who expresses movement or lack of movement where it is most intimately felt, in her rhythms. She can also write speedy, jingly lines, as for the nimble goblins. But most frequently she makes speed express perpetual motion more hectic than exhilarating. To this effect a poem on the restless wind uses a short, two-beat line, nearly unrelieved repetition of pairs of participles, and sameness of rhymes: "Whistling and moaning / Ever beginning / Ending, repeating / Hinting and dinning / Lagging and fleeting". The point here is that the wind always seems to be saying something important, but it never amounts to a clear message. Only a sort of nagging commotion comes across. Another poem uses the fast flow of a regular and internally-balanced line to express a cycle with no sense of upshot: "The stream moaneth as it floweth, / The wind sigheth as it bloweth, / Leaves are falling, Autumn goeth, / Winter cometh back again". **"Vigil of the Annunciation"** brilliantly contrasts speed with solemn pacing as the difference between earth and heaven:

> All weareth, all wasteth,
> All flitteth, all hasteth,
> All of flesh and time:—
> Sound, sweet heavenly chime,
> Ring in the unutterable eternal prime.

Lines one and two are jingles of two unstress/stress/unstress feet, rhythmically regular and syntactically symmetrical. Line three provides a transition. It uses the same first word "All" but shifts to an iamb, so that "All" is stressed rather than unstressed, and there are three beats to the line. The pace is no longer rushing but deliberate and emphatic, the more so because the short foot makes the opening a strong beat, and the now "masculine" ending closes the line with a strong beat; the colon and dash also signal this full close. Line four has four beats and tolls with spondees, like the bells it describes. The last line takes its dignified time, now up to five beats, freed from monotonous metrical predictability. It makes the earthly jogtrot of short lines, regular metre, reiterated words and syntactical units, and unemphatic "feminine" endings sound merely repetitious and trivial.

However, if lagging suspense or cyclical, reiterative time tires Christina Rossetti, standstill can be worse. An emblem for this condition is a landscape. The prince of **"The Prince's Progress"** encounters it, and it appears also in the distressing poem **"Cobwebs"** (1855). The landscape distresses by lack of change. No night and day, no seasons, no waxing and waning moon, no ebbing and flowing tide relieve the monotony. Even such aimless fluctuation would enliven this stagnant, sluggish, brooding plain. There is no past or future. Without time there is no fear either, says the poem's last line, which I find interesting, because it prefers to barren changelessness the time line implied even by fear.

Rossetti is in one mode a poet of unbearable stoppage, expressed in sound as well as conceptually and visually. A powerful example comes from Sonnet 26 of her double sonnet sequence **"Later Life"** (before 1882). It begins, "This Life is full of numbness and of balk. / Of haltingness and baffled shortcoming". A word could hardly stop shorter than "balk", in meaning and in the abruptness of the explosive "k" after the continuant "l". It is a hard-to-say word. "l" before certain consonants comes so hard that it often tends to be elided (as in "calm" and "walk"), but in "balk" it demands full pronunciation. "Balk" is here appropriately end-stopped. Early in the next line the slant-rhyming "halt" reinforces its meaning. It accumulates stress by the yielded stress of "and", as strict iambic pentameter gives way to speech rhythm. "Baffled shortcoming" also perfectly baffles the ostensible metre; it stops it short. This line has ten syllables and can be read with five beats, but it generates no flow at all, since "short" and "come" form a spondee, leaving the iamb and the "ing" nowhere. The "led" in "baffled" is one of those stillborn mutters of English hard to dignify into a syllable, further frustrating the iamb and almost making "baffled short" into a spondee. All this stoppage at the end discourages any impulse to lilt "haltingness", which would mean forcing normal speech rhythm anyway, so that the line really comes out with four beats instead of five, three of them displaced. It is no wonder that Christina Rossetti found admirers not only in the mellifluous Swinburne but also in the more unorthodox and wrenching Gerard Manley Hopkins. Her lines could be very meaningfully sprung. She possesses sensitivity to time counted syllabically and quantitatively too, though she never imitates Greek versification. For instance, she remarks that "Autumn" is a "slow name". The same could be said of "numbness" in my example.

Rossetti's heaven contradicts itself in a way that comments on her earth and time and song. She says heaven enjoys exemption from variability. The apocalyptic sea of glass does not ebb and flow. In contrast to the world, which is "this near-at-hand-land [that] breeds pain by measure", heaven sheds pain by shedding measure. But since this life is as dreadful when it seems to stop as when it rushes in aimless circles or drags on, awaiting consummation, she elsewhere restores time to heaven. According to *Time Flies,* no monotony or tedium troubles heaven because of the change, succession, and variety supplied by music. Bliss dispenses with time yet keeps it. A perfect casting of the paradox appears in the poem **"Young Death"**, which makes heaven a place where there is "no more . . . cadence in the song". Oxymoronic song without cadence is heaven. There are cadences in Rossetti's songs.

Her obsession with time makes her an intensely musical poet, but since earth's time is long drawn out in suspense, fretfully fluctuating, or balked, so is her music. Critics have disagreed as to whether to consider her an imperfect and irregular poet or a technical virtuoso, and even when her technique is admired it may seem to serve mere dreariness and monotony of material. Ruskin complained about Rossetti's metrical irregularity, but Geoffrey Grigson has compared the poetic gifts of Christina and Dante Gabriel Rossetti in her favour. C. M. Bowra and K. E. Janowitz appreciate formal elements—restricted phrasal emphasis, long vowel sounds, heavy caesuras, tolling regularity of beat, anaphora, and other kinds of repetition—for their fine adjustment to content. Stuart Curran is impatient with this content, which he finds too penurious to justify the rich technical skill. He finds Rossetti's outlook, in fact, too modest and too feminine. I think he is right about the modesty and femininity, except in supposing that these aren't enough to sustain poetic worth, and that fineness of finish only cloaks an underlying poverty. Rather, I think the poetry is fine for giving voice to qualities necessarily muted.

It is true that one must develop an ear for Christina Rossetti because her subject won't bear eloquent assertion, or tough wit, tautness and compression, Curran's desired "masculine force". Neither would it bear the sort of liquid loveliness Ruskin presumably wanted when he told her to smooth out her metre. What would either toughness or smooth charm have to do with the worn-out, waiting princess? Mostly, Christina Rossetti is left to be famous in name and a few children's and anthology pieces. Criticism is scanty, but I think we shall be able to appreciate her more than Ruskin or Curran or most others if we can appreciate Virginia Woolf's comment: "Modest as you were, still you were drastic."

Re-evaluation of Rossetti is beginning among feminist critics. Still, her effects *are* drastic and not guaranteed to please either fanciers of a virile style or feminists, who may grow dispirited and find fault with work which expresses neither women's fulfilment nor even much anger at its lack. In their influential *Madwoman in the Attic,* Sandra Gilbert and Susan Gubar judge a poetry of renunciation to be necessarily a renunciation of poetry. Their theoretical base is a post-Freudian linking of "the self-gratifications of art and sensuality". They assume the fusion into a single force of the "poetic/sexual life of self-assertion". For them, **"Goblin Market"** tells its author's story. To remain unsatisfied by the goblins' erotic fruits means to forfeit fruits of knowledge (by a problematical analogy with the fruit Eve ate) and hence to forfeit fruits of language and poetry. Gilbert and Gubar think that Rossetti bowed to the balking of desire and, in so doing, buried herself alive as a poet. But in my view poetry may be made of love's deferral as well as its consummation.

In some cases, certainly, Rossetti's poems react against deferral in non-acceptance and anger, utter giving up, or imagined fulfilment and release. Some turn a critical eye on the woman who lives to wait. However, the proportions of the work remain such that the reactions only serve to set off the usual long-suffering.

"Another Spring" offers a rare example of refusal to accept "hope deferred". The speaker says she should have seized the day. For once, she wishes she had not waited, and a touch of anger accompanies the thought of lost chances. Anger grows stronger in **"An Old World Thicket"** (before 1882). Here a dreamer is galled by the discrepancy between the springtime jubilee of a dream landscape and the blankness of her own feelings. She shifts from sadness and dejection to revolt, "That kicks and breaks itself against the bolt / Of an imprisoning fate, / And vainly shakes, and cannot shake the gate". Diction and syntax beautifully enforce the idea of vainness in the last line. Anger and quenching occur simultaneously, for the same verb takes affirmative and negative forms. Action is exactly nullified; shaking happens and doesn't happen.

Sometimes Rossetti contemplates just giving up, "Faithless and hopeless turning to the wall". On the other hand, when lowered energy is allowed to soar, the relief is wonderful. Her prayer is heard, "Re-energise my will", and then the "long-drawn straining effort" ceases. Instead, "I will arise and run", "horses of sheer fire / Whirling me home to heaven". "Joy speaks in praises there, and sings and flies". **"In Progress"** achieves the tremendous energy of its last lines by juxtaposition with earlier heaviness. A woman's life passes in review, calm, dim, exhausted, slow-speaking, silent, grave, monotonous, drudging, patient, wearied, but "Sometimes I fancy we may one day see / Her head shoot forth seven stars from where they lurk". "Shoot" quite astonishes, and the seven stars take one's breath away.

Other poems look for release. **"Acme"** (1856) proposes two different kinds. One is sleep, unconsciousness: "Sleep awhile: / Make even awhile as though I might forget". The other is the opposite of not feeling the pain. It seeks to feel it acutely and definitely, waking "To quickened torture and a subtler edge. / The wrung cord snaps at last: beneath the wedge / The toughest oak groans long but rends at length". "Snaps" is sharply, explosively right, especially after "wring", and "at last" exactly makes the point. But I can't help wondering if the oak that groans long but rends at length qualifies the relief of release, like the sleep that only soothes "as though" it brought forgetfulness. "Rends" lacks the suddenness and finality of "snaps", both in idea and sound. "At length" differs from "at last"; it can mean "over a long period", which returns us to Rossetti's usual experience. Quick, sharp, final pain merely stakes a boundary defining, like release through sleep, or fruition in heaven or on earth, or hopeless turning to the wall, or angry revolt, Rossetti's imaginative centre: a sense of life a long time enduring: "I wish it were over the terrible pain, / Pang after pang again and again: / First the shattering ruining blow, / Then the probing steady and slow".

She can define her position by self-criticism too, obliquely or more directly. The poem **"Repining"** (1847) pre-sents a figure of restlessness and fatigue, a woman spinning. The endless thread and the wearily turning wheel suggest time passing without arriving: "The long thread seemed to increase / Even while she spun and did not cease". This woman wants something to happen to save her from her ennui. Typically, she wants a lover to come, but the poem subjects her hope to the disillusioning test of fulfilment. A lover does come, he materialises as a kind of angel, but it turns out he does not save her. She leaves with him, but her journey satisfies her no more than sitting still because in the world she surveys only deathly horrors, an avalanche, a shipwreck, a city on fire, a battlefield. No finality graces the coming of the angel/ lover. The journey leads nowhere except to her wish to go back to where she came from, that is, to her repining.

"Day-Dreams" (1857) also treats the characteristic Christina Rossetti experience in a characteristic figure, the woman waiting. It is an interesting and unusual poem because it employs a male voice, using this to give a critique of feminine lassitude. The speaker is the lover who comes to woo this archetypal Rossetti maiden who sits gazing and gazing through her chamber window, dreaming, silent, still, gradually dying. The last two stanzas describe her burial, but the poem doesn't explain why she dies; in fact, the speaker is bemused by her perplexing attrition. When he strews flowers before his beloved, she just sits there. He gets no answers from her, and no response to his passion: "Cold she sits through all my kindling". The poem stands in ironic relation to **"Goblin Market"** and **"The Prince's Progress"**. Laura in **"Goblin Market"** is in too much of a hurry for sensuous/erotic consummation—joys brides hope to have. In **"The Prince's Progress"** the bride waits for her tardy bridegroom as long as she must and can. But in this poem love is at hand, and it is not goblin-tainted, yet the lady makes no move. With an ennui grown constitutional like Maude's, this lady's state resembles that described in **"Repining"**. The awaited angel/lover arrives, but it makes no difference, and the repining goes on. This is a poem of renunciation without a reason and waiting without an object. Postponement here becomes truly the "self-postponement" of William Michael Rossetti's phrase. He so characterises his sister's life not exactly with disapproval but not with out-and-out relish either. He doesn't quite know what to think.

And in the poem the speaker doesn't know what his lady is waiting for. Her long watch perpetuates itself inexplicably, and she seems to fix her expectations on the ultimate consummation of oblivion. He is baffled and also exasperated: "Who can guess or read the spirit / Shrined within her eyes?" "Now if I could guess her secret, / Were it worth the guess?" Full of vague longing and languor, the lady "wastes" her lover's strength and his nights and days. She defers hope and love until he no longer cares for her answer. She dies a mystery that went on too long: "I will give her stately burial, / Stately willow-branches bent: / Have her carved in alabaster, / As she dreamed and leant / While I wondered what she meant". Through this nonplussing damozel Christina Rossetti comments critically on the morbidity that many have complained about in her own poems. But in morbidity a poet can find material for eloquence, and of self-postponement she can make art. Emblematic of this art is the figure of a woman whose love vigil extends itself in perpetuity, a woman a man finds hard to understand.

Constance W. Hassett (essay date 1986)

SOURCE: "Christina Rossetti and the Poetry of Reticence," in *Philological Quarterly,* Vol. 65, No. 4, Fall, 1986, pp. 495-514.

[*In the following essay, Hassett argues that Rossetti uses a variety of techniques to emphasize the concepts that are hinted at and alluded to in her poetry.*]

Christina Rossetti is a reserved poet. Against the pressure of her guardedness, her writer's impulse resolves itself into shaped stanzas, deflected understatements, and quieted rhythms. Her laconic style is the result of a deeply private dialectic between verbal evasion and aesthetic control. The paradox of Rossetti's art is that the withholding of speech is constitutive. She bends an instinct to silence, avoidance, and mute watchfulness into a distinctive style.

Not surprisingly, Rossetti's struggle into articulateness becomes her subject. Diffidence and brave reticence are treated overtly in her text. In the confrontation-scene of **"Goblin Market,"** Rossetti contrives matters so that "Lizzie uttered not a word" (1:22). In a highly typical gesture, one Rossetti female turns "in silence to the wall" (1:154); another retreats from a quarrel and does "not answer him again" (1:137). Rossetti's characters often feel "brimful of words" (2:150) and truths "which had to stay unsaid" (1:167). While such instances of verbal avoidance and suppression could be multiplied, the best single example is **"May."**

> I cannot tell you how it was;
> But this I know: it came to pass
> Upon a bright and breezy day
> When May was young. . . .
>
> I cannot tell you what it was;
> But this I know: it did but pass.
> It passed away with sunny May. . . .
>
>   (1:51)

Not only does this poem plead an inability to specify its subject, "I cannot tell you what it was," it relies on punningly evasive phrasing, "passed away," to regret a loss it never concretely identifies. As often in Rossetti's poetry, conspicuous avoidance is pure gain. By suppressing its apparent subject, **"May"** seems to make only modest claims for the importance of the event it records, while at the same time suggesting an impressively large and ineluctable emotion. In effect, what might be called Rossetti's decorum of omission blocks intepretation and thus protects her Wordsworthian theme. No particular loss, but rather, the enigma of loss, the mysteriousness of life's

"fallings from us, vanishings," remains the poem's undiminished concern.

"May" also exhibits Rossetti's distinctive way with detail. Although the poem works principally by withholding information, it is by no means vaguely bereft of particulars. On the contrary, there is a nearly inverse relation between significant omission and fine distinctions. Rossetti approaches her avoided subject by surrounding the unnamed "it" with specification. She localizes its arrival, for example, within the boundaries of May: "As yet the poppies were not born / Between the blades of tender corn" (1:51). The displaced precision of these lines—with their yet-to-be-born poppies among discrete blades of grain—creates an impression of accuracy that works to heighten Rossettian reticence. Inclusions signal exclusions and the pressure of something left out is intensified. "It" becomes a present-absence, and authorial reticence begins to solicit attention as reticence. In short, the play of detail contributes to Rossetti's poetics of the known-but-unmentioned. In general, the minutiae Rossetti selects tend to be of a particular class. Her clear-eyed notice is not so much microscopic as it is attentive to the elusive and half-hidden. Typical observations attend to the way ripples cause reflections to "flow, / One moment joined, to vanish out of reach" and how violets lie hidden in a "double shade of leaves, / Their own and others dropped down withering" (1:194).

Rossetti's details have been appreciated before, of course, but their effect has been somewhat misrepresented. The notion prevails that Rossetti is a highly pictorial poet, one who offers "richly colored scenes in the authentic Pre-Raphaelite mode" [Lionel Stevenson, *The Pre-Raphaelite Poets,* 1972]. This evaluation, however, is not strictly accurate. Rossetti's representation of flowers is an illuminating case in point. Although she frequently mentions them, she does not attempt the high-realization of the dandelion puff in Hunt's *Rienzi* (his first PRB painting) or the violets, field roses and purple loosestrife in Millais's splendid *Ophelia.* And if one avoids cross-genre comparisons and looks instead to contemporary Victorian poetry, the conclusion is the same. Rossetti's appealing phrase, "chill-veined snowdrops" (1:48), does not exhibit the "remarkable visual precision" of Tennyson's description of the "lines of green that streak the white / Of the first snowdrop's inner leaves." Nor is there anything to match Rossetti's own prose comments in *Called to be Saints:*

> The Snowdrop . . . droops its head like an icicle. That which is not white in its blossom, is green; with a deep-set yellow centre, like a hint rather than a touch of sunshine. . . . its leaves grow in pairs, slim as grass, pointing upwards: every vein of each leaf tends straight upwards, without twists or retrogression of curves. Its stalk is green and bowing at the summit, whence hangs the bell-shaped flower, composed of six petals in a twofold arrangement: near that point where the stalk curves downwards a green tip extends as if to shelter the blossom, and within the bell are lodged six fruitful stamens.

As a poet, Rossetti simply does not indulge in this degree of visual particularity. And yet the impression of an "authentic Pre-Raphaelite" style is not entirely unfounded. While Rossetti does not offer startlingly full or fresh pictures, she does convey the sense of intense, habitual attentiveness. That she seems to make "the minuter discriminations" derives from the manner of her observation: her poetry singles out the objects of her notice. Undaunted by the profusion nature presents to one's field of vision, Rossetti's keen eye locates uncurling seams of new growth and cleanly delimited edges. Her habit is to discriminate the margin, edge, tip, periphery and "boundary shore" (1:191). She sees the "rock girt" sea (1:194), the "outskirts" of a pool (1:221), the "topmost edge of waves" (2: 145), and the "skirt" of a "riven" cloud (1:214). And because there is no straining in such observations— because they are underdeveloped as pictures—they create the cumulative impression of accustomed, accurate watchfulness. One can hypothesize, too, that there is a deep connection between Rossetti's instinctive attention to margins and her personal sense of barriers, exclusions, and self-contained isolation. For her, the notion of physical limits easily slips over into existential metaphor: thus her lovers find themselves doubly edged, "on the water's brink, / As on the brink of parting"; isolation is a matter of having "hedged me with a thorny hedge" (1:192); and heaven is "accessible tho' fenced" (2:285).

Since Rossetti achieves intensity by means of inexplicitness, the proliferation of techniques for under-specifying might well be considered her hallmark. Sometimes, her recoil from a topic can be measured by the studied shyness of the diction: "Something this foggy day, a something which / Is neither of this fog nor of today / Has set me dreaming" (2:145); "Where my heart is (wherever that may be) / Might I but follow!" (1:212). In a well-wrought artistic context, such understated passages acquire the prominence of anti-style. They register as evasions and hint at motives behind their blandness. Such purposeful haziness even warrants renaming. Upon publication, **"A Prospective Meeting"** was given the vague new title **"Somewhere or Other"** (1:161, 290). One hardly knows what to expect of a work so-named and yet such uncertainty is highly apropos. The poem concerns the pain of imprecision, the difference between focused expectation and achingly unfocused desire. In the course of three stanzas, the title phrase accrues ominous and ironic meanings; the prospective meeting might occur in an as yet unknown "somewhere," or an "other" where that is nowhere, or after death in the "other" world. As possibilities multiply, it becomes clear that the wide spectrum of interpretation is the very cause of the poem's distinctive uneasiness. The vague phrasing turns out to be essential as both means and meaning; it is the method that enables the unnerved poem to hold its fears in suspension, to avoid and yet to probe a source of anxiety.

Another of Rossetti's many ways of saying little yet intimating much is her use of beguilingly familiar motifs. Her poetic economy exploits the associations that a traditional image carries. She allows narrative and thematic anticipations to create a context against which incongruities—sometimes very slight ones—register strongly. When the tension between the expected fit and the actual pres-

sure of a detail becomes apparent, Rossetti's effect is largely achieved. **"An Apple-Gathering"** is a good example of the way such adjustments function. In this poem the plucking of blossoms forestalls the bearing of fruit, an action that seems to imply the early and unwise conferring of sexual favors. But Rossetti's poem is not the obvious one it appears to be. Instead of the predictable contrast between the premature and the timely, **"An Apple-Gathering"** turns on the difference between blossom and apple, i.e., between pre-sexual love and mature appetite. The quality of feeling is the issue. When the heroine is abandoned for a woman with a "basket full" of apples, Rossetti's unexpected point emerges:

> Ah Willie, Willie, was my love less worth
>   Than apples with their green leaves piled above?
> I counted rosiest apples on the earth
>   Of far less worth than love.
>
>   (1:44)

In the procreative and carnal scheme of things, virginal love—chaste pre-sexual feeling—is unfruitful. This cruel lesson, the girl's discovery that she is considered unappealing and unnatural, is not the poem's only point, however. Rossetti's dislocation of the apple-metaphor yields a further irony: society's identification of the virgin with her opposite. Because the heroine has resisted the fall into ripened sexuality, she is rejected by her community: "My neighbors mocked me while they saw me pass / So empty-handed back" (1:43). Rossetti's startling point is that protracted innocence leaves the heroine an outcast as surely as if she were seduced—as surely as if she were the fallen woman the reader initially takes her to be. Rossetti's use of a familiar motif thus impels the reader to enact—and presumably to reject—an identification that the poem obliquely protests.

If the reaction to Rossetti's misleading technique is a slight discomfort at having been led, a more lasting consequence is an intensification of attention. The Rossettian manner, like that of all ironists, creates Rossettian readers. Having been compelled to revise an interpretation, one learns to look for certain strategies in the poems. One becomes alerted to indirection and understatement. Occasionally Rossetti offers extra encouragement to those who would track her dislocations. In **"After Death,"** she subverts a traditional scenario while offering rubrics for interpretation:

> The curtains were half drawn, the floor was
>   swept
>   And strewn with rushes, rosemary and may
>   Lay thick upon the bed on which I lay,
> Where thro' the lattice ivy-shadows crept.
> He leaned above me, thinking that I slept
>   And could not hear him; but I heard him say:
>   "Poor child, poor child:" and as he turned away
> Came a deep silence, and I knew he wept.
> He did not touch the shroud, or raise the fold
>   That hid my face, or take my hand in his,
>   Or ruffle the smooth pillows for my head:
>   He did not love me living; but once dead

He pitied me; and very sweet it is
To know he still is warm tho' I am cold.

(1:37-38)

The appeal of this frequently anthologized sonnet has much to do with Rossetti's skill at representing preternatural sensitivity. The dead woman comprehends, though she cannot see, the thick layer of herbs and the motion of shadows. Such subtlety of perception establishes her as a model for the reader. Moreover, in an obliquely cautionary way, the poem dramatizes the possibility of impercipience. When the viewing male assumes that there is no intelligence beneath the shroud, his mistake hardly matters in death—but it is the kind of error that certainly matters in life. The poem assumes, and exposes, his misinterpretation of the living woman.

It is important to see, too, that Rossetti is concerned with aesthetic as well as social mis-reading. Her poem can even be said to anticipate its own history in the hands of commentators. That is to say, **"After Death"** has often been considered maudlin and self-pitying, but such a view is not necessarily accurate. Rossetti prepares her conclusion by reporting a series of withheld touches: the man does not touch the shroud, raise the cloth, take her hand, or smooth her pillow. This litany manqué catalogs the denying actions of a non-lover, but it is also a caveat to the reader. Its warning is to look beneath the surface, to "lift the fold"; it virtually requires the uncovering of subversive readings. Thus urged, the reader does well to probe the final lines: "but once dead / He pitied me; and very sweet it is / To know he still is warm tho' I am cold." The viewed woman may be expressing gratitude for the viewer's pity, but vengefulness is also possible: the man is warm with life, but often "life is not sweet" (1:155) in Rossetti's poetry. Scorn is likely too: the man is warm with belated feeling, but it is a tepid and perhaps contemptible lukewarmness. Rossetti's technique does not require a settling on one correct interpretation, so much as an awareness that the superficial and sentimental interpretation has become unsettled. Her point is made when the reader becomes conscious of competing readings. To "lift the fold" of Rossetti's conclusion is to become less confident about what the final conjunction of "sweet" and "cold" reveals about the woman's feelings. The possibilities run the gamut from gratitude to magisterial imperturbability.

This last emotion is recurrent in Rossetti's art. Sometimes it is named in elegantly falling rhythm, "a passionless sadness without dread." Frequently it is represented as a condition of suspended animation. The poet who makes an art of what is not said describes her preferred world in terms of what is not sensed. Rossetti's blissful Persephone-figure hears "as through a veil":

She cannot see the grain
Ripening on hill and plain,

She cannot feel the rain
Upon her hand.

(1:27)

The fortunate dead do not see

[The] grass grow long above our heads and feet,
Nor hear the happy lark that soars sky high,
Nor sigh that spring is fleet and summer fleet,
Nor mark the waxing wheat. . . .

(1:155)

The unimpeded rhythm and soothing anaphora of such lines mime the neutralized and evened emotion Rossetti admires. The condition of her dead represents a hypothesis about a perfected life; their **"Dream Land"** ease is a comment on the strains of duration. That the words "long" and "longing" recur with extraordinary frequency in Rossetti's poetry underscores her view that time-bound life is a sequence of yearning episodes:

Come back to me, who wait and watch for
you:—
Or come not yet, for it is over then,
And long it is before you come again.

(2:86)

It is possible, of course, to treat desire as a vivid and vitalizing ardor, and Rossetti occasionally does so. The moon, in one instance, is represented as "a fire of pale desire in incompleteness" (2:273); the saints are "desirous still with still-fulfilled desire" (2:289). More characteristic, however, is the equation of longing with organic disorder; it is a dis-ease or "yearning palsy" (2:125), an unrelenting addiction:

Sometimes I said: This thing shall be no more;
My expectation wearies and shall cease;
I will resign it now and be at peace:
Yet never gave it o'er.

(1:52)

However strong the wish to become "wishless" (2:283), desire creeps in and destroys peace. The refractory, craving self is its own worst enemy, "self stabbing self with keen lack-pity knife" (2:125). In this polarized context of ease and dis-ease, Rossetti's Persephone-figure, her literally unfeeling heroine, is an icon of composure; her unresponsiveness emblematizes wholeness and autonomy.

Rossetti's death-loving poems are best understood, therefore, in relation to the works that liberate their characters from "cankerous" longing (1:19). They are informed by the same values that locate Laura and Lizzie in their imperturbable idyll at the conclusion of **"Goblin Market."** That familiar tale is surely to be read as a myth of quelled yearning. With Laura cheated into a condition of "baulked desire" (1:18), Rossetti effects—through Lizzie's strenuous efforts—the equivalent of an interior act of pained, hard-won detachment. Henceforth Laura is able to suspend the longing that harms her. What happens in **"Goblin Market"** is akin to what might have occurred in

"Mariana" if Tennyson had sprung his heroine out of her despair—but without having Angelo arrive as in Measure for Measure. Fulfillment is not Rossetti's solution; her fantasy is one of release, of irrevocable and unembittered freedom from desire.

The conviction that **"Dream Land"** and **"Goblin Market"** carry is derived, in part, from Rossetti's understanding of the difference between idyllic and actual emotion. She can idealize the triumph over passion because she knows so well the grief of restraint and the secret cost of detachment. The dismay of the virginally rejected heroine of **"An Apple-Gathering"** is much to the point, as is the sorrow of **"Memory."** This highly elusive poem begins, "I nursed it in my bosom while it lived, / I hid it in my heart when it was dead" (1:147). If "it" can be nursed, die, and be mourned, perhaps "it" is like (or is) a child. But a later stanza offers an unsettling metaphor:

> None know the choice I made; I make it still.
>   None know the choice I made and broke my
>   heart,
> Breaking mine idol: I have braced my will
>   Once, chosen for once my part.
>
>   (1:148)

The metaphor of deliberate idol-breaking is clear enough in isolation, but lingering impressions from stanza one allow a disturbing after-image—a destroyed idol/child. In her covert way, Rossetti conveys the anxiety of elective childlessness. The passionless "braced" will forestalls the love that can (in another poem) "fill thy girth / And . . . make fat thy dearth" (1:155). **"Memory"** ends with the ticking of the biological clock, "the time grows old, / Grows old, in which I grieve" (1:148).

In addition to the pathos of childlessness, Rossetti recognizes that passionlessness may be too near-allied to nervelessness. She knows that the impossible wish to be tranquilly whole and composed can decline into a damaging wish to be merely closed off and inert. In **"By the Sea"** she plays her own best critic by exploring the nuances, both positive and negative, of her favorite imagery of insentience.

> Why does the sea moan evermore?
>   Shut out from heaven it makes its moan,
> It frets against the boundary shore;
>   All earth's full rivers cannot fill
>   The sea, that drinking thirsteth still.
>
> Sheer miracles of loveliness
>   Lie hid in its unlooked-on bed:
> Anemones, salt, passionless,
>   Blow flower-like; just enough alive
>   To blow and multiply and thrive.
>
> Shells quaint with curve, or spot, or spike,
>   Encrusted live things argus-eyed,
> All fair alike, yet all unlike,

> Are born without a pang, and die
> Without a pang, and so pass by.
>
>   (1:191)

To be "unlike" and "unlooked-on" is appealing. To live "without a pang" is more attractive still. And yet, to be "just enough alive . . . to thrive" seems inadequate; these sea creatures may be, as Rossetti writes elsewhere, "short of life" (1:29).

This gem of a poem provides a striking example of Rossetti's skill at omission. The reserve that determines so many aspects of her art enables her to pare down her draft by half. The manuscript of **"By the Sea"** has two extra opening stanzas and an additional concluding stanza that is ruinously explicit:

> I would I lived without a pang:
>   Oh happy they who day by day
> Quiescent neither sobbed nor sang;
>   Unburdened with a what or why
>   They live and die and so pass by.
>
>   (1:298)

This clear choice in favor of "unburdened" pre-consciousness is uninterestingly reductive. But in cropped form, the poem allows opposing feelings to remain in suspension. Individuated but preconscious, beautiful but ephemeral: these paired qualities evoke contending responses that are more powerful for being unresolved. Rossetti also revises with an ear to correlations between theme and rhythm. The manuscript line, "Salt passionless anemones" (1:298), is printed as "Anemones, salt, passionless." The final version, with its medial pauses and abutting stresses, is considerably stiffened. Instead of sliding by in alternating rhythm the key word "passionless" now feels chosen—oddly less "passionless"—and placed with Rossettian tact. Such deftness justifies a plea for closer attention to Rossetti's skill as a metrist. Admiring but also dismissive, the assessment of Rossetti's formal accomplishment tends to rest at the adjectival stage. Her lyrics are said to be careful, decorative, easy, firm, natural, pellucid, polished, pure, simple, and apparently or genuinely spontaneous. The occasional technical comment notes the presence of alliteration, feminine endings, monorhyme and other "characteristics which are alike obvious to vigilance and carelessness." And once noted, such features are said to be "not without effect" or "no accident" and passed over. It should be granted that underdeveloped appreciation of Rossetti's "perfect" craft is not entirely the individual commentator's fault. The methods of textual analysis favor a poetry that is compressed, arresting, and highly-textured. Critical vocabulary prefers effects that are counterpointed and paradoxical and is ill-equipped to comment on the rhythmic practice of an apparently plain-speaking stanzaic poet. Nonetheless, Rossetti's style is distinguishable and its means do yield to scrutiny. The subdued quality of many poems, for example, is a matter of stress adjustment. A speaker is made to sound retiring by rhythmically weakening the lines. Thus the revenant in **"At Home,"** does not say of her friends, "They sang, they jested, kissed and laughed." The rollicking levity of four stressed verbs is not true to her excluded condition as an onlooker. Instead she comments, "They sang, they jested, and they laughed" (1:28). The slightly hesitant rhythm—caused by the demoted third stress and the repeated "they"—marks her non-participation. An equally reticent effect is achieved by the nearly opposite technique of impeding a fully-stressed line. The printed version of **"May"** inserts commas in the final verse: "And left me old, and cold, and grey" (1:51). By separating the adjectives, the punctuation suggests a slowed performance of the line and creates the impression of gradually expanding thought. Because the speaker finds that no single word is severe enough for her condition, she accumulates the terms of her grief. Both the wish to specify and the reluctance are felt in the rhythm. Many of Rossetti's adjustments of tempo are reserved for final lines. The intensity of the quiet close is one of her favorite devices. **"Touching 'Never'"** imagines conceding a point: "I would have owned the point you pressed on me, / Was possible, or probable, or true" (2:102). The rhythm of complete concession is achieved by allowing only three full stresses and by pairing the falling rhythm of the polysyllables against a terminal monosyllable. The final "true" is simultaneously slight and heavy, literally understated and yet weightily emphatic. In short, Rossetti's reserved art owes much to the variety of her restrained rhythms.

Rossetti's poetry is all of a piece but not all in the same tone. There are buoyant poems like **"No, Thank You, John"** which vigorously rejects a suitor. To emphasize her heroine's firmness, Rossetti exploits the imperative: "Use your own common sense," "Don't call me false," "Rise above / Quibbles" (1:50, 51). Such briskness foils the wheedling strategies of the suitor whose polite formulas have become a "weariness." The poem, it turns out, is as much a criticism of John's rhetoric as a refusal of marriage. It exposes the obliging manner that attempts to obligate and the strategy of misconstruing another's silences. The heroine resists the suitor with a blunt insistence on the integrity of the unsaid: "I never said I loved you, John." When overt agreeableness masks coerciveness, Rossetti's solution is to insist on the absoluteness of one's verbal abstentions. Occasionally Rossetti's tone is harsh and her sedate irony gives way to open scorn. **"A Triad"** is fierce in its representation of women who are famished for, shamed or vulgarized by love. **"Light Love"** is chilled with anger. Cast as a parting dialogue between an unwed mother and her faithless lover, the poem bristles with tense exchanges. As one after another of the male's exit strategies fail, his manner declines from pretended solicitude through demeaning innuendo to crass insult. The poem is keenly interested in the psychology of this seducer. As he talks of his new love, he gloats over signs of her growing sexual responsiveness:

> Ripe-blooming she, my rose, my peach;
>   She wooes me day and night:
> I watch her tremble in my reach;
>   She reddens, my delight;
>   She ripens, reddens in my sight.
>
>   (1:138)

Such voyeuristic attention to a maiden's trembling sensitivity, such prying regard for this "peach" on her "guarded tree," amounts to a violation of the *hortus conclusus*. In her compelling article on Rossetti's **"Inward Pose,"** Dolores Rosenblum calls attention to Rossetti's thematic "preoccupation with being looked at." She considers Rossetti's "special experience as an artist's model" to have contributed to her "persistent awareness of being scrutinized." The article is too detailed to summarize here; one wants merely to note that Rosenblum's central insight is confirmed in **"Light Love"** and to add a further point. Rossetti's complex reaction to scrutiny is of a piece with her poetics. Her ironies and understatements as well as the chosen restraints of her formal technique manifest an impulse to reveal—but in a manner that is veiled. Even her editorial deletions from volume to volume can be seen as a narrow application of this general tendency. When a poem is too pointed, with a theme in high relief, she withdraws it from view. Such is the case with **"Light Love."** Rossetti probably came to feel exposed by her exposure of caddishness for she excluded it from her 1875 volume. By her usual standards, certainly, the poem is far too explicit in its case against prying eyes.

It is a distinctive feature of Rossetti's art that one of her bitterest moods appears to be her mildest. Her betrayed characters are capable of reproachfulness, yet have remarkably gentle ways of lodging their complaints. Her revenants, in particular, are notably diffident. In numerous poems these forgotten dead return, lament their exclusion, and then withdraw. Some, indeed, make no moan at all and entirely forgo the ghostly privilege of disturbing the living. One such visitant "shivered comfortless, but cast / No chill" on the festivities **"At Home"** (1:28). So retiring are these shades, one must look for some additional motive, one that reinforces reticence, in order to explain their chastened emotion. Rossetti's attitude towards faithlessness is a determining factor here; she regards forgetfulness, inattention, and subtler forms of rejection as no more than ordinarily banal. When, for example, the ghost of a loved woman returns to fetch her beloved, his refusal is represented as wholly intelligible. In lines that echo the marriage vow, he protests his fidelity "for life" and "thro' sickness;" but, he concludes, "death mars all" (1:121). He prefers now to mourn rather than join her, to tend her grave where he has "planted a violet / Which the wind waves, which the dew makes wet" (1:121). This mortal's self-concern is hardly admirable, but its very ordinariness dulls the keenness of one's indignation.

Thus it happens that Rossetti's dying do not weep. They anticipate neglect and sometimes go so far as to absolve the living in advance of their defections:

> When I am dead, my dearest,
> Sing no sad songs for me;
> Plant thou no roses at my head,
>   Nor shady cypress tree:
> Be the green grass above me
>   With showers and dewdrops wet;
> And if thou wilt, remember,
> And if thou wilt, forget.
>
>   (1:58)

Such lyricism is not the result of saintly self-effacement or generosity. It is—as the startling final lines reveal—an expression of anticipated detachment: "Haply I may remember, / And haply may forget." The poem practices immunity from the pain of being forgotten.

There is a peculiar but real satisfaction in such a rehearsal. For the duration that one becomes a ghost, inhabiting one's world like a revenant, life hurts less. To face the present as if it were irrevocably past is to force betrayals into the distance and to muffle resentment. Imagined relocations are not, of course, unique to Rossetti. Tennyson uses a similar device in "Enoch Arden" when he allows the returned sailor to view his own life as it is being lived by another. And a journal entry from Thomas Hardy's *Life* might well serve as a gloss on both poets. Hardy reports actually playing the revenant.

> For my part, if there is any way of getting a melancholy satisfaction out of life it lies in dying, so to speak, before one is out of the flesh; by which I mean putting on the manners of ghosts, wandering in their haunts, and taking their views of surrounding things. To think of life as passing away is a sadness; to think of it as past is at least tolerable. Hence even when I enter into a room to pay a simple morning call I have unconsciously the habit of regarding the scene as if I were a spectre not solid enough to influence my environment; only fit to behold and say, as another spectre said: "Peace be unto you!"

Hardy, like Rossetti, tries to visit the present from a perspective beyond desire. The danger of such a strategy is a self-indulgent dourness that Rossetti, Tennyson and Hardy have each been accused of but, rightly practiced, it becomes a means of autonomy. In Rossetti's case, it makes the experience of self less susceptible to the inconstancy of others.

An understanding of Rossettian ghostliness provides a useful tool for assessing the related strategy of self-effacement. Just as Rossetti's dying prepare to be unremembered, her living often try to be unseen and unheard. If blushes are observed by "pitiless eyes" (1:219), secrets will be no less callously treated. One's recourse is to veil both the flush and the private meanings. Sometimes this wisdom of reserve is projected in seasonal terms. In **"Winter: My Secret,"** Rossetti writes that "spring's an expansive time" (1:47) but warns against any vernal / verbal revelation. As the title suggests, the speaker has a secret, but it is tauntingly withheld: "my secret's mine, and I won't tell." This discrepancy between the poem's actual reticence and its speaker's flaunting manner is conspicuous and fully deliberate; the difference is Rossetti's way of enacting her poem's own counsel against transparency and self-exposure. One of Rossetti's most perceptive admirers has noted this connection: "The indirectness of this subtle poem is part of its strategy for preserving the integrity of its 'secret,' and hence for maintaining the very possibility of integrity and truth in speech." He adds that in Rossetti's poetry generally, secrecy is symbolic and "a sign of the presence of individuality. Independence is a function of the ability to have a secret which

the sanctioned forces of society cannot invade" [Jerome McGann, *Victorian Studies* 23 (1980)].

This observation can be expanded; Rossetti's instinct against parading meanings yields a sub-genre of poems that solicit guesses at meanings that remain undisclosed:

> So she sits and doth not answer
>   With her dreaming eyes,
> With her languid look delicious
>   Almost paradise,
> Less than happy, over-wise
> Now if I could guess her secret,
>   Were it worth the guess?—

Poems often turn on the fact that others do not know an important truth. The lady of **"Monna Innominata"** is perhaps the most striking instance of a character who is defined by communal unknowing, but the card-playing winner of **"The Queen of Hearts"** is a related figure. The object of her "lynx-eyed" rival's watchfulness, Flora sustains the other's "scrutinizing gaze" (1:132-33). She cannot be found out and her "ways are secret still." Such unfathomableness elicits an inverted form of tribute as Flora's interrogator hints at "arts unknown." Should Flora explain her winning technique, there would be no more intimations of mysterious "craft." The irony here is that reticence per se conveys a kind of power. Rossetti's insight in the **"Winter: My Secret," "Monna Innominata,"** and **"The Queen of Hearts"** is that opacity, a well-maintained reserve, is authoritative. Well might each of these ladies scoff: "let them prate; who know not what we knew" (2:91).

Part of the special pleasure of **"The Queen of Hearts"** is the way Rossetti's stanza form dramatizes the speaker's assaults and failures. Pentameter lines indicate a strategy for penetrating Flora's secret, and trimeters reveal consequences:

> I've scanned you with a scrutinizing gaze,
> Resolved to fathom these your secret ways:
>   But, sift them as I will,
>   Your ways are secret still.
>
>   (1:132)

The expansion and contraction of lines, what Rossetti refers to as the "inning and outing," enact the surge and fall of competitive hope. Once the alternation of couplet lengths is felt as a pattern, it comes to be wittily predictive. The diminishment, the shaped appearance of the stanzas on the page, confirms what the opening lines assert: Flora "invariably" wins and baffles. But to point out Rossetti's skill in molding **"The Queen of Hearts"** is a trifle misleading, for such imitative sculpting is not her usual practice. Ordinarily her verse forms should be read not as mimesis, but as restraint. Instead of the flow of blank verse or the suavity of pentameter couplets, Rossetti chooses the confinement of discrete, matched stanzas. Her preference for short measures and full stops confers a high degree of line-integrity; so skilled is her exploitation of the "margin of silence" that simple enjambments come to seem something of a special effect:

> I all-forgotten shivered, sad
>   To stay and yet to part how loth.
>
> (1:28)

The caesura isolates "sad" on the near-side of the line break. But with the next verse, the syntax reorganizes itself so that "sad" is pulled across the gap thereby enacting its own drama of reluctant lingering. Historically, Rossetti's stanzas often derive from ballad forms with their distinct rhythm of stresses and suppressed fourth beats. This last feature is exploited most noticeably in those tetrameter stanzas where a final trimeter isolates itself as a discrete line:

> Their life stood full at blessed noon;
>   I, only I, had passed away:
> "Tomorrow and today," they cried:
>   I was of yesterday.
>
> (1:28)

> So now in patience I possess
>   My soul year after tedious year,
> Content to take the lowest place,
>   The place asigned me here.
>
> (1:207)

The recurrence of such lines can still an entire poem's momentum. But Rossetti can achieve the same patient effect with a sequence of trimeters:

> Where sunless rivers weep
> Their waves into the deep,
> She sleeps a charmed sleep.
>
> (1:27)

Here the triple rhyme and circular syntax (sleeps a . . . sleep) contribute to the lines' inertia so that all seems reluctant to advance. In general, the organization of Rossetti's art is like that of her visual field; she perceives and re-presents not in terms of luxuriant wholes, but with respect to cleanly delimited edges.

Rossetti's poems also demonstrate the perils of communicativeness. The speaker of **"Queen of Hearts,"** for example, seems unaware of the back-stabbing emotion revealed by her admission about card-marking: "I cheated once; I made a private notch / In Heart-Queen's back" (1:133). Such transparency is clearly a liability in a competitor. In other poems Rossetti explores the futility of plain-speaking. When any utterance can be willfully misconstrued as nagging—"Now never teaze me . . . he said in scorn" (1:137)—or when the terms of an argument are degraded, one can refuse to speak at all. The best recourse is "irresponsive" silence: "Aloof, aloof, we stand aloof, so stand / Thou too aloof bound with the flawless band / Of inner solitude" (2:122).

And yet Rossetti does not recommend verbal cowardice. Nor does the demise of her most forthright heroine imply a disapproving or punitive attitude on Rossetti's part. An interesting example of the complexities of reticence, **"Jessie Cameron"** is emphatic about Jessie's uninhibited speech.

> She was a careless, fearless girl,
>   And made her answer plain,
> Outspoken she to earl or churl,
>   Kindhearted in the main,
> But somewhat heedless with her tongue
>   And apt at causing pain.
>
> (1:117)

When Jessie handles an importunate suitor ungently, their verbal stand-off becomes a literal one, and the unyielding pair drown in the incoming tide. But to discover Rossetti's attitude toward Jessie's calamitous plain-speaking requires a look at the poem's long denouement. The remaining six stanzas (out of ten) record folk speculations about Jessie's suitor, the couple's final disposition, and the haunting consequences of their deaths. These stanzas are a virtual anthology of closure devices. By invoking the convention of garrulous, anonymous "watchers," Rossetti multiplies motifs until the over-abundant possibilities collapse into one another. Finally, all are irrelevant to the single, looming fact of Jessie's strong resistance. The more "some say" about the episode, the less telling each version becomes:

> Whether he helped or hindered her,
>   Threw up his life or lost it well,
> The troubled sea for all its stir
>   Finds no voice to tell.
>
> (1:119)

By disallowing the hypotheses that might close Jessie's story, Rossetti shows that fearless speech remains an unresolved issue. Indeed, the final inexplicitness of **"Jessie Cameron"** holds out the possibility of subversive reading. Rossetti is not transparent or effusive, but she plainly invites the reader to "lift the fold" of her poem's reserve and see that her narrative guardedness protects a tale of unguarded utterance.

In the last analysis, Rossettian reticence is the opposite of evasiveness. Her withholdings have the feel of potential communications. Hovering between expression and non-expression, they serve as intimations to be pursued. By insisting vividly on what is not felt, not said, not revealed, not narrated, Rossetti engages the reader while she herself appears to disengage. Operating like an absent-presence, she directs attention, orchestrates experience, and invulnerably annotates our shared vulnerability. Like her own Persephones, ghosts, and secret-keepers, she establishes her distance. But it is a strategic distance. Rightly understood, Rossetti's remoteness is participatory; her abstentions are the means of her special intensity.

Roderick McGillis (essay date 1987)

SOURCE: "Simple Surfaces: Christina Rossetti's Work for Children," in *The Achievement of Christina Rossetti,* edited by David A. Kent, Cornell, 1987, pp. 208-30.

[*In the following essay, McGillis analyzes Rossetti's works for children, arguing that these works offer lessons and insights for adults as well as children.*]

In almost everything Christina Rossetti wrote for young readers we hear an authorial voice strong in ambiguity, whispering secrets beneath what Jerome J. McGann calls "those deceptively simple poetic surfaces" [Jerome J. McGann, "Christina Rossetti's Poems: A New Edition and a Revaluation," *Victorian Studies* 23 (1980)]. As we allow our minds to play upon the surfaces, what appears straightforward becomes richly complex, so much so that meaning often becomes of doubtful certainty and of less importance than the simple surfaces themselves. We look less for meaning in this work than for the subtleties of form and language. In other words, Rossetti's work for children treats its readers to an experience of the high morality of art, thus offering them the opportunity for freeplay, for participation in imaginative understanding. The function of fantasy in works such as *Goblin Market* (1862), *Sing-Song* (1872), and *Speaking Likenesses* (1874) is to deconstruct allegoric and didactic meaning; the characteristic psychological tension in Victorian fantasy, the pull of both duty and desire, is evident in Rossetti's work, but its implications go beyond simple dichotomy. It posits a reader capable of comprehending and accepting this uncertain world as a schoolhouse where we prepare for a certain world yet to come.

Rossetti's works for children include *Maude: Prose and Verse,* written in 1850, but not published until 1897, three years after her death. Maude's story lacks the vibrancy of Rossetti's other works for children, and it has not reached the audience Rossetti had in mind. *Goblin Market, Sing-Song,* and *Speaking Likenesses* are much more successful works for children. *Goblin Market* and *Sing-Song* continue to appear in children's lists. *Speaking Likenesses* has not received the same approval as the two earlier works, but it deserves attention because of its intricate form. In the following discussion I examine the three works in the chronological order in which they appeared to show that Rossetti's interest in language and form does not alter radically from work to work.

Criticism has had less to say about *Sing-Song* and *Speaking Likenesses* than about *Goblin Market* (I, 11-26), for reasons that are not difficult to imagine. Rossetti did not, in fact, write *Goblin Market* for children, and therefore the poem invites the attention of a mature reader; *Goblin Market* manifestly contains the theme of sexual frustration, a sure hook for academic readers; and finally the poem satisfies the critic's desire to allegorize. As McGann has noted, despite Rossetti's claim that *Goblin Market* is not an allegory, readers refuse to take her at her word. Even a sympathetic reader, Rossetti's brother William Michael, reports in one sentence his sister's repeated assertion that, as he puts it, the poem "is not a moral apologue consistently carried out in detail," and in the next asserts: "I find at times that people do not see the central point of the story, such as the authoress intended it: and she has expressed it too, but perhaps not with due emphasis." Critics have proposed various allegoric inter-

pretations for *Goblin Market:* Christian, sexual, psychological, social, artistic, subversive. Most critics are not as candid as A. A. DeVitis, who sees "the essential meaning of the poem" revealed by "an interpretation of the symbolism and an appreciation of the imagery." If other readers are not as forthright as DeVitis, they nonetheless imply they have grasped the poem's "essential meaning."

Even when a reading formally deconstructs the poem's stated meaning, we are not left in doubt as to its real meaning. Jeanie Watson, in the most recent essay on *Goblin Market,* analyzes Rossetti's use of the "interplay between moral tale and fairy tale that allows [the poem] to be utterly subversive and yet ultimately moral" [*Children's Literature* 12 (1984)]. In this poem "the immoral moral triumphs," and the reader learns that "maidens have the right to buy the fruit of Goblin Market." In short, Watson allegorizes the poem as a Romantic text that calls for "perception and participation in whole vision." *Goblin Market* becomes, in effect, a sequel to *The Book of Thel,* only in Rossetti's poem the female does not retreat from experience. In Watson's reading, Lizzie and Laura repudiate the "fruits of knowledge," but the reader remains unconvinced that they are right in doing so: "Laura and Lizzie are saved to their damnation, and we and Christina Rossetti know it, even if they do not." Reading this interpretation, I find it difficult to understand the "discomfort" the ending of the poem communicates, since Rossetti (apparently) and Watson had no difficulty accepting the subversion of the poem's ostensible moral.

But Laura and Lizzie are manifestly not "saved to their damnation." Not only does Laura come through her experience young and refreshed, but years later she tells her children the story of her relations with goblin men. Questions come to mind, among them: who are the men Laura and Lizzie marry? and why does Laura, not Lizzie, become a story-teller? But answers are as stubbornly irretrievable (or perhaps irrelevant) as the questions are insistent. The poem's subversive power derives from its refusal to offer pat morals of any sort; it refuses allegory. When Watson says the two sisters are saved only to be damned, she bases her argument on the idea that Laura and Lizzie accept convention and mouth familiar Victorian pieties regarding sisterly love and the avoidance of experience. In this view Laura, after tasting the fruits of experience and later falling into a trance, awakes renewed; apparently she has retreated to innocence.

The result of Laura's long night of senselessness certainly gives the impression of a return to innocence:

> Laura awoke as from a dream,
> Laughed in the innocent old way,
> Hugged Lizzie but not twice or thrice;
> Her gleaming locks showed not one thread of
>   grey,
> Her breath was sweet as May
> And light danced in her eyes.
>
> [ll. 537-42]

Laura's awakening is reminiscent of the scene in the *Odyssey* in which Odysseus' sailors return to human form after Odysseus has overpowered Circe. Transformed, the sailors "not only became men again but looked younger and much handsomer and taller than before." Their experience has proved efficacious; they seem rejuvenated. We understand the sailors' fall into bestiality as transitional. If their renewal is a renewal of innocence, however, it is closer to what in Blake's terms is organized innocence than to unorganized innocence. Laura's trial is similarly renovating. She wakes "as from a dream." Her experience is perhaps as inevitable as dreaming, for it is a mental or psychological event. When she laughs in the "innocent old way," we can hear (helped by the emphasis on "old way") an ambiguity. She laughs in the *manner* of her former innocence; she laughs in an innocent, yet aged, wise, old way. Laura, however, is not so much renewed as she is transfigured: her hair "gleams" and light dances in her eyes.

Transfiguration, of course, is not simply transformation; Rossetti's values are not Homer's. Laura's awakening has Christian import. She rises in the early morning as

> early reapers plodded to the place
> Of golden sheaves,
> And dew-wet grass
> Bowed in the morning winds so brisk to pass,
> And new buds with new day
> Opened of cup-like lilies on the stream
>
> [ll. 531-36]

The language here resonates with biblical echoes. In Psalm 126, for example, the Lord turns "the captivity of Zion" and fills the Israelites' "mouth . . . with laughter, and [their] tongue with singing"; they "were like them that dream." Similarly, on a fresh harvest morning, Laura wakes from her dream to laugh. The psalm tells us that he who "goeth forth and weepeth, bearing precious seed, shall doubtless come again with rejoicing, bringing his sheaves with him." And Isaiah 18:4 tells us that the Lord's dwelling place is "like a cloud of dew in the heat of harvest." Finally, the lilies, as Dante Gabriel Rossetti's *The Girlhood of Mary Virgin* (1849) and *Ecce Ancilla Domini!* (1850) remind us, represent purity and virginity. The "golden sheaves," "new buds," "new day," and "cup-like lilies" in *Goblin Market* suggest not only harvest but also revelation, the uncovering of a better world. Rossetti's description, then, suggests a spiritual awakening, an awakening of almost apocalyptic import. The revelation that has come to Laura has come after her soul's sleep. The soul's sleep, as McGann points out, is a "peculiar millenarian and Anabaptist doctrine," and "the single most important enabling principle in Rossetti's poetry" [Jerome McGann, "The Religious Poetry of Christina Rossetti," *Critical Inquiry* 10 (1983)]. The soul's sleep is a "waiting time" between death and judgment, a time during which the soul can dream of or catch glimpses of paradise. In *Goblin Market* Laura experiences the soul's sleep after receiving the "fiery antidote" (l. 559) from Lizzie. We do not know what passed in her mind during that long night, but we do know Laura was "past" both pleasure and anguish. "Is it death or is it life?" asks the mysterious narrator. Whichever state it is, the result is "life out of death" (ll. 522-25). The life Laura returns to on the harvest morning brings her marriage and children; more important, she becomes a storyteller.

We might recall that after eating the goblin fruit Laura becomes silent: "She said not one word in her heart's sore ache" (l. 261). She lies awake "silent till Lizzie slept," and then she rises to weep and gnash her teeth "for baulked desire" (ll. 265, 267). For days, she watches "in sullen silence of exceeding pain" (l. 271). The goblin men have effectively silenced Laura; in accepting their fruit she has lost her voice. In this world men are the rhymers, the speakers, the storytellers, the merchants. Before Lizzie starts out to meet the goblin men on their own terms, with a "silver penny in her purse," she remembers Jeanie

> Who should have been a bride;
> But who for joys brides hope to have
> Fell sick and died
> In her gay prime,
> In earliest Winter time,
> With the first glazing rime,
> With the first snow-fall of crisp Winter time.
>
> [ll. 313-19]

It is not too much to imagine that the goblins' "sugar-baited words" (l. 234), their glazing rhymes, silenced Jeanie because she, like Laura, paid the goblin price: "a golden curl" (l. 125). Lizzie refuses this price and tosses her penny to the goblins. Taking part in the market place as an equal, Lizzie confounds the goblins:

> They began to scratch their pates,
> No longer wagging, purring,
> But visibly demurring,
> Grunting and snarling.
>
> [ll. 390-93]

They then buffet and batter her until her resistance wearies them. Flinging back her penny and kicking their fruits, the goblins disappear into the ground, into the brook, or into the air. They are incorporated into three of the four elements.

The fourth element—fire—remains for Laura. She receives the "fiery antidote" (l. 559) from Lizzie, and this brings her release from the goblin bondage and its accompanying release of language. Bondage to goblin men is replaced by maternal bonding. Laura and Lizzie are bound up in their children, their "mother-hearts beset with fears" (l. 546). The word "beset" suggests not only that fears assail them from all sides but also that the fears brace those hearts with maternal care. For Laura this care includes telling the story of her experience with the goblin men; she repeats her history in words and transforms this history into fiction, into fairy tale. She gathers "the [not "her"] little ones" about her and tells them "of her early prime" (ll. 548-49). She would tell of

> Those pleasant days long gone
> Of not-returning time:
> Would talk about the haunted glen,
> The wicked, quaint fruit-merchant men,
> Their fruit like honey to the throat
> But poison in the blood . . .
>
> [ll. 550-55]

It is notable that Laura recalls her past experiences as "pleasant," a strange adjective in light of her listlessness and frustration after she ate the goblin fruit. But in the form of narrative those experiences *are* pleasant. And what Laura is now capable of seeing is the worth of her early fall from innocence. She now perceives the nature of the goblins' wickedness: their perversion of language.

Laura not only calls the goblins "wicked," she also calls them "quaint," which indicates the goblins are strange in appearance, as indeed they are. But "quaint" also refers to their cleverness with language; they are quaint orators, cunningly reversing what we know: "One parrot-voiced and jolly / Cried 'Pretty Goblin' still for 'Pretty Polly'" (ll. 112-13). One of them speaks in "tones as smooth as honey" (l. 108), a metaphor that appears again in Laura's narrative when she describes the goblin fruits as "honey to the throat / But poison in the blood" (ll. 554-55). This line echoes Revelation 10:8-10, in which an angel commands John to take the "little book" that the angel holds and to "eat it up," and, John says, "it was in my mouth sweet as honey: as soon as I had eaten it, my belly was bitter." In other words, Laura's experience is revelatory; she has become a seer and sayer free of the earthbound goblins who would silence her and confine her to a sterile natural cycle. Yet without the goblins, without the nameless bitterness, she would not be free to speak.

We might conjecture that Laura, speaking as she does to an audience of children, chooses the fairy tale as her form of utterance. As many commentators have pointed out, *Goblin Market* is a fairy tale. Alan Barr compares the poem to "Snow White," in which the beautiful girl who eats a poisoned apple can be revived from her deadly sleep only by a prince. Dorothy Mermin speaks of Rossetti's story as "a transformation of a traditional fairy tale," but, unlike Snow White (whom Mermin does not mention), Laura is not "cured" by a prince; her cure comes when she "ceases to want him." According to Mermin, Lizzie, who not only brings the antidote to Laura but who also "*is* the antidote," is the "folktale heroine," since she outwits the goblins, "getting their treasure without paying their price."

That Rossetti has the fairy tale tradition in mind is hardly questionable, and that she is aware of the fairy tales' understanding of female identity and the demands made upon it by a patriarchal society (especially as presented by the Brothers Grimm) seems just as clear. In many of the tales females are robbed of their identity and pushed

to the edge of hysteria by male attitudes and male tyranny (see, for example, "The Rabbit's Bride" or "Fred and Kate"). In *Goblin Market* Laura speaks of stealing from the goblins: "Good Folk, I have no coin, / To take were to purloin" (ll. 116-17). Ironically, it is the goblins who "purloin"; they steal Laura's identity—her voice, her lock of golden hair, her maidenhood. The goblins do not show "all good fidelity"; truly they do not sell such fruit in any town, since once paid with that which is most precious, they depart. In actuality, because of Lizzie's efforts, the goblins do not accomplish the theft of Laura's identity. Lizzie and Laura are perhaps "two sides of a single individual" [Alan Barr, "Sensuality Survived: Christina Rossetti's *Goblin Market*," *English Miscellany* 28-29 (1979-1980)] and, after Lizzie's successful confrontation with the goblins, Laura's identity is restored.

If there is one fairy tale from which *Goblin Market* derives, it surely must be "The Robber Bridegroom." In this story a father offers his younger daughter in marriage to a stranger, despite the fact that his daughter does not love him "as a bride ought to love her bridegroom." The girl visits her prospective husband only to learn that he is the leader of a band of robbers. An old woman in the robber's house warns her that her "wedding can only be with Death." Hiding behind a large cask, the girl witnesses a gruesome scene: the robber with his henchmen returns with another young girl "that had been ensnared like the bride." The robbers kill the young girl. One tries to remove a ring from one of the dead girl's fingers (in some translations he chops off the finger), and the ring flips behind the cask. The robbers soon fall asleep; the girl escapes. When the bridegroom comes for his bride, a feast is set and the guests tell stories. When the bride's turn comes she tells of her "dream" in which she describes the events she had witnessed in the robber's house. She tells her tale carefully, building up to the moment when she reveals the ring. The bridegroom and his gang of thieves are executed. In this story the murdered young girl, like Jeanie in *Goblin Market,* illustrates the fate of the female who accepts male domination. The old woman, whose role is like Lizzie's but without the implications of Christian sacrifice, assists the bride in avoiding the usual female fate. The bride becomes master of her fate.

McGann points out that "personal independence" is one of Rossetti's "central subjects," and to the extent that Laura and Lizzie are free of the goblin menace, they become independent. Apparently, however, the two girls do not (as Mermin suggests Laura does) cease to desire a male. Whom they marry remains a mystery, but it is certain that they become "wives / With children of their own." Marriage is in keeping with the biblical overtones of the poem and in Rossetti's poetry often represents "wholeness, sanity, and integration." We might recall "Snow White" or especially "Sleeping Beauty," in which the marriage signals a renewal of the kingdom, a recovery of the land. Or we might recall "The Frog Prince," in which, paradoxically, the ugliness of sex, when rejected, is transformed into the lineaments of gratified desire. Perhaps Rossetti (in *Goblin Market* at least) is not so much "ambivalent about the sensual joys of this world" as she is aware of the fairy tale attitudes to marriage and to male-female relationships generally. Perhaps she goes farther and plays with the form. McGann speaks of *Goblin Market* as exhibiting "the disarming formal appearance of a children's fairy story."

It is true, I think, that *Goblin Market* troubles the reader through its formal as well as its thematic ambiguities. The poem teases us out of thought; it plays with our reactions and expectations; it shifts our understanding of language. It might not be too much to say that the poem is about its own form, its language. Like the fairy tale, *Goblin Market* foregrounds design and language. The opening announces this formal interest:

> Morning and evening
> Maids heard the goblins cry:
> "Come buy our orchard fruits,
> Come buy, come buy:
> Apples and quinces,
> Lemons and oranges,
> Plump unpecked cherries,
> Melons and raspberries,
> Bloom-down-cheeked peaches,
> Swart-headed mulberries,
> Wild freè-born cranberries,
> Crab-apples, dewberries,
> Pine-apples, blackberries,
> Apricots, strawberries;—
> All ripe together
> In summer weather . . .
>
> [ll. 1-16]

And the catalogue continues for fifteen more lines. These lines establish, as Barr says, "the obvious tone of wonder and fairy-tale like fantasy" and also a "strongly commercial aspect of the language." What Barr does not point out is that fairy tale language and commercial language are opposites, just as morning and evening are opposites. The reader immediately learns to be wary of goblin language; goblins are hawkers, double talkers. Why, for example, need they say "orchard fruits" rather than simply "fruits" (the third line would then scan the same as the fourth line)? What the goblins are selling is language; they take a familiar patterning of language in children's literature—the list or catalogue—and charm Laura with it ("Their offers should not charm us"). They "suck" her in, although it is she who "sucked until her lips were sore" (l. 136).

The verbal stream at the beginning of the poem is, of course, a lie. Instead of freeing language and releasing passion, the goblin words fix, enclose, suspend, and exhaust those who listen to them with eager curiosity. The thirty-one-line opening bark of the goblins begins and ends with the exhortation to "come buy." In all, there are only six different rhymes in this passage. The rhyme on "buy" ("cry," "fly," "by," "try," and "eye") sounds at the beginning, middle, and end of the passage, effectively enclosing and fixing it. Further, the most frequently repeated rhyme, on "berries," clogs these lines. The goblins

sound sweet "cooing all together" (l. 78); they sound "kind and full of loves" (l. 79), but their sound is deceiving, cloying. Tucked into the middle of this list of fruits is the familiar *carpe diem* warning: "Morns that pass by, / Fair eves that fly" (ll. 17-18). Here is the nub of the goblins' argument: come buy before it is too late. But the roll call of fruits from apples to citrons mutes this hint of change and decay. The catalogue fills the mind with the fullness of nature, yet it, like innocence, can deceive. Nursery rhyme and fairy tale unlock the word hoard and play with language; the goblins' list purports to do the same, while in truth it is merely a huckster's cry. The language the goblins sell betrays the sense of community that fairy tales and nursery rhymes promote. Laura restores this sense of community at the end when she gathers the little ones about her and bids "them cling together" (l. 561). The final words of the poem, Laura's words, are often thought to be overly didactic, but they speak of brotherhood—or, in this case, sisterhood—of the importance of friendship and community. The poem has shown, through its similes, through its repetition, through its verbal echoes, that "sister" is as much figurative as actual.

Finally, then, *Goblin Market* is a poem of figuration. Its surface dazzles with similes (there are forty in all), accented rhythms, and intricate rhymes. Its verbal ingenuity turns a "kernel-stone" (l. 281) into a "carnal" stone and the act of sucking becomes a draining of the self, a shrinking into the self. Clearly, it is not by eating but by being eaten that one comes closest to the soul of another. Clearly, it is by perceiving nature as figuring a higher reality and not as a reality in itself that we free ourselves from the tyranny of material things. Laura's mistake is in accepting the goblin fruit as literal; she buys from the goblins a language without polysemy. The result is a craving for more and more, a carnality that cannot be satisfied, at least not until Lizzie returns home and offers herself to her sister: "Laura, make much of me" (l. 472). And the reader must make much of *Goblin Market*. Language is untrustworthy when we fail to make enough from it. The fall from innocence is a verbal fall as much as anything else, and if children are not to experience language only as the hectoring babble of the market place they must be prepared at an early age to appreciate the play inherent in it.

This emphasis on the imaginative possibilities of language informs Rossetti's first published work for children, *Sing-Song*. *Sing-Song* is a book of nursery rhymes, as the subtitle informs us, but these rhymes are acutely aware of the verbal world children live in, and they encourage children to enjoy the play of language. Some rhymes are obviously playful:

> A city plum is not a plum;
> A dumb-bell is no bell, though dumb;
> A party rat is not a rat;
> A sailor's cat is not a cat;
> A soldier's frog is not a frog;
> A captain's log is not a log.
>
> [ll, 21]

That words are not so much referential as they are met-aphoric is clear. A city plum is and is not a plum, but a plum, whether city or otherwise, *is* dumb. Words in po-etic discourse move in the direction of sound play and their semantic meanings loosen. A frog may sit on a log, although a soldier's frog more appropriately sits on a shoulder. And it has nothing whatever to do with a cap-tain's log. A captain's log, although not a log, is probably made from one. In Saussurian terms the signifiers are not at one with the signifieds; instead, Rossetti's rhyme points out how in poetic discourse metaphor detaches us from the one-dimensional relationship between word and con-cept. In other words, poetic language need not refer to a direct reality. The purpose of "A city plum is not a plum" is not, as R. Loring Taylor suggests, to give information or to teach children "basic skills." As Anthony Easthope says,

> The language of a poem may aim for transparency but this does not make a poem referential. Transparency, a certain relation of signifier and signified, is not the same thing as reference, which is a relation between signified and reality . . . in all discourse the signifier precedes the signified and no discourse is by nature transparent. But this fact does not preclude there being a discourse which gives knowledge by referring to a reality. It does mean that discourse providing such knowledge depends upon the reader being positioned so as to read the discourse as transparent and treat it as referential. On this basis the study of poetry can give knowledge of poetry by referring to it accurately [Anthony Easthope, *Poetry as Discourse,* 1983].

The poems in *Sing-Song* (at least a great many of them) give pleasure in the way all nursery songs give pleasure, through their rhyme, their rhythms, and their metaphors; they teach children to understand, and to have fun with, the play of language. In these poems, as in *Goblin Mar-ket,* Rossetti emphasizes sound, repetition, and the heavi-ly accentual line. Meaning emerges from the reader's engaging the poem as discourse, that is, as a form of communication that differs from statement. Any prose statement we might produce from our reading of Rosset-ti's poems derives from formal elements. Take for exam-ple this poem:

> "Kookoorookoo! kookoorookoo!"
> Crows the cock before the morn;
> "Kikirikee! kikirikee!"
> Roses in the east are born.
>
> "Kookoorookoo! kookoorookoo!"
>   Early birds begin their singing;
> "Kikirikee! kikirikee!:
>   The day, the day, the day is springing.
>
> [Il, 20]

More obviously than other poems in the book, this poem derives from nursery rhymes such as "Cock-a-doddle doo! My dame has lost her shoe," "Titty cum tawtay," and "Bow, wow, wow." The voice that speaks the poem pro-duces two sound words that are similar yet opposite. The consonants are the same, but the vowel sounds differ. In the first stanza this pattern raises the question: if cocks crow "kookoorookoo," then who or what cries "kikiri-kee"? The second stanza might indicate that early birds sing "kikirikee," but the semicolon at the end of the sec-ond line (in both stanzas) works against this reading. If we allow the semicolon to divide each stanza in half, then the "kikirikee" is a general sound communicating the energy and life of the new day. The last line with its three repetitions of "day" reinforces this sense of vitality. So too do the alliteration and assonance: "crows cock before morn kee east roses born."

The word "springing" not only supports the energetic bounce of the poem's rhythm and the liveliness of the new morn, it also suggests springtime and that pastoral freshness so pervasive in *Sing-Song*. A hint of this qual-ity is perhaps evident in the roses that have their birth in the east. Rossetti delicately shades her meaning so that pastoral freshness is inseparable from spiritual celebra-tion. Georgina Battiscombe notes that *Sing-Song* contains "no mention of God, or of the Christian stories so famil-iar to Victorian children, or indeed, of religion in any form" [Georgina Battiscombe, *Christina Rossetti: A Di-vided Life,* 1981]. Yet angels, the Maker, heaven, faith, hope, love—all these appear in *Sing-Song*. An aura of spirituality is apparent both in this poem and throughout *Sing-Song*. We begin to suspect there is a spiritual mean-ing in the line "Roses in the east are born," especially when we consider that roses and other flowers appear as figures in at least fifteen poems in the volume. The poem, then, is a celebration of birth, a new morning, spiritual vitality, and natural harmony. The "kookoorookoo" and "kikirikee" do not belong exclusively to specific birds, and the speaker of the poem is not a specific individual. This verse, like all nursery rhymes, is a collective song, only here the song is a collective hymn of praise to a world that reflects the divine.

But this reading presents only half the story. "Kook-oorookoo, kookoorookoo" is but one poem of many in this volume. We experience *Sing-Song* as we experi-ence Blake's *Songs of Innocence and Experience,* as a coherent text; and, Battiscombe points out, "even in these childlike verses for and about children Christina cannot forget the great central themes of her poetry, love, death, and parting." In other words, there is a dark side to the pastoral innocence of *Sing-Song*. The reader learns that spring blossoms and youth are frail and that today and tomorrow are brief; in one poem the poet exhorts three children not to "wait for roses" (II, 26) and so lose the day. We might recall the opposition of vowel sounds in "kookoorookoo" and "kikirikee." Add to this the oppo-sition (in the same poem) of bird and flower, active verb and passive verb in the first stanza, and we might catch a hint of deeper, unstated opposites: east and morning imply west and evening, birth leads to death, and what springs up must come down.

One of the best-known poems in *Sing-Song* reflects the presence of the divine. **"Who has seen the wind"** gives simple, yet intense, expression to the numinous:

Who has seen the wind?
  Neither I nor you:
But when the leaves hang trembling
  The wind is passing thro'.

Who has seen the wind?
  Neither you nor I:
But when the trees bow down their heads
  The wind is passing by.

                          [ll. 42]

The movement from three to two to four to three stress lines in the first stanza accurately suggests the passing wind, and the half stress on "hang" effectively modulates the breeze. Line three of the second stanza has five stresses to convey the strength of the wind that bends the branches. The sense of the wind as *inspiritus,* the breath of the divine, comes through in the word "trembling"; the leaves that tremble express awe. Reverence is in the line: "But when the trees bow down their heads." And the two words "thro'" and "by" convey the spiritual power to penetrate or to brush by. In other poems, too, Rossetti uses the wind as an image of divine immanence and power both to emphasize the pastoral harmony of her world and to show the darker side of pastoral innocence. **"O wind, where have you been"** and **"O wind, why do you never rest"** depict sweetness and restlessness. In **"The wind has such a rainy sound,"** wind and sea combine to present an evocation of death.

It is fair to say, however, that joy dominates here and throughout **Sing-Song**. Even when their theme is clearly death and parting, the poems express an element of joy:

"Goodbye in fear, goodbye in sorrow,
  Goodbye, and all in vain,
Never to meet again, my dear—'
  Never to part again."
"Goodbye today, goodbye tomorrow,
  Goodbye till earth shall wane,
Never to meet again, my dear—"
  Never to part again."

                          [ll. 49]

Two voices speak. One voice, that which speaks the first three lines of each quatrain, is melancholy and negative. The second voice, however, transforms the first speaker's negative into a positive. Like the child in Wordsworth's "We Are Seven," the second speaker does not accept discontinuity. In its verbal repetition and its complicated interlocking rhymes, the poem centers on form; the two quatrains draw together. Although the implication here is not exactly that "death is the bringer of joy," in **Sing-Song** as a whole Rossetti presents death as a positive aspect of life. In part, she accomplishes this transformation by identifying death as one point in a larger pattern, and as a natural event. A child may die, but the child is a rose: "I have but one rose in the world, / And my one rose stands a-drooping" (II, 39). Ships may go down, but they do so like apples in the orchard tumbling from their tree. A baby dies making father and mother sigh; flowers also "bloom to die" and they ask not why: they accept the

way of things, especially since "if all were sun and never rain, / There'd be no rainbow still" (II, 24). Finally, death is soul's sleep: "Our little baby fell asleep, / And may not wake again / For days and days, and weeks and weeks" (II, 20). But the poem assures us he will "wake again." Death sends a child's soul "home to Paradise" and leaves his "body waiting here" (II, 22).

Throughout **Sing-Song** death is an imaginative idea, not a sign of closure. In other words, just as Rossetti's poems delight in word play and intricacy of form and allusion, her notion of death is equally fertile and equally at variance with discontinuity and finality. Rossetti's concern with death and attention to poetic form is perhaps best summarized in the volume's final poem:

Lie a-bed,
Sleepy head,
Shut up eyes, bo-peep;
Till daybreak
Never wake:—
Baby, sleep.

                          [ll. 51]

Taylor finds an "alarming ambiguity" in this lullaby, and he also finds "disconcerting" a "tendency to equate sleep

Frontispiece to Speaking Likenesses, *drawn by Arthur Hughes.*

with death" in *Sing-Song* generally. The sleep that is death, however, is Rossetti's depiction of the soul's sleep, that comforting time of preparation and waiting for a grand new morning. In **"Lie a-bed"** the masculine rhymes and strong end-stops at the third and last lines signal finality, closure, death. But the two halves of the little poem are hooked together with the rhyme of "bo-peep" and "sleep." "Bo-peep" reminds us we are in the world of nursery rhyme where rhyme is strongly musical; the words have a nonreferential significance and power. If we catch a somber note here, as Taylor does, if we allow our minds to play on the meaning of "wake" and consider its two senses—emerging from sleep and watching over the body of a dead person—we might also consider the wake of the poem as the track it leaves behind, the residue in the mind. We might hear that coupling of "peep" and "sleep," an aural connection that suggests a seeing in sleep. During the soul's sleep we catch glimpses of the greater reality to come; we peep into the future. During our nightly dreams we peep into our unconscious. This little lullaby allows us a peep into the mystery of sleep both in its nightly and in its premillenarian aspects. This baby will not sleep the sleep of death, but this baby may or may not sleep until the next morning or the final morning. The sense of closure in all lullabies is premature, since there is always more to come, more to sing.

Sing-Song contains many themes: death, mother love, pastoral delicacy, desire, class divisions, suffering, the importance of family, love, and fantasy. There are lessons in arithmetic, time, money, and color. Even in these teaching poems we can discern play with closure and its opposite. The poem explaining time, for example, begins with the smallest unit of clock time: "How many seconds in a minute? / Sixty, and no more in it." The sense of closure is blunt: "and no more in it." Time circumscribes experience; we have twenty-four hours in a day "for work and play," and the almanac "makes clear" there are twelve months in a year. Yet time cannot circumscribe experience, as the poem's final couplet makes clear: "How many ages in time? / No one knows the rhyme" (II, 30). "Time" and "rhyme"—the two words are united and remind us that neither completes anything. Rhyme is part of a poem's time, its musical beat, but it has nothing to do with measurable clock or seasonal time. Rhyme is as timeless as language and sound. Time, on the other hand, is rhymeless in the sense that it cannot be packaged in a couplet, since "no one knows the rhyme"; paradoxically, time and rhyme perform this coupling which the poem says is impossible.

Sing-Song, like *Goblin Market,* is less concerend with allegory or didacticism than it is with intensity of both form and language. Rossetti chooses her forms—fairy tale and nursery rhyme—carefully. These forms foregound play, repetition, song, and language. What Douglas Kneale says in the context of Wordsworth's *Prelude* applies here: "The question of what a text is 'about' . . . shifts from a concern with historical or referential meaning to a concern with rhetorical or semiological foregrounding." This concern is nowhere more apparent than in Rossetti's last book for children, *Speaking Likenesses,* the only prose

work Rossetti published for children. *Speaking Likenesses* is a fantasy consisting of three stories held together by the framing device of an aunt who tells the stories to five sisters while they sew, draw, or darn. The first story, by far the longest, tells of little Flora's eighth birthday and the dream she has during the afternoon. The second story tells of a girl named Edith who attempts vainly to boil a kettle. The last story takes place on Christmas Eve, and it concerns the night journey of Maggie to the country house of a doctor. The first and third stories contain frightening and disturbing images and action. This is probably why the *Times Literary Supplement* called *Speaking Likenesses* "a peculiarly revolting book" (May 29, 1959, p. xi). Taylor too finds the stories in *Speaking Likenesses* self-defeating and "unclear"; rather than a children's book Rossetti has written "a sad and sometimes bitter parable of a lonely lady." But in this book too Rossetti's concerns are playful. Her narrator, for example, is a source of fun, and we should be careful not to conclude that this "aunt" speaks for Christina Rossetti. True, the narrator's "didactic stance permeates the book," but the children who are her audience manage to undercut her didacticism.

Clara, Jane, Laura, Ella, and Maude continually interrupt the narrator's storytelling. They comment on the oddness of a name, they ask for clarification, or they point out improbable assertions. The cumulative effect is to point out the difference between the irritable, presumptuous, and matter-of-fact aunt from the curious children who are receptive to fancy and wonder. For example, when, in the first of the three stories, the narrator describes the sunny afternoon of Flora's birthday, she remarks that "bell flowers rang without clappers." Before she can complete her sentence, Maude interrupts to ask whether bell flowers can ring without clappers. The narrator shrugs the question off with the reply: "Well, not exactly, Maude: but you're coming to much more wonderful matters!" In other words, don't ask difficult questions and attend to the rest of my story.

Yet the narrator's attitude to storytelling is rather strange: she urges her listeners to occupy themselves with sewing, painting, or darning while they listen. When Jane and Laura appear to become engrossed in the fantastic room with animated furniture, the narrator admonishes them not to "*quite* forget the pocket handkerchiefs you sat down to hem." Sitting down to hear a story is apparently too idle an occupation for this aunt. Like many other writers for children in the nineteenth century, Rossetti, through her narrator, expresses a distrust of fantasy, of make-believe, of story for its own sake. When Jane asks whether the furniture that arranges itself flat against the walls also flattens itself across the door, her aunt answers briskly: "Why, yes, I suppose it may have done so, Jane. . . . At any rate, as this is all make-believe, I say No. Attention!" At one point in the third story the narrator interrupts herself to ask the children if they know what would happen to the heroine of her story (a girl named Maggie) if she were to sleep out in the cold winter weather. This interruption allows the narrator to speak of death.

This is the last interruption that occurs. The book ends without a return to its narrative frame. Each of the first two stories ends abruptly, followed, apparently a day later, by a conversation between the children and their aunt concerning the next story. What are we to assume at the end of the third story? That there is no next day? The disjunction between the opening, where the narrator tells the "dear little girls" to gather round her, and the end, where Maggie and her Granny go quietly to bed, is clear. The book begins with a call to story, and it ends within the world of story. What matters is story, not the narrator's lessons on acoustics or her warning that one should never put an empty kettle on a fire. The children's interruptions show their interest in and engagement with the stories; they ask for details when their aunt appears insufficiently clear or niggardly with detail. In short, they ask with Laura, "And please, Aunt, be wonderful."

Just as the narrative frame draws attention to the act of storytelling—to the notion that details impede linearity of plot, to the fact that the reading experience involves the interruption of narrative—the stories themselves draw attention to form, to the play of allusion, to impediments to linearity. The second story, the account of Edith's failure to boil a kettle, can serve as an illustration for them all. Edith and the kettle are "spending one warm afternoon together in a wood," which has, "by some freak," one vine that grows among the beech trees and silver birches and that "dangled bunches of pale purple grapes among its leaves and twisted tendrils." Just where the vine grows a party is to take place, and Edith decides to take the kettle there and light the fire to boil it. First, however, she eyes the grapes and longs to grasp a cluster. Then she turns her attention to the fire; she fails with her six matches to start the fire, and her helpers, various animals, also fail. Just before the project is brought to an end by the arrival of Nurse, a fox bustles up, brushes the dust from Edith's frock, attempts in vain to reach the grapes and then trots away muttering "they must be sour." The allusion is clearly to Aesop. If we look for a moral in this story of Edith and the kettle, Aesop's famous fable provides one. The fox does not worry about not reaching the grapes; Edith is in "despair" and sits down to cry: some people blame circumstances when they fail through their own incapacity, while others take disappointment with indifference. Edith, however, does neither. Rossetti inverts Aesop's moral.

Yet to point such a moral contrast is to ignore the story's more obvious nonsense. While Rossetti inverts Aesop's fable, her story does not suggest a more acute moral. She simply plays with the form of fable. The fox trots into the scene and out again, and what he signals is first the unexpected and then "fable." The fable's primary function is fun, and as several versions of Aesop indicate (most notably the 1692 translation by Roger L'Estrange), the moral explanation simply refuses to satisfy, or in some cases even to apply. Indeed, Rossetti's whole story is free association, made up as the aunt speaks (she states at the beginning that she does not know the story of the frog who couldn't boil the kettle but that she will try to tell it anyway). What ultimately matters in her story is this frog, the toad whose father lived in a stone, and the other animals who try to help so ineffectually. In short, behind

Speaking Likenesses lies an impulse to the condition of Lewis Carroll. Rossetti wrote to her brother Dante Gabriel that *Speaking Likenesses* was "merely a Christmas trifle, would-be in the *Alice* style." Most readers have found the book a pale shade of *Alice,* yet the two works do have certain similarities: the atmosphere of dream, fantastic creatures and talking animals, animated objects, the uncovering of desire, and the nakedness of fear.

The first story in *Speaking Likenesses,* that of eight-year-old Flora and her birthday party, presents the clearest parallel to Carroll's own "Alice style." Flora, who is irritated at the manner in which her birthday party is passing and not interested in listening to a story, falls asleep and dreams about another birthday party where furniture comes to life and the children's bodies consist of hooks, angles, or slime. These quaint children in Flora's dream, the boys Hooks, Angles, and Quills, and the girls Sticky, Slime, and Queen, play two games: "Hunt the Pincushion" and "Self-help." The nightmare quality some readers perceive in *Alice's Adventures in Wonderland* is also evident in Rossetti's story in these two games that reveal a deep fear of sexual violence and a disturbing disrespect for humanity. The first game treats human beings as objects, things without feeling or dignity; it reverses the fairy tale convention of imagining inanimate objects as human. This mis-imagining is Rossetti's point. In Carroll's first *Alice* book inanimate objects such as mallets and balls become hedgehogs and flamingos. The Queen of Hearts presides over a lively game in which there are no rules and no ill consequences. "Hunt the Pincushion," however, reverses this situation. The hunt is no longer an innocent search for an object; it is a bloodsport. Rossetti clarifies the sexual implications of the game and draws attention to its nastier aspects. Through her representation of this game, as well as the second game, "Self-help," Rossetti provides a criticism of her culture. In modern terms, this is a feminist criticism. Players of "Hunt the Pincushion" select "the smallest and weakest player (if possible let her be fat: a hump is best of all)," and they "chase her round and round the room." The pincushion is female. In "Self-help" the "boys were players, the girls were played," and in describing this game, Rossetti satirizes the whole notion of self-help, made popular in the mid-century by Samuel Smiles's *Self-Help* (1859). The unpleasant implications for females in Smiles's assertion that "energy of will may be defined to be the very central power of character in a man" are uncovered in Rossetti's imagined game. In Flora's dream "self-help" comes to mean a male helping himself at the expense of the female.

Most readers of *Speaking Likenesses* will be brought up short by Rossetti's descriptions of these games. Plot and linearity are irrelevant. Satire and innuendo halt—or should halt—the reader. Rossetti herself indicates the proper response by having her narrator interrupt the narrative to say, "Don't look shocked, dear Ella, at my choice of words. . . ." What these shocking words are we can only suppose, but since the description of "Self-help" that immediately precedes this interruption is harmless enough, we can imagine Ella (and the other girls) registering a growing amazement as the story proceeds.

Certainly, the description of "Hunt the Pincushion" contains shocking words:

> Quills with every quill erect tilted against her, and needed not a pin: but Angles whose corners almost cut her, Hooks who caught and slit her frock, Slime who slid against her and passed her, Sticky who rubbed off on her neck and plump bare arms, the scowling Queen, and the whole laughing scolding pushing troop, all wielded longest sharpest pins, and all by turns overtook her.

The passage that follows, in which the narrator reflects on the effect of the game upon the "stickers," combines colloquial expression ("cutting corners") with tautology ("pricking quills, catching hooks") and alliterative effect ("particular personal pangs"). In short, the narrator directs our attention to vocabulary and to stylistic effects, and in so doing she impedes the narrative. The story is not the thing; words become things.

Christina Rossetti's work for children, then, is difficult only in the sense that the reader who expects simple narrative or clear didacticism will be surprised. The three works I have discussed do appear conventionally didactic and traditionally narrative in impulse (*Sing-Song's* traditional quality is in its nursery rhyme simplicity). Yet they are also disturbing and confusing. What appears straightforward is, upon reflection, askew. The reader confronts nursery rhyme and fairy tale in a new guise, and so discovers Rossetti's conscious playing with form and traditional themes. Even the shortest rhyme in *Sing-Song* is an exercise in stylistics: "Motherless baby and babyless mother, / Bring them together to love one another" (II, 50). The first line is an example of antimetabole, a repetition of words (here with morphological change) in reverse order. The second line overcomes the first in that the negative "less" gives way to the positive "to" (together, to love). Opposites come together in this rhyme, opposites that are not, in fact, so opposite to begin with. The disturbing fact of death, the uncertainty of life—these are defeated by the stronger sense of continuity: the continuing mystery of mother love, of human relationships, and of a language strong enough to communicate these mysteries.

Because children's literature generally appears simple, unconcerned in its content with the complexities and vagaries of human emotion, thought, and psychology, it has attracted little critical scrutiny. Because serious literary commentary has never allowed children's literature a canonical status, it has remained outside the great tradition. Rossetti's *Goblin Market,* however, has been embraced by critics and anthologists as a children's poem precisely because it invites the kind of literary debate they are hard-pressed to generate from works more forthrightly presented as children's literature—even though *Goblin Market* finds its formal impetus in the same tradition that informs the more obviously childlike *Sing-Song* and *Speaking Likenesses:* the tradition of fable, fairy tale, and nursery rhyme. These forms derive their power from ellipsis and symbol and freedom from the

contingencies that govern realistic and referential forms of literature. By using these forms, Rossetti—like many other women writers of the Victorian period who wrote for children—was able to voice her desires and her feminine concerns at once openly and secretly. Thus a child can read these works for the adventures of plot and language; an adult may look for the edifying lessons in behavior that will benefit a child; and the careful reader will discern the desire of a passionate woman who wanted to express her identity as a woman and to create an art that was truly personal and yet truly representative of humanity's possibilities. Clearly, if we have eyes to see and ears to hear, the deceptively simple surfaces of Rossetti's art reveal secret delights and imaginative truth.

W. David Shaw (essay date 1990)

SOURCE: "Meaning More Than Is Said: Sources of Mystery in Christina Rossetti and Arnold," in *Victorians and Mystery: Crises of Representation,* Cornell, 1990, pp. 251-75.

[*In the following excerpt, Shaw discusses Rossetti's reserved and tentative style, arguing that her language and poetic techniques reveal her religious beliefs.*]

[Christina Rossetti] is a heroic knower: to cross the divide that separates knowledge from belief, she must make such mystery words as "God" and "heart" mean more than she can hope to say. Rather than profane a mystery by scaling it down reductively, as Matthew Arnold tries to do when redefining religion, she prefers to be silent like Clough. Only "love," says Rossetti, can understand "the mystery, whereof / We can but spell a surface history" (**"Judge nothing before the time,"** ll. 1-2; 2:295). By "mystery" she means something like a secret science or withheld truth, as Newman defines these difficult ideas in his Oxford sermons. In her sonnet **"Cardinal Newman,"** Rossetti commends Newman's doctrine of reserve, praising him for choosing "love not in the shallows but the deep." As God speaks less openly the more he promises, so Rossetti speaks more obliquely the more she has to say. Less reserve might have exposed her harrowed heart to the sport of scoffing and insult, to which Newman says any high road open to all men would have exposed the mysteries of religious faith.

George Steiner has argued that language "borders on three other modes of statement—light, music, and silence." Like Vaughan's "great ring of pure and endless light," the fourth act of Shelley's *Prometheus Unbound* has much in common with an overexposed negative; and Swinburne's poetry often sounds like music for which readers are asked to supply a libretto. Rossetti, by contrast, tends to find silence at the limits of language, or else some simple but powerful gesture like the offering of her heart. Rather than saying less about God than she means to say, she prefers to say nothing. To intimate more than she is able to say, Rossetti keeps using dashes and elisions. Often she presents mere deleted fragments of a text she has censored. Such a text may survive only in manuscript or in its resourceful reconstruction by an editor-critic. Her inventive use of repetition and metaphors of situation also confers elusive contextual definitions upon the dictionary meaning of so simple but mysterious a word as "heart" or "love." Finding refuge in muteness, Rossetti draws upon tautologies and tropes of reserve. The signature of her skepticism is a use of elisions, dashes, and caesural breaks, which remind us that she means more than she says. The signature of her faith, by contrast, is a heroic use of chiasmus. This trope of crossing over allows Rossetti to say all that she means. It helps her cross the divide between life and death, knowledge and ignorance, in an ironic double movement that is sanctioned ultimately by the perfect chiasmus of the Cross.

Though deeply personal suffering nourishes many of Rossetti's best lyric poems, we can best grasp her uncanny power to mean more than she says when that suffering has been most carefully displaced, as in the lyric **"Listening."** Originally the poem was part of a longer lyric called **"Two Choices,"** whose canceled sixth and seventh stanzas contained the following desolating lines:

> He chose a love-warm priceless heart,
>   And I a cold bare dignity . . .
> I chose a tedious dignity
>   As cold as cold as snow; . . .
> I chose a barren wilderness
>   Whose buds died years ago.

The graceful bough and tendrils of the vine to which the modern Eve is now compared (ll. 7-8) were initially harrowing metaphors, harsh images of barrenness and waste, prompting the thought that the buds in Rossetti's wilderness died years ago. Her loss is more painful when contrasted with the Eden of delights and refreshing waters—the paradise of soul's sleep—from which Rossetti, while alive, has chosen to remove herself. The husband has chosen in his cushat dove the kind of wife Rossetti could never consent to become. From possible wisdom she declines to cold dignity, then to mere tedious dignity, which is cold as snow. Once we restore the deleted stanzas of **"Listening,"** we realize that its vision of a domestic Eden is the vision of an outsider. Only a study of the poem's revisions can reveal how harrowing is its crisis of representation. The half-satirical portrait of the "cushat dove" discloses the "listening" of a soul in hell, or else the dream of someone who is sleeping at last.

Though the poet's self-censorship is strict, her heartbreaking pain cannot be permanently repressed. Indeed, in the next poem Rossetti wrote, the sonnet **"Dead before death"** (1:59), all the displaced suffering surges forth. Its bitter outburst appalled William Michael Rossetti. "I am unable to say," he admits in a perplexed tone, "what gave rise to this very intense and denunciatory outpouring." William Michael might better have appreciated the cause of his sister's acrimony had he consulted the manuscript notebook in his possession, which reveals how the domestic paradise of **"Listening"** had originally been disturbed by countervailing impressions of chaos and hell. We expect the sestet of a Petrarchan sonnet such as **"Dead before**

death" to resolve or at least mute the despair of its octave. But the sestet of this sonnet uses the echoing vault of the poet's despair to set up new linkages of desolating sound. Indeed, this sonnet refuses to honor, as it were, its own generic promise. Even after the expression of despair ought formally to conclude, at the end of the octave, the echoes of desolation continue to sound through the last six lines:

> All fallen the blossom that no fruitage bore,
>   All lost the present and the future time,
> All lost, all lost, the lapse that went before:
> So lost till death shut-to the opened door,
>   So lost from chime to everlasting chime,
> So cold and lost for ever evermore.
>   **("Dead before death,"** ll. 9-14)

The harshness of the anaphoric triads (ll. 9-11) is relieved only by the reverberating wail of open vowels. "Evermore" answers "everlasting" and "for ever," and "So" and "cold" answer a series of other open sounds; "Ah," "All," and "lost" (ll. 1, 9-11, 14). While the triadic "So," "So," "So" (ll. 12-14) remains rigid, the echoing "lost"s huddle close together (l. 11), then become predictably expansive. The contraction of the chiming "ever"s, converging in the final "for ever evermore," reverses this expanding pattern. Because the speaker's despair persists "from chime to everlasting chime," even after we expect it to be resolved at the end of the octave, we find these echoes that refuse to cease are not crowded with meaning but are mere hollow sounds like the echo of Sin's words in *Paradise Lost,* a reverberation of loss, desolation, and death: "I fled, and cry'd out DEATH; / Hell trembl'd at the hideous Name, and sigh'd / From all her Caves, and back resounded DEATH" (*Paradise Lost,* 2.787-89).

To turn the hell of a stony heart into an Eden of renewal or rebirth, Rossetti will sometimes make literal losses figurative. In the revised version of the lyric entitled **"May"** ("Sweet Life is dead."—"Not so"), Rossetti replaces an active first-person use of the verb "build" with a noncommittal passive form of the verb "freeze."

> 'Twixt him and me a wall
> Was frozen of earth-like stone
> With brambles overgrown:
>   **("May,"** ll. 17-19)

The lyric was originally titled **"A Colloquy."** In the extensively revised second stanza we can see most clearly how a love lyric has been turned into a nature poem. Initially, in building a wall of stone between herself and her lover, Rossetti had only her own stony heart to blame for their separation and estrangement:

> But love is dead to me;
>   I watched his funeral:
>   Cold poplars stood up tall
> While yewtrees crouched to see
> And fair vines bowed the knee

> Twixt him and me a wall
> I built of cold hard stone
>   With brambles overgrown;
> Chill darkness wraps him like a pall
> And I am left alone.

The funeral she watched in the original version was not just the funeral of the "worn-out year" (l. 12) but the funeral of a lover for whose death she seemed personally responsible. By contrast, in the revised version the colloquy between two voices evokes an unlocalized event, which cannot be given just one name, as it could in the first version where a specific lover had died. In the dividing wall of frozen "earth-like stone" (l. 18) there is something now that exceeds the picture of a literal wall as a riddle exceeds its solution.

> But Life is dead to me:
> The worn-out year was failing,
> West winds took up a wailing
> To watch his funeral:
>   Bare poplars shivered tall
> And lank vines stretched to see.
>   Twixt him and me a wall
> Was frozen of earth-like stone
>   With brambles overgrown:
> Child darkness wrapped him like a pall,
> And I am left alone.
>   ("May," ll. 11-21)

If the masculine third-person pronouns in this stanza refer not just to **"Life"** but to a lover who has died or from whom Rossetti is actually estranged, then the "earth-like stone" is less an image than a phantasm. The pictures in the stanza possess hallucinatory power. Their obsession with wailing winds, shivering trees, stretching vines, and earthlike stone is indeed strange. But as tokens of estranged and suppressed guilt, these dark phantasms dramatize a crisis of knowing: it is no wonder Rossetti can never quite shake them off. By turning a poem about thwarted love and guilt into a triumphal nature lyric, however, she is able to displace self-blame. Restorative power comes not in the form of another lover but as a life force from nowhere, catching the poet off guard.

> I meet him day by day,
> Where bluest fountains flow
> And trees are white as snow
>
>   . . . . .
>
> He makes my branch to bud and bear,
>   And blossoms where I tread.
>   ("May," ll. 2-4, 30-31)

Stirred into being by pregnant caesural pauses between "branch," "bud," and "bear" (l. 30), and by strong rhymes such as "flow" and "snow" (ll. 3-4), as compared with the weakly trailing feminine rhymes "failing," "wailing" (ll. 12-13), this new power imposes itself stealthily but irresistibly. Bound by obligation and love to the springtime

scene as she never could be bound to another heart, Rossetti finds that her throttled affections also start to bud and grow.

Originally, the mother in the ballad **"Seeking Rest"** was not a literal mother but Mother Earth. In its earlier version, preserved in Bodleian Library MS. Don. e, notebook 6, fols. 22-26, the ballad opened with the following words of the child: "She knocked at the Earth's greening door. / O Mother, let me in." In seeking the greater objectivity of a ballad, Rossetti decides to delete the child's suicidal longing and her powerful echo of the old man's petition in "The Pardoner's Tale": "And on the ground which is my modres gate / I knokke . . . / and saye, 'Leve moder, leet me in'" (ll. 441-43). But in no sense are the silences of the final version marked by neatness and composure.

> My Mother said: "The child is changed
>   That used to be so still;
> All the day long she sings and sings,
>   And seems to think no ill;
> She laughs as if some inward joy
>   Her heart would overfill."
>
> My Sisters said: "Now prythee tell
>   Thy secret unto us:
> Let us rejoice with thee; for all
>   Is surely prosperous,
> Thou art so merry: tell us, Sweet:
>   We had not used thee thus."
>
> My Mother says: "What ails the child
>   Lately so blythe of cheer?
> Art sick or sorry? Nay, it is
>   The winter of the year;
> Wait till the Springtime comes again,
>   And the sweet flowers appear."
>
> My Sisters say: "Come, sit with us,
>   That we may weep with thee:
> Show us thy grief that we may grieve:
>   Yea haply, if we see
> Thy sorrow, we may ease it; but
>   Shall share it certainly."
>
> How should I share my pain, who kept
>   My pleasure all my own?
> My Spring will never come again;
>   My pretty flowers have blown
> For the last time; I can but sit
>   And think and weep alone.
>   ("Seeking Rest")

"Seeking Rest" is a deeply disturbing ballad, partly because of what it leaves out. The breaks at the end of the poem, "I can but sit / And think and weep alone" (ll. 29-30), are too sharply and strikingly placed to be only rhythmic breaks. Like the breaks between the stanzas, especially between stanzas 2 and 3, where incommunicable joy turns to equally unfathomable grief, the caesuras are designed to juxtapose actions and thus avoid plot and explanation. The child is autistic. In her inexplicable joys she is as totally isolated from her mother and her sisters as she is strictly alone in her immedicable woes. These are "woes that nothing can be done for," as Frost would say, the woes of someone for whom "spring will never come again" (l. 27), "woes flat and final." Though grief is merely a blank in this ballad—the absence of a joy that has been—enough of the original loss survives to unnerve the reader and intimate an absence that is expressed in silence, a silence of private mourning and unshakable reserve. Contrary to what the mother and sisters assume, the silences do not result from the absence of something nameable such as spring. The child is silent because she has a mute sense of the larger strangenesses of life. She is also in the presence of a nothingness, a void, that successive stanzas of the ballad forcefully intimate but that no inquiry or surmise of the mother and the sisters can successfully explain.

Like the child in **"Seeking Rest,"** Rossetti finds there are mysteries about which she can either say nothing or say too much. In **"Winter, my secret"** cutting, eliding, and covering up are all means of preserving silence about such mysteries. Volleys of multiple rhymes set off humorous chain reactions in the poem.

> Perhaps some day, who knows?
> But not to-day; it froze, and blows, and snows
>   . . . . .
>
> Come bounding and surrounding me,
> Come buffeting, astounding me
>   (ll. 2-3, 15-16)

By the time we reach the fourth internal rhyme in the second example, however, the joking has ceased to be merely amusing. Prying readers may be less hostile or bitter than the fierce Russian snows, but Rossetti prefers to leave that assumption untested. Winter destroys, she muses, and springtime renewals are precarious at best. Perhaps the only time to reveal secrets like hers is late midsummer. These seasonal images are nonnaming figures for the secrets of Rossetti's inner weather. As charades for the mysteries Rossetti has locked up, these figures betray a Zenlike propensity to tease the reader. Rossetti jokes about what frightens her and coyly hints that her secret may be the absence of any secret after all. The poem means more than it says because it keeps postponing its disclosures. Like all the lyrics examined so far, it appears to present a mere deleted fragment of some less withholding testament Rossetti has chosen to suppress.

In other groups of poems Rossetti contrives to mean more than she says by creating elusive contextual definitions for the dictionary meaning of so apparently simple a word as "heart." Each metaphor of situation that Rossetti uses points enigmatically to a mysterious "overmeaning" for "heart" that she is unable to dramatize fully in any single situation in the poems. One of the most potent of these definitions comes at the end of "A Christmas carol" ("In

the bleak mid-winter") (1:216-17). The sudden exaltation of the lowly "maiden" (l. 30) prepares for Rossetti's insistence at the end of the carol on the sufficiency of a single unadorned word—the poet's "heart." The gifts of the Magi and of the heavenly cherubim and the gifts of the poor coexist, both plainly established, now without conflict and in reciprocal dignity.

> What can I give Him,
>   Poor as I am?
> If I were a shepherd
>   I would bring a lamb,
> If I were a wise man
>   I would do my part,—
> Yet what I can I give Him,
>   Give my heart.
>   (**"In the bleak mid-winter,"** ll. 33-40)

After the dash, the poet catches her breath before offering her heart. She drops the "I" and repeats the verb. The poet is poorer than a shepherd, who at least could bring a lamb. And like Mary, she has no wisdom. But at the end of the carol Rossetti's intimate offerings of her heart and her art are wholly congruent. The confidence sponsored by this congruence can be felt in the lyricism of the last verse, which implicitly rebukes the stiffness of the bleak opening stanzas. Its trochees are at once rigid and lilting, spare and weighted. As one of those rare lyrics in which apparent artlessness seems the greatest achievement of the poet's art, **"In the bleak and mid-winter"** is really a response to Mary's directive in the sonnet **"All Saints."** The greatest gift Rossetti can give is poetry of etched austerity and unadorned words, a poetry expressing her love of God—an art of the heart.

Contributing to our sense that by "heart" Rossetti means something more than she can say is her use of a different situation to define the word in the lyric beginning "Lord, when my heart was whole I kept it back" ("Afterward he repented, and went,'"). In this lyric, now that her heart is broken, Rossetti wonders whether she can ever achieve at-onement with God. Why should God be expected to accept damaged goods? And yet God operates by love and is not bound by logic, she reflects. The broken heart she offers may be most like God's, since his too was once broken on a cross.

In another lyric, **"A heavy heart,"** the heart is at first the ponderous grammatical object of a transitive verb: "I offer Thee this heavy heart of me" (l. 2). In the last stanza the lightened heart is lifted, and it becomes grammatical subject instead of object.

> Lifted to Thee my heart weights not so heavy,
>   It leaps and lightens lifted up to Thee.
> (ll. 11-12)

In the final line, "Thy Face, me loving, for Thou lovest me," the first-person pronoun is twice framed by the divine "Thou" in an empathic merging of persons. The mirroring effect of the midline caesura and the chiasmus of "me loving, . . . lovest me" are devices of a poet who knows how to use the chiasmus of the Cross and who loves to handle varied grammatical elements, turning them over with fond and exact scrutiny. In finding the proper language of prayerful petition in **"Sursam Corda"** (2:311-12), Rossetti also finds the means to lift up her heart, an action she is powerless to perform at the beginning of the lyric: "I cannot, Lord, lift up my heart to Thee" (l. 2). The proximity of "Lord" and "lift" and the remoteness of "I" and "lift" suggest who the real agent of the lifting must be. In a powerful chiasmus and an increasingly intimate progression of principal verbs, Rossetti implores God to take what she is powerless either to keep or to give away: "Stoop, Lord, and hearken, hearken, Lord, and do, / And take my will, and take my heart, and take me too" (**"Sursam Corda,"** ll. 8-9).

Of all Rossetti's poems on bruised or broken hearts that seek at-onement with God, the lyric **"Twice"** (1:124-26) is most affecting. It condenses most powerfully the repressions of both human and divine love and is therefore the riskiest of Rossetti's experiments in this genre. There is always a disquieting possibility that in experiencing the disappointment of her earthly love, Rossetti is simply rehearsing for a disappointment after death. Can religion entirely overcome the exhaustion, despair, and suffering reiterated in her secular lyrics? If God is as cruelly stringent as Rossetti, will her afterlife not be as resolutely chastened and impoverished as her present life? These are fearful questions for Rossetti to ask. She has staked all on God's love for *her:* she does not want to lose a wager twice.

"Twice" establishes a precarious but potent relation between the "You" of the first half of the lyric and the "Thou" of the second. Is God going to be any more generous or loving than the contemptuous "You" who coldly studied then rejected the proffered heart as he might have studied, then discarded, a flawed work of art?

> You took my heart in your hand
>   With a friendly smile,
> With a critical eye you scanned,
>   Then set it down,
> And said: It is unripe . . .
>
>   (**"Twice,"** ll. 9-13)

As in **"A Fisher-Wife"** (2:109), in which the "heart sits leaden" in the fisher-wife's "breast" until brought into her "mouth" (ll. 4, 8), there is in this lyric a powerful interaction between figurative and literal meanings. Part of the human anatomy can be made to achieve metonymically what the whole body can never achieve: "You took my heart in your hand / . . . Then set it down, / . . . As you set it down it broke" (ll. 9, 12, 17). As the critical friend, who cannot really have loved Rossetti, handles the heart as he might handle a piece of pottery, the metonymy is made to come to life with shocking literalness and force.

The last three stanzas repeat the drama for a second time: two of the agents—Rossetti and her proffered heart—are the same, but God is substituted for the critical lover.

> This contemned of a man,
>   This marred one heedless day,
> This heart take Thou to scan
>
>   . . . . .
>
> I take my heart in my hand—
>   I shall not die, but live—
> Before Thy face I stand;
>   I, for Thou callest such:
> All that I have I bring,
>   All that I am I give,
> Smile Thou and I shall sing,
>   But shall not question much.
>
>   (**"Twice,"** ll. 33-35, 41-48)

In revising the original version of line 33, "this heart, contemned of man," Rossetti seems too ashamed even to name her proffered gift and deletes the word "heart" (1:273). In the final version the heart becomes nothing more distinctive than a displaced object, a mere demonstrative pronoun detached for three lines from its proper referent: "This contemned . . . , / this marred . . . , / this heart take Thou to scan" (ll. 33-35). But even while intensifying the shock and pain of her earlier rejections, Rossetti now uses the altered refrain ("You took my heart in your hand" [l. 9], "I take my heart in my hand" [ll. 25, 41]), the new form of scanning and criticizing (which is now refining, not dismissive), the smile of God, which replaces the cold stare of the friend, and the "I"'s singing instead of questioning, to recall and correct other uses—not only in this lyric but also in other poems on bruised or broken hearts. "All that I am I give" (l. 46) harks back to the ending of "A Christmas carol": "I would do my part,—/ Yet what I can I give Him, / Give my heart" (ll. 38-40). As Rossetti in her carol falters after the dash, she wonders if she will be able to make her offering and complete her song. Will the whole enterprise totter and come to ruin, as her heart has so often faltered and failed her? Even in the poem **"Twice"** the dash after "live" (l. 42) puts the outcome in doubt.

But Rossetti is saved by devices that are now familiar. In **"A Christmas carol"** the remote is made homely, an art of the heart, as biblical commonplaces are renewed and the ordinary becomes miraculous again. And in **"Twice"** the poet's simple promise to "sing" (l. 47) reverses the bleak ending of the third stanza: "Nor sung with the singing bird" (l. 24). Even the last line recalls and completes the meaning of line 22: "nor questioned since." Though the poet refuses to question in both instances, she does so for opposite reasons. "To question" in the third stanza was to be self-critical, or perhaps to question God's justice. Originally Rossetti had lacked the heart to examine her own heart; she had not enough courage to be critical of others. Now she "shall not question much," not because she is afraid of any injustice she may expose, but because she is confident God's treatment of her will be just.

In refusing to close the divide that separates her faith in God from her understanding of him, Rossetti is simply refusing to reduce deity to the compass of her own imperfect mind and heart. To pretend that the gap does not exist, as a reductionist like Arnold does when he redefines God as the higher self, is simply to annihilate that distinction between nature and grace—that divide between God and man—that any heroic theory of knowledge and faith must struggle to preserve as its precondition and sine qua non. Her skepticism is inseparable, then, from the ironic double movement that reinstates faith at the moment of doubt, when caesural breaks inflict wounds on her poetry and God comes to life in the silence of a dash or a negation—at the very site of fracture or loss.

This skepticism is most apparent in lyrics that use tautologies, depleted diction, and tropes of reserve. In one of her most exacting lyrics of depletion, for example, "'A bruised reed shall he not break'" (1:67-68), Rossetti makes the end lines of successive stanzas decline from the modest to the minimal: "Alas, I cannot will" (l. 8), "I cannot wish, alas!" (l. 16), "I do not deprecate" (l. 24). Each time the soul seems capable of doing less. But at least the final negation is an affirmation in disguise. To deprecate is to negate, but to negate that negation is already to prepare for a reversal of the soul's will-less state. Though no self-activity may be possible, Rossetti can at least anticipate the first faint stirring of affective life.

We think that God will appeal to the soul's memory of the Crucifixion as a way of restoring the poet's love. He will chastise her by asking, How can *you* forget? But this is not what Rossetti's God says. Rather, if God was crucified for this will-less (though not unwilling) soul, the question to be asked is: How can *I* forget?

> For thee I hung upon the cross in pain,
>   How then can I forget?
> If thou as yet dost neither love, nor hate,
>   Nor choose, nor wish,—resign thyself, be still
> Till I infuse love, hatred, longing, will.—
>   I do not deprecate.
> ("'**A bruised reed shall he not break**,'" ll. 19-24)

Over the expected platitude Rossetti has inscribed her own censorship of platitude. On behalf of the poet's bruised and damaged soul, God has already suffered too much to forget her now. Nor does he presume to criticize or minimize her anguish, for he has known the same anguish himself.

Everything depends on the power of contraction. The final line is the most contracted of all, for here the utterance of both speakers—God and the soul—is gathered into a single concentrated phrase. Indeed, for the first time in the poem God and the soul are able to speak in unison. The last line, "I do not deprecate," is equally in character for either speaker. Though readers are shocked, I think, to find "hatred" included in the catalog of affective states God chooses to "infuse"—love, hatred, longing, will—it is part of Rossetti's honesty that she should

make God the author of her hatred of himself. "All poetry is difficult," as T. S. Eliot reminds us, "almost impossible, to write: and one of the great permanent causes of error in writing poetry is the difficulty of distinguishing between what one really feels and what one would like to feel." In this lyric about bruised and broken hearts Rossetti is trying to find in life's most minimal offerings something residual that will suffice. In examining the depletions of a skeletal life—the renunciations of a soul that has perhaps renounced too much, Rossetti contracts language to the vanishing point. But even as the refrains decline from the modest to the minimal, Rossetti shows how the last trace of a false refuge or comfort must be broken down and abandoned. Her exacting honesty makes her exhaustion and depleted diction harrowing, but that honesty is part of her greatness as a poet.

In another of her most charged but depleted lyrics, **"All heaven is blazing yet,"** Rossetti manages to mean more than she says by using many connecting strategies that are all part of the verbal sleight-of-hand and the contrived economy of means. The tremor of open vowels, including the four exclamatory "O"s, sends a quaver of barely suppressed emotion down these lines. The tones range from hopeful to despairing. Linking patterns of similar length and shape invite the reader to compare "O hope deferred, be still' (l. 12) with "O hope deferred, hope still" (l. 16). Lines 4 and 12 have the same shape, as do lines 5 and 6 and lines 13 and 14. Even the rhyme words in these similar pairs are nearly identical: "choose," "Will" (ll. 13, 14) and "chose," "will" (ll. 5, 6). The huddling together of repeated sounds is the shudder of a soul that laments what it has lost but that also resolves to gather up and concentrate its now diminished powers.

> All heaven is blazing yet
>   With the meridian sun:
> Make haste, unshadowing sun, make haste to set;
>   O lifeless life, have done.
> I choose what once I chose;
>   What once I willed, I will:
> Only the heart its own bereavement knows;
>   O clamorous heart, lie still
>
> That which once I chose, I choose;
>   That which I willed, I will;
> That which I once refused, I still refuse:
>   O hope deferred, be still.
> That which I chose and choose
>   And will is Jesus' Will:
> He hath not lost his life who seems to lose:
>   O hope deferred, hope still.
>   ("**All heaven is blazing yet**")

Linkages of shape and sound are most arresting when there is some disproportion between the members. Thus there are slight variations in the rhyme words, and the pattern of syntax in "be still" and "hope still" (ll. 12, 16) is only apparently identical. The first "still" is an adjective, meaning "quiet" or "serene," and the second "still" is an adverb, a synonym for "perpetually" or "nevertheless." Lines 5 and 6 are almost tautologies: "I choose what once I chose; / What once I willed, I will." Tautology is the most withholding of tropes, and part of Rossetti's private theology of reserve: it enables her to mean more than she says. But in lines 13 and 14, which bear a deceptive similarity to these analytic statements, the poet switches to a synthetic judgment. Now she adds in the predicate a meaning not given in the subject, an identification of the poet's will with Jesus' will.

The rhyme words "will," "still," "chose," and "choose" recur ten times in a sixteen-line poem. The shadow of depletion is on such chastened diction. It is as if a computer had been given a limited number of rhymes and instructed to produce a minimal narrative. The austere poetic economy extends to individual words such as "only," which pack maximum meaning into Rossetti's unlavish idiom by looking two ways at once. "Only" (l. 7) might mean "were it not for the fact that the heart in its aloneness is clamorous and unruly." Or it might mean that the heart and nothing but the heart "its own bereavement knows." Lines 5 and 6 produce chiastic inversions of each other: "I choose what once I chose; / What once I willed, I will." Lines 9 and 10 repeat the same syntactic pattern as lines 5 and 6 but use different accusative forms. Line 11 has approximately the same semantic shape, but there is some disproportion now in its greater length: "That which I once refused, I still refuse." Coincidence of syntactic units and line lengths concentrates the energy with astonishing economy of means. The final "hope deferred" (l. 16) is the hope of earthly joy, but what it hopes "still" is the hope of Paul. Renunciation and deferral are made more acceptable when they allow Rossetti to cross the divide that separates hope from Hope, the second of Paul's three Christian virtues.

Closely allied to such lyrics of tautology and depleted diction are oracular poems that manage to mean more than they say by hiding thought in multiple or punning uses of a single word. Ordinarily, the comfort provided by a predictable refrain helps protect the mind against invasions of powers it is helpless to control. But when a familiar phrase takes on unpredictable new meanings, as does the phrase "Astonished Heaven" in Rossetti's lyric **"Her seed; it shall bruise thy head,"** the comfort of a limit is continually being broken down. By using changing grammatical functions of "astonished" Rossetti can create an *experience* of that very astonishment that is evoked by what is indefinite, unlimited—ultimately beyond the power of any single word to define.

Refrains are a familiar form of domesticating mystery, of trying to bring the strange into the orbit of the commonplace and known. First heaven is astonished at the miracle of man's creation: "Astonished Heaven looked on when man was made" (l. 1). This is merely conventional wonder and is appropriately conveyed by an adjective modifying a noun. But the oracle about the second Adam astonishes heaven in a different sense. To define the typological mystery of the lyric's title, which prefigures the victory of the second Adam over Satan, Rossetti seems to use "astonished" as a transitive verb

that turns "heaven" from a grammatical subject into an object:

> Surely that oracle of hope first said,
>   Astonished Heaven.
> **("Her seed; it shall bruise thy head,"** ll. 3-4)

But how can "heaven," as the author of "that oracle," be astonished by its own invention? The absence of any commas in the 1892 version of line 3, the use of two commas in the 1904 version, one before "first" and one after "said," and the use of only one comma in the version preferred by R. W. Crump, which is the version I have quoted (2:455), suggests the grammatical instability of the lines, which waver in emphasis between the effect on heaven of the oracle's pronouncement and the burden of the oracle itself. If we register the latter emphasis, it is as if the stanza's last line circles back on the opening phrase, making the oracle's content nothing less than the first quatrain of Rossetti's poem.

Most astonishing is the third use of "astonished." In confronting the mystery of a final transformation we might expect Rossetti to use a subjunctive verb: "Till one last trump shake earth, and" astonish Heaven. Instead, she writes "and undismayed / Astonished Heaven" (ll. 10-11). Perhaps in the eyes of God the Last Judgment has already occurred. Or is the past tense of "astonished" used to remind the reader of the instability of all time indicators? "Astonished Heaven" may simply be a nominative absolute construction, syntactically severed from the phrases that precede, as the soul that awakes at the end of time is astonished to find a disintegrating world fall away around it. Or is "Heaven," along with "earth," another direct object of the verb "shake"?

> Till one last trump shake earth, and undismayed
>   Astonished Heaven.
> **("Her seed; it shall bruise thy head,"** ll. 10-11)

If so, why is there a comma after "earth"? And if Rossetti is saying that the trump did not dismay "Astonished Heaven," why does she use the past tense to describe a future action? David A. Kent reminds me that the active grammar may restore to life a buried pun in "undismayed." The trump that "unmakes" earth is able to astonish but not undo an "un-dis-made" or undismantled heaven, invulnerable, at the end, to the grand annihilation. The ever-present alternatives to any single interpretation come from Rossetti's conviction that God's vision of the end of time is not her own, and that each renewed insight about change will disclose deeper problems concerning a mystery she can never quite adjust to, a strangeness she continues to ponder with fresh wonder.

In the lyric **"Praying Always,"** it is the mystery of "forever," already latent in the commonplace adverb "always," that is first being limited to the measurement of a clock, then imperceptibly transformed into something immeasurable. The repeating phrase "The clock strikes one" (ll.

2, 7) is a time indicator that localizes events "after midnight" and "after mid-day." But the third use of "one" terminates the action like a stopwatch "after noon and night" (l. 11) when, in the final stanza, time stops altogether. Although the preposition "after" appears to be used similarly in all three phrases, there is in fact a profound disparity between the first two "after"s and the final one. The first phrase of stanza 3, "After noon and night," is not another adverbial phrase like "after midnight" (l. 1) or "after mid-day" (l. 6). Because this third phrase is introduced by a nontemporal preposition, by an "after" *after* all befores and afters, its meaning is not to be found in any dictionary.

> After noon and night, one day
>   For ever one
>   Ends not, once begun.
> Whither away,
> O brothers and O sisters? Pause and pray.
> **("Praying Always,"** ll. 11-15)

Like Arthur Hallam's summons to Tennyson from "that deep dawn behind the tomb" (*In Memoriam,*) the summons to all brothers and sisters is a summons that speaks to Rossetti from the other side of silence.

If tautologies, depleted diction, and a punning or oracular multiple use of words are the signatures in Rossetti's verse of her skeptical conviction that meaning is always in excess of anything she can say, her heroic use of chiasmus is the signature of her equally strong conviction that mysterious truths, though beyond the power of words to compass fully, can at least be *intimated*. In poems of heroic crossing between doubt and faith, death and life, Rossetti combines two attitudes to God that are seldom found together. She speaks as if there were a divine attribute of justice that must be appeased. But she also shares the mystic's sense that the only atonement she has need of is an atonement or becoming one with the divine nature. Too often in seeking the comfort of a limit, Rossetti builds a wall between herself and God. This wall can be broken down only when the poet learns to tutor her heart and discipline her affections. Though the simultaneous search for limits and for something unlimited or boundless precipitates a crisis in representation, Rossetti finds that only by achieving at-onement with God in the mystic's sense can she understand how atonement in the traditional sense is possible.

In **"Weary in well-doing"** (1:182) Rossetti must learn to make her life a chiasmus, a crossing-over from despair to hope, from brokenness and fragmentation to at-onement with God. But this crossing is at first a mere vexing: God simply crosses her will.

> I would have gone; God bade me stay:
>   I would have worked; God bade me rest.
>   . . . . .
> Now I would stay; God bids me go:
>   Now I would rest; God bids me work.
> **("Weary in well-doing,"** ll. 1-2, 6-7)

The first two lines of the second stanza are the chiastic inversion of the first two lines of the first stanza. God's will seems an arbitrary reversal of everything Rossetti seeks. With the predictable midline caesuras in the first two lines and the strong breaks at the end of line 3 and 4, "He broke my will from day to day, / He read my yearnings unexpressed / And said them nay . . . " (**"Weary in well-doing,"** ll. 3-5), Rossetti's emphatically rhymed tetrameters and dimeters compose a sequence of pauses filled by words. The caesuras are more than just breaks. They are cuts, deliberately inflicted to batter down and wound the heart. As Rossetti's broken will turns into a broken heart "tost to and fro" like damaged merchandise (l. 8), the mere deciphering of unexpressed desires becomes the more frightening terror of the doubting soul, who begins to question her faith in God.

The true chiasmus of a crossing-over from emptiness to plenitude, from brokenness to true communion, comes only as a different kind of crossing—as a crossing of the line lengths in the final question:

> I go, Lord, where Thou sendest me;
>   Day after day I plod and moil:
> But, Christ my God, when will it be
> That I may let alone my toil
>   And rest with Thee?
> **("Weary in well-doing,"** ll. 11-15)

In the first three lines of stanzas 1 and 2, semantic units and line lengths coincide. The one-line units tend at first to isolate the "I" as a mere cipher confined to singular statements. But in the last stanza the line lengths of the semantic units begin to expand. The pattern of lines per semantic unit is 1, 1, 3 instead of 1, 1, 1, 2. The movement into the more spacious three-line unit provides a crossover from the individual to God. Through a slight augmentation of the two-line unit Rossetti shows how a soul that is broken and not at one strives for wholeness and at-onement.

In another lyric of crossing-over, **"Love is strong as death,"** the soul's initial neglect of God—it has not sought, found, or thirsted for God—sets the metaphorical terms for its own recovery of at-onement. So appropriate is the changed perspective in the second stanza to both the transformed soul and God that by the end of the lyric the poet and God, locked together by three binding verbs—"look and see / And clasp" (ll. 11-12)—can slip into each other. Lost in a coupling of pronouns, God and the soul are no longer divided as they were at the end of the first stanza: "Thy perishing me." Instead, their union is celebrated by a syntactic convergence, by a fusing of "thee . . . Me" (l. 12) in an empathic merging of persons.

Poems of quarreling and fractious debate usually set the terms of their own resolution. A lyric of crossed wills may turn into a lyric of genuine crossing, but only if the poet's aimless questioning has a destination as well as a destiny. Even in a lyric such as **"Up-Hill"** the reader has a sense that the pilgrim's questions and the stranger's answers could go on forever. The inn is said to contain "beds for all who come" partly because the pilgrim is eager for rest and frames the appropriate question: "Will there be beds for me and all who seek?" (l. 15). Like a skilled Socratic ironist, the stranger withholds information. Instead of consolidating the mental level on which the pilgrim's questions are asked, the stranger's laconic answers are only as satisfactory as the pilgrim's questions. Better and fuller answers must await better questions.

The soul's ability to set the terms of its own recovery is nowhere more evident than in another poem of anguished crossing-over, the sonnet **"Have I not striven, my God, and watched and prayed?"**, which rivals in intensity and despair the dark sonnets of Hopkins. The triad of alliterating verbs in the middle of the sonnet, "I grope and grasp not; gaze, but cannot see" (l. 7), recalls the leveling hammer blows of the opening line, with its polysyndeton and harsh triple stresses on the past participles: "Have I not striven, my God, and wátched and práyed?" But this triad allows Rossetti to launch her final fearful question. When she is herself as God is now, out of sight and reach, will the God who has reduced her to nothingness in every other sense reduce to nothingness her shame as well? If so, the loneliness that has contracted her soul in the one-line questions of the sestet, generating the near insolence of her query "Is Thine Arm shortened that Thou canst not aid?" (l. 4), has still to achieve that curious blend of intimacy and reverence that by the end of the sonnet must once more make her whole.

> Have I not striven, my God, and watched and
>   prayed?
>   Have I not wrestled in mine agony?
>   Wherefore still turn Thy Face of Grace from
>   me?
> Is Thine Arm shortened that Thou canst not aid?
> Thy silence breaks my heart: speak tho' to
>   upbraid,
>   For Thy rebuke yet bids us follow Thee.
>   I grope and grasp not; gaze, but cannot see.
> When out of sight and reach my bed is made,
> And piteous men and women cease to blame
> Whispering and wistful of my gain or loss;
> Thou Who for my sake once didst feel the
>   Cross,
>   Lord, wilt Thou turn and look upon me then,
> And in Thy Glory bring to nought my shame,
>   Confessing me to angels and to men?

One of this sonnet's curious features is the way it breaks at the end of the seventh line. The querulous self at the beginning is given only seven of the octave's normal eight lines, while the drive toward at-onement occupies exactly half the sonnet. The spacious expansion of the final question, which occupies one more line than a conventional sestet, hesitatingly sets forth the search for wholeness. After the broken, halting syntax of the first seven lines, where the one-line anaphoric questions collapse into elliptical half-line confessions of heartbreak and despair, Rossetti is able to cross by the bold bridge of her spa-

A chalk drawing of Rossetti in 1877, by Dante Gabriel Rossetti.

cious seven-line question to an imagined state of recovered wholeness and simplicity. This striking dramatic effect is lost in the sonnet's original manuscript version. Initially, the premature crossover at the end of line 5 made Rossetti's indictment of God too studied and rhetorical.

> Or is the load of one more sinner laid
>   On Thee, too heavy a load for even Thee?
>   (ll. 5-6)

This original version, which appears in the manuscript notebook in the British Library, is recorded by R. W. Crump. But in the revised version, the anger is more desolating and is allowed to break out into stark bereavement: "Thy silence breaks my heart." It then turns into an oddly abased but still reproachful prayer: "speak tho' to upbraid, / For Thy rebuke yet bids us follow Thee." In the final version all the steps of feeling are embodied in the short clauses, the sharp midline break after "heart" (l. 5), and in the strong end-line pauses. The chiasmus of the sonnet's last two lines, which encloses the phrases "my shame" and "me" between God's "glory" and the approval of his angelic witnesses, is a climactic crossing-over from nothing to all. The crossover ratifies and puts its seal, so to speak, on the syntactic and semantic drive of the brokenhearted petitioner who, though shattered and unwhole, also rediscovers the meaning of again being one with God.

Rossetti's best lyrics of elegiac crossing combine so many forms of mystery that each time we read them they reveal a different facet to the mind. Some readers may feel that, in crossing over from human to divine love, a lyric such as **"Twice,"** which I have examined as an example of conferring contextual definition upon the word "heart," should culminate in an act more impressive and less homely than the poet's taking her heart in her hand. But then, one realizes, this is an exact and powerful gesture. The offering of her heart is the most important gift she can make. The plain honesty of statement, intimating an almost mute depth of feeling, reverberates with the last line of **"A Christmas carol"** and has the same reassuring ordinariness and truth. More immediate and poignant than the solemnities of her marriage feast in **"Revelation"** is Rossetti's vision in **"Twice"** of a divine lover, capable of picking up her broken heart and offering it such solace as he can. When the devotional poet stops looking at her brokenness and looks instead at the wholeness of Christ, she has already set the conditions for her recovery. Instead of remaining self-abased and depleted, Rossetti must learn to merge with God: she must trust that her broken heart will be acceptable to him and that she can find in her at-onement with him all the heart can wish.

In order to mean more than she says, it is important that Rossetti, even in crossing the divide between death and life, doubt and faith, human and divine love, should continue to use withholding tautologies and tropes of reserve. Rossetti worries more than most poets about what cannot be said, about the places in personal life where hope winds down and possibilities of renovation seem to die. Her tentativeness can be more compelling than positiveness, and her most weighted moments are emphasized by lack of insistence. Even when recorded in little operettas or domestic melodramas of the soul, Rossetti's losses are a touching memento of human limits, a reminder of all that can never be fully grasped or loved or said. I suspect this is another way of saying that Rossetti's art of reserve is simply human in the fullest sense.

Antony H. Harrison (essay date 1990)

SOURCE: "Christina Rossetti and the Sage Discourse of Feminist High Anglicanism," in *Victorian Sages and Cultural Discourse: Renegotiating Gender and Power,* edited by Thais E. Morgan, Rutgers University Press, 1990, pp. 87-104.

[*In the following essay, Harrison explores the feminist leanings in Rossetti's works.*]

> [W]hile knowledge runs apace, ignorance keeps ahead of knowledge: and all which the deepest students know proves to themselves, yet more convincingly than to others, that

much more exists which still they know not. As saints in relation to spiritual wisdom, so sages in relation to intellectual wisdom, eating they yet hunger and drinking they yet thirst.

> It may never indeed in this world be [God's] pleasure to grant us previsions of seers and forecastings of prophets: but He will assuredly vouchsafe us so much foresight and illumination as should suffice to keep us on the watch with loins girded and lamps burning; not with hearts meanwhile failing us.

> —Christina Rossetti, *Seek and Find*

Three months before she died of cancer, Christina Rossetti wrote to her close friend Frederick Shields in order to bid "good-bye for this life" and request his "prayers for a poor sinful woman who has dared to speak to others and is herself what God knows her to be." Ironically, by the date of this letter (5 September 1894) Rossetti had a reputation in both England and America as a saintly, reclusive writer of highly wrought and effective poems (both secular and devotional) as well as six widely read books of religious commentary. In all of these works she "dared to speak to others" in a characteristically humble, but nonetheless firmly sagacious, indeed often prophetic, voice. Commentators toward the end of the century commonly acknowledge the power of Rossetti's work which for them is inseparable from her religious piety. "She is an inspired prophetess or priestess," according to one reviewer [*Catholic World* 24 (Oct. 1876)]. For another, she is a "poet and saint" who "lived a life of sacrifice . . . [and] unreluctantly endured the pains of her spirituality" [Alice Meynell, *New Review* 12 (Feb. 1895)]. One eulogy acknowledges that "her language was always that of Christian assurance and of simple . . . faith in her Saviour. . . . [H]er life was one of transcendent humility" [*Times* (London), January 7, 1895]. After the turn of the century, we are told that Rossetti "needed not to pray, for her life was an unbroken communion with God" [Paul Elmer More, *Atlantic Monthly* 94 (Dec. 1904)].

Rossetti's reputation as a devout "prophetess" and saintly woman, along with consistently strong reviews of her work (especially her devotional poems and prose), attracted a remarkable audience, as other commentators late in her career indicate. A long essay in *Harper's* for May 1888 insists that "Christina Rossetti's deeply spiritual poems are known even more widely than those of her more famous brother." Two years earlier William Sharp had acknowledged that "the youngest of the Rossetti family has, as a poet, a much wider reputation and a much larger circle of readers than even her brother Gabriel, for in England, and much more markedly in America, the name of Christina Rossetti is known intimately where perhaps that of the author of the *House of Life* is but a name and nothing more." Reviewing Mackenzie Bell's biography of Rossetti in 1898, a writer for *The Nation* noted that her income rapidly increased during the last years of her life "less because of a growing appreciation of her poetry than because of her manuals of piety" which "secured her an extensive following." And a writer for *The Dial* remarked that Rossetti's "devotional books . . . have both found and deserved a large and appreciative audience." Such observations appear to confirm a widespread agreement among the Victorian reading public that "[T]here is no higher form [of Christianity] than that of a highly educated, devout English woman."

As these commentaries also suggest, Rossetti's work is most often patently didactic. In that respect it resembles the sage discourse of Carlyle, Ruskin, and even Arnold at times, but the language she speaks, the stances she most often adopts, and her intended audience are uniquely "feminine" (according to Victorian stereotypes) and otherworldly. These latter traits afford Rossetti a perspective on the values and behavior of her contemporaries that is unavailable to male writers of the era and enable her to launch a quietly comprehensive attack on the entire network of patriarchal values which even the most stringent social critics of her day normally accept without question. Surprisingly, and it may seem, paradoxically, Rossetti is able to accomplish this goal by positioning herself as a devout adherent of High Anglican religious doctrine and, ostensibly, as an advocate of the more widespread Victorian ideology of "woman's sphere." By embracing religious values with a uniquely radical fervor, however, Rossetti's work undercuts the domestic ideology of middle and upper-class Victorians, and functions to subvert both the patriarchal values that governed Victorian England and their extension in industrial capitalism.

Historically, criticism of Rossetti has properly emphasized her renunciatory mindset. *Vanitas mundi* is her most frequent theme, and no work better illustrates her employment of it than the sonnet **"The World"** (1854):

> By day she wooes me, soft, exceeding fair:
>   But all night as the moon so changeth she;
>   Loathsome and foul with hideous leprosy
> And subtle serpents gliding in her hair.
> By day she wooes me to the outer air,
>   Ripe fruits, sweet flowers, and full satiety:
>   But thro' the night, a beast she grins at me,
> A very monster void of love and prayer.
> By day she stands a lie; by night she stands
>   In all the naked horror of the truth
> With pushing horns and clawed and clutching
>   hands.
> Is this a friend indeed; that I should sell
>   My soul to her, give her my life and youth,
> Till my feet, cloven too, take hold on hell?

Rossetti's use of image patterns from religious and classical sources here is striking, as is her craftsmanship. But the fact that Rossetti personifies as a duplicitous woman the world she repudiates is of even greater interest because her procedure in this poem is typical of her poetry as well as of her prose works. Rossetti appropriates traditional antifeminist (that is, Medusan) iconography in order to highlight its patriarchal origins by conflating the image of the "foul" seductress with her male counterpart from Christian tradition, Satan. The speaker employs these representational traditions of "the world" not only to ex-

pose the materialism, hedonism, and false amatory ideologies that they serve, but also to renounce the degraded constructions of woman's nature and her accepted roles that these ideologies depend upon and perpetuate. Clearly, the wholly fallen, "loathsome and foul," world that is disparaged includes the stereotypes that have been associated with duplicity and corruption ever since the myths of Medusa and Eve were generated within patriarchal cultures.

Much of Rossetti's poetry and, more significantly, all of her devotional writings are designed for a female audience and exploit an array of assumptions about women's social and moral roles that were fundamental to the Victorian ideology of the "woman's sphere." This domestic ideology insisted that a middle-class woman, as a leisured Angel in the House, occupy herself by ministering to the moral and spiritual needs of her husband and children while undertaking tasks (embroidering, arranging flowers, playing music) that were largely ornamental. Retaining her spiritual purity by transcending, or at least remaining oblivious to, all worldly—that is economic, political, or in any sense utilitarian—concerns was essential to the Victorian woman's success as a spiritual minister. Joan Burstyn has explained usefully a rationale for the inculcation of this stereotype and the assumptions on which it was based:

> [According] to this ideal, women played a crucial part in providing stability for men who were torn by doubts and faced by insoluble problems. Few people were prepared to confront social, economic and intellectual changes in society by changing their own terms of thought, which was what the psychological crisis of the age called for; most Victorians turned, instead, to an intensification of personal relationships and an exaggerated adherence to domestic virtues. Religious writers, in their exaggeration of domestic virtues, described women as saviours of society. Men might be assailed by religious scepticism, but women never.

Rossetti's work consistently engages this ideology in its clear connections with the material seductions of the world, and insists, in effect, that both be renounced. In the work of less radical writers, commentaries like Rossetti's would appear merely to reinforce middle-class Victorian ideals of the woman's sphere. But, as I will demonstrate, the stance that she takes regarding worldly renunciation is far more militant than that of most of her contemporaries, and ultimately undercuts the material assumptions upon which the stereotypical roles of middle-class women were based.

One aim of the domestic ideology in Victorian England was to compensate for the almost complete usurpation by men of economic activities (such as spinning, sewing, and other domestic labors) previously undertaken by women of all classes. These activities had provided women with social status and a degree of economic independence unavailable to them in Victorian England. Judith Lowder Newton has examined how "the ideology of woman's sphere . . . served the interests of industrial capitalism by insuring the continuing domination of middle-class women by middle-class men and, through its mitigation of the harshness of economic transition, by insuring the continuing domination of male bourgeoisie in relation to working-class men and women as a whole." The domestic ideology assured women "that they *did* have work, power, and status" in the world after all. Through her insistent advocacy of worldly renunciation, Rossetti implicitly repudiates the fundamental economic and political values of industrial capitalism and thus subverts the ideology of the "woman's sphere" which operated in the service of those values.

Rossetti's most fervent monitions are associated, in the predictably orthodox manner of **"The World,"** with the figure of Satan. In *Time Flies* (1885), for instance, she decries the fact that, "over and over again we are influenced and constrained by the hollow momentary world we behold . . . while utterly obtuse as regards the substantial eternal world no less present around us though disregarded." At one point, she compares this "hollow momentary world" to a funnel-shaped spider's web: "it exhibits beauty, ingenuity, intricacy. Imagine it in the early morning jewelled with dewdrops, and each of these at sunny moments a spark of light or a section of rainbow. Woven, too, as no man could weave it, fine and flexible, frail and tenacious. Yet are its beauties of brilliancy and colour no real part of it. The dew evaporates, the tints and sparkle vanish, the tenacity remains, and at the bottom of all lurks a spider." The spider is, of course, Satan who, according to Rossetti's theological literalism, owns this world: "it must be perilously difficult to set up one's tent amid Satan's own surroundings and continue in no way the worse for that neighborhood. The world and the flesh flaunt themselves in very uncompromising forms in the devil's own territory. And all the power and the glory of them set in array before a man whose work forces him to face and sift them day and night, may well make such an one tremble." In the event,

> Earth is half spent and rotting at the core,
> Here hollow death's-heads mock us with a
>   grin,
> Here heartiest laughter leaves us tired and sore.
> Men heap up pleasures and enlarge desire,
> Outlive desire, and famished evermore
> Consume themselves within the undying fire.

In order to assist readers in avoiding such a fate, Rossetti typically presents them with parables. In the approximately two thousand pages of devotional commentary she published between 1874 and 1892, Rossetti instructively discusses an extraordinary range of topics from the perspective of a fervent adherent of the High Anglican devotionalist doctrine. These include such matters as what and how to read; the probability of Christian election; the possibilities for self-perfection through the imitation of Christ; prospects for immortality; varieties of love; the necessity of patience, obedience, and humility; the maintenance of moral purity, or the controversy over virginity; the need for empathy and charity; the problems of knowing truth in a fallen world; the achievement of harmony with the divine will; the necessity of faith; the inevitabil-

ity of suffering; the multitude of temptations in the world (especially the problem of vanity); and the constitution of true happiness. Rossetti usually approaches such issues through an analysis of religious texts, the lives of saints, or personal experiences rendered figuratively. Because Rossetti clearly anticipated a female audience for her devotional works, the treatment of all these subjects bears ultimately on her perception of the prescribed roles for Victorian women.

Early in *Seek and Find* (1879) Rossetti makes explicit her intent to address a variety of issues derived from the Benedicte primarily in connection with "the feminine lot." Here, as elsewhere throughout her devotional prose, Rossetti insists upon the spiritual superiority of women by comparing expectations of their behavior with the example of Christ. More complexly, however, she is able to reconcile herself to women's subordination to men in worldly affairs only by looking forward to an eventual equality of the sexes in heaven.

> In many points the feminine lot copies very closely the voluntarily assumed position of our Lord and Pattern. Woman must obey: and Christ "learned obedience" (Gen. 3. 16; Heb. 5. 8). She must be fruitful, but in sorrow: and He, symbolised by a corn of wheat, had not brought forth much fruit except He had died (Gen. 3. 16; St. John 12. 24). She by natural constitution is adapted not to assert herself, but to be subordinate: and He came not to be ministered unto but to minister; He was among His own "as he that serveth" (1 St. Peter 3. 7; 1 Tim. 2. 2, 12; St. Mark 10. 45; St. Luke 22. 27). Her office is to be man's helpmeet: and concerning Christ God saith, "I have laid help upon One that is mighty" (Gen. 2. 18, 21, 22; Ps. 89. 19). And well may she glory, inasmuch as one of the tenderest of divine promises takes (so to say) the feminine form: "As one whom his mother comforteth, so will I comfort you" (Is. 66. 13)

> In the case of the twofold Law of Love, we are taught to call one Commandment "first and great," yet to esteem the second as "like unto it" (St. Matt. 22. 37-39). The man is the head of the woman, the woman the glory of the man (1 Cor. 11. 3, 7). . . . But if our [pride] will after all not be stayed, or at any rate not be allayed (for stayed [it] must be) by the limit of God's ordinance governing our sex, one final consolation yet remains to careful and troubled hearts: in Christ there is neither male nor female, for we are all one (Gal. 3. 28). (30-32)

Clearly Rossetti herself has a "careful and troubled" heart when considering these vexed matters. I quote this lengthy passage in full because its rhetorical strategies mark a conflict within the patriarchal religious doctrine to which Rossetti subscribes. Repeatedly in her poetry, her prose works, and her letters, she wrestles with the glaring contradiction between her culture's insistence upon the inferior social status of women and their spiritual exaltation. She obediently and humbly claims to accept the illogic of this contradiction. But, as in this passage, her ultimate subordination of power relations in this world to expectations for the afterlife subverts the domestic ideology that her exegetical discourse would appear to serve. The final purpose of her prose works is to insure that women, deemed "last" in the affairs of this world, will be "first" in heaven, and thereby to inspire each of her female readers to give "all diligence to make her own personal calling and election sure." Rossetti's general procedure is to translate "symbols, parables, analogies, inferences" into "words of the wise which are as goads." Her aim is that, as a result of such efforts as her own, "we" women "shall demean ourselves charitably, decorously according to our station; we shall reflect honour on those from whom we derive honour; out of the abundance of our heart our mouth will speak wisdom; kindness will govern our tongue, and justice our enactments;—thus shall it be with us even now, and much more in the supreme day of rising up, the Day of Resurrection."

This passage and many of her poems—from **"Goblin Market," "A Triad,"** and **"Maude Clare"** to **"The Lowest Room," "The Prince's Progress,"** and **"Monna Innominata"**—adapt the discourse of gender-marked power struggles to the language and formulae of religious doctrine. That is, within the conventional language of such passages that clearly accepts the patriarchally ordained position of women, a deliberate subtext of resistance to cultural determinations operates. Such a strategy appears again in *Time Flies* in the entry for March 23: "In common parlance Strong and Weak are merely relative terms: thus the 'strong' of one sentence will be the 'weak' of another. We behold the strong appointed to help the weak: Angels who 'excel in strength,' men. And equally the weak the strong: woman 'the weaker vessel,' man. This, though it should not inflate any, may fairly buoy us all up." Ultimately, Rossetti believed in the potential of all women to be "elect," as the title of her volume published in 1881, *Called to Be Saints,* indicates. In *The Face of the Deep* (1892) she explains, "now the saints are they who know not their names, however they name each other. Thus *Patience* will not discern herself, but will identify a neighbour as *Charity,* who in turn will recognize not herself, but mild Patience; and they both shall know some fellow Christian, as *Hope* or *Prudence* or *Faith;* and every one of these shall be sure of the others, only not of herself."

Very often in Rossetti's work, as in the passages I have cited, the rhetoric of orthodoxy and acquiescence gradually becomes a rhetoric of resistance. This writing is "a mode of social strategy" and "a form of struggle"—as Newton has described certain Victorian novels—directed to a specific literary and religious subculture in Victorian England that, by extension and projection, assumes a degree of solidarity and sisterhood. Elaine Showalter was the first to discuss this "feminist" phenomenon in connection with the literature of Victorian England, emphasizing that "it is important to understand the female subculture not only as . . . a set of opinions, prejudices, tastes, and values prescribed for a subordinate group to perpetuate its subordination—but also as a thriving and positive entity." Rossetti's position illustrates Nancy Cott's view that "women's group consciousness [is] a subculture uniquely divided against itself by ties to the dominant culture. While the ties to the dominant culture are the

informing and restricting ones, they provoke within the subculture certain strengths as well as weaknesses, enduring values as well as accommodations." In assaulting her dominant culture's primary social and material value systems through a critique based in the religious beliefs that traditionally complemented and served those systems, Rossetti deploys subversive strategies of extraordinary power and complexity.

In order fully to understand the operations of these strategies, it is crucial to explore the particular sociohistorical contexts of her work. Rossetti's adherence to Victorian High Anglicanism, as a culturally specific and unique system of religious values, actually reinforced the femininist subversiveness of her writing.

As is evident from even the most cursory reading of Rossetti's poetry and devotional prose, her work finds its primary inspiration in her High Anglican religious beliefs. Her agnostic brother W. M. Rossetti described her as "an Anglo-Catholic, and, among Anglo-Catholics, a Puritan." In this century, Raymond Chapman has successfully argued a case "for seeing Christina Rossetti as directly and fully a product of the Oxford Movement," and he insists that she is "the true inheritor of the Tractarian devotional mode in poetry." More recently, George B. Tennyson and others have extended Chapman's argument, and the history of Rossetti's involvement with High Anglican churches and church figures has been documented thoroughly by her biographers. In 1843, at the impressionable age of twelve, Rossetti began regular attendance at Christ Church, Albany Street, "noted at the time for the incendiary sermons of the Reverend William Dodsworth, one of the chief preachers of the Oxford Movement, a man closely associated with both [John Henry] Newman and [Edward] Pusey." As Lona Mosk Packer notes, citing an article from the *Edinburgh Review,* this church was becoming "a principal centre of High Church religionism in the metropolis." Rossetti's early religious education in this environment and her lifelong involvement with major figures from the later days of High Anglicanism profoundly influenced her particular appropriations of a system of religious beliefs that pervaded every aspect of her existence. Rossetti's most recent biographer, Georgina Battiscombe, insists that "for [Rossetti] this form of religion came to be, quite simply and without question, the most important thing in her life."

Readers of Rossetti's works today tend to forget the extent to which Anglo-Catholicism was perceived in mid-century as a radical movement. As Packer explains, "this exhilarating . . . Tractarian Renascence" was "an avant-garde movement accepted alike by the Regent's Park worthies and the Albany Street literati." Rossetti's involvement with the institutional extensions of this movement continued and deepened throughout her life. All but one of her books of devotional prose were published by the Society for Promoting Christian knowledge, a press with close ties to Anglo-Catholicism.

More significantly, Rossetti developed important connections with the High Anglican movement to resurrect sisterhoods, conventual institutions that many Victorians found threatening because they undercut the roles and functions widely accepted for middle-class women. One Anglican convent opened about 1850 a few doors from Christ Church:

> founded and directed by Dr. Pusey, who chose the Albany Street church as the scene of a novel ex-periment, . . . the religious community of women caused amazement and consternation even in a parish as radical as [William] Dodsworth's. 'The special vocation of a Sister,' wrote Pusey's biographer, 'the character involved and the claims of such a character, were altogether unknown. . . . That young ladies [of good families] should shrink from society, and entertain thoughts of a vow of celibacy in the face of an eligible marriage was almost inconceivable.'

In 1874, Rossetti's sister Maria, to whom she was extremely close, joined the All Saints' Sisterhood in Margaret Street. Yet already two decades earlier Rossetti had been composing poems, such as **"Three Nuns"** and **"The Convent Threshold,"** that clearly reflect her fascination with these new institutions that liberated women from the temptations of "the world," especially the world of the Victorian marriage market (attacked parodically in **"Goblin Market"**) and the domestic ideology of which they were a crucial component.

In her sonnet **"A Triad"** Rossetti concisely exposes the unsatisfactory vocational alternatives for Victorian women.

> Three sang of love together; one with lips
>   Crimson, with cheeks and bosom in a glow,
> Flushed to the yellow hair and finger tips;
>   And one there sang who soft and smooth as snow
>   Bloomed like a tinted hyacinth at a show;
> And one was blue with famine after love,
>   Who like a harpstring snapped rang harsh and low
> The burden of what those were singing of.
> One shamed herself in love; one temperately
>   Grew gross in soulless love, a sluggish wife;
> One famished died for love. Thus two of three
>   Took death for love and won him after strife;
>   All on threshold, yet all short of life.

For Rossetti, becoming a bride of Christ was the only vital alternative to the stereotypical roles of prostitute, wife, and lovelorn spinster, and it is one she advocates repeatedly in her poems and devotional works, sometimes with extraordinary passion. Renunciation of the world, with all its misguided social institutions and material temptations, is the unique route to self-fulfillment, as is made clear in **"A Better Resurrection"**:

> My life is like a faded leaf,
>   My harvest dwindled to a husk;
> Truly my life is void and brief
>   And tedious in the barren dusk;
> My life is like a frozen thing,

> No bud nor greenness can I see:
> Yet rise it shall—the sap of Spring;
>   O Jesus, rise in me.
> My life is like a broken bowl,
>   A broken bowl that cannot hold
> One drop of water for my soul
>   Or cordial in the searching cold;
> Cast in the fire the perished thing,
>   Melt and remould it, till it be
> A royal cup for Him my King:
>   O Jesus, drink of me.

Rossetti herself never joined a sisterhood, in part because of a compulsion to exercise whatever influence she could through her writings in order to expose and to subvert the system of cultural values that denied genuine fulfillment for women. She did so by advocating strict, devotional alternatives. (Unexpectedly, at one point in *Time Flies* she wryly interjects, "But Bishops should write for me, not I for Bishops!"). Rossetti did, nonetheless, become an associate at one of the many Anglican Church-related homes founded at mid-century for the redemption of prostitutes, working regularly at St. Mary Magdalene's on Highgate Hill until her health broke down in the late 1860s. As Martha Vicinus has observed, the "reform of fallen women" was one of the three major tasks undertaken by the Anglican sisterhood. Rossetti's involvement in it had visible effects on her many poems about fallen women (including **"Goblin Market," "The Convent Threshold,"** and **"An Apple-Gathering"**) as well as on her devotional prose works.

Rossetti's intimate connections with the newly developing Anglican sisterhoods, although she remained outside their conventual restrictions, gave her a unique position from which freely to present a critique of her society. These institutions, conservative as they might appear in the late twentieth century, were, in fact, radically liberating for the women who became involved with them. As an extension of the Oxford Movement, the convents "played an important initial role in the emancipation of women in England," presenting "a wide variety of opportunities to women in the fields of teaching, nursing, social work, and community organization." Vicinus has traced the origins, development, and social influence of the Anglican sisterhoods, emphasizing the extent to which they empowered Victorian women: the "sisters carved out an area of expertise and power within their male-dominated churches. . . . [They] were clearly in the vanguard of women's single-sex organizations, in both their organizational autonomy and their insistence upon women's right to a separate religious life." Vicinus also remarks upon the varieties of freedom offered to Victorian women through the sisterhoods, which were among "the most important women's communities in the nineteenth century":

> They were among the first to insist upon a woman's right to choose celibacy, to live communally, and to do meaningful work. They demanded and received great loyalty from their members and were in turn deeply supportive of each other . . . [T]he orders maintained

a very high standard of religious life, proving convincingly that women could lead women, live together, and work for the greater good of the church, the people, and God.

One sister's commentary suggests the radicalism of the Anglican sisterhood movement: "It was a wonderful thing at that period to be young among young comrades. . . . It was an era of religion and faith, and at the same time of intellectual challenge. We read, discussed, debated and experimented and felt that all life lay before us to be changed and moulded by our vision and desire."

Rossetti could not have been unaware of the potentially liberating effects of Anglican sisterhoods upon Victorian women, and of the fact that these sisterhoods were perceived by many to be disturbingly subversive of dominant patriarchal ideologies, including that of the woman's sphere. John Shelton Reed has recently discussed the public controversy that swirled around the sisterhoods. He explains that "there was widespread uneasiness about the development of sisterhoods" because they clearly presented an "affront to Victorian family values." For instance, "Prebendary Gresley of Lichfield, a sober Tractarian . . . gave the anglo-catholic view when he remarked matter-of-factly that 'Home and comfort have been too long the idols of Englishmen, a settlement and establishment in life the *summum bonum* of Englishwomen. It is a great point to have it admitted that there may be something nobler and more desirable than these acknowledged blessings.'" Earlier, Florence Nightingale, a heroine of Rossetti's early adulthood, had described the Victorian domestic ideology derisively as a "Fetich": "'Family'—the idol they have made of it. It is a kind of Fetichism. . . . They acknowledge no God, for all they say to the contrary, but this Fetich." Sisterhoods strongly threatened this idol. Conventual life "took women out of their homes. It gave important work and sometimes great responsibility. It replaced their ties to fathers, husbands, and brothers by loyalties to church and sisterhood. It demonstrated that there were callings for women of the upper and middle classes other than those of wife, daughter, and 'charitable spinster,'" offering "an alternative to a life of idleness or drudgery—exotic, but safely exotic, and cloaked in the respectability of religion."

But as Reed has demonstrated, the sisterhood was only one of many Anglo-Catholic innovations that threatened the social and economic values of the Victorian patriarchy. The revival of auricular confession and the establishment of "free and open seating" in the churches (as opposed to private family pews), among other Anglo-Catholic alterations of church ritual, were also seen as powerfully subversive, especially because these changes were strongly supported by women who, as most observers agreed, were drawn to Anglo-Catholicism in disproportionate numbers. One commentator complained that "The Ritual movement is a lay movement . . . but it is more than that; it is a female movement. . . . The Ritualistic clergyman is led, or rather misled, by a few ladies." In fact, the religious movement to which Rossetti fervently committed herself and the audience to whom she directed her devotional prose commentaries and poems must finally be seen as feminist:

> By its sometimes studied disregard for conventional standards of manliness and by its revaluation of celibacy, the movement issued a series of subtle but continual challenges to received patriarchal values. That these challenges were heard and understood by the movement's male opponents is evident in their denigration of women's part in the movement, and in the alarm and contempt evoked in them by the movement's 'effeminacy.'

As I have already remarked, the quality of Rossetti's own devotionalist feminism is complicated and often disguised by her ostensible subscription to orthodox notions of male supremacy, especially in her prose writings. (Her poems, however, are full of male villains.) But a number of passages from her devotional books, letters, and unpublished remarks expose a radically femininist bent. Rossetti's insistence that women patiently endure this life in expectation of the life to come upholds the dogmas of the patriarchy, but only in anticipation of the ultimate dissolution of these dogmas in that afterlife which is a "flowering land of love" where men and women will be "happy equals" (**"Monna Innominata"**). Typical is Rossetti's modulation (in a discussion of St. Hilary) from an acceptance of an "unknown" wife's subordinate position in matters of worldly reputation to an insistence on her ultimate equality with her spouse: "now of St. Hilary's wife I read nothing further, beyond such a hint of her career as is involved in that of her husband. Wherefore of her I am free to think of as one 'unknown and yet well known'; on earth of less dignified name than her husband. . . . in Paradise it may well be of equal account" (*Time Flies*).

Rossetti's discussions of marriage and of the marital relations between the sexes are, in her devotional works, most often cautiously critical. Her poems almost never broach the topic, except to renounce the prospects of marital union, to depict betrayed or disappointed love, or to celebrate the prospect of marital union with Christ in the afterlife. (In the preface to **"Monna Innominata"** she goes so far as to suggest that Elizabeth Barrett Browning would have written better sonnets had she been "unhappy, rather than happy in love". Because worldly marriages for Rossetti most often require that women "grow gross in soulless love," she often implicitly disdains the institution. In one passage from *Letter and Spirit* she obediently acknowledges that "A wife's paramount duty is indeed to her husband, superseding all other human obligations." But she immediately proceeds to subvert the patriarchal ideology underlying that dogma: "yet to assume this duty, free-will has first stepped in with its liability to err; in this connexion woman has to reap as she has sown, be the crop what it may: while in the filial relation all is safe and flawless, for all is of Divine ordaining."

When discussing prospects for immortality in particular, or moral virtue and purity in general, Rossetti frequently recurs to Christ's commandments regarding marriage:

> Change and vicissitude are confined to this life and this world: once safe in the next world the saved are safe for ever and ever. So our Lord deigned to effect to teach us all, when answering certain Saducees, He said: "The children of this world marry, and are given in marriage: but they which shall be accounted worthy to obtain that world, and the resurrection from the dead, neither marry, nor are given in marriage: neither can they die any more: for they are equal unto the angels. . . ." And further we gather hence by implication that not all shall "obtain . . . the resurrection from the dead." (*Face of the Deep*).

The clear implication here is that the unmarried are more likely to be saved than those who succumb to this worldly institution. Earlier in *The Face of the Deep,* when discussing how "the precarious purity of mortal life shall become the indefectible purity of the immortal," Rossetti compares the individual who succumbs to the world's temptations to trodden snow which turns to mud. By contrast, those who remain pure are like "snow on mountain summits" that "endures alone": "Even so chaste virgins choose solitude for a bower." Such implicit attacks upon marriage in Rossetti's work must finally be seen discursively to reify the subversion of patriarchal social values—especially the "Fetich" of the family and its extension in the ideology of the "woman's sphere"—a revolt that took on institutional form in the revival of the Anglican sisterhoods.

Because Rossetti strategically positions herself on the margins of "the world" in her prose works, focusing her commentaries on preparing for the afterlife, she rarely presents cultural critiques that do not take on circumspect, parabolic forms. In her secular poems, however, especially the dozens that expose patriarchal amatory ideologies that victimize women, she is more outspoken; but even many of these works (including **"Goblin Market,"** **"The Prince's Progress,"** and **"Dream-Love"**) are allegorical. Occasionally, Rossetti's letters also demonstrate the feminist directions of her thought quite explicitly. One in particular, written to the widely published suffragist Augusta Webster, reveals Rossetti's view of sexual roles as artificial "barriers" that are exclusively this-worldly in their provenance. Rossetti is apparently responding to a request from Webster that she support the suffragist movement. "You express yourself with such cordial openness that I feel encouraged to endeavour also after self-expression," Rossetti explains candidly, as she begins a discussion of the appointed roles of the sexes that modulates into a speculation on their power relations. I quote the rest of this extraordinary letter in full:

> Does it not appear as if the Bible was based upon an understood unalterable distinction between men and women, their position, duties, privileges? Not arrogating to myself but most earnestly desiring to attain to the character of a humble orthodox Xian, so it does appear to me; not merely under the Old but also under the New Dispensation. The fact of the Priesthood being exclusively man's, leaves me in no doubt that the highest functions are not *in this world* open to both sexes: and if not all, then a selection must be made

and a line drawn somewhere.—On the other hand if female rights are sure to be overborne for lack of female voting influence, then I confess I feel disposed to shoot ahead of my instructresses, and to assert that female *M.P.'s* are only right and reasonable. Also I take exceptions at the exclusion of married women from the suffrage,—for who so apt as Mothers—all previous arguments allowed for the moment—to protect the interests of themselves and of their offspring? I do think if anything ever does sweep away the barrier of sex, and make the female not a giantess or a heroine but at once and full grown a hero and giant, it is that mighty maternal love which makes little birds and little beasts as well as little women matches for very big adversaries.

Rossetti begins with an unquestioning acceptance of the dogmas of patriarchal orthodoxy. But her fear—irrepressible in this letter as in so many of her poems—that men cannot be expected, finally, to protect "female rights" inspires her to take a line that is, even at the end of the century, distinctly radical.

That radical line emerges in part from Rossetti's customary exaltation of motherhood, her significantly *partial* acceptance of the ideology of the "woman's sphere." (Most often in her work, Rossetti elides any discussion of husbands and marriage as a necessary institutional prelude to the production of children.) But her radicalism also results from a literal acceptance of a basic premise of the domestic ideology: that men are inevitably seduced and sullied by involvement with "the world." Although Rossetti acknowledges that women are men's helpmates (the "weaker vessels" appointed to assist "the strong"), it becomes clear in this letter and throughout her secular poetry that "goblin" men will prove difficult, if not impossible, to redeem, participating as they do in the "loathsome and foul" world controlled by Satan. Hence, the most consistently positive relationships among characters in Rossetti's poems are between mothers and daughters or between sisters. These relationships reinforce a spirit of subcultural solidarity that, ultimately, can deal with "the world" only by wholly renouncing it.

Thus, Rossetti's sage discourse always advocates renunciation and resistance. Addressing a female audience whose values, like her own, had been molded primarily by patriarchal religious, amatory, and domestic ideologies, she consistently appropriates elements of those ideologies in order to expose their inability to fulfill the spiritual, moral, and even intellectual needs of Victorian women. In response to the misguided values of "the world," she urges the acceptance of alternative, radically devotionalist values whose origins are avowedly patriarchal but whose otherworldly goal for adherents is an eventual assumption into a genderless, egalitarian utopia—Paradise.

Despite the unwavering strength of her faith and the consistency of her vision of the fallen world, Rossetti was characteristically humble and cautious, especially in her prose works, when she assumed the authoritative role of sage that her reformist ambitions demanded of her. In *The Face of the Deep,* her last work, she comes to final terms with the spiritual dangers and ideological difficuties facing any Victorian woman who engaged in sage discourse. As usual, however, a prospectively feminist self-confidence emerges in the very act of self-effacement:

> Far be it from me to think to unfold mysteries or interpret prophecies. But I trust that to gaze in whatever ignorance on what God reveals, is so far to do His will. If ignorance breed humility, it will not debar from wisdom. If ignorance betake itself to prayer, it will lay hold on grace. . . . [A]t least I . . . may deepen awe, and stir up desire by a contemplation of things inevitable, momentous, transcendent.

Jan Marsh on Rossetti's life and achievement:

There is today no prospect of Christina Rossetti being forgotten, but we are only beginning to understand her complex and contradictory personality, and the experiences that led her to choose a narrow way. Her harvest, in terms of poetry, was both full and lasting; it was also of greater range and depth than has commonly been thought. The combination of emotional pain and literary talent gave her life and work a unique quality. As both a woman and a writer she deserves remembrance.

FURTHER READING

Bibliography

Addison, Jane. "Christina Rossetti Studies, 1974-1991: A Checklist and Synthesis." *Bulletin of Bibliography* 52, No. 1 (March 1995): 73-93.
    Biographical sketch and extensive bibliography of writings about Rossetti from 1974 to 1991.

Crump, R. W. *Christina Rossetti: A Reference Guide.* Boston: G. K. Hall & Co., 1976, 172 p.
    Bibliography of writings about Rossetti from 1862 to 1973.

Biography

Battiscombe, Georgina. *Christina Rossetti: A Divided Life.* New York: Holt, Rinehart and Winston, 1981, 233 p.
    Biography focussing on the conflict between the outward calm of Rossetti's life and her internal emotional turmoil.

Jones, Kathleen. *Learning Not to Be First: The Life of

Christina Rossetti. Gloucestershire, England: Windrush Press, 1991, 252 p.
    Biography in which the critic argues that earlier accounts of Rossetti's life were overly speculative in nature.
Marsh, Jan. *Christina Rossetti: A Literary Biography.* New York: Viking Penguin, 1995, 640 p.
    Complete, feminist interpretation of Rossetti's life.

Parker, Lona Mosk. *Christina Rossetti.* Berkeley and Los Angeles: University of California Press, 1963, 459 p.
    Biography concentrating on Rossetti's emotional life.

Rossetti, Geoffrey W. "Christina Rossetti." *The Criterion* X, No. XXXVIII (October 1930): 95-117.

    Biographical essay by Rossetti's nephew which includes excerpts from the poet's poems and letters.

Rossetti, William Michael. "Memoir." In *The Poetical Works of Christina Georgina Rossetti,* by Christina Georgina Rossetti, edited by William Michael Rossetti, pp. xiv-lxxi. New York: Macmillan Co., 1904.
    Biographical essay by Rossetti's brother.

Saunders, Mary F. *The Life of Christina Rossetti.* London: Hutchinson & Co., n.d., 291 p.
    Biography based partly on previously unpublished materials and interviews with Rossetti's associates.

Thomas, Eleanor Walter. *Christina Georgina Rossetti.* New York: Columbia University Press, 1931, 229 p.
    A critical biography in which Thomas examines the relationship between Rossetti's work and the literature of her time.

Thomas, Frances. *Christina Rossetti.* Worcestershire: Self Publishing Association, 1992, 446 p.
    Comprehensive biography of Rossetti with an introduction that provides an overview of Rossetti's literary achievements.

Criticism

Adlard, John. "Christina Rossetti: Strategies of Loneliness." In *The Contemporary Review* 221, No. 1280 (September 1972): 146-50.
    Analysis of Rossetti's *Goblin Market* focussing on the adult themes of the work.

Armstrong, Isobel. "Christina Rossetti: Diary of a Feminist Reading." In *Women Reading Women's Writing,* edited by Sue Roe, pp. 115-37. Brighton, England: Harvester Press, 1987.
    Discusses Rossetti's place in the literary canon from a feminist perspective.

Charles, Edna Kotin. *Christina Rossetti: Critical Perspectives, 1862-1982.* Selinsgrove, Pa.: Susquehana University Press, 1985, 187 p.
    Reviews and explains the scholarship and criticism of Rossetti's works from 1862 to 1982.

D'Amico, Diane. Review of *The Complete Poems of Christina Rossetti: A Variorum Edition,* Vol. 3, by Christina Rossetti, edited by R. W. Crump. In *Victorian Poetry* 30, No. 1 (Spring 1992): 87-91.

> Discusses the importance of Crump's variorum edition of Rossetti's poetry in prompting reevaluations of Rossetti's significance.

Forman, H. Buxton. "Christina Gabriela Rossetti." In *Our Living Poets: An Essay in Criticism,* pp. 231-53. London: Tinsley Brothers, 1871.

> Provides an early critical assessment of Rossetti as a significant contributor to "real poetry" and the "history of female literature."

Gilbert, Sandra M. and Susan Gubar. "The Aesthetics of Renunciation." In *The Madwoman in the Attic: The Woman Writer and the Nineteenth-Century Literary Imagination,* pp. 539-80. New Haven: Yale University Press, 1979.

> Examines the work of Rossetti and that of other female poets, such as Emily Dickinson and Virginia Woolf, in the context of the argument that women writers have experienced difficulty in sustaining an image of them-selves as poets—that, in fact, they have been forced to "renounce" themselves.

Harrison, Antony H. "Christina Rossetti: The Poetic Vocation." *Texas Studies in Language and Literature* 27, No. 3 (Fall 1985): 225-48.

> Argues that an examination of Rossetti's methods of composition and aesthetic principles reveals the seriousness of her dedication to her poetic works.

Knoepflmacher, U. C. "Avenging Alice: Christina Rossetti and Lewis Carroll." *Nineteenth-Century Literature* 41, No. 3 (December 1986): 299-328.

> Explores the connection between Rossetti's *Speaking Likenesses* and Carroll's *Alice in Wonderland* in the context of the relationship between Rossetti and Carroll.

McGann, Jerome. "The Religious Poetry of Christina Rossetti." *Critical Inquiry* 10, No. 1 (September 1983): 127-44.

> Explores the neglect of Rossetti's religious poetry by early twentieth-century proponents of the New Critical movement.

Morrill, David F. "'Twilight is not good for maidens': Uncle Polidori and the Psychodynamics of Vampirism in *Goblin Market.*" *Victorian Poetry* 28, No. 1 (Spring 1990): 1-16.

> Suggests the influence of John Polidori's *The Vampyre* on Rossetti's "Goblin Market."

Woolf, Virginia. "I Am Christina Rossetti." In *Collected Essays, Vol. IV.* New York: Harcourt, Brace & World, 1967, pp. 54-60.

> Originally written to commemorate the one-hundredth anniversary of Rossetti's birth, this essay offers a positive assessment of Rossetti's work.

Harriet Beecher Stowe

Uncle Tom's Cabin; or, Life among the Lowly

The following entry presents criticism of Stowe's novel *Uncle Tom's Cabin; or, Life among the Lowly* (1852). For a discussion of Stowe's complete career, see *NCLC*, Volume 3.

INTRODUCTION

Uncle Tom's Cabin, the book that Abraham Lincoln reportedly claimed started the Civil War, was one of the most widely read and profoundly influential works of the nineteenth century. Its anti-slavery message, in direct response to the Fugitive Slave Act of 1850, provoked unprecedented levels of critical disagreement throughout the North and South, serving as a catalyst for sectional conflict. Following the war and the end of slavery, the novel—and its numerous stage adaptations—continued to serve as a focal point for discussions of race in America well into the twentieth century. While usually recognized for its historical contributions, *Uncle Tom's Cabin* has also played an important role in shaping American literature and is noted for its influence on many prominent writers, ranging from Sarah Orne Jewett to Richard Wright and Ishmael Reed.

Biographical Information

When the first installment of *Uncle Tom's Cabin* appeared in the abolitionist magazine *The National Era* in June 1851, Stowe had a modest reputation as a writer of didactic fiction, having published *The Mayflower*, a collection of sentimental short stories and sketches. The daughter of a prominent Presbyterian theologian, her income garnered from writing supplemented her preacher husband's paltry salary. Stowe often claimed that the writing of her most famous work was aided by the hand of God, tracing its inspiration to a Brunswick communion service in which she tried to imagine the death of a pious slave at the hands of a white master. Following the tremendous success of the novel, Stowe published *A Key to Uncle Tom's Cabin* (1853), in which she defended the novel against Southern critiques. Although she continued to write prolifically for several more years, none of her later works achieved the success of her first novel.

Plot and Major Characters

Uncle Tom's Cabin chronicles the life and death of the title character, a black slave known for his reliability and Christian virtue. Beset by financial problems, Mr. Shelby, a Kentucky plantation owner, is forced to sell Tom and Harry, the young son of Eliza, Mrs. Shelby's slave, to a trader. Eliza, however, flees with her son, jumping from one ice floe to another across the Ohio River and narrowly escaping the pursuing slave dealer and his dogs.

Later she is reunited with her husband, George Harris, a highly intelligent escaped slave, in the home of a Quaker family; with the help of the Underground Railroad, they eventually secure their freedom in Canada. While aboard a ship destined for a New Orleans slave market, Tom saves the life of a young girl named Eva, who later convinces her father, Augustine St. Clare, to purchase her heroic rescuer and friend. Tom quickly gains the affection of everyone on the plantation. He forms a close bond with little Eva, who befriends a young, unmanageable slave girl named Topsy before becoming ill and dying. Tom also discusses Christianity with St. Clare, who promises to set him free but is killed in a brawl, enabling Mrs. St. Clare to sell him to the cruel and sadistic Simon Legree, a plantation owner from the North. Intending to make Tom overseer of the other slaves, Legree orders him to flog a sick, weak woman for not working hard enough. After refusing, Tom himself is beaten by Legree's two black henchmen, Sambo and Quimbo. Legree's mistress, Cassy, a refined quadroon whose daughter had been torn from her and sold into slavery, attends to Tom's injuries and tries to enlist his help in murdering their master. But Tom, a model of Christian forgiveness, refuses and convinces her to abort her plan. Later, when Cassy and her daughter, Emmeline, pretend to escape by hiding in the attic that Legree believes to be haunted, Tom refuses to reveal their whereabouts and is again severely beaten. Two days later, after George Shelby, the son of Tom's first master, returns to buy him back, Tom dies with words of Christ's love on his lips. Shortly after Tom's death, Cassy and Emmeline finally make their escape, eventually joining the Harrises in Canada, where it is revealed that Eliza is Cassy's lost daughter.

Major Themes

Stowe wrote the novel for the specific purpose of ending slavery, but her portrayal of domestic values and her characterization of African Americans has continued to interest critics long after emancipation. The novel, as several commentators have observed, casts the "peculiar institution" as a crime against home, family, and true Christian values. Not only is slavery shown destroying familial relationships and morality within the slave community, it is depicted as a threat to the homes of all Americans, in both the South and the North. Many modern readers, however, have found in her antislavery arguments a critique against "masculine" values of individualism, competition, and the marketplace—and a concomitant affirmation of "feminine" values of community, love, and domesticity. Interpretations of Stowe's portrayal of Tom have also undergone considerable revision. While many contemporary readers identified him as a model of Christian virtue, modern readers have often viewed him as a symbol of African-American subordination to white authority.

Critical Reception

Some of the most hotly contested debates in American literary history have surrounded Stowe's monumental work. In the antebellum years, the controversy focused primarily on her antislavery arguments and her depiction of the South. The first American book to sell more than a million copies, *Uncle Tom's Cabin* was well received in the North, despite the arguments of some abolitionists who felt she was too lenient; however, Southern reviewers accused her of slander, and dozens of "anti-Tom" novels soon appeared. After the Civil War, white critics in the North and South, for the most part, came to agree with Stowe's position on slavery, but many took issue with her presentation of African-American characters, claiming that they were depicted in too positive a manner. In the post-World War II years, however, the opposite view prevailed. Reviewers such as African-American novelist James Baldwin found in Stowe's portrayal of Tom a negative stereotype of servility and impotence. While "Uncle Tom" has remained a pejorative term, several scholars since the mid-1980s have vigorously defended both the political message and the artistic merit of the novel. Largely through the efforts of feminist and historically based critics who have focused on Stowe's attention to the domestic culture of her nineteenth-century female audience, *Uncle Tom's Cabin* has once again become the subject of serious academic study.

CRITICISM

David Levin (essay date 1971)

SOURCE: "American Fiction as Historical Evidence: Reflections on *Uncle Tom's Cabin,*" in *Forms of Uncertainty: Essays in Historical Criticism,* University Press of Virginia, 1992, pp. 249-59.

[*In the excerpt that follows, originally from an essay published in 1971, Levin addresses Stowe's treatment of various social issues in* Uncle Tom's Cabin *from a historical perspective, concluding that Stowe should be commended for her often-overlooked, complex intellectual statement.*]

The historical document known as *Uncle Tom's Cabin* illustrates a truth that has been known to American historians ever since Washington Irving published Knickerbocker's *History of New York:* that contemporary experience of historians alters the evidence they study. My earliest recollection of that humbling but challenging truth is a high school history teacher's warning in 1939 that we ought not to choose *Uncle Tom's Cabin* as collateral reading, because (he said) Mrs. Stowe depicts slave owners and slavery too critically. Thirty years later I find that

my most difficult problem as a teacher centers on the same book, which many students now reject as James Baldwin rejected it, for combining sentimentality and racial condescension with vindictive stereotypes in a way that deserves the scornful title, "Everybody's Protest Novel." Some of my students declare that Mrs. Stowe "knows nothing about black people," and that for knowledge of conventional characters we might as well read instead a few original radio scripts for *Amos 'n Andy.* One graduate student in history insists that Mrs. Stowe practices cruel deception by inventing the loving family of Uncle Tom and Aunt Chloe, because the Moynihan Report, Stanley Elkins's book on *Slavery,* and a number of other sociological projections depict the slave family as matriarchal. A few students, whose feelings I respect, find it unbearable to read seriously beyond the obvious signals that this is a book written for an Anglo-Saxon Us (however culpably aggressive) about an intellectually and energetically inferior (albeit an admirably patient and peaceful) African Them. Whatever the context, a sensitive young reader must develop an extraordinary capacity for detachment in order to read beyond the narrator's many variations on this kind of statement: "Now there is no more use in making believe be angry with a negro than with a child; both instinctively see the true state of the case, through all attempts to affect the contrary."

Against most of these limited readings I have appealed to a small group of excellent critical essays about *Uncle Tom's Cabin*—commentaries by Edmund Wilson, Charles Foster, Kenneth Lynn, Alice Crozier, Cushing Strout, and Howard Mumford Jones—because all these writers acknowledge the book's literary value as well as its documentary importance for American literary and social history, and they all recognize some connection between the documentary importance and Mrs. Stowe's literary skill. I have also appealed to historical authorities, including a not wholly facetious declaration by Kenneth Stampp that *Uncle Tom's Cabin* is one of the best books ever written about American slavery. And now some genuinely new historical research has put new life into the old book. Professor Herbert Gutman has blasted the foundations of the matriarchy by demonstrating that in all parts of the United States, during the last years of slavery, black children, whether slaves or free, were just about as likely as lower-class white children to grow up in two-parent households. And he has demonstrated that black Americans emerged from slavery with the two-parent, patriarchal household as the norm of family life. Gutman's full study has not yet been published, but in a recent issue of the *New York Review of Books* Eugene Genovese has built a long speculative essay on Gutman's fine work and on insights that were already explicit in the novels, psychiatric studies, and histories of Albion Tourgee, Ralph Ellison, Margaret Walker, Robert Coles, and C. L. R. James. Genovese asks us to study Afro-American strengths and human triumphs under American slavery, as well as the suffering and degradation.

With such encouragement, I confess that my interest in romantic histories and historical romances leads me to read *Uncle Tom's Cabin* as a romance of manners written by an extremely perceptive, intelligent woman. As we read it retrospectively, aware of subsequent history and literature, we see not only Mrs. Stowe's anticipation of other authors' themes, character types, and issues, but also her remarkable understanding of them. If God did write the book for her, as she is said to have claimed years afterward, he made more use of her social intelligence than her emphasis on his inspiration would seem to allow, and he let her see how to make the sentimental romance an especially appropriate instrument of that intelligence. I should like to concentrate my remarks on what Mrs. Stowe saw truly about the nature of her society, and how she strengthened her book with some of her most valuable perceptions. . . .

It seems to me likely that the extraordinary popular success of *Uncle Tom's Cabin* may owe as much to the book's intellectual power as to its strong sentiment. Whether or not my conjecture persuades you, the examples I am about to discuss ought to demonstrate that a sentimental romancer in the early 1850s explicitly delineated relationships that we too often credit to the original discovery of recent historians. When properly understood, moreover, the literary genre in which she cast her reflections proves capable, despite its obvious weaknesses, of expressing an admirably complex statement of American social contradictions. I cannot give here all the evidence to justify my admiration for the book, but the argument can safely rest on the following discussion of manners, Christianity, and nonviolence. I shall spend most of my time on manners.

Mrs. Stowe sees the complexity of American slavery, and she makes admirable use of literary and racial stereotypes to reveal it. Her opening scene confronts us with three male characters, a gentleman, a vulgar slave trader, and a black child (Harry) whom the planter calls Jim Crow and commands to dance for the two men. The child dutifully plays the comic role of Jim Crow. He obeys a command to imitate "old Uncle Cudjoe with the rheumatism" and "Elder Robbins reading a psalm," whereupon the trader decides to buy the child, along with Uncle Tom, the best hand on the plantation. One feels an unsettling ambiguity about Mrs. Stowe's attitude during this and the subsequent episodes that set the entire plot in motion, for she evidently prefers Mr. Shelby's gentlemanly manners to the bluntness and the social presumptuousness of Haley, the trader, and she apparently believes that black children were born to dance. Her triumph is nonetheless clear. She shows us that the gentleman and the trader were bound together in selling and buying black talent, black childhood, black joy. Later on, she gives the repulsive trader the line that explicitly identifies the two classes with each other: when Shelby's son condemns Haley for "buying men and women, and chaining them like cattle," Haley replies: "So long as your grand folks want to buy men and women, I'm as good as they is; 'tain't any meaner sellin' on 'em than 'tis buyin.'" Even more brilliantly, moreover, Mrs. Stowe's dramatic action highlights one major function of the grand folks' superior manners: to protect gentlemen from direct recognition of the brutal reality that makes them as mean as traders. Mrs. Stowe

may prefer the gentleman to the slave trader, but when Haley understandably complains that Eliza's escape has cheated him out of his investment in her son, Shelby demands that he "observe something of the decorum of a gentleman" in the presence of Mrs. Shelby; and when Haley persists, Shelby retreats into an even more pompous declaration that the family honor has been impugned. The pomposity is as unmistakably there in his language as in some of the preposterous diction that William Faulkner later gave Thomas Sutpen in *Absalom, Absalom!* The threat of a challenge cows the vulgar trader. So much for the function of honor. Haley's only revenge is to pronounce the ugly truth to young George Shelby and to elicit in reply a vow that George will never buy or sell people. Only a few hours after his father's threatening appeal to honor, George admits to Haley that for the first time in his life he feels ashamed to be a Kentuckian.

Manners function in the same intricate way among the black characters. A century before Stanley Elkins, Mrs. Stowe echoed Frederick Douglass's argument that plantations like Simon Legree's brutalized field hands, if not in the way of Nazi concentration camps, which weren't yet available, then at least in the way of English and American factories. But she avoids Elkins's erroneous claim that male self-respect was virtually impossible because there was no black male authority. Even on Legree's plantation and especially on the property of Uncle Tom's other two owners Mrs. Stowe creates a variety of functions and degrees of authority, rivalry, respect. Uncle Tom is not merely Mr. Shelby's best hand, "a large, broad-chested, powerfully-made man, of a full glossy black," with a "truly African face" that expresses grave and steady good sense along with benevolence. He is also the central authority among Shelby's slaves, the leader of prayer meetings, the wise man consulted in crises. When he decides to let himself be sold rather than run away, he offers as his explicit reason the given condition on which the plot originally moves: that if he doesn't go with Haley the entire plantation and all the slaves will go to Haley by default. Tom does follow this argument with an appeal to true honor (as distinct from Shelby's class honor), and he soon insists on the kind of Christian forgiveness and trust in Providence with which his name is unpleasantly associated in our language; but in this context it is especially important to notice that both these appeals follow from the inevitable condition—either he goes or everyone goes—and that even in his most magnificent insistence on forgiveness he is in absolute command of his cabin. Aunt Chloe expresses the fiery response of intelligent human nature, blaming Mr. Shelby, begging her "old man" to flee, and wishing all slave traders in hell: "lor, if the devil don't get 'em, what's he good for?" But Tom is in command, and his wife defers to his forgiveness, his misplaced faith in Shelby, and his practical good sense of the common danger. This is a patriarchal, two-parent household, and the young children in it know that the father who loves them enough to weep at the prospect of leaving them is strong enough to enforce his domestic authority.

There is no need or time to discuss here the entire range

of black characters on the several plantations, from the hired-out mechanic and inventor George Harris and Eliza, his serving-maid wife, to Legree's slave drivers and the various antecedents of Faulkner's Dilsey who preside over the Kentucky and New Orleans kitchens. I do need to say a few words about Sam and Andy, the two slaves whose adroit bungling, manipulation, and psychology delay Haley long enough to insure Eliza's miraculous escape across the Ohio. Mrs. Stowe's clumsy efforts to condescend into the comically political mind of Sam are technically and racially embarrassing, but she carries off his actions and his treatment of the master class with brilliant success. She shows Sam and Andy elaborating the kind of role in which Haley had originally found Eliza's little boy so adaptable. These grown men, however, use the role assigned to them by white men; they use it to thwart a white man's will and to play off one master against another. In a burlesque of Anglo-Saxon bustle and efficiency they deftly mismanage the chase as white stereotyping says that a black man would, and in the same way they trick Haley into commanding them to take the wrong road. At the end their loud, ambiguous laughter completes the burlesque; we hear some of their actual, unmistakable words, but Haley hears the laughter that masks even as it expresses their contempt. It is the same laughter that makes young Thomas Sutpen want to strike out at the fantastic balloon-face in Faulkner's *Absalom, Absalom!,* and Haley reacts with a foreshadowing of Sutpen's anger.

In praising Mrs. Stowe's portrayal of Sam and Andy, I don't mean to contradict my students' judgment that Mrs. Stowe had little understanding of black people. I do believe that she understood a great deal about people's relationships with one another and about how conventional literary characters and sociological stereotypes or roles express genuinely human qualities. Topsy's perception of Miss Ophelia's revulsion from the physical touch of black people, and Topsy's willingness to adapt to the expectations of her owners, are deeply true even though the characterization often seems to me hopelessly limited (in a way that Eva St. Clare's is not) by Mrs. Stowe's inability to write from inside the black child's mind. For me it is the functioning of manners that overcomes the faults. The white characters discuss Topsy in her presence as if she were not there, and her alert response reveals the depth of their misunderstanding and the intelligence of her own observation. For me this kind of relationship does more than the most fervently explicit pleas to establish Mrs. Stowe's genuine appreciation of her central contention: that black men and women are thoroughly human.

In view of this purpose, as several critics have seen in different ways, Mrs. Stowe's heavy emphasis on sentiment is itself an intelligent comment on her society. The Ohio senator's wife who shelters Eliza and her son in defiance of the Fugitive Slave Law exemplifies the critics' judgment when she appeals to a mother's feelings against her husband's cautious reasoning on "great public interests": "I *hate* reasoning, John—especially reasoning on such subjects." Earlier, when Mrs. Shelby learns that Eliza's son and Uncle Tom must be sold to save the rest

of the estate, she reminds her husband that her "common sense" has always told her slavery could come to no good. By calling your attention to the pervasiveness of reasonable analysis that underlies this appeal to universal sentiment, I hope to give a clearer idea of the book's sociological range and historical insight. Repeatedly Mrs. Stowe shows us a situation in which logic has gone wild. Like the creator of Jason Compson, she has an astonishingly fine ear for the language of racism and the fundamental contradictions embraced by men who must defend slavery. She begins with our old friend Haley, who argues with unexpected persuasiveness that it is more humane not to bring up slaves to expect humane treatment. "You mean well by 'em," he concedes, "but tan't no real kindness, after all . . . I think I treat niggers just about as well as it's ever worth while to treat 'em." Mrs. Stowe makes devastating use of other slogans. "It's a free country," declares George Harris's owner when the man to whom George has been hired out tries to dissuade him from spitefully demoting George to field labor; "It's a free country. The man's *mine,* and I do what I please with him." When reminded of George's laborsaving invention the same man replies that it is just like "a nigger" to invent something that will avoid work. "They are all labor-saving machines themselves, every one of 'em!" Americans in the free states praise Hungarian rebels as heroes but hunt fugitive southern slaves for bounty, dead or alive. Even Augustine St. Clare, the most intelligent commentator and to my mind the finest characterization in the book, fails to see until Uncle Tom forces him to see the logic of all his own thorough arguments against slavery, for St. Clare is astonished and hurt to learn that Tom would rather be free than owned by the kindest master. In the end, then, we observe Simon Legree, who claims to run his plantation merely on the economic principle that it is cheaper to work slaves into the ground and then buy new ones than it would be to care for individual health and welfare. Legree contradicts his own principle by beating poor Tom to death—supposedly in order to preserve his authority, but the action, like the entire system, is essentially self-defeating.

In the face of such reasoning Mrs. Stowe implies that the only reasonable hope lies in a primary appeal to feeling and common sense. For thirty years before the composition of *Uncle Tom's Cabin,* romances had often opposed the natural hearts of heroes and heroines against the formal restrictions of civilized law and historical tradition. Whether or not *Uncle Tom's Cabin* helped to cause the Civil War, the author does in effect foresee the catastrophe. In her last direct address to the reader, she insists that "there is one thing" besides prayer "that *every* individual can do" to oppose slavery: "they can see to it *that they feel right.*" She entreats her readers to "*feel* strongly, healthily, and justly, on the great interests of humanity" against "the sophistries of worldly policy." Her last warning is biblical, apocalyptic, but also worldly wise. Years of wrath were coming.

As every reader must quickly perceive (among the white characters, at least), it is the women in the book who most clearly represent the supremacy of right feeling. But it would be a mistake to assume that the women's authority rests on sentiment and intuition alone. Here again Mrs. Stowe's sharp observation of manners penetrates so deeply beyond the obvious contrasts that defects in characterization are overcome by social understanding. Mrs. Shelby's rebuke of her husband brings out woman's role among American aristocrats and businessmen. Both the husband and the wife see that woman is the moral authority and that, in effect, her moral purity is maintained by ignorance and irrelevance. Both Shelby and the Ohio senator leave moral and religious questions to their wives, and thus declare that in the real world moral and religious questions are unimportant. What I want to stress here is a perception of Mrs. Stowe's that is rarely noticed. Repeatedly in this book, the women with the most powerful moral sentiments also develop extremely intelligent arguments. Mrs. Shelby points the lesson when she says that she *could* understand her husband's affairs if he didn't keep her in such ignorance of them; and it is she and Aunt Chloe who eventually begin to execute reasonably practical plans for redeeming Tom. Aunt Chloe gives Tom a series of unanswerable arguments to show that Mr. Shelby doesn't deserve Tom's loyalty, and little Eva herself—too often dismissed in our day as "sugary confection"—sees that her father's desire to shield her from knowledge of miserable suffering is a selfish way of defending the cruel system. She ought to know the real horrors, she insists, and she ought to feel about them. She sees, beyond his childish assurance that his kindness will protect his slaves, the need for a system that won't depend on one man's kindness.

With Eva, then, we come to the question of Christianity. I pass over the central function of Tom's and Eva's piety; it is no less important for being obvious, but in this final set of examples I wish to show the primacy of Mrs. Stowe's social intelligence even on the one subject that is closer to her heart than the domestic sentiments of women. She knows that Uncle Tom is "a moral miracle." She shows us in the opening pages her awareness that true Christianity often plays into the hands of the exploiters. We are told explicitly that Tom's extraordinary trustworthiness—or at least Shelby's extraordinary financial trust in him—began just after Tom's conversion at a camp meeting. "Why, last fall," Shelby says to Haley, "I let him go to Cincinnati alone, to do business for me, and bring home five hundred dollars. 'Tom,' says I to him, 'I trust you, because I think you're a Christian—I know you wouldn't cheat.' Tom comes back, sure enough; *I knew he would.*" Haley, too, says that he values religion in a nigger, "when it's the real *article.*" This kind of perception, so economically dramatized and so heavily freighted with commercial diction, goes a long way toward authenticating Mrs. Stowe's conception of Tom's saintly resistance to Simon Legree. I assent to her conception of the moral miracle because she knows that trustworthiness is valued by genuine Christians and commercial exploiters of the genuine article. She knows that the moral miracle brings a high price in the market because he is not only strong but obedient. And she highlights his most saintly qualities by contrasting them in action to equally powerful black rejections of Christian principles. I have already

mentioned Aunt Chloe's passionate refusal to forgive Mr. Shelby and her desire to send all slave traders to the devil. In the same spirit George Harris renounces the country, the race, and for a time the God of his father and, though white enough to pass, wishes he himself were "two shades darker, rather than one lighter." And when Tom refuses to help Cassy murder Simon Legree, because (he says) "The Lord hasn't *called* us to wrath. We must suffer, and wait his time"—then Cassy replies with the powerful arguments that our outraged contemporaries have so often used in recent years:

> "Wait! . . . Haven't I waited?—waited till my head is dizzy and my heart sick? What has he made me suffer? What has he made hundreds of poor creatures suffer? Isn't he wringing the life-blood out of *you?* I'm called on; *they* call me! His time's come, and I'll have his heart's blood."

Tom, of course, wins that argument, but we must remember that Mrs. Stowe wrote both speeches. Speaking in her own voice, after all, our author has directly warned us several hundred pages earlier that "you [like the slave trader] can get used to such [horrible] things, too, my friend; and it is the great object of recent efforts to make our whole northern community used to them, for the glory of the Union." If we read only Uncle Tom's appeal to Cassy, we will tend to agree with some of the most disgusted of my students about the book; if we read only Mrs. Stowe's remarks about the horrors, we may adopt my high school teacher's opinion. To see the richness of the historical evidence in *Uncle Tom's Cabin,* as in less topical works of fiction, we must study the complex reality of the whole book.

Ernest Cassara (essay date 1973)

SOURCE: "The Rehabilitation of Uncle Tom: Significant Themes in Mrs. Stowe's Antislavery Novel," in *CLA Journal,* Vol. XVII, No. 2, December, 1973, pp. 230-40.

[*In the excerpt that follows, Cassara outlines the features that make Tom a heroic figure, in contrast to those who view him as the obsequious character from which the pejorative term "Uncle Tom" has derived.*]

The expression "Uncle Tom" in the context of today's racial tensions has come to stand for a servile, cringing, hypocritical Negro who is willing to accommodate to the white power structure and to a less-than-equal place in American society. The melodramatic stage adaptation of *Uncle Tom's Cabin* by George L. Aiken in 1852 contributed to this misunderstanding of the character of Uncle Tom, as did a long line of successors in the form of the "Tom shows" which pictured Uncle Tom writhing at the feet of the whip-wielding Simon Legree. This stereotypical Uncle Tom could not have been further from the mind of Harriet Beecher Stowe when she created the character around whom the story of her best-selling novel revolves. For Mrs. Stowe, Tom is a man of heroic proportions.

It is appropriate that the central figure of the book should be a man who, against overwhelming brutality, struggles through to a Christian victory. Mrs. Stowe, after all, on a number of occasions was to indicate that God was the real author of the book. One need not take this statement literally to understand what was behind the thought. The central message of the book is that spiritual strength, born of Christian conviction, can triumph over the worst example of man's inhumanity to man. In the character of Uncle Tom are portrayed Mrs. Stowe's beliefs concerning the nature of true Christianity. She may have been stretching a point in claiming God's authorship for the work, but the claim is understandable as a product of her intense conviction that the institution of slavery involved America in deep sin against God and man. The intensity of the conviction was the motive power behind her writing of the novel and provided the vision for the development of the story.

Mrs. Stowe was anything but a religious fanatic, however. She was a hard-headed, practical observer of the nineteenth-century American scene. A reading of *The Key to Uncle Tom's Cabin* with its irony and pungent sarcastic commentary on the hypocritical defense of the slave system by American society, the churches in particular, should be enough to dispel any such notion. Her hard-headedness is further displayed in her "concluding remarks" in *Uncle Tom's Cabin* where in discussing the Negro's aptitudes she shows a keen appreciation for the kind of argument that will impress her American reader. No matter what she may have to say about the Negro's emotional make-up, his sensitivity to rhythm, his childlikeness, and so forth, in the body of the novel, and was later to say in her antislavery novel *Dred* (1856), she knew that money-conscious Americans would judge the black man by his ability to compete in the market place. Drawing on the information provided by her husband, Professor Calvin Stowe, she was able to report several cases of free blacks who had succeeded in business in Cincinnati where the Stowes had lived for almost two decades. The success of these former slaves, furthermore, could be measured in dollars and cents and she did not hesitate to give their worth in these terms. For example,

> G——. Full black; coal-dealer; about thirty years old; worth eighteen thousand dollars; paid for himself twice, being once defrauded to the amount of sixteen hundred dollars; made all his money by his own efforts,—much of it while a slave, hiring his time of his master, and doing business for himself; a fine, gentlemanly fellow.

This was the ultimate proof that a Negro, given a chance to take his place as a free man in American society could more than hold his own in the rough-and-tumble of the market.

Mrs. Stowe's hero in the novel, however, was of a different make. No matter what American society may think, for her the ideal man is he who can put into practice in his life the precepts of Jesus Christ. Tom, for Mrs. Stowe, was not an "Uncle Tom" in the sense in which the expression is used currently. It may be that the degeneration of the term was inevitable since the Uncle Tom of the novel cannot be measured by the standards of a post-Christian age in which the idea of turning the other cheek even unto death is an antique, quaint notion. Mrs. Stowe's Uncle Tom must be measured by other standards.

In sketching the character and tracing the development of Tom in the novel, Mrs. Stowe is preparing him, and the reader, for a struggle of titanic proportions against the forces of evil. Tom is a man of a simple, loving nature, but, in Mrs. Stowe's view, he is no simpleton. He has self-respect and a sense of honor. When Master Arthur Shelby decides to sell Tom, one of the greatest assets on his plantation, to help relieve a debt which threatens to ruin him, Tom refuses to consider the alternative of running away. Tom had reared his master, the young child having been placed in his arms when he was just a baby. Tom was a trusted member of the Shelby family, with a great responsibility on his shoulders. Tom's sense of honor, fostered by his study of Christianity, would not allow him to run or to do anything that would hurt the man who had placed his faith in him.

Tom, according to Arthur Shelby in his negotiations with Haley the slave trader, had "got religion at a camp-meeting, four years ago. . . ." From that point on Shelby had placed complete trust in him to manage his Kentucky plantation—"money, house, horses"—and allowed him complete freedom of movement. Tom had proved a competent manager of the farm and completely trustworthy. He had become so dedicated to his master and the other members of the plantation, white and black, that he preferred the heavy burden of separation from them and his wife Chloe and their children than to see the plantation broken up and all of them dispersed.

Mrs. Stowe pictures Tom's growth in religion as an evolutionary process. From the time of his conversion he became anxious to learn to read the Bible so that he could make out God's message for himself. With the help of young Master George Shelby he struggled with the laborious process—he, after all was in middle age before he began to read—and as time passed marked out for himself certain stories and favorite passages in the Scriptures from which he derived instruction and comfort. Tom became "a sort of minister" among the plantation slaves. He engaged in exhortations in the "meetings" that were held in his cabin. "Nothing," writes Mrs. Stowe, "could exceed the touching simplicity, the childlike earnestness of his prayer, enriched with the language of Scripture, which seemed so entirely to have wrought itself into his being, as to have become a part of himself, and to drop from his lips unconsciously. . . ."

The ministerial role of Tom was enhanced in his new setting in New Orleans. As a member of the household of Augustine St. Clare he was the constant companion of the incredibly saint-like Little Eva St. Clare, but also, especially after the child's death, the confidant of his master. Tom was troubled by the life-style of St. Clare who, trapped in an unhappy marriage and in the sin of the slave system which he detested, devoted his days to a worldly self-indulgence. Tom strives to convert him, to bring him from his disillusioned outlook to the Christian faith, encouraging him to become a force for good in society. St. Clare, shaken by the death of his beloved Eva, impressed by the earnest simplicity of Uncle Tom, is on the verge of succumbing, when—for the sake of Mrs. Stowe's story line—he is killed trying to separate the contenders in a coffee-house brawl. As St. Clare lies dying it is to Tom he turns for consolation, calling on him to pray.

> St. Clare could say but little; he lay with his eyes shut, but it was evident that he wrestled with bitter thoughts. After a while, he laid his hand on Tom's, who was kneeling beside him, and said, "Tom! poor fellow!"
>
> "What, Mas'r?" said Tom, earnestly.
>
> "I am dying!" said St. Clare, pressing his hand; "pray!"
>
> "If you would like a clergyman"—said the physician.
>
> St. Clare hastily shook his head, and said again to Tom, more earnestly, "Pray!"
>
> And Tom did pray, with all his mind and strength, for the soul that was passing,—the soul that seemed looking so steadily and mournfully from those large, melancholy blue eyes. It was literally prayer offered with strong crying and tears.
>
> When Tom ceased to speak, St. Clare reached out and took his hand, looking earnestly at him, but saying nothing. He closed his eyes, but still retained his hold; for, in the gates of eternity, the black hand and the white hold each other with an equal clasp.

It was with a break-up of the St. Clare household that Tom fell into the clutches of that reprobate son of New England, Simon Legree, proprietor of a run-down plantation at an isolated spot up the Red River. Legree purchased Tom with the intention of making him overseer of his fellow slaves. Part of the on-the-job training for this position involves the flogging of old, weak Lucy who was not picking her daily quota of cotton. When Tom refuses to take up the lash, he is set on a collision course with the adamant Legree, who, in a rage, determines that he shall bend to his command or die.

This is the setting for the final stage in Tom's developing Christian ministry, his martyrdom. No amount of beating at the hands of Legree's black henchmen, Sambo and Quimbo, will ring from Tom his assent to indulge in such inhumanity. He senses his contest of wills with the depraved Legree can lead to one thing only. He refuses to run away, however, for he has now become committed to minister to his fellow slaves. These poor wretches, despairing in this seemingly god-forsaken place, respond to Tom's loving concern, expressed in words and in continuing acts of kindness.
Tom's fate is sealed when he refuses to betray to the

wrathful Legree the whereabouts of Legree's mulatto concubine Cassy who, with the young Emmeline, purchased by Legree with similar intentions, is in hiding in preparation for escape.

Tom's dedication to his fellow blacks and his decision to die rather than betray Cassy and Emmeline was not taken without internal struggle. Tom reached the lowest point of physical and emotional exhaustion at the hands of Legree and despaired of ever seeing his wife Chloe and his children again. Tom wondered if he could hold out any longer, but victory was snatched from defeat by the intervention of Christ.

> When a heavy weight presses the soul to the lowest level at which endurance is possible, there is an instant and desperate effort of every physical and moral nerve to throw off the weight; and hence the heaviest anguish often precedes a return tide of joy and courage. So was it now with Tom. The atheistic taunts of his cruel master sunk his before dejected soul to the lowest ebb; and, though the hand of faith still held to the eternal rock, it was with a numb, despairing grasp. Tom sat, like one stunned, at the fire. Suddenly everything around him seemed to fade, and a vision rose before him of one crowned with thorns, buffeted and bleeding. Tom gazed, in awe and wonder, at the majestic patience of the face; the deep, pathetic eyes thrilled him to his inmost heart; his soul woke, as, with floods of emotion, he stretched out his hands and fell upon his knees,— when, gradually, the vision changed: the sharp thorns became rays of glory; and, in splendor inconceivable, he saw that same face bending compassionately towards him, and a voice said, "He that overcometh shall sit down with me on my throne, even as I also overcame, and am set down with my Father on his throne."
>
> How long Tom lay there he knew not. When he came to himself, the fire was gone out, his clothes were wet with the chill and drenching dews; but the dread soul-crisis was past, and, in the joy that filled him, he no longer felt hunger, cold, degradation, disappointment, wretchedness. From his deepest soul, he that hour loosed and parted from every hope in the life that now is, and offered his own will an unquestioning sacrifice to the Infinite. . . .
>
> Those who have been familiar with the religious histories of the slave population know that relations like what we have narrated are very common among them. We have heard some from their own lips, of a very touching and affecting character. The psychologist tells us of a state, in which the affections and images of the mind become so dominant and overpowering, that they press into their service the outward senses, and make them give tangible shape to the inward imagining. Who shall measure what an all-pervading Spirit may do with these capabilities of our mortality, or the ways in which he may encourage the desponding souls of the desolate? If the poor forgotten slave believes that Jesus hath appeared and spoken to him, who shall contradict him? Did He not say that his mission, in all ages, was to bind up the broken-hearted, and set at liberty them that are bruised?

For Mrs. Stowe, the true hero is an Uncle Tom who embodies in himself the primitive Christian virtues of returning love for evil and hate and a willingness to give his life rather than become an accomplice to evil. In this, Tom is walking in the footsteps of his real Master who centuries before had refused to take up arms in self-defense and had taken up instead a cross rather than perpetuate evil in the world by his own actions.

Like Jesus, Tom refused to collaborate with the forces of evil. The odds were overwhelmingly against him but in his Golgotha he was perfected in his weakness. He came out of that experience with the conviction St. Paul was sure he had received of the Lord: "My grace is sufficient for you, for my power is made perfect in weakness." It is with Pauline conviction that Tom, at the door of death, tells young Master George Shelby (who has found him too late),

> Don't call me poor fellow! . . . I *have* been poor fellow; but that's all past and gone, now. I'm right in the door, going into glory! Oh, Mas'r George! *Heaven has come!* I've got the victory!—the Lord Jesus has given it to me! Glory be to his name! . . . Oh, Mas'r George, what a thing 'tis to be a Christian!

The relationship of Legree to his slaves was that classically set forth by Thomas Jefferson in 1784 in his *Notes on, Virginia:*

> The whole commerce between master and slave is a perpetual exercise of the most boisterous passions, the most unremitting despotism on the one part, and degrading submissions on the other. Our children see this, and learn to imitate it; for man is an imitative animal. . . . The parent storms, the child looks on, catches the lineaments of wrath, puts on the same airs in the circle of smaller slaves, gives a loose to the worst of passions, and thus nursed, educated, and daily exercised in tyranny, cannot but be stamped by it with odious peculiarities. The man must be a prodigy who can retain his manners and morals undepraved by such circumstances.

Jefferson sounded what was to be a persistent theme in antislavery literature. These evil passions let loose by the master-slave relationship was a major concern of Theodore Weld in *American Slavery As It Is: The Testimony of a Thousand Witnesses,* a book which had an abiding influence on Mrs. Stowe and which she cites several times in her *Key to Uncle Tom's Cabin*. It was this brutalizing aspect of slavery—as damaging to the emotional make-up of the white master as to the emotional and physical make-up of the black slave—that is represented most dramatically in the Legree-Uncle Tom relationship but which emerges several times elsewhere in *Uncle Tom's Cabin,* in *Dred,* and in an extended discussion in the *Key to Uncle Tom's Cabin.*

For Mrs. Stowe slavery is not a regional matter. The blackguard Simon Legree is a New Englander in origin, Edward Clayton the hero of *Dred,* who attempts to educate his slaves in preparation for freedom, is a Southerner, as is the humane, indulgent Augustine St. Clare. Her antislavery books are not attacks on the South but on a system

which brings out the most base aspects of man's nature. She is convinced that absolute power can corrupt any man.

The Vermont branch of the St. Clare family (in New England spelled Sinclair) was headed by a domineering patriarch. A brother with the same personality traits settled in New Orleans. There the institution of slavery allowed an expression of these traits which was not possible to a Northern St. Clare. A tyranny or despotism unrestrained by public opinion—especially in the more remote areas, and the plantations were inevitably extensive,—developed in many of the whites in their dealings with slaves. These traits are clearly a part of the make-up of Augustine St. Clare's brother Alfred and we observe them and their destructive potential in the dealings of Alfred's young son Henrique with his black attendant. Augustine St. Clare had no stomach for such a life. Mrs. Stowe indicates that his well-developed sense of irony and his indulgent tolerance of, indeed pampering of, his slaves, is due to the impact of his mother on his personality, an influence apparently not felt by brother Alfred.

This propensity to dominate led to tremendous abuse of the slave. No matter what the proponents of slavery might say about the protective statutes designed to regulate the relationships of master and slave and to set limits to the control of the former over the latter, Mrs. Stowe, as did Weld before her, attempted to show that they were quite unprotective. Instead, a barbarous atmosphere prevailed in many places with abuse and murder of slaves by Legree-type masters who were, in effect, beyond the law. Any petty despot can become a slave master, no one asks his qualifications.

> To the Pirate Legree the law gives a power which no man of woman born, save One, ever was good enough to exercise.

> Are there such men as Legree? Let any one go into the low districts and dens of New York, let them go into some of the lanes and alleys of London, and will they not there see many Legrees? Nay, take the purest district of New England, and let people cast about in their memory and see if there have not been men there, hard, coarse, unfeeling, brutal, who, if they had possessed the absolute power of Legree, would have used it in the same way; and that there should be Legrees in the Southern States, is only saying that human nature is the same there that it is everywhere. The only difference is this—that in free States Legree is chained and restrained by law; in the slave States, the law makes him an absolute, irresponsible despot.

In the mind of Harriet Beecher Stowe Tom was a true Christian because he refused to react to Legree as most men would have in such a situation. He would bear up under all manner of tribulation because of his conviction that this was the true Christian way. He refused to strike back, preferring, in effect, to turn the other cheek. When offered the opportunity by Cassy to murder Legree in his drunken stupor, Tom recoiled in horror. As much as he might value freedom he chose the risk of almost certain death rather than betray his real Master in heaven and risk being with Him in eternity. Tom responded to Legree's taunting malignity as he believed Jesus would, with love. For Mrs. Stowe Tom's response is heroic because it is motivated not by fear but by concern for the fate of the soul of Simon Legree as well as of his own. Tom pitied Legree as a poor benighted person, lost in the darkness of hate.

Tom becomes a model to the slaves who had been living bestial, hate-filled lives. His patience under the scorn of Legree, his teaching of religion and ministering to their needs, even at the risk of further enraging Legree, had brought them a hope which had completely fled from their lives. Even the black rogues, Sambo and Quimbo, so imitative of Legree in their vileness, are overcome by Tom's acceptance of what turns out to be the fatal beating, come to him as he lay dying, asking for forgiveness and some words of hope that they are not spiritually doomed.

Critics have noted a certain condescension in Mrs. Stowes' attitude toward the Negro. This impression is given by passages in her antislavery works which speak of the simple, child-like nature, which responds more than white folks to rhythm, color, etc. There are also indications that she believes that colonization is the ultimate solution of the black problem in the United States. She, however, is not consistent in this attitude. As noted above, she sought to demonstrate that the black was perfectly capable of success in the white man's world of business. In *Uncle Tom's Cabin* she represents George Harris as a talented inventor who obviously has more ability than his spiteful master (who wants to keep him "in his place") and the man to whom he is hired out. Harry in *Dred* is a capable manager of Nina Gordon's plantation. It may be objected that both George Harris and Harry have a good percentage of white blood and that is why they are so represented. But, such is not the case with Mrs. Stowe's prime hero, Tom. He is a black of the blacks. In his lack of education and in his simplicity, Tom is more representative of the state of the slaves as they were known to Mrs. Stowe. One is led to suspect that Mrs. Stowe believed it was easier for the Negro slave to live a true Christian life because he had known suffering as had the early followers of Christ. He had not been corrupted by the leisure and sophistication of the white man's society. He was closer to the natural state of children. Mrs. Stowe's Christianity put great stock in the biblical passage [in Mark 10:14-15] in which Jesus is reported to have said, "Suffer the little children to come unto me, and forbid them not: for of such is the kingdom of God. Verily I say unto you, Whoever shall not receive the kingdom of God as a little child, he shall not enter therein."

Mrs. Stowe has been criticized for not proposing a solution to the problem of slavery. The criticism does not take into account that she was a child of evangelical Christianity in a day when the Social Gospel had yet to be preached. Improvements were thought to be accomplished by the awakening of conscience in the individual Christian who in turn would revitalize the churches and society. She made an extended criticism, quite bitterly ironic, of the failure of the churches to respond to the slavery issue in the *Key to Uncle Tom's Cabin* and that book and her novels contain many sharp barbs directed at those clergymen who served as apologists for slavery. She sought in her way to awaken Christian America to the barbarities of the slave system in the conviction that quickened consciences would lead to a new awakening. It was her hope that that day was not far off.

> Is it not evident to everyone who takes enlarged views of human society that a gentle but irresistible influence is pervading the human race, prompting groanings, and longings, and dim aspirations for some coming era of good? Worldly men read the signs of the times, and call this power the Spirit of the Age—but should not the Church acknowledge it as the Spirit of God?

Elizabeth Ammons (essay date 1977)

SOURCE: "Heroines in *Uncle Tom's Cabin*," in *American Literature,* Vol. XLIX, No. 2, May, 1977, pp. 161-79.

[*In the following excerpt, Ammons discusses various feminist themes in* Uncle Tom's Cabin, *suggesting that Stowe replaces masculine values with feminine and maternal ones.*]

Late in the nineteenth century Harriet Beecher Stowe announced that God wrote *Uncle Tom's Cabin* (1852). The novel by then seemed too monumental even to its author to have been imagined by one woman. Earlier in her life, in contrast, Stowe had no doubt that she wrote the subversive book or that she was inspired to write it, despite marital and household irritations, precisely because she was a woman.

In a letter to her husband ten years before the publication of the novel, and almost ninety years before Virginia Woolf's famous declaration of independence on behalf of all women writers in *A Room of One's Own* (1929), Harriet Beecher Stowe said: "There is one thing I must suggest. If I am to write, I must have a room to myself, which shall be *my* room." With her room came the mission to write what became America's best-known novel, and the mission fell to her, she believed, because she was a mother. She recalled for one of her grown children, "I well remember the winter you were a baby and I was writing 'Uncle Tom's Cabin.' My heart was bursting with the anguish excited by the cruelty and injustice our nation was showing to the slave, and praying God to let me do a little and to cause my cry for them to be heard. I remember many a night weeping over you as you lay sleeping beside me, and I thought of the slave mothers whose babies were torn from them." One of her seven children died while still an infant. She says: "It was at his dying bed and at his grave that I learned what a poor slave mother may feel when her child is torn away from her." Authors' remarks on the genesis of their work sometimes prove misleading, but not in this case. Stowe's insistence on maternal experience as the generative principle of *Uncle Tom's Cabin* identifies the ethical center of the novel, and helps explain the unusual, and often misunderstood, characterization of Tom.

Stowe's protagonist is gentle, pious, chaste, domestic, long-suffering and self-sacrificing. In a nineteenth-century heroine, those attributes would not seem strange. Associate them, however, with the hero of an American novel, a genre sifted for its Adamic rebels, and readers' complacence can evaporate. Indeed, the farther *Uncle Tom's Cabin* has moved in time from the historical reality of chattel slavery, the more obvious and the more criticized "effeminate" Tom has become; and whether it is stated in so many words or not, often what is objected to is the fact that Stowe makes him a heroine instead of a hero. That deliberate feminization of Tom, and the way Stowe links him to Eva and them both to a constellation of mothers, black and white, are what I wish to discuss.

The importance of women in Stowe's novel has attracted critical notice. Edward Wagenknecht remarks [in *Harriet Beecher Stowe: The Known and the Unknown*, 1965] that "the great evangelists in her fiction are all female—some of them little girls like . . . Eva in *Uncle Tom's Cabin,* who saves Topsy by embodying the power of Jesus's love." Donald K. Pickens, who maintains [in *Negro American Literature Forum*, Vol. 3, 1969] that Tom is "admirable in spite of Mrs. Stowe's racist inclinations," bluntly states: *"Uncle Tom's Cabin* is subversive. It is a feminist tract. The men are not attractive. . . . Women, in counter distinction, are upright and true to their inner selves." Alice C. Crozier explains [in *The Novels of Harriet Beecher Stowe*, 1969] that the novel characterizes mothers as "the real saviors of society," and she points out some similarities between Stowe's mothers and Uncle Tom on the one hand and little Eva on the other. What needs discussion is the nature of Stowe's feminism in the novel and her odd equation of mothers/Eva/Tom, an equation which, if followed through to its logical conclusion, argues the radical substitution of feminine and maternal for masculine values.

Stowe's treatment of maternal values may at a glance look unremarkable. Nearly every page of *Uncle Tom's Cabin* hymns the virtues of Mother, the revered figure whose benign influence over domestic life in the nineteenth century was conveniently supposed, and promoted, to redress the abuses against humanity engendered in the masculine, money-making realm. Stowe, however, refuses to appoint Mother the handmaiden of Mammon in *Uncle Tom's Cabin*. Instead, she enlists the cult of motherhood in the unorthodox cause of challenging, not accommodating, the patriarchal status quo. Like her sister Catharine Beecher, Harriet Beecher Stowe displays in *Uncle Tom's Cabin* a facility for converting essentially repressive concepts of femininity into a positive (and activist) alternative system of values in which woman figures not merely as the moral superior of man, his inspirer, but as the model for him in the new millennium about to dawn.

In the novel Stowe accepts the definition of woman pop-
ular at the midcentury. She recognizes that two "spheres" exist, one masculine and commercial, the other feminine and domestic, and has no quarrel with the set of qualities commonly partitioned to the left-hand "sphere." For her, femininity—true womanliness—means unshakable allegiance to the Christian virtues of faith, hope, charity, mercy, and self-sacrifice; purity in body and mind; ethical dependence more on emotion than on reason; submission to mundane authority except when it violates higher laws; and protection of the home as a sacred and inviolable institution. Moreover, these stereotypically feminine attributes are in Stowe's opinion the only worthwhile human ones because they place the welfare of the group, of the whole human family, before that of self. Her ideal person, therefore, is a heroine, and a completely conventional one: pious, pure, noncompetitive, unselfish, emotional, domestic, and outwardly submissive. Yet Stowe uses the conventional in unconventional ways in *Uncle Tom's Cabin*. Her novel proposes as the foundation for a new democratic era, in place of masculine authority, feminine nurture: a type of love epitomized in the Christlike girl-child, Eva, whose name calls to mind the Edenic mother of the race. Figuring as Eva's adult counterparts are several mothers and one man: sweet-tempered black Tom, meek like Christ yet fiercely loyal to a domestic set of values. The author's obvious contradiction of gender in the Eva/Christ and Tom/heroine associations, both of which serve as savior analogues in the novel, animates her conviction, as she later stated it plainly [in *Religious Studies*, 1877], that "there was in Jesus more of the pure feminine element than in any other man." The feminine Christ is no figure of speech for Stowe. It is a concept that guides characterization and inspires the maternal-feminist cast to her vision of ethical revolution in *Uncle Tom's Cabin*. The Redeemer from the sins of the fathers in the novel is not, as traditional theology puts it, a second Adam (an emblem utterly familiar of course to anyone who was the daughter, sister, and wife of ministers), but as Stowe would put it, a second Eve.

The opening episode of *Uncle Tom's Cabin* introduces Stowe's argument by portraying mothers, black and white, as active opponents of slavery. The system itself, this first scene makes clear, is basically masculine: white men buy and sell black people while the white woman stands by powerless to intervene. This may not be the pattern in every case but, in Stowe's opinion, it is the model, as her prime and detailed treatment of it suggests. When the slave-holder, Mr. Shelby, gets himself into debt and decides that he must sell some property, he settles on Eliza's son, Harry, and Uncle Tom. Shelby, it is true, does not *want* to sell the pretty child or the kind man who raised him from a boy; but sell he does, and to a trader he knows to be so callous, so "'alive to nothing but trade and profit . . . [that] he'd sell his own mother at a good per centage.'" Figuratively Shelby would do the same, as his selling of Tom demonstrates, and Stowe emphasizes how fine the line is that separates the "benevolent" planter Shelby and the coarse trader Haley, whose favorite topic of conversation (to Shelby's discomfort) always has to do with slave mothers' aggravating attachment to their children, whom Haley is in the business of selling away from them. Shelby is in the same business, one step removed, but would rather not admit it. His wife confronts him. Although helpless to overrule him legally, she cries out against his refined brutality, calling slavery "'a bitter, bitter, most accursed thing!—a curse to the master and a curse to the slave! I was a fool to think I could make anything good out of such a deadly evil. . . . I never thought that slavery was right—never felt willing to own slaves.'" When her mate suggests they sneak off on a trip to avoid witnessing the black families' grief at separation, her resistance crystallizes. "'No, no,' said Mrs. Shelby; 'I'll be in no sense accomplice or help in this cruel business.'" Likewise Tom's wife, Aunt Chloe, reacts rebelliously, supporting Eliza in her decision to run away with her child and urging Tom to go with her. These two maternal antagonists of slavery secure Eliza's flight. Because Mrs. Shelby surreptitiously encourages the slaves to sabotage the search for Eliza, and because Aunt Chloe stalls the pursuit by producing culinary disasters which keep the search party at dinner for hours, Eliza is able to make her break for freedom across the frozen Ohio, baby in arms.

Due to the conspiracy of the two mothers, one white and one black, followed by the equally crucial assistance of stalwart Mrs. Bird, wife of a wrong-headed Ohio Senator and herself a recently bereaved mother, Eliza and child arrive safely at a Quaker station on the route to Canada. The community serves as a hint of the ideal in *Uncle Tom's Cabin*. It is family-centered, nonviolent, egalitarian; and especially impressive among its members are two hearty matrons, significantly named Ruth and Rachel. Stowe remarks: "So much has been said and sung of beautiful young girls, why don't somebody wake up to the beauty of old women?" For Stowe Rachel Halliday's beauty issues from her perfection as a mother and from the way she uses her power in what is in practice a matriarchal (because completely home-centered) community. Stowe plays with the idea of Rachel as a mother-goddess, calling her a figure much more worthy of a "cestus" than the overrated Venus whom "bards" like to sing about, and then immediately follows that remark with a glimpse of Rachel's husband happily "engaged in the anti-patriarchal operation of shaving." Of course, Stowe is being whimsical here, but only in the sense that she is too confident a Christian to need to appeal seriously to pagan concepts to express the principle incarnate in Rachel, whose earthy maternal love Stowe will bring to transfigured life in the two unlikely but motherly Christ-figures, Eva and Tom. As a matter of fact the Quaker community is "anti-patriarchal" in its pacifism and its matrifocal social structure, and that is its beauty for Stowe. "Rachel never looked so truly and benignly happy as at the head of her table. There was so much motherliness and full-heartedness even in the way she passed a plate of cakes or poured a cup of coffee, that it seemed to put a spirit into the food and drink she offered." Rachel Halliday, sitting at the head of her family's table in a scene that brings to mind Christ's ministry at the Last Supper, illustrates how humane and spiritually nourishing mother-rule might be.

Eliza and her family escape their white masters. Most slaves did not, and Harriet Beecher Stowe places particular emphasis on the horrors suffered by the system's maternal victims. The first slave auction in the book focuses on an aged mother and teen-aged son who are sold apart over the old woman's pleas and sobs. A young black woman whose baby is stolen and sold drowns herself in the Mississippi, her only obituary an entry in a slave trader's ledger under "losses." A middle-aged slave, her twelve children auctioned away, drinks to silence memory of her thirteenth baby who was starved to death; drunk once too often, the woman is locked in a cellar until the smell of her corpse satisfies her owners' wrath. The degradation of Cassy, Simon Legree's chattel concubine, began with a white lover's clandestine sale of her two small children. Cassy spared her next baby; in her own words, "'I took the little fellow in my arms, when he was two weeks old, and kissed him, and cried over him; and then I gave him laudanum, and held him close to my bosom, while he slept to death. . . . I am not sorry, to this day; he, at least, is out of pain.'" These cruelly severed ties between mothers and children recur throughout Stowe's exposé of slavery for several reasons: to stir Abolitionist passion within parents in Stowe's audience, to assert the humanity of the black race in the face of racist myths that blacks do not share the emotions of whites, to show that women suffer horrible tortures in the midst of a society boastful about its chivalry toward the "gentle sex," and—most important—to dramatize the root evil of slavery: the displacement of life-giving maternal values by a profit-hungry masculine ethic that regards human beings as marketable commodities. Planters, traders, drivers, bounty hunters, judges, voters—all are white, all are men, all are responsible; and the mothers and motherless children in *Uncle Tom's Cabin* show the human cost of the system.

No character illustrates Stowe's charge more starkly than Topsy. Motherless all her young life and systematically kept ignorant by whites, what can the child believe except that she "just growed"? It is a miracle that she has managed that. For years her owners have routinely beaten her with chains and fireplace pokers, starved her, and locked her in closets until she can respond to nothing but pain and violent abuse. The child has been crippled psychologically by an entire social structure purposely designed to strip her (and her black brothers) of all sense of human selfhood. Stowe defends Topsy as a credible character in *A Key to Uncle Tom's Cabin* (1853): "Does any one wish to know what is inscribed on the seal which keeps the great stone over the sepulchre of African mind? It is this,—which was so truly said by poor Topsy,—'NOTHING BUT A NIGGER!' It is this, burnt into the soul by the branding-iron of cruel and unchristian scorn, that is a sorer and deeper wound than all the physical evils of slavery together. There never was a slave who did not feel it."

It is significant that only Evangeline St. Clare can dress Topsy's "wound" and awaken in the motherless black girl feelings of tenderness, trust, and self-respect. To understand the ethereal blonde child's life-renewing influence, one must take seriously the unearthly qualities Stowe attaches to Eva. She is not a realistic character any more than Hawthorne's preternatural Pearl in *The Scarlet Letter* (1850) or Melville's Pip in *Moby Dick* (1851). Stowe, too, relies on Romantic convention in *Uncle Tom's Cabin,* first published serially in 1851-52. She consistently describes Eva as dreamy, buoyant, inspired, cloudlike, spotless; and flatly states that this child has an "aerial grace, such as one might dream of for some mythic and allegorical being." Stowe is clear that her mythic and allegorical character resembles Jesus. Tom, who "almost worshipped her as something heavenly and divine," often gazes on Eva "as the Italian sailor gazes on his image of the child Jesus,—with a mixture of reverence and tenderness." Eva's Mammy considers her a "blessed lamb" not destined to live long. Stowe calls her a "dove" and associates her with the morning star. Ophelia describes her as "Christ-like" and hopes that she has learned "something of the love of Christ from her." Tom, before her death, visualizes Eva's face among the angels; and after she is gone he has a dream-vision of the saintly child reading Christ's words to him, words of comfort which end with "'I am the Lord thy God, the Holy One of Israel, thy Saviour.'" Even while alive Eva's selflessness seems supranatural. Sights and stories of slavery's atrocity make "her large, mystic eyes dilate with horror" and move her to lay her hands on her breast and sigh profoundly. She explains, "'these things *sink into my heart.*'" The child identifies with the slaves' misery, telling Tom finally: "'I can understand why Jesus *wanted* to die for us. . . . I *would die* for them, Tom, if I could.'" On the figurative level—the only level on which Eva makes sense—she gets her wish. Stowe contrives her death to demonstrate that there is no life for a pure, Christlike spirit in the corrupt plantation economy the book attacks.

None of this means that Eva "is" Christ. But I think it does mean that she reflects by way of her name a type of Christ, and Stowe's unusual typology vivifies the moral center of *Uncle Tom's Cabin.* As Ursula Brumm explains of typology in general in *American Thought and Religious Typology:* "Typology is a pattern for construing the world's events as leading toward redemption. . . . The type is not a symbol of Christ. It is a definite historical person or event of the Old Testament that prefigures Christ, yet exists with its own independent meaning and justification." The most common type has always been Adam-Christ; just as the race was born in Adam, so it is reborn in Christ, the new Adam. Stowe suggests a different type: Eve-Christ. (It is worth noting that Marie, Eva's mother, in name—though in nothing else—helps strengthen the Christ portion of the emblem.) Eva is no ordinary personification of Christian love, even in nineteenth-century literature which is full of saintly tubercular children and incredibly virtuous heroines impedestaled as the spiritual betters of their less perfect men. One critic [J. C. Furnas, in *Goodbye to Uncle Tom,* 1956] laughs at Stowe for the ignorant blunder of making the child "a sort of paper-doll Christ of the wrong sex." Paper-doll she might seem; mythic and allegorical beings are not easy to bring to life. But there is no mistake in gender. Stowe creates a girl and names her for Eve as a prefigure of Christ because she believes, as is everywhere obvious in *Uncle Tom's Cabin,* that the Savior's love is that of woman, especially

mothers. Stowe said of the novel a couple of years after its publication, "This story is to show how Jesus Christ, who liveth and was dead, and now is alive and forevermore, has still a mother's love for the poor and lowly." To personify Christ's maternal love in the novel Stowe alludes to the biblical mother of all people, Eve, whom she implicitly resurrects from infamy in the person of an innocent child. Her unfallen Eva yokes the two Testaments: she is "'one of the roses of Eden that the Lord has dropped down expressly for the poor and lowly,'" at the same time that the motherly little girl is the living image of a dead Grandmother (also named Evangeline) who was "'a direct embodiment and personification of the New Testament.'" The idea of woman as evangelist and even as a new and better Eve working with the Redeemer to reclaim the world from its modern corruption was not unique with Stowe. But her suggestion of an Eve-Christ typology is not common, and it is used to original purpose. Stowe makes her Christlike "'evangel'" of a new, democratic millennium an Eve/angel—a female spirit who links the gospel of Jesus with the mother of the race—to offer an unmasculine ideal for all human behavior.

Tom embodies that ideal. As the title of the book indicates, home and family matter most to him. He first appears at his and Chloe's cabin, surrounded by children, and the first thing we hear about this man who has "a voice as tender as a woman's" is that he is "'an uncommon fellow.'" St. Clare pronounces him a "'moral miracle,'" and Stowe tells us that, in addition to his "remarkably inoffensive and quiet character," he is blessed "to the full [with] the gentle, domestic heart, which, woe for them! has been a peculiar characteristic of his unhappy race." Stowe offers the generalization admiringly. Sold, Tom hovers over his sleeping children for the last time in a scene the author makes memorable by refusing to paint a portrait of masculine reserve. "Sobs, heavy, hoarse and loud, shook the chair [Tom leaned over], and great tears fell through his fingers on the floor." Tom makes no effort to hide his emotion, and he weeps more for his children than for himself. That is characteristic. Tom always places the well-being of others first. He goes peaceably with the slave trader Haley because he knows that if he runs away a large number of slaves will be sold to match the price Shelby can get for him. He can even forgive Shelby and continue to love the cruel man he cared for from infancy, much (Stowe implies) as Christ forgave his oppressors or a mother can continue to love the grown child who breaks her heart. The reason Stowe gives for such amazingly generous behavior is simple. Tom, like most women but few men in the novel, really tries to live according to the Gospel's injunction to love his neighbor as himself.

Structure in *Uncle Tom's Cabin* emphasizes that Harriet Beecher Stowe knows how unusual a "hero" she draws in Tom. He is the central character in the book, yet, though mentioned and glimpsed in the early chapters, he does not enter the action fully until Chapter 10, then to disappear for one chapter and reappear in Chapter 12, disappearing in Chapter 13 and finally reentering the action for sustained treatment in Chapter 14. Two devices are at work here. First, Stowe delays Tom's story until after Eliza's and George Harris's successful escapes from slavery have been assured. Their action shows Stowe's approval of courageous rebellion against slavery and, in the character of proud George Harris, her respect for conventionally manly defiance of injustice and enforced submission. Thus, by the time Uncle Tom's story becomes central, it should be clear that the author feminizes him not because she is unable to make him assertively masculine but because she does not wish to do so. Second, Stowe arranges Tom's sustained entrance into the action, Chapter 14, to associate him with maternal figures: Rachel Halliday in Chapter 13 followed by the motherly child Eva St. Clare in Chapter 14. Stowe's strategy is clearcut. She presents Rachel in all her warm maternal glory, switches to Tom reading his Bible forlorn and family-less on a southbound steamboat, then introduces the "sunbeam" Eva whose image refreshes Tom and whom Stowe immediately identifies as mythic and allegorical. This progression from Rachel to Tom and Eva marks a turning point in the novel. It sets the stage for Tom's story, a course of events inaugurated by his and Eva's immersion together in the Mississippi (the figurative baptism signifies their oneness in Christ, which will eventuate in their similarly redemptive, sacrificial deaths); and it serves as an interpretive crux. The three juxtaposed characters—the earthy mother, the gentle black man, and the ethereal girl-child—embody in different yet complementary ways the redemptive feminine-Christ principle that informs *Uncle Tom's Cabin*.

Action as well as structure accentuates Tom's feminine character. He tearfully watches a mother's grief over the theft and sale of her baby, and

> to him, it looked like something unutterably horrible and cruel, because, poor, ignorant black soul! he had not learned to generalize, and to take enlarged views. If he had only been instructed by certain ministers of Christianity, he might have thought better of it, and seen in it an every-day incident of a lawful trade; a trade which is the vital support of an institution which some American divines tell us has no evils but such as are inseparable from any other relations in social and domestic life. But Tom, as we see, being a poor, ignorant fellow, whose reading had been confined entirely to the New Testament, could not comfort and solace himself with views like these.

The author's mock contempt gets heavy-handed here, but her point about Tom is important. He reacts to the horror of slavery as Stowe's heroines do: from the heart. Empathy, compassion, comfort, practical assistance, psychological support—these dispositions describe Stowe's Uncle Tom just as they do most of her admirable women. The passivity which popular culture chooses to remember is not his dominant attribute; whenever possible (which is infrequent, given his slave status) Tom does take action. But he is always nonviolent and patient. At Legree's plantation, a microcosm of the commercial white ethic Stowe indicts, Tom's "tenderness of feeling, a commiseration for his fellow-sufferers, strange and new to them" so infuriates grotesquely masculine Simon Legree that he becomes obsessed with the challenge of making Tom

"hard"—brutal, callous, authoritarian: a fit candidate for overseer. But no amount of torture can make Tom agree to flog his fellow slaves. Legree cannot harden him. To the end Tom remains soft, sacrificing himself rather than betray the hiding place of two fugitive slave women.

Stowe displays shrewd political strategy in choosing to characterize her hero as a stereotypical Victorian heroine: pious, domestic, self-sacrificing, emotionally uninhibited in response to people and ethical questions. Not only does the characterization make Tom unthreatening in any literal way that would play into the hands of belligerently racist whites who maintained that blacks were brutes who must be oppressed; the characterization insinuates Tom into the nineteenth-century idolatry of feminine virtue, sentimentalized in young girls and sacrosanct in Mother. Stowe's genius as a propagandist is that she exploits both conventions—the former in Eva and the latter in a panorama of mothers of both races (especially Rachel Halliday)—and then, having captured her audience's allegiance, extends that allegiance to Tom by making him, a black man, the supreme heroine of the book. Implicitly the novel asks who, without forsaking reverence for Mother and the sanctity of the Home, could fail to champion Tom's right to liberty for himself and his family and, by extension, that same right for all slaves?

Stowe's feminization of Tom also is important because it argues her case for nonviolent resistance to the corrupting influence of slavery as the only hope for the permanent eradication of a system based on violence. In Stowe's view, ten years before the Civil War, the solution to slavery does not lie in armed rebellion, meeting violence with violence (though she sympathizes with that reaction in the character of George Harris and returns to the idea of black counter-aggression four years later in her antislavery novel inspired by the Nat Turner rebellion: *Dred, A Tale of the Great Dismal Swamp* [1856]). In 1852 Stowe, thoroughly Romantic in this, locates the solution to slavery in a revolution of white values which will honor emotional verities above rationalized materialist schemes. Nurturant values in her opinion have been, but should not be, shunted off by men into the safekeeping of women; truths of the heart are considered feminine and therefore fit to govern only the domestic "sphere" of life. In *A Key to Uncle Tom's Cabin* Stowe comments on the worldly drive "to be above others in power, rank and station" and says: "If there is anything which distinguishes man from other creatures, it is that he is *par excellence* an *oppressive animal*. On this principle . . . all empires have been founded; and the ideal of founding a kingdom in any other way had not even been thought of when Jesus of Nazareth appeared"; she says that "Jesus Christ alone founded his empire upon LOVE." This opposition between power and love as possible foundations for social organization appears in *Uncle Tom's Cabin* as the alternatives of aristocracy or democracy and, in economic terms, capitalism or cooperativism. Stowe so obviously criticizes the first half of each antithesis (she uses the womanish spokesman Augustine St. Clare, Eva's father, to articulate her case) that Charles H. Foster [in *The Rungless Ladder: Harriet Beecher Stowe and New England Puritanism,*

1954] does not distort the book by discussing it in a Marxian light. Foster is mistaken, however, when he concludes that Stowe's attack on laissez-faire capitalism provides "the masculine edge, the intellectual bite of *Uncle Tom's Cabin*." Quite the contrary. Stowe's criticism of the profit motive reveals the distinctly feminine, specifically maternal, heart of her argument against what she and others referred to as "the patriarchal institution," slavery. She insists that love is more important than power; and *Uncle Tom's Cabin* endorses a domestic ideology, especially in the person of its gentle male protagonist, to make the point that home and mother must not figure as sanctuaries from the world but as imperative models for its reconstruction. The task of feminizing or Christianizing dominant human values will not be easy. White men hold all worldly power; and until they undergo a radical change of heart, Stowe realistically believes, no fundamental change will occur. Nevertheless she argues, or one might more accurately say hopes, that radical yet peaceful change can take place. In the novel Tom's unbelligerent character provokes his murder, and that causes George Shelby, the son of Tom's original owner, to free the Shelby slaves when he returns to the Kentucky plantation. That is, Tom's martyrdom at the hands of brutal Simon Legree inspires limited but concrete social change, a change that begins in one young man's heart and radiates from there to bring one small segment of the social order in line with the values of Mrs. rather than Mr. Shelby, the mother rather than the father.

Finally Tom's character is important because it demonstrates Stowe's belief that a man can live admirably in accord with her nineteenth-century maternal ideal. Tom's sensitivity and gentleness do not in her opinion make him a weak character. Instead, they combine with his traditionally attractive male strength and courage to create a morally superior and more loving than average man in the America she fictionalizes. (Stowe does at times condescend to lowly, ignorant, black Tom. The other side of that controversy, however, is the fact that she makes the worthiest man in the novel black, and her commitment is genuine.)

One could argue that the purpose of *Uncle Tom's Cabin,* a book confident about what comprises true womanliness, is to define true manliness. Stowe gives her verdict on crude masculinity in the characters of Haley, Marks, Loker, Skeggs, and Simon Legree, who are all antisocial, misogynist, and dealers in death. Legree, with his bullet head and iron knuckles, is a caricature, and a very serious one, of supermasculinity, which Stowe associates with the devil, Christ's antagonist. Legree's plantation is the hell of *Uncle Tom's Cabin* because it is built on antifeminine, antimaternal, antifamily principles, as Stowe emphasizes by making Legree's one terror his horror of the feminine. He is defenseless against the coil of Eva's hair that reminds him of his mother, and the softness of Tom's character maddens him. At the other end of the spectrum are white men like Senator Bird or Mr. Symmes and Mr. Wilson whose susceptibility to feminine influence or impulses makes them potentially admirable, but only potentially, because they defy the masculine, commercial ethic se-

cretly and with a sense of guilt rather than doing so publicly and conscientiously like the maternally guided Quaker men. In between the poles stand Mr. Shelby, who is for all his refinement a man closer to Legree than to his wife, and Augustine St. Clare, the most tortured white man in the book. In his heart he subscribes to feminine, Christian values, as his verbal opposition to slavery and his dying word *"Mother!"* testify; but his will is impotent. In some ways St. Clare is a more terrifying example of masculine privilege and power than Legree: he knows what is right, he has the power to act on that knowledge at least with respect to his own slaves, but he invokes an arrogant paternalism to justify his refusal to act. If Legree represents one face of the problem, brute masculine oppression, St. Clare represents another: pathetic masculine sophistry.

Stowe's indictment of masculine ethics does not mean that all of the women in *Uncle Tom's Cabin* deserve admiration. Ophelia earns our regard only after she has confronted her own racism, and Eva's mother remains viciously self-centered to the end. (Stowe does extenuate her cruelty by including its pathology, but the woman is still a destructive person.) Nor are all white men villains—though most of them are. Yet this is not misandry. Stowe does not condemn white men for themselves but for the exploitive and inhumane values they live by and enforce as the ruling class in America. A disenchanted planter states Stowe's criticism directly in *Dred,* the novel that followed *Uncle Tom's Cabin:* "'As matters are going on now in our country, I must either lower my standard of right and honor, and sear my soul in all its nobler sensibilities, or I must be what the world calls an unsuccessful man. There is no path in life, that I know of, where . . . a man can make the purity of his moral nature the first object.'" This man's sister, in contrast, denounces slavery "with that straight-out and generous indignation which belongs to women, who, generally speaking, are ready to follow their principles to any result with more inconsiderate fearlessness than men." Women, excluded from the white masculine "success" ethic, had little or no power to begin with and could therefore in Stowe's view place principle before prestige or profit when confronted with the immorality of slavery. Consequently they do not figure as conservers of the status quo in her antislavery fiction. Most of them stand as models of an alternative, humane ethic which Stowe envisions as the foundation for an enlightened and equitable new era.

The architecture of the concluding chapters of *Uncle Tom's Cabin* underscores Stowe's vision, her wish that masculinity be defined along more feminine lines for the reformation of society. The final chapters provide three positive male models and, finally, one female model. Foremost is Tom, an ideal. Stowe presents his death as a Christlike victory of the feminine principle over satanic Simon Legree. Then she presents George Harris. She makes him an eloquent spokesman for the proud, free, black man, whose understandable bitterness is tempered by his devotion to healing feminine values, such as Eliza's. His white counterpart, significantly named George as well, is the freed planter, young Shelby; he renounces his father as a model by emancipating the family's slaves, an action his mother has always favored. These three men—Tom, George Harris, George Shelby—illustrate Stowe's belief that the male of the species can be as beautiful morally as the female but only if old models of masculinity are radically revised.

To describe how that change of masculine heart might come about, Stowe reserves the last chapter of *Uncle Tom's Cabin* for herself. She presents the last model in the book and offers the last testimony, and it is as a woman that she testifies. She admits that she was afraid of her subject. Slavery was too huge, too horrible for a woman to write about. But, then, if a woman, a mother, would not speak out, would anyone? She makes an impassioned appeal to white Americans, devoting a few lines to sailors, ship-owners, and farmers, and then addresses her vanguard:

> Mothers of America,—you, who have learned, by the cradles of your own children, to love and feel for all mankind,—by the sacred love you bear your child; by your joy in his beautiful, spotless infancy; by the motherly pity and tenderness with which you guide his growing years; by the anxieties of his education; by the prayers you breathe for his soul's eternal good;—I beseech you, pity the mother who has all your affections, and not one legal right to protect, guide, or educate, the child of her bosom! By the sick hour of your child; by those dying eyes, which you can never forget; by those last cries, that wrung your heart when you could neither help nor save; by the desolation of that empty cradle, that silent nursery,—I beseech you, pity those mothers who are constantly made childless by the American slave-trade! And say, mothers of America, is this a thing to be defended, sympathized with, passed over in silence?

She asks, "What can any individual do?" and concludes: "There is one thing that every individual can do,—they can see to it that *they feel right.* . . . The man or woman who *feels* strongly, healthily and justly, on the great interests of humanity, is a constant benefactor to the human race. See, then, to your sympathies in this matter! Are they in harmony with the sympathies of Christ? or are they swayed and perverted by the sophistries of worldly policy?" Stowe's appeal is unabashedly emotional, and her vision of reform can be criticized as nothing more than an adjustment of personal sentiment. But precisely that admission of emotion—being unafraid to feel and profess one's feelings—is for her the first step to Abolition and thus the motivating aesthetic of *Uncle Tom's Cabin.* One heroine protests when her cerebral husband says "'You allow yourself to feel too much'" on the issue of slavery: "'Feel too much! Am not I a woman,—a mother?'" Stowe writes to make all Americans "feel too much" with her white women, her black slaves, and her children—legally nonexistent, "feminine" people who are still alive to natural feelings because they are untrained in the masculine discipline of automatically subordinating emotion to reason, the discipline responsible in Stowe's opinion for legalized slavery. Like her older sister Catharine Beecher, Stowe turns a handicap into an asset.

Lowly feminine feeling can revolutionize man's world.

Harriet Beecher Stowe stopped short of the radical feminism of her younger sister, Isabella Beecher Hooker, who became an avid follower of Victoria Woodhull. At least publicly, Harriet did not declare with Isabella the belief that "the Millennium was close at hand [when] the whole world would soon become a single matriarchy—a 'maternal government,' as Isabella called it." Nor do I find Harriet Beecher Stowe commenting anywhere on her sister's conviction that she, Isabella, was destined to rule in the Matriarchy as Christ's vice-regent. Harriet Beecher Stowe was more moderate. For instance, she supported but did not actively campaign for woman's suffrage, let alone agree with Victoria Woodhull on the subject of free love. Nevertheless *Uncle Tom's Cabin* shows the Beecher half-sisters closer ideologically than biographers, convinced that Isabella was mad, like to imply. Both women associated Christ with woman, defined the coming Millennium in matrifocal terms, and looked to feminine values as the foundation for ethical revolution in America. Clearly impatient by 1870, Harriet Beecher Stowe [in *My wife and I; or, Henry Henderson's History,* 1871] had a sympathetic character pronounce on the issue of women's rights: "The woman question of our day, as I understand it is this—Shall MOTHERHOOD ever be felt in the public administration of the affairs of state?" Stowe had reason to sound impatient. She had asked America that same question twenty years earlier in *Uncle Tom's Cabin* with its purposefully odd, maternal-yet-Christlike characters, Uncle Tom and Eva, as well as a variety of literal mothers, black and white.

Cushing Strout (essay date 1981)

SOURCE: "*Uncle Tom's Cabin* and the Portent of Millennium," in *The Veracious Imagination: Essays on American History, Literature, and Biography,* Wesleyan University Press, 1981, pp. 59-69.

[*In the following excerpt, Strout examines the nineteenth-century theological traditions that informed the writing of* Uncle Tom's Cabin, *defending Stowe against modernist critics who accuse her of racism.*]

"Everybody's Protest Novel," James Baldwin called it in 1949, in order to condemn it and its descendants. Looking at it through the eyes of a modern Negro, he found it a hysterically moralistic melodrama of stereotypes with a cast of genteel mulattoes and quadroons whose lightness of color betrayed Harriet Beecher Stowe's revulsion against blackness. "Tom, therefore, her only black man," he asserts, "has been robbed of his humanity and divested of his sex. It is the price for that darkness with which he has been branded." Her fear of the dark, Baldwin charges, is "a theological terror, the terror of damnation; and the spirit that breathes in this book, hot, self-righteous, fearful, is not different from that spirit of medieval times which sought to exorcise evil by burning witches; and is not different from that terror which activates a lynch mob." The bill as drawn is as plausible as it is unhistorical, as provocative as it is astigmatic—half right for all the wrong reasons.

It is true that Stowe was hot about the crime of slavery and fearful of the doom of her country, as Baldwin is hot and fearful with equally good reason about the race problem today, but her novel deliberately aimed to undercut self-righteous moralizing. While she succumbed in part to the sentimental tradition of the paternalistic plantation with its childlike slaves and their indulgent owner, she did not blink the fact that the inept benevolence of her planter St. Clare could not prevent his wife from selling his slaves down the river. Baldwin takes Miss Ophelia from New England as the author's mouthpiece forgetting that Stowe has St. Clare accuse her of a Yankee prejudice against Negroes, "wanting them out of your sight and smell." The author's postscript lays the heaviest burden of guilt for slavery on the "people of the free states" who have "defended, encouraged, and participated, and are more guilty for it, before God, than the South, in that they have *not* the apology of education or custom." Her fabled villain, Simon Legree, is a Yankee. If she stacked the cards, she did not deal all the good ones to any section or group, particularly not to her own.

Reading Stowe out of her context, Baldwin misses the relevance of the relative whiteness of her blacks in the novel. Their color dramatizes Stowe's sense of the great horror of slavery—the breaking up of families for exploitative reasons. In a culture which idealized the home as much as hers did, the sexual crossing of the color line, promoted by the system of slavery, was a vivid symbol of evil because the white man who exploited a black woman violated the integrity of two families, his own and hers. It is the tragedy of Misse Cassy, Legree's mulatto mistress, that she has been sold by a white man whom she loved and by whom she bore two children. The planter St. Clare suffers from an unhappy marriage to a coldly respectable woman who breaks up the family life of his slaves, and that sugary confection, little Eva, prefers the Southern plantation to Vermont because "it makes so many more round you to love, you know." The mulatto George, Eliza's husband, begins to recover his faith in the justice of God only when he lives for a while in the Quaker home of Rachel Halliday, who had "so much motherliness and full-heartedness even in the way she passed a plate of cakes or poured a cup of coffee, that it seemed to put a spirit into the food and drink she offered." Stowe gives her the accolade: "This, indeed, was a home,—*home,* a word that George had never yet known a meaning for." Trust in God's providence soon begins to "encircle his heart, as with a golden cloud of protection and confidence." St. Clare on his deathbed, envisioning "the gates of eternity," knows he has come "Home, at last," and his final word is *"Mother!"* This unpalatably Victorian cult of the family gags the contemporary reader, but its power to move her audience had much to do with the effectiveness of Stowe's indictment of slavery as an institution which deprived Negroes of their rights to recognized marriage and a stable family. The paleness of her Negro characters dramatically underlined this connection, a heritage from slavery which the controversial Moynihan

Report (1965) to President Lyndon Johnson emphasized in the unsentimental sociological language of our own culture.

Baldwin is understandably appalled by Stowe's sentimentality, but he entirely loses sight of the sources of it. This "ostentatious parading of excessive and spurious emotion," he concludes, is "the mask of cruelty," a propensity proved by the fact that her sometimes terrifying story is a "catalog of violence." The linkage of sentimentality and cruelty is common in those journalistic exposés which contrive to titillate the feelings they editorially censor; but the violence in *Uncle Tom's Cabin* has an extremely realistic basis. Stowe not only relied on documentary accounts of the horrors of slavery, but she was familiar at first hand with the violence of her own period of history. Edmund Wilson points out that on the day her father and her husband were read out of the Presbyterian Church for heresy by the General Assembly in Philadelphia, one of the city's new buildings, dedicated to abolitionism, was burned down by a mob. In 1841 when Harriet began writing stories, a man hiding a runaway slave attacked the owner, a local farmer was murdered by Negro thieves, a white woman was raped, and race riots erupted for a week. When a cholera epidemic broke out in Cincinnati, Harriet lost her most recent baby. She later recalled that it was at his grave that she learned "what a poor slave a mother may feel when her child is torn from her." Much that is in *Uncle Tom's Cabin,* she felt, "had its root in the awful scenes and bitter sorrows of that summer." Violence was not something she vicariously experienced through her writing; it was part of her life which served her imagination as a writer. Wilson puts it with his usual felicity: "*Uncle Tom,* with its lowering threats and its harassing persecutions, its impotence of well-meaning people, its outbreaks of violence and its sudden bereavements, had been lived in the Beecher home, where the trials and tribulations, as they used to be called, of the small family world inside were involved with, were merged in, the travail of the nation to which it belonged."

These qualifications, however, do not strike at the heart of Baldwin's misreading of the story as social propaganda with its theological meaning reduced to a medieval terror of witches. Wilson comes much closer to the truth in *Patriotic Gore* when he points out that the tale "has registered the moment when the Civil War was looming as something already felt but not yet clearly foreseen: an ambiguous promise and menace, the fulfillment of some awful prophecy which had never quite been put into words." Wilson does not extend this crucial insight to the details of the story itself, but he puts the reader on the right track by observing that millennial expectations of a religious nature "blazed up against the twilight of the Calvinist faith, at the beginning of the Civil War." *Uncle Tom's Cabin* is a great document of the millennial temper of American Protestantism in the first half of the nineteenth century, a prime source for understanding its philosophy of history and revivalist theology.

Traditional Calvinism predicted great trials for the church before the millennium, which would be inaugurated by the Second Coming of Christ. Jonathan Edwards and his New England followers, Joseph Bellamy, Timothy Dwight, and Samuel Hopkins, preached instead the more radical doctrine of a golden age on earth to be fulfilled before Christ came to earth in order to wind things up for the Last Judgment. This more optimistic postmillennial view of the Second Coming was, as Stowe wrote in *Poganuc People,* "the star of hope in the eyes of the New England clergy; their faces were set eastward, towards the dawn of that day, and the cheerfulness of those anticipations illuminated the hard tenets of their theology with a rosy glow." This "little bit of a woman, about as thin and dry as a pinch of snuff," as she described herself, grew up in this New England world of modified Edwardsianism. Appropriately, her preface foresees "another and better day dawning," foreshadowed by the signs that "the hand of benevolence is everywhere stretched out." The contemporary movement for humanitarian reform which linked the ideals of piety and benevolence was augury of a coming millennium. The turbulent current of the Mississippi River in *Uncle Tom's Cabin* symbolized the "headlong tide of business" on which her countrymen were afloat, carrying with it "a more fearful freight, the tears of the oppressed, the sighs of the helpless, the bitter prayers of the poor, ignorant hearts to an unknown God—unknown, unseen and silent, but who will yet come out of his place to save all the poor of the earth!" Her passionate faith in the Second Coming wavered between the optimistic hopes of the postmillennialists and the apocalyptic fears of the premillennialists, but the eschatological expectation is always present as a reverberating note of the novel's major thematic chords.

In her pages Negro Christians live in hope, whites live in fear. St. Clare's mother told him of a millennium that was coming, "when Christ should reign, and all men should be free and happy." He concludes that "all this sighing and groaning, and stirring among the dry bones foretells what she used to tell me was coming." He reads the signs in "a mustering among the masses, the world over," a singular observation for a plantation master. St. Clare wonders: "But who may abide the day of His appearing?" His creator completes the portentous quotation in her postscript: "for that day shall burn as an oven: and he shall appear as swift witness against those that oppress the hireling in his wages, the widow and the fatherless, and that *turn aside the stranger in his right:* and he shall break in pieces the oppressor." Christians might pray for the coming Kingdom, but they should remember in fear and trembling that in this last convulsion "prophecy associates, in dread fellowship, the *day of vengeance* with the year of his redeemed." The rhetoric is, of course, like that of the storefront Negro churches in Baldwin's *Go Tell It on the Mountain,* and its judgment on inhumanity is kin to his own apocalyptic preaching in *The Fire Next Time.*

Stowe was no Calvinist, despite the fact that Calvin was the name of her husband, a professor of biblical literature at Lane Theological Seminary which her father had founded in Cincinnati. Her novel was in large part a protest against the Calvinist doctrine of human inability to merit salvation. One of her brothers had been deeply disturbed

by Jonathan Edwards's case against free will, and her sister Catharine had suffered badly from the doctrine of predestined election of the saints. Harriet herself agonized over the fate of the unregenerate soul of her drowned son. By the time the novel was written, the influential revivalist preacher, Charles G. Finney, had assimilated Calvinism to an optimistic Arminianism, emphasizing human ability to work out one's salvation, that would have seemed both heretical and sentimental to Jonathan Edwards. Finney thought men could become converted "in the space of a few minutes" if they only listened to the promptings of the heart instead of to the voice of theological reason. This voluntaristic emotional Protestantism saved Stowe and suffused her story.

The unlettered faith of Uncle Tom, who got religion at a camp-meeting revival, is the true hero of her book. "We does for the Lord when we does for his critturs," he says in the spirit of Finney himself. When Misse Cassy, imprisoned on Legree's brutal plantation, asks why the Lord should have put some people in a situation where "we can't help but sin," Tom replies, "I think we can help it." Even Legree was almost once persuaded by good angels: "his heart inly relented,—there was a conflict,—but sin got the victory, and he set all the force of his rough nature against the conviction of his conscience." Swift conversion, in Finney's fashion, is part of the sentimentality of the novel. Eliza's husband George finds, again in the Quaker house of Rachel Halliday, that there his "dark, misanthropic, pining atheistic doubts, and fierce despair, melted before the light of a living Gospel, breathed in living faces." Tom's faith not only converts St. Clare to a pledge of manumission, but four pages later, suffering from a knife wound inflicted during a tavern brawl, the former agnostic dies with a hymn on his lips and Tom's hand in his own. When Tom himself dies from his beatings, like "One whose suffering changed an instrument of torture, degradation and shame, into a symbol of glory, honor, and immortal life," his triumphant Christian victory over sin and death instantly converts two of the "imbruted blacks" on the plantation belonging to the atheist Simon Legree. The spiritual discipline of Calvinism had become too intellectually rigorous and morally severe for a sentimental people. Stowe's book exemplified the convergence of the popular cults of home, love, and instant salvation which transformed protestantism into a culture-religion.

Baldwin finds in her instead that same "medieval spirit" which burns witches and activates a lynch mob. Stowe's simplistic conception of villainy is exemplified in her picture of Legree as an atheistic, profit-minded, slave-holding alcoholic, a catalog of sins out of the Protestant tracts of her own day. But, though she believed the Bible provided the faithful with an absolute morality, she rose above the tractarian limits of her material in her portrait of the amiable skeptic St. Clare, who complains that "this whole business of human virtue is poor mean trash," because it is "a mere matter, for the most part, of latitude and longitude, and geographical position, acting with natural temperament." As for her superstition, it is Legree's literal fear of the dark which the author exploits as a means to engineer the escape of the slave girls from his plantation. Playing the part of ghosts, they terrify him into his fatal alcoholism, which seemed "to throw the lurid shadows of a coming retribution back into the present life." It is indeed that shadow, which menaces her readers as well for their complicity in the guilt of slavery, that saves her novel from being swamped in the milk of Finney's revivalistic benevolence. Her eschatology strikes the note of judgment which broods over the story, linking it to the Calvinism she hated.

Surprisingly, Baldwin misses his one chance to score directly on target with his charge of a "fear of the dark." He does not relate it to her concluding plea for colonization of the freed Negro in Africa. Stowe's abolitionism was far more conservative than that of her colleagues in the antislavery movement. The churches of the North, she urged, should defy the Fugitive Slave Law of 1850 by taking upon their shoulders the Christian duty of educating escaped slaves until they had sufficient "moral and intellectual maturity" to be assisted in their passage to Liberia, where they could "put in practice the lessons they have learned in America." This morally evasive solution conveniently suited a society in which racial prejudice against freed Negroes was strong everywhere in the Union. Stowe's rejection of "integration" was rationalized on the ground that while American Negroes as an injured group *ought* to have "*more* than the rights of common men," only a nation of blacks could have the power which effectively would "break their chains." This argument seemingly prefigures the Black Nationalism of Marcus Garvey in the 1920s and of the Black Muslims in the 1960s, but Stowe believed with Eliza's husband that "'a nation has a right to argue, remonstrate, implore, and present the cause of its race,—which an individual has not.'" Only black power could *justify* Negro protest.

Unlike her distant descendants' views, Stowe's Black Nationalism was linked to her identification of the Negroes with Christian virtues of suffering and tenderness. For this reason "the highest form of the peculiarly *Christian life*" would be exhibited in Africa when God had chosen it, "in the furnace of affliction, to make her the highest and noblest in that kingdom which he will set up, when every other kingdom has been tried and failed; for the first shall be last, and the last first." Liberia was to be the fulfillment of the expectations which little Eva and Uncle Tom dreamed of in their devoted reading of Revelation or of Tom's heavily marked passage from Matthew describing the Second Coming and the Last Judgment, which inspires his master to manumission and conversion. The dated, conservative policy of colonization was thus buttressed with the radical doctrine of the millennium and rationalized by an inverted racist division between "the hot and hasty Saxon," who would dominate America, and the "affectionate, magnanimous, and forgiving" Negro, who would build a Christian republic in Liberia. This mixture of sentimental piety, millennial hope, romantic racism, and political conservatism not only helps to explain the novel's enormous appeal, but marks its distance from the framework in which responsible thinking about the Negro's position in America must be done

today. It is understandable why "Uncle Tom" has become the stereotype of the submissive Negro who plays the role acceptable to his oppressors, rather than the Christian hero who conquers sin and death by the power of his faith, just as it is understandable that the movement which is closest to her ethics of piety and benevolence, Martin Luther King's Christian nonviolent reformers, should heroically struggle for the integration of Negro Americans into their native society. It is in her policy of exporting free Negroes, which Lincoln also accepted, that she betrays a moral evasion of the deeper dilemmas inherent in the history of American race relations.

Protest novels, in Baldwin's phrase, "are a mirror of our confusion, dishonesty, panic, trapped and immobilized in the sunlit prison of the American dream." For the historian such confusion, however, can be of enormous documentary value. To misread *Uncle Tom's Cabin* is not to commit an aesthetic crime, but it is to suffer a major failure of historical comprehension. Baldwin warns us to remember, in defiance of the conventions of protest novels, that "the oppressed and the oppressor are bound together within the same society; they accept the same criteria, they share the same beliefs, they both alike depend upon the same reality." That awareness is precisely the strength of Stowe's novel and the source of its author's agony. Her story dramatizes the confused anxieties of her time with genuine power. She idealized a dream of domesticity which miscegenation and the slave trade ruthlessly violated. As a Christian she responded to the opposite ideal, however, of the hymn sung by slaves on Legree's plantation: "O there'll be mourning, mourning, mourning, at the judgment-seat of Christ! Parents and children there shall part! parents and children there shall part!" For true believers natural bonds, like racial differences, mean nothing. "In the gates of eternity," she believed, "the black hand and the white hold each other with an equal clasp"; yet in this world, she concluded, Negroes must find their home in a separate nation of believers. George, Eliza, and Cassy excite the reader's sympathy by their struggles to escape from slavery; yet Uncle Tom is honored above all for his stoically resigned acceptance of his sufferings. The vector of these contrary forces and feelings is Stowe's escapist dream of a Christian republic in Liberia which will make faith and freedom inseparably one. The postmillennialists were confident of a coming utopia. Stowe fervently hoped it would come, but she transferred it to Africa, fearing in her own country a vast convulsion as punishment for "unredressed injustice."

Stowe's millennialism would in a few years after the publication of her novel be set to martial music in "The Battle Hymn of the Republic" as Yankee soldiers sang of "the glory of the coming of the Lord" who had "trampled out the vineyards where the grapes of wrath are stored." That "fateful lightning of His terrible swift sword," which she had dreaded, was loosed at Fort Sumter. In the beginning it was more like the apocalyptic pessimism of traditional Protestantism than the post-millennial optimism of the religion of her day. Yet the end of the war did bring an end to slavery. The ambivalence in her sense of the future was justified. Now that our own present seems to hold the same ambivalent possibilities of fulfillment or destruction, reinforced by the nuclear dilemma, perhaps we can afford to read her with some sympathy for the poignant tension in which her novel holds conflicting anxieties in dramatic solution. To do so, however, we shall have to be as willing to reconstruct historically her religious tradition as she was anxious to bring it to bear upon the dilemma of slavery in a presumedly Christian and democratic society.

This much historical sympathy may have the paradoxical effect of freeing us from our own tendency, which Baldwin himself has succumbed to, of indulging in apocalyptic thinking. The substitution of abstractions for characters is not the result of what Baldwin calls her "fear of the dark"; it is implicit instead in the eschatological effort to transcend the concrete limitations and responsibilities of the specific demands of the historical hour. To read *Uncle Tom's Cabin* in this critical way is to see that its confused anxieties and emotional power, as well as its intellectual limitations, stem not from racial prejudice but from the ambivalent encounter of the American Protestant imagination with history. *Uncle Tom's Cabin* is not "Everybody's Protest Novel"; it is rather the expression of a specific religious imagination in its desperate attempt both to meet and to escape the dilemmas of American culture in the antebellum years. Baldwin connects it with *Little Women, Gentlemen's Agreement,* and *Native Son.* But Stowe's "intense theological preoccupations," as he quite correctly calls them, connect her novel much more relevantly to *The Pilgrim's Progress.* Read in this light, *Uncle Tom's Cabin* is not a fantasy, "connecting nowhere with reality," as Baldwin charges, for its images, rhetoric, and ideas are deeply connected with the ideological tensions of the most critical period of our history. The immense popularity of the novel is not only testimony to its power to make slavery a religious and moral issue in antebellum terms. It is proof as well of the pressure Americans felt—and still feel—to exaggerate their guilt, while minimizing their political responsibility, through a vision of history which wavers between a nightmare of doom and a dream of utopia. In this sense *Uncle Tom's Cabin* is surely one of the most American books in our literature and Baldwin is finally right—for the wrong reasons—in connecting it with our panic and confusion in "the sunlit prison of the American dream."

Leslie Fiedler (essay date 1982)

SOURCE: "Home as Heaven, Home as Hell: Uncle Tom's Canon," in *Rewriting the Dream: Reflections on the Changing American Literary Canon,* edited by W. M.; Verhoeven, Rodopi, 1992, pp. 22-42.

[*An American critic, novelist, short story writer, essayist, poet, and editor, Fiedler is a commentator on American literature who has generated a great deal of controversy. Using primarily Marxist and Freudian perspectives, he attempts to uncover the origins of modern literature and show how myth is used in literature today. In the excerpt* that follows, from an essay originally published in 1982, Fiedler discusses the myth of marriage and parenthood shared by Stowe's female audience, examining its role in her antislavery argument and its influence on the novel's critical reception.]

The myth which informs *Uncle Tom's Cabin* . . . , in which home, marriage, and mother are postulated as the greatest goods, belongs *only* to what I had been taught to regard as "subliterature"; so that indeed I may have failed to do it justice less because of male chauvinism than elitist snobbery. It is true, in any event, that I gave even scanter consideration than I had to Mrs. Stowe and her sisters to male writers of great mythopoeic powers whose fantasies were based on macho myths that similarly found no echo in High Literature. In my compendious study of American fiction from 1789 to 1959, I ignored completely, for instance, the two greatest exploiters of the Darwinian *mythos* of survival of the fittest, both proud of being "manly" men. I did not even mention the name of either the resolutely "lowbrow" Edgar Rice Burroughs (who wanted to call himself "Normal Bean" on the title page of his first novel) or that marginal "middlebrow" Jack London.

I have begun recently to try to come to terms with the first, and I keep promising myself that someday I will deal at length with the second, to whom I still do not quite understand my response. Yet, though *Tarzan of the Apes* and *The Call of the Wild* titillated my deep fantasy as a boy, and I can return to them still with a pleasure more than merely nostalgic, the archetypes they embody threaten always to turn into stereotypes, and they seem to me in any case unreliable clues to the nature of the deep American psyche. Certainly they are less central, less illuminating, than the myth of interethnic male bonding, which I have been exploring with almost monomaniacal exclusivity for all of my critical career.

There is, however, a second myth of equal importance, to which I regret having paid so little attention for so long; because without fully understanding it, I have come to realize, it is impossible fully to understand the first, with which it exists in dialectical tension. What I am talking about is the myth classically formulated in *Uncle Tom's Cabin* (let us call it the myth of Home as Heaven), which—without at first being aware of what I was up to—I have been learning to take seriously, for the last fifteen or more years. *Re*-learning to take it seriously, I suppose I should say, as I had been able to do as a child, but could not do as an adult until I had unlearned literary "standards," by measuring them against Mrs. Stowe's novel rather than it against them.

Once I had begun to do so, it became clear that the American books which, according to those standards, were clearly superior to hers were not only more elegantly structured and textured, more ideologically dense, more overtly subversive—more difficult and challenging, in short— but they almost invariably celebrated the flight from civilization and the settlement, church and school, from everything which had survived (under female auspices) of

Christian humanism in the New World—thus reinforcing the myth of Home as Hell.

The uniquely American hero/anti-hero of such books rescues no maiden, like Perseus, kills no dragon, like St. George, discovers no treasure, like Beowulf or Siegfried; he does not even manage at long last to get back to his wife, like Odysseus. He is, in fact, an anti-Odysseus, who finds his identity by *running away from home.* This may seem a boyish notion of heroism; yet it is first embodied in Rip Van Winkle, who enters the scene already mature and leaves it a grizzled old man, while Rip's immediate successor, Natty Bumppo, makes his central appearance even older. But he grows younger and younger, as his author dreams a dream in which time runs backward from civilization to virgin wilderness. Here the new Eve, the WASP wife, has not yet been created, and the new Adam lives in an innocent anti-marriage with a Noble Red Man, called Chingachgook or the Great Serpent, quite like Satan, the primordial enemy of Woman.

It was Cooper who first realized that the anti-wife must be nonwhite as well as nonfemale, and mythically it seems scarcely to matter what hue of nonwhite. He can be brown like Melville's Queequeg or black like Twain's Nigger Jim; but at the moment he becomes a Negro, his runaway mate turns into the boy who will not grow up, which is to say, Huck Finn, and the myth achieves its final form. Later, the wilderness lovers undergo even stranger transmogrifications, but two essential elements of the myth never change: the nightmare of misogyny and the dream of racial reconciliation.

It is, however, misogyny in a peculiarly American form: a view of women which identifies them with everything that must be escaped in order to be free. Even in the dying twentieth century such latter-day avatars of the "runaway boy" as R. P. McMurphy in Ken Kesey's *One Flew Over the Cuckoo's Nest* continue to repeat in their own words the cry of Huckleberry Finn, "Aunt Sally, she wants to adopt me and civilize me . . . but I been there before." Actually, Twain had first written, "*They* want to adopt me and civilize me," but his sure instinct led him to revise it to "Aunt Sally, *she*. . . ."

All Americans, therefore (including girls and women, who also grew up reading Mark Twain), at levels deeper than ideology perceive white women as the enemy, which may explain why even the most enlightened of us, male and female alike, end up cheering McMurphy's attempted rape-murder of Big Nurse at the movies, and why, after all, ERA may never become part of the Constitution. How can it be, we ask ourselves, between waking and sleeping, that our mythical oppressors now consider themselves, claim to have considered themselves all along, the oppressed? But, of course, the myth of the wilderness companions represents also the male ex-European's dream of effecting—behind the backs of white women, as it were—a reconciliation with those fellow males we know we have really, *really* oppressed.

That reconciliation does not, however, envisage a mar-

riage in the flesh. Only in the spirit can white and non-white become one. Our anti-heroes do not flee white women to beget on red/brown/black/yellow ones children neither white nor nonwhite. *The Leatherstocking Tales* are haunted by a horror of miscegenation; so that just as white girls flee the threat of Indian rape, Natty recoils in dismay when asked to mate with a "squaw." "There's no cross in my blood," he cries, and he prefers to die without issue rather than father an heir unable to make the same boast.

In later versions of the myth, like *Moby Dick* and *Huckleberry Finn,* the threat of miscegenation is scarcely permitted to cross the threshold of consciousness. Yet we know from Melville's *Typee* and Twain's *Pudd'nhead Wilson* that their authors too were possessed by a fear of "blood pollution," which, indeed, it may be a convert function of the myth of male bonding to exorcise. But in the favorite books of the wives and mothers left behind by Rip, Natty, Ishmael and Huck, that nightmare horror is openly exploited. It represents, in fact, the dark underside of their counter-myth, in which home is portrayed as the earthly paradise, and marriage and integration into the family not as a fate to be fled for the sake of freedom, but as one to be sought in quest of maturity, responsibility and Christian salvation.

Precisely for this reason, perhaps, the pop novels which exploit the counter-myth have been able to deal, in a way in which the "classics" of male bonding have not, with traumatic historical events climaxing in the Civil War and its tragic aftermath. Surrendering these events, along with the nightmare images of black-white rape and flogging, which are their mythic context, to the domestic romancers, our "classic" male novelists have ended by substituting nostalgia for history. Mark Twain, for instance, retreating to his own antebellum boyhood, makes of slavery an occasion for paeans to transcendent homoerotic love, when he does not travesty it in heartless burlesque. And Walt Whitman converts the War Between the States into a backdrop for the masochistic adventures of a wound-dresser among beautiful, maimed young men.

Only William Faulkner, last heir to the tradition of misogyny and male bonding, confronts head-on the nightmare terror of miscegenation. But this is because, straddling the line between High Literature and pop, he draws also on the tradition which begins with Harriet Beecher Stowe. Certain lines, for instance, spoken by Dilsey in *The Sound and the Fury* could be transferred, without jarring the reader, to Uncle Tom. But the stylistic context in which they appear, modeled on elitist European novels like Joyce's *Ulysses,* has alienated the majority audience that responded passionately to a series of truly popular works, which begins with Mrs. Stowe's book and the "Tom plays" into which it was almost immediately translated, and is continued in Thomas Dixon, Jr.'s *The Leopard's Spots* and *The Clansman* (along with *The Birth of a Nation,* a film derived from them by D. W. Griffith), Margaret Mitchell's *Gone With the Wind* (both as a novel and a movie) and Alex Haley's *Roots* (in all of its pop versions, from the predigested book selection to what threatened for a while to become an endlessly continued TV series).

Read as a single work composed over more than a century, in many media and by many hands, these constitute a hitherto unperceived "epic," embodying a myth of our history unequaled in scope and resonance by any work of High Art. No epic, however, was ever created so inadvertently, so improbably, arising out of a tradition at once disreputable and genteel, which seemed destined forever to produce not literature of high seriousness, "doctrinal to a nation," but only ephemeral best sellers. Yet precisely for this reason they have been loved by the majority audience, which considers them not epical at all (the very word turns them off) but "good reads." And indeed they are, singly and compositely, a "good read": not merely celebrating domesticity, but moving inexorably to their expected "happy endings," permitting easy identification with their sympathetic protagonists, and providing along the way opportunities for shudders and thrills, laughter and tears.

The archetypal ancestry of this fictional mode goes back as far as the fairy tale—"Cinderella," in particular—and in other cultures it has been adopted by writers as distinguished as Samuel Richardson and Charles Dickens. But in America it was from the start the almost exclusive province of the unpretentious authors of "best sellers," particularly women writing for women. Beginning with Susanna Rowson, whose *Charlotte Temple* appeared before the end of the eighteenth century, their line continued with what Hawthorne in the mid-nineteenth (envious of their sales, perhaps, as well as contemptuous of their values) called the "horde of damned female scribblers." And they have, in fact, kept "scribbling" down to our time, including in their numbers Susan Warner, Mrs. E.D.E.N. Southworth, Louisa May Alcott, Helen Hunt Jackson, Alice Hegan Rice, Edna Ferber, Fannie Hurst, Taylor Caldwell, etc., etc.

In the post-print media, the laureates of the domestic myth have fared even better, winning equal time with the makers of the wilderness myth. Until very recently, however, they were kept separate and distinct, programs of the first kind being shown on television only during the hours when men were traditionally in the office and the shop rather than at home. But with the shift in gender roles begotten by the latest wave of the women's movement, they have begun to invade the evening hours. Yet by and large, each day until dusk our TV screens are still possessed by the daytime serials, the so-called soap operas, whose family crises are typically acted out in enclosed spaces: living rooms, bedrooms, kitchens or offices, from which the characters, usually related by blood or marriage, escape occasionally to hospital rooms, psychiatric wards, prison cells or courtrooms—sometimes even to exotic resorts in Jamaica or Bermuda.

More often than not, in any case, the action is framed by three walls of a set (whose closure is completed by the fourth wall behind our heads), not so much a home away from home as a home continuous with the one in which we watch. Seldom does anyone ride a horse, a car, a plane on screen, and no one ever floats down the Mississippi on a raft or sails off on a whaling ship. Nor is anyone ever alone willingly or for long, for all aspire to heterosexual bonding, marriage, children, integration into the family. To be sure, no marriage lasts long; not because the wedded state is despised, but precisely because it is the sole conceivable Happy Ending, and the soap opera can never end. Only begin again, which is to say, move toward another marriage, and another, and another . . . doomed sometimes, quasi-incestuous always, but never, never joining together the races, never breaching the miscegenation taboo.

Once night falls, however (and amidst the encroaching after-dark soaps and soft-porn sitcoms), the westerns, the cop shows, the s.f. spectaculars reassert their dominance and we head out for the Territory once more—riding the range, prowling the streets of the urban jungle, penetrating outer space. And wherever long-term bonding occurs it is likely to involve a pair of ethnically disparate bachelors: the Jew Starsky and the Gentile Hutch, the black Tenspeed and the white Brownshoe, the earthling Captain Kirk and the Vulcan Mr. Spock. But they are being driven from the air these days, these descendants of Natty Bumppo and Chingachgook—attacked from all sides, presumably because of the ambience of violence in which alone their love can flourish. One suspects that on a deeper level the hostility to them is rooted in a distrust of interethnic male bonding itself.

If, however, as TV programming suggests, the American mind is possessed by a pair of antithetical myths, split down the middle in a kind of institutionalized ambivalence (since, of course, men watch soaps and women cop shows), we would never guess it when we leave television for the classroom—and begin the required reading of the "masterworks of our tradition," as defined by the Guardians of High Culture. These guardians have traditionally been white Anglo-Saxon Protestants, more often than not genteel, almost invariably straight males or closet gays. Even when vulgarians of lesser breeds or women have more recently begun to make it into the Old Boys Club, they have done so by introjecting the values of their predecessors, proving, therefore, quite as incapable of judging fairly works produced by and for culturally marginal groups in our society, including those to which they themselves belong.

Only *Uncle Tom's Cabin* among the books best loved by such groups has seemed at least problematical to those guardians—much abused, but a contender still for inclusion in a misogynist canon, which extends from Washington Irving to Saul Bellow ("What do they want?" he asks about women through the protagonist of *Herzog*. "They eat green salad and they drink blood"). It is, therefore, with that book that any attempt to redeem the feminine pop tradition and its essential archetype must begin.

It is scarcely surprising that *Uncle Tom's Cabin, or Life Among the Lowly* should contain the most compendious gallery of homes in all American literature, ranging from the humble Kentucky habitation which gives the novel its name ("In one corner of it stood a bed, covered neatly with a snowy spread. . . . The wall over the fireplace was adorned with some very brilliant scriptural prints, and a portrait of General Washington") to the elegant New Orleans summer villa of the St. Clares ("The common sitting room opened on to a large garden, fragrant with every picturesque plant and flower of the tropics"), and from the prim New England farmhouse of Miss Ophelia's family ("Within . . . wide clean rooms, where nothing seems to be doing or going to be done, where everything is once and forever rigidly in place") to the squalid and decayed mansion of Simon Legree ("The wallpaper was defaced in spots with slops of beer and wine and garnished with . . . long sums footed up, as if somebody had been practicing arithmetic there").

After all, Harriet Beecher Stowe had been a lifelong homemaker, who was to publish in 1865 a kind of domestic guidebook called *House and Home Papers* and to co-author four years later with her sister Catharine *American Woman's Home,* dedicated to "THE WOMEN OF AMERICA, in whose hands rest the real destinies of the Republic, as moulded by early training and preserved amid the maturer influences of home." It seems inevitable, then, that even in a novel dealing with the larger problems of slavery and states' rights (but also addressed to women) the myth of the Utopian Household appears—receiving, indeed, its classic formulation.

The earthly paradise which Mrs. Stowe describes is presumably an ordinary Quaker household, maternal, nurturing, almost edible, and—be it noted—*all white* except for the temporary residents, Eliza, a black mother fleeing to save her child, and George, her bitter and troubled husband, who rejoins her there by happy chance. The names of the inhabitants, however, are allegorical (the presiding matriarch is called, for instance, Rachel Halliday, in memory of the Old Testament mother forever weeping for her children and refusing to be comforted), and the archetypal implications of the scene are reinforced by references to an unfallen Eden in which an aging and chaste Venus peacefully reigns.

> . . . all moved obediently to Rachel's gentle "Hadn't thee better?" on the work of getting breakfast; for a breakfast in the luxurious valleys of Indiana is a thing complicated and multi-form, and like picking up the rose-leaves . . . in Paradise, asking other hands than those of the original mother. . . . Bards have written of the cestus of Venus, that turned the heads of all the world in successive generations. We had rather, for our part, have the cestus of Rachel Halliday, that kept heads from being turned, and made everything go on harmoniously. We think it is more suited to our modern days, decidedly.

More resonant mythologically than the classical or biblical names, however, are the words "mother" and "home" which echo and re-echo through the passage:

> Rachel never looked so truly and benignly happy as at the head of her table. There was so much motherliness

and full-heartedness even in the way she passed a plate of cakes or poured a cup of coffee, that it seemed to put a spirit into the food and drink she offered. . . . This, indeed, was a home—*home*. . . .

It was the assimilation of the slavery issue into so homely a scene which won the hearts of the readers of "female" best sellers, ordinarily indifferent to the world of "male" politics, persuading them that the "patriarchal institution," as Mrs. Stowe called slavery—not quite aware, I think, of the full implications of the metaphor—was a threat to Home and Mother and Family. Once freed, she suggested, black Americans would aspire to the kind of "happy ending" which she and her genteel audience demanded of their favorite novels: the reunion of parents and children, husbands and wives, in monogamous Christian households.

Just such a household she describes at the Dickens-like tearful-cheerful conclusion of her book, when George and Eliza, safe across the Canadian border, gather together with their son and daughter, plus a miraculously preserved and rediscovered mother and sister, in a truly Pickwickian love feast.

> The scene now changes to a small, neat tenement, in the outskirts of Montreal; the time, evening. A cheerful fire blazes on the hearth; a tea-table, covered with a snowy cloth, stands prepared for the evening meal. . . . But to return to our friends, whom we left wiping their eyes, and recovering from too great and sudden a joy. They are now seated around the social board, and are getting decidely companionable.

If George, the new head of his own house, dreams of a further emigration to Africa, it is not in order to "light out for the territory ahead of the rest," like Huckleberry Finn, to whom domestic "civilization" seems the end rather than the beginning of freedom; much less is it to search for his "roots," like some late twentieth-century black nationalist. Far from desiring to find an alternative to the Christian culture which has enslaved and unmanned him, a way of life based on polytheism, tribalism, polygamy or free sexuality, he plans to spread the Christian gospel to his unredeemed brethren on the Dark Continent: "As a Christian patriot, a teacher of Christianity, I go to *my country,*" he writes to a friend; and doubtless Mrs. Stowe's first fans dreamed of his bringing to the benighted not just literacy and "the sublime doctrine of love and forgiveness," but "small, neat tenements" and "snowy table-cloths" as well.

Not even those mothers, however, whom Mrs. Stowe continually addresses in asides ("If it were *your* Harry, mother, or your Will, that were going to be torn from you . . . tomorrow morning . . .") seem to have been much moved by the evocation of the servantless Quaker household, in which order is so effortlessly preserved and even the furniture is motherly; nor have the loving but desexed characters who inhabit it lived on among their dearest memories. What has continued to survive in the imagination not just of mothers but the whole world is what is truly mythic in *Uncle Tom's Cabin.*

In the Quaker household, we are dealing not with myth but mythology—contrived, self-conscious, verging on allegory—a fantasy arising not out of the public nightmares of race and sex which Mrs. Stowe shared with her contemporaries in a nation moving toward total war, but out of her personal insecurities: her fear of growing old, her conviction that she was not beautiful, her inability to control her children (a favorite son would become an alcoholic and drift from sight) or to keep her house in order, though she in fact always had servants, some of them black and all apparently as inefficient as she. Writing of a typical day in her own nonutopian household, Mrs. Stowe walks the thin line between hilarity and despair:

> This meal being cleared away, Mr. Stowe dispatched to market with various memoranda of provisions, etc., and baby being washed and dressed, I begin to think what next must be done. I start to cut out some little dresses . . . when Master Henry makes a doleful lip and falls to crying with might and main. I catch him up, and, turning around, see one of his sisters flourishing the things out of my workbox in fine style. Moving it away and looking the other side, I see the second little mischief seated by the hearth chewing coals and scraping up ashes with great apparent relish. Grandmother lays hold upon her and charitably offers to endeavor to quiet baby while I go on with my work. I set at it again . . . measure them once more to see which is the right one, and proceed . . . when I see the twins on the point of quarreling with each other. Number one pushes number two over. Number two screams: that frightens the baby, and he joins in. I call number one a naughty girl, take the persecuted one in my arms, and endeavor to comfort her. . . .

How different the Hallidays—Rachel, her impotent and scarcely visible husband, her incredibly cheerful and co-operative children—are not just from Mrs. Stowe, her husband and their children, but even more from others of her characters, mysteriously known even to those who have never read Mrs. Stowe's novel: Uncle Tom, Eliza, Topsy, Little Eva and Simon Legree. Primordial images rather than living persons, they emerge mysteriously from the collective unconscious and pass, scarcely mediated by her almost transparent text, into the public domain, to which, like all authentic popular literature, they properly belong.

Similarly, the scenes which stay with us forever seem as archetypal and oneiric as those protagonists: Eliza leaping from ice floe to ice floe in pursuit of freedom, or Eva, on the verge of maturity, dying a death lingering enough not just to convert her demure black anti-type, Topsy, and her Byronic father, but to extort tears from generations of readers. Eliza's scene is shorter than we can believe—like a fragmentary dream dreamed in the moment before waking—while Eva's is described in considerable detail; but both have the realer-than-real vividness of hallucinations:

> There was a sound in that chamber, first of one who stepped quickly. It was Miss Ophelia, who had resolved to sit up all night with her little charge, and who, at

the turn of the night, had discerned what experienced nurses significantly call "a change." The outer door was quickly opened, and Tom, who was watching outside, was on the alert, in a moment.

"Go for the doctor, Tom! lose not a moment," said Miss Ophelia; and, stepping across the room, she rapped at St. Clare's door.

"Cousin," she said, "I wish you would come."

Those words fell on his heart like clods upon a coffin. Why did they? He was up and in the room in an instant, and bending over Eva, who still slept.

What was it he saw that made his heart stand still? Why was no word spoken between the two? Thou canst say, who hast seen that same expression on the face dearest to thee;—that look indescribable, hopeless, unmistakable, that says to thee that thy beloved is no longer thine.

On the face of the child, however, there was no ghastly imprint—only a high and almost sublime expression—the over-shadowing presence of spiritual natures, the dawning of immortal life in that childish soul. . . .

. . . The child lay panting on her pillows, as one exhausted—the large clear eyes rolled up and fixed. Ah, what said those eyes, that spoke so much of heaven? Earth was past, and earthly pain; but so solemn, so mysterious, was the triumphant brightness of that face, that it checked even the sobs of sorrow. They pressed around her, in breathless stillness.

"Eva," said St. Clare, gently.

She did not hear.

"O, Eva, tell us what you see? What is it?" said her father.

A bright, a glorious smile passed over her face, and she said, brokenly—"O! love—joy—peace!" gave one sigh, and passed from death unto life!

"Farewell, beloved child! the bright, eternal doors have closed after thee; we shall see thy sweet face no more. O, woe for them who watched thy entrance into heaven, when they shall wake and find only the cold gray sky of daily life, and thou gone forever."

What haunts us most deeply, however, is the scene of Uncle Tom being beaten to death by Simon Legree, flanked by his black henchmen Sambo and Quimbo. Rooted in history, as Mrs. Stowe understands it, they seem less historical figures than projections of a misandry otherwise difficult for a dutiful wife, sister and daughter of strong pious males to confess. Yet the white Vermonter Legree embodies the kind of macho Yankee inflexibility she must have known from earliest childhood, while the other two, with "their coarse, heavy features; their great eyes, rolling enviously . . . their barbarous, guttural, half-brute, intonation," seem figments of the fear of black phallic power which Mrs. Stowe took such pains elsewhere to euphemize or deny. It is the first, the New Englander, however, who performs the deed of darkness, while his dusky overseers merely stand by—yet are party to the total horror all the same:

> Legree drew in a long breath; and, suppressing his rage, took Tom by the arm, and, approaching his face almost to his, said, in a terrible voice, "Hark'e, Tom!—ye think, 'cause I've let you off before, I don't mean what I say; but this time, I've *made up my mind* and counted the cost. You've always stood it out agin' me: now, I'll *conquer ye, or kill ye!*—one or t'other. I'll count every drop of blood there is in you, and take'em, one by one, till ye give up!"

It is an encounter which lives on in the depths of my own mind with hallucinatory vividness, as seems appropriate enough in light of the fact that it originally came to Mrs. Stowe as a hallucination. To me, moreover, as to her and her readers, early and late, both that event and the gothic swampland plantation on which it occurs represent (whatever demurrers the conscious mind may make) the quintessential, the archetypal Deep South. Yet, of course, she had never known that region at first hand, so that it remains as imaginary and symbolic as the "Europe" of Poe's tales of terror. "Dark Places," she calls the chapter in which Uncle Tom first sees the infernal landscape of "Down the River," adding the epigraph: "The dark places of the earth are full of the habitations of cruelty"; then describes for us the "dreary pine barrens, where the wind whispered mournfully . . . the doleful trees rising out of the slimy, spongy ground, hung with long wreaths of funereal black moss, while ever and anon the loathsome form of the moccasin snake might be seen sliding among broken stumps."

Oddly enough, her vision of Tom's death in the bayous of Louisiana came to her in polar New England, rather than when she was as close to the real South as she ever got, which is to say, in Cincinnati, just across the river from slaveholding Kentucky. She had, in fact, just moved to snowbound Bowdoin, Maine, where her husband had been appointed professor of theology at the local college, when her imagination began to be possessed of images of black field hands toiling and suffering in cotton fields under a sweltering sun. At first, as December storms shook the house around her and she lay sleepless beside her half-frozen babies, she thought only of the blizzards of her Connecticut childhood, her parents struggling homeward through mounting drifts. But seated at a communion service in the college church in February 1852, she saw before her, lit by a meridional glare brighter than the dim northern light at the windows, the bloody and broken body of an old black man beaten to death by his white master. And barely repressing her tears, she rushed home to write down (the words are her son's, remembering, echoing hers years afterward) "the vision which had been blown into her mind as by a mighty wind."

Then, the ink scarcely dry, she read the first installment of what was to become *Uncle Tom's Cabin* aloud to her children, who "broke into convulsions of weeping," and only when they were asleep did she permit herself to give way to tears. "I remember," she wrote to one of her sons a quarter of a century later, " . . . weeping over you as you lay sleeping beside me, and I thought of the slave mothers whose babies were torn from them." But surely she was thinking too of the child she had lost before leaving Cincinnati, the son she always referred to as "the most beautiful and beloved" of all her brood, since elsewhere—indeed, more than once—she noted for posterity that "it was at his dying bed that I learned what a poor slave mother may feel when her child is torn away from her." And she added, "I felt that I could never be consoled for it, unless this crushing of my own heart might enable me to work out some great good to others."

That "great good" turned out to be, of course, *Uncle Tom's Cabin,* whose serial publication she began almost immediately, not quite knowing at first where she was going or how long it would take her—but sustained, it would appear, by other hallucinations as vivid as the first. Moreover, as she sought to make of these images a popular fiction (her family was financially dependent at this point on her earnings as a writer), it occurred to her that it would not be sufficient merely to portray the suffering of a black male under the lash. To move as well as convince American mothers, and through them their husbands and sons, it was necessary also to portray slavery as an offense against the Family, the Utopian Household, Motherhood itself.

Contemporary accounts written by fugitive male slaves often tell of their being driven to resistance and flight by separation from their male buddies, but such stories had, for Mrs. Stowe, no mythic resonance. Or perhaps she was dimly aware that to have portrayed slavery as an offense against male bonding rather than marriage and parenthood would have meant falling out of the myth she shared with her female audience. She actually made one small concession to her masculine readers by introducing a minor subplot involving the tender relationship between Tom and young "Marse George," the son of his original master. But though that white boy pledges eternal love to the old black slave and keeps the faith, he finds him again too late to save him from the fury of Simon Legree and has to content himself (how reading the book at the age of seven or eight, I thrilled to that scene) with knocking Legree to the ground.

It was a compromise with her own pacifist principles that Mrs. Stowe was willing to make, knowing that some of her readers, especially the boys and men among them, would not be content with Tom's passive Christian "victory" over his oppressor, for whom he prays with his dying breath. She was, however, unwilling (and for this the small boy in me has never quite forgiven her) to let any love but that of Christ triumph over oppression and death. She never managed to describe the horror she saw at the communion rail as well as she did George's punching-out of Legree. But it survives in our memories, all the same, like the other key scenes of the book, as image or icon rather than text.

The words she finds or does not find simply do not matter, since even when she does find them (as in the description of Eva's death), they are woefully inadequate by conventional literary "standards." Her most mythically resonant tableaus are in fact usually the "worst" written: shrill to the point of hysteria, sickly-sweet to the verge of nausea, yet somehow so magically moving that they transcend not just the criteria of taste but credibility itself. It must be remembered, moreover, that the text we read has already been much edited, indeed almost rewritten. Like Emily Dickinson, Mrs. Stowe used in place of most other marks of punctuation an all-purpose dash: a characteristic, it would seem, of mid-nineteenth-century ladies' epistolary style. But her editors not only repunctuated her manuscripts, they "corrected" them.

William Dean Howells, who worked with her when she was already a practiced old hand at her craft, was moved to comment in this regard: "As for the author of *Uncle Tom's Cabin* her syntax was such a snare to her that it sometimes needed the combined skill of all the proofreaders and the assistant editor to extricate her." Then he added, to make clear the limits of editorial revision: "Of course, nothing was ever written into her work, but in changes of diction, in correction of solecisms, in transposition of phrases, the text was largely rewritten on the margin of her proofs. The soul of her art was present, but the form was so often absent, that when it was clothed on anew, it would have been hard to say whose cut the garment was of in many places."

It is pointless, then, to treat her as if she were *mutatis mutandis* another Flaubert, and misleading to insist on her radical difference from the hacks who translated her works to the stage. It was not they who invented the character whom a squeamish latter-day admirer of the "true" Mrs. Stowe, Ellen Moers, refers to as "tractly Little Eva." Consequently, it is impossible after the fact to edit out of her text Eva's embarrassing "Christian" defense of slavery: "It makes for so many more around to love." Like the equally soupy pious last words which Uncle Tom breathes into the ear of the boy, who arrives just too late to save him ("I love every creatur', every what!—it's nothing *but* love! O Mas'r George! what a thing 'tis to be a Christian!"), it belongs to the "soul" of her art, however great a stumbling block it may be to modernist critics.

Even harder for them to accept are certain of Mrs. Stowe's assumptions about the nature and destiny of black Americans, since she was what we call nowadays a "racist," which is to say, one who believes that whites and blacks are intrinsically different. Yet three of the enduring archetypal characters in her novel are Afro-Americans, as seems only fair in light of the fact that, for better or worse, it was she who invented American blacks for the imagination of the whole world, converting them from facts of history, demography and economics to avatars and archetypes.

She was not the first American author to have created Negro characters. They had appeared earlier in novels and stories by such eminent writers as James Fenimore Cooper, Edgar Allan Poe and Herman Melville, but somehow they had remained archetypally inert, refusing to leap from the printed page to the public domain. And though the long-lived minstrel show had begun to invent its pervasive stereotypes of plantation life before Mrs. Stowe ever set pen to paper, they too failed to kindle the imagination of the world. To be sure, Mrs. Stowe herself was influenced by them, so that before we learn the real name of George and Eliza Harris' small son, Harry, we hear him hailed as "Jim Crow." Moreover, many of the minor blacks who surround her serious protagonists are modeled on the clowns in blackface who cracked jokes with a white interlocutor.

But clearly, images of black Americans could not stir an emotional response adequate to the horrors of slavery so long as they remained merely comic. Small wonder, then, that Mr. Bones retreated to the wings once Topsy had revealed the pathos beneath the burlesque, once Eliza had fled the bloodhounds on the ice (though only in the dramatic version) and Uncle Tom had been beaten to death in full view of a weeping household. Nor is it surprising that the figure of the martyred black slave under the lash, too old to be a sexual threat, too pious to evoke fears of violent revenge, captured the deep fantasy of a white world, haunted (since the Haitian revolt at least) with nightmares of black insurrection, and needing therefore to be assured that tears rather than blood would be sufficient to erase their guilt.

There are, to be sure, standard minstrel-show types among the astonishing array of Afro-American characters who move through the crowded pages of *Uncle Tom's Cabin,* comic darkies brought on for comic relief. Others represent stereotypes of other kinds, ranging from the faithful servant to the naked victim on the slave block, while a few, like Augustine St. Clare's spoiled and vain Creole valet, "Mr. Adolph," are rendered with the objective "realism" of a social observer. But only Eliza, Topsy and Tom, pressing on toward their foreknown endings—a bittersweet martyrdom, a breathless escape to freedom, an improbable conversion to a lifetime of Christian service— mysteriously survive outside the fiction in which they were born.

It is they alone who have become models, archetypal grids through which we have for so long perceived the Negroes around us and they themselves that, desiring to change the relationship of blacks and whites in the "real" world, we discover that we must deal with those deep images as well as laws and social custom. But, of course, most potent of the three in this regard is Uncle Tom. Indeed, among the "good niggers" of our literature, only Mark Twain's Jim has achieved a comparable mythological status, the wilderness companion of the white runaway from civilization, originally conceived as a red man but transformed in *Huckleberry Finn* into a black man.

Walter Benn Michaels (essay date 1983)

SOURCE: "Romance and Real Estate," in *The Gold Standard and the Logic of Naturalism: American Literature at the Turn of the Century,* University of California Press, 1987, pp. 85-112.

[*In the following excerpt from an essay originally published in 1983, Michaels examines the economic themes of* Uncle Tom's Cabin, *focusing on the role of slavery in the marketplace.*]

. . . . The conjunction of death and secure property has its place in [*Uncle Tom's Cabin,* a text] intended not as a romance but, in its author's words [in *A Key to Uncle Tom's Cabin,* 1853], as a "representation . . . of real incidents, of actions really performed, of words and expressions really uttered." Riding by his slave quarters late at night, Simon Legree hears the singing of a "musical tenor voice": "'When I can read my title clear / To mansions in the skies,'" Uncle Tom sings," 'I'll bid farewell to every fear / And wipe my weeping eyes.'" Tom is preparing for the martyrdom toward which Legree will soon help him, and his sense of heaven as a "home" to which he has clear title is barely metaphoric. Slaves, of course, were forbidden to own property, but Stowe thought of them as, by definition, the victims of theft. Slavery, "appropriating one set of human beings to the use and improvement of another," robbed a man of himself, and so freedom involved above all the restitution of property. Only in death did the slave's title to himself become "sure"; only in death did Uncle Tom's cabin actually become his.

It is not, in itself, surprising that freedom in the mid-nineteenth century, the period that C. B. Macpherson [in *Possessive Individualism,* 1964] has called the "zenith" of "possessive market society," should be understood as essentially a property relation, but it does provide in *Uncle Tom's Cabin* some unexpected and little-noted points of emphasis. When, for example, George Shelby frees his slaves, he tells them that their lives will go on pretty much as before but with the "advantage" that, in case of his "getting in debt or dying," they cannot be "taken up and sold." The implication here is that Shelby himself would never sell them, and in fact, voluntary sales play a comparatively minor role in Stowe's depiction of the evils of slavery. A paragraph from [William] Goodell's *The American Slave Code* [1853] helps explain why: "This feature of liability to seizure for the master's debt," Goodell writes,

> is, in many cases, more terrific to the slave than that which subjects him to the master's voluntary sale. The slave may be satisfied that his master is not willing to sell him—that it is not for his interest or convenience to do so. He may be conscious that he is, in a manner, necessary to his master or mistress. . . . He may even confide in their Christian benevolence and moral principle, or promise that they would not sell him. . . . But all this affords him no security or ground of assurance that his master's creditor will not seize him . . . against even his master's entreaties. Such occurrences are too common to be unnoticed or out of mind.

According to Goodell, then, the slave, whose condition consists in being subordinated to the absolute power of his master, may in the end be less vexed by the absoluteness of that power than by its ultimate incompleteness. It is as if the greatest danger to the slave is not his master's power but his impotence. Thus, Eliza and little Harry flee the Shelbys because, although the Shelbys were "kind," they also "were owing money" and were being forced to sell Harry—"they couldn't," she says, "help themselves." And when Augustine St. Clare dies, his entire household is overwhelmed not so much by grief as by "terror and consternation" at being left "utterly unprotected."

What the slaves fear, of course, is being taken from a kind master to a cruel one; this threat, Goodell thinks, makes them constantly insecure, and the mechanics of this insecurity are the plot mechanism that sells Uncle Tom down the river. But in describing the reaction of St. Clare's slaves to his death, Stowe indirectly points toward a logic of slavery that runs deeper than the difference between good and bad masters, deeper even than the master-slave relation itself. As a matter of course, she notes, the slave is "devoid of rights"; the only "acknowledgment" of his "longings and wants" as a "human and immortal creature" that he ever receives comes to him "through the sovereign and irresponsible will of his master; and when that master is stricken down, nothing remains." The point here is not that one man in the power of another may be subjected to the most inhumane cruelties; nor is it the more subtle point that the power of even a humane master dehumanizes the slave—for Stowe, the power of the kind master and the cruel master both can be tolerated, since even a Legree, refusing Tom his every want and longing, at least acknowledges those wants by refusing them and thus acknowledges his humanity. Rather, the most terrifying spectacle slavery has to offer is the spectacle of slaves *without masters.* Since the "only possible acknowledgment" of the slave as a "human and immortal creature" is through his master's "will," when in debt or in death the master's will is extinguished, the slave's humanity is extinguished also. The slave without a master stands revealed as nothing more than "a bale of merchandise," inhuman testimony to the absolute transformation of a personal relation into a market relation.

Stowe, like most of her contemporaries, customarily understood slavery as "a relic of a barbarous age." The conflict between the "aristocratic" "Slave Power" and "republican" "free labor" would prove "irrepressible," William Seward proclaimed in a tremendously influential speech, and the supposed "feudalism" of the South was a northern byword. More recently, Eugene Genovese [in *The Political Economy of Slavery,* 1967], reviving the irrepressible-conflict interpretation of the Civil War, has described the slave-holding planters as the "closest thing to feudal lords imaginable in a nineteenth-century bourgeois republic" and has argued that the South was a fundamentally precapitalist society. But, as we have begun to see, Stowe was basically more horrified by the bourgeois elements of slavery than by the feudal ones. She and Goodell both were struck by the insecurity of the slave's life, and she, in particular, saw that insecurity as the inevitable fate of property in a free market. The evil of slavery lies, then, not in its reversion to a barbaric paternalism but in its uncanny way of epitomizing the market society to which she herself belongs. Rejecting the claims of southern apologists that slavery provides a social and economic refuge from capitalism, Stowe imagines it instead as a mirror of the social and economic relations coming to the fore in the bourgeois North.

Hence the slave trade, what she calls the "great Southern slave-market," dominates her picture of the South, and, despite their feudal status, the slaves in her writings share the anxious lives of Hawthorne's "republican" northerners—"somebody is always at the drowning-point." The "fluctuations of hope, and fear, and desire" they experience appear now as transformations of their market value. Their emotions represent their status as the objects of speculation. "Nothing is more fluctuating than the value of slaves," remarks a Virginia legislator in *The Key to Uncle Tom's Cabin*. A recent Louisiana law had reduced their value: Texas's imminent admission to the Union as a slave state would increase it. The Virginians speak of their "slave-breeding" as a kind of agriculture and of their female slaves as "brood-mares," but Stowe penetrates more deeply into the nature of the commodity by imagining the product without any producer. What everybody knows about the "goblin-like" Topsy, that she just "grow'd," is only part of the answer to a series of questions asked her by Miss Ophelia: "'Do you know who made you? . . . Tell me where you were born, and who your father and mother were.'" "'Never was born,'" Topsy replies, "'never had no father nor mother. . . . I was raised by a speculator.'" If production in *The House of the Seven Gables* is done with mirrors, production in *Uncle Tom's Cabin* is an equally demonic magic trick, substituting the speculator for the parent and utterly effacing any trace of labor, human or divine.

Kristen Herzog (essay date 1983)

SOURCE: "Harriet Beecher Stowe's *Uncle Tom's Cabin:* Women and Blacks Revolutionizing Society," in *Women, Ethnics, and Exotics: Images of Power in Mid-Nineteenth-Century American Fiction,* The University of Tennessee Press, Knoxville, 1983, pp. 102-20.

[*In the excerpt that follows, Herzog discusses the women and African-American characters in* Uncle Tom's Cabin, *focusing on their role in the author's vision of a new religious and political order.*]

A well-known social history of the nineteenth-century South [William R. Taylor's *Cavalier and Yankee*] features a chapter entitled "Women and Negroes: One and Inseparable." Certainly women and blacks in the Old South shared an inferior social status. Both groups, along with whites of ethnic descent, were subservient to an empowered group of cavalier gentlemen of English ancestry and unmixed blood. But women and blacks were also believed to have an affinity of character: "Let women and negroes alone, and instead of quacking with them [by giving them

education] physic your own diseases. Leave them in their humility, their grateful affection, their self-renouncing loyalty, their subordination of the heart." In Harriet Beecher Stowe's fiction blacks and women are almost interchangeable in the hierarchy of values. Both [according to Jean Willoughby Ashton's *Harriet Beecher Stowe: A Reference Guide,* 1977] "achieve moral triumphs in spite of or perhaps because of the oppressions of a predominantly masculine and commercial world."

How does the constellation of blacks and women in the woman's world of Stowe relate to the very different world of Hawthorne and Melville? The two great representatives of the American Renaissance rediscovered the power of the primitive human impulse which in women, as well as in ethnic and exotic characters, had not been as suppressed by the processes of civilization as it had in most Western males. Hawthorne's women and Melville's primitives represent demonic impulses as well as vital innocence. Harriet Beecher Stowe is more directly interested in the "primitive Christian" values of women and blacks than in their primitive human qualities. For Stowe these two groups embody Christian faith more convincingly than authoritarian white males do and therefore they have the potential to revitalize society. Although critics have frequently assumed that she finds only submissive innocence in blacks and women and that she glorifies black accommodation and female devotion to home and hearth, recent scholarship has corrected this view.

Stowe's shortcomings are obvious. Not only did she occasionally use the same clichés in style, plot, and setting as most of the historical romancers in the first half of the nineteenth century, but she reacted against the popular version of a terrifying Puritan God by proclaiming a God of love whose image often verged on the sentimental.

Stowe's weaknesses as a writer, however, partly due to her family's Puritan prejudices against the arts and partly to her burdens as a wife and a mother of seven children, were also her strengths. She was, and still is, able to affect an immensely diversified spectrum of readers in every corner of the globe through *Uncle Tom's Cabin*. The almost incredible publication history of this novel is well known. The book was such a literary freak that Henry James called it "a wonderful 'leaping fish.'" One hundred thousand books were sold in less than two months after publication in March 1852. By November, twenty different editions could be found in English bookstores. Before the decade was over, innumerable translations had appeared around the world.

As a woman, Stowe provided a "feminine" point of view which in most of the less intelligent "scribbling women" despised by Hawthorne degenerated into a flood of clichés. As a person "unrefined" by the literary circles of her time, she stands out as the only important writer of the mid-nineteenth-century to address openly and critically the "peculiar institution" of slavery. [According to Elizabeth Ammons's essay "Heroines in *Uncle Tom's Cabin*," in *Critical Essays on Harriet Beecher Stowe,* 1980] "Stowe turns a handicap into an asset. Lowly feminine feeling can revolutionize man's world." Although Stowe's insistence on feeling reflected an intriguing feminism, she has been accused of vindicating women in a costly way. "She had to debase all that was best in her religious heritage, repress all that was strongest in her own creativity—and then, boast of it." The question is whether Stowe's "feminization" of religion is a sentimental dilution or a true transformation. Are blacks in *Uncle Tom's Cabin* shown as "feminine" in a negative sense and women as glorious domestic priestesses or angels? And how are both supposed to reform society?

Women and blacks are shown in astonishing diversity in *Uncle Tom's Cabin*. This lively variety of characters surprises many readers who associate the book with the character types derived from the minstrel Tom plays or who know the novel only through the sentimental excerpts which are frequently anthologized. [According to Kenneth S. Lynn's 1962 introduction to the novel,] "Those critics who label *Uncle Tom's Cabin* good propaganda but bad art cannot have given sufficient time to the novel to meet its inhabitants. If they should ever linger over it long enough to take in the shrewdness, the energy, the truly Balzacian variousness of Mrs. Stowe's characterizations, they would surely cease to perpetuate one of the most unjust clichés of American criticism." "In *Uncle Tom's Cabin* (and even more in *Dred,* her second slavery novel) Mrs. Stowe provides extremely interesting material about the regional laws and customs, about the differing skills and trades and occupations, about the African tribal origins and American family trees that made one black American different from another in the midcentury," [stated Ellen Moers in *Harriet Beecher Stowe and American Literature,* 1978]. Edmund Wilson [in *Patriotic Gore: Studies in the Literature of the American Civil War,* 1962] found a startling "eruptive force" in the work: "Out of the background of undistinguished narrative, inelegantly and carelessly written, the characters leap into being with a vitality that is all the more striking for the ineptitude of the prose that presents them." Although Wilson mentions her inept style, another critic [Alice C. Crozier, in *The Novels of Harriet Beecher Stowe,* 1969] maintains that "from the merely artistic point of view, *Uncle Tom's Cabin* is an achievement of great subtlety and originality." And Ellen Moers, seeking to put an end to the idea that the novel belongs only to American history, vigorously declared, "My intention is to put *Uncle Tom's Cabin* back in American literature where it belongs, for I think it is a great novel."

> Harriet Beecher Stowe was different because she was a woman writer, not a man writer. As a woman writer she was obsessed with money and work because . . . she had to earn a living for her large family. As a woman, she was concerned with "Life among the Lowly," the subtitle of *Uncle Tom's Cabin,* because she was used to hard manual labor, and she had no property rights. As a woman she was a disruptive radical, because she had nothing to gain from political patronage. As a woman she felt close ties to the literature of England and Europe, because prominent women writers of the nineteenth century made her feel at least as much at home there as here. As a woman

she had no control over her place of residence. . . . But when young, as a spinster daughter, she was picked up and moved . . . out West to the frontier city of Cincinnati. . . . Harriet Beecher Stowe was thus the only writer of the American Renaissance really to encounter the fugitive slave. . . . No wonder *Uncle Tom's Cabin* was different.

Although in the popular imagination Uncle Tom is taken to be sickeningly submissive, Stowe's actual characterization of Tom surpasses her stereotypical generalizations about the "African race." Uncle Tom is a man of "truly African features," a "large, broad-chested, powerfully made man," self-respecting, dignified, expressing "grave and steady good sense," and "humble simplicity." He is a loving family father, "a sort of patriarch in religious matters," a slave so loyal that he "would lay down his life" for his master. He excuses his master, Mr. Shelby, for selling him because "Mas'r couldn't help hisself." He has the "gentle domestic heart, which . . . has been a peculiar characteristic of his unhappy race," and he is "African" also in being "naturally patient, timid and unenterprising"; yet he shows "heroic courage" when faced with the prospect of being sold down the river. His little weakness consists in being "rather proud of his honesty," since he does not have much else to be proud of compared with people of the higher walks of society. Having read only the New Testament, "he had not learned to generalize and to take enlarged views," that is, he had not been instructed by Christian ministers who regard the buying and selling of slaves as nothing but a lawful trade. The remark about Tom's learning is biting in its irony, one of many which serve to offset the sentimental episodes.

Under his easy-going master St. Clare, a mixture of Byronic aristocrat and Hamlet, Tom is "ever quiet and obliging," showing "apparent contentment." Since his "kindly race" is "ever yearning toward the simple and childlike," little Eva appears to Tom as "almost divine"; "he half believed that he saw one of the angels stepped out of his New Testament." For the kindly St. Clare, as earlier for Mr. Shelby, Tom would lay down his life, not only to protect the physical life of his master but "to see Mas'r a Christian." In contrast to the slave Tom in William Gilmore Simms's *Woodcraft,* Uncle Tom wants his legal freedom desperately, even though he has an unusually kind master and a comfortable life. Under the vicious Legree and his henchmen, Tom acts at first "submissively," but in helping a slave woman fill her basket with cotton, even though he risks brutal punishment by the overseer, and in refusing to beat other slaves or to reveal Cassy's and Emmeline's hiding place, he is a strong and courageous man, an extremely virtuous but not an impossible character. He is more a type than an individual, but so are characters in Cooper, Scott, or Dickens. If he is something of a stereotype, so are the white Yankee Legree, the white Marie St. Clare, and the angelic Eva. Moreover, he is intended to be a type or symbol, for Stowe expresses through him, as through other black characters, her Christian conviction that God lives "among the lowly." "He hides from the wise and prudent, and reveals unto babes."

The modern reader who resents *Uncle Tom's Cabin* "has small reason to resent Tom specifically. He was dutiful to his master and forgiving unto seventy times seven, not because of truckling instincts but because he was a true Christian. Present-day Negro distaste for him means only current lack of sympathy with Christian values," [stated J. C. Furnas in *Goodbye to Uncle Tom*, 1956]." In spite of voicing some of the racial prejudices of her day in describing the "African race," Stowe is aware of the rich cultural heritage of Africa. "Tom looked respectable enough to be a Bishop of Carthage, as men of his color were, in other ages." He is no self-conscious martyr, and his acceptance of torture and death does not show that he lacks a desire for freedom. He keeps hoping "that some way of escape might yet be opened to him," but he feels a commitment to those around him. Legree resents Tom's "commiseration for his fellow-sufferers." When Cassy begs him to help her kill Legree he refuses. He also does not want to join in Cassy's and Emmeline's escape because he feels "the Lord's given me a work among these yer poor souls." He advises the two, however, to flee because "it's more'n you can stand,—and you'd better go, if you can." His refusal to flee has been viewed [by Jean Yellin in *Intricate Knot: Black Figures in American Literature, 1776-1863*, 1972] as a resignation to his condition:

> Tom's refusal to obey his master in obedience to a higher law was a truly revolutionary position in the midcentury America of Thoreau and John Brown, as it has been in Jefferson's time, and is in our own. . . . But the way in which Tom acts out his refusal has in recent years turned his name into a curse. While the mulatto fugitives and their white abolitionist allies portrayed in the novel practice resistance, both passive and active, black Uncle Tom practices Christian resignation.

Tom's nonviolent resistance for the purpose of arousing a tyrant's conscience should not be viewed as resignation. Rather, Uncle Tom is a person "who refuses to acknowledge that he is a thing and who maintains his integrity as a human being against every assault of uninhibited perverse power" [according to Moody E. Prior in "Mrs. Stowe's Uncle Tom," *Critical Inquiry*, Vol. 5, 1979].

Stowe has been accused of other stereotypes in her characterization of blacks. Did she really, unlike the writers of slave narratives and unlike Richard Hildreth in *Archy Moore*, show only submissive blacks and resisting mulattoes? Do the black people in *Uncle Tom's Cabin* always show their true faces to their masters? Is there "no irony" in the black characters of the novel because they are all "static and straightforward"? A look at a wide range of Stowe's black characters will help to answer these questions, and it will also show the "feminine" nature of these figures.

The most outstanding male black character in *Uncle Tom's Cabin* besides Tom himself is George Harris. He expresses more doubt than Christian faith; he resents the patience and obedience toward his master which his wife, Eliza, considers necessary, and he would rather be killed than remain a slave. He and his companion Jim do not hesitate to carry pistols and, after George's "declaration of independence," to shoot anybody who fires at them and their family. George is thus a complete contrast to Tom. In fact, in many of his words and actions he seems almost like a twentieth-century Black Power advocate or Pan-Africanist. Although other abolitionist authors suggest that mulattoes excel and rebel only because of their white heritage of pride and intellect, nowhere does Harriet Beecher Stowe rate white blood higher than black. She lets St. Clare speak of "all our haughty feelings" which burn in the veins of white fathers' sons; and George Harris declares, "If I wished anything, I would wish myself two shades darker, rather than one lighter." She shows the conceitedness of Rosa and Jane, the mulatto chambermaids, who feel far above "low niggers" like Topsy, and many of her all-black characters have much more integrity and strength than the effete, servile, and arrogant mulatto Adolph, although the author evokes sympathy for him also.

George Harris may be modelled after Frederick Douglass, who was also of mixed heritage, and to whom Harriet Beecher Stowe wrote for guidance while composing *Uncle Tom's Cabin,* probably after having read his autobiography. That the fugitives in her novel are mostly mulattoes can be explained by the large percentage of successful fugitives from slavery whose escape through the Southern states was possible only because of their light skin. Moreover, in *Uncle Tom's Cabin* as well as in *Dred,* Stowe illustrates "the enormous importance of nurture in shaping the individual. Although she does not ignore the relevance of hereditary factors, she states unequivocally that training will determine the direction in which an individual's talents will develop." When she describes George Harris as beautiful and daring, she takes over the stereotype used by other abolitionists who portrayed persons of mixed blood favorably; but whereas they usually imagined the heroic mulatto's beauty and intelligence to be in constant conflict with the savage primitivism inherited from his or her black ancestors, George Harris proudly identifies himself with Africans.

The character of Sam, like Tom and George, disproves the premise that the all-black characters of the novel are submissive, that they always show their true faces to their masters, and that they are portrayed without irony. On one level Sam is a stereotype from the minstrel tradition. To please "Missis" he tricks the slave trader Haley by causing repeated delays and frustrations, thereby allowing Eliza to escape. But much more is involved in this comic interlude. "No American author before Mrs. Stowe had realized that the comic inefficiency of a Black Sam could constitute a studied insult to the white man's intelligence," [stated Kenneth S. Lynn]. The images used to describe Sam suggest a defiant hero. His palm-leaf hat is his special symbol; its braids are coming apart and the strands are standing upright, giving it "a blazing air of freedom and defiance, quite equal to that of any Fejee chief." He pretends eager attempts to catch Haley's horse so the chase can begin but actually drives the animal crazy by hiding a sharp little nut under the saddle and brushing the palm-leaf "inadvertently" in its face. "Like the sword of Coeur de Lion, which always blazed in the front and thickest of the battle, Sam's palm-leaf was to be seen everywhere when there was the least danger that a horse could be caught." The imagery is mock-heroic, and yet Sam's ability to talk Haley into taking the wrong route is so cunning that the white trader is made fun of, not the slave. Sam is ridiculed for his vanity as a self-styled politician and orator and his insistence on "principles" because he actually considers only which side his bread is buttered on. But Sam is seen more seriously in his likeness to Senator Bird, who "liked the idea of considering himself a sacrifice to his country." Although the senator helped to pass the Fugitive Slave Law, he shows a kind heart and a helping hand when he is confronted with the fugitive Eliza. In the case of both the black slave and the white senator, their concrete actions are better, more ingenious, and more courageous than their shallow principles.

Sam is not the only black character who puts on a mask before a white master and who is treated ironically by the author. Aunt Chloe supports Sam's game by delaying the dinner for Haley in any way possible. She "warn't a going to have raw gravy on the table, to help nobody's catchings." She also cannot agree with some of Tom's piety. When Tom suggests they should pray even for mean slave catchers, she decides, "Lor, it's too tough! I can't pray for 'em."

Other portrayals of all-black characters are extremely sober. The tragic Prue is driven to despair and alcohol because she is abused as a breeder. Dreams of angelic realms do not sustain her as they do Eva and Tom. Prue does not want to go to heaven because she expects to find white people there. No tearful death scene is painted for her. The brutality of her life and death is consummated in a sentence: "[F]lies had got her,—and she's dead!"

The slave Topsy has been called [in Ellen Moers's *Literary Women*, 1977] Stowe's "most brilliant original creation." The famous catechism scene (which possibly owes something to the similar scene with Pearl in *The Scarlet Letter*) is an ingenious exposure of the lack of understanding of middle-class society and the church for the realities of slave life. "I spect I grow'd. Don't think nobody never made me," declares Topsy in answer to the question of who made her. There is no sentimental fluff in Topsy, at least not until Eva's death. Topsy represents the nihilistic consequences of slavery as much as "the indomitable free spirit of the mischievous, deceitful, troublesome, eternal American child." In a bright touch by the author, the black child exposes the theological absurdity of an absolute predestination for either heaven or hell. "I's so awful wicked there can't nobody do nothin' with me." There is much irony and "masking" in Topsy's behavior. That she ends up as missionary to Africa appears to be a pious cliché, but Stowe makes a good point in a heavy-handed way: there is no racial trait that cannot be changed by environment.

The variety of black characters that surround the famous

Uncle Tom put him in perspective. Many of the strong characters in **Uncle Tom's Cabin,** and in *Dred*, are all-black. Tom's choice of patient suffering is one among many other desperate answers to a desperate situation. His serious treatment stands in contrast to the comedy, irony, and masking in other characters. His "feminine" traits are not meant to illustrate weakness but uncommon strength. This point is also made in St. Clare's story of the slave Scipio. "A powerful, gigantic fellow" and "a native-born African," Scipio has "the rude instinct of freedom in him to an uncommon degree." This "regular African lion" knocked down an overseer, escaped into the swamps, gallantly fought the dogs that hunted him down and finally fell to a gun shot. St. Clare, having laid a wager that he could "break" the man, claimed the wounded slave, nursed him in his own room, set him legally free, and told him he could go wherever he liked. Scipio stayed with him, became a Christian and "gentle as a child," and finally died of cholera after having worked "like a giant" to nurse the cholera-stricken St. Clare back to health. Scipio shows that Stowe's concept of "gentle" Christianity does not connote weakness.

In addition to the wide array of male black images **Uncle Tom's Cabin** offers some outstanding women. Lucy, the suicide, has "grit"; Dinah, the cook, is disorderly but talented and common-sensical; and the mulatto women, Eliza, Cassy, and Emmeline, are especially powerful. These women prove, like the men, that Stowe's portraits of black characters by far transcend her general theoretical statements about racial traits.

The slave Eliza shows strength and daring in her escape from slavery. Her feat of leaping over the icy river seems "impossible to anything but madness and despair." In her later escape to Canada, she dresses up like a man. [As John William Ward stated in *Red, White, and Blue: Men, Books, and Ideas in American Culture,* 1969], "whether Mrs. Stowe was aware of the implications of her decision to put Eliza in the disguise of a man . . . the implications for the meaning of what the woman stands for in **Uncle Tom's Cabin** are immense. The patient, submissive character, ennobled by feeling and symbolized most by the good woman, is simply ineffective."

A much more complex character is Cassy, the quadroon mistress of Legree who later turns out to be Eliza's mother. Whereas mulattoes were invisible in plantation fiction, the abolitionists elevated them to the special role of heroic victim. Their beauty and intelligence were supposed to elicit sympathy from white readers. Stowe alters the stereotype of the beautiful victim in several ways. When the reader meets Cassy, she is no longer beautiful. "Her face was deeply wrinkled with lines of pain." She is not submissive but "blazing with rage and scorn." Showing none of the proverbial piety and patience of so many tragic mulattoes, she is convinced that "the Lord never visits these parts" and that all of Legree's slaves have become cruel to each other beyond redemption. As she relates her painful history to Tom, all the while nursing his wounds, the separation from her children stands out as her most unbearable experience, and she is filled with the desire for revenge. Legree, meanwhile, has come to prefer the newly arrived Emmeline to Cassy, and Cassy knows he will soon ruin the lovely fifteen-year-old girl. "I'll send him where he belongs,—a short way, too—one of these nights, if they burn me alive for it!" She finally begs Tom to help her kill Legree, and when he refuses she insists on doing it on her own. He persuades her to flee instead with Emmeline, and she manages to fool the superstitious Legree with tremendous ingenuity.

The white women of *Uncle Tom's Cabin* are almost as varied as the black. Marie St. Clare appears mostly as the stereotype of the spoiled Southern belle who turns into a sickly and finally vicious planter's wife. Her character is sometimes tiresome, but her exasperating ways make St. Clare's cynicism more plausible. She foreshadows Faulkner's Mrs. Compson, and her inefficiency makes the "Mammy" of the house stand out as forcefully and nobly as the Compsons' Dilsey. Ironically, Marie St. Clare draws a comparison between her lot and that of the slaves, which was not uncommon in the mid-nineteenth-century South but sounds absurd coming from the mouth of the pampered Marie: "It's we mistresses that are the slaves, down here."

A striking contrast to Marie is Miss Ophelia, St. Clare's New England cousin who comes to take care of everything which is left undone by the genteel Marie St. Clare. Ophelia's portrait is an important one in the novel. Her exasperating efficiency points up what she considers to be Southern shiftlessness, and she is a parody of the cold correctness and narrow-mindedness of the New Englander who would rather send missionaries to Africa than touch a black child. In the character of Ophelia, as well as Marie St. Clare, Stowe satirizes those who concentrate only on what slavery does to the soul. Marie admits that black people have immortal souls, but for her that belief does not mean they are equal to whites; and Ophelia for a long time cannot bear the touch of Topsy, but she works on her soul from the first moment of meeting her. Ophelia can look "like one of the Fates." Her management of the house is a "regency." Her progressive attempts at systematic order are doomed by Dinah's clinging to old-fashioned inconveniences and time-honored clutter, out of which she creates "glorious dinners." Miss Ophelia's "labors in all departments that depended on the cooperation of servants were like those of Sisyphus or the Danaides." When Marie St. Clare, "in a faint and lady-like voice, like the last dying breath of an Arabian jessamine," begins to complain about her husband, Ophelia knits energetically and looks "about as sympathizing as a stone lion." Stowe's images for women are varied; there is nothing like a general femininity in her female characters.

Mrs. Shelby, Eliza's beloved mistress, and Mrs. Bird, the Senator's wife, are also individualized. Both are sensitive, kind, trapped by the evils of slavery, and eager to alleviate at least its worst abuses. Eliza calls Mrs. Shelby "a Christian and an angel." Mr. Shelby thinks that his wife suddenly has turned into an abolitionist because Eliza's and Tom's fate has opened her eyes to the fact that slavery cannot be gilded over by pious sermons and kind deeds. She secretly supports Eliza's escape and later manages through Chloe to raise money to buy Tom back. Mr. Shelby thinks that women, including his wife, "don't understand business . . . never do, and never can," but he himself goes into heavy debt, and he keeps his wife from earning money by giving music lessons, an occupation he considers degrading for a lady.

Mrs. Bird is also a woman thought by her husband to undergo a change in attitude. He sees her turning into a politician because she gives a spirited interpretation of the cruelties and absurdities inherent in the Fugitive Slave Law. She is a "timid, blushing little woman . . . with mild blue eyes . . . ; as for courage, a moderate-sized cock turkey had been known to put her to rout at the very first gobble. . . . There was only one thing capable of arousing her . . . ; anything in the shape of cruelty would throw her into a passion." She is determined to break the new law "the first time I get a chance." Soon afterwards when the Senator ignores the law he helped to pass in order to assist Eliza, the author gives us an insight into Mrs. Bird's wifely wisdom: "Now, little Mrs. Bird was a discreet woman,—a woman who never in her life said, 'I told you so!' and, on the present occasion, though pretty well aware of the shape her husband's meditations were taking, she very prudently forbore to meddle with them, only sat very quietly in her chair, and looked quite ready to hear her liege lord's intentions, when he should think proper to utter them." Clearly the woman and the slave are confronted with the same problem: how to circumvent an abstract, inhuman form of government which the "patriarchal institution" of slavery (so called by its supporters) is based on; how to break out of the stifling cash nexus and the pretensions of social class. Women and slaves historically were often united in the same cause. Many planters' wives felt a special resentment for the system of slavery because they were forced to tolerate their husbands' black mistresses and mulatto children. Stowe did not dare to touch on this issue although she herself had an aunt (Mary Foote) who married a West Indian planter and was greeted at his island home by a horde of her husband's mulatto children. From then on she was unhappy, became ill, returned home, and wasted away until her death in the Beecher home when Harriet was two years old.

The white woman whose image touches upon the leitmotif of the novel is Rachel Halliday. Her "face and form . . . made 'mother' seem the most natural word in the world." A Quaker woman, Rachel is motherhood personified. On her "high, placid forehead . . . time had written no inscription, except peace on earth, good will to men, and beneath shone a large pair of clear, honest, loving brown eyes. . . . So much has been said and sung of beautiful young girls, why don't somebody wake up to the beauty of old women?" All the boys and girls of the Quaker settlement "moved obediently to Rachel's gentle 'Thee had better,' or more gentle 'Hadn't thee better?'"

Motherhood of this kind is "the still point of the turning world" of Harriet Beecher Stowe. The religion of love was best expressed in the life of the home and in the mother-child relationship. The authors of the sentimental domestic novels had painted idyllic home scenes or the tragic effects of intemperance on the home, but none had dared to describe the anarchy of the slave's home life. The separation of mother and child, expressed both by the physical separation of slave families at the auction block and by spiritual alienation of white people like St. Clare and Legree, became the central topic of Stowe's novel. Loving relationships are at the heart of the story. The family, especially, is the core of the social community. The focus on "love" often strikes us as sentimental, especially in Eva's pious words. Dying children, however, were not only a staple in nineteenth-century fiction; they were also a heartbreaking reality for mothers in an age that did not have inoculations, antiseptic hospital rooms, and modern medical techniques. (Stowe herself had lost her baby Charles to cholera in 1849.) Moreover, "love" is for Stowe as much a quality of the mind as an emotion. In a letter she writes, "I check myself when expressing feelings like this, so much has been said of it by the sentimental. . . . Love after all is the life blood, the existence, the all in all of mind."

The cult of motherhood was almost sacred in mid-nineteenth-century America: "Books on mothers of famous men, especially Mary Washington . . . poured from the presses in the 1840s and 1850s; their message was that men achieved greatness because of the instruction and inspiration they received from their mothers." In Harriet Beecher, the daughter of the minister Lyman Beecher, the importance of motherhood and women's guiding role receives an added twist. She later wrote in *Oldtown Folks*:

> Woman's nature has never been consulted in theology. Theologic systems, as to the expression of their great body of ideas, have, as yet, been the work of man alone. They have had their origin, as in St. Augustine, with men who were utterly ignorant of moral and intellectual companionship with woman, looking on her only in her animal nature as a temptation and a snare. . . .

> Plato says somewhere that the only perfect human thinker and philosopher who will ever arise will be the MAN-WOMAN, or a human being who unites perfectly the nature of the two sexes.

Stowe believes that woman's nature can be an influence in theological matters and thereby in the reordering of society. As Christian mothers are the true spiritual guides, so God is seen as a loving parent. "We must see what generosity, what tenderness, what magnanimity can be in man and woman, and believe all that and more in God. All that there is in the best fathers and best mothers must be in him." In Harriet Beecher Stowe's works "women are the true spiritual guides." "She never bowed down to the clergy. She was the daughter, the wife, the mother of a clergyman, and the sister of seven clergymen—she understood that breed only too well. But the insight of a Christian mother—ah! that is the norm by which she tests everything."

Women, however, are not the only group which can save society from patriarchy, commercialism, and injustice. Many black people have the same spiritual superiority as women in Stowe's world. This view has been called "romantic racialism." It is based partly on German romanticism and partly on the teaching of Alexander Kinmont, a leading Midwestern exponent of Swedenborgianism, who delivered a series of lectures in Cincinnati in 1837-38 which Stowe may have attended. (Stowe also may have read his works.) The German philosopher Johann Gottfried von Herder emphasized the value and uniqueness of a wide variety of cultural groups, not just four or five biological races. Romantic racialists following Herder saw the black person's innocence and childlike nature as different and beautiful. "To attribute to someone the simplicity of a child . . . especially in the middle of the nineteenth century, was a compliment of the first order," [stated George M. Fredrickson in *The Black Image in the White Mind*, 1971]. The virtues of black people were then further identified with true Christianity. Especially in Stowe's novel *The Minister's Wooing* "women and Negroes are almost interchangeable when it comes to their natural virtues."

Since women and blacks both suffered similar social constraints, feminism and abolitionism were closely allied. While Harriet Beecher Stowe had many reservations about the leading white feminists of her time, she greatly admired the black feminist Sojourner Truth. It is not surprising, then, that the slave Milly in *Dred* and the black Candace in *The Minister's Wooing* are the greatest redemptive characters in her novels. What is surprising is that Uncle Tom is a man. In a letter of 1853 Stowe says of the baby boy she lost through cholera, "It was at his dying bed and at his grave that I learned what a poor slave mother may feel when her child is torn away from her." [According to Elizabeth Ammons] "Stowe's insistence on maternal experience as the generative principle of *Uncle Tom's Cabin* identifies the ethical center of the novel, and helps explain the unusual, and often misunderstood, characterization of Tom." Tom has the traditional virtues of a heroine, of an American Eve, not an American Adam, and he is linked to the girl Eva as well as to a variety of black and white mothers. Everything that is good and true in St. Clare is grounded in the memory of his mother. "Mother" is his last word before his death. Cassy can deceive Legree because she plays the haunting ghost of his mother whose guidance he did not follow. Tom, before he is sold away from the Shelbys, advises young George Shelby, "Al'ays keep close to yer mother. . . . The Lord gives good many things twice over; but he don't give ye a mother but once." Rachel Halliday's motherliness provides George Harris with the first real "home" in his lifetime. Even the rough slave catcher Tom Loker, wounded and abandoned by his fickle friends, remembers the warnings of his mother. But these mothers are not the decorative figures that women usually are in antebellum fiction. They are not pleasing and accommodating but guiding and goading. Although women's virtues are the stereotypical ones of piety, purity, noncompetitiveness, and unselfishness, Stowe's novel [stated Ammons] "proposes as the foundation for a new democratic era, in place of masculine authority, feminine nurture." There is an "obvious contradiction of gender in the Eva/Christ and Tom/heroine associations. . . . The Redeemer from the sins of the fathers in the novel is not, as traditional theology puts it, a second Adam (an emblem utterly familiar of course to anyone who was the daughter, sister, and wife of ministers), but . . . a second Eve."

The traditional understanding of feminine spirituality is satirized through the character of Mr. Shelby. "He really seemed somehow or other to fancy that his wife had piety and benevolence enough for two—to indulge a shadowy expectation of getting into heaven through her superabundance of qualities to which he made no particular pretension." Stowe paints in these lines the picture of the popular "gentleman" of nineteenth-century fiction, but the important question in *Uncle Tom's Cabin* is, "Who can be a *gentle man* in a system where human beings are only things?" The values of maternal nurturing and "feminine" sensitivity to injustice are not, in *Uncle Tom's Cabin,* relegated to the domestic realm of women. In fact, Stowe suggests that if they are—for example, if men like Senator Bird do not practice in politics what they practice under the influence of their wives at home,—then some day "the masses are to rise," as St. Clare puts it. The novelist Lydia Maria Child writes in her *Letters from New York* in 1843:

When Christ said, "Blessed are the meek," did he preach to women only?

Whatsoever can be named as loveliest, best, and most graceful in woman, would likewise be good and graceful in man. You will perhaps remind me of courage. If you use the word in its highest signification . . . woman, above others, has abundant need of it in her pilgrimage. . . . If you mean mere animal courage, that is not mentioned in the Sermon on the Mount.

For Melville neither nonwhites nor women had a specific voice. He represented the injustice done to them mostly by pointing to their silence. Harriet Beecher Stowe indicates in *Uncle Tom's Cabin* that these masses, female and black, are rising, apocalyptically if not democratically, and that the values usually demanded of blacks and women will be healing and saving if all human beings make them their own. "There is a mustering among the masses, the world over; and there is a *dies irae* coming on, sooner or later." "And this, oh Afrika! latest called of nations,—called to the crown of thorns, the scourge, the bloody sweat, the cross of agony,—this is to be thy victory; by this shalt thou reign with Christ when his kingdom shall come on earth."

When Harriet Beecher Stowe was seven years old, her father proudly declared she was a genius, but he immediately qualified the statement by saying that he wished she had been a boy—he would give a hundred dollars if she could be a boy. "The highest compliment which Lyman paid to his daughters was to tell them they were like boys," [stated Gayle Kimball in "Harriet Beecher Stowe's Revision of New England Theology," in the *Journal of*

Presbyterian History, Vol. 58, 1980]. She grew up to be a woman and an artist "whose achievement was to beat daddy at his own game, and, more importantly, to realize far more fully than he the meaning of the religious vocabulary they both employed." The "feminization" of Beecher Calvinism, though often sentimental in vocabulary and imagery, can be understood as a radical reordering of values in which primitive Christianity is rediscovered in those to whom male politicians, church leaders, and "cavaliers" had relegated it: women and blacks. If these two groups are considered primitive, Stowe seems to say, let them show what strength they possess in their powerlessness. A similar point can be made about feminine religion in the nineteenth century in general:

The giving over of religion to women, in its content and in its membership, provided a repository for these female values during the period when the business of building the nation did not immediately require them. . . . The family, popular culture, and religion were the vehicles by which feminine virtues were translated into values.

The constant identification of woman with virtue and with religion reenforced her own belief in her power to overcome obstacles. . . . Religion in its emphasis on the brotherhood of man developed in women a conscious sense of sisterhood, a quality absolutely essential for any kind of meaningful woman's movement.

In some respects, the saving of the world in *Uncle Tom's Cabin* depends on the individualistic, emotional principle of "feeling right": "If the mothers of the free states had all felt as they should, in times past, the sons of the free states would not have been the holders, and, proverbially, the hardest masters of slaves." Yet the new world which the values of the heart would usher in can only be achieved by legal and political means. "One man can do nothing, against the whole action of a community. Education, to do anything, must be a state education; or there must be enough agreed in it to make a current." George Harris knows he cannot change society on his own; therefore he chooses to go to Liberia. "Do you say that I am deserting my enslaved brethren? I think not. If I forget them one hour, one moment of my life, so may God forget me. But, what can I do for them, here? Can I break their chains? No, not as an individual; but let me go and form part of a nation, which shall have a voice in the Councils of nations, and then we can speak." Stowe could never talk about "feeling right" without emphasizing its radical social and political implications. Her very conservatism is a revolutionary force. *Uncle Tom's Cabin* is "the *summa theologica* of nineteenth-century America's religion of domesticity, a brilliant redaction of the culture's favorite story about itself—the story of salvation through motherly love. Out of the ideological materials they had at their disposal, the sentimental novelists elaborated a myth that gave women the central position of power and authority in the culture, and of these efforts Uncle Tom's Cabin is the most dazzling exemplar," [stated Jane P. Tompkins in "Sentimental Power: *Uncle Tom's Cabin* and the Politics of Literary History," *Glyph,* Vol. 8, 1981]. Stowe showed that not only women but also blacks embodied a power that could transform society. Those who were excluded from decision making, the "lowly" of her subtitle, had the greatest understanding of the primitive Christian insight that the meek will inherit the earth, not the submissive meek but the tough meek who, like Uncle Tom, refuse to submit.

Stowe was a democrat. She considered certain Calvinistic tendencies to be simply religious versions of patriarchal order and antiquated royal absolutism claiming "divine right." But another strand of New England Calvinism emphasized the virtues of the heart, the simplicity of the saints, and the genuinely Protestant idea that the most uneducated believer might interpret the Scriptures more accurately than state and church authorities. This conviction led Stowe to celebrate the intuitive strengths and communal instincts of women and slaves who expressed the "sympathies of Christ" as opposed to the "sophistries of worldly policy." It was from the lowly of her society that she expected a new religious and political order to emerge.

Minrose C. Gwin (essay date 1985)

SOURCE: "'A Lie More Palatable than the Truth': Fictional Sisterhood in a Fictional South," in *Black and White Women of the Old South: The Peculiar Sisterhood in American Literature,* The University of Tennessee Press, Knoxville, 1985, pp. 19-43.

[*In the following excerpt, Gwin discusses the relationships between white and black female characters in* Uncle Tom's Cabin, *emphasizing the strength of these bonds against the threat of slavery.*]

In *Uncle Tom's Cabin,* where slavery is linked to the male sphere, the bonds between white and black women not only provide succor but can generate enormous power against that sphere. The bonds between Mrs. Shelby and two of her female slaves, Eliza and Aunt Chloe, provide a literal and metaphorical frame for the novel. All three women characters are stereotypes. Stowe herself acknowledged Mrs. Shelby as "a fair type of the very best class of Southern women"—and the Shelbys' Kentucky farm as "the fairest side of slave-life, where easy indulgence and good-natured forbearance are tempered by just discipline and religious instruction, skilfully and judiciously imparted." Eliza is, of course, the beleaguered mulatta; and Chloe, like Eastman's Phillis, the mammy with the strength to move mountains.

Yet again the real wonder of the novel is that Stowe can bring these women characters to life. Where they operate most dramatically and most believably is in their relationships with one another. This is true even in relationships between women of the same race; one of the most moving relationships in the book is between Cassy, who is looking for a child, and young Emmeline, who needs the protection of a mother. Although many of the interracial

female relationships also are based on the maternal impulse, others are developed in an acknowledgment of common womanhood and common humanistic values. The importance of these female bonds cannot be overstated. More than anything else, they show the generative power of love and devastatingly delineate by contrast the rapacity of a system that tallies human life in profit and loss columns.

The opposition of female and male values becomes immediately apparent in the opening scene of *Uncle Tom's Cabin.* Mr. Shelby's willingness to sell Uncle Tom, his valued faithful slave, is contrasted with his acknowledgment to the trader of Mrs. Shelby's ties with Eliza. The fact that Mrs. Shelby cannot believe that her husband would ever agree to sell Eliza's child ("I would as soon have one of my own children sold," she tells Eliza) reflects not only her attachment to the beautiful quadroon whom she has herself nurtured but the vast gulf between the female and male views of responsibility to valued chattels. Unlike her husband, Mrs. Shelby has committed herself to a parental role which she cannot dismiss merely because there are money troubles.

Even though such a role as conceived by Stowe is surely based on racist presumptions, the bond between the Kentucky mistress and Eliza is described in warm maternal terms. Mrs. Shelby has protected the young beautiful girl from sexual abuse, acted as matchmaker "to unite her handsome favorite with one of her own class who seemed in every way suited to her," adorned Eliza's hair with flowers on her wedding day, and arranged to have her married in her own parlor. In the past she tried to comfort Eliza upon the loss of two infants and "directed her naturally passionate feeling within the bounds of reason and religion." Obviously Stowe couches her description of the mistress-slave relationship in the premise of white superiority; still, there is stark and chilling contrast between Mrs. Shelby's loyalty to Eliza, reflected in her horror at having to sell little Harry—"If I could only at least save Eliza's child, I would sacrifice anything I have," she mourns—and Mr. Shelby's matter-of-fact attitude about selling Tom and Harry: " . . . the price of these two was needed to make up the balance, and I had to give them up."

Mrs. Shelby's loyalty to Eliza actually supersedes her loyalty to her own husband. She is glad when Eliza runs away. To prevent the slave woman's capture, Mrs. Shelby joins the slaves in league against her husband and Haley the trader. She directs Sam and Andy to "lose" the horses; she and Chloe conspire to make dinner late. Once the meal is on the table, she detains the trader "by every female artifice." Her bond with Eliza makes her "feel too much," as her husband says—"an awful feeling of guilt" for having pushed the desperate slave woman to the extreme of risking her life and that of her child on the treacherous ice floes of the frigid Ohio River. Her reaction to the news that Eliza made it to the other side of the river is in ironic contrast to her husband's response. "Are we not both responsible to God for this poor girl? My God! lay not this sin to our charge," she says, to which

Mr. Shelby responds, "What sin, Emily? You see yourself that we have only done what we were obliged to." Likewise, her outraged response to the sale of Eliza's Harry and her willingness to take responsibility for what she considers to be an immoral act against the slave woman contrast sharply with Shelby's lack of emotion and his refusal to take moral responsibility for the selling of Tom. Shelby, never one to accept guilt, absents himself from the farm on the day his loyal slave is to be taken so "that he might not witness the unpleasant scenes of the consummation" of his own act of separating Tom from his family.

Stowe herself maintained [in *A Key to Uncle Tom's Cabin*] that "the worst abuse" of slavery was "its outrage on the family"; and generally she saw women, white and black, as the keepers of moral virtues and domestic values. It is *because* of this ideal of woman as upholder of right action that Marie St. Clare becomes, by contrast, such a despicable character and that Ophelia's racism is so shocking. It is also this maternal, familial ideal that makes Cassy's protectiveness of Emmeline believable and moving. Similarly Chloe's passionate refusal to forgive Mr. Shelby and her wish to send all slave-traders to hell is not so much a black rejection of Christian principles, as David Levin has suggested [in "American Fiction," *Negro American Literature Forum*, Vol. 5, 1972], as a female rejection of the male sphere, which buys and sells human beings for profit and callously disregards familial ties. In *Uncle Tom's Cabin,* then, the bonding of white and black women against the dehumanizing greed of a male marketplace has enormous thematic force.

The plot reverberates with that force. Mr. Shelby's decision to sell Tom and little Harry breaks up two families. Stowe's purpose was, of course, to muster sympathy for black families who lived under the specter of slavery; and her story shows women, black and white, reacting in dismay and rage at the destruction of these families. Eliza, with Aunt Chloe's and Mrs. Shelby's help, flees to safety after her treacherous journey across the ice. The slave woman, who responds with active rebellion to her son's imminent sale, is happily reunited with her husband George in Canada. Meanwhile, Tom's misfortune increases after being separated from his family, going from the relatively easy existence he finds on the Louisiana plantation of the humane Augustine St. Clare to actual torment at the hands of Simon Legree. Although Stowe seems to praise Tom's long-suffering Christianity, his downward plunge in fortune to eventual death shows, interestingly, that his passivity gets him nowhere. He dies, the victim of his own goodness. His relationships with little angelic Eva St. Clare and Legree's mistress Cassy are full of love and tenderness; yet in the end he is, in many ways, beaten by the institution of slavery and the cruelty and inhumanity of its perpetrators Marie St. Clare and Simon Legree. His willingness to suffer and to die contrasts sharply to the active efforts of his wife Chloe to save him by earning money to buy him back. In their denial of passivity, the cross-racial female relationships in the book reflect the implication of plot in *Uncle Tom's Cabin*—that those who do not fight a rapacious system ultimately lose themselves to it.

Stowe's development of women's cross-racial bonds here (and later in *Dred*) has obvious implications for the abolitionist cause: if mistresses and their female slaves can be friends and work toward the same goals, then they may be seen to share a common humanity and a common morality. This relationship also implies a connection in Stowe's mind between feminism and abolitionism. Certainly in the popular mind of the period there resided a strong connection between such "similar repressions" and the submissive virtues of women and blacks. John R. Adams [in his biography *Harriet Beecher Stowe*] and others have suggested that Stowe's sympathy with slaves might be traced to her own experiences with the servitude of domesticity. She was the mother of seven children, one of whom died in infancy. Her professor husband, Calvin, was absent for long periods, and the family often was pinched for money.

As to her feminist views, or lack of them, Stowe has most recently been placed somewhere between what feminist critics and historians call the "domestic feminism" of her older sister Catharine Beecher, who wrote books and articles on the stabilizing influence of women upon society, and the radical feminism of her youngest sister, Isabella Beecher Hooker, who became an avid follower of Victoria Woodhull and who was convinced that the world was soon to become a matriarchy and that she, Isabella, would rule as Christ's vice-regent. Perhaps the single most visceral connection in Stowe's mind between feminism and abolitionism was her intense admiration for Sojourner Truth, the powerful black spokeswoman for human rights during the fifties. Truth, a freed slave who traveled through America in behalf of women's rights and abolition, visited the Stowes in 1853 and won whole-hearted admiration from the whole family. "There was both power and sweetness in that great warm soul and that vigorous frame," Stowe later wrote of "The Libyan Sibyl."

Stowe's moderation in such issues as women's suffrage— she supported but did not actively campaign for the vote— may be due partly to the fact that she was perhaps more concerned about extending the realm of the domestic sphere with its humanistic values into the world around it than moving women out of that sphere into the world of male materialism. Yet, Severn Duvall [in *"Uncle Tom's Cabin*: The Sinister Side of Patriarchy," *New England Quarterly,* Vol. 36, 1963] points to the immense threat that *Uncle Tom's Cabin* and Stowe posed to the southern patriarchy. Like the slave, the white woman had her proper place "on the scale of Nature" and thus in the antebellum familial hierarchy. White southerners were horrified at a woman "unsexing herself" enough to write a novel on slavery, perhaps because for the first time masculine dominance of the southern social order was being challenged publicly.

The antislavery movement, like moral reform and temperance, was at its core in a very deep sense a woman's issue. Northern women were urged to "rise up in the moral power of womanhood; and give utterance to the voice of outraged mercy" and to hear "the sighs, the groans, the death-like struggles of scourged sisters at the South." Theodore Weld's *American Slavery As It Is,* which Stowe claimed to have kept under her pillow during the writing of *Uncle Tom's Cabin,* listed incident after incident of the sexual degradation and physical abuse of slave women. During the 1830s and 1840s thousands of northern and western women formed antislavery societies, and their activism carried them into state and national politics, making them "subjects of intense controversy." The bonding of white and black women in an abolitionist novel and the feminist implications of these fictional cross-racial relationships should not be surprising, then.

It is the relationship between Mrs. Shelby and Chloe which provides the most insight into Stowe's emphasis on the strength of female values and female bonds. Uncle Tom is the submissive Christian; his wife is the Christian warrior. He accepts inhumanity; she rejects it. Together Chloe and Mrs. Shelby become a Christian chorus of remonstration and reproof. The beginning of the book shows them brilliantly playing the womanly roles expected of them in order to save Eliza: Mrs. Shelby is the gracious southern lady making witty conversation at the dinner table to detain the slave trader Haley from taking up the chase; Chloe is the energetic mammy laboring to prepare what *must* be the quintessence of dinners for the white gentleman at that table. Theirs is a concerted effort to save another woman and her child—an effort which probably would have failed had it not *been* concerted. This is perhaps one of the few places in the novel where race becomes unimportant. An invisible, powerful, yet unspoken thread runs from kitchen to table and back; both women work desperately within their own spheres to buy Eliza time, yet their efforts blend and merge into a wonderful, peculiarly female mire of food and talk which engulfs Haley's efforts to take up the chase.

Behind this humorous account of Chloe's bad gravy and Mrs. Shelby's chatter are an intense urgency and an electrifying three-way connection between the two black women and their mistress. There are two integral dramas played out in Eliza's behalf as she frantically races against the clock in her movements across the countryside: Chloe slows time, dragging it out with methodical preparations of "watching and stirring with dogged precision"; and Mrs. Shelby's pleasant cultured voice chats and drones, compartmentalizing the moments, making them fly lightly, imperceptibly. Linked by their manipulations of the same unit of time, the three women challenge male attitudes and actions: Mrs. Shelby circumvents her husband's decision to sell Harry; Chloe rejects Tom's passivity; Eliza rebels against a white, male-controlled system that counts slave children as so many cattle. Stowe shows the strength of this three-way female bond and its humanistic challenge to a dehumanizing system as the epitome of courageous, active love, a balance for Tom's passive Christian response to Legree's evil.

These active women in *Uncle Tom's Cabin* may in fact provide a strong counterargument to the moral and critical dissatisfaction which has given the term *Uncle Tom*

its pejorative sense. In depicting Eliza's escape, Stowe has pitted three women, two of them black, against the white male world—and she has allowed them to win. Nor is it any accident that it is often women—the hostess of the public house, the Quakers, Mrs. Bird—who respond to Eliza's desperation and who actively assist her. While Tom's willingness to endure cruelty and tragedy is in some sense a grand defiance, these women respond against slavery practically and actively. Like Chloe, they decry the system and they cripple it by helping others escape its clutches. It is interesting generally that Stowe chose to make so many of her female characters so active, perhaps with the exceptions of Eva and Marie St. Clare, and so many of her white and black males—Mr. Shelby, Tom, St. Clare—so passive. Only the young men, George Shelby and George Harris, seem to have much force to their personalities.

Throughout the novel, Chloe and Mrs. Shelby continue to cooperate in an actively ongoing effort to return Tom to his home. Mrs. Shelby, who has sworn to repurchase Tom, soon finds that she cannot count on her husband to make any effort to save money toward that end. Possessor of "a clear, energetic, practical mind, and a force of character every way superior to that of her husband," she rejoices in Chloe's proposition that the black cook hire herself out. Together they figure how long Chloe will have to work at the bakery for four dollars a week to save enough to buy Tom back and Mrs. Shelby promises to save what she can to add to Chloe's earnings. Significantly, the scene in which Chloe and her mistress make these arrangements is preceded by one in which Mrs. Shelby begs her husband to straighten out his financial matters by selling some of his horses or farms. When he refuses (we are given the distinct feeling that Mr. Shelby could have sold something besides Uncle Tom to even up his debts) and she suggests that she herself earn money by giving music lessons, he reacts with indignation: "You wouldn't degrade yourself that way, Emily? I never could consent to it." We are reminded of his horrified response to Eliza's escape after he has promised Harry to the slave trader: "It touches my honor!" Mr. Shelby's concern with his "honor" seems to supersede all moral obligations. His negative response to his wife's pleadings is thus a strong contrast to her own affirmative response to Chloe's request, which will leave the Shelby household without a cook.

Actually Mrs. Shelby and Chloe seem closer emotionally and ideologically than either woman does to her own husband. Though both are fond of their husbands—Chloe is certainly heartbroken over the sale of Tom—they refuse to share their husbands' attitudes toward slavery. Just as Mrs. Shelby cannot accept her husband's idea of slaves as convenient means of settling debts, so Chloe rejects Tom's Christian acceptance of his fate. " . . . de Lord lets drefful things happen, sometimes," she says. "I don't seem to get no comfort dat way." Despite Tom's protests, she places blame where it is due—directly upon Mr. Shelby. "Mas'r never ought ter left it so that ye *could* be took for his debts. . . . Them as sells heart's love and heart's blood, to get out thar scrapes, de Lord'll be up to 'em!" Unlike their husbands, both women hold individuals morally accountable for their actions.

The tie that binds Chloe and Mrs. Shelby is further strengthened by their joint role as a chorus of lamentation at what Stowe felt to be the central evil of slavery—the disruption of family ties. Twice Mrs. Shelby shares Chloe's grief, first when Tom is sold away and finally at the end of the book, when George comes home without Tom. Unrealistic as these scenes are, there is a sense in both of shared female outrage. Interestingly, in each scene Chloe is presented as first rejecting Mrs. Shelby's displays of mutual sorrow, and then accepting the white woman as fellow mourner. Stowe was aware, seemingly, that the black woman may resent a white woman's intrusion into her own peculiar realm of despair. When, as she is preparing Tom's belongings for his journey, Chloe receives word that "Missis" is coming, she immediately retorts, "She can't do no good; what's she coming for?" When Mrs. Shelby enters her cabin, Chloe sets a chair for her "in a manner decidedly gruff and crusty." It is only when Mrs. Shelby sits down and begins to sob that Chloe ceases to associate her mistress with Mr. Shelby's devastating decision to sell Tom, accepts her common grief, and finally weeps with her.

Likewise, when Chloe is told of her husband's death, she deals Mrs. Shelby a gesture of rejection by giving her the money she had earned for Tom's freedom: "'Thar,' said she, gathering it up, and holding it, with a trembling hand, to her mistress, 'don't never want to see nor hear on 't again. Jist as I knew 't would be,—sold, and murdered on dem ar' old plantations!'" But when Mrs. Shelby responds only with sympathy and grief—"My poor, good Chloe!"—the black woman accepts her as a fellow mourner and again all weep together and lament Tom's death and the system that caused it. This mutuality of grief, though limited always by the fact that Mrs. Shelby and Chloe are stereotypes based on racial myth, is nonetheless moving. We are reminded of archetypal scenes of women throughout history weeping for their lost men and lamenting the loss of peace and harmony among men. To have black and white women join in this timeless chorus of grief extends the dimensions of the novel from the polemic to the mythic.

These dynamic female bonds also define the concept of motherhood in *Uncle Tom's Cabin*. Since what it means to be a mother is so closely tied in the novel to what it means to be a true Christian and a caring human being, the process of defining a good mother becomes a basic pattern that knits the novel together. Weaving in and out of the relationships between black and white women, the maternal impulse, or lack of it, becomes a criterion upon which to judge their humanity. Mrs. Shelby teaches Eliza how to be a good mother. Mammy mothers Eva when the child's own mother, Marie St. Clare, shows no maternal interest in her daughter. Eva mothers Topsy when Ophelia's racism precludes such nurture. The depravity of Prue's mistress is felt so intensely because she interferes with Prue's maternal impulses; she refuses to give the black woman milk to feed her starving infant. As Elizabeth Ammons points out [in "Heroines in *Uncle Tom's Cabin*," *Critical Essays on Harriet Beecher Stowe*, 1980], the cruel separations between mothers and children in *Uncle Tom's Cabin* dramatize "the root evil of slavery: the displacement of life-giving maternal values by a profit-hungry masculine ethic; . . . mothers and motherless children show the human cost of the system." Stowe herself says that she wrote *Uncle Tom's Cabin* because of her own empathy with slave mothers. After the death of her infant son, she writes, "at his grave . . . I learned what a poor slave mother may feel when her child is torn away from her."

The discrepancy between Marie's selfishness and indifference to maternal obligation and Mammy's loving maternal nurture is meant to be particularly acute. Marie's relationships both to her own daughter and to her black servant illuminate the white mother's egocentric corruption and illustrate Stowe's thesis that total power breeds evil. Unlike Mrs. Shelby, who is described by the author as "a fair type of the very best class of Southern women," Marie St. Clare is "the type of a class of women not peculiar to any latitude, nor any condition of society." In the North, Stowe writes, such a woman has "no end to her troubles" in retaining servants, whom she invariably overworks and underpays. But with the absolute control which slavery permits her, the southern Marie becomes an unleashed fury who can do as she wills to whom she likes and inflict "the most disgraceful and violent punishments." More subtle torture she measures out upon Mammy, keeping the black woman at her beck and call every night and then complaining at Mammy's "selfishness" in sleeping so soundly. Like Prue's mistress, Marie shows her inhumanity by denying Mammy her own children. Marie is characterized as less than a whole woman, having "no heart," thoroughly selfish. Her relationship with black women—her inhumane treatment of Mammy and later sending Rosa to be whipped—serves as an index of her total corruption, as does her marked lack of interest in her own daughter.

In contrast, Mammy's love for Eva and her nurture of the white child show the black woman's humanity and unselfishness. The scene in which Eva returns home with her father and Ophelia reveals the vast difference between Marie's and Mammy's responses to the child. Stowe draws the distinction heavy-handedly. When Eva kisses her mother, Marie's response is half-hearted: "'That'll do,—take care, child,—don't you make my head ache,' said the mother, after she had languidly kissed her." But as Eva kisses Mammy, Stowe writes, "this woman did not tell her that she made her head ache, but on the contrary, she hugged her, and laughed, and cried, till her sanity was a thing to be doubted of. . . ." While Marie takes no notice of the child's declining health and strength, Mammy is acutely aware of Eva's oncoming death. More than that, Mammy, like Tom, intuitively knows Eva for who she is—a rare and mysterious good spirit whose time on earth is limited. Like Tom, who sees "the Lord's mark in her forehead," Mammy knows Eva "wasn't never like a child that's to live—there was allers something deep in her eyes."

Marie is obviously jealous of Mammy and Eva's closeness. One of her most despicable acts is to keep the black woman away from Eva's deathbed with her own incessant demands, "so that stolen interviews and momentary glimpses" of Eva are all Mammy can obtain. The relationship between Marie and Mammy is characterized by the white woman's constraints upon the black woman's maternal feelings. Marie denies Mammy her own children and later her surrogate child. Though these denials are only one facet of Marie's egocentricity, they are telling ones. Marie is not only a bad mother herself; she forces Mammy to be one as well. Stowe shows in this relationship the institution of slavery at its worst. It is the system which permits Marie to control Mammy's maternal impulses—surely a power no woman should have over another.

Just as Marie will not fulfill her maternal obligations, Ophelia's antipathy for blacks makes her unwilling to provide much-needed nurture for Topsy. Interestingly, Eva, who is denied the same nurturance by her own mother but given it freely by Mammy, steps into that role with Topsy, who has internalized much of the racial hatred directed toward her during her short life. In a most significant way, Eva becomes the force which moves Topsy from self-hate and forces Ophelia to see the psychological destructiveness of her own racism. While Mammy provides the positive maternal force in the Marie-Mammy-Eva relationship, Eva is the sustainer of true motherhood in the Ophelia-Eva-Topsy triangle. With a childish mother herself, Eva takes on the cloak of motherhood that saves Topsy. Although the scene is overdone, Eva's "burst of feeling" and her pronouncement of love are moving in that they seem to engender in Topsy, for the first time in her life, a sense of self-worth and a realization that she was wrong in thinking "there can't nobody love niggers, and niggers can't do nothin'!" Though as children they are mirror images, Eva saves Topsy by mothering her. The vitality and all-encompassing nature of this motherlove give the black girl peace and wholeness. It also shows Ophelia the psychological destruction caused by racism and helps her overcome her aversion to Topsy so that she can learn to be a true mother to the child.

True motherhood is often denied the slave women of the novel. Nowhere is this denial felt more deeply than in Prue's story. Simon Legree's cruelty seems mild compared to that of Prue's mistress, who refuses to buy milk for the slave mother to feed her starving infant. When the child "cried, and cried, and cried, day and night," the white woman forces Prue to put the infant away in a garret where it starves to death, wailing continuously. Prue's misery at the child's murder makes her wish for her own death, which—grotesque though it is—puts her at last out of imaginary earshot of her dying infant's crying. The white woman's denial of food for the child is worsened by the fact that Prue's own milk dried up as the result of a fever contracted by nursing her mistress.

In the shadowy character of this villainous mistress surely Stowe, whose own children were so important to her, was

sketching the worst that could be said of slavery. When white women embrace the materialistic dehumanization of slavery, depicted as a male attitude in this novel, they seem to become so warped and twisted by absolute power that they deny the maternal bonds that link them to all women (those that Mrs. Shelby, Eliza, and Chloe feel so deeply), and become asexual monsters who destroy human lives and psyches more out of pique and carelessness than conscious cruelty. In this fiction, slavery generates such female monsters, and they are best shown through their relationships with those over whom they exert the most power, yet with whom they should feel the most common bond—black women.

Yet these relationships in *Uncle Tom's Cabin* most often show white and black women in a peculiarly female and often powerful opposition to the materialism of slavery; as such, these bonds reveal the vast gulf between humanistic values and materialistic assessments of human life. What it means to be human in the profoundest sense is often connected to what it means to be truly maternal—to nurture others, as Eva does Topsy, and so to encourage generative growth in lives other than one's own. Motherhood and Christian nurture are closely associated. In a sense, then, Marie St. Clare and Prue's mistress become in their relationships with their black women slaves more evil than Legree himself. They deny their own maternal impulses as well as those of their slaves; they are thus doubly evil. Yet they demand maternal nurture for themselves from those same women. In their relationships with black women, they become children and evil ones at that, whose behavior shows above all the sinful nature of all human beings, and the horrifying consequences of allowing that sinful nature full rein.

George Goodin (essay date 1985)

SOURCE: "The Virtuous Victim: *Les Misérables, Billy Budd, The Power and the Glory, Uncle Tom's Cabin*," in *The Poetics of Protest: Literary Form and Political Implication in the Victim-of-Society Novel,* Southern Illinois University Press, 1985, pp. 51-86.

[*In the following excerpt, Goodin discusses the characterization of Tom and the ending of the novel in relation to themes of resistance and community.*]

As [Stowe's] title ought to suggest, [*Uncle Tom's Cabin*] is largely the story of a community. According to Stowe's 1878 essay "The Story of *Uncle Tom's Cabin*," the novel's animus was the Fugitive Slave Law of 1850, which required even the citizens of the Free North to consider slaves merely as property by turning them in if they escaped from their masters. Its germ was a story about a young slave woman who escaped with her child by leaping from one ice floe to another on the Ohio River, and the story of another slave who would not escape because he would not violate the trust his master had bestowed on him. It is the story, then, of escape and the refusal to escape, of the Harris family and of Uncle Tom, two different virtuous victims.

Eliza Harris shuns the very idea of escape until threatened with the sale of her son Harry to a trader who has admired the boy's intelligence. Her husband, George, has already decided to escape because his master's envy of his learning and inventiveness has led to a systematic attempt to degrade him. He decides to be free, and from the moment of his decision he is because he is willing to fight to death for his freedom. The successful escape and reunion of his family dominate the first quarter of the novel. Even afterwards, it occasionally counterpoints the sufferings of Tom.

Tom is sold away from his family because he is more valuable than the other slaves. He permits himself to be sold, instead of escaping as he encourages others to do, not because he is the abject and passive Christian darky that James Baldwin and others have seen in him, but because his alternative is to see many of his fellow slaves sold down the river to pay his master's debt. In this respect Stowe varied the story from her original germ. She showed him refusing to escape not out of loyalty to his master, but out of loyalty to his own community. Undoubtedly, she confronted him with such drastic alternatives because it is difficult to write a novel about life under slavery without some characters who do not escape from it.

The stories of Uncle Tom and the Harrises permit Stowe to present an extremely wide array of antagonists throughout the middle of the novel. Tom Loker is a brutal slave-catcher and Marks a canting one who pretends to be humane in order to keep from decreasing the value of those he pursues. Slave masters likewise range from negative to positive antagonists, with a higher proportion of the latter so that Stowe can show slavery at its best and still show it wrong as a system. By showing its terrible effects on masters as well as slaves, she raises the grim possibility that this enormous legalized injustice served no one's real interests. It is this great range and complexity that led Edmund Wilson to count himself with Henry James among the novel's admirers: "The farther one reads in *Uncle Tom,* the more one becomes aware that a critical mind is at work, which has the complex situation in a very firm grip and which, no matter how vehement the characters become, is controlling and coordinating their interrelations." The novel achieves whatever literary value one might assign it largely because of the propagandistic purpose and political passion of its writer, casting great doubt on the presumption that literary and political values must always conflict. And if the story is true that Abraham Lincoln saluted Stowe as the one who brought on the Civil War, then—even allowing for presidential hyperbole—the novel casts doubt too on the presumption that social protest novels have no liberating effects on politics.

The ending of *Uncle Tom's Cabin* was written first, and everything leads to it. In it . . . , we can see the shape of the beginning of the virtuous victim's story, the initial conversion reported but not presented. Tom is sold from the estate to St. Claire, the most positive of the novel's antagonists, to Simon Legree, the most negative. Like

Claggart, Legree has a "native antipathy of bad to good." He too operates by trying to subvert social bonds.

> Legree, like some potentates we read of in history, governed his plantation by a sort of resolution of forces. Sambo and Quimbo cordially hated each other; the plantation hands, one and all, cordially hated them; and, by playing off one against another, he was pretty sure, through one or the other of the three parties, to get informed of whatever was on foot in the place.

He is a northerner who has given up his puritanical religion and channeled its intensity into moneymaking. He is a test case for the anti-abolitionist view that masters would take care of their slaves out of their own self-interest. His own is a slender reed bending to an irrationality which ruins not only others but also himself.

Legree buys Tom to use him as a driver, an instrument for oppressing his fellows. When Tom insists on helping a weak mulatto woman, Legree orders him to flog her instead. When Tom refuses, he himself is beaten. He is befriended by Cassy, who urges him to give in.

> "It's no use, my poor fellow!" she broke out at last, "it's of no use, this you've been trying to do. You were a brave fellow,—you had the right on your side; but it's all in vain, and out of the question, for you to struggle. You are in the devil's hands;—he is the strongest, and you must give up!" . . .

> "There's no law here, of God or man, that can do you, or any one of us, the least good; and, this man! there's no earthly thing that he's too good to do. I could make any one's hair rise, and their teeth chatter, if I should only tell what I've seen and been knowing to, here,— and it's no use resisting."

Tom continues to resist Legree, but becomes despondent and enters a dark night of the soul.

Legree comes to pressure him anew. He is desperate because of Tom's resistance. He wants to crush it and substitute himself for the church that sustains it, but he shows Tom all too clearly the alternatives.

> When a heavy weight presses the soul to the lowest level at which endurance is possible, there is an instant and desperate effort of every physical and moral nerve to throw off the weight; and hence the heaviest anguish often precedes a return tide of joy and courage. So was it now with Tom. The atheistic taunts of his cruel master sunk his dejected soul to the lowest ebb; and, though the hand of faith still held to the eternal rock, it was with a numb, despairing grasp. Tom sat, like one stunned, at the fire. Suddenly everything around him seemed to fade, and a vision rose before him of one crowned with thorns, buffeted and bleeding. Tom gazed, in awe and wonder, at the majestic patience of the face; the deep, pathetic eyes thrilled him to his inmost heart; his soul woke, as, with floods of emotion, he stretched out his hands and fell upon his knees,— when, gradually, the vision changed: the sharp thorns became rays of glory.

This reaffirmation of an earlier conversion makes clear the values of resistance and community which motivate Tom throughout the novel. Legree's power starts to break, and Tom becomes a center holding the slaves together. He can encourage others to escape and help them, but he cannot leave his beleaguered community. For helping others, he is killed by Legree, and the novel shifts to the survivors, including the Harrises. Once more, a double ending serves to contrast not passivity and activity but the death of an individual and the survival of his community. The community survival in the end is immanent in the invulnerability it lends the hero; the death of the individual in the end is immanent throughout in his selflessness. It is a fall, but not entirely a defeat.

Jane Tompkins (essay date 1985)

SOURCE: "Sentimental Power: *Uncle Tom's Cabin* and the Politics of Literary History," in *Sensational Designs: The Cultural Work of American Fiction, 1790-1860,* Oxford University Press, Inc., 1985, pp. 122-46.

[*In the following excerpt, Tompkins defends the value of* Uncle Tom's Cabin *as a work of sentimental fiction, discussing Stowe's attention to nineteenth-century women's culture and her vision of social reform.*]

[The] popular domestic novel of the nineteenth century represents a monumental effort to reorganize culture from the woman's point of view; that this body of work is remarkable for its intellectual complexity, ambition, and resourcefulness; and that, in certain cases, it offers a critique of American society far more devastating than any delivered by better-known critics such as Hawthorne and Melville. Finally, it suggests that the enormous popularity of these novels, which has been cause for suspicion bordering on disgust, is a reason for paying close attention to them. *Uncle Tom's Cabin* was, in almost any terms one can think of, the most important book of the century. It was the first American novel ever to sell over a million copies and its impact is generally thought to have been incalculable. Expressive of and responsible for the values of its time, it also belongs to a genre, the sentimental novel, whose chief characteristic is that it is written by, for, and about women. In this respect, *Uncle Tom's Cabin* is not exceptional but representative. It is the *summa theologica* of nineteenth-century America's religion of domesticity, a brilliant redaction of the culture's favorite story about itself—the story of salvation through motherly love. Out of the ideological materials at their disposal, the sentimental novelists elaborated a myth that gave women the central position of power and authority in the culture; and of these efforts *Uncle Tom's Cabin* is the most dazzling exemplar.

I have used words like "monumental" and "dazzling" to describe Stowe's novel and the tradition of which it is a part because they have for too long been the casualties of a set of critical attitudes that equate intellectual merit with a certain kind of argumentative discourse and certain kinds of subject matter. A long tradition of academic parochi-alism has enforced this sort of discourse through a series of cultural contrasts: light "feminine" novels vs. tough-minded intellectual treatises; domestic "chattiness" vs. serious thinking; and summarily, the "damned mob of scribbling women" vs. a few giant intellects, unappreciated and misunderstood in their time, struggling manfully against a flood of sentimental rubbish.

The inability of twentieth-century critics either to appreciate the complexity and scope of a novel like Stowe's, or to account for its enormous popular success, stems from their assumptions about the nature and function of literature. In modernist thinking, literature is by definition a form of discourse that has no designs on the world. It does not attempt to change things, but merely to represent them, and it does so in a specifically literary language whose claim to value lies in its uniqueness. Consequently, works whose stated purpose is to influence the course of history, and which therefore employ a language that is not only not unique but common and accessible to everyone, do not qualify as works of art. Literary texts, such as the sentimental novel, that make continual and obvious appeals to the reader's emotions and use technical devices that are distinguished by their utter conventionality, epitomize the opposite of everything that good literature is supposed to be. "For the literary critic," writes J. W. Ward [in *Red, White, and Blue: Men, Books, and Ideas in American Culture*, 1961], summing up the dilemma posed by *Uncle Tom's Cabin,* "the problem is how a book so seemingly artless, so lacking in apparent literary talent, was not only an immediate success but has endured."

How deep the problem goes is illustrated dramatically by George F. Whicher's discussion of Stowe's novel in *The Literary History of the United States* [1963]. Reflecting the consensus view on what good novels are made of, Whicher writes: "Nothing attributable to Mrs. Stowe or her handiwork can account for the novel's enormous vogue; its author's resources as a purveyor of Sunday-school fiction were not remarkable. She had at most a ready command of broadly conceived melodrama, humor, and pathos, and of these popular elements she compounded her book." At a loss to understand how a book so compounded was able to "convulse a mighty nation," Whicher concludes—incredibly—that Stowe's own explanation that "God wrote it" "solved the paradox." Rather than give up his bias against "melodrama," "pathos," and "Sunday-school fiction," Whicher takes refuge in a solution that, even according to his lights, is patently absurd. And no wonder. The modernist literary aesthetic cannot account for the unprecedented and persistent popularity of a book like *Uncle Tom's Cabin,* for this novel operates according to principles quite other than those that have been responsible for determining the currently sanctified American literary classics.

It is not my purpose, however, to drag Hawthorne and Melville from their pedestals, nor to claim that the novels of Stowe, Fanny Fern, and Elizabeth Stuart Phelps are good in the same way that *Moby-Dick* and *The Scarlet Letter* are; rather, I will argue that the work of the sentimental writers is complex and significant in ways other than those that characterize the established masterpieces. I will ask the reader to set aside some familiar categories for evaluating fiction—stylistic intricacy, psychological subtlety, epistemological complexity—and to see the sentimental novel not as an artifice of eternity answerable to certain formal criteria and to certain psychological and philosophical concerns, but as a political enterprise, halfway between sermon and social theory, that both codifies and attempts to mold the values of its time.

The power of a sentimental novel to move its audience depends upon the audience's being in possession of the conceptual categories that constitute character and event. That storehouse of assumptions includes attitudes toward the family and toward social institutions; a definition of power and its relation to individual human feeling; notions of political and social equality; and above all, a set of religious beliefs that organizes and sustains the rest. Once in possession of the system of beliefs that undergirds the patterns of sentimental fiction, it is possible for modern readers to see how its tearful episodes and frequent violations of probability were invested with a structure of meanings that fixed these works, for nineteenth-century readers, not in the realm of fairy tale or escapist fantasy, but in the very bedrock of reality. I do not say that we can read sentimental fiction exactly as Stowe's audience did—that would be impossible—but that we can and should set aside the modernist prejudices which consign this fiction to oblivion, in order to see how and why it worked for its readers, in its time, with such unexampled effect.

Let us consider the episode in *Uncle Tom's Cabin* most often cited as the epitome of Victorian sentimentalism— the death of little Eva—because it is the kind of incident most offensive to the sensibilities of twentieth-century academic critics. It is on the belief that this incident is nothing more than a sob story that the whole case against sentimentalism rests. Little Eva's death, so the argument goes, like every other sentimental tale, is awash with emotion but does nothing to remedy the evils it deplores. Essentially, it leaves the slave system and the other characters unchanged. This trivializing view of the episode is grounded in assumptions about power and reality so common that we are not even aware they are in force. Thus generations of critics have commented with condescending irony on little Eva's death. But in the system of belief that undergirds Stowe's enterprise, dying is the supreme form of heroism. In *Uncle Tom's Cabin,* death is the equivalent not of defeat but of victory; it brings an access of power, not a loss of it; it is not only the crowning achievement of life, it is life, and Stowe's entire presentation of little Eva is designed to dramatize this fact.

Stories like the death of little Eva are compelling for the same reason that the story of Christ's death is compelling; they enact a philosophy, as much political as religious, in which the pure and powerless die to save the powerful and corrupt, and thereby show themselves more powerful than those they save. They enact, in short, a *theory* of power in which the ordinary or "common sense" view of what is efficacious and what is not (a view to which most

modern critics are committed) is simply reversed, as the very possibility of social action is made dependent on the action taking place in individual hearts. Little Eva's death enacts the drama of which all the major episodes of the novel are transformations, the idea, central to Christian soteriology, that the highest human calling is to give one's life for another. It presents one version of the ethic of sacrifice on which the entire novel is based and contains in some form all of the motifs that, by their frequent recurrence, constitute the novel's ideological framework.

Little Eva's death, moreover, is also a transformation of a story circulating in the culture at large. It may be found, for example, in a dozen or more versions in the evangelical sermons of the Reverend Dwight Lyman Moody which he preached in Great Britain and Ireland in 1875. In one version it is called "The Child Angel" and it concerns a beautiful golden-haired girl of seven, her father's pride and joy, who dies and, by appearing to him in a dream in which she calls to him from heaven, brings him salvation. The tale shows that by dying even a child can be the instrument of redemption for others, since in death she acquires a spiritual power over those who loved her beyond what she possessed in life.

The power of the dead or the dying to redeem the unregenerate is a major theme of nineteenth-century popular fiction and religious literature. Mothers and children are thought to be uniquely capable of this work. In a sketch entitled **"Children,"** published the year after *Uncle Tom* came out, Stowe writes: "Wouldst thou know, o parent, what is that faith which unlocks heaven? Go not to wrangling polemics, or creeds and forms of theology, but draw to thy bosom thy little one, and read in that clear trusting eye the lesson of eternal life." If children because of their purity and innocence can lead adults to God while living, their spiritual power when they are dead is greater still. Death, Stowe argues in a pamphlet entitled *Ministration of Departed Spirits,* enables the Christian to begin his "real work." God takes people from us sometimes so that their "ministry can act upon us more powerfully from the unseen world."

> The mother would fain electrify the heart of her child. She yearns and burns in vain to make her soul effective on its soul, and to inspire it with a spiritual and holy life; but all her own weaknesses, faults and mortal cares, cramp and confine her till death breaks all fetters; and then, first truly alive, risen, purified, and at rest, she may do calmly, sweetly, and certainly, what, amid the tempest and tossings of her life, she labored for painfully and fitfully.

When the spiritual power of death is combined with the natural sanctity of childhood, the child becomes an angel endowed with salvific force.

Most often, it is the moment of death that saves, when the dying child, glimpsing for a moment the glory of heaven, testifies to the reality of the life to come. Uncle Tom knows that this will happen when little Eva dies, and explains it to Miss Ophelia as follows:

"You know it says in Scripture, 'At midnight there was a great cry made. Behold the bridegroom cometh.' That's what I'm spectin now, every night, Miss Feely,—and I could n't sleep out o' hearin', no ways."

"Why, Uncle Tom, what makes you think so?"

"Miss Eva, she talks to me. The Lord, he sends his messenger in the soul. I must be thar, Miss Feely; for when that ar blessed child goes into the kingdom, they'll open the door so wide, we'll all get a look in at the glory, Miss Feely."

Little Eva does not disappoint them. She exclaims at the moment when she passes "from death unto life": "O, love,—joy,—peace!" And her exclamation echoes those of scores of children who die in Victorian fiction and sermon literature with heaven in their eyes. Dickens' Paul Dombey, seeing the face of his dead mother, dies with the words: "The light about the head is shining on me as I go!" The fair, blue-eyed young girl in Lydia Sigourney's *Letters to Mothers,* "death's purple tinge upon her brow," when implored by her mother to utter one last word, whispers "Praise!"

Of course, it could be argued by critics of sentimentalism that the prominence of stories about the deaths of children is precisely what is wrong with the literature of the period; rather than being cited as a source of strength, the presence of such stories in **Uncle Tom's Cabin** could be regarded as an unfortunate concession to the age's fondness for lachrymose scenes. But to dismiss such scenes as "all tears and flapdoodle" is to leave unexplained the popularity of the novels and sermons that are filled with them, unless we choose to believe that a generation of readers was unaccountably moved to tears by matters that are intrinsically silly and trivial. That popularity is better explained, I believe, by the relationship of these scenes to a pervasive cultural myth which invests the suffering and death of an innocent victim with just the kind of power that critics deny to Stowe's novel: the power to work in, and change, the world.

This is the kind of action that little Eva's death in fact performs. It proves its efficacy not through the sudden collapse of the slave system, but through the conversion of Topsy, a motherless, godless black child who has up until that point successfully resisted all attempts to make her "good." Topsy will not be "good" because, never having had a mother's love, she believes that no one can love her. When Eva suggests that Miss Ophelia would love her if only she were good, Topsy cries out: "No; she can't bar me, 'cause I'm a nigger!—she'd's soon have a toad touch her! There can't nobody love niggers, and niggers can't do nothin'! *I* don't care."

"O, Topsy, poor child, *I* love you!" said Eva, with a sudden burst of feeling, and laying her little thin, white hand on Topsy's shoulder; "I love you, because you have n't had any father, or mother, or friends;—because you've been a poor, abused child! I love you, and I want you to be good. I am very unwell, Topsy, and I think I shan't live a great while; and it really grieves

me, to have you be so naughty. I wish you would try to be good, for my sake;—it's only a little while I shall be with you."

The round, keen eyes of the black child were overcast with tears;—large, bright drops rolled heavily down, one by one, and fell on the little white hand. Yes, in that moment, a ray of real belief, a ray of heavenly love, had penetrated the darkness of her heathen soul! She laid her head down between her knees, and wept and sobbed,—while the beautiful child, bending over her, looked like the picture of some bright angel stooping to reclaim a sinner.

The rhetoric and imagery of this passage—its little white hand, its ray from heaven, bending angel, and plentiful tears—suggest a literary version of the kind of polychrome religious picture that hangs on Sunday-school walls. Words like "kitsch," "camp," and "corny" come to mind. But what is being dramatized here bears no relation to these designations. By giving Topsy her love. Eva initiates a process of redemption whose power, transmitted from heart to heart, can change the entire world. And indeed the process has begun. From that time on, Topsy is "different from what she used to be" (eventually she will go to Africa and become a missionary to her entire race), and Miss Ophelia, who overhears the conversation, is different, too. When little Eva is dead and Topsy cries out "ther an't *nobody* left now," Miss Ophelia answers her in Eva's place:

"Topsy, you poor child," she said, as she led her into her room, "don't give up! *I* can love you, though I am not like that dear little child. I hope I've learnt something of the love of Christ from her. I can love you; I do, and I'll try to help you to grow up a good Christian girl."

Miss Ophelia's voice was more than her words, and more than that were the honest tears that fell down her face. From that hour, she acquired an influence over the mind of the destitute child that she never lost.

The tears of Topsy and of Miss Ophelia, which we find easy to ridicule, are the sign of redemption in **Uncle Tom's Cabin;** not words, but the emotions of the heart bespeak a state of grace, and these are known by the sound of a voice, the touch of a hand, but chiefly, in moments of greatest importance, by tears. When Tom lies dying on the plantation on the Red River, the disciples to whom he has preached testify to their conversion by weeping.

Tears had fallen on that honest, insensible face,—tears of late repentance in the poor, ignorant heathen, whom his dying love and patience had awakened to repentance. . . .

Even the bitter and unregenerate Cassy, moved by "the sacrifice that had been made for her," breaks down; "moved by the few last words which the affectionate soul had yet strength to breathe, . . . the dark, despairing woman had wept and prayed." When George Shelby, the son of

Tom's old master, arrives too late to free him, "tears which did honor to his manly heart fell from the young man's eyes as he bent over his poor friend." And when Tom realizes who is there, "the whole face lighted up, the hard hands clasped, and tears ran down the cheeks." The vocabulary of clasping hands and falling tears is one which we associate with emotional exhibitionism, with the overacting that kills off true feeling through exaggeration. But the tears and gestures of Stowe's characters are not in excess of what they feel; if anything they fall short of expressing the experiences they point to—salvation, communion, reconciliation.

If the language of tears seems maudlin and little Eva's death ineffectual, it is because both the tears and the redemption that they signify belong to a conception of the world that is now generally regarded as naive and unrealistic. Topsy's salvation and Miss Ophelia's do not alter the anti-abolitionist majority in the Senate or prevent southern plantation owners and northern investment bankers from doing business to their mutual advantage. Because most modern readers regard such political and economic facts as final, it is difficult for them to take seriously a novel that insists on religious conversion as the necessary precondition for sweeping social change. But in Stowe's understanding of what such change requires, it is the *modern* view that is naive. The political and economic measures that constitute effective action for us, she regards as superficial, mere extensions of the worldly policies that produced the slave system in the first place. Therefore, when Stowe asks the question that is in every reader's mind at the end of the novel—namely, "what can any individual do?"—she recommends not specific alterations in the current political and economic arrangements, but rather a change of heart.

> There is one thing that every individual can do—they can see to it that *they feel right.* An atmosphere of sympathetic influence encircles every human being; and the man or woman who *feels* strongly, healthily and justly, on the great interests of humanity, is a constant benefactor to the human race. See, then, to your sympathies in this matter! Are they in harmony with the sympathies of Christ? or are they swayed and perverted by the sophistries of worldly policy?

Stowe is not opposed to concrete measures such as the passage of laws or the formation of political pressure groups, it is just that, by themselves, such actions would be useless. For if slavery *were* to be abolished by these means, the moral conditions that produced slavery in the first place would continue in force. The choice is not between action and inaction, programs and feelings; the choice is between actions that spring from the "sophistries of worldly policy" and those inspired by the "sympathies of Christ." Reality, in Stowe's view, cannot be changed by manipulating the physical environment; it can only be changed by conversion in the spirit because it is the spirit alone that is finally real.

The notion that historical change takes place only through religious conversion, which is a theory of power as old as

Christianity itself, is dramatized and vindicated in *Uncle Tom's Cabin* by the novel's insistence that all human events are organized, clarified, and made meaningful by the existence of spiritual realities. The novel is packed with references to the four last things—Heaven, Hell, Death, and Judgment—references which remind the reader constantly that historical events can only be seen for what they are in the light of eternal truths. When St. Clare stands over the grave of little Eva, unable to realize "that it was his Eva that they were hiding from his sight," Stowe interjects, "Nor was it!—not Eva, but only the frail seed of that bright, immortal form with which she shall yet come forth, in the day of the Lord Jesus!" And when Legree expresses satisfaction that Tom is dead, she turns to him and says: "Yes, Legree; but who shall shut up that voice in thy soul? that soul, past repentance, past prayer, past hope, in whom the fire that never shall be quenched is already burning!" These reminders come thick and fast; they are present in Stowe's countless quotations from Scripture—introduced at every possible opportunity, in the narrative, in dialogue, in epigraphs, in quotations from other authors; they are present in the Protestant hymns that thread their way through scene after scene, in asides to the reader, apostrophes to the characters, in quotations from religious poetry, sermons, and prayers, and in long stretches of dialogue and narrative devoted to the discussion of religious matters. Stowe's narrative stipulates a world in which the facts of Christ's death and resurrection and coming day of judgment are never far from our minds because it is only within this frame of reference that she can legitimately have Tom claim, as he dies, "I've got the victory!"

The eschatological vision, by putting all individual events in relation to an order that is unchanging, collapses the distinctions among them so that they become interchangeable representations of a single timeless reality. Groups of characters blend into the same character, while the plot abounds with incidents that mirror one another. These features are the features, not of classical nineteenth-century fiction, but of typological narrative. It is this tradition rather than that of the English novel that *Uncle Tom's Cabin* reproduces and extends; for this novel does not simply quote the Bible, it rewrites the Bible as the story of a Negro slave. Formally and philosophically, it stands opposed to works like *Middlemarch* and *The Portrait of a Lady* in which everything depends on human action and decision unfolding in a temporal sequence that withholds revelation until the final moment. The truths that Stowe's narrative conveys can only be reembodied, never discovered, because they are already revealed from the beginning. Therefore, what seem from a modernist point of view to be gross stereotypes in characterization and a needless proliferation of incident, are essential properties of a narrative aimed at demonstrating that human history is a continual reenactment of the sacred drama of redemption. It is the novel's reenactment of this drama that made it irresistible in its day.

Uncle Tom's Cabin retells the culture's central religious myth—the story of the crucifixion—in terms of the nation's greatest political conflict—slavery—and of its most cherished social beliefs—the sanctity of motherhood and the family. It is because Stowe is able to combine so many of the culture's central concerns in a narrative that is immediately accessible to the general population that she is able to move so many people so deeply. The novel's typological organization allows her to present political and social situations both as themselves and as transformations of a religious paradigm which interprets them in a way that readers can both understand and respond to emotionally. For the novel functions both as a means of describing the social world and as a means of changing it. It not only offers an interpretive framework for understanding the culture, and, through the reinforcement of a particular code of values, recommends a strategy for dealing with cultural conflict, but it is itself an agent of that strategy, putting into practice the measures it prescribes. As the religious stereotypes of "Sunday-school fiction" define and organize the elements of social and political life, so the "melodrama" and "pathos" associated with the underlying myth of crucifixion put the reader's heart in the right place with respect to the problems the narrative defines. Hence, rather than making the enduring success of *Uncle Tom's Cabin* inexplicable, these popular elements which puzzled Whicher and have puzzled so many modern scholars—melodrama, pathos, Sunday-school fiction—are the *only* terms in which the book's success can be explained.

The nature of these popular elements also dictates the terms in which any full-scale analysis of *Uncle Tom's Cabin* must be carried out. As I have suggested, its distinguishing features, generically speaking, are not those of the realistic novel, but of typological narrative. Its characters, like the figures in an allegory, do not change or develop, but reveal themselves in response to the demands of a situation. They are not defined primarily by their mental and emotional characteristics—that is to say, psychologically—but soteriologically, according to whether they are saved or damned. The plot, likewise, does not unfold according to Aristotelian standards of probability, but in keeping with the logic of a preordained design, a design which every incident is intended, in one way or another, to enforce. The setting does not so much describe the features of a particular time and place as point to positions on a spiritual map. In *Uncle Tom's Cabin* the presence of realistic detail tends to obscure its highly programmatic nature and to lull readers into thinking that they are in an everyday world of material cause and effect. But what pass for realistic details—the use of dialect, the minute descriptions of domestic activity—are in fact performing a rhetorical function dictated by the novel's ruling paradigm; once that paradigm is perceived, even the homeliest details show up not as the empirically observed facts of human existence but as the expressions of a highly schematic intent.

This schematization has what one might call a totalizing effect on the particulars of the narrative, so that every character in the novel, every scene, and every incident, comes to be apprehended in terms of every *other* character, scene, and incident: all are caught up in a system of endless cross-references in which it is impossible to refer to one without referring to all the rest. To demonstrate what I mean by this kind of narrative organization—a demonstration which will have to stand in lieu of a full-scale reading of the novel—let me show how it works in relation to a single scene. Eva and Tom are seated in the garden of St. Clare's house on the shores of Lake Pontchartrain.

It was Sunday evening, and Eva's Bible lay open on her knee. She read,—"And I saw a sea of glass, mingled with fire."

"Tom," said Eva, suddenly stopping, and pointing to the lake, "there 'tis."

"What, Miss Eva?"

"Don't you see,—there?" said the child, pointing to the glassy water, which, as it rose and fell, reflected the golden glow of the sky.

"There's a 'sea of glass, mingled with fire.'"

"True enough, Miss Eva," said Tom; and Tom sang—

"O, had I the wings of the morning,
I'd fly away to Canaan's shore;
Bright angels should convey me home,
To the new Jerusalem."

"Where do you suppose new Jerusalem is, Uncle Tom?" said Eva.

"O, up in the clouds, Miss Eva."

"Then I think I see it," said Eva. "Look in those clouds!—they look like great gates of pearl; and you can see beyond them—far, far off—it's all gold. Tom, sing about 'spirits bright.'"

Tom sung the words of a well-known Methodist hymn,

"I see a band of spirits bright,
That taste the glories there;
They all are robed in spotless white,
And conquering palms they bear."

"Uncle Tom, I've seen *them,*" said Eva. . . .

"They come to me sometimes in my sleep, those spirits"; and Eva's eyes grew dreamy, and she hummed, in a low voice,

"They are all robed in spotless white,
And conquering palms they bear."

"Uncle Tom," said Eva, "I'm going there."

"Where, Miss Eva?"

The child rose, and pointed her little hand to the sky; the glow of evening lit her golden hair and flushed cheek with a kind of unearthly radiance, and her eyes were bent earnestly on the skies.

> "I'm going *there*," she said, "to the spirits bright, Tom; *I'm going, before long.*"

The iterative nature of this scene presents in miniature the structure of the whole novel. Eva reads from her Bible about a "sea of glass, mingled with fire," then looks up to find one before her. She reads the words aloud a second time. They remind Tom of a hymn which describes the same vision in a slightly different form (Lake Pontchartrain and the sea of glass become "Canaan's shore" and the "new Jerusalem") and Eva sees what he has sung, this time in the clouds, and offers her own description. Eva asks Tom to sing again and his hymn presents yet another form of the same vision, which Eva again says she has seen: the spirits bright come to her in her sleep. Finally, Eva repeats the last two lines of the hymn and declares that she is going "there"—to the place which has now been referred to a dozen times in this passage. Stowe follows with another description of the golden skies and then with a description of Eva as a spirit bright, and closes the passage with Eva's double reiteration that she is going "there."

The entire scene itself is a re-presentation of others that come before and after. When Eva looks out over Lake Pontchartrain, she sees the "Canaan of liberty" Eliza saw on the other side of the Ohio River, and the "eternal shore" Eliza and George Harris will reach when they cross Lake Erie in the end. Bodies of water mediate between worlds: the Ohio runs between the slave states and the free; Lake Erie divides the United States from Canada, where runaway slaves cannot be returned to their masters; the Atlantic Ocean divides the North American continent from Africa, where Negroes will have a nation of their own; Lake Pontchartrain shows Eva the heavenly home to which she is going soon; the Mississippi River carries slaves from the relative ease of the middle states to the grinding toil of the southern plantations; the Red River carries Tom to the infernal regions ruled over by Simon Legree. The correspondences between the episodes I have mentioned are themselves based on correspondences between earth and heaven (or hell). Ohio, Canada, and Liberia are related to one another by virtue of their relationship to the one "bright Canaan" for which they stand; the Mississippi River and the Ohio are linked by the Jordan. (Ultimately, there are only three places to be in this story: heaven, hell, or Kentucky, which represents the earthly middle ground in Stowe's geography.)

Characters in the novel are linked to each other in exactly the same way that places are—with reference to a third term that is the source of their identity. The figure of Christ is the common term which unites all of the novel's good characters, who are good precisely in proportion as they are imitations of him. Eva and Tom head the list (she reenacts the last supper and he the crucifixion), but they are also linked to most of the slaves, women, and children in the novel by the characteristics they all share: piety, impressionability, spontaneous affection—and victimiza-

tion. In this scene, Eva is linked with the "spirits bright" (she later becomes a "bright, immortal form") both because she can see them and is soon to join them, and because she, too, always wears white and is elsewhere several times referred to as an "angel." When Eva dies, she will join her father's mother, who was also named Evangeline, and who herself always wore white, and who, like Eva, is said to be "a direct embodiment and personification of the New Testament." And this identification, in its turn, refers back to Uncle Tom who is "all the moral and Christian virtues bound in black morocco, complete." The circularity of this train of association is typical of the way the narrative doubles back on itself: later on, Cassy, impersonating the ghost of Legree's saintly mother, will wrap herself in a white sheet.

The scene I have been describing is a node within a network of allusion in which every character and event in the novel has a place. The narrative's rhetorical strength derives in part from the impression it gives of taking every kind of detail in the world into account, from the preparation of breakfast to the orders of the angels, and investing those details with a purpose and a meaning which are both immediately apprehensible and finally significant. The novel reaches out into the reader's world and colonizes it for its own eschatology: that is, it not only incorporates the homely particulars of "Life among the Lowly" into its universal scheme, but it gives them a power and a centrality in that scheme, thereby turning the sociopolitical order upside down. The totalizing effect of the novel's iterative organization and its doctrine of spiritual redemption are inseparably bound to its political purpose: to bring in the day when the meek—which is to say, women—will inherit the earth.

The specifically political intent of the novel is apparent in its forms of address. Stowe addresses her readers not simply as individuals but as citizens of the United States: "to you, generous, noble-minded men and women, of the South," "farmers of Massachusetts, of New Hampshire, of Vermont," "brave and generous men of New York," "and you, mothers of America." She speaks to her audience directly in the way the Old Testament prophets spoke to Israel, exhorting, praising, blaming, warning of the wrath to come. "This is an age of the world when nations are trembling and convulsed. A mighty influence is abroad, surging and heaving the world, as with an earthquake. And is America safe? . . . O, Church of Christ, read the signs of the times!" Passages like these, descended from the revivalist rhetoric of "Sinners in the Hands of an Angry God," are intended, in the words of a noted scholar, "to direct an imperiled people toward the fulfillment of their destiny, to guide them individually towards salvation, and collectively toward the American city of God."

These words are from Sacvan Bercovitch's *The American Jeremiad,* an influential work of modern scholarship which, although it completely ignores Stowe's novel, makes us aware that **Uncle Tom's Cabin** is a jeremiad in the fullest and truest sense. A jeremiad, in Bercovitch's definition, is "a mode of public exhortation . . . designed to join social criticism to spiritual renewal, public to private identity, the shifting 'signs of the times' to certain traditional metaphors, themes, and symbols." Stowe's novel provides the most obvious and compelling instance of the jeremiad since the Great Awakening, and its exclusion from Bercovitch's book is a striking instance of how totally academic criticism has foreclosed on sentimental fiction; for, because *Uncle Tom's Cabin* is absent from the canon, it isn't "there" to be referred to even when it fulfills a man's theory to perfection. Hence its exclusion from critical discourse is perpetuated automatically, and absence begets itself in a self-confirming cycle of neglect. Nonetheless, Bercovitch's characterization of the jeremiad provides an excellent account of how *Uncle Tom's Cabin* actually worked: among its characters, settings, situations, symbols, and doctrines, the novel establishes a set of correspondences which unite the disparate realms of experience Bercovitch names—social and spiritual, public and private, theological and political—*and,* through the vigor of its representations, attempts to move the nation as a whole toward the vision it proclaims.

The tradition of the jeremiad throws light on *Uncle Tom's Cabin* because Stowe's novel was political in exactly the same way the jeremiad was: both were forms of discourse in which "theology was wedded to politics and politics to the progress of the kingdom of God." The jeremiad strives to persuade its listeners to a providential view of human history which serves, among other things, to maintain the Puritan theocracy in power. Its fusion of theology and politics is not only doctrinal—in that it ties the salvation of the individual to the community's historical enterprise—it is practical as well, for it reflects the interests of Puritan ministers in their bid to retain spiritual and secular authority. The sentimental novel, too, is an act of persuasion aimed at defining social reality; the difference is that the jeremiad represents the interests of Puritan ministers, while the sentimental novel represents the interests of middle-class women. But the relationship between rhetoric and history in both cases is the same. In both cases it is not as if rhetoric and history stand opposed, with rhetoric made up of wish fulfillment and history made up of recalcitrant facts that resist rhetoric's onslaught. Rhetoric *makes* history by shaping reality to the dictates of its political design; it makes history by convincing the people of the world that its description of the world is the true one. The sentimental novelists make their bid for power by positing the kingdom of heaven on earth as a world over which women exercise ultimate control. If history did not take the course these writers recommended, it is not because they were not political, but because they were insufficiently persuasive.

Uncle Tom's Cabin, however, unlike its counterparts in the sentimental tradition, was spectacularly persuasive in conventional political terms: it helped convince a nation to go to war and to free its slaves. But in terms of its own conception of power, a conception it shares with other sentimental fiction, the novel was a political failure. Stowe conceived her book as an instrument for bringing about the day when the world would be ruled not by force, but by Christian love. The novel's deepest political aspirations are expressed only secondarily in its devastating

attack on the slave system; the true goal of Stowe's rhetorical undertaking is nothing less than the institution of the kingdom of heaven on earth. Embedded in the world of *Uncle Tom's Cabin,* which is the fallen world of slavery, there appears an idyllic picture, both utopian and Arcadian, of the form human life would assume if Stowe's readers were to heed her moral lesson. In this vision, described in the chapter entitled "The Quaker Settlement," Christian love fulfills itself not in war, but in daily living, and the principle of sacrifice is revealed not in crucifixion, but in motherhood. The form that Stowe's utopian society takes bears no resemblance to the current social order. Man-made institutions—the church, the courts of law, the legislatures, the economic system—are nowhere in sight. The home is the center of all meaningful activity; women perform the most important tasks; work is carried on in a spirit of mutual cooperation; and the whole is guided by a Christian woman who, through the influence of her "loving words," "gentle moralities," and "motherly loving kindness," rules the world from her rocking-chair.

> For why? for twenty years or more, nothing but loving words, and gentle moralities, and motherly loving kindness, had come from that chair;—head-aches and heart-aches innumerable had been cured there,—difficulties spiritual and temporal solved there,—all by one good, loving woman, God bless her!

The woman in question *is* God in human form. Seated in her kitchen at the head of her table, passing out coffee and cake for breakfast, Rachel Halliday, the millenarian counterpart of little Eva, enacts the redeemed form of the last supper. This is holy communion as it will be under the new dispensation: instead of the breaking of bones, the breaking of bread. The preparation of breakfast exemplifies the way people will work in the ideal society; there will be no competition, no exploitation, no commands. Motivated by self-sacrificing love, and joined to one another by its cohesive power, people will perform their duties willingly and with pleasure: moral suasion will take the place of force.

> All moved obediently to Rachel's gentle "Thee had better," or more gentle "Hadn't thee better?" in the work of getting breakfast.... Everything went on so sociably, so quietly, so harmoniously, in the great kitchen,—it seemed so pleasant to every one to do just what they were doing, there was such an atmosphere of mutual confidence and good fellowship everywhere. . . .

The new matriarchy which Isabella Beecher Hooker had dreamed of leading, pictured here in the Indiana kitchen ("for a breakfast in the luxurious valleys of Indiana is . . . like picking up the rose-leaves and trimming the bushes in Paradise," constitutes the most politically subversive dimension of Stowe's novel, more disruptive and far-reaching in its potential consequences than even the starting of a war or the freeing of slaves. Nor is the ideal of matriarchy simply a daydream; Catharine Beecher, Stowe's elder sister, had offered a ground plan for the realization of such a vision in her *Treatise on Domestic Economy* (1841), which the two sisters republished in an enlarged version entitled *The American Woman's Home* in 1869. Dedicated "To the Women of America, in whose hands rest the real destinies of the republic," this is an instructional book on homemaking in which a wealth of scientific information and practical advice are pointed toward a millenarian goal. Centering on the home, for these women, is not a way of indulging in narcissistic fantasy, as critics have argued, or a turning away from the world into self-absorption and idle reverie; it is the prerequisite of world conquest—defined as the reformation of the human race through proper care and nurturing of its young. Like *Uncle Tom's Cabin, The American Woman's Home* situates the minutiae of domestic life in relation to their soteriological function: "What, then, is the end designed by the family state which Jesus Christ came into this world to secure? It is to provide for the training of our race . . . by means of the self-sacrificing labors of the wise and good . . . with chief reference to a future immortal existence." "The family state," the authors announce at the beginning, "is the aptest earthly illustration of the heavenly kingdom, and . . . woman is its chief minister." In the body of the text, the authors provide women with everything they need to know for the proper establishment and maintenance of home and family, from the construction of furniture ("The [bed] frame is to be fourteen inches from the floor . . . and three inches in thickness. At the head, and at the foot, is to be screwed a notched two-inch board, three inches wide, as in Fig. 8," [30]), to architectural plans, to chapters of instruction on heating, ventilation, lighting, healthful diet, preparation of food, cleanliness, the making and mending of clothes, the care of the sick, the organization of routines, financial management, psychological health, the care of infants, the managing of young children, home amusement, the care of furniture, planting of gardens, the care of domestic animals, the disposal of waste, the cultivation of fruit, and providing for the "Homeless, the Helpless, and the Vicious." After each of these activities has been treated in detail, they conclude by describing the ultimate aim of the domestic enterprise. The founding of a "truly 'Christian family'" will lead to the gathering of a "Christian neighborhood." This "cheering example," they continue,

> would soon spread, and ere long colonies from these prosperous and Christian communities would go forth to shine as "lights of the world" in all the now darkened nations. Thus the "Christian family" and "Christian neighborhood" would become the grand ministry, as they were designed to be, in training our whole race for heaven.

The imperialistic drive behind the encyclopedism and determined practicality of this household manual flatly contradicts the traditional derogations of the American cult of domesticity as a "mirror-phenonenon," "self-immersed" and "self-congratulatory." *The American Woman's Home* is a blueprint for colonizing the world in the name of the "family state" under the leadership of Christian women. What is more, people like Stowe and Catharine Beecher were speaking not simply for a set of

moral and religous values. In speaking for the home, they speak for an economy—a hosehold economy—which had supported New England life since its inception. The home, rather than representing a retreat or refuge from a crass industrial-commercial world, offers an economic *alternative* to that world, one which calls into question the whole structure of American society which was growing up in response to the increase in trade and manufacturing. Stowe's image of a utopian community as presented in Rachel Halliday's kitchen is not simply a Christian dream of a communitarian cooperation and harmony; it is a reflection of the real communitarian practices of village life, practices which depended upon cooperation, trust, and a spirit of mutual supportiveness which characterize the Quaker community of Stowe's novel.

One could argue, then, that for all its revolutionary fervor, *Uncle Tom's Cabin* is a conservative book, because it advocates a return to an older way of life—household economy—in the name of the nation's most cherished social and religious beliefs. Even the emphasis on the woman's centrality might be seen as harking back to the "age of Homespun" when the essential goods were manufactured in the home and their production was carried out and guided by women. But Stowe's very conservatism—her reliance on established patterns of living and traditional beliefs—is precisely what gives her novel its revolutionary potential. By pushing those beliefs to an extreme and by insisting that they be applied universally, not just to one segregated corner of civil life, but to the conduct of all human affairs, Stowe means to effect a radical transformation of her society. The brilliance of the strategy is that it puts the central affirmations of a culture into the service of a vision that would destroy the present economic and social institutions; by resting her case, absolutely, on the saving power of Christian love and on the sanctity of motherhood and the family, Stowe relocates the center of power in American life, placing it not in the government, nor in the courts of law, nor in the factories, nor in the marketplace, but in the kitchen. And that means that the new society will not be controlled by men, but by women. The image of the home created by Stowe and Beecher in their treatise on domestic science is in no sense a shelter from the stormy blast of economic and poolitical life, a haven from reality divorced from fact which allows the machinery of industrial capitalism to grind on; it is conceived as a dynamic center of activity, physical and spiritual, economic and moral, whose influence spreads out in ever-widening circles. To this activity—and this is the crucial innovation—men are incidental. Although the Beecher sisters pay lip service on occasion to male supremacy, women's roles occupy virtually the whole of their attention and dominate the scene. Male provender is deemphasized in favor of female processing. Men provide the seed, but women bear and raise the children. Men provide the flour, but women bake the bread and get the breakfast. The removal of the male from the center to the periphery of the human sphere is the most radical component of this millenarian scheme, which is rooted so solidly in the most traditional values— religion, motherhood, home, and family. Exactly what position men will occupy in the millennium is specified by a detail inserted casually into Stowe's description of the Indiana kitchen. While the women and children are busy preparing breakfast, Simeon Halliday, the husband and father, stands "in his shirt-sleeves before a little looking-glass in the corner, engaged in the anti-patriarchal operation of shaving."

With this detail, so innocently placed, Stowe reconceives the role of men in human history: while Negroes, children, mothers, and grandmothers do the world's primary work, men groom themselves contentedly in a corner. The scene, as critics have noted is often the case in sentimental fiction, is "intimate," the backdrop is "domestic," the tone at times is even "chatty" but the import, as critics have failed to recognize, is world-shaking. The enterprise of sentimental fiction, as Stowe's novel attests, is anything but domestic, in the sense of being limited to purely personal concerns. Its mission, on the contrary, is global and its interests identical with the interests of the race. If the fiction written in the nineteenth century by women whose works sold in the hundreds of thousands has seemed narrow and parochial to the critics of the twentieth century, that narrowness and parochialism belong not to these works nor to the women who wrote them; they are the beholders' share.

Jean Fagan Yellin (essay date 1986)

SOURCE: "Doing It Herself: *Uncle Tom's Cabin* and Woman's Role in the Slavery Crisis," in *New Essays on "Uncle Tom's Cabin,"* edited by Eric J. Sundquist, Cambridge University Press, 1986, pp. 85-105.

[*In the following essay, Yellin discusses the influence of mid-nineteenth-century feminist thought on the writing of* Uncle Tom's Cabin, *emphasizing the roles that Angelina E. Grimké and Catharine Beecher had on the creation of Stowe's female characters.*]

> The trembling earth, the low-murmuring thunders, already admonish us of our danger; and if females can exert any saving influence in this emergency, it is time for them to awake.
>
> -Catharine E. Beecher

> But, what can any individual do?
>
> -Harriet Beecher Stowe

The question the narrator of *Uncle Tom's Cabin* posed to her audience—whom she repeatedly addressed as "mother"—was not new. By 1851, the debate over what American women could do to end chattel slavery had raged for more than a decade. The major positions had been staked out in the 1830s by the abolitionists Sarah and Angelina Grimké and their opponent, Harriet Beecher Stowe's sister, the educator Catharine Beecher. Organization of a feminist movement in 1848 and passage of a new fugitive slave law requiring northerners to cooperate in the capture of fugitive slaves in 1850 gave the inquiry new significance.

Uncle Tom's Cabin is primarily a Christian novel; most importantly, it frames the mundane struggle for black emancipation in the United States in the universal spiritual struggle for Christian salvation. In contrast to the slave narratives, which focus on the efforts of *black* people to achieve freedom, Stowe's novel explores the moral dilemma of *white* Americans who must decide how to act in the face of the 1850 Fugitive Slave Law: whether to obey the law and apprehend escaped slaves or to act on their feelings of charity, help the fugitives, and break the law. Repeatedly, the free white individuals faced with these moral dilemmas are women. This essay explores the ways in which *Uncle Tom's Cabin,* written three years after the meeting at Seneca Falls where feminists had spelled out their demands for full participation in American life, dramatizes women's roles in the fight against chattel slavery in America.

In 1836, public debate over the place of women in the life of the young republic was transformed when Angelina E. Grimké, youngest daughter of an aristocratic slaveholding Charleston family, identified herself with the Garrisonian abolitionists and published *An Appeal to the Christian Women of the South.* Almost immediately, her effort to assume the leadership of American women was challenged by the northern educator Catharine Beecher. In *An Essay on Slavery and Abolitionism, with Reference to the Duty of American Females, Addressed to A. E. Grimké,* Beecher presented the basic tenets of an ideology that she developed to counter Grimké, an ideology historian Kathryn Sklar has dubbed "domestic feminism." The Garrisonian abolitionists Angelina Grimké and her sister and co-worker Sarah responded with three polemics spelling out the basic tenets of nineteenth-century American feminism. By the time Stowe wrote her novel, the ideas on both sides had been elaborated. In her *Treatise on Domestic Economy* and elsewhere, Beecher had developed the notion of the moral superiority of females and the argument that by dominating domestic life, women could redeem American culture. Followers of the Grimkés' doctrine of sexual equality had organized the woman's rights movement, implementing their belief that women should reform American life by acting within the public sphere as well as within the home.

The polemics by the Grimké sisters and Catharine Beecher agree on a number of points. All concur that slavery is a sin, that America is in danger, that Christian women have the power to end slavery and save the nation, and that they have a duty to act in this crisis. They clash, however, when they discuss how and where women should act. Their dispute is grounded not only in differing ideas about race and abolitionism but also in their divergent ideas about women and American democracy.

In her *Appeal to the Christian Women of the South,* Grimké had suggested that free white southern women oppose slavery by performing a series of unexceptional private acts within the domestic circle—reading, praying, being kind, convincing the males in their families that slavery is wrong, and persuading the slaves to remain submissive. But she had also urged these southern women to perform exceptional acts—to break state laws and emancipate their slaves, pay them wages, and teach them to read and write. She had proposed that these women flaunt the statutes forbidding emancipation and literacy in obedience to a Higher Law, and counseled that, if apprehended, they should practice the doctrine of Christian resignation: "If a law commands me to *sin I will break it;* if it calls me to *suffer,* I will let it take its course *unresistingly.*" Suggesting that southern women pattern themselves on the biblical Queen Esther and on the members of contemporary British Ladies' Anti-Slavery Societies, Grimké urged them specifically to risk engaging in political action and appealing to their legislators to end chattel slavery.

Catharine Beecher, asked to circulate the *Appeal* and learning of Grimké's plans to organize northern women in the abolitionist cause, responded by challenging Grimké directly. Postulating an aristocratic order in which "Heaven has appointed to one sex the superior, and to the other the subordinate station," and asserting that "woman holds a subordinate relation in society to the other sex," in a pamphlet framed as a letter to Grimké, Beecher defines the appropriate behavior for women:

> A man may act on society by the collision of intellect, in public debate; he may urge his measures by a sense of shame, by fear and by personal interest; he may coerce by the combination of public sentiment; he may drive by physical force, and he does not outstep the boundaries of his sphere. But all the power, and all the conquests that are lawful to women, are those only which appeal to the kindly, generous, peaceful and benevolent principles.

> Woman is to win every thing by peace and love. . . . But this is to all be accomplished in the domestic and social sphere.

Accordingly, Beecher asserts that women should limit the expression of their opposition to slavery to the domestic circle, where they should use their influence to mediate between opponents and advocates of slavery. Predictably, she is "entirely opposed to the plan of arraying females in any Abolition movement."

As for Grimké's proposal that southern women petition their legislators to end slavery, Beecher asserts that "in this country, petitions to Congress . . . seem IN ALL CASES, to fall entirely without the sphere of female duty." Arguing that the crucial need is not for women to exert political power but to use their female force to promote a national "spirit of candour, forbearance, charity, and peace," Beecher urges Christian women to recognize their true calling as the guardians of American morals and American youth. By assuming this role, she argues, they can "exert a wise and appropriate influence, and one which will most certainly tend to bring an end, not only of slavery, but unnumbered other evils and wrongs."

The Grimkés responded in three polemics setting forth the basic ideas of nineteenth-century American feminism. Grounding their arguments in the philosophy of natural rights and in a radical reading of the Bible, they assert woman's equal role with man as God's reasonable creature and as citizen of the Republic.

The cover of *An Appeal to the Women of the Nominally Free States,* their first pamphlet, suggests both its connections to and its quarrels with Beecher's polemic. Her call for women to respond to the current crisis is quoted, but her conclusions are countered by a text urging women to become abolitionist partisans within the political arena; an antislavery quatrain by the black poet Sarah Forten signals that instead of ignoring the role of black women, as Beecher had, this polemic pleads for unity among women of all races. It proposes that white women end their prejudice and urges black women to "mingle with us *whilst* we have the prejudice, because it is only by associating with you that we shall ever be able to overcome it."

Angelina Grimké's fullest answer to Beecher, however, is *Letters to Catharine E. Beecher, in Reply to An Essay on Slavery and Abolitionism, Addressed to A. E. Grimké.* Written as Grimké was traveling on her historic lecture tour during the summer of 1837, this polemic radiates the energy sparked by her controversy with Beecher and fueled by her encounters with "promiscuous" audiences of men and women throughout New England. Grimké concludes with three essays on woman's role in the national struggle against chattel slavery and white racism. Presenting a natural rights argument that "woman's rights are . . . an integral part of her moral being" and asserting that "the mere circumstance of sex does not give to man higher rights and responsibilities than to women," she reasons that "whatever it is morally right for a man to do, it is morally right for a woman to do." It follows that women, like men, have a duty to end the sin of slavery by acting within both the domestic and public spheres. Similarly, women, like men, can appropriately engage in sharp argument, and they most certainly should join the abolitionists' petition campaigns:

> The right of petition is the only political right that women have. . . . Surely, we ought to be permitted at least to remonstrate against every political measure that may tend to injure or oppress our sex.

Attacking Beecher's *Letters* as an effort "to quench the flame of sympathy in the hearts of their fathers, husbands, brothers and sons," Grimké accuses her of lacking "deep sympathy for thy sister in bonds." "Where, oh where," she asks—exposing the raw nerve joining feminist politics and female culture—"are the outpourings of a soul overwhelmed with a sense of the heinous crimes of our nation, and the necessity of immediate repentance?"

This polemic inspired two others. Sarah Grimké expanded its discussion of women into a comprehensive argument in *Letters on the Equality of the Sexes and the Condition of Woman,* the fullest statement of American feminism to precede the Declaration of Sentiments adopted at Seneca Falls in 1848. In addition, the Grimké sisters, working with Angelina's husband, Theodore Weld, apparently used its inclusion of southerners' descriptions of slavery as a model for *American Slavery As It Is: Testimony of a Thousand Witnesses.* Composed of clippings from southern newspapers and statements from observers of southern slavery, this best-selling abolitionist fact book became an effective weapon in the abolitionist campaign for signatures on antislavery petitions to Congress.

American Slavery As It Is fulfilled an additional function: Harriet Beecher Stowe later wrote that she kept it "in her work basket by day, and slept with it under her pillow by night, till its facts crystallized into Uncle Tom."

The women Stowe portrays in **Uncle Tom's Cabin** do not merely exist within the system of chattel slavery; they are largely defined by their various relationships to this system. Repeatedly—inevitably—they make choices and engage in actions that relate to the slavery question. In the beginning, these dramas of moral choice are acted out by Emily Shelby and Marie St. Clare, free white "Christian women of the South"; they are later reenacted by Mary Bird and Rachel Halliday, white women of the "nominally free states." Although Stowe includes among her characters female slaves—mulatto women like Eliza Harris and Cassy and black females like Aunt Chloe and Topsy—she does not present them with similar moral seriousness.

Because slavery determines the texture of their home life, Stowe's white southern ladies need not stray beyond their own walls to engage in this drama of moral choice. Mrs. Shelby is seated at her dressing table when she learns, from her husband's sale of Eliza's little Harry and Uncle Tom, the lesson she could have learned by reading Angelina Grimké's *Appeal to the Christian Women of the South.* She learns that slavery is

> "A bitter, bitter, most accursed thing!—a curse to the master and a curse to the slave! I was a fool to think I could make anything good out of such a deadly evil. It is a sin. . . . but I thought I could gild it over,— I thought, by kindness, and care, and instruction, I could make the condition of mine better than freedom,—fool that I was!"

Watching her efforts to oppose these slave sales, we see an equivocal dramatization of Catharine Beecher's program. As if following Beecher's restrictions, Emily Shelby temperately asks permission to intercede for the slaves within her own home. But she is unsuccessful (and, in her distress, sounds the harsh tones of abolitionist reprovers, as her husband notes). Mrs. Shelby, although a member of the slaveholding class, as a married woman is powerless to prevent these sales. Forbidden by her husband from using her "practical mind" to right their financial affairs and to buy Tom back, only after Mr. Shelby's death is she able to settle the debts and try to redeem the old slave. It is Mrs. Shelby's son, young Mas'r George (whom she has raised to be a Christian), who then plays the role of the earthly emancipator of the Shelby slaves, but he has learned his part from his Christian mother. Although

Mrs. Shelby fails to influence her husband—thus setting into motion the events of the novel—she persists in following Beecher's instructions and succeeds at last by influencing her son, who completes the action.

It has been pointed out that **Uncle Tom's Cabin** develops according to a typological pattern. Stowe presents a series of free white Christian mothers (including St. Clare's and Legree's) who, in accordance with Beecher's restrictions, attempt to influence their sons' actions in regard to slavery. What is striking is not that this pattern is repeated but that their influence is sometimes effective and sometimes not. This fact, centrally dramatized in the uncertainty of Mrs. Shelby's influence on her husband and son, resonates with significance. Is the problem of slavery in **Uncle Tom's Cabin** finally inseparable from the problem of women's political impotence? Is a hidden issue in the novel the feminist issue of political power for women?

The example of Marie St. Clare suggests that the problem of slavery in **Uncle Tom's Cabin** cannot be resolved by a simple shift of power to women because—unlike Emily Shelby, who has always felt that slavery is wrong—Marie St. Clare has always felt it to be right. In the world of **Uncle Tom's Cabin,** although Christianity and sin are shown in active and deadly opposition, although most women appear to be morally superior to most men, and although women bear the responsibility of instilling Christian values in their sons, husbands, and slaves, Christian sympathy is not gender specific. Both women and men are capable of Christian feeling and its opposite. Marie's false religion and callousness toward her female slaves echo Angelina and Sarah Grimké's testimony about female slaveholders in *American Slavery As It Is;* she would whip a whole plantation of slaves if her husband did not prevent her. Although it is true that the idyllic center of Stowe's novel is the Quaker matriarchate of Rachel Halliday's kitchen, it is not only some men (like the reformed slave catcher Tom Loker) who fail to develop the morality essential for participation in such a society; Marie St. Clare dramatizes that women, too, can be immoral.

Marie St. Clare and Emily Shelby are not, however, the only female members of the slaveholding class in **Uncle Tom's Cabin**. Little Eva, whose drama fundamentally addresses the issue of spiritual salvation rather than earthly emancipation, is another—perhaps surprising—member of this group. (Stowe implicitly admits this kinship when she makes Little Eva assert her preference for the southern way of life over that of New England: "it makes so many more round you to love, you know.") The uniqueness of Evangeline's character as a member of this class is underscored by the fact that she lacks the guidance of a Christian mother. The St. Clare ménage, like the Legree plantation, is an antihome. Until the advent of Miss Ophelia, it had contained no woman who organized its kitchen and ordered its morals; Marie's refusal to do the former is directly related to her inability to do the latter. Although the "shiftless" chaos of Aunt Dinah's kitchen is countered by Mammy's warmth and "respectability"—and although Mammy is a Christian—neither of these women of color functions as a center in this mistressless house.

Uncle Tom, who remains uncorrupted by slavery, is not the only "moral miracle" in Stowe's book. As her father states, Little Eva, who rises above her domestic environment and who remains uncorrupted by mastery, is another.

Although it is perhaps difficult to conceive of any development in Little Eva's character, she is not a completely static figure. We first see her acting out Grimké's suggestions to Christian female slaveholders, going among the slaves on the riverboat "with her hands full of candy, nuts, and oranges, which she would distribute joyfully to them." Two years later, a slightly more mature Eva responds differently to the evils of slavery. Learning to read, she comes to love the Bible, and she develops her antislavery sympathies into antislavery proposals. Eva voices her belief that slaves should be taught to read Scripture; then she wishes she had money to "buy a place in the free states, and take all our people there, and hire teachers, to teach them to read and write." Powerless to effect this modest program for emancipation and literacy, she nonetheless teaches Mammy her letters. When exposed to her cousin's tyrannical actions toward his slave, she confronts Henrique and condemns him: "How could you be so cruel and wicked to poor Dodo?" "I don't want you to call me dear Eva, when you do so." Later, physically ill but spiritually ecstatic, Eva "had vague longings to do something for . . . [the slaves], to bless and save not only them, but all in their condition."

Addressing Uncle Tom, the child speaks in the classic phrases of a martyr: "I would be glad to die, if my dying could stop all this misery. I *would die* for them, Tom, if I could." Talking with her father, however, Eva outlines a more prudential plan to end slavery in America. Explaining that she is sad "for our poor people" and wishes "they were all *free*," Eva proposes that St. Clare become an antislavery leader (one who does not, like William Lloyd Garrison, denounce his opponents):

> "Papa, you are such a good man, and so noble, and kind, and you always have a way of saying things that is so pleasant, couldn't you go all round and try to persuade people to do right about this? When I am dead, papa, then you will think of me, and do it for my sake."

She then announces,

> "I would do it, if I could."

Eva's distressed reactions to the slave culture in which she lives recall the agonies of Angelina Grimké's South Carolina childhood—which she and other abolitionists had publicized widely. In *American Slavery As It Is,* Grimké had written that she had "fainted away" at the age of thirteen, after seeing a boy whose head had been shaved and who had been "dreadfully whipped," and that a slave woman's accounts of whippings at the work house "smote me with such horror that my limbs could hardly sustain me." She wrote she had prayed that she might be permit-

ted to be sacrificed to end slavery, and she believed it "the Lord's doing" that she "did not become totally hardened, under the daily operation of the system." Passionately, she recounted "the recollections of my childhood, and the effaceless imprint upon my riper years, with the breaking of my heart-strings," and recorded her misery when finally she recognized herself "powerless to shield the victims" of slavery.

Like the juvenile Angelina, Stowe's little Evangeline—whose given name suggests Grimké's—is mentally and emotionally tortured by the violence of slavery that surrounds her. Are we to read her announcement that "I would do it, if I could" to mean that she would become an antislavery lecturer if she were an adult male like her father? Or does Stowe here more radically imply that if Eva were to grow into womanhood, she herself would become an antislavery lecturer—like Angelina Grimké, that other young Christian girl who, although a member of the slaveholding aristocracy, was also physically and mentally sickened by slavery?

Stowe's characterization invites such conjecture. Eva is (as her mother laments) hopelessly democratic. Always seeming "somehow to put herself on an equality with every creature that comes near her," she embodies an egalitarian Christian love. Her vision undermines the authoritarian religiosity endorsed by Marie's proslavery minister, who preaches that "all the orders and distinctions in society came from God; and that it was so appropriate, you know, and beautiful, that some should be high and some low, and that some were born to rule and some to serve, and all that, you know." Although addressing the issues of race and slavery and not the condition of women, this celebration of aristocracy recalls the hierarchical postulates of Catharine Beecher. If Little Eva's radically egalitarian Christianity encompasses issues of sex and gender as well as race and class—if in her eyes, as in Angelina Grimké's, social "orders and distinctions" concerning women are as ungodly as those concerning nonwhites and slaves—then, perhaps, had she lived, Eva might have assumed the role she proposes to St. Clare. She might, like Angelina Grimké, "go all around and try to persuade people to do right about this."

Stowe's illustrators implied the connections between Eva and the antislavery activists by rendering her conversion of Topsy in terms of an emblem the abolitionists had popularized showing a standing neoclassical figure of Justice as a white-skinned, white-gowned female rescuing a black female supplicant. But Little Eva's importance rests elsewhere. She lives and dies a divine child. Powerless on earth, powerful in heaven, Stowe's female exemplar is less an advocate of mundane emancipation than a model of heavenly salvation. As her conversion of Topsy demonstrates, she is a spiritual, not a political, liberator.

Uncle Tom is Stowe's martyr. His tortured figure does not—like Eva's—recall the sacrificial aristocratic white Christian female Angelina Grimké had evoked in her first *Appeal*. Tom's passion echoes instead Sarah Grimké's testimony in *American Slavery As It Is*. She reported that a male black South Carolina slave had refused to deny Christ when ordered by his master as a test of his religious sincerity. Although "terribly whipped, the fortitude of the sufferer was not to be shaken; he nobly rejected the offer of exemption from further punishment at the expense of destroying his soul, and this blessed martyr *died*."

Raised in what the Grimkés called a "nominally free state," Miss Ophelia seems a more likely candidate than Little Eva for the role of female abolitionist. But as the action unfolds, it becomes clear that Ophelia St. Clare is not representative of the northern women the Grimkés had recruited into female antislavery societies, much less of those who had joined the "promiscuous" abolitionist organizations composed of both men and women, and who had recently endorsed the feminist convention at Seneca Falls.

Although she deplored slavery, in Vermont Miss Ophelia had not been a member of the local abolitionist society. As a guest in the St. Clare household, she initially follows Beecher's advice by restricting her activities to the domestic sphere and attempting to moderate the inflammatory opinions around her. But her discussions parody the dialogues Beecher had projected. Ophelia's mildest comments enflame Marie's advocacy of slavery, and her debate with St. Clare becomes an occasion for him to echo the denunciatory testimonials of antislavery southerners in *American Slavery As It Is*. In **Uncle Tom's Cabin**, slavery is condemned by a southern male, not a northern female; when Miss Ophelia attempts to soften St. Clare's militant male rhetoric, she is vitiating a southerner's attack on slavery.

Her relationship with Topsy, however, recalls *An Appeal to the Women of the Nominally Free States;* as the Grimkés' second polemic had argued, the northern woman's racism is a crucial problem. Indeed, the sign of Miss Ophelia's conversion after Eva's death is her eradication of this bias.

When Miss Ophelia gains legal title to Topsy, she is transformed from a representative "woman of the nominally free states" into a slaveholding "Christian woman of the South." In her role as slaveholder, Ophelia St. Clare appears to conform to the outlines Grimké had suggested in her first *Appeal:* She converts and educates her slave. Further, as a Christian slaveholding woman, Miss Ophelia shows that she has learned the lesson that Mrs. Shelby left unlearned until too late: that it is futile to educate and Christianize her slave unless she can also guarantee emancipation. Because Miss Ophelia has absorbed this lesson (and because, although a woman, she has control of her property), Topsy will never be persecuted like Emily Shelby's Eliza.

But because Ophelia takes Topsy with her to the free North, it becomes unnecessary for her to act out the more radical program Grimké had proposed to slaveholding women: to break the laws forbidding education and emancipation. Miss Ophelia succeeds in converting, educating, and emancipating Topsy without following either Grimké's

radical proposal to southern women that they violate unjust laws or Grimké's radical proposal to northern women that they enter the political arena. In the world of Stowe's novel, the example of Miss Ophelia appears to validate Beecher's argument that women can work effectively against slavery within the domestic circle.

Although Ophelia St. Clare may serve as a model for southern women by Christianizing, educating, and emancipating her slave, and for northern women by overcoming her racism, perhaps Mary Bird is the most important model for Stowe's readers among women of "the nominally free states" whose involvement with slaves and slavery was less intimate. Stowe's dramatization of the invasion of Mrs. Bird's Ohio home by slavery's evil presence demonstrates that slavery shapes not only southern homes like the Shelbys' and the St. Clares' but also northern domestic life. In this scene, Stowe's narrator expresses surprise at Mrs. Bird's abrupt first words to her husband: "and what have they been doing in the Senate?" In apparent approval of the housewife's characteristic lack of involvement with the political sphere, she comments:

> Now, it was a very unusual thing for gentle little Mrs. Bird ever to trouble her head with what was going on in the house of the state, very wisely considering that she had enough to do to mind her own.

Nevertheless, Mrs. Bird persists in questioning her husband about the passage of a new fugitive slave law, explaining, when he accuses her of "getting to be a politician, all at once," that her concern is not political, but spiritual:

> "I wouldn't give a fig for all your politics, generally, but I think this is something downright cruel and unchristian."

Although Senator Bird asserts that because the abolitionists have been harrassing Kentucky slaveholders, the fugitive slave law seemed "necessary . . . to quiet the excitement," his wife condemns the measure and—defying Beecher's warning—attacks her husband's political position in the clear accents of a "reprover": "You ought to be ashamed, John! . . . It's a shameful, wicked, abominable law."

Nor does she stop there. Mary Bird announces her intention to follow the radical path Angelina Grimké had urged:

> "I'll break it, for one, the first time I get a chance; and I hope I *shall* have a chance, I do!"

Refusing to take seriously her husband's arguments and explanations, Mrs. Bird rests her case like Grimké solely on Holy Scriptures, asserting, "Now, John, I don't know anything about politics, but I can read my Bible; and there I see that I must feed the hungry, clothe the naked, and comfort the desolate; and that Bible I mean to follow." Not satisfied with proclaiming her defiance, she attacks her husband's position until an interruption signals the appearance of the runaway Eliza and her son. It is only after the female fugitive has successfully appealed to the northern woman for protection, only after the free woman and the female fugitive slave have established their sisterhood as bereaved mothers, that the senator suggests a plan for Eliza's escape. Although Stowe's treatment of Mrs. Bird follows Catharine Beecher's strictures that women should act within the domestic sphere, Mary Bird's condemnations of the attempts by her husband (and the rest of the Senate) to mediate between the proslavery and antislavery forces, her proclamation of her defiance of unjust laws, and her actual defiance of them are contrary to Beecher's instructions.

But the world of *Uncle Tom's Cabin* is a fortunate world for northern white women who oppose chattel slavery within the domestic sphere. Mrs. Bird's husband, swayed by her argument, her actions, or Eliza's desperate situation, does not oppose his wife. Neither slave catchers nor United States marshals arrive at her door. Mrs. Bird is not forced to take the next step Grimké had outlined; she is not judged a criminal. Like the women of the slaveholding states, this northern woman encounters slavery in her home. Stowe shows her remaining there, permits her to take a moral antislavery position and—despite the immorality of this world—to avoid suffering any adverse consequences whatever.

Catharine Beecher's pamphlet had ignored the presence of women of color in the struggle against slavery. Although in her first *Appeal* Angelina Grimké had simply counseled both male and female slaves to be patient, in the second she had urged free Afro-American women to participate in the abolitionist movement despite its racism. Stowe's *Uncle Tom's Cabin* includes a number of nonwhite female characters—slave, fugitive, and free— but although it follows their physical actions with some attention, it expresses little interest in their moral choices. Indeed, in *Uncle Tom's Cabin* neither male nor female nonwhite characters are seriously treated as rational creatures engaged in the human activity of making moral choices, but instead are seen as natural creatures reacting to events. Like all of Stowe's characters, however, they have the duty to be Christians and to help others follow Christ.

Accordingly, Eliza Harris is shown as a Christian wife and mother who influences the spiritual salvation of her husband and children. In relation to the issue of earthly emancipation, her role is less clear. While a slave, Eliza first echoes Grimké's advice by counseling her outraged husband to be patient; when her little son Harry is threatened, she automatically obeys the voice of nature and attempts his rescue; finally free and safe, after converting her husband to Christianity, she happily follows him to Africa in an effort to save the pagans. In the process, we are presented with a detailed description of her efforts to elude her catchers. But we are not shown Eliza agonizing over her decisions; these are presented as simple reactions, not reasoned moral choices. Even Cassy, the prototypical "tragic mulatto" on the Legree place who, maddened by sexual abuse, once killed her baby to save him

from a life of slavery, receives similar treatment. Although it is this dark female who tempts Tom to abandon his faith, her abrupt conversion occurs within the space of a single sentence.

Stowe consistently presents her blacker female figures with even less complexity. Although Topsy and Aunt Chloe, the most important ones, are first seen as comic and then shown as Christians, the moral choices inevitably involved in their transformations are scanted. Stowe's serious concern with the morality of free white aristocratic "Christian women of the South" and free white "women of the nominally free states"—women like Emily Shelby, Marie St. Clare, Ophelia St. Clare, Mary Bird and Rachael Halliday—contrasts dramatically with her summary treatment of the moral conflicts of black and mulatto female characters like the hard-working Chloe, the battered child Topsy, the heroic slave mother Eliza, and even the sexually abused Cassy.

> There is one thing that every individual can do,—they can see to it that *they feel right.*

Uncle Tom's Cabin, it has been pointed out, is a jeremiad. Harriet Beecher Stowe's narrator does not assume "the office of a mediator," presenting herself as "the advocate of charity and peace," as one who takes "every possible means to soothe exasperated feelings, and . . . [avoids] all those offensive peculiarities that in their nature tend to inflame and offend," as Beecher said females should. Instead (although she is not, as her enemies charged, a "reprover" of the South), Stowe's narrator certainly is a reprover; she exacerbates the slavery issue—as Beecher charged the abolitionists did, and as she asserted women must not do.

Further, although writing in a literary form traditional to women and addressing a female audience (who surely read her words within the domestic sphere), Stowe echoed the Grimkés and other abolitionist-feminists by raising her woman's voice on the most volatile political issue of the day; and she compounded this brazenness by serializing her novel in the pages of an antislavery newspaper. Clearly, her intention was to politicize a female audience. But in this, she echoed not only the feminist Grimkés; she also repeated a contradiction at the heart of her sister's *Letters.* Immediately after their appearance, the Grimkés' defenders had pointed out that Beecher violated her own strictures on female behavior by engaging in public debate on a political issue.

In *Uncle Tom's Cabin,* none of the characters—black, mulatto or white, male or female—becomes involved in the public struggle against slavery, as Grimké had urged. Although both Miss Ophelia and Mrs. Bird refuse to obey unjust laws, the New Englander simply takes her slave north, where slavery is illegal and education available, and proceeds to conform to the enlightened local statutes. Although the Ohioan does indeed run a risk by violating the new fugitive slave law, she fortunately escapes apprehension and punishment, as do Rachel and the other members of the Quaker community. If there are any legal consequences for the Kentuckian Mrs. Shelby caused by the actions of her son George, who plays the role of southern emancipator Grimké had urged on her female audience, we never hear of them. In contrast to the fugitive, emancipated, and freeborn Afro-American participants in the Convention of American Women Against Slavery whom Grimké had addressed in her second *Appeal,* Stowe's free black and mulatto women—Eliza Harris, Cassy, even Topsy—embrace colonization and become expatriates.

The narrator's announcement that her objective is "to awaken sympathy and feeling for the African race, as they exist among us," suggests that sympathy is a force essentially destructive of human injustice. Despite the negative example of Marie St. Clare (who is incapable of sympathizing with anyone), both the action and the narration of the novel demonstrate that women have easy access to this revolutionary power. Yet none of Stowe's female characters uses it, as had the Grimkés and their followers, collectively to challenge institutionalized injustice in the public sphere. Instead, *Uncle Tom's Cabin* shows individual women using the power of sympathy to enable them to act effectively in private against slavery when the servile institution threatens the domestic sphere. Stowe's female Christians act successfully against slavery without walking out of their own front doors.

To the extent that, within the process of defending Christian domestic values, Stowe's emphasis on individual sympathy and on the doctrine of Higher Laws functions not only as a critique of chattel slavery but also as a critique of racist patriarchal capitalist culture in America, and to the extent that it suggests an alternative society grounded in egalitarian Christianity and proposes a loving maternal ethic in opposition to patriarchal values, *Uncle Tom's Cabin* endorses nineteenth-century radical ideas.

In this regard, the crucial connections between sex and race in *Uncle Tom's Cabin* demand examination. The primary distinctions in Stowe's book are between non-Christians and Christians. Stowe assigns intellectual superiority and worldly power to the first group and spiritual superiority and otherworldly power—seen as infinitely more important—to the second. In the process, she conflates race and sex. Her first group consists primarily of white males. Her second group includes essentially white females and all nonwhites.

The connections between Uncle Tom, the cultural type of the True Woman, and Stowe's view of Jesus Christ have been repeatedly noted. But these connections involve more than Stowe's black martyr; in her book, nonwhites as a group, like women as a group, possess special religious attributes. In *Letters to Catharine E. Beecher,* Grimké had articulated her awareness of parallels between the oppression of slaves and the oppression of women, announcing that "the investigation of the rights of the slave has led to a better understanding of my own." Stowe's novel echoes other nineteenth-century analyses, however, in connecting "women and Negroes" not only in terms of

their earthly powerlessness, but also as the reservoirs of a sympathy that signals their heavenly power and revolutionary potential. To the extent that we take seriously the radical implications of Stowe's book, we can perhaps take seriously the connections between her divine child Evangeline and her feminist antiracist contemporary Angelina Grimké, and find in Stowe's heavenly child a budding social activist.

At issue here is not how forceful and revolutionary we judge the power of sympathy to be: Stowe echoes both Beecher and the Grimkés in dramatizing its regenerative force. At issue here is how Christians should use that power.

A dozen years ago, writing in the shadow of the modern freedom movement and examining *Uncle Tom's Cabin* as a response to the 1850 Fugitive Slave Law, I concluded that Stowe's "sentimentalized racialism" (the term is George Fredrickson's) opposed the active resistance of black and white abolitionists and insurrectionists. Created in the context of radical abolitionist and insurrectionist responses to the 1850 Fugitive Slave Law, Stowe's book apotheosizes a black man who triumphs in heaven after practicing Christian resignation when tortured on earth (and pointing others toward eternal salvation) while celebrating more ordinary slaves who escape and expatriate themselves to Africa. Today, writing in the midst of the modern feminist movement and examining the treatment of female characters in *Uncle Tom's Cabin* as a response to the 1848 Seneca Falls Convention, I can only conclude that Stowe makes a similar move in relation to women. Created in the context of feminist demands for equal rights for women, Stowe's book apotheosizes a juvenile white female who triumphs in heaven after practicing Christian charity on earth, ameliorating the suffering of the slaves (and pointing them toward eternal salvation) while celebrating more ordinary women who practice not feminism and abolitionism but "domestic feminism" and colonization.

Although on a spiritual level Stowe's attack on the patriarchal institution challenges all oppressive earthly authority, ultimately both the spiritual and the mundane dramas in *Uncle Tom's Cabin* counter the practical measures urged by the black and white activists following the Grimkés' lead—women like Abby Kelley Foster and Sojourner Truth, who, for more than a decade, had been invading American public life, going "all around" trying "to persuade people to do right about this." Catharine Beecher must have been pleased.

Notes

1 *An Essay on Slavery and Abolitionism, with Reference to the Duty of American Females, Addressed to A. E. Grimké,* (Philadelphia: Henry Perkins; Boston: Perkins & Marvin, 1837); quoted in [A. E. Grimké et al], *An Appeal to the Women of the Nominally Free States,* Issued by an Anti-Slavery Convention of American Women (New York: W. S. Dorr, 1837).

2 *Uncle Tom's Cabin* appeared as a serial in the *National*

Era, June 3, 1851-April 2, 1852, and was published in book form in 1852. Parenthetical references in my text refer to the edition edited by Kenneth Lynn (Cambridge, Mass.: Harvard University Press, 1962); the passage quoted is in chap. 45.

3 Angelina Grimké, *Appeal to the Christian Women of the South, The Anti-Slavery Examiner* 1 (September 1836): [1]-35. For the Grimké sisters, see Gerda Lerner, *The Grimké Sisters from South Carolina* (1967; rpt. New York: Schocken Books, 1971); and Katharine Du Pre Lumpkin, *The Emancipation of Angelina Grimké* (Chapel Hill: University of North Carolina Press, 1974). For the situation of women, see, for example, Barbara Welter, "The Cult of True Womanhood," *American Quarterly* 18 (1966): 151-74; Nancy Cott, *The Bonds of Womanhood* (New Haven, Conn.: Yale University Press, 1977); and Linda Kerber, *Women of the Republic* (Chapel Hill: University of North Carolina Press, 1980).

4 Kathryn Kish Sklar, *Catharine Beecher: A Study in American Domesticity* (New Haven, Conn.: Yale University Press, 1973).

5 See *An Appeal to the Women of the Nominally Free States,* which appeared as a statement of the 1837 Convention of American Women Against Slavery; A. E. Grimké, *Letters to Catharine E. Beecher, in Reply to An Essay on Slavery and Abolitionism, Addressed to A. E. Grimké* (Boston: Isaac Knapp, 1838); and Sarah Grimké's *Letters on the Equality of the Sexes and the Condition of Women, Addressed to Mary S. Parker, President of the Boston Female Anti-Slavery Society* (Boston: Isaac Knapp, 1838). Catharine Beecher's *Treatise on Domestic Economy for the Use of Young Ladies at Home and at School* (Boston: t. H. Webb, 1834), revised by Beecher and Stowe, appeared as *The American Woman's Home, or Principles of domestic Science* (New York: J. B. Ford, 1869). For recent controversy concerning feminism and female culture in nineteenth-century America, see Ellen DuBois, M. J. Buhle, T. Kaplan, G. Lerner, and C. Smith-Rosenberg, "Politics and Culture in Women's History: A Symposium," *Feminist Studies* 6 (Spring 1980): 26-64. Although sensitive to the problems of terminology raised in these comments, in this essay I use "feminist" when referring both to supporters of the nineteenth-century women's rights movement who were essentially reformist and to those radicals who proposed an end to patriarchy. I do so because my purpose here is simply to differentiate between the Grimkés' "feminism" and Beecher's "domestic feminism," a crucial distinction inexplicably ignored in Ann Douglas's Introduction to a recent edition of *Uncle Tom's Cabin* (New York: Penguin Books, 1981).

6 Grimké, *Appeal to the Christian Women of the South,* p. 20.

7 Beecher, *An Essay on Slavery and Abolitionism,* pp. 99-100.

8 *Ibid.,* pp. 104, 128, 145. Further, Beecher implicitly attacks Grimké's efforts to win northern women to abolitionism by attacking the proposal that women lecture in public. Her revulsion at Fanny Wright's public appearances was surely telling in a pamphlet addressed to Grimké, newest and most prominent of the female speakers: "If the female advocate chooses to come upon a stage, and expose her person . . . it is . . . right to express disgust at whatever is offensive or indecorous" (p. 121).

9 [Grimké et al,] *Appeal to the Women of the Nominally Free States,* p. 61.

10 Grimké, *Letters to Catharine E. Beecher,* pp. 108, 115, 112, 128-29.

11 For *Letters on the Equality of the Sexes,* see note 5. *American Slavery As It Is: Testimony of a Thousand Witnesses* (New York: American Anti-slavery Society, 1839).

12 From an unpublished manuscript by Sarah Weld of reminiscences of her mother, Angelina Grimké Weld, quoted in Gilbert Hobbs Barnes, *The Antislavery Impulse, 1830-44* (1933; rpt. New York: Harcourt, Brace & World, 1964), p. 231.

13 See *Uncle Tom's Cabin,* chap. 19, and *American Slavery As It Is,* pp. 56, 24. For the matriarchal utopian impulse in *Uncle Tom's Cabin,* see Elizabeth Ammons, "Heroines in Uncle Tom's Cabin," *American Literature* 49 (May 1977): 161-79; also see Gillian Brown, "Getting in the Kitchen with Dinah: Domestic Politics in Uncle Tom's Cabin," *American Quarterly* 36 (Fall 1984): 503-23.

14 *American Slavery As It Is,* pp. 53, 55; also see Grimké's letter to William Lloyd Garrison, August 30, 1835, published in the Liberator and widely reprinted, and the many press reports of Grimké's speeches describing her childhood suffering.

15 *American Slavery As It Is,* p. 24.

16 For a different view of Eliza, see Nina Baym, *Woman's Fiction* (Ithaca, N.Y.: Cornell University Press, 1978), p. 16; for Cassy as a quintessential figure in woman's fiction, see Sandra Gilbert and S. Gubar, *The Madwoman in the Attic* (New Haven, Conn.: Yale University Press, 1979), pp. 533-35.

17 See Jane Tomkins, *Sensational Designs: The Cultural Work of American Fiction 1790-1860* (New York: Oxford University Press, 1985), pp. 122-46; cf. also Sacvan Bercovitch, *The American Jeremiad* (Madison: University of Wisconsin Press, 1978).

18 Beecher, *Essay on Slavery and Abolitionism,* pp. 128, 129, 138-39.

20 Preface to *Uncle Tom's Cabin,* ed. Lynn.

21 Grimké, *Letters to Catharine E. Beecher,* p. 114. The issue of the commonality of the oppressed is complex.

Grimké, for one, did not confuse the brutality of black slavery with the condition of free women like herself in noting that the former led her to examine the latter. For the complicated comment of another antislavery feminist, see L. Maria Child, "The African Race," *National Anti-Slavery Standard,* April 27, 1843, p. 187: "In comparison with the Caucasian race, I have often said that they [the Africans] are what woman is in comparison with man. The comparison between women and the colored race as classes is striking. Both are exceedingly adhesive in their attachments; both, comparatively speaking, have a tendency to submission; and hence, both have been kept in subjection by physical force, and considered rather in the light of property, than as individuals." For an interpretation asserting the radical character of sentiment that argues *Uncle Tom's Cabin* subverts the patriarchy, see Tompkins, *Sensational Designs.*

22 Jean Fagan Yellin, *The Intricate Knot* (New York: New York University Press, 1972), chap. 7; George Fredrickson, *The Black Image in the White Mind* (New York: Harper & Row, 1971).

Stephen J. DeCanio (essay date 1990)

SOURCE: "*Uncle Tom's Cabin:* A Reappraisal," in *The Centennial Review,* Vol. XXXIV, No. 4, Fall, 1990, pp. 587-93.

[*In the following excerpt, DeCanio examines the philosophical questions underlying* Uncle Tom's Cabin, *suggesting that Stowe's treatment of religion and faith has as much relevance for a modern audience as her commentary on gender and ethnicity.*]

Uncle Tom's Cabin, the main work for which Harriet Beecher Stowe is now remembered, is enjoying a rebirth. With the received "canon" of American literature under attack as elitist, racist, and sexist, it is not surprising that an authentic anti-slavery novel, written by a nineteenth-century radical abolitionist woman, should be viewed with new favor. In truth, *Uncle Tom's Cabin* has been a neglected classic. What is ironic, however, is that the book is intriguing not primarily because of the gender of its author or the ethnicity of its characters, but because of the philosophical problem it poses. Strangest of all, this problem involves a subject—religion—that is among those least likely to be perceived as central to the reconstruction of the literary canon. . . .

Uncle Tom's Cabin is rich in subplots, and its many characters span the range from angelic to degenerate. Before discussing the content of the novel in any more detail, however, it is necessary to address the book's treatment of the two issues, race and gender, that animate much of the current debate over the literary canon. Stowe's treatment of these delicate subjects is instructive without being enlightening. *Uncle Tom's Cabin* is rife with racial stereotypes and caricatures. "Negroes" are "not naturally daring and enterprising, but home-loving and affectionate." Tom "had the soft, impressible nature of his kindly

race, ever yearning toward the simple and childlike." Cooking was "an indigenous talent of the African race." Eva and Topsy are compared as "the representatives of their races. The Saxon, born of ages of cultivation, command, education, physical and moral eminence; the Afric, born of ages of oppression, submission, ignorance, toil, and vice!" These examples suffice, with the added note that Stowe casually denigrates other ethnic groups, with negative comments about Italians and Jews.

Despite these instances of irredeemable stereotyping, Stowe fundamentally adhered to an environmental explanation for what she perceived as behavioral deficiencies of the slaves. If slaves were brutish, it was because they were treated brutally. Stowe recognized that blacks in the past had achieved high culture, and that in the future, "the Negro race, no longer despised and trodden down, will, perhaps, show forth some of the latest and most magnificent revelations of human life." In this same passage, Stowe speculates that perhaps God has "chosen poor Africa in the furnace of affliction, to make her the highest and noblest in that kingdom which he will set up. . . ." Thus to some extent, Stowe was able to transcend the prejudices of her time. Nevertheless, the pervasiveness of stock characterizations is disconcerting. Given that Stowe was one of the most radical of abolitionists, it is sobering to contemplate the general level of racial prejudice that must have prevailed in the North at the time of her writing.

However, if Stowe advances an argument for the culture and personalities of blacks based on "nurture," there is no hint of a similar consciousness in her treatment of women. The tone is set in the opening pages, when George Shelby addresses his wife as "Emily," and she addresses him as "Mr. Shelby." Stowe recognizes that women may be more capable than men (Mrs. Shelby is superior to her husband in business acumen as well as in moral development), but she never questions their specialized role as mothers and wives. Some of the most vivid characters in *Uncle Tom's Cabin* are women, and these women are not portrayed as intellectually inferior to men in any respect. Yet their social subordination to men is intrinsic.

Similarly, Stowe's attitudes towards sex can colloquially be described as "Victorian." In *Uncle Tom's Cabin,* the ultimate degradation of a slave woman is to be sexually exploited by her owner. However, this crime is condemned not explicitly as a form of rape (as it would be today), but rather because of its destruction of the chastity and virtue of the woman. Legitimate sex and marriage are inseparable, although the former is unmentionable. The splitting up of slave marriages by separate sales wrecks nuclear families characterized by a high degree of fidelity, affection, and internal stability. Such family breakups are horrible not because they condemn the former spouses to a loss of intimacy, but because they lead to sexual encounters with new partners.

Thus, while there is an abundance of material pertinent to cultural history in Stowe's novel, the book itself does not make any fundamental contribution to the current debates on ethnicity and gender. Stowe's views on race are embarrassing. She gives no inkling of the discontents of Victorian marriage. Her ideal domestic arrangement is entirely independent of time, place, culture, or personality. On these issues, *Uncle Tom's Cabin* at best provides an insight into the anachronistic mentality of a certain class of nineteenth-century American intellectuals.

Nevertheless, *Uncle Tom's Cabin* presents serious philosophical and moral challenges. The central problem posed by Stowe is how religious faith can be maintained in the face of seemingly overwhelming evil. This problem is very much alive today. It is not solved in *Uncle Tom's Cabin,* even though the novel leaves no doubt about Stowe's own views. Her ostensible Christianity is evident throughout the book, in authorial asides as well as in the development of plot and characters. In Stowe's moral universe, virtue is synonymous with Christianity. Tom is the hero because he achieves the ideal of true martyrdom.

However, Stowe subverts the overt "message" of her text in several significant ways. First, although advocating a particular version of Christianity, she recognizes the existence of one of the basic puzzles of all religions: how can God permit an evil such as slavery to continue? Stowe asks this question repeatedly, and Tom wrestles with it during the dark nights on the Legree plantation: "The gloomiest problem of this mysterious life was constantly before his eyes,—souls crushed and ruined, evil triumphant, and God silent."

This ancient problem of evil is raised at the very moment when Tom is driven to the brink of despair by exhaustion and abuse. He is saved from the abyss only by a *mystical vision of the Savior,* an experience that overwhelms his doubts and makes him finally immune to any pain Legree can inflict. The key point is that Tom's faith and resolve are held together by an experience that cannot be communicated. By acts of kindness towards his fellow slaves and his refusal to obey Legree's orders to harm others, Tom's actions are able to reflect his inner state of being. Nevertheless, the vision that provides his final line of spiritual defense is not based on reason, and cannot be transmitted through the language of logical discourse. By definition, a mystical experience is intrinsically personal and internal. Stowe must rely on revelation as the ultimate arbiter of Tom's truth.

The undermining of Stowe's Christian ideal extends beyond the story of Tom himself. Indeed, the parallel plot of George, Eliza, and Harry may be seen as a counterpoint to Tom's pilgrimage to martyrdom. Tom loses everything in this world because of his obedience and acquiescence. George and Eliza choose escape and rebellion rather than suffering the injustices of slavery, *and they succeed.* Their escape is aided by Quakers who defy the law (the Fugitive Slave Act). George, Eliza, and Harry (along with two other runaway slaves) are dogged by professional slave-catchers. After many days of being chased, the runaways are finally cornered. At this critical moment, George proclaims that he will die fighting before allowing his family and himself to be recaptured. He then shoots one of the bounty hunters, and puts the others to flight. His willingness to use deadly force is decisive for the success of the escape.

Stowe is clearly uncomfortable with this denouement. She prettifies the incident as much as possible: the chief slave catcher is only wounded, not killed; he is abandoned by his accomplices and rescued by the escapees themselves; he is nursed back to health by a wise Quaker grandmother; his experience leads him to give up his evil profession. George himself is converted to Christianity through the piety of his wife, but only *after* they reach Canada. However, the justice of George's resistance cannot logically stand or fall on the random path of a pistol ball.

Nor is the thrilling story of George and Eliza the only challenge to Tom's Christianity. One of the most harrowing characters in the novel is Cassy, a beautiful slave who has been forced to be Legree's mistress. Cassy makes what she can of the situation, walking a tightrope between sanity and madness as she lives out her days in self-loathing and disgust. She is finally driven to action by the arrival of Tom and Emmeline, a fifteen-year-old girl Legree has purchased to be the new victim of his attentions. Cassy is motivated by Legree's inhuman treatment of Tom rather than by any threat to her own hated position. She decides to kill Legree and free his slaves. She induces Legree to drink himself unconscious, then asks Tom to wield the waiting axe. Tom refuses. Cassy is insistent:

> But think of these poor creatures [Legree's slaves]. . . . We might set them all free, and go somewhere in the swamps, and find an island, and live by ourselves; I've heard of its being done. Any life is better than this.

When Tom is adamant, Cassy declares that she will do the deed herself. Tom pleads with her, and barely persuades her to let Legree live. Instead, Tom urges her to escape with Emmeline. Tom views escape not as a good thing in itself, but as an alternative for Cassy that will free her from the continuing temptation to murder Legree.

These conflicting currents (including Augustine St. Clare's agonized inability to devise a way out of the dilemma of the decent slave owner) are what make *Uncle Tom's Cabin* fascinating to the modern reader. Few today find Stowe's outward professions of religious faith persuasive. There is good reason for skepticism. Organized (and unorganized) Christianity has proved to be a weak barrier against the barbarisms that have haunted the world during the twentieth century. Renunciation and self-sacrifice of the extreme variety exhibited by Tom have always been implausible. Even holding up these qualities as *ideals* may be morally wrong, when faced with regimes more hideous than anything Stowe could have imagined.

The problem of "evil triumphant, and God silent" is more acute now than it was during the 1850s. Within living memory, Simon Legree has been reincarnated in a more frightening form, with the powers of the technologically advanced police state at his command. The Nazism of Hitler and the Communism of Stalin have transformed entire countries into Legree plantations. When Legree challenges Tom by telling him, *"I'm your church now! You understand,—you've got to be as I say,"* he is enunciating the central principle of the totalitarian state. Tom is surely right to resist Legree's demand for his soul; what is not convincing is Stowe's belief that Tom is right to acquiesce in Legree's demand for his body.

In summary, **Uncle Tom's Cabin** warrants the renewed attention it is receiving. Reevaluation is justified not only because of the gender of its author, and not because the book unearths unpleasant realities of slavery that have been covered up by establishment critics and historians. From the beginning, some observers (not least of which were the slaves themselves) knew slavery for what it was. Stowe deserves our attention because her great anti-slavery epic presages a dilemma of our own time. For believers and unbelievers alike, denial of the claims of the Leviathan state is a moral imperative. Stowe's religion could not specify the course of most effective resistance in the 1850s, and her pieties have become even less sustainable as the events of our own century have taken their terrible toll.

Stephen Railton (essay date 1991)

SOURCE: "Mothers, Husbands, and an Uncle: Stowe's *Uncle Tom's Cabin,"* in *Authorship and Audience: Literary Performance in the American Renaissance,* Princeton University Press, 1991, pp. 74-89.

[*In the following excerpt, Railton focuses on Stowe's relationship to her audience, contending that* Uncle Tom's Cabin *is both a radical novel of social protest and a conventional recording of genteel Victorian preconceptions.*]

There are still two good reasons to read **Uncle Tom's Cabin:** for its radicalism, and for its conventionality. As a novel of social protest, it generates so much passion within its own pages that, although the particular evil it indicts has given way to other forms of injustice, its power remains largely intact. In this respect it is like *The Grapes of Wrath,* which is deeply indebted to Stowe's archetypal work. As one of the three best-selling novels of mid-nineteenth-century America, it is also a perfect mirror of genteel Victorian preconceptions, a wide-ranging guide to the tastes and values of the audience for which contemporaries like Hawthorne and Melville, as struggling professional novelists, tried to write. Powerfully radical and perfectly conventional: it might sound as if I mean two different books. But while Stowe does not finally manage to reconcile these antithetical qualities, in **Uncle Tom's Cabin** she does enable them to live together—as husband and wife.

Stowe's work first appeared serially, between June 1851 and April 1852, in *The National Era,* a weekly abolitionist paper. Almost exactly in the middle of its run, *Moby-Dick* was published in New York. It took about a decade to sell the first printing of Melville's book; just over three-fourths of those two thousand copies were sold within a year. By comparison, Hawthorne's *House of the Seven Gables,* also published in 1851, did better: it sold about seven thousand copies its first year. According to her own subsequent account of writing the novel, Stowe felt the same anxiety of performance that all writers experience. "A feeling of profound discouragement came over her," she says about the moment when the manuscript was finished, but not yet published as a book; "Would anybody read it?" She did not have to worry for long. Appearing in two volumes in 1852, **Uncle Tom's Cabin** sold five thousand copies in two days, fifty thousand in six weeks, well over three hundred thousand by the end of the year, and more than half a million before the panic of 1857 depressed the book market. Her novel may not ultimately have done quite as well as Susan Warner's *Wide, Wide World* (1850) or Maria Cummins's *Lamplighter* (1854)— probably the most popular of all nineteenth-century American novels—but as the first novel that Stowe ever wrote, it was an inspired work. She liked to suggest that God had inspired it and dictated it to her scene by scene, but the wondrous way her novel worked on its contemporary audience is not as mysterious as that. Stowe had great gifts as a novelist; they were, however, those of a Victorian American woman who knew her reading public.

The National Era's subtitle promised "Original Sketches and Tales for Home Reading," a phrase that locates that public very accurately. But Stowe herself regularly addresses her readers, and two of her formulas are equally revealing: "my lady readers" and "our refined and Christian readers." As Ann Douglas and Henry Nash Smith have recently reminded us, the audience for fiction in Stowe's America was broadly middle class, at least nominally Christian, and overwhelmingly female. It is hard to say precisely how female, but since more than thirty copies of Warner's novel were sold for every one, say, of *Some Adventures of Captain Simon Suggs* (1845), among the most successful of the books by the Southwestern Humorists who wrote for male readers, it is clear that "Home Reading" almost invariably meant the parlor, not the den. And adjectives like *lady, refined,* and *Christian* point to the needlepoint mottoes that were likely to be hanging on those parlor walls, the pieties by which the female American novel reader understood the world, and her place in it.

Harriet Beecher Stowe believed in those pieties. Her novel about slavery professes to realism; on her first pages she announces "the desire to be graphic in our account," in her last chapter she iterates her "desire to exhibit [slavery] in a *living dramatic reality,"* and when introducing her titular character, she does so in the guise of a nineteenth-century realist: "At this table was seated Uncle Tom . . . who, as he is to be the hero of our story, we must daguerreotype for our readers." Contemporary Southern critics accused her of lying, but more conspicuous is the pervasive way her vision of "reality" was determined by the assumptions about the world she shared with her American readers. The subtitle of her novel, for example, is "Life Among the Lowly," a phrase that sufficiently indicates the class-conscious perspective within which all the characters of the novel are placed. While as a Christian she believes in the equality of every soul before God, and as an opponent of slavery she insists that the slave is endowed with a fully human capacity to love and suffer ("For, sir, he was a man,—and you are but another man,") as a dramatic novelist she preserves the social distinctions between her characters as carefully as Fielding or Austen ever did. In fact, Stowe displays even more firmness on this point, for the American bourgeoisie can never take its status for granted. Haley, the slave trader, is not just morally evil; socially, he is an affront to the "well-furnished dining parlor" in which he sits: "He was a short, thick-set man, with coarse, commonplace features, and that swaggering air of pretension which marks a low man who is trying to elbow his way upward in the world." Treating coarse and commonplace as synonyms is hardly democratic, but if sainthood is a role all have an equal opportunity to apply for, "gentleman" is a title Stowe explicitly reserves for men of property and manners.

Stowe's ear for dialect was almost as fine as Mark Twain's. But Murray's Grammar, which Haley defies, was one of her fixed points of cultural reference, and she never allows her narrator's voice to speak in any but the most refined accents. The linguistic line between genteel whites and lowly blacks is held in place through all her attempts to expand the boundaries of middle-class sympathy to include the slave. At times there is a noticeable schizophrenia in this mixture of egalitarian intentions and snobbish means, as in this passage that treats all races as one, but not all modes of speech: "Black Sam, upon this, scratched his woolly pate, which, if it did not contain very profound wisdom, still contained a great deal of a particular species much in demand among politicians of all complexions and countries, and vulgarly denominated 'knowing which side the bread is buttered.'" The need for quotation marks here to preserve her distance from the vernacular is symptomatic of the aesthetic way she treats the "vulgar" throughout. Like Jay Gatsby, Fitzgerald's parvenu, she picks her words with a care that betrays the anxiety as well as the allegiance she and her readers shared as a class.

Two of her allegiances, however, inform the novel still more fundamentally than class. These are anchored to a pair of comparably sacred, omnipotent authorities: mothers and the New Testament. Indeed, often it is impossible to tell them apart. "*She* was *divine!*" is what Augustine St. Clare says about his mother; "She was a direct embodiment and personification of the New Testament." St. Clare, Tom's master during the novel's middle portions, is a middle-aged, well-traveled sophisticate whom worldly experience has turned into a cynical aesthete. But Tom's faith, coupled to the example of his own little daughter, brings him home to Christianity, and in this Victorian version of the parable of the prodigal son, home is presided over by a doting mother—and so, apparently, is heaven, as we learn at St. Clare's death bed:

"His mind is wandering," said the doctor.

"No! it is coming HOME, at last!" said St. Clare. . . .

So he lay for a few moments. They saw that the mighty hand was on him. Just before the spirit parted, he opened his eyes, with a sudden light, as of joy and recognition, and said *"Mother!"* and then he was gone.

The might of a mother's hand is underscored by Simon Legree's bad dreams, which are haunted by the holy ghost of his doting mother. Evil, Stowe reminds her readers, is an alchemist that can convert "things sweetest and holiest to phantoms of horror and affright." To Legree's "demoniac heart of sin," his mother's "forgiving love" becomes the "fiery" proof of his damnation; he is as terrified of a lock of golden hair that recalls his mother as a vampire is of the Cross. At night, it seems, grown men go back to that state St. Clare arrives at on the verge of death: "that of a wearied child who sleeps." The way Legree's Victorian mother, American ancestor of Portnoy's Jewish one, reigns over his pre-Freudian nightmares makes him pathetic rather than villainous, but Stowe cannot imagine an adversary more potent than mother love. Tom's parting advice to George Shelby, young son of his first master, is Stowe's revision of the first commandment: "Don't be gettin" into any of them foolish ways boys has of gettin' too big to mind their mothers." As a means of salvation, minding your mother almost makes God and the Bible superfluous.

This idolatry of motherhood might seem out of place in a devoutly Protestant novel, but the thematic prominence Stowe gives mothers and the way she regularly treats "maternal love" as a "supernatural power" are not the consequences of her theology. They are the first principles of her cultural faith. Stowe and her readers were nowhere more deeply in agreement, nor more apparently sure of themselves, than in their assumptions about the way the hand that rocked the cradle did indeed rule the world. As the recent feminist revisioning of the genteel tradition has noted, this belief can be seen as a fantasy by which women sought to compensate for the changing patterns of nineteenth-century American life; as the growth of a capitalist marketplace economy marginalized women, as they felt increasingly excluded from socially productive roles, they converted their place in the home's domestic "economy" into a moral and emotional throne. Maternal "power" was "supernatural" precisely because it was not political, or even real. That this was a form of fantasy, however, just increased the need middle-class women felt to insist on it, especially in the pages of the books, magazines, and annuals that were admitted into the home.

What kind of reverence and respect was due to mothers is what we hear in the archly smug tone of Stowe's voice when she talks about Rachel Halliday, the woman whose "face and form . . . made 'mother' seem the most natural word in the world": "Bards have written of the cestus of Venus, that turned the heads of all the world in successive generations. We had rather, for our part, have the cestus of Rachel Halliday, that kept heads from being turned, and made everything go on harmoniously. We

think it is more suited to our modern days, decidedly."
Eros is thus replaced by mother love, and even *caritas* is
made to wear Rachel's apron. As Rachel's son says,
"Mother can do almost everything"; when she presides
over breakfast, not only do the chicken and ham seem
glad to be sizzling in the pan ("as if they rather enjoyed
being cooked than otherwise"!), but also the "dark, misanthropic, pining, atheistic doubts" of George Harris, an
embittered runaway slave, "melt away" before the unction of her "motherliness." No scene in *Uncle Tom's Cabin*
is set in a church, but there are many that take place in
various kitchens, where the table supplants the altar, and
a mother's cooking becomes the eucharist. At Rachel's
table this is made explicit: "There was so much motherliness and full-heartedness even in the way she passed a
plate of cakes or poured a cup of coffee, that it seemed
to put a spirit into the food and drink she offered." Where
institutional Christianity puts the wine and wafer, where
Emerson put instead the orator's eloquence, Stowe (and
her readers) put homemade cakes and coffee.

Stowe's self-gratulatory celebration of home and mother
does serve her polemical purpose. The most persistent
way she dramatizes the evil of slavery is to describe its
brutal impact on family life; there are only a few chapters
that do not at least refer to the forced separation of mother and child by the slave trader or on the auction block,
and more than a few times that rending is described in
detail. In that famous scene when Eliza flees across the
ice on the Ohio River, she is presented not as a woman
escaping the personal horror or injustice of slavery but as
a mother desperately trying to keep her child. One lesson
that Stowe learned from Charles Dickens was that the
mass audience could be made to feel an injustice more
readily than it could be logically convinced of one. Given
her audience of "home readers," the most effective heart-
string for her to tug at was the maternal one. Susan Warner
had already demonstrated the potency of this motif: in
The Wide, Wide World all the emotional urgency of the
story derives from the fact that little Ellen Montgomery is
forced to leave her mother. They are separated by an act
of God—Mrs. Montgomery's failing health. Stowe's novel, while often fully as sentimental, deserves credit for
exploiting this motif for socially redeeming purposes. In
her novel, mothers and children are separated by the remediable acts of men.

Yet if motherhood as an abstract value dominates Stowe's
portrayal of slavery, so does Christianity. That modicum
of romantic love that has not been displaced onto maternal instinct, for instance, is transposed into the all-inclusive terms of the New Testament: "And your loving me,"
George Harris tells his wife, "why, it was almost like
raising one from the dead! I've been a new man ever
since!" Throughout the novel Stowe keeps two plot lines
in motion; both begin in Kentucky, then move in opposite
directions. The Harrises head north, to Canada, freedom,
and family reunion; Tom is carried south, to a lonely
death at Legree's hands. It would, however, be heretical
to decide that Tom's story ends any less happily than
Eliza and George's. Here is Stowe's own coercive synopsis of that story, offered just before Tom is killed:

The longest way must have its close,—the gloomiest
night will wear on to a morning. An eternal, inexorable
lapse of moments is ever hurrying the day of the evil
to an eternal night, and the night of the just to an
eternal day. We have walked with our humble friend
thus far in the valley of slavery; first through flowery
fields of ease and indulgence, then through heart-
breaking separation from all that man holds dear.
Again, we have waited with him in a sunny island,
where generous hands concealed his chains with
flowers; and, lastly, we have followed him when the
last rays of earthly hope went out in the night, and
seen how, in the blackness of earthly darkness, the
firmament of the unseen has blazed with stars of new
and significant lustre.

It is fair to say that Tom's movement southward does
work to initiate Stowe's readers into the true horror of
slavery, the institutional realities that always underlay the
benign appearance slavery assumed at the Shelby plantation. As a secular movement, Tom's journey is a fall:
from a type of paradise to an unmistakable inferno; in her
descriptions of Legree's plantation, Stowe uses the whole
glossary of Christian melodrama: "sooty," "diabolical,"
"fiendish," and so on.

But at the same time, when we consider the journey of
Tom's soul through that emblematic valley, we see that
he has not been moving downward at all, but upward, to
heaven. And the diction and imagery of Stowe's synopsis
require us to set his story in this allegorical context, where
worldly night translates as eternal day. Four times in her
novel she specifically mentions *Pilgrim's Progress,* the
definitive Protestant account of a soul's pilgrimage to
salvation. There were probably almost as many copies of
Bunyan's book in Victorian America as there were parlors; it is the book that Huck Finn, unacculturated as he
is, tries to read at the Grangerford plantation on the Mississippi just about the time that Tom would have passed
by on his way south. Brought up outside the pale of genteel Christianity, Huck does not know how to interpret
the allegory: it was "about a man that left his family it
didn't say why." But Stowe's readers knew why: because
in the Gospels Jesus had said that to be worthy of the
kingdom of heaven, a man must leave everything, even
sons and daughters, to follow him. Because it dramatized
the precepts of the New Testament so vividly, and thus
made theology entertaining to the mass public that read
novels, Bunyan's allegory supplied the popular writers of
mid-nineteenth-century America with their essential plot.
Homelessness, pilgrimage, suffering, trial, growing through
adversity toward God—these are the basics of Uncle Tom's
story, and Ellen Montgomery's, and Gerty Flint's, the
central character of *The Lamplighter*.

Ellen and Gerty are young, female, white, Anglo-Saxon
Protestants. Certainly Stowe displays a large amount of
sociological courage in stepping outside this pattern of
narcissistic self-reinforcement to put a black male slave at
the center of her novel. The most daring aspect of the
novel, probably, is the way that in the central chapters
she spiritually "marries" Tom to the book's heroine, Eva
St. Clare, who is young, female, white, and so on. As

Stowe points out through the character of Miss Ophelia, even in the free North the prejudice against blacks was deeply rooted. And as she reminds us many times, the official attitude toward Tom labeled him "chattel property." To refute both private prejudices and legalistic dehumanization, she gives Tom not just an immortal soul but a beautiful, redemptive one. By the end he becomes a black Christ, crucified by Legree yet able to forgive his oppressors. We may feel, however, that it would have been better for the cause of the slaves she is pleading so earnestly if she had made less of Tom as a Christian and more of him as a man, because the terrible paradox of Christianity is that it is precisely through suffering and submission that one earns immortal glory. Each third of her novel contains a character who resists or even rebels against fate. George Harris is prepared to kill for his and his family's freedom. Augustine St. Clare cannot accept the death of his daughter. Cassy—to the modern reader probably the most compelling character in the book—is Stowe's version of the Romantic dark heroine, within whose black eyes can be read a history of sexual oppression and abuse (which, needless to say, Stowe leaves largely unwritten) and fierce contempt for both her master and for the God who permits a man like Legree to exist. Cassy, as we first meet her, belongs in the company of Hawthorne's Hester Prynne and Melville's Ahab and Pierre. But doctrinally, resisting fate is rejecting Providence. "Bitter" is the adjective Stowe repeatedly, even obsessively, uses to describe these characters, all of whom must finally be soothed and tamed; the only response to personal suffering that Stowe's Christianity permits is the posture of resignation that has made Tom infamous:

> "O, Ma'r [he tells St. Clare], when I was sold away from my old woman and the children, I was jest a'most broke up. I felt as if there warn't nothin' left; and then the good Lord, he stood by me, and he says, 'Fear not, Tom;' and he brings light and joy into a poor feller's soul,—makes all peace; and I's so happy, and loves everybody, and feels willin' jest to be the Lord's and have the Lord's will done, and be put jest where the Lord wants to put me."

Uncle Tom does not actually deserve the particular reputation that he has. Although he is willing to be a good and faithful servant wherever the Lord puts him, he never ceases to want his own freedom; he tells Cassy that she should escape from Legree because her soul is imperiled; and in fact he dies because he will not betray where she and a fellow slave are hiding. The quarrel with Tom as a stereotype of the happy darky should more properly be with Stowe's Victorian Christianity, which thematically subordinates her concern with this life to the next. This might even seem to imply that slavery, by institutionalizing suffering and submission, is good for the slave's salvation, just as in Warner's novel several people point out to Ellen that it is for the best that she has been separated from her mother, else she might not have come to Him on whom her eternal happiness depends. "It is through suffering only," Cummins insists in *The Lamplighter,* that "we are made perfect." Like Bunyan's Christian, Tom attains a "Victory" within the novel, but it is not over

slavery. It is over religious doubt and his stubbornly human heart. Stowe's valuations become particularly problematic at the end of Tom's life, when he instructs young George Shelby, the son of his first master who finds Tom dying at Legree's, to tell his family and fellow slaves back in Kentucky "'to follow me—follow me!'" He even rebukes George's moral rage against Legree: "'He an't done me no real harm,—only opened the gate of the kingdom for me; that's all!'"

This missionary zeal for martyrdom seems to put much too high a price on the next world, and to sell one's claims in this world much too cheaply. As a protest novel designed to indict the "living dramatic reality" of slavery, ***Uncle Tom's Cabin*** is undermined by its other identity as an allegory about "a Christian soul goin' to glory," for there living realities are referred to higher, scriptural meanings. But of course, although she is writing on their behalf, Stowe is not writing for the slaves.

Her literary priorities—seeing reality through the eyes of a mother who cherishes the New Testament—reach a quintessentially Victorian-American apotheosis in the figure of Evangeline St. Clare, the blue-eyed, blond-haired little girl whose exemplary life and death define the spiritual dimensions that even a character like Cassy must be humanly diminished to fit. Eva is an impossible child, more attractive than Ellen or Gerty only because, though the daughter of slaveholders, she nonetheless feels deeply the wrongs of slavery. Yet what is most amazing about her is that, while Stowe and her readers agreed that Eva was too good, too innocent, too saintly to live very long in this polluted world, they would have been astounded at the thought that little Eva is too good to be true. To realize how thoroughly conditioned ***Uncle Tom's Cabin*** is by genteel ideals, we need only quote Stowe's first description of Eva, which doubtless was intended to "daguerreotype" her as well:

> Her face was remarkable less for its perfect beauty of feature than for a singular and dreamy earnestness of expression, which made the ideal start when they looked at her, and by which the dullest and most literal were impressed, without exactly knowing why. The shape of her head and the turn of her neck and bust was peculiarly noble, and the long golden-brown hair that floated like a cloud around it, the deep spiritual gravity of her violet blue eyes, shaded by heavy fringes of golden brown———

Enough. No picture emerges from this mélange of euphemism (bust), cliché (like a cloud), Sunday school eloquence (spiritual gravity), and abstraction (noble, beauty), but then again, the passage explicitly devalues a literal sensibility. Stowe and her readers united in prizing the ability to see the reality that was not there, whether that was the hand of Providence, maternal sovereignty, or little Eva. They read this passage and *saw* someone, but only because they had agreed beforehand on the meaning and validity of these terms. We read this passage, and all we can see is the pattern of pieties by which they understood reality.

This description is typical of Stowe's diction throughout, which linguistically leaves the ideals of her refined, Christian, lady readers snugly in place. Yet those contemporary readers were unaware of the way Stowe reconfirms their preconceptions, were instead roused by her book to a passionate conviction that something had to be changed. What remains for us to note is the equally consistent way Stowe puts her novel in opposition to American culture. In this context, even diction becomes a polemical resource. We could look, for example, at the dialogue in chapter 9, "In Which It Appears That a Senator Is But a Man." That title itself suggests one of Stowe's most incisive moral arguments: that man's existence in society is a fallen one, that the social roles he plays alienate him from his individual humanity. This was one of the cardinal points Emerson made in his transcendentalist attack on society: "Whoso would be a man, must be a nonconformist." The conversation Stowe records between Senator Bird and his wife further measures the distance between the statehouse, where laws are enacted, and a mother's home, where life is lived, and shows as clearly as Orwell would how the official language of politics serves to obscure the truth. The husband has just returned from Columbus, where he has helped pass a law "'forbidding people to help off the slaves'" as a means of "'quieting the excitement'" stirred up by "'these reckless Abolitionists'" and reassuring "'our brethren in Kentucky.'" The verbal distinctions here between slaves and people, reckless and brotherly, were exactly the ones by which politicians sought to preserve the status quo. Mrs. Bird sees through them in eloquently plain language:

> "And what is the law? It don't forbid us to shelter these poor creatures a night, does it, and to give 'em something comfortable to eat, and a few old clothes, and send them quietly about their business."

> "Why, yes, my dear; that would be aiding and abetting, you know."

"Aiding and abetting" is the legal abstraction Bird relies on to obfuscate the Christian virtues of love and charity. Stowe's contempt for the politic desire to play this game with matters of conscience is no mere liberal one. By the end of the chapter, after Senator Bird, brought face to face with the breathing reality of slavery, has helped Eliza to evade Haley's pursuit, he has become more than a man, more even than a nonconformist. He is now an outlaw.

As an exhortation toward "Civil Disobedience," Stowe's novel is as radical as Thoreau's essay. Her desire to write it may have been initially prompted by the passage of the Fugitive Slave Law, which made the North an accomplice in the business of catching and keeping slaves. But her indictment of American society—North and South—is far more sweeping. Again and again she attacks and subverts the "constitutional relations" of the United States. Alongside her consoling Christian moralism one finds her scathing treatment of institutional Christianity in America: "the dead sea of respectable churches" in which the values of the New Testament are

disgraced by the very "ministers of Christianity." Every figure in the novel is defined by his or her relationship to Jesus, but the only white Christians about whom Stowe has no reservations are the Quakers, a group that has embraced St. Clare's subversive conclusion about the antisocial consequences of true Christianity: "'My view of Christianity is such,' he added, 'that I think no man can consistently profess it without throwing the whole weight of his being against this monstrous system of injustice that lies at the foundation of all our society.'" The foundation of all society: St. Clare includes the wage relations between employer and laborer in exactly the same moral category as the chattel relationship between master and slave, thus lining Stowe's novel up with the *Communist Manifesto* Marx had published three years earlier.

Indeed, the business of catching slaves is only the most visible part of the complicity that, in Stowe's account, despite the protestations of her southern critics, binds North and South together in a monstrous system of evil—the very "business" of slavery. Perhaps her most radical, most tough-minded assault is the case she draws up against "business" itself, though that too is certainly a cherished American piety. She uses the word repetedly. Aptly, it is spoken first in the novel by Haley, the slave trader: "Well, I've got just as much conscience as any man in business can afford to keep." It is mentioned frequently in a later conversation between him and two other slave traders as they draw up a contract for running down Eliza and her son. Stowe expands her use of the word until one begins to feel that business in America is inseparable from this trade in human flesh. When, for instance, the steamboat, carrying Tom to market in New Orleans and proudly flying the American flag reaches the Mississippi, Stowe offers a culturally panoramic view:

> What other river of the world bears on its bosom to the ocean the wealth and enterprise of such another country?—a country whose products embrace all between the tropics and the poles! Those turbid waters, hurrying, foaming, tearing along, an apt resemblance of that headlong tide of business which is poured along its wave by a race more vehement and energetic than any the old world ever saw. . . .

These sentences are further proof of Stowe's brilliant ear for dialect, in this case the tub-thumping bombast of America's chambers of commerce. But with one sentence more she erases this materialist complacency; precisely because of its produce, the Mississippi is a river of tears that may yet be a river of fire:

> Ah! would that they did not also bear along a more fearful sight,—the tears of the oppressed, the sighs of the helpless, the bitter prayers of poor, ignorant hearts to an unknown God—unknown, unseen and silent, but who will yet "come out of his place to save all the poor of the earth!"

And when still later she recounts how a young quadroon named Emmeline is sold away from her mother to Simon

Legree to satisfy her owner's creditor, "the respectable firm of B. & Co., in New York," Stowe pointedly establishes the economic bond between business offices and Legree's plantation in the swamp. Like the slave trader, Brother B. has just as much conscience as any man in business can afford: "He didn't like trading in slaves . . . but, then, there were thirty thousand dollars in the case; and that was rather too much money to be lost for a principle."

As Stowe continues, through forty-five chapters, to point with irony and indignation at such "Select Incidents of Lawful Trade," her book gathers enormous moral force. It becomes a jeremiad as rhetorically compelling as any ever preached. The expression she puts on her prose evokes the look that Moses must have had on his face, fresh from his communion with God, holding the Ten Commandments in his hand and watching Israel worshipping the golden calf. The America she observes every day, in its constitutional relations, in its business affairs, from its legislatures and pulpits as well as on its plantations, damns itself. It is found in default of its political principles, as embodied in the Declaration of Independence, and its professed moral laws, as laid down in the New Testament. Like a swollen river, it is rushing toward Armageddon, for the New Testament whose values she defers to is a gospel of wrath as well as love. Even little Eva's favorite chapter is the Book of Revelation, and it is on a sustained note of apocalyptic urgency, a kind of moral wail, that Stowe ends her own "Concluding Remarks." "Christians!" she cries, leaving her audience without a shred of complacency to consider the last judgment of the new world, "every time that you pray that the kingdom of Christ may come, can you forget that prophecy associates, in dread fellowship, the *day of vengeance* with the year of his redeemed?"

Thus this book is split down the middle between confirming and condemning Victorian America. Stowe hangs "God will damn our country" right next to the sampler that says "God bless our home." It is time to note where she draws the line. While her critique of capitalism, like her portrayal of Tom's journey as a pilgrimage, is made sub specie aeternitatis, there is a still more striking dichotomy in the novel than the one between secular and spiritual realms. Unconsciously, Stowe segregates the culture she reflects into two worlds. As in that conversation between Mr. and Mrs. Bird, what is smugly affirmed throughout the novel is the world of women—home, mothers, gentility. What is radically attacked is the world of men—business, law, politics. Even Christianity is divided between the domestic and the institutional, the kitchen table and the pulpit, where the crucial but unacknowledged distinction is again the sexual one. It is frustrating to realize that Stowe, despite her moral clarity and sheer brilliance as a polemicist, never notices this split. There is one sentence in her last chapter that tries to make a connection: "If the mothers of the free states had all felt as they should, in times past, the sons of the free states would not have been the holders, and, proverbially, the hardest masters of slaves." Potentially this taps a reservoir of maternal guilt at least

as vast as that of maternal love she had drawn on so often earlier, but it alone cannot reconcile the two halves of the book.

Nowhere is this split clearer than at the end of the plot line that follows the Harrises to Canada. There the tone is very different from the fury Stowe whips up in her concluding exhortation; warmth and coziness prevail:

> The scene now changes to a small, neat tenement, in the outskirts of Montreal; the time, evening. A cheerful fire blazes on the hearth; a tea-table, covered with a snowy cloth, stands prepared for the evening meal. In one corner of the room was a table covered with a green cloth, where was an open writing-desk, pens, paper, and over it a shelf of well-selected books.
>
> This was George's study. . . .
>
> At this present time, he is seated at the table, making notes from a volume of the family library he has been reading.
>
> "Come, George," says Eliza, "you've been gone all day. Do put down that book, and let's talk, while I'm getting tea,—do."
>
> And little Eliza seconds the effort, by toddling up to her father, and trying to pull the book out of his hand, and install herself on his knee as a substitute.
>
> "O, you little witch!" says George, yielding, as, in such circumstances, man always must.

To Stowe and her readers this genteel setting, complete with cheerful hearth, tea-table and well-selected books, presided over by women, regulated by what Hawthorne called "homely witchcraft," was the full secular equivalent to the heaven that Tom attains in death. To be sure, there is one sharp irony in Stowe's account of it: only in Canada can these Americans be free to be a family; in a stunning reversal of America's self-serving mythology, she had earlier described the joy with which the Harrises had hailed "the blessed English shores." But the more urgent irony Stowe wholly misses. To be genteel, tea-tables must be covered with a snowy cloth; study tables, with a green one. And where did the cloths that Eliza doubtless washes and irons and keeps very neat come from? Perhaps the very cotton field where Uncle Tom died.

This is the point that Thoreau makes in *Walden,* his antislavery work. John Field, an Irish immigrant struggling toward gentility through his own Slough of Despond,

> rated it as a gain in coming to America, that here you could get tea, and coffee, and meat every day. But the only true America is that country where you are at liberty to pursue such a mode of life as may enable you to do without these, and where the state does not endeavor to compel you to sustain the slavery and war and other superfluous expenses which directly or indirectly result from the use of such things.

What Thoreau saw, but Stowe remains blind to, is that it was Victorian habits of consumption as much as male business practices that caused the economic and moral injustices she protests. *Walden* has many affinities with **Uncle Tom's Cabin,** including a narrative reliance on the plot of *Pilgrim's Progress* (though Thoreau applies the terms of Christianity to what Carlyle called natural supernaturalism). But Thoreau's emphasis is on white slavery, on how an individual's mind is trapped by the dominant prejudices of his culture. Harriet Beecher Stowe is a case in point. Making money is tainted, but spending it tastefully on decorous superfluities is a sacramental act. Little Eva must be daintily dressed—"always in white"—though it never occurs to Stowe, as it would to Thoreau, to count the number of slave hours that were spent picking the cotton to make her wardrobe. The "graceful," "beautiful," "elegant," "exquisite" furnishings in Eva's bedroom are described with a lavish and doting detail that is the narrative equivalent to a shopping spree. Rachel's table must groan with food. Even an ex-slave like Eliza needs an elaborate set of cotton tablecloths. These are the feminine pieties her book never challenges. Indeed, her tribute to them is as heartfelt as any part of her protest.

When Stowe's novel was published, its immediate popularity alarmed the guardians of the status quo because it seemed like a wedge driven between the North and the South. To anyone interested in American culture it is still a disconcerting document for the way it reflects a kind of Mason-Dixon line between the sexes. By the mid-nineteenth century, apparently, American husbands and American wives lived culturally at such extremes that "home" and "the wide, wide world" might as well have been located on two different planets. The only link between them, it seems, was the relationship between mothers and sons, which was consequently made to bear a huge and suffocating burden. To the student of American literature, however, there is one further consequence to note. If Stowe's endorsement of conventional gentility hobbled her as a social critic, it nonetheless gave her great freedom as a novelist. Because unconsciously she could divorce the essentially male evil she was attacking from the essentially female audience she was addressing, she felt invited to use all her powers as a writer, all the resources of popular fiction. That is why **Uncle Tom's Cabin** is the most Dickensian of all Victorian American novels. For Dickens identified the social evils he wanted to attack chiefly with the neofeudal aristocracy of rank and wealth; thus he could use his genius to entertain as well as instruct his middle-class reading public without feeling as though he were violating his integrity either as a writer or as a critic. The gender division served Stowe the same way this class division served Dickens: she and her home readers were on the same side.

This was an encouragement to expression that her male contemporaries never felt. Hawthorne's work makes a number of concessions to Victorian appetites and expectations. His light heroines—Phoebe, Priscilla, Hilda—resemble Eva, Ellen, and Gerty in ways that often make modern readers wince; two of the twenty-four chapters in *The Scarlet Letter* dramatically recount the threat of the Puritan patriarchs to separate Hester and her little daughter Pearl; his most popular story, "The Gentle Boy" (1832), is unfortunately one that Susan Warner would have been proud to have written herself. On the whole, though, as I shall discuss later, Hawthorne managed brilliantly to write for his audience without sacrificing his vision and to enjoy at least a moderate degree of success. Yet it did not seem so to him. In 1855, while everyone around him was reading *The Lamplighter,* he wrote a friend to complain bitterly about "that damned mob of scribbling women" who wrote the most popular stories of his time. "I should have no chance of success," he went on, "while the public taste is preoccupied with their trash—and I should be ashamed of myself if I did succeed."

Melville's fate reveals still more poignantly the cost of a novelist's ambivalence toward his or her prospective audience and misgivings about potential success. In the middle of his short, anguished career, Melville wrote "Hawthorne and His Mosses" (1850) to plead with the American public to nurture the American writer, and the audience to whom he looks is, like Stowe's, an explicitly maternal one: "Let America then prize and cherish her writers . . . she has good kith and kin of her own, to take to her bosom." Yet for Melville, as for Thoreau, this audience defined reality by the very preconceptions from which he was trying to struggle free. Thus Melville could not decide whether to write *for* or *at* those readers with whom Stowe felt so much at home; any desire to please them seemed to him a temptation to betray himself. His works too are split down the middle, but we have to draw the line in a different place—where Melville did: between himself and his only available audience. "What I feel most moved to write," he told Hawthorne, "that is banned,—it will not pay. Yet, altogether, write the *other* way I cannot. So the product is a final hash, and all my books are botches." He began *Pierre* (1852) determined to bridge these two extremes, and he began aptly, telling how Pierre Glendenning was driven away from his mother into the wider world. But as he narrated the tragedy of Pierre's naive attempt to be a writer, all his own accumulated resentments returned. Near the end, just before Pierre spits on his manuscript, Melville disgustedly repudiates his responsibilities as a narrator: "Nor does any canting showman here stand by." This is a rejection of more than the culture. It dismisses the very role that Dickens and Stowe could play as novelists. Any attempt to communicate with, much less to entertain the public, turns language into cant, and the writer into a debased showman.

Thoreau came to the same disgusted conclusion: "If you would get money as a writer or lecturer, you must be popular, which is to go down perpendicularly." Yet there is a better reason than money to seek popularity. In keeping with Romantic and Victorian notions of aesthetics, both Stowe and Melville gave the novelist a prophetic office. Fiction was a means, not an end; ultimately, it was a way to tell the truth. Pierre speaks for both when he declares that his ambition as a writer is to "gospelize the world anew!" But the Old Testament prophets were commissioned directly by God. Stowe put in a claim for that sanction, yet finally, of course, the novelist as prophet—

if her words are to have any larger authority, if his vision is to matter in the world—has to depend upon the appreciation of an audience. In his unwillingness to concede to the expectations of the American public, Melville lost, though just as unwillingly, his chance to arouse or redeem them, to tell them anything at all. Thoreau similarly sacrificed any opportunity to reach his contemporaries to his need to define himself. He could jokingly refer to the "mothers" in the audience of *Walden,* but he could only write for them by casting them into a role they could never have been expected to accept. In her first novel, on the other hand, Stowe became the only American novelist of her generation to cross the gap between great and popular fiction, although she was able to do so only because of the other great divide in her culture. What she felt moved to write was a vehement condemnation of American society. No one can doubt her sincerity, or her book's literary and moral power. But at the same time she wrote a best-selling novel that paid very well and deeply satisfied its reader's tastes—because the society she attacked was off at the office, while the one that bought books stayed home to read them.

Winfried Fluck (essay date 1992)

SOURCE: "The Power and Failure of Representation in Harriet Beecher Stowe's *Uncle Tom's Cabin,"* in *New Literary History,* Vol. 23, No. 2, Spring, 1992, pp. 319-38.

[*In the following excerpt, Fluck examines* Uncle Tom's Cabin *in terms of various definitions of sentimentalism, discussing both its cultural importance and its aesthetic limitations.*]

Reacting against a long history of neglect, current revisionist studies of American literature have drawn our attention to Harriet Beecher Stowe's *Uncle Tom's Cabin* as an especially rich and powerful example of sentimentality in the novel. Such attempts to make sense of materials which critics drawing on formalist and modernist models of the literary text are no longer able to read redress a long-standing imbalance in American literary history. As is well known, American literary history has almost always been uneasy with *Uncle Tom's Cabin,* as it has been with sentimentality in general. On the one hand, no critic can completely ignore the fact that *Uncle Tom's Cabin* is "probably the most influential book ever written by an American." On the other hand, the explicit or implicit aesthetic criteria governing literary histories in the period of high modernism do not provide for a principle according to which the novel could be discussed in any meaningful way. J. W. Ward [in *Red, White, and Blue: Men, Books, and Ideas in American Culture,* 1969] has put the case so well that his characterization of the ensuing dilemma necessitates another quotation: "For the literary critic, the problem is simply how a book so seemingly artless, so lacking in apparent literary talent, was not only an immediate success but has endured." One solution to this problem has been to acknowledge the

novel, somewhat grudgingly, as an important cultural and political event, whose deplorable aesthetic strategies might be excused for once, since they served a good purpose after all—namely that of mobilizing the American public against slavery. In this way, cultural and aesthetic functions are separated, as if they were not inevitably linked in the emergence and formation of meaning. In contrast, one of the purposes of the new revisionism and historicism in the study of American literature is to bridge this gap between a culturally oriented and an aesthetically oriented reading of fictional texts in order to permit an understanding of sentimentality as both a cultural and an aesthetic strategy.

In the following interpretation I want to draw on some of the results of these new readings of *Uncle Tom's Cabin,* and I shall then try to supplement and extend them. For it still seems that in talking about the sentimental in literature there is an apparently unavoidable tendency to be stuck with one of two choices: either to criticize sentimental fiction as a text that fails, or to explain and defend it by recovering its former cultural function. The two approaches, although strikingly different in emphasis, remain surprisingly similar in structure: both remain within a dichotomous mode of argumentation and cannot acknowledge any interplay between weaknesses and strengths. Thus, while in the first case the critic will be almost exclusively interested in the text's failures, in the second, the goal must be to secure the consistency of an assumed inner cultural and aesthetic logic of the sentimental text—an approach that, useful as it is, is often in danger of a gesture of mere inversion, because it assumes that to point out the potential cultural function of a literary text can also serve as an explanation of aesthetic effect.

As discussions of the problem have indicated again and again, however, the phenomenon of the sentimental in literature may be more complex than a primarily dichotomous model of argumentation suggests. Instead of opting for either the party of failure or for that of success, it seems more helpful and productive to me to relate these opposing perspectives with one another and to bring them thus into a dialogue. It will be my assumption in the following discussion that the two views sketched out are not necessarily mutually exclusive—for to assume so would also mean to assume that the other side is simply ignorant or blind. Rather, they can be seen to highlight different aspects of the same phenomenon—aspects which should both be taken into account and negotiated in one comprehensive reading. The task, in this case, would be to do both: to make an attempt to understand the inner working principles and cultural logic of sentimental fiction, and yet to account also for a modern feeling of discrepancy, excess, and exaggeration in parts of the novel that seems to be widespread.

For such a deliberately interactionist approach it is indispensable to keep the major possibilities of defining the sentimental in literature in mind, instead of opting for any single definition. This seems especially pertinent, since the concept of sentimentality, through its long and varied history, has assumed such a high degree of instability that, along with the word *realism,* it has almost become a "floating signifier" which no single definition can hope to tie down and anchor. Still, it seems useful to outline the three major approaches which definitions of the sentimental take: (1) the definition of sentimentality in literature in philosophical or cultural terms, that is, as a new epistemology or a system of cultural beliefs which developed in the eighteenth century and played an important role in American culture of the nineteenth century; (2) the definition of sentimentality in literature in terms of genre, that is, in terms of certain dominant narrative patterns, established, in essence, by Richardson and the sentimental novel of the eighteenth century; (3) the definition of sentimentality in fiction in a more narrowly formal and aesthetic sense, as a rhetorical strategy, or, as one might also say, as a mode of representation marked by gestures of rhetorical excess and exaggeration—an aspect of the text which, in contrast to the culture of sentimentality and the sentimental narrative, one could call sentimental rhetoric.

II

It has been one strategy of those literary and cultural critics who have retained an interest in **Uncle Tom's Cabin** even in the era of high modernism to emphasize the unusual scope and depth of its social analysis. In its attempt to present the slavery issue in all of its various forms and manifestations, the novel covers a wide range of social life, not only of the American South, but, where necessary, even beyond.

The depth of the novel's social analysis is most apparent in its deliberate attempts to provide a comprehensive picture of how slavery affects the American South: After being exposed first to the still paternal and relatively mild forms of slavery that prevail in the gentry household of the Shelbys in Kentucky, we are then taken further South, first to the aristocratic plantation of the St. Clares, with its alternating rhythm of fastidiousness and cruel neglect; until finally, in a further geographical and moral descent, we have to witness the debased forms of merciless exploitation and physical torture which prevail in the swamp land of Louisiana. In order to avoid the possibility that her case against slavery would be reduced to a discussion of particular instances and environments, Beecher Stowe obviously aimed at a fictional representation of slavery in its totality—which also meant to introduce elements of social and cultural differentiation between the various regional and social segments of the American South.

On the other hand, it is quite obvious that such sociological and realistic tendencies remain under the firm control of an unswerving moral perspective. Had sociological explanation and differentiation been carried too far, this would have invited the kind of rationalization and moral relativism by means of which the males of the novel, even such men of undeniable integrity as Shelby and St. Clare, manage to arrange themselves with the moral scandal of slavery. In order to counter similar rationalizations

in the reader, the novel had to insist on the priority of a single, superior moral criterion for dealing with the problem of slavery: As numerous critics have shown, it is this the power of the heart, of natural emotion and moral sentiment, to penetrate to the perception of a moral order—a sentimental epistemology which also has the effect of putting women in the position of superior moral authority.

On the whole, this characterization already points to a first tension or dilemma in the novel. On the one hand, the potential national novel has to sentimentalize itself in order to discuss the national disgrace from a truly moral perspective; while the sentimental novel, on the other hand, sociologizes and radicalizes itself in order to embrace questions of national self-definition. It is one explanation for the singular status of **Uncle Tom's Cabin** in American literary history that the novel must be considered an unusual, hybrid mixture of the social and the moral, of the potential of the historical and social novel linked with the strategies of sentimental fiction.

It may be helpful at this point to contrast this project of a national novel which tries to address a crucial question of American history from the perspective of sentimental fiction with another version of the literary genre which played such a prominent part in the attempts at a national self-definition which dominated the first half of the nineteenth century in the United States. Under the influence of Scott and starting with the work of Cooper, the historical novel had become one of the dominant genres in the development of American fiction. Designed to account for the historical emergence, social variety, and moral quality of a civilization, the genre seemed ideally suited for an examination of the new social order established in America. The guiding question in such books as, for example, Cooper's first Leatherstocking tale *The Pioneers,* clearly is to what extent this social order had already fulfilled the promise of a new and superior stage of civilization associated with the idea of America from its very beginning. In exemplary acts of conversion or rejection, of integration or symbolic expulsion, *The Pioneers* is therefore trying to use fiction as a testing ground for the symbolic reconstruction of a new social order in which the social and the moral would finally coalesce. For Cooper, at least the Cooper of *The Pioneers,* such a reunion can still be confidently envisioned—all that is required in order to effect a moral regeneration is a firm hand in controlling and, where necessary, eliminating the savage elements on the fringes of civilization.

In the hierarchical world of *The Pioneers,* divided into an upper world of civilizing forces and a nether world of savage elements, slavery does not yet pose a problem; in fact, Cooper does not even seem to be aware of its moral dimension. In contrast, Beecher Stowe sees the central moral problem endangering the promise of a new and morally regenerated American civilization not on its borders, but at the very heart of civilized society itself. If the social fabric is crucially contaminated by slavery, however, then such a defect can no longer be regarded as a temporary threat which can be safely entrusted to society's pioneers. What generates and shapes *Uncle Tom's Cabin* as a novel, in other words, is a fundamental split between the social and the moral order which threatens to undermine American civilization. Such a view must have been especially disheartening, since American society had based its self-definition on the prospect of establishing a new stage in the development of human civilization—which included the promise that the social and the moral which had fallen apart in a corrupt Old World could be successfully reunited in the New. The growing awareness of the problem of slavery, on the other hand, must have raised the terrible suspicion of a permanent split between the two orders. If something was to be done against this frightful prospect, then it had to be of a sweeping and sufficiently radical nature, transcending the carefully controlled rationality of the customary discussions of the issue. It is in this situation, as Philip Fisher has shown, that Beecher Stowe reappropriated the literary genre which is traditionally concerned with—in fact, seems to be brought into existence by—the conflict between the social and the moral: that of sentimental fiction.

My starting point, then, for the following discussion of *Uncle Tom's Cabin* is the assumption that sentimental fiction takes its departure from a rupture between the social and moral order which threatens to become permanent. In this it can be seen as a reaction to a historical moment in which the reality and superiority of the moral order can no longer be taken for granted and must be recuperated in a gesture of often violent reunification and reaffirmation. Such a view of the sentimental as being generated by, among other things, the fear of a permanent split between the social and the moral can help to explain two of its most obvious and enduring features. To start with, sentimental fiction is always constituted by a violation of the moral order, by an often violent separation of a person from his/her object of affection. The ensuing task of overcoming this fear of separation by reaffirming the seemingly endangered moral order at all costs, may provide a first suggestion for understanding the often forced and exaggerated nature of the sentimental reconciliation of the moral and the social.

The need for reaffirmation, in turn, draws attention to what I see as the basic problem of narrative representation in the sentimental text. If sentimental fiction wants to respond to the threat of a split between the two realms by reaffirming the reality and superiority of the moral order, then it has to find ways of representing this order in especially convincing and moving ways. Sentimental fiction can thus be regarded as a specific symbolic strategy to make an increasingly elusive order "visible" again. As the history and changing fortunes of sentimental fiction demonstrate, this has also remained its biggest problem. For since the values which it wants to elevate and represent in fiction are, by definition, immaterial and of a "merely" spiritual or emotional nature, the sentimental text has to rely on equivalents or analogies (if not allegories) for the moral realm. And this, in turn, may provide an explanation for both our positive and negative reac-

tions to sentimentality. On the one hand, the reader may experience the deliberate and emphatic channeling of emotions into an object of social analysis in positive ways, as a kind of recharging of the social world with moral meaning. Wherever he or she is, on the other hand, not convinced by the analogy for fusing the social and the moral, there will be the impression of a forced way of creating meaning.

III

The beginning of a novel is usually an especially important and instructive moment for understanding the project that is getting underway. Uncle Tom's Cabin begins with the description of a conversation between Tom's master, the gentleman farmer Shelby, and the slave trader Haley:

> Late in the afternoon of a chilly day in February, two gentlemen were sitting alone over their wine, in a well-furnished dining parlor, in the town of P——, in Kentucky. There were no servants present, and the gentlemen, with chairs closely approaching, seemed to be discussing some subject with great earnestness.

> For convenience sake, we have said, hitherto, two *gentlemen*. One of the parties, however, when critically examined, did not seem, strictly speaking, to come under the species. He was a short, thick-set man, with coarse, commonplace features, and that swaggering air of pretension which marks a low man who is trying to elbow his way upward in the world. He was much over-dressed, in a gaudy vest of many colors, a blue neckerchief, bedropped gayly with yellow spots, and arranged with a flaunting tie, quite in keeping with the general air of the man. His hands, large and coarse, were plentifully bedecked with rings; and he wore a heavy gold watch-chain, with a bundle of seals of portentious size. . . .

Two things may be noted for the purposes of our discussion. First, it is at this point still the authorial voice which is the main source of moral meaning for a reader who is placed in a safe position outside of the book. And second, the authorial voice can provide these moral meanings because signs can still be counted upon to represent the moral dimension of reality in a reliable way: the fact that Haley elbowed his way upward in the world and thus obviously violated the moral and social equilibrium (the image is of pushing others aside) is plainly visible in the embarrassing, almost grotesque violations of taste and proportion which characterize his outer appearance. The authorial voice can thus be quite confident that in piling up instances of such disproportion, it will be able to establish a consensus with the reader about the deplorable lack of a moral dimension in Haley's character. Ironically enough, however, it is this mode of representation, in which linguistic and visual signs do still have a stable moral referent, which also poses the main problem for the novel. This becomes obvious when the two men begin to talk about Tom:

> "Why, the fact is, Haley, Tom is an uncommon fellow; he is certainly worth that sum anywhere,—steady, honest, capable, manages my whole farm like a clock."

> "You mean honest, as niggers go," said Haley, helping himself to a glass of brandy.

> "No; I mean, really, Tom is a good, steady, sensible, pious fellow. He got religion at a camp-meeting, four years ago; and I believe he really *did* get it. I've trusted him, since then, with everything I have,—money, house, horses,—and let him come and go round the country; and I always found him true and square in everything."

The phrase "you mean honest, as niggers go" draws attention to the problem which Beecher Stowe had to overcome: within the dominant cultural convention, blackness may have held connotations of various possibilities, but not that of genuine morality. While all other signs can, in other words, be relied upon to represent a moral dimension of reality, in the case of the "black," this moral dimension is suppressed by the cultural semantics of blackness. What the novel thus has to do, if its argument is to be successful, is to transform and resemanticize the meaning of the sign "black" by moving it, as Yuri Lotman would put it, from one semantic field—which comprises all characters and settings linked by their lack of a genuine moral dimension—to the semantic field informed by genuine morality. Or, to put it differently, the fact that the public meaning of the sign "black" misrepresents Tom as a person does not lead the novel to a deliberate foregrounding of the tyranny of signs (as would be the case in high modernism and postmodernism), but to a concerted effort to resemanticize this one sign within a cultural system and mode of literary representation which the novel wants to strengthen, not to question, in order to achieve its own cultural and political goals. For this goal of a resemanticization, however, the comments of the authorial voice alone are obviously not strong enough, at least not for establishing and making visible a version of the moral order by which our feelings could be sufficiently engaged. If *Uncle Tom's Cabin* would have to rely on the narrator's power of persuasion alone, it would remain a form of mere preaching. The novel has to draw on other narrative devices such as, for example, melodramatic plot patterns, and of these the repositioning of the reader may be the most important and the most effective. Significantly, it is at the moment in which Mr. Shelby confesses that he has sold Tom and Eliza's child that the novel begins to move away from the Shelbys and, with it, from the gentry world of refined and enlightened society members, and begins to take the side of the victim:

> There was one listener to this conversation whom Mr. and Mrs. Shelby little suspected.

> Communicating with their apartment was a large closet, opening by a door into the outer passage. When Mrs. Shelby had dismissed Eliza for the night, her feverish and excited mind had suggested the idea of this closet; and she had hidden herself there, and, with her ear pressed close against the crack of the door, had lost not a word of the conversation.

> When the voice died into silence, she rose and crept stealthily away. Pale, shivering, with rigid features and compressed lips, she looked an entirely altered being from the soft and timid creature she had been hitherto.

By shifting to the perspective of one of the potential victims, the novel manages to transform us from an imaginary participant in a conversation with the authorial voice—and thus from the position of a social equal—to the stance of a helpless onlooker who can only compensate for his or her own helplessness by an intensification of emotional involvement. This is, of course, the basic transformation that the novel wants to achieve in the reader and on which it bases its whole theory of effect. The drama of separation, loss, and reunion, is thus repeated on the formal level of the text: sentimental texts want to eliminate aesthetic distance, but in order to achieve this, they first have to make us experience such distance as painful.

Yet the skillful narrative evocation of a fear of painful separation must be placed within the larger context of a moral order if it is to be effective. If the reader is to be shocked into an awareness of the vulnerability of the moral order, he or she must also be confronted with an image of that which is threatened; in other words, with versions of an intact order that can serve as a norm and countermodel for the staging of its possible breakup. It is here that sentimentality in the sense of a specific system of cultural values and beliefs comes into play, for it provides Beecher Stowe with powerful images for a still successful blending of the social and the moral realm. Significantly, Eliza is not only a woman but a mother; the fear of separation with which the novel begins is caused by the threat of a family breakup. In a typical sequence of events and chapters, the fear of separation created in the first three chapters is thus contrasted with a description of that idyll and institution which is threatened most in the novel, that of home and family. As Fisher has shown convincingly, it is the depiction of the family which provides the main metaphor for a still intact version of social and moral order in *Uncle Tom's Cabin*—at least at its beginning. This is not, as Fisher rightly asserts, to be understood as a retreat from the realm of the political. On the contrary, as long as we insist on seeing it that way, we will overlook the larger political and cultural implication of the move, that of a far-reaching dehierarchization and democratization. For, clearly, what the metaphor of the family does is to redefine a character such as Tom in a new social role: instead of emphasizing his ethnic identity, he is now presented in the roles of father, husband, and especially that of uncle, which establishes, in the very title of the book, a family relation between white and black. In emphasizing social rather than ethnic aspects of identity, a common emotional bond is thus created in order to encourage the reader to invest emotions which would otherwise be held back.

In view of the available options, this is a shrewd and effective strategy of humanization. Other metaphors of the nation—for example that of the ship—inevitably imply functional hierarchies. The family, on the other hand, was reconceptualized in the eighteenth century as the one social group which is held together by an emotional bond and thus entitles each of its members to a just share of solidarity and protection. As Ellen Goodman points out, the "family is formed not for the survival of the fittest, but for that of the weakest"; it is, beginning with the eighteenth century, no longer a primarily economic unit, but an emotional one. In consequence, the family emerges in *Uncle Tom's Cabin* as the most important barrier to a final split between the social and the moral which threatens the nation. Seen in this context, the sentimental discourse within the novel must be considered as a strategy by which the segregated black becomes a member of a nation redefined as family, and should thus be treated on the basis of a common emotional and social bond.

Such a strategy, which for the first time in American history may have managed to make the black visible as a moral being, was preceded by two similar acts of dehierarchization and democratization. The first wave of sentimental fiction established by Richardson in the eighteenth century can be seen as an attempt to elevate woman to the level of a socially equal and morally superior participant is social life. In the early nineteenth century, this sentimental claim is then further extended to include the figure of the child. And in *Uncle Tom's Cabin,* Beecher Stowe adds another link to this chain, and she does so by linking the figure of the black with that of the child—above all, with that of Little Eva who is a supreme example of all the sentimental idealizations of the child in the nineteenth century. The crucial argument which the novel levels against slavery is therefore not based on primarily political or philosophical considerations. Instead, the novel asserts the priority and necessity of a moral perspective. The most devastating argument against slavery is that it tears apart the one social body in which the social and the moral is still happily united, that of the family.

If the novel is to be effective in its argument, however, then it has to extend the sentimental chain to include yet another figure as part of the family, namely the reader himself. In a historical novel such as *The Pioneers,* the reader is still addressed as a primarily public self who is to be drawn into an ongoing dialogue on the nature and quality of American civilization. In *Uncle Tom's Cabin,* in contrast, the reader is urged to give priority to the private self and to overcome his or her rational distance in order to join the national family. For only as a person who relies on his or her own feelings and emotional responses as the primary source of knowledge will the reader be able to realize the full moral dimension of what is going on; only if the reader is willing to act and feel toward the victimized characters as if they were his or her own kin, will he or she be able to develop an intense feeling of moral responsibility.

It is within this context of a transformation of the reader that the role and significance of the melodramatic ele-
ments of the novel have to be seen. Quite obviously, they are sentimentality's other side of the coin. They provide the necessary dimension of threat and fear of separation—of which death is only the most spectacular and final—which is a necessary precondition for the forceful sentimental reaffirmation of union and togetherness. This function is already apparent in the very first scene of the novel in which our anxieties about the possible breakup of the social and moral fabric are evoked skillfully. This first threat of separation, melodramatically staged in the slave trader's offer to buy Eliza's little boy, marks the beginning of an endlessly repeated cycle of painful separations and happy reunions, of unbelievable streaks of misfortune and the most fortunate coincidences, of ever-renewed persecution and last-minute escapes. In both Tom's and Eliza's story, experiences of threat, loss, separation, and victimization form the center of the narrative. And in both cases, we can observe a basic interaction between melodramatic threat and sentimental reaffirmation. As a rule, it can be said that the stronger the melodramatic staging of loss, the stronger the sentimental reaffirmation following it. To give but three of the most obvious examples: the climax of Eliza's story and one of the most thrilling scenes of the novel, her hair-breadth escape over the raging river on its dangerously drifting pieces of ice, is soon followed by the heavily idealized picture of the major model family of the novel, that of the Quaker household. Similarly, the approaching deaths of Little Eva and Tom seem to increase the deliberately sentimental evocation of a higher link and purpose in their fates. Not accidentally, critics who dislike the novel have focussed on these scenes as the most problematical.

The melodramatic discourse thus plays its own role in the strategy of emotional activation and participation which the novel pursues. It is primarily responsible for putting the reader into the position of a family member who is cut off from his or her own relatives, longing for reunion. And this drama gains a special intensity and meaning, I think, because it is designed to act out a terrible suspicion: amid the constantly renewed cycles of misfortunes and unfortunate accidents, the impression must grow that the incessant violations of the moral order are committed without due punishment and proper moral retribution. The melodrama can thus be seen as that discourse in which the moral order has assumed an increasingly enigmatic dimension, and in which its very existence is questioned. The fear that it evokes is that the characters with which the reader sympathizes might have been left alone and deserted in a hostile universe. Its deeply disturbing events seem to defy the belief in a benevolent moral order governing our lives.

If all of this is correct, however, if the implied reader of the melodramatic discourse is that of a separated private self shaken by fears of loss, then this melodramatic element can also develop a tendency to work against the very discourse which it is designed to support, the sentimental affirmation of family and togetherness. For, as a rule, the melodrama has a built-in tendency to maximize its effects of victimization until the very last minute and thus to delay the moment of reassurance. The sentimental celebration of the idea of the family, on which Beecher Stowe bases her strategy, must be interested, on the other hand, in providing as many model images of the saving power of the family as possible. This is quite obvious (and works quite well) in the first half of the novel, where an alternating narrative rhythm between the melodramatic disturbance of the family and its sentimental reaffirmation prevails: the threat to Eliza and her family is followed by the description of Tom's idyllic family life; her narrow escape over the river is succeeded by the glowing idealization of the Quaker family. But as the novel progresses and shifts its narrative focus increasingly to the Tom plotline, the suspicion seems to increase that the family may not be strong enough after all to carry the full burden of a scenario of national regeneration. The two basic elements of the narrative, the melodramatic disturbance of a moral order and its sentimental reaffirmation, are thus in danger of falling further and further apart; which in turn means that if the novel wants to continue to provide effective images of reunion, it has to move to another analogy or, as Jane Tompkins puts it very fittingly, to another storehouse of commonly held assumptions.

In reaction, a third discourse within the novel becomes stronger and stronger—significantly at a moment in which the description of the family life at the St. Clares sharpens our sensibility that the family as a social body and cultural institution may not be strong enough to provide a real alternative to the social forces which have created and maintained slavery as a social institution. As a consequence, Little Eva, who is no longer at home in this earthly family, has to be moved to another, this time transcendent family, the celestial community of saints and innocents. And the problem increases even further as the novel moves on to the perverted, family-less world of the bachelor Legree, where a moral redemption of Tom's terrible fate can only be found in the analogy to the story of Christ. In both cases, that of Little Eva as well as that of Tom, the sentimental affirmation has thus to turn to the level of typological thought, that is, to a method of interpretation which gives moral meaning to characters and events by drawing on analogies to the Bible. At a moment of increasing threat that can no longer be controlled by the up to then prevalent forms of sentimental reaffirmation, the typological discourse provides a new stability to the semantic fields of the novel which have been destabilized by the extended melodramatic discourse; it thus makes it possible once again to know and judge with confidence.

Typological references can be found in the novel from the start. One of her (reluctant) black pursuers, for example, relates Eliza's miraculous flight over the river to the crossing of the river Jordan; similarly, the home, for example that of the Quaker family, can be seen as a type of Paradise to come. But such typological references remain dominated in the first part of the novel by the powerful enactment of its many melodramatic plot elements and by the richness of its social and political analysis. In the subplot around Eliza people may suffer, but they also find ways to escape and to rebuild their lives. In contrast, Little Eva and Tom become supreme examples of the

innocent, defenseless victim for whom Christ's redemption through sacrifice is used as a type. By this strategy, the novel gradually replaces one model of the moral order, that of the family, by another, that of the Bible as the highest authority on questions of moral justice and providence, of guilt and redemption, which we have in our Western civilization. In other words, in response to a growing doubt and anxiety about the existence of a moral order, the novel shows an unmistakable tendency to dissolve the sentimental discourse into the typological; or, to put it differently, to stabilize the increasingly difficult sentimental affirmation by reference to a holy text that can serve as supreme evidence of the existence of a moral order.

Not surprisingly, it is this level of typological reference with which modern readers have had the greatest difficulties. In fact, I think it is fair to say that for the modern reader the novel becomes increasingly difficult to handle the more it typologizes itself. For while the analogy of the family is still familiar and can be revived and reimbued with meaning, as Fisher's essay has shown, the typological affirmation of a moral order, as Jane Tompkins [in *Sensational Designs: The Cultural Work of American Fiction, 1790-1860,* 1985] in turn has shown, is no longer a code on which the modern reader can or wants to draw. (Significantly, the typological dimension of the novel is not even mentioned in Fisher's argument.) The gradual disregard of the typological dimension of the novel is already apparent in its immensely popular stage adaptations in the second half of the nineteenth century. What must have been an essential source of the novel's enormous impact and popularity at the time of its publication—its skillful blending of social analysis, melodramatic plot patterns, and sentimental affirmation of the family into the all-embracing context of a typological redefinition of the national dilemma, in other words, its extension of national history into eschatological vision—quite obviously poses the main problem for the novel's modern reception.

And this, I think, can provide some further insight into the problems with sentimentality which we may have as modern readers. For if sentimental fiction is indeed an attempt to reconcile the social and the moral, if it is, in other words, trying to make something visible that seems to have become increasingly enigmatic, then its success as a cultural strategy does not depend primarily on its rhetorical force, but on the familiarity, plausibility, and cultural authority of the analogies which it introduces for its own purposes of a literary representation of the threatened moral order. The often amazing impact of sentimental fiction can be explained by the fact that it has the courage to foreground those hidden models and metaphors through which we keep our faith, however tenuous it may be, in a form of life that still has a moral structure—metaphors such as the family, the collective, the loving couple. On the other hand, we will hold a strongly negative and maybe even derogatory view of sentimentality wherever we have the impression that the text wants to manipulate us into the acknowledgment of a value or metaphor which we are no longer willing to accept as a convincing configuration of union. With the loss of the cultural authority of the models and metaphors on which it bases its confidence in the possibility and power of literary representation, the literary text also loses its power to represent a moral order convincingly. What occurs as a result is a shift between levels of definition: instead of being an emotionally engaging literary representation of a system of cultural beliefs (definition 1), sentimentality in literature turns into only another case of rhetorical excess (definition 3).

IV

Such observations can lead back to a reconsideration of sentimental fiction as a mode of literary representation. Fiction can, by definition, be seen as that kind of discourse which tries to express something otherwise "unnameable" or "inexpressible." The story of the changing concepts of this otherwise inaccessible dimension of meaning is also a story of constant retreat: in nineteenth-century organicism, it is still a condensed essence which only great philosophical and artistic works can grasp; in twentieth-century formalism, it is the pressure of the artistic form that transforms the semantics of everyday language into a meaning that can no longer be retranslated into other forms of discourse; while in poststructuralism, meaning can no longer be grasped even as a somewhat elusive *Gestalt* configuration, but can only be conceptualized as a constant process of deferral and dissemination. In comparison—and this, I think, lies at the bottom of our contemporary distrust of the sentimental—sentimental fiction promises to do the impossible: it is still insisting on its ability to represent an invisible order in writing by drawing on a certain system of gestures and narrative devices, while modernism as an avant-garde movement has gone exactly in the opposite direction, namely to question the literary representation of authentic values by creating a carefully controlled system of ambiguities and indeterminacies that, at least in theory, would allow the reader to be part of that process of exploration which literature is supposed to initiate.

The aesthetic problem surrounding sentimental fiction would, in this case, not be its lack of rhetorical restraint, but its insistence on an idea of literary representation which disregards our modern awareness of the arbitrariness and inherently supplementary character of the process of signification. As we have seen in our interpretation of *Uncle Tom's Cabin,* however, sentimental fiction can indirectly acknowledge this inherent instability by gradually transforming itself in the process of its own, inner, narrative eventfulness. And this, in turn, can provide us with an additional explanation for the seemingly irrepressible tendency of the sentimental text to plunge into what the modern reader, as a rule, experiences as "excessive" representation. This excessive gesture, so all-pervasive on all narrative levels of sentimental fiction, can best be understood, I think, as an attempt to recuperate its own power of representation and thus to counter the fears of a failure or even breakdown of its own project of reuniting the social and the moral. A strange irony is at work here: the

more the sentimental text becomes afraid of failing, the more it strains itself; the more it strains itself, however, the more it begins to undermine its own premise that an adequate representation of the moral order is still possible; and the more it undermines itself, the more it can be reappropriated by a postmodern sensibility.

From this perspective, sentimental fiction can be seen as a mode of representation generated by a profound anxiety about its own moral referent, which in turn pressures the text toward a permanent surplus of signification. The sentimental text, however, is not a postmodern text and it would be inappropriate to turn it into one—especially in the case of *Uncle Tom's Cabin*. Instead, it seems more adequate to say that in our contemporary reception sentimental fiction is distinguished by the fact that it occupies something like a middle ground between two possibilities and functions of fiction. On the one hand, the sentimental text tries hard to retain the moral referent which it is trying to represent. In other words, an aspect of the "real," or, at least, the fiction of it, is maintained, which modernism and postmodernism tries to question. And this also means that of all the genres based on the idea of a possibility of representation, the sentimental text may work hardest against a technique of self-reflexive distancing which leaves us emotionally "flat." Instead it deliberately and unashamedly invites us to fuel our emotions and desires (for union) by projecting them into a system of signs and images. Since what we experience as rhetorical excess has a tendency to draw our attention to the text's failure of representation, we are, on the other hand, reluctant to accept this fiction of the "real" as authentic, but remain aware of its fictionality. In our contemporary reception we are thus caught in the middle, or, to be more precise, we are constantly moving between emotional involvement and a mode of ironic distancing (something, by the way, that seems also typical of our contemporary attitude toward the opera). Ironically enough then, it is in this sense of a permanent interaction between stances that seem mutually exclusive, between a constant breakdown of the power of representation into a failure of representation which foregrounds itself, that a sentimental novel such as *Uncle Tom's Cabin* can gain new power and aesthetic interest.

To speak of a failure of representation, however, may not appear to be the best way to support a renewed interest in the novel and may irritate those who want to argue for the strength of the book's social analysis. For even though I have tried to distinguish the text from consistently postmodern modes of signification, one may still claim that I have submitted the novel to a kind of indirect "postmodernization" by pointing out its instability of meaning and the ensuing inner "eventfulness" of its representation. This instability, however, is confirmed by the very readings, most of them of a revisionist or "historicist" kind, which want to deny it. The pattern of substitution of a moral referent which we observed in the novel itself is reenacted by current revisionist criticism; taken together, it inevitably mimics the novel's sequence of substitutions, because the moral referent which the novel is supposed to represent can never be prescribed satisfactorily. On the contrary, it is constantly redefined in terms of the various views of social relevance which can be found in revisionist criticism: in Fisher's reading the moral meaning of the novel is derived from a benign populism developed through the analysis of Cooper's work, while for Tompkins the novel represents an idealized version of female communality which she derives from her reading of the domestic novel. For W. B. Michaels [in *The American Renaissance Reconsidered*, 1985], the novel represents a fear and critique of market relations, whereas Gillian Brown [in "Getting in the Kitchen with Dinah: Domestic Politics in *Uncle Tom's Cabin, American Quarterly*, Vol. 36, 1984] sees it as both a representation of domestic values and their utopian rehabilitation through a critique of male hegemony; for this "activist female model Stowe proposes," which marks the "arrival of woman as a revisionary social critics," Cassy becomes the role model. Jean Fagan Yellin [*New Essays on "Uncle Tom's Cabin,"* 1986], on the other hand, who examines the novel from the point of view of Angelika Grimké's feminism, fails to see such a critique and finds the only saving grace in certain similarities between Little Eva's and Grimké's lives, which establish Eva as a "budding social activist." And while Brown and Yellin emphasize a certain degree of ambivalence in the novel's discussion of domesticity, Elizabeth Ammons [in *New Essays on Uncle Tom's Cabin*, 1986] celebrates it as a successful affirmation of "matrifocal values." Such a list could be extended.

Had the novel managed to represent its model of social and moral order successfully, then this constant substitution of a moral referent would neither be possible nor necessary; in fact, it would have to be considered as a diffusion of the novel's message. Thus, revisionist critical practice, like any other interpretive practice, is made possible by a lack which, on the overt level of argumentation, it tends to deny in its attempt to complement the text with that historical or feminist subtext which would supposedly be able finally to make the novel's process of signification stable and transparent. One may argue, however, that, far from being a shortcoming, it is the very "failure" of representation which, in a strange paradox characteristic of fiction, secures the novel's effectiveness: if the text—as might be the case, for example, if it were exclusively typological—had not left any space for that ongoing process of imaginary supplementation in which current revisionism, although it may not like to acknowledge this, still partakes, then *Uncle Tom's Cabin* would not have been able to affect as many readers as it did, nor would it have been able to become meaningful again for contemporary readers, including those who have recovered important dimensions of its meaning and have therefore added to our understanding of the novel and its cultural impact.

Jennifer L. Jenkins (essay date 1992)

SOURCE: "Failed Mothers and Fallen Houses: The Crisis of Domesticity in *Uncle Tom's Cabin,"* in *ESQ: A Journal of the American Renaissance*, Vol. 38, No. 2, Second Quarter, 1992, pp. 161-87.

[*In the following excerpt, Jenkins examines race, sexuality, and motherhood in* Uncle Tom's Cabin, *tracing what she contends is the collapse of Stowe's domestic plot.*]

So this is the little lady who made this big war.
—Abraham Lincoln

Harriet Beecher Stowe viewed slavery primarily as a domestic issue. From her childbed she thought of it, at her kitchen table she wrote of it, and her novel of slavery reflects this domestic atmosphere. For Stowe, slavery threatened the integrity of the family, and with a domestic tale she might best illustrate this danger. Thus, in her fiction mothers represent the domestic realm and guard the home against worldly contaminations. In *Uncle Tom's Cabin,* however, that reforming maternal force fails. As the novel moves along its agenda of illustrating the evils of slavery, the corresponding narrative deviates from its original form. Political concerns exaggerate all aspects of domestic life, in some cases transforming the benign into the horrific, the loving mother into the angel of death. The progressive collapse of domesticity in the novel enacts the failure of Stowe's domestic novel as such: as the scenes move from hearth to hell, the narrative shifts from domestic to gothic. *Uncle Tom's Cabin* so politicizes both story and telling that only failed mothers, fallen houses, and a fractured domestic plot remain.

The Stowe-ic philosophy is a fatal contamination to woman.
—George Holmes, *Southern Literary Messenger*

Stowe insists in *Uncle Tom's Cabin* that the divisive culture and politics of mid-nineteenth-century America are merely symptoms of a troubled family. Preoccupied with home and family in her own life, she proposes these two forces as common elements in both black and white life in her fictional antebellum South. In *American Woman's Home* (1869) she would promote a domestic separation of labor, in which men build houses and women oversee the households: "The family state then, is the aptest earthly illustration of the heavenly kingdom, and in it woman is its chief minister. . . . To man is appointed the out-door labor." Woman, the "chief minister," rules this domestic heaven, while man is expelled from the maternal "kingdom" to the world of work. Male guilt for abandoning religion and family in favor of trade, according to Barbara Welter [in *Dimity Convictions: The American Woman in the Nineteenth Century*, 1976] produced this ministerial ideal of the feminine: "He could salve his conscience," she argues, "by reflecting that he had left behind a hostage, not only to fortune, but to all the values which he held so dear and treated so lightly. Woman, in the cult of True Womanhood presented by the women's magazines, gift annuals and religious literature of the nineteenth century, was the hostage in the home." This "cult of True Womanhood" or "cult of domesticity" idealized a pious indoor life of refinement and efficiency designed to please the master, and to transform the mistress into an "angel in the house."

Like any cult, however, domesticity had its dangers.

Though the house could symbolize inherited identity for a man, for a woman it often threatened identity itself. With the rise of manufacturing and city-based industry, women, who had once shared pioneer life out-of-doors with men, increasingly were sent to their rooms. For women writers, in particular, the house became an utterly other sort of icon. Built by father, brother or husband, the house could soon prove prison, madhouse, seraglio, or charnel house to its female inhabitants. By the nineteenth century, the enclosure of frontier forests had given way to equally oppressive walls and roofs. Small wonder, then, that houses could become places of some distaste and horror in the female imagination. In *Uncle Tom's Cabin* domestic confinement produces uncanny tendencies both in houses and in the women who run them. So, while Stowe subscribes to contemporary sentimental ideologies of domesticity, her novel actually posits domestic space as a gothic site.

As in most domestic novels, mothers are the agents of power in *Uncle Tom's Cabin*. Stowe contends polemically that motherly love is sacred, demonstrated in pity, tenderness, and prayers—an argument consistent with her image of a domestic heaven. Appropriating this trope, Jane Tompkins has argued [in *Sensational Design: The Cultural Work of American Fiction, 1790-1860,* 1985] that *Uncle Tom's Cabin* offers to "reorganize culture from a woman's point of view," and thus becomes a feminine hagiography of sorts: "It is the *summa theologica* of nineteenth-century America's religion of domesticity, a brilliant redaction of the culture's favorite story about itself—the story of salvation through motherly love. Out of the ideological materials at their disposal, the sentimental novelists elaborated a myth that gave women the central position of power and authority in the culture." This good, Christian mother is the maternal type that Tompkins has found to be a compelling icon in American culture. Indeed, Stowe herself attributed such motherliness to women of all classes and races.

Yet the mothers of *Uncle Tom's Cabin* appropriate this position of authority not by means of love, but of fear. As Julia Kristeva notes, the Christianized notion of maternal love offers "the whole range of love-types from sublimation to asceticism and masochism." One loving, harmless mother does appear in the novel: the Quaker Rachel Halliday. She stands as the cultural ideal of motherhood against which all other mothers in the novel may be measured. When Stowe's women deviate from this benign stereotype they become gothic images of the feminine, and degenerate into extremes: either the madwoman-vampire, or the self-sacrificing mamma who obsessively loves her children to death. The good mothers become particularly horrible, due to the suffocating intensity of their maternal love. The effect of this ambivalent maternal force is sameness: the vampire and the angel become indistinguishable. From Mrs. Shelby to Mrs. Legree, Stowe's mothers neglect, deceive, or abuse their offspring. As the plot of the novel moves the characters from one mother to the next, an encyclopedia of domestic collapse takes shape. Angelic but insidious mammas meet the underground railroad, while the river journeys on the

Mississippi and the Red carry Tom from termagant to shrew to madwoman. Such domestic disruption and collapse fractures the plot and subverts the narrative of *Uncle Tom's Cabin*.

2

> For abjection, when all is said and done, is the other facet of religious, moral, and ideological codes on which rest the sleep of individuals and the breathing spells of society.
>
> —Julia Kristeva, *Powers of Horror*

Chapter 2 introduces Eliza Harris, ostensibly the subject of its title—"The Mother." The opening statement leaves that role ambiguous, however, for Mrs. Shelby does the active mothering: "Eliza had been brought up by her mistress, from girlhood, as a petted and indulged favorite." Despite marriage and motherhood, the doll-like Eliza remains an innocent. Battered by the forces of nature and humanity, she will face her greatest perils alone, and only at the very end of the novel will she demonstrate any behavior that links her with the mothers of the story. Although driven by "maternal love" to escape across the ice floes, Eliza functions in the novel much as Eva does: as a pure, Christian child.

Despite her title of "missis," Emily Shelby's behavior towards Eliza is distinctly maternal. She gives Eliza the room next to her own, keeping her "safe under the protecting care of her mistress." Eliza grows up in "the house" rather than in a cabin, learning the manners and speech of a white family member. The motherly hand of Mrs. Shelby even touches Eliza's marriage to George Harris:

> With a little *womanly complacency* in match-making, [Mrs. Shelby] felt pleased to unite her handsome favorite with one of her own class who seemed in every way suited to her; and so they were married in her mistress' great parlor, and her mistress herself adorned the bride's beautiful hair with orange-blossoms, and threw over it the bridal veil. . . . For a year or two Eliza saw her husband frequently, and there was nothing to interrupt their happiness, except the loss of two infant children, to whom she was passionately attached, and whom she mourned with a grief so intense as to call for a gentle remonstrance from her mistress, who sought, *with maternal anxiety,* to direct her naturally passionate feelings within the bounds of reason and religion. (emphases added)

Plainly treating Eliza as a daughter—overseeing the wedding, comforting her through the sorrows of infant mortality, and worrying over her morbidness—Mrs. Shelby even allows herself the conceit of attributing Eliza's skin color to "class" rather than race. Remembering that Eliza has "that peculiar air of refinement, that softness of voice and manner, which seems in many cases to be a particular gift to the quadroon and mulatto women," Mrs. Shelby's motherliness may be more than a convenient fiction. Eliza may be more a part of the white family than we know. Mary Chesnut's contemporary remark is wryly to the point: "Any lady is ready to tell you who is the father of all the mulatto children in everybody's house but her own. Those, she seems to think, drop from the clouds." Suggestively, Mrs. Shelby tries to calm Eliza's justified fears for her son Harry by emphasizing, "'I would as soon have one of my own children sold.'"

Yet Mrs. Shelby's solicitude may also veil a prevailing cultural anxiety toward mulatto sexuality. Chesnut's comment on mulatto children is not exceptional; mixed-race women proved a definite threat to white female sexuality and property rights. Edward Said [in *Orientalism,* 1978] describes a popular white conception of women of color: "[They] are usually the creatures of a male power-fantasy. They express unlimited sensuality, they are more or less stupid, and above all they are willing." Such an image could prove extremely worrisome to white women who were bound by stricter cultural laws of religion and dress than their exotic sisters. Kristin Herzog [in *Women, Ethnics, and Exotics: Images of Power in Mid-Nineteenth Century American Fiction,* 1983] reports of the American domestic novel that "while exotics were seen as passionate, . . . ethnic characters closer to home were more likely to be considered submissive." Herzog makes a polarity out of a situation that was undoubtedly causal: *because* exotics were seen as passionate, those close to home were more likely to be submissive, or made so by their mistresses. That "particular gift" (that is, submissive refinement) of mulatto and quadroon women may account for Eliza's very presence on the Shelby place; it may also explain her mistress's determination to have Eliza married and Christianized. Mrs. Shelby's "complacency in match-making," then, may have much to do with the motherly rewards of veiling Eliza's mark of sensuality— her "beautiful hair"—and of channeling Eliza's sexuality into a union "with one of her own class" (i.e., not a white man). In [*White Over Black: American Attitudes Toward the Negro, 1550-1812,* 1968] his landmark study of attitudes toward race, Winthrop D. Jordan explains the convenience of merging class and race:

> The colonist on the American continent . . . remained firm in his rejection of the mulatto, in his categorization of mixed-bloods as belonging to the lower caste. . . . Interracial propagation was a constant reproach that he was failing to be true to himself. . . . For the separation of slaves from free men depended on a clear demarcation of the races, and the presence of mulattoes blurred this essential distinction. Accordingly he made every effort to nullify the effects of racial intermixture. By classifying the mulatto as a Negro he was in effect denying that intermixture had occurred at all.

Along with keeping Eliza in her own "class," Mrs. Shelby attempts to "direct her naturally passionate feelings within the bounds of reason and religion." By defining Eliza as a child, a wife, and a Christian, Mrs. Shelby may successfully guard against an outburst of the mulatto's "naturally passionate feelings," while ensuring their existence as a mark of difference. Eliza must not be white, but she must not be too exotically nonwhite, either. Although Mr. Shelby's vices run toward fiscal rather than sexual promiscuity, his wife forestalls any opportunity for the denial of racial difference that Stowe counsels in her novel's

preface. Mrs. Shelby fulfills the cultural trope of the sentimental mother, but Stowe's language seems to suggest, albeit unwittingly, that such a trope is pure masquerade.

Thus, Mrs. Shelby's maternal bounty is superficial at best. She contrives a filial relationship which exists largely for the sake of appearances. While not malicious, her treatment of Eliza is indeed thoughtless. With the sale of Tom and Harry confirmed, Emily Shelby's initial thoughts are not those of a surrogate mother and grandmother; but rather (like her husband), she fears that her authority has been challenged. Concerned first for her own credibility, she asks: "'How can I ever hold up my head again among them, if, for the sake of a little paltry gain, we sell [them] . . . how can I bear to have this *open acknowledgment* that we care for no tie, no duty, no relation, however sacred, compared with money? . . . how will she [Eliza] believe me . . . ?'" (emphasis added). The "open acknowledgment" of the Shelbys' true relation to their slaves holds far more horror for Mrs. Shelby than does the actual sale of these two purported members of the family. Mrs. Shelby's passivity—or cowardice or neglect—precipitates Eliza's escape and, subsequently, the famous flight across the ice floes to Ohio. Eliza leaves behind domestic arrangements on the Shelby plantation which are largely illusory, for the actual "family" shrinks (and pales) when put to the test.

The treacherous route north carries the narrative from a domestic setting into the realm of erotic terror. The hunt for Eliza involves the capture of a "treasure," and Stowe's narrative repeatedly describes Eliza as not only pricey but toothsome. The Quaker Phineas Fletcher overhears bounty hunters say that "two of them were going to run [her] down to New Orleans to sell, on their own account, and they calculated to get sixteen or eighteen hundred dollars for her." The lip-licking slave-catcher Marks, "his sharp eyes, nose and mouth, all alive with enterprise," says that she is "'white and handsome.'" Should Eliza be captured, her body and her virtue will almost certainly suffer for her escape. Eliza's flight has a dimension of erotic suspense that appears in many sentimental novels: an innocent woman flees horsemen armed with whips and guns. Predatory descriptions of her pursuers dominate the narration. Haley chases her to the Ohio riverbank "like a hound after a deer"; similarly bestial descriptions characterize Loker and Marks in the riverside tavern in Kentucky. Loker resembles a "bull-dog come unto man's estate" in whom "brutal and unhesitating violence was in a state of the highest possible development." His companion Marks, the feline "mousing man," has "a long, thin hand, like a raven's claw."

While these sadistic and cannibalistic slave-catchers are trying to make good for the trader Haley on the sale of little Harry, they are also symbolic agents of the Shelbys. For Eliza, they constitute an immediate sexual threat as well as an implicit rebuke for leaving Mrs. Shelby. In the scenes of pursuit of Eliza, Stowe mixes the threat of parental power with sexual danger. The two combine to punish Eliza for running away and for her exotic sexuality, both violations of the white mother's power. This threatening combination of the domestic and sadistic wrenches the narrative away from the theme of motherly love, exposing the tenuousness of the domestic plot and identifying the slaveowning home as a gothic site.

3

He maketh a barren woman to keep house,
and to be a joyful mother of children.
—Psalm 113

Benign mothers are scarce in the South to which Haley takes Tom. New Orleans, site of the most debased mothers in the novel, lies at the end of a long, muddy river, and is a town of mysterious, alluring, flower-filled compounds. The Mississippi River functions for Tom as the Ohio does for Eliza: as a physical and psychological border. While Eliza's crossing is an escape and a rebirth, Stowe implies that Tom's passage to New Orleans is, both geographically and politically, a descent. His journey south on "those turbid waters" of the Mississippi carries him through "the shivery canes, and the tall, dark cypress, hung with wreaths of dark, funereal moss" to the decadent, feminized city of mixed races and religions. Stowe emphasizes the spooky nature of the landscape, playing on the "funeral" atmosphere of the South to make her point about its uncanny ways. The conditions described in Tom's tale are even more gothic than those of Eliza's flight, perhaps because Stowe was imagining terrain which she had never seen.

The St. Clare mansion houses an extreme of Southern decadence and ennui, displayed in its "Moorish" architecture and "picturesque and voluptuous ideality." The entire compound abounds in eastern, "arabesque" and exotic details and plantings. Stowe emphasizes the exotic and non-Christian dimension of life in her imaginary South, listing the "Moorish" and "Arabian" elements of the garden's design and plantings, and associating them with the time of "oriental romance in Spain." By conflating the Orient, the Moors, and Spain, Stowe constructs a body of images that, for her, describe the nonwhite, non-American, non-Calvinist world. Indeed, the novel's representative New Englander, Ophelia St. Clare (pronounced "Sinclair" at home in Protestant Vermont), labels Eva's "'own dear, darling home'" "'rather old and heathenish.'" Thus Stowe draws her South as not only more European than American but even more Oriental than European. Coincidentally, Karen Halttunen finds a very similar garden in Henry Ward Beecher's gothic "The Strange Woman," a lecture on the evils of "the prostitute's 'house of death.'" Reverend Beecher placed in his imagined house a seductive mistress, a woman who, like the dissipated Marie St. Clare, feeds on life and casts aside the bodies.

Stowe's imaginative descriptions of the South demonstrate the same sensationalism that Said finds in many Western treatments of the Orient. Said notes that within the binary opposition of Europe and Asia, "it is Europe that articulates the Orient; this articulation is the prerogative, not of a puppet master, but of a genuine creator, whose life-giving power represents, animates, constitutes the otherwise silent and dangerous space beyond familiar boundaries." From Brunswick, Maine, Stowe set out to follow her sister-in-law's advice, and "write something that will make this whole nation feel what an accursed thing slavery is," and in the process did indeed become "a genuine creator" of the "otherwise silent and dangerous space beyond [the] familiar boundaries" of the Ohio River. Her portrait of the South emphasizes the same sort of detail that Said identifies in the various European creations of the Orient: "It is their vacillations, their tempting suggestiveness, their capacity for entertaining and confusing the mind, that are interesting." In describing a virtual terra incognita, Stowe alternates her emphasis on the domestic with exotic details. While Tom's journey from cabin to mansion contains no overt element of sexual danger, the lushness and sensuality of the South do create a picture of a seductively, dangerously feminized and decadent place. Such an environment, Stowe suggests, can only produce corrupt and horrific versions of the family.

Marie St. Clare dominates the New Orleans section of **Uncle Tom's Cabin.** Enclosed in the Moorish, flower-filled decadence of the St. Clare mansion, this "tall, dark-eyed, sallow woman" rules her home through hypochondria and peevishness. Marie is a domestic tyrant who bullies her family and complains that she has not the strength to beat her servants. Her maternal instincts are all directed inward, to indulging her own hypochondria. Stowe shrewdly assesses her condition: "There is not on earth a more merciless exactor of love from others than a thoroughly selfish woman; and the more unlovely she grows, the more jealously and scrupulously she exacts love, to the uttermost farthing." Marie's version of motherhood inverts Stowe's traditional notion of maternal sacrifice, for she must be the center of attention, servants and children deferring to her needs. Indeed, her character is the antithesis of that which Stowe and her sister Catharine Beecher would promote as womanly in their **American Woman's Home** two decades later:

> Woman's profession embraces the care and nursing of the body in the critical periods of infancy and sickness, the training of the human mind in the most impressible period of childhood, the instruction and control of servants, and most of the government and economies of the family state. These duties of woman are as sacred and important as any ordained to man.

There is no danger that Marie St. Clare will perform any of these sacred duties. She redirects all nursing, training of children, and instruction of servants toward fulfilling her own whims. Instead of nurturing those around her, she feeds off the entire household. Antebellum sociologist George Fitzhugh [in *Sociology for the South,* 1854] hailed this type of woman as proper and seemly: "So long as she is nervous, fickle, capricious, delicate, diffident and dependent, man will worship and adore her. Her weakness is her strength, and her true art is to cultivate and improve that weakness." However seemly her condition, Marie sucks the life out of her family with her petty demands and capricious fits of "sick-headache." The narrator notes, apparently without irony, that Marie's parasitical nature developed in part as a result of motherhood:

> A life of constant inaction, bodily and mental,—the friction of ceaseless ennui and discontent, united to the ordinary weakness which attended the period of maternity,—in course of a few years changed the blooming young belle into a yellow, faded, sickly woman, whose time was divided among a variety of fanciful diseases, and who considered herself, in every sense, the most ill-used and suffering person in existence.

Expanding her postpartum confinement into a way of life, Marie becomes nearly vampiric in her habits. Bright light and activity drive her to inhabit shuttered rooms. Reclining behind curtains and veils, her body covered by rugs and draperies, she torments Mammy and St. Clare with selfish demands and petulance. She warns, "The least breath disturbs me; and a strange hand about me would drive me absolutely frantic." Marie even appropriates Eva's tuberculosis, energetically claiming the bloodless and ethereal condition as her own.

Yet, as the angelic Eva grows pale and weakens, her mother conversely gains the strength and will to indulge in repeated fits of "violent hysterics" which almost certainly contribute to Eva's death. Marie diverts attention from Eva to herself, declaring that "the state of her mind was such, it was impossible for her to rest"—the narrator adding, "and, of course, it was against her principles to let any one else rest." These bursts of hypochondria absorb the attention and energies of the household to such a degree "that many of the servants really thought that Missis was the principal sufferer in the case." Marie then seizes the occasion of her daughter's death to conduct a grand opera of grief: "and Marie's room was darkened, and she lay on the bed, sobbing and moaning in uncontrollable grief, and calling every moment for the attentions of all of her servant." Eva's death serves as the turning point for the fortunes of most of the novel's characters, and is often interpreted as portraying the novel's true message—that Christian conversion is the only answer to slavery. For example, Eric J. Sundquist argues: "Subsuming the failed power of institutional religion into the realm of sentimental social reform, Eva's death belongs to the period's enormous literature of mourning and consolation but transcends its simple pieties as Stowe seeks out a new world of power by reconceiving Christian man in the image of a beatific child-woman." Yet the effects of Eva's death are largely negative, even in Stowe's terms: Topsy learns not to be good, but to be a good slave, and the abolitionist Ophelia becomes a slaveowner; Tom is not freed; St. Clare is not converted. Meanwhile, the vampiric Marie's strength grows with each new tragedy, as if Eva's failures were her own triumphs.

Throughout this middle part of the novel, Stowe repeatedly associates Eva with St. Clare's mother. Both are pious, angelic, other-wordly creatures whom St. Clare adores. His mother "had been a woman of uncommon elevation and purity of character, and he gave to this child [Eva] his mother's name, fondly fancying that she would prove a reproduction of her image," a fact that Marie notes with jealousy. On the night of his death, Augustine muses: "'I don't know what makes me think of my mother so much, tonight. . . . I have a strange kind of feeling, as if she were near me.'" This premonition heralds his passing. Before his conversion, before Tom's manumission, and before Marie's temper has been salved, St. Clare is fatally stabbed. The chapter that leads to his "Reunion" with his little Evangeline ends with his vision of "joy and recognition" in which St. Clare cries *"'Mother!'"* with his dying breath. Even this mother, whose influence was notably pious and chaste, returns as an angel of death.

In contrast to such white mothers is the Negro Prue, whose mistress forces her to abandon her baby to starvation. Prue had been a breed-slave in Kentucky, and was sold to a New Orleans man who allowed her to keep one last child. His wife, however, demanded such nursing and attention that the infant was neglected, with the horrifying result that

> "Missis got sot agin it, and she said 't wan't nothin' but crossness. She wished it was dead, she said; and she would n't let me have it o' nights, cause, she said, it kept me awake, and made me good for nothing. She made me sleep in her room; and I had to put it away off in a little kind o' garret, and thar it cried itself to death, one night. It did; and I tuck to drinkin', to keep its crying out of my ears! I did,—and I will drink! I will, if I do go to torment for it!"

Prue's own death echoes her child's, for she is locked away in the cellar after repeated beatings for drunkenness. Thus, her mistress repeats the infanticide by effectively killing one who stands in a loosely filial relation to her. Marie St. Clare similarly refused to let Mammy bring her two "little dirty things" to New Orleans, and is equally impatient with her slave's "sulkiness." Although mistresses like Mrs. Shelby seem benign in comparison to these women, the common principle remains: slaves are treated as members of the white family until they become troublesome, and then they are sacrificed or abandoned by their white "mothers." This treatment, in turn, produces particularly debased slave mothers, who are forced by their mistresses to abandon and sacrifice their own children. Gillian Brown examines what she calls the "promiscuous housekeeping" at the St. Clare mansion, and finds as its cause the chaotic disruption that slavery inflicts on the domestic economy: "This failure of domestic practices to sustain both black family unity and the white mistress's authority points not only to the slave economy's disregard of domestic values but to domesticity's dependence on the whims of whatever economic practice it adjoins." In Brown's astute reading, only a domestic economy ordered by women can soothe the chaos and abolish slavery. As I read it, however, the matriarchal solution signals only collapse and crisis and the return of the domestically repressed, as played out in the final third of the novel.

4

But in America feelings vehement and absorbing . . .
become still more deep, morbid, and impassioned by
the constant habits of self-government which the rigid
forms of our society demand. They are repressed, and
they burn inward till they burn the very soul, leaving
only dust and ashes.

—Harriet Beecher Stowe to Georgiana May, May
1833

Simon Legree's Louisiana plantation reflects the absolute
collapse of domesticity, as Stowe indicates by entitling
the first chapter of the Red River section of her novel
"Dark Places." She offers the epigraph from Psalm 74 for
emphasis: "The dark places of the earth are full of the
habitations of cruelty." The cruelty of this habitation is a
direct result, Stowe implies, of Legree's rapacious attitude toward slavery. His policy of "use up, and buy more"
extends to the condition of the house and its garden. The
St. Clare garden was exotic and oriental, like the benevolent household of pampered mulattoes. Legree's garden
is reverting to wildness:

> What once was a large garden was now all grown over
> with weeds, through which, here and there, some
> solitary exotic reared its forsaken head. What had been
> a conservatory had now no window-sashes, and on the
> mouldering shelves stood some dry, forsaken flower-
> pots, with sticks in them, whose dried leaves showed
> they had once been plants.

This physical invasion of nature over culture forecasts the
devolution of the inhabitants of this plantation. In the
main house, the half-mad Cassy and the trembling Emmeline provide a minor strain of the mixed-race exoticism prevalent in the St. Clare establishment. These "solitary exotic[s]" are indeed forsaken, for Legree owns both
light-skinned women, as Cassy herself states, "body and
soul." The ravaged conservatory has a human correlative
in the slave cabins, which house "sullen, scowling, imbruted men, and feeble, discouraged women, or women
that were not women . . . who, treated in every way like
brutes, had sunk as nearly to their level as it was possible
for human beings to do." "Women that were not women"
mark the devastation that slavery has inflicted upon the
black family. For Stowe, conditions that produce unwomanly women subvert the natural order of things, for without women in their proper place as administrators of the
home, the rest of society cannot function. Thus we see
Legree's field hands forced to hand-grind and cook their
own corn for supper each day, and the big house shows
no evidence of housekeeping. While house-slaves do appear in the narrative, their effects are certainly absent;
Legree's plantation simply does not contain a domestic
contingent.

The ravaged condition of Legree's house and the absence
of any semblance of housekeeping signal the final corruption of domesticity in the novel. No domestic tie is
recognized, and no domestic activity occurs. The house is
decrepit; there are no regular meals. Far from the chaos

of the St. Clare kitchen, this house appears to have no
kitchen at all. The decay in which Legree lives is an
extension of Stowe's eerie Southern landscape:

> The sitting-room of Legree's establishment was a large,
> long room, with a wide, ample fireplace. It had once
> been hung with a showy and expensive paper, which
> now hung mouldering, torn and discolored, from the
> damp walls. The place had that peculiar sickening,
> unwholesome smell, compounded of mingled damp,
> dirt and decay, which one often notices in close old
> houses. The wall-paper was defaced, in spots, by slops
> of beer and wine; or garnished with chalk
> memorandums, and long sums footed up, as if
> somebody had been practising arithmetic there.

The damp walls and the molding, defaced wallpaper produce a "sickening, unwholesome smell" of decay, another
mark of domestic failure on Legree's plantation. The smell
in the big house, like the condition of the garden, directly
reflects Legree's "godless and cruel" nature. In *House
and Home Papers* (1865) Stowe would insist that "no
other gift of God, so precious, so inspiring, is treated with
such utter irreverence and contempt in the calculations of
us mortals as this same air of heaven. A sermon on ox-
ygen . . . might do more to repress sin than the most
orthodox discourse to show when and how and why sin
came." Similarly, the writing on the stained and spotted
wall foretells Legree's destruction. His calculations of
profit in human souls recall part of the prophetic message
Daniel interpreted for Belshazzar: "God hath numbered
thy kingdom and finished it" (Dan. 5:26). But arithmetic
is not all that is practiced here. The house itself seems to
conjure a repressed mother to avenge Legree's domestic
abuses.

Halttunen has found that the haunted, decaying house is
a familiar trope in writings by other Beecher family members. Both Stowe's father, Lyman Beecher, and her brother, Henry Ward Beecher, used the haunted house as a
rhetorical device in their respective reformist tracts, *Six
Sermons on Intemperance* (1826), and *Seven Lectures to
Young Men* (1844). Of particular interest here is "The
Strange Woman," in which Henry Ward Beecher equates
feminine sexuality with danger and a house where 'sickly
fumes' fill the air, 'the naked walls drip filth,' and the
room 'echoes with mirth concealing hideous misery.'" As
Halttunen observes, the imagery is surprisingly similar in
the male Beecher hauntings and Stowe's Legree house.
Simon Legree's ruined mansion houses not just intemperance and sexual dominance but slavery as well; little
wonder that the wallpaper is peeling.

Cassy's story combines all of the abuses that are practiced upon slave women throughout the novel, and exhibits all of the resulting corruptions of the domestic ideal.
Like Henry Ward Beecher's "strange woman" of sin, Cassy
makes the house into a dangerous, uncanny place; yet she
is both victim and perpetrator. While her brother found
feminine sexuality to be merely dangerous, Stowe suggests that such sexuality is empowering. Cassy represents
the extreme condition of a mother debased by slavery.
She is the product of many fallen houses, the first of

which is her white father's. Upon his death she is sold to a young man who fathers her children and treats her like a wife until his gambling debts get out of hand. Her third owner sells away her children and finally sells Cassy herself when she tries to knife her son's new owner. A fourth owner fathers another child, whom she overdoses with laudanum to spare it the fate of her older children. On Legree's ruined plantation Cassy lives as a gothic madwoman, the "forsaken exotic" who rules the house through her fearsome strangeness. Her past life and present conditions combine to produce in her an "irritability [which], at times, broke out into raving insanity; and this liability made her a sort of object of dread to Legree, who had that superstitious horror of insane persons which is common to coarse and uninstructed minds." Cassy's madness is the force that controls this house, and it is a force of subverted and corrupted sexuality and domesticity. Because of her exotic mixed blood, she was betrayed, prostituted, and forced into infanticide by the very ones who named her exotic in the first place. Because of that same exoticism, Cassy cannot be domesticated: she always represents Said's "silent and dangerous space beyond familiar boundaries." The legal destruction of this mother's dignity and integrity, Stowe suggests, is a primary horror of slavery; such perversions of the domestic can only produce an uncanny figure of madness, sexuality, and revenge. Here the novel becomes a gothic narrative, itself a corruption of the domestic plot.

Madness, sexuality, and revenge combine in the gothic scenes involving Legree's mother to reveal what Kristeva has called "the two-sided sacred," a formulation of sanctity in which "one aspect is defensive and socializing, the other shows fear and indifferentiation." In Mother Legree, Stowe's ideal of the sacred mother displays both socializing and fearsome aspects. As a "good" mother like Rachel Halliday or Mrs. Senator Bird, Mrs. Legree had lived the role of the defensive and socializing mother, who "trained her only son, with long, unwearied love, and patient prayers." Yet she soon became an object of terror for Legree. Having left his New England home for the sea, he returned once, only to spurn his fair-haired mother. He learned of her death in a letter which contained her forgiveness and a serpentine "lock of long, curling hair" which "twined about his fingers" in a manner as cloying to him as his mother had been in life. While Legree's mother was the innocent victim of a brutal husband and an equally brutal son, in this narrative she has become monstrous. Her goodness and patience and tolerance become horrifying in their intensity, which of course increases after her death. Stowe freely states that the best of mothers may have dire effects on their children: "There is a dread, unhallowed necromancy of evil, that turns things sweetest and holiest to phantoms of horror and affright. That pale, loving mother,—her dying prayers, her forgiving love,—wrought in that demoniac heart of sin only as a damning sentence, bringing with it a fearful looking for of judgment and fiery indignation." This fearsome, necromantic quality, which Kristeva associates with abjection, appears in Legree's mother as a natural counterpart to her excessive goodness. Once Cassy dons the shroud of this spurned mother, Stowe's mater-

nal ideal becomes inverted, and another angelic mother returns as an angel of death.

The ghostly figure of a wronged mother is an appropriate mistress for Legree's house, with its utter dearth of housekeeping and domestic comfort. She seems to return to avenge the corruption wrought on the house and its inhabitants by Legree's neglect of domestic concerns. Cassy appropriates this spirit of Legree's mother in order to free herself from her devastated surroundings. Her impersonation of Legree's mother's ghost allows Cassy to amplify motherly duties both of protection and of punishment— the two faces of the sacred. Having suffered at Legree's hands herself, Cassy takes the new concubine Emmeline under her protection, and ministers to Tom, who has been beaten for refusing to strike another slave. When "all the smouldering embers of womanly feeling flash . . . up in the worn heart of Cassy," an accidental discovery allows her to care for the unprotected by terrorizing Legree. With "perfect amazement" she notes his reaction to the talismanic lock of Eva's hair. The "'witch thing'" found on Tom provokes both suspicion and terror in Legree, and echoes Legree's last contact with his mother: "There dropped out of it . . . a long, shining curl of fair hair,— hair which, like a living thing, twined itself round Legree's fingers." The animation of this dead lock of hair throws him into a fit of terror, in which he screams to "'take it off—burn it up!—burn it up!'" The sinuous twining of the hair of a young girl around the finger of a man is suggestive, to say the least, and recalls the predatory attentions of Legree toward Emmeline. Yet in the case of Eva's curl, the power relation is inverted: this talisman of an innocent child's love fills Legree with revulsion and horror. Legree is truly spooked by this symbol of the sentimental feminine, which becomes as fearsome to him as he was to the type of women it represents. Thus, ironically, darling Eva has become a purveyor of erotic terror and an agent of Legree's own monstrous mother.

This entire episode of domestic vengeance contains an erotic dimension that signals the narrative shift away from a simple domestic novel. When Cassy dons the maternal shroud for nightly visitations, the fusion of mistress and mother in the same terrifying figure evokes incest taboos that daunt even Legree. The sweetness of his living mother was a torment to Legree; the persistence of her deathly form leaves him sleepless, dissipated, and raving. His impression that his mother has replaced his lover as ghostly mistress of the house (when in fact his mistress has replaced his mother as ghost) raises all of the terrors of racial indifferentiation that Winthrop Jordan catalogues. The very presence of mulattoes, Jordan argues, "blurred this essential distinction" between slaves and free men. In that sense, Cassy represents the slipperiness of race: once the absolute distinctions between black and white fade, all other distinctions collapse. This indifferentiation is, of course, one side of Kristeva's dual sacred. When the exotic, sensual, mad mulatto becomes indistinguishable from the white, pure, Christian mother, the true dangers of interracial intercourse come to light. If Cassy and Mother cannot be told apart, Cassy might *be* Mother.

One outcome of this horror of the feminine is the brutal beating of Tom. Tom knows of Cassy's escape plans, and admits that knowledge to Legree, but refuses to tell the details. Overwrought by his nights with Mother, Legree vows to "'count every drop of blood there is in you, and take 'em, one by one.'" Tom's passivity—like that of Legree's living mother—drives Legree, finally, to beat him to death. Kristeva explains how this sort of violence may be a reaction to the sacred:

> This is precisely where we encounter the *rituals of defilement* and their derivatives, which, based on the feeling of abjection and all *converging on the maternal*, attempt to symbolize the other threat to the subject: that of being swamped by the dual relationship, thereby risking the loss not of a part (castration) but of the totality of his living being.

Legree's fear of "being swamped" by his mother appears in his phobic response to Eva's curl, and in the "ritual of defilement" that ends Tom's life. While critics have commented upon the sado-masochistic and bloodthirsty nature of Legree's contact with the passive Tom, the intensity and frantic nature of Legree's cruelty indicate that he is fighting demons other than those of Tom's Methodism (it is worth remembering here, too, that Stowe's germinal vision of this scene came to her during a communion service, a ritual that sanctifies a certain type of cannibalism). Curiously, the very evils practiced by the monstrous mothers in the novel are reproduced in Legree's reactions to the image of his mother.

Following Tom's death, Stowe reports, ghost stories "were uncommonly rife" on the plantation. She then tells "An Authentic Ghost Story" about Legree:

> Well, he slept, for he was tired,—slept soundly. But, finally, there came over his sleep a shadow, a horror, an apprehension of something dreadful hanging over him. It was his mother's shroud, he thought; but Cassy had it, holding it up, and showing it to him. . . .

> It was a cloudy, misty, moonlight, and there he saw it!—something white, gliding in! He heard the still rustle of its ghostly garments. It stood still by his bed;—a cold hand touched his; a voice said, three times, in a low, fearful whisper, "Come! come! come!"

The erotic implications of the ghost's command aside, the image of Cassy holding up his mother's shroud does threaten the loss of the "totality of his living being." This is clearly more than a castration dream, for Legree is encouraged to manifest sexual power in the face of an absorbing and totalizing force, the ghost of his mother. The fact that Cassy now has the shroud, and specifically shows it to him, indicates again a blurring of mother and lover, white and black, now with the implication that the opposition of master and slave is by no means stable. Having lost all ability to make the distinctions that his mastery depends upon, Legree becomes another victim of a maternal angel of death, dying in a ruined house with the "stern, white, inexorable figure" at his bedside.

In her "Concluding Remarks" to the novel, Stowe remonstrates with Northern women for lapses in their sacred motherly reponsibility, and describes the profane result:

> If the mothers of the free states had all felt as they should, in times past, the sons of the free states would not have been the holders, and, proverbially, the hardest masters of slaves; the sons of the free states would not have connived at the extension of slavery, in our national body; the sons of the free states would not, as they do, trade the souls and bodies of men as an equivalent to money, in their mercantile dealings.

Lack of proper maternal feeling, Stowe argues, cultivates slavery and produces those most hideous of offspring, Northern slaveholders and brokers like Simon Legree. For her, only restoration of the family and a return to domestic order will heal the ills of the slave trade. Yet when we examine the family and domestic order that Stowe chooses to restore at the end of the novel, we find much to give us pause.

The shift into eroticism and horror at the end of the novel marks Stowe's abandonment of the domestic plot. The Southern story ends with Tom's death and George Shelby's fulfillment of his promise of manumission. Yet Uncle Tom's cabin is not restored, and the domestic model that replaces it is quite untraditional. Eliza crops her hair and dresses like a man to cross Lake Erie; she is so changed that little Harry does not know her, although George finds her unsexing strangely attractive. The Harrises' northward journey resolves in a chance reunion with Cassy (Eliza's mother) and Madame de Thoux (George's sister). This tidy restoration of the mulatto family tries to contain the women's exoticism in domesticity and confine George's intellect to the nonwhite, non-American venue of Liberia. The cross-dressing of the exotic Eliza and the establishment of the mad Cassy as matriarch, however, reinforce the novel's fascination with the mixed-race, sexual mother. Meanwhile, the white domestic models are dispersed or forgotten. The Quakers are left behind and not mentioned again; Mrs. Legree, a woman who "felt as [she] should," produces the heinous Simon and then haunts him by racial and sexual proxy. Race, sexuality, and motherhood fracture Stowe's domestic plot into images of failed mothers and fallen houses, leaving a new family model based on gender confusion and madness.

FURTHER READING

Criticism

Crozier, Alice C. "*Uncle Tom's Cabin*; or, History in the Making." In her *The Novels of Harriet Beecher Stowe*, pp. 3-33. New York: Oxford, 1969.

A broad analysis of themes, characters, and nineteenth-century culture that addresses the novel as a historically accurate "picture of Southern society."

Furnas, J. C. *Goodbye to Uncle Tom*. New York: Sloane, 1956, 435 p.

Condemns the novel for inaccurate and condescending portrayals of African Americans that have fostered the growth of twentieth-century racial stereotypes.

Gardiner, Jane. "The Assault Upon Uncle Tom: Attempts of Pro-Slavery Novelists to Answer *Uncle Tom's Cabin*, 1852-1860." *Southern Humanities Review* 12 (1978): 313-24.

Summarizes various arguments mounted by Northern and Southern writers to counter *Uncle Tom's Cabin*, concluding that their works, for the most part, were "unbought, unread, and unknown, even in the South."

————. "Pro-Slavery Propaganda in Fiction Written in Answer to *Uncle Tom's Cabin*, 1852-1861: An Annotated Checklist." *Resources for American Literary Study* 7 (1977): 201-09.

A brief survey of 25 works of fiction written by pro-slavery sympathizers to refute Stowe's arguments.

Goodman, Charlotte. "From *Uncle Tom's Cabin* to Vyry's Kitchen: The Black Female Folk Tradition in Margaret Walker's *Jubilee*." In *Tradition and the Talents of Women*, edited by Florence Howe, pp. 328-37. Urbana: University of Chicago Press, 1991.

Suggests that Walker's 1966 novel serves as a "countertext" to *Uncle Tom's Cabin* by providing a "richly imagined and carefully documented representation of the community of black women," depicting a world that the critic finds "virtually invisible" in Stowe's masterwork.

Gossett, Thomas F. "Critical Reception of *Uncle Tom's Cabin*: 1941 to the Present." In his *"Uncle Tom's Cabin" and American Culture*, pp. 388-408. Dallas: Southern Methodist University Press, 1985.

Broad survey covering both positive and negative post-World War II reactions to the novel, featuring comments from such notable authors and critics as James Baldwin and William Faulkner.

Graham, Thomas. "Memoranda and Documents: Harriet Beecher Stowe and the Question of Race." *New England Quarterly* (1973): 614-22.

Discusses Stowe's anti-slavery writings, her humanitarian efforts, and her views on race, providing a counterpoint to J. C. Furnas's influential 1956 critique of the novel in *Goodbye to Uncle Tom*.

Grinstein, Alexander. "*Uncle Tom's Cabin* and Harriet Beecher Stowe: Beating Fantasies and Thoughts of Dying." *American Imago* 40 (1983): 115-44.

Examines some of the "underlying psychological themes" of the novel in conjunction with various biographical materials on Stowe.

Hirsch, Stephen A. "Uncle Tomitudes: The Popular Reaction to *Uncle Tom's Cabin*." In *Studies in the American Renaissance*, edited by Joel Myerson, pp. 303-30. Boston: Twayne, 1978.

Surveys various positive and negative contemporary reviews of the novel.

Hudson, Benjamin F. "Another View of 'Uncle Tom.'" *Phylon* (1963): 79-87.

Defends Stowe's characterization of Tom by comparing him to the Stoic philosopher Epictetus, arguing that the name "Uncle Tom" should "epitomize dignity, self respect, and love for all mankind."

Krog, Carl E. "Women, Slaves, and Family in *Uncle Tom's Cabin*: Symbolic Battleground in Antebellum America." *The Midwest Quarterly* 31 (1990): 252-69

Supplements an analysis of Stowe's portrayal of slaves, women, and family with a survey of various Southern responses to the novel.

Levine, Robert S. "*Uncle Tom's Cabin* in *Frederick Douglass' Paper*: An Analysis of Reception." *American Literature* 64 (1992): 71-93.

Places modern critical responses to the novel within a historical context by focusing on the reception given the novel in Douglass' black abolitionist newspaper during the early 1850s.

McConnell, Frank D. "Uncle Tom and the Avant-Garde." *Massachusetts Review* 16 (1975): 732-45.

Places the novel in the category of works that "provide the psychic context" of classic American literature, drawing comparisons with such writers as Walt Whitman, Gertrude Stein, and Norman Mailer.

Riggio, Thomas P. "*Uncle Tom* Reconstructed: A Neglected Chapter in the History of a Book." *American Quarterly* 28 (1976): 56-70.

Examines the role of the novel in Southern Reconstruction fiction, particularly in the work of Thomas Dixon, and the influence of stage plays "in the shaping of Uncle Tom's contemporary image."

Spillers, Hortense J. "Changing the Letter: The Yokes, the Jokes of Discourse, or, Mrs. Stowe, Mr. Reed." In *Slavery and the Literary Imagination*, edited by Deborah E. McDowell and Arnold Rampersad, pp. 25-61. Baltimore: Johns Hopkins University Press, 1987.

Compares Stowe to late twentieth-century African American novelist and satirist Ishmael Reed, outlining the different strategies each brings to their discussions of slavery.

Van Buren, Jane Silverman. "*Uncle Tom's Cabin*: A Myth of Familial Relations." In her *The Modernist Madonna: Semiotics of the Maternal Metaphor*, pp. 64-95. Bloomington, Indiana: Indiana University Press, 1989.

Draws from the criticism and theoretical work of Claude Levi-Strauss, Joseph Campbell, and others in arguing that the powerful attraction to the novel can be found in its articulation of several myths of mother-child-father relations.

Wasserstrom, William. "Abandoned in Providence: Harriet Beecher Stowe, Howells, Henry James." In his *The Ironies*

of Progress: Henry Adams and the American Dream, pp. 51-
76. Carbondale: Southern Illinois University Press, 1984.
     A comparison of *Uncle Tom's Cabin* with various works
by Howells and James, addressing each author's portrayal
of the American home and family.

Additional coverage of Stowe's life and career is contained in the following source published by Gale Research: *Nineteenth-Century Literature Criticism*, **Vol. 3;** *World Literature Criticism; DISCovering Authors; Junior DISCovering Authors; Dictionary of Literary Biography*, **Vols. 1, 12, 42, 74;** *Concise Dictionary of American Literary Biography, 1865-1917; Major Authors and Illustrators for Children and Young Adults;* **and** *Yesterday's Authors of Books for Children*, **Vol. 1.**

Nineteenth-Century Literature Criticism

Cumulative Indexes
Volumes 1-50

Auel, Jean M(arie) 1936- . . . . CLC 31
See also AAYA 7; BEST 90:4; CA 103;
CANR 21

Auerbach, Erich 1892-1957 . . . . . . TCLC 43
See also CA 118

Augier, Emile 1820-1889 . . . . NCLC 31

August, John
See De Voto, Bernard (Augustine)

Augustine, St. 354-430 . . . . CMLC 6

Aurelius
See Bourne, Randolph S(illiman)

Austen, Jane
1775-1817 . . . . . NCLC 1, 13, 19, 33, 51;
DA; WLC
See also CDBLB 1789-1832; DLB 116

Auster, Paul 1947- . . . . CLC 47
See also CA 69-72; CANR 23

Austin, Frank
See Faust, Frederick (Schiller)

Austin, Mary (Hunter)
1868-1934 . . . . TCLC 25
See also CA 109; DLB 9, 78

Autran Dourado, Waldomiro
See Dourado, (Waldomiro Freitas) Autran

Averroes 1126-1198 . . . . CMLC 7
See also DLB 115

Avison, Margaret 1918- . . . . CLC 2, 4
See also CA 17-20R; DLB 53; MTCW

Axton, David
See Koontz, Dean R(ay)

Ayckbourn, Alan
1939- . . . . CLC 5, 8, 18, 33, 74
See also CA 21-24R; CANR 31; DLB 13;
MTCW

Aydy, Catherine
See Tennant, Emma (Christina)

Ayme, Marcel (Andre) 1902-1967 . . . CLC 11
See also CA 89-92; CLR 25; DLB 72

Ayrton, Michael 1921-1975 . . . . CLC 7
See also CA 5-8R; 61-64; CANR 9, 21

Azorin . . . . CLC 11
See also Martinez Ruiz, Jose

Azuela, Mariano
1873-1952 . . . . TCLC 3; HLC
See also CA 104; 131; HW; MTCW

Baastad, Babbis Friis
See Friis-Baastad, Babbis Ellinor

Bab
See Gilbert, W(illiam) S(chwenck)

Babbis, Eleanor
See Friis-Baastad, Babbis Ellinor

Babel, Isaak (Emmanuilovich)
1894-1941(?) . . . . . . TCLC 2, 13; SSC 16
See also CA 104

Babits, Mihaly 1883-1941 . . . . TCLC 14
See also CA 114

Babur 1483-1530 . . . . LC 18

Bacchelli, Riccardo 1891-1985 . . . . . CLC 19
See also CA 29-32R; 117

Bach, Richard (David) 1936- . . . . CLC 14
See also AITN 1; BEST 89:2; CA 9-12R;
CANR 18; MTCW; SATA 13

Bachman, Richard
See King, Stephen (Edwin)

Bachmann, Ingeborg 1926-1973 . . . . . CLC 69
See also CA 93-96; 45-48; DLB 85

Bacon, Francis 1561-1626 . . . . LC 18
See also CDBLB Before 1660; DLB 151

Bacon, Roger 1214(?)-1292 . . . . . . CMLC 14
See also DLB 115

Bacovia, George . . . . TCLC 24
See also Vasiliu, Gheorghe

Badanes, Jerome 1937- . . . . CLC 59

Bagehot, Walter 1826-1877 . . . . . . NCLC 10
See also DLB 55

Bagnold, Enid 1889-1981 . . . . CLC 25
See also CA 5-8R; 103; CANR 5, 40;
DLB 13; MAICYA; SATA 1, 25

Bagritsky, Edvard 1895-1934 . . . . . TCLC 60

Bagrjana, Elisaveta
See Belcheva, Elisaveta

Bagryana, Elisaveta . . . . CLC 10
See also Belcheva, Elisaveta
See also DLB 147

Bailey, Paul 1937- . . . . CLC 45
See also CA 21-24R; CANR 16; DLB 14

Baillie, Joanna 1762-1851 . . . . NCLC 2
See also DLB 93

Bainbridge, Beryl (Margaret)
1933- . . . . CLC 4, 5, 8, 10, 14, 18, 22, 62
See also CA 21-24R; CANR 24; DLB 14;
MTCW

Baker, Elliott 1922- . . . . CLC 8
See also CA 45-48; CANR 2

Baker, Nicholson 1957- . . . . CLC 61
See also CA 135

Baker, Ray Stannard 1870-1946 . . . TCLC 47
See also CA 118

Baker, Russell (Wayne) 1925- . . . . . . CLC 31
See also BEST 89:4; CA 57-60; CANR 11,
41; MTCW

Bakhtin, M.
See Bakhtin, Mikhail Mikhailovich

Bakhtin, M. M.
See Bakhtin, Mikhail Mikhailovich

Bakhtin, Mikhail
See Bakhtin, Mikhail Mikhailovich

Bakhtin, Mikhail Mikhailovich
1895-1975 . . . . CLC 83
See also CA 128; 113

Bakshi, Ralph 1938(?)- . . . . CLC 26
See also CA 112; 138

Bakunin, Mikhail (Alexandrovich)
1814-1876 . . . . NCLC 25

Baldwin, James (Arthur)
1924-1987 . . . . . . CLC 1, 2, 3, 4, 5, 8, 13,
15, 17, 42, 50, 67; BLC; DA; DC 1;
SSC 10; WLC
See also AAYA 4; BW 1; CA 1-4R; 124;
CABS 1; CANR 3, 24;
CDALB 1941-1968; DLB 2, 7, 33;
DLBY 87; MTCW; SATA 9;
SATA-Obit 54

Ballard, J(ames) G(raham)
1930- . . . . CLC 3, 6, 14, 36; SSC 1
See also AAYA 3; CA 5-8R; CANR 15, 39;
DLB 14; MTCW

Balmont, Konstantin (Dmitriyevich)
1867-1943 . . . . TCLC 11
See also CA 109

Balzac, Honore de
1799-1850 . . . . NCLC 5, 35; DA; SSC 5;
WLC
See also DLB 119

Bambara, Toni Cade
1939- . . . . CLC 19, 88; BLC; DA
See also AAYA 5; BW 2; CA 29-32R;
CANR 24; DLB 38; MTCW

Bamdad, A.
See Shamlu, Ahmad

Banat, D. R.
See Bradbury, Ray (Douglas)

Bancroft, Laura
See Baum, L(yman) Frank

Banim, John 1798-1842 . . . . NCLC 13
See also DLB 116

Banim, Michael 1796-1874 . . . . . . NCLC 13

Banks, Iain
See Banks, Iain M(enzies)

Banks, Iain M(enzies) 1954- . . . . CLC 34
See also CA 123; 128

Banks, Lynne Reid . . . . CLC 23
See also Reid Banks, Lynne
See also AAYA 6

Banks, Russell 1940- . . . . CLC 37, 72
See also CA 65-68; CAAS 15; CANR 19;
DLB 130

Banville, John 1945- . . . . CLC 46
See also CA 117; 128; DLB 14

Banville, Theodore (Faullain) de
1832-1891 . . . . NCLC 9

Baraka, Amiri
1934- . . . . CLC 1, 2, 3, 5, 10, 14, 33;
BLC; DA; PC 4
See also Jones, LeRoi
See also BW 2; CA 21-24R; CABS 3;
CANR 27, 38; CDALB 1941-1968;
DLB 5, 7, 16, 38; DLBD 8; MTCW

Barbauld, Anna Laetitia
1743-1825 . . . . NCLC 50

Barbellion, W. N. P. . . . . TCLC 24
See also Cummings, Bruce F(rederick)

Barbera, Jack (Vincent) 1945- . . . . . . CLC 44
See also CA 110; CANR 45

Barbey d'Aurevilly, Jules Amedee
1808-1889 . . . . NCLC 1; SSC 17
See also DLB 119

Barbusse, Henri 1873-1935 . . . . TCLC 5
See also CA 105; DLB 65

Barclay, Bill
See Moorcock, Michael (John)

Barclay, William Ewert
See Moorcock, Michael (John)

Barea, Arturo 1897-1957 . . . . TCLC 14
See also CA 111

Barfoot, Joan 1946- . . . . CLC 18
See also CA 105

Beerbohm, Max
See Beerbohm, Henry Maximilian

Beer-Hofmann, Richard
1866-1945 .... TCLC 60
See also DLB 81

Begiebing, Robert J(ohn) 1946-..... CLC 70
See also CA 122; CANR 40

Behan, Brendan
1923-1964 .... CLC 1, 8, 11, 15, 79
See also CA 73-76; CANR 33;
CDBLB 1945-1960; DLB 13; MTCW

Behn, Aphra
1640(?)-1689 .... LC 1; DA; DC 4;
PC 12; WLC
See also DLB 39, 80, 131

Behrman, S(amuel) N(athaniel)
1893-1973 .... CLC 40
See also CA 13-16; 45-48; CAP 1; DLB 7,
44

Belasco, David 1853-1931 .... TCLC 3
See also CA 104; DLB 7

Belcheva, Elisaveta 1893- .... CLC 10
See also Bagryana, Elisaveta

Beldone, Phil "Cheech"
See Ellison, Harlan (Jay)

Beleno
See Azuela, Mariano

Belinski, Vissarion Grigoryevich
1811-1848 .... NCLC 5

Belitt, Ben 1911-................. CLC 22
See also CA 13-16R; CAAS 4; CANR 7;
DLB 5

Bell, James Madison
1826-1902 .... TCLC 43; BLC
See also BW 1; CA 122; 124; DLB 50

Bell, Madison (Smartt) 1957- ...... CLC 41
See also CA 111; CANR 28

Bell, Marvin (Hartley) 1937-..... CLC 8, 31
See also CA 21-24R; CAAS 14; DLB 5;
MTCW

Bell, W. L. D.
See Mencken, H(enry) L(ouis)

Bellamy, Atwood C.
See Mencken, H(enry) L(ouis)

Bellamy, Edward 1850-1898 ...... NCLC 4
See also DLB 12

Bellin, Edward J.
See Kuttner, Henry

Belloc, (Joseph) Hilaire (Pierre)
1870-1953 .... TCLC 7, 18
See also CA 106; DLB 19, 100, 141;
YABC 1

Belloc, Joseph Peter Rene Hilaire
See Belloc, (Joseph) Hilaire (Pierre)

Belloc, Joseph Pierre Hilaire
See Belloc, (Joseph) Hilaire (Pierre)

Belloc, M. A.
See Lowndes, Marie Adelaide (Belloc)

Bellow, Saul
1915- ...... CLC 1, 2, 3, 6, 8, 10, 13, 15,
25, 33, 34, 63, 79; DA; SSC 14; WLC
See also AITN 2; BEST 89:3; CA 5-8R;
CABS 1; CANR 29; CDALB 1941-1968;
DLB 2, 28; DLBD 3; DLBY 82; MTCW

Belser, Reimond Karel Maria de
See Ruyslinck, Ward

Bely, Andrey .... TCLC 7; PC 11
See also Bugayev, Boris Nikolayevich

Benary, Margot
See Benary-Isbert, Margot

Benary-Isbert, Margot 1889-1979... CLC 12
See also CA 5-8R; 89-92; CANR 4;
CLR 12; MAICYA; SATA 2;
SATA-Obit 21

Benavente (y Martinez), Jacinto
1866-1954 .... TCLC 3
See also CA 106; 131; HW; MTCW

Benchley, Peter (Bradford)
1940- .... CLC 4, 8
See also AAYA 14; AITN 2; CA 17-20R;
CANR 12, 35; MTCW; SATA 3

Benchley, Robert (Charles)
1889-1945 .... TCLC 1, 55
See also CA 105; DLB 11

Benda, Julien 1867-1956 .... TCLC 60
See also CA 120

Benedict, Ruth 1887-1948 .... TCLC 60

Benedikt, Michael 1935- .... CLC 4, 14
See also CA 13-16R; CANR 7; DLB 5

Benet, Juan 1927-................. CLC 28
See also CA 143

Benet, Stephen Vincent
1898-1943 .... TCLC 7; SSC 10
See also CA 104; DLB 4, 48, 102; YABC 1

Benet, William Rose 1886-1950 ... TCLC 28
See also CA 118; DLB 45

Benford, Gregory (Albert) 1941-.... CLC 52
See also CA 69-72; CANR 12, 24;
DLBY 82

Bengtsson, Frans (Gunnar)
1894-1954 .... TCLC 48

Benjamin, David
See Slavitt, David R(ytman)

Benjamin, Lois
See Gould, Lois

Benjamin, Walter 1892-1940 ..... TCLC 39

Benn, Gottfried 1886-1956........ TCLC 3
See also CA 106; DLB 56

Bennett, Alan 1934-........... CLC 45, 77
See also CA 103; CANR 35; MTCW

Bennett, (Enoch) Arnold
1867-1931 .... TCLC 5, 20
See also CA 106; CDBLB 1890-1914;
DLB 10, 34, 98

Bennett, Elizabeth
See Mitchell, Margaret (Munnerlyn)

Bennett, George Harold 1930-
See Bennett, Hal
See also BW 1; CA 97-100

Bennett, Hal .... CLC 5
See also Bennett, George Harold
See also DLB 33

Bennett, Jay 1912-............... CLC 35
See also AAYA 10; CA 69-72; CANR 11,
42; JRDA; SAAS 4; SATA 41;
SATA-Brief 27

Bennett, Louise (Simone)
1919- .... CLC 28; BLC
See also BW 2; DLB 117

Benson, E(dward) F(rederic)
1867-1940 .... TCLC 27
See also CA 114; DLB 135

Benson, Jackson J. 1930-......... CLC 34
See also CA 25-28R; DLB 111

Benson, Sally 1900-1972 .... CLC 17
See also CA 19-20; 37-40R; CAP 1;
SATA 1, 35; SATA-Obit 27

Benson, Stella 1892-1933........ TCLC 17
See also CA 117; DLB 36

Bentham, Jeremy 1748-1832 ..... NCLC 38
See also DLB 107

Bentley, E(dmund) C(lerihew)
1875-1956 .... TCLC 12
See also CA 108; DLB 70

Bentley, Eric (Russell) 1916-....... CLC 24
See also CA 5-8R; CANR 6

Beranger, Pierre Jean de
1780-1857 .... NCLC 34

Berendt, John (Lawrence) 1939-.... CLC 86
See also CA 146

Berger, Colonel
See Malraux, (Georges-)Andre

Berger, John (Peter) 1926- ...... CLC 2, 19
See also CA 81-84; DLB 14

Berger, Melvin H. 1927-.......... CLC 12
See also CA 5-8R; CANR 4; CLR 32;
SAAS 2; SATA 5

Berger, Thomas (Louis)
1924- .... CLC 3, 5, 8, 11, 18, 38
See also CA 1-4R; CANR 5, 28; DLB 2;
DLBY 80; MTCW

Bergman, (Ernst) Ingmar
1918- .... CLC 16, 72
See also CA 81-84; CANR 33

Bergson, Henri 1859-1941........ TCLC 32

Bergstein, Eleanor 1938-........... CLC 4
See also CA 53-56; CANR 5

Berkoff, Steven 1937-............. CLC 56
See also CA 104

Bermant, Chaim (Icyk) 1929- ...... CLC 40
See also CA 57-60; CANR 6, 31

Bern, Victoria
See Fisher, M(ary) F(rances) K(ennedy)

Bernanos, (Paul Louis) Georges
1888-1948 .... TCLC 3
See also CA 104; 130; DLB 72

Bernard, April 1956- .... CLC 59
See also CA 131

Berne, Victoria
See Fisher, M(ary) F(rances) K(ennedy)

Bernhard, Thomas
1931-1989 .... CLC 3, 32, 61
See also CA 85-88; 127; CANR 32;
DLB 85, 124; MTCW

Berriault, Gina 1926-............. CLC 54
See also CA 116; 129; DLB 130

Berrigan, Daniel 1921-............. CLC 4
See also CA 33-36R; CAAS 1; CANR 11,
43; DLB 5

Berrigan, Edmund Joseph Michael, Jr.
1934-1983
See Berrigan, Ted
See also CA 61-64; 110; CANR 14

Berrigan, Ted . . . . **CLC 37**
See also Berrigan, Edmund Joseph Michael, Jr.
See also DLB 5

Berry, Charles Edward Anderson 1931-
See Berry, Chuck
See also CA 115

Berry, Chuck . . . . **CLC 17**
See also Berry, Charles Edward Anderson

Berry, Jonas
See Ashbery, John (Lawrence)

Berry, Wendell (Erdman)
1934- . . . . **CLC 4, 6, 8, 27, 46**
See also AITN 1; CA 73-76; DLB 5, 6

Berryman, John
1914-1972 . . . . . . **CLC 1, 2, 3, 4, 6, 8, 10, 13, 25, 62**
See also CA 13-16; 33-36R; CABS 2; CANR 35; CAP 1; CDALB 1941-1968; DLB 48; MTCW

Bertolucci, Bernardo 1940- . . . . **CLC 16**
See also CA 106

Bertrand, Aloysius 1807-1841 . . . . **NCLC 31**

Bertran de Born c. 1140-1215 . . . . . **CMLC 5**

Besant, Annie (Wood) 1847-1933 . . . **TCLC 9**
See also CA 105

Bessie, Alvah 1904-1985 . . . . **CLC 23**
See also CA 5-8R; 116; CANR 2; DLB 26

Bethlen, T. D.
See Silverberg, Robert

Beti, Mongo . . . . **CLC 27; BLC**
See also Biyidi, Alexandre

Betjeman, John
1906-1984 . . . . **CLC 2, 6, 10, 34, 43**
See also CA 9-12R; 112; CANR 33; CDBLB 1945-1960; DLB 20; DLBY 84; MTCW

Bettelheim, Bruno 1903-1990 . . . . . **CLC 79**
See also CA 81-84; 131; CANR 23; MTCW

Betti, Ugo 1892-1953 . . . . **TCLC 5**
See also CA 104

Betts, Doris (Waugh) 1932- . . . . **CLC 3, 6, 28**
See also CA 13-16R; CANR 9; DLBY 82

Bevan, Alistair
See Roberts, Keith (John Kingston)

Bialik, Chaim Nachman
1873-1934 . . . . **TCLC 25**

Bickerstaff, Isaac
See Swift, Jonathan

Bidart, Frank 1939- . . . . **CLC 33**
See also CA 140

Bienek, Horst 1930- . . . . **CLC 7, 11**
See also CA 73-76; DLB 75

Bierce, Ambrose (Gwinett)
1842-1914(?) . . . . . . **TCLC 1, 7, 44; DA; SSC 9; WLC**
See also CA 104; 139; CDALB 1865-1917; DLB 11, 12, 23, 71, 74

Billings, Josh
See Shaw, Henry Wheeler

Billington, (Lady) Rachel (Mary)
1942- . . . . **CLC 43**
See also AITN 2; CA 33-36R; CANR 44

Binyon, T(imothy) J(ohn) 1936- . . . . **CLC 34**
See also CA 111; CANR 28

Bioy Casares, Adolfo
1914- . . . **CLC 4, 8, 13, 88; HLC; SSC 17**
See also CA 29-32R; CANR 19, 43; DLB 113; HW; MTCW

Bird, Cordwainer
See Ellison, Harlan (Jay)

Bird, Robert Montgomery
1806-1854 . . . . **NCLC 1**

Birney, (Alfred) Earle
1904- . . . . **CLC 1, 4, 6, 11**
See also CA 1-4R; CANR 5, 20; DLB 88; MTCW

Bishop, Elizabeth
1911-1979 . . . . . . **CLC 1, 4, 9, 13, 15, 32; DA; PC 3**
See also CA 5-8R; 89-92; CABS 2; CANR 26; CDALB 1968-1988; DLB 5; MTCW; SATA-Obit 24

Bishop, John 1935- . . . . **CLC 10**
See also CA 105

Bissett, Bill 1939- . . . . **CLC 18**
See also CA 69-72; CAAS 19; CANR 15; DLB 53; MTCW

Bitov, Andrei (Georgievich) 1937- . . . **CLC 57**
See also CA 142

Biyidi, Alexandre 1932-
See Beti, Mongo
See also BW 1; CA 114; 124; MTCW

Bjarme, Brynjolf
See Ibsen, Henrik (Johan)

Bjornson, Bjornstjerne (Martinius)
1832-1910 . . . . **TCLC 7, 37**
See also CA 104

Black, Robert
See Holdstock, Robert P.

Blackburn, Paul 1926-1971 . . . . . . **CLC 9, 43**
See also CA 81-84; 33-36R; CANR 34; DLB 16; DLBY 81

Black Elk 1863-1950 . . . . **TCLC 33**
See also CA 144; NNAL

Black Hobart
See Sanders, (James) Ed(ward)

Blacklin, Malcolm
See Chambers, Aidan

Blackmore, R(ichard) D(oddridge)
1825-1900 . . . . **TCLC 27**
See also CA 120; DLB 18

Blackmur, R(ichard) P(almer)
1904-1965 . . . . **CLC 2, 24**
See also CA 11-12; 25-28R; CAP 1; DLB 63

Black Tarantula, The
See Acker, Kathy

Blackwood, Algernon (Henry)
1869-1951 . . . . **TCLC 5**
See also CA 105

Blackwood, Caroline 1931- . . . . **CLC 6, 9**
See also CA 85-88; CANR 32; DLB 14; MTCW

Blade, Alexander
See Hamilton, Edmond; Silverberg, Robert

Blaga, Lucian 1895-1961 . . . . **CLC 75**

Blair, Eric (Arthur) 1903-1950
See Orwell, George
See also CA 104; 132; DA; MTCW; SATA 29

Blais, Marie-Claire
1939- . . . . **CLC 2, 4, 6, 13, 22**
See also CA 21-24R; CAAS 4; CANR 38; DLB 53; MTCW

Blaise, Clark 1940- . . . . **CLC 29**
See also AITN 2; CA 53-56; CAAS 3; CANR 5; DLB 53

Blake, Nicholas
See Day Lewis, C(ecil)
See also DLB 77

Blake, William
1757-1827 . . . . **NCLC 13, 37; DA; PC 12; WLC**
See also CDBLB 1789-1832; DLB 93; MAICYA; SATA 30

Blasco Ibanez, Vicente
1867-1928 . . . . **TCLC 12**
See also CA 110; 131; HW; MTCW

Blatty, William Peter 1928- . . . . **CLC 2**
See also CA 5-8R; CANR 9

Bleeck, Oliver
See Thomas, Ross (Elmore)

Blessing, Lee 1949- . . . . **CLC 54**

Blish, James (Benjamin)
1921-1975 . . . . **CLC 14**
See also CA 1-4R; 57-60; CANR 3; DLB 8; MTCW; SATA 66

Bliss, Reginald
See Wells, H(erbert) G(eorge)

Blixen, Karen (Christentze Dinesen)
1885-1962
See Dinesen, Isak
See also CA 25-28; CANR 22; CAP 2; MTCW; SATA 44

Bloch, Robert (Albert) 1917-1994 . . . **CLC 33**
See also CA 5-8R; 146; CAAS 20; CANR 5; DLB 44; SATA 12

Blok, Alexander (Alexandrovich)
1880-1921 . . . . **TCLC 5**
See also CA 104

Blom, Jan
See Breytenbach, Breyten

Bloom, Harold 1930- . . . . **CLC 24**
See also CA 13-16R; CANR 39; DLB 67

Bloomfield, Aurelius
See Bourne, Randolph S(illiman)

Blount, Roy (Alton), Jr. 1941- . . . . . **CLC 38**
See also CA 53-56; CANR 10, 28; MTCW

Bloy, Leon 1846-1917 . . . . **TCLC 22**
See also CA 121; DLB 123

Blume, Judy (Sussman) 1938- . . . **CLC 12, 30**
See also AAYA 3; CA 29-32R; CANR 13, 37; CLR 2, 15; DLB 52; JRDA; MAICYA; MTCW; SATA 2, 31, 79

Blunden, Edmund (Charles)
1896-1974 . . . . **CLC 2, 56**
See also CA 17-18; 45-48; CAP 2; DLB 20, 100; MTCW

Bly, Robert (Elwood)
1926- . . . . CLC 1, 2, 5, 10, 15, 38
See also CA 5-8R; CANR 41; DLB 5;
MTCW

Boas, Franz   1858-1942. . . . . TCLC 56
See also CA 115

Bobette
See Simenon, Georges (Jacques Christian)

Boccaccio, Giovanni
1313-1375 . . . . CMLC 13; SSC 10

Bochco, Steven   1943- . . . . CLC 35
See also AAYA 11; CA 124; 138

Bodenheim, Maxwell   1892-1954 . . . TCLC 44
See also CA 110; DLB 9, 45

Bodker, Cecil   1927- . . . . CLC 21
See also CA 73-76; CANR 13, 44; CLR 23;
MAICYA; SATA 14

Boell, Heinrich (Theodor)
1917-1985 . . . . CLC 2, 3, 6, 9, 11, 15, 27,
32, 72; DA; WLC
See also CA 21-24R; 116; CANR 24;
DLB 69; DLBY 85; MTCW

Boerne, Alfred
See Doeblin, Alfred

Boethius   480(?)-524(?) . . . . CMLC 15
See also DLB 115

Bogan, Louise
1897-1970 . . . . . . CLC 4, 39, 46; PC 12
See also CA 73-76; 25-28R; CANR 33;
DLB 45; MTCW

Bogarde, Dirk . . . . CLC 19
See also Van Den Bogarde, Derek Jules
Gaspard Ulric Niven
See also DLB 14

Bogosian, Eric   1953- . . . . CLC 45
See also CA 138

Bograd, Larry   1953- . . . . CLC 35
See also CA 93-96; SATA 33

Boiardo, Matteo Maria   1441-1494 . . . . LC 6

Boileau-Despreaux, Nicolas
1636-1711 . . . . LC 3

Boland, Eavan (Aisling)   1944- . . . CLC 40, 67
See also CA 143; DLB 40

Bolt, Lee
See Faust, Frederick (Schiller)

Bolt, Robert (Oxton)   1924- . . . . CLC 14
See also CA 17-20R; CANR 35; DLB 13;
MTCW

Bombet, Louis-Alexandre-Cesar
See Stendhal

Bomkauf
See Kaufman, Bob (Garnell)

Bonaventura. . . . . NCLC 35
See also DLB 90

Bond, Edward   1934- . . . . CLC 4, 6, 13, 23
See also CA 25-28R; CANR 38; DLB 13;
MTCW

Bonham, Frank   1914-1989. . . . . CLC 12
See also AAYA 1; CA 9-12R; CANR 4, 36;
JRDA; MAICYA; SAAS 3; SATA 1, 49;
SATA-Obit 62

Bonnefoy, Yves   1923- . . . . CLC 9, 15, 58
See also CA 85-88; CANR 33; MTCW

Bontemps, Arna(ud Wendell)
1902-1973 . . . . CLC 1, 18; BLC
See also BW 1; CA 1-4R; 41-44R; CANR 4,
35; CLR 6; DLB 48, 51; JRDA;
MAICYA; MTCW; SATA 2, 44;
SATA-Obit 24

Booth, Martin   1944- . . . . CLC 13
See also CA 93-96; CAAS 2

Booth, Philip   1925- . . . . CLC 23
See also CA 5-8R; CANR 5; DLBY 82

Booth, Wayne C(layson)   1921- . . . . . CLC 24
See also CA 1-4R; CAAS 5; CANR 3, 43;
DLB 67

Borchert, Wolfgang   1921-1947 . . . . . TCLC 5
See also CA 104; DLB 69, 124

Borel, Petrus   1809-1859. . . . . NCLC 41

Borges, Jorge Luis
1899-1986 . . . CLC 1, 2, 3, 4, 6, 8, 9, 10,
13, 19, 44, 48, 83; DA; HLC; SSC 4;
WLC
See also CA 21-24R; CANR 19, 33;
DLB 113; DLBY 86; HW; MTCW

Borowski, Tadeusz   1922-1951 . . . . . . TCLC 9
See also CA 106

Borrow, George (Henry)
1803-1881 . . . . NCLC 9
See also DLB 21, 55

Bosman, Herman Charles
1905-1951 . . . . TCLC 49

Bosschere, Jean de   1878(?)-1953. . . TCLC 19
See also CA 115

Boswell, James
1740-1795 . . . . LC 4; DA; WLC
See also CDBLB 1660-1789; DLB 104, 142

Bottoms, David   1949- . . . . CLC 53
See also CA 105; CANR 22; DLB 120;
DLBY 83

Boucicault, Dion   1820-1890 . . . . . . NCLC 41

Boucolon, Maryse   1937-
See Conde, Maryse
See also CA 110; CANR 30

Bourget, Paul (Charles Joseph)
1852-1935 . . . . TCLC 12
See also CA 107; DLB 123

Bourjaily, Vance (Nye)   1922- . . . . CLC 8, 62
See also CA 1-4R; CAAS 1; CANR 2;
DLB 2, 143

Bourne, Randolph S(illiman)
1886-1918 . . . . TCLC 16
See also CA 117; DLB 63

Bova, Ben(jamin William)   1932- . . . . CLC 45
See also CA 5-8R; CAAS 18; CANR 11;
CLR 3; DLBY 81; MAICYA; MTCW;
SATA 6, 68

Bowen, Elizabeth (Dorothea Cole)
1899-1973 . . . . . . CLC 1, 3, 6, 11, 15, 22;
SSC 3
See also CA 17-18; 41-44R; CANR 35;
CAP 2; CDBLB 1945-1960; DLB 15;
MTCW

Bowering, George   1935- . . . . CLC 15, 47
See also CA 21-24R; CAAS 16; CANR 10;
DLB 53

Bowering, Marilyn R(uthe)   1949- . . . CLC 32
See also CA 101

Bowers, Edgar   1924- . . . . CLC 9
See also CA 5-8R; CANR 24; DLB 5

Bowie, David . . . . CLC 17
See also Jones, David Robert

Bowles, Jane (Sydney)
1917-1973 . . . . CLC 3, 68
See also CA 19-20; 41-44R; CAP 2

Bowles, Paul (Frederick)
1910- . . . . CLC 1, 2, 19, 53; SSC 3
See also CA 1-4R; CAAS 1; CANR 1, 19;
DLB 5, 6; MTCW

Box, Edgar
See Vidal, Gore

Boyd, Nancy
See Millay, Edna St. Vincent

Boyd, William   1952- . . . . CLC 28, 53, 70
See also CA 114; 120

Boyle, Kay
1902-1992 . . . . . CLC 1, 5, 19, 58; SSC 5
See also CA 13-16R; 140; CAAS 1;
CANR 29; DLB 4, 9, 48, 86; DLBY 93;
MTCW

Boyle, Mark
See Kienzle, William X(avier)

Boyle, Patrick   1905-1982. . . . . CLC 19
See also CA 127

Boyle, T. C.
See Boyle, T(homas) Coraghessan

Boyle, T(homas) Coraghessan
1948- . . . . CLC 36, 55; SSC 16
See also BEST 90:4; CA 120; CANR 44;
DLBY 86

Boz
See Dickens, Charles (John Huffam)

Brackenridge, Hugh Henry
1748-1816 . . . . NCLC 7
See also DLB 11, 37

Bradbury, Edward P.
See Moorcock, Michael (John)

Bradbury, Malcolm (Stanley)
1932- . . . . CLC 32, 61
See also CA 1-4R; CANR 1, 33; DLB 14;
MTCW

Bradbury, Ray (Douglas)
1920- . . . CLC 1, 3, 10, 15, 42; DA; WLC
See also AITN 1, 2; CA 1-4R; CANR 2, 30;
CDALB 1968-1988; DLB 2, 8; MTCW;
SATA 11, 64

Bradford, Gamaliel   1863-1932. . . . . TCLC 36
See also DLB 17

Bradley, David (Henry, Jr.)
1950- . . . . CLC 23; BLC
See also BW 1; CA 104; CANR 26; DLB 33

Bradley, John Ed(mund, Jr.)
1958- . . . . CLC 55
See also CA 139

Bradley, Marion Zimmer   1930- . . . . . CLC 30
See also AAYA 9; CA 57-60; CAAS 10;
CANR 7, 31; DLB 8; MTCW

Bradstreet, Anne
1612(?)-1672 . . . . LC 4; DA; PC 10
See also CDALB 1640-1865; DLB 24

Brady, Joan   1939- . . . . CLC 86
See also CA 141

Bragg, Melvyn 1939- . . . . CLC 10
See also BEST 89:3; CA 57-60; CANR 10;
DLB 14

Braine, John (Gerard)
1922-1986 . . . . CLC 1, 3, 41
See also CA 1-4R; 120; CANR 1, 33;
CDBLB 1945-1960; DLB 15; DLBY 86;
MTCW

Brammer, William 1930(?)-1978 . . . . CLC 31
See also CA 77-80

Brancati, Vitaliano 1907-1954 . . . . . TCLC 12
See also CA 109

Brancato, Robin F(idler) 1936- . . . . . CLC 35
See also AAYA 9; CA 69-72; CANR 11,
45; CLR 32; JRDA; SAAS 9; SATA 23

Brand, Max
See Faust, Frederick (Schiller)

Brand, Millen 1906-1980 . . . . CLC 7
See also CA 21-24R; 97-100

Branden, Barbara . . . . CLC 44

Brandes, Georg (Morris Cohen)
1842-1927 . . . . TCLC 10
See also CA 105

Brandys, Kazimierz 1916- . . . . CLC 62

Branley, Franklyn M(ansfield)
1915- . . . . CLC 21
See also CA 33-36R; CANR 14, 39;
CLR 13; MAICYA; SAAS 16; SATA 4,
68

Brathwaite, Edward Kamau 1930- . . . CLC 11
See also BW 2; CA 25-28R; CANR 11, 26,
47; DLB 125

Brautigan, Richard (Gary)
1935-1984 . . . . CLC 1, 3, 5, 9, 12, 34, 42
See also CA 53-56; 113; CANR 34; DLB 2,
5; DLBY 80, 84; MTCW; SATA 56

Braverman, Kate 1950- . . . . CLC 67
See also CA 89-92

Brecht, Bertolt
1898-1956 . . . . . . TCLC 1, 6, 13, 35; DA;
DC 3; WLC
See also CA 104; 133; DLB 56, 124; MTCW

Brecht, Eugen Berthold Friedrich
See Brecht, Bertolt

Bremer, Fredrika 1801-1865 . . . . . NCLC 11

Brennan, Christopher John
1870-1932 . . . . TCLC 17
See also CA 117

Brennan, Maeve 1917- . . . . CLC 5
See also CA 81-84

Brentano, Clemens (Maria)
1778-1842 . . . . NCLC 1
See also DLB 90

Brent of Bin Bin
See Franklin, (Stella Maraia Sarah) Miles

Brenton, Howard 1942- . . . . CLC 31
See also CA 69-72; CANR 33; DLB 13;
MTCW

Breslin, James 1930-
See Breslin, Jimmy
See also CA 73-76; CANR 31; MTCW

Breslin, Jimmy . . . . CLC 4, 43
See also Breslin, James
See also AITN 1

Bresson, Robert 1907- . . . . CLC 16
See also CA 110

Breton, Andre 1896-1966 . . . CLC 2, 9, 15, 54
See also CA 19-20; 25-28R; CANR 40;
CAP 2; DLB 65; MTCW

Breytenbach, Breyten 1939(?)- . . CLC 23, 37
See also CA 113; 129

Bridgers, Sue Ellen 1942- . . . . CLC 26
See also AAYA 8; CA 65-68; CANR 11,
36; CLR 18; DLB 52; JRDA; MAICYA;
SAAS 1; SATA 22

Bridges, Robert (Seymour)
1844-1930 . . . . TCLC 1
See also CA 104; CDBLB 1890-1914;
DLB 19, 98

Bridie, James . . . . TCLC 3
See also Mavor, Osborne Henry
See also DLB 10

Brin, David 1950- . . . . CLC 34
See also CA 102; CANR 24; SATA 65

Brink, Andre (Philippus)
1935- . . . . CLC 18, 36
See also CA 104; CANR 39; MTCW

Brinsmead, H(esba) F(ay) 1922- . . . . CLC 21
See also CA 21-24R; CANR 10; MAICYA;
SAAS 5; SATA 18, 78

Brittain, Vera (Mary)
1893(?)-1970 . . . . CLC 23
See also CA 13-16; 25-28R; CAP 1; MTCW

Broch, Hermann 1886-1951 . . . . TCLC 20
See also CA 117; DLB 85, 124

Brock, Rose
See Hansen, Joseph

Brodkey, Harold 1930- . . . . CLC 56
See also CA 111; DLB 130

Brodsky, Iosif Alexandrovich 1940-
See Brodsky, Joseph
See also AITN 1; CA 41-44R; CANR 37;
MTCW

Brodsky, Joseph . . CLC 4, 6, 13, 36, 50; PC 9
See also Brodsky, Iosif Alexandrovich

Brodsky, Michael Mark 1948- . . . . . . CLC 19
See also CA 102; CANR 18, 41

Bromell, Henry 1947- . . . . CLC 5
See also CA 53-56; CANR 9

Bromfield, Louis (Brucker)
1896-1956 . . . . TCLC 11
See also CA 107; DLB 4, 9, 86

Broner, E(sther) M(asserman)
1930- . . . . CLC 19
See also CA 17-20R; CANR 8, 25; DLB 28

Bronk, William 1918- . . . . CLC 10
See also CA 89-92; CANR 23

Bronstein, Lev Davidovich
See Trotsky, Leon

Bronte, Anne 1820-1849 . . . . NCLC 4
See also DLB 21

Bronte, Charlotte
1816-1855 . . . NCLC 3, 8, 33; DA; WLC
See also CDBLB 1832-1890; DLB 21

Bronte, (Jane) Emily
1818-1848 . . . . NCLC 16, 35; DA; PC 8;
WLC
See also CDBLB 1832-1890; DLB 21, 32

Brooke, Frances 1724-1789 . . . . LC 6
See also DLB 39, 99

Brooke, Henry 1703(?)-1783 . . . . LC 1
See also DLB 39

Brooke, Rupert (Chawner)
1887-1915 . . . . TCLC 2, 7; DA; WLC
See also CA 104; 132; CDBLB 1914-1945;
DLB 19; MTCW

Brooke-Haven, P.
See Wodehouse, P(elham) G(renville)

Brooke-Rose, Christine 1926- . . . . . . CLC 40
See also CA 13-16R; DLB 14

Brookner, Anita 1928- . . . . . . CLC 32, 34, 51
See also CA 114; 120; CANR 37; DLBY 87;
MTCW

Brooks, Cleanth 1906-1994 . . . . . CLC 24, 86
See also CA 17-20R; 145; CANR 33, 35;
DLB 63; DLBY 94; MTCW

Brooks, George
See Baum, L(yman) Frank

Brooks, Gwendolyn
1917- . . . . . . CLC 1, 2, 4, 5, 15, 49; BLC;
DA; PC 7; WLC
See also AITN 1; BW 2; CA 1-4R;
CANR 1, 27; CDALB 1941-1968;
CLR 27; DLB 5, 76; MTCW; SATA 6

Brooks, Mel . . . . CLC 12
See also Kaminsky, Melvin
See also AAYA 13; DLB 26

Brooks, Peter 1938- . . . . CLC 34
See also CA 45-48; CANR 1

Brooks, Van Wyck 1886-1963 . . . . . . CLC 29
See also CA 1-4R; CANR 6; DLB 45, 63,
103

Brophy, Brigid (Antonia)
1929- . . . . CLC 6, 11, 29
See also CA 5-8R; CAAS 4; CANR 25;
DLB 14; MTCW

Brosman, Catharine Savage 1934- . . . . CLC 9
See also CA 61-64; CANR 21, 46

Brother Antoninus
See Everson, William (Oliver)

Broughton, T(homas) Alan 1936- . . . CLC 19
See also CA 45-48; CANR 2, 23

Broumas, Olga 1949- . . . . CLC 10, 73
See also CA 85-88; CANR 20

Brown, Charles Brockden
1771-1810 . . . . NCLC 22
See also CDALB 1640-1865; DLB 37, 59,
73

Brown, Christy 1932-1981 . . . . CLC 63
See also CA 105; 104; DLB 14

Brown, Claude 1937- . . . . CLC 30; BLC
See also AAYA 7; BW 1; CA 73-76

Brown, Dee (Alexander) 1908- . . CLC 18, 47
See also CA 13-16R; CAAS 6; CANR 11,
45; DLBY 80; MTCW; SATA 5

Brown, George
See Wertmueller, Lina

Brown, George Douglas
1869-1902 . . . . TCLC 28

Brown, George Mackay 1921- . . . . CLC 5, 48
See also CA 21-24R; CAAS 6; CANR 12,
37; DLB 14, 27, 139; MTCW; SATA 35

Brown, (William) Larry 1951-...... **CLC 73**
See also CA 130; 134

Brown, Moses
See Barrett, William (Christopher)

Brown, Rita Mae 1944-..... **CLC 18, 43, 79**
See also CA 45-48; CANR 2, 11, 35;
MTCW

Brown, Roderick (Langmere) Haig-
See Haig-Brown, Roderick (Langmere)

Brown, Rosellen 1939-............ **CLC 32**
See also CA 77-80; CAAS 10; CANR 14, 44

Brown, Sterling Allen
1901-1989 .... **CLC 1, 23, 59; BLC**
See also BW 1; CA 85-88; 127; CANR 26;
DLB 48, 51, 63; MTCW

Brown, Will
See Ainsworth, William Harrison

Brown, William Wells
1813-1884 .... **NCLC 2; BLC; DC 1**
See also DLB 3, 50

Browne, (Clyde) Jackson 1948(?)-... **CLC 21**
See also CA 120

Browning, Elizabeth Barrett
1806-1861 ..... **NCLC 1, 16; DA; PC 6;**
WLC
See also CDBLB 1832-1890; DLB 32

Browning, Robert
1812-1889 .... **NCLC 19; DA; PC 2**
See also CDBLB 1832-1890; DLB 32;
YABC 1

Browning, Tod 1882-1962 .... **CLC 16**
See also CA 141; 117

Brownson, Orestes (Augustus)
1803-1876 .... **NCLC 50**

Bruccoli, Matthew J(oseph) 1931- .. **CLC 34**
See also CA 9-12R; CANR 7; DLB 103

Bruce, Lenny.................... **CLC 21**
See also Schneider, Leonard Alfred

Bruin, John
See Brutus, Dennis

Brulard, Henri
See Stendhal

Brulls, Christian
See Simenon, Georges (Jacques Christian)

Brunner, John (Kilian Houston)
1934-.................... **CLC 8, 10**
See also CA 1-4R; CAAS 8; CANR 2, 37;
MTCW

Bruno, Giordano 1548-1600........ **LC 27**

Brutus, Dennis 1924- .... **CLC 43; BLC**
See also BW 2; CA 49-52; CAAS 14;
CANR 2, 27, 42; DLB 117

Bryan, C(ourtlandt) D(ixon) B(arnes)
1936-....................... **CLC 29**
See also CA 73-76; CANR 13

Bryan, Michael
See Moore, Brian

Bryant, William Cullen
1794-1878 .... **NCLC 6, 46; DA**
See also CDALB 1640-1865; DLB 3, 43, 59

Bryusov, Valery Yakovlevich
1873-1924 .... **TCLC 10**
See also CA 107

Buchan, John 1875-1940 .... **TCLC 41**
See also CA 108; 145; DLB 34, 70; YABC 2

Buchanan, George 1506-1582 .... **LC 4**

Buchheim, Lothar-Guenther 1918- ... **CLC 6**
See also CA 85-88

Buchner, (Karl) Georg
1813-1837 .... **NCLC 26**

Buchwald, Art(hur) 1925-......... **CLC 33**
See also AITN 1; CA 5-8R; CANR 21;
MTCW; SATA 10

Buck, Pearl S(ydenstricker)
1892-1973 .... **CLC 7, 11, 18; DA**
See also AITN 1; CA 1-4R; 41-44R;
CANR 1, 34; DLB 9, 102; MTCW;
SATA 1, 25

Buckler, Ernest 1908-1984........ **CLC 13**
See also CA 11-12; 114; CAP 1; DLB 68;
SATA 47

Buckley, Vincent (Thomas)
1925-1988 .... **CLC 57**
See also CA 101

Buckley, William F(rank), Jr.
1925- .... **CLC 7, 18, 37**
See also AITN 1; CA 1-4R; CANR 1, 24;
DLB 137; DLBY 80; MTCW

Buechner, (Carl) Frederick
1926-................. **CLC 2, 4, 6, 9**
See also CA 13-16R; CANR 11, 39;
DLBY 80; MTCW

Buell, John (Edward) 1927-........ **CLC 10**
See also CA 1-4R; DLB 53

Buero Vallejo, Antonio 1916- ... **CLC 15, 46**
See also CA 106; CANR 24; HW; MTCW

Bufalino, Gesualdo 1920(?)-........ **CLC 74**

Bugayev, Boris Nikolayevich 1880-1934
See Bely, Andrey
See also CA 104

Bukowski, Charles
1920-1994 .... **CLC 2, 5, 9, 41, 82**
See also CA 17-20R; 144; CANR 40;
DLB 5, 130; MTCW

Bulgakov, Mikhail (Afanas'evich)
1891-1940 .... **TCLC 2, 16; SSC 18**
See also CA 105

Bulgya, Alexander Alexandrovich
1901-1956 .... **TCLC 53**
See also Fadeyev, Alexander
See also CA 117

Bullins, Ed 1935- .... **CLC 1, 5, 7; BLC**
See also BW 2; CA 49-52; CAAS 16;
CANR 24, 46; DLB 7, 38; MTCW

Bulwer-Lytton, Edward (George Earle Lytton)
1803-1873 .... **NCLC 1, 45**
See also DLB 21

Bunin, Ivan Alexeyevich
1870-1953 .... **TCLC 6; SSC 5**
See also CA 104

Bunting, Basil 1900-1985.... **CLC 10, 39, 47**
See also CA 53-56; 115; CANR 7; DLB 20

Bunuel, Luis 1900-1983 .. **CLC 16, 80; HLC**
See also CA 101; 110; CANR 32; HW

Bunyan, John 1628-1688 .. **LC 4; DA; WLC**
See also CDBLB 1660-1789; DLB 39

Burckhardt, Jacob (Christoph)
1818-1897 .... **NCLC 49**

Burford, Eleanor
See Hibbert, Eleanor Alice Burford

Burgess, Anthony
CLC 1, 2, 4, 5, 8, 10, 13, 15, 22, 40, 62,
81
See also Wilson, John (Anthony) Burgess
See also AITN 1; CDBLB 1960 to Present;
DLB 14

Burke, Edmund
1729(?)-1797 .... **LC 7; DA; WLC**
See also DLB 104

Burke, Kenneth (Duva)
1897-1993 .... **CLC 2, 24**
See also CA 5-8R; 143; CANR 39; DLB 45,
63; MTCW

Burke, Leda
See Garnett, David

Burke, Ralph
See Silverberg, Robert

Burney, Fanny 1752-1840 .... **NCLC 12**
See also DLB 39

Burns, Robert 1759-1796............ **PC 6**
See also CDBLB 1789-1832; DA; DLB 109;
WLC

Burns, Tex
See L'Amour, Louis (Dearborn)

Burnshaw, Stanley 1906-..... **CLC 3, 13, 44**
See also CA 9-12R; DLB 48

Burr, Anne 1937-................. **CLC 6**
See also CA 25-28R

Burroughs, Edgar Rice
1875-1950 .... **TCLC 2, 32**
See also AAYA 11; CA 104; 132; DLB 8;
MTCW; SATA 41

Burroughs, William S(eward)
1914-....... **CLC 1, 2, 5, 15, 22, 42, 75;**
DA; WLC
See also AITN 2; CA 9-12R; CANR 20;
DLB 2, 8, 16, 152; DLBY 81; MTCW

Burton, Richard F. 1821-1890.... **NCLC 42**
See also DLB 55

Busch, Frederick 1941- ... **CLC 7, 10, 18, 47**
See also CA 33-36R; CAAS 1; CANR 45;
DLB 6

Bush, Ronald 1946- .... **CLC 34**
See also CA 136

Bustos, F(rancisco)
See Borges, Jorge Luis

Bustos Domecq, H(onorio)
See Bioy Casares, Adolfo; Borges, Jorge
Luis

Butler, Octavia E(stelle) 1947- ..... **CLC 38**
See also BW 2; CA 73-76; CANR 12, 24,
38; DLB 33; MTCW

Butler, Robert Olen (Jr.) 1945-..... **CLC 81**
See also CA 112

Butler, Samuel 1612-1680 .... **LC 16**
See also DLB 101, 126

Butler, Samuel
1835-1902 ...... **TCLC 1, 33; DA; WLC**
See also CA 143; CDBLB 1890-1914;
DLB 18, 57

Butler, Walter C.
See Faust, Frederick (Schiller)

Author Index

Conroy, Pat 1945-............ **CLC 30, 74**
See also AAYA 8; AITN 1; CA 85-88;
CANR 24; DLB 6; MTCW

Constant (de Rebecque), (Henri) Benjamin
1767-1830 .... **NCLC 6**
See also DLB 119

Conybeare, Charles Augustus
See Eliot, T(homas) S(tearns)

Cook, Michael 1933-............ **CLC 58**
See also CA 93-96; DLB 53

Cook, Robin 1940-.............. **CLC 14**
See also BEST 90:2; CA 108; 111;
CANR 41

Cook, Roy
See Silverberg, Robert

Cooke, Elizabeth 1948-........... **CLC 55**
See also CA 129

Cooke, John Esten 1830-1886..... **NCLC 5**
See also DLB 3

Cooke, John Estes
See Baum, L(yman) Frank

Cooke, M. E.
See Creasey, John

Cooke, Margaret
See Creasey, John

Cooney, Ray .... **CLC 62**

Cooper, Douglas 1960-........... **CLC 86**

Cooper, Henry St. John
See Creasey, John

Cooper, J. California.............. **CLC 56**
See also AAYA 12; BW 1; CA 125

Cooper, James Fenimore
1789-1851 .... **NCLC 1, 27**
See also CDALB 1640-1865; DLB 3;
SATA 19

Coover, Robert (Lowell)
1932-.. **CLC 3, 7, 15, 32, 46, 87; SSC 15**
See also CA 45-48; CANR 3, 37; DLB 2;
DLBY 81; MTCW

Copeland, Stewart (Armstrong)
1952- .... **CLC 26**

Coppard, A(lfred) E(dgar)
1878-1957 .... **TCLC 5**
See also CA 114; YABC 1

Coppee, Francois 1842-1908 ...... **TCLC 25**

Coppola, Francis Ford 1939-....... **CLC 16**
See also CA 77-80; CANR 40; DLB 44

Corbiere, Tristan 1845-1875 ..... **NCLC 43**

Corcoran, Barbara 1911-.......... **CLC 17**
See also AAYA 14; CA 21-24R; CAAS 2;
CANR 11, 28; DLB 52; JRDA; SAAS 20;
SATA 3, 77

Cordelier, Maurice
See Giraudoux, (Hippolyte) Jean

Corelli, Marie 1855-1924........ **TCLC 51**
See also Mackay, Mary
See also DLB 34

Corman, Cid..................... **CLC 9**
See also Corman, Sidney
See also CAAS 2; DLB 5

Corman, Sidney 1924-
See Corman, Cid
See also CA 85-88; CANR 44

Cormier, Robert (Edmund)
1925- .... **CLC 12, 30; DA**
See also AAYA 3; CA 1-4R; CANR 5, 23;
CDALB 1968-1988; CLR 12; DLB 52;
JRDA; MAICYA; MTCW; SATA 10, 45

Corn, Alfred (DeWitt III) 1943-.... **CLC 33**
See also CA 104; CANR 44; DLB 120;
DLBY 80

Corneille, Pierre 1606-1684........ **LC 28**

Cornwell, David (John Moore)
1931- .... **CLC 9, 15**
See also le Carre, John
See also CA 5-8R; CANR 13, 33; MTCW

Corso, (Nunzio) Gregory 1930-... **CLC 1, 11**
See also CA 5-8R; CANR 41; DLB 5, 16;
MTCW

Cortazar, Julio
1914-1984 ...... **CLC 2, 3, 5, 10, 13, 15,**
33, 34; HLC; SSC 7
See also CA 21-24R; CANR 12, 32;
DLB 113; HW; MTCW

Corwin, Cecil
See Kornbluth, C(yril) M.

Cosic, Dobrica 1921- .... **CLC 14**
See also CA 122; 138

Costain, Thomas B(ertram)
1885-1965 .... **CLC 30**
See also CA 5-8R; 25-28R; DLB 9

Costantini, Humberto
1924(?)-1987 .... **CLC 49**
See also CA 131; 122; HW

Costello, Elvis 1955-.............. **CLC 21**

Cotter, Joseph Seamon Sr.
1861-1949 .... **TCLC 28; BLC**
See also BW 1; CA 124; DLB 50

Couch, Arthur Thomas Quiller
See Quiller-Couch, Arthur Thomas

Coulton, James
See Hansen, Joseph

Couperus, Louis (Marie Anne)
1863-1923 .... **TCLC 15**
See also CA 115

Coupland, Douglas 1961-.......... **CLC 85**
See also CA 142

Court, Wesli
See Turco, Lewis (Putnam)

Courtenay, Bryce 1933-........... **CLC 59**
See also CA 138

Courtney, Robert
See Ellison, Harlan (Jay)

Cousteau, Jacques-Yves 1910-...... **CLC 30**
See also CA 65-68; CANR 15; MTCW;
SATA 38

Coward, Noel (Peirce)
1899-1973 .... **CLC 1, 9, 29, 51**
See also AITN 1; CA 17-18; 41-44R;
CANR 35; CAP 2; CDBLB 1914-1945;
DLB 10; MTCW

Cowley, Malcolm 1898-1989 .... **CLC 39**
See also CA 5-8R; 128; CANR 3; DLB 4,
48; DLBY 81, 89; MTCW

Cowper, William 1731-1800....... **NCLC 8**
See also DLB 104, 109

Cox, William Trevor 1928- ... **CLC 9, 14, 71**
See also Trevor, William
See also CA 9-12R; CANR 4, 37; DLB 14;
MTCW

Coyne, P. J.
See Masters, Hilary

Cozzens, James Gould
1903-1978 .... **CLC 1, 4, 11**
See also CA 9-12R; 81-84; CANR 19;
CDALB 1941-1968; DLB 9; DLBD 2;
DLBY 84; MTCW

Crabbe, George 1754-1832....... **NCLC 26**
See also DLB 93

Craig, A. A.
See Anderson, Poul (William)

Craik, Dinah Maria (Mulock)
1826-1887 .... **NCLC 38**
See also DLB 35; MAICYA; SATA 34

Cram, Ralph Adams 1863-1942.... **TCLC 45**

Crane, (Harold) Hart
1899-1932 .... **TCLC 2, 5; DA; PC 3;**
WLC
See also CA 104; 127; CDALB 1917-1929;
DLB 4, 48; MTCW

Crane, R(onald) S(almon)
1886-1967 .... **CLC 27**
See also CA 85-88; DLB 63

Crane, Stephen (Townley)
1871-1900 .... **TCLC 11, 17, 32; DA;**
SSC 7; WLC
See also CA 109; 140; CDALB 1865-1917;
DLB 12, 54, 78; YABC 2

Crase, Douglas 1944-............. **CLC 58**
See also CA 106

Crashaw, Richard 1612(?)-1649...... **LC 24**
See also DLB 126

Craven, Margaret 1901-1980....... **CLC 17**
See also CA 103

Crawford, F(rancis) Marion
1854-1909 .... **TCLC 10**
See also CA 107; DLB 71

Crawford, Isabella Valancy
1850-1887 .... **NCLC 12**
See also DLB 92

Crayon, Geoffrey
See Irving, Washington

Creasey, John 1908-1973.......... **CLC 11**
See also CA 5-8R; 41-44R; CANR 8;
DLB 77; MTCW

Crebillon, Claude Prosper Jolyot de (fils)
1707-1777 .... **LC 28**

Credo
See Creasey, John

Creeley, Robert (White)
1926- ..... **CLC 1, 2, 4, 8, 11, 15, 36, 78**
See also CA 1-4R; CAAS 10; CANR 23, 43;
DLB 5, 16; MTCW

Crews, Harry (Eugene)
1935- .... **CLC 6, 23, 49**
See also AITN 1; CA 25-28R; CANR 20;
DLB 6, 143; MTCW

Davies, (William) Robertson
1913- ..... CLC 2, 7, 13, 25, 42, 75; DA;
WLC
See also BEST 89:2; CA 33-36R; CANR 17,
42; DLB 68; MTCW

Davies, W(illiam) H(enry)
1871-1940 .... TCLC 5
See also CA 104; DLB 19

Davies, Walter C.
See Kornbluth, C(yril) M.

Davis, Angela (Yvonne) 1944- ...... CLC 77
See also BW 2; CA 57-60; CANR 10

Davis, B. Lynch
See Bioy Casares, Adolfo; Borges, Jorge
Luis

Davis, Gordon
See Hunt, E(verette) Howard, (Jr.)

Davis, Harold Lenoir 1896-1960.... CLC 49
See also CA 89-92; DLB 9

Davis, Rebecca (Blaine) Harding
1831-1910 .... TCLC 6
See also CA 104; DLB 74

Davis, Richard Harding
1864-1916 .... TCLC 24
See also CA 114; DLB 12, 23, 78, 79

Davison, Frank Dalby 1893-1970 ... CLC 15
See also CA 116

Davison, Lawrence H.
See Lawrence, D(avid) H(erbert Richards)

Davison, Peter (Hubert) 1928- ..... CLC 28
See also CA 9-12R; CAAS 4; CANR 3, 43;
DLB 5

Davys, Mary 1674-1732............. LC 1
See also DLB 39

Dawson, Fielding 1930- .... CLC 6
See also CA 85-88; DLB 130

Dawson, Peter
See Faust, Frederick (Schiller)

Day, Clarence (Shepard, Jr.)
1874-1935 .... TCLC 25
See also CA 108; DLB 11

Day, Thomas 1748-1789............. LC 1
See also DLB 39; YABC 1

Day Lewis, C(ecil)
1904-1972 .... CLC 1, 6, 10; PC 11
See also Blake, Nicholas
See also CA 13-16; 33-36R; CANR 34;
CAP 1; DLB 15, 20; MTCW

Dazai, Osamu .... TCLC 11
See also Tsushima, Shuji

de Andrade, Carlos Drummond
See Drummond de Andrade, Carlos

Deane, Norman
See Creasey, John

de Beauvoir, Simone (Lucie Ernestine Marie
Bertrand)
See Beauvoir, Simone (Lucie Ernestine
Marie Bertrand) de

de Brissac, Malcolm
See Dickinson, Peter (Malcolm)

de Chardin, Pierre Teilhard
See Teilhard de Chardin, (Marie Joseph)
Pierre

Dee, John 1527-1608 .... LC 20

Deer, Sandra 1940-............... CLC 45

De Ferrari, Gabriella .... CLC 65

Defoe, Daniel
1660(?)-1731 .... LC 1; DA; WLC
See also CDBLB 1660-1789; DLB 39, 95,
101; JRDA; MAICYA; SATA 22

de Gourmont, Remy
See Gourmont, Remy de

de Hartog, Jan 1914- .... CLC 19
See also CA 1-4R; CANR 1

de Hostos, E. M.
See Hostos (y Bonilla), Eugenio Maria de

de Hostos, Eugenio M.
See Hostos (y Bonilla), Eugenio Maria de

Deighton, Len .... CLC 4, 7, 22, 46
See also Deighton, Leonard Cyril
See also AAYA 6; BEST 89:2;
CDBLB 1960 to Present; DLB 87

Deighton, Leonard Cyril 1929-
See Deighton, Len
See also CA 9-12R; CANR 19, 33; MTCW

Dekker, Thomas 1572(?)-1632....... LC 22
See also CDBLB Before 1660; DLB 62

de la Mare, Walter (John)
1873-1956 .. TCLC 4, 53; SSC 14; WLC
See also CDBLB 1914-1945; CLR 23;
DLB 19; SATA 16

Delaney, Franey
See O'Hara, John (Henry)

Delaney, Shelagh 1939- .... CLC 29
See also CA 17-20R; CANR 30;
CDBLB 1960 to Present; DLB 13;
MTCW

Delany, Mary (Granville Pendarves)
1700-1788 .... LC 12

Delany, Samuel R(ay, Jr.)
1942- .... CLC 8, 14, 38; BLC
See also BW 2; CA 81-84; CANR 27, 43;
DLB 8, 33; MTCW

De La Ramee, (Marie) Louise 1839-1908
See Ouida
See also SATA 20

de la Roche, Mazo 1879-1961...... CLC 14
See also CA 85-88; CANR 30; DLB 68;
SATA 64

Delbanco, Nicholas (Franklin)
1942- .... CLC 6, 13
See also CA 17-20R; CAAS 2; CANR 29;
DLB 6

del Castillo, Michel 1933- .... CLC 38
See also CA 109

Deledda, Grazia (Cosima)
1875(?)-1936 .... TCLC 23
See also CA 123

Delibes, Miguel .... CLC 8, 18
See also Delibes Setien, Miguel

Delibes Setien, Miguel 1920-
See Delibes, Miguel
See also CA 45-48; CANR 1, 32; HW;
MTCW

DeLillo, Don
1936- ..... CLC 8, 10, 13, 27, 39, 54, 76
See also BEST 89:1; CA 81-84; CANR 21;
DLB 6; MTCW

de Lisser, H. G.
See De Lisser, Herbert George
See also DLB 117

De Lisser, Herbert George
1878-1944 .... TCLC 12
See also de Lisser, H. G.
See also BW 2; CA 109

Deloria, Vine (Victor), Jr. 1933-.... CLC 21
See also CA 53-56; CANR 5, 20; MTCW;
NNAL; SATA 21

Del Vecchio, John M(ichael)
1947- .... CLC 29
See also CA 110; DLBD 9

de Man, Paul (Adolph Michel)
1919-1983 .... CLC 55
See also CA 128; 111; DLB 67; MTCW

De Marinis, Rick 1934-........... CLC 54
See also CA 57-60; CANR 9, 25

Demby, William 1922-....... CLC 53; BLC
See also BW 1; CA 81-84; DLB 33

Demijohn, Thom
See Disch, Thomas M(ichael)

de Montherlant, Henry (Milon)
See Montherlant, Henry (Milon) de

Demosthenes 384B.C.-322B.C. .... CMLC 13

de Natale, Francine
See Malzberg, Barry N(athaniel)

Denby, Edwin (Orr) 1903-1983..... CLC 48
See also CA 138; 110

Denis, Julio
See Cortazar, Julio

Denmark, Harrison
See Zelazny, Roger (Joseph)

Dennis, John 1658-1734............ LC 11
See also DLB 101

Dennis, Nigel (Forbes) 1912-1989.... CLC 8
See also CA 25-28R; 129; DLB 13, 15;
MTCW

De Palma, Brian (Russell) 1940-.... CLC 20
See also CA 109

De Quincey, Thomas 1785-1859 ... NCLC 4
See also CDBLB 1789-1832; DLB 110; 144

Deren, Eleanora 1908(?)-1961
See Deren, Maya
See also CA 111

Deren, Maya .... CLC 16
See also Deren, Eleanora

Derleth, August (William)
1909-1971 .... CLC 31
See also CA 1-4R; 29-32R; CANR 4;
DLB 9; SATA 5

Der Nister 1884-1950........... TCLC 56

de Routisie, Albert
See Aragon, Louis

Derrida, Jacques 1930-........ CLC 24, 87
See also CA 124; 127

Derry Down Derry
See Lear, Edward

Dersonnes, Jacques
See Simenon, Georges (Jacques Christian)

Desai, Anita 1937- .... CLC 19, 37
See also CA 81-84; CANR 33; MTCW;
SATA 63

de Saint-Luc, Jean
See Glassco, John

de Saint Roman, Arnaud
See Aragon, Louis

Descartes, Rene 1596-1650 . . . . **LC 20**

De Sica, Vittorio 1901(?)-1974 . . . . . **CLC 20**
See also CA 117

Desnos, Robert 1900-1945 . . . . **TCLC 22**
See also CA 121

Destouches, Louis-Ferdinand
1894-1961 . . . . **CLC 9, 15**
See also Celine, Louis-Ferdinand
See also CA 85-88; CANR 28; MTCW

Deutsch, Babette 1895-1982 . . . . **CLC 18**
See also CA 1-4R; 108; CANR 4; DLB 45;
SATA 1; SATA-Obit 33

Devenant, William 1606-1649 . . . . **LC 13**

Devkota, Laxmiprasad
1909-1959 . . . . **TCLC 23**
See also CA 123

De Voto, Bernard (Augustine)
1897-1955 . . . . **TCLC 29**
See also CA 113; DLB 9

De Vries, Peter
1910-1993 . . . . **CLC 1, 2, 3, 7, 10, 28, 46**
See also CA 17-20R; 142; CANR 41;
DLB 6; DLBY 82; MTCW

Dexter, Martin
See Faust, Frederick (Schiller)

Dexter, Pete 1943- . . . . **CLC 34, 55**
See also BEST 89:2; CA 127; 131; MTCW

Diamano, Silmang
See Senghor, Leopold Sedar

Diamond, Neil 1941- . . . . **CLC 30**
See also CA 108

di Bassetto, Corno
See Shaw, George Bernard

Dick, Philip K(indred)
1928-1982 . . . . **CLC 10, 30, 72**
See also CA 49-52; 106; CANR 2, 16;
DLB 8; MTCW

Dickens, Charles (John Huffam)
1812-1870 . . . . . . **NCLC 3, 8, 18, 26, 37,
50; DA; SSC 17; WLC**
See also CDBLB 1832-1890; DLB 21, 55,
70; JRDA; MAICYA; SATA 15

Dickey, James (Lafayette)
1923- . . . . **CLC 1, 2, 4, 7, 10, 15, 47**
See also AITN 1, 2; CA 9-12R; CABS 2;
CANR 10; CDALB 1968-1988; DLB 5;
DLBD 7; DLBY 82, 93; MTCW

Dickey, William 1928-1994 . . . . . **CLC 3, 28**
See also CA 9-12R; 145; CANR 24; DLB 5

Dickinson, Charles 1951- . . . . **CLC 49**
See also CA 128

Dickinson, Emily (Elizabeth)
1830-1886 . . **NCLC 21; DA; PC 1; WLC**
See also CDALB 1865-1917; DLB 1;
SATA 29

Dickinson, Peter (Malcolm)
1927- . . . . **CLC 12, 35**
See also AAYA 9; CA 41-44R; CANR 31;
CLR 29; DLB 87; JRDA; MAICYA;
SATA 5, 62

Dickson, Carr
See Carr, John Dickson

Dickson, Carter
See Carr, John Dickson

Diderot, Denis 1713-1784 . . . . **LC 26**

Didion, Joan 1934- . . . . . **CLC 1, 3, 8, 14, 32**
See also AITN 1; CA 5-8R; CANR 14;
CDALB 1968-1988; DLB 2; DLBY 81,
86; MTCW

Dietrich, Robert
See Hunt, E(verette) Howard, (Jr.)

Dillard, Annie 1945- . . . . **CLC 9, 60**
See also AAYA 6; CA 49-52; CANR 3, 43;
DLBY 80; MTCW; SATA 10

Dillard, R(ichard) H(enry) W(ilde)
1937- . . . . **CLC 5**
See also CA 21-24R; CAAS 7; CANR 10;
DLB 5

Dillon, Eilis 1920- . . . . **CLC 17**
See also CA 9-12R; CAAS 3; CANR 4, 38;
CLR 26; MAICYA; SATA 2, 74

Dimont, Penelope
See Mortimer, Penelope (Ruth)

Dinesen, Isak . . . . **CLC 10, 29; SSC 7**
See also Blixen, Karen (Christentze
Dinesen)

Ding Ling . . . . **CLC 68**
See also Chiang Pin-chin

Disch, Thomas M(ichael) 1940- . . . **CLC 7, 36**
See also CA 21-24R; CAAS 4; CANR 17,
36; CLR 18; DLB 8; MAICYA; MTCW;
SAAS 15; SATA 54

Disch, Tom
See Disch, Thomas M(ichael)

d'Isly, Georges
See Simenon, Georges (Jacques Christian)

Disraeli, Benjamin 1804-1881 . . **NCLC 2, 39**
See also DLB 21, 55

Ditcum, Steve
See Crumb, R(obert)

Dixon, Paige
See Corcoran, Barbara

Dixon, Stephen 1936- . . . . . **CLC 52; SSC 16**
See also CA 89-92; CANR 17, 40; DLB 130

Dobell, Sydney Thompson
1824-1874 . . . . **NCLC 43**
See also DLB 32

Doblin, Alfred . . . . **TCLC 13**
See also Doeblin, Alfred

Dobrolyubov, Nikolai Alexandrovich
1836-1861 . . . . **NCLC 5**

Dobyns, Stephen 1941- . . . . **CLC 37**
See also CA 45-48; CANR 2, 18

Doctorow, E(dgar) L(aurence)
1931- . . . . . **CLC 6, 11, 15, 18, 37, 44, 65**
See also AITN 2; BEST 89:3; CA 45-48;
CANR 2, 33; CDALB 1968-1988; DLB 2,
28; DLBY 80; MTCW

Dodgson, Charles Lutwidge 1832-1898
See Carroll, Lewis
See also CLR 2; DA; MAICYA; YABC 2

Dodson, Owen (Vincent)
1914-1983 . . . . **CLC 79; BLC**
See also BW 1; CA 65-68; 110; CANR 24;
DLB 76

Doeblin, Alfred 1878-1957 . . . . **TCLC 13**
See also Doblin, Alfred
See also CA 110; 141; DLB 66

Doerr, Harriet 1910- . . . . **CLC 34**
See also CA 117; 122; CANR 47

Domecq, H(onorio) Bustos
See Bioy Casares, Adolfo; Borges, Jorge
Luis

Domini, Rey
See Lorde, Audre (Geraldine)

Dominique
See Proust, (Valentin-Louis-George-Eugene-)
Marcel

Don, A
See Stephen, Leslie

Donaldson, Stephen R. 1947- . . . . **CLC 46**
See also CA 89-92; CANR 13

Donleavy, J(ames) P(atrick)
1926- . . . . **CLC 1, 4, 6, 10, 45**
See also AITN 2; CA 9-12R; CANR 24;
DLB 6; MTCW

Donne, John
1572-1631 . . . . **LC 10, 24; DA; PC 1**
See also CDBLB Before 1660; DLB 121,
151

Donnell, David 1939(?)- . . . . **CLC 34**

Donoghue, P. S.
See Hunt, E(verette) Howard, (Jr.)

Donoso (Yanez), Jose
1924- . . . . **CLC 4, 8, 11, 32; HLC**
See also CA 81-84; CANR 32; DLB 113;
HW; MTCW

Donovan, John 1928-1992 . . . . **CLC 35**
See also CA 97-100; 137; CLR 3;
MAICYA; SATA 72; SATA-Brief 29

Don Roberto
See Cunninghame Graham, R(obert)
B(ontine)

Doolittle, Hilda
1886-1961 . . . . . **CLC 3, 8, 14, 31, 34, 73;
DA; PC 5; WLC**
See also H. D.
See also CA 97-100; CANR 35; DLB 4, 45;
MTCW

Dorfman, Ariel 1942- . . . . **CLC 48, 77; HLC**
See also CA 124; 130; HW

Dorn, Edward (Merton) 1929- . . . **CLC 10, 18**
See also CA 93-96; CANR 42; DLB 5

Dorsan, Luc
See Simenon, Georges (Jacques Christian)

Dorsange, Jean
See Simenon, Georges (Jacques Christian)

Dos Passos, John (Roderigo)
1896-1970 . . . . . . **CLC 1, 4, 8, 11, 15, 25,
34, 82; DA; WLC**
See also CA 1-4R; 29-32R; CANR 3;
CDALB 1929-1941; DLB 4, 9; DLBD 1;
MTCW

Dossage, Jean
See Simenon, Georges (Jacques Christian)

Dostoevsky, Fedor Mikhailovich
1821-1881 ...... NCLC 2, 7, 21, 33, 43;
DA; SSC 2; WLC

Doughty, Charles M(ontagu)
1843-1926 .... TCLC 27
See also CA 115; DLB 19, 57

Douglas, Ellen .... CLC 73
See also Haxton, Josephine Ayres;
Williamson, Ellen Douglas

Douglas, Gavin 1475(?)-1522........ LC 20

Douglas, Keith 1920-1944 .... TCLC 40
See also DLB 27

Douglas, Leonard
See Bradbury, Ray (Douglas)

Douglas, Michael
See Crichton, (John) Michael

Douglass, Frederick
1817(?)-1895 .... NCLC 7; BLC; DA;
WLC
See also CDALB 1640-1865; DLB 1, 43, 50,
79; SATA 29

Dourado, (Waldomiro Freitas) Autran
1926- .... CLC 23, 60
See also CA 25-28R; CANR 34

Dourado, Waldomiro Autran
See Dourado, (Waldomiro Freitas) Autran

Dove, Rita (Frances)
1952- .... CLC 50, 81; PC 6
See also BW 2; CA 109; CAAS 19;
CANR 27, 42; DLB 120

Dowell, Coleman 1925-1985........ CLC 60
See also CA 25-28R; 117; CANR 10;
DLB 130

Dowson, Ernest Christopher
1867-1900 .... TCLC 4
See also CA 105; DLB 19, 135

Doyle, A. Conan
See Doyle, Arthur Conan

Doyle, Arthur Conan
1859-1930 .... TCLC 7; DA; SSC 12;
WLC
See also AAYA 14; CA 104; 122;
CDBLB 1890-1914; DLB 18, 70; MTCW;
SATA 24

Doyle, Conan
See Doyle, Arthur Conan

Doyle, John
See Graves, Robert (von Ranke)

Doyle, Roddy 1958(?)- .... CLC 81
See also AAYA 14; CA 143

Doyle, Sir A. Conan
See Doyle, Arthur Conan

Doyle, Sir Arthur Conan
See Doyle, Arthur Conan

Dr. A
See Asimov, Isaac; Silverstein, Alvin

Drabble, Margaret
1939- .... CLC 2, 3, 5, 8, 10, 22, 53
See also CA 13-16R; CANR 18, 35;
CDBLB 1960 to Present; DLB 14;
MTCW; SATA 48

Drapier, M. B.
See Swift, Jonathan

Drayham, James
See Mencken, H(enry) L(ouis)

Drayton, Michael 1563-1631......... LC 8

Dreadstone, Carl
See Campbell, (John) Ramsey

Dreiser, Theodore (Herman Albert)
1871-1945 .... TCLC 10, 18, 35; DA;
WLC
See also CA 106; 132; CDALB 1865-1917;
DLB 9, 12, 102, 137; DLBD 1; MTCW

Drexler, Rosalyn 1926- .... CLC 2, 6
See also CA 81-84

Dreyer, Carl Theodor 1889-1968.... CLC 16
See also CA 116

Drieu la Rochelle, Pierre(-Eugene)
1893-1945 .... TCLC 21
See also CA 117; DLB 72

Drinkwater, John 1882-1937...... TCLC 57
See also CA 109; DLB 10, 19, 149

Drop Shot
See Cable, George Washington

Droste-Hulshoff, Annette Freiin von
1797-1848 .... NCLC 3
See also DLB 133

Drummond, Walter
See Silverberg, Robert

Drummond, William Henry
1854-1907 .... TCLC 25
See also DLB 92

Drummond de Andrade, Carlos
1902-1987 .... CLC 18
See also Andrade, Carlos Drummond de
See also CA 132; 123

Drury, Allen (Stuart) 1918-....... CLC 37
See also CA 57-60; CANR 18

Dryden, John
1631-1700 ... LC 3, 21; DA; DC 3; WLC
See also CDBLB 1660-1789; DLB 80, 101,
131

Duberman, Martin 1930-........... CLC 8
See also CA 1-4R; CANR 2

Dubie, Norman (Evans) 1945-...... CLC 36
See also CA 69-72; CANR 12; DLB 120

Du Bois, W(illiam) E(dward) B(urghardt)
1868-1963 ...... CLC 1, 2, 13, 64; BLC;
DA; WLC
See also BW 1; CA 85-88; CANR 34;
CDALB 1865-1917; DLB 47, 50, 91;
MTCW; SATA 42

Dubus, Andre 1936- ... CLC 13, 36; SSC 15
See also CA 21-24R; CANR 17; DLB 130

Duca Minimo
See D'Annunzio, Gabriele

Ducharme, Rejean 1941- .... CLC 74
See also DLB 60

Duclos, Charles Pinot 1704-1772 ..... LC 1

Dudek, Louis 1918- .... CLC 11, 19
See also CA 45-48; CAAS 14; CANR 1;
DLB 88

Duerrenmatt, Friedrich
1921-1990 ...... CLC 1, 4, 8, 11, 15, 43
See also CA 17-20R; CANR 33; DLB 69,
124; MTCW

Duffy, Bruce (?)-................ CLC 50

Duffy, Maureen 1933- .... CLC 37
See also CA 25-28R; CANR 33; DLB 14;
MTCW

Dugan, Alan 1923- .... CLC 2, 6
See also CA 81-84; DLB 5

du Gard, Roger Martin
See Martin du Gard, Roger

Duhamel, Georges 1884-1966 .... CLC 8
See also CA 81-84; 25-28R; CANR 35;
DLB 65; MTCW

Dujardin, Edouard (Emile Louis)
1861-1949 .... TCLC 13
See also CA 109; DLB 123

Dumas, Alexandre (Davy de la Pailleterie)
1802-1870 .... NCLC 11; DA; WLC
See also DLB 119; SATA 18

Dumas, Alexandre
1824-1895 .... NCLC 9; DC 1

Dumas, Claudine
See Malzberg, Barry N(athaniel)

Dumas, Henry L. 1934-1968..... CLC 6, 62
See also BW 1; CA 85-88; DLB 41

du Maurier, Daphne
1907-1989 ...... CLC 6, 11, 59; SSC 18
See also CA 5-8R; 128; CANR 6; MTCW;
SATA 27; SATA-Obit 60

Dunbar, Paul Laurence
1872-1906 ...... TCLC 2, 12; BLC; DA;
PC 5; SSC 8; WLC
See also BW 1; CA 104; 124;
CDALB 1865-1917; DLB 50, 54, 78;
SATA 34

Dunbar, William 1460(?)-1530(?) .... LC 20
See also DLB 132, 146

Duncan, Lois 1934-............... CLC 26
See also AAYA 4; CA 1-4R; CANR 2, 23,
36; CLR 29; JRDA; MAICYA; SAAS 2;
SATA 1, 36, 75

Duncan, Robert (Edward)
1919-1988 .... CLC 1, 2, 4, 7, 15, 41, 55;
PC 2
See also CA 9-12R; 124; CANR 28; DLB 5,
16; MTCW

Duncan, Sara Jeannette
1861-1922 .... TCLC 60
See also DLB 92

Dunlap, William 1766-1839 .... NCLC 2
See also DLB 30, 37, 59

Dunn, Douglas (Eaglesham)
1942- .... CLC 6, 40
See also CA 45-48; CANR 2, 33; DLB 40;
MTCW

Dunn, Katherine (Karen) 1945-..... CLC 71
See also CA 33-36R

Dunn, Stephen 1939- .... CLC 36
See also CA 33-36R; CANR 12; DLB 105

Dunne, Finley Peter 1867-1936.... TCLC 28
See also CA 108; DLB 11, 23

Dunne, John Gregory 1932-........ CLC 28
See also CA 25-28R; CANR 14; DLBY 80

Dunsany, Edward John Moreton Drax
Plunkett 1878-1957
See Dunsany, Lord
See also CA 104; DLB 10

Elliott, William
See Bradbury, Ray (Douglas)

Ellis, A. E. . . . . **CLC 7**

Ellis, Alice Thomas . . . . **CLC 40**
See also Haycraft, Anna

Ellis, Bret Easton 1964- . . . . **CLC 39, 71**
See also AAYA 2; CA 118; 123

Ellis, (Henry) Havelock
1859-1939 . . . . **TCLC 14**
See also CA 109

Ellis, Landon
See Ellison, Harlan (Jay)

Ellis, Trey 1962- . . . . **CLC 55**

Ellison, Harlan (Jay)
1934- . . . . **CLC 1, 13, 42; SSC 14**
See also CA 5-8R; CANR 5, 46; DLB 8;
MTCW

Ellison, Ralph (Waldo)
1914-1994 . . . . **CLC 1, 3, 11, 54, 86;**
BLC; DA; WLC
See also BW 1; CA 9-12R; 145; CANR 24;
CDALB 1941-1968; DLB 2, 76;
DLBY 94; MTCW

Ellmann, Lucy (Elizabeth) 1956- . . . . **CLC 61**
See also CA 128

Ellmann, Richard (David)
1918-1987 . . . . **CLC 50**
See also BEST 89:2; CA 1-4R; 122;
CANR 2, 28; DLB 103; DLBY 87;
MTCW

Elman, Richard 1934- . . . . **CLC 19**
See also CA 17-20R; CAAS 3; CANR 47

Elron
See Hubbard, L(afayette) Ron(ald)

Eluard, Paul . . . . **TCLC 7, 41**
See also Grindel, Eugene

Elyot, Sir Thomas 1490(?)-1546 . . . . . **LC 11**

Elytis, Odysseus 1911- . . . . **CLC 15, 49**
See also CA 102; MTCW

Emecheta, (Florence Onye) Buchi
1944- . . . . **CLC 14, 48; BLC**
See also BW 2; CA 81-84; CANR 27;
DLB 117; MTCW; SATA 66

Emerson, Ralph Waldo
1803-1882 . . . . . . **NCLC 1, 38; DA; WLC**
See also CDALB 1640-1865; DLB 1, 59, 73

Eminescu, Mihail 1850-1889 . . . . . **NCLC 33**

Empson, William
1906-1984 . . . . **CLC 3, 8, 19, 33, 34**
See also CA 17-20R; 112; CANR 31;
DLB 20; MTCW

Enchi Fumiko (Ueda) 1905-1986 . . . . **CLC 31**
See also CA 129; 121

Ende, Michael (Andreas Helmuth)
1929- . . . . **CLC 31**
See also CA 118; 124; CANR 36; CLR 14;
DLB 75; MAICYA; SATA 61;
SATA-Brief 42

Endo, Shusaku 1923- . . . . . **CLC 7, 14, 19, 54**
See also CA 29-32R; CANR 21; MTCW

Engel, Marian 1933-1985 . . . . **CLC 36**
See also CA 25-28R; CANR 12; DLB 53

Engelhardt, Frederick
See Hubbard, L(afayette) Ron(ald)

Enright, D(ennis) J(oseph)
1920- . . . . **CLC 4, 8, 31**
See also CA 1-4R; CANR 1, 42; DLB 27;
SATA 25

Enzensberger, Hans Magnus
1929- . . . . **CLC 43**
See also CA 116; 119

Ephron, Nora 1941- . . . . **CLC 17, 31**
See also AITN 2; CA 65-68; CANR 12, 39

Epsilon
See Betjeman, John

Epstein, Daniel Mark 1948- . . . . **CLC 7**
See also CA 49-52; CANR 2

Epstein, Jacob 1956- . . . . **CLC 19**
See also CA 114

Epstein, Joseph 1937- . . . . **CLC 39**
See also CA 112; 119

Epstein, Leslie 1938- . . . . **CLC 27**
See also CA 73-76; CAAS 12; CANR 23

Equiano, Olaudah
1745(?)-1797 . . . . **LC 16; BLC**
See also DLB 37, 50

Erasmus, Desiderius 1469(?)-1536 . . . . **LC 16**

Erdman, Paul E(mil) 1932- . . . . **CLC 25**
See also AITN 1; CA 61-64; CANR 13, 43

Erdrich, Louise 1954- . . . . **CLC 39, 54**
See also AAYA 10; BEST 89:1; CA 114;
CANR 41; DLB 152; MTCW; NNAL

Erenburg, Ilya (Grigoryevich)
See Ehrenburg, Ilya (Grigoryevich)

Erickson, Stephen Michael 1950-
See Erickson, Steve
See also CA 129

Erickson, Steve . . . . **CLC 64**
See also Erickson, Stephen Michael

Ericson, Walter
See Fast, Howard (Melvin)

Eriksson, Buntel
See Bergman, (Ernst) Ingmar

Ernaux, Annie 1940- . . . . **CLC 88**

Eschenbach, Wolfram von
See Wolfram von Eschenbach

Eseki, Bruno
See Mphahlele, Ezekiel

Esenin, Sergei (Alexandrovich)
1895-1925 . . . . **TCLC 4**
See also CA 104

Eshleman, Clayton 1935- . . . . **CLC 7**
See also CA 33-36R; CAAS 6; DLB 5

Espriella, Don Manuel Alvarez
See Southey, Robert

Espriu, Salvador 1913-1985 . . . . **CLC 9**
See also CA 115; DLB 134

Espronceda, Jose de 1808-1842 . . . **NCLC 39**

Esse, James
See Stephens, James

Esterbrook, Tom
See Hubbard, L(afayette) Ron(ald)

Estleman, Loren D. 1952- . . . . **CLC 48**
See also CA 85-88; CANR 27; MTCW

Eugenides, Jeffrey 1960(?)- . . . . **CLC 81**
See also CA 144

Euripides c. 485B.C.-406B.C. . . . . **DC 4**
See also DA

Evan, Evin
See Faust, Frederick (Schiller)

Evans, Evan
See Faust, Frederick (Schiller)

Evans, Marian
See Eliot, George

Evans, Mary Ann
See Eliot, George

Evarts, Esther
See Benson, Sally

Everett, Percival L. 1956- . . . . **CLC 57**
See also BW 2; CA 129

Everson, R(onald) G(ilmour)
1903- . . . . **CLC 27**
See also CA 17-20R; DLB 88

Everson, William (Oliver)
1912-1994 . . . . **CLC 1, 5, 14**
See also CA 9-12R; 145; CANR 20; DLB 5,
16; MTCW

Evtushenko, Evgenii Aleksandrovich
See Yevtushenko, Yevgeny (Alexandrovich)

Ewart, Gavin (Buchanan)
1916- . . . . **CLC 13, 46**
See also CA 89-92; CANR 17, 46; DLB 40;
MTCW

Ewers, Hanns Heinz 1871-1943 . . . **TCLC 12**
See also CA 109

Ewing, Frederick R.
See Sturgeon, Theodore (Hamilton)

Exley, Frederick (Earl)
1929-1992 . . . . **CLC 6, 11**
See also AITN 2; CA 81-84; 138; DLB 143;
DLBY 81

Eynhardt, Guillermo
See Quiroga, Horacio (Sylvestre)

Ezekiel, Nissim 1924- . . . . **CLC 61**
See also CA 61-64

Ezekiel, Tish O'Dowd 1943- . . . . **CLC 34**
See also CA 129

Fadeyev, A.
See Bulgya, Alexander Alexandrovich

Fadeyev, Alexander . . . . **TCLC 53**
See also Bulgya, Alexander Alexandrovich

Fagen, Donald 1948- . . . . **CLC 26**

Fainzilberg, Ilya Arnoldovich 1897-1937
See Ilf, Ilya
See also CA 120

Fair, Ronald L. 1932- . . . . **CLC 18**
See also BW 1; CA 69-72; CANR 25;
DLB 33

Fairbairns, Zoe (Ann) 1948- . . . . **CLC 32**
See also CA 103; CANR 21

Falco, Gian
See Papini, Giovanni

Falconer, James
See Kirkup, James

Falconer, Kenneth
See Kornbluth, C(yril) M.

Falkland, Samuel
See Heijermans, Herman

Fallaci, Oriana 1930-............. **CLC 11**
See also CA 77-80; CANR 15; MTCW

Faludy, George 1913-.............. **CLC 42**
See also CA 21-24R

Faludy, Gyoergy
See Faludy, George

Fanon, Frantz 1925-1961..... **CLC 74; BLC**
See also BW 1; CA 116; 89-92

Fanshawe, Ann 1625-1680.......... **LC 11**

Fante, John (Thomas) 1911-1983 ... **CLC 60**
See also CA 69-72; 109; CANR 23;
DLB 130; DLBY 83

Farah, Nuruddin 1945-....... **CLC 53; BLC**
See also BW 2; CA 106; DLB 125

Fargue, Leon-Paul 1876(?)-1947 ... **TCLC 11**
See also CA 109

Farigoule, Louis
See Romains, Jules

Farina, Richard 1936(?)-1966 .... **CLC 9**
See also CA 81-84; 25-28R

Farley, Walter (Lorimer)
1915-1989 .... **CLC 17**
See also CA 17-20R; CANR 8, 29; DLB 22;
JRDA; MAICYA; SATA 2, 43

Farmer, Philip Jose 1918-....... **CLC 1, 19**
See also CA 1-4R; CANR 4, 35; DLB 8;
MTCW

Farquhar, George 1677-1707........ **LC 21**
See also DLB 84

Farrell, J(ames) G(ordon)
1935-1979 .... **CLC 6**
See also CA 73-76; 89-92; CANR 36;
DLB 14; MTCW

Farrell, James T(homas)
1904-1979 .... **CLC 1, 4, 8, 11, 66**
See also CA 5-8R; 89-92; CANR 9; DLB 4,
9, 86; DLBD 2; MTCW

Farren, Richard J.
See Betjeman, John

Farren, Richard M.
See Betjeman, John

Fassbinder, Rainer Werner
1946-1982 .... **CLC 20**
See also CA 93-96; 106; CANR 31

Fast, Howard (Melvin) 1914- ...... **CLC 23**
See also CA 1-4R; CAAS 18; CANR 1, 33;
DLB 9; SATA 7

Faulcon, Robert
See Holdstock, Robert P.

Faulkner, William (Cuthbert)
1897-1962 ..... **CLC 1, 3, 6, 8, 9, 11, 14,
18, 28, 52, 68; DA; SSC 1; WLC**
See also AAYA 7; CA 81-84; CANR 33;
CDALB 1929-1941; DLB 9, 11, 44, 102;
DLBD 2; DLBY 86; MTCW

Fauset, Jessie Redmon
1884(?)-1961 .... **CLC 19, 54; BLC**
See also BW 1; CA 109; DLB 51

Faust, Frederick (Schiller)
1892-1944(?) .... **TCLC 49**
See also CA 108

Faust, Irvin 1924-................ **CLC 8**
See also CA 33-36R; CANR 28; DLB 2, 28;
DLBY 80

Fawkes, Guy
See Benchley, Robert (Charles)

Fearing, Kenneth (Flexner)
1902-1961 .... **CLC 51**
See also CA 93-96; DLB 9

Fecamps, Elise
See Creasey, John

Federman, Raymond 1928- ...... **CLC 6, 47**
See also CA 17-20R; CAAS 8; CANR 10,
43; DLBY 80

Federspiel, J(uerg) F. 1931-........ **CLC 42**

Feiffer, Jules (Ralph) 1929-.... **CLC 2, 8, 64**
See also AAYA 3; CA 17-20R; CANR 30;
DLB 7, 44; MTCW; SATA 8, 61

Feige, Hermann Albert Otto Maximilian
See Traven, B.

Feinberg, David B. 1956-.......... **CLC 59**
See also CA 135

Feinstein, Elaine 1930-............ **CLC 36**
See also CA 69-72; CAAS 1; CANR 31;
DLB 14, 40; MTCW

Feldman, Irving (Mordecai) 1928-.... **CLC 7**
See also CA 1-4R; CANR 1

Fellini, Federico 1920-1993 ..... **CLC 16, 85**
See also CA 65-68; 143; CANR 33

Felsen, Henry Gregor 1916- ...... **CLC 17**
See also CA 1-4R; CANR 1; SAAS 2;
SATA 1

Fenton, James Martin 1949-....... **CLC 32**
See also CA 102; DLB 40

Ferber, Edna 1887-1968.......... **CLC 18**
See also AITN 1; CA 5-8R; 25-28R; DLB 9,
28, 86; MTCW; SATA 7

Ferguson, Helen
See Kavan, Anna

Ferguson, Samuel 1810-1886..... **NCLC 33**
See also DLB 32

Fergusson, Robert 1750-1774 .... **LC 29**
See also DLB 109

Ferling, Lawrence
See Ferlinghetti, Lawrence (Monsanto)

Ferlinghetti, Lawrence (Monsanto)
1919(?)- .... **CLC 2, 6, 10, 27; PC 1**
See also CA 5-8R; CANR 3, 41;
CDALB 1941-1968; DLB 5, 16; MTCW

Fernandez, Vicente Garcia Huidobro
See Huidobro Fernandez, Vicente Garcia

Ferrer, Gabriel (Francisco Victor) Miro
See Miro (Ferrer), Gabriel (Francisco
Victor)

Ferrier, Susan (Edmonstone)
1782-1854 .... **NCLC 8**
See also DLB 116

Ferrigno, Robert 1948(?)-.......... **CLC 65**
See also CA 140

Feuchtwanger, Lion 1884-1958 ..... **TCLC 3**
See also CA 104; DLB 66

Feuillet, Octave 1821-1890 ...... **NCLC 45**

Feydeau, Georges (Leon Jules Marie)
1862-1921 .... **TCLC 22**
See also CA 113

Ficino, Marsilio 1433-1499 .... **LC 12**

Fiedeler, Hans
See Doeblin, Alfred

Fiedler, Leslie A(aron)
1917-.................. **CLC 4, 13, 24**
See also CA 9-12R; CANR 7; DLB 28, 67;
MTCW

Field, Andrew 1938-.............. **CLC 44**
See also CA 97-100; CANR 25

Field, Eugene 1850-1895 .... **NCLC 3**
See also DLB 23, 42, 140; MAICYA;
SATA 16

Field, Gans T.
See Wellman, Manly Wade

Field, Michael .... **TCLC 43**

Field, Peter
See Hobson, Laura Z(ametkin)

Fielding, Henry
1707-1754 .... **LC 1; DA; WLC**
See also CDBLB 1660-1789; DLB 39, 84,
101

Fielding, Sarah 1710-1768.......... **LC 1**
See also DLB 39

Fierstein, Harvey (Forbes) 1954- ... **CLC 33**
See also CA 123; 129

Figes, Eva 1932-.................. **CLC 31**
See also CA 53-56; CANR 4, 44; DLB 14

Finch, Robert (Duer Claydon)
1900-....................... **CLC 18**
See also CA 57-60; CANR 9, 24; DLB 88

Findley, Timothy 1930- .... **CLC 27**
See also CA 25-28R; CANR 12, 42;
DLB 53

Fink, William
See Mencken, H(enry) L(ouis)

Firbank, Louis 1942-
See Reed, Lou
See also CA 117

Firbank, (Arthur Annesley) Ronald
1886-1926 .... **TCLC 1**
See also CA 104; DLB 36

Fisher, M(ary) F(rances) K(ennedy)
1908-1992 .... **CLC 76, 87**
See also CA 77-80; 138; CANR 44

Fisher, Roy 1930-................ **CLC 25**
See also CA 81-84; CAAS 10; CANR 16;
DLB 40

Fisher, Rudolph
1897-1934 .... **TCLC 11; BLC**
See also BW 1; CA 107; 124; DLB 51, 102

Fisher, Vardis (Alvero) 1895-1968.... **CLC 7**
See also CA 5-8R; 25-28R; DLB 9

Fiske, Tarleton
See Bloch, Robert (Albert)

Fitch, Clarke
See Sinclair, Upton (Beall)

Fitch, John IV
See Cormier, Robert (Edmund)

Fitzgerald, Captain Hugh
See Baum, L(yman) Frank

FitzGerald, Edward 1809-1883 .... **NCLC 9**
See also DLB 32

Fitzgerald, F(rancis) Scott (Key)
    1896-1940 ...... **TCLC 1, 6, 14, 28, 55;**
                   DA; SSC 6; WLC
    See also AITN 1; CA 110; 123;
      CDALB 1917-1929; DLB 4, 9, 86;
      DLBD 1; DLBY 81; MTCW

Fitzgerald, Penelope 1916-... **CLC 19, 51, 61**
    See also CA 85-88; CAAS 10; DLB 14

Fitzgerald, Robert (Stuart)
    1910-1985 .... **CLC 39**
    See also CA 1-4R; 114; CANR 1; DLBY 80

FitzGerald, Robert D(avid)
    1902-1987 .... **CLC 19**
    See also CA 17-20R

Fitzgerald, Zelda (Sayre)
    1900-1948 .... **TCLC 52**
    See also CA 117; 126; DLBY 84

Flanagan, Thomas (James Bonner)
    1923- .... **CLC 25, 52**
    See also CA 108; DLBY 80; MTCW

Flaubert, Gustave
    1821-1880 .... **NCLC 2, 10, 19; DA;**
                    SSC 11; WLC
    See also DLB 119

Flecker, (Herman) James Elroy
    1884-1915 .... **TCLC 43**
    See also CA 109; DLB 10, 19

Fleming, Ian (Lancaster)
    1908-1964 .... **CLC 3, 30**
    See also CA 5-8R; CDBLB 1945-1960;
      DLB 87; MTCW; SATA 9

Fleming, Thomas (James) 1927- .... **CLC 37**
    See also CA 5-8R; CANR 10; SATA 8

Fletcher, John Gould 1886-1950 ... **TCLC 35**
    See also CA 107; DLB 4, 45

Fleur, Paul
    See Pohl, Frederik

Flooglebuckle, Al
    See Spiegelman, Art

Flying Officer X
    See Bates, H(erbert) E(rnest)

Fo, Dario 1926-.................. **CLC 32**
    See also CA 116; 128; MTCW

Fogarty, Jonathan Titulescu Esq.
    See Farrell, James T(homas)

Folke, Will
    See Bloch, Robert (Albert)

Follett, Ken(neth Martin) 1949- .... **CLC 18**
    See also AAYA 6; BEST 89:4; CA 81-84;
      CANR 13, 33; DLB 87; DLBY 81;
      MTCW

Fontane, Theodor 1819-1898 ..... **NCLC 26**
    See also DLB 129

Foote, Horton 1916-.............. **CLC 51**
    See also CA 73-76; CANR 34; DLB 26

Foote, Shelby 1916- .... **CLC 75**
    See also CA 5-8R; CANR 3, 45; DLB 2, 17

Forbes, Esther 1891-1967......... **CLC 12**
    See also CA 13-14; 25-28R; CAP 1;
      CLR 27; DLB 22; JRDA; MAICYA;
      SATA 2

Forche, Carolyn (Louise)
    1950- .... **CLC 25, 83, 86; PC 10**
    See also CA 109; 117; DLB 5

Ford, Elbur
    See Hibbert, Eleanor Alice Burford

Ford, Ford Madox
    1873-1939 .... **TCLC 1, 15, 39, 57**
    See also CA 104; 132; CDBLB 1914-1945;
      DLB 34, 98; MTCW

Ford, John 1895-1973............. **CLC 16**
    See also CA 45-48

Ford, Richard 1944-.............. **CLC 46**
    See also CA 69-72; CANR 11, 47

Ford, Webster
    See Masters, Edgar Lee

Foreman, Richard 1937-.......... **CLC 50**
    See also CA 65-68; CANR 32

Forester, C(ecil) S(cott)
    1899-1966 .... **CLC 35**
    See also CA 73-76; 25-28R; SATA 13

Forez
    See Mauriac, Francois (Charles)

Forman, James Douglas 1932-...... **CLC 21**
    See also CA 9-12R; CANR 4, 19, 42;
      JRDA; MAICYA; SATA 8, 70

Fornes, Maria Irene 1930-...... **CLC 39, 61**
    See also CA 25-28R; CANR 28; DLB 7;
      HW; MTCW

Forrest, Leon 1937- .... **CLC 4**
    See also BW 2; CA 89-92; CAAS 7;
      CANR 25; DLB 33

Forster, E(dward) M(organ)
    1879-1970 ..... **CLC 1, 2, 3, 4, 9, 10, 13,**
               15, 22, 45, 77; DA; WLC
    See also AAYA 2; CA 13-14; 25-28R;
      CANR 45; CAP 1; CDBLB 1914-1945;
      DLB 34, 98; DLBD 10; MTCW;
      SATA 57

Forster, John 1812-1876 .... **NCLC 11**
    See also DLB 144

Forsyth, Frederick 1938-...... **CLC 2, 5, 36**
    See also BEST 89:4; CA 85-88; CANR 38;
      DLB 87; MTCW

Forten, Charlotte L. .... **TCLC 16; BLC**
    See also Grimke, Charlotte L(ottie) Forten
    See also DLB 50

Foscolo, Ugo 1778-1827......... **NCLC 8**

Fosse, Bob .... **CLC 20**
    See also Fosse, Robert Louis

Fosse, Robert Louis 1927-1987
    See Fosse, Bob
    See also CA 110; 123

Foster, Stephen Collins
    1826-1864 .... **NCLC 26**

Foucault, Michel
    1926-1984 .... **CLC 31, 34, 69**
    See also CA 105; 113; CANR 34; MTCW

Fouque, Friedrich (Heinrich Karl) de la Motte
    1777-1843 .... **NCLC 2**
    See also DLB 90

Fourier, Charles 1772-1837 ...... **NCLC 51**

Fournier, Henri Alban 1886-1914
    See Alain-Fournier
    See also CA 104

Fournier, Pierre 1916- .... **CLC 11**
    See also Gascar, Pierre
    See also CA 89-92; CANR 16, 40

Fowles, John
    1926- ...... **CLC 1, 2, 3, 4, 6, 9, 10, 15,**
                   33, 87
    See also CA 5-8R; CANR 25; CDBLB 1960
      to Present; DLB 14, 139; MTCW;
      SATA 22

Fox, Paula 1923-................ **CLC 2, 8**
    See also AAYA 3; CA 73-76; CANR 20,
      36; CLR 1; DLB 52; JRDA; MAICYA;
      MTCW; SATA 17, 60

Fox, William Price (Jr.) 1926- ..... **CLC 22**
    See also CA 17-20R; CAAS 19; CANR 11;
      DLB 2; DLBY 81

Foxe, John 1516(?)-1587 .... **LC 14**

Frame, Janet .... **CLC 2, 3, 6, 22, 66**
    See also Clutha, Janet Paterson Frame

France, Anatole .... **TCLC 9**
    See also Thibault, Jacques Anatole Francois
    See also DLB 123

Francis, Claude 19(?)- .... **CLC 50**

Francis, Dick 1920- .... **CLC 2, 22, 42**
    See also AAYA 5; BEST 89:3; CA 5-8R;
      CANR 9, 42; CDBLB 1960 to Present;
      DLB 87; MTCW

Francis, Robert (Churchill)
    1901-1987 .... **CLC 15**
    See also CA 1-4R; 123; CANR 1

Frank, Anne(lies Marie)
    1929-1945 .... **TCLC 17; DA; WLC**
    See also AAYA 12; CA 113; 133; MTCW;
      SATA-Brief 42

Frank, Elizabeth 1945-............ **CLC 39**
    See also CA 121; 126

Franklin, Benjamin
    See Hasek, Jaroslav (Matej Frantisek)

Franklin, Benjamin 1706-1790... **LC 25; DA**
    See also CDALB 1640-1865; DLB 24, 43,
      73

Franklin, (Stella Maraia Sarah) Miles
    1879-1954 .... **TCLC 7**
    See also CA 104

Fraser, (Lady) Antonia (Pakenham)
    1932- .... **CLC 32**
    See also CA 85-88; CANR 44; MTCW;
      SATA-Brief 32

Fraser, George MacDonald 1925-.... **CLC 7**
    See also CA 45-48; CANR 2

Fraser, Sylvia 1935-.............. **CLC 64**
    See also CA 45-48; CANR 1, 16

Frayn, Michael 1933-...... **CLC 3, 7, 31, 47**
    See also CA 5-8R; CANR 30; DLB 13, 14;
      MTCW

Fraze, Candida (Merrill) 1945- ..... **CLC 50**
    See also CA 126

Frazer, J(ames) G(eorge)
    1854-1941 .... **TCLC 32**
    See also CA 118

Frazer, Robert Caine
    See Creasey, John

Frazer, Sir James George
    See Frazer, J(ames) G(eorge)

Frazier, Ian 1951-................ **CLC 46**
    See also CA 130

Frederic, Harold 1856-1898...... **NCLC 10**
    See also DLB 12, 23

Frederick, John
See Faust, Frederick (Schiller)

Frederick the Great 1712-1786 . . . . . . **LC 14**

Fredro, Aleksander 1793-1876. . . . . **NCLC 8**

Freeling, Nicolas 1927- . . . . **CLC 38**
See also CA 49-52; CAAS 12; CANR 1, 17;
DLB 87

Freeman, Douglas Southall
1886-1953 . . . . **TCLC 11**
See also CA 109; DLB 17

Freeman, Judith 1946- . . . . **CLC 55**

Freeman, Mary Eleanor Wilkins
1852-1930 . . . . **TCLC 9; SSC 1**
See also CA 106; DLB 12, 78

Freeman, R(ichard) Austin
1862-1943 . . . . **TCLC 21**
See also CA 113; DLB 70

French, Albert 1943- . . . . **CLC 86**

French, Marilyn 1929- . . . . . . **CLC 10, 18, 60**
See also CA 69-72; CANR 3, 31; MTCW

French, Paul
See Asimov, Isaac

Freneau, Philip Morin 1752-1832 . . **NCLC 1**
See also DLB 37, 43

Freud, Sigmund 1856-1939 . . . . **TCLC 52**
See also CA 115; 133; MTCW

Friedan, Betty (Naomi) 1921- . . . . . . **CLC 74**
See also CA 65-68; CANR 18, 45; MTCW

Friedman, B(ernard) H(arper)
1926- . . . . **CLC 7**
See also CA 1-4R; CANR 3

Friedman, Bruce Jay 1930- . . . . **CLC 3, 5, 56**
See also CA 9-12R; CANR 25; DLB 2, 28

Friel, Brian 1929- . . . . **CLC 5, 42, 59**
See also CA 21-24R; CANR 33; DLB 13;
MTCW

Friis-Baastad, Babbis Ellinor
1921-1970 . . . . **CLC 12**
See also CA 17-20R; 134; SATA 7

Frisch, Max (Rudolf)
1911-1991 . . . . . **CLC 3, 9, 14, 18, 32, 44**
See also CA 85-88; 134; CANR 32;
DLB 69, 124; MTCW

Fromentin, Eugene (Samuel Auguste)
1820-1876 . . . . **NCLC 10**
See also DLB 123

Frost, Frederick
See Faust, Frederick (Schiller)

Frost, Robert (Lee)
1874-1963 . . . . **CLC 1, 3, 4, 9, 10, 13, 15,**
26, 34, 44; DA; PC 1; WLC
See also CA 89-92; CANR 33;
CDALB 1917-1929; DLB 54; DLBD 7;
MTCW; SATA 14

Froude, James Anthony
1818-1894 . . . . **NCLC 43**
See also DLB 18, 57, 144

Froy, Herald
See Waterhouse, Keith (Spencer)

Fry, Christopher 1907- . . . . **CLC 2, 10, 14**
See also CA 17-20R; CANR 9, 30; DLB 13;
MTCW; SATA 66

Frye, (Herman) Northrop
1912-1991 . . . . **CLC 24, 70**
See also CA 5-8R; 133; CANR 8, 37;
DLB 67, 68; MTCW

Fuchs, Daniel 1909-1993 . . . . **CLC 8, 22**
See also CA 81-84; 142; CAAS 5;
CANR 40; DLB 9, 26, 28; DLBY 93

Fuchs, Daniel 1934- . . . . **CLC 34**
See also CA 37-40R; CANR 14

Fuentes, Carlos
1928- . . . . . . **CLC 3, 8, 10, 13, 22, 41, 60;**
DA; HLC; WLC
See also AAYA 4; AITN 2; CA 69-72;
CANR 10, 32; DLB 113; HW; MTCW

Fuentes, Gregorio Lopez y
See Lopez y Fuentes, Gregorio

Fugard, (Harold) Athol
1932- . . . . **CLC 5, 9, 14, 25, 40, 80; DC 3**
See also CA 85-88; CANR 32; MTCW

Fugard, Sheila 1932- . . . . **CLC 48**
See also CA 125

Fuller, Charles (H., Jr.)
1939- . . . . **CLC 25; BLC; DC 1**
See also BW 2; CA 108; 112; DLB 38;
MTCW

Fuller, John (Leopold) 1937- . . . . **CLC 62**
See also CA 21-24R; CANR 9, 44; DLB 40

Fuller, Margaret . . . . **NCLC 5, 50**
See also Ossoli, Sarah Margaret (Fuller
marchesa d')

Fuller, Roy (Broadbent)
1912-1991 . . . . **CLC 4, 28**
See also CA 5-8R; 135; CAAS 10; DLB 15,
20

Fulton, Alice 1952- . . . . **CLC 52**
See also CA 116

Furphy, Joseph 1843-1912 . . . . **TCLC 25**

Fussell, Paul 1924- . . . . **CLC 74**
See also BEST 90:1; CA 17-20R; CANR 8,
21, 35; MTCW

Futabatei, Shimei 1864-1909 . . . . . . **TCLC 44**

Futrelle, Jacques 1875-1912 . . . . . . **TCLC 19**
See also CA 113

Gaboriau, Emile 1835-1873 . . . . . . **NCLC 14**

Gadda, Carlo Emilio 1893-1973 . . . . **CLC 11**
See also CA 89-92

Gaddis, William
1922- . . . . . **CLC 1, 3, 6, 8, 10, 19, 43, 86**
See also CA 17-20R; CANR 21; DLB 2;
MTCW

Gaines, Ernest J(ames)
1933- . . . . **CLC 3, 11, 18, 86; BLC**
See also AITN 1; BW 2; CA 9-12R;
CANR 6, 24, 42; CDALB 1968-1988;
DLB 2, 33, 152; DLBY 80; MTCW

Gaitskill, Mary 1954- . . . . **CLC 69**
See also CA 128

Galdos, Benito Perez
See Perez Galdos, Benito

Gale, Zona 1874-1938 . . . . **TCLC 7**
See also CA 105; DLB 9, 78

Galeano, Eduardo (Hughes) 1940- . . . **CLC 72**
See also CA 29-32R; CANR 13, 32; HW

Galiano, Juan Valera y Alcala
See Valera y Alcala-Galiano, Juan

Gallagher, Tess 1943- . . . . **CLC 18, 63; PC 9**
See also CA 106; DLB 120

Gallant, Mavis
1922- . . . . **CLC 7, 18, 38; SSC 5**
See also CA 69-72; CANR 29; DLB 53;
MTCW

Gallant, Roy A(rthur) 1924- . . . . **CLC 17**
See also CA 5-8R; CANR 4, 29; CLR 30;
MAICYA; SATA 4, 68

Gallico, Paul (William) 1897-1976 . . . **CLC 2**
See also AITN 1; CA 5-8R; 69-72;
CANR 23; DLB 9; MAICYA; SATA 13

Gallup, Ralph
See Whitemore, Hugh (John)

Galsworthy, John
1867-1933 . . . . **TCLC 1, 45; DA; WLC 2**
See also CA 104; 141; CDBLB 1890-1914;
DLB 10, 34, 98

Galt, John 1779-1839 . . . . **NCLC 1**
See also DLB 99, 116

Galvin, James 1951- . . . . **CLC 38**
See also CA 108; CANR 26

Gamboa, Federico 1864-1939 . . . . . . **TCLC 36**

Gandhi, M. K.
See Gandhi, Mohandas Karamchand

Gandhi, Mahatma
See Gandhi, Mohandas Karamchand

Gandhi, Mohandas Karamchand
1869-1948 . . . . **TCLC 59**
See also CA 121; 132; MTCW

Gann, Ernest Kellogg 1910-1991 . . . . **CLC 23**
See also AITN 1; CA 1-4R; 136; CANR 1

Garcia, Cristina 1958- . . . . **CLC 76**
See also CA 141

Garcia Lorca, Federico
1898-1936 . . . . **TCLC 1, 7, 49; DA;**
DC 2; HLC; PC 3; WLC
See also CA 104; 131; DLB 108; HW;
MTCW

Garcia Marquez, Gabriel (Jose)
1928- . . . . **CLC 2, 3, 8, 10, 15, 27, 47, 55,**
68; DA; HLC; SSC 8; WLC
See also AAYA 3; BEST 89:1, 90:4;
CA 33-36R; CANR 10, 28; DLB 113;
HW; MTCW

Gard, Janice
See Latham, Jean Lee

Gard, Roger Martin du
See Martin du Gard, Roger

Gardam, Jane 1928- . . . . **CLC 43**
See also CA 49-52; CANR 2, 18, 33;
CLR 12; DLB 14; MAICYA; MTCW;
SAAS 9; SATA 39, 76; SATA-Brief 28

Gardner, Herb . . . . **CLC 44**

Gardner, John (Champlin), Jr.
1933-1982 . . . . . **CLC 2, 3, 5, 7, 8, 10, 18,**
28, 34; SSC 7
See also AITN 1; CA 65-68; 107;
CANR 33; DLB 2; DLBY 82; MTCW;
SATA 40; SATA-Obit 31

Gardner, John (Edmund) 1926- . . . . . **CLC 30**
See also CA 103; CANR 15; MTCW

Gardner, Noel
  See Kuttner, Henry

Gardons, S. S.
  See Snodgrass, W(illiam) D(e Witt)

Garfield, Leon 1921- .... CLC 12
  See also AAYA 8; CA 17-20R; CANR 38,
  41; CLR 21; JRDA; MAICYA; SATA 1,
  32, 76

Garland, (Hannibal) Hamlin
  1860-1940 .... TCLC 3; SSC 18
  See also CA 104; DLB 12, 71, 78

Garneau, (Hector de) Saint-Denys
  1912-1943 .... TCLC 13
  See also CA 111; DLB 88

Garner, Alan 1934- .... CLC 17
  See also CA 73-76; CANR 15; CLR 20;
  MAICYA; MTCW; SATA 18, 69

Garner, Hugh 1913-1979 .... CLC 13
  See also CA 69-72; CANR 31; DLB 68

Garnett, David 1892-1981 .... CLC 3
  See also CA 5-8R; 103; CANR 17; DLB 34

Garos, Stephanie
  See Katz, Steve

Garrett, George (Palmer)
  1929- .... CLC 3, 11, 51
  See also CA 1-4R; CAAS 5; CANR 1, 42;
  DLB 2, 5, 130, 152; DLBY 83

Garrick, David 1717-1779 .... LC 15
  See also DLB 84

Garrigue, Jean 1914-1972 .... CLC 2, 8
  See also CA 5-8R; 37-40R; CANR 20

Garrison, Frederick
  See Sinclair, Upton (Beall)

Garth, Will
  See Hamilton, Edmond; Kuttner, Henry

Garvey, Marcus (Moziah, Jr.)
  1887-1940 .... TCLC 41; BLC
  See also BW 1; CA 120; 124

Gary, Romain .... CLC 25
  See also Kacew, Romain
  See also DLB 83

Gascar, Pierre .... CLC 11
  See also Fournier, Pierre

Gascoyne, David (Emery) 1916- .... CLC 45
  See also CA 65-68; CANR 10, 28; DLB 20;
  MTCW

Gaskell, Elizabeth Cleghorn
  1810-1865 .... NCLC 5
  See also CDBLB 1832-1890; DLB 21, 144

Gass, William H(oward)
  1924- ... CLC 1, 2, 8, 11, 15, 39; SSC 12
  See also CA 17-20R; CANR 30; DLB 2;
  MTCW

Gasset, Jose Ortega y
  See Ortega y Gasset, Jose

Gates, Henry Louis, Jr. 1950- ...... CLC 65
  See also BW 2; CA 109; CANR 25; DLB 67

Gautier, Theophile 1811-1872 ..... NCLC 1
  See also DLB 119

Gawsworth, John
  See Bates, H(erbert) E(rnest)

Gaye, Marvin (Penze) 1939-1984 ... CLC 26
  See also CA 112

Gebler, Carlo (Ernest) 1954- .... CLC 39
  See also CA 119; 133

Gee, Maggie (Mary) 1948- .... CLC 57
  See also CA 130

Gee, Maurice (Gough) 1931- .... CLC 29
  See also CA 97-100; SATA 46

Gelbart, Larry (Simon) 1923- ... CLC 21, 61
  See also CA 73-76; CANR 45

Gelber, Jack 1932- .... CLC 1, 6, 14, 79
  See also CA 1-4R; CANR 2; DLB 7

Gellhorn, Martha (Ellis) 1908- .. CLC 14, 60
  See also CA 77-80; CANR 44; DLBY 82

Genet, Jean
  1910-1986 ... CLC 1, 2, 5, 10, 14, 44, 46
  See also CA 13-16R; CANR 18; DLB 72;
  DLBY 86; MTCW

Gent, Peter 1942- .... CLC 29
  See also AITN 1; CA 89-92; DLBY 82

Gentlewoman in New England, A
  See Bradstreet, Anne

Gentlewoman in Those Parts, A
  See Bradstreet, Anne

George, Jean Craighead 1919- ...... CLC 35
  See also AAYA 8; CA 5-8R; CANR 25;
  CLR 1; DLB 52; JRDA; MAICYA;
  SATA 2, 68

George, Stefan (Anton)
  1868-1933 .... TCLC 2, 14
  See also CA 104

Georges, Georges Martin
  See Simenon, Georges (Jacques Christian)

Gerhardi, William Alexander
  See Gerhardie, William Alexander

Gerhardie, William Alexander
  1895-1977 .... CLC 5
  See also CA 25-28R; 73-76; CANR 18;
  DLB 36

Gerstler, Amy 1956- .... CLC 70

Gertler, T. .... CLC 34
  See also CA 116; 121

Ghalib 1797-1869 .... NCLC 39

Ghelderode, Michel de
  1898-1962 .... CLC 6, 11
  See also CA 85-88; CANR 40

Ghiselin, Brewster 1903- .... CLC 23
  See also CA 13-16R; CAAS 10; CANR 13

Ghose, Zulfikar 1935- .... CLC 42
  See also CA 65-68

Ghosh, Amitav 1956- .... CLC 44

Giacosa, Giuseppe 1847-1906 ...... TCLC 7
  See also CA 104

Gibb, Lee
  See Waterhouse, Keith (Spencer)

Gibbon, Lewis Grassic .... TCLC 4
  See also Mitchell, James Leslie

Gibbons, Kaye 1960- .... CLC 50, 88

Gibran, Kahlil
  1883-1931 .... TCLC 1, 9; PC 9
  See also CA 104

Gibson, William 1914- .... CLC 23; DA
  See also CA 9-12R; CANR 9, 42; DLB 7;
  SATA 66

Gibson, William (Ford) 1948- ... CLC 39, 63
  See also AAYA 12; CA 126; 133

Gide, Andre (Paul Guillaume)
  1869-1951 .... TCLC 5, 12, 36; DA;
                   SSC 13; WLC
  See also CA 104; 124; DLB 65; MTCW

Gifford, Barry (Colby) 1946- .... CLC 34
  See also CA 65-68; CANR 9, 30, 40

Gilbert, W(illiam) S(chwenck)
  1836-1911 .... TCLC 3
  See also CA 104; SATA 36

Gilbreth, Frank B., Jr. 1911- .... CLC 17
  See also CA 9-12R; SATA 2

Gilchrist, Ellen 1935- .. CLC 34, 48; SSC 14
  See also CA 113; 116; CANR 41; DLB 130;
  MTCW

Giles, Molly 1942- .... CLC 39
  See also CA 126

Gill, Patrick
  See Creasey, John

Gilliam, Terry (Vance) 1940- .... CLC 21
  See also Monty Python
  See also CA 108; 113; CANR 35

Gillian, Jerry
  See Gilliam, Terry (Vance)

Gilliatt, Penelope (Ann Douglass)
  1932-1993 .... CLC 2, 10, 13, 53
  See also AITN 2; CA 13-16R; 141; DLB 14

Gilman, Charlotte (Anna) Perkins (Stetson)
  1860-1935 .... TCLC 9, 37; SSC 13
  See also CA 106

Gilmour, David 1949- .... CLC 35
  See also CA 138

Gilpin, William 1724-1804 .... NCLC 30

Gilray, J. D.
  See Mencken, H(enry) L(ouis)

Gilroy, Frank D(aniel) 1925- .... CLC 2
  See also CA 81-84; CANR 32; DLB 7

Ginsberg, Allen
  1926- ...... CLC 1, 2, 3, 4, 6, 13, 36, 69;
                 DA; PC 4; WLC 3
  See also AITN 1; CA 1-4R; CANR 2, 41;
  CDALB 1941-1968; DLB 5, 16; MTCW

Ginzburg, Natalia
  1916-1991 .... CLC 5, 11, 54, 70
  See also CA 85-88; 135; CANR 33; MTCW

Giono, Jean 1895-1970 .... CLC 4, 11
  See also CA 45-48; 29-32R; CANR 2, 35;
  DLB 72; MTCW

Giovanni, Nikki
  1943- ...... CLC 2, 4, 19, 64; BLC; DA
  See also AITN 1; BW 2; CA 29-32R;
  CAAS 6; CANR 18, 41; CLR 6; DLB 5,
  41; MAICYA; MTCW; SATA 24

Giovene, Andrea 1904- .... CLC 7
  See also CA 85-88

Gippius, Zinaida (Nikolayevna) 1869-1945
  See Hippius, Zinaida
  See also CA 106

Giraudoux, (Hippolyte) Jean
  1882-1944 .... TCLC 2, 7
  See also CA 104; DLB 65

Gironella, Jose Maria 1917- .... CLC 11
  See also CA 101

Gissing, George (Robert)
1857-1903 . . . . TCLC 3, 24, 47
See also CA 105; DLB 18, 135

Giurlani, Aldo
See Palazzeschi, Aldo

Gladkov, Fyodor (Vasilyevich)
1883-1958 . . . . TCLC 27

Glanville, Brian (Lester) 1931- . . . . . . CLC 6
See also CA 5-8R; CAAS 9; CANR 3;
DLB 15, 139; SATA 42

Glasgow, Ellen (Anderson Gholson)
1873(?)-1945 . . . . TCLC 2, 7
See also CA 104; DLB 9, 12

Glaspell, Susan (Keating)
1882(?)-1948 . . . . TCLC 55
See also CA 110; DLB 7, 9, 78; YABC 2

Glassco, John 1909-1981 . . . . CLC 9
See also CA 13-16R; 102; CANR 15;
DLB 68

Glasscock, Amnesia
See Steinbeck, John (Ernst)

Glasser, Ronald J. 1940(?)- . . . . CLC 37

Glassman, Joyce
See Johnson, Joyce

Glendinning, Victoria 1937- . . . . CLC 50
See also CA 120; 127

Glissant, Edouard 1928- . . . . CLC 10, 68

Gloag, Julian 1930- . . . . CLC 40
See also AITN 1; CA 65-68; CANR 10

Glowacki, Aleksander
See Prus, Boleslaw

Glueck, Louise (Elisabeth)
1943- . . . . CLC 7, 22, 44, 81
See also CA 33-36R; CANR 40; DLB 5

Gobineau, Joseph Arthur (Comte) de
1816-1882 . . . . NCLC 17
See also DLB 123

Godard, Jean-Luc 1930- . . . . CLC 20
See also CA 93-96

Godden, (Margaret) Rumer 1907- . . . CLC 53
See also AAYA 6; CA 5-8R; CANR 4, 27,
36; CLR 20; MAICYA; SAAS 12;
SATA 3, 36

Godoy Alcayaga, Lucila 1889-1957
See Mistral, Gabriela
See also BW 2; CA 104; 131; HW; MTCW

Godwin, Gail (Kathleen)
1937- . . . . CLC 5, 8, 22, 31, 69
See also CA 29-32R; CANR 15, 43; DLB 6;
MTCW

Godwin, William 1756-1836 . . . . . . NCLC 14
See also CDBLB 1789-1832; DLB 39, 104,
142

Goethe, Johann Wolfgang von
1749-1832 . . . . NCLC 4, 22, 34; DA;
PC 5; WLC 3
See also DLB 94

Gogarty, Oliver St. John
1878-1957 . . . . TCLC 15
See also CA 109; DLB 15, 19

Gogol, Nikolai (Vasilyevich)
1809-1852 . . . . NCLC 5, 15, 31; DA;
DC 1; SSC 4; WLC

Goines, Donald
1937(?)-1974 . . . . CLC 80; BLC
See also AITN 1; BW 1; CA 124; 114;
DLB 33

Gold, Herbert 1924- . . . . . . CLC 4, 7, 14, 42
See also CA 9-12R; CANR 17, 45; DLB 2;
DLBY 81

Goldbarth, Albert 1948- . . . . CLC 5, 38
See also CA 53-56; CANR 6, 40; DLB 120

Goldberg, Anatol 1910-1982 . . . . CLC 34
See also CA 131; 117

Goldemberg, Isaac 1945- . . . . CLC 52
See also CA 69-72; CAAS 12; CANR 11,
32; HW

Golding, William (Gerald)
1911-1993 . . . . CLC 1, 2, 3, 8, 10, 17, 27,
58, 81; DA; WLC
See also AAYA 5; CA 5-8R; 141;
CANR 13, 33; CDBLB 1945-1960;
DLB 15, 100; MTCW

Goldman, Emma 1869-1940 . . . . . . TCLC 13
See also CA 110

Goldman, Francisco 1955- . . . . CLC 76

Goldman, William (W.) 1931- . . . . CLC 1, 48
See also CA 9-12R; CANR 29; DLB 44

Goldmann, Lucien 1913-1970 . . . . . . CLC 24
See also CA 25-28; CAP 2

Goldoni, Carlo 1707-1793 . . . . LC 4

Goldsberry, Steven 1949- . . . . CLC 34
See also CA 131

Goldsmith, Oliver
1728-1774 . . . . LC 2; DA; WLC
See also CDBLB 1660-1789; DLB 39, 89,
104, 109, 142; SATA 26

Goldsmith, Peter
See Priestley, J(ohn) B(oynton)

Gombrowicz, Witold
1904-1969 . . . . CLC 4, 7, 11, 49
See also CA 19-20; 25-28R; CAP 2

Gomez de la Serna, Ramon
1888-1963 . . . . CLC 9
See also CA 116; HW

Goncharov, Ivan Alexandrovich
1812-1891 . . . . NCLC 1

Goncourt, Edmond (Louis Antoine Huot) de
1822-1896 . . . . NCLC 7
See also DLB 123

Goncourt, Jules (Alfred Huot) de
1830-1870 . . . . NCLC 7
See also DLB 123

Gontier, Fernande 19(?)- . . . . CLC 50

Goodman, Paul 1911-1972 . . . . CLC 1, 2, 4, 7
See also CA 19-20; 37-40R; CANR 34;
CAP 2; DLB 130; MTCW

Gordimer, Nadine
1923- . . . . CLC 3, 5, 7, 10, 18, 33, 51, 70;
DA; SSC 17
See also CA 5-8R; CANR 3, 28; MTCW

Gordon, Adam Lindsay
1833-1870 . . . . NCLC 21

Gordon, Caroline
1895-1981 . . . CLC 6, 13, 29, 83; SSC 15
See also CA 11-12; 103; CANR 36; CAP 1;
DLB 4, 9, 102; DLBY 81; MTCW

Gordon, Charles William 1860-1937
See Connor, Ralph
See also CA 109

Gordon, Mary (Catherine)
1949- . . . . CLC 13, 22
See also CA 102; CANR 44; DLB 6;
DLBY 81; MTCW

Gordon, Sol 1923- . . . . CLC 26
See also CA 53-56; CANR 4; SATA 11

Gordone, Charles 1925- . . . . CLC 1, 4
See also BW 1; CA 93-96; DLB 7; MTCW

Gorenko, Anna Andreevna
See Akhmatova, Anna

Gorky, Maxim . . . . TCLC 8; WLC
See also Peshkov, Alexei Maximovich

Goryan, Sirak
See Saroyan, William

Gosse, Edmund (William)
1849-1928 . . . . TCLC 28
See also CA 117; DLB 57, 144

Gotlieb, Phyllis Fay (Bloom)
1926- . . . . CLC 18
See also CA 13-16R; CANR 7; DLB 88

Gottesman, S. D.
See Kornbluth, C(yril) M.; Pohl, Frederik

Gottfried von Strassburg
fl. c. 1210- . . . . CMLC 10
See also DLB 138

Gould, Lois . . . . CLC 4, 10
See also CA 77-80; CANR 29; MTCW

Gourmont, Remy de 1858-1915 . . . . TCLC 17
See also CA 109

Govier, Katherine 1948- . . . . CLC 51
See also CA 101; CANR 18, 40

Goyen, (Charles) William
1915-1983 . . . . CLC 5, 8, 14, 40
See also AITN 2; CA 5-8R; 110; CANR 6;
DLB 2; DLBY 83

Goytisolo, Juan
1931- . . . . CLC 5, 10, 23; HLC
See also CA 85-88; CANR 32; HW; MTCW

Gozzano, Guido 1883-1916 . . . . PC 10
See also DLB 114

Gozzi, (Conte) Carlo 1720-1806 . . NCLC 23

Grabbe, Christian Dietrich
1801-1836 . . . . NCLC 2
See also DLB 133

Grace, Patricia 1937- . . . . CLC 56

Gracian y Morales, Baltasar
1601-1658 . . . . LC 15

Gracq, Julien . . . . CLC 11, 48
See also Poirier, Louis
See also DLB 83

Grade, Chaim 1910-1982 . . . . CLC 10
See also CA 93-96; 107

Graduate of Oxford, A
See Ruskin, John

Graham, John
See Phillips, David Graham

Graham, Jorie 1951- . . . . CLC 48
See also CA 111; DLB 120

Graham, R(obert) B(ontine) Cunninghame
See Cunninghame Graham, R(obert)
B(ontine)
See also DLB 98, 135

Graham, Robert
See Haldeman, Joe (William)

Graham, Tom
See Lewis, (Harry) Sinclair

Graham, W(illiam) S(ydney)
1918-1986 .... **CLC 29**
See also CA 73-76; 118; DLB 20

Graham, Winston (Mawdsley)
1910- .... **CLC 23**
See also CA 49-52; CANR 2, 22, 45;
DLB 77

Grant, Skeeter
See Spiegelman, Art

Granville-Barker, Harley
1877-1946 .... **TCLC 2**
See also Barker, Harley Granville
See also CA 104

Grass, Guenter (Wilhelm)
1927- ..... **CLC 1, 2, 4, 6, 11, 15, 22, 32,**
49, 88; DA; WLC
See also CA 13-16R; CANR 20; DLB 75,
124; MTCW

Gratton, Thomas
See Hulme, T(homas) E(rnest)

Grau, Shirley Ann
1929- .... **CLC 4, 9; SSC 15**
See also CA 89-92; CANR 22; DLB 2;
MTCW

Gravel, Fern
See Hall, James Norman

Graver, Elizabeth 1964- .... **CLC 70**
See also CA 135

Graves, Richard Perceval 1945- .... **CLC 44**
See also CA 65-68; CANR 9, 26

Graves, Robert (von Ranke)
1895-1985 ...... **CLC 1, 2, 6, 11, 39, 44,**
45; PC 6
See also CA 5-8R; 117; CANR 5, 36;
CDBLB 1914-1945; DLB 20, 100;
DLBY 85; MTCW; SATA 45

Gray, Alasdair (James) 1934- ...... **CLC 41**
See also CA 126; CANR 47; MTCW

Gray, Amlin 1946- .... **CLC 29**
See also CA 138

Gray, Francine du Plessix 1930-.... **CLC 22**
See also BEST 90:3; CA 61-64; CAAS 2;
CANR 11, 33; MTCW

Gray, John (Henry) 1866-1934 .... **TCLC 19**
See also CA 119

Gray, Simon (James Holliday)
1936- .... **CLC 9, 14, 36**
See also AITN 1; CA 21-24R; CAAS 3;
CANR 32; DLB 13; MTCW

Gray, Spalding 1941- .... **CLC 49**
See also CA 128

Gray, Thomas
1716-1771 ...... **LC 4; DA; PC 2; WLC**
See also CDBLB 1660-1789; DLB 109

Grayson, David
See Baker, Ray Stannard

Grayson, Richard (A.) 1951- .... **CLC 38**
See also CA 85-88; CANR 14, 31

Greeley, Andrew M(oran) 1928- .... **CLC 28**
See also CA 5-8R; CAAS 7; CANR 7, 43;
MTCW

Green, Brian
See Card, Orson Scott

Green, Hannah
See Greenberg, Joanne (Goldenberg)

Green, Hannah .... **CLC 3**
See also CA 73-76

Green, Henry................... **CLC 2, 13**
See also Yorke, Henry Vincent
See also DLB 15

Green, Julian (Hartridge) 1900-
See Green, Julien
See also CA 21-24R; CANR 33; DLB 4, 72;
MTCW

Green, Julien .... **CLC 3, 11, 77**
See also Green, Julian (Hartridge)

Green, Paul (Eliot) 1894-1981 ...... **CLC 25**
See also AITN 1; CA 5-8R; 103; CANR 3;
DLB 7, 9; DLBY 81

Greenberg, Ivan 1908-1973
See Rahv, Philip
See also CA 85-88

Greenberg, Joanne (Goldenberg)
1932- .... **CLC 7, 30**
See also AAYA 12; CA 5-8R; CANR 14,
32; SATA 25

Greenberg, Richard 1959(?)- .... **CLC 57**
See also CA 138

Greene, Bette 1934- .... **CLC 30**
See also AAYA 7; CA 53-56; CANR 4;
CLR 2; JRDA; MAICYA; SAAS 16;
SATA 8

Greene, Gael .... **CLC 8**
See also CA 13-16R; CANR 10

Greene, Graham
1904-1991 .... **CLC 1, 3, 6, 9, 14, 18, 27,**
37, 70, 72; DA; WLC
See also AITN 2; CA 13-16R; 133;
CANR 35; CDBLB 1945-1960; DLB 13,
15, 77, 100; DLBY 91; MTCW; SATA 20

Greer, Richard
See Silverberg, Robert

Greer, Richard
See Silverberg, Robert

Gregor, Arthur 1923- .... **CLC 9**
See also CA 25-28R; CAAS 10; CANR 11;
SATA 36

Gregor, Lee
See Pohl, Frederik

Gregory, Isabella Augusta (Persse)
1852-1932 .... **TCLC 1**
See also CA 104; DLB 10

Gregory, J. Dennis
See Williams, John A(lfred)

Grendon, Stephen
See Derleth, August (William)

Grenville, Kate 1950- .... **CLC 61**
See also CA 118

Grenville, Pelham
See Wodehouse, P(elham) G(renville)

Greve, Felix Paul (Berthold Friedrich)
1879-1948
See Grove, Frederick Philip
See also CA 104; 141

Grey, Zane 1872-1939 .... **TCLC 6**
See also CA 104; 132; DLB 9; MTCW

Grieg, (Johan) Nordahl (Brun)
1902-1943 .... **TCLC 10**
See also CA 107

Grieve, C(hristopher) M(urray)
1892-1978 .... **CLC 11, 19**
See also MacDiarmid, Hugh
See also CA 5-8R; 85-88; CANR 33;
MTCW

Griffin, Gerald 1803-1840 .... **NCLC 7**

Griffin, John Howard 1920-1980.... **CLC 68**
See also AITN 1; CA 1-4R; 101; CANR 2

Griffin, Peter 1942- .... **CLC 39**
See also CA 136

Griffiths, Trevor 1935-......... **CLC 13, 52**
See also CA 97-100; CANR 45; DLB 13

Grigson, Geoffrey (Edward Harvey)
1905-1985 .... **CLC 7, 39**
See also CA 25-28R; 118; CANR 20, 33;
DLB 27; MTCW

Grillparzer, Franz 1791-1872...... **NCLC 1**
See also DLB 133

Grimble, Reverend Charles James
See Eliot, T(homas) S(tearns)

Grimke, Charlotte L(ottie) Forten
1837(?)-1914
See Forten, Charlotte L.
See also BW 1; CA 117; 124

Grimm, Jacob Ludwig Karl
1785-1863 .... **NCLC 3**
See also DLB 90; MAICYA; SATA 22

Grimm, Wilhelm Karl 1786-1859 .. **NCLC 3**
See also DLB 90; MAICYA; SATA 22

Grimmelshausen, Johann Jakob Christoffel
von 1621-1676 .... **LC 6**

Grindel, Eugene 1895-1952
See Eluard, Paul
See also CA 104

Grisham, John 1955- .... **CLC 84**
See also AAYA 14; CA 138; CANR 47

Grossman, David 1954- .... **CLC 67**
See also CA 138

Grossman, Vasily (Semenovich)
1905-1964 .... **CLC 41**
See also CA 124; 130; MTCW

Grove, Frederick Philip .... **TCLC 4**
See also Greve, Felix Paul (Berthold
Friedrich)
See also DLB 92

Grubb
See Crumb, R(obert)

Grumbach, Doris (Isaac)
1918- .... **CLC 13, 22, 64**
See also CA 5-8R; CAAS 2; CANR 9, 42

Grundtvig, Nicolai Frederik Severin
1783-1872 .... **NCLC 1**

Grunge
See Crumb, R(obert)

Grunwald, Lisa 1959- .... **CLC 44**
See also CA 120

Guare, John 1938- .... **CLC 8, 14, 29, 67**
See also CA 73-76; CANR 21; DLB 7;
MTCW

Gudjonsson, Halldor Kiljan 1902-
See Laxness, Halldor
See also CA 103

Guenter, Erich
See Eich, Guenter

Guest, Barbara 1920- .... **CLC 34**
See also CA 25-28R; CANR 11, 44; DLB 5

Guest, Judith (Ann) 1936- .... **CLC 8, 30**
See also AAYA 7; CA 77-80; CANR 15;
MTCW

Guevara, Che .... **CLC 87; HLC**
See also Guevara (Serna), Ernesto

Guevara (Serna), Ernesto 1928-1967
See Guevara, Che
See also CA 127; 111; HW

Guild, Nicholas M. 1944- .... **CLC 33**
See also CA 93-96

Guillemin, Jacques
See Sartre, Jean-Paul

Guillen, Jorge 1893-1984 .... **CLC 11**
See also CA 89-92; 112; DLB 108; HW

Guillen (y Batista), Nicolas (Cristobal)
1902-1989 ..... **CLC 48, 79; BLC; HLC**
See also BW 2; CA 116; 125; 129; HW

Guillevic, (Eugene) 1907- .... **CLC 33**
See also CA 93-96

Guillois
See Desnos, Robert

Guiney, Louise Imogen
1861-1920 .... **TCLC 41**
See also DLB 54

Guiraldes, Ricardo (Guillermo)
1886-1927 .... **TCLC 39**
See also CA 131; HW; MTCW

Gumilev, Nikolay Stepanovich
1886-1921 .... **TCLC 60**

Gunn, Bill .... **CLC 5**
See also Gunn, William Harrison
See also DLB 38

Gunn, Thom(son William)
1929- .... **CLC 3, 6, 18, 32, 81**
See also CA 17-20R; CANR 9, 33;
CDBLB 1960 to Present; DLB 27;
MTCW

Gunn, William Harrison 1934(?)-1989
See Gunn, Bill
See also AITN 1; BW 1; CA 13-16R; 128;
CANR 12, 25

Gunnars, Kristjana 1948- .... **CLC 69**
See also CA 113; DLB 60

Gurganus, Allan 1947- .... **CLC 70**
See also BEST 90:1; CA 135

Gurney, A(lbert) R(amsdell), Jr.
1930- .... **CLC 32, 50, 54**
See also CA 77-80; CANR 32

Gurney, Ivor (Bertie) 1890-1937 ... **TCLC 33**

Gurney, Peter
See Gurney, A(lbert) R(amsdell), Jr.

Guro, Elena 1877-1913 .... **TCLC 56**

Gustafson, Ralph (Barker) 1909- .... **CLC 36**
See also CA 21-24R; CANR 8, 45; DLB 88

Gut, Gom
See Simenon, Georges (Jacques Christian)

Guthrie, A(lfred) B(ertram), Jr.
1901-1991 .... **CLC 23**
See also CA 57-60; 134; CANR 24; DLB 6;
SATA 62; SATA-Obit 67

Guthrie, Isobel
See Grieve, C(hristopher) M(urray)

Guthrie, Woodrow Wilson 1912-1967
See Guthrie, Woody
See also CA 113; 93-96

Guthrie, Woody .... **CLC 35**
See also Guthrie, Woodrow Wilson

Guy, Rosa (Cuthbert) 1928- .... **CLC 26**
See also AAYA 4; BW 2; CA 17-20R;
CANR 14, 34; CLR 13; DLB 33; JRDA;
MAICYA; SATA 14, 62

Gwendolyn
See Bennett, (Enoch) Arnold

H. D. .... **CLC 3, 8, 14, 31, 34, 73; PC 5**
See also Doolittle, Hilda

H. de V.
See Buchan, John

Haavikko, Paavo Juhani
1931- .... **CLC 18, 34**
See also CA 106

Habbema, Koos
See Heijermans, Herman

Hacker, Marilyn 1942- .... **CLC 5, 9, 23, 72**
See also CA 77-80; DLB 120

Haggard, H(enry) Rider
1856-1925 .... **TCLC 11**
See also CA 108; DLB 70; SATA 16

Hagiwara Sakutaro 1886-1942 .... **TCLC 60**

Haig, Fenil
See Ford, Ford Madox

Haig-Brown, Roderick (Langmere)
1908-1976 .... **CLC 21**
See also CA 5-8R; 69-72; CANR 4, 38;
CLR 31; DLB 88; MAICYA; SATA 12

Hailey, Arthur 1920- .... **CLC 5**
See also AITN 2; BEST 90:3; CA 1-4R;
CANR 2, 36; DLB 88; DLBY 82; MTCW

Hailey, Elizabeth Forsythe 1938- ... **CLC 40**
See also CA 93-96; CAAS 1; CANR 15

Haines, John (Meade) 1924- .... **CLC 58**
See also CA 17-20R; CANR 13, 34; DLB 5

Haldeman, Joe (William) 1943- ..... **CLC 61**
See also CA 53-56; CANR 6; DLB 8

Haley, Alex(ander Murray Palmer)
1921-1992 .... **CLC 8, 12, 76; BLC; DA**
See also BW 2; CA 77-80; 136; DLB 38;
MTCW

Haliburton, Thomas Chandler
1796-1865 .... **NCLC 15**
See also DLB 11, 99

Hall, Donald (Andrew, Jr.)
1928- .... **CLC 1, 13, 37, 59**
See also CA 5-8R; CAAS 7; CANR 2, 44;
DLB 5; SATA 23

Hall, Frederic Sauser
See Sauser-Hall, Frederic

Hall, James
See Kuttner, Henry

Hall, James Norman 1887-1951 ... **TCLC 23**
See also CA 123; SATA 21

Hall, (Marguerite) Radclyffe
1886(?)-1943 .... **TCLC 12**
See also CA 110

Hall, Rodney 1935- .... **CLC 51**
See also CA 109

Halleck, Fitz-Greene 1790-1867 .. **NCLC 47**
See also DLB 3

Halliday, Michael
See Creasey, John

Halpern, Daniel 1945- .... **CLC 14**
See also CA 33-36R

Hamburger, Michael (Peter Leopold)
1924- .... **CLC 5, 14**
See also CA 5-8R; CAAS 4; CANR 2, 47;
DLB 27

Hamill, Pete 1935- .... **CLC 10**
See also CA 25-28R; CANR 18

Hamilton, Alexander
1755(?)-1804 .... **NCLC 49**
See also DLB 37

Hamilton, Clive
See Lewis, C(live) S(taples)

Hamilton, Edmond 1904-1977 .... **CLC 1**
See also CA 1-4R; CANR 3; DLB 8

Hamilton, Eugene (Jacob) Lee
See Lee-Hamilton, Eugene (Jacob)

Hamilton, Franklin
See Silverberg, Robert

Hamilton, Gail
See Corcoran, Barbara

Hamilton, Mollie
See Kaye, M(ary) M(argaret)

Hamilton, (Anthony Walter) Patrick
1904-1962 .... **CLC 51**
See also CA 113; DLB 10

Hamilton, Virginia 1936- .... **CLC 26**
See also AAYA 2; BW 2; CA 25-28R;
CANR 20, 37; CLR 1, 11; DLB 33, 52;
JRDA; MAICYA; MTCW; SATA 4, 56,
79

Hammett, (Samuel) Dashiell
1894-1961 .... **CLC 3, 5, 10, 19, 47;**
SSC 17
See also AITN 1; CA 81-84; CANR 42;
CDALB 1929-1941; DLBD 6; MTCW

Hammon, Jupiter
1711(?)-1800(?) .... **NCLC 5; BLC**
See also DLB 31, 50

Hammond, Keith
See Kuttner, Henry

Hamner, Earl (Henry), Jr. 1923- ... **CLC 12**
See also AITN 2; CA 73-76; DLB 6

Hampton, Christopher (James)
1946- .... **CLC 4**
See also CA 25-28R; DLB 13; MTCW

Hamsun, Knut .... **TCLC 2, 14, 49**
See also Pedersen, Knut

Handke, Peter 1942- .. **CLC 5, 8, 10, 15, 38**
See also CA 77-80; CANR 33; DLB 85,
124; MTCW

Hanley, James 1901-1985 ... **CLC 3, 5, 8, 13**
See also CA 73-76; 117; CANR 36; MTCW

Hannah, Barry 1942- .... **CLC 23, 38**
See also CA 108; 110; CANR 43; DLB 6;
MTCW

Hannon, Ezra
See Hunter, Evan

Hansberry, Lorraine (Vivian)
1930-1965 ...... **CLC 17, 62; BLC; DA;
DC 2**
See also BW 1; CA 109; 25-28R; CABS 3;
CDALB 1941-1968; DLB 7, 38; MTCW

Hansen, Joseph 1923-............ **CLC 38**
See also CA 29-32R; CAAS 17; CANR 16,
44

Hansen, Martin A. 1909-1955..... **TCLC 32**

Hanson, Kenneth O(stlin) 1922- .... **CLC 13**
See also CA 53-56; CANR 7

Hardwick, Elizabeth 1916- .... **CLC 13**
See also CA 5-8R; CANR 3, 32; DLB 6;
MTCW

Hardy, Thomas
1840-1928 ...... **TCLC 4, 10, 18, 32, 48,
53; DA; PC 8; SSC 2; WLC**
See also CA 104; 123; CDBLB 1890-1914;
DLB 18, 19, 135; MTCW

Hare, David 1947- .... **CLC 29, 58**
See also CA 97-100; CANR 39; DLB 13;
MTCW

Harford, Henry
See Hudson, W(illiam) H(enry)

Hargrave, Leonie
See Disch, Thomas M(ichael)

Harjo, Joy 1951- .... **CLC 83**
See also CA 114; CANR 35; DLB 120;
NNAL

Harlan, Louis R(udolph) 1922-..... **CLC 34**
See also CA 21-24R; CANR 25

Harling, Robert 1951(?)- .... **CLC 53**

Harmon, William (Ruth) 1938-..... **CLC 38**
See also CA 33-36R; CANR 14, 32, 35;
SATA 65

Harper, F. E. W.
See Harper, Frances Ellen Watkins

Harper, Frances E. W.
See Harper, Frances Ellen Watkins

Harper, Frances E. Watkins
See Harper, Frances Ellen Watkins

Harper, Frances Ellen
See Harper, Frances Ellen Watkins

Harper, Frances Ellen Watkins
1825-1911 .... **TCLC 14; BLC**
See also BW 1; CA 111; 125; DLB 50

Harper, Michael S(teven) 1938- .. **CLC 7, 22**
See also BW 1; CA 33-36R; CANR 24;
DLB 41

Harper, Mrs. F. E. W.
See Harper, Frances Ellen Watkins

Harris, Christie (Lucy) Irwin
1907- .... **CLC 12**
See also CA 5-8R; CANR 6; DLB 88;
JRDA; MAICYA; SAAS 10; SATA 6, 74

Harris, Frank 1856(?)-1931 .... **TCLC 24**
See also CA 109

Harris, George Washington
1814-1869 .... **NCLC 23**
See also DLB 3, 11

Harris, Joel Chandler
1848-1908 .... **TCLC 2; SSC 19**
See also CA 104; 137; DLB 11, 23, 42, 78,
91; MAICYA; YABC 1

**Harris, John (Wyndham Parkes Lucas)
Beynon** 1903-1969
See Wyndham, John
See also CA 102; 89-92

Harris, MacDonald................. **CLC 9**
See also Heiney, Donald (William)

Harris, Mark 1922- .... **CLC 19**
See also CA 5-8R; CAAS 3; CANR 2;
DLB 2; DLBY 80

Harris, (Theodore) Wilson 1921-.... **CLC 25**
See also BW 2; CA 65-68; CAAS 16;
CANR 11, 27; DLB 117; MTCW

Harrison, Elizabeth Cavanna 1909-
See Cavanna, Betty
See also CA 9-12R; CANR 6, 27

Harrison, Harry (Max) 1925-...... **CLC 42**
See also CA 1-4R; CANR 5, 21; DLB 8;
SATA 4

Harrison, James (Thomas)
1937- .... **CLC 6, 14, 33, 66; SSC 19**
See also CA 13-16R; CANR 8; DLBY 82

Harrison, Jim
See Harrison, James (Thomas)

Harrison, Kathryn 1961- .... **CLC 70**
See also CA 144

Harrison, Tony 1937-............. **CLC 43**
See also CA 65-68; CANR 44; DLB 40;
MTCW

Harriss, Will(ard Irvin) 1922-...... **CLC 34**
See also CA 111

Harson, Sley
See Ellison, Harlan (Jay)

Hart, Ellis
See Ellison, Harlan (Jay)

Hart, Josephine 1942(?)- .... **CLC 70**
See also CA 138

Hart, Moss 1904-1961 .... **CLC 66**
See also CA 109; 89-92; DLB 7

Harte, (Francis) Bret(t)
1836(?)-1902 .... **TCLC 1, 25; DA;
SSC 8; WLC**
See also CA 104; 140; CDALB 1865-1917;
DLB 12, 64, 74, 79; SATA 26

Hartley, L(eslie) P(oles)
1895-1972 .... **CLC 2, 22**
See also CA 45-48; 37-40R; CANR 33;
DLB 15, 139; MTCW

Hartman, Geoffrey H. 1929-....... **CLC 27**
See also CA 117; 125; DLB 67

Hartmann von Aue
c. 1160-c. 1205 .... **CMLC 15**
See also DLB 138

Haruf, Kent 19(?)- .... **CLC 34**

Harwood, Ronald 1934-.......... **CLC 32**
See also CA 1-4R; CANR 4; DLB 13

Hasek, Jaroslav (Matej Frantisek)
1883-1923 .... **TCLC 4**
See also CA 104; 129; MTCW

Hass, Robert 1941-............ **CLC 18, 39**
See also CA 111; CANR 30; DLB 105

Hastings, Hudson
See Kuttner, Henry

Hastings, Selina................... **CLC 44**

Hatteras, Amelia
See Mencken, H(enry) L(ouis)

Hatteras, Owen................... **TCLC 18**
See also Mencken, H(enry) L(ouis); Nathan,
George Jean

Hauptmann, Gerhart (Johann Robert)
1862-1946 .... **TCLC 4**
See also CA 104; DLB 66, 118

Havel, Vaclav 1936-........ **CLC 25, 58, 65**
See also CA 104; CANR 36; MTCW

Haviaras, Stratis................... **CLC 33**
See also Chaviaras, Strates

Hawes, Stephen 1475(?)-1523(?) ..... **LC 17**

Hawkes, John (Clendennin Burne, Jr.)
1925- ...... **CLC 1, 2, 3, 4, 7, 9, 14, 15,
27, 49**
See also CA 1-4R; CANR 2, 47; DLB 2, 7;
DLBY 80; MTCW

Hawking, S. W.
See Hawking, Stephen W(illiam)

Hawking, Stephen W(illiam)
1942- .... **CLC 63**
See also AAYA 13; BEST 89:1; CA 126;
129

Hawthorne, Julian 1846-1934 ..... **TCLC 25**

Hawthorne, Nathaniel
1804-1864 ...... **NCLC 39; DA; SSC 3;
WLC**
See also CDALB 1640-1865; DLB 1, 74;
YABC 2

Haxton, Josephine Ayres 1921-
See Douglas, Ellen
See also CA 115; CANR 41

Hayaseca y Eizaguirre, Jorge
See Echegaray (y Eizaguirre), Jose (Maria
Waldo)

Hayashi Fumiko 1904-1951....... **TCLC 27**

Haycraft, Anna
See Ellis, Alice Thomas
See also CA 122

Hayden, Robert E(arl)
1913-1980 ...... **CLC 5, 9, 14, 37; BLC;
DA; PC 6**
See also BW 1; CA 69-72; 97-100; CABS 2;
CANR 24; CDALB 1941-1968; DLB 5,
76; MTCW; SATA 19; SATA-Obit 26

Hayford, J(oseph) E(phraim) Casely
See Casely-Hayford, J(oseph) E(phraim)

Hayman, Ronald 1932-............ **CLC 44**
See also CA 25-28R; CANR 18

Haywood, Eliza (Fowler)
1693(?)-1756 .... **LC 1**

Hazlitt, William 1778-1830 ...... **NCLC 29**
See also DLB 110

Hazzard, Shirley 1931- .... **CLC 18**
See also CA 9-12R; CANR 4; DLBY 82;
MTCW

Head, Bessie 1937-1986... **CLC 25, 67; BLC**
See also BW 2; CA 29-32R; 119; CANR 25;
DLB 117; MTCW

Headon, (Nicky) Topper 1956(?)- ... **CLC 30**

Heaney, Seamus (Justin)
1939- .... **CLC 5, 7, 14, 25, 37, 74**
See also CA 85-88; CANR 25;
CDBLB 1960 to Present; DLB 40;
MTCW

Hearn, (Patricio) Lafcadio (Tessima Carlos)
1850-1904 .... **TCLC 9**
See also CA 105; DLB 12, 78

Hearne, Vicki 1946-.............. **CLC 56**
See also CA 139

Hearon, Shelby 1931-............. **CLC 63**
See also AITN 2; CA 25-28R; CANR 18

Heat-Moon, William Least. .... **CLC 29**
See also Trogdon, William (Lewis)
See also AAYA 9

Hebbel, Friedrich 1813-1863..... **NCLC 43**
See also DLB 129

Hebert, Anne 1916- .... **CLC 4, 13, 29**
See also CA 85-88; DLB 68; MTCW

Hecht, Anthony (Evan)
1923- .... **CLC 8, 13, 19**
See also CA 9-12R; CANR 6; DLB 5

Hecht, Ben 1894-1964 .... **CLC 8**
See also CA 85-88; DLB 7, 9, 25, 26, 28, 86

Hedayat, Sadeq 1903-1951........ **TCLC 21**
See also CA 120

Hegel, Georg Wilhelm Friedrich
1770-1831 .... **NCLC 46**
See also DLB 90

Heidegger, Martin 1889-1976 ...... **CLC 24**
See also CA 81-84; 65-68; CANR 34;
MTCW

Heidenstam, (Carl Gustaf) Verner von
1859-1940 .... **TCLC 5**
See also CA 104

Heifner, Jack 1946-.............. **CLC 11**
See also CA 105; CANR 47

Heijermans, Herman 1864-1924 ... **TCLC 24**
See also CA 123

Heilbrun, Carolyn G(old) 1926-..... **CLC 25**
See also CA 45-48; CANR 1, 28

Heine, Heinrich 1797-1856 .... **NCLC 4**
See also DLB 90

Heinemann, Larry (Curtiss) 1944- .. **CLC 50**
See also CA 110; CANR 31; DLBD 9

Heiney, Donald (William) 1921-1993
See Harris, MacDonald
See also CA 1-4R; 142; CANR 3

Heinlein, Robert A(nson)
1907-1988 ...... **CLC 1, 3, 8, 14, 26, 55**
See also CA 1-4R; 125; CANR 1, 20;
DLB 8; JRDA; MAICYA; MTCW;
SATA 9, 69; SATA-Obit 56

Helforth, John
See Doolittle, Hilda

Hellenhofferu, Vojtech Kapristian z
See Hasek, Jaroslav (Matej Frantisek)

Heller, Joseph
1923- .... **CLC 1, 3, 5, 8, 11, 36, 63; DA;**
WLC
See also AITN 1; CA 5-8R; CABS 1;
CANR 8, 42; DLB 2, 28; DLBY 80;
MTCW

Hellman, Lillian (Florence)
1906-1984 ...... **CLC 2, 4, 8, 14, 18, 34,**
44, 52; DC 1
See also AITN 1, 2; CA 13-16R; 112;
CANR 33; DLB 7; DLBY 84; MTCW

Helprin, Mark 1947- ..... **CLC 7, 10, 22, 32**
See also CA 81-84; CANR 47; DLBY 85;
MTCW

Helvetius, Claude-Adrien
1715-1771 .... **LC 26**

Helyar, Jane Penelope Josephine 1933-
See Poole, Josephine
See also CA 21-24R; CANR 10, 26

Hemans, Felicia 1793-1835 ...... **NCLC 29**
See also DLB 96

Hemingway, Ernest (Miller)
1899-1961 .... **CLC 1, 3, 6, 8, 10, 13, 19,**
30, 34, 39, 41, 44, 50, 61, 80; DA; SSC 1;
WLC
See also CA 77-80; CANR 34;
CDALB 1917-1929; DLB 4, 9, 102;
DLBD 1; DLBY 81, 87; MTCW

Hempel, Amy 1951-.............. **CLC 39**
See also CA 118; 137

Henderson, F. C.
See Mencken, H(enry) L(ouis)

Henderson, Sylvia
See Ashton-Warner, Sylvia (Constance)

Henley, Beth .... **CLC 23**
See also Henley, Elizabeth Becker
See also CABS 3; DLBY 86

Henley, Elizabeth Becker 1952-
See Henley, Beth
See also CA 107; CANR 32; MTCW

Henley, William Ernest
1849-1903 .... **TCLC 8**
See also CA 105; DLB 19

Hennissart, Martha
See Lathen, Emma
See also CA 85-88

Henry, O. .... **TCLC 1, 19; SSC 5; WLC**
See also Porter, William Sydney

Henry, Patrick 1736-1799 .... **LC 25**

Henryson, Robert 1430(?)-1506(?).... **LC 20**
See also DLB 146

Henry VIII 1491-1547.............. **LC 10**

Henschke, Alfred
See Klabund

Hentoff, Nat(han Irving) 1925-..... **CLC 26**
See also AAYA 4; CA 1-4R; CAAS 6;
CANR 5, 25; CLR 1; JRDA; MAICYA;
SATA 42, 69; SATA-Brief 27

Heppenstall, (John) Rayner
1911-1981 .... **CLC 10**
See also CA 1-4R; 103; CANR 29

Herbert, Frank (Patrick)
1920-1986 ...... **CLC 12, 23, 35, 44, 85**
See also CA 53-56; 118; CANR 5, 43;
DLB 8; MTCW; SATA 9, 37;
SATA-Obit 47

Herbert, George 1593-1633 .... **LC 24; PC 4**
See also CDBLB Before 1660; DLB 126

Herbert, Zbigniew 1924- .... **CLC 9, 43**
See also CA 89-92; CANR 36; MTCW

Herbst, Josephine (Frey)
1897-1969 .... **CLC 34**
See also CA 5-8R; 25-28R; DLB 9

Hergesheimer, Joseph
1880-1954 .... **TCLC 11**
See also CA 109; DLB 102, 9

Herlihy, James Leo 1927-1993 ...... **CLC 6**
See also CA 1-4R; 143; CANR 2

Hermogenes fl. c. 175- .... **CMLC 6**

Hernandez, Jose 1834-1886...... **NCLC 17**

Herrick, Robert
1591-1674 .... **LC 13; DA; PC 9**
See also DLB 126

Herring, Guilles
See Somerville, Edith

Herriot, James 1916-1995 .... **CLC 12**
See also Wight, James Alfred
See also AAYA 1; CANR 40

Herrmann, Dorothy 1941-......... **CLC 44**
See also CA 107

Herrmann, Taffy
See Herrmann, Dorothy

Hersey, John (Richard)
1914-1993 .... **CLC 1, 2, 7, 9, 40, 81**
See also CA 17-20R; 140; CANR 33;
DLB 6; MTCW; SATA 25;
SATA-Obit 76

Herzen, Aleksandr Ivanovich
1812-1870 .... **NCLC 10**

Herzl, Theodor 1860-1904........ **TCLC 36**

Herzog, Werner 1942-............. **CLC 16**
See also CA 89-92

Hesiod c. 8th cent. B.C.- .... **CMLC 5**

Hesse, Hermann
1877-1962 .... **CLC 1, 2, 3, 6, 11, 17, 25,**
69; DA; SSC 9; WLC
See also CA 17-18; CAP 2; DLB 66;
MTCW; SATA 50

Hewes, Cady
See De Voto, Bernard (Augustine)

Heyen, William 1940- .... **CLC 13, 18**
See also CA 33-36R; CAAS 9; DLB 5

Heyerdahl, Thor 1914-............. **CLC 26**
See also CA 5-8R; CANR 5, 22; MTCW;
SATA 2, 52

Heym, Georg (Theodor Franz Arthur)
1887-1912 .... **TCLC 9**
See also CA 106

Heym, Stefan 1913-.............. **CLC 41**
See also CA 9-12R; CANR 4; DLB 69

Heyse, Paul (Johann Ludwig von)
1830-1914 .... **TCLC 8**
See also CA 104; DLB 129

Hood, Hugh (John Blagdon)
    1928- . . . . CLC 15, 28
  See also CA 49-52; CAAS 17; CANR 1, 33;
    DLB 53

Hood, Thomas 1799-1845 . . . . NCLC 16
  See also DLB 96

Hooker, (Peter) Jeremy 1941- . . . . . . CLC 43
  See also CA 77-80; CANR 22; DLB 40

Hope, A(lec) D(erwent) 1907- . . . . CLC 3, 51
  See also CA 21-24R; CANR 33; MTCW

Hope, Brian
  See Creasey, John

Hope, Christopher (David Tully)
    1944- . . . . CLC 52
  See also CA 106; CANR 47; SATA 62

Hopkins, Gerard Manley
    1844-1889 . . . . NCLC 17; DA; WLC
  See also CDBLB 1890-1914; DLB 35, 57

Hopkins, John (Richard) 1931- . . . . . . CLC 4
  See also CA 85-88

Hopkins, Pauline Elizabeth
    1859-1930 . . . . TCLC 28; BLC
  See also BW 2; CA 141; DLB 50

Hopkinson, Francis 1737-1791 . . . . . . LC 25
  See also DLB 31

Hopley-Woolrich, Cornell George 1903-1968
  See Woolrich, Cornell
  See also CA 13-14; CAP 1

Horatio
  See Proust, (Valentin-Louis-George-Eugene-)
    Marcel

Horgan, Paul 1903-1995 . . . . CLC 9, 53
  See also CA 13-16R; CANR 9, 35;
    DLB 102; DLBY 85; MTCW; SATA 13

Horn, Peter
  See Kuttner, Henry

Hornem, Horace Esq.
  See Byron, George Gordon (Noel)

Hornung, E(rnest) W(illiam)
    1866-1921 . . . . TCLC 59
  See also CA 108; DLB 70

Horovitz, Israel (Arthur) 1939- . . . . . CLC 56
  See also CA 33-36R; CANR 46; DLB 7

Horvath, Odon von
  See Horvath, Oedoen von
  See also DLB 85, 124

Horvath, Oedoen von 1901-1938 . . . TCLC 45
  See also Horvath, Odon von
  See also CA 118

Horwitz, Julius 1920-1986 . . . . CLC 14
  See also CA 9-12R; 119; CANR 12

Hospital, Janette Turner 1942- . . . . . CLC 42
  See also CA 108

Hostos, E. M. de
  See Hostos (y Bonilla), Eugenio Maria de

Hostos, Eugenio M. de
  See Hostos (y Bonilla), Eugenio Maria de

Hostos, Eugenio Maria
  See Hostos (y Bonilla), Eugenio Maria de

Hostos (y Bonilla), Eugenio Maria de
    1839-1903 . . . . TCLC 24
  See also CA 123; 131; HW

Houdini
  See Lovecraft, H(oward) P(hillips)

Hougan, Carolyn 1943- . . . . CLC 34
  See also CA 139

Household, Geoffrey (Edward West)
    1900-1988 . . . . CLC 11
  See also CA 77-80; 126; DLB 87; SATA 14;
    SATA-Obit 59

Housman, A(lfred) E(dward)
    1859-1936 . . . . . . TCLC 1, 10; DA; PC 2
  See also CA 104; 125; DLB 19; MTCW

Housman, Laurence 1865-1959 . . . . . TCLC 7
  See also CA 106; DLB 10; SATA 25

Howard, Elizabeth Jane 1923- . . . CLC 7, 29
  See also CA 5-8R; CANR 8

Howard, Maureen 1930- . . . . . CLC 5, 14, 46
  See also CA 53-56; CANR 31; DLBY 83;
    MTCW

Howard, Richard 1929- . . . . . . CLC 7, 10, 47
  See also AITN 1; CA 85-88; CANR 25;
    DLB 5

Howard, Robert Ervin 1906-1936 . . . TCLC 8
  See also CA 105

Howard, Warren F.
  See Pohl, Frederik

Howe, Fanny 1940- . . . . CLC 47
  See also CA 117; SATA-Brief 52

Howe, Irving 1920-1993 . . . . CLC 85
  See also CA 9-12R; 141; CANR 21;
    DLB 67; MTCW

Howe, Julia Ward 1819-1910 . . . . . TCLC 21
  See also CA 117; DLB 1

Howe, Susan 1937- . . . . CLC 72
  See also DLB 120

Howe, Tina 1937- . . . . CLC 48
  See also CA 109

Howell, James 1594(?)-1666 . . . . LC 13
  See also DLB 151

Howells, W. D.
  See Howells, William Dean

Howells, William D.
  See Howells, William Dean

Howells, William Dean
    1837-1920 . . . . TCLC 7, 17, 41
  See also CA 104; 134; CDALB 1865-1917;
    DLB 12, 64, 74, 79

Howes, Barbara 1914- . . . . CLC 15
  See also CA 9-12R; CAAS 3; SATA 5

Hrabal, Bohumil 1914- . . . . CLC 13, 67
  See also CA 106; CAAS 12

Hsun, Lu . . . . TCLC 3
  See also Shu-Jen, Chou

Hubbard, L(afayette) Ron(ald)
    1911-1986 . . . . CLC 43
  See also CA 77-80; 118; CANR 22

Huch, Ricarda (Octavia)
    1864-1947 . . . . TCLC 13
  See also CA 111; DLB 66

Huddle, David 1942- . . . . CLC 49
  See also CA 57-60; CAAS 20; DLB 130

Hudson, Jeffrey
  See Crichton, (John) Michael

Hudson, W(illiam) H(enry)
    1841-1922 . . . . TCLC 29
  See also CA 115; DLB 98; SATA 35

Hueffer, Ford Madox
  See Ford, Ford Madox

Hughart, Barry 1934- . . . . CLC 39
  See also CA 137

Hughes, Colin
  See Creasey, John

Hughes, David (John) 1930- . . . . CLC 48
  See also CA 116; 129; DLB 14

Hughes, (James) Langston
    1902-1967 . . . . . CLC 1, 5, 10, 15, 35, 44;
      BLC; DA; DC 3; PC 1; SSC 6; WLC
  See also AAYA 12; BW 1; CA 1-4R;
    25-28R; CANR 1, 34; CDALB 1929-1941;
    CLR 17; DLB 4, 7, 48, 51, 86; JRDA;
    MAICYA; MTCW; SATA 4, 33

Hughes, Richard (Arthur Warren)
    1900-1976 . . . . CLC 1, 11
  See also CA 5-8R; 65-68; CANR 4;
    DLB 15; MTCW; SATA 8;
    SATA-Obit 25

Hughes, Ted
    1930- . . . . CLC 2, 4, 9, 14, 37; PC 7
  See also CA 1-4R; CANR 1, 33; CLR 3;
    DLB 40; MAICYA; MTCW; SATA 49;
    SATA-Brief 27

Hugo, Richard F(ranklin)
    1923-1982 . . . . CLC 6, 18, 32
  See also CA 49-52; 108; CANR 3; DLB 5

Hugo, Victor (Marie)
    1802-1885 . . NCLC 3, 10, 21; DA; WLC
  See also DLB 119; SATA 47

Huidobro, Vicente
  See Huidobro Fernandez, Vicente Garcia

Huidobro Fernandez, Vicente Garcia
    1893-1948 . . . . TCLC 31
  See also CA 131; HW

Hulme, Keri 1947- . . . . CLC 39
  See also CA 125

Hulme, T(homas) E(rnest)
    1883-1917 . . . . TCLC 21
  See also CA 117; DLB 19

Hume, David 1711-1776 . . . . LC 7
  See also DLB 104

Humphrey, William 1924- . . . . CLC 45
  See also CA 77-80; DLB 6

Humphreys, Emyr Owen 1919- . . . . . CLC 47
  See also CA 5-8R; CANR 3, 24; DLB 15

Humphreys, Josephine 1945- . . . . CLC 34, 57
  See also CA 121; 127

Hungerford, Pixie
  See Brinsmead, H(esba) F(ay)

Hunt, E(verette) Howard, (Jr.)
    1918- . . . . CLC 3
  See also AITN 1; CA 45-48; CANR 2, 47

Hunt, Kyle
  See Creasey, John

Hunt, (James Henry) Leigh
    1784-1859 . . . . NCLC 1

Hunt, Marsha 1946- . . . . CLC 70
  See also BW 2; CA 143

Hunt, Violet 1866-1942 . . . . TCLC 53

Hunter, E. Waldo
  See Sturgeon, Theodore (Hamilton)

James, Montague (Rhodes)
1862-1936 .... **TCLC 6; SSC 16**
See also CA 104

James, P. D. .... **CLC 18, 46**
See also White, Phyllis Dorothy James
See also BEST 90:2; CDBLB 1960 to
Present; DLB 87

James, Philip
See Moorcock, Michael (John)

James, William 1842-1910..... **TCLC 15, 32**
See also CA 109

James I 1394-1437 .... **LC 20**

Jameson, Anna 1794-1860 ...... **NCLC 43**
See also DLB 99

Jami, Nur al-Din 'Abd al-Rahman
1414-1492 .... **LC 9**

Jandl, Ernst 1925- .... **CLC 34**

Janowitz, Tama 1957- .... **CLC 43**
See also CA 106

Jarrell, Randall
1914-1965 .... **CLC 1, 2, 6, 9, 13, 49**
See also CA 5-8R; 25-28R; CABS 2;
CANR 6, 34; CDALB 1941-1968; CLR 6;
DLB 48, 52; MAICYA; MTCW; SATA 7

Jarry, Alfred 1873-1907....... **TCLC 2, 14**
See also CA 104

Jarvis, E. K.
See Bloch, Robert (Albert); Ellison, Harlan
(Jay); Silverberg, Robert

Jeake, Samuel, Jr.
See Aiken, Conrad (Potter)

Jean Paul 1763-1825 .... **NCLC 7**

Jefferies, (John) Richard
1848-1887 .... **NCLC 47**
See also DLB 98, 141; SATA 16

Jeffers, (John) Robinson
1887-1962 .... **CLC 2, 3, 11, 15, 54; DA;
WLC**
See also CA 85-88; CANR 35;
CDALB 1917-1929; DLB 45; MTCW

Jefferson, Janet
See Mencken, H(enry) L(ouis)

Jefferson, Thomas 1743-1826 .... **NCLC 11**
See also CDALB 1640-1865; DLB 31

Jeffrey, Francis 1773-1850....... **NCLC 33**
See also DLB 107

Jelakowitch, Ivan
See Heijermans, Herman

Jellicoe, (Patricia) Ann 1927- ...... **CLC 27**
See also CA 85-88; DLB 13

Jen, Gish .... **CLC 70**
See also Jen, Lillian

Jen, Lillian 1956(?)-
See Jen, Gish
See also CA 135

Jenkins, (John) Robin 1912- .... **CLC 52**
See also CA 1-4R; CANR 1; DLB 14

Jennings, Elizabeth (Joan)
1926- .... **CLC 5, 14**
See also CA 61-64; CAAS 5; CANR 8, 39;
DLB 27; MTCW; SATA 66

Jennings, Waylon 1937-........... **CLC 21**

Jensen, Johannes V. 1873-1950.... **TCLC 41**

Jensen, Laura (Linnea) 1948- ...... **CLC 37**
See also CA 103

Jerome, Jerome K(lapka)
1859-1927 .... **TCLC 23**
See also CA 119; DLB 10, 34, 135

Jerrold, Douglas William
1803-1857 .... **NCLC 2**

Jewett, (Theodora) Sarah Orne
1849-1909 .... **TCLC 1, 22; SSC 6**
See also CA 108; 127; DLB 12, 74;
SATA 15

Jewsbury, Geraldine (Endsor)
1812-1880 .... **NCLC 22**
See also DLB 21

Jhabvala, Ruth Prawer
1927- .... **CLC 4, 8, 29**
See also CA 1-4R; CANR 2, 29; DLB 139;
MTCW

Jiles, Paulette 1943-........... **CLC 13, 58**
See also CA 101

Jimenez (Mantecon), Juan Ramon
1881-1958 .... **TCLC 4; HLC; PC 7**
See also CA 104; 131; DLB 134; HW;
MTCW

Jimenez, Ramon
See Jimenez (Mantecon), Juan Ramon

Jimenez Mantecon, Juan
See Jimenez (Mantecon), Juan Ramon

Joel, Billy .... **CLC 26**
See also Joel, William Martin

Joel, William Martin 1949-
See Joel, Billy
See also CA 108

John of the Cross, St. 1542-1591 .... **LC 18**

Johnson, B(ryan) S(tanley William)
1933-1973 .... **CLC 6, 9**
See also CA 9-12R; 53-56; CANR 9;
DLB 14, 40

Johnson, Benj. F. of Boo
See Riley, James Whitcomb

Johnson, Benjamin F. of Boo
See Riley, James Whitcomb

Johnson, Charles (Richard)
1948- .... **CLC 7, 51, 65; BLC**
See also BW 2; CA 116; CAAS 18;
CANR 42; DLB 33

Johnson, Denis 1949-............. **CLC 52**
See also CA 117; 121; DLB 120

Johnson, Diane 1934-....... **CLC 5, 13, 48**
See also CA 41-44R; CANR 17, 40;
DLBY 80; MTCW

Johnson, Eyvind (Olof Verner)
1900-1976 .... **CLC 14**
See also CA 73-76; 69-72; CANR 34

Johnson, J. R.
See James, C(yril) L(ionel) R(obert)

Johnson, James Weldon
1871-1938 .... **TCLC 3, 19; BLC**
See also BW 1; CA 104; 125;
CDALB 1917-1929; CLR 32; DLB 51;
MTCW; SATA 31

Johnson, Joyce 1935-............. **CLC 58**
See also CA 125; 129

Johnson, Lionel (Pigot)
1867-1902 .... **TCLC 19**
See also CA 117; DLB 19

Johnson, Mel
See Malzberg, Barry N(athaniel)

Johnson, Pamela Hansford
1912-1981 .... **CLC 1, 7, 27**
See also CA 1-4R; 104; CANR 2, 28;
DLB 15; MTCW

Johnson, Samuel
1709-1784 .... **LC 15; DA; WLC**
See also CDBLB 1660-1789; DLB 39, 95,
104, 142

Johnson, Uwe
1934-1984 .... **CLC 5, 10, 15, 40**
See also CA 1-4R; 112; CANR 1, 39;
DLB 75; MTCW

Johnston, George (Benson) 1913- ... **CLC 51**
See also CA 1-4R; CANR 5, 20; DLB 88

Johnston, Jennifer 1930-........... **CLC 7**
See also CA 85-88; DLB 14

Jolley, (Monica) Elizabeth
1923- .... **CLC 46; SSC 19**
See also CA 127; CAAS 13

Jones, Arthur Llewellyn 1863-1947
See Machen, Arthur
See also CA 104

Jones, D(ouglas) G(ordon) 1929-.... **CLC 10**
See also CA 29-32R; CANR 13; DLB 53

Jones, David (Michael)
1895-1974 .... **CLC 2, 4, 7, 13, 42**
See also CA 9-12R; 53-56; CANR 28;
CDBLB 1945-1960; DLB 20, 100; MTCW

Jones, David Robert 1947-
See Bowie, David
See also CA 103

Jones, Diana Wynne 1934- .... **CLC 26**
See also AAYA 12; CA 49-52; CANR 4,
26; CLR 23; JRDA; MAICYA; SAAS 7;
SATA 9, 70

Jones, Edward P. 1950-.......... **CLC 76**
See also BW 2; CA 142

Jones, Gayl 1949-.......... **CLC 6, 9; BLC**
See also BW 2; CA 77-80; CANR 27;
DLB 33; MTCW

Jones, James 1921-1977.... **CLC 1, 3, 10, 39**
See also AITN 1, 2; CA 1-4R; 69-72;
CANR 6; DLB 2, 143; MTCW

Jones, John J.
See Lovecraft, H(oward) P(hillips)

Jones, LeRoi .... **CLC 1, 2, 3, 5, 10, 14**
See also Baraka, Amiri

Jones, Louis B. .... **CLC 65**
See also CA 141

Jones, Madison (Percy, Jr.) 1925- ... **CLC 4**
See also CA 13-16R; CAAS 11; CANR 7;
DLB 152

Jones, Mervyn 1922- .... **CLC 10, 52**
See also CA 45-48; CAAS 5; CANR 1;
MTCW

Jones, Mick 1956(?)- .... **CLC 30**

Jones, Nettie (Pearl) 1941-........ **CLC 34**
See also BW 2; CA 137; CAAS 20

Jones, Preston 1936-1979 .... **CLC 10**
See also CA 73-76; 89-92; DLB 7

Jones, Robert F(rancis) 1934- . . . . CLC 7
See also CA 49-52; CANR 2

Jones, Rod 1953- . . . . CLC 50
See also CA 128

Jones, Terence Graham Parry
1942- . . . . CLC 21
See also Jones, Terry; Monty Python
See also CA 112; 116; CANR 35

Jones, Terry
See Jones, Terence Graham Parry
See also SATA 67; SATA-Brief 51

Jones, Thom 1945(?)- . . . . CLC 81

Jong, Erica 1942- . . . . . . CLC 4, 6, 8, 18, 83
See also AITN 1; BEST 90:2; CA 73-76;
CANR 26; DLB 2, 5, 28, 152; MTCW

Jonson, Ben(jamin)
1572(?)-1637 . . . . LC 6; DA; DC 4; WLC
See also CDBLB Before 1660; DLB 62, 121

Jordan, June 1936- . . . . CLC 5, 11, 23
See also AAYA 2; BW 2; CA 33-36R;
CANR 25; CLR 10; DLB 38; MAICYA;
MTCW; SATA 4

Jordan, Pat(rick M.) 1941- . . . . CLC 37
See also CA 33-36R

Jorgensen, Ivar
See Ellison, Harlan (Jay)

Jorgenson, Ivar
See Silverberg, Robert

Josephus, Flavius c. 37-100 . . . . . . CMLC 13

Josipovici, Gabriel 1940- . . . . CLC 6, 43
See also CA 37-40R; CAAS 8; CANR 47;
DLB 14

Joubert, Joseph 1754-1824 . . . . NCLC 9

Jouve, Pierre Jean 1887-1976 . . . . . . CLC 47
See also CA 65-68

Joyce, James (Augustine Aloysius)
1882-1941 . . . . . . TCLC 3, 8, 16, 35, 52;
DA; SSC 3; WLC
See also CA 104; 126; CDBLB 1914-1945;
DLB 10, 19, 36; MTCW

Jozsef, Attila 1905-1937 . . . . TCLC 22
See also CA 116

Juana Ines de la Cruz 1651(?)-1695 . . . LC 5

Judd, Cyril
See Kornbluth, C(yril) M.; Pohl, Frederik

Julian of Norwich 1342(?)-1416(?) . . . . LC 6
See also DLB 146

Just, Ward (Swift) 1935- . . . . CLC 4, 27
See also CA 25-28R; CANR 32

Justice, Donald (Rodney) 1925- . . CLC 6, 19
See also CA 5-8R; CANR 26; DLBY 83

Juvenal c. 55-c. 127 . . . . CMLC 8

Juvenis
See Bourne, Randolph S(illiman)

Kacew, Romain 1914-1980
See Gary, Romain
See also CA 108; 102

Kadare, Ismail 1936- . . . . CLC 52

Kadohata, Cynthia . . . . CLC 59
See also CA 140

Kafka, Franz
1883-1924 . . . . TCLC 2, 6, 13, 29, 47, 53;
DA; SSC 5; WLC
See also CA 105; 126; DLB 81; MTCW

Kahanovitsch, Pinkhes
See Der Nister

Kahn, Roger 1927- . . . . CLC 30
See also CA 25-28R; CANR 44; SATA 37

Kain, Saul
See Sassoon, Siegfried (Lorraine)

Kaiser, Georg 1878-1945 . . . . TCLC 9
See also CA 106; DLB 124

Kaletski, Alexander 1946- . . . . CLC 39
See also CA 118; 143

Kalidasa fl. c. 400- . . . . CMLC 9

Kallman, Chester (Simon)
1921-1975 . . . . CLC 2
See also CA 45-48; 53-56; CANR 3

Kaminsky, Melvin 1926-
See Brooks, Mel
See also CA 65-68; CANR 16

Kaminsky, Stuart M(elvin) 1934- . . . CLC 59
See also CA 73-76; CANR 29

Kane, Paul
See Simon, Paul

Kane, Wilson
See Bloch, Robert (Albert)

Kanin, Garson 1912- . . . . CLC 22
See also AITN 1; CA 5-8R; CANR 7;
DLB 7

Kaniuk, Yoram 1930- . . . . CLC 19
See also CA 134

Kant, Immanuel 1724-1804 . . . . . . NCLC 27
See also DLB 94

Kantor, MacKinlay 1904-1977 . . . . . . CLC 7
See also CA 61-64; 73-76; DLB 9, 102

Kaplan, David Michael 1946- . . . . . . CLC 50

Kaplan, James 1951- . . . . CLC 59
See also CA 135

Karageorge, Michael
See Anderson, Poul (William)

Karamzin, Nikolai Mikhailovich
1766-1826 . . . . NCLC 3
See also DLB 150

Karapanou, Margarita 1946- . . . . . . CLC 13
See also CA 101

Karinthy, Frigyes 1887-1938 . . . . . . TCLC 47

Karl, Frederick R(obert) 1927- . . . . . CLC 34
See also CA 5-8R; CANR 3, 44

Kastel, Warren
See Silverberg, Robert

Kataev, Evgeny Petrovich 1903-1942
See Petrov, Evgeny
See also CA 120

Kataphusin
See Ruskin, John

Katz, Steve 1935- . . . . CLC 47
See also CA 25-28R; CAAS 14; CANR 12;
DLBY 83

Kauffman, Janet 1945- . . . . CLC 42
See also CA 117; CANR 43; DLBY 86

Kaufman, Bob (Garnell)
1925-1986 . . . . CLC 49
See also BW 1; CA 41-44R; 118; CANR 22;
DLB 16, 41

Kaufman, George S. 1889-1961 . . . . . CLC 38
See also CA 108; 93-96; DLB 7

Kaufman, Sue . . . . CLC 3, 8
See also Barondess, Sue K(aufman)

Kavafis, Konstantinos Petrou 1863-1933
See Cavafy, C(onstantine) P(eter)
See also CA 104

Kavan, Anna 1901-1968 . . . . . . CLC 5, 13, 82
See also CA 5-8R; CANR 6; MTCW

Kavanagh, Dan
See Barnes, Julian

Kavanagh, Patrick (Joseph)
1904-1967 . . . . CLC 22
See also CA 123; 25-28R; DLB 15, 20;
MTCW

Kawabata, Yasunari
1899-1972 . . . . . CLC 2, 5, 9, 18; SSC 17
See also CA 93-96; 33-36R

Kaye, M(ary) M(argaret) 1909- . . . . . CLC 28
See also CA 89-92; CANR 24; MTCW;
SATA 62

Kaye, Mollie
See Kaye, M(ary) M(argaret)

Kaye-Smith, Sheila 1887-1956 . . . . . TCLC 20
See also CA 118; DLB 36

Kaymor, Patrice Maguilene
See Senghor, Leopold Sedar

Kazan, Elia 1909- . . . . CLC 6, 16, 63
See also CA 21-24R; CANR 32

Kazantzakis, Nikos
1883(?)-1957 . . . . TCLC 2, 5, 33
See also CA 105; 132; MTCW

Kazin, Alfred 1915- . . . . CLC 34, 38
See also CA 1-4R; CAAS 7; CANR 1, 45;
DLB 67

Keane, Mary Nesta (Skrine) 1904-
See Keane, Molly
See also CA 108; 114

Keane, Molly . . . . CLC 31
See also Keane, Mary Nesta (Skrine)

Keates, Jonathan 19(?)- . . . . CLC 34

Keaton, Buster 1895-1966 . . . . CLC 20

Keats, John
1795-1821 . . . NCLC 8; DA; PC 1; WLC
See also CDBLB 1789-1832; DLB 96, 110

Keene, Donald 1922- . . . . CLC 34
See also CA 1-4R; CANR 5

Keillor, Garrison . . . . CLC 40
See also Keillor, Gary (Edward)
See also AAYA 2; BEST 89:3; DLBY 87;
SATA 58

Keillor, Gary (Edward) 1942-
See Keillor, Garrison
See also CA 111; 117; CANR 36; MTCW

Keith, Michael
See Hubbard, L(afayette) Ron(ald)

Keller, Gottfried 1819-1890 . . . . NCLC 2
See also DLB 129

Kellerman, Jonathan 1949- . . . . CLC 44
See also BEST 90:1; CA 106; CANR 29

Kleist, Heinrich von
1777-1811 . . . . NCLC 2, 37
See also DLB 90

Klima, Ivan 1931- . . . . CLC 56
See also CA 25-28R; CANR 17

Klimentov, Andrei Platonovich 1899-1951
See Platonov, Andrei
See also CA 108

Klinger, Friedrich Maximilian von
1752-1831 . . . . NCLC 1
See also DLB 94

Klopstock, Friedrich Gottlieb
1724-1803 . . . . NCLC 11
See also DLB 97

Knebel, Fletcher 1911-1993 . . . . CLC 14
See also AITN 1; CA 1-4R; 140; CAAS 3;
CANR 1, 36; SATA 36; SATA-Obit 75

Knickerbocker, Diedrich
See Irving, Washington

Knight, Etheridge
1931-1991 . . . . CLC 40; BLC
See also BW 1; CA 21-24R; 133; CANR 23;
DLB 41

Knight, Sarah Kemble 1666-1727 . . . . . LC 7
See also DLB 24

Knister, Raymond 1899-1932 . . . . . . TCLC 56
See also DLB 68

Knowles, John
1926- . . . . CLC 1, 4, 10, 26; DA
See also AAYA 10; CA 17-20R; CANR 40;
CDALB 1968-1988; DLB 6; MTCW;
SATA 8

Knox, Calvin M.
See Silverberg, Robert

Knye, Cassandra
See Disch, Thomas M(ichael)

Koch, C(hristopher) J(ohn) 1932- . . . CLC 42
See also CA 127

Koch, Christopher
See Koch, C(hristopher) J(ohn)

Koch, Kenneth 1925- . . . . CLC 5, 8, 44
See also CA 1-4R; CANR 6, 36; DLB 5;
SATA 65

Kochanowski, Jan 1530-1584 . . . . LC 10

Kock, Charles Paul de
1794-1871 . . . . NCLC 16

Koda Shigeyuki 1867-1947
See Rohan, Koda
See also CA 121

Koestler, Arthur
1905-1983 . . . . CLC 1, 3, 6, 8, 15, 33
See also CA 1-4R; 109; CANR 1, 33;
CDBLB 1945-1960; DLBY 83; MTCW

Kogawa, Joy Nozomi 1935- . . . . CLC 78
See also CA 101; CANR 19

Kohout, Pavel 1928- . . . . CLC 13
See also CA 45-48; CANR 3

Koizumi, Yakumo
See Hearn, (Patricio) Lafcadio (Tessima
Carlos)

Kolmar, Gertrud 1894-1943 . . . . . . TCLC 40

Komunyakaa, Yusef 1947- . . . . CLC 86
See also DLB 120

Konrad, George
See Konrad, Gyoergy

Konrad, Gyoergy 1933- . . . . . . CLC 4, 10, 73
See also CA 85-88

Konwicki, Tadeusz 1926- . . . . . CLC 8, 28, 54
See also CA 101; CAAS 9; CANR 39;
MTCW

Koontz, Dean R(ay) 1945- . . . . CLC 78
See also AAYA 9; BEST 89:3, 90:2;
CA 108; CANR 19, 36; MTCW

Kopit, Arthur (Lee) 1937- . . . . CLC 1, 18, 33
See also AITN 1; CA 81-84; CABS 3;
DLB 7; MTCW

Kops, Bernard 1926- . . . . CLC 4
See also CA 5-8R; DLB 13

Kornbluth, C(yril) M. 1923-1958 . . . . TCLC 8
See also CA 105; DLB 8

Korolenko, V. G.
See Korolenko, Vladimir Galaktionovich

Korolenko, Vladimir
See Korolenko, Vladimir Galaktionovich

Korolenko, Vladimir G.
See Korolenko, Vladimir Galaktionovich

Korolenko, Vladimir Galaktionovich
1853-1921 . . . . TCLC 22
See also CA 121

Kosinski, Jerzy (Nikodem)
1933-1991 . . . . CLC 1, 2, 3, 6, 10, 15, 53,
70
See also CA 17-20R; 134; CANR 9, 46;
DLB 2; DLBY 82; MTCW

Kostelanetz, Richard (Cory) 1940- . . CLC 28
See also CA 13-16R; CAAS 8; CANR 38

Kostrowitzki, Wilhelm Apollinaris de
1880-1918
See Apollinaire, Guillaume
See also CA 104

Kotlowitz, Robert 1924- . . . . CLC 4
See also CA 33-36R; CANR 36

Kotzebue, August (Friedrich Ferdinand) von
1761-1819 . . . . NCLC 25
See also DLB 94

Kotzwinkle, William 1938- . . . CLC 5, 14, 35
See also CA 45-48; CANR 3, 44; CLR 6;
MAICYA; SATA 24, 70

Kozol, Jonathan 1936- . . . . CLC 17
See also CA 61-64; CANR 16, 45

Kozoll, Michael 1940(?)- . . . . CLC 35

Kramer, Kathryn 19(?)- . . . . CLC 34

Kramer, Larry 1935- . . . . CLC 42
See also CA 124; 126

Krasicki, Ignacy 1735-1801 . . . . NCLC 8

Krasinski, Zygmunt 1812-1859 . . . . NCLC 4

Kraus, Karl 1874-1936 . . . . TCLC 5
See also CA 104; DLB 118

Kreve (Mickevicius), Vincas
1882-1954 . . . . TCLC 27

Kristeva, Julia 1941- . . . . CLC 77

Kristofferson, Kris 1936- . . . . CLC 26
See also CA 104

Krizanc, John 1956- . . . . CLC 57

Krleza, Miroslav 1893-1981 . . . . CLC 8
See also CA 97-100; 105; DLB 147

Kroetsch, Robert 1927- . . . . . . CLC 5, 23, 57
See also CA 17-20R; CANR 8, 38; DLB 53;
MTCW

Kroetz, Franz
See Kroetz, Franz Xaver

Kroetz, Franz Xaver 1946- . . . . CLC 41
See also CA 130

Kroker, Arthur 1945- . . . . CLC 77

Kropotkin, Peter (Aleksieevich)
1842-1921 . . . . TCLC 36
See also CA 119

Krotkov, Yuri 1917- . . . . CLC 19
See also CA 102

Krumb
See Crumb, R(obert)

Krumgold, Joseph (Quincy)
1908-1980 . . . . CLC 12
See also CA 9-12R; 101; CANR 7;
MAICYA; SATA 1, 48; SATA-Obit 23

Krumwitz
See Crumb, R(obert)

Krutch, Joseph Wood 1893-1970 . . . . CLC 24
See also CA 1-4R; 25-28R; CANR 4;
DLB 63

Krutzch, Gus
See Eliot, T(homas) S(tearns)

Krylov, Ivan Andreevich
1768(?)-1844 . . . . NCLC 1
See also DLB 150

Kubin, Alfred 1877-1959 . . . . TCLC 23
See also CA 112; DLB 81

Kubrick, Stanley 1928- . . . . CLC 16
See also CA 81-84; CANR 33; DLB 26

Kumin, Maxine (Winokur)
1925- . . . . CLC 5, 13, 28
See also AITN 2; CA 1-4R; CAAS 8;
CANR 1, 21; DLB 5; MTCW; SATA 12

Kundera, Milan
1929- . . . . CLC 4, 9, 19, 32, 68
See also AAYA 2; CA 85-88; CANR 19;
MTCW

Kunene, Mazisi (Raymond) 1930- . . . CLC 85
See also BW 1; CA 125; DLB 117

Kunitz, Stanley (Jasspon)
1905- . . . . CLC 6, 11, 14
See also CA 41-44R; CANR 26; DLB 48;
MTCW

Kunze, Reiner 1933- . . . . CLC 10
See also CA 93-96; DLB 75

Kuprin, Aleksandr Ivanovich
1870-1938 . . . . TCLC 5
See also CA 104

Kureishi, Hanif 1954(?)- . . . . CLC 64
See also CA 139

Kurosawa, Akira 1910- . . . . CLC 16
See also AAYA 11; CA 101; CANR 46

Kushner, Tony 1957(?)- . . . . CLC 81
See also CA 144

Kuttner, Henry 1915-1958 . . . . TCLC 10
See also CA 107; DLB 8

Kuzma, Greg 1944- . . . . CLC 7
See also CA 33-36R

Kuzmin, Mikhail 1872(?)-1936 . . . . TCLC 40

Author Index

Llewellyn Lloyd, Richard Dafydd Vivian
    1906-1983 . . . . **CLC 7, 80**
    See also Llewellyn, Richard
    See also CA 53-56; 111; CANR 7;
    SATA 11; SATA-Obit 37

Llosa, (Jorge) Mario (Pedro) Vargas
    See Vargas Llosa, (Jorge) Mario (Pedro)

Lloyd Webber, Andrew 1948-
    See Webber, Andrew Lloyd
    See also AAYA 1; CA 116; SATA 56

Llull, Ramon c. 1235-c. 1316. . . . . **CMLC 12**

Locke, Alain (Le Roy)
    1886-1954 . . . . **TCLC 43**
    See also BW 1; CA 106; 124; DLB 51

Locke, John 1632-1704 . . . . **LC 7**
    See also DLB 101

Locke-Elliott, Sumner
    See Elliott, Sumner Locke

Lockhart, John Gibson
    1794-1854 . . . . **NCLC 6**
    See also DLB 110, 116, 144

Lodge, David (John) 1935-. . . . . **CLC 36**
    See also BEST 90:1; CA 17-20R; CANR 19;
    DLB 14; MTCW

Loennbohm, Armas Eino Leopold 1878-1926
    See Leino, Eino
    See also CA 123

Loewinsohn, Ron(ald William)
    1937- . . . . **CLC 52**
    See also CA 25-28R

Logan, Jake
    See Smith, Martin Cruz

Logan, John (Burton) 1923-1987. . . . . **CLC 5**
    See also CA 77-80; 124; CANR 45; DLB 5

Lo Kuan-chung 1330(?)-1400(?). . . . . . **LC 12**

Lombard, Nap
    See Johnson, Pamela Hansford

London, Jack. . **TCLC 9, 15, 39; SSC 4; WLC**
    See also London, John Griffith
    See also AAYA 13; AITN 2;
    CDALB 1865-1917; DLB 8, 12, 78;
    SATA 18

London, John Griffith 1876-1916
    See London, Jack
    See also CA 110; 119; DA; JRDA;
    MAICYA; MTCW

Long, Emmett
    See Leonard, Elmore (John, Jr.)

Longbaugh, Harry
    See Goldman, William (W.)

Longfellow, Henry Wadsworth
    1807-1882 . . . . **NCLC 2, 45; DA**
    See also CDALB 1640-1865; DLB 1, 59;
    SATA 19

Longley, Michael 1939-. . . . . **CLC 29**
    See also CA 102; DLB 40

Longus fl. c. 2nd cent. - . . . . **CMLC 7**

Longway, A. Hugh
    See Lang, Andrew

Lopate, Phillip 1943- . . . . **CLC 29**
    See also CA 97-100; DLBY 80

Lopez Portillo (y Pacheco), Jose
    1920- . . . . **CLC 46**
    See also CA 129; HW

Lopez y Fuentes, Gregorio
    1897(?)-1966 . . . . **CLC 32**
    See also CA 131; HW

Lorca, Federico Garcia
    See Garcia Lorca, Federico

Lord, Bette Bao 1938- . . . . **CLC 23**
    See also BEST 90:3; CA 107; CANR 41;
    SATA 58

Lord Auch
    See Bataille, Georges

Lord Byron
    See Byron, George Gordon (Noel)

Lorde, Audre (Geraldine)
    1934-1992 . . . . **CLC 18, 71; BLC; PC 12**
    See also BW 1; CA 25-28R; 142; CANR 16,
    26, 46; DLB 41; MTCW

Lord Jeffrey
    See Jeffrey, Francis

Lorenzo, Heberto Padilla
    See Padilla (Lorenzo), Heberto

Loris
    See Hofmannsthal, Hugo von

Loti, Pierre . . . . **TCLC 11**
    See also Viaud, (Louis Marie) Julien
    See also DLB 123

Louie, David Wong 1954- . . . . **CLC 70**
    See also CA 139

Louis, Father M.
    See Merton, Thomas

Lovecraft, H(oward) P(hillips)
    1890-1937 . . . . **TCLC 4, 22; SSC 3**
    See also AAYA 14; CA 104; 133; MTCW

Lovelace, Earl 1935-. . . . . **CLC 51**
    See also BW 2; CA 77-80; CANR 41;
    DLB 125; MTCW

Lovelace, Richard 1618-1657. . . . . . . **LC 24**
    See also DLB 131

Lowell, Amy 1874-1925 . . **TCLC 1, 8; PC 12**
    See also CA 104; DLB 54, 140

Lowell, James Russell 1819-1891 . . **NCLC 2**
    See also CDALB 1640-1865; DLB 1, 11, 64,
    79

Lowell, Robert (Traill Spence, Jr.)
    1917-1977 . . . **CLC 1, 2, 3, 4, 5, 8, 9, 11,**
                 15, 37; DA; PC 3; WLC
    See also CA 9-12R; 73-76; CABS 2;
    CANR 26; DLB 5; MTCW

Lowndes, Marie Adelaide (Belloc)
    1868-1947 . . . . **TCLC 12**
    See also CA 107; DLB 70

Lowry, (Clarence) Malcolm
    1909-1957 . . . . **TCLC 6, 40**
    See also CA 105; 131; CDBLB 1945-1960;
    DLB 15; MTCW

Lowry, Mina Gertrude 1882-1966
    See Loy, Mina
    See also CA 113

Loxsmith, John
    See Brunner, John (Kilian Houston)

Loy, Mina . . . . **CLC 28**
    See also Lowry, Mina Gertrude
    See also DLB 4, 54

Loyson-Bridet
    See Schwob, (Mayer Andre) Marcel

Lucas, Craig 1951- . . . . **CLC 64**
    See also CA 137

Lucas, George 1944-. . . . . **CLC 16**
    See also AAYA 1; CA 77-80; CANR 30;
    SATA 56

Lucas, Hans
    See Godard, Jean-Luc

Lucas, Victoria
    See Plath, Sylvia

Ludlam, Charles 1943-1987. . . . . **CLC 46, 50**
    See also CA 85-88; 122

Ludlum, Robert 1927- . . . . **CLC 22, 43**
    See also AAYA 10; BEST 89:1, 90:3;
    CA 33-36R; CANR 25, 41; DLBY 82;
    MTCW

Ludwig, Ken. . . . . **CLC 60**

Ludwig, Otto 1813-1865. . . . . **NCLC 4**
    See also DLB 129

Lugones, Leopoldo 1874-1938 . . . . . **TCLC 15**
    See also CA 116; 131; HW

Lu Hsun 1881-1936 . . . . **TCLC 3**

Lukacs, George . . . . **CLC 24**
    See also Lukacs, Gyorgy (Szegeny von)

Lukacs, Gyorgy (Szegeny von) 1885-1971
    See Lukacs, George
    See also CA 101; 29-32R

Luke, Peter (Ambrose Cyprian)
    1919- . . . . **CLC 38**
    See also CA 81-84; DLB 13

Lunar, Dennis
    See Mungo, Raymond

Lurie, Alison 1926-. . . . . **CLC 4, 5, 18, 39**
    See also CA 1-4R; CANR 2, 17; DLB 2;
    MTCW; SATA 46

Lustig, Arnost 1926-. . . . . **CLC 56**
    See also AAYA 3; CA 69-72; CANR 47;
    SATA 56

Luther, Martin 1483-1546. . . . . **LC 9**

Luzi, Mario 1914-. . . . . **CLC 13**
    See also CA 61-64; CANR 9; DLB 128

Lynch, B. Suarez
    See Bioy Casares, Adolfo; Borges, Jorge
    Luis

Lynch, David (K.) 1946-. . . . . **CLC 66**
    See also CA 124; 129

Lynch, James
    See Andreyev, Leonid (Nikolaevich)

Lynch Davis, B.
    See Bioy Casares, Adolfo; Borges, Jorge
    Luis

Lyndsay, Sir David 1490-1555 . . . . . . **LC 20**

Lynn, Kenneth S(chuyler) 1923- . . . . **CLC 50**
    See also CA 1-4R; CANR 3, 27

Lynx
    See West, Rebecca

Lyons, Marcus
    See Blish, James (Benjamin)

Lyre, Pinchbeck
    See Sassoon, Siegfried (Lorraine)

Lytle, Andrew (Nelson) 1902-. . . . . . **CLC 22**
    See also CA 9-12R; DLB 6

Lyttelton, George 1709-1773. . . . . . . **LC 10**

Maas, Peter 1929- .... CLC 29
See also CA 93-96

Macaulay, Rose 1881-1958 ..... TCLC 7, 44
See also CA 104; DLB 36

Macaulay, Thomas Babington
1800-1859 .... NCLC 42
See also CDBLB 1832-1890; DLB 32, 55

MacBeth, George (Mann)
1932-1992 .... CLC 2, 5, 9
See also CA 25-28R; 136; DLB 40; MTCW;
SATA 4; SATA-Obit 70

MacCaig, Norman (Alexander)
1910- .... CLC 36
See also CA 9-12R; CANR 3, 34; DLB 27

MacCarthy, (Sir Charles Otto) Desmond
1877-1952 .... TCLC 36

MacDiarmid, Hugh
.... CLC 2, 4, 11, 19, 63; PC 9
See also Grieve, C(hristopher) M(urray)
See also CDBLB 1945-1960; DLB 20

MacDonald, Anson
See Heinlein, Robert A(nson)

Macdonald, Cynthia 1928- ...... CLC 13, 19
See also CA 49-52; CANR 4, 44; DLB 105

MacDonald, George 1824-1905 ..... TCLC 9
See also CA 106; 137; DLB 18; MAICYA;
SATA 33

Macdonald, John
See Millar, Kenneth

MacDonald, John D(ann)
1916-1986 .... CLC 3, 27, 44
See also CA 1-4R; 121; CANR 1, 19;
DLB 8; DLBY 86; MTCW

Macdonald, John Ross
See Millar, Kenneth

Macdonald, Ross..... CLC 1, 2, 3, 14, 34, 41
See also Millar, Kenneth
See also DLBD 6

MacDougal, John
See Blish, James (Benjamin)

MacEwen, Gwendolyn (Margaret)
1941-1987 .... CLC 13, 55
See also CA 9-12R; 124; CANR 7, 22;
DLB 53; SATA 50; SATA-Obit 55

Macha, Karel Hynek 1810-1846.. NCLC 46

Machado (y Ruiz), Antonio
1875-1939 .... TCLC 3
See also CA 104; DLB 108

Machado de Assis, Joaquim Maria
1839-1908 .... TCLC 10; BLC
See also CA 107

Machen, Arthur.................. TCLC 4
See also Jones, Arthur Llewellyn
See also DLB 36

Machiavelli, Niccolo 1469-1527 .. LC 8; DA

MacInnes, Colin 1914-1976...... CLC 4, 23
See also CA 69-72; 65-68; CANR 21;
DLB 14; MTCW

MacInnes, Helen (Clark)
1907-1985 .... CLC 27, 39
See also CA 1-4R; 117; CANR 1, 28;
DLB 87; MTCW; SATA 22;
SATA-Obit 44

Mackay, Mary 1855-1924
See Corelli, Marie
See also CA 118

Mackenzie, Compton (Edward Montague)
1883-1972 .... CLC 18
See also CA 21-22; 37-40R; CAP 2;
DLB 34, 100

Mackenzie, Henry 1745-1831 .... NCLC 41
See also DLB 39

Mackintosh, Elizabeth 1896(?)-1952
See Tey, Josephine
See also CA 110

MacLaren, James
See Grieve, C(hristopher) M(urray)

Mac Laverty, Bernard 1942- .... CLC 31
See also CA 116; 118; CANR 43

MacLean, Alistair (Stuart)
1922-1987 .... CLC 3, 13, 50, 63
See also CA 57-60; 121; CANR 28; MTCW;
SATA 23; SATA-Obit 50

Maclean, Norman (Fitzroy)
1902-1990 .... CLC 78; SSC 13
See also CA 102; 132

MacLeish, Archibald
1892-1982 ....CLC 3, 8, 14, 68
See also CA 9-12R; 106; CANR 33; DLB 4,
7, 45; DLBY 82; MTCW

MacLennan, (John) Hugh
1907-1990 .... CLC 2, 14
See also CA 5-8R; 142; CANR 33; DLB 68;
MTCW

MacLeod, Alistair 1936- .... CLC 56
See also CA 123; DLB 60

MacNeice, (Frederick) Louis
1907-1963 .... CLC 1, 4, 10, 53
See also CA 85-88; DLB 10, 20; MTCW

MacNeill, Dand
See Fraser, George MacDonald

Macpherson, James 1736-1796 ...... LC 29
See also DLB 109

Macpherson, (Jean) Jay 1931-...... CLC 14
See also CA 5-8R; DLB 53

MacShane, Frank 1927-........... CLC 39
See also CA 9-12R; CANR 3, 33; DLB 111

Macumber, Mari
See Sandoz, Mari(e Susette)

Madach, Imre 1823-1864........ NCLC 19

Madden, (Jerry) David 1933- .... CLC 5, 15
See also CA 1-4R; CAAS 3; CANR 4, 45;
DLB 6; MTCW

Maddern, Al(an)
See Ellison, Harlan (Jay)

Madhubuti, Haki R.
1942- .... CLC 6, 73; BLC; PC 5
See also Lee, Don L.
See also BW 2; CA 73-76; CANR 24;
DLB 5, 41; DLBD 8

Maepenn, Hugh
See Kuttner, Henry

Maepenn, K. H.
See Kuttner, Henry

Maeterlinck, Maurice 1862-1949 ... TCLC 3
See also CA 104; 136; SATA 66

Maginn, William 1794-1842...... NCLC 8
See also DLB 110

Mahapatra, Jayanta 1928-......... CLC 33
See also CA 73-76; CAAS 9; CANR 15, 33

Mahfouz, Naguib (Abdel Aziz Al-Sabilgi)
1911(?)-
See Mahfuz, Najib
See also BEST 89:2; CA 128; MTCW

Mahfuz, Najib .... CLC 52, 55
See also Mahfouz, Naguib (Abdel Aziz
Al-Sabilgi)
See also DLBY 88

Mahon, Derek 1941-.............. CLC 27
See also CA 113; 128; DLB 40

Mailer, Norman
1923- ...... CLC 1, 2, 3, 4, 5, 8, 11, 14,
28, 39, 74; DA
See also AITN 2; CA 9-12R; CABS 1;
CANR 28; CDALB 1968-1988; DLB 2,
16, 28; DLBD 3; DLBY 80, 83; MTCW

Maillet, Antonine 1929-........... CLC 54
See also CA 115; 120; CANR 46; DLB 60

Mais, Roger 1905-1955 .... TCLC 8
See also BW 1; CA 105; 124; DLB 125;
MTCW

Maistre, Joseph de 1753-1821.... NCLC 37

Maitland, Sara (Louise) 1950-...... CLC 49
See also CA 69-72; CANR 13

Major, Clarence
1936- .... CLC 3, 19, 48; BLC
See also BW 2; CA 21-24R; CAAS 6;
CANR 13, 25; DLB 33

Major, Kevin (Gerald) 1949-....... CLC 26
See also CA 97-100; CANR 21, 38;
CLR 11; DLB 60; JRDA; MAICYA;
SATA 32

Maki, James
See Ozu, Yasujiro

Malabaila, Damiano
See Levi, Primo

Malamud, Bernard
1914-1986 ...... CLC 1, 2, 3, 5, 8, 9, 11,
18, 27, 44, 78, 85; DA; SSC 15; WLC
See also CA 5-8R; 118; CABS 1; CANR 28;
CDALB 1941-1968; DLB 2, 28, 152;
DLBY 80, 86; MTCW

Malaparte, Curzio 1898-1957 ..... TCLC 52

Malcolm, Dan
See Silverberg, Robert

Malcolm X.................. CLC 82; BLC
See also Little, Malcolm

Malherbe, Francois de 1555-1628..... LC 5

Mallarme, Stephane
1842-1898 .... NCLC 4, 41; PC 4

Mallet-Joris, Francoise 1930-...... CLC 11
See also CA 65-68; CANR 17; DLB 83

Malley, Ern
See McAuley, James Phillip

Mallowan, Agatha Christie
See Christie, Agatha (Mary Clarissa)

Maloff, Saul 1922-................ CLC 5
See also CA 33-36R

Malone, Louis
See MacNeice, (Frederick) Louis

Malone, Michael (Christopher)
1942- . . . . **CLC 43**
See also CA 77-80; CANR 14, 32

Malory, (Sir) Thomas
1410(?)-1471(?) . . . . **LC 11; DA**
See also CDBLB Before 1660; DLB 146;
SATA 59; SATA-Brief 33

Malouf, (George Joseph) David
1934- . . . . **CLC 28, 86**
See also CA 124

Malraux, (Georges-)Andre
1901-1976 . . . . . . **CLC 1, 4, 9, 13, 15, 57**
See also CA 21-22; 69-72; CANR 34;
CAP 2; DLB 72; MTCW

Malzberg, Barry N(athaniel) 1939-... **CLC 7**
See also CA 61-64; CAAS 4; CANR 16;
DLB 8

Mamet, David (Alan)
1947- . . . . **CLC 9, 15, 34, 46; DC 4**
See also AAYA 3; CA 81-84; CABS 3;
CANR 15, 41; DLB 7; MTCW

Mamoulian, Rouben (Zachary)
1897-1987 . . . . **CLC 16**
See also CA 25-28R; 124

Mandelstam, Osip (Emilievich)
1891(?)-1938(?) . . . . **TCLC 2, 6**
See also CA 104

Mander, (Mary) Jane 1877-1949... **TCLC 31**

Mandiargues, Andre Pieyre de. . . . . . . **CLC 41**
See also Pieyre de Mandiargues, Andre
See also DLB 83

Mandrake, Ethel Belle
See Thurman, Wallace (Henry)

Mangan, James Clarence
1803-1849 . . . . **NCLC 27**

Maniere, J.-E.
See Giraudoux, (Hippolyte) Jean

Manley, (Mary) Delariviere
1672(?)-1724 . . . . **LC 1**
See also DLB 39, 80

Mann, Abel
See Creasey, John

Mann, (Luiz) Heinrich 1871-1950... **TCLC 9**
See also CA 106; DLB 66

Mann, (Paul) Thomas
1875-1955 . . . . **TCLC 2, 8, 14, 21, 35, 44,
60; DA; SSC 5; WLC**
See also CA 104; 128; DLB 66; MTCW

Manning, David
See Faust, Frederick (Schiller)

Manning, Frederic 1887(?)-1935... **TCLC 25**
See also CA 124

Manning, Olivia 1915-1980 . . . . . . **CLC 5, 19**
See also CA 5-8R; 101; CANR 29; MTCW

Mano, D. Keith 1942- . . . . **CLC 2, 10**
See also CA 25-28R; CAAS 6; CANR 26;
DLB 6

Mansfield, Katherine
. . . . **TCLC 2, 8, 39; SSC 9; WLC**
See also Beauchamp, Kathleen Mansfield

Manso, Peter 1940- . . . . **CLC 39**
See also CA 29-32R; CANR 44

Mantecon, Juan Jimenez
See Jimenez (Mantecon), Juan Ramon

Manton, Peter
See Creasey, John

Man Without a Spleen, A
See Chekhov, Anton (Pavlovich)

Manzoni, Alessandro 1785-1873... **NCLC 29**

Mapu, Abraham (ben Jekutiel)
1808-1867 . . . . **NCLC 18**

Mara, Sally
See Queneau, Raymond

Marat, Jean Paul 1743-1793 . . . . **LC 10**

Marcel, Gabriel Honore
1889-1973 . . . . **CLC 15**
See also CA 102; 45-48; MTCW

Marchbanks, Samuel
See Davies, (William) Robertson

Marchi, Giacomo
See Bassani, Giorgio

Margulies, Donald. . . . . **CLC 76**

Marie de France c. 12th cent. -.... **CMLC 8**

Marie de l'Incarnation 1599-1672.... **LC 10**

Mariner, Scott
See Pohl, Frederik

Marinetti, Filippo Tommaso
1876-1944 . . . . **TCLC 10**
See also CA 107; DLB 114

Marivaux, Pierre Carlet de Chamblain de
1688-1763 . . . . **LC 4**

Markandaya, Kamala . . . . **CLC 8, 38**
See also Taylor, Kamala (Purnaiya)

Markfield, Wallace 1926-. . . . . **CLC 8**
See also CA 69-72; CAAS 3; DLB 2, 28

Markham, Edwin 1852-1940 . . . . . . **TCLC 47**
See also DLB 54

Markham, Robert
See Amis, Kingsley (William)

Marks, J
See Highwater, Jamake (Mamake)

Marks-Highwater, J
See Highwater, Jamake (Mamake)

Markson, David M(errill) 1927- . . . . **CLC 67**
See also CA 49-52; CANR 1

Marley, Bob. . . . . **CLC 17**
See also Marley, Robert Nesta

Marley, Robert Nesta 1945-1981
See Marley, Bob
See also CA 107; 103

Marlowe, Christopher
1564-1593 . . . . . **LC 22; DA; DC 1; WLC**
See also CDBLB Before 1660; DLB 62

Marmontel, Jean-Francois
1723-1799 . . . . **LC 2**

Marquand, John P(hillips)
1893-1960 . . . . **CLC 2, 10**
See also CA 85-88; DLB 9, 102

Marquez, Gabriel (Jose) Garcia
See Garcia Marquez, Gabriel (Jose)

Marquis, Don(ald Robert Perry)
1878-1937 . . . . **TCLC 7**
See also CA 104; DLB 11, 25

Marric, J. J.
See Creasey, John

Marrow, Bernard
See Moore, Brian

Marryat, Frederick 1792-1848 . . . . **NCLC 3**
See also DLB 21

Marsden, James
See Creasey, John

Marsh, (Edith) Ngaio
1899-1982 . . . . **CLC 7, 53**
See also CA 9-12R; CANR 6; DLB 77;
MTCW

Marshall, Garry 1934- . . . . **CLC 17**
See also AAYA 3; CA 111; SATA 60

Marshall, Paule
1929- . . . . **CLC 27, 72; BLC; SSC 3**
See also BW 2; CA 77-80; CANR 25;
DLB 33; MTCW

Marsten, Richard
See Hunter, Evan

Martha, Henry
See Harris, Mark

Martial c. 40-c. 104 . . . . **PC 10**

Martin, Ken
See Hubbard, L(afayette) Ron(ald)

Martin, Richard
See Creasey, John

Martin, Steve 1945- . . . . **CLC 30**
See also CA 97-100; CANR 30; MTCW

Martin, Violet Florence
1862-1915 . . . . **TCLC 51**

Martin, Webber
See Silverberg, Robert

Martindale, Patrick Victor
See White, Patrick (Victor Martindale)

Martin du Gard, Roger
1881-1958 . . . . **TCLC 24**
See also CA 118; DLB 65

Martineau, Harriet 1802-1876 . . . . **NCLC 26**
See also DLB 21, 55; YABC 2

Martines, Julia
See O'Faolain, Julia

Martinez, Jacinto Benavente y
See Benavente (y Martinez), Jacinto

Martinez Ruiz, Jose 1873-1967
See Azorin; Ruiz, Jose Martinez
See also CA 93-96; HW

Martinez Sierra, Gregorio
1881-1947 . . . . **TCLC 6**
See also CA 115

Martinez Sierra, Maria (de la O'LeJarraga)
1874-1974 . . . . **TCLC 6**
See also CA 115

Martinsen, Martin
See Follett, Ken(neth Martin)

Martinson, Harry (Edmund)
1904-1978 . . . . **CLC 14**
See also CA 77-80; CANR 34

Marut, Ret
See Traven, B.

Marut, Robert
See Traven, B.

Marvell, Andrew
1621-1678 . . . . . **LC 4; DA; PC 10; WLC**
See also CDBLB 1660-1789; DLB 131

Marx, Karl (Heinrich)
  1818-1883 .... NCLC 17
  See also DLB 129

Masaoka Shiki. .... TCLC 18
  See also Masaoka Tsunenori

Masaoka Tsunenori 1867-1902
  See Masaoka Shiki
  See also CA 117

Masefield, John (Edward)
  1878-1967 .... CLC 11, 47
  See also CA 19-20; 25-28R; CANR 33;
  CAP 2; CDBLB 1890-1914; DLB 10, 19;
  MTCW; SATA 19

Maso, Carole 19(?)- .... CLC 44

Mason, Bobbie Ann
  1940- .... CLC 28, 43, 82; SSC 4
  See also AAYA 5; CA 53-56; CANR 11,
  31; DLBY 87; MTCW

Mason, Ernst
  See Pohl, Frederik

Mason, Lee W.
  See Malzberg, Barry N(athaniel)

Mason, Nick 1945- .... CLC 35

Mason, Tally
  See Derleth, August (William)

Mass, William
  See Gibson, William

Masters, Edgar Lee
  1868-1950 ...... TCLC 2, 25; DA; PC 1
  See also CA 104; 133; CDALB 1865-1917;
  DLB 54; MTCW

Masters, Hilary 1928- .... CLC 48
  See also CA 25-28R; CANR 13, 47

Mastrosimone, William 19(?)- ...... CLC 36

Mathe, Albert
  See Camus, Albert

Matheson, Richard Burton 1926- ... CLC 37
  See also CA 97-100; DLB 8, 44

Mathews, Harry 1930- .... CLC 6, 52
  See also CA 21-24R; CAAS 6; CANR 18,
  40

Mathews, John Joseph 1894-1979... CLC 84
  See also CA 19-20; 142; CANR 45; CAP 2;
  NNAL

Mathias, Roland (Glyn) 1915- ...... CLC 45
  See also CA 97-100; CANR 19, 41; DLB 27

Matsuo Basho 1644-1694. .... PC 3

Mattheson, Rodney
  See Creasey, John

Matthews, Greg 1949- .... CLC 45
  See also CA 135

Matthews, William 1942- .... CLC 40
  See also CA 29-32R; CAAS 18; CANR 12;
  DLB 5

Matthias, John (Edward) 1941- ...... CLC 9
  See also CA 33-36R

Matthiessen, Peter
  1927- .... CLC 5, 7, 11, 32, 64
  See also AAYA 6; BEST 90:4; CA 9-12R;
  CANR 21; DLB 6; MTCW; SATA 27

Maturin, Charles Robert
  1780(?)-1824 .... NCLC 6

Matute (Ausejo), Ana Maria
  1925- .... CLC 11
  See also CA 89-92; MTCW

Maugham, W. S.
  See Maugham, W(illiam) Somerset

Maugham, W(illiam) Somerset
  1874-1965 ...... CLC 1, 11, 15, 67; DA;
                               SSC 8; WLC
  See also CA 5-8R; 25-28R; CANR 40;
  CDBLB 1914-1945; DLB 10, 36, 77, 100;
  MTCW; SATA 54

Maugham, William Somerset
  See Maugham, W(illiam) Somerset

Maupassant, (Henri Rene Albert) Guy de
  1850-1893 .... NCLC 1, 42; DA; SSC 1;
                               WLC

  See also DLB 123

Maurhut, Richard
  See Traven, B.

Mauriac, Claude 1914- .... CLC 9
  See also CA 89-92; DLB 83

Mauriac, Francois (Charles)
  1885-1970 .... CLC 4, 9, 56
  See also CA 25-28; CAP 2; DLB 65;
  MTCW

Mavor, Osborne Henry 1888-1951
  See Bridie, James
  See also CA 104

Maxwell, William (Keepers, Jr.)
  1908- .... CLC 19
  See also CA 93-96; DLBY 80

May, Elaine 1932- .... CLC 16
  See also CA 124; 142; DLB 44

Mayakovski, Vladimir (Vladimirovich)
  1893-1930 .... TCLC 4, 18
  See also CA 104

Mayhew, Henry 1812-1887 ...... NCLC 31
  See also DLB 18, 55

Maynard, Joyce 1953- .... CLC 23
  See also CA 111; 129

Mayne, William (James Carter)
  1928- .... CLC 12
  See also CA 9-12R; CANR 37; CLR 25;
  JRDA; MAICYA; SAAS 11; SATA 6, 68

Mayo, Jim
  See L'Amour, Louis (Dearborn)

Maysles, Albert 1926- .... CLC 16
  See also CA 29-32R

Maysles, David 1932- .... CLC 16

Mazer, Norma Fox 1931- .... CLC 26
  See also AAYA 5; CA 69-72; CANR 12,
  32; CLR 23; JRDA; MAICYA; SAAS 1;
  SATA 24, 67

Mazzini, Guiseppe 1805-1872 .... NCLC 34

McAuley, James Phillip
  1917-1976 .... CLC 45
  See also CA 97-100

McBain, Ed
  See Hunter, Evan

McBrien, William Augustine
  1930- .... CLC 44
  See also CA 107

McCaffrey, Anne (Inez) 1926- ...... CLC 17
  See also AAYA 6; AITN 2; BEST 89:2;
  CA 25-28R; CANR 15, 35; DLB 8;
  JRDA; MAICYA; MTCW; SAAS 11;
  SATA 8, 70

McCall, Nathan 1955(?)- .... CLC 86
  See also CA 146

McCann, Arthur
  See Campbell, John W(ood, Jr.)

McCann, Edson
  See Pohl, Frederik

McCarthy, Charles, Jr. 1933-
  See McCarthy, Cormac
  See also CANR 42

McCarthy, Cormac 1933- ..... CLC 4, 57, 59
  See also McCarthy, Charles, Jr.
  See also DLB 6, 143

McCarthy, Mary (Therese)
  1912-1989 ... CLC 1, 3, 5, 14, 24, 39, 59
  See also CA 5-8R; 129; CANR 16; DLB 2;
  DLBY 81; MTCW

McCartney, (James) Paul
  1942- .... CLC 12, 35

McCauley, Stephen (D.) 1955- ..... CLC 50
  See also CA 141

McClure, Michael (Thomas)
  1932- .... CLC 6, 10
  See also CA 21-24R; CANR 17, 46;
  DLB 16

McCorkle, Jill (Collins) 1958- ...... CLC 51
  See also CA 121; DLBY 87

McCourt, James 1941- .... CLC 5
  See also CA 57-60

McCoy, Horace (Stanley)
  1897-1955 .... TCLC 28
  See also CA 108; DLB 9

McCrae, John 1872-1918. .... TCLC 12
  See also CA 109; DLB 92

McCreigh, James
  See Pohl, Frederik

McCullers, (Lula) Carson (Smith)
  1917-1967 .... CLC 1, 4, 10, 12, 48; DA;
                               SSC 9; WLC
  See also CA 5-8R; 25-28R; CABS 1, 3;
  CANR 18; CDALB 1941-1968; DLB 2, 7;
  MTCW; SATA 27

McCulloch, John Tyler
  See Burroughs, Edgar Rice

McCullough, Colleen 1938(?)- ...... CLC 27
  See also CA 81-84; CANR 17, 46; MTCW

McElroy, Joseph 1930- .... CLC 5, 47
  See also CA 17-20R

McEwan, Ian (Russell) 1948- ... CLC 13, 66
  See also BEST 90:4; CA 61-64; CANR 14,
  41; DLB 14; MTCW

McFadden, David 1940- .... CLC 48
  See also CA 104; DLB 60

McFarland, Dennis 1950- .... CLC 65

McGahern, John
  1934- .... CLC 5, 9, 48; SSC 17
  See also CA 17-20R; CANR 29; DLB 14;
  MTCW

McGinley, Patrick (Anthony)
  1937- .... CLC 41
  See also CA 120; 127

McGinley, Phyllis 1905-1978 ...... **CLC 14**
See also CA 9-12R; 77-80; CANR 19;
DLB 11, 48; SATA 2, 44; SATA-Obit 24

McGinniss, Joe 1942- .... **CLC 32**
See also AITN 2; BEST 89:2; CA 25-28R;
CANR 26

McGivern, Maureen Daly
See Daly, Maureen

McGrath, Patrick 1950- .... **CLC 55**
See also CA 136

McGrath, Thomas (Matthew)
1916-1990 .... **CLC 28, 59**
See also CA 9-12R; 132; CANR 6, 33;
MTCW; SATA 41; SATA-Obit 66

McGuane, Thomas (Francis III)
1939- .... **CLC 3, 7, 18, 45**
See also AITN 2; CA 49-52; CANR 5, 24;
DLB 2; DLBY 80; MTCW

McGuckian, Medbh 1950- .... **CLC 48**
See also CA 143; DLB 40

McHale, Tom 1942(?)-1982 ...... **CLC 3, 5**
See also AITN 1; CA 77-80; 106

McIlvanney, William 1936- .... **CLC 42**
See also CA 25-28R; DLB 14

McIlwraith, Maureen Mollie Hunter
See Hunter, Mollie
See also SATA 2

McInerney, Jay 1955- .... **CLC 34**
See also CA 116; 123; CANR 45

McIntyre, Vonda N(eel) 1948- ..... **CLC 18**
See also CA 81-84; CANR 17, 34; MTCW

McKay, Claude ..... **TCLC 7, 41; BLC; PC 2**
See also McKay, Festus Claudius
See also DLB 4, 45, 51, 117

McKay, Festus Claudius 1889-1948
See McKay, Claude
See also BW 1; CA 104; 124; DA; MTCW;
WLC

McKuen, Rod 1933- .... **CLC 1, 3**
See also AITN 1; CA 41-44R; CANR 40

McLoughlin, R. B.
See Mencken, H(enry) L(ouis)

McLuhan, (Herbert) Marshall
1911-1980 .... **CLC 37, 83**
See also CA 9-12R; 102; CANR 12, 34;
DLB 88; MTCW

McMillan, Terry (L.) 1951- ..... **CLC 50, 61**
See also BW 2; CA 140

McMurtry, Larry (Jeff)
1936- .... **CLC 2, 3, 7, 11, 27, 44**
See also AITN 2; BEST 89:2; CA 5-8R;
CANR 19, 43; CDALB 1968-1988;
DLB 2, 143; DLBY 80, 87; MTCW

McNally, T. M. 1961- .... **CLC 82**

McNally, Terrence 1939- ...... **CLC 4, 7, 41**
See also CA 45-48; CANR 2; DLB 7

McNamer, Deirdre 1950- .... **CLC 70**

McNeile, Herman Cyril 1888-1937
See Sapper
See also DLB 77

McPhee, John (Angus) 1931- ...... **CLC 36**
See also BEST 90:1; CA 65-68; CANR 20,
46; MTCW

McPherson, James Alan
1943- .... **CLC 19, 77**
See also BW 1; CA 25-28R; CAAS 17;
CANR 24; DLB 38; MTCW

McPherson, William (Alexander)
1933- .... **CLC 34**
See also CA 69-72; CANR 28

Mead, Margaret 1901-1978 .... **CLC 37**
See also AITN 1; CA 1-4R; 81-84;
CANR 4; MTCW; SATA-Obit 20

Meaker, Marijane (Agnes) 1927-
See Kerr, M. E.
See also CA 107; CANR 37; JRDA;
MAICYA; MTCW; SATA 20, 61

Medoff, Mark (Howard) 1940- ... **CLC 6, 23**
See also AITN 1; CA 53-56; CANR 5;
DLB 7

Medvedev, P. N.
See Bakhtin, Mikhail Mikhailovich

Meged, Aharon
See Megged, Aharon

Meged, Aron
See Megged, Aharon

Megged, Aharon 1920- .... **CLC 9**
See also CA 49-52; CAAS 13; CANR 1

Mehta, Ved (Parkash) 1934- .... **CLC 37**
See also CA 1-4R; CANR 2, 23; MTCW

Melanter
See Blackmore, R(ichard) D(oddridge)

Melikow, Loris
See Hofmannsthal, Hugo von

Melmoth, Sebastian
See Wilde, Oscar (Fingal O'Flahertie Wills)

Meltzer, Milton 1915- .... **CLC 26**
See also AAYA 8; CA 13-16R; CANR 38;
CLR 13; DLB 61; JRDA; MAICYA;
SAAS 1; SATA 1, 50, 80

Melville, Herman
1819-1891 ..... **NCLC 3, 12, 29, 45, 49;**
DA; SSC 1, 17; WLC
See also CDALB 1640-1865; DLB 3, 74;
SATA 59

Menander
c. 342B.C.-c. 292B.C. .... **CMLC 9; DC 3**

Mencken, H(enry) L(ouis)
1880-1956 .... **TCLC 13**
See also CA 105; 125; CDALB 1917-1929;
DLB 11, 29, 63, 137; MTCW

Mercer, David 1928-1980. .... **CLC 5**
See also CA 9-12R; 102; CANR 23;
DLB 13; MTCW

Merchant, Paul
See Ellison, Harlan (Jay)

Meredith, George 1828-1909 ... **TCLC 17, 43**
See also CA 117; CDBLB 1832-1890;
DLB 18, 35, 57

Meredith, William (Morris)
1919- .... **CLC 4, 13, 22, 55**
See also CA 9-12R; CAAS 14; CANR 6, 40;
DLB 5

Merezhkovsky, Dmitry Sergeyevich
1865-1941 .... **TCLC 29**

Merimee, Prosper
1803-1870 .... **NCLC 6; SSC 7**
See also DLB 119

Merkin, Daphne 1954- .... **CLC 44**
See also CA 123

Merlin, Arthur
See Blish, James (Benjamin)

Merrill, James (Ingram)
1926-1995 .... **CLC 2, 3, 6, 8, 13, 18, 34**
See also CA 13-16R; CANR 10; DLB 5;
DLBY 85; MTCW

Merriman, Alex
See Silverberg, Robert

Merritt, E. B.
See Waddington, Miriam

Merton, Thomas
1915-1968 .. **CLC 1, 3, 11, 34, 83; PC 10**
See also CA 5-8R; 25-28R; CANR 22;
DLB 48; DLBY 81; MTCW

Merwin, W(illiam) S(tanley)
1927- ... **CLC 1, 2, 3, 5, 8, 13, 18, 45, 88**
See also CA 13-16R; CANR 15; DLB 5;
MTCW

Metcalf, John 1938- .... **CLC 37**
See also CA 113; DLB 60

Metcalf, Suzanne
See Baum, L(yman) Frank

Mew, Charlotte (Mary)
1870-1928 .... **TCLC 8**
See also CA 105; DLB 19, 135

Mewshaw, Michael 1943- .... **CLC 9**
See also CA 53-56; CANR 7, 47; DLBY 80

Meyer, June
See Jordan, June

Meyer, Lynn
See Slavitt, David R(ytman)

Meyer-Meyrink, Gustav 1868-1932
See Meyrink, Gustav
See also CA 117

Meyers, Jeffrey 1939- .... **CLC 39**
See also CA 73-76; DLB 111

Meynell, Alice (Christina Gertrude Thompson)
1847-1922 .... **TCLC 6**
See also CA 104; DLB 19, 98

Meyrink, Gustav .... **TCLC 21**
See also Meyer-Meyrink, Gustav
See also DLB 81

Michaels, Leonard
1933- .... **CLC 6, 25; SSC 16**
See also CA 61-64; CANR 21; DLB 130;
MTCW

Michaux, Henri 1899-1984 ...... **CLC 8, 19**
See also CA 85-88; 114

Michelangelo 1475-1564. .... **LC 12**

Michelet, Jules 1798-1874 .... **NCLC 31**

Michener, James A(lbert)
1907(?)- .... **CLC 1, 5, 11, 29, 60**
See also AITN 1; BEST 90:1; CA 5-8R;
CANR 21, 45; DLB 6; MTCW

Mickiewicz, Adam 1798-1855 ..... **NCLC 3**

Middleton, Christopher 1926- ...... **CLC 13**
See also CA 13-16R; CANR 29; DLB 40

Middleton, Richard (Barham)
1882-1911 .... **TCLC 56**

Middleton, Stanley 1919- .... **CLC 7, 38**
See also CA 25-28R; CANR 21, 46;
DLB 14

Moorcock, Michael (John)
1939- .... CLC **5, 27, 58**
See also CA 45-48; CAAS 5; CANR 2, 17,
38; DLB 14; MTCW

Moore, Brian
1921- .... CLC **1, 3, 5, 7, 8, 19, 32**
See also CA 1-4R; CANR 1, 25, 42; MTCW

Moore, Edward
See Muir, Edwin

Moore, George Augustus
1852-1933 .... TCLC **7**; SSC **19**
See also CA 104; DLB 10, 18, 57, 135

Moore, Lorrie .... CLC **39, 45, 68**
See also Moore, Marie Lorena

Moore, Marianne (Craig)
1887-1972 .... CLC **1, 2, 4, 8, 10, 13, 19,
47; DA; PC 4**
See also CA 1-4R; 33-36R; CANR 3;
CDALB 1929-1941; DLB 45; DLBD 7;
MTCW; SATA 20

Moore, Marie Lorena   1957-
See Moore, Lorrie
See also CA 116; CANR 39

Moore, Thomas   1779-1852....... NCLC **6**
See also DLB 96, 144

Morand, Paul   1888-1976 .... CLC **41**
See also CA 69-72; DLB 65

Morante, Elsa   1918-1985 .... CLC **8, 47**
See also CA 85-88; 117; CANR 35; MTCW

Moravia, Alberto .... CLC **2, 7, 11, 27, 46**
See also Pincherle, Alberto

More, Hannah   1745-1833 .... NCLC **27**
See also DLB 107, 109, 116

More, Henry   1614-1687............. LC **9**
See also DLB 126

More, Sir Thomas   1478-1535 .... LC **10**

Moreas, Jean.................... TCLC **18**
See also Papadiamantopoulos, Johannes

Morgan, Berry   1919- .... CLC **6**
See also CA 49-52; DLB 6

Morgan, Claire
See Highsmith, (Mary) Patricia

Morgan, Edwin (George)   1920- ..... CLC **31**
See also CA 5-8R; CANR 3, 43; DLB 27

Morgan, (George) Frederick
1922- .... CLC **23**
See also CA 17-20R; CANR 21

Morgan, Harriet
See Mencken, H(enry) L(ouis)

Morgan, Jane
See Cooper, James Fenimore

Morgan, Janet   1945- .... CLC **39**
See also CA 65-68

Morgan, Lady   1776(?)-1859...... NCLC **29**
See also DLB 116

Morgan, Robin   1941-.............. CLC **2**
See also CA 69-72; CANR 29; MTCW;
SATA 80

Morgan, Scott
See Kuttner, Henry

Morgan, Seth   1949(?)-1990 .... CLC **65**
See also CA 132

Morgenstern, Christian
1871-1914 .... TCLC **8**
See also CA 105

Morgenstern, S.
See Goldman, William (W.)

Moricz, Zsigmond   1879-1942 ..... TCLC **33**

Morike, Eduard (Friedrich)
1804-1875 .... NCLC **10**
See also DLB 133

Mori Ogai .... TCLC **14**
See also Mori Rintaro

Mori Rintaro   1862-1922
See Mori Ogai
See also CA 110

Moritz, Karl Philipp   1756-1793 ...... LC **2**
See also DLB 94

Morland, Peter Henry
See Faust, Frederick (Schiller)

Morren, Theophil
See Hofmannsthal, Hugo von

Morris, Bill   1952-................ CLC **76**

Morris, Julian
See West, Morris L(anglo)

Morris, Steveland Judkins   1950(?)-
See Wonder, Stevie
See also CA 111

Morris, William   1834-1896 .... NCLC **4**
See also CDBLB 1832-1890; DLB 18, 35, 57

Morris, Wright   1910-... CLC **1, 3, 7, 18, 37**
See also CA 9-12R; CANR 21; DLB 2;
DLBY 81; MTCW

Morrison, Chloe Anthony Wofford
See Morrison, Toni

Morrison, James Douglas   1943-1971
See Morrison, Jim
See also CA 73-76; CANR 40

Morrison, Jim .... CLC **17**
See also Morrison, James Douglas

Morrison, Toni
1931- .... CLC **4, 10, 22, 55, 81, 87;
BLC; DA**
See also AAYA 1; BW 2; CA 29-32R;
CANR 27, 42; CDALB 1968-1988;
DLB 6, 33, 143; DLBY 81; MTCW;
SATA 57

Morrison, Van   1945- .... CLC **21**
See also CA 116

Mortimer, John (Clifford)
1923- .... CLC **28, 43**
See also CA 13-16R; CANR 21;
CDBLB 1960 to Present; DLB 13;
MTCW

Mortimer, Penelope (Ruth)   1918-.... CLC **5**
See also CA 57-60; CANR 45

Morton, Anthony
See Creasey, John

Mosher, Howard Frank   1943-...... CLC **62**
See also CA 139

Mosley, Nicholas   1923-........ CLC **43, 70**
See also CA 69-72; CANR 41; DLB 14

Moss, Howard
1922-1987 .... CLC **7, 14, 45, 50**
See also CA 1-4R; 123; CANR 1, 44;
DLB 5

Mossgiel, Rab
See Burns, Robert

Motion, Andrew   1952-........... CLC **47**
See also DLB 40

Motley, Willard (Francis)
1909-1965 .... CLC **18**
See also BW 1; CA 117; 106; DLB 76, 143

Motoori, Norinaga   1730-1801.... NCLC **45**

Mott, Michael (Charles Alston)
1930- .... CLC **15, 34**
See also CA 5-8R; CAAS 7; CANR 7, 29

Moure, Erin   1955- .... CLC **88**
See also CA 113; DLB 60

Mowat, Farley (McGill)   1921- ..... CLC **26**
See also AAYA 1; CA 1-4R; CANR 4, 24,
42; CLR 20; DLB 68; JRDA; MAICYA;
MTCW; SATA 3, 55

Moyers, Bill   1934-.............. CLC **74**
See also AITN 2; CA 61-64; CANR 31

Mphahlele, Es'kia
See Mphahlele, Ezekiel
See also DLB 125

Mphahlele, Ezekiel   1919-..... CLC **25**; BLC
See also Mphahlele, Es'kia
See also BW 2; CA 81-84; CANR 26

Mqhayi, S(amuel) E(dward) K(rune Loliwe)
1875-1945 .... TCLC **25**; BLC

Mr. Martin
See Burroughs, William S(eward)

Mrozek, Slawomir   1930-........ CLC **3, 13**
See also CA 13-16R; CAAS 10; CANR 29;
MTCW

Mrs. Belloc-Lowndes
See Lowndes, Marie Adelaide (Belloc)

Mtwa, Percy   (?)-................. CLC **47**

Mueller, Lisel   1924-........... CLC **13, 51**
See also CA 93-96; DLB 105

Muir, Edwin   1887-1959 .... TCLC **2**
See also CA 104; DLB 20, 100

Muir, John   1838-1914 .... TCLC **28**

Mujica Lainez, Manuel
1910-1984 .... CLC **31**
See also Lainez, Manuel Mujica
See also CA 81-84; 112; CANR 32; HW

Mukherjee, Bharati   1940-......... CLC **53**
See also BEST 89:2; CA 107; CANR 45;
DLB 60; MTCW

Muldoon, Paul   1951-.......... CLC **32, 72**
See also CA 113; 129; DLB 40

Mulisch, Harry   1927-............. CLC **42**
See also CA 9-12R; CANR 6, 26

Mull, Martin   1943-.............. CLC **17**
See also CA 105

Mulock, Dinah Maria
See Craik, Dinah Maria (Mulock)

Munford, Robert   1737(?)-1783 .... LC **5**
See also DLB 31

Mungo, Raymond   1946-........... CLC **72**
See also CA 49-52; CANR 2

Munro, Alice
1931- .... CLC **6, 10, 19, 50**; SSC **3**
See also AITN 2; CA 33-36R; CANR 33;
DLB 53; MTCW; SATA 29

Nin, Anais
1903-1977 ...... **CLC 1, 4, 8, 11, 14, 60;**
SSC 10
See also AITN 2; CA 13-16R; 69-72;
CANR 22; DLB 2, 4, 152; MTCW

Nissenson, Hugh 1933- .... **CLC 4, 9**
See also CA 17-20R; CANR 27; DLB 28

Niven, Larry .... **CLC 8**
See also Niven, Laurence Van Cott
See also DLB 8

Niven, Laurence Van Cott 1938-
See Niven, Larry
See also CA 21-24R; CAAS 12; CANR 14,
44; MTCW

Nixon, Agnes Eckhardt 1927- ...... **CLC 21**
See also CA 110

Nizan, Paul 1905-1940 .... **TCLC 40**
See also DLB 72

Nkosi, Lewis 1936- .... **CLC 45; BLC**
See also BW 1; CA 65-68; CANR 27

Nodier, (Jean) Charles (Emmanuel)
1780-1844 .... **NCLC 19**
See also DLB 119

Nolan, Christopher 1965- .... **CLC 58**
See also CA 111

Norden, Charles
See Durrell, Lawrence (George)

Nordhoff, Charles (Bernard)
1887-1947 .... **TCLC 23**
See also CA 108; DLB 9; SATA 23

Norfolk, Lawrence 1963- .... **CLC 76**
See also CA 144

Norman, Marsha 1947- .... **CLC 28**
See also CA 105; CABS 3; CANR 41;
DLBY 84

Norris, Benjamin Franklin, Jr.
1870-1902 .... **TCLC 24**
See also Norris, Frank
See also CA 110

Norris, Frank
See Norris, Benjamin Franklin, Jr.
See also CDALB 1865-1917; DLB 12, 71

Norris, Leslie 1921- .... **CLC 14**
See also CA 11-12; CANR 14; CAP 1;
DLB 27

North, Andrew
See Norton, Andre

North, Anthony
See Koontz, Dean R(ay)

North, Captain George
See Stevenson, Robert Louis (Balfour)

North, Milou
See Erdrich, Louise

Northrup, B. A.
See Hubbard, L(afayette) Ron(ald)

North Staffs
See Hulme, T(homas) E(rnest)

Norton, Alice Mary
See Norton, Andre
See also MAICYA; SATA 1, 43

Norton, Andre 1912- .... **CLC 12**
See also Norton, Alice Mary
See also AAYA 14; CA 1-4R; CANR 2, 31;
DLB 8, 52; JRDA; MTCW

Norton, Caroline 1808-1877 ...... **NCLC 47**
See also DLB 21

Norway, Nevil Shute 1899-1960
See Shute, Nevil
See also CA 102; 93-96

Norwid, Cyprian Kamil
1821-1883 .... **NCLC 17**

Nosille, Nabrah
See Ellison, Harlan (Jay)

Nossack, Hans Erich 1901-1978 ..... **CLC 6**
See also CA 93-96; 85-88; DLB 69

Nostradamus 1503-1566 .... **LC 27**

Nosu, Chuji
See Ozu, Yasujiro

Notenburg, Eleanora (Genrikhovna) von
See Guro, Elena

Nova, Craig 1945- .... **CLC 7, 31**
See also CA 45-48; CANR 2

Novak, Joseph
See Kosinski, Jerzy (Nikodem)

Novalis 1772-1801 .... **NCLC 13**
See also DLB 90

Nowlan, Alden (Albert) 1933-1983 .. **CLC 15**
See also CA 9-12R; CANR 5; DLB 53

Noyes, Alfred 1880-1958 .... **TCLC 7**
See also CA 104; DLB 20

Nunn, Kem 19(?)- .... **CLC 34**

Nye, Robert 1939- .... **CLC 13, 42**
See also CA 33-36R; CANR 29; DLB 14;
MTCW; SATA 6

Nyro, Laura 1947- .... **CLC 17**

Oates, Joyce Carol
1938- ...... **CLC 1, 2, 3, 6, 9, 11, 15, 19,**
33, 52; DA; SSC 6; WLC
See also AITN 1; BEST 89:2; CA 5-8R;
CANR 25, 45; CDALB 1968-1988;
DLB 2, 5, 130; DLBY 81; MTCW

O'Brien, Darcy 1939- .... **CLC 11**
See also CA 21-24R; CANR 8

O'Brien, E. G.
See Clarke, Arthur C(harles)

O'Brien, Edna
1936- ... **CLC 3, 5, 8, 13, 36, 65; SSC 10**
See also CA 1-4R; CANR 6, 41;
CDBLB 1960 to Present; DLB 14;
MTCW

O'Brien, Fitz-James 1828-1862... **NCLC 21**
See also DLB 74

O'Brien, Flann .... **CLC 1, 4, 5, 7, 10, 47**
See also O Nuallain, Brian

O'Brien, Richard 1942- .... **CLC 17**
See also CA 124

O'Brien, Tim 1946- .... **CLC 7, 19, 40**
See also CA 85-88; CANR 40; DLB 152;
DLBD 9; DLBY 80

Obstfelder, Sigbjoern 1866-1900 ... **TCLC 23**
See also CA 123

O'Casey, Sean
1880-1964 ...... **CLC 1, 5, 9, 11, 15, 88**
See also CA 89-92; CDBLB 1914-1945;
DLB 10; MTCW

O'Cathasaigh, Sean
See O'Casey, Sean

Ochs, Phil 1940-1976 .... **CLC 17**
See also CA 65-68

O'Connor, Edwin (Greene)
1918-1968 .... **CLC 14**
See also CA 93-96; 25-28R

O'Connor, (Mary) Flannery
1925-1964 .... **CLC 1, 2, 3, 6, 10, 13, 15,**
21, 66; DA; SSC 1; WLC
See also AAYA 7; CA 1-4R; CANR 3, 41;
CDALB 1941-1968; DLB 2, 152;
DLBD 12; DLBY 80; MTCW

O'Connor, Frank .... **CLC 23; SSC 5**
See also O'Donovan, Michael John

O'Dell, Scott 1898-1989 .... **CLC 30**
See also AAYA 3; CA 61-64; 129;
CANR 12, 30; CLR 1, 16; DLB 52;
JRDA; MAICYA; SATA 12, 60

Odets, Clifford 1906-1963 .... **CLC 2, 28**
See also CA 85-88; DLB 7, 26; MTCW

O'Doherty, Brian 1934- .... **CLC 76**
See also CA 105

O'Donnell, K. M.
See Malzberg, Barry N(athaniel)

O'Donnell, Lawrence
See Kuttner, Henry

O'Donovan, Michael John
1903-1966 .... **CLC 14**
See also O'Connor, Frank
See also CA 93-96

Oe, Kenzaburo 1935- .... **CLC 10, 36, 86**
See also CA 97-100; CANR 36; MTCW

O'Faolain, Julia 1932- .... **CLC 6, 19, 47**
See also CA 81-84; CAAS 2; CANR 12;
DLB 14; MTCW

O'Faolain, Sean
1900-1991 .... **CLC 1, 7, 14, 32, 70;**
SSC 13
See also CA 61-64; 134; CANR 12;
DLB 15; MTCW

O'Flaherty, Liam
1896-1984 .... **CLC 5, 34; SSC 6**
See also CA 101; 113; CANR 35; DLB 36;
DLBY 84; MTCW

Ogilvy, Gavin
See Barrie, J(ames) M(atthew)

O'Grady, Standish James
1846-1928 .... **TCLC 5**
See also CA 104

O'Grady, Timothy 1951- .... **CLC 59**
See also CA 138

O'Hara, Frank
1926-1966 .... **CLC 2, 5, 13, 78**
See also CA 9-12R; 25-28R; CANR 33;
DLB 5, 16; MTCW

O'Hara, John (Henry)
1905-1970 .... **CLC 1, 2, 3, 6, 11, 42;**
SSC 15
See also CA 5-8R; 25-28R; CANR 31;
CDALB 1929-1941; DLB 9, 86; DLBD 2;
MTCW

O Hehir, Diana 1922- .... **CLC 41**
See also CA 93-96

Okigbo, Christopher (Ifenayichukwu)
1932-1967 ..... **CLC 25, 84; BLC; PC 7**
See also BW 1; CA 77-80; DLB 125;
MTCW

461

Petrov, Evgeny .... TCLC 21
See also Kataev, Evgeny Petrovich

Petry, Ann (Lane) 1908- ...... CLC 1, 7, 18
See also BW 1; CA 5-8R; CAAS 6;
CANR 4, 46; CLR 12; DLB 76; JRDA;
MAICYA; MTCW; SATA 5

Petursson, Halligrimur 1614-1674 .... LC 8

Philipson, Morris H. 1926- .... CLC 53
See also CA 1-4R; CANR 4

Phillips, David Graham
1867-1911 .... TCLC 44
See also CA 108; DLB 9, 12

Phillips, Jack
See Sandburg, Carl (August)

Phillips, Jayne Anne
1952- .... CLC 15, 33; SSC 16
See also CA 101; CANR 24; DLBY 80;
MTCW

Phillips, Richard
See Dick, Philip K(indred)

Phillips, Robert (Schaeffer) 1938-... CLC 28
See also CA 17-20R; CAAS 13; CANR 8;
DLB 105

Phillips, Ward
See Lovecraft, H(oward) P(hillips)

Piccolo, Lucio 1901-1969......... CLC 13
See also CA 97-100; DLB 114

Pickthall, Marjorie L(owry) C(hristie)
1883-1922 .... TCLC 21
See also CA 107; DLB 92

Pico della Mirandola, Giovanni
1463-1494 .... LC 15

Piercy, Marge
1936- .... CLC 3, 6, 14, 18, 27, 62
See also CA 21-24R; CAAS 1; CANR 13,
43; DLB 120; MTCW

Piers, Robert
See Anthony, Piers

Pieyre de Mandiargues, Andre 1909-1991
See Mandiargues, Andre Pieyre de
See also CA 103; 136; CANR 22

Pilnyak, Boris .... TCLC 23
See also Vogau, Boris Andreyevich

Pincherle, Alberto 1907-1990 ... CLC 11, 18
See also Moravia, Alberto
See also CA 25-28R; 132; CANR 33;
MTCW

Pinckney, Darryl 1953-........... CLC 76
See also BW 2; CA 143

Pindar 518B.C.-446B.C......... CMLC 12

Pineda, Cecile 1942-............. CLC 39
See also CA 118

Pinero, Arthur Wing 1855-1934 ... TCLC 32
See also CA 110; DLB 10

Pinero, Miguel (Antonio Gomez)
1946-1988 .... CLC 4, 55
See also CA 61-64; 125; CANR 29; HW

Pinget, Robert 1919- .... CLC 7, 13, 37
See also CA 85-88; DLB 83

Pink Floyd
See Barrett, (Roger) Syd; Gilmour, David;
Mason, Nick; Waters, Roger; Wright,
Rick

Pinkney, Edward 1802-1828 ..... NCLC 31

Pinkwater, Daniel Manus 1941- .... CLC 35
See also Pinkwater, Manus
See also AAYA 1; CA 29-32R; CANR 12,
38; CLR 4; JRDA; MAICYA; SAAS 3;
SATA 46, 76

Pinkwater, Manus
See Pinkwater, Daniel Manus
See also SATA 8

Pinsky, Robert 1940-........ CLC 9, 19, 38
See also CA 29-32R; CAAS 4; DLBY 82

Pinta, Harold
See Pinter, Harold

Pinter, Harold
1930- ..... CLC 1, 3, 6, 9, 11, 15, 27, 58,
73; DA; WLC
See also CA 5-8R; CANR 33; CDBLB 1960
to Present; DLB 13; MTCW

Pirandello, Luigi
1867-1936 ..... TCLC 4, 29; DA; DC 5;
WLC
See also CA 104

Pirsig, Robert M(aynard)
1928-.................. CLC 4, 6, 73
See also CA 53-56; CANR 42; MTCW;
SATA 39

Pisarev, Dmitry Ivanovich
1840-1868 .... NCLC 25

Pix, Mary (Griffith) 1666-1709 ...... LC 8
See also DLB 80

Pixerecourt, Guilbert de
1773-1844 .... NCLC 39

Plaidy, Jean
See Hibbert, Eleanor Alice Burford

Planche, James Robinson
1796-1880 .... NCLC 42

Plant, Robert 1948-.............. CLC 12

Plante, David (Robert)
1940-.................. CLC 7, 23, 38
See also CA 37-40R; CANR 12, 36;
DLBY 83; MTCW

Plath, Sylvia
1932-1963 ..... CLC 1, 2, 3, 5, 9, 11, 14,
17, 50, 51, 62; DA; PC 1; WLC
See also AAYA 13; CA 19-20; CANR 34;
CAP 2; CDALB 1941-1968; DLB 5, 6,
152; MTCW

Plato 428(?)B.C.-348(?)B.C.... CMLC 8; DA

Platonov, Andrei .... TCLC 14
See also Klimentov, Andrei Platonovich

Platt, Kin 1911- .... CLC 26
See also AAYA 11; CA 17-20R; CANR 11;
JRDA; SAAS 17; SATA 21

Plick et Plock
See Simenon, Georges (Jacques Christian)

Plimpton, George (Ames) 1927-..... CLC 36
See also AITN 1; CA 21-24R; CANR 32;
MTCW; SATA 10

Plomer, William Charles Franklin
1903-1973 .... CLC 4, 8
See also CA 21-22; CANR 34; CAP 2;
DLB 20; MTCW; SATA 24

Plowman, Piers
See Kavanagh, Patrick (Joseph)

Plum, J.
See Wodehouse, P(elham) G(renville)

Plumly, Stanley (Ross) 1939- ...... CLC 33
See also CA 108; 110; DLB 5

Plumpe, Friedrich Wilhelm
1888-1931 .... TCLC 53
See also CA 112

Poe, Edgar Allan
1809-1849 ..... NCLC 1, 16; DA; PC 1;
SSC 1; WLC
See also AAYA 14; CDALB 1640-1865;
DLB 3, 59, 73, 74; SATA 23

Poet of Titchfield Street, The
See Pound, Ezra (Weston Loomis)

Pohl, Frederik 1919- .... CLC 18
See also CA 61-64; CAAS 1; CANR 11, 37;
DLB 8; MTCW; SATA 24

Poirier, Louis 1910-
See Gracq, Julien
See also CA 122; 126

Poitier, Sidney 1927-............. CLC 26
See also BW 1; CA 117

Polanski, Roman 1933- .... CLC 16
See also CA 77-80

Poliakoff, Stephen 1952-.......... CLC 38
See also CA 106; DLB 13

Police, The
See Copeland, Stewart (Armstrong);
Summers, Andrew James; Sumner,
Gordon Matthew

Polidori, John William
1795-1821 .... NCLC 51
See also DLB 116

Pollitt, Katha 1949-............. CLC 28
See also CA 120; 122; MTCW

Pollock, (Mary) Sharon 1936-...... CLC 50
See also CA 141; DLB 60

Polo, Marco 1254-1324 .... CMLC 15

Pomerance, Bernard 1940-........ CLC 13
See also CA 101

Ponge, Francis (Jean Gaston Alfred)
1899-1988 .... CLC 6, 18
See also CA 85-88; 126; CANR 40

Pontoppidan, Henrik 1857-1943 ... TCLC 29

Poole, Josephine .... CLC 17
See also Helyar, Jane Penelope Josephine
See also SAAS 2; SATA 5

Popa, Vasko 1922- .... CLC 19
See also CA 112

Pope, Alexander
1688-1744 .... LC 3; DA; WLC
See also CDBLB 1660-1789; DLB 95, 101

Porter, Connie (Rose) 1959(?)- ..... CLC 70
See also BW 2; CA 142; SATA 81

Porter, Gene(va Grace) Stratton
1863(?)-1924 .... TCLC 21
See also CA 112

Porter, Katherine Anne
1890-1980 ...... CLC 1, 3, 7, 10, 13, 15,
27; DA; SSC 4
See also AITN 2; CA 1-4R; 101; CANR 1;
DLB 4, 9, 102; DLBD 12; DLBY 80;
MTCW; SATA 39; SATA-Obit 23

Porter, Peter (Neville Frederick)
1929- .... CLC 5, 13, 33
See also CA 85-88; DLB 40

Porter, William Sydney 1862-1910
　See Henry, O.
　See also CA 104; 131; CDALB 1865-1917;
　　DA; DLB 12, 78, 79; MTCW; YABC 2

Portillo (y Pacheco), Jose Lopez
　See Lopez Portillo (y Pacheco), Jose

Post, Melville Davisson
　1869-1930 . . . . TCLC 39
　See also CA 110

Potok, Chaim 1929- . . . . CLC 2, 7, 14, 26
　See also AITN 1, 2; CA 17-20R; CANR 19,
　　35; DLB 28, 152; MTCW; SATA 33

Potter, Beatrice
　See Webb, (Martha) Beatrice (Potter)
　See also MAICYA

Potter, Dennis (Christopher George)
　1935-1994 . . . . CLC 58, 86
　See also CA 107; 145; CANR 33; MTCW

Pound, Ezra (Weston Loomis)
　1885-1972 . . . . . . CLC 1, 2, 3, 4, 5, 7, 10,
　　　　　　　　　13, 18, 34, 48, 50; DA; PC 4; WLC
　See also CA 5-8R; 37-40R; CANR 40;
　　CDALB 1917-1929; DLB 4, 45, 63;
　　MTCW

Povod, Reinaldo 1959-1994 . . . . CLC 44
　See also CA 136; 146

Powell, Anthony (Dymoke)
　1905- . . . . CLC 1, 3, 7, 9, 10, 31
　See also CA 1-4R; CANR 1, 32;
　　CDBLB 1945-1960; DLB 15; MTCW

Powell, Dawn 1897-1965 . . . . CLC 66
　See also CA 5-8R

Powell, Padgett 1952-. . . . . CLC 34
　See also CA 126

Powers, J(ames) F(arl)
　1917- . . . . CLC 1, 4, 8, 57; SSC 4
　See also CA 1-4R; CANR 2; DLB 130;
　　MTCW

Powers, John J(ames) 1945-
　See Powers, John R.
　See also CA 69-72

Powers, John R. . . . . CLC 66
　See also Powers, John J(ames)

Pownall, David 1938-. . . . . CLC 10
　See also CA 89-92; CAAS 18; DLB 14

Powys, John Cowper
　1872-1963 . . . . CLC 7, 9, 15, 46
　See also CA 85-88; DLB 15; MTCW

Powys, T(heodore) F(rancis)
　1875-1953 . . . . TCLC 9
　See also CA 106; DLB 36

Prager, Emily 1952-. . . . . CLC 56

Pratt, E(dwin) J(ohn)
　1883(?)-1964 . . . . CLC 19
　See also CA 141; 93-96; DLB 92

Premchand. TCLC 21
　See also Srivastava, Dhanpat Rai

Preussler, Otfried 1923-. . . . . CLC 17
　See also CA 77-80; SATA 24

Prevert, Jacques (Henri Marie)
　1900-1977 . . . . CLC 15
　See also CA 77-80; 69-72; CANR 29;
　　MTCW; SATA-Obit 30

Prevost, Abbe (Antoine Francois)
　1697-1763 . . . . LC 1

Price, (Edward) Reynolds
　1933- . . . . CLC 3, 6, 13, 43, 50, 63
　See also CA 1-4R; CANR 1, 37; DLB 2

Price, Richard 1949- . . . . CLC 6, 12
　See also CA 49-52; CANR 3; DLBY 81

Prichard, Katharine Susannah
　1883-1969 . . . . CLC 46
　See also CA 11-12; CANR 33; CAP 1;
　　MTCW; SATA 66

Priestley, J(ohn) B(oynton)
　1894-1984 . . . . CLC 2, 5, 9, 34
　See also CA 9-12R; 113; CANR 33;
　　CDBLB 1914-1945; DLB 10, 34, 77, 100,
　　139; DLBY 84; MTCW

Prince 1958(?)- . . . . CLC 35

Prince, F(rank) T(empleton) 1912- . . CLC 22
　See also CA 101; CANR 43; DLB 20

Prince Kropotkin
　See Kropotkin, Peter (Aleksieevich)

Prior, Matthew 1664-1721. . . . . LC 4
　See also DLB 95

Pritchard, William H(arrison)
　1932- . . . . CLC 34
　See also CA 65-68; CANR 23; DLB 111

Pritchett, V(ictor) S(awdon)
　1900- . . . . CLC 5, 13, 15, 41; SSC 14
　See also CA 61-64; CANR 31; DLB 15,
　　139; MTCW

Private 19022
　See Manning, Frederic

Probst, Mark 1925- . . . . CLC 59
　See also CA 130

Prokosch, Frederic 1908-1989. . . . CLC 4, 48
　See also CA 73-76; 128; DLB 48

Prophet, The
　See Dreiser, Theodore (Herman Albert)

Prose, Francine 1947-. . . . . CLC 45
　See also CA 109; 112; CANR 46

Proudhon
　See Cunha, Euclides (Rodrigues Pimenta) da

Proulx, E. Annie 1935- . . . . CLC 81

Proust, (Valentin-Louis-George-Eugene-)
　Marcel
　1871-1922 . . . TCLC 7, 13, 33; DA; WLC
　See also CA 104; 120; DLB 65; MTCW

Prowler, Harley
　See Masters, Edgar Lee

Prus, Boleslaw 1845-1912 . . . . TCLC 48

Pryor, Richard (Franklin Lenox Thomas)
　1940- . . . . CLC 26
　See also CA 122

Przybyszewski, Stanislaw
　1868-1927 . . . . TCLC 36
　See also DLB 66

Pteleon
　See Grieve, C(hristopher) M(urray)

Puckett, Lute
　See Masters, Edgar Lee

Puig, Manuel
　1932-1990 . . . CLC 3, 5, 10, 28, 65; HLC
　See also CA 45-48; CANR 2, 32; DLB 113;
　　HW; MTCW

Purdy, Al(fred Wellington)
　1918- . . . . CLC 3, 6, 14, 50
　See also CA 81-84; CAAS 17; CANR 42;
　　DLB 88

Purdy, James (Amos)
　1923- . . . . CLC 2, 4, 10, 28, 52
　See also CA 33-36R; CAAS 1; CANR 19;
　　DLB 2; MTCW

Pure, Simon
　See Swinnerton, Frank Arthur

Pushkin, Alexander (Sergeyevich)
　1799-1837 . . . . NCLC 3, 27; DA; PC 10;
　　　　　　　　　　　　　　　　　　　　　　　WLC
　See also SATA 61

P'u Sung-ling 1640-1715 . . . . LC 3

Putnam, Arthur Lee
　See Alger, Horatio, Jr.

Puzo, Mario 1920-. . . . . CLC 1, 2, 6, 36
　See also CA 65-68; CANR 4, 42; DLB 6;
　　MTCW

Pym, Barbara (Mary Crampton)
　1913-1980 . . . . CLC 13, 19, 37
　See also CA 13-14; 97-100; CANR 13, 34;
　　CAP 1; DLB 14; DLBY 87; MTCW

Pynchon, Thomas (Ruggles, Jr.)
　1937- . . . . . CLC 2, 3, 6, 9, 11, 18, 33, 62,
　　　　　　　　　　　72; DA; SSC 14; WLC
　See also BEST 90:2; CA 17-20R; CANR 22,
　　46; DLB 2; MTCW

Qian Zhongshu
　See Ch'ien Chung-shu

Qroll
　See Dagerman, Stig (Halvard)

Quarrington, Paul (Lewis) 1953-. . . . CLC 65
　See also CA 129

Quasimodo, Salvatore 1901-1968 . . . CLC 10
　See also CA 13-16; 25-28R; CAP 1;
　　DLB 114; MTCW

Queen, Ellery. . . . . CLC 3, 11
　See also Dannay, Frederic; Davidson,
　　Avram; Lee, Manfred B(ennington);
　　Sturgeon, Theodore (Hamilton); Vance,
　　John Holbrook

Queen, Ellery, Jr.
　See Dannay, Frederic; Lee, Manfred
　　B(ennington)

Queneau, Raymond
　1903-1976 . . . . CLC 2, 5, 10, 42
　See also CA 77-80; 69-72; CANR 32;
　　DLB 72; MTCW

Quevedo, Francisco de 1580-1645. . . . LC 23

Quiller-Couch, Arthur Thomas
　1863-1944 . . . . TCLC 53
　See also CA 118; DLB 135

Quin, Ann (Marie) 1936-1973 . . . . CLC 6
　See also CA 9-12R; 45-48; DLB 14

Quinn, Martin
　See Smith, Martin Cruz

Quinn, Simon
　See Smith, Martin Cruz

Quiroga, Horacio (Sylvestre)
　1878-1937 . . . . TCLC 20; HLC
　See also CA 117; 131; HW; MTCW

Quoirez, Francoise 1935-.......... CLC 9
See also Sagan, Francoise
See also CA 49-52; CANR 6, 39; MTCW

Raabe, Wilhelm 1831-1910 .... TCLC 45
See also DLB 129

Rabe, David (William) 1940-... CLC 4, 8, 33
See also CA 85-88; CABS 3; DLB 7

Rabelais, Francois
1483-1553 .... LC 5; DA; WLC

Rabinovitch, Sholem 1859-1916
See Aleichem, Sholom
See also CA 104

Racine, Jean 1639-1699 .... LC 28

Radcliffe, Ann (Ward) 1764-1823 .. NCLC 6
See also DLB 39

Radiguet, Raymond 1903-1923 .... TCLC 29
See also DLB 65

Radnoti, Miklos 1909-1944 .... TCLC 16
See also CA 118

Rado, James 1939-.............. CLC 17
See also CA 105

Radvanyi, Netty 1900-1983
See Seghers, Anna
See also CA 85-88; 110

Rae, Ben
See Griffiths, Trevor

Raeburn, John (Hay) 1941-........ CLC 34
See also CA 57-60

Ragni, Gerome 1942-1991 .... CLC 17
See also CA 105; 134

Rahv, Philip 1908-1973 .... CLC 24
See also Greenberg, Ivan
See also DLB 137

Raine, Craig 1944-.............. CLC 32
See also CA 108; CANR 29; DLB 40

Raine, Kathleen (Jessie) 1908- ... CLC 7, 45
See also CA 85-88; CANR 46; DLB 20;
MTCW

Rainis, Janis 1865-1929 .... TCLC 29

Rakosi, Carl................... CLC 47
See also Rawley, Callman
See also CAAS 5

Raleigh, Richard
See Lovecraft, H(oward) P(hillips)

Rallentando, H. P.
See Sayers, Dorothy L(eigh)

Ramal, Walter
See de la Mare, Walter (John)

Ramon, Juan
See Jimenez (Mantecon), Juan Ramon

Ramos, Graciliano 1892-1953 ..... TCLC 32

Rampersad, Arnold 1941-.......... CLC 44
See also BW 2; CA 127; 133; DLB 111

Rampling, Anne
See Rice, Anne

Ramsay, Allan 1684(?)-1758 .... LC 29
See also DLB 95

Ramuz, Charles-Ferdinand
1878-1947 .... TCLC 33

Rand, Ayn
1905-1982 ..... CLC 3, 30, 44, 79; DA;
WLC
See also AAYA 10; CA 13-16R; 105;
CANR 27; MTCW

Randall, Dudley (Felker)
1914- .... CLC 1; BLC
See also BW 1; CA 25-28R; CANR 23;
DLB 41

Randall, Robert
See Silverberg, Robert

Ranger, Ken
See Creasey, John

Ransom, John Crowe
1888-1974 .... CLC 2, 4, 5, 11, 24
See also CA 5-8R; 49-52; CANR 6, 34;
DLB 45, 63; MTCW

Rao, Raja 1909- .... CLC 25, 56
See also CA 73-76; MTCW

Raphael, Frederic (Michael)
1931- .... CLC 2, 14
See also CA 1-4R; CANR 1; DLB 14

Ratcliffe, James P.
See Mencken, H(enry) L(ouis)

Rathbone, Julian 1935- .... CLC 41
See also CA 101; CANR 34

Rattigan, Terence (Mervyn)
1911-1977 .... CLC 7
See also CA 85-88; 73-76;
CDBLB 1945-1960; DLB 13; MTCW

Ratushinskaya, Irina 1954- .... CLC 54
See also CA 129

Raven, Simon (Arthur Noel)
1927- .... CLC 14
See also CA 81-84

Rawley, Callman 1903-
See Rakosi, Carl
See also CA 21-24R; CANR 12, 32

Rawlings, Marjorie Kinnan
1896-1953 .... TCLC 4
See also CA 104; 137; DLB 9, 22, 102;
JRDA; MAICYA; YABC 1

Ray, Satyajit 1921-1992........ CLC 16, 76
See also CA 114; 137

Read, Herbert Edward 1893-1968.... CLC 4
See also CA 85-88; 25-28R; DLB 20, 149

Read, Piers Paul 1941- ...... CLC 4, 10, 25
See also CA 21-24R; CANR 38; DLB 14;
SATA 21

Reade, Charles 1814-1884 .... NCLC 2
See also DLB 21

Reade, Hamish
See Gray, Simon (James Holliday)

Reading, Peter 1946- .... CLC 47
See also CA 103; CANR 46; DLB 40

Reaney, James 1926- .... CLC 13
See also CA 41-44R; CAAS 15; CANR 42;
DLB 68; SATA 43

Rebreanu, Liviu 1885-1944 .... TCLC 28

Rechy, John (Francisco)
1934- .... CLC 1, 7, 14, 18; HLC
See also CA 5-8R; CAAS 4; CANR 6, 32;
DLB 122; DLBY 82; HW

Redcam, Tom 1870-1933 .... TCLC 25

Reddin, Keith..................... CLC 67

Redgrove, Peter (William)
1932- .... CLC 6, 41
See also CA 1-4R; CANR 3, 39; DLB 40

Redmon, Anne................... CLC 22
See also Nightingale, Anne Redmon
See also DLBY 86

Reed, Eliot
See Ambler, Eric

Reed, Ishmael
1938- ... CLC 2, 3, 5, 6, 13, 32, 60; BLC
See also BW 2; CA 21-24R; CANR 25;
DLB 2, 5, 33; DLBD 8; MTCW

Reed, John (Silas) 1887-1920 ...... TCLC 9
See also CA 106

Reed, Lou....................... CLC 21
See also Firbank, Louis

Reeve, Clara 1729-1807 .... NCLC 19
See also DLB 39

Reich, Wilhelm 1897-1957........ TCLC 57

Reid, Christopher (John) 1949-..... CLC 33
See also CA 140; DLB 40

Reid, Desmond
See Moorcock, Michael (John)

Reid Banks, Lynne 1929-
See Banks, Lynne Reid
See also CA 1-4R; CANR 6, 22, 38;
CLR 24; JRDA; MAICYA; SATA 22, 75

Reilly, William K.
See Creasey, John

Reiner, Max
See Caldwell, (Janet Miriam) Taylor
(Holland)

Reis, Ricardo
See Pessoa, Fernando (Antonio Nogueira)

Remarque, Erich Maria
1898-1970 .... CLC 21; DA
See also CA 77-80; 29-32R; DLB 56;
MTCW

Remizov, A.
See Remizov, Aleksei (Mikhailovich)

Remizov, A. M.
See Remizov, Aleksei (Mikhailovich)

Remizov, Aleksei (Mikhailovich)
1877-1957 .... TCLC 27
See also CA 125; 133

Renan, Joseph Ernest
1823-1892 .... NCLC 26

Renard, Jules 1864-1910 .... TCLC 17
See also CA 117

Renault, Mary.............. CLC 3, 11, 17
See also Challans, Mary
See also DLBY 83

Rendell, Ruth (Barbara) 1930- .. CLC 28, 48
See also Vine, Barbara
See also CA 109; CANR 32; DLB 87;
MTCW

Renoir, Jean 1894-1979 .... CLC 20
See also CA 129; 85-88

Resnais, Alain 1922-............. CLC 16

Reverdy, Pierre 1889-1960 .... CLC 53
See also CA 97-100; 89-92

Rexroth, Kenneth
1905-1982 ...... **CLC 1, 2, 6, 11, 22, 49**
See also CA 5-8R; 107; CANR 14, 34;
CDALB 1941-1968; DLB 16, 48;
DLBY 82; MTCW

Reyes, Alfonso 1889-1959 .... **TCLC 33**
See also CA 131; HW

Reyes y Basoalto, Ricardo Eliecer Neftali
See Neruda, Pablo

Reymont, Wladyslaw (Stanislaw)
1868(?)-1925 .... **TCLC 5**
See also CA 104

Reynolds, Jonathan 1942- .... **CLC 6, 38**
See also CA 65-68; CANR 28

Reynolds, Joshua 1723-1792 .... **LC 15**
See also DLB 104

Reynolds, Michael Shane 1937- .... **CLC 44**
See also CA 65-68; CANR 9

Reznikoff, Charles 1894-1976 .... **CLC 9**
See also CA 33-36; 61-64; CAP 2; DLB 28,
45

Rezzori (d'Arezzo), Gregor von
1914- .... **CLC 25**
See also CA 122; 136

Rhine, Richard
See Silverstein, Alvin

Rhodes, Eugene Manlove
1869-1934 .... **TCLC 53**

R'hoone
See Balzac, Honore de

Rhys, Jean
1890(?)-1979 .... **CLC 2, 4, 6, 14, 19, 51**
See also CA 25-28R; 85-88; CANR 35;
CDBLB 1945-1960; DLB 36, 117; MTCW

Ribeiro, Darcy 1922- .... **CLC 34**
See also CA 33-36R

Ribeiro, Joao Ubaldo (Osorio Pimentel)
1941- .... **CLC 10, 67**
See also CA 81-84

Ribman, Ronald (Burt) 1932- .... **CLC 7**
See also CA 21-24R; CANR 46

Ricci, Nino 1959- .... **CLC 70**
See also CA 137

Rice, Anne 1941- .... **CLC 41**
See also AAYA 9; BEST 89:2; CA 65-68;
CANR 12, 36

Rice, Elmer (Leopold)
1892-1967 .... **CLC 7, 49**
See also CA 21-22; 25-28R; CAP 2; DLB 4,
7; MTCW

Rice, Tim(othy Miles Bindon)
1944- .... **CLC 21**
See also CA 103; CANR 46

Rich, Adrienne (Cecile)
1929- .... **CLC 3, 6, 7, 11, 18, 36, 73, 76;
PC 5**
See also CA 9-12R; CANR 20; DLB 5, 67;
MTCW

Rich, Barbara
See Graves, Robert (von Ranke)

Rich, Robert
See Trumbo, Dalton

Richard, Keith .... **CLC 17**
See also Richards, Keith

Richards, David Adams 1950- ...... **CLC 59**
See also CA 93-96; DLB 53

Richards, I(vor) A(rmstrong)
1893-1979 .... **CLC 14, 24**
See also CA 41-44R; 89-92; CANR 34;
DLB 27

Richards, Keith 1943-
See Richard, Keith
See also CA 107

Richardson, Anne
See Roiphe, Anne (Richardson)

Richardson, Dorothy Miller
1873-1957 .... **TCLC 3**
See also CA 104; DLB 36

Richardson, Ethel Florence (Lindesay)
1870-1946
See Richardson, Henry Handel
See also CA 105

Richardson, Henry Handel .... **TCLC 4**
See also Richardson, Ethel Florence
(Lindesay)

Richardson, Samuel
1689-1761 .... **LC 1; DA; WLC**
See also CDBLB 1660-1789; DLB 39

Richler, Mordecai
1931- .... **CLC 3, 5, 9, 13, 18, 46, 70**
See also AITN 1; CA 65-68; CANR 31;
CLR 17; DLB 53; MAICYA; MTCW;
SATA 44; SATA-Brief 27

Richter, Conrad (Michael)
1890-1968 .... **CLC 30**
See also CA 5-8R; 25-28R; CANR 23;
DLB 9; MTCW; SATA 3

Riddell, J. H. 1832-1906 .... **TCLC 40**

Riding, Laura .... **CLC 3, 7**
See also Jackson, Laura (Riding)

Riefenstahl, Berta Helene Amalia 1902-
See Riefenstahl, Leni
See also CA 108

Riefenstahl, Leni .... **CLC 16**
See also Riefenstahl, Berta Helene Amalia

Riffe, Ernest
See Bergman, (Ernst) Ingmar

Riggs, (Rolla) Lynn 1899-1954 .... **TCLC 56**
See also CA 144; NNAL

Riley, James Whitcomb
1849-1916 .... **TCLC 51**
See also CA 118; 137; MAICYA; SATA 17

Riley, Tex
See Creasey, John

Rilke, Rainer Maria
1875-1926 .... **TCLC 1, 6, 19; PC 2**
See also CA 104; 132; DLB 81; MTCW

Rimbaud, (Jean Nicolas) Arthur
1854-1891 ..... **NCLC 4, 35; DA; PC 3;
WLC**

Rinehart, Mary Roberts
1876-1958 .... **TCLC 52**
See also CA 108

Ringmaster, The
See Mencken, H(enry) L(ouis)

Ringwood, Gwen(dolyn Margaret) Pharis
1910-1984 .... **CLC 48**
See also CA 112; DLB 88

Rio, Michel 19(?)- .... **CLC 43**

Ritsos, Giannes
See Ritsos, Yannis

Ritsos, Yannis 1909-1990 ..... **CLC 6, 13, 31**
See also CA 77-80; 133; CANR 39; MTCW

Ritter, Erika 1948(?)- .... **CLC 52**

Rivera, Jose Eustasio 1889-1928 ... **TCLC 35**
See also HW

Rivers, Conrad Kent 1933-1968 ...... **CLC 1**
See also BW 1; CA 85-88; DLB 41

Rivers, Elfrida
See Bradley, Marion Zimmer

Riverside, John
See Heinlein, Robert A(nson)

Rizal, Jose 1861-1896 .... **NCLC 27**

Roa Bastos, Augusto (Antonio)
1917- .... **CLC 45; HLC**
See also CA 131; DLB 113; HW

Robbe-Grillet, Alain
1922- ...... **CLC 1, 2, 4, 6, 8, 10, 14, 43**
See also CA 9-12R; CANR 33; DLB 83;
MTCW

Robbins, Harold 1916- .... **CLC 5**
See also CA 73-76; CANR 26; MTCW

Robbins, Thomas Eugene 1936-
See Robbins, Tom
See also CA 81-84; CANR 29; MTCW

Robbins, Tom .... **CLC 9, 32, 64**
See also Robbins, Thomas Eugene
See also BEST 90:3; DLBY 80

Robbins, Trina 1938- .... **CLC 21**
See also CA 128

Roberts, Charles G(eorge) D(ouglas)
1860-1943 .... **TCLC 8**
See also CA 105; CLR 33; DLB 92;
SATA-Brief 29

Roberts, Kate 1891-1985 .... **CLC 15**
See also CA 107; 116

Roberts, Keith (John Kingston)
1935- .... **CLC 14**
See also CA 25-28R; CANR 46

Roberts, Kenneth (Lewis)
1885-1957 .... **TCLC 23**
See also CA 109; DLB 9

Roberts, Michele (B.) 1949- .... **CLC 48**
See also CA 115

Robertson, Ellis
See Ellison, Harlan (Jay); Silverberg, Robert

Robertson, Thomas William
1829-1871 .... **NCLC 35**

Robinson, Edwin Arlington
1869-1935 .... **TCLC 5; DA; PC 1**
See also CA 104; 133; CDALB 1865-1917;
DLB 54; MTCW

Robinson, Henry Crabb
1775-1867 .... **NCLC 15**
See also DLB 107

Robinson, Jill 1936- .... **CLC 10**
See also CA 102

Robinson, Kim Stanley 1952- ...... **CLC 34**
See also CA 126

Robinson, Lloyd
See Silverberg, Robert

Robinson, Marilynne 1944- .... **CLC 25**
See also CA 116

Robinson, Smokey.................. CLC 21
See also Robinson, William, Jr.

Robinson, William, Jr.   1940-
See Robinson, Smokey
See also CA 116

Robison, Mary   1949-............. CLC 42
See also CA 113; 116; DLB 130

Rod, Edouard   1857-1910 .... TCLC 52

Roddenberry, Eugene Wesley   1921-1991
See Roddenberry, Gene
See also CA 110; 135; CANR 37; SATA 45;
SATA-Obit 69

Roddenberry, Gene .... CLC 17
See also Roddenberry, Eugene Wesley
See also AAYA 5; SATA-Obit 69

Rodgers, Mary   1931-.............. CLC 12
See also CA 49-52; CANR 8; CLR 20;
JRDA; MAICYA; SATA 8

Rodgers, W(illiam) R(obert)
1909-1969 .... CLC 7
See also CA 85-88; DLB 20

Rodman, Eric
See Silverberg, Robert

Rodman, Howard   1920(?)-1985..... CLC 65
See also CA 118

Rodman, Maia
See Wojciechowska, Maia (Teresa)

Rodriguez, Claudio   1934-......... CLC 10
See also DLB 134

Roelvaag, O(le) E(dvart)
1876-1931 .... TCLC 17
See also CA 117; DLB 9

Roethke, Theodore (Huebner)
1908-1963 ...... CLC 1, 3, 8, 11, 19, 46
See also CA 81-84; CABS 2;
CDALB 1941-1968; DLB 5; MTCW

Rogers, Thomas Hunton   1927-..... CLC 57
See also CA 89-92

Rogers, Will(iam Penn Adair)
1879-1935 .... TCLC 8
See also CA 105; 144; DLB 11; NNAL

Rogin, Gilbert   1929-.............. CLC 18
See also CA 65-68; CANR 15

Rohan, Koda .... TCLC 22
See also Koda Shigeyuki

Rohmer, Eric.................... CLC 16
See also Scherer, Jean-Marie Maurice

Rohmer, Sax .... TCLC 28
See also Ward, Arthur Henry Sarsfield
See also DLB 70

Roiphe, Anne (Richardson)
1935-..................... CLC 3, 9
See also CA 89-92; CANR 45; DLBY 80

Rojas, Fernando de   1465-1541 ..... LC 23

Rolfe, Frederick (William Serafino Austin
Lewis Mary)   1860-1913...... TCLC 12
See also CA 107; DLB 34

Rolland, Romain   1866-1944....... TCLC 23
See also CA 118; DLB 65

Rolvaag, O(le) E(dvart)
See Roelvaag, O(le) E(dvart)

Romain Arnaud, Saint
See Aragon, Louis

Romains, Jules   1885-1972 .... CLC 7
See also CA 85-88; CANR 34; DLB 65;
MTCW

Romero, Jose Ruben   1890-1952 ... TCLC 14
See also CA 114; 131; HW

Ronsard, Pierre de
1524-1585 .... LC 6; PC 11

Rooke, Leon   1934-............. CLC 25, 34
See also CA 25-28R; CANR 23

Roper, William   1498-1578......... LC 10

Roquelaure, A. N.
See Rice, Anne

Rosa, Joao Guimaraes   1908-1967... CLC 23
See also CA 89-92; DLB 113

Rose, Wendy   1948-........ CLC 85; PC 12
See also CA 53-56; CANR 5; NNAL;
SATA 12

Rosen, Richard (Dean)   1949-...... CLC 39
See also CA 77-80

Rosenberg, Isaac   1890-1918...... TCLC 12
See also CA 107; DLB 20

Rosenblatt, Joe .... CLC 15
See also Rosenblatt, Joseph

Rosenblatt, Joseph   1933-
See Rosenblatt, Joe
See also CA 89-92

Rosenfeld, Samuel   1896-1963
See Tzara, Tristan
See also CA 89-92

Rosenthal, M(acha) L(ouis)   1917-... CLC 28
See also CA 1-4R; CAAS 6; CANR 4;
DLB 5; SATA 59

Ross, Barnaby
See Dannay, Frederic

Ross, Bernard L.
See Follett, Ken(neth Martin)

Ross, J. H.
See Lawrence, T(homas) E(dward)

Ross, Martin
See Martin, Violet Florence
See also DLB 135

Ross, (James) Sinclair   1908-....... CLC 13
See also CA 73-76; DLB 88

Rossetti, Christina (Georgina)
1830-1894 ..... NCLC 2, 50; DA; PC 7;
WLC
See also DLB 35; MAICYA; SATA 20

Rossetti, Dante Gabriel
1828-1882 .... NCLC 4; DA; WLC
See also CDBLB 1832-1890; DLB 35

Rossner, Judith (Perelman)
1935-................... CLC 6, 9, 29
See also AITN 2; BEST 90:3; CA 17-20R;
CANR 18; DLB 6; MTCW

Rostand, Edmond (Eugene Alexis)
1868-1918 .... TCLC 6, 37; DA
See also CA 104; 126; MTCW

Roth, Henry   1906-............ CLC 2, 6, 11
See also CA 11-12; CANR 38; CAP 1;
DLB 28; MTCW

Roth, Joseph   1894-1939......... TCLC 33
See also DLB 85

Roth, Philip (Milton)
1933-...... CLC 1, 2, 3, 4, 6, 9, 15, 22,
31, 47, 66, 86; DA; WLC
See also BEST 90:3; CA 1-4R; CANR 1, 22,
36; CDALB 1968-1988; DLB 2, 28;
DLBY 82; MTCW

Rothenberg, Jerome   1931-....... CLC 6, 57
See also CA 45-48; CANR 1; DLB 5

Roumain, Jacques (Jean Baptiste)
1907-1944 .... TCLC 19; BLC
See also BW 1; CA 117; 125

Rourke, Constance (Mayfield)
1885-1941 .... TCLC 12
See also CA 107; YABC 1

Rousseau, Jean-Baptiste   1671-1741 ... LC 9

Rousseau, Jean-Jacques
1712-1778 .... LC 14; DA; WLC

Roussel, Raymond   1877-1933 ..... TCLC 20
See also CA 117

Rovit, Earl (Herbert)   1927-......... CLC 7
See also CA 5-8R; CANR 12

Rowe, Nicholas   1674-1718........... LC 8
See also DLB 84

Rowley, Ames Dorrance
See Lovecraft, H(oward) P(hillips)

Rowson, Susanna Haswell
1762(?)-1824 .... NCLC 5
See also DLB 37

Roy, Gabrielle   1909-1983....... CLC 10, 14
See also CA 53-56; 110; CANR 5; DLB 68;
MTCW

Rozewicz, Tadeusz   1921-........ CLC 9, 23
See also CA 108; CANR 36; MTCW

Ruark, Gibbons   1941- .... CLC 3
See also CA 33-36R; CANR 14, 31;
DLB 120

Rubens, Bernice (Ruth)   1923-... CLC 19, 31
See also CA 25-28R; CANR 33; DLB 14;
MTCW

Rudkin, (James) David   1936- ...... CLC 14
See also CA 89-92; DLB 13

Rudnik, Raphael   1933-............. CLC 7
See also CA 29-32R

Ruffian, M.
See Hasek, Jaroslav (Matej Frantisek)

Ruiz, Jose Martinez .... CLC 11
See also Martinez Ruiz, Jose

Rukeyser, Muriel
1913-1980 .... CLC 6, 10, 15, 27; PC 12
See also CA 5-8R; 93-96; CANR 26;
DLB 48; MTCW; SATA-Obit 22

Rule, Jane (Vance)   1931-.......... CLC 27
See also CA 25-28R; CAAS 18; CANR 12;
DLB 60

Rulfo, Juan   1918-1986.... CLC 8, 80; HLC
See also CA 85-88; 118; CANR 26;
DLB 113; HW; MTCW

Runeberg, Johan   1804-1877...... NCLC 41

Runyon, (Alfred) Damon
1884(?)-1946 .... TCLC 10
See also CA 107; DLB 11, 86

Rush, Norman   1933-.............. CLC 44
See also CA 121; 126

Saroyan, William
1908-1981 ..... **CLC 1, 8, 10, 29, 34, 56;
DA; WLC**
See also CA 5-8R; 103; CANR 30; DLB 7,
9, 86; DLBY 81; MTCW; SATA 23;
SATA-Obit 24

Sarraute, Nathalie
1900- .... **CLC 1, 2, 4, 8, 10, 31, 80**
See also CA 9-12R; CANR 23; DLB 83;
MTCW

Sarton, (Eleanor) May
1912- .... **CLC 4, 14, 49**
See also CA 1-4R; CANR 1, 34; DLB 48;
DLBY 81; MTCW; SATA 36

Sartre, Jean-Paul
1905-1980 .... **CLC 1, 4, 7, 9, 13, 18, 24,
44, 50, 52; DA; DC 3; WLC**
See also CA 9-12R; 97-100; CANR 21;
DLB 72; MTCW

Sassoon, Siegfried (Lorraine)
1886-1967 .... **CLC 36; PC 12**
See also CA 104; 25-28R; CANR 36;
DLB 20; MTCW

Satterfield, Charles
See Pohl, Frederik

Saul, John (W. III) 1942- .... **CLC 46**
See also AAYA 10; BEST 90:4; CA 81-84;
CANR 16, 40

Saunders, Caleb
See Heinlein, Robert A(nson)

Saura (Atares), Carlos 1932- .... **CLC 20**
See also CA 114; 131; HW

Sauser-Hall, Frederic 1887-1961.... **CLC 18**
See also Cendrars, Blaise
See also CA 102; 93-96; CANR 36; MTCW

Saussure, Ferdinand de
1857-1913 .... **TCLC 49**

Savage, Catharine
See Brosman, Catharine Savage

Savage, Thomas 1915- .... **CLC 40**
See also CA 126; 132; CAAS 15

Savan, Glenn 19(?)- .... **CLC 50**

Sayers, Dorothy L(eigh)
1893-1957 ....**TCLC 2, 15**
See also CA 104; 119; CDBLB 1914-1945;
DLB 10, 36, 77, 100; MTCW

Sayers, Valerie 1952-............. **CLC 50**
See also CA 134

Sayles, John (Thomas)
1950- .... **CLC 7, 10, 14**
See also CA 57-60; CANR 41; DLB 44

Scammell, Michael .... **CLC 34**

Scannell, Vernon 1922- .... **CLC 49**
See also CA 5-8R; CANR 8, 24; DLB 27;
SATA 59

Scarlett, Susan
See Streatfeild, (Mary) Noel

Schaeffer, Susan Fromberg
1941- .... **CLC 6, 11, 22**
See also CA 49-52; CANR 18; DLB 28;
MTCW; SATA 22

Schary, Jill
See Robinson, Jill

Schell, Jonathan 1943-............ **CLC 35**
See also CA 73-76; CANR 12

Schelling, Friedrich Wilhelm Joseph von
1775-1854 .... **NCLC 30**
See also DLB 90

Schendel, Arthur van 1874-1946... **TCLC 56**

Scherer, Jean-Marie Maurice 1920-
See Rohmer, Eric
See also CA 110

Schevill, James (Erwin) 1920-....... **CLC 7**
See also CA 5-8R; CAAS 12

Schiller, Friedrich 1759-1805 .... **NCLC 39**
See also DLB 94

Schisgal, Murray (Joseph) 1926-..... **CLC 6**
See also CA 21-24R

Schlee, Ann 1934-................. **CLC 35**
See also CA 101; CANR 29; SATA 44;
SATA-Brief 36

Schlegel, August Wilhelm von
1767-1845 .... **NCLC 15**
See also DLB 94

Schlegel, Friedrich 1772-1829 .... **NCLC 45**
See also DLB 90

Schlegel, Johann Elias (von)
1719(?)-1749 .... **LC 5**

Schlesinger, Arthur M(eier), Jr.
1917- .... **CLC 84**
See also AITN 1; CA 1-4R; CANR 1, 28;
DLB 17; MTCW; SATA 61

Schmidt, Arno (Otto) 1914-1979.... **CLC 56**
See also CA 128; 109; DLB 69

Schmitz, Aron Hector 1861-1928
See Svevo, Italo
See also CA 104; 122; MTCW

Schnackenberg, Gjertrud 1953-..... **CLC 40**
See also CA 116; DLB 120

Schneider, Leonard Alfred 1925-1966
See Bruce, Lenny
See also CA 89-92

Schnitzler, Arthur
1862-1931 .... **TCLC 4; SSC 15**
See also CA 104; DLB 81, 118

Schopenhauer, Arthur
1788-1860 .... **NCLC 51**
See also DLB 90

Schor, Sandra (M.) 1932(?)-1990 ... **CLC 65**
See also CA 132

Schorer, Mark 1908-1977 .... **CLC 9**
See also CA 5-8R; 73-76; CANR 7;
DLB 103

Schrader, Paul (Joseph) 1946-...... **CLC 26**
See also CA 37-40R; CANR 41; DLB 44

Schreiner, Olive (Emilie Albertina)
1855-1920 .... **TCLC 9**
See also CA 105; DLB 18

Schulberg, Budd (Wilson)
1914- .... **CLC 7, 48**
See also CA 25-28R; CANR 19; DLB 6, 26,
28; DLBY 81

Schulz, Bruno
1892-1942 .... **TCLC 5, 51; SSC 13**
See also CA 115; 123

Schulz, Charles M(onroe) 1922- .... **CLC 12**
See also CA 9-12R; CANR 6; SATA 10

Schumacher, E(rnst) F(riedrich)
1911-1977 .... **CLC 80**
See also CA 81-84; 73-76; CANR 34

Schuyler, James Marcus
1923-1991 .... **CLC 5, 23**
See also CA 101; 134; DLB 5

Schwartz, Delmore (David)
1913-1966 ... **CLC 2, 4, 10, 45, 87; PC 8**
See also CA 17-18; 25-28R; CANR 35;
CAP 2; DLB 28, 48; MTCW

Schwartz, Ernst
See Ozu, Yasujiro

Schwartz, John Burnham 1965- .... **CLC 59**
See also CA 132

Schwartz, Lynne Sharon 1939-..... **CLC 31**
See also CA 103; CANR 44

Schwartz, Muriel A.
See Eliot, T(homas) S(tearns)

Schwarz-Bart, Andre 1928-........ **CLC 2, 4**
See also CA 89-92

Schwarz-Bart, Simone 1938-........ **CLC 7**
See also BW 2; CA 97-100

Schwob, (Mayer Andre) Marcel
1867-1905 .... **TCLC 20**
See also CA 117; DLB 123

Sciascia, Leonardo
1921-1989 .... **CLC 8, 9, 41**
See also CA 85-88; 130; CANR 35; MTCW

Scoppettone, Sandra 1936-......... **CLC 26**
See also AAYA 11; CA 5-8R; CANR 41;
SATA 9

Scorsese, Martin 1942- .... **CLC 20**
See also CA 110; 114; CANR 46

Scotland, Jay
See Jakes, John (William)

Scott, Duncan Campbell
1862-1947 .... **TCLC 6**
See also CA 104; DLB 92

Scott, Evelyn 1893-1963........... **CLC 43**
See also CA 104; 112; DLB 9, 48

Scott, F(rancis) R(eginald)
1899-1985 .... **CLC 22**
See also CA 101; 114; DLB 88

Scott, Frank
See Scott, F(rancis) R(eginald)

Scott, Joanna 1960- .... **CLC 50**
See also CA 126

Scott, Paul (Mark) 1920-1978.... **CLC 9, 60**
See also CA 81-84; 77-80; CANR 33;
DLB 14; MTCW

Scott, Walter
1771-1832 ...... **NCLC 15; DA; PC 12;
WLC**
See also CDBLB 1789-1832; DLB 93, 107,
116, 144; YABC 2

Scribe, (Augustin) Eugene
1791-1861 .... **NCLC 16; DC 5**

Scrum, R.
See Crumb, R(obert)

Scudery, Madeleine de 1607-1701..... **LC 2**

Scum
See Crumb, R(obert)

Scumbag, Little Bobby
See Crumb, R(obert)

Seabrook, John
See Hubbard, L(afayette) Ron(ald)

Sealy, I. Allan 1951- .... **CLC 55**

Search, Alexander
See Pessoa, Fernando (Antonio Nogueira)

Sebastian, Lee
See Silverberg, Robert

Sebastian Owl
See Thompson, Hunter S(tockton)

Sebestyen, Ouida 1924- .... **CLC 30**
See also AAYA 8; CA 107; CANR 40;
CLR 17; JRDA; MAICYA; SAAS 10;
SATA 39

Secundus, H. Scriblerus
See Fielding, Henry

Sedges, John
See Buck, Pearl S(ydenstricker)

Sedgwick, Catharine Maria
1789-1867 .... **NCLC 19**
See also DLB 1, 74

Seelye, John 1931- .... **CLC 7**

Seferiades, Giorgos Stylianou 1900-1971
See Seferis, George
See also CA 5-8R; 33-36R; CANR 5, 36;
MTCW

Seferis, George .... **CLC 5, 11**
See also Seferiades, Giorgos Stylianou

Segal, Erich (Wolf) 1937- .... **CLC 3, 10**
See also BEST 89:1; CA 25-28R; CANR 20,
36; DLBY 86; MTCW

Seger, Bob 1945- .... **CLC 35**

Seghers, Anna .... **CLC 7**
See also Radvanyi, Netty
See also DLB 69

Seidel, Frederick (Lewis) 1936- ..... **CLC 18**
See also CA 13-16R; CANR 8; DLBY 84

Seifert, Jaroslav 1901-1986 ..... **CLC 34, 44**
See also CA 127; MTCW

Sei Shonagon c. 966-1017(?) ...... **CMLC 6**

Selby, Hubert, Jr. 1928- ..... **CLC 1, 2, 4, 8**
See also CA 13-16R; CANR 33; DLB 2

Selzer, Richard 1928- .... **CLC 74**
See also CA 65-68; CANR 14

Sembene, Ousmane
See Ousmane, Sembene

Senancour, Etienne Pivert de
1770-1846 .... **NCLC 16**
See also DLB 119

Sender, Ramon (Jose)
1902-1982 .... **CLC 8; HLC**
See also CA 5-8R; 105; CANR 8; HW;
MTCW

Seneca, Lucius Annaeus
4B.C.-65. .... **CMLC 6; DC 5**

Senghor, Leopold Sedar
1906- .... **CLC 54; BLC**
See also BW 2; CA 116; 125; CANR 47;
MTCW

Serling, (Edward) Rod(man)
1924-1975 .... **CLC 30**
See also AAYA 14; AITN 1; CA 65-68;
57-60; DLB 26

Serna, Ramon Gomez de la
See Gomez de la Serna, Ramon

Serpieres
See Guillevic, (Eugene)

Service, Robert
See Service, Robert W(illiam)
See also DLB 92

Service, Robert W(illiam)
1874(?)-1958 ...... **TCLC 15; DA; WLC**
See also Service, Robert
See also CA 115; 140; SATA 20

Seth, Vikram 1952- .... **CLC 43**
See also CA 121; 127; DLB 120

Seton, Cynthia Propper
1926-1982 .... **CLC 27**
See also CA 5-8R; 108; CANR 7

Seton, Ernest (Evan) Thompson
1860-1946 .... **TCLC 31**
See also CA 109; DLB 92; JRDA; SATA 18

Seton-Thompson, Ernest
See Seton, Ernest (Evan) Thompson

Settle, Mary Lee 1918- .... **CLC 19, 61**
See also CA 89-92; CAAS 1; CANR 44;
DLB 6

Seuphor, Michel
See Arp, Jean

**Sevigne, Marie (de Rabutin-Chantal) Marquise
de** 1626-1696 .... **LC 11**

Sexton, Anne (Harvey)
1928-1974 .... **CLC 2, 4, 6, 8, 10, 15, 53;
DA; PC 2; WLC**
See also CA 1-4R; 53-56; CABS 2;
CANR 3, 36; CDALB 1941-1968; DLB 5;
MTCW; SATA 10

Shaara, Michael (Joseph Jr.)
1929-1988 .... **CLC 15**
See also AITN 1; CA 102; DLBY 83

Shackleton, C. C.
See Aldiss, Brian W(ilson)

Shacochis, Bob .... **CLC 39**
See also Shacochis, Robert G.

Shacochis, Robert G. 1951-
See Shacochis, Bob
See also CA 119; 124

Shaffer, Anthony (Joshua) 1926- .... **CLC 19**
See also CA 110; 116; DLB 13

Shaffer, Peter (Levin)
1926- .... **CLC 5, 14, 18, 37, 60**
See also CA 25-28R; CANR 25, 47;
CDBLB 1960 to Present; DLB 13;
MTCW

Shakey, Bernard
See Young, Neil

Shalamov, Varlam (Tikhonovich)
1907(?)-1982 .... **CLC 18**
See also CA 129; 105

Shamlu, Ahmad 1925- .... **CLC 10**

Shammas, Anton 1951- .... **CLC 55**

Shange, Ntozake
1948- .... **CLC 8, 25, 38, 74; BLC; DC 3**
See also AAYA 9; BW 2; CA 85-88;
CABS 3; CANR 27; DLB 38; MTCW

Shanley, John Patrick 1950- .... **CLC 75**
See also CA 128; 133

Shapcott, Thomas William 1935- ... **CLC 38**
See also CA 69-72

Shapiro, Jane .... **CLC 76**

Shapiro, Karl (Jay) 1913- .. **CLC 4, 8, 15, 53**
See also CA 1-4R; CAAS 6; CANR 1, 36;
DLB 48; MTCW

Sharp, William 1855-1905 .... **TCLC 39**

Sharpe, Thomas Ridley 1928-
See Sharpe, Tom
See also CA 114; 122

Sharpe, Tom. .... **CLC 36**
See also Sharpe, Thomas Ridley
See also DLB 14

Shaw, Bernard. .... **TCLC 45**
See also Shaw, George Bernard
See also BW 1

Shaw, G. Bernard
See Shaw, George Bernard

Shaw, George Bernard
1856-1950 .... **TCLC 3, 9, 21; DA; WLC**
See also Shaw, Bernard
See also CA 104; 128; CDBLB 1914-1945;
DLB 10, 57; MTCW

Shaw, Henry Wheeler
1818-1885 .... **NCLC 15**
See also DLB 11

Shaw, Irwin 1913-1984...... **CLC 7, 23, 34**
See also AITN 1; CA 13-16R; 112;
CANR 21; CDALB 1941-1968; DLB 6,
102; DLBY 84; MTCW

Shaw, Robert 1927-1978 .... **CLC 5**
See also AITN 1; CA 1-4R; 81-84;
CANR 4; DLB 13, 14

Shaw, T. E.
See Lawrence, T(homas) E(dward)

Shawn, Wallace 1943- .... **CLC 41**
See also CA 112

Shea, Lisa 1953- .... **CLC 86**

Sheed, Wilfrid (John Joseph)
1930- .... **CLC 2, 4, 10, 53**
See also CA 65-68; CANR 30; DLB 6;
MTCW

Sheldon, Alice Hastings Bradley
1915(?)-1987
See Tiptree, James, Jr.
See also CA 108; 122; CANR 34; MTCW

Sheldon, John
See Bloch, Robert (Albert)

Shelley, Mary Wollstonecraft (Godwin)
1797-1851 .... **NCLC 14; DA; WLC**
See also CDBLB 1789-1832; DLB 110, 116;
SATA 29

Shelley, Percy Bysshe
1792-1822 ...... **NCLC 18; DA; WLC**
See also CDBLB 1789-1832; DLB 96, 110

Shepard, Jim 1956- .... **CLC 36**
See also CA 137

Shepard, Lucius 1947- .... **CLC 34**
See also CA 128; 141

Shepard, Sam
1943- .... **CLC 4, 6, 17, 34, 41, 44; DC 5**
See also AAYA 1; CA 69-72; CABS 3;
CANR 22; DLB 7; MTCW

Shepherd, Michael
See Ludlum, Robert

Sinyavsky, Andrei (Donatevich)
1925- .... CLC **8**
See also CA 85-88

Sirin, V.
See Nabokov, Vladimir (Vladimirovich)

Sissman, L(ouis) E(dward)
1928-1976 .... CLC **9, 18**
See also CA 21-24R; 65-68; CANR 13;
DLB 5

Sisson, C(harles) H(ubert) 1914- ..... CLC **8**
See also CA 1-4R; CAAS 3; CANR 3;
DLB 27

Sitwell, Dame Edith
1887-1964 .... CLC **2, 9, 67**; PC **3**
See also CA 9-12R; CANR 35;
CDBLB 1945-1960; DLB 20; MTCW

Sjoewall, Maj 1935- .... CLC **7**
See also CA 65-68

Sjowall, Maj
See Sjoewall, Maj

Skelton, Robin 1925- .... CLC **13**
See also AITN 2; CA 5-8R; CAAS 5;
CANR 28; DLB 27, 53

Skolimowski, Jerzy 1938- .... CLC **20**
See also CA 128

Skram, Amalie (Bertha)
1847-1905 .... TCLC **25**

Skvorecky, Josef (Vaclav)
1924- .... CLC **15, 39, 69**
See also CA 61-64; CAAS 1; CANR 10, 34;
MTCW

Slade, Bernard .... CLC **11, 46**
See also Newbound, Bernard Slade
See also CAAS 9; DLB 53

Slaughter, Carolyn 1946- .... CLC **56**
See also CA 85-88

Slaughter, Frank G(ill) 1908- ...... CLC **29**
See also AITN 2; CA 5-8R; CANR 5

Slavitt, David R(ytman) 1935- .... CLC **5, 14**
See also CA 21-24R; CAAS 3; CANR 41;
DLB 5, 6

Slesinger, Tess 1905-1945 .... TCLC **10**
See also CA 107; DLB 102

Slessor, Kenneth 1901-1971........ CLC **14**
See also CA 102; 89-92

Slowacki, Juliusz 1809-1849 ..... NCLC **15**

Smart, Christopher
1722-1771 .... LC **3**; PC **12**
See also DLB 109

Smart, Elizabeth 1913-1986........ CLC **54**
See also CA 81-84; 118; DLB 88

Smiley, Jane (Graves) 1949- .... CLC **53, 76**
See also CA 104; CANR 30

Smith, A(rthur) J(ames) M(arshall)
1902-1980 .... CLC **15**
See also CA 1-4R; 102; CANR 4; DLB 88

Smith, Anna Deavere 1950-........ CLC **86**
See also CA 133

Smith, Betty (Wehner) 1896-1972... CLC **19**
See also CA 5-8R; 33-36R; DLBY 82;
SATA 6

Smith, Charlotte (Turner)
1749-1806 .... NCLC **23**
See also DLB 39, 109

Smith, Clark Ashton 1893-1961 .... CLC **43**
See also CA 143

Smith, Dave .... CLC **22, 42**
See also Smith, David (Jeddie)
See also CAAS 7; DLB 5

Smith, David (Jeddie) 1942-
See Smith, Dave
See also CA 49-52; CANR 1

Smith, Florence Margaret 1902-1971
See Smith, Stevie
See also CA 17-18; 29-32R; CANR 35;
CAP 2; MTCW

Smith, Iain Crichton 1928- .... CLC **64**
See also CA 21-24R; DLB 40, 139

Smith, John 1580(?)-1631 .... LC **9**

Smith, Johnston
See Crane, Stephen (Townley)

Smith, Lee 1944-.............. CLC **25, 73**
See also CA 114; 119; CANR 46; DLB 143;
DLBY 83

Smith, Martin
See Smith, Martin Cruz

Smith, Martin Cruz 1942-......... CLC **25**
See also BEST 89:4; CA 85-88; CANR 6,
23, 43; NNAL

Smith, Mary-Ann Tirone 1944-..... CLC **39**
See also CA 118; 136

Smith, Patti 1946- .... CLC **12**
See also CA 93-96

Smith, Pauline (Urmson)
1882-1959 .... TCLC **25**

Smith, Rosamond
See Oates, Joyce Carol

Smith, Sheila Kaye
See Kaye-Smith, Sheila

Smith, Stevie .... CLC **3, 8, 25, 44**; PC **12**
See also Smith, Florence Margaret
See also DLB 20

Smith, Wilbur (Addison) 1933- ..... CLC **33**
See also CA 13-16R; CANR 7, 46; MTCW

Smith, William Jay 1918- .... CLC **6**
See also CA 5-8R; CANR 44; DLB 5;
MAICYA; SATA 2, 68

Smith, Woodrow Wilson
See Kuttner, Henry

Smolenskin, Peretz 1842-1885.... NCLC **30**

Smollett, Tobias (George) 1721-1771 .. LC **2**
See also CDBLB 1660-1789; DLB 39, 104

Snodgrass, W(illiam) D(e Witt)
1926- .... CLC **2, 6, 10, 18, 68**
See also CA 1-4R; CANR 6, 36; DLB 5;
MTCW

Snow, C(harles) P(ercy)
1905-1980 .... CLC **1, 4, 6, 9, 13, 19**
See also CA 5-8R; 101; CANR 28;
CDBLB 1945-1960; DLB 15, 77; MTCW

Snow, Frances Compton
See Adams, Henry (Brooks)

Snyder, Gary (Sherman)
1930- .... CLC **1, 2, 5, 9, 32**
See also CA 17-20R; CANR 30; DLB 5, 16

Snyder, Zilpha Keatley 1927- ...... CLC **17**
See also CA 9-12R; CANR 38; CLR 31;
JRDA; MAICYA; SAAS 2; SATA 1, 28,
75

Soares, Bernardo
See Pessoa, Fernando (Antonio Nogueira)

Sobh, A.
See Shamlu, Ahmad

Sobol, Joshua.................... CLC **60**

Soderberg, Hjalmar 1869-1941 .... TCLC **39**

Sodergran, Edith (Irene)
See Soedergran, Edith (Irene)

Soedergran, Edith (Irene)
1892-1923 .... TCLC **31**

Softly, Edgar
See Lovecraft, H(oward) P(hillips)

Softly, Edward
See Lovecraft, H(oward) P(hillips)

Sokolov, Raymond 1941-........... CLC **7**
See also CA 85-88

Solo, Jay
See Ellison, Harlan (Jay)

Sologub, Fyodor .... TCLC **9**
See also Teternikov, Fyodor Kuzmich

Solomons, Ikey Esquir
See Thackeray, William Makepeace

Solomos, Dionysios 1798-1857 ... NCLC **15**

Solwoska, Mara
See French, Marilyn

Solzhenitsyn, Aleksandr I(sayevich)
1918- ...... CLC **1, 2, 4, 7, 9, 10, 18, 26,
34, 78**; DA; WLC
See also AITN 1; CA 69-72; CANR 40;
MTCW

Somers, Jane
See Lessing, Doris (May)

Somerville, Edith 1858-1949 ...... TCLC **51**
See also DLB 135

Somerville & Ross
See Martin, Violet Florence; Somerville,
Edith

Sommer, Scott 1951- .... CLC **25**
See also CA 106

Sondheim, Stephen (Joshua)
1930- .... CLC **30, 39**
See also AAYA 11; CA 103; CANR 47

Sontag, Susan 1933-... CLC **1, 2, 10, 13, 31**
See also CA 17-20R; CANR 25; DLB 2, 67;
MTCW

Sophocles
496(?)B.C.-406(?)B.C..... CMLC **2**; DA;
DC **1**

Sordello 1189-1269............. CMLC **15**

Sorel, Julia
See Drexler, Rosalyn

Sorrentino, Gilbert
1929- .... CLC **3, 7, 14, 22, 40**
See also CA 77-80; CANR 14, 33; DLB 5;
DLBY 80

Soto, Gary 1952-........ CLC **32, 80**; HLC
See also AAYA 10; CA 119; 125; DLB 82;
HW; JRDA; SATA 80

Stern, Gerald 1925- .... CLC 40
See also CA 81-84; CANR 28; DLB 105

Stern, Richard (Gustave) 1928-... CLC 4, 39
See also CA 1-4R; CANR 1, 25; DLBY 87

Sternberg, Josef von 1894-1969..... CLC 20
See also CA 81-84

Sterne, Laurence
1713-1768 .... LC 2; DA; WLC
See also CDBLB 1660-1789; DLB 39

Sternheim, (William Adolf) Carl
1878-1942 .... TCLC 8
See also CA 105; DLB 56, 118

Stevens, Mark 1951- .... CLC 34
See also CA 122

Stevens, Wallace
1879-1955 .... TCLC 3, 12, 45; DA;
PC 6; WLC
See also CA 104; 124; CDALB 1929-1941;
DLB 54; MTCW

Stevenson, Anne (Katharine)
1933- .... CLC 7, 33
See also CA 17-20R; CAAS 9; CANR 9, 33;
DLB 40; MTCW

Stevenson, Robert Louis (Balfour)
1850-1894 .... NCLC 5, 14; DA;
SSC 11; WLC
See also CDBLB 1890-1914; CLR 10, 11;
DLB 18, 57, 141; JRDA; MAICYA;
YABC 2

Stewart, J(ohn) I(nnes) M(ackintosh)
1906- .... CLC 7, 14, 32
See also CA 85-88; CAAS 3; CANR 47;
MTCW

Stewart, Mary (Florence Elinor)
1916- .... CLC 7, 35
See also CA 1-4R; CANR 1; SATA 12

Stewart, Mary Rainbow
See Stewart, Mary (Florence Elinor)

Stifle, June
See Campbell, Maria

Stifter, Adalbert 1805-1868...... NCLC 41
See also DLB 133

Still, James 1906- .... CLC 49
See also CA 65-68; CAAS 17; CANR 10,
26; DLB 9; SATA 29

Sting
See Sumner, Gordon Matthew

Stirling, Arthur
See Sinclair, Upton (Beall)

Stitt, Milan 1941-............... CLC 29
See also CA 69-72

Stockton, Francis Richard 1834-1902
See Stockton, Frank R.
See also CA 108; 137; MAICYA; SATA 44

Stockton, Frank R............... TCLC 47
See also Stockton, Francis Richard
See also DLB 42, 74; SATA-Brief 32

Stoddard, Charles
See Kuttner, Henry

Stoker, Abraham 1847-1912
See Stoker, Bram
See also CA 105; DA; SATA 29

Stoker, Bram .... TCLC 8; WLC
See also Stoker, Abraham
See also CDBLB 1890-1914; DLB 36, 70

Stolz, Mary (Slattery) 1920-....... CLC 12
See also AAYA 8; AITN 1; CA 5-8R;
CANR 13, 41; JRDA; MAICYA;
SAAS 3; SATA 10, 71

Stone, Irving 1903-1989........... CLC 7
See also AITN 1; CA 1-4R; 129; CAAS 3;
CANR 1, 23; MTCW; SATA 3;
SATA-Obit 64

Stone, Oliver 1946-.............. CLC 73
See also CA 110

Stone, Robert (Anthony)
1937- .... CLC 5, 23, 42
See also CA 85-88; CANR 23; DLB 152;
MTCW

Stone, Zachary
See Follett, Ken(neth Martin)

Stoppard, Tom
1937- ...... CLC 1, 3, 4, 5, 8, 15, 29, 34,
63; DA; WLC
See also CA 81-84; CANR 39;
CDBLB 1960 to Present; DLB 13;
DLBY 85; MTCW

Storey, David (Malcolm)
1933- .... CLC 2, 4, 5, 8
See also CA 81-84; CANR 36; DLB 13, 14;
MTCW

Storm, Hyemeyohsts 1935-......... CLC 3
See also CA 81-84; CANR 45; NNAL

Storm, (Hans) Theodor (Woldsen)
1817-1888 .... NCLC 1

Storni, Alfonsina
1892-1938 .... TCLC 5; HLC
See also CA 104; 131; HW

Stout, Rex (Todhunter) 1886-1975 ... CLC 3
See also AITN 2; CA 61-64

Stow, (Julian) Randolph 1935- .. CLC 23, 48
See also CA 13-16R; CANR 33; MTCW

Stowe, Harriet (Elizabeth) Beecher
1811-1896 ...... NCLC 3, 50; DA; WLC
See also CDALB 1865-1917; DLB 1, 12, 42,
74; JRDA; MAICYA; YABC 1

Strachey, (Giles) Lytton
1880-1932 .... TCLC 12
See also CA 110; DLB 149; DLBD 10

Strand, Mark 1934- ...... CLC 6, 18, 41, 71
See also CA 21-24R; CANR 40; DLB 5;
SATA 41

Straub, Peter (Francis) 1943- ...... CLC 28
See also BEST 89:1; CA 85-88; CANR 28;
DLBY 84; MTCW

Strauss, Botho 1944- .... CLC 22
See also DLB 124

Streatfeild, (Mary) Noel
1895(?)-1986 .... CLC 21
See also CA 81-84; 120; CANR 31;
CLR 17; MAICYA; SATA 20;
SATA-Obit 48

Stribling, T(homas) S(igismund)
1881-1965 .... CLC 23
See also CA 107; DLB 9

Strindberg, (Johan) August
1849-1912 ...... TCLC 1, 8, 21, 47; DA;
WLC
See also CA 104; 135

Stringer, Arthur 1874-1950 .... TCLC 37
See also DLB 92

Stringer, David
See Roberts, Keith (John Kingston)

Strugatskii, Arkadii (Natanovich)
1925-1991 .... CLC 27
See also CA 106; 135

Strugatskii, Boris (Natanovich)
1933- .... CLC 27
See also CA 106

Strummer, Joe 1953(?)- .... CLC 30

Stuart, Don A.
See Campbell, John W(ood, Jr.)

Stuart, Ian
See MacLean, Alistair (Stuart)

Stuart, Jesse (Hilton)
1906-1984 .... CLC 1, 8, 11, 14, 34
See also CA 5-8R; 112; CANR 31; DLB 9,
48, 102; DLBY 84; SATA 2;
SATA-Obit 36

Sturgeon, Theodore (Hamilton)
1918-1985 .... CLC 22, 39
See also Queen, Ellery
See also CA 81-84; 116; CANR 32; DLB 8;
DLBY 85; MTCW

Sturges, Preston 1898-1959 ...... TCLC 48
See also CA 114; DLB 26

Styron, William
1925- .... CLC 1, 3, 5, 11, 15, 60
See also BEST 90:4; CA 5-8R; CANR 6, 33;
CDALB 1968-1988; DLB 2, 143;
DLBY 80; MTCW

Suarez Lynch, B.
See Bioy Casares, Adolfo; Borges, Jorge
Luis

Su Chien 1884-1918
See Su Man-shu
See also CA 123

Suckow, Ruth 1892-1960
See also CA 113; DLB 9, 102; SSC 18

Sudermann, Hermann 1857-1928 .. TCLC 15
See also CA 107; DLB 118

Sue, Eugene 1804-1857 .... NCLC 1
See also DLB 119

Sueskind, Patrick 1949-........... CLC 44
See also Suskind, Patrick

Sukenick, Ronald 1932-..... CLC 3, 4, 6, 48
See also CA 25-28R; CAAS 8; CANR 32;
DLBY 81

Suknaski, Andrew 1942- .... CLC 19
See also CA 101; DLB 53

Sullivan, Vernon
See Vian, Boris

Sully Prudhomme 1839-1907...... TCLC 31

Su Man-shu .... TCLC 24
See also Su Chien

Summerforest, Ivy B.
See Kirkup, James

Summers, Andrew James 1942-..... CLC 26

Summers, Andy
See Summers, Andrew James

Summers, Hollis (Spurgeon, Jr.)
1916- .... CLC 10
See also CA 5-8R; CANR 3; DLB 6

Summers, (Alphonsus Joseph-Mary Augustus)
    Montague 1880-1948 . . . . **TCLC 16**
    See also CA 118

Sumner, Gordon Matthew 1951- . . . . **CLC 26**

Surtees, Robert Smith
    1803-1864 . . . . **NCLC 14**
    See also DLB 21

Susann, Jacqueline 1921-1974 . . . . . . **CLC 3**
    See also AITN 1; CA 65-68; 53-56; MTCW

Suskind, Patrick
    See Sueskind, Patrick
    See also CA 145

Sutcliff, Rosemary 1920-1992 . . . . . **CLC 26**
    See also AAYA 10; CA 5-8R; 139;
        CANR 37; CLR 1, 37; JRDA; MAICYA;
        SATA 6, 44, 78; SATA-Obit 73

Sutro, Alfred 1863-1933 . . . . **TCLC 6**
    See also CA 105; DLB 10

Sutton, Henry
    See Slavitt, David R(ytman)

Svevo, Italo . . . . **TCLC 2, 35**
    See also Schmitz, Aron Hector

Swados, Elizabeth 1951- . . . . **CLC 12**
    See also CA 97-100

Swados, Harvey 1920-1972 . . . . **CLC 5**
    See also CA 5-8R; 37-40R; CANR 6;
        DLB 2

Swan, Gladys 1934- . . . . **CLC 69**
    See also CA 101; CANR 17, 39

Swarthout, Glendon (Fred)
    1918-1992 . . . . **CLC 35**
    See also CA 1-4R; 139; CANR 1, 47;
        SATA 26

Sweet, Sarah C.
    See Jewett, (Theodora) Sarah Orne

Swenson, May
    1919-1989 . . . . **CLC 4, 14, 61; DA**
    See also CA 5-8R; 130; CANR 36; DLB 5;
        MTCW; SATA 15

Swift, Augustus
    See Lovecraft, H(oward) P(hillips)

Swift, Graham (Colin) 1949- . . . . **CLC 41, 88**
    See also CA 117; 122; CANR 46

Swift, Jonathan
    1667-1745 . . . . . . **LC 1; DA; PC 9; WLC**
    See also CDBLB 1660-1789; DLB 39, 95,
        101; SATA 19

Swinburne, Algernon Charles
    1837-1909 . . . . . . **TCLC 8, 36; DA; WLC**
    See also CA 105; 140; CDBLB 1832-1890;
        DLB 35, 57

Swinfen, Ann . . . . **CLC 34**

Swinnerton, Frank Arthur
    1884-1982 . . . . **CLC 31**
    See also CA 108; DLB 34

Swithen, John
    See King, Stephen (Edwin)

Sylvia
    See Ashton-Warner, Sylvia (Constance)

Symmes, Robert Edward
    See Duncan, Robert (Edward)

Symonds, John Addington
    1840-1893 . . . . **NCLC 34**
    See also DLB 57, 144

Symons, Arthur 1865-1945 . . . . **TCLC 11**
    See also CA 107; DLB 19, 57, 149

Symons, Julian (Gustave)
    1912- . . . . **CLC 2, 14, 32**
    See also CA 49-52; CAAS 3; CANR 3, 33;
        DLB 87; DLBY 92; MTCW

Synge, (Edmund) J(ohn) M(illington)
    1871-1909 . . . . **TCLC 6, 37; DC 2**
    See also CA 104; 141; CDBLB 1890-1914;
        DLB 10, 19

Syruc, J.
    See Milosz, Czeslaw

Szirtes, George 1948- . . . . **CLC 46**
    See also CA 109; CANR 27

Tabori, George 1914- . . . . **CLC 19**
    See also CA 49-52; CANR 4

Tagore, Rabindranath
    1861-1941 . . . . **TCLC 3, 53; PC 8**
    See also CA 104; 120; MTCW

Taine, Hippolyte Adolphe
    1828-1893 . . . . **NCLC 15**

Talese, Gay 1932- . . . . **CLC 37**
    See also AITN 1; CA 1-4R; CANR 9;
        MTCW

Tallent, Elizabeth (Ann) 1954- . . . . . **CLC 45**
    See also CA 117; DLB 130

Tally, Ted 1952- . . . . **CLC 42**
    See also CA 120; 124

Tamayo y Baus, Manuel
    1829-1898 . . . . **NCLC 1**

Tammsaare, A(nton) H(ansen)
    1878-1940 . . . . **TCLC 27**

Tan, Amy 1952- . . . . **CLC 59**
    See also AAYA 9; BEST 89:3; CA 136;
        SATA 75

Tandem, Felix
    See Spitteler, Carl (Friedrich Georg)

Tanizaki, Jun'ichiro
    1886-1965 . . . . **CLC 8, 14, 28**
    See also CA 93-96; 25-28R

Tanner, William
    See Amis, Kingsley (William)

Tao Lao
    See Storni, Alfonsina

Tarassoff, Lev
    See Troyat, Henri

Tarbell, Ida M(inerva)
    1857-1944 . . . . **TCLC 40**
    See also CA 122; DLB 47

Tarkington, (Newton) Booth
    1869-1946 . . . . **TCLC 9**
    See also CA 110; 143; DLB 9, 102;
        SATA 17

Tarkovsky, Andrei (Arsenyevich)
    1932-1986 . . . . **CLC 75**
    See also CA 127

Tartt, Donna 1964(?)- . . . . **CLC 76**
    See also CA 142

Tasso, Torquato 1544-1595 . . . . **LC 5**

Tate, (John Orley) Allen
    1899-1979 . . . . **CLC 2, 4, 6, 9, 11, 14, 24**
    See also CA 5-8R; 85-88; CANR 32;
        DLB 4, 45, 63; MTCW

Tate, Ellalice
    See Hibbert, Eleanor Alice Burford

Tate, James (Vincent) 1943- . . . **CLC 2, 6, 25**
    See also CA 21-24R; CANR 29; DLB 5

Tavel, Ronald 1940- . . . . **CLC 6**
    See also CA 21-24R; CANR 33

Taylor, C(ecil) P(hilip) 1929-1981 . . . **CLC 27**
    See also CA 25-28R; 105; CANR 47

Taylor, Edward 1642(?)-1729 . . . . **LC 11; DA**
    See also DLB 24

Taylor, Eleanor Ross 1920- . . . . **CLC 5**
    See also CA 81-84

Taylor, Elizabeth 1912-1975 . . . **CLC 2, 4, 29**
    See also CA 13-16R; CANR 9; DLB 139;
        MTCW; SATA 13

Taylor, Henry (Splawn) 1942- . . . . . . **CLC 44**
    See also CA 33-36R; CAAS 7; CANR 31;
        DLB 5

Taylor, Kamala (Purnaiya) 1924-
    See Markandaya, Kamala
    See also CA 77-80

Taylor, Mildred D. . . . . **CLC 21**
    See also AAYA 10; BW 1; CA 85-88;
        CANR 25; CLR 9; DLB 52; JRDA;
        MAICYA; SAAS 5; SATA 15, 70

Taylor, Peter (Hillsman)
    1917- . . . . . . **CLC 1, 4, 18, 37, 44, 50, 71;
                                                  SSC 10**
    See also CA 13-16R; CANR 9; DLBY 81,
        94; MTCW

Taylor, Robert Lewis 1912- . . . . **CLC 14**
    See also CA 1-4R; CANR 3; SATA 10

Tchekhov, Anton
    See Chekhov, Anton (Pavlovich)

Teasdale, Sara 1884-1933 . . . . **TCLC 4**
    See also CA 104; DLB 45; SATA 32

Tegner, Esaias 1782-1846 . . . . **NCLC 2**

Teilhard de Chardin, (Marie Joseph) Pierre
    1881-1955 . . . . **TCLC 9**
    See also CA 105

Temple, Ann
    See Mortimer, Penelope (Ruth)

Tennant, Emma (Christina)
    1937- . . . . **CLC 13, 52**
    See also CA 65-68; CAAS 9; CANR 10, 38;
        DLB 14

Tenneshaw, S. M.
    See Silverberg, Robert

Tennyson, Alfred
    1809-1892 . . **NCLC 30; DA; PC 6; WLC**
    See also CDBLB 1832-1890; DLB 32

Teran, Lisa St. Aubin de . . . . **CLC 36**
    See also St. Aubin de Teran, Lisa

Terence 195(?)B.C.-159B.C. . . . . . . **CMLC 14**

Teresa de Jesus, St. 1515-1582 . . . . . . **LC 18**

Terkel, Louis 1912-
    See Terkel, Studs
    See also CA 57-60; CANR 18, 45; MTCW

Terkel, Studs . . . . **CLC 38**
    See also Terkel, Louis
    See also AITN 1

Terry, C. V.
    See Slaughter, Frank G(ill)

Terry, Megan 1932- . . . . CLC 19
    See also CA 77-80; CABS 3; CANR 43;
    DLB 7

Tertz, Abram
    See Sinyavsky, Andrei (Donatevich)

Tesich, Steve 1943(?)- . . . . CLC 40, 69
    See also CA 105; DLBY 83

Teternikov, Fyodor Kuzmich 1863-1927
    See Sologub, Fyodor
    See also CA 104

Tevis, Walter 1928-1984 . . . . CLC 42
    See also CA 113

Tey, Josephine . . . . TCLC 14
    See also Mackintosh, Elizabeth
    See also DLB 77

Thackeray, William Makepeace
    1811-1863 . . . . NCLC 5, 14, 22, 43; DA;
                                                        WLC
    See also CDBLB 1832-1890; DLB 21, 55;
        SATA 23

Thakura, Ravindranatha
    See Tagore, Rabindranath

Tharoor, Shashi 1956- . . . . CLC 70
    See also CA 141

Thelwell, Michael Miles 1939- . . . . . CLC 22
    See also BW 2; CA 101

Theobald, Lewis, Jr.
    See Lovecraft, H(oward) P(hillips)

Theodorescu, Ion N. 1880-1967
    See Arghezi, Tudor
    See also CA 116

Theriault, Yves 1915-1983 . . . . CLC 79
    See also CA 102; DLB 88

Theroux, Alexander (Louis)
    1939- . . . . CLC 2, 25
    See also CA 85-88; CANR 20

Theroux, Paul (Edward)
    1941- . . . . CLC 5, 8, 11, 15, 28, 46
    See also BEST 89:4; CA 33-36R; CANR 20,
        45; DLB 2; MTCW; SATA 44

Thesen, Sharon 1946- . . . . CLC 56

Thevenin, Denis
    See Duhamel, Georges

Thibault, Jacques Anatole Francois
    1844-1924
    See France, Anatole
    See also CA 106; 127; MTCW

Thiele, Colin (Milton) 1920- . . . . CLC 17
    See also CA 29-32R; CANR 12, 28;
        CLR 27; MAICYA; SAAS 2; SATA 14,
        72

Thomas, Audrey (Callahan)
    1935- . . . . CLC 7, 13, 37
    See also AITN 2; CA 21-24R; CAAS 19;
        CANR 36; DLB 60; MTCW

Thomas, D(onald) M(ichael)
    1935- . . . . CLC 13, 22, 31
    See also CA 61-64; CAAS 11; CANR 17,
        45; CDBLB 1960 to Present; DLB 40;
        MTCW

Thomas, Dylan (Marlais)
    1914-1953 . . . TCLC 1, 8, 45; DA; PC 2;
                                                SSC 3; WLC
    See also CA 104; 120; CDBLB 1945-1960;
        DLB 13, 20, 139; MTCW; SATA 60

Thomas, (Philip) Edward
    1878-1917 . . . . TCLC 10
    See also CA 106; DLB 19

Thomas, Joyce Carol 1938- . . . . CLC 35
    See also AAYA 12; BW 2; CA 113; 116;
        CLR 19; DLB 33; JRDA; MAICYA;
        MTCW; SAAS 7; SATA 40, 78

Thomas, Lewis 1913-1993 . . . . CLC 35
    See also CA 85-88; 143; CANR 38; MTCW

Thomas, Paul
    See Mann, (Paul) Thomas

Thomas, Piri 1928- . . . . CLC 17
    See also CA 73-76; HW

Thomas, R(onald) S(tuart)
    1913- . . . . CLC 6, 13, 48
    See also CA 89-92; CAAS 4; CANR 30;
        CDBLB 1960 to Present; DLB 27;
        MTCW

Thomas, Ross (Elmore) 1926- . . . . . . CLC 39
    See also CA 33-36R; CANR 22

Thompson, Francis Clegg
    See Mencken, H(enry) L(ouis)

Thompson, Francis Joseph
    1859-1907 . . . . TCLC 4
    See also CA 104; CDBLB 1890-1914;
        DLB 19

Thompson, Hunter S(tockton)
    1939- . . . . CLC 9, 17, 40
    See also BEST 89:1; CA 17-20R; CANR 23,
        46; MTCW

Thompson, James Myers
    See Thompson, Jim (Myers)

Thompson, Jim (Myers)
    1906-1977(?) . . . . CLC 69
    See also CA 140

Thompson, Judith . . . . CLC 39

Thomson, James 1700-1748 . . . . . . LC 16, 29
    See also DLB 95

Thomson, James 1834-1882 . . . . . . NCLC 18
    See also DLB 35

Thoreau, Henry David
    1817-1862 . . . . . . NCLC 7, 21; DA; WLC
    See also CDALB 1640-1865; DLB 1

Thornton, Hall
    See Silverberg, Robert

Thurber, James (Grover)
    1894-1961 . . . CLC 5, 11, 25; DA; SSC 1
    See also CA 73-76; CANR 17, 39;
        CDALB 1929-1941; DLB 4, 11, 22, 102;
        MAICYA; MTCW; SATA 13

Thurman, Wallace (Henry)
    1902-1934 . . . . TCLC 6; BLC
    See also BW 1; CA 104; 124; DLB 51

Ticheburn, Cheviot
    See Ainsworth, William Harrison

Tieck, (Johann) Ludwig
    1773-1853 . . . . NCLC 5, 46
    See also DLB 90

Tiger, Derry
    See Ellison, Harlan (Jay)

Tilghman, Christopher 1948(?)- . . . . . CLC 65

Tillinghast, Richard (Williford)
    1940- . . . . CLC 29
    See also CA 29-32R; CANR 26

Timrod, Henry 1828-1867 . . . . NCLC 25
    See also DLB 3

Tindall, Gillian 1938- . . . . CLC 7
    See also CA 21-24R; CANR 11

Tiptree, James, Jr. . . . . CLC 48, 50
    See also Sheldon, Alice Hastings Bradley
    See also DLB 8

Titmarsh, Michael Angelo
    See Thackeray, William Makepeace

Tocqueville, Alexis (Charles Henri Maurice
        Clerel Comte) 1805-1859 . . . . . NCLC 7

Tolkien, J(ohn) R(onald) R(euel)
    1892-1973 . . . . CLC 1, 2, 3, 8, 12, 38;
                                                        DA; WLC
    See also AAYA 10; AITN 1; CA 17-18;
        45-48; CANR 36; CAP 2;
        CDBLB 1914-1945; DLB 15; JRDA;
        MAICYA; MTCW; SATA 2, 32;
        SATA-Obit 24

Toller, Ernst 1893-1939 . . . . TCLC 10
    See also CA 107; DLB 124

Tolson, M. B.
    See Tolson, Melvin B(eaunorus)

Tolson, Melvin B(eaunorus)
    1898(?)-1966 . . . . CLC 36; BLC
    See also BW 1; CA 124; 89-92; DLB 48, 76

Tolstoi, Aleksei Nikolaevich
    See Tolstoy, Alexey Nikolaevich

Tolstoy, Alexey Nikolaevich
    1882-1945 . . . . TCLC 18
    See also CA 107

Tolstoy, Count Leo
    See Tolstoy, Leo (Nikolaevich)

Tolstoy, Leo (Nikolaevich)
    1828-1910 . . . . . . TCLC 4, 11, 17, 28, 44;
                                                DA; SSC 9; WLC
    See also CA 104; 123; SATA 26

Tomasi di Lampedusa, Giuseppe 1896-1957
    See Lampedusa, Giuseppe (Tomasi) di
    See also CA 111

Tomlin, Lily . . . . CLC 17
    See also Tomlin, Mary Jean

Tomlin, Mary Jean 1939(?)-
    See Tomlin, Lily
    See also CA 117

Tomlinson, (Alfred) Charles
    1927- . . . . CLC 2, 4, 6, 13, 45
    See also CA 5-8R; CANR 33; DLB 40

Tonson, Jacob
    See Bennett, (Enoch) Arnold

Toole, John Kennedy
    1937-1969 . . . . CLC 19, 64
    See also CA 104; DLBY 81

Toomer, Jean
    1894-1967 . . . . . . CLC 1, 4, 13, 22; BLC;
                                                PC 7; SSC 1
    See also BW 1; CA 85-88;
        CDALB 1917-1929; DLB 45, 51; MTCW

Torley, Luke
    See Blish, James (Benjamin)

Tornimparte, Alessandra
    See Ginzburg, Natalia

Torre, Raoul della
    See Mencken, H(enry) L(ouis)

Torrey, E(dwin) Fuller   1937-....... **CLC 34**
See also CA 119

Torsvan, Ben Traven
See Traven, B.

Torsvan, Benno Traven
See Traven, B.

Torsvan, Berick Traven
See Traven, B.

Torsvan, Berwick Traven
See Traven, B.

Torsvan, Bruno Traven
See Traven, B.

Torsvan, Traven
See Traven, B.

Tournier, Michel (Edouard)
1924- .... **CLC 6, 23, 36**
See also CA 49-52; CANR 3, 36; DLB 83;
MTCW; SATA 23

Tournimparte, Alessandra
See Ginzburg, Natalia

Towers, Ivar
See Kornbluth, C(yril) M.

Towne, Robert (Burton)   1936(?)-.... **CLC 87**
See also CA 108; DLB 44

Townsend, Sue   1946-............ **CLC 61**
See also CA 119; 127; MTCW; SATA 55;
SATA-Brief 48

Townshend, Peter (Dennis Blandford)
1945- .... **CLC 17, 42**
See also CA 107

Tozzi, Federigo   1883-1920....... **TCLC 31**

Traill, Catharine Parr
1802-1899 .... **NCLC 31**
See also DLB 99

Trakl, Georg   1887-1914.......... **TCLC 5**
See also CA 104

Transtroemer, Tomas (Goesta)
1931- .... **CLC 52, 65**
See also CA 117; 129; CAAS 17

Transtromer, Tomas Gosta
See Transtroemer, Tomas (Goesta)

Traven, B.   (?)-1969............. **CLC 8, 11**
See also CA 19-20; 25-28R; CAP 2; DLB 9,
56; MTCW

Treitel, Jonathan   1959- .... **CLC 70**

Tremain, Rose   1943-.............. **CLC 42**
See also CA 97-100; CANR 44; DLB 14

Tremblay, Michel   1942-........... **CLC 29**
See also CA 116; 128; DLB 60; MTCW

Trevanian....................... **CLC 29**
See also Whitaker, Rod(ney)

Trevor, Glen
See Hilton, James

Trevor, William
1928- .... **CLC 7, 9, 14, 25, 71**
See also Cox, William Trevor
See also DLB 14, 139

Trifonov, Yuri (Valentinovich)
1925-1981 .... **CLC 45**
See also CA 126; 103; MTCW

Trilling, Lionel   1905-1975 .... **CLC 9, 11, 24**
See also CA 9-12R; 61-64; CANR 10;
DLB 28, 63; MTCW

Trimball, W. H.
See Mencken, H(enry) L(ouis)

Tristan
See Gomez de la Serna, Ramon

Tristram
See Housman, A(lfred) E(dward)

Trogdon, William (Lewis)   1939-
See Heat-Moon, William Least
See also CA 115; 119; CANR 47

Trollope, Anthony
1815-1882 ...... **NCLC 6, 33; DA; WLC**
See also CDBLB 1832-1890; DLB 21, 57;
SATA 22

Trollope, Frances   1779-1863 ..... **NCLC 30**
See also DLB 21

Trotsky, Leon   1879-1940........ **TCLC 22**
See also CA 118

Trotter (Cockburn), Catharine
1679-1749 .... **LC 8**
See also DLB 84

Trout, Kilgore
See Farmer, Philip Jose

Trow, George W. S.   1943-......... **CLC 52**
See also CA 126

Troyat, Henri   1911-.............. **CLC 23**
See also CA 45-48; CANR 2, 33; MTCW

Trudeau, G(arretson) B(eekman)   1948-
See Trudeau, Garry B.
See also CA 81-84; CANR 31; SATA 35

Trudeau, Garry B................. **CLC 12**
See also Trudeau, G(arretson) B(eekman)
See also AAYA 10; AITN 2

Truffaut, Francois   1932-1984...... **CLC 20**
See also CA 81-84; 113; CANR 34

Trumbo, Dalton   1905-1976 .... **CLC 19**
See also CA 21-24R; 69-72; CANR 10;
DLB 26

Trumbull, John   1750-1831....... **NCLC 30**
See also DLB 31

Trundlett, Helen B.
See Eliot, T(homas) S(tearns)

Tryon, Thomas   1926-1991 .... **CLC 3, 11**
See also AITN 1; CA 29-32R; 135;
CANR 32; MTCW

Tryon, Tom
See Tryon, Thomas

Ts'ao Hsueh-ch'in   1715(?)-1763....... **LC 1**

Tsushima, Shuji   1909-1948
See Dazai, Osamu
See also CA 107

Tsvetaeva (Efron), Marina (Ivanovna)
1892-1941 .... **TCLC 7, 35**
See also CA 104; 128; MTCW

Tuck, Lily   1938-................. **CLC 70**
See also CA 139

Tu Fu   712-770.................... **PC 9**

Tunis, John R(oberts)   1889-1975 ... **CLC 12**
See also CA 61-64; DLB 22; JRDA;
MAICYA; SATA 37; SATA-Brief 30

Tuohy, Frank.................... **CLC 37**
See also Tuohy, John Francis
See also DLB 14, 139

Tuohy, John Francis   1925-
See Tuohy, Frank
See also CA 5-8R; CANR 3, 47

Turco, Lewis (Putnam)   1934- ... **CLC 11, 63**
See also CA 13-16R; CANR 24; DLBY 84

Turgenev, Ivan
1818-1883 ...... **NCLC 21; DA; SSC 7;**
WLC

Turgot, Anne-Robert-Jacques
1727-1781 .... **LC 26**

Turner, Frederick   1943-.......... **CLC 48**
See also CA 73-76; CAAS 10; CANR 12,
30; DLB 40

Tutu, Desmond M(pilo)
1931- .... **CLC 80; BLC**
See also BW 1; CA 125

Tutuola, Amos   1920- ... **CLC 5, 14, 29; BLC**
See also BW 2; CA 9-12R; CANR 27;
DLB 125; MTCW

Twain, Mark
..... **TCLC 6, 12, 19, 36, 48, 59; SSC 6;**
WLC
See also Clemens, Samuel Langhorne
See also DLB 11, 12, 23, 64, 74

Tyler, Anne
1941- .... **CLC 7, 11, 18, 28, 44, 59**
See also BEST 89:1; CA 9-12R; CANR 11,
33; DLB 6, 143; DLBY 82; MTCW;
SATA 7

Tyler, Royall   1757-1826.......... **NCLC 3**
See also DLB 37

Tynan, Katharine   1861-1931 .... **TCLC 3**
See also CA 104

Tyutchev, Fyodor   1803-1873 ..... **NCLC 34**

Tzara, Tristan .... **CLC 47**
See also Rosenfeld, Samuel

Uhry, Alfred   1936-............... **CLC 55**
See also CA 127; 133

Ulf, Haerved
See Strindberg, (Johan) August

Ulf, Harved
See Strindberg, (Johan) August

Ulibarri, Sabine R(eyes)   1919- ..... **CLC 83**
See also CA 131; DLB 82; HW

Unamuno (y Jugo), Miguel de
1864-1936 .... **TCLC 2, 9; HLC; SSC 11**
See also CA 104; 131; DLB 108; HW;
MTCW

Undercliffe, Errol
See Campbell, (John) Ramsey

Underwood, Miles
See Glassco, John

Undset, Sigrid
1882-1949 .... **TCLC 3; DA; WLC**
See also CA 104; 129; MTCW

Ungaretti, Giuseppe
1888-1970 .... **CLC 7, 11, 15**
See also CA 19-20; 25-28R; CAP 2;
DLB 114

Unger, Douglas   1952-............. **CLC 34**
See also CA 130

Unsworth, Barry (Forster)   1930-.... **CLC 76**
See also CA 25-28R; CANR 30

Warner, Sylvia Townsend
  1893-1978 .... CLC **7, 19**
  See also CA 61-64; 77-80; CANR 16;
  DLB 34, 139; MTCW

Warren, Mercy Otis 1728-1814... NCLC **13**
  See also DLB 31

Warren, Robert Penn
  1905-1989 .... CLC **1, 4, 6, 8, 10, 13, 18,
        39, 53, 59; DA; SSC 4; WLC**
  See also AITN 1; CA 13-16R; 129;
  CANR 10, 47; CDALB 1968-1988;
  DLB 2, 48, 152; DLBY 80, 89; MTCW;
  SATA 46; SATA-Obit 63

Warshofsky, Isaac
  See Singer, Isaac Bashevis

Warton, Thomas 1728-1790........ LC **15**
  See also DLB 104, 109

Waruk, Kona
  See Harris, (Theodore) Wilson

Warung, Price 1855-1911........ TCLC **45**

Warwick, Jarvis
  See Garner, Hugh

Washington, Alex
  See Harris, Mark

Washington, Booker T(aliaferro)
  1856-1915 .... TCLC **10; BLC**
  See also BW 1; CA 114; 125; SATA 28

Washington, George 1732-1799...... LC **25**
  See also DLB 31

Wassermann, (Karl) Jakob
  1873-1934 .... TCLC **6**
  See also CA 104; DLB 66

Wasserstein, Wendy
  1950- .... CLC **32, 59; DC 4**
  See also CA 121; 129; CABS 3

Waterhouse, Keith (Spencer)
  1929-...................... CLC **47**
  See also CA 5-8R; CANR 38; DLB 13, 15;
  MTCW

Waters, Frank (Joseph) 1902-...... CLC **88**
  See also CA 5-8R; CAAS 13; CANR 3, 18;
  DLBY 86

Waters, Roger 1944-.............. CLC **35**

Watkins, Frances Ellen
  See Harper, Frances Ellen Watkins

Watkins, Gerrold
  See Malzberg, Barry N(athaniel)

Watkins, Paul 1964-.............. CLC **55**
  See also CA 132

Watkins, Vernon Phillips
  1906-1967 .... CLC **43**
  See also CA 9-10; 25-28R; CAP 1; DLB 20

Watson, Irving S.
  See Mencken, H(enry) L(ouis)

Watson, John H.
  See Farmer, Philip Jose

Watson, Richard F.
  See Silverberg, Robert

Waugh, Auberon (Alexander) 1939-.. CLC **7**
  See also CA 45-48; CANR 6, 22; DLB 14

Waugh, Evelyn (Arthur St. John)
  1903-1966 ..... CLC **1, 3, 8, 13, 19, 27,
        44; DA; WLC**
  See also CA 85-88; 25-28R; CANR 22;
  CDBLB 1914-1945; DLB 15; MTCW

Waugh, Harriet 1944- .... CLC **6**
  See also CA 85-88; CANR 22

Ways, C. R.
  See Blount, Roy (Alton), Jr.

Waystaff, Simon
  See Swift, Jonathan

Webb, (Martha) Beatrice (Potter)
  1858-1943 .... TCLC **22**
  See also Potter, Beatrice
  See also CA 117

Webb, Charles (Richard) 1939-...... CLC **7**
  See also CA 25-28R

Webb, James H(enry), Jr. 1946-.... CLC **22**
  See also CA 81-84

Webb, Mary (Gladys Meredith)
  1881-1927 .... TCLC **24**
  See also CA 123; DLB 34

Webb, Mrs. Sidney
  See Webb, (Martha) Beatrice (Potter)

Webb, Phyllis 1927-.............. CLC **18**
  See also CA 104; CANR 23; DLB 53

Webb, Sidney (James)
  1859-1947 .... TCLC **22**
  See also CA 117

Webber, Andrew Lloyd............. CLC **21**
  See also Lloyd Webber, Andrew

Weber, Lenora Mattingly
  1895-1971 .... CLC **12**
  See also CA 19-20; 29-32R; CAP 1;
  SATA 2; SATA-Obit 26

Webster, John 1579(?)-1634(?) .... DC **2**
  See also CDBLB Before 1660; DA; DLB 58;
  WLC

Webster, Noah 1758-1843 .... NCLC **30**

Wedekind, (Benjamin) Frank(lin)
  1864-1918 .... TCLC **7**
  See also CA 104; DLB 118

Weidman, Jerome 1913-............ CLC **7**
  See also AITN 2; CA 1-4R; CANR 1;
  DLB 28

Weil, Simone (Adolphine)
  1909-1943 .... TCLC **23**
  See also CA 117

Weinstein, Nathan
  See West, Nathanael

Weinstein, Nathan von Wallenstein
  See West, Nathanael

Weir, Peter (Lindsay) 1944- .... CLC **20**
  See also CA 113; 123

Weiss, Peter (Ulrich)
  1916-1982 .... CLC **3, 15, 51**
  See also CA 45-48; 106; CANR 3; DLB 69,
  124

Weiss, Theodore (Russell)
  1916-.................. CLC **3, 8, 14**
  See also CA 9-12R; CAAS 2; CANR 46;
  DLB 5

Welch, (Maurice) Denton
  1915-1948 .... TCLC **22**
  See also CA 121

Welch, James 1940-......... CLC **6, 14, 52**
  See also CA 85-88; CANR 42; NNAL

Weldon, Fay
  1933- .... CLC **6, 9, 11, 19, 36, 59**
  See also CA 21-24R; CANR 16, 46;
  CDBLB 1960 to Present; DLB 14;
  MTCW

Wellek, Rene 1903- .... CLC **28**
  See also CA 5-8R; CAAS 7; CANR 8;
  DLB 63

Weller, Michael 1942-......... CLC **10, 53**
  See also CA 85-88

Weller, Paul 1958-.............. CLC **26**

Wellershoff, Dieter 1925-.......... CLC **46**
  See also CA 89-92; CANR 16, 37

Welles, (George) Orson
  1915-1985 .... CLC **20, 80**
  See also CA 93-96; 117

Wellman, Mac 1945- .... CLC **65**

Wellman, Manly Wade 1903-1986 .. CLC **49**
  See also CA 1-4R; 118; CANR 6, 16, 44;
  SATA 6; SATA-Obit 47

Wells, Carolyn 1869(?)-1942 ...... TCLC **35**
  See also CA 113; DLB 11

Wells, H(erbert) G(eorge)
  1866-1946 .... TCLC **6, 12, 19; DA;
        SSC 6; WLC**
  See also CA 110; 121; CDBLB 1914-1945;
  DLB 34, 70; MTCW; SATA 20

Wells, Rosemary 1943-............ CLC **12**
  See also AAYA 13; CA 85-88; CLR 16;
  MAICYA; SAAS 1; SATA 18, 69

Welty, Eudora
  1909-...... CLC **1, 2, 5, 14, 22, 33; DA;
        SSC 1; WLC**
  See also CA 9-12R; CABS 1; CANR 32;
  CDALB 1941-1968; DLB 2, 102, 143;
  DLBD 12; DLBY 87; MTCW

Wen I-to 1899-1946 .... TCLC **28**

Wentworth, Robert
  See Hamilton, Edmond

Werfel, Franz (V.) 1890-1945 ...... TCLC **8**
  See also CA 104; DLB 81, 124

Wergeland, Henrik Arnold
  1808-1845 .... NCLC **5**

Wersba, Barbara 1932-............ CLC **30**
  See also AAYA 2; CA 29-32R; CANR 16,
  38; CLR 3; DLB 52; JRDA; MAICYA;
  SAAS 2; SATA 1, 58

Wertmueller, Lina 1928- .... CLC **16**
  See also CA 97-100; CANR 39

Wescott, Glenway 1901-1987....... CLC **13**
  See also CA 13-16R; 121; CANR 23;
  DLB 4, 9, 102

Wesker, Arnold 1932- .... CLC **3, 5, 42**
  See also CA 1-4R; CAAS 7; CANR 1, 33;
  CDBLB 1960 to Present; DLB 13;
  MTCW

Wesley, Richard (Errol) 1945-....... CLC **7**
  See also BW 1; CA 57-60; CANR 27;
  DLB 38

Wessel, Johan Herman 1742-1785 .... LC **7**

West, Anthony (Panther)
1914-1987 . . . . CLC 50
See also CA 45-48; 124; CANR 3, 19;
DLB 15

West, C. P.
See Wodehouse, P(elham) G(renville)

West, (Mary) Jessamyn
1902-1984 . . . . CLC 7, 17
See also CA 9-12R; 112; CANR 27; DLB 6;
DLBY 84; MTCW; SATA-Obit 37

West, Morris L(anglo)   1916- . . . . . CLC 6, 33
See also CA 5-8R; CANR 24; MTCW

West, Nathanael
1903-1940 . . . . . TCLC 1, 14, 44; SSC 16
See also CA 104; 125; CDALB 1929-1941;
DLB 4, 9, 28; MTCW

West, Owen
See Koontz, Dean R(ay)

West, Paul   1930- . . . . CLC 7, 14
See also CA 13-16R; CAAS 7; CANR 22;
DLB 14

West, Rebecca   1892-1983 . . CLC 7, 9, 31, 50
See also CA 5-8R; 109; CANR 19; DLB 36;
DLBY 83; MTCW

Westall, Robert (Atkinson)
1929-1993 . . . . CLC 17
See also AAYA 12; CA 69-72; 141;
CANR 18; CLR 13; JRDA; MAICYA;
SAAS 2; SATA 23, 69; SATA-Obit 75

Westlake, Donald E(dwin)
1933- . . . . CLC 7, 33
See also CA 17-20R; CAAS 13; CANR 16,
44

Westmacott, Mary
See Christie, Agatha (Mary Clarissa)

Weston, Allen
See Norton, Andre

Wetcheek, J. L.
See Feuchtwanger, Lion

Wetering, Janwillem van de
See van de Wetering, Janwillem

Wetherell, Elizabeth
See Warner, Susan (Bogert)

Whalen, Philip   1923- . . . . CLC 6, 29
See also CA 9-12R; CANR 5, 39; DLB 16

Wharton, Edith (Newbold Jones)
1862-1937 . . . . . . TCLC 3, 9, 27, 53; DA;
SSC 6; WLC
See also CA 104; 132; CDALB 1865-1917;
DLB 4, 9, 12, 78; MTCW

Wharton, James
See Mencken, H(enry) L(ouis)

Wharton, William (a pseudonym)
. . . . CLC 18, 37
See also CA 93-96; DLBY 80

Wheatley (Peters), Phillis
1754(?)-1784 . . . . LC 3; BLC; DA; PC 3;
WLC
See also CDALB 1640-1865; DLB 31, 50

Wheelock, John Hall   1886-1978 . . . . CLC 14
See also CA 13-16R; 77-80; CANR 14;
DLB 45

White, E(lwyn) B(rooks)
1899-1985 . . . . CLC 10, 34, 39
See also AITN 2; CA 13-16R; 116;
CANR 16, 37; CLR 1, 21; DLB 11, 22;
MAICYA; MTCW; SATA 2, 29;
SATA-Obit 44

White, Edmund (Valentine III)
1940- . . . . CLC 27
See also AAYA 7; CA 45-48; CANR 3, 19,
36; MTCW

White, Patrick (Victor Martindale)
1912-1990 . . CLC 3, 4, 5, 7, 9, 18, 65, 69
See also CA 81-84; 132; CANR 43; MTCW

White, Phyllis Dorothy James   1920-
See James, P. D.
See also CA 21-24R; CANR 17, 43; MTCW

White, T(erence) H(anbury)
1906-1964 . . . . CLC 30
See also CA 73-76; CANR 37; JRDA;
MAICYA; SATA 12

White, Terence de Vere
1912-1994 . . . . CLC 49
See also CA 49-52; 145; CANR 3

White, Walter F(rancis)
1893-1955 . . . . TCLC 15
See also White, Walter
See also BW 1; CA 115; 124; DLB 51

White, William Hale   1831-1913
See Rutherford, Mark
See also CA 121

Whitehead, E(dward) A(nthony)
1933- . . . . CLC 5
See also CA 65-68

Whitemore, Hugh (John)   1936- . . . . . CLC 37
See also CA 132

Whitman, Sarah Helen (Power)
1803-1878 . . . . NCLC 19
See also DLB 1

Whitman, Walt(er)
1819-1892 . . . . . NCLC 4, 31; DA; PC 3;
WLC
See also CDALB 1640-1865; DLB 3, 64;
SATA 20

Whitney, Phyllis A(yame)   1903- . . . . CLC 42
See also AITN 2; BEST 90:3; CA 1-4R;
CANR 3, 25, 38; JRDA; MAICYA;
SATA 1, 30

Whittemore, (Edward) Reed (Jr.)
1919- . . . . CLC 4
See also CA 9-12R; CAAS 8; CANR 4;
DLB 5

Whittier, John Greenleaf
1807-1892 . . . . NCLC 8
See also CDALB 1640-1865; DLB 1

Whittlebot, Hernia
See Coward, Noel (Peirce)

Wicker, Thomas Grey   1926-
See Wicker, Tom
See also CA 65-68; CANR 21, 46

Wicker, Tom . . . . CLC 7
See also Wicker, Thomas Grey

Wideman, John Edgar
1941- . . . . CLC 5, 34, 36, 67; BLC
See also BW 2; CA 85-88; CANR 14, 42;
DLB 33, 143

Wiebe, Rudy (Henry)   1934- . . . CLC 6, 11, 14
See also CA 37-40R; CANR 42; DLB 60

Wieland, Christoph Martin
1733-1813 . . . . NCLC 17
See also DLB 97

Wiene, Robert   1881-1938 . . . . TCLC 56

Wieners, John   1934- . . . . CLC 7
See also CA 13-16R; DLB 16

Wiesel, Elie(zer)
1928- . . . . CLC 3, 5, 11, 37; DA
See also AAYA 7; AITN 1; CA 5-8R;
CAAS 4; CANR 8, 40; DLB 83;
DLBY 87; MTCW; SATA 56

Wiggins, Marianne   1947- . . . . CLC 57
See also BEST 89:3; CA 130

Wight, James Alfred   1916-
See Herriot, James
See also CA 77-80; SATA 55;
SATA-Brief 44

Wilbur, Richard (Purdy)
1921- . . . . CLC 3, 6, 9, 14, 53; DA
See also CA 1-4R; CABS 2; CANR 2, 29;
DLB 5; MTCW; SATA 9

Wild, Peter   1940- . . . . CLC 14
See also CA 37-40R; DLB 5

Wilde, Oscar (Fingal O'Flahertie Wills)
1854(?)-1900 . . . . TCLC 1, 8, 23, 41; DA;
SSC 11; WLC
See also CA 104; 119; CDBLB 1890-1914;
DLB 10, 19, 34, 57, 141; SATA 24

Wilder, Billy . . . . CLC 20
See also Wilder, Samuel
See also DLB 26

Wilder, Samuel   1906-
See Wilder, Billy
See also CA 89-92

Wilder, Thornton (Niven)
1897-1975 . . . . . . CLC 1, 5, 6, 10, 15, 35,
82; DA; DC 1; WLC
See also AITN 2; CA 13-16R; 61-64;
CANR 40; DLB 4, 7, 9; MTCW

Wilding, Michael   1942- . . . . CLC 73
See also CA 104; CANR 24

Wiley, Richard   1944- . . . . CLC 44
See also CA 121; 129

Wilhelm, Kate . . . . CLC 7
See also Wilhelm, Katie Gertrude
See also CAAS 5; DLB 8

Wilhelm, Katie Gertrude   1928-
See Wilhelm, Kate
See also CA 37-40R; CANR 17, 36; MTCW

Wilkins, Mary
See Freeman, Mary Eleanor Wilkins

Willard, Nancy   1936- . . . . CLC 7, 37
See also CA 89-92; CANR 10, 39; CLR 5;
DLB 5, 52; MAICYA; MTCW;
SATA 37, 71; SATA-Brief 30

Williams, C(harles) K(enneth)
1936- . . . . CLC 33, 56
See also CA 37-40R; DLB 5

Williams, Charles
See Collier, James L(incoln)

Williams, Charles (Walter Stansby)
1886-1945 . . . . TCLC 1, 11
See also CA 104; DLB 100

Williams, (George) Emlyn
    1905-1987 .... **CLC 15**
    See also CA 104; 123; CANR 36; DLB 10,
    77; MTCW

Williams, Hugo 1942-............ **CLC 42**
    See also CA 17-20R; CANR 45; DLB 40

Williams, J. Walker
    See Wodehouse, P(elham) G(renville)

Williams, John A(lfred)
    1925- .... **CLC 5, 13; BLC**
    See also BW 2; CA 53-56; CAAS 3;
    CANR 6, 26; DLB 2, 33

Williams, Jonathan (Chamberlain)
    1929- .... **CLC 13**
    See also CA 9-12R; CAAS 12; CANR 8;
    DLB 5

Williams, Joy 1944-.............. **CLC 31**
    See also CA 41-44R; CANR 22

Williams, Norman 1952- .... **CLC 39**
    See also CA 118

Williams, Tennessee
    1911-1983 ..... **CLC 1, 2, 5, 7, 8, 11, 15,
        19, 30, 39, 45, 71; DA; DC 4; WLC**
    See also AITN 1, 2; CA 5-8R; 108;
    CABS 3; CANR 31; CDALB 1941-1968;
    DLB 7; DLBD 4; DLBY 83; MTCW

Williams, Thomas (Alonzo)
    1926-1990 .... **CLC 14**
    See also CA 1-4R; 132; CANR 2

Williams, William C.
    See Williams, William Carlos

Williams, William Carlos
    1883-1963 .... **CLC 1, 2, 5, 9, 13, 22, 42,
        67; DA; PC 7**
    See also CA 89-92; CANR 34;
    CDALB 1917-1929; DLB 4, 16, 54, 86;
    MTCW

Williamson, David (Keith) 1942-.... **CLC 56**
    See also CA 103; CANR 41

Williamson, Ellen Douglas 1905-1984
    See Douglas, Ellen
    See also CA 17-20R; 114; CANR 39

Williamson, Jack.................. **CLC 29**
    See also Williamson, John Stewart
    See also CAAS 8; DLB 8

Williamson, John Stewart 1908-
    See Williamson, Jack
    See also CA 17-20R; CANR 23

Willie, Frederick
    See Lovecraft, H(oward) P(hillips)

Willingham, Calder (Baynard, Jr.)
    1922-1995 .... **CLC 5, 51**
    See also CA 5-8R; CANR 3; DLB 2, 44;
    MTCW

Willis, Charles
    See Clarke, Arthur C(harles)

Willy
    See Colette, (Sidonie-Gabrielle)

Willy, Colette
    See Colette, (Sidonie-Gabrielle)

Wilson, A(ndrew) N(orman) 1950- .. **CLC 33**
    See also CA 112; 122; DLB 14

Wilson, Angus (Frank Johnstone)
    1913-1991 .... **CLC 2, 3, 5, 25, 34**
    See also CA 5-8R; 134; CANR 21; DLB 15,
    139; MTCW

Wilson, August
    1945- .. **CLC 39, 50, 63; BLC; DA; DC 2**
    See also BW 2; CA 115; 122; CANR 42;
    MTCW

Wilson, Brian 1942-.............. **CLC 12**

Wilson, Colin 1931-............. **CLC 3, 14**
    See also CA 1-4R; CAAS 5; CANR 1, 22,
    33; DLB 14; MTCW

Wilson, Dirk
    See Pohl, Frederik

Wilson, Edmund
    1895-1972 .... **CLC 1, 2, 3, 8, 24**
    See also CA 1-4R; 37-40R; CANR 1, 46;
    DLB 63; MTCW

Wilson, Ethel Davis (Bryant)
    1888(?)-1980 .... **CLC 13**
    See also CA 102; DLB 68; MTCW

Wilson, John 1785-1854.......... **NCLC 5**

Wilson, John (Anthony) Burgess 1917-1993
    See Burgess, Anthony
    See also CA 1-4R; 143; CANR 2, 46;
    MTCW

Wilson, Lanford 1937-....... **CLC 7, 14, 36**
    See also CA 17-20R; CABS 3; CANR 45;
    DLB 7

Wilson, Robert M. 1944-......... **CLC 7, 9**
    See also CA 49-52; CANR 2, 41; MTCW

Wilson, Robert McLiam 1964-..... **CLC 59**
    See also CA 132

Wilson, Sloan 1920-.............. **CLC 32**
    See also CA 1-4R; CANR 1, 44

Wilson, Snoo 1948-............... **CLC 33**
    See also CA 69-72

Wilson, William S(mith) 1932- ..... **CLC 49**
    See also CA 81-84

Winchilsea, Anne (Kingsmill) Finch Counte
    1661-1720 .... **LC 3**

Windham, Basil
    See Wodehouse, P(elham) G(renville)

Wingrove, David (John) 1954-...... **CLC 68**
    See also CA 133

Winters, Janet Lewis .... **CLC 41**
    See also Lewis, Janet
    See also DLBY 87

Winters, (Arthur) Yvor
    1900-1968 .... **CLC 4, 8, 32**
    See also CA 11-12; 25-28R; CAP 1;
    DLB 48; MTCW

Winterson, Jeanette 1959-......... **CLC 64**
    See also CA 136

Wiseman, Frederick 1930-......... **CLC 20**

Wister, Owen 1860-1938 .... **TCLC 21**
    See also CA 108; DLB 9, 78; SATA 62

Witkacy
    See Witkiewicz, Stanislaw Ignacy

Witkiewicz, Stanislaw Ignacy
    1885-1939 .... **TCLC 8**
    See also CA 105

Wittgenstein, Ludwig (Josef Johann)
    1889-1951 .... **TCLC 59**
    See also CA 113

Wittig, Monique 1935(?)-.......... **CLC 22**
    See also CA 116; 135; DLB 83

Wittlin, Jozef 1896-1976 .... **CLC 25**
    See also CA 49-52; 65-68; CANR 3

Wodehouse, P(elham) G(renville)
    1881-1975 ... **CLC 1, 2, 5, 10, 22; SSC 2**
    See also AITN 2; CA 45-48; 57-60;
    CANR 3, 33; CDBLB 1914-1945;
    DLB 34; MTCW; SATA 22

Woiwode, L.
    See Woiwode, Larry (Alfred)

Woiwode, Larry (Alfred) 1941-... **CLC 6, 10**
    See also CA 73-76; CANR 16; DLB 6

Wojciechowska, Maia (Teresa)
    1927- .... **CLC 26**
    See also AAYA 8; CA 9-12R; CANR 4, 41;
    CLR 1; JRDA; MAICYA; SAAS 1;
    SATA 1, 28

Wolf, Christa 1929- .... **CLC 14, 29, 58**
    See also CA 85-88; CANR 45; DLB 75;
    MTCW

Wolfe, Gene (Rodman) 1931-....... **CLC 25**
    See also CA 57-60; CAAS 9; CANR 6, 32;
    DLB 8

Wolfe, George C. 1954-........... **CLC 49**

Wolfe, Thomas (Clayton)
    1900-1938 ... **TCLC 4, 13, 29; DA; WLC**
    See also CA 104; 132; CDALB 1929-1941;
    DLB 9, 102; DLBD 2; DLBY 85; MTCW

Wolfe, Thomas Kennerly, Jr. 1931-
    See Wolfe, Tom
    See also CA 13-16R; CANR 9, 33; MTCW

Wolfe, Tom .... **CLC 1, 2, 9, 15, 35, 51**
    See also Wolfe, Thomas Kennerly, Jr.
    See also AAYA 8; AITN 2; BEST 89:1;
    DLB 152

Wolff, Geoffrey (Ansell) 1937- ..... **CLC 41**
    See also CA 29-32R; CANR 29, 43

Wolff, Sonia
    See Levitin, Sonia (Wolff)

Wolff, Tobias (Jonathan Ansell)
    1945- .... **CLC 39, 64**
    See also BEST 90:2; CA 114; 117; DLB 130

Wolfram von Eschenbach
    c. 1170-c. 1220 .... **CMLC 5**
    See also DLB 138

Wolitzer, Hilma 1930-............ **CLC 17**
    See also CA 65-68; CANR 18, 40; SATA 31

Wollstonecraft, Mary 1759-1797...... **LC 5**
    See also CDBLB 1789-1832; DLB 39, 104

Wonder, Stevie .... **CLC 12**
    See also Morris, Steveland Judkins

Wong, Jade Snow 1922-........... **CLC 17**
    See also CA 109

Woodcott, Keith
    See Brunner, John (Kilian Houston)

Woodruff, Robert W.
    See Mencken, H(enry) L(ouis)

Woolf, (Adeline) Virginia
    1882-1941 ...... TCLC 1, 5, 20, 43, 56;
                              DA; SSC 7; WLC
    See also CA 104; 130; CDBLB 1914-1945;
    DLB 36, 100; DLBD 10; MTCW

Woollcott, Alexander (Humphreys)
    1887-1943 .... TCLC 5
    See also CA 105; DLB 29

Woolrich, Cornell   1903-1968 .... CLC 77
    See also Hopley-Woolrich, Cornell George

Wordsworth, Dorothy
    1771-1855 .... NCLC 25
    See also DLB 107

Wordsworth, William
    1770-1850 .... NCLC 12, 38; DA; PC 4;
                                          WLC
    See also CDBLB 1789-1832; DLB 93, 107

Wouk, Herman   1915- .... CLC 1, 9, 38
    See also CA 5-8R; CANR 6, 33; DLBY 82;
    MTCW

Wright, Charles (Penzel, Jr.)
    1935- .... CLC 6, 13, 28
    See also CA 29-32R; CAAS 7; CANR 23,
    36; DLBY 82; MTCW

Wright, Charles Stevenson
    1932- .... CLC 49; BLC 3
    See also BW 1; CA 9-12R; CANR 26;
    DLB 33

Wright, Jack R.
    See Harris, Mark

Wright, James (Arlington)
    1927-1980 .... CLC 3, 5, 10, 28
    See also AITN 2; CA 49-52; 97-100;
    CANR 4, 34; DLB 5; MTCW

Wright, Judith (Arandell)
    1915- .... CLC 11, 53
    See also CA 13-16R; CANR 31; MTCW;
    SATA 14

Wright, L(aurali) R.   1939- .... CLC 44
    See also CA 138

Wright, Richard (Nathaniel)
    1908-1960 .... CLC 1, 3, 4, 9, 14, 21, 48,
                              74; BLC; DA; SSC 2; WLC
    See also AAYA 5; BW 1; CA 108;
    CDALB 1929-1941; DLB 76, 102;
    DLBD 2; MTCW

Wright, Richard B(ruce)   1937- ...... CLC 6
    See also CA 85-88; DLB 53

Wright, Rick   1945- .... CLC 35

Wright, Rowland
    See Wells, Carolyn

Wright, Stephen Caldwell   1946- .... CLC 33
    See also BW 2

Wright, Willard Huntington   1888-1939
    See Van Dine, S. S.
    See also CA 115

Wright, William   1930- .... CLC 44
    See also CA 53-56; CANR 7, 23

Wu Ch'eng-en   1500(?)-1582(?) .... LC 7

Wu Ching-tzu   1701-1754 .... LC 2

Wurlitzer, Rudolph   1938(?)- ... CLC 2, 4, 15
    See also CA 85-88

Wycherley, William   1641-1715 .... LC 8, 21
    See also CDBLB 1660-1789; DLB 80

Wylie, Elinor (Morton Hoyt)
    1885-1928 .... TCLC 8
    See also CA 105; DLB 9, 45

Wylie, Philip (Gordon)   1902-1971 ... CLC 43
    See also CA 21-22; 33-36R; CAP 2; DLB 9

Wyndham, John .... CLC 19
    See also Harris, John (Wyndham Parkes
    Lucas) Beynon

Wyss, Johann David Von
    1743-1818 .... NCLC 10
    See also JRDA; MAICYA; SATA 29;
    SATA-Brief 27

Yakumo Koizumi
    See Hearn, (Patricio) Lafcadio (Tessima
    Carlos)

Yanez, Jose Donoso
    See Donoso (Yanez), Jose

Yanovsky, Basile S.
    See Yanovsky, V(assily) S(emenovich)

Yanovsky, V(assily) S(emenovich)
    1906-1989 .... CLC 2, 18
    See also CA 97-100; 129

Yates, Richard   1926-1992 ..... CLC 7, 8, 23
    See also CA 5-8R; 139; CANR 10, 43;
    DLB 2; DLBY 81, 92

Yeats, W. B.
    See Yeats, William Butler

Yeats, William Butler
    1865-1939 ..... TCLC 1, 11, 18, 31; DA;
                                          WLC
    See also CA 104; 127; CANR 45;
    CDBLB 1890-1914; DLB 10, 19, 98;
    MTCW

Yehoshua, A(braham) B.
    1936- .... CLC 13, 31
    See also CA 33-36R; CANR 43

Yep, Laurence Michael   1948- ...... CLC 35
    See also AAYA 5; CA 49-52; CANR 1, 46;
    CLR 3, 17; DLB 52; JRDA; MAICYA;
    SATA 7, 69

Yerby, Frank G(arvin)
    1916-1991 .... CLC 1, 7, 22; BLC
    See also BW 1; CA 9-12R; 136; CANR 16;
    DLB 76; MTCW

Yesenin, Sergei Alexandrovich
    See Esenin, Sergei (Alexandrovich)

Yevtushenko, Yevgeny (Alexandrovich)
    1933- .... CLC 1, 3, 13, 26, 51
    See also CA 81-84; CANR 33; MTCW

Yezierska, Anzia   1885(?)-1970 ..... CLC 46
    See also CA 126; 89-92; DLB 28; MTCW

Yglesias, Helen   1915- .... CLC 7, 22
    See also CA 37-40R; CAAS 20; CANR 15;
    MTCW

Yokomitsu Riichi   1898-1947 ...... TCLC 47

Yonge, Charlotte (Mary)
    1823-1901 .... TCLC 48
    See also CA 109; DLB 18; SATA 17

York, Jeremy
    See Creasey, John

York, Simon
    See Heinlein, Robert A(nson)

Yorke, Henry Vincent   1905-1974 ... CLC 13
    See also Green, Henry
    See also CA 85-88; 49-52

Yosano Akiko   1878-1942 .. TCLC 59; PC 11

Yoshimoto, Banana .... CLC 84
    See also Yoshimoto, Mahoko

Yoshimoto, Mahoko   1964-
    See Yoshimoto, Banana
    See also CA 144

Young, Al(bert James)
    1939- .... CLC 19; BLC
    See also BW 2; CA 29-32R; CANR 26;
    DLB 33

Young, Andrew (John)   1885-1971 .... CLC 5
    See also CA 5-8R; CANR 7, 29

Young, Collier
    See Bloch, Robert (Albert)

Young, Edward   1683-1765 .... LC 3
    See also DLB 95

Young, Marguerite   1909- .... CLC 82
    See also CA 13-16; CAP 1

Young, Neil   1945- .... CLC 17
    See also CA 110

Yourcenar, Marguerite
    1903-1987 .... CLC 19, 38, 50, 87
    See also CA 69-72; CANR 23; DLB 72;
    DLBY 88; MTCW

Yurick, Sol   1925- .... CLC 6
    See also CA 13-16R; CANR 25

Zabolotskii, Nikolai Alekseevich
    1903-1958 .... TCLC 52
    See also CA 116

Zamiatin, Yevgenii
    See Zamyatin, Evgeny Ivanovich

Zamyatin, Evgeny Ivanovich
    1884-1937 .... TCLC 8, 37
    See also CA 105

Zangwill, Israel   1864-1926 .... TCLC 16
    See also CA 109; DLB 10, 135

Zappa, Francis Vincent, Jr.   1940-1993
    See Zappa, Frank
    See also CA 108; 143

Zappa, Frank .... CLC 17
    See also Zappa, Francis Vincent, Jr.

Zaturenska, Marya   1902-1982 .... CLC 6, 11
    See also CA 13-16R; 105; CANR 22

Zelazny, Roger (Joseph)   1937- ...... CLC 21
    See also AAYA 7; CA 21-24R; CANR 26;
    DLB 8; MTCW; SATA 57;
    SATA-Brief 39

Zhdanov, Andrei A(lexandrovich)
    1896-1948 .... TCLC 18
    See also CA 117

Zhukovsky, Vasily   1783-1852 .... NCLC 35

Ziegenhagen, Eric .... CLC 55

Zimmer, Jill Schary
    See Robinson, Jill

Zimmerman, Robert
    See Dylan, Bob

Zindel, Paul   1936- ... CLC 6, 26; DA; DC 5
    See also AAYA 2; CA 73-76; CANR 31;
    CLR 3; DLB 7, 52; JRDA; MAICYA;
    MTCW; SATA 16, 58

Zinov'Ev, A. A.
    See Zinoviev, Alexander (Aleksandrovich)

Zinoviev, Alexander (Aleksandrovich)
1922- . . . . CLC 19
See also CA 116; 133; CAAS 10

Zoilus
See Lovecraft, H(oward) P(hillips)

Zola, Emile (Edouard Charles Antoine)
1840-1902 . . . . . . TCLC 1, 6, 21, 41; DA;
WLC
See also CA 104; 138; DLB 123

Zoline, Pamela 1941- . . . . CLC 62

Zorrilla y Moral, Jose 1817-1893 . . NCLC 6

Zoshchenko, Mikhail (Mikhailovich)
1895-1958 . . . . TCLC 15; SSC 15
See also CA 115

Zuckmayer, Carl 1896-1977 . . . . CLC 18
See also CA 69-72; DLB 56, 124

Zuk, Georges
See Skelton, Robin

Zukofsky, Louis
1904-1978 . . . . CLC 1, 2, 4, 7, 11, 18;
PC 11
See also CA 9-12R; 77-80; CANR 39;
DLB 5; MTCW

Zweig, Paul 1935-1984 . . . . CLC 34, 42
See also CA 85-88; 113

Zweig, Stefan 1881-1942 . . . . TCLC 17
See also CA 112; DLB 81, 118

Literary Criticism Series
Cumulative Topic Index

This index lists all topic entries in Gale's *Classical and Medieval Literature Criticism, Contemporary Literary Criticism, Literature Criticism from 1400 to 1800, Nineteenth-Century Literature Criticism,* and *Twentieth-Century Literary Criticism.*

Topic Index

NCLC Cumulative Nationality Index

Nationality Index

NCLC-50 Title Index

495

ISBN 0-8103-9291-7